COMMON ELEMENTS

Name	*Symbol*	*Approx. at. wt.*	*Common ox. nos.*	*Name*	*Symbol*	*Approx. at. wt.*	*Common ox. nos.*
aluminum	Al	27.0	+3	magnesium	Mg	24.3	+2
antimony	Sb	121.8	+3, +5	manganese	Mn	54.9	+2, +4, +7
arsenic	As	74.9	+3, +5	mercury	Hg	200.6	+1, +2
barium	Ba	137.3	+2	nickel	Ni	58.7	+2
bismuth	Bi	209.0	+3	nitrogen	N	14.0	−3, +3, +5
bromine	Br	79.9	−1, +5	oxygen	O	16.0	−2
calcium	Ca	40.1	+2	phosphorus	P	31.0	+3, +5
carbon	C	12.0	+2, +4	platinum	Pt	195.1	+2, +4
chlorine	Cl	35.5	−1, +5, +7	potassium	K	39.1	+1
chromium	Cr	52.0	+2, +3, +6	silicon	Si	28.1	+4
cobalt	Co	58.9	+2, +3	silver	Ag	107.9	+1
copper	Cu	63.5	+1, +2	sodium	Na	23.0	+1
fluorine	F	19.0	−1	strontium	Sr	87.6	+2
gold	Au	197.0	+1, +3	sulfur	S	32.1	−2, +4, +6
hydrogen	H	1.0	−1, +1	tin	Sn	118.7	+2, +4
iodine	I	126.9	−1, +5	titanium	Ti	47.9	+3, +4
iron	Fe	55.8	+2, +3	tungsten	W	183.8	+6
lead	Pb	207.2	+2, +4	zinc	Zn	65.4	+2

COMMON IONS AND THEIR CHARGES

Name	*Symbol*	*Charge*	*Name*	*Symbol*	*Charge*
aluminum	Al^{+++}	+3	lead(II)	Pb^{++}	+2
ammonium	NH_4^+	+1	magnesium	Mg^{++}	+2
barium	Ba^{++}	+2	mercury(I)	Hg_2^{++}	+2
calcium	Ca^{++}	+2	mercury(II)	Hg^{++}	+2
chromium(III)	Cr^{+++}	+3	nickel(II)	Ni^{++}	+2
cobalt(II)	Co^{++}	+2	potassium	K^+	+1
copper(I)	Cu^+	+1	silver	Ag^+	+1
copper(II)	Cu^{++}	+2	sodium	Na^+	+1
hydronium	H_3O^+	+1	tin(II)	Sn^{++}	+2
iron(II)	Fe^{++}	+2	tin(IV)	Sn^{++++}	+4
iron(III)	Fe^{+++}	+3	zinc	Zn^{++}	+2
acetate	$C_2H_3O_2^-$	−1	hydrogen sulfate	HSO_4^-	−1
bromide	Br^-	−1	hydroxide	OH^-	−1
carbonate	CO_3^{--}	−2	hypochlorite	ClO^-	−1
chlorate	ClO_3^-	−1	iodide	I^-	−1
chloride	Cl^-	−1	nitrate	NO_3^-	−1
chlorite	ClO_2^-	−1	nitrite	NO_2^-	−1
chromate	CrO_4^{--}	−2	oxide	O^{--}	−2
cyanide	CN^-	−1	perchlorate	ClO_4^-	−1
dichromate	$Cr_2O_7^{--}$	−2	permanganate	MnO_4^-	−1
fluoride	F^-	−1	peroxide	O_2^{--}	−2
hexacyanoferrate(II)	$Fe(CN)_6^{----}$	−4	phosphate	PO_4^{---}	−3
hexacyanoferrate(III)	$Fe(CN)_6^{---}$	−3	sulfate	SO_4^{--}	−2
hydride	H^-	−1	sulfide	S^{--}	−2
hydrogen carbonate	HCO_3^-	−1	sulfite	SO_3^{--}	−2

modern chemistry

H. Clark Metcalfe John E. Williams Joseph F. Castka

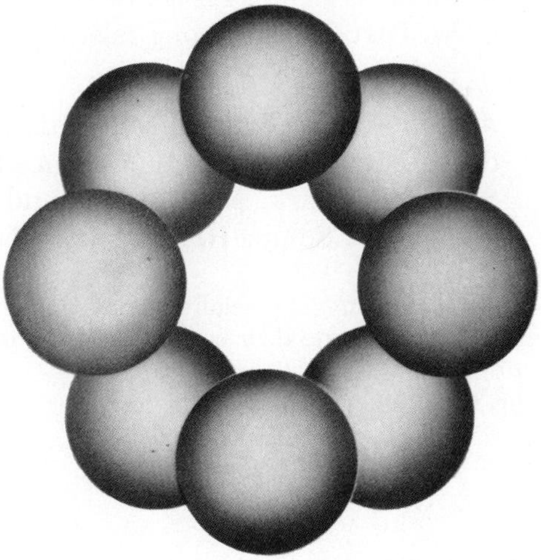

HOLT, RINEHART AND WINSTON, PUBLISHERS
New York—London—Toronto—Sydney

THE HOLT MODERN CHEMISTRY PROGRAM

Metcalfe, Williams, and Castka
Modern Chemistry (Student Text)
Modern Chemistry (Teacher's Edition)
Laboratory Experiments in Chemistry
Exercises and Experiments in Chemistry
Tests in Chemistry (Duplicating Masters)

H. Clark Metcalfe

P.O. Box V2, Wickenburg, Arizona, 85358; formerly teacher of chemistry at Winchester-Thurston School, Pittsburgh, Pennsylvania, and Head of the Science Department, Wilkinsburg Senior High School, Wilkinsburg, Pennsylvania.

John E. Williams

Formerly teacher of chemistry and physics at Newport Harbor High School, Newport Beach, California, and Head of the Science Department, Broad Ripple High School, Indianapolis, Indiana.

Joseph F. Castka

Formerly Assistant Principal for the Supervision of Physical Science, Martin Van Buren High School, New York City; and Adjunct Associate Professor of General Science and Chemistry, C. W. Post College, Long Island University, New York.

Charles E. Dull

Author of the original editions of MODERN CHEMISTRY, deceased, was Head of the Science Department, West Side High School, Newark, New Jersey, and was Supervisor of Science, Junior and Senior High Schools, Newark, New Jersey.

The cover photograph of specially formulated polyethylene powders flowing through funnels to demonstrate their consistency is courtesy of Union Carbide Corporation.

Credits for photographs used in the text are given on page 666.

ISBN: 0-03-019816-X
4 039 11

PREFACE

MODERN CHEMISTRY is a textbook that fulfills various curriculum requirements for an introductory course in chemistry. Teachers will find ample material in MODERN CHEMISTRY for an outstanding college-preparatory program. For those students who do not plan to go further in science, there is sufficient elementary theory and interest-arousing descriptive information for a complete general course of study. The Teacher's Edition for MODERN CHEMISTRY gives suggestions for implementing both types of chemistry courses and suggestions for an advanced course as well.

It has been the authors' purpose to include in the text more than can be covered in one year. This wealth of material permits a wide choice of topics and allows for selective emphasis. Teachers should choose those topics that best meet their needs.

In MODERN CHEMISTRY, the subject matter of chemistry is organized in a logical, workable sequence. Descriptive and theoretical topics are alternated to provide classroom variety and a well-correlated laboratory program. Special attention has been given to the introduction of technical vocabulary words. Each of these words is printed in the text in ***bold-face italics*** and is carefully defined where it is first used. Refresher definitions of these words occur at appropriate intervals in the text.

Significant content changes in this edition of MODERN CHEMISTRY include the following: new introductory material on the atomic theory; an expansion of the treatment of electron affinity; reorganization of the topic of chemical bonding to improve its teachability; information on new synthetic elements, including Element 107, and on elements and compounds on other planets and in outer space; inclusion of a new chapter on oxygen, ozone, hydrogen, and deuterium; new information on hydrogen bonds and their relation to the properties of solvents; a thorough revision of the chapter on ionization to include the most up-to-date concepts; a revised description of acids and bases, which includes historical, Brønsted, and Lewis definitions; simplification of the organic chemistry unit and inclusion of information on energy sources; a revised section on reaction energy; changes in the descriptive chemistry of metallic and nonmetallic elements to include modern recovery processes and uses; more extensive use of marginal notes for reference, review, and supplementary information; and many minor changes that improve the clarity and readability of the text.

The material for each chapter includes Sample Problems where appropriate. At the end of each chapter there is a Summary, followed by suitable Questions and Problems. The Questions, which are based on the text itself, are graded according to difficulty in Groups A and B. The Problems are similary graded. The average student should master all the Group A Questions and Problems; the better student will be able to do both. In the back of the book are a Mathematics Refresher, Data Tables, a Glossary, and an Index.

Because of their clarity and great learning value, line drawings are used extensively. The text is also illustrated with many fine photographs. The illustration at the top of each chapter opener page is specifically designed to relate chemistry with the environment or with a familiar human activity or situation not usually associated with science. These illustrations are made meaningful by assigning a thought or essay-type question in the Questions section at the end of the chapter. The reference to this question is made in the parenthesis of the illustration's caption. There is also a series of Photo Essays where pictorial material is used to highlight special topics and careers in chemistry that are of current interest.

The text was written by H. Clark Metcalfe and John E. Williams. Joseph F. Castka was mainly responsible for the preparation of all supplementary materials to accompany the text, including the Teacher's Edition, EXERCISES AND EXPERIMENTS IN CHEMISTRY, LABORATORY EXPERIMENTS IN CHEMISTRY, and TESTS IN CHEMISTRY.

The following persons have assisted in preparing this revision by their helpful criticism: R. J. Friesen, Assistant Professor, Chemistry Department, University of Waterloo, Waterloo, Ontario, Canada; Gilbert P. Haight, Jr., Professor, University of Illinois, Urbana, Illinois; Kenneth W. May, Teacher of Chemistry, Camden High School, Camden, New York; Jeffrey May, Research Chemist, Molecular Corporation, Cambridge, Massachusetts; and P. Calvin Maybury, Professor of Chemistry, University of South Florida, Tampa, Florida.

The authors also acknowledge with thanks the work of Felix Cooper, who prepared the text illustrations, and FINE LINE ILLUSTRATIONS, INC., for rendering new art work. Our thanks to Arthur Rondeau of White Plains High School, White Plains, New York, and to Dr. Sol Charney of New Rochelle High School, New Rochelle, New York, for providing the facilities for the special color photographs of students and laboratory activities.

H. Clark Metcalfe, John E. Williams, Joseph F. Castka

CONTENTS

ARM &
HAMMER
AKING SODA
RYEA'S
N STARCH
A
B

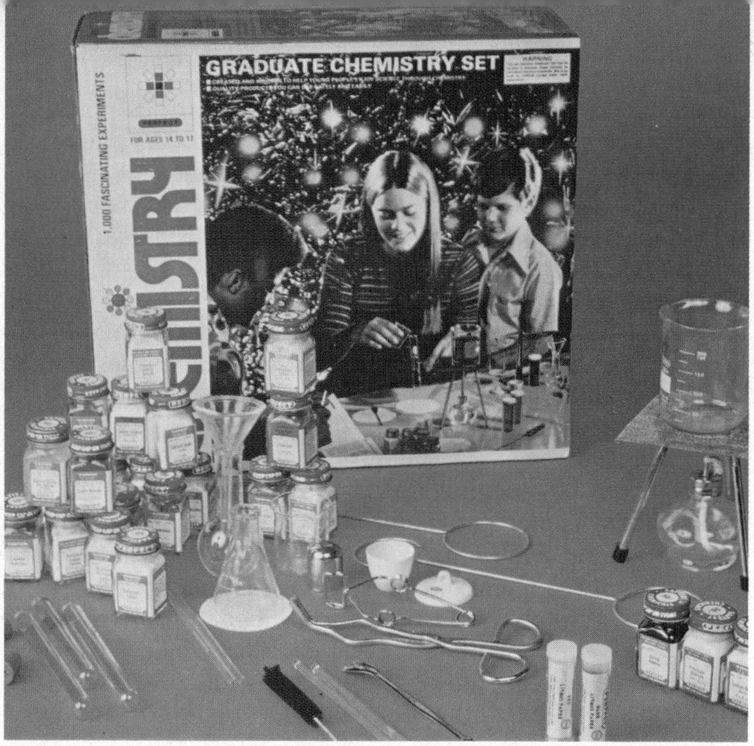

chapter 1

THE SCIENCE OF CHEMISTRY

Perhaps your study of chemistry began with a hobby chemistry set. (See Question 20 on page 20.)

Introduction

1.1 Chemistry is a laboratory science

Have you ever been curious enough about something to ask yourself "I wonder how this works?" Then, did you follow through by making a few simple tests? If you have, you acted like a scientist. Scientists search for relationships that can be used to explain and predict the behavior of things. They often answer their questions from the results of their experiments.

Part of the satisfaction of science is trying things for yourself —experimenting. Chemistry is a laboratory science. You will have an opportunity to try things for yourself—to experiment in the chemistry laboratory. You will find it interesting to identify chemical substances. One of your first experiments will require you to test some common household chemicals. The results will help you learn something about these substances from the way they behave. By doing other experiments you will learn how to use laboratory equipment and various techniques in handling chemicals safely. You will understand more clearly what chemistry, as a science, is all about. You will begin to appreciate the skills and attitudes that chemists must develop.

Fig. 1-1. In the experiment shown on the opposite page, students are learning to identify some common household chemicals from the way they behave.

1.2 A discovery

In 1856, 18-year-old William Henry Perkin was studying chemistry under August von Hofmann. In the course of his studies, Perkin became interested in an important chemical derived from the tropical cinchona tree. This substance was quinine, widely used at the time to treat malaria patients. Malaria claimed many lives and quinine was very much in demand. The supply, however, was limited. With the information and chemical know-how he got from von Hofmann, young Perkin decided to experiment on his own to find a substitute for quinine. His search began by treating one of the substances derived from coal tar, a sticky waste product resulting from the decomposition of soft coal by heat. Von Hofmann had already shown that some of the coal tar derivatives he had found resemble quinine.

After several failures, Perkin discovered a brilliant purple substance. This was not the quinine substitute he set out to discover, but he recognized that this new substance had real possibilities. The purple material became the foundation of a very successful dye industry. Young Perkin became wealthy as a result of his work and sharp mind. As Pasteur once said, "Chance favors the prepared mind." Coal tar became the source for many other products. Detergents, food flavorings, explosives, and plastics are all direct descendants of Perkin's chemical success with the sticky reject from the coal industry.

1.3 Chemistry affects our lives

The word *chemistry* is used in two ways. It is used to describe the activity of chemists, or what chemists do. The word *chemistry* also means the chemical knowledge resulting from the activities of chemists.

Chemistry affects our lives in many ways. When you are sick, the physician prescribes a drug discovered and produced by chemists. Chemical research is responsible for synthetic fibers, plastics, and synthetic rubber used in the tires and other parts of automobiles. Synthetic fertilizers that increase the yield of food from each acre of land were developed in the chemistry laboratory. So were the insecticides that prevent destruction of crops by insects. Almost every product you can think of has been affected in some way by chemists.

Fig. 1-2. Chemists have produced many materials that have improved the usefulness of many common products.

The production of some of these beneficial materials, however, has affected plant, animal, and human life in harmful ways. Poisonous wastes from a chemical plant in Japan found their way into fish living in the nearby waters. Many persons eating the fish died as a result of the poison. Industrial wastes released into the Hudson River have collected in the bodies of fish living in these waters, making them inedible. The air around some manufacturing plants may also become unfit to breathe as a result of industrial pollution. Streams, rivers, and lakes have become unfit for human use because of industrial pollution.

Manufacture of some products has created new and unexpected problems. Lead from the exhaust of automobiles released into the air has been carried all over the earth by

Fig. 1-3. An earth-resources satellite (Landsat) photograph of New York harbor. The S-shaped pattern just outside the harbor entrance shows acid wastes being dumped.

Fig. 1-4. This gasoline has a chemical in it that contains lead. When the gasoline is burned in the car's engine, the lead is released to the atmosphere from the car's exhaust.

currents in the atmosphere. It has even been found in ice at the North Pole. Its presence in the air is one more health hazard affecting animal and human life.

The manufacture of chemicals intended for beneficial purposes has not been without mishap. A drug called thalidomide, used by some pregnant women to help them sleep, resulted in deformities in their babies. The insecticide DDT nearly caused the extinction of several species of birds, including the eagle, before it was banned by law.

Why, then, did these harmful products reach the consumer? One reason is that scientific knowledge is, at best, incomplete. Scientists cannot always tell in advance what effects new products may have once they are widely used. A second reason is that some products do not reveal their harmful effects until after a long period of time. Asbestos is a good example. Asbestos is a rock fiber whose fire-proof property makes it useful in many products such as automobile brake linings and nonflammable insulation. It was discovered only recently that asbestos may cause lung cancer if the lungs are exposed to asbestos fibers for a long period of time. Some people are just now getting the disease after working for a short time in an asbestos factory as long as 20 years ago. Some adults now have the disease because, when they were children, they were exposed to the asbestos dust from their parent's clothes. No one suspected this danger in the early years of the use of asbestos fibers.

The Environmental Protection Agency is set up to control pollution and the Pure Food and Drug Administration to regulate the release of new products. Are we, then, adequately protected? Consumer and environmental protection advocates point to instances where controls have been inadequate. On the other hand, manufacturers say that most products prove to be safe, and that stricter rules would affect the release of useful and beneficial products. A better understanding of the arguments for and against the manufacture and use of consumer goods is one more reason for studying chemistry.

Fig. 1-5. The insecticide DDT endangered several species of birds, including the eagle.

doing chemistry

1

2

7

Chemists do many things. Chemical engineers build plants (1). Physical chemists test a new product (2). A biochemist tests for cancer-producing chemicals (3). Analytical chemists determine the composition of substances: Nitrogen in petroleum (4), exhaust fumes (5). Analytical chemists in government laboratories test food for rat filth (6), or test for pollution (7). Some chemists work in unusual places. An analytical instrument, a mass spectrometer is being installed in a hydrolab (8). Some chemists such as the inorganic chemist, Marie Curie (9), or the biomedical chemist Marjory Horning (10), have done fundamental research in university laboratories. Marie Curie discovered and separated new elements. For her discoveries, she received the best-known award given to scientists—the Nobel Prize. Dr. Horning studied the way drugs affect humans.

4

5

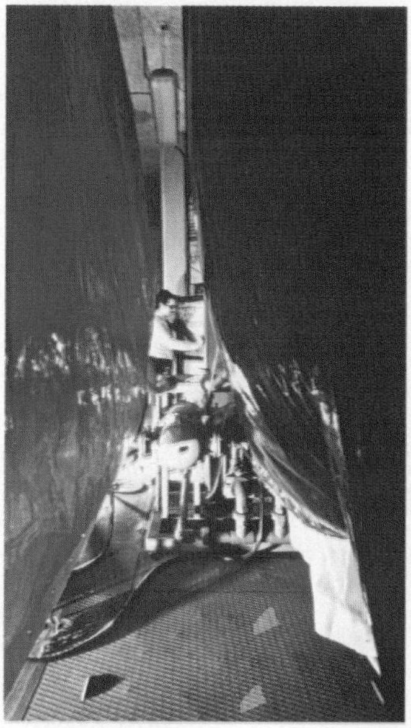

6

9

10

Matter and Energy

Fig. 1-6. Cleaner air, the result of air pollution control devices at a steel-making plant.

1.4 Matter

All materials about us consist of matter. With our senses of sight, touch, taste, and smell, we recognize various kinds of matter. This book, your desk, the air you breathe, the water you drink are examples of matter. You can see some of these examples easily. You can hold a rock or a stick of wood in your hand. Other kinds of matter, such as air, are more difficult to see. You ride on compressed air in automobile tires. You can see the tremendous damage caused by the fast-moving air in a tornado or hurricane. We say that ***matter*** *is anything that occupies space and has mass.*

Matter may be acted upon by *forces* that set it in motion, or change its motion. *The resistance that matter offers to change of position or motion is a property called* ***inertia.*** A baseball and

A B

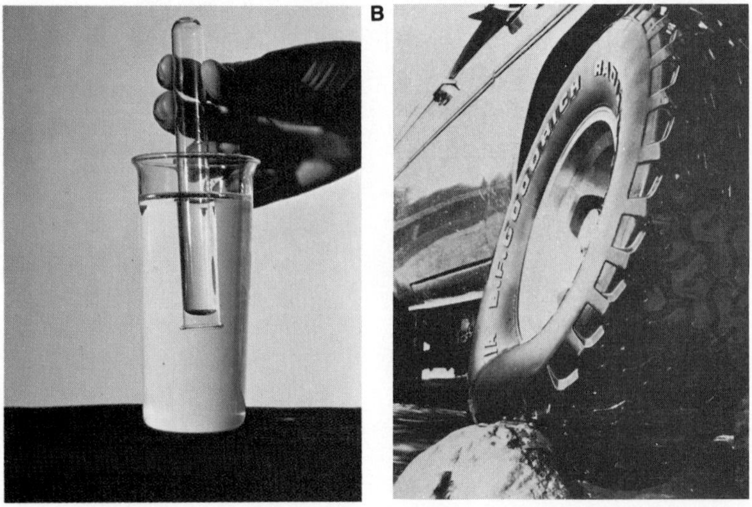

Fig. 1-7. **(A)** What keeps the water from entering the test tube? **(B)** What property of air makes it useful in automobile tires?

a cannonball of the same size do not have the same inertia. Much more force is needed to hurl the cannonball with the same speed as a pitched baseball. You can easily imagine what would happen to a bat making contact with a cannonball at this speed. Or to a catcher's hand trying to stop this fast-moving metal ball instead of a baseball.

Fig. 1-8. What property of matter makes bricks useful in building construction?

1.5 Three phases of matter

Under ordinary conditions of temperature and pressure, matter may exist in three *phases:* solid, liquid, and gas. Sometimes these phases are referred to as the three states of matter.

A *solid* retains its size and shape. It has a definite volume. Most solids cannot be reduced to a smaller volume. They are said, then, to be *incompressible.* Some things are rigid like solids, but can be compressed. Though it appears to be a solid, a dry sponge can be compressed.

A *liquid* is not rigid. To retain a liquid, you must keep it in a container. The surface of an *undisturbed* liquid is level, even if its container is tilted. Beneath its surface, a liquid always takes the shape of its container. A liquid also has a definite volume.

A *gas* is easily compressed. It does not have a definite shape or volume. A gas acquires the shape of its container and evenly fills the entire space of the container, no matter how big or small. You can squeeze the air in a balloon into many shapes. By compressing the air, you can make it fit into a slightly smaller volume. With the hose stopped up, the air in a bicycle pump can be reduced to a fraction of its original volume.

A "phase" is a uniform part of a system separated from other uniform parts by boundary faces.

Ice in water represents a two-phase system, a solid phase and a liquid phase.

1.6 Properties of matter

A scientist identifies matter and determines its usefulness by studying its properties. Many liquids, including water, are colorless. Some liquids, such as ether, have distinctive odors; others, like water, are odorless. Since no two liquids boil at the same temperature and freeze at the same temperature, these characteristics may be used to identify unknown liquids.

Properties that are useful in identifying matter are called *specific* or *characteristic properties.* The most useful are those that can be measured and expressed as quantities (numbers) with units. Thus, the freezing point of water is a more useful property of water than its color.

Characteristic properties can be separated into two general groups: physical properties and chemical properties. ***Physical properties*** *are those that can be determined without changing the identity of the material.* For example, when water is cooled sufficiently, it reaches a point where it becomes ice, a solid. The appearance of the water changes, but not its identity. Thus, the freezing point of water is a physical property. Physical properties include color, odor, and hardness. Some

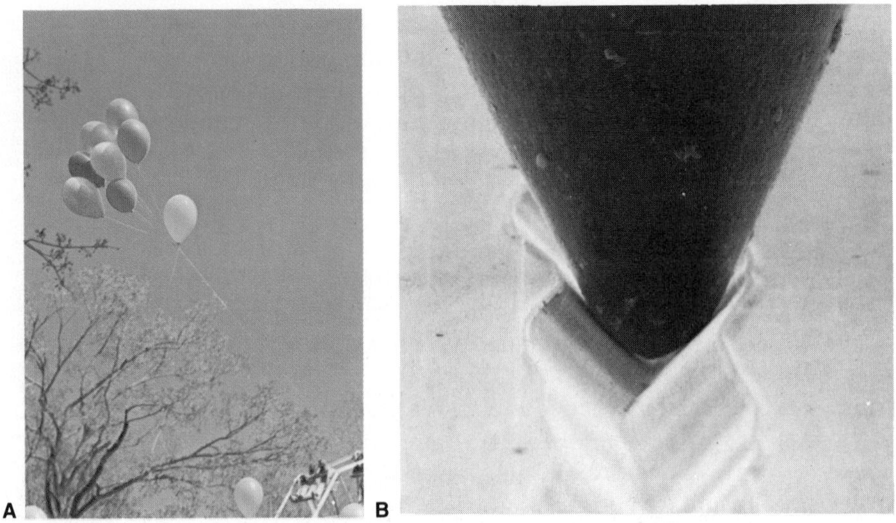

Fig. 1-9. (A) What property of the gas in these balloons makes them rise? (B) What physical property of diamond makes it useful as the tip of a phonograph needle?

Fig. 1-10. An example of a chemical reaction. Not all chemical reactions are this spectacular.

other physical properties that you will become familiar with are density, solubility, and crystalline form.

Chemical properties *are those that describe the behavior of a material in reactions that change its identity.* Whether or not a material burns in air is an example of a chemical property. If a material is tested by burning it in air, not only is its appearance changed but its identity also is changed. A process that changes the chemical identity of a material is called a *chemical reaction.*

1.7 Basic units of measurement

There are several quantities associated with matter that can be measured directly by comparison with basic units of measurement. Among these are the fundamental quantities, *length, mass, temperature,* and *time.* They are the basis for many scientific measurements. Other quantities of matter such as area, volume, density, and heat are measured by using a combination of these basic quantities. The volume of a rectangular box, for example, is determined by multiplying three length measurements. This is usually expressed in a mathematical equation

$$\textbf{Volume} = \textbf{length} \times \textbf{width} \times \textbf{height}$$

The product of this equation is an example of a *derived* measurement. Later on in this chapter, the derived quantities of density and heat will be developed, since they are used extensively in the chemistry laboratory.

Length *is the shortest distance between two points.* On a plane surface, this distance is a straight line. It is usually measured by comparison with a standard distance. For this purpose, the meter has been adopted as the standard unit of length in scientific measurement. The distance between two

A

B

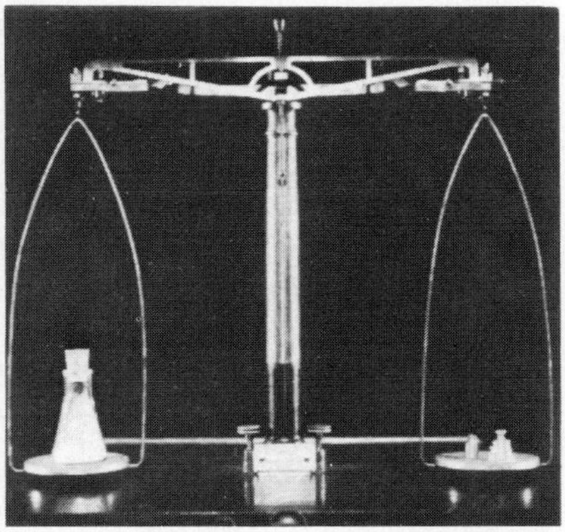

C

Fig. 1-11. **(A)** A balance used about 4000 years ago. **(B)** The horizontal beam at the top of this balance is supported at the center. The pans, hung at each end of the beam, are at equal distances from the center support. When equal masses are placed on each pan, the beam balances. **(C)** With this precision balance, differences of 1/100,000,000 of a kilogram can be measured.

points is then measured by the number of times this standard length is contained between the two points.

Mass *is a measure of the amount or quantity of matter contained in an object.* This measurement is made by comparing the object to be measured with a standard mass. In the laboratory, this is usually done by balancing the quantity of matter being measured with the required number of standard mass units on a balance. You will do this in the laboratory.

Mass is also responsible for the weight of a body. ***Weight*** *is a measure of the force of attraction between the earth and a body.* This attraction is usually measured as the amount of stretch in the spring of a spring balance. The stretching force, the force due to gravity, is slightly less at high altitudes than at sea level. The reason for this difference is that the force of gravity depends upon the distance between the earth's center and the center of the object when the object is on or above the earth's surface. The object's mass, however, remains unchanged despite change of location. *The mass of a body is constant.*

Time *is duration of an event, a quantity usually measured with some sort of clock.* Measurement of time is commonly based on the period of the earth's rotation. This interval has been assigned the quantity of 24 hours. One hour is divided into 60 minutes, and one minute is further divided into 60 seconds. Since the actual time for the earth's rotation is changing, scientists today use a far more precise time standard. This standard is based on the frequency of light emitted from a special lamp.

Fig. 1-12. This astronaut is weightless in space. Is he also massless?

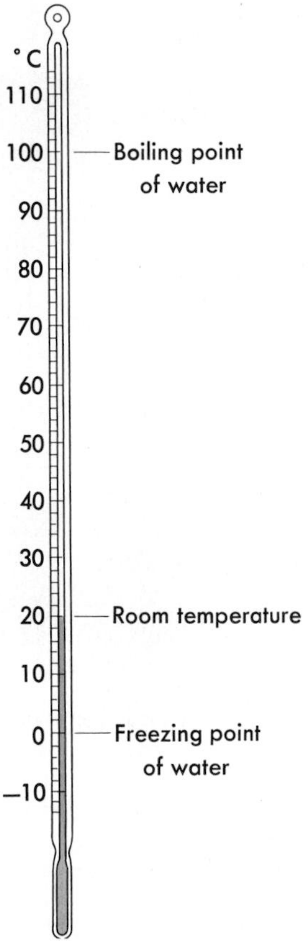

Fig. 1-13. The Celsius thermometer is widely used in scientific work. What is the temperature on the Fahrenheit thermometer of the temperatures shown here?

Temperature *is the degree of hotness or coldness that can be sensed in an object.* Just as an object may be pushed or pulled to estimate its mass, or lifted to estimate its weight, an object's temperature may be determined by touching it. The sensation may be described as hot, warm, cool, or cold. Temperature is a physical property of matter.

Our temperature sense, while generally useful, may be unreliable under some conditions. If you place one hand in cold water and then in cool water, the cool water feels warm by comparison. If your hand has been in hot water first, however, the cool water feels cold.

Instead of relying on our temperature sense, we use instruments. Temperature is generally measured with a thermometer. One form of this instrument is a glass tube partly filled with a liquid. The liquid used is usually mercury (or alcohol dyed red to make it more visible). When this mercury or alcohol is heated, its volume increases; when cooled, its volume decreases. The corresponding change in volume makes the level of the liquid rise or fall inside the glass tube. A convenient scale is marked along the length of the tube to measure the change of level and accordingly the change of temperature.

Thermometers for scientific use are commonly marked with the Celsius temperature scale. This scale was devised by a Swedish astronomer, Anders Celsius. He established his thermometer scale by defining two *fixed points* and dividing the interval between them into 100 equal parts or *degrees*.

Celsius selected the normal freezing point of water as the lower fixed point and marked it 0. He used the normal boiling point of water as the upper fixed point and marked it 100. By extending the same scale divisions beyond the two fixed points, he could measure temperatures below 0° and above 100°. See Figure 1-13.

Fig. 1-14. The change of phase from ice to water occurs at 0°C.

1.8 Intensive and extensive properties

All the measurable properties of matter fall into one of two categories: *extensive* properties and *intensive* properties. The value of a measurement of an extensive property depends on *how much* matter is being considered. Mass, length, and volume are extensive properties. More matter means more mass. Values for extensive quantities can be added together. Two identical blocks each with the same mass will have a combined mass which is the sum of the two separate masses. The space occupied by any two blocks is the sum of the volumes of the two individual blocks. The value of an extensive quantity depends on the *extent (size) of matter.*

The measured value of an *intensive property does not depend* on how much matter is being considered. Temperature is an intensive property. Suppose you have two equal amounts of water, each at exactly the same temperature. Unlike mass and volume, if you combine these two to make a single quantity of water, *the temperature of the combined water is still the same as it was before.* Temperature is *not* additive. Even if you combine equal volumes of water that are at two different temperatures, the final temperature would *not* be the sum of the original temperatures. The final temperature would be somewhere between the two original temperatures.

1.9 The metric system of measurement

The *metric system* of measurement was developed in France near the end of the eighteenth century. It is used in scientific work throughout the world. It is in general use in practically all countries except the United States, Great Britain, and some other English-speaking countries. Great Britain is in the midst of a long-range program for conversion to metric measurements. Australia, New Zealand, and Canada are also moving from English to metric. The United States was formally committed by the Metric Conversion Act of 1975 to encourage the changeover. As part of this change, you have probably noticed that the weight of some food is given in both the metric and English systems on the package. Also, in some places, the distances on highway signs are given in both miles (mi) and kilometers (km), a metric unit of distance.

Many American industries that participate in foreign markets have already adopted the metric system. This move was necessary if they were to remain competitive in those markets, which are almost entirely metric.

The metric system is a decimal system similar to our money system. To make calculations easy, the relationships between units are multiples of 10. Our basic unit of money is the dol-

Fig. 1-15. If the air pressure in the large truck tire is the same as the air pressure in the bicycle tire, is pressure an intensive or extensive property?

Fig. 1-16. The quantity of many products is indicated on the label in both English and metric units.

Fig. 1-17. Since any bar of metal may change slightly in length, the standard meter is now defined as 1,650,763.73 wavelengths of the red-orange line of krypton 86. If a beam of light is split into two paths, then reunited, a pattern of light and dark circles results. Each circle represents a wavelength. Distances can be measured by lengthening one path length and counting the changes in the pattern of circles. Use red-orange krypton-86 light, count 1,650,763.73 changes, and you've got a meter.

lar. One tenth of a dollar is a dime ($0.10). In the metric system, the units that are 1/10 of the basic unit have the prefix *deci-*. Length in the metric system is measured in meters. Thus, *one tenth of a meter is a decimeter* (0.10 m).

In our money system, the unit that is 1/100 of a dollar is a cent ($0.01). In the metric system, the units that are 1/100 of the basic unit have the prefix *centi-*. Thus, a *centimeter is one hundredth of a meter* (0.01 m).

Even though it isn't commonly used, the unit that is 1/1000 of a dollar is called the *mill*. In the metric system, the units that are 1/1000 of the basic unit have the prefix *milli-*. Thus, a *millimeter is one thousandth of a meter* (0.001 m).

A commonly used prefix indicating 1000 of the basic units is *kilo-*. In countries using the metric system, distances are usually given in kilometers (km). The speedometers of cars indicate speed in kilometers per hour.

The quantity of a liquid or a gas is usually measured by the space it takes up in the container holding it. In the metric system, the standard measure of quantity is the liter. One liter is the amount of space enclosed within the walls of a cube measuring 10 centimeters on each edge. The volume of this cube is 10 cm × 10 cm × 10 cm = 1000 cubic centimeters. ($1000\ cm^3 = 1$ liter). Since the quantities of liquids measured in the chemistry laboratory are comparatively small, one thousandth of a liter, or one milliliter (1 ml), is used as a more convenient unit for most purposes.

The mass of 1000 cubic centimeters (cm^3) of water at 4° Celsius is one kilogram. (Later in the course you will learn why water at 4° Celsius was chosen as the standard.) Since $1\ cm^3 = 1$ ml, a liter (1000 ml) of water at 4°C has a mass of 1000 grams (g), or 1 kilogram (kg). A standard metal kilogram cylinder is kept at the International Bureau of Weights and Measures. Mass is measured by comparing with this standard mass, or reproductions of it. In the chemistry laboratory, the gram (1/1000 of a kilogram) is more frequently used to measure mass since the amounts of chemicals used are usually small.

Fig. 1-18. A cube 10 cm on an edge contains 1000 cm^3.

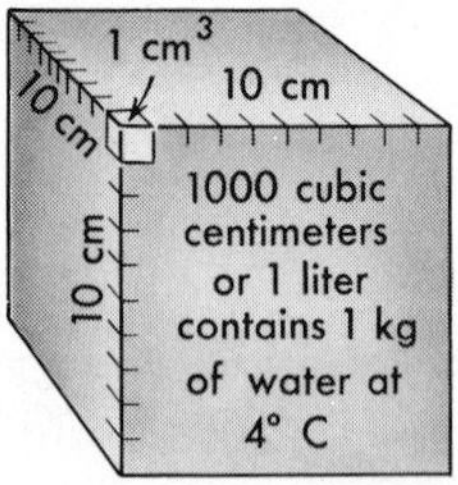

1.10 Density—an intensive property of matter

A useful relationship in chemistry is the one that combines two extensive properties of matter, namely, mass and volume. This relationship is called density. When equal volumes of different kinds of matter are compared, a characteristic number results. For example, one cubic centimeter of lead has a mass of 11.34 grams; one cubic centimeter of mercury has a mass of 13.59 grams. The density of lead, then, is 11.34 grams per cubic centimeter, and the density of mercury is 13.59 grams per cubic centimeter. ***Density*** *is defined as the*

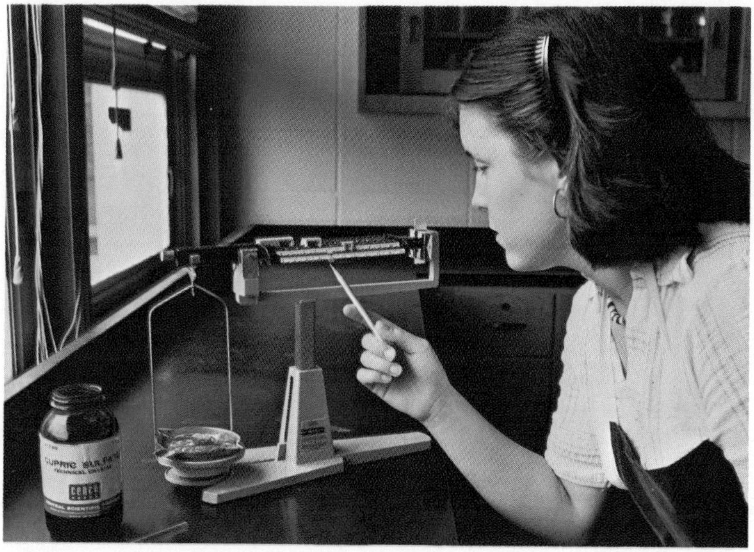

Fig. 1-19. This student is determining the mass of a chemical using a laboratory balance.

mass per unit volume of a substance. This definition is expressed in simple algebraic equation

$$D = \frac{m}{V}$$

where D represents density, m is mass, and V is volume. In this text, the unit of mass used in this ratio is the gram, and the unit of volume is either the cubic centimeter for the density of solids or liquids, or liter for the density of gases. Density in the tables will then read accordingly as grams per cubic centimeter (g/cm^3), or grams per liter (g/liter).

If you are asked to identify a certain chunk of metal in the laboratory, one of the properties that might help you is the metal's density. You would measure its mass on a platform balance, and its volume by measuring the water displaced by the metal in a graduated cylinder. Dividing the mass by the volume will give you the density. Density is an intensive property; therefore it does not depend on the amount of substance you use to determine it.

Fig. 1-20. The cork floats because it is less dense than the liquid. The metal key sinks because it is denser than the liquid. If steel is denser than sea water, why do steel ships float?

1.11 Energy

In Section 1.4, inertia was described as a property of matter. The inertia of the cannonball was greater than that of the baseball. Therefore, it takes more force to pitch the cannonball at a given speed. *When a force affects the motion of an object, work is done.* You do more work pitching a cannonball than pitching a baseball at the same speed.

This idea of work is related to the idea of energy. ***Energy*** *is defined as the capacity for doing work.* Before pitching the cannonball, you had the ability to do work stored in you. *Stored energy is called* ***potential energy.*** As you do work moving the cannonball, the potential energy in your muscles is changed into ***kinetic energy,*** *the energy of motion.*

The idea of kinetic and potential energy can be further used to interpret the behavior of matter. Water held behind a dam has potential energy because of its raised position. As the water is released from behind the dam, some of its potential energy becomes kinetic energy because of its falling motion. This falling water, if run through a turbine or over a water wheel, has the capacity to do useful work whether it is generating electricity or grinding grain. A wound watch spring also has potential energy. It stores the energy it received when it was wound. It releases this energy in the form of kinetic energy as it turns the hands of the watch.

Lifting the lid of a pot requires work. When water boils in a pot with a tight-fitting lid, the steam forces the lid open. Work is done by the steam. To do this work the following energy changes took place. The stored or potential energy of the fuel in the stove was changed to the heat energy of the flame. This heat energy was transferred to the water. The rapidly moving and close particles of water became rapidly moving and more widely separated particles of steam. The kinetic energy of steam then forced the lid open.

In the early part of the nineteenth century, horses supplied the work to bore cannon barrels. Count Rumford, an observant scientist, was in charge of making cannons for the Bavarian army. He noticed that the temperature increase of a cannon barrel as it was being bored depended upon how hard the horses worked. James Prescott Joule, another scientist, determined the exact relationship between heat energy and work. A specific amount of heat is produced by a given amount of work. This relationship supports the idea, which is now widely accepted, that the total amount of energy remains constant when it is changed from one form to another.

Fig. 1-21. At the moment when this ball changes direction, most of its kinetic energy is changed to potential energy. How is the potential energy stored?

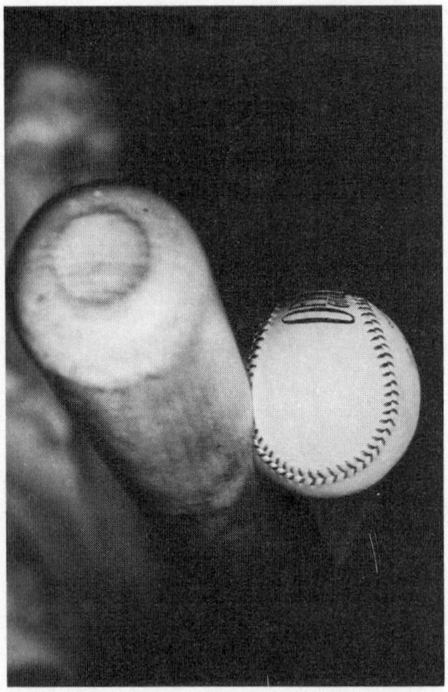

Scientists have identified other forms of energy. Visible, infrared, and ultraviolet light are forms of radiant energy we receive from the sun. Microwave radiation used in cooking, and X rays are also forms of radiant energy.

Millions of years ago, radiant energy from the sun was stored in matter by growing plants. These plants died and were converted beneath the earth's surface into the fossil fuels we use today—natural gas, crude oil, and coal. Fossil fuels are a source of chemical energy, another form of potential energy. Burning these fossil fuels releases energy directly as heat. This heat can be used to do work. Gasoline, made from crude oil, is burned in the engine of a car. The heat energy produced and converted to kinetic energy does useful work moving the car. When the car stops, the brakes convert kinetic energy into heat. Similarly, energy can be traced through changes from a source to its final form as heat.

1.12 Heat

From common experience you know that if you hold a pan of water over a source of heat energy such as a flame, the temperature of the pan and of the water rises. How could you measure the amount of heat produced when a particular substance burns? Suppose as a source of heat energy, you burn a piece of potato chip having a mass of 1.5 g. If in some way you can transfer the potato chip's heat to a given mass of water, the temperature of the water will increase. The increase in temperature is a measure of how much heat energy went into the water. However, the amount of the temperature increase is affected by the mass of water you use. If you add the potato chip's heat energy to a large mass of water, the temperature rise will be less than if you add it to a small mass of water. If you used 500 g of water and assumed that all the heat from the burning potato chip went into the water, you might find the water temperature increased from 20°C to 36°C. The increase in temperature was 36°C − 20°C = 16°C. Such an experiment reveals that measuring the amount of heat released when a substance burns requires that you know the mass of water heated and the water temperature change that takes place. The combination of these two measured quantities now gives a new, derived quantity. In the metric system, this quantity is called the *calorie*.

Why must you make this assumption?

In order to measure changes in or transfer of heat energy, the *calorie* is used as a convenient standard and will be used in this text. *The **calorie** is defined as the quantity of heat required to raise the temperature of 1 gram of water through 1 Celsius degree.* When the potato chip referred to above was burned, it raised the temperature of 500 g of water 16°C. Since each gram of water required 16 calories for the 16°C temperature rise, 500 grams of water will require 500 × 16 or 8000 calories. Thus, 8000 calories of chemical potential energy were changed to heat energy when the 1.5 grams of potato chips burned.

A larger unit of heat energy is the kilocalorie or large calorie (Calorie). 1 Cal = 1 kcal = 1000 cal. The Calorie is commonly used to indicate the energy value of foods. The heat energy given off by the potato chip was 8 Cal.

Fig. 1-22. The burning potato chip heats the water in the container. By knowing the mass of water and the temperature change, the amount of heat taken in by the water can be calculated. How do you think the design of this experiment could be improved?

1.13 Temperature and heat

Temperature and heat are different but related physical quantities. Temperature is the property that determines the direction of heat transfer. If a system, *a body of matter,* has a higher temperature than its surroundings, energy is lost by the system. For example, if you heat an iron nail in a flame, it cools to room temperature when you remove it from the flame. If the temperature of a system is lower than its surroundings, energy is gained by the system. For example, if you bring a glass of cold milk from the refrigerator into a warm room, the milk will gradually warm to room temperature.

When two systems with different temperatures are in contact, the warmer system cools as it gives up heat and the cooler system warms as it acquires heat (as long as neither system experiences a change of phase). As an example, if a heated nail is dropped into a beaker of water, the nail will cool and the water will warm until they both are the same temperature. When the temperatures of the two systems are equal, no further net transfer of heat occurs. The two systems are said to be in *thermal (heat) equilibrium. It follows that systems in thermal equilibrium have the same temperature.*

Heat flows from a region of high heat intensity to a region of low heat intensity.

In Section 1.8, we said that temperature is an intensive property of a system. A small glass of water can have the same temperature as a large body of water. If you want to cool water, however, you must remove heat from the water. The amount of heat you must remove to produce a desired temperature change depends upon the amount of water present. To reduce the temperature of 1 gram of water from 21°C to 20°C, you must remove one calorie of heat. To reduce the temperature of 1000 grams of water from 21°C to 20°C requires the removal of 1000 calories of heat. From this example you can see that heat is an extensive property.

Methods of Science

1.14 Uncertainty in measurement

Suppose all the members of your class measured the object shown in the illustration in the margin with a metric ruler. You probably would all agree that its length is between 7.1 cm and 7.2 cm. However, you might not all agree on the value of the next digit. Some of you might say it looks like 0.07 cm, others 0.08 cm, still others 0.09 cm. The last digit, then, is uncertain. Even so, it represents useful information. It tells us that the object is longer than 7.1 cm but shorter than 7.2 cm. We might record this value as 7.18 cm, understanding that there is uncertainty in the last digit of the measurement. The recorded value consists of figures that have physical significance. We call these digits *significant figures*. In a number, ***significant figures*** *are all digits known with certainty along with the first digit that is uncertain.*

Fig. 1-23. This student is measuring the width of a block of wood. The 1 cm mark is lined up with one edge of the block. The distance is read on the scale at the other edge. Then, 1 cm is subtracted from the distance read. Why do you think the student followed this procedure?

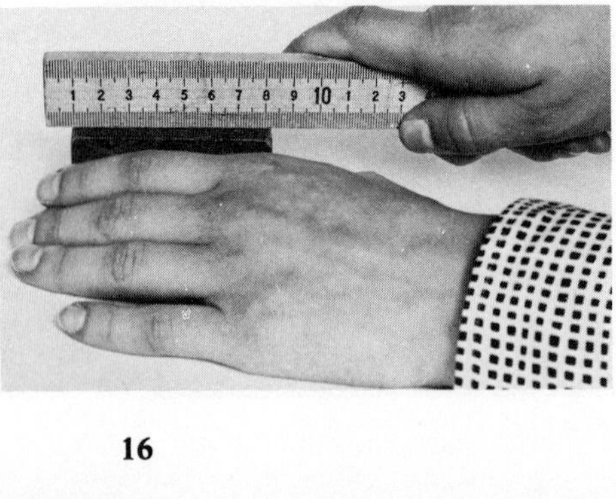

Many of you will probably use calculators in doing problems in chemistry. A calculation such as a division or multiplication may produce digits all the way across the readout of your calculator. You must keep in mind that all those numbers are not significant figures. The results of a multiplication or a division should include no more figures than the least number of significant figures in your original data.

If you use a micrometer to measure the diameter of a small metal cylinder, your results might be 6.531 mm with the last digit uncertain. Using a ruler for the same measurement, only one digit is certain. With the micrometer, three digits are certain. The certainty of a measurement depends upon the instrument you use.

Suppose you took several measurements of the cylinder's diameter at the same spot on the object using a micrometer each time in exactly the same way. These values for the diameter of the object might be 6.533 mm, 6.530 mm, 6.532 mm, 6.532 mm. ***Precision** is the agreement between numerical values of two or more measurements that have been made in the same way.* Precision refers to the reproducibility of measurement data. When you buy a measuring instrument, its precision is often indicated in some way.

If you compare your measurements with those of another student who measured the same object using an equally precise micrometer, you might find that your results disagree. Either one or both of your micrometers might not be accurate. ***Accuracy** means the nearness of a measurement to its accepted value.* To settle your disagreement, you could compare each micrometer with an accepted standard for a millimeter or a centimeter. In this way you could be sure that your micrometers are accurate.

The terms *accuracy* and *precision* are often confused in common usage. In science, however, it is important to make a clear distinction between them. You should learn to use these terms correctly.

No measurement of a physical quantity is absolutely certain.

1.15 Scientific laws and theories

The word *law* is commonly used in several ways. Human laws are rules of conduct enforced by some authority. If you break a traffic law, you can expect to get a ticket and suffer some penalty. In science, a ***law (or principle)** is a generalization that describes behavior in nature.* For example, suppose you observe that every time you take a definite mass of iron and combine it chemically with sulfur, a definite mass of sulfur is used. Suppose you observe that many other substances behave in the same way. You might state this relationship as a law of definite composition: Every compound has a definite composition by mass. In Section 2.10, you will study this law, which was first observed by Louis Proust.

Scientists are often interested in explaining how a set of observations occur. *A reasonable explanation of observations is called a **theory.*** John Dalton's atomic theory was used to explain the law of definite composition and other chemical laws. You will study the atomic theory in Chapter 3.

Theories often involve the use of an imaginary model, or a mental picture, that helps scientists explain the observed behavior. In Dalton's atomic theory, matter is pictured as made of small particles called atoms. If the theory is true, matter should behave in certain predictable ways. Experiments based upon these predictions test the theory. For example, based upon the atomic theory, Dalton predicted the law of multiple proportions. (You will study this law in Section 7.10.) He then experimented and discovered his prediction was right. If his predictions had not been right, his experiment might have been at fault. Or his theory might have needed changing. However, experimental support for his theory is one reason it was quickly accepted by other scientists.

1.16 Certainty in science

Albert Einstein's idea that matter and energy are different forms of the same thing led to the development of nuclear power. When asked how scientists work, he replied, "If you want to know the essence of scientific method, don't listen to what a scientist may tell you. Watch what he does."

If you took Einstein's advice, you would probably see that most scientists start solving a problem by going to the library. They start by finding out what other scientists have written about the problem. This step is important because it reduces duplication of effort. Some other scientist may already have solved the problem. If that is the case, the scientist may check the other scientist's results and go on to another problem. However, if the problem has not been solved, the scientist may experiment. At this point, the scientist would probably try to think of possible solutions to the problem. *Possible solutions are called **hypotheses**.* The scientist then experiments to test each hypothesis. After completing their experiments, most scientists publish a report of what they did and their results, for study by other scientists.

Science is a way of finding out about nature. It involves creative thinking and imagination as well as collecting facts and doing experiments. It is a way of doing things so as to reduce human errors as much as possible. Even so, some mistakes are made. For example, there is the case of polywater. Suppose all the clear, liquid water around you turned to a thick syrupy liquid that didn't boil or freeze. In 1962, Russian scientists reported that they had discovered just such a strange form of water. At first, the news was not taken seriously. Then in 1969, an American, repeating the Russian experiment, obtained similar results. He named the new liquid *polywater.*

Fig. 1-24. Photograph of polywater that appeared in a scientific magazine.

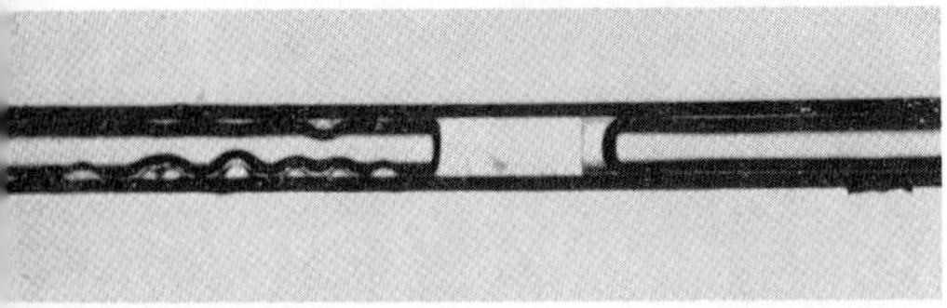

Hundreds of scientists became involved in studying polywater. Many articles on the subject were published in scientific journals. In the case of polywater, the idea was so sensational that even popular newspapers carried such stories as, "Polywater Threatening Life on Earth?"

Looking back, these results were suspicious. There was little agreement between different scientists' results. Some had trouble making polywater. Those who succeeded found that its physical properties varied according to who had prepared it and how it was prepared. But supporters of the polywater idea said there was reason for disagreement. Polywater was made in small quantities in thin tubes. Each tube had a hole down the center finer than a human hair. It was nearly impossible to remove the thick liquid from these tubes.

More and more scientists suspected that they were mistaken about polywater. When samples were tested carefully, varying amounts of impurities such as salt, sweat, and grease were found in all samples. When scientists took great precautions to avoid all contamination, they could not prepare polywater.

Finally, the American and Russian scientists who originated the idea were convinced that they had been mistaken. In 1973, they published the results of experiments that led them to their new conclusions. The idea of polywater went down the drain.

SUMMARY

Chemistry is what chemists do. Chemistry is also the body of chemical knowledge resulting from the activities of chemists. Useful chemical products may prove to be harmful because they endanger the health of individuals or pollute the environment. Protective agencies have been set up as one form of control.

Matter is anything that occupies space and has mass. Inertia is a property of matter that tends to resist a change in its position or motion. Under ordinary conditions of temperature and pressure, matter exists in three phases: solid, liquid, or gas.

Physical properties are those that can be determined without changing the identity of the material. Chemical properties are those that describe the behavior of materials in chemical reactions. Chemical reactions are processes that change the chemical identity of materials.

Length is the measure of the shortest distance between two points. Mass is the measure of the quantity of matter. Weight is a measure of the force of attraction between a body and the earth. Time is the duration of an event. Temperature measures the heat intensity or degree of hotness or coldness of matter.

Extensive properties of matter are additive. They depend on the quantities being measured. Examples are mass, length, and volume. Intensive properties are not additive. They *do not* depend on the quantities of matter being measured. Examples are temperature and density.

The metric system of measurement is a decimal system used in scientific work. In this system, the basic unit of length is the meter; the basic unit of mass is the gram. The volumes of liquids and gases are commonly measured in liters. A system of prefixes is used to provide larger and smaller units of measure.

Density of matter is mass per unit volume. In chemistry, the densities of solids and liquids are usually expressed in g/cm^3; the densities of gases are expressed in g/liter.

Energy is the capacity for doing work. Potential energy is the work capacity stored in matter owing to its position or orientation in space, or because of its chemical composition. Kinetic energy is the work capacity of matter owing to its motion.

Heat is a form of energy. Temperature (heat intensity) is measured in degrees Celsius. The quantity of heat is measured in calories. A calorie is the quantity of heat required to raise the temperature of one gram of water one Celsius degree. Heat flows from a body of higher temperature to one of lower temperature. Thermal equilibrium is established in a system when all parts reach the same temperature.

Significant figures are all the digits of a measurement known with certainty along with one digit that is estimated or uncertain. Precision is the agreement between measurements that have been made in the same way. Accuracy is the nearness of a measurement to an accepted value.

In science, a law or principle is a generalization that describes behavior in nature. A theory is a reasonable explanation of observed behavior in nature. An hypothesis is a supposition of how matter or energy behaves that is based on limited observations or incomplete information.

QUESTIONS

Group A

1. In your own words, write what the word *chemistry* means to you. Compare your definition with what you read in the second paragraph of Section 1.1.
2. Briefly state your own reasons why chemistry is important as a part of your education.
3. Make a list of careers that require knowledge of chemistry that are not included in the photo essay on pages 4 and 5.
4. What is the purpose of an experiment in science?
5. What distinguishes (*a*) a solid from a liquid? (*b*) a liquid from a gas?
6. List some properties of materials that are classified as physical properties.
7. List some properties of materials that are classified as chemical properties.
8. What are four fundamental quantities used in chemistry, and in what basic metric unit is each measured?
9. What metric prefixes are commonly used in chemistry?
10. What disadvantages may be encountered in your everyday use of the metric system instead of the English system of weights and measures?
11. What are the advantages of the metric system over the English system of measurement in scientific work?
12. (*a*) What is the distinction between heat and temperature? (*b*) In what unit is each measured?

Group B

13. Prepare a list of new chemical products that you have read about in newspapers or magazines.
14. (*a*) List five common materials used in the kitchen of your home. (*b*) What properties does each have that makes it suitable for its particular use?
15. When a porous solid like a sponge is compressed, what actually occurs?
16. What determines whether a certain property of a material is classified as physical or chemical?
17. Why does the sense of touch give the most direct evidence of the existence of matter?
18. Volume is a property of a material. (*a*) Is it a specific property? (*b*) Is mass a specific property? (*c*) Is the ratio of mass to volume a specific property? Explain.
19. Distinguish between an intensive and an extensive property of matter.
20. The hobby chemistry set has introduced chemistry to many young people long before high school days. Can you present arguments for and against the use of such sets? How would you advise a younger member of the family in the use of chemicals? Before you attempt to answer these two questions, review the Techniques and Safety Sketches in your laboratory book shown on the two pages that precede the first experiment for some suggestions.

unmixing mixtures, 1

Often in your laboratory experiments you will need to separate mixtures. Some mixtures of liquids can be separated by distillation. This method is frequently used by research chemists to separate the products of a reaction (1). A mixture of two solids can be separated by using some difference in physical properties. A mixture of iron and sulfur (2) can be separated by a magnet because iron is attracted and sulfur is not (3).

1

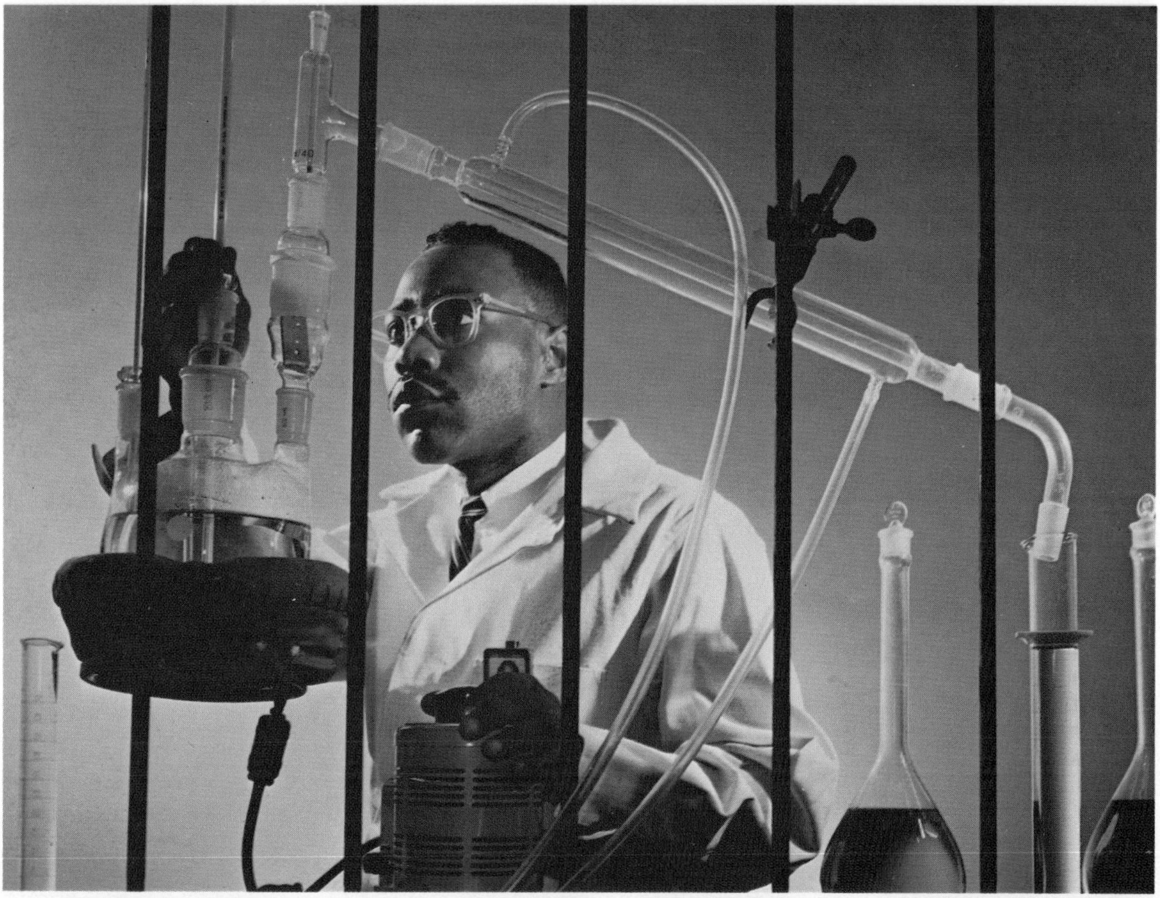

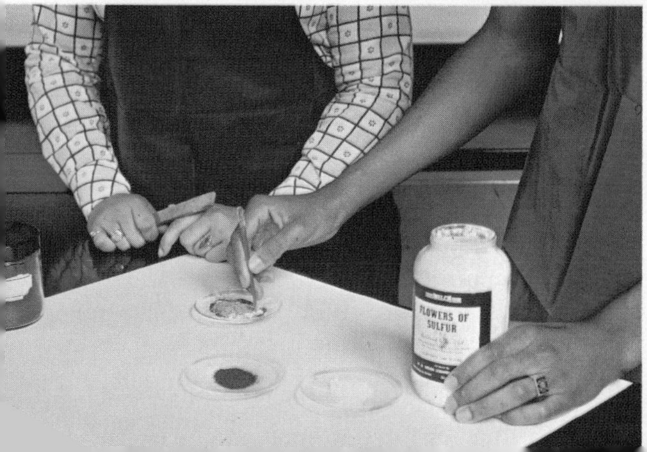

3

If one solid melts at a different temperature from the other, one can be melted and poured off (4) without disturbing the settled solid. Notice that the glass rod is used correctly to guide the flow of liquid. Two solids can be separated by shaking them with a solvent that dissolves one of them (5). Even if neither solid is soluble in a liquid, two solids can be separated if they settle at different rates (6).

Fine particles of an insoluble solid can be separated from a liquid by filtration. The black solid (7) is stopped by the filter paper while the blue solution passes through. A solid dissolved in a liquid can be recovered by evaporation (8). A dissolved solid can be separated from a liquid by distillation (9). Both the solid and the liquid can be recovered.

4

5

6

7

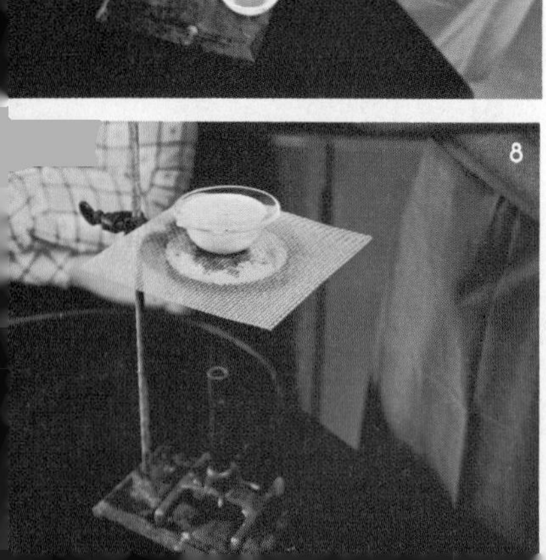
8

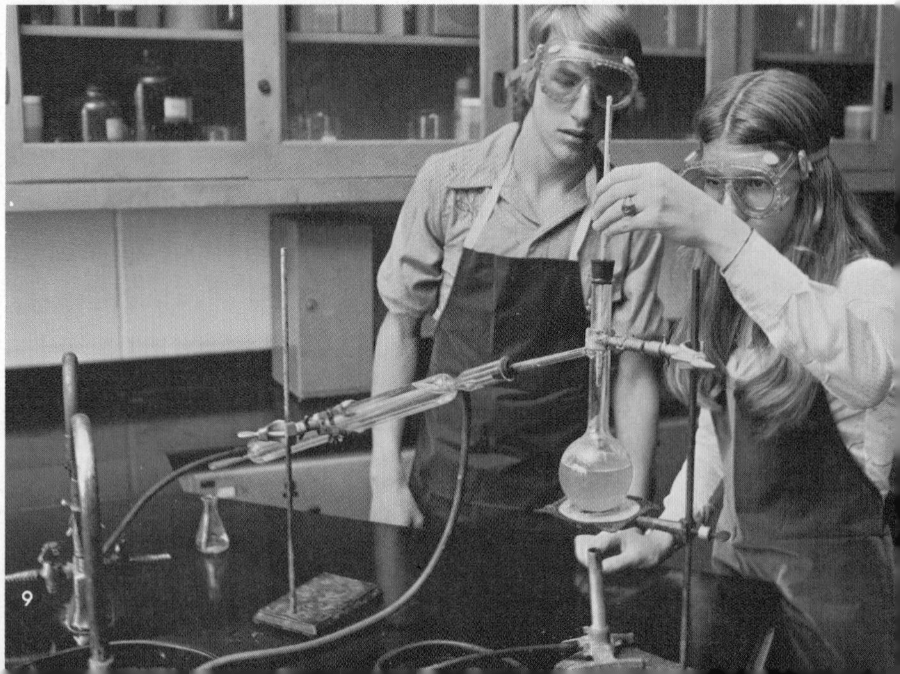
9

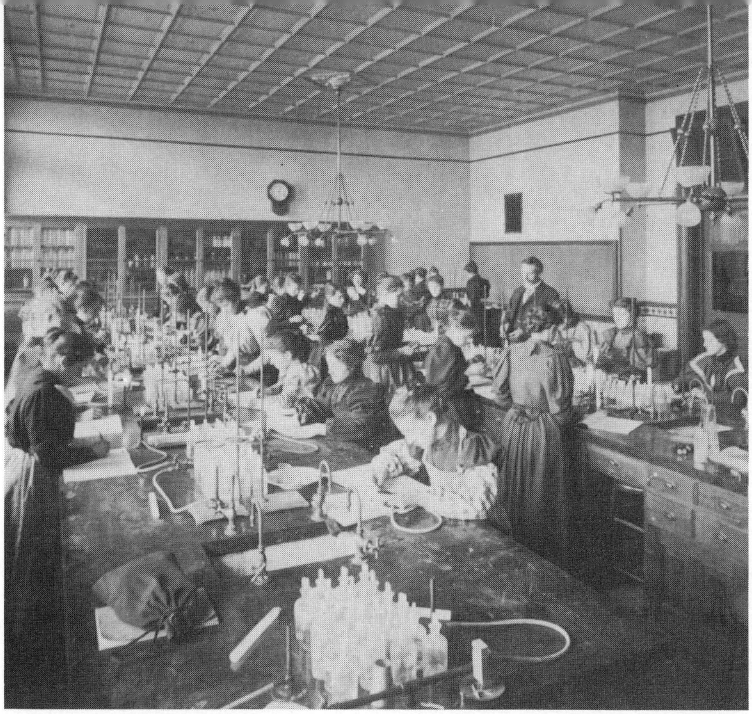

chapter 2

MATTER AND ITS CHANGES

The way it was. A typical chemistry laboratory scene around 1899. (See Question 36 on page 39.)

Composition of Matter

2.1 Classes of matter

The first chapter gave you some idea of what chemistry is all about. You saw how it developed as an experimental science. The basic tools and methods used in chemistry were briefly described there. In more specific language, however, chemistry is the study of (*1*) the structure and composition of matter, (*2*) the changes that occur in the composition of this matter, and (*3*) the mechanisms that bring about these changes. Since the subject of the study is matter, let us first concern ourselves with what matter is and go on from there.

Matter is anything that occupies space and has mass. It includes all materials found in nature. Some materials are made up of parts that are not alike. How they differ may or may not be readily apparent. *Matter that has parts with different properties is* ***heterogeneous*** (het-er-oh-*jee*-nee-us). Granite, a common rock, is heterogeneous in this sense. Distinctly different parts are easily observed.

Other materials appear uniform throughout—all parts are alike. The properties of any one part are similar to the properties of all other parts. *Matter that has similar properties throughout is* ***homogeneous*** (hoh-muh-*jee*-nee-us). Sugar and ordinary table salt are examples of homogeneous materials.

The many different kinds of matter in the world around us are the materials with which chemists work. It would be very difficult and time-consuming to study materials without first organizing them into similar groups. We already know that matter exists in three different phases as solids, liquids, and

Fig. 2-1. Both heterogeneous and homogeneous materials are shown in this geode. The outer crust is a mixture of many materials. The inner crystals are quartz, a pure substance.

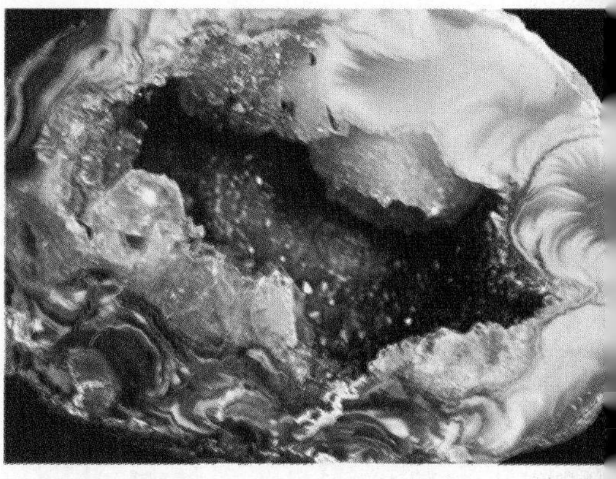

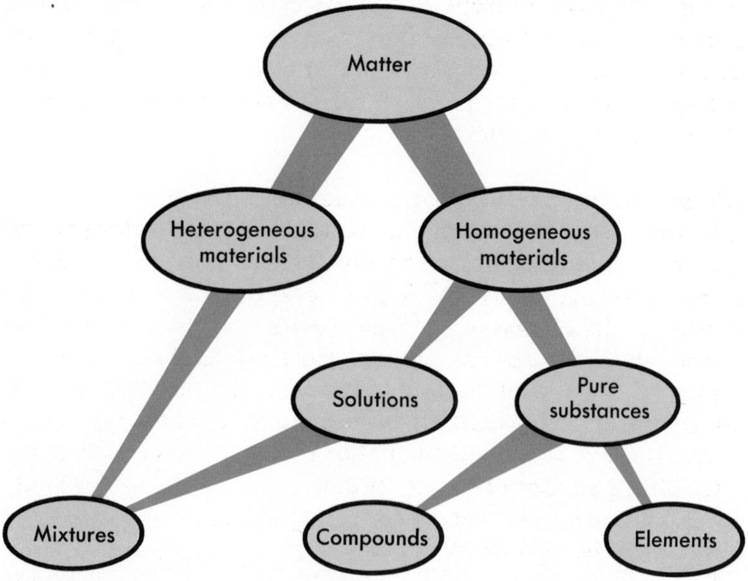

Fig. 2-2. All matter is divided into three general classes: elements, compounds, and mixtures. Solutions are homogeneous mixtures.

gases. Materials may also be grouped into three general classes on the basis of their properties. These classes are *elements, compounds,* and *mixtures.* These and other ways of classifying matter make the study of chemistry easier. See Figure 2-2. This diagram will be helpful as you study Sections 2.2 and 2.3.

2.2 Mixtures

Suppose we examine a piece of granite closely with a hand lens. Three different crystalline materials can be seen. They are quartz, feldspar, and mica. The properties of each differ greatly. Granite is a heterogeneous material, having parts with different properties. It is a *mixture.* One part of a piece of quartz has the same properties as every other part. This fact is also true of feldspar and of mica. Each of these components of granite is a homogeneous material. Heterogeneous materials are mixtures of homogeneous materials.

Heterogeneous materials are mixtures.

A mixture does not have a set of unique properties. Instead, its properties are a combination of the properties of its homogeneous parts. But all mixtures are not heterogeneous. When sugar is dissolved in water, the resulting solution has similar properties throughout. Thus the solution is homogeneous. The amount of sugar or water may be increased, but we will still have a homogeneous mixture of the two materials. The solution has the sweet taste of the sugar it contains. The water may be removed by evaporation and the sugar recovered in its original form. Solutions are homogeneous mixtures.

Some homogeneous materials are mixtures.

Air is a solution of gases. It is a mixture composed principally of nitrogen, oxygen, argon, carbon dioxide, and water

Solutions are mixtures that are homogeneous.

vapor. Each gas present in the air displays its own unique properties. Alloys, combinations of metals (or certain nonmetals), are usually solid solutions. *A **mixture** is a material consisting of two or more kinds of matter, each retaining its own characteristic properties.*

2.3 Substances include compounds and elements

It has already been stated that materials with similar properties throughout are homogeneous. In chemistry, such homogeneous materials are called *pure substances,* or simply *substances. A **substance** is a homogeneous material consisting of one particular kind of matter.* Both the sugar and the water of a sugar-water solution are substances in this sense. Granite is not a substance because it has a combination of the properties of quartz, feldspar, and mica. On the other hand, the properties of sugar cannot be attributed to anything but the sugar itself. They stem from its particular composition. *A substance has a definite chemical composition.*

Mixtures are not substances in a chemical sense. Elements and compounds are.

Suppose we place a small quantity of sugar in a test tube and heat it over a low flame. The substance melts and changes color. Finally a black residue remains in the bottom of the test tube. Drops of a clear colorless liquid appear around the cool open end. The black substance has the properties of carbon and the liquid has the properties of water. The properties of the sugar no longer exist. In fact, the sugar no longer exists. Instead, we have two different substances, carbon and water.

The decomposition of sugar by heat is an example of a chemical process.

Each time the experiment is repeated, the sugar decomposes in the same way yielding the same proportions of carbon and water. Sugar is recognized as a complex substance showing a consistent composition. It is an example of a *compound. A **compound** is a substance that may be decomposed into two or more simpler substances by ordinary chemical means.*

Chemists are able to decompose water into two simpler substances, hydrogen and oxygen. Thus water is also a compound. Chemists have not succeeded in decomposing carbon, hydrogen, or oxygen into any simpler substances. We conclude that these are elementary substances or *elements. **Elements** are substances that cannot be further decomposed by ordinary chemical means.* Elementary substances cannot be broken down or simplified by the usual methods used to cause chemical reactions. These methods include application of heat, light, or electric energy.

Fig. 2-3. Plutonium being prepared for fabrication into atomic reactor fuel.

2.4 The known elements

One of the fascinating facts of science is that all known matter is composed of approximately 100 elements. A few elementary substances, such as gold, silver, copper, and sulfur, have been known since ancient times. During the Middle Ages and the Renaissance, more elements were discovered. Through the

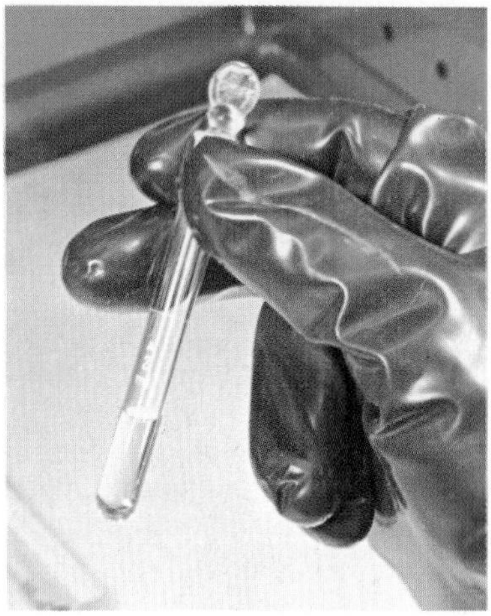

Fig. 2-4. A vial containing californium, element number 98. This transuranium element is produced by bombarding plutonium with neutrons in a nuclear reactor.

Fig. 2-5. James Harris, a chemist at the Lawrence Radiation Laboratory in California, prepares target material for the creation of element 104.

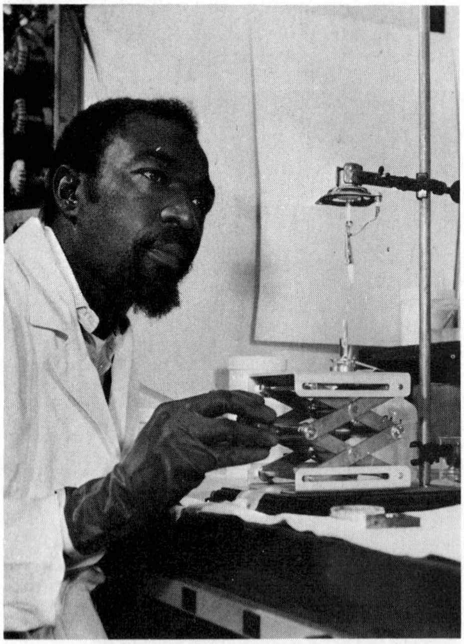

years, improved research techniques have enabled scientists to add to the list of elements.

There are 106 known elements at the time of this writing. In 1976, a group of Russian scientists announced their discovery (by synthesis) of element 107. This claim has not been verified by other scientists and is viewed with skepticism by American scientists who have specialized in the search for new elements. The 92 elements ranging from hydrogen to uranium are traditionally known as *natural* elements. They make up the pre-Atomic Age list of known elements.

In the decade before World War II, a great experimental study of atomic structure was undertaken. Enrico Fermi, an Italian theoretical physicist, stated that it should be possible to prepare the ninety-third and ninety-fourth elements from uranium. Element 93 was first produced in the laboratories of the University of California, Berkeley, in 1940. It was named *neptunium* for the planet Neptune. This planet is beyond the planet Uranus just as element 93 is beyond uranium (element 92) on the list of elements. Later, element 94 was produced in the same laboratories. It was given the name *plutonium* for the planet Pluto, which is beyond Neptune.

These triumphs were followed by the production of *americium* (am-er-*ih*-see-um) named for America, *curium* (*ku*-ree-um) named in honor of Marie Curie, *berkelium* (*berk*-lee-um) for Berkeley (the site of the University of California), and *californium* for the University and the State. More recently *einsteinium* named after Albert Einstein, *fermium* named for Enrico Fermi, and *mendelevium* (men-del-*ev*-eeum) named for Dmitri Mendeleyev brought the total to 101.

In 1957, a team of American, British, and Swedish scientists working at the Nobel Institute in Sweden announced the discovery of element 102. They suggested the name *nobelium*. Careful experiments by other scientists, however, failed to confirm their discovery.

In 1958, a research group at Lawrence Radiation Laboratory of the University of California produced *nobelium* and identified it by chemical means. This group retained the name *nobelium* for element 102, to honor Alfred Nobel. Nobel made a significant contribution to the advancement of science through his Nobel Prizes.

In 1961, element 103 was produced by scientists at the Lawrence Radiation Laboratory. The name *lawrencium* has been assigned to element 103. It honors Dr. Ernest O. Lawrence, the inventor of the cyclotron (a kind of "atom smasher") and founder of the laboratory in which the element was first produced.

Russian scientists reported the production of element 104 in 1964. They suggested the name *kurchatovium* for the Russian physicist I. V. Kurchatov. However, other scientists have not succeeded in duplicating the Russian experiments and so the report remains unverified. The Lawrence Radiation Laboratory group produced element 104 in 1968 by several different methods. They proposed the name *rutherfordium* after Ernest Rutherford, a British atomic scientist. Both *kurchatovium* and *rutherfordium* are unofficial names for element 104. A permanent name will be assigned when it is determined which group of scientists actually first produced the element.

A similar situation exists at the time of this writing with respect to elements 105 and 106. In February 1970, Russian scientists reported the synthesis of element 105. They proposed the name *niels bohrium* after Niels Bohr, a Danish atomic scientist. In April of that same year, American scientists at the Lawrence Radiation Laboratory reported the synthesis of element 105. The American group proposed the name *hahnium* after Otto Hahn, a German physical chemist who was one of the discoverers of nuclear fission. *Hahnium* and *niels bohrium* are unofficial names for element 105.

In 1974, the Russian group claimed the discovery of element 106. A counterclaim to the synthesis of element 106 was entered by the American group. To date, neither team has proposed a name for this element.

Fig. 2-6. Sulfur (top) is a nonmetallic element that occurs as yellow rhombic crystals in its ordinary form. The metallic element gallium (center) occurs as gray-black orthorhombic crystals. Mercury (bottom) is the only metallic element that is liquid at room temperature.

2.5 Two general classes of elements

Elements differ enough in their properties so that chemists recognize two general classes, *metals* and *nonmetals*.

Metals. Some elements have a *luster* (shine like silver). They reflect heat and light readily. They conduct heat and electricity remarkably well. Some are *ductile* (can be drawn into wire). Some are *malleable* (can be hammered into thin sheets). Elements that have such properties are known as **metals.** Some examples of metals are gold, silver, copper, zinc, sodium, potassium, titanium, magnesium, calcium, and aluminum. At room temperature, mercury is a liquid metal.

Nonmetals. These elements are usually poor conductors of heat and electricity. They cannot be hammered into sheets or drawn into wire because they are usually too brittle. Sulfur is an example of a nonmetal. Some nonmetals such as iodine, carbon, and phosphorus are solid at room temperature. Bromine is a liquid nonmetal. Others, such as oxygen, nitrogen, chlorine, and neon are gases.

Some elements have certain properties characteristic of metals and other properties characteristic of nonmetals. Arsenic, antimony, silicon, and germanium are examples. They are sometimes called ***metalloids.***

2.6 Chemical symbols

Jöns Jaköb Berzelius (1779–1848), a Swedish chemist, was the first to use letters as symbols for elements. These letter sym-

The first letter of a symbol is always capitalized.

The second letter of a two-letter symbol is never capitalized.

bols replaced the small circles containing identifying marks which John Dalton used to indicate different elements. Berzelius used the first letter of the name of an element as its symbol. For example, the letter **O** is the symbol for oxygen, and the letter **H** is the symbol for hydrogen.

There are over 100 elements and only 26 letters in our alphabet. Thus, the names of several elements must begin with the same letter. In such cases, Berzelius added a second letter whose sound is conspicuous when the name of the element is pronounced. For example, the symbol for carbon is **C;** for calcium, **Ca;** for chlorine, **Cl;** for chromium, **Cr;** and for cobalt, **Co.** The first letter of a symbol is *always* capitalized, but the second letter of a symbol is *never* capitalized. For example, **Co** is the symbol for cobalt; CO is the formula for a compound called carbon monoxide. This compound is composed of the elements carbon and oxygen.

In several cases, the symbol for an element is derived from the Latin name of the element. For example, the symbol for iron is **Fe,** from the Latin *ferrum.* **Pb,** the symbol for lead, comes from the Latin *plumbum.* The symbols for silver, **Ag,** and sodium, **Na,** come from the Latin, *argentum* and *natrium.* Some common elements and their symbols are listed in Table 2-1.

Table 2-1

COMMON ELEMENTS AND THEIR SYMBOLS

Name	Symbol
aluminum	Al
antimony	Sb
arsenic	As
barium	Ba
bismuth	Bi
bromine	Br
calcium	Ca
carbon	C
chlorine	Cl
chromium	Cr
cobalt	Co
copper	Cu
fluorine	F
gold	Au
hydrogen	H
iodine	I
iron	Fe
lead	Pb
magnesium	Mg
manganese	Mn
mercury	Hg
nickel	Ni
nitrogen	N
oxygen	O
phosphorus	P
platinum	Pt
potassium	K
silicon	Si
silver	Ag
sodium	Na
strontium	Sr
sulfur	S
tin	Sn
titanium	Ti
tungsten	W
zinc	Zn

2.7 Significance of a symbol

A chemical symbol is more than an abbreviation; it contains quantitative information. When we use the symbol **K,** it not only means potassium but also stands for *one atom* of potassium. The expression **2K** means 2 atoms of potassium; **5K** means 5 atoms of potassium. Similarly, **Fe** means 1 atom of iron; **3Fe,** 3 atoms of iron; and **10Fe,** 10 atoms of iron. The atom is the smallest unit of an element that can enter into combination with other elements. The chemist uses different kinds of atoms to build chemical compounds. The symbol of an element will acquire additional meaning for you as your study of chemistry progresses.

2.8 The earth's elemental composition

Approximately 90 elements are known to occur in a free or combined state in the earth's crust in measurable amounts. The atmosphere consists almost entirely of two elements, nitrogen and oxygen. Water, which covers a great portion of the surface of the earth, is a compound of hydrogen and oxygen. Natural water also contains many dissolved substances.

Only about 30 elements are fairly common. Table 2-2 shows the relative distribution (by weight) of the 10 most abundant elements in the atmosphere, lakes, rivers, oceans, and the solid earth's crust.

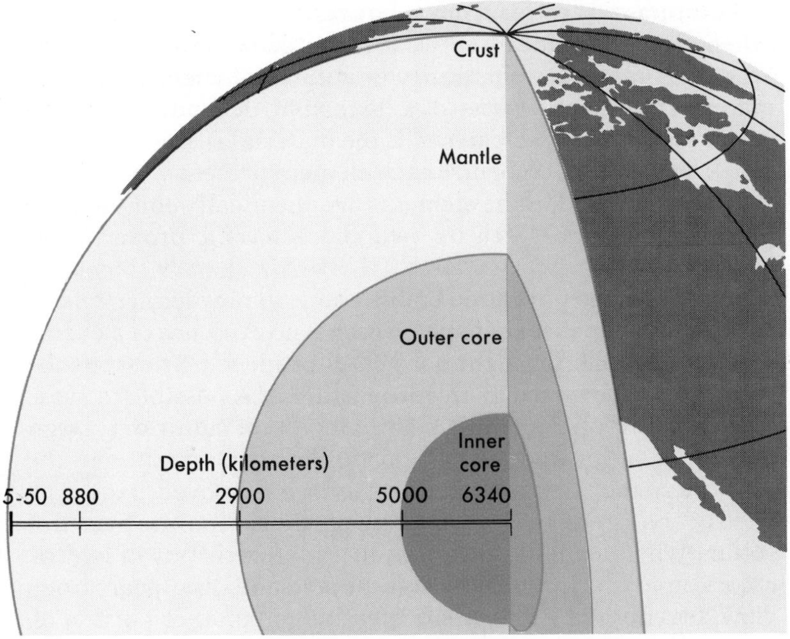

Fig. 2-7. Regions of the interior of the earth.

Table 2-2

COMPOSITION OF SURFACE ENVIRONMENT	
Element	Distribution (by weight)
oxygen	49.5%
silicon	25.8%
aluminum	7.5%
iron	4.7%
calcium	3.4%
sodium	2.6%
potassium	2.4%
magnesium	1.9%
hydrogen	0.9%
titanium	0.6%
all other elements	0.7%

Some elements in Table 2-2 would change positions relative to other elements if the table were based on factors other than weight. On a basis of relative number of particles, for example, hydrogen would appear ahead of aluminum.

The solid crust of the earth is the foundation of all of human existence. Yet it makes up only about 0.4% of the total mass of the earth and less than 1% of its volume. See Figure 2-7. The mantle accounts for about 67.2% and the core 32.4% of the earth's total mass.

The two major elements in the solid crust are oxygen and silicon (in combined form). Together they account for almost 75% of the weight of the continental crust. Eight elements (in combined form) make up over 98% of the weight of the continental crust. These are listed in Table 2-3 on the next page.

These eight common elements, along with the less common ones, combine in many ways to produce the more than 2000 different minerals that are found in the solid earth's crust.

Scientists of the Smithsonian Institution have estimated that five elements account for more than 94% of the weight of the total solid earth. (This includes the continental crust, mantle, and core.) These elements are given in Table 2-4.

The mantle is believed to consist almost entirely of compounds of four elements—magnesium, iron, silicon, and oxygen. Most earth scientists agree that the earth's core contains about 85% elemental iron, about 7% nickel, and 8% of a mixture of silicon, cobalt, and sulfur.

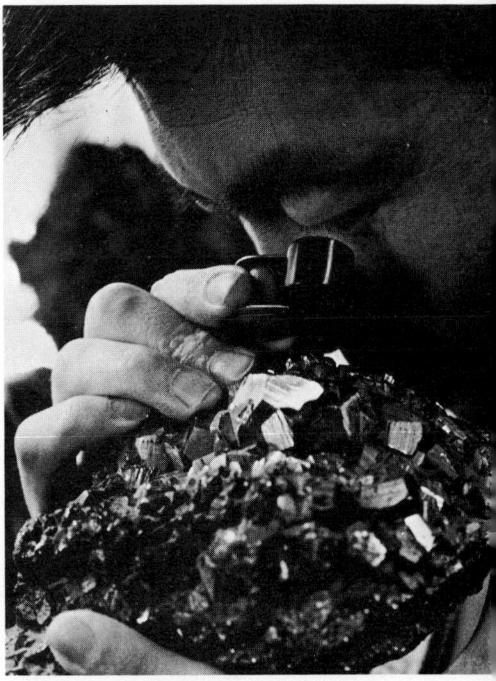

Fig. 2-8. The earth's crust contains more than 2000 different minerals. A Stanford University scientist uses a hand lens to examine the surface features of pyrite (FeS_2), the most common iron sulfide mineral.

Table 2-3

COMPOSITION OF THE CONTINENTAL CRUST	
Element	Distribution (by weight)
oxygen	46.6%
silicon	27.7%
aluminum	8.1%
iron	5.0%
calcium	3.6%
sodium	2.8%
potassium	2.6%
magnesium	2.1%

Table 2-4

COMPOSITION OF THE SOLID EARTH	
Element	Distribution (by weight)
iron	34.6%
oxygen	29.5%
silicon	15.2%
magnesium	12.7%
nickel	2.4%

2.9 Compounds differ from mixtures

When matter is made up of two or more elements, the elements are either mixed mechanically or combined chemically. The material is either a *mixture* or a *compound,* depending on what has happened to the elements. If the material is a mixture, the properties used to recognize each element present will persist. On the other hand, if the elements are chemically combined, a complex substance with its own characteristic properties is observed.

Suppose some powdered sulfur and iron powder are mixed thoroughly on a sheet of paper. There is no evidence of a chemical reaction; neither light nor heat is produced. The two substances may be mixed in any proportion. It is possible to use a large amount of iron and a small amount of sulfur or a large portion of sulfur and a small portion of iron.

As the paper containing this mixture is moved back and forth over a strong magnet, the iron particles separate from the sulfur. When a small portion of the mixture is put in hydrochloric acid, the iron reacts with the acid and disappears from view, leaving the sulfur unaffected. When another portion of the mixture is put in liquid carbon disulfide, the sulfur dissolves leaving the iron powder unchanged.

In each of these tests, the properties of iron and sulfur persist. This is typical of a mixture; the *components* (substances of which it is made) do not lose their identity. They may be mixed in any proportion without showing any evidence of chemical activity.

It is possible to cause the iron and sulfur to react chemically and form a compound. Suppose these two elements are mixed in the ratio of 7 g iron to 4 g sulfur and the mixture is heated strongly in a test tube over a Bunsen burner flame. With a rise in temperature the mixture begins to glow. Even after its removal from the flame, the mixture continues to react and the whole mass soon becomes red hot. *Both heat and light are produced during the chemical reaction in which sulfur and iron combine and form a compound.*

After the reaction has ceased and the product has been removed, careful examination shows that it no longer resembles either the iron or the sulfur. Each element has lost its characteristic properties. The iron cannot be removed by a magnet. The sulfur cannot be dissolved out of the product with carbon disulfide. In the original mixture, hydrochloric acid reacted chemically with the iron and odorless hydrogen gas was produced. Hydrochloric acid also reacts chemically with this new product and a gas is again produced. However, in this reaction, the gas is distinctly different from that formed in the previous reaction. This gas has an odor. It is *hydrogen sulfide,* a poisonous gas that is notorious for its rotten-egg odor. This different product gives evidence that a new substance with a new set of

Table 2-5

DIFFERENCES BETWEEN A MIXTURE AND A COMPOUND	
Mixture	Compound
1. In a mixture, the components may be present in any proportion.	1. In a compound, the constituents always have a definite proportion by weight.
2. In the preparation of a mixture, there is no evidence of any chemical action taking place.	2. In the preparation of a compound, evidence of chemical action is usually apparent (light, heat, etc.)
3. In a mixture, the components do not lose their identity. They may be separated by physical means.	3. In a compound, the constituents lose their identity. They can be separated by chemical means only.

properties was formed during the reaction between the iron and sulfur.

Each time this reaction occurs between iron and sulfur, the same new substance is formed. It is found by chemical analysis to consist of iron and sulfur in the same weight relationship. *A compound is always composed of the same elements in a definite proportion by weight.* For example, the compound we are now discussing, which is called *iron sulfide,* is composed of 63.5% iron and 36.5% sulfur. This composition represents a weight ratio of seven parts iron to four parts sulfur. If we had started the reaction with eight parts of iron and four parts of sulfur, one part by weight of iron would remain as an unused surplus after the reaction was completed. Differences between mixtures and compounds are summarized in Table 2-5.

Analysis is the process of identifying the kind and quantity of each element in a compound.

2.10 Law of definite composition

Louis Proust (1755–1826), a French chemist, was one of the first to observe that elements combine with one another in a definite ratio by weight. About 50 years later, Jean Servais Stas, a Belgian chemist, performed a series of precise experiments which confirmed this observation. We now call Proust's observation the ***law of definite composition:*** *Every compound has a definite composition by weight.*

Using the law of definite composition, a manufacturer of chemical compounds can determine precisely the quantity of each constituent required to prepare a specific compound.

2.11 Common examples of mixtures and compounds

In Section 2.2, we described air as a mixture. Its composition varies somewhat in different localities. Other familiar examples of mixtures include substances such as baking powders, concrete, and various kinds of soil. There is practically no limit to the number of possible mixtures. They may be made up of two or more elements, of two or more compounds, or of both elements and compounds. For example, brass is a mix-

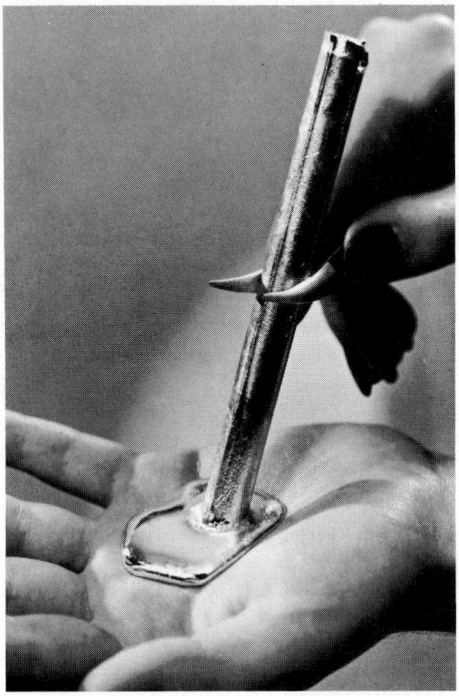

Fig. 2-9. The metallic element gallium will melt in your hand but will not boil until heated to about 2000°C.

ture of two elements, copper and zinc. Common gunpowder is a mixture of two elements, carbon and sulfur, with a compound, potassium nitrate. A solution of common salt is a mixture of two compounds, sodium chloride and water.

A large dictionary may define almost a half-million words. All of these words are formed from one or more of the 26 letters of our alphabet. Try to imagine the number of compounds possible from different combinations of 100 or more elements. Of course, some elements do not unite readily with others and form compounds. Helium is an element that exists only in the free state. It forms no compounds whatever. Enough elements do combine, however, to make possible several million compounds known to chemists. Water, table salt, sugar, alcohol, baking soda, ether, glycerol, cellulose, nitric acid, and sulfuric acid are some examples of common compounds.

The simplest compounds are made up of two different elements. Iron sulfide is such a compound. Carbon dioxide is composed only of carbon and oxygen. Table salt consists of sodium combined with chlorine. Sodium is an active metallic element that must be protected from contact with air and water. Chlorine is a poisonous gas. But when combined chemically, the two elements form common table salt.

Many compounds are composed of no more than three different elements. Carbon, hydrogen, and oxygen are the elements that make up sugar. These same three elements occur combined in different proportions in many other compounds having decidedly different properties.

Changes in Matter

2.12 Physical changes

Ice melts, water boils, liquids freeze, glass breaks, and sugar dissolves in water. We may heat a wire made of the metal platinum until it glows. In all these cases, matter undergoes some change and some quantity of energy is involved. The form of the matter may be different or it may have experienced a change of phase. However, in no case has the matter lost its identity. In some cases, a reversal of the action that caused the change restores the material to its original form. Then its identifying properties are again readily recognized. An example is the case of water that changes to steam when heated. If the steam loses heat, it returns to the original liquid form and the properties of water are again recognized.

These examples illustrate *physical changes*. In such changes, only physical properties are altered. No new substances are formed. ***Physical changes*** *are those in which the identifying properties of substances remain unchanged.*

Modern ideas concerning solutions suggest that some types of physical changes may involve intermediate processes that are not physical in nature. These ideas will be treated in Chapter 13.

2.13 Chemical changes

You know that wood burns, iron rusts, silver tarnishes, milk sours, plants decay, and acids react with metals. In these reactions, the identifying properties of the original substances disappear. New substances with different properties are formed. Changes occur which alter the composition of matter. ***Chemical changes*** *are those in which different substances with new properties are formed.*

Chemical changes may involve *1.* forming compounds from elementary substances, *2.* breaking down complex substances into simpler compounds or into the elements that compose them. Compounds may react with other compounds or elements. New and different compounds are then formed. To recognize and control these processes, chemists need to understand chemical reactions. What they usually observe are changes in the properties of substances in bulk. They try to interpret and understand these changes in terms of the behavior of the particles of the substances involved.

2.14 Chemical reactions involve energy

Every change in matter, physical or chemical, involves energy. Thus, chemical reactions are always accompanied by energy changes. Substances possess energy because of their composition and structure. This is a kind of potential energy which chemists generally refer to as *chemical energy.* The products of chemical reactions are different in composition and structure from the original substances. Consequently, they have larger or smaller amounts of chemical energy than the original substances. If the amount is smaller, energy is given up or *liberated* during the reaction. Usually this energy is in the form of heat. If the amount of chemical energy is larger, energy is *absorbed* during the reaction.

Calcium carbide, a compound formed of the elements calcium and carbon, is produced in the intense heat of an electric furnace. The compound carbon disulfide is formed when hot sulfur vapor is passed over white-hot carbon in an electric furnace. Heat energy is absorbed continuously while these chemical reactions are taking place. *Any process that absorbs energy as it progresses is said to be* ***endothermic.***

Some chemical reactions are important because of their products. Others are important because of the energy that is released. When fuels are burned, large amounts of heat energy are released rapidly. Many similar reactions occur in nature but take place so slowly that the release of heat is not noticed. *Any process that liberates energy as it proceeds is said to be* ***exothermic.*** Most, but not all, chemical reactions that occur spontaneously in nature are exothermic. One important exception is photosynthesis. In this process, which occurs in the leaves of green plants in the presence of sunlight, carbon

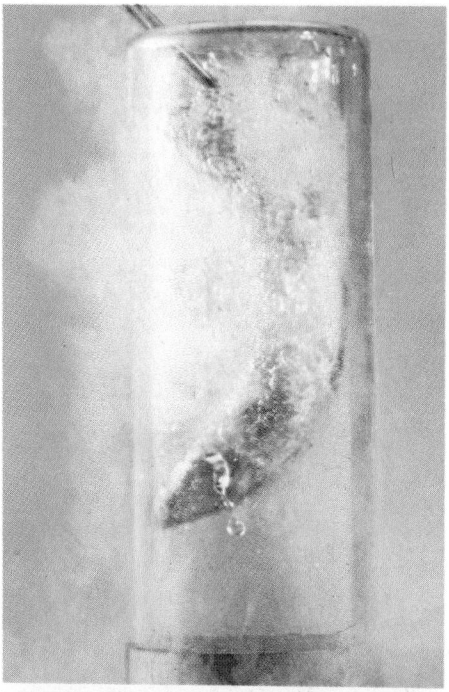

Fig. 2-10. After a banana is dipped in liquid nitrogen at −195.8°C, it can be used as a hammer.

Energy is absorbed in endothermic reactions.

Energy is released in exothermic reactions.

dioxide and water are changed to a simple sugar. Photosynthesis is an endothermic reaction. Radiant energy from the sun is stored as chemical energy in the sugar.

When fuels are burned, light energy usually accompanies the release of heat. A photoflash lamp is designed to release a maximum amount of energy as light. The final proof that a chemical reaction has taken place rests with the analysis of the products. However, the evolution of heat and light usually indicates that a chemical reaction is taking place.

The explosion of dynamite or gunpowder is an exothermic chemical reaction that is used to produce *mechanical energy*. Similarly, burning a mixture of gasoline vapor and air in the cylinder of an automobile engine produces mechanical energy.

In a flashlight cell, the zinc cup is involved in a chemical reaction when the cell is in use. *Electric energy* is produced by this reaction. The electric current gives evidence of the chemical reaction taking place within the cell.

Fig. 2-11. The elements, sulfur and zinc, mixed in the evaporating dish at room temperature (A) do not react until the temperature of the mixture is raised (B). Once started, the reaction gives off energy.

(A)

(B)

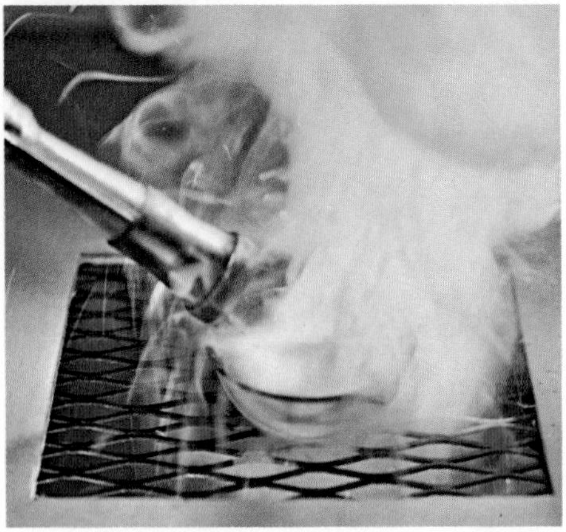

The *production of a gas* usually indicates that a chemical reaction is taking place. However, we must avoid mistaking a boiling liquid, a dissolved gas escaping from a solution, or gas escaping from the surface of a solid as evidence of a chemical reaction.

In many cases when one solution is added to another, an *insoluble* solid (one that is not dissolved in the liquid) is formed. *Such an insoluble solid is called a* ***precipitate.*** Formation of a precipitate may show that a chemical reaction has taken place as the solutions are mixed.

Chemists use several agents to bring about chemical reactions or to control those that have already started. Some form of energy is often involved.

1. *Heat energy.* A match is kindled by rubbing it over a rough surface to warm it by friction. By holding the lighted match to a piece of paper, we may start the paper burning. The heat from the burning match is used to start this chemical reaction. Once started, however, the combustion is an exothermic reaction. We do not need to continue furnishing heat in order to keep the paper burning. Many chemical reactions that occur in the preparation of foods are endothermic. Heat is supplied to keep these reactions going. As a rule, increasing temperature increases the rate of chemical reactions. *Each increase in temperature of 10 C° approximately doubles the rate of many chemical reactions.*

2. *Light energy.* The process of photosynthesis, by which green plants manufacture food, requires light energy. When we open the shutter of a camera for only a fraction of a second, light falls on the sensitive film. This exposure to light forms an invisible image on the film by a chemical reaction. From this image we can then develop a picture at some later time.

3. *Electric energy.* If a direct current of electricity is passed through water containing a little acid, the water decomposes into hydrogen and oxygen. We use this method of bringing about a chemical reaction when we charge a storage battery. Electric energy is used in plating one metal on another. It is used in extracting aluminum and other metals from their ores, and in purifying some metals. Electric energy is also used to produce heat for thermal processes. The use of an electric furnace in the production of calcium carbide and carbon disulfide was mentioned earlier in this section.

4. *Solution in water.* Baking powder is a mixture of two or more compounds. No chemical reaction occurs as long as the powder is kept *dry*. However, when water is added to baking powder, a chemical reaction begins immediately and a gas is released. Many chemicals that do not react in the *dry* state begin to react as soon as they are dissolved in water.

5. *Catalysis* (kuh-*tal*-uh-sis). Some chemical reactions are promoted by *catalysts* (*kat*-uh-lists). These are specific agents which promote reactions that would otherwise be difficult or impractical to carry out. A catalyst does not start a chemical reaction that would not occur of itself. For example, oxygen can be prepared in the laboratory by heating a mixture of potassium chlorate and manganese dioxide. Without the manganese dioxide, the preparation would have to be carried out at a higher temperature. Also, the gas would be produced more slowly. The manganese dioxide aids the reaction by its presence. It can be recovered in its original form at the conclusion of the experiment. *A **catalyst** is a substance or combination of substances that increases the rate of a chemical reaction without itself being permanently changed.*

Many chemical processes, such as the production of vegetable shortening, the manufacture of synthetic rubber, and the preparation of high-octane gasoline, depend on catalysis for their successful operation.

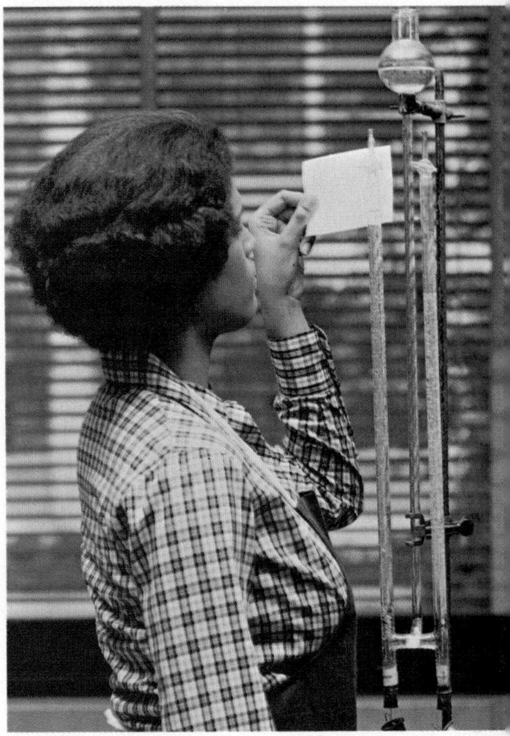

Fig. 2-12. Electric energy can be used to decompose water into hydrogen and oxygen.

2.15 Reaction tendencies

We are not surprised to see a ball roll unaided down an incline. This is just what would be expected. The ball gives up potential energy in this process and achieves a more stable condition at a lower energy level. We would be surprised, however, if the ball rolled up the incline by and of itself. Our experiences with nature have taught us to recognize a basic rule for natural processes: *There is a tendency for processes to occur that lead to a lower energy state.* This tendency in nature is toward greater *stability* (resistance to change) of a system.

The great majority of chemical reactions in nature are exothermic. Energy is liberated as they proceed and the products have less energy than the original *reactants* or starting substances. With the above rule in mind, we expect exothermic

Spontaneous chemical reactions are self-acting because of the properties of the system.

reactions *to occur spontaneously.* That is, we expect them *to have the potential to proceed without outside help.*

It should follow that endothermic reactions, in which energy is absorbed, would not occur spontaneously. They would proceed only with outside help. Certainly, we must expend energy on the ball to roll it up the incline. At the top of the incline its potential energy is high and its stability is low.

We do not have to look very far to find endothermic reactions, which take place spontaneously with the absorption of energy. For example, when steam is passed over hot carbon, carbon monoxide and hydrogen gases are produced. Heat is absorbed and the products are in a higher energy state than the reactants. The spontaneous reaction is endothermic and our rule appears to have failed. Apparently the tendency of a reaction to proceed spontaneously is not determined exclusively by this energy-change rule.

An ice cube melts spontaneously at room temperature. Heat is transferred from the air to the ice. As the ice melts, the absorbed energy is contained in the water formed. The well-ordered structure of the ice crystal is lost. The less orderly liquid water, a phase of higher energy content, is formed. Why does this change occur?

What we observe here is a tendency for the ice to move into the less orderly liquid phase. This observation suggests a second basic rule for natural processes: *There is a tendency for processes to occur that lead to a less orderly or a more disordered state.* This tendency in nature is toward greater disorder in a

Fig. 2-13. Changes of phase.

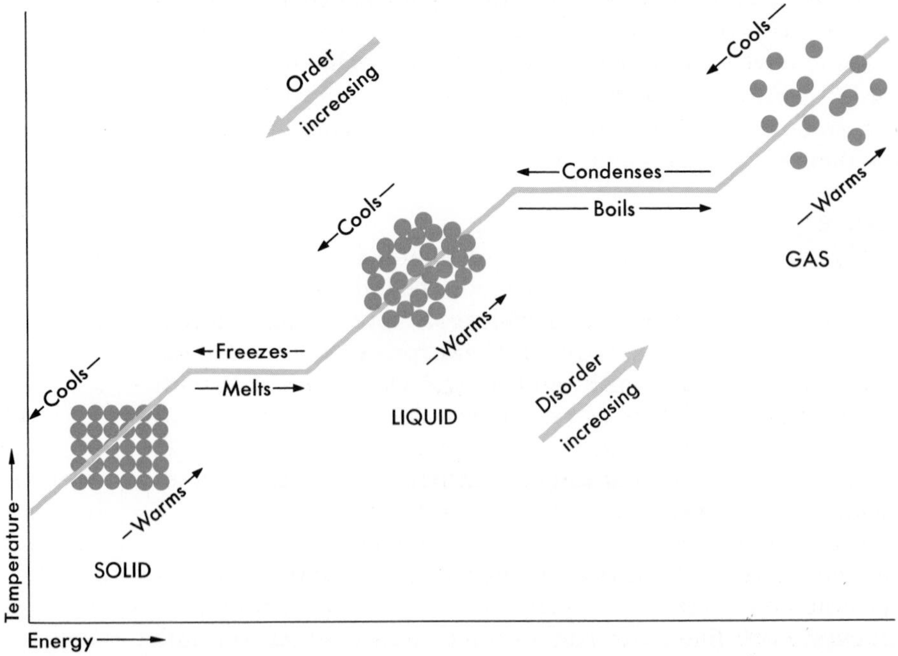

system. A disordered system is one that lacks a regular arrangement of its parts. *That property which describes the disorder of a sytem is called* ***entropy.*** The more disordered or random the state, the *higher* is the entropy. Liquid water has higher entropy than ice.

Entropy is a measure of the disorder of a system.

Thus, processes in nature are driven in two ways: toward *lowest* energy and toward *highest* entropy. Where these two oppose each other, the dominant factor determines the direction of the spontaneous change. In the steam-plus-hot-carbon reaction, the temperature is high enough that the entropy factor overcomes the unfavorable energy-change factor. The spontaneous endothermic reaction occurs.

If the ice cube is subjected to a temperature below 0°C, it will not melt. Liquid water placed in this environment freezes. The temperature is low enough that the energy-change factor overcomes the entropy-change factor. Heat is given up by the water (lower energy) and the well-ordered ice crystal is formed (lower entropy). Entropy as a factor in reaction systems will be considered in more detail in Section 20.7

2.16 Nuclear changes

New substances are produced during a chemical reaction by rearranging the atoms of the original substances. In a *nuclear change,* new substances with new properties are also produced. There is a difference, however. *In a* ***nuclear change,*** *the new substances are formed by changes in the identity of the atoms themselves.*

In nature, some nuclear changes take place spontaneously. Radium atoms break apart in successive stages, finally becoming lead. Scientists are able to bring about many important nuclear changes. The elements beyond uranium named in Section 2.4 are products of nuclear changes. Nuclear reactions, both natural and artificial, will be discussed in Chapter 30.

SUMMARY

Matter is classified as a mixture or a pure substance. Pure substances are homogeneous and are either compounds or elements. Compounds can be decomposed into two or more simpler substances by ordinary chemical means. Elements cannot be further decomposed by ordinary chemical means. Mixtures are composed of two or more kinds of matter, each retaining its own characteristic properties.

Of the 107 known or reported elements, the 92 ranging from hydrogen to uranium represent the pre-Atomic Age list of elements. Approximately 90 of these elements occur free or combined in the earth's crust. Only about 30 elements are fairly common. Elements are recognized as metals or nonmetals based on their properties. Some elements have certain properties characteristic of metals and other properties characteristic of nonmetals. These elements are called metalloids.

Symbols are used to represent elements. The symbol of an element stands for one atom of that element. The atom is the smallest particle of an element that can enter into combination with other elements. Compounds are composed of two or more elements. Every compound has a definite composition by weight.

Physical changes are those in which the identifying properties of a substance remain unchanged. Examples are freezing, boiling, and dissolving. Chemical changes are those in which different substances with new properties are formed. Reactions that absorb energy as they proceed are endothermic. Reactions that liberate energy are exothermic. The rates of some chemical reactions can be accelerated by catalysts.

There is a basic tendency for processes to occur in nature that lead to a lower energy state. A second basic tendency is for processes to occur that lead to a more disordered or more random state. Entropy is the property that describes the disorder of a system. The more disordered the system, the higher the entropy.

QUESTIONS

Group A

1. What are the three general classes of matter?
2. Distinguish between matter and a substance.
3. Distinguish between a complex substance and an elementary substance.
4. (*a*) What are the two general classes of elements? (*b*) Do all elements fit definitely into one of these classes?
5. Distinguish between a compound and a mixture.
6. What are the five most abundant elements in the earth's surface environment?
7. (*a*) What are the properties of metals? (*b*) of nonmetals?
8. (*a*) How many elements are known? (*b*) How many were known prior to the beginning of the Atomic Age?
9. What is the meaning of a chemical symbol?
10. (*a*) List five familiar substances that are elements. (*b*) List five that are compounds. (*c*) List five familiar mixtures.
11. What is the difference between a physical change and a chemical reaction?
12. How can a chemist usually increase the speed of a chemical change?
13. If two or more elements have symbols beginning with the same letter, how do we distinguish them?
14. If a symbol has two letters, (*a*) what is always true of the first letter? (*b*) What is always true of the second letter?
15. Write the names (spelled correctly) of the elements represented by the following symbols: (*a*) S; (*b*) Zn; (*c*) K; (*d*) N; (*e*) Ni; (*f*) Co; (*g*) Ba; (*h*) Fe; (*i*) Cl; (*j*) Cr; (*k*) Mg; (*l*) Mn; (*m*) As; (*n*) Pb; (*o*) Na.
16. Write the symbols for the following elements: (*a*) aluminum; (*b*) tungsten; (*c*) mercury; (*d*) carbon; (*e*) bromine; (*f*) silicon; (*g*) tin; (*h*) hydrogen; (*i*) gold; (*j*) silver; (*k*) fluorine; (*l*) strontium; (*m*) calcium; (*n*) phosphorus; (*o*) bismuth.
17. Distinguish between exothermic and endothermic processes.

Group B

18. What difference in the properties of white sand and sugar enables you to separate a mixture of the two substances?
19. How would you carry out the separation of the sand-sugar mixture of Question 18?
20. Why is a solution recognized as a mixture?

21. What is the meaning of the phrase "definite composition by weight"?
22. Why is the law of definite composition very important to chemists?
23. Consult the complete list of known elements in Table 4, Appendix B, and compile a list of those about which you already have some knowledge. Give the name, symbol, and the pertinent bit of knowledge in column form.
24. Given two liquids, one a solution and the other a compound, how would you distinguish the solution from the compound?
25. Suppose you heat three different solids in open vessels and then allow them to cool. The first gains weight, the second loses weight, and the third remains the same. How can you reconcile these facts with the generalization that, in an ordinary chemical reaction, the total mass of the reacting materials is equal to the total mass of the products?
26. How can you explain the fact that gold, silver, and copper were known long before such metals as iron and aluminum?
27. Suppose you were given a sample of iodine crystals, a sample of antimony metal, and a sample of a mixture of iodine and antimony, which had been ground together to form a fine powder of uniform consistency. Look up the physical and chemical properties of both iodine and antimony. Then list those properties of each element that you believe would be useful in separating and recovering them from the mixture. On the basis of these properties, devise a procedure that would enable you to separate the two elements from the mixture and recover the separate elements.
28. Which of these changes are physical and which are chemical? (*a*) burning coal; (*b*) tarnishing silver; (*c*) magnetizing steel; (*d*) exploding gunpowder; (*e*) boiling water; (*f*) melting shortening.
29. Which of the chemical changes listed in Question 28 are also exothermic?
30. Show by example how each form of energy produces chemical changes: (*a*) heat energy; (*b*) light energy; (*c*) electric energy.
31. What evidences usually indicate chemical reaction?
32. Can you suggest a reason why iron and sulfur unite in definite proportions when iron sulfide is formed?
33. How do you decide whether a certain change is physical or chemical?
34. What two basic tendencies in nature appear to influence reaction processes?
35. An ice cube melts at room temperature and water freezes at temperatures below 0°C. From these facts, what can you infer concerning the relationship between the temperature of a system and the influence of the entropy factor on the change that the system undergoes?
36. The photograph of a typical turn-of-the-century high school chemistry laboratory on page 23 omits a routine safety measure in today's chemistry laboratory. Can you tell what is missing?

evidence of atoms

Chemistry experiments in the early 1800's supported Dalton's atomic theory. Physics experiments in the late 1800's provided more evidence of atoms. When most of the air is pumped from a glass tube and it is connected to a source of electricity, rays are given off by the negatively charged electrode, called the cathode. Sir William Crookes by 1885, thoroughly studied these cathode rays using specially designed tubes (1). He concluded that cathode rays travel in straight lines like light. But, unlike light, these cathode rays have enough mass to move a paddle wheel (2) and are affected by a magnet (3). J. J. Thomson's experiments in 1897 (4) provided evidence that cathode rays are the negatively charged particles we now call electrons. Positively charged particles were also first detected using specially designed tubes.

Evidence of atomic structure came from studying the light given off when an element is excited by electricity in a tube or is heated. This student (5) is using a spectroscope to examine the light given off by the electrically excited gas glowing in the tube. Other instruments such as X—ray spectrographs and mass spectrographs (6) have increased our knowledge of atoms.

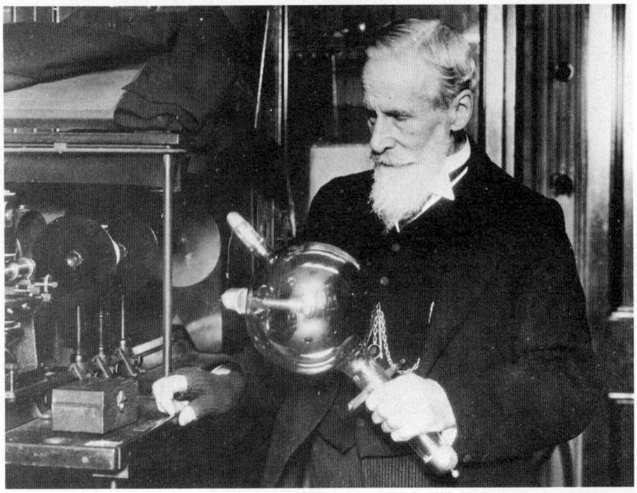

1

2

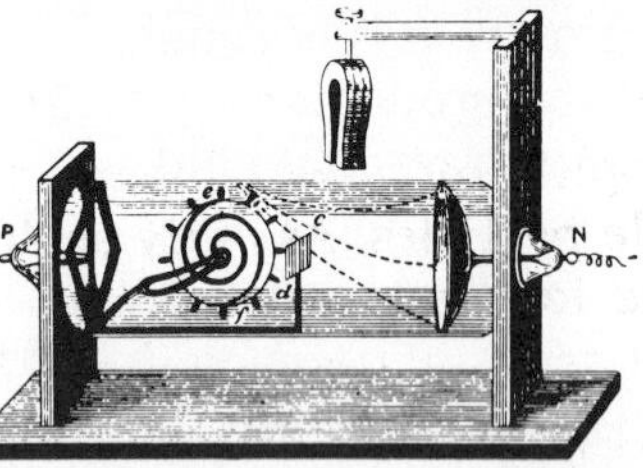

3

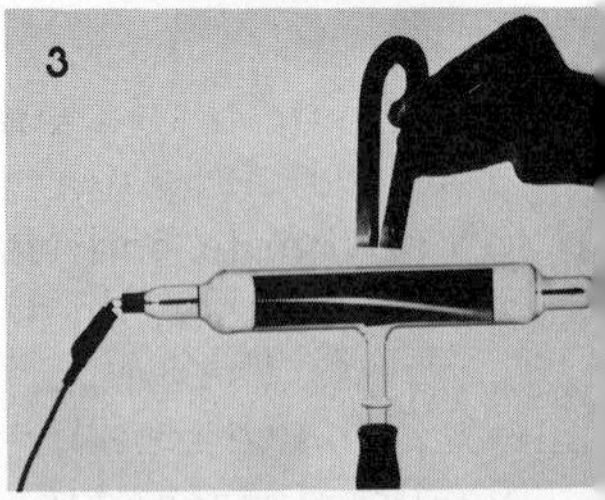

4

5

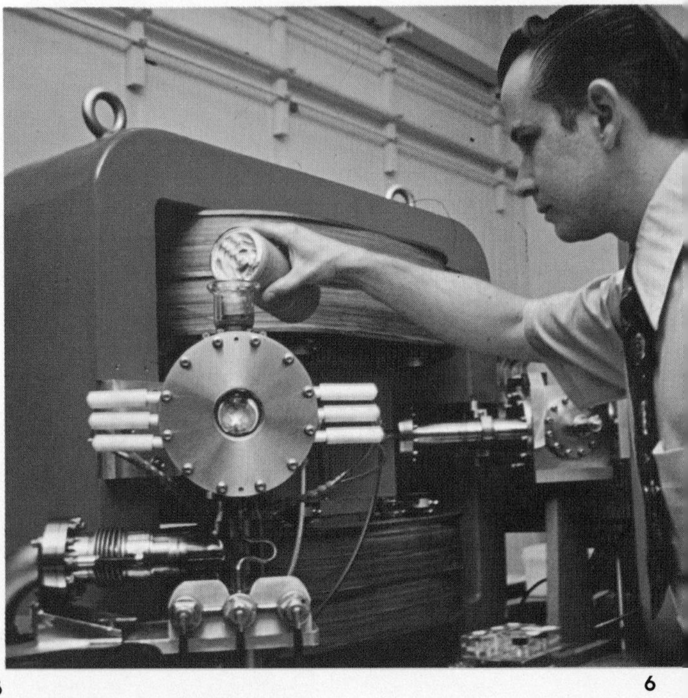

6

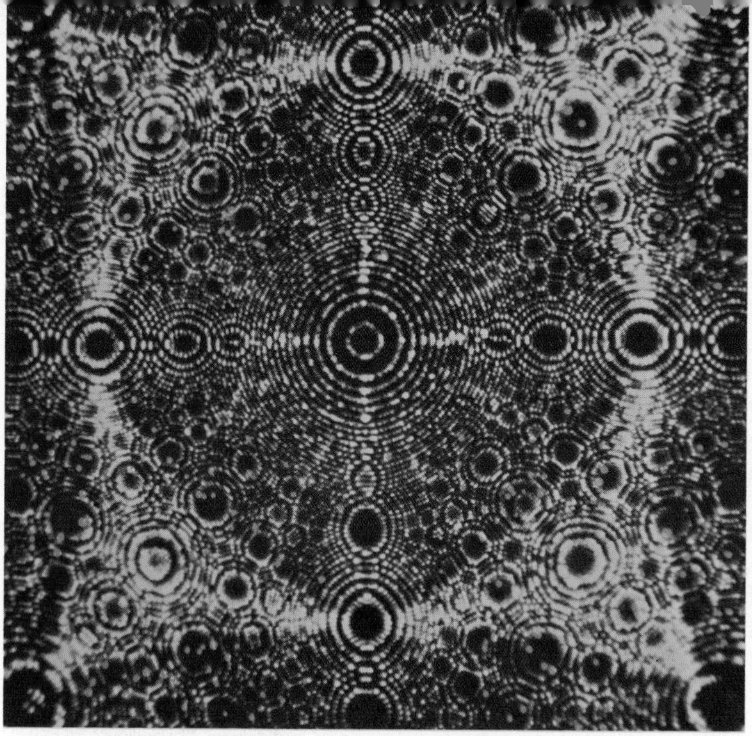

chapter 3

ATOMIC STRUCTURE

A field-ion micrograph of platinum-iridium alloy. (See Question 33 on page 56.)

3.1 Particles of matter

For a very long time people have believed that matter is made up of simple, indivisible particles. As early as 400 B.C. some Greek thinkers had the idea that matter could not be destroyed. They believed that matter could be divided into smaller and smaller particles until a basic particle of matter would be reached that could not be divided further. Such basic particles were thought to be the smallest particles of matter that existed. Democritus called them *atoms*. The word "atom" is from the Greek word meaning "indivisible."

Democritus (deh-mock-writ-us) (460–370 B.C.) was a Greek thinker. He believed that the hard atoms of the four primitive elements (earth, air, water, and fire) moved in a vacuum. The shape and size of these atoms explained some of their properties. For example, the atoms of fire were tiny spheres. Because of their smooth surfaces, they did not link with the atoms of the other elements. The atoms of earth, air, and water had shapes that enabled them to connect with each other and form visible matter.

When you crush a lump of sugar, you can see that it is made up of many small particles of sugar. You may grind these particles into very fine powder, but each tiny piece is still sugar. Now suppose you dissolve the sugar in water. The tiny particles disappear completely. Even if you look at the sugar-water solution through a microscope, you cannot see any sugar particles. However, if you taste the solution, you know that the sugar is still there.

If you open a laboratory gas valve, you can smell the escaping gas. Yet you cannot see gas particles in the air of the room, even if you use the most powerful microscope. These observations and many others like them have led scientists to believe that the basic particles of matter must be very, very small.

3.2 The atomic theory

Invention of the chemical balance gave chemists a tool for studying the composition of substances quantitatively. Chem-

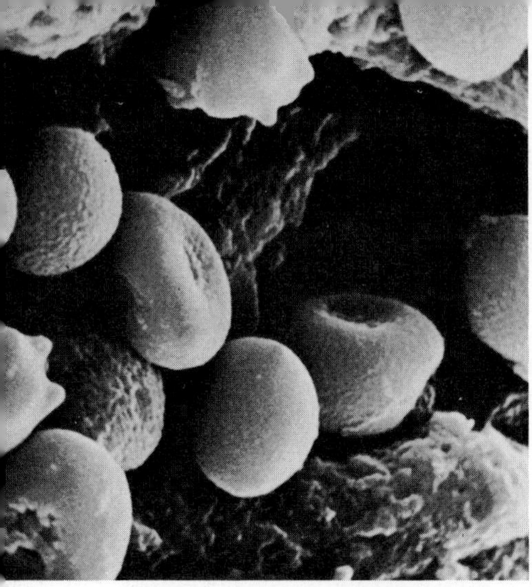

Fig. 3-1. These red blood cells are enlarged about 1200 times. In a progression toward smaller and smaller objects, compare these cells with the virus below (enlarged about 80,000 times), and the representation of an arrangement of atoms on the facing page.

John Dalton (1766–1844) was an English schoolmaster. He was interested in the composition and properties of the gases in the atmosphere. He kept a daily record of the weather from 1787 until 1844.

Fig. 3-2. A bacterial virus, or phage, is shown "exploded" so its central core of DNA is visible as a single strand. A simple virus may be thought of as a giant protein molecule.

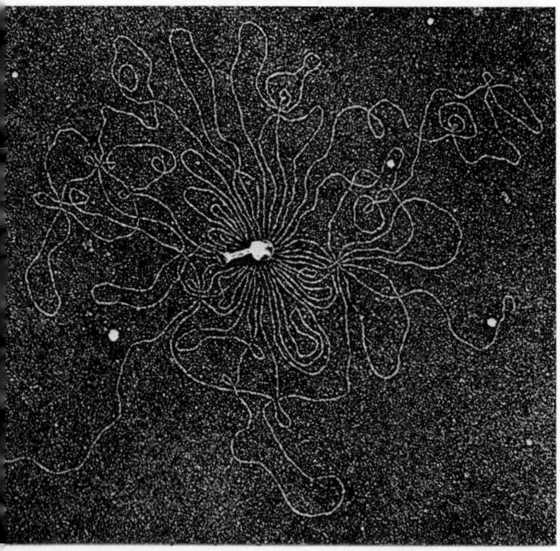

ists showed, in the half-century prior to the year 1800, that substances they investigated are chemical combinations of a fairly small number of elements. They learned much about how elements combine and form compounds and how compounds can be broken down into their constituent elements. From this knowledge they formulated several quantitative laws of chemical combination, such as Proust's law of definite composition (See Section 2.10).

John Dalton's atomic theory, first conceived in 1803 and published in 1808–1810, was ultimately accepted because it satisfactorily explained these laws. It forms the basis of our modern atomic theory.

In science, a theory is never secure. Each new observation tests it. If the theory does not explain the new observation satisfactorily, the theory is either rejected or revised. Thus far, the atomic theory has stood the test of time. It has satisfactorily explained observations and laws in many different fields. It now includes information about

1. the structure and properties of atoms;
2. the kinds of compounds that atoms form;
3. the properties of compounds that atoms form;
4. the mass, volume, and energy relations of reactions between atoms.

An ***atom*** *is the smallest unit of an element that can exist either alone or in combination with other atoms like it or different from it.* With increased knowledge, Dalton's original statements have had to be revised. For example, Dalton thought that atoms of the same element were identical in all respects, particularly mass. But, we now have evidence that the mass of each atom of an element is not exactly the same. Sources of this evidence are described in the Photo Essay that precedes this section: Evidence of Atoms. The chemical and physical properties of matter lead scientists to make the following statements about atoms and their properties:

1. All matter is made up of very small particles called *atoms.*

2. Atoms of the *same element* are *chemically alike;* atoms of *different elements* are *chemically different.*

3. Individual atoms of an element may not all have the same mass. However, *the atoms of an element,* as it occurs naturally, *have,* for practical purposes, *a definite average mass that is characteristic of the element.*

4. Individual atoms of different elements may have nearly identical masses. However, *the atoms of different naturally occurring elements have different average masses.*

5. Atoms are not subdivided in *chemical reactions.*

Right now, statements 3 and 4 may be a bit puzzling. Later, in Section 3.14, we shall make their meaning clearer.

3.3 The structure of the atom

For nearly 100 years, scientists have been gathering evidence about the structure of atoms. Some of this evidence has come from the study of radioactive elements such as radium and uranium. Particle accelerators, the mass spectrograph, the X-ray tube, the spectroscope, and a variety of other electronic devices have given additional information. From all this information scientists have developed a theory of atomic structure. This theory includes an explanation of the observed phenomena in terms of a model with familiar properties. This atomic structure model will be described in the following sections of this chapter and in Chapter 4. Remember, as you read, that this explanation is based on the best present understanding of experiments on atomic structure. Further experiments may make changes in the model necessary.

At the present time, scientists know that atoms are not simple indivisible particles. Instead, they are composed of several different kinds of still smaller particles arranged in a rather complex way.

Fig. 3-3. The point of a tungsten needle as viewed through a field-ion microscope. This instrument magnifies objects up to 3,000,000 diameters and shows the regular arrangement of tungsten atoms in the metal.

An atom consists of two main parts. *The positively charged central part is called the* ***nucleus.*** It is very small and very dense. Its diameter is about 10^{-12} cm. Its density is about 20 metric tn/cm^3.

A more useful unit for atomic sizes is the angstrom.

$$\textbf{1 angstrom (Å)} = \mathbf{10^{-8}}\ \textbf{cm}$$

To get some idea of the extreme smallness of the angstrom, consider the fact that 1 cm is the same fractional part of 10^3 km (about 600 miles) as 1 Å is of 1 cm.

We have just given the diameter of a nucleus as about 10^{-12} cm, or about 10^{-4} Å. This is about one ten-thousandth of the diameter of the atom itself, since atoms range from 1 Å to 5 Å in diameter.

The idea that an atom has a nucleus was the result of experiments conducted about 1910. These experiments were under the direction of the English physicist Ernest Rutherford (1871–1937). Rutherford used an evacuated tube (a tube from which the gas has been pumped). In it, a beam of high-speed positively charged particles was aimed at a thin sheet of gold. Most of the particles passed straight through the gold. A few were slightly deflected (turned away from a straight course) as they passed through the gold. A very few were greatly deflected back from the gold. These very few great deflections were explained by means of an assumption. It was assumed that the positively charged particles were bounced back if they approached a positively charged atomic nucleus head-on. The few slight deflections were explained by assuming that the particles were turned from their paths in near misses of nuclei. But most of the particles passed straight through the gold foil.

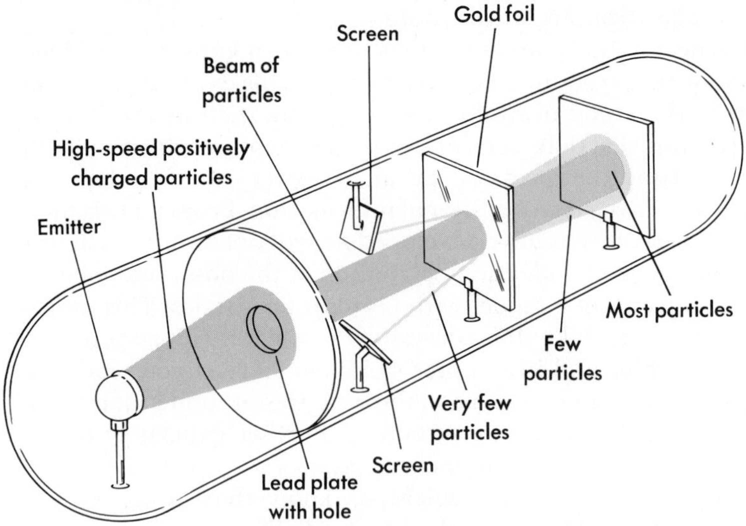

Fig. 3-4. A schematic diagram of Rutherford's experiment. High-speed positively charged particles are given off in many directions by the emitter. The hole in the lead plate allows a beam of particles moving toward the gold foil to pass through. The solid portion of the lead plate absorbs the other particles. Most of the high-speed positively charged particles in the beam passed through the gold foil. A few were slightly deflected, while a very few were very greatly deflected. The screens emit a flash of light when struck by a charged particle.

Therefore, the experimenters reasoned, most of an atom must consist of space through which such particles could move readily. In fact, since a vast majority of the particles went undeflected, the nucleus must occupy a very, very small portion of the volume of an atom.

The other part of the atom lies outside the central nucleus. It is made up of negatively charged particles called *electrons*. Electrons move about the nucleus with different energies. Several electrons having similar energies comprise a ***shell*** and are said to be in the same ***energy level.***

About 1913, the Danish scientist Niels Bohr (1885–1962) compared the movement of electrons about the nucleus of an atom with the revolution of the planets around the sun. The paths of the electrons are now believed to be much less definite than the orbits of the planets. Electrons move about the nucleus of an atom much as bees move about in the area near their hive. Sometimes the electrons are near the nucleus; sometimes they are farther away. In this way, the electrons seem to occupy the relatively vast empty space around the nucleus. The positions of the electrons may be visualized as an electron cloud about the nucleus. This electron cloud gives the atom its volume and keeps out other atoms.

Each atom is electrically neutral. This electric neutrality shows that the total positive charge of the nucleus must equal the total negative charge of the electrons in the shells or energy levels. The experimental evidence for the existence of electrons and for their location and motion within atoms will be described in Sections 3.4 and 4.3.

3.4 The characteristics of electrons

Electrons *are negatively charged particles with a mass of 9.110* $\times 10^{-28}$ *g.* The mass of an electron is $\frac{1}{1837}$ of the mass of the most common type of hydrogen atom. The most common type of hydrogen atom has the simplest structure and the least mass of any atom.

The electron is a very small particle. Its radius is 2.818×10^{-13} cm, or 2.818×10^{-5} Å. Electrons are negatively charged particles. No smaller quantity of electric charge than that on one electron has ever been found. Regardless of the atom of which an electron is a part, *all electrons are identical.*

Electrons were discovered in 1897 by an English scientist, J. J. Thomson (1856–1940). This discovery was the result of investigations of the flow of electricity through a glass tube from which most of the gas had been pumped.

3.5 The nucleus of the atom

The nuclei of atoms of different elements are different. The amounts of positive charge are always different. The nuclei of atoms of different elements also have different masses, although the difference in mass is sometimes very slight. Except for the simplest type of hydrogen atom, a nucleus is made up of two kinds of particles, *protons* and *neutrons.*

***Protons** are positively charged particles with a mass of 1.673×10^{-24} g.* This mass is $\frac{1836}{1837}$ of the mass of the simplest type of hydrogen atom. This atom consists of a single-proton nucleus with a single electron moving about it. Most of the mass of the simplest type of hydrogen atom is due to the mass of the proton. While a proton has much more mass than an electron, it is believed to be smaller. The electric charge on the proton has the same magnitude as that on an electron but is positive in sign. In any atom, the number of electrons and protons is equal. Since protons and electrons have equal but opposite electric charges, an atom is electrically neutral.

Protons were discovered in the early years of this century during the investigation of "positive rays." Such rays appear when electricity flows through specially designed glass tubes from which most of the gas has been pumped.

***Neutrons** are neutral particles with a mass of 1.675×10^{-24} g,* which is about the same mass as a proton. They have no electric charge.

Neutrons were discovered by the English scientist, James C. Chadwick (1891–1974), in 1932. The experiment during which this discovery was made is described in Sec. 30.13.

Particles that have the same electric charge generally repel one another. Nevertheless, as many as 100 protons can exist close together in a nucleus. This close existence of protons in the nucleus can occur when up to about 150 neutrons are also present. When a proton and a neutron are very close to each other, there is a strong attraction between them. Proton-proton attractive forces and neutron-neutron attractive forces exist when such pairs of particles are very close together. These short-range proton-neutron, proton-proton, and neutron-neutron forces hold the nuclear particles together. They are referred to as *nuclear forces.*

In nuclear changes, particles in addition to protons and neutrons come from the nucleus. We shall describe some of these in Chapter 30. We do not need to know about these particles now to understand atomic structure and chemical changes.

Table 3-1

PARTICLES IN AN ATOM

Name	Mass	Atomic Mass (See Section 3.12)	Mass Number (See Section 3.6)	Charge
electron	9.110×10^{-28} g	0.0005486	0	−1
proton	1.673×10^{-24} g	1.007277	1	+1
neutron	1.675×10^{-24} g	1.008665	1	0

3.6 Hydrogen atoms

The most common type of hydrogen is sometimes called *protium* (*pro*-tee-um). Its atoms have the simplest possible composition. The nucleus of a protium atom consists of one proton. This proton has one electron moving about it. This electron could most probably be found at a distance from the nucleus corresponding to the innermost shell, or lowest energy level, which an electron can have. This shell or energy level is called the ***K shell*** or ***1st energy level.*** Scientists discover how electrons are arranged in atoms of an element by studying the chemical properties of the element and its spectrum. An illustration may help you to understand the sizes and distances between the particles of the protium atom better. Picture the nucleus (a proton) as being 1 cm in diameter (about the diameter of the end of your little finger). Comparatively, the electron, which is somewhat larger, moves about this nucleus at an average distance of about 48 m. (The 48-m distance is about one-half the length of a football field.) The electron moves rapidly about the nucleus, effectively occupying the surrounding space.

*The **atomic number** of an atom is the number of protons in the nucleus of that atom.* An element consists of atoms all of which have the same number of protons in each nucleus. Hence, all atoms of the same element have the same atomic number. (All unexcited neutral atoms of an element have the same arrangement of electrons about their nuclei, too.) The atoms of the element hydrogen have one proton in each nucleus. Their atomic number, therefore, is 1. Any atom having the atomic number 1 contains one proton in its nucleus and is a hydrogen atom.

In addition to protium, which makes up 99.985% of naturally occurring hydrogen, there are two other known forms of hydrogen atoms. One of these is *deuterium* (dyou-*tir*-ee-um), which occurs to the extent of 0.015% in nature. Each deuterium atom has a nucleus containing one proton and one neutron, with one electron moving about it.

The third form of hydrogen is *tritium* (*trit*-ee-um). Tritium is a radioactive form. It exists in nature in very small amounts but can be prepared artificially by a nuclear reaction. Each tritium atom has a nucleus composed of one proton and two neutrons, with one electron moving about it.

These three kinds of atoms are all hydrogen atoms, since each has a nucleus containing one proton. The atomic number of each is 1. However, because their nuclei contain different numbers of neutrons, these atoms have different masses. *Atoms of the same element which have different masses are called* ***isotopes.***

All elements have two or more isotopes. Isotopes of an element may occur naturally, or they may be prepared artificial-

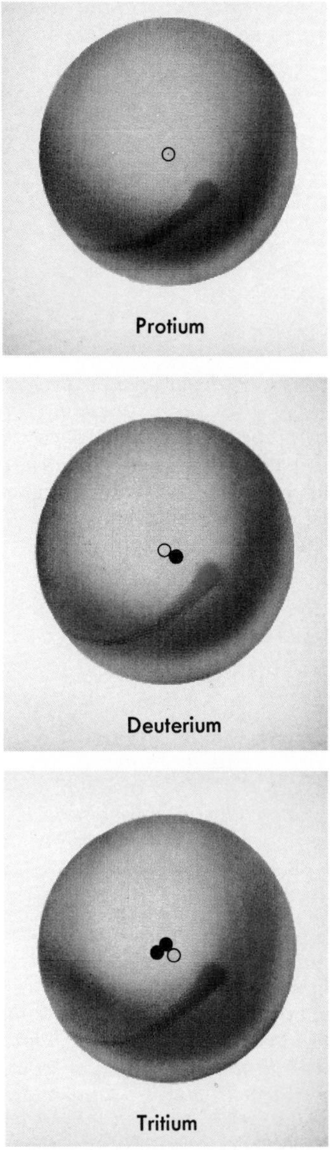

Fig. 3-5. Tentative models of the three isotopes of hydrogen: protium, deuterium, and tritium. Each has one proton in the nucleus and one electron moving about the nucleus in the 1st energy level. The only structural difference between them is the number of neutrons in the nucleus of each atom. In these diagrams, the nuclei are enlarged in proportion to the size of the atom to show their composition.

ly. While isotopes have different masses, they do not differ significantly in chemical properties. See Appendix, Table 2, for a list of natural and radioactive isotopes of some of the elements.

Each different variety of atom as determined by the number of protons and number of neutrons in its nucleus is called a ***nuclide.*** Nuclides having *the same number of protons* (the same atomic number) are *isotopes.* The three hydrogen isotopes are the nuclides: protium, deuterium, and tritium.

In addition to their names, hydrogen nuclides may also be distinguished by their *mass numbers. The* ***mass number*** *of an atom is the sum of the number of protons and neutrons in its nucleus.* The mass number of protium is 1 (1 proton + 0 neutron). That of deuterium is 2 (1 proton + 1 neutron). That of tritium is 3 (1 proton + 2 neutrons). Sometimes these isotopes are named hydrogen-1, hydrogen-2, and hydrogen-3, respectively.

3.7 Elements in atomic number order

At the time of this writing, 107 different elements are known or reported to exist. Their atomic numbers range from 1 to 107. The elements may be arranged in the order of increasing atomic number. This arrangement simplifies the understanding of atomic structure. If the elements are arranged in this way, the nuclei of the atoms of one element differ from those of the preceding element by one additional proton per nucleus. (The number of neutrons per nucleus may or may not change from atom to atom.)

3.8 Helium atoms

The second element in order of complexity is helium. Since each helium nucleus contains two protons, the atomic number of helium is 2. Natural helium exists as a mixture of two isotopes. Helium-3 occurs to the extent of $1.34 \times 10^{-4}\%$. Helium-4 accounts for practically 100% of natural helium. These helium nuclides respectively contain 1 neutron and 2 neutrons per nucleus. (Note that the number of neutrons in the nucleus of an atom may be determined by subtracting the atomic number from the mass number.) Moving about each helium nucleus are two electrons, both in the ***1st energy level.*** The chemical properties and spectrum of helium indicate that the 1st energy level may contain a *maximum* of two electrons. Thus, helium atoms have a *filled* 1st energy level.

The atoms of hydrogen have one 1st-energy level electron. The atoms of helium have two (the maximum number). Hydrogen and helium, then, form the first *series* of elements.

Fig. 3-6. Tentative model of a helium-4 atom. Its nucleus consists of two protons and two neutrons. Its two electrons move about this nucleus and completely fill the 1st energy level of the atom.

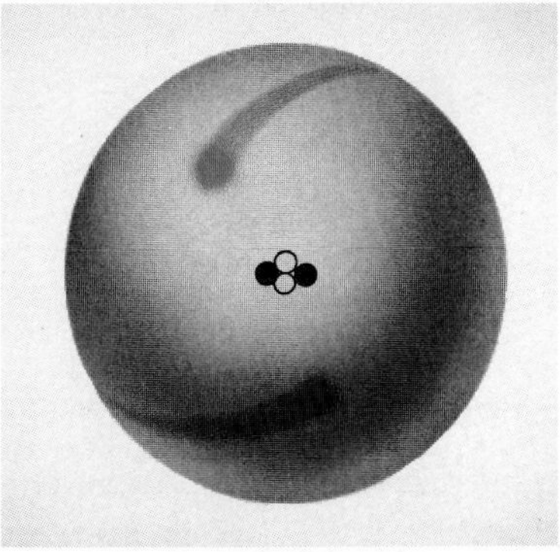

3.9 Lithium atoms

Lithium exists in nature as two isotopes. Each atom of one isotope contains 3 protons, 3 neutrons, and 3 electrons. Each

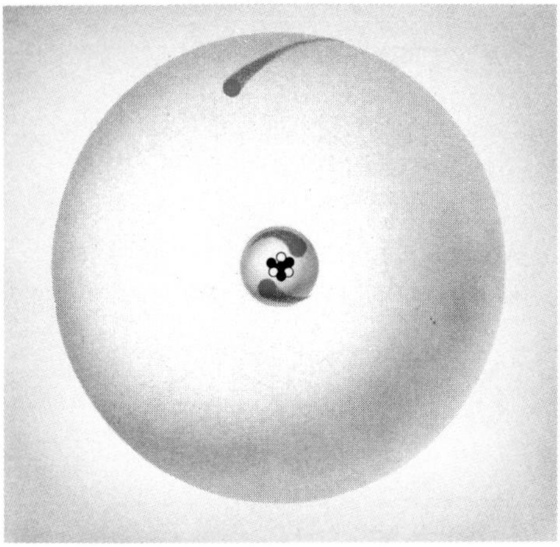

Fig. 3-7. Tentative model of a lithium-7 atom. This atom has a nucleus consisting of three protons and four neutrons. Two electrons are in the 1st energy level and one is in the 2nd energy level. Lithium is the first element in the second series.

atom of the other isotope contains 3 protons, 4 neutrons, and 3 electrons. By the composition of these atoms, we know that the atomic number of lithium is 3 (3 protons). The mass number of the first isotope is 6 (3 protons + 3 neutrons). The mass number of the second isotope is 7 (3 protons + 4 neutrons). These isotopes are lithium-6 and lithium-7.

The chemical properties of lithium and a study of its spectrum help us learn its electron arrangement. Two of the three electrons in a lithium atom move in the 1st energy level. The third moves about the nucleus at a greater distance and with higher energy than the other two. It moves in the next larger shell or next higher energy level. This is called the ***L-shell*** or ***2nd energy level.*** The 1st energy level contains no more than two electrons. When it has this maximum of two electrons, additional electrons occupy higher energy levels at greater distances from the nucleus.

3.10 Other atoms of the second series

The element with atomic number 4 is beryllium. Naturally occurring beryllium consists of only one nuclide, beryllium-9. Beryllium nuclei consist of four protons and five neutrons. The four electrons are arranged with two in the 1st energy level and two in the 2nd energy level. Next in order of atomic structure are the elements boron, carbon, nitrogen, oxygen, fluorine, and neon. The atoms of each successive element have one additional proton per nucleus and may have one or two additional neutrons per nucleus. Each successive element has one additional electron in the 2nd energy level of each of its atoms. The atoms of the element neon have eight electrons in the 2nd energy level. The chemical properties and spectrum of neon indicate that the 2nd energy level may contain a maximum of eight electrons. So neon completes the second series of elements.

Table 3-2 contains information about the composition of the nuclei and electron configurations (arrangements) of atoms in the first and second series.

3.11 The atoms of the third series

The elements in the third series are sodium, magnesium, aluminum, silicon, phosphorus, sulfur, chlorine, and argon. The atoms of these elements have a filled 1st energy level of two electrons and a filled 2nd energy level of eight electrons. Successive electrons occupy the ***M shell*** or ***3rd energy level.*** This level contains eight electrons in the atoms of argon.

3.12 Atomic mass

Atomic masses are measured using a mass spectrograph. This device was developed by F. W. Aston, an English scientist, in 1919.

The actual mass of a single atom is very small. An atom of oxygen-16 has a mass of 2.65×10^{-23} g. A hydrogen-1 atom has a mass of 1.67×10^{-24} g. These numbers are not very easy to use in chemical arithmetic problems. Therefore, a system

Table 3-2

Name of Nuclide	Abundance	Atomic Number	Mass Number	Composition of Nucleus		Electron Configuration	
				Protons	Neutrons	1st energy level (K shell)	2nd energy level (L shell)
hydrogen-1 (protium)	99.985%	1	1	1	0	1	
hydrogen-2 (deuterium)	0.015%	1	2	1	1	1	
helium-3	0.00013%	2	3	2	1	2	
helium-4	99.99987%	2	4	2	2	2	
lithium-6	7.42%	3	6	3	3	2	1
lithium-7	92.58%	3	7	3	4	2	1
beryllium-9	100%	4	9	4	5	2	2
boron-10	19.78%	5	10	5	5	2	3
boron-11	80.22%	5	11	5	6	2	3
carbon-12	98.89%	6	12	6	6	2	4
carbon-13	1.11%	6	13	6	7	2	4
nitrogen-14	99.63%	7	14	7	7	2	5
nitrogen-15	0.37%	7	15	7	8	2	5
oxygen-16	99.759%	8	16	8	8	2	6
oxygen-17	0.037%	8	17	8	9	2	6
oxygen-18	0.204%	8	18	8	10	2	6
fluorine-19	100%	9	19	9	10	2	7
neon-20	90.92%	10	20	10	10	2	8
neon-21	0.257%	10	21	10	11	2	8
neon-22	8.82%	10	22	10	12	2	8

NATURALLY OCCURRING NUCLIDES (First and Second Series of Elements)

has been worked out for expressing the masses of atoms in numbers on a relative scale. These relative numbers are easier to use.

A relative scale consists of numbers without units. These relative-scale numbers must also be directly proportional to the magnitude of some property of matter we can measure. An example will make this definition clearer. Suppose we wish to set up a relative scale of weights of the members of your class. First, we must select the weight of one member of the class and give this weight a simple numerical value. In theory, it does not make any difference whose weight we select or what numerical value we assign to this weight. In practice, our choices should be made on the basis of convenience and usefulness.

Suppose we select the weight of a 125-lb (pound) pupil and assign this weight a value of 5.00. Now we may calculate the

Zeros to the right of a nonzero digit, but to the left of an understood decimal point, are not significant unless specifically indicated to be significant. The rightmost such zero that is significant is indicated by a bar placed above it.

relative weights of the other members of the class by comparing their *actual* weights with that of the 125-lb pupil. A $15\bar{0}$-lb pupil has a weight that is $\frac{15\bar{0}\text{ lb}}{125\text{ lb}}$ or 1.20 times that of the 125-lb pupil. Since the 125-lb pupil has an assigned weight of 5.00 on our relative weight scale, the $15\bar{0}$-lb pupil will have a relative weight of $1.20 \times 5.00 = 6.00$. We could have calculated this relative weight in one step by using the expression $\frac{15\bar{0}\text{ lb}}{125\text{ lb}} \times 5.00 = 6.00$. Similarly, the weight of a $20\bar{0}$-lb pupil will have a value of $\frac{20\bar{0}\text{ lb}}{125\text{ lb}} \times 5.00 = 8.00$ on the relative scale. The weight of a $10\bar{0}$-lb pupil will have a value of $\frac{10\bar{0}\text{ lb}}{125\text{ lb}} \times 5.00 = 4.00$ on the relative scale. These relative weights, 5.00, 6.00, 8.00, and 4.00, are directly proportional to the actual weights of 125 lb, $15\bar{0}$ lb, $20\bar{0}$ lb, and $10\bar{0}$ lb, respectively. If we are concerned only with *relationships* between these weights, it does not matter whether we use the actual weights or the relative weights. In the example we have given, the actual weights and the relative weights are probably equally convenient to use. But the very small numbers which express the actual masses of atoms in grams are not convenient to use.

In order to set up a relative scale of masses of atoms, one atom is chosen and assigned a relative mass value. The masses of all other atoms are then expressed in relation to this defined relative mass. Such a system of relative masses was set up by the world organizations of chemists and physicists. In this system, the carbon-12 atom was chosen and assigned a relative mass of exactly 12. An atom such as the hydrogen-1 atom has a mass about $\frac{1}{12}$ that of the carbon-12 atom. So it has a relative mass of about $\frac{1}{12}$ of 12 or about 1. The accurate value for the relative mass of hydrogen-1 atoms is 1.007825. *The mass of an atom expressed relative to the "carbon-12 = exactly 12" scale is called the* ***atomic mass*** *of the atom.* Thus, 1.007825 is the atomic mass of hydrogen-1.

The mass of a hydrogen-2 atom is about $\frac{1}{6}$ that of a carbon-12 atom. Its atomic mass has been measured to be 2.01410. An oxygen-16 atom has about $\frac{4}{3}$ the mass of a carbon-12 atom. Careful measurements show its atomic mass to be 15.99491. The mass of a magnesium-24 atom is found to be slightly less than double that of a carbon-12 atom. Its accurate atomic mass is 23.98504. In the same way the atomic mass of any nuclide is determined by comparison with the mass of a carbon-12 atom. Atomic masses are very accurately known, as the values given as examples above indicate. We have learned that the *mass number* is the total number of protons and neutrons in the nucleus of an atom. We can now see that it is also *the whole number closest to the atomic mass.*

The masses of the subatomic particles may also be expressed

on the atomic-mass scale. The atomic mass of the electron is 0.0005486. That of the proton is 1.007277 and that of the neutron is 1.008665.

3.13 The Avogadro number and the mole

The number of atoms in the atomic mass of a nuclide taken in grams is an important unit of measure in chemistry. This is the number of carbon-12 atoms in exactly 12 grams of this nuclide. It is also the number of atoms in 1.007825 g of hydrogen-1. It is also the number of atoms in 15.99491 g of oxygen-16. You should recognize that the number of atoms in these three cases must be identical. This is true because atomic masses are directly proportional to actual masses of nuclides.

Scientists have developed many direct and indirect ways for determining this number. Its best present value is 6.022094×10^{23}. This means that there are 6.022094×10^{23} carbon-12 atoms in exactly 12 g of this nuclide; 6.022094×10^{23} hydrogen-1 atoms in 1.007825 g of hydrogen-1; 6.022094×10^{23} oxygen-16 atoms in 15.99491 g of oxygen-16; and so on. This quantity, 6.022094×10^{23}, is so important in science that it has been given a special name. It is called the ***Avogadro number,*** honoring an Italian chemist and physicist, Amedeo Avogadro (1776–1856). This constant is quite useful and should be remembered to at least three significant figures: 6.02×10^{23}.

The amount of substance containing the Avogadro number of any kind of chemical unit is called a ***mole*** *of that substance.* Thus, exactly 12 g of carbon-12 is a mole of carbon-12 atoms; 1.007825 g of hydrogen-1 is a mole of hydrogen-1 atoms; 15.99491 g of oxygen-16 is a mole of oxygen-16 atoms; and so on. Note that *mole* is the name of the quantity containing a convenient number (6.02×10^{23}) of chemical units. Here the chemical unit is the atom. "Mole" is used by chemists the way a grocer uses "dozen" or a stationer uses "gross." A dozen eggs is the quantity 12 eggs; a gross of pencils is the quantity 144 pencils; a mole of atoms is the quantity 6.02×10^{23} atoms. The mole is a very important unit of measure in chemistry. It will be used throughout this text. See Table 3-3.

Fig. 3-8. The mass in grams of one mole of atoms of an element, 6.02×10^{23} atoms, is the gram-atomic weight of the element. The numerical portion of this quantity is the atomic weight of the element.

Table 3-3

MOLAR QUANTITIES OF NUCLIDES

Nuclide	Atomic Mass	Molar Quantity	Number of Atoms	Mass
C-12	12 exactly	1 mole	6.02×10^{23}	12 g exactly
H-1	1.007825	1 mole	6.02×10^{23}	1.007825 g
O-16	15.99491	1 mole	6.02×10^{23}	15.99491 g

To help you understand the enormous number of units in one mole, imagine this situation. Suppose everyone living today on the earth (4 billion people) were to help count the atoms in one mole of an element (copper, for instance). If each person counted continuously at the rate of one atom per second, it would require about 5 million years for all the atoms to be counted.

3.14 Atomic weight

Naturally occurring elements usually exist as a mixture of several isotopes. The percentage of each isotope in the naturally occurring element is nearly always the same, no matter where the element is found. Hence, the mass in grams of one mole of the *naturally occurring atoms* of an element indicates the average relative mass of these atoms on the same "carbon-12 = exactly 12" scale used for atomic masses. *The mass in grams of one mole of naturally occurring atoms of an element is called the* ***gram-atomic weight*** *of the element. The numerical portion of this quantity is the* ***atomic weight*** *of the element.*

Naturally occurring hydrogen consists of 99.985% hydrogen-1 atoms, atomic mass 1.007825; and 0.015% hydrogen-2 atoms, atomic mass 2.01410. In one mole of atoms of this mixture of isotopes, there will be 0.99985 mole of hydrogen-1 atoms and 0.00015 mole of hydrogen-2 atoms. The mass of 0.99985 mole of hydrogen-1 atoms is

$$\mathbf{0.99985\ mole \times \frac{1.007825\ g}{1\ mole} = 1.00767\ g}$$

and the mass of 0.00015 mole of hydrogen-2 atoms is

$$\mathbf{0.00015\ mole \times \frac{2.01410\ g}{1\ mole} = 0.00030\ g}$$

The mass of one mole of atoms of this mixture is therefore

$$\mathbf{1.00767\ g + 0.00030\ g = 1.00797\ g}$$

This mass is the gram-atomic weight of hydrogen. The numerical portion, 1.00797, is the atomic weight of hydrogen. Similarly, naturally occurring carbon consists of 98.89% carbon-12, atomic mass exactly 12 (by definition), and 1.11% carbon-13, atomic mass 13.00335. One mole of atoms of this mixture has a mass of 12.01115 g. Thus, 12.01115 g is the gram-atomic weight of carbon and 12.01115 is its atomic weight.

Atomic weights are important to the chemist because they indicate relative mass relationships between reacting elements. They enable the chemist to predict the quantities of materials that will be involved in chemical reactions.

Atomic weights appear in the periodic table on the inside back cover of this book and in Table 4 in the Appendix. They include the most recent accurate figures. They are still revised occasionally when new data become available. You need not memorize them. Approximate atomic weights are given on the inside of the front cover (and in Table 5 of the Appendix). These are accurate enough for use in solving problems in high school chemistry. For more advanced chemical work, the accurate atomic weights in the periodic table or Table 4 of the Appendix must always be used.

SAMPLE PROBLEM

What is the mass in grams of 3.50 moles of copper atoms?

SOLUTION

The atomic weight of copper from the table inside the back cover or from Appendix, Table 4 is 63.546. Therefore, the gram-atomic weight of copper, or the mass of one mole of copper atoms, is 63.546 g. The mass of 3.50 moles of copper atoms is

$$\mathbf{3.50\ moles \times \frac{63.546\ g\ Cu}{mole} = 222\ g\ Cu}$$

Since the number of moles of copper atoms is expressed in the problem to only three significant figures, the approximate atomic weight of copper found in the table inside the front cover or in Appendix, Table 5, 63.5 could have been used in the solution. The same answer is obtained.

$$\mathbf{3.50\ moles \times \frac{63.5\ g\ Cu}{mole} = 222\ g\ Cu}$$

SAMPLE PROBLEM

How many moles of atoms are there in 6.195 g of phosphorus?

SOLUTION

Since the mass of phosphorus is given to four significant figures, we must use the atomic weight of phosphorus given in the table inside the back cover to at least four significant figures. Rounded to four significant figures, 30.9738 is 30.97. Thus, there is one mole of phosphorus atoms in 30.97 g of phosphorus. Then 6.195 g of phosphorus contains

$$\mathbf{6.195\ g\ P \times \frac{1\ mole}{30.97\ g\ P} = 0.2000\ mole}$$

Note that significant-figure rules permit an answer calculated to four significant figures.

SUMMARY

The idea that matter consists of simple, indivisible, indestructible particles called atoms was proposed by Greek thinkers as early as 400 B.C. John Dalton, between 1803 and 1808, was the first to realize that the nature and properties of atoms could explain the concept stated in the law of definite composition, and also the way and the proportions in which substances react with one another.

An atom is the smallest unit of an element that can exist either alone or in combination with other atoms like it or different from it. The atomic theory states that

1. All matter is made up of very small particles called atoms.

2. Atoms of the same element are chemically alike; atoms of different elements are chemically different.

3. Individual atoms of an element may not all have the same mass. The atoms of an element, as it occurs naturally, have a definite average mass that is characteristic of the element.

4. Individual atoms of different elements may have nearly identical masses. The atoms of different naturally occurring elements have different average masses.

5. Atoms are not subdivided in chemical reactions.

An atom consists of a positively charged central part called the nucleus and negatively charged particles called electrons, which move about the nucleus in shells or energy levels. Atoms are electrically neutral. Particles in the nucleus are positively charged protons and neutral neutrons. These are held together in the nucleus by very short-range forces.

The hydrogen atom has a nucleus made up of one proton. One electron moves about this nucleus in the K shell or 1st energy level. Three isotopes of hydrogen (protium, deuterium, and tritium) are possible with nuclei containing, respectively, no neutron, one neutron, and two neutrons. Isotopes are atoms of the same element that have different masses. The atomic number of an atom is the number of protons in the nucleus of that atom. The atomic number of hydrogen is 1.

Each different variety of atom as determined by the number of protons and number of neutrons in its nucleus is called a nuclide. The mass number of an atom is the sum of the number of protons and neutrons in its nucleus.

The K shell or 1st energy level may contain a maximum of two electrons. The L shell or 2nd energy level may contain a maximum of eight electrons. Argon, the final element in the third series, has eight electrons in the M shell or 3rd energy level.

The mass of an atom expressed relative to the "carbon-12 = exactly 12" scale is called the atomic mass of the atom. The whole number closest to the atomic mass is also the mass number of the atom.

The amount of substance containing an Avogadro number of any kind of chemical unit is called a mole of that substance. The Avogadro number is 6.02×10^{23}.

The mass in grams of one mole of naturally occurring atoms of an element is called the gram-atomic weight of the element. The numerical portion of this quantity is the atomic weight of the element.

QUESTIONS

Group A

1. What evidence is there that the particles of matter are very small?
2. What topics in chemistry are today included in the atomic theory?
3. What general statements may be made about the atoms of the elements and their properties?
4. (*a*) What are the main parts of an atom? (*b*) What particles are found in each part? (*c*) Describe each type of particle.
5. How does the size of the nucleus of an atom compare with the size of an atom?

6. What is a shell or energy level?
7. Describe the movement of electrons about the nucleus of an atom.
8. Describe the structure of each of the three isotopes of hydrogen.
9. (*a*) What is the atomic number of an atom? (*b*) How is it related to the number of electrons in a neutral atom?
10. (*a*) What are nuclides? (*b*) What are isotopes?
11. If you know the number and kinds of particles in an atom, how can you calculate its mass number?
12. An atomic nucleus that contains 8 protons and 9 neutrons is surrounded by 8 electrons: 2 in the 1st energy level and 6 in the 2nd energy level. (*a*) What is the atomic number of this nuclide? (*b*) What is its mass number? (*c*) What is the name of this nuclide?
13. Which among the first ten elements exist naturally as a single nuclide?
14. What is the atomic mass of an atom?
15. (*a*) How many atoms are there in exactly 12 g of carbon-12? (*b*) What name is given to this number? (*c*) What name is given to the amount of substance containing this number of chemical units?
16. What is the atomic weight of an element?
17. What nuclide is the standard for the atomic weight scale?
18. Why are atomic weights important to the chemist?
19. From the Table of Atomic Weights, find the atomic numbers and atomic weights of: (*a*) silver; (*b*) gold; (*c*) copper; (*d*) sulfur; (*e*) uranium.
20. What is the mass in grams of: (*a*) 2.00 moles of helium atoms; (*b*) 5.00 moles of boron atoms; (*c*) 0.500 mole of neon atoms; (*d*) 0.250 mole of magnesium atoms; (*e*) 0.100 mole of silicon atoms? Use the Table of Atomic Weights and follow the rules for significant figure calculations.
21. How many moles of atoms are there in: (*a*) 20.823 g of lithium; (*b*) 160.93 g of sodium; (*c*) 3.995 g of argon; (*d*) 8.016 g of sulfur; (*e*) 20.24 g of aluminum?

Group B

22. What two observations about matter did Dalton believe could be explained by the nature and properties of atoms?
23. In one of the Rutherford experiments, it was found that 1 high-speed positively charged particle in 8000 was deflected by 90° or more when directed at a thin sheet of platinum. What does this observation indicate about the structure of platinum atoms?
24. If you arrange the elements in order of increasing atomic number, how do the atoms of successive elements differ in (*a*) number of protons? (*b*) number of electrons? (*c*) number of neutrons?
25. Describe the electron configurations of atoms in elements of the second series.
26. Copy and complete the following table *on a separate sheet of paper.*

Name of Nuclide	Atomic Number	Mass Number	Composition of Nucleus		Electron Configuration		
			Protons	Neutrons	K	L	M
sodium-23	11						
magnesium-24	12						
aluminum-27	13						
silicon-28	14						
phosphorus-31	15						
sulfur-32	16						
chlorine-35	17						
argon-40	18						

27. Chlorine exists in nature as chlorine-35, atomic mass 34.96885, and chlorine-37, atomic mass 36.96590. Its atomic weight is 35.453. What must be the approximate abundance in nature of these two isotopes?
28. The elements sodium, aluminum, and phosphorus have only one naturally occurring nuclide. How will the atomic mass of this nuclide and the atomic weight of the element compare?
29. (*a*) What is the relationship between an atom containing 10 protons, 10 neutrons, and 10 electrons, and one containing 10 protons, 11 neutrons, and 10 electrons? (*b*) What is the relationship between an atom containing 10 protons, 11 neutrons, and 10 electrons, and one containing 11 protons, 10 neutrons, and 11 electrons?
30. How can the mass in grams of a single atom of a nuclide be calculated if the atomic mass of the nuclide is known?
31. What is the significance of the quotient obtained by dividing the gram-atomic weight of an element by the Avogadro number?
32. Calculate the atomic weight of oxygen. The naturally occurring element consists of 99.759% O-16, atomic mass 15.99491; 0.037% O-17, atomic mass 16.99914; and 0.204% O-18, atomic mass 17.99916.
33. What evidence does the field-ion micrograph on page 41 give concerning the structure of platinum-iridium alloy?

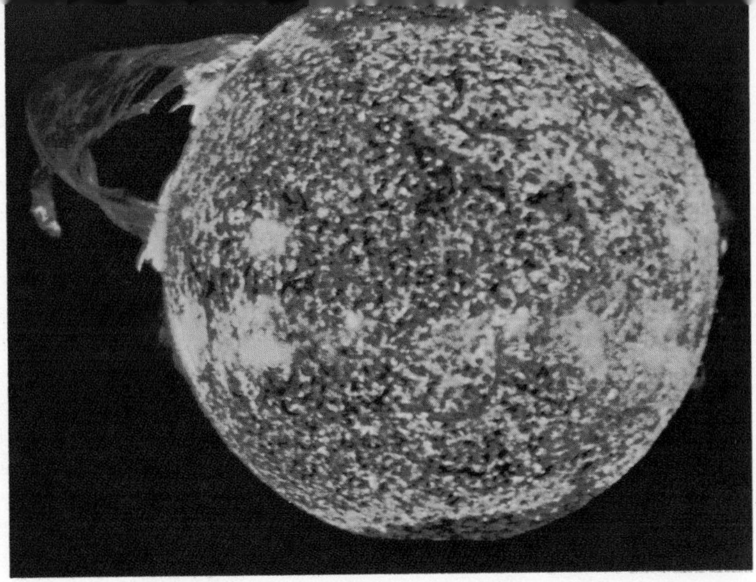

chapter 4

ARRANGEMENT OF ELECTRONS IN ATOMS

HELIUM

Helium was first discovered in the sun. (See Question 29 on page 70.)

4.1 The nucleus and moving electrons

In Chapter 3, you learned about the particles that make up atoms. The atom was described as a nucleus, containing protons and usually neutrons, surrounded by electrons. The electrons in an atom move about the nucleus. The regions where the electrons move are called shells or energy levels. Now you must learn more about the structure of atoms. You must find out how the electrons are arranged and held within the atom.

Recall that the nucleus has a positive charge because of its protons. Also, a neutral atom contains an equal number of protons and negatively charged electrons. Thus we might expect electrons to be held in an atom by the attraction between oppositely charged particles. This arrangement would be similar to the orbiting of a satellite around the earth. Instead of gravitational attraction, which holds a satellite in orbit, the attraction of oppositely charged particles would hold an electron in its path.

However, scientists have observed that electrically charged particles moving in curved paths give off energy. If an electron moving about a nucleus continually gave off energy, it should slow down. It should gradually move nearer to the nucleus and eventually fall into it. This behavior would be like the slowing down of a satellite by friction with the earth's upper atmosphere. As this slowing down occurs, the satellite falls toward the earth and eventually burns up in the earth's atmosphere. But we know that atoms do not collapse. Electrons do not fall into the nucleus. Thus, the attraction of oppositely charged

Fig. 4-1. Both waves are traveling toward the right at the same speed. Let us assume they travel the distance shown in 1 sec. Then the frequency of the top wave is 5 waves/sec and the frequency of the bottom wave is 10 waves/sec. The top wave has a wavelength twice that of the bottom wave. The wavelength is inversely proportional to the frequency. The top wave has a lower frequency and a longer wavelength. The bottom wave has a higher frequency and a shorter wavelength.

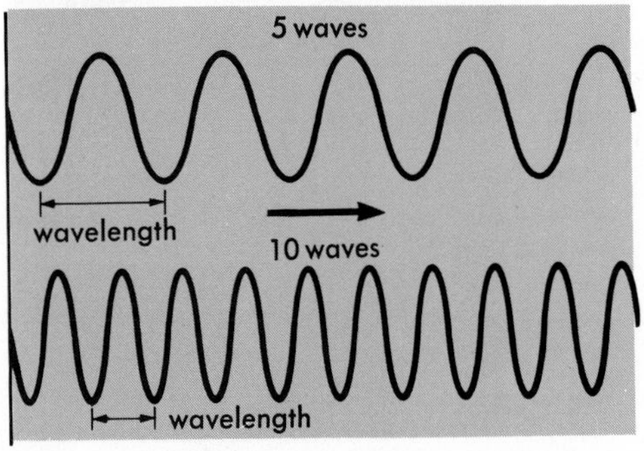

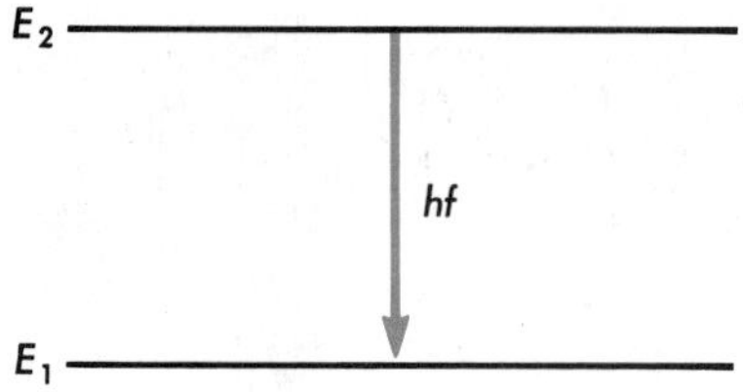

Fig. 4-2. When an excited atom with energy E_2 returns to energy E_1, it gives off a photon having energy $E_2 - E_1 = E = hf$.

Fig. 4-3. Hydrogen atoms are excited when high-voltage electricity is passed through a glass tube containing hydrogen gas. The lavender glow is characteristic of hydrogen.

particles may partly explain how electrons are held by the nucleus of an atom. But it is not satisfactory for explaining the motion of electrons about the nucleus.

4.2 Electromagnetic radiation

Visible light is one kind of electromagnetic radiation. Other kinds of electromagnetic radiation are X rays, ultraviolet and infrared light, and radio waves. Electromagnetic radiations are forms of energy that travel through space as waves. They move at the rate of 3.00×10^8 m/sec, the speed of light in a vacuum. For any wave motion, the speed equals the product of the *frequency* (the number of waves passing a given point in one second) and the *wavelength*. For electromagnetic radiation

$$c = f\lambda$$

where c is the speed of light, f is the frequency, and λ (lambda) is the wavelength. Since c is the same for all electromagnetic radiation, the product $f\lambda$ is a constant; and λ is inversely proportional to f. (See Figure 4-1 on preceding page.)

Electromagnetic radiation, in addition to its wave characteristics, also has some properties of particles. Electromagnetic radiation is transferred to matter in units or *quanta* of energy called ***photons.*** The energy of a photon is proportional to the frequency of the radiation. Thus, the energy of a photon and the frequency of the radiation are related by

$$E = hf$$

Here, E is the energy of the photon, h is a proportionality constant called *Planck's constant,* and f is the frequency of the radiation. Planck's constant is the same for all types of electromagnetic radiation. Since f multiplied by Planck's constant equals E, f and E are directly proportional.

We have already stated that energy is transferred to matter in photon units. Therefore, the absorption of a photon by an atom increases its energy by a definite quantity, hf. An atom that has absorbed energy in this way is called an *excited* atom. When excited atoms radiate energy, the radiation must be given off in photon units also. (See Figure 4-2.)

4.3 Spectra of atoms

Atoms may be excited by heating them in a flame or in an electric arc. Such excited atoms give off light of a characteristic color as they return to their normal energy states. An example is the yellow-orange light given off by sodium atoms in a glass rod heated in a burner flame. Atoms of gases can be excited by passing high-voltage electricity through the gas contained inside a glass tube. The red light of neon advertising signs is a familiar example. If hydrogen gas is used in such a tube, it glows with a characteristic lavender color. (See Figure 4-3.)

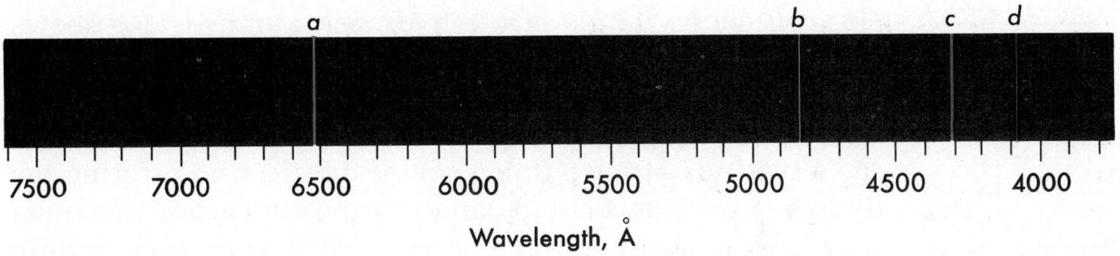

Fig. 4-4. The visible bright-line spectrum of hydrogen seen through a spectroscope.

The continuous spectrum at the top of page 505 shows the relationship between wavelength and color of light.

See Question 15 at the end of this chapter.

When observed through a spectroscope, the lavender-colored light of hydrogen gas reveals lines of particular colors as shown in Figure 4-4. Such a spectrum is called a bright-line spectrum. It indicates that the light given off by excited atoms has only certain wavelengths. Light of a particular wavelength has a definite *frequency* ($c = f\lambda$) and a characteristic color. A definite frequency also means a definite energy ($E = hf$). Hence the bright-line hydrogen spectrum shows that excited hydrogen atoms emit (give off) photons having only certain energies. Now, recall the proportionality relationship between λ, f, and E described in Section 4.2. Because of this relationship, a long wavelength is associated with less energy and a short wavelength is associated with more energy.

It has been found that emitted photons have only certain energies. Further, these energies represent differences between the energies of atoms before and after radiation. Therefore, these energies of atoms are *fixed and definite quantities.* And because each species of atom has its own characteristic spectrum, each atom must have its own characteristic energy possibilities. This evidence also means that the energy changes that occur from time to time within an atom involve definite amounts of energy rather than a continuous flow of energy.

It has been found that the energy changes of an excited atom returning to its normal energy state are actually changes in the energy of its electrons. Therefore, a diagram that shows the electron energy levels of the atom can be devised. Since the hydrogen atom is a simple atom with a simple spectrum, it was thoroughly studied in the early years of this century. Figure 4-6 includes lines in the ultraviolet and infrared regions of the hydrogen spectrum. Figure 4-7 gives the corresponding

Fig. 4-5. In addition to telescopes for visible light, astronomers use radio telescopes to estimate the amount and the distribution of hydrogen in the universe.

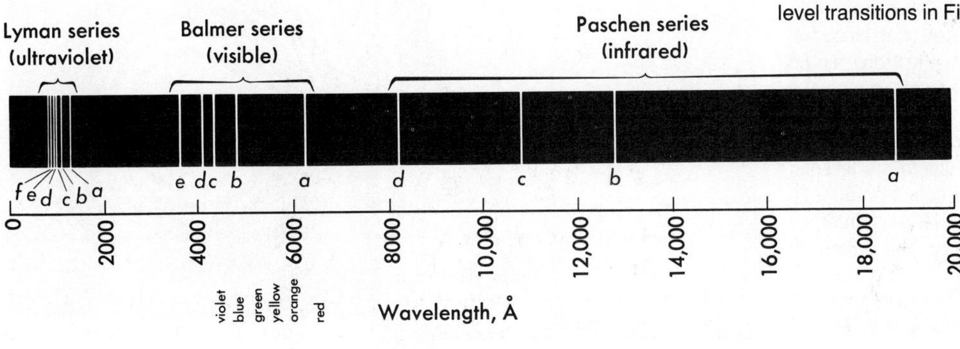

Fig. 4-6. Representative lines in the hydrogen spectrum. The small letter below each line indicates which of the energy-level transitions in Figure 4-7 produces it.

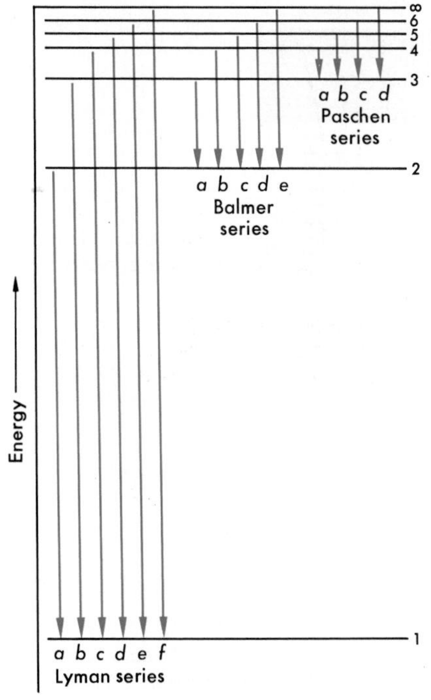

Fig. 4-7. An electron energy-level diagram for hydrogen showing some of the transitions that are possible in this atom. Transitions that leave an electron in a particular final energy level belong to a particular spectral series. Some of these series are named for the people who discovered them.

electron energy levels of the hydrogen atom. It also shows some of the electron transitions that are possible in this atom.

The idea of electron energy levels in the hydrogen atom was developed by Niels Bohr in 1913. The definite energy levels of the atom indicate two things about the electron orbiting the hydrogen nucleus. First, it can move only at certain distances from the nucleus. Second, it can move with only certain speeds. Bohr's theory states that electrons do not give off energy when they remain in given energy levels. They only give off energy when they change to lower energy levels. This helps explain why electrons in atoms do not lose energy, fall into the nucleus, and cause the atom to collapse.

This model works well in explaining the spectra of one-electron particles like the hydrogen atom. But it does not explain satisfactorily the spectra of more complex atoms.

4.4 Wave-mechanics concept of an atom

During the past half century, the work of theoretical physicists, including Heisenberg, de Broglie, and Schrödinger, helped develop a theory of atomic structure based on wave mechanics. The basic ideas of wave mechanics are beyond the scope of a high school chemistry course. It will be useful, however, to consider some of its conclusions.

The motion of an electron about an atom is not in a definite path like that of the earth about the sun. In fact, it is impossible to determine an electron's path without changing that path. So we can give an electron's location only in terms of probabilities. This location is described by a *space orbital.* A space orbital may be thought of as a highly probable location in which an electron may be found. The path of the single hydrogen electron creates a spherical *electron cloud* surrounding the nucleus. This cloud has a maximum density at the most probable distance of the electron from the nucleus. (See Figure 4-9.) In the hydrogen atom, this most probable distance of the electron agrees very well with the distance predicted by the

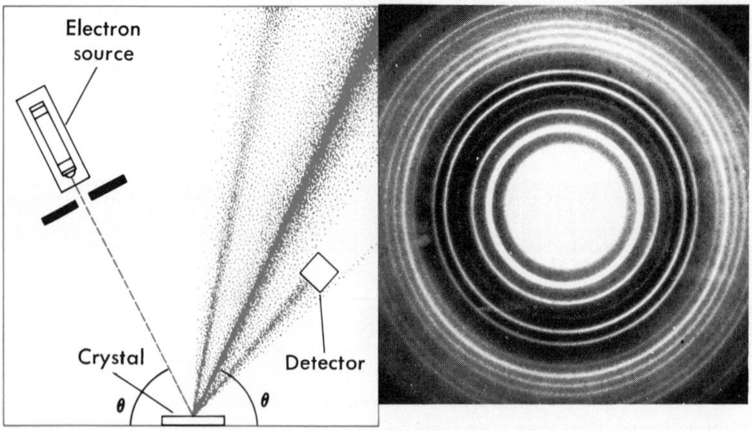

Fig. 4-8. In 1927, C. J. Davisson and L. H. Germer demonstrated that electrons show wave properties. Electrons aimed at the orderly layers of atoms in a crystal are detected at angles other than the ordinary angle of reflection, θ. These extra electron beams are similar to interference patterns produced by electromagnetic waves, such as light and X rays. Interference is a wave property. The pattern at the right, also similar to that produced by X rays, was produced by electrons aimed directly at a thin sheet of aluminum.

Bohr theory. The electron cloud gives size and shape to an atom. It also prevents two free atoms (or portions of free atoms) from occupying the same space.

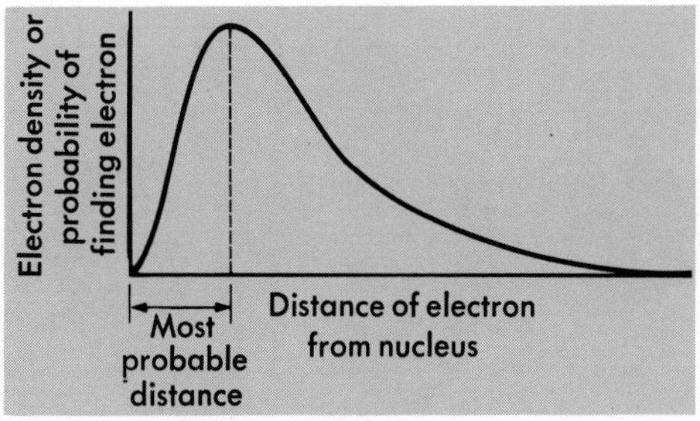

Fig. 4-9. A graph showing the probability of finding the single hydrogen electron as its distance from the nucleus varies.

4.5 Quantum numbers

The mathematics of wave mechanics shows that the energy state of an electron in an atom may be described by a set of four numbers. These are called *quantum numbers.* These quantum numbers describe the space orbital in which the electron moves in terms of (1) distance from the nucleus, (2) shape, (3) position with respect to the three axes in space, and (4) the direction of spin of the electron in the orbital.

The *principal quantum number,* symbolized by n, indicates the most probable distance of the electron from the nucleus of the atom. It is a positive whole number, having values 1, 2, 3, and so on. The principal quantum number is the main energy-level designation, or identifying number, of an orbital. The 1st energy level is closest to the nucleus with others at increasing distances. Electrons in the 1st energy level have the lowest energies. Electrons in higher energy levels have increasingly greater energies. Sometimes, the energy levels are designated by letters instead of numbers. These designations are K shell, L shell, M shell, N shell, O shell, etc.

The *orbital quantum number* indicates the shape of the orbital in which the electron moves. The number of possible shapes is equal to the value of the principal quantum number. In the 1st energy level, an orbital of only one shape is possible. In the 2nd energy level, orbitals of two shapes are possible. In

Table 4-1

QUANTUM NUMBER RELATIONSHIPS IN ATOMIC STRUCTURE

Principal Quantum Number (energy level) (n)	Orbital Quantum Number (n orbital shapes) (n sublevels)	Number of Orbitals per Sublevel	Number of Orbitals per Energy Level (n^2)	Number of Electrons per Sublevel	Number of Electrons per Energy Level ($2n^2$)
1	*s*	1	1	2	2
2	*s* *p*	1 3	4	2 6	8
3	*s* *p* *d*	1 3 5	9	2 6 10	18
4	*s* *p* *d* *f*	1 3 5 7	16	2 6 10 14	32

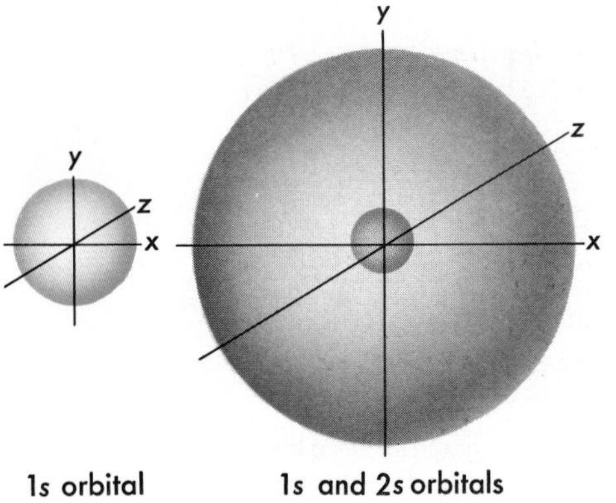

Fig. 4-10. Position in the space about the nucleus of *s* orbitals.

Fig. 4-11. The three spatial positions of *p* orbitals.

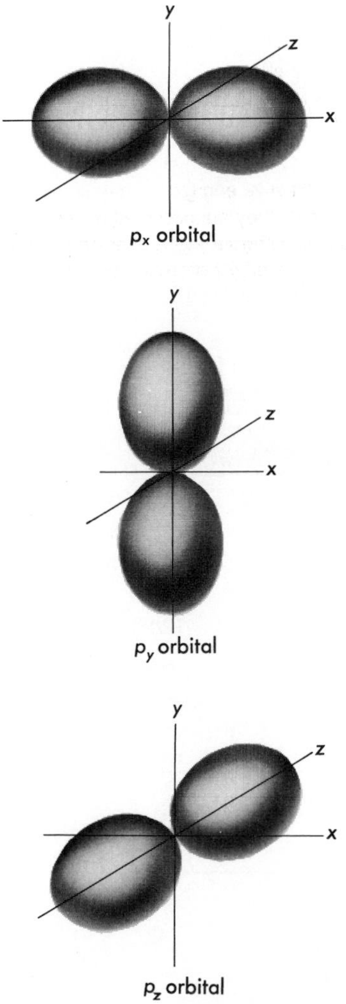

the 3rd energy level, orbitals of three shapes are possible. In the *n*th energy level, orbitals of *n* shapes are possible. The letter designations for the first four orbital quantum numbers are *s, p, d,* and *f.* These are listed in order of ascending energies. For a particular energy level, the *s* orbital has the lowest energy. The *p* orbitals have higher energy than the *s* orbitals, the *d* orbitals have higher energy than the *p* orbitals, and so on. Sometimes the *s* orbital is called the *s* sublevel, the *p* orbitals the *p* sublevel, the *d* orbitals the *d* sublevel, etc.

The *magnetic quantum number* indicates the position about the three axes in space of the orbital. There is only one position in the space around the nucleus for an *s* orbital. There are three positions for a *p* orbital, five positions for a *d* orbital, and seven positions for an *f* orbital. See Figures 4-10 and 4-11.

The *spin quantum number* indicates a property of the electron described by just two conditions. These conditions may be thought of as being like the right-handed or left-handed conditions of a glove. By similarity with the earth-sun system, this property is called *electron spin.* Scientists often refer to the two possibilities for spin as clockwise and counterclockwise. Thus, each of the *positions of orbitals in the space around the nucleus* described by the first three quantum numbers can be occupied by only two electrons and these must have opposite spins. No two electrons in an atom therefore can have exactly the same set of four quantum numbers. This agrees with the observation that no two electrons in an atom have exactly the same energy.

4.6 Electron configuration of atoms of first three series

The quantum numbers that describe the arrangement of electrons about an atom are related to the energies of the electrons. The energies associated with the various electron orbitals as they become occupied by electrons are shown in Figure 4-12. The most stable state of an atom is called its *ground state* In this condition, the electrons have the lowest possible energies. If we know the number of electrons in an atom, we can describe the arrangement of electrons, or the *electron configuration,* of its ground state. We can do this because electrons occupy the various orbitals in a reasonably definite order starting with those of lowest energy.

Hydrogen atoms have only one electron. In the ground state this electron moves in the 1*s* sublevel, the *s* sublevel of the 1st energy level. The two electrons of helium atoms both occupy the 1*s* sublevel. This may be shown in *orbital notation* as

	1*s*		1*s*
H	$\oslash$	**He**	$\otimes$

Here, the occupation of a space orbital by one electron is represented as $\oslash$. The occupation of a space orbital by two electrons is represented as ⊗. An empty circle, ○, indicates an unoccupied space orbital. The two helium electrons occupying the same space orbital must have opposite spins. Two such electrons of opposite spin in the same space orbital are called an *electron pair.*

In *electron-configuration notation* hydrogen has the designation $1s^1$. This designation shows that hydrogen has one electron (represented by the superscript) in the *s* sublevel of the 1st energy level. Helium's electron structure is represented as $1s^2$. This means that helium has two electrons (represented by the superscript) in the *s* sublevel of the 1st energy level.

In *electron-dot notation,* hydrogen and helium are designated as

H·　　He:

In this notation, the symbol represents the element, and the dots indicate the number of outer-shell electrons. Two dots written together, as in the helium notation, represent an *electron pair.*

The elements in the second series have electrons occupying the 2nd energy level. Their ground-state electron arrangements may be represented by orbital notation, electron-configuration notation, and electron-dot notation as shown in Table 4-2 on the following page. Note that the orbital notations and electron-configuration notations show *all* of the electrons in the atom. However, the electron-dot notations show only the electrons in the *outer* (highest numbered) energy level or shell. (See Figure 4-13.)

Note that in Figure 4-10 on the opposite page, the s *orbitals are spherical in shape. In Figure 4-11 below it, the* p *orbitals are shaped like a pair of ellipsoids tangent at points of greatest curvature at the nucleus. They are oriented long the three axes in space. The superposition of the three* p *orbitals produces a spherical electron cloud.*

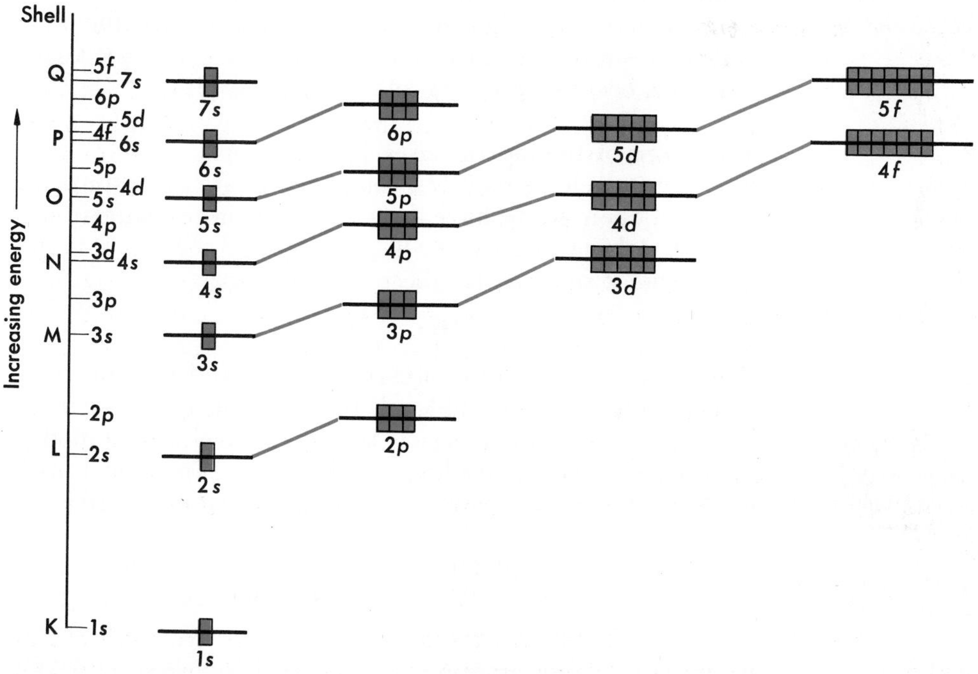

Fig. 4-12. This chart shows the approximate relative energies of the atomic sublevels as they are occupied by electrons. Note how the sublevels of an energy level vary in energy and that the sublevels of higher energy levels overlap.

Table 4-2

ELECTRON NOTATIONS OF ATOMS IN THE SECOND SERIES

	Orbital Notation 1s	2s	2p	Electron-configuration Notation	Electron-dot Notation
Li	⊗	⊘	○ ○ ○	$1s^2 2s^1$	Li·
Be	⊗	⊗	○ ○ ○	$1s^2 2s^2$	Be:
B	⊗	⊗	⊘ ○ ○	$1s^2 2s^2 2p^1$	Ḃ:
C	⊗	⊗	⊘ ⊘ ○	$1s^2 2s^2 2p^2$	·Ċ:
N	⊗	⊗	⊘ ⊘ ⊘	$1s^2 2s^2 2p^3$	·Ṇ̇:
O	⊗	⊗	⊗ ⊘ ⊘	$1s^2 2s^2 2p^4$	·Ọ̈:
F	⊗	⊗	⊗ ⊗ ⊘	$1s^2 2s^2 2p^5$	:Ḟ̣̈:
Ne	⊗	⊗	⊗ ⊗ ⊗	$1s^2 2s^2 2p^6$	:N̤̈e:

Observe that electrons do not pair up in *p* orbitals until each of the three *p* space orbitals is occupied by a single electron. These single electrons also have parallel spins. An atom such as the neon atom has the *s* and *p* sublevels of its outer (highest numbered) energy level filled with eight electrons. Thus, it is said to have an outer shell consisting of an *octet*.

See Question 20 at the end of this chapter.

The electron configurations of the elements of the third series are similar to those of the second series with successive electrons occupying the 3*s* and 3*p* space orbitals.

4.7 Atoms of the fourth series

The first two elements in the fourth series are potassium and calcium. Their atoms have the same electron configuration in the first three energy levels as argon, $1s^2 2s^2 2p^6 3s^2 3p^6$. Electron-dot symbols for these elements are

K· Ca:

These symbols show the presence of one and two electrons respectively in the 4*s* sublevel. In the atoms of the next ten elements of this fourth series, the 3*d* sublevel is occupied in successive steps by the addition of electrons. The distribution of electrons in the ground state of these atoms is given in Table 4-3.

Half-filled or completely filled sublevels have extra stability. The structures of both the chromium and copper atoms given in Table 4-3 appear to be irregular. Chromium would be expected to have four 3*d* electrons and two 4*s* electrons. Instead,

6 3
4 Sym- 2
7 bol 1
5 8

Fig. 4-13. The order of placing electron dots, which represent outer-shell electrons. If there is only one dot in a position, it is centered. Dots 1 and 2 represent *s* electrons. Dots 3 through 8 represent *p* electrons. The *p* electrons do not form pairs until the three *p* orbitals have one electron each. An atom with electrons in all eight positions has an outer shell consisting of an octet.

in the ground state, chromium atoms have five 3*d* electrons and one 4*s* electron. This $3d^5 4s^1$ structure must have higher stability and lower energy than the expected $3d^4 4s^2$ structure. (The $3d^4 4s^2$ configuration can occur in excited chromium atoms.) Apparently a half-filled 3*d* sublevel provides greater stability than a 3*d* sublevel with only four electrons. This greater stability occurs even though the electron-pair in the 4*s* sublevel is broken up. Copper would be expected to have nine 3*d* electrons and two 4*s* electrons. Instead, in the ground state, it has ten 3*d* electrons and one 4*s* electron. Here the filled 3*d* sublevel provides greater stability. (The $3d^9 4s^2$ configuration can occur in excited copper atoms.)

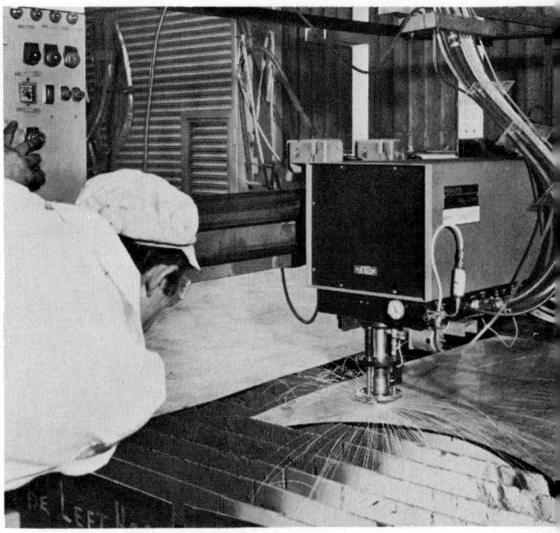

Fig. 4-14. A high energy CO_2 laser is being used to cut a piece of metal.

With the element zinc, the 3rd energy level is completely filled. Also there are two electrons in the 4th energy level. The remaining six elements in the fourth series are gallium, germanium, arsenic, selenium, bromine, and krypton. They all have completely filled 1st, 2nd, and 3rd energy levels. The electrons in the 4*s* and 4*p* sublevels are shown in these electron-dot symbols:

Ga: ·Ge: ·As: ·Se: :Br: :Kr:

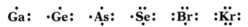

Krypton is the last member of the fourth series. It is a gas that has an octet (two *s* and six *p* electrons) in its 4th energy level. Its electron-configuration notation is $1s^2 2s^2 2p^6 3s^2 3p^6 3d^{10}$-$4s^2 4p^6$. Observe that in this notation all the sublevels of an energy level are grouped together in *s*, *p*, *d*, and *f* order.

Table 4-3

STRUCTURE OF ATOMS IN THE FOURTH SERIES

Name	Symbol	Atomic Number	Number of Electrons in Sublevels							
			1*s*	2*s*	2*p*	3*s*	3*p*	3*d*	4*s*	4*p*
potassium	K	19	2	2	6	2	6		1	
calcium	Ca	20	2	2	6	2	6		2	
scandium	Sc	21	2	2	6	2	6	1	2	
titanium	Ti	22	2	2	6	2	6	2	2	
vanadium	V	23	2	2	6	2	6	3	2	
chromium	Cr	24	2	2	6	2	6	5	1	
manganese	Mn	25	2	2	6	2	6	5	2	
iron	Fe	26	2	2	6	2	6	6	2	
cobalt	Co	27	2	2	6	2	6	7	2	
nickel	Ni	28	2	2	6	2	6	8	2	
copper	Cu	29	2	2	6	2	6	10	1	
zinc	Zn	30	2	2	6	2	6	10	2	
gallium	Ga	31	2	2	6	2	6	10	2	1
germanium	Ge	32	2	2	6	2	6	10	2	2
arsenic	As	33	2	2	6	2	6	10	2	3
selenium	Se	34	2	2	6	2	6	10	2	4
bromine	Br	35	2	2	6	2	6	10	2	5
krypton	Kr	36	2	2	6	2	6	10	2	6

Table 4-4

STRUCTURE OF ATOMS IN THE FIFTH SERIES													
Name	Symbol	Atomic Number	Number of Electrons in Sublevels										
			1*s*	2*s*	2*p*	3*s*	3*p*	3*d*	4*s*	4*p*	4*d*	5*s*	5*p*
rubidium	Rb	37	2	2	6	2	6	10	2	6		1	
strontium	Sr	38	2	2	6	2	6	10	2	6		2	
yttrium	Y	39	2	2	6	2	6	10	2	6	1	2	
zirconium	Zr	40	2	2	6	2	6	10	2	6	2	2	
niobium	Nb	41	2	2	6	2	6	10	2	6	4	1	
molybdenum	Mo	42	2	2	6	2	6	10	2	6	5	1	
technetium	Tc	43	2	2	6	2	6	10	2	6	5	2	
ruthenium	Ru	44	2	2	6	2	6	10	2	6	7	1	
rhodium	Rh	45	2	2	6	2	6	10	2	6	8	1	
palladium	Pd	46	2	2	6	2	6	10	2	6	10		
silver	Ag	47	2	2	6	2	6	10	2	6	10	1	
cadmium	Cd	48	2	2	6	2	6	10	2	6	10	2	
indium	In	49	2	2	6	2	6	10	2	6	10	2	1
tin	Sn	50	2	2	6	2	6	10	2	6	10	2	2
antimony	Sb	51	2	2	6	2	6	10	2	6	10	2	3
tellurium	Te	52	2	2	6	2	6	10	2	6	10	2	4
iodine	I	53	2	2	6	2	6	10	2	6	10	2	5
xenon	Xe	54	2	2	6	2	6	10	2	6	10	2	6

4.8 Atoms of the fifth series

The fifth series of elements, like the fourth, consists of 18 elements. The first two of these are rubidium and strontium. These elements have inner shells like krypton, and one and two electrons respectively in the 5*s* sublevel.

Rb·   Sr:

In the atoms of the next ten elements, the five 4*d* sublevel orbitals become occupied by the successive addition of electrons to the atom structure.

The atoms of the element cadmium have completely filled 1st, 2nd, and 3rd energy levels. The 4*s*, 4*p*, and 4*d* sublevels are also filled, and there are two electrons in the 5*s* sublevel. The atoms of the remaining six elements of the fifth series are indium, tin, antimony, tellurium, iodine, and xenon. The first four energy levels of these elements are similar to those of cadmium, but successive electrons occupy the 5*p* sublevel, which has the next higher energy.

In: ·Sn: ·Sb: ·Te: :I: :Xe:

Thus the addition of electrons to sublevels of two different energy levels proceeds in the fifth series as it did in the fourth series. Xenon, the last member of the series, has an octet in its 5th energy level, and 4*s*, 4*p*, and 4*d* sublevels filled.

4.9 Atoms of the sixth series

The sixth series of atoms is much longer than the others. It consists of 32 elements. The atoms of the first two, cesium and barium, have inner energy levels like xenon and successive electrons in the 6*s* sublevel.

Cs· Ba:

At lanthanum, the lowest energy *d*-sublevel (here 5*d*) begins to fill, as 4*d* began to fill at yttrium and 3*d* began to fill at scandium. But with the very next element, cerium, something different happens. In the atoms of cerium and the next 12 elements of the sixth series, the 7 orbitals of the 4*f* sublevel are occupied by the addition of successive electrons. In atoms of

Table 4-5

STRUCTURE OF ATOMS IN THE SIXTH SERIES

Name	Symbol	Atomic Number		Number of Electrons in Sublevels						
				4*d*	4*f*	5*s*	5*p*	5*d*	6*s*	6*p*
cesium	Cs	55		10		2	6		1	
barium	Ba	56		10		2	6		2	
lanthanum	La	57		10		2	6	1	2	
cerium	Ce	58		10	2	2	6		2	
praseodymium	Pr	59		10	3	2	6		2	
neodymium	Nd	60		10	4	2	6		2	
promethium	Pm	61		10	5	2	6		2	
samarium	Sm	62		10	6	2	6		2	
europium	Eu	63		10	7	2	6		2	
gadolinium	Gd	64		10	7	2	6	1	2	
terbium	Tb	65		10	9	2	6		2	
dysprosium	Dy	66		10	10	2	6		2	
holmium	Ho	67		10	11	2	6		2	
erbium	Er	68	krypton	10	12	2	6		2	
thulium	Tm	69	structure	10	13	2	6		2	
ytterbium	Yb	70	plus	10	14	2	6		2	
lutetium	Lu	71		10	14	2	6	1	2	
hafnium	Hf	72		10	14	2	6	2	2	
tantalum	Ta	73		10	14	2	6	3	2	
tungsten	W	74		10	14	2	6	4	2	
rhenium	Re	75		10	14	2	6	5	2	
osmium	Os	76		10	14	2	6	6	2	
iridium	Ir	77		10	14	2	6	7	2	
platinum	Pt	78		10	14	2	6	9	1	
gold	Au	79		10	14	2	6	10	1	
mercury	Hg	80		10	14	2	6	10	2	
thallium	Tl	81		10	14	2	6	10	2	1
lead	Pb	82		10	14	2	6	10	2	2
bismuth	Bi	83		10	14	2	6	10	2	3
polonium	Po	84		10	14	2	6	10	2	4
astatine	At	85		10	14	2	6	10	2	5
radon	Rn	86		10	14	2	6	10	2	6

the element ytterbium, the 4th energy level has all of its sublevels filled with 32 electrons.

The atoms of the next ten elements of the sixth series have successive electrons occupying the five orbitals of the 5*d* sublevel, which have the next higher energies.

The atoms of the remaining six elements of this series are thallium, lead, bismuth, polonium, astatine, and radon. They have the first four energy levels complete, and filled 5*s*, 5*p*, and 5*d* sublevels. The 6*s* and 6*p* electrons are shown in these electron-dot symbols:

Ṫl: ·Ṗb: ·Bi: ·Po: :At: :Rn:

Radon, the last member of the sixth series, has an octet in its 6th energy level, and 5*s*, 5*p*, and 5*d* sublevels filled.

4.10 Atoms of the seventh series

The seventh series of elements is an incomplete series of which only 21 elements are known. Table 4-6 shows what is believed to be the arrangement of electrons in the 5th, 6th, and 7th energy levels. Appendix Table 7, Electronic Arrangement of the Elements, gives the complete electron configurations for all of the elements.

Table 4-6

STRUCTURE OF ATOMS IN THE SEVENTH SERIES

Name	Symbol	Atomic Number		Number of Electrons in Sublevels						
				4f	*5d*	*5f*	*6s*	*6p*	*6d*	*7s*
francium	Fr	87		14	10		2	6		1
radium	Ra	88		14	10		2	6		2
actinium	Ac	89		14	10		2	6	1	2
thorium	Th	90		14	10		2	6	2	2
protactinium	Pa	91		14	10	2	2	6	1	2
uranium	U	92		14	10	3	2	6	1	2
neptunium	Np	93		14	10	4	2	6	1	2
plutonium	Pu	94	xenon	14	10	6	2	6		2
americium	Am	95	structure	14	10	7	2	6		2
curium	Cm	96	plus	14	10	7	2	6	1	2
berkelium	Bk	97		14	10	8	2	6	1	2
californium	Cf	98		14	10	10	2	6		2?
einsteinium	Es	99		14	10	11	2	6		2?
fermium	Fm	100		14	10	12	2	6		2?
mendelevium	Md	101		14	10	13	2	6		2?
nobelium	No	102		14	10	14	2	6		2?
lawrencium	Lr	103		14	10	14	2	6	1	2?
		104		14	10	14	2	6	2	2?
		105		14	10	14	2	6	3	2?
		106		14	10	14	2	6	4	2?
		107		14	10	14	2	6	5	2?

SUMMARY

Electromagnetic radiations are forms of energy that travel through space as waves. The frequency of a wave and its wavelength are inversely proportional. Electromagnetic radiation also has some properties of particles. Electromagnetic radiation is transferred to matter in photon units. The energy of a photon is directly proportional to the frequency of the radiation. An atom that has absorbed energy is called an excited atom. When excited atoms radiate energy, the radiation is given off in photon units.

The bright-line spectra of atoms show that energy changes involving only fixed and definite quantities of energy may occur within atoms. This is evidence for electron energy levels in atoms.

A space orbital is a highly probable location in which an electron may be found. The energy state of an electron in an atom may be described by four quantum numbers. The principal quantum number indicates the most probable distance of the electron from the nucleus of the atom. The orbital quantum number indicates the shape of the orbital in which the electron moves. The magnetic quantum number indicates the position about the three axes in space of the orbital. The spin quantum number indicates the direction of spin of the electron. No two electrons in an atom can have exactly the same set of quantum numbers.

The most stable state of an atom is its ground state. If we know the number of electrons in an atom, we can describe its electron configuration because electrons occupy the various orbitals in a reasonably definite order. Electron configurations can be described by orbital notation, electron-configuration notation, and electron-dot notation. Two electrons of opposite spin in the same space orbital are an electron pair. An atom with only the *s* and *p* orbitals of its outer energy level filled with eight electrons is said to have an outer shell consisting of an octet. Seven series of atoms have been identified. The final element in each series has an octet in its outer shell.

QUESTIONS

Group A

1. (*a*) What are electromagnetic radiations? (*b*) Give examples of forms of electromagnetic radiation.
2. (*a*) In what form do electromagnetic radiations travel through space? (*b*) In what form are they transferred to matter?
3. How is an excited atom produced?
4. (*a*) The red line in the visible spectrum of hydrogen has a wavelength of 6563 Å. From Figures 4-6 and 4-7 identify the electron-energy-level transition that produces this line. (*b*) Which electron-energy-level transition produces the blue line having a wavelength of 4861 Å?
5. What are the principal characteristics of the Bohr model of the hydrogen atom?
6. What is a space orbital?
7. (*a*) What is an electron cloud? (*b*) What properties does it give an atom?
8. What are the four kinds of quantum numbers and what does each indicate?
9. (*a*) What is the shape of an *s* orbital? (*b*) How many *s* orbitals can there be in an energy level? (*c*) How many electrons can occupy such an orbital? (*d*) What characteristic must these electrons have? (*e*) Which is the lowest energy level having an *s* orbital?
10. (*a*) What is the shape of a *p* orbital? (*b*) How many *p* orbitals can there be in an energy level? (*c*) How are they

arranged with respect to one another? (*d*) Which is the lowest energy level having *p* orbitals?

11. (*a*) May two electrons in the same atom have exactly the same set of quantum numbers? (*b*) May two electrons occupy the same space orbital in an atom? (*c*) Under what conditions?
12. Distinguish between an atom in its ground state and an excited atom.
13. (*a*) What is an electron pair? (*b*) What is an octet?

Group B

14. What aspect of the attraction between oppositely charged particles makes it unsatisfactory for explaining how electrons move in an atom?
15. Derive the relationship between λ and E for electromagnetic radiation.
16. Why must energy transitions within an atom occur in definite amounts rather than as a continuous flow?
17. (*a*) From Figures 4-6 and 4-7, determine the approximate wavelength of the radiation produced by an electron transition in a hydrogen atom from the 4th energy level to the 1st energy level; (*b*) from the 4th energy level to the 3rd energy level.
18. (*a*) How many *d* orbitals can there be in an energy level? (*b*) How many *d* electrons can there be in an energy level? (*c*) Which is the lowest energy level having *d* orbitals?
19. (*a*) How many *f* orbitals can there be in an energy level? (*b*) How many *f* electrons can there be in an energy level? (*c*) Which is the lowest energy level having *f* orbitals?
20. How many electron pairs are there in the outer shell of each of the following atoms: (*a*) carbon; (*b*) krypton; (*c*) oxygen; (*d*) arsenic; (*e*) iodine?
21. Which of the atoms in Question 20 has an octet as an outer shell?
22. On a separate sheet of paper copy and complete the following table for the atoms in the third series. *Do not write in this book.*

Chemical Symbol	Orbital Notation	Electron-configuration Notation	Electron-dot Notation
Na			
Mg			
Al			
Si			
P			
S			
Cl			
Ar			

23. How many energy levels are partially or fully occupied in the mendelevium atom?
24. Why do the fourth and fifth series of elements contain 18 elements, rather than 8 as in the second and third series?
25. Why does the sixth series of elements contain 32 elements, rather than 18 as in the fourth and fifth series?
26. (*a*) Which energy level corresponds to the N shell? (*b*) What types of space orbitals can be found in this energy level? (*c*) How many of each type? (*d*) How many electrons can occupy each of these types of space orbitals? (*e*) How many electrons are needed to completely fill the N shell?
27. Which sublevels of the 3rd energy level are filled (*a*) in the element argon; (*b*) in the element krypton?
28. What is a probable electron configuration for element 109?
29. Read the article on helium in an encyclopedia. How can you relate the photograph of the sun with the spectrum of helium shown with it?

chapter 5

THE PERIODIC LAW

One of the Group VIII elements displaying its most popular use. (See Question 35 on page 90.)

5.1 Mendeleyev's periodic table

Suppose for an elementary knowledge of chemistry, you had to study separately the properties of each of the known chemical elements. This would be a very great task. But suppose some of the elements had similar properties. And, if these elements could be placed in groups, it would not be too difficult to remember the distinguishing properties of each group. It might even be possible to remember how the properties varied among the members of the group, if the variations occurred fairly regularly.

About 1869, the Russian chemist Dmitri Mendeleyev (men-deh-*lay*-eff) (1834–1907) devised a useful classification system for the elements. Mendeleyev called this classification system the *Periodic Table of the Elements.* In this table, consisting of rows and columns, elements are placed in order. The sequence is like that of words on a printed page, left to right, top to bottom. The particular order Mendeleyev used was that of increasing atomic weight. He selected the width of the table (the number of columns) so that elements with similar properties occupied positions in the same column. The periodic tables we use today have evolved from the pioneer work done by Mendeleyev.

Fig. 5-1. Dmitri Mendeleyev, a Russian chemist, worked out the first useful periodic table of the chemical elements.

When Mendeleyev first prepared his periodic table, he realized that all the elements were probably not yet discovered. For example, the elements scandium, gallium, and germanium were unknown in Mendeleyev's day. He carefully studied the properties of the known elements. Based upon

You may be interested in looking up the chemical element classifications of J. W. Dobereiner, J. A. Newlands, and L. Meyer.

his study, Mendeleyev left gaps in his table and predicted that new elements would be discovered that would fill these gaps. He also predicted the properties of these new elements. His predictions were later found to be very accurate when compared with the actual properties of these elements.

Mendeleyev noticed that when the elements are arranged in order of increasing atomic weight, their chemical properties follow a pattern. Similar chemical properties occur again at definite intervals. Mendeleyev concluded that "the properties of the elements are in periodic dependence on their atomic weights."

In Mendeleyev's table, the first two rows (or *series*, or *periods*) had seven elements before elements with similar properties occurred again. In the third and fourth periods, Mendeleyev found that there were 17 elements before similar properties occurred again. The noble gases, neon, argon, krypton, and xenon, were discovered by Sir William Ramsay (1852–1916) during the 1890's. Another noble gas, helium, was discovered on the sun in 1868. It was not really accepted as an element until it was found on the earth in 1895. These noble gases added an element to each period of the periodic table.

Fig. 5-2. Even though Mendeleyev's original periodic table appears quite different from the one we use today, there are similarities. How many elements can you find that we now classify as belonging in the same groups? Which elements did Mendeleyev predict would be discovered?

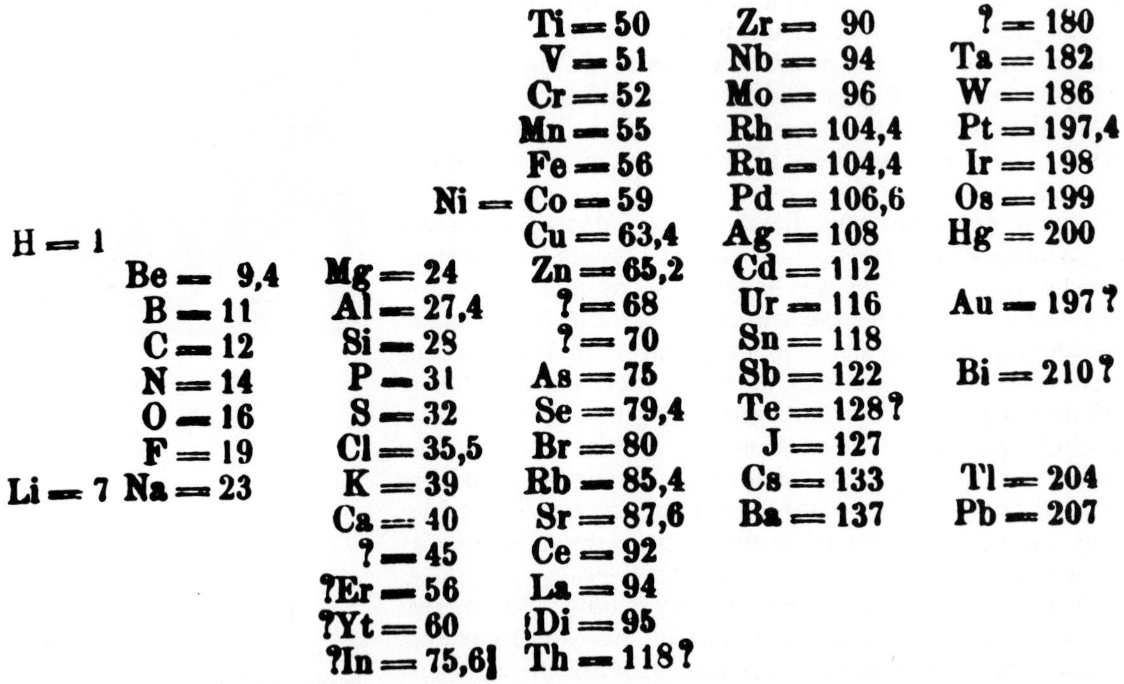

			Ti = 50	Zr = 90	? = 180
			V = 51	Nb = 94	Ta = 182
			Cr = 52	Mo = 96	W = 186
			Mn = 55	Rh = 104,4	Pt = 197,4
			Fe = 56	Ru = 104,4	Ir = 198
			Ni = Co = 59	Pd = 106,6	Os = 199
H = 1			Cu = 63,4	Ag = 108	Hg = 200
	Be = 9,4	Mg = 24	Zn = 65,2	Cd = 112	
	B = 11	Al = 27,4	? = 68	Ur = 116	Au = 197?
	C = 12	Si = 28	? = 70	Sn = 118	
	N = 14	P = 31	As = 75	Sb = 122	Bi = 210?
	O = 16	S = 32	Se = 79,4	Te = 128?	
	F = 19	Cl = 35,5	Br = 80	J = 127	
Li = 7	Na = 23	K = 39	Rb = 85,4	Cs = 133	Tl = 204
		Ca = 40	Sr = 87,6	Ba = 137	Pb = 207
		? = 45	Ce = 92		
		?Er = 56	La = 94		
		?Yt = 60	Di = 95		
		?In = 75,6	Th = 118?		

Mendeléev's periodic table as it appeared in the* Zeitschrift für Chemie *for 1869

5.2 Moseley determines atomic numbers

About 45 years after Mendeleyev's work on the periodic table, an important discovery was made which helped improve the classification of the elements. In Chapter 3, it was stated that the atomic number of an element indicates the number of protons in the nuclei of its atoms. Henry Gwyn-Jeffreys Moseley (1887–1915), an English scientist, performed some X-ray experiments that showed how the number of protons per nucleus varied progressively from element to element.

X rays are electromagnetic radiations. Light is another form of electromagnetic radiation. But, unlike light, *X rays are not visible and are of higher frequency and shorter wavelength than light.* X rays are produced when high-speed electrons strike a metal target in an evacuated tube (one from which the gas has been pumped). Moseley found that the wavelengths of the X rays produced depend on the kind of metal used as the target. He used as targets various metals ranging in atomic weight from aluminum to gold. He found that the wavelengths of X rays became shorter as he used elements with more protons in their nuclei. The higher the atomic number of an element, the shorter the wavelength of the X rays produced when that element is used as the target in an X-ray tube.

Moseley found in some cases an unusual variation in the wavelengths of X rays between two successive elements. The variation was twice as great as his calculations indicated. He concluded that in such cases an element was missing from the periodic table. Several elements have since been discovered which fill the gaps that Moseley indicated.

5.3 The periodic law

When the elements in a periodic table are placed in the order of increasing atomic numbers instead of increasing atomic weights, some of the problems of arrangement disappear. Arranged according to increasing atomic weights, potassium precedes argon. Yet, when arranged according to properties in the table, potassium follows argon. This is in agreement with the atomic numbers: argon, 18, and potassium, 19. A similar case is that of tellurium, 52, and iodine, 53.

As stated in Section 5.1, Mendeleyev concluded that the properties of elements are related in a periodic way to their atomic weights. Today, evidence shows that atomic numbers are better standards for establishing the order of the elements. Mendeleyev's conclusion is now restated as the ***periodic law:*** *The physical and chemical properties of the elements are periodic functions of their atomic numbers.* In other words, (1) the properties of elements go through a pattern of change; (2) elements of similar properties occur at certain intervals, provided the elements are arranged in a periodic table in the order of increasing atomic number.

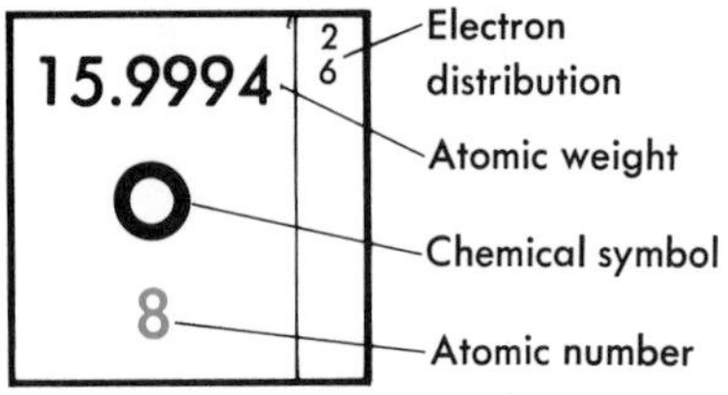

Fig. 5-3. This figure shows the position of information found in each block of the periodic table.

One unique property of hydrogen atoms is their single electron. If an electron is removed from a hydrogen atom, only the nucleus, one ten-thousandth the diameter of the atom, remains.

Fig. 5-4(A). The first four elements of period three of the periodic table.

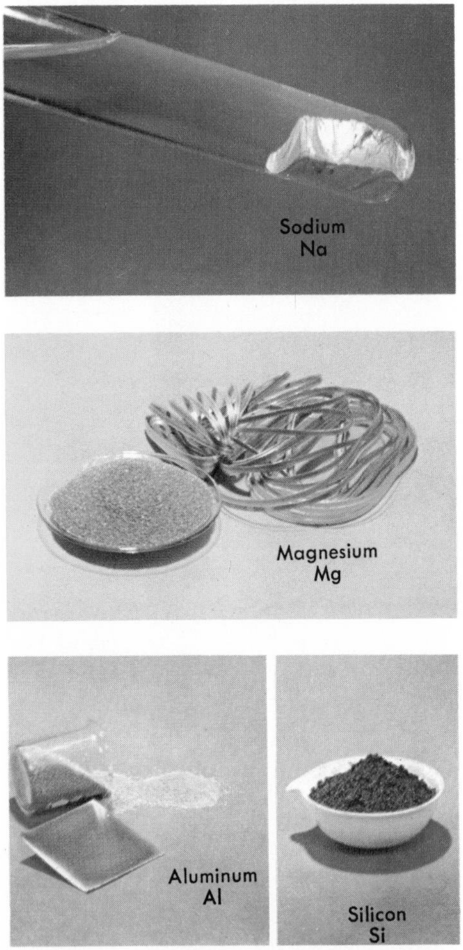

5.4 Arrangement of the modern periodic table

The modern periodic table is shown on pages 76–77. Frequent reference to these pages as you study this section will help you to understand the periodic table and its importance in chemistry.

Each element is assigned a separate block in the table. (See Figure 5-3.) In the center of the block is the chemical symbol for the element. Below the symbol is the atomic number of the element. Above the symbol is the atomic weight. To the right of each symbol are numbers. These numbers indicate the distribution of electrons in the shells of the atoms of this element. A horizontal row of blocks on the table is called a ***period*** or ***series.*** A vertical column is called a ***group*** or ***family.***

Hydrogen, atomic number 1, is placed at the top of the table by itself because of its many unique properties. It is in the first column at the left of the table because its atoms have one electron in the outermost shell. Helium, atomic number 2, is at the top of the extreme right-hand column. Helium is classified as an inert gas because it does not react with other elements. It is the simplest member of the group of elements known as the *noble gases.* Note that helium atoms have two electrons in the K shell or 1st energy level, and that with these two electrons, the K shell is complete. Hydrogen and helium compose the first period of elements.

The second period consists of eight elements: (1) *Lithium,* a soft, silvery, active metal, whose atoms have one electron in their outer shell, the L shell or 2nd energy level. (2) *Beryllium,* a silvery metal, less active than lithium, whose atoms have two electrons in their L shell. (3) *Boron,* a black solid with some nonmetallic properties, whose atoms have three electrons in their L shell. (4) *Carbon,* a solid element with very distinctive chemical properties intermediate between those of metals and nonmetals, four electrons in the L shell. (5) *Nitrogen,* a colorless gas, nonmetallic properties, five electrons in the L shell. (6) *Oxygen,* a colorless gas, strong nonmetallic properties, six electrons in the L shell. (7) *Fluorine,* a pale-yellow gas, very strong nonmetallic properties, seven electrons in the L shell. (8) *Neon,* a colorless, inert (unreactive) gas, eight electrons in the L shell. Refer to Appendix Table 7, Electron Arrangement of the Elements.

It should be noted that these elements range from an active metallic element (Li) through two metalloids (Be and B, whose properties are between those of the typical metal and nonmetal) to an active nonmetallic element (F), while the last element in the period (Ne) is inert. This variation in properties from metallic through metalloidal to nonmetallic is accompanied by an increase in the number of L-shell electrons from 1 to 7. The inert element neon has 8 electrons, an octet, in the L shell.

The third period also consists of eight elements: (1) *Sodium,* a soft, silvery, active metal similar to lithium, one electron in the outermost shell, the M shell or 3rd energy level. (2) *Magnesium,* a silvery metal similar in properties to beryllium, two electrons in the M shell. (3) *Aluminum,* a silvery metal with some nonmetallic properties, three electrons in the M shell. (4) *Silicon,* a dark-colored nonmetallic element with some properties resembling carbon, four electrons in the M shell. (5) *Phosphorus,* a nonmetallic solid element that forms compounds similar to those of nitrogen, five electrons in the M shell. (6) *Sulfur,* a yellow nonmetallic solid element, six electrons in the M shell. (7) *Chlorine,* a yellow-green gas with strong nonmetallic properties resembling those of fluorine, seven electrons in the M shell. (8) *Argon,* a colorless, inert gas, eight electrons in the M shell. Figure 5-4 illustrates the variations in the properties of these third-period elements. Again the elements range from active metallic through metalloidal to active nonmetallic properties as the number of electrons in the outer shell varies from 1 to 7. The element with an octet as its outer shell is a noble gas.

Elements with similar properties have a similar arrangement of outer-shell electrons. They fall into the same group in the periodic table.

In Group I of the periodic table, we find the *sodium family,* a group of six similar, very active, metallic elements. Their atoms all have only one electron in the outermost shell. *Francium* is the most complex member of the sodium family. The position of francium in the periodic table indicates that it is probably the most active metal.

Group II also consists of six active metals whose chemical properties are very much alike. The atoms of each have two electrons in their outer shell. This is the *calcium family.* The most chemically active member of this family is *radium.*

The properties of elements in Group III vary from nonmetallic to metallic as the atoms become larger and heavier. The atoms of this group have three electrons in their outer shell.

The elements of Group IV vary in similar fashion. Their atoms have four electrons in the outer shell. Atoms of elements in both Group III and Group IV have very stable inner shells.

Group V is the *nitrogen family. Nitrogen* and *phosphorus,* the elements in this family at the top of the table, are nonmetallic. The element *bismuth* at the bottom of the table is metallic. *Arsenic* and *antimony* exhibit both metallic and nonmetallic properties. The atoms of each of these elements have five electrons in the outer shell and have very stable inner shells.

Group VI is the *oxygen family.* The properties of elements in this family vary from active nonmetallic to metallic as the

Fig. 5-4(B). The last four elements of period three of the periodic table.

PERIODIC TABLE

METALS

TRANSITION ELEMENTS

	I	II							
1	1.0080 **H** 1 1								
2	6.941 **Li** 3 2 1	9.01218 **Be** 4 2 2							
3	22.9898 **Na** 11 2 8 1	24.305 **Mg** 12 2 8 2							
4	39.102 **K** 19 2 8 8 1	40.08 **Ca** 20 2 8 8 2	44.9559 **Sc** 21 2 8 9 2	47.90 **Ti** 22 2 8 10 2	50.9414 **V** 23 2 8 11 2	51.996 **Cr** 24 2 8 13 1	54.9380 **Mn** 25 2 8 13 2	55.847 **Fe** 26 2 8 14 2	58.9332 **Co** 27 2 8 15 2
5	85.4678 **Rb** 37 2 8 18 8 1	87.62 **Sr** 38 2 8 18 8 2	88.9059 **Y** 39 2 8 18 9 2	91.22 **Zr** 40 2 8 18 10 2	92.9064 **Nb** 41 2 8 18 12 1	95.94 **Mo** 42 2 8 18 13 1	98.9062 **Tc** 43 2 8 18 13 2	101.07 **Ru** 44 2 8 18 15 1	102.9055 **Rh** 45 2 8 18 16 1
6	132.9055 **Cs** 55 2 8 18 18 8 1	137.34 **Ba** 56 2 8 18 18 8 2	Lanthanide Series 174.97 **Lu** 71 2 8 18 32 9 2	178.49 **Hf** 72 2 8 18 32 10 2	180.9479 **Ta** 73 2 8 18 32 11 2	183.85 **W** 74 2 8 18 32 12 2	186.2 **Re** 75 2 8 18 32 13 2	190.2 **Os** 76 2 8 18 32 14 2	192.22 **Ir** 77 2 8 18 32 15 2
7	[223] **Fr** 87 2 8 18 32 18 8 1	226.0254 **Ra** 88 2 8 18 32 18 8 2	Actinide Series [257] **Lr** 103 2 8 18 32 32 9 2	[261] 104 2 8 18 32 32 10 2	[260] 105 2 8 18 32 32 11 2	[263] 106 2 8 18 32 32 12 2	[261] 107 2 8 18 32 32 13 2		

Lanthanide Series	138.9055 **La** 57 2 8 18 18 9 2	140.12 **Ce** 58 2 8 18 20 8 2	140.9077 **Pr** 59 2 8 18 21 8 2	144.24 **Nd** 60 2 8 18 22 8 2	[147] **Pm** 61 2 8 18 23 8 2	150.4 **Sm** 62 2 8 18 24 8 2	151.96 **Eu** 63 2 8 18 25 8 2
Actinide Series	[227] **Ac** 89 2 8 18 32 18 9 2	232.0381 **Th** 90 2 8 18 32 18 10 2	231.0359 **Pa** 91 2 8 18 32 20 9 2	238.029 **U** 92 2 8 18 32 21 9 2	237.0482 **Np** 93 2 8 18 32 22 9 2	[244] **Pu** 94 2 8 18 32 24 8 2	[243] **Am** 95 2 8 18 32 25 8 2

OF THE ELEMENTS

NON METALS

			III	IV	V	VI	VII	Noble gases VIII
								4.00260 **He** 2 (2)
			10.81 **B** 5 (2, 3)	12.011 **C** 6 (2, 4)	14.0067 **N** 7 (2, 5)	15.9994 **O** 8 (2, 6)	18.9984 **F** 9 (2, 7)	20.179 **Ne** 10 (2, 8)
			26.9815 **Al** 13 (2, 8, 3)	28.086 **Si** 14 (2, 8, 4)	30.9738 **P** 15 (2, 8, 5)	32.06 **S** 16 (2, 8, 6)	35.453 **Cl** 17 (2, 8, 7)	39.948 **Ar** 18 (2, 8, 8)
58.71 **Ni** 28 (2, 8, 16, 2)	63.546 **Cu** 29 (2, 8, 18, 1)	65.37 **Zn** 30 (2, 8, 18, 2)	69.72 **Ga** 31 (2, 8, 18, 3)	72.59 **Ge** 32 (2, 8, 18, 4)	74.9216 **As** 33 (2, 8, 18, 5)	78.96 **Se** 34 (2, 8, 18, 6)	79.904 **Br** 35 (2, 8, 18, 7)	83.80 **Kr** 36 (2, 8, 18, 8)
106.4 **Pd** 46 (2, 8, 18, 18, 0)	107.868 **Ag** 47 (2, 8, 18, 18, 1)	112.40 **Cd** 48 (2, 8, 18, 18, 2)	114.82 **In** 49 (2, 8, 18, 18, 3)	118.69 **Sn** 50 (2, 8, 18, 18, 4)	121.75 **Sb** 51 (2, 8, 18, 18, 5)	127.60 **Te** 52 (2, 8, 18, 18, 6)	126.9045 **I** 53 (2, 8, 18, 18, 7)	131.30 **Xe** 54 (2, 8, 18, 18, 8)
195.09 **Pt** 78 (2, 8, 18, 32, 17, 1)	196.9665 **Au** 79 (2, 8, 18, 32, 18, 1)	200.59 **Hg** 80 (2, 8, 18, 32, 18, 2)	204.37 **Tl** 81 (2, 8, 18, 32, 18, 3)	207.2 **Pb** 82 (2, 8, 18, 32, 18, 4)	208.9806 **Bi** 83 (2, 8, 18, 32, 18, 5)	[210] **Po** 84 (2, 8, 18, 32, 18, 6)	[210] **At** 85 (2, 8, 18, 32, 18, 7)	[222] **Rn** 86 (2, 8, 18, 32, 18, 8)

RARE EARTH ELEMENTS

157.25 **Gd** 64 (2, 8, 18, 25, 9, 2)	158.9254 **Tb** 65 (2, 8, 18, 27, 8, 2)	162.50 **Dy** 66 (2, 8, 18, 28, 8, 2)	164.9303 **Ho** 67 (2, 8, 18, 29, 8, 2)	167.26 **Er** 68 (2, 8, 18, 30, 8, 2)	168.9342 **Tm** 69 (2, 8, 18, 31, 8, 2)	173.04 **Yb** 70 (2, 8, 18, 32, 8, 2)
[245] **Cm** 96 (2, 8, 18, 32, 25, 9, 2)	[247] **Bk** 97 (2, 8, 18, 32, 26, 9, 2)	[249] **Cf** 98 (2, 8, 18, 32, 28, 8, 2)	[254] **Es** 99 (2, 8, 18, 32, 29, 8, 2)	[255] **Fm** 100 (2, 8, 18, 32, 30, 8, 2)	[256] **Md** 101 (2, 8, 18, 32, 31, 8, 2)	[254] **No** 102 (2, 8, 18, 32, 32, 8, 2)

A value given in brackets denotes the mass number of the isotope of longest known half-life.

atoms become larger and heavier. The atoms of each of these elements have six electrons in the outer shell and they have very stable inner shells.

The elements in Group VII, the *halogen family*, are very active nonmetals. Their atoms each have seven electrons in the outer shell and have very stable inner shells. The most active member of the halogen family is its simplest element, *fluorine*.

Group VIII is the *noble-gas family*. With the exception of *helium* atoms, which have a pair of electrons as their outer shell, atoms of these elements have an octet as their outer shell. This is the greatest number of electrons found in an outer shell. No compounds of helium, neon, and argon are known. A few compounds of krypton, xenon, and radon have been prepared. The low atomic weight noble gases are not considered in a discussion of activity because they form no compounds. Thus, we see that the activity of the elements ranges from the most active metal at the lower left corner of the periodic table to the most active nonmetal at the upper right corner.

Fig. 5-5. The periodic table consists essentially of blocks of elements whose structures add support to our modern atomic theory.

SUBLEVEL BLOCKS OF THE PERIODIC TABLE

s sublevel block

TRANSITION ELEMENTS *d* sublevel block

p sublevel block

Period	Sublevels being filled	I	II											III	IV	V	VI	VII	VIII
1	1s	H 1	He 2																
2	2*s* 2*p*	Li 3	Be 4											B 5	C 6	N 7	O 8	F 9	Ne 10
3	3*s* 3*p*	Na 11	Mg 12											Al 13	Si 14	P 15	S 16	Cl 17	Ar 18
4	4*s* 3*d* 4*p*	K 19	Ca 20	Sc 21	Ti 22	V 23	Cr 24	Mn 25	Fe 26	Co 27	Ni 28	Cu 29	Zn 30	Ga 31	Ge 32	As 33	Se 34	Br 35	Kr 36
5	5*s* 4*d* 5*p*	Rb 37	Sr 38	Y 39	Zr 40	Nb 41	Mo 42	Tc 43	Ru 44	Rh 45	Pd 46	Ag 47	Cd 48	In 49	Sn 50	Sb 51	Te 52	I 53	Xe 54
6	6*s* 4*f* 5*d* 6*p*	Cs 55	Ba 56	Lu 71	Hf 72	Ta 73	W 74	Re 75	Os 76	Ir 77	Pt 78	Au 79	Hg 80	Tl 81	Pb 82	Bi 83	Po 84	At 85	Rn 86
7	7*s* 5*f* 6*d* 7*p*	Fr 87	Ra 88	Lr 103	104	105	106	107											

RARE EARTH ELEMENTS *f* sublevel block

Period	Sublevels	Series													
6	4*f*	Lanthanide series	La 57	Ce 58	Pr 59	Nd 60	Pm 61	Sm 62	Eu 63	Gd 64	Tb 65	Dy 66	Ho 67	Er 68	Tm 69	Yb 70
7	5*f*	Actinide series	Ac 89	Th 90	Pa 91	U 92	Np 93	Pu 94	Am 95	Cm 96	Bk 97	Cf 98	Es 99	Fm 100	Md 101	No 102

The fourth period consists of 18 elements. It is the first long period. In addition to the eight elements in Groups I to VIII, there are also ten ***transition elements.*** These are metallic elements whose atoms have one or two electrons in the outer shell. Successive electrons usually occupy the group of 5 space orbitals of the 3*d* sublevel.

The fifth period also consists of 18 elements. It includes ten transition elements, in which successive electrons occupy the group of 5 space orbitals of the 4*d* sublevel. The transition elements are all metals.

The sixth period consists of 32 elements. In addition to the elements in Groups I to VIII and the ten transition elements, there is a group of 14 ***rare earth elements.*** These elements have almost identical chemical properties. They compose the *lanthanide series.* The two outer shells of these atoms are almost the same. The outermost shell contains two electrons. The next-inner shell contains either eight or nine electrons. Successive electrons occupy the group of 7 space orbitals of the 4*f* sublevel, as the number of electrons in the 4th energy level increases from 18 to 32.

The seventh period of elements is at present an incomplete period. It is assumed to be similar to the sixth period. The rare earth elements in this period compose the *actinide series.* At present, 21 members of the seventh period are known or reported.

In the periodic table, the elements are roughly divided into metals, nonmetals, and noble gases. The line separating the metals from the nonmetals is a zigzag line. It runs diagonally down and to the right near the right end of the table. The elements that border this zigzag line are the *metalloids.* These elements show both metallic and nonmetallic properties under different conditions.

5.5 Size of atoms: a periodic property

We recognized in Chapter 3 that an atom consists of a central nucleus with electrons moving about it. It was noted that the nucleus has a diameter which is about one ten-thousandth that of the atom. Most of the volume of an atom is occupied by moving electrons. The complex motion of the negatively charged electrons makes the atoms appear as spheres even though they are mostly empty space. The spherical electron cloud gives an atom its volume and excludes other atoms.

The volume of an atom is not a completely definite quantity because the boundary of an atom's electron cloud is not a distinct surface. Rather, it is somewhat fuzzy and indefinite. An atom may be rather easily distorted when it combines with other atoms. But very great force must be used if it is to be compressed.

The reported "size" of an atom varies somewhat with the

dimension measured and the method used to measure it. Scientists have measured the distance between adjacent nuclei in the crystalline forms of elements and in the molecules of gaseous elements. One-half of this distance is used, with slight correction, as the radius of one atom. The radius of an atom, and thus its volume, do *not* increase regularly with atomic number. Such an increase might be expected from the regular addition of an electron in successive elements. But atomic size varies in a periodic fashion as shown in Figure 5-6. This figure is a miniature periodic table with element symbols and atomic numbers in black. Atomic radii are shown in color. The radii of atoms of the elements are given in angstroms. Figure 5-7 shows the atomic radius plotted as a function of the atomic number.

From this chart and graph two conclusions about the relationship between atomic radius and the periodic table may be drawn:

1. The atomic radius generally increases with atomic number in a particular group or family of elements. Each element

Fig. 5-6. Periodic table showing radii of the atoms of the elements in angstrom units.

PERIODIC TABLE OF ATOMIC RADII

I	II											III	IV	V	VI	VII	VIII
0.32 **H** 1																	0.31 **He** 2
1.23 **Li** 3	0.89 **Be** 4											0.82 **B** 5	0.77 **C** 6	0.75 **N** 7	0.73 **O** 8	0.72 **F** 9	0.71 **Ne** 10
1.54 **Na** 11	1.36 **Mg** 12											1.18 **Al** 13	1.11 **Si** 14	1.06 **P** 15	1.02 **S** 16	0.99 **Cl** 17	0.98 **Ar** 18
2.03 **K** 19	1.74 **Ca** 20	1.44 **Sc** 21	1.32 **Ti** 22	1.22 **V** 23	1.18 **Cr** 24	1.17 **Mn** 25	1.17 **Fe** 26	1.16 **Co** 27	1.15 **Ni** 28	1.17 **Cu** 29	1.25 **Zn** 30	1.26 **Ga** 31	1.22 **Ge** 32	1.20 **As** 33	1.17 **Se** 34	1.14 **Br** 35	1.12 **Kr** 36
2.16 **Rb** 37	1.91 **Sr** 38	1.62 **Y** 39	1.45 **Zr** 40	1.34 **Nb** 41	1.30 **Mo** 42	1.27 **Tc** 43	1.25 **Ru** 44	1.25 **Rh** 45	1.28 **Pd** 46	1.34 **Ag** 47	1.48 **Cd** 48	1.44 **In** 49	1.40 **Sn** 50	1.40 **Sb** 51	1.36 **Te** 52	1.33 **I** 53	1.31 **Xe** 54
2.35 **Cs** 55	1.98 **Ba** 56	1.56 **Lu** 71	1.44 **Hf** 72	1.34 **Ta** 73	1.30 **W** 74	1.28 **Re** 75	1.26 **Os** 76	1.27 **Ir** 77	1.30 **Pt** 78	1.34 **Au** 79	1.49 **Hg** 80	1.48 **Tl** 81	1.47 **Pb** 82	1.46 **Bi** 83	1.46 **Po** 84	1.45 **At** 85	**Rn** 86
Fr 87	2.20 **Ra** 88	**Lr** 103	104	105	106	107											

1.69 **La** 57	1.65 **Ce** 58	1.64 **Pr** 59	1.64 **Nd** 60	1.63 **Pm** 61	1.62 **Sm** 62	1.85 **Eu** 63	1.62 **Gd** 64	1.61 **Tb** 65	1.60 **Dy** 66	1.58 **Ho** 67	1.58 **Er** 68	1.58 **Tm** 69	1.70 **Yb** 70
2.0 **Ac** 89	1.65 **Th** 90	**Pa** 91	1.42 **U** 92	**Np** 93	**Pu** 94	**Am** 95	**Cm** 96	**Bk** 97	**Cf** 98	**Es** 99	**Fm** 100	**Md** 101	**No** 102

Atomic radii mostly from R.T. Sanderson, INORGANIC CHEMISTRY, Reinhold Publishing Corporation, New York, 1967

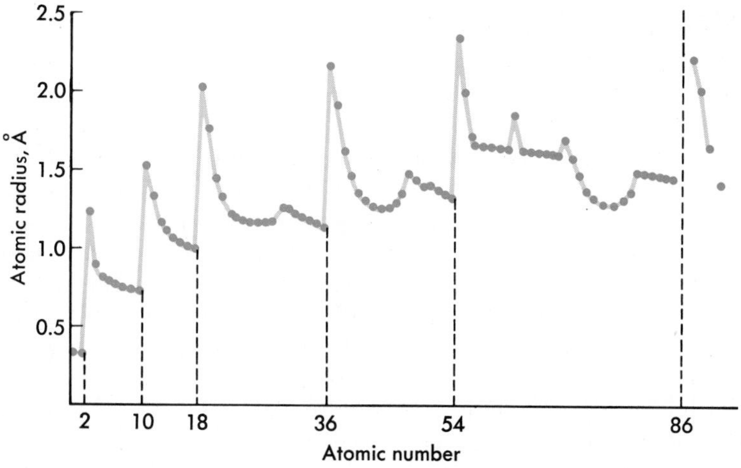

Fig. 5-7. Graph showing atomic radius plotted as a function of atomic number.

in a group has one more shell or energy level than the element above it. The increased nuclear charge decreases the radii of the electron shells by drawing them closer. But the addition of a shell more than counteracts this effect.

2. From Group I to Group VIII in a period, there is a general decrease in the atomic radii of the elements. Each element has a greater positive nuclear charge than the one before it. This greater charge results in a greater total force of attraction between the electrons and the nucleus. This greater force of attraction may explain why the electrons of the elements across a period are successively closer to the nucleus.

Since the number of protons in the nucleus of the elements increases in any one period from left to right, so does the number of electrons in the outermost orbitals about the nucleus. As the number of electrons increases, the force of repulsion between them also increases. Irregularities in the atomic radius pattern may be caused by patterns in this force of repulsion.

5.6 Ionization energy

A negatively charged electron is held in an atom by the attraction of the positively charged protons in the nucleus. By supplying energy, it is possible to remove an electron from an atom. Suppose we use **A** as a symbol for an atom of any element and → to mean "yields." Then this electron removal may be shown in equation form as

$$\mathbf{A} + \mathbf{energy} \rightarrow \mathbf{A^+} + \mathbf{e^-}$$

The particle, $\mathbf{A^+}$, remaining after the removal of an electron, e^-, is an *ion* with a single positive charge. *An* ***ion*** *is an atom* (or sometimes a group of atoms) *which has a net positive or negative charge.* This net charge results from unequal numbers of positively charged protons and negatively charged

PERIODIC TABLE OF FIRST IONIZATION ENERGIES

I	II											III	IV	V	VI	VII	VIII
314 **H** 1																	567 **He** 2
124 **Li** 3	215 **Be** 4											191 **B** 5	$\overline{260}$ **C** 6	335 **N** 7	314 **O** 8	402 **F** 9	497 **Ne** 10
119 **Na** 11	176 **Mg** 12											138 **Al** 13	188 **Si** 14	242 **P** 15	239 **S** 16	299 **Cl** 17	363 **Ar** 18
$\overline{100}$ **K** 19	141 **Ca** 20	151 **Sc** 21	157 **Ti** 22	155 **V** 23	156 **Cr** 24	171 **Mn** 25	181 **Fe** 26	181 **Co** 27	176 **Ni** 28	178 **Cu** 29	217 **Zn** 30	138 **Ga** 31	182 **Ge** 32	226 **As** 33	225 **Se** 34	272 **Br** 35	323 **Kr** 36
96 **Rb** 37	131 **Sr** 38	147 **Y** 39	158 **Zr** 40	159 **Nb** 41	164 **Mo** 42	168 **Tc** 43	$\overline{170}$ **Ru** 44	172 **Rh** 45	192 **Pd** 46	175 **Ag** 47	207 **Cd** 48	133 **In** 49	169 **Sn** 50	199 **Sb** 51	208 **Te** 52	241 **I** 53	$\overline{280}$ **Xe** 54
$\overline{90}$ **Cs** 55	$\overline{120}$ **Ba** 56	125 **Lu** 71	161 **Hf** 72	182 **Ta** 73	184 **W** 74	182 **Re** 75	201 **Os** 76	$\overline{210}$ **Ir** 77	208 **Pt** 78	213 **Au** 79	241 **Hg** 80	141 **Tl** 81	171 **Pb** 82	168 **Bi** 83	196 **Po** 84	**At** 85	248 **Rn** 86
Fr 87	122 **Ra** 88	**Lr** 103	104	105	106	107											

129 **La** 57	126 **Ce** 58	125 **Pr** 59	127 **Nd** 60	128 **Pm** 61	$\overline{130}$ **Sm** 62	131 **Eu** 63	142 **Gd** 64	135 **Tb** 65	137 **Dy** 66	139 **Ho** 67	141 **Er** 68	143 **Tm** 69	144 **Yb** 70
159 **Ac** 89	**Th** 90	**Pa** 91	**U** 92	**Np** 93	134 **Pu** 94	138 **Am** 95	**Cm** 96	**Bk** 97	**Cf** 98	**Es** 99	**Fm** 100	**Md** 101	**No** 102

Fig. 5-8. Periodic table showing first ionization energies of the elements in kilocalories per mole.

electrons. *The energy required to remove an electron from an atom is its* ***ionization energy.*** The chart, Figure 5-8, shows the ionization energy required to remove one electron from an atom of each element. One unit in which ionization energy is expressed is kcal/mole. The first ionization energy of oxygen, for example, is 314 kcal/mole. This means that 314 kcal of energy must be supplied to remove one electron from each atom in one mole of oxygen atoms. (Recall that one mole of oxygen atoms is 6.02×10^{23} atoms.) Figure 5-9 is a graph showing first ionization energy plotted as a function of atomic number. From Figures 5-8 and 5-9, the following conclusions can be drawn:

1. Low ionization energy is characteristic of a metal. *High ionization energy* is characteristic of a nonmetal. The chemical inertness of the noble gases is strong evidence for the unusual stability, or resistance to change, of the outer-shell octet. As might be expected, the noble gases have unusually high ionization energies.

2. Within a group of nontransition elements, the ionization energy generally decreases with increasing atomic number.

This is because, within such groups, increasing atomic number is accompanied by increasing atomic radius. The outer-shell electrons of the elements of higher atomic number within a group are farther from the nucleus. Thus, these electrons are attracted less by the nucleus. The ionization energy for removal of one outer-shell electron is therefore less as the atomic number of the atom is greater. This reasoning does not hold true for the transition elements.

3. Ionization energy does not vary uniformly from element to element within a series. Instead, it is a *periodic* property. In each series or period, the ionization energy increases from Group I to Group VIII. But the increase is not regular. There is a decrease in ionization energies between Groups II and III in Periods 2 and 3. This decrease occurs as the *s* sublevel is filled and the *p* sublevel is started. In these periods, there is also a decrease between Groups V and VI as the *p* sublevel becomes half-filled. In Periods 4, 5, and 6, there is a sharp decrease in the ionization energy between the last transition element and Group III. This decrease occurs as the *d* sublevel has become filled and the *p* sublevel is started. These irregularities apparently are related to the extra stability of completed and half-completed sublevels.

5.7 Ionization energy to remove successive electrons

It is, of course, possible to remove more than one electron from many-electron atoms.

$$\textbf{Na} + \textbf{ionization energy 1st electron} \rightarrow \textbf{Na}^{+} + e^{-}$$

$$\textbf{Na}^{+} + \textbf{ionization energy 2nd electron} \rightarrow \textbf{Na}^{++} + e^{-}$$

$$\textbf{Na}^{++} + \textbf{ionization energy 3rd electron} \rightarrow \textbf{Na}^{+++} + e^{-}$$

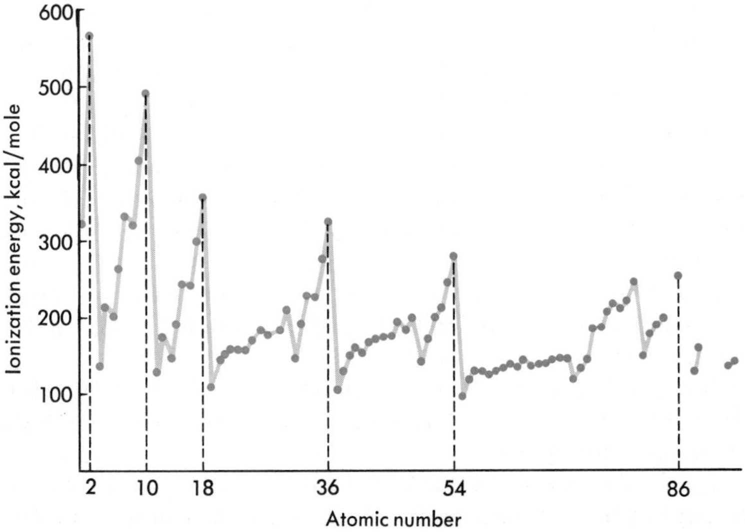

Fig. 5-9. Graph showing first ionization energy as a function of atomic number.

Table 5-1

ELECTRON CONFIGURATIONS AND IONIZATION ENERGIES OF SODIUM, MAGNESIUM, AND ALUMINUM					
Elements	Electron Configuration	Ionization Energy (kcal/mole)			
		1st electron	2nd electron	3rd electron	4th electron
Na	$1s^2 2s^2 2p^6 3s^1$	119	$109\bar{0}$	1652	2281
Mg	$1s^2 2s^2 2p^6 3s^2$	176	347	1848	2519
Al	$1s^2 2s^2 2p^6 3s^2 3p^1$	138	434	656	2767

Table 5-1 shows the electron configurations of sodium, magnesium, and aluminum atoms. It also gives the ionization energies required to remove successive electrons from atoms of these elements. Notice the increase in energy for each successive electron removed.

It is not surprising that the ionization energy increases with each electron removed from an atom. After all, each successive electron must be removed from a particle with an increasingly greater net positive charge. But let us examine the variation in ionization energies still more closely.

For sodium atoms, there is a great increase between the first and second ionization energies. The first electron, a 3*s* electron, is rather easily removed. But to remove the second electron, almost ten times as much energy is needed. This increase occurs because the second electron is a 2*p* electron in a much lower energy level. The lower the energy level, the greater the energy needed to remove an electron from the attraction of the nucleus. See Figure 5-10.

Fig. 5-10. Energy-level transitions for the removal of successive electrons from sodium, magnesium, and aluminum atoms.

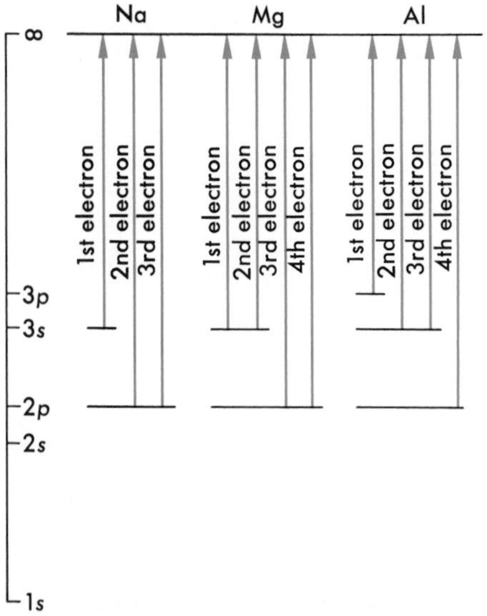

The removal of electrons from magnesium atoms requires little ionization energy for the first two electrons, since both are 3*s* electrons. More energy is required to remove the first 3*s* electron from magnesium atoms than the first 3*s* electron from sodium atoms. This increase occurs because the magnesium atoms have a greater nuclear charge and the 3*s* electrons are closer to the nucleus. But to remove the third electron from magnesium atoms requires between five and six times as much energy as is needed to remove the second. This increase occurs because the third electron is a 2*p* electron. Since 2*p* electrons of magnesium are at a much lower energy level than 3*s* electrons, there is a great increase in ionization energy.

It is easy to remove the first three electrons from aluminum atoms. In fact, it is easier to remove the first electron from aluminum atoms than it is to remove the first electron from magnesium atoms. A look at the electron configuration indicates that the first aluminum electron is a 3*p* electron. It is in a slightly higher energy sublevel than the first magnesium electron, which is a 3*s* electron. There is a great increase in ionization energy between the third and fourth aluminum electrons. This increase is explained by the fact that the fourth electron is a 2*p* electron. This electron is in a much lower energy level than the first three electrons, which were all 3rd energy-level electrons.

The order in which electrons are removed from atoms by ionization is not the same as the order in which electrons occupy orbitals in the structures described in Sections 4.6–4.10. This difference is caused by the shifting of the relative positions of energy sublevels as they are occupied by electrons. Electrons are removed from atoms by ionization in the reverse of the order given by the electron-configuration notation. The electron-configuration notation of iron is $1s^2 2s^2 2p^6$-$3s^2 3p^6 3d^6 4s^2$. The first electron removed from iron atoms is a 4*s* electron. So is the second. The third electron is a 3*d* electron. So are the fourth, fifth, sixth, and so on.

See Question 28 at the end of this chapter.

5.8 Electron affinity

Neutral atoms can acquire additional electrons. The measure of this tendency is *electron affinity*. ***Electron affinity*** *is the energy change that occurs when an electron is acquired by a neutral atom.* When an electron is added to a neutral atom, an ion with a single negative charge is formed. An amount of energy, the electron affinity, is either released or absorbed.

For most atoms, the electron affinity is energy that is released. In equation form, the acquiring of an electron and the release of energy may be expressed as follows:

$$\mathbf{A + e^- \rightarrow A^- + energy} \qquad \textbf{(Equation 1)}$$

Since energy is released, the change is exothermic. The negative ion will be more stable than the neutral atom. Because the energy, the electron affinity, is released, it is given a positive sign as shown in Equation 1. Like ionization energy, electron affinity may be measured in kcal/mole. The electron affinity indicates how tightly an additional electron is bound to an atom. If the electron affinity is positive and low, the electron is weakly bound. If the electron affinity is positive and high, the electron is strongly bound.

It may be helpful to review Sections 2.14 and 2.15.

For some atoms, the electron affinity is energy that is absorbed. In equation form, this change may be expressed

$$\mathbf{A + e^- + energy \rightarrow A^-}$$

Since energy is absorbed, the change is endothermic. A more useful form of this equation is similar to Equation 1, with the energy term to the right of the "yields" sign:

$$\mathbf{A + e^- \rightarrow A^- - energy} \qquad \textbf{(Equation 2)}$$

In the case of an endothermic reaction, the energy change, the electron affinity, is given a negative sign as shown in Equation 2. If the electron affinity is negative, energy must be used in forming the negative ion. The negative ion, consequently, will be less stable than the neutral atom.

Figure 5-11 gives the known experimental values for electron affinities in kilocalories per mole of atoms. Estimated values are given for some of the other atoms. These data are graphed in Figure 5-12. From these figures we can make several observations.

The Group II elements, the elements of the zinc subfamily (Zn, Cd, Hg), and the noble gases have zero or negative electron affinities. This is evidence that the atoms of these elements have filled outermost *s* or *p* sublevels, and stable inner energy levels. An electron can be added to such atoms only by supplying energy. The addition of an electron to these atoms produces a singly charged negative ion that is less stable than the atom.

Fig. 5-11. Periodic table showing the electron affinities of the elements in kilocalories per mole. The values in parentheses are estimated.

PERIODIC TABLE OF ELECTRON AFFINITIES

I	II											III	IV	V	VI	VII	VIII
17.4 **H** 1																	(−5.1) **He** 2
14.3 **Li** 3	(−58) **Be** 4											6.5 **B** 5	29.3 **C** 6	0.0 **N** 7	33.8 **O** 8	78.4 **F** 9	(−6.9) **Ne** 10
12.6 **Na** 11	(−55) **Mg** 12											11 **Al** 13	31.9 **Si** 14	17.2 **P** 15	47.9 **S** 16	83.4 **Cl** 17	(−8.3) **Ar** 18
11.6 **K** 19	(−37.4) **Ca** 20	(−17) **Sc** 21	(5) **Ti** 22	(12) **V** 23	15 **Cr** 24	(−25) **Mn** 25	3.2 **Fe** 26	(20) **Co** 27	26.5 **Ni** 28	29.4 **Cu** 29	(0) **Zn** 30	(8.5) **Ga** 31	27.7 **Ge** 32	18 **As** 33	46.6 **Se** 34	77.6 **Br** 35	(−9.2) **Kr** 36
11.2 **Rb** 37	(−40.1) **Sr** 38	(0) **Y** 39	(10) **Zr** 40	23 **Nb** 41	23 **Mo** 42	(20) **Tc** 43	(25) **Ru** 44	(28) **Rh** 45	(10) **Pd** 46	30.0 **Ag** 47	(−6) **Cd** 48	8.1 **In** 49	28.8 **Sn** 50	24.2 **Sb** 51	45.4 **Te** 52	70.6 **I** 53	(−9.7) **Xe** 54
10.9 **Cs** 55	(−12) **Ba** 56	**Lu** 71	(−17) **Hf** 72	20 **Ta** 73	10 **W** 74	3.5 **Re** 75	(25) **Os** 76	(37) **Ir** 77	49.1 **Pt** 78	53.2 **Au** 79	(−2) **Hg** 80	10 **Tl** 81	24.2 **Pb** 82	24.2 **Bi** 83	(42) **Po** 84	(65) **At** 85	(−9.7) **Rn** 86
(10.5) **Fr** 87	**Ra** 88	**Lr** 103	104	105	106	107											

(10) **La** 57	**Ce** 58	**Pr** 59	**Nd** 60	**Pm** 61	**Sm** 62	**Eu** 63	**Gd** 64	**Tb** 65	**Dy** 66	**Ho** 67	**Er** 68	**Tm** 69	**Yb** 70
Ac 89	**Th** 90	**Pa** 91	**U** 92	**Np** 93	**Pu** 94	**Am** 95	**Cm** 96	**Bk** 97	**Cf** 98	**Es** 99	**Fm** 100	**Md** 101	**No** 102

Values in parentheses are estimated.

Data compiled by E.C.M. Chen and W.E. Wentworth, *J. Chem. Ed.*, August 1975 and private communication

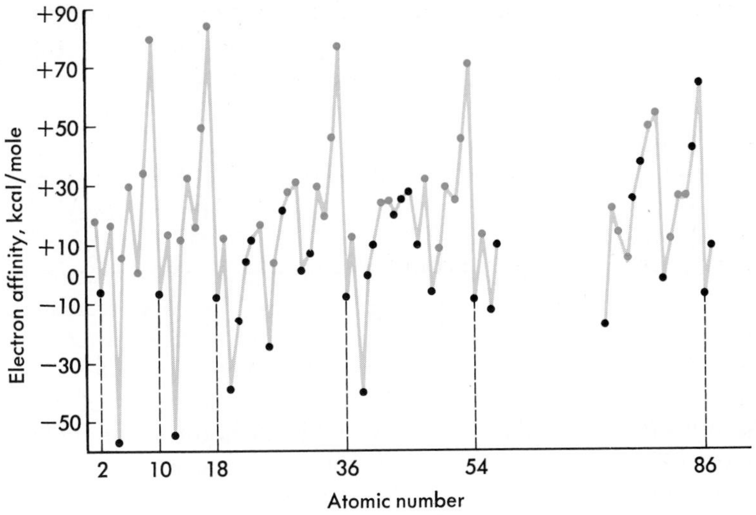

Fig. 5-12. Graph showing electron affinity as a function of atomic number. Experimental data are shown by dots in color; estimated data are shown by black dots.

If only the experimental values are considered, we see that there is usually a decrease in electron affinity in the numbered families from the third through the sixth periods. The added electron takes a position in the atom farther from the nucleus. Not as much energy is released; the electron is not as strongly held.

For the Group I elements there is a decrease in electron affinity between the second and third periods. But for Groups III, IV, V, VI, and VII, there is an increase between the second and third periods. The Period Two elements are small in size and frequently show irregularities in properties when compared with other elements in their group.

There is an increase in electron affinity between Groups III and IV. The addition of an electron to a Group III atom results in an ion with 2 electrons in the outer *p* sublevel. The addition of an electron to a Group IV atom results in an ion with 3 electrons in the outer *p* sublevel, a half-filled *p* sublevel. The greater amount of energy released when an electron is added to a Group IV atom than to a Group III atom is evidence of the greater stability of a half-filled *p* sublevel than one with only 2 electrons.

There is a decrease in electron affinity between Groups IV and V. The Group V atoms have half-filled *p* sublevels, and there is little attraction for another electron.

There is a general increase in electron affinity among the atoms of Groups V, VI, and VII. The addition of electrons in turn to Group V, VI, and VII atoms produces ions with increasingly stable outer shells. The addition of an electron to a Group VII atom produces an ion with an outer-shell octet. The quite high electron affinities of the halogens is additional evidence for the stability of outer-shell octets.

The concepts of ionization energy and electron affinity are

helpful in understanding how compounds are formed from atoms of metallic and nonmetallic elements. This topic is discussed in greater detail in parts of Chapter 6.

5.9 Value of the periodic table

In former years, the periodic table served as a check on atomic weight determinations. It also was used in the prediction of new elements. These uses are now outdated. Today, the periodic table serves as a useful and systematic classification of elements according to their properties. The occurrence at regular intervals of properties such as atomic size, ionization energy, and electron affinity has already been described. This information is valuable in determining the types of compounds that certain elements form. The periodic table, though not perfect, makes the study of chemistry easier.

SUMMARY

About 1869, Mendeleyev classified the elements according to physical and chemical properties by arranging them in the order of increasing atomic weight. He concluded that the properties of elements are in periodic dependence on their atomic weights.

Moseley found that X rays could be used to determine the atomic number of an element. An increase in the number of protons in the nucleus of atoms of the metal used as the target in an X-ray tube shortens the wavelength of the X rays it produces. When elements are arranged in the order of their atomic numbers, some discrepancies in Mendeleyev's arrangement disappear. As a result of this discovery, the periodic law is now stated as follows: The physical and chemical properties of the elements are periodic functions of their atomic numbers.

In the modern periodic table, the families of elements with similar properties, or groups, are in vertical columns. Each element in a family has a similar number of electrons in its outer shell. At the left of the table, the most active elements are at the bottom. At the right of the table, they are at the top. A row of elements is called a period. In a given period, the properties of the elements gradually pass from strong metallic to strong nonmetallic nature, with the last member of a period being a noble gas. Atomic size, ionization energy, and electron affinity vary from element to element in a periodic fashion.

QUESTIONS

Group A

1. (*a*) On what basis did Mendeleyev arrange the elements in his periodic table? (*b*) On what basis are they arranged today?
2. What use did Mendeleyev make of his study of the known elements?
3. How are X rays used to determine the atomic number of an element?
4. What is the periodic law?
5. (*a*) What information is given in each block of the periodic table? (*b*) How are these data arranged in each block?
6. (*a*) What is a group or family of elements? (*b*) What position does a family occupy in the periodic table?
7. (*a*) What is a series or period of elements? (*b*) What position does a period occupy in the periodic table?

8. (*a*) Name the elements in the second period. (*b*) How does the number of electrons in the outer shell vary in these elements? (*c*) How do their properties compare?
9. What is similar about the electron configurations of elements with similar properties?
10. How do the elements at the left of the periodic table vary in activity?
11. How do the elements in Group VII vary in activity?
12. What name is given to the elements that border the line dividing the metals from the nonmetals?
13. Why is the radius of an atom not a definitely fixed quantity?
14. (*a*) How do the atomic radii of the Group I elements compare with the radii of other elements of their period? (*b*) For what structural characteristic of these atoms is this evidence?
15. (*a*) Write an equation to represent the removal of the single outer-shell electron from a potassium atom. (*b*) Write an equation to represent the addition of an electron to a neutral bromine atom. (*c*) What particles are produced from the neutral atoms by these reactions?
16. (*a*) What does the low ionization energy of metals tell us about their atomic structure? (*b*) What does the high ionization energy of nonmetals tell us about their atomic structure?
17. What is electron affinity?
18. Write an equation to represent (*a*) the addition of an electron to a sodium atom; (*b*) the addition of an electron to a chlorine atom; (*c*) the addition of an electron to an argon atom. (*d*) Compare the strength with which the electron is bound in the three ions formed.

Group B

19. What family of elements was missing from Mendeleyev's periodic table?
20. (*a*) What are X rays? (*b*) How are they produced?
21. (*a*) How did Mendeleyev know where to leave gaps for undiscovered elements in his periodic table? (*b*) How did Moseley know where to leave gaps for undiscovered elements?
22. (*a*) Why is hydrogen placed separately in the periodic table? (*b*) Why is it placed above Group I?
23. (*a*) What are transition elements? (*b*) In which periods of elements do they appear?
24. (*a*) What are rare earth elements? (*b*) In which periods of elements do they appear?
25. (*a*) How does atomic size vary with atomic number within a family of elements? (*b*) How does our explanation of atomic structure account for this variation?
26. (*a*) How does atomic size generally vary with atomic number within a period of elements? (*b*) How does our explanation of atomic structure account for this variation?
27. (*a*) How would you expect the ionization energies of two atoms of about equal size but different atomic number to compare? (*b*) Why?
28. (*a*) If energy must be supplied to remove an outer-shell electron from an atom, which is more stable, the atom or the resulting ion? (*b*) If energy is released during the addition of an electron to a neutral atom, which is more stable, the atom or the resulting ion?
29. The Group II and Group VIII elements have negative electron affinities. To what structural features of these atoms is this related?
30. There is a decrease in electron affinity between Groups IV and V. For what structural characteristic of atoms is this evidence?
31. What determines the number of elements in each period of the periodic table?
32. How many 5th energy-level orbitals would be filled theoretically in element 118?

33. What is the present value of the periodic table?
34. On a separate sheet of paper, copy and complete the following table. *Do not write in this book.*
On the basis of the electron configuration, explain the variation in ionization energies for successive electrons for the atoms given.
35. The neon sign like the one shown at the top of page 71 is used extensively for indoor and outdoor advertising displays. The neon gas enclosed in the glass tubing glows with a characteristic orange-red light when high voltage electricity from a transformer excites the atoms of neon. What is the source of this orange-red light? (Refer to Section 4.3.)

Chemical Element	Electron-configuration Notation	Ionization Energy (kcal/mole)			
		1st electron	2nd electron	3rd electron	4th electron
K		100	729	1054	1405
Ca		141	274	1174	1547
Ga		138	473	708	1470

unmixing mixtures, 2

1

Often chemists need to separate mixtures. Many methods they use depend upon properties that result from bond polarity differences. For example, substances in general, dissolve in liquids with similar bond polarity. A liquid is used in which that component is as soluble as possible. Shaking the sample with a series of fresh samples of that liquid will remove the component. This process is called extraction. Pictured is an apparatus that can do several dozen extractions at the same time (1).

Chromatography is a separation method that also depends upon differences in bond polarity. A mixture is added to the top of a column packed evenly with a solid. A liquid is used to wash components of the mixture down the column. Separation results from differences in attraction between each component, the column, and the solvent (2).

2

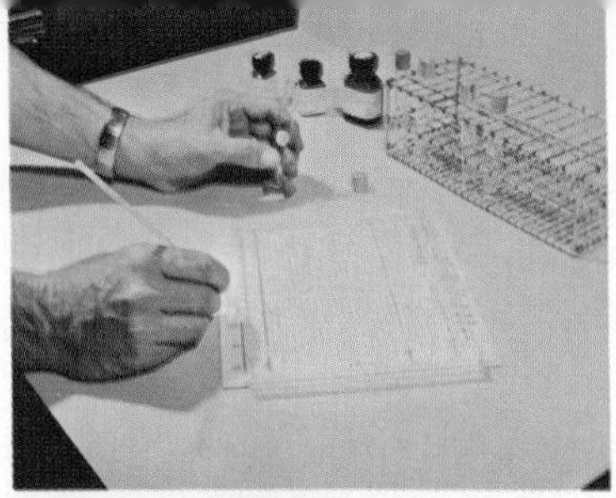
3

4

5

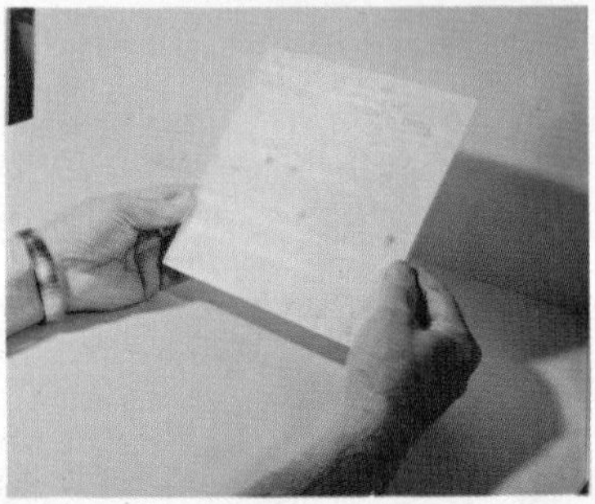
6

7

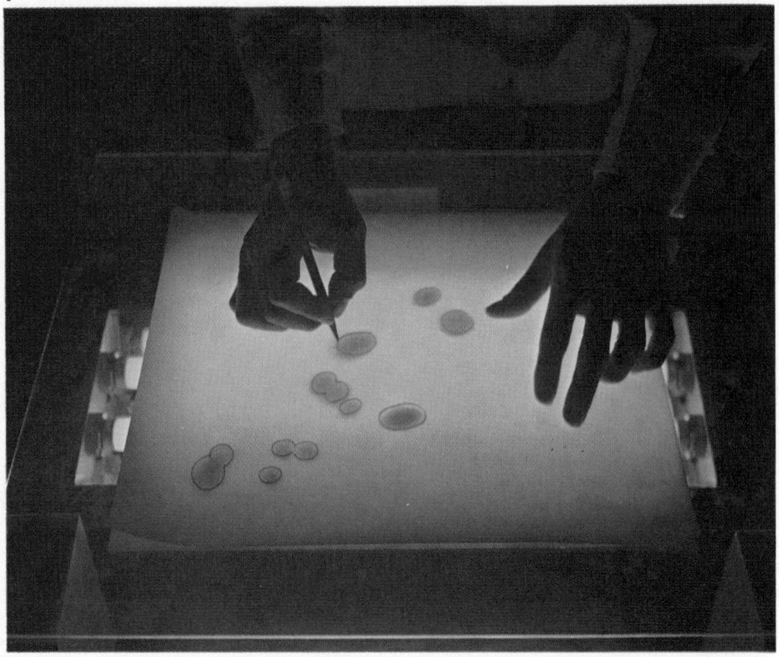

A sheet of filter paper or a thin layer of material on a glass plate may be used instead of the column. Different mixtures are spotted at identifiable places along one edge (3). The plate is placed in a jar so that the liquid just touches the bottom edge (4). The jar is covered to prevent evaporation of the liquid. As capillary action moves the liquid up the plate, the components are separated. The plate is sprayed with a chemical that makes each component visible (5). The chemist then interprets the results (6). Sometimes ultraviolet light helps make components visible (7).

In gas chromatography, a small sample is injected ahead of the column (8). A gas such as nitrogen sweeps the components through the column. A detector at the end indentifies each component. This system is used to analyze Olympic athletes for any one of two hundred banned drugs. The characteristic pattern of each drug is fed into a computer. A sample from the athlete is injected into the gas chromatograph. A mass spectrometer analyzes each component. The computer compares the sample's pattern with the pattern for banned drugs (9).

8

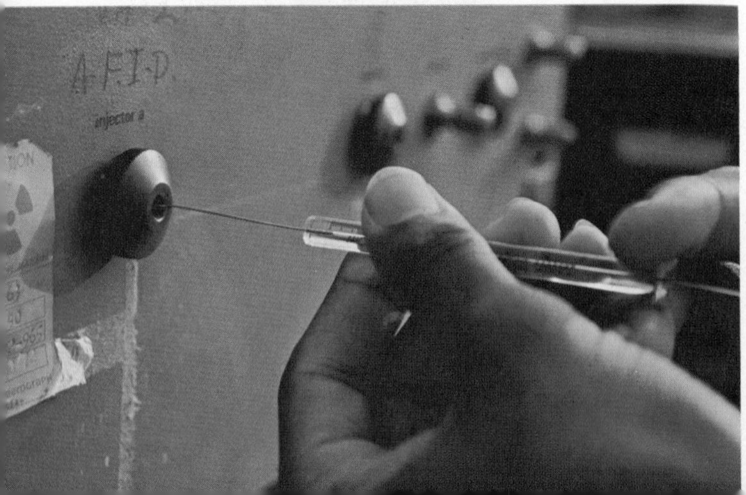

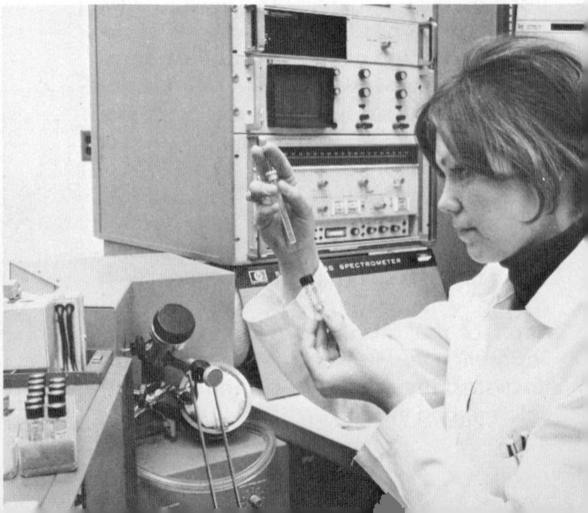

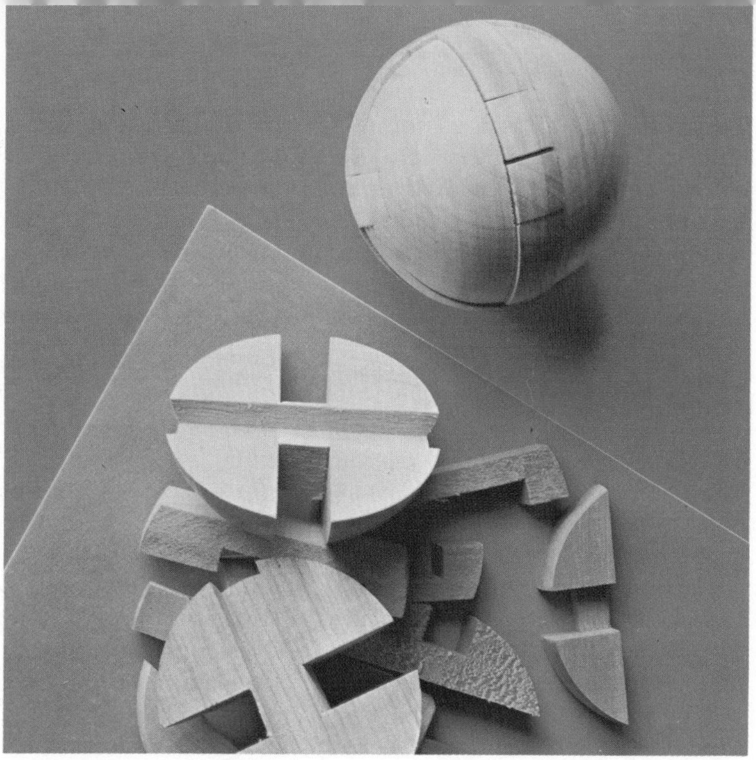

chapter 6

CHEMICAL BONDS

There is only one way that the pieces fit together. (See Question 41 on page 120.)

6.1 Elements form compounds

In Chapter 2 you learned about the process of chemical change. Forming compounds from elements is one kind of chemical change. In the following chapters the theory of the structure of the atoms of the elements was described. In this chapter, atomic theory will be used to explain *how* atoms combine and form the other particles of substances. You will learn what these particles are, how atoms are held together in these particles, and how these particles vary in size and shape.

Here is a series of chemical formulas for some well-known compounds:

$\mathbf{HCl}$	$\mathbf{NaCl}$
$\mathbf{H_2O}$	$\mathbf{CaCl_2}$
$\mathbf{NH_3}$	$\mathbf{AlCl_3}$
$\mathbf{CH_4}$	$\mathbf{CCl_4}$

These formulas were originally established by chemical analysis. Analysis means the separation of a material into its component parts to determine its composition. Methods of working out chemical formulas from the results of analyses are described in Chapters 7 and 11. Ways in which these compounds are formed are described in Chapter 8 and later chapters throughout this book. It is not necessary at this point to know how these compounds are formed or how these formulas are determined.

Notice that each formula in the left column contains hydrogen. The first formula shows that one atom of hydrogen combines with one atom of chlorine. The second formula shows that two atoms of hydrogen combine with one atom of oxygen. The third and fourth formulas show that three atoms of hydrogen combine with one atom of nitrogen, but four atoms of hydrogen combine with one atom of carbon. In the four formulas, different numbers of hydrogen atoms combine with one atom of other elements.

Now look at the second column. Each formula contains chlorine. One chlorine atom combines with one sodium atom.

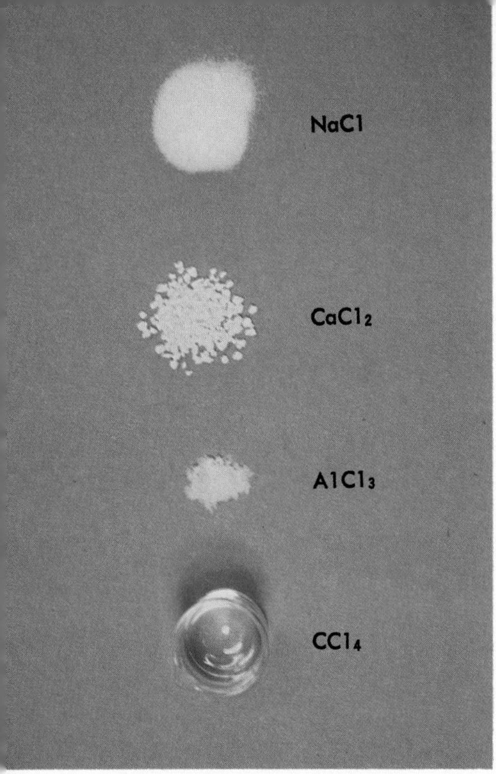

Fig. 6-1. In these compounds, different numbers of chlorine atoms combine with single atoms of other elements.

Two chlorine atoms combine with one calcium atom. Three chlorine atoms combine with one aluminum atom, but four chlorine atoms combine with one carbon atom. Different numbers of chlorine atoms combine with one atom of other elements. Why is there this difference in the number of hydrogen and chlorine atoms that will combine with a single atom of another element? Is there any relation between the structure of an atom and the number of other atoms with which it will combine?

6.2 Valence electrons and chemical bonds

The electrons in the outermost shell of an atom play a very important part in the formation of compounds. The electrons in an *incomplete* outer shell are called ***valence electrons.*** The remainder of the atom, excluding the valence electrons, is called the ***kernel*** of the atom. In the formation of chemical compounds from the elements, *valence electrons are usually either transferred from the outer shell of one atom to the outer shell of another atom, or shared among the outer shells of the combining atoms.* This transfer or sharing of electrons produces ***chemical bonds.*** (The formation of some chemical bonds by atoms of transition and rare-earth elements involves not only outer shell electrons but also those of an incomplete next inner shell.)

Electron transfer results in ***ionic bonding*** *while electron sharing* produces ***covalent bonding.*** When an atom of one element combines chemically with an atom of another element, both atoms usually attain a stable outer shell having a noble-gas configuration. *This kind of electron structure has chemical stability.*

Electron-dot symbols for the noble gases showing their outer-shell configurations are

$$\text{He:}\ \ \text{:}\ddot{\underset{\cdot\cdot}{\text{Ne}}}\text{:}\ \ \text{:}\ddot{\underset{\cdot\cdot}{\text{Ar}}}\text{:}\ \ \text{:}\ddot{\underset{\cdot\cdot}{\text{Kr}}}\text{:}\ \ \text{:}\ddot{\underset{\cdot\cdot}{\text{Xe}}}\text{:}\ \ \text{:}\ddot{\underset{\cdot\cdot}{\text{Rn}}}\text{:}$$

Energy changes are always involved in the process of electron transfer or electron sharing. In *most* cases, when compounds are formed from the elements, energy is given off. The process of electron transfer is *always* exothermic and that of electron sharing is *usually* exothermic. In a *few* cases of compound formation by electron sharing, energy is absorbed. The process of electron sharing may sometimes be endothermic.

Recall from Section 2.15 that the products of exothermic reactions have less energy and are more stable than the reactants. The products of endothermic reactions have more energy and are less stable than the reactants.

6.3 Ionic bonding (electrovalence)

In the formation of a compound by ionic bonding, electrons are actually transferred from the outer shell of one atom to the outer shell of a second atom. By this process both atoms usually attain completed outer shells with noble-gas configurations. For example, sodium reacts with chlorine and forms sodium chloride. The single 3*s* electron of a sodium atom is transferred to the singly occupied 3*p* orbital of a chlorine atom.

Some experimental evidence for electron transfer is described in Section 22.6.

	1*s*	2*s*	2*p*	3*s*	3*p*
Na	⊗	⊗	⊗⊗⊗	⊘	○○○
Cl	⊗	⊗	⊗⊗⊗	⊗	⊗⊗⊘

The sodium, now deficient in one electron, has the stable electron configuration of neon. The chlorine, now with one excess electron, has the stable electron configuration of argon. Only 1 atom of each element is required for the electron transfer that produces these stable electron configurations. Thus, the *formula* of the compound is **NaCl.** *A* ***chemical formula*** *is a shorthand method of using chemical symbols to represent the composition of a substance.*

The particles produced by this transfer of an electron are no longer electrically neutral atoms of sodium and chlorine. They are: (1) a *sodium ion* with a single excess positive charge, and (2) a *chloride* ion with a single excess negative charge.

	1*s*	2*s*	2*p*	3*s*	3*p*
Na^+	⊗	⊗	⊗⊗⊗	○	○○○
Cl^-	⊗	⊗	⊗⊗⊗	⊗	⊗⊗⊗

These ions are arranged systematically in crystals of sodium chloride in the ratio of 1 sodium ion to 1 chloride ion. See Figure 6-3.

The formula NaCl, which represents the composition of the compound, sodium chloride, is an ***empirical formula.*** An empirical formula indicates (1) the kinds of atoms in the compound formed, and (2) the simplest whole-number ratio of the atoms in the compound. The formula $Na_{17}Cl_{17}$ shows the kinds and ratio of atoms that make up the compound, sodium chloride. But the empirical formula NaCl represents this information in the simplest way.

Table 6-1 shows the number of protons and electrons in the atoms and ions of sodium and chlorine and the charges that result. It also shows their electrovalent symbols, and their radii in angstroms.

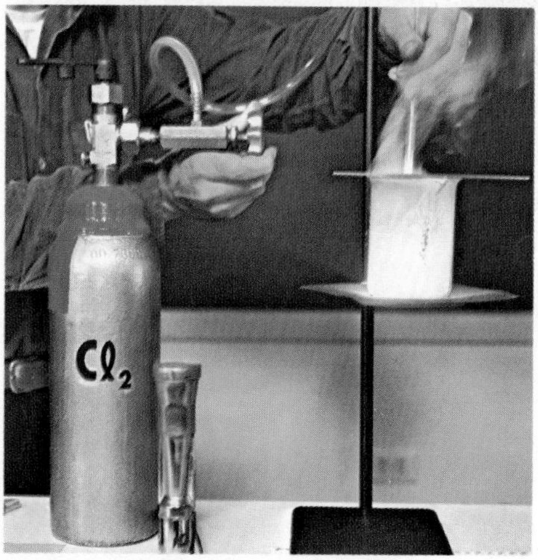

Fig. 6-2. Sodium metal, heated in the beaker, combines directly with chlorine gas and forms the compound sodium chloride.

Fig. 6-3. This diagram shows the arrangement of the sodium and chloride ions in a portion of a sodium chloride crystal.

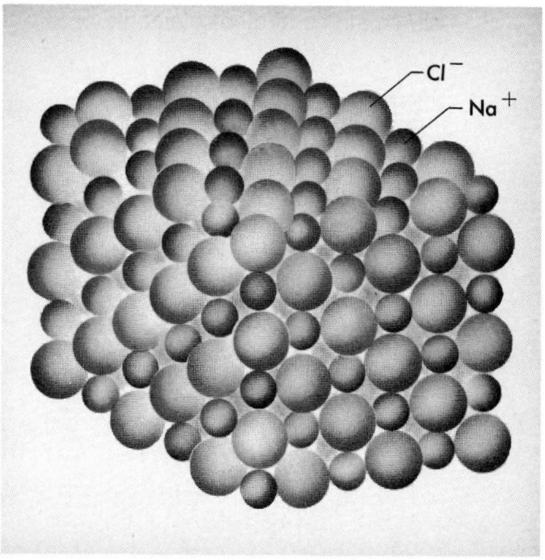

Table 6-1

DATA ON ATOMS AND IONS OF SODIUM AND CHLORINE

	Sodium Atom	Sodium Ion	Chlorine Atom	Chloride Ion
number of protons	11	11	17	17
number of electrons	11	10	17	18
net charge	0	+1	0	−1
symbol	Na	Na^+	Cl	Cl^-
radius, Å	1.54	0.97	0.99	1.81

Using only the 3rd energy level electrons, the electron-dot symbol for an atom of sodium is

$$\mathbf{Na}^{\circ}$$

That for an atom of chlorine is

$$\cdot\underset{\cdot\cdot}{\overset{\cdot\cdot}{\mathbf{Cl}}}:$$

Fig. 6-4. The regular shape of a naturally formed crystal of sodium chloride results from the regular arrangement of sodium ions and chloride ions in the crystal.

When these atoms react, sodium atoms become sodium ions. The electron-dot symbol for a sodium ion is

$$\mathbf{Na}^{+}$$

The chlorine atoms become chloride ions, which have the electron-dot symbol

$$\overset{\circ}{\cdot}\underset{\cdot\cdot}{\overset{\cdot\cdot}{\mathbf{Cl}}}:^{-}$$

These ions form the compound sodium chloride. The electron-dot formula for sodium chloride may be written as

$$\mathbf{Na}^{+}\ \overset{\circ}{\cdot}\underset{\cdot\cdot}{\overset{\cdot\cdot}{\mathbf{Cl}}}:^{-}$$

or as a simpler ionic formula, $\mathbf{Na^{+}Cl^{-}}$.

Note the symbols for electrons ◦ and •, which are used here and in other electron-dot formulas in this chapter. These symbols are used only to show the origin of the electrons in the completed shells. They *do not mean* that electrons from different atoms are different from each other. All electrons, regardless of the atom from which they originate, are identical. However, when two electrons occupy the same space orbital, we can tell something more about them because of electron spin. If the orbital is to be occupied in a stable way, the electrons must have opposite spins.

6.4 Energy change in ionic bonding

Sodium ions and chloride ions in a common salt crystal can be formed from widely separated sodium and chlorine atoms. In order *to study the energy change involved,* this chemical change can be assumed to consist of three separate reactions. The first reaction, the removal of one electron from each sodium atom, is endothermic. The amount of energy required is the *ionization energy* of sodium. For one mole of sodium atoms,

Ionization energy was explained in Section 5.6.

$$\mathbf{1\ mole\ Na + 119\ kcal \rightarrow 1\ mole\ Na^{+} + 1\ mole\ e^{-}}$$

Only one electron can be readily removed from each sodium atom because a great increase in ionization energy occurs between the first and second electrons. (See Section 5.7.)

The second reaction is the addition of one electron to each neutral chlorine atom. This reaction is exothermic. The energy given off is the *electron affinity* of chlorine. For one mole of chlorine atoms,

Electron affinity was explained in Section 5.8.

$$\textbf{1 mole Cl + 1 mole } e^- \rightarrow \textbf{1 mole } Cl^- \textbf{ + 83 kcal}$$

The third reaction is that in which the oppositely charged sodium ions and chloride ions take up their positions in the sodium chloride crystal. This reaction is also exothermic.

$$\textbf{1 mole } Na^+ \textbf{ + 1 mole } Cl^- \rightarrow \textbf{1 mole } Na^+Cl^- \textbf{ + 189 kcal}$$

The first reaction requires energy (119 kcal). This is less than the sum of the energies given off in the second and third reactions (83 kcal and 189 kcal). The overall effect is that energy is given off. [(83 kcal + 189 kcal) – (119 kcal) = 153 kcal]. The summation of these three separate reactions is

$$\begin{array}{llll}
\text{1 mole Na} + \text{119 kcal} & \rightarrow \cancel{\text{1 mole } Na^+} & & + \cancel{\text{1 mole } e^-} \\
\text{1 mole Cl} & + \cancel{\text{1 mole } e^-} \rightarrow \cancel{\text{1 mole Cl}} & & + \text{83 kcal} \\
\cancel{\text{1 mole } Na^+} & + \cancel{\text{1 mole } Cl^-} \rightarrow \text{1 mole } Na^+Cl^- & & + \text{189 kcal} \\
\hline
\text{1 mole Na} & + \text{1 mole Cl} \rightarrow \text{1 mole } Na^+Cl^- & & + \text{153 kcal}
\end{array}$$

The net process of electron transfer is exothermic. The formation of all ionic compounds from their elements is exothermic.

6.5 Oxidation and reduction

Let us now consider still another aspect of the reactions by which sodium ions and chloride ions are produced. We may consider the formation of a sodium ion from a sodium atom to involve the loss of an electron, and we might write the equation for this change this way:

$$Na - e^- \rightarrow Na^+$$

However, chemists prefer to show only the substances entering a reaction at the left of the "yields" sign. The substances formed by the reaction are written at the right of the "yields" sign. Consequently, we should rewrite the equation showing the formation of a sodium ion from a sodium atom this way:

$$Na \rightarrow Na^+ + e^- \quad \textbf{(Loss of electron: Oxidation)}$$

Any chemical reaction that involves the loss of one or more electrons by an atom or ion is called ***oxidation.*** The particle that loses the electron(s) is said to be *oxidized.* In the reaction above, the sodium atom is oxidized to a sodium ion, since it loses one electron. The reaction is an *oxidation.*

The *oxidation state* of an element is represented by a signed number, called an ***oxidation number.*** This number indicates the number of electrons that can be assumed to be lost, gained, or shared by an atom in forming a compound. Oxidation numbers are assigned according to a set of seven rules. These rules will be introduced as needed in this chapter.

Rule 1: *The oxidation number of an atom of a free element is zero.*

Rule 2: *The oxidation number of a monatomic (one-atomed) ion is equal to its charge.*

From these rules we see (1) The oxidation number of elementary sodium is zero: $\overset{0}{\mathbf{Na}}$. (2) The oxidation number of sodium ion is plus one: $\overset{+1}{\mathbf{Na}}{}^{+}$. Note that an oxidation number is written above a symbol, while an ion charge is written as a right superscript.

The formation of a chloride ion from a chlorine atom involves the gain of an electron:

$$\mathbf{Cl + e^- \rightarrow Cl^-} \quad \textbf{(Gain of electron: Reduction)}$$

A chemical reaction that involves the gain of one or more electrons by an atom or ion is called ***reduction.*** The particle that gains the electron(s) is said to be *reduced.* The chlorine atom is reduced to a chloride ion since it gains an electron. The reaction is a *reduction.* The oxidation number of elementary chlorine is zero: $\overset{0}{\mathbf{Cl}}$ (Rule 1). The oxidation number of chloride ion is minus one: $\overset{-1}{\mathbf{Cl}}{}^{-}$ (Rule 2).

In the reaction

$$\overset{0}{\mathbf{Na}} + \overset{0}{\mathbf{Cl}} \rightarrow \overset{+1}{\mathbf{Na}}{}^{+}\overset{-1}{\mathbf{Cl}}{}^{-}$$

elementary sodium is oxidized and elementary chlorine is reduced. *The substance that is reduced* has received electrons from the oxidized substance and is called the ***oxidizing agent.*** (In the reaction represented by the equation, chlorine is the oxidizing agent.) At the same time, *the substance that is oxidized* has transferred electrons to the reduced substance and is called the ***reducing agent.*** (Sodium is the reducing agent in this reaction.) **NaCl** is the correct empirical formula for the compound sodium chloride. Note that the algebraic sum of the oxidation numbers written above this formula is zero.

Rule 3: *The algebraic sum of the oxidation numbers of all the atoms in the formula of a compound is zero.*

Fig. 6-5. Magnesium and bromine react vigorously and form magnesium bromide.

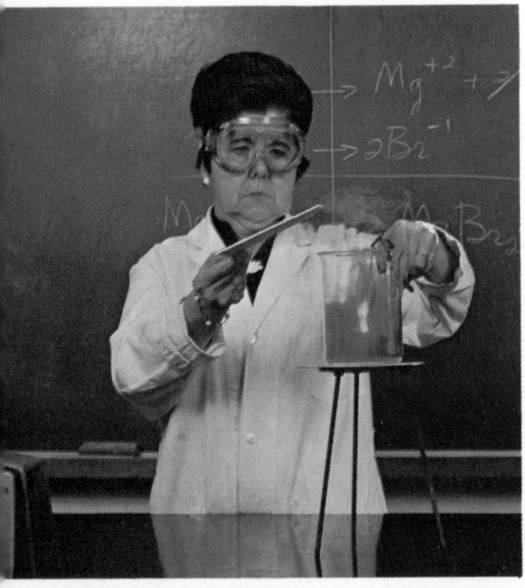

6.6 Formation of magnesium bromide from its elements

In the formation of magnesium bromide, the two 3*s* electrons of the magnesium are transferred. *Both* 3*s* electrons must be transferred if magnesium is to acquire the stable electron configuration of the noble gas, neon. Recall that the ionization energies of the two 3*s* electrons in magnesium are low. But there is a great increase in ionization energy between the second and third electrons. Hence, only two electrons may be removed chemically. The 4th energy level of the bromine atom already contains seven electrons. (Eight, of course, is the number needed for a noble-gas configuration.) Thus, a single bromine atom has a place for only one of the two electrons that the magnesium atom transfers. So two bromine atoms are needed to react with one magnesium atom. Each bromine atom gains one electron. See diagram below

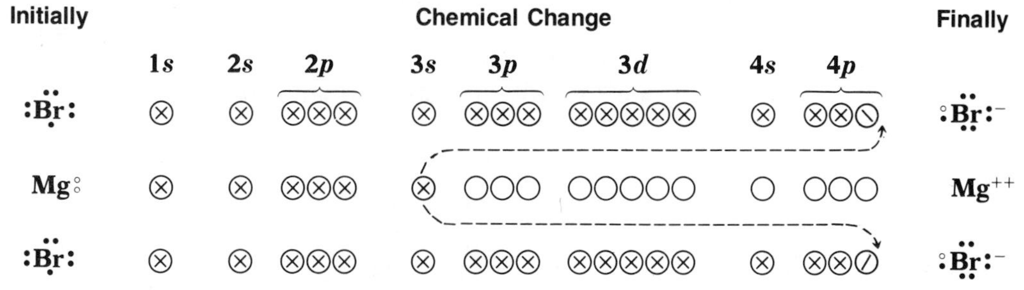

The empirical formula for the compound magnesium bromide is $\mathbf{MgBr_2}$. The magnesium ions in this compound each have two excess positive charges. The bromide ions each have a single excess negative charge. These particles are arranged in orderly fashion in crystals of magnesium bromide. The ratio of the particles is 2 bromide ions to 1 magnesium ion (see Table 6-2 and also Figure 6-6). The subscript $_2$ following Br in the formula indicates that there are two bromide ions to each magnesium ion in the compound. When no subscript is used, as with Mg, one atom or monatomic ion is understood.

The electron-dot symbols for atoms of magnesium and bromine are

Mg: **·Br:**

and for magnesium ion and bromide ion are

$\mathbf{Mg^{++}}$ **:Br:**$^-$

The electron-dot formula for magnesium bromide is then

:Br:$^-$ $\mathbf{Mg^{++}}$ **:Br:**$^-$

and the ionic formula is $\mathbf{Mg^{++}Br_2^-}$. Note that in the formula $\mathbf{Mg^{++}Br_2^-}$ the subscript $_2$ applies to *both* the symbol **Br** and its

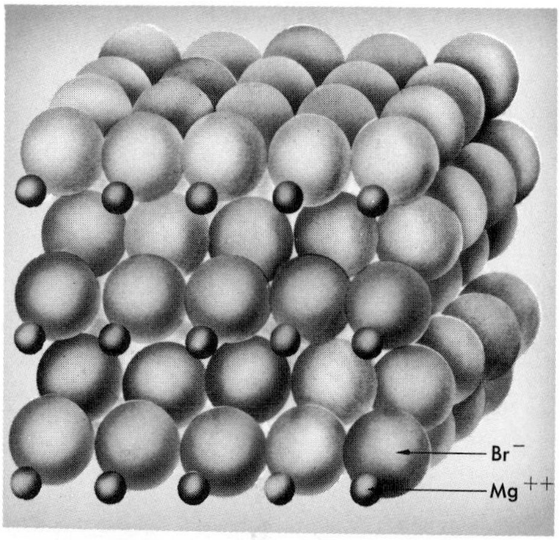

Fig. 6-6. This diagram shows the arrangement of the magnesium and bromide ions in a portion of a magnesium bromide crystal.

Table 6-2

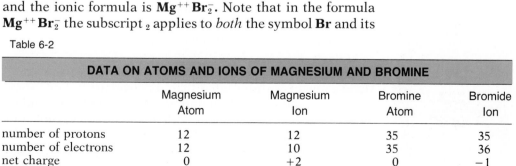

DATA ON ATOMS AND IONS OF MAGNESIUM AND BROMINE

	Magnesium Atom	Magnesium Ion	Bromine Atom	Bromide Ion
number of protons	12	12	35	35
number of electrons	12	10	35	36
net charge	0	+2	0	−1
symbol	Mg	Mg^{++}	Br	Br^-
radius, Å	1.36	0.66	1.14	1.96

charge $^-$. It shows that there are two $\mathbf{Br^-}$ ions with each $\mathbf{Mg^{++}}$ ion in the formula.

Energy is required to remove two electrons from one magnesium atom. But this energy is less than the electron affinity of two bromine atoms plus the energy released when one magnesium ion and two bromide ions take up their positions in a magnesium bromide crystal. Thus, the formation of the compound magnesium bromide from widely separated magnesium and bromine atoms is another example of the exothermic nature of electron transfer.

See Problem 3 at the end of the chapter.

In forming the compound magnesium bromide, elemental magnesium atoms are oxidized from $\overset{0}{\mathbf{Mg}}$ to $\overset{+2}{\mathbf{Mg}}{}^{++}$.

$$\overset{0}{\mathbf{Mg}} \rightarrow \overset{+2}{\mathbf{Mg}}{}^{++} + \mathbf{2e^-}$$

At the same time, for each magnesium atom oxidized, two elemental bromine atoms are reduced from $\overset{0}{\mathbf{Br}}$ to $\overset{-1}{\mathbf{Br}}{}^-$.

$$\mathbf{2}\,\overset{0}{\mathbf{Br}} + \mathbf{2e^-} \rightarrow \mathbf{2}\,\overset{-1}{\mathbf{Br}}{}^-$$

Bromine is the oxidizing agent; magnesium is the reducing agent.

You should also recognize that when oxidation occurs, the element oxidized undergoes an algebraic increase in oxidation number. When magnesium atoms are *oxidized* to magnesium ions, the oxidation number of magnesium *increases* from 0 to +2.

Fig. 6-7. Compounds of transition metals have different colors depending on their oxidation states. See Questions 35 and 36 at the end of this chapter.

When reduction occurs, the element reduced undergoes an algebraic decrease in oxidation number. When bromine atoms are *reduced* to bromide ions, the oxidation number of bromine *decreases* from 0 to −1.

In the formula $\overset{+2}{\mathbf{Mg}}{}^{++}\overset{-1}{\mathbf{Br}}{}_2^-$ the algebraic sum of +2 and 2(−1) equals zero. Note how the algebraic sum of the oxidation numbers of the atoms in a formula is determined. Each oxidation number must be multiplied by the number of atoms or monatomic ions having that oxidation number. The formulas of ionic compounds merely indicate the relative numbers of positive and negative ions that combine. Therefore, *all formulas for ionic compounds are empirical.*

6.7 Elements with several oxidation numbers

Many elements exhibit more than one oxidation state. Some differences in the oxidation number of an element depend on the kind of bond that it forms with other elements. However, another factor is important. Transition elements, with four or five electron energy levels, can readily transfer the electrons in the outermost level. Many of them, with very little additional energy, can also transfer one or two electrons from the next-to-outermost level. The electrons in excess of an octet in the next-to-outermost energy level are those available for transfer. Iron is such a transition element. In forming compounds, it can transfer two 4*s* electrons. Sometimes, in more energetic reactions, a 3*d* electron can also be transferred. Thus its oxidation number can be +2 or +3. This variable number of transferable electrons accounts for the variable oxidation state of many of the transition metals. The table of Common Elements inside the front cover and Table 5 in the Appendix, lists common oxidation numbers.

6.8 Relative sizes of atoms and ions

Once again, look at Tables 6-1 and 6-2 accompanying Sections 6.3 and 6.6. These tables give the radii of the atoms and ions of sodium, magnesium, chlorine, and bromine. Notice the great difference in radius between an atom and the ion formed from it.

It is characteristic of metals to form positive ions. *Positive ions are called* ***cations.*** It is to be expected that metallic ions would be smaller than the corresponding metallic atoms since the outer shell electrons are no longer present. As a result, the remaining electrons are drawn closer to the nucleus by its unbalanced positive charge.

Nonmetallic elements form negative ions. *Negative ions are called* ***anions.*** Nonmetallic ions are larger than the corresponding nonmetallic atoms. Electrons have been added, making the outer shell an octet. Since the total positive charge of the nucleus remains the same, the average force of attraction for each electron decreases because there are more electrons.

Table 6-3 shows the sizes of representative atoms and ions. From these data and the generalizations given above, it will be seen that

1. Within a group or family of elements, the ion size increases with atomic number because of shell addition.

Table 6-3

RADII OF REPRESENTATIVE ATOMS AND IONS IN ANGSTROMS

	Group I		Group II		Group III		Group VI		Group VII	
Period 2	Li Li^+	1.23 0.68	Be Be^{++}	0.89 0.35	B B^{+++}	0.82 0.23	O O^{--}	0.73 1.40	F F^-	0.72 1.33
Period 3	Na Na^+	1.54 0.97	Mg Mg^{++}	1.36 0.66	Al Al^{+++}	1.18 0.51	S S^{--}	1.02 1.84	Cl Cl^-	0.99 1.81
Period 4	K K^+	2.03 1.33	Ca Ca^{++}	1.74 0.99	Ga Ga^{+++}	1.26 0.62	Se Se^{--}	1.17 1.98	Br Br^-	1.14 1.96
Period 5	Rb Rb^+	2.16 1.47	Sr Sr^{++}	1.91 1.12	In In^{+++}	1.44 0.81	Te Te^{--}	1.36 2.21	I I^-	1.33 2.20
Period 6	Cs Cs^+	2.35 1.67	Ba Ba^{++}	1.98 1.34	Tl Tl^{+++}	1.48 0.95				

2. Within a period of elements, the Group I, II, and III cations show a sharp decrease in size. On the other hand, the Group VII anion is only slightly smaller than the Group VI anion. Group I and II cations have the same electron configurations, but the Group II cation's greater nuclear charge draws the electrons much closer. Group VI and VII anions have identical electron configurations, too. The Group VII anion's greater nuclear charge draws the electrons closer.

Figures 6-3 and 6-6 show the arrangement of ions in crystals of the compounds sodium chloride and magnesium bromide. Such arrangements depend on the relative numbers and sizes of each kind of ion present. Crystals are described in more detail in Chapter 12.

6.9 Covalent bonding (covalence): hydrogen molecules

In covalent bonding, electrons are not transferred from one atom to another. Instead, they are *shared* by the bonded atoms. In forming a single covalent bond, two atoms mutually share one of their electrons. These two shared electrons (with opposite spins) effectively fill an orbital in each atom. They make up a *covalent electron pair* that forms the bond between these two atoms.

The atoms of the common elemental gases, hydrogen, oxygen, nitrogen, fluorine, and chlorine, form stable diatomic (two-atomed) *molecules* by covalent bonding. *A* ***molecule*** *is the smallest chemical unit of a substance that is capable of stable independent existence.* For these elemental gases, the smallest chemical units capable of stable independent existence are diatomic units. Single atoms of the five gases listed above are chemically unstable under most conditions. Hence, these diatomic units make up molecules of these gases.

In diatomic hydrogen molecules, each hydrogen atom shares its single 1*s* valence electron with the other. These two electrons move about both nuclei, so that each atom, in effect, has its 1*s* orbital filled. In effect, each hydrogen atom has the stable electron configuration of a helium atom.

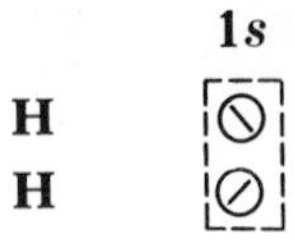

The *electron-dot formula* for a molecule of hydrogen is

H:H

Frequently chemists indicate a shared pair of electrons by a dash (—) instead of the symbol (:). Thus the formula for a molecule of hydrogen may be written

H—H

This type of formula is called a *structural formula*.

The *molecular formula* for hydrogen is $\mathbf{H_2}$. The numerical subscript indicates the number of atoms per molecule. *A formula that indicates the actual composition of a molecule is called a* ***molecular formula.***

Hydrogen molecules are linear (straight-line) as shown in Figure 6-8.

Hydrogen molecules have greater stability than separate hydrogen atoms. This statement is supported by the fact that energy is given off in the reaction

$$\textbf{2 moles H atoms} \rightarrow \textbf{1 mole } \mathbf{H_2} \textbf{ molecules} + \textbf{104 kcal energy}$$

One mole of H_2 molecules has lower energy and is therefore more stable than two moles of uncombined H atoms. The reverse reaction is that of separating hydrogen molecules into the atoms that make them up. Energy must be supplied for this reaction.

$$\textbf{1 mole } \mathbf{H_2} + \textbf{104 kcal} \rightarrow \textbf{2 moles H}$$

The energy required, 104 kcal/mole, is called the *bond energy* of the **H—H** bond. ***Bond energy*** *is the energy required to break chemical bonds*. It is usually expressed in kcal per mole of bonds broken.

Diatomic molecules of elements are considered to be free elements. Thus, each atom in the molecule may be assigned a zero oxidation number (Rule 1).

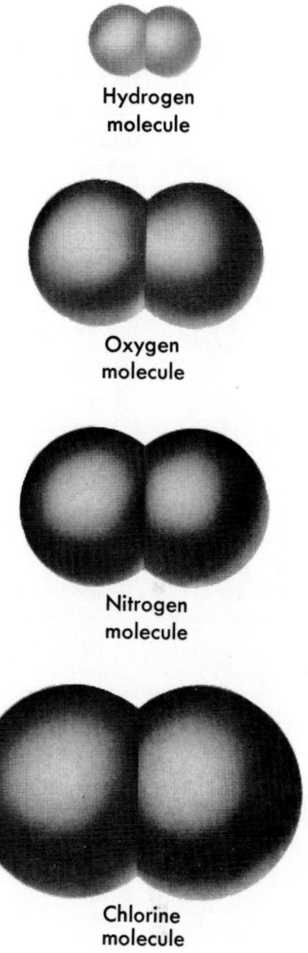

Fig. 6-8. The molecules of the common gases, such as those of hydrogen, nitrogen, oxygen, and chlorine represented here, consist of two atoms joined by covalent bonding. These are all linear molecules.

6.10 Chlorine molecules

Diatomic chlorine molecules can be formed in the same manner as hydrogen molecules. Each atom shares one electron with the other, filling, in effect, an incomplete 3*p* orbital in each. This gives both atoms the stable electron arrangement of the noble gas, argon. Both atoms have, in effect, an octet in the 3rd energy level.

	1*s*	2*s*	2*p*	3*s*	3*p*
Cl	⊗	⊗	⊗⊗⊗	⊗	⊗⊗ ⦸
Cl	⊗	⊗	⊗⊗⊗	⊗	⊗⊗ ⊘

The electron-dot formula for a molecule of chlorine is

$$\overset{\circ\circ}{\underset{\circ\circ}{{}^{\circ}_{\circ}\mathrm{Cl}}}{}^{\circ}_{\bullet}\overset{\bullet\bullet}{\underset{\bullet\bullet}{\mathrm{Cl}}}{}^{\bullet}_{\bullet}$$

Its structural formula is

$$\mathbf{Cl—Cl}$$

and its molecular formula is $\mathbf{Cl_2}$. Chlorine molecules are linear (straight-line) like those of hydrogen. (See Figure 6-8.)

Energy is required to separate chlorine molecules into chlorine atoms.

$$\textbf{1 mole } \mathbf{Cl_2} + \textbf{58 kcal} \rightarrow \textbf{2 moles Cl}$$

Table 6-4

BOND ENERGIES

Bond	Energy (kcal/mole)
H—H	104
N—N	37
N≡N	227
O—O	34
O═O	119
Cl—Cl	58
Br—Br	46
I—I	36
C—H	98
N—H	92
O—H	111
Cl—H	103
Br—H	87
I—H	71
C—Cl	78
C—Br	66

Hence, the bond energy of the **Cl—Cl** bond is 58 kcal/mole, and the chlorine molecules are more stable than separate chlorine atoms.

Diatomic molecules of the other halogens have similar formulas and shapes. Their bond energies are given in Table 6-4.

6.11 Oxygen molecules

Oxygen also exists as diatomic molecules. But the bonding in an oxygen molecule is rather complex. It is not shown very satisfactorily by orbital and electron-dot formulas. A possible orbital notation for an oxygen molecule is

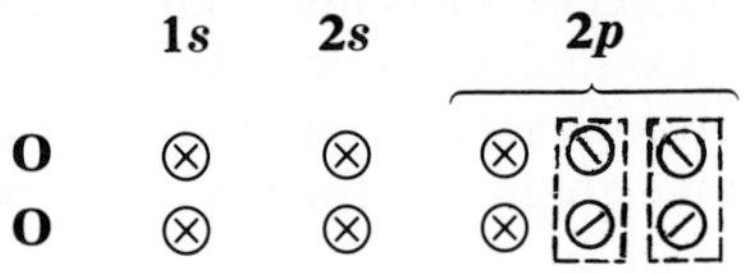

The corresponding electron-dot formula is

Its structural formula is

O═O

and its molecular formula is $\mathbf{O_2}$.

Note that *two pairs* of electrons are shared in the oxygen molecule. This sharing of two electron pairs makes a *double covalent bond.* A double covalent bond is represented in a structural formula by a double dash. The oxygen molecule is linear. The bond energy of the **O═O** bond is 119 kcal/mole. Oxygen molecules are more stable than separate oxygen atoms.

6.12 Nitrogen molecules

The structure of the nitrogen molecule indicates the sharing of *three pairs* of electrons. Nitrogen molecules contain a *triple covalent bond.*

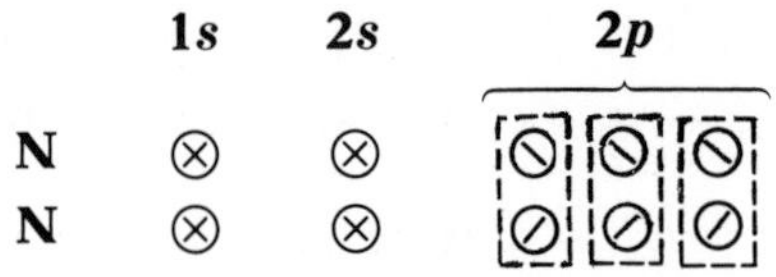

The electron-dot formula for the nitrogen molecule is

Its structural formula is

N≡N

and its molecular formula is $\mathbf{N_2}$. Note that a triple covalent bond is represented in a structural formula by a triple dash.

Nitrogen molecules are linear molecules. The bond energy of the **N≡N** bond is 227 kcal/mole. With such a high bond energy, nitrogen molecules are much more stable than individual atoms.

6.13 Covalent bonding of unlike atoms: hydrogen chloride molecules

Atoms of different elements may combine by covalent bonding. A hydrogen atom and a chlorine atom combine by covalent bonding and form a hydrogen chloride molecule. In this molecule, the 1*s* hydrogen electron and a 3*p* chlorine electron complete a space orbital, as shown below.

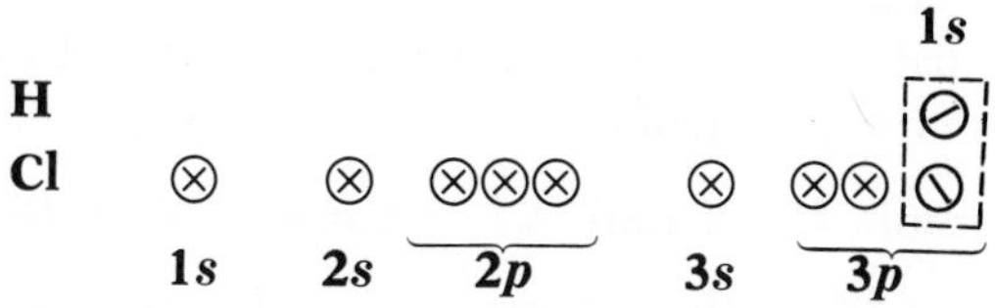

The electron-dot formula for hydrogen chloride is

$$\mathrm{H{:}\underset{..}{\overset{..}{Cl}}{:}}$$

Its structural formula is

H—Cl

and its molecular formula is **HCl.** The HCl molecule is linear as shown in Figure 6-9.

To separate HCl molecules into H and Cl atoms requires energy.

1 mole HCl + 103 kcal → 1 mole H + 1 mole Cl

Hence, hydrogen chloride molecules are more stable than separate hydrogen and chlorine atoms. The bond energy of the **H—Cl** bond is 103 kcal/mole.

Rule 4: *In compounds, the oxidation number of hydrogen is +1.*

For review purposes, use the statement of this rule in Section 6.25 since an exception is described later in this chapter.

By Rule 4, the oxidation number of hydrogen in hydrogen chloride is +1. By Rule 3 (Section 6.5) the oxidation number of chlorine must be −1.

Bond energies can be used to calculate the approximate energy of a chemical reaction. (See Table 6-4.) This method of calculation assumes that the energy change in a reaction is the net result of the breaking and making of chemical bonds.

The reaction for the formation of one mole of hydrogen chloride molecules may be used as an example. One-half mole of hydrogen molecules and one-half mole of chlorine molecules combine as follows:

$$\tfrac{1}{2}\ \text{mole}\ H_2 + \tfrac{1}{2}\ \text{mole}\ Cl_2 \rightarrow 1\ \text{mole HCl}$$

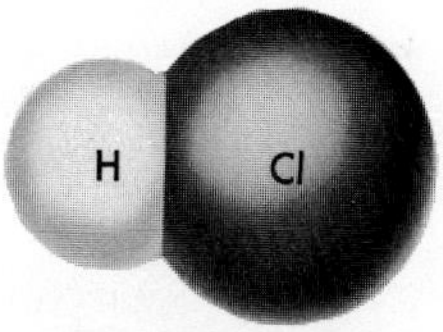

Hydrogen chloride molecule

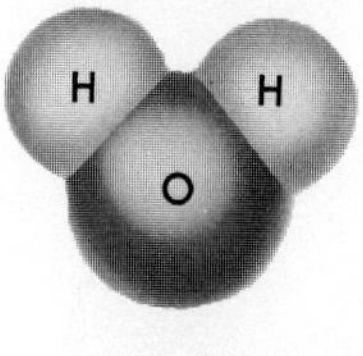

Water molecule

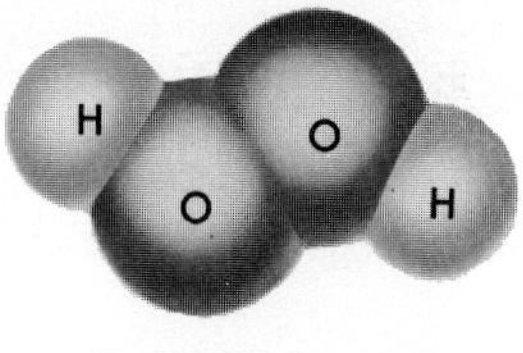

Hydrogen peroxide molecule

Fig. 6-9. Hydrogen chloride, water, and hydrogen peroxide are compounds whose simplest particles are molecules composed of covalently bonded atoms. Hydrogen chloride molecules are linear; water molecules are bent molecules; hydrogen peroxide molecules are double-bent molecules.

Fig. 6-10. Hydrogen burns in chlorine and forms hydrogen chloride, a colorless gas.

This reaction may be considered for calculation purposes to occur in three steps. The first step is the breaking of bonds in one-half mole of hydrogen molecules:

$$\tfrac{1}{2}\ \textbf{mole}\ \mathbf{H_2} + \textbf{52 kcal} \rightarrow \textbf{1 mole H}$$

(The equation is written for one-half mole of H_2 molecules. The energy needed is one-half the bond energy per mole, 104 kcal.)

The second step is the breaking of bonds in one-half mole of chlorine molecules:

$$\tfrac{1}{2}\ \textbf{mole}\ \mathbf{Cl_2} + \textbf{29 kcal} \rightarrow \textbf{1 mole Cl}$$

(Again the energy involved is one-half the bond energy per mole, 58 kcal.)

The third reaction is the reverse of the **H—Cl** bond energy reaction written earlier in this section:

$$\textbf{1 mole H} + \textbf{1 mole Cl} \rightarrow \textbf{1 mole HCl} + \textbf{103 kcal}$$

Combining these three equations and adding them algebraically,

$$\begin{array}{lll} \tfrac{1}{2}\ \text{mole}\ H_2 + 52\ \text{kcal} & \rightarrow & \cancel{1\ \text{mole H}} \\ \tfrac{1}{2}\ \text{mole}\ Cl_2 + 29\ \text{kcal} & \rightarrow & \cancel{1\ \text{mole Cl}} \\ \cancel{1\ \text{mole H}} + \cancel{1\ \text{mole Cl}} & \rightarrow & 1\ \text{mole HCl} + 103\ \text{kcal} \\ \hline \tfrac{1}{2}\ \text{mole}\ H_2 + \tfrac{1}{2}\ \text{mole}\ Cl_2 & \rightarrow & 1\ \text{mole HCl} + \ \ 22\ \text{kcal} \end{array}$$

Thus, we see that the reaction is exothermic. The amount of energy released is 22 kcal.

6.14 Water molecules

The common compound, water, consists of molecules formed by covalent bonding of two hydrogen atoms with one oxygen atom. The orbital representation of this bonding is shown in the margin at the left.

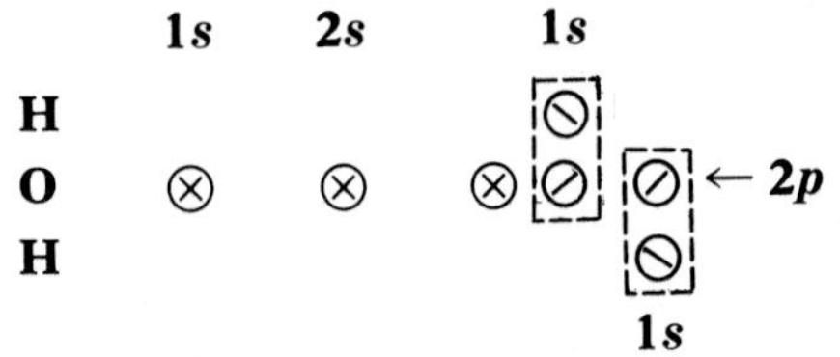

The electron-dot formula for water is

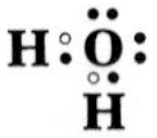

Its structural formula is

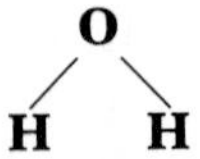

and its molecular formula is $\mathbf{H_2O}$.

A molecule containing three atoms can have one of only two shapes. Either (1) the atoms lie on the same straight line and form a linear molecule, or (2) the atoms do not lie on one straight line and form a bent molecule. Figure 6-9 shows that the hydrogen atoms and oxygen atom in a water molecule do not lie on the same straight line. Water molecules are bent molecules. Very careful measurements reveal that the distances between the oxygen atom and each of the two hydrogen atoms are the same. This evidence suggests that the two hydrogen atoms act the same way in the molecule.

Energy is required to break up water molecules into the atoms of which they are made.

$$\textbf{1 mole } H_2O + \textbf{222 kcal} \rightarrow \textbf{2 moles H} + \textbf{1 mole O}$$

Water molecules, therefore, have lower energy and are more stable than separate hydrogen and oxygen atoms. Two **H—O** bonds are broken per molecule of water decomposed. Therefore, the **H—O** bond energy is 111 kcal/mole or one-half that shown in the equation.

6.15 Hydrogen peroxide molecules

It is possible for more than one kind of molecule to be formed from the same kinds of atoms. A second compound that may be formed from hydrogen and oxygen is hydrogen peroxide, a well-known bleaching and oxidizing agent. The orbital notation of hydrogen peroxide is shown in the margin.

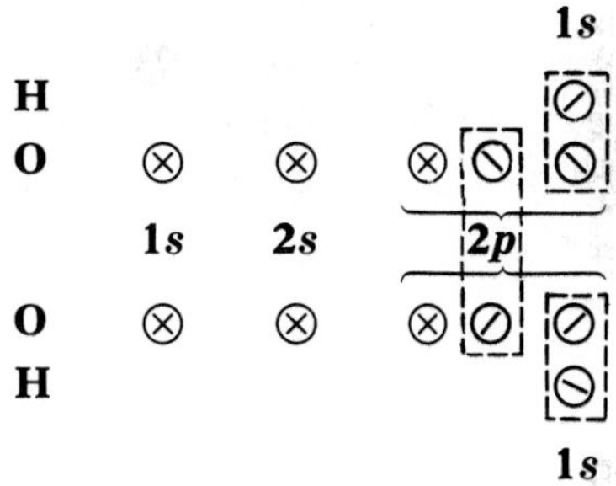

Its electron-dot formula is

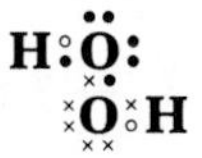

Its structural formula is

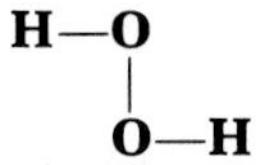

Its molecular formula is H_2O_2. Experimental evidence indicates that the hydrogen peroxide molecule is a double-bent shaped molecule. (See Figure 6-9.)

Rule 5: *In compounds, the oxidation number of oxygen is* -2.

For review purposes, use the statement of this rule in Section 6.25 since a further exception is discussed later in this chapter.

One exception to this rule is that, in peroxides, the oxidation number of oxygen is -1. Thus we see that, in water, the oxidation number of hydrogen is $+1$ and of oxygen is -2. On the other hand, in hydrogen peroxide, the oxidation number of hydrogen is $+1$, and of oxygen is -1. (Use Rule 3 to check this result.)

6.16 Other molecules containing hydrogen

Table 6-5 on the next page gives some examples of covalent bonding between hydrogen and nitrogen, and between hydrogen and carbon. The oxidation number of hydrogen in each molecule is $+1$. But note that the oxidation numbers of nitrogen and carbon vary from molecule to molecule.

Ammonia, NH_3, molecules have three hydrogen atoms so

spaced about a nitrogen atom that the molecule has the shape of a pyramid. Think of the hydrogen atoms as forming the base of the pyramid, with the nitrogen atom at the peak. In methane, CH_4, the hydrogen atoms are symmetrically spaced in three dimensions about the carbon atom. Methane molecules have a regular tetrahedral shape. A regular tetrahedron is a solid figure that has four sides, each side an equilateral triangle.

Consider the examples of covalent bonding illustrated thus far. Except for hydrazine (Table 6-5), all of the bonded atoms are more stable because they have filled orbitals. They have lower energy than the unbonded atoms. Thus, the reactions in which these molecules are formed from atoms are exothermic. Only the combination of nitrogen and hydrogen atoms forming hydrazine, N_2H_4, is endothermic.

The neutral particle that results from the covalent bonding of atoms is a molecule. Its composition is represented by a molecular formula.

6.17 Hybridization

In a methane molecule, CH_4, one carbon atom is covalently bonded to four hydrogen atoms. The hydrogen atoms are symmetrically arranged as if at the vertices of a regular tetrahedron with the carbon atom at the center. The carbon-hydrogen bond angles in this molecule are all 109.5°. See Figure 6-11.

Table 6-5

DATA ON SOME REPRESENTATIVE MOLECULES

	Ammonia	Hydrazine	Methane	Ethane
molecular formula	NH_3	N_2H_4	CH_4	C_2H_6
structural formula	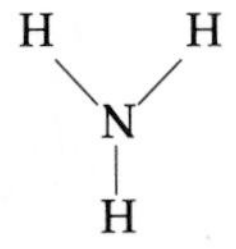	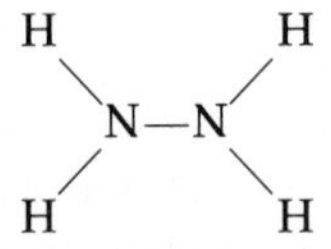	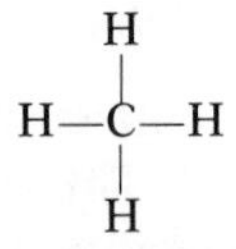	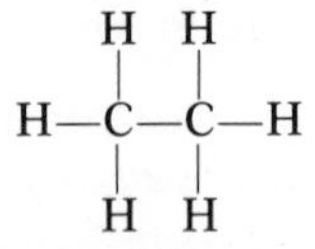
electron-dot formula	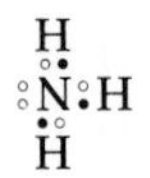		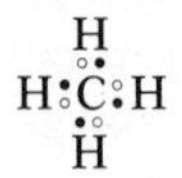	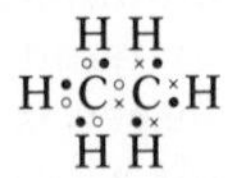
oxidation numbers	H = +1 N = −3	H = +1 N = −2	H = +1 C = −4	H = +1 C = −3
model of molecule		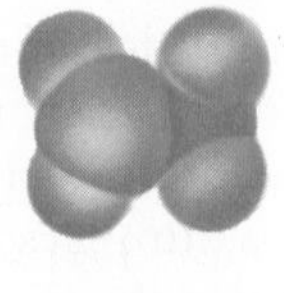		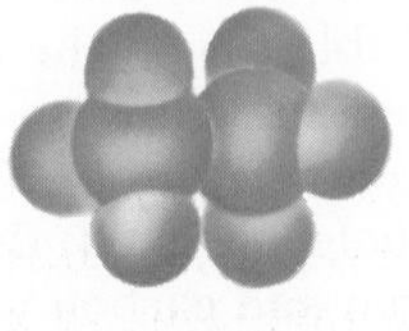

In orbital notation, carbon atoms are represented

	1s	**2s**	**2p**
C	⊗	⊗	⦸⦸○

This notation indicates that the valence electrons should be two 2*s* and two 2*p* electrons. However, when carbon atoms combine, it is believed that one of the 2*s* electrons acquires enough energy to occupy a 2*p* orbital. This structure may be represented

	1s	**2s**	**2p**
C	⊗	⦸	⦸⦸⦸

Thus, the bonding electrons of a carbon atom are one 2*s* electron and three 2*p* electrons. A carbon atom, therefore, can form four covalent bonds, as it does with hydrogen atoms in the methane molecule.

We have noted that one of the valence electrons of the carbon atom is a 2*s* electron and the other three are 2*p* electrons. Hence, we might expect one of the carbon-hydrogen bonds in methane to be different from the other three. Experimentally, however, this is not the case. All the bonds are equivalent. We can explain this difference by assuming that *hybridization* of the one 2*s* and three 2*p* orbitals occurs. Four equivalent orbitals are produced.

Hybridization *is the combining of two or more orbitals of nearly the same energy into new orbitals of equal energy.* The hybrid orbitals of the carbon atom are called sp^3 (read *sp*-three) orbitals. Hybrid orbitals result from the combination of one *s* orbital and three *p* orbitals. In orbital notation, we may show the effect of hybridization this way:

	1s	**2sp³**
C	⊗	⦸⦸⦸⦸

As mentioned, these four sp^3 orbitals point toward the corners of a regular tetrahedron from the carbon atom at their center. This arrangement permits the maximum separation of four orbitals grouped about a given point. This arrangement accounts for the regular tetrahedral shape of methane molecules.

The idea of hybrid tetrahedral orbitals can also account for the observed shape of the ammonia molecule. This is true even though ammonia has only three hydrogen atoms attached to a central nitrogen atom. The electron-dot symbol for a nitrogen atom is

$$\cdot\dot{\underset{\cdot}{\mathrm{N}}}:$$

Let us imagine that the electrons in the four positions about the symbol are distributed among four equivalent tetrahedral orbitals. This arrangement gives one orbital with a pair of

Fig. 6-11. In the methane molecule, CH_4, a carbon atom is covalently and symmetrically bonded to four hydrogen atoms. The tetrahedral shape is the result of sp^3 hybridization of the carbon-atom orbitals.

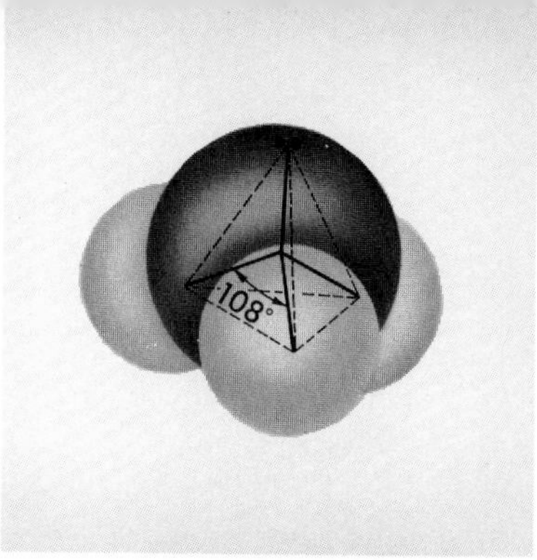

Fig. 6-12. The pyramidal shape of the ammonia molecule, NH_3, may be explained by the sp^3 hybridization of nitrogen-atom orbitals.

electrons and three orbitals with single electrons which can be shared with the electron from each of three hydrogen atoms. The result is a structure that resembles a pyramid as shown in Figure 6-12. The three hydrogen atoms form the base of the pyramid. The unshared pair of nitrogen electrons forms the peak. The angles between the **N—H** bonds in ammonia are known to be 108°. This agrees well with the tetrahedral angle of 109.5°.

We may extend this idea to the structure of the water molecule. The electron-dot formula for this molecule is

$$\begin{array}{c} \cdot\cdot \\ \mathbf{H}\!:\!\mathbf{O}\!: \\ \cdot\cdot \\ \mathbf{H} \end{array}$$

Here we may imagine four tetrahedral hybrid orbitals. Two of these form the oxygen-hydrogen bonds. The other two are each a pair of unshared oxygen electrons. See Figure 6-13. The bond angle in the water molecule is only 105°. The unshared electron pairs on the oxygen atom tend to repel each other more than the shared electrons repel each other. These unequal opposing repulsions make the angle between the shared pairs decrease slightly in size.

Other types of hybridization are described in Chapter 18.

Fig. 6-13. The bent shape of the water molecule, H_2O, may be explained by the considerable sp^3 hybridization of oxygen-atom orbitals.

6.18. Size of molecules

Molecules are very small. It is estimated that if a drop of water could be magnified to the size of the earth, the molecules composing it would be about one meter in diameter. But molecules vary greatly in size. The simple molecules of gases, consisting of one, two, or three atoms, have diameters of about 3×10^{-8} cm. Some virus protein molecules consist of about 7.5×10^5 atoms and have diameters of about 2.3×10^{-6} cm. These molecules have been photographed with an electron microscope. On the angstrom scale, this range of molecular diameters is from 3 Å to 230 Å.

Fig. 6-14. An electron photomicrograph of a cold virus, about 205,000 magnification.

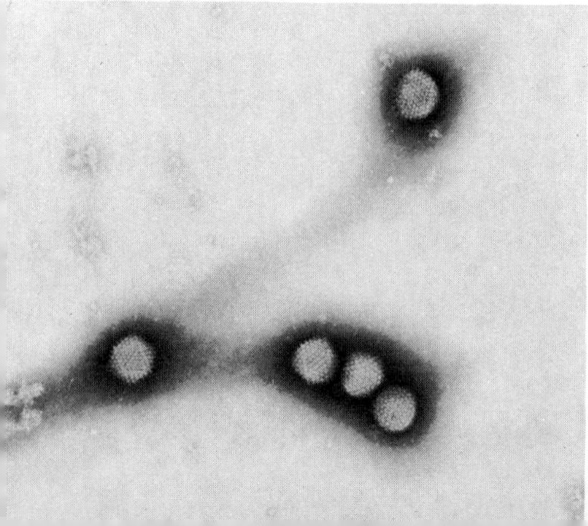

6.19 Electronegativity

In ionic bonding, electrons are *completely transferred* from the outer shells of metallic atoms to the outer shells of nonmetallic atoms. In covalent bonding, electrons are *shared* in the outer shells of the bonded atoms.

If two covalently bonded atoms are alike, their attractions for the shared electrons are equal. The electrons are most probably distributed equally about both atoms. Each atom remains electrically neutral, even though they are bonded together. *A covalent bond in which there is an equal attraction for the shared electrons and a resulting balanced distribution of charge is called a* ***pure, or nonpolar, covalent bond.*** If two different atoms are covalently bonded, one atom may attract the shared electron pair more strongly than the other atom does. Then, the electrons are not equally shared but are more closely held by the atom with stronger attraction. This atom is not electrically neutral. Instead it is slightly negative, though not as negative as a singly charged anion. The other atom is then left slightly positive, though not as positive as a singly charged cation. *A covalent bond in which there is an unequal attraction for the shared electrons and a resulting unbalanced distribution of charge is called a* ***polar covalent bond.*** Polar covalent bonds thus are intermediate in nature between ionic bonds and pure covalent bonds. In ionic bonds, electron transfer is complete. In pure covalent bonds, electron sharing is equal. Polar covalent bonds are part covalent and part ionic in character.

Ionization energy is a measure of the strength with which a neutral atom holds an outer-shell electron. Electron affinity indicates the strength of the attraction between a neutral atom and an additional electron. Linus Pauling (b. 1901) and other chemists considered these two values, together with certain properties of molecules. They derived an arbitrary scale which indicates *the attraction of an atom for the shared electrons forming a bond between it and another atom. This property is called* ***electronegativity.*** Atoms with high electronegativity have a strong attraction for electrons they share with another atom. Atoms with low electronegativity have a weak attraction for electrons they share with another atom. The relative electronegativities of two atoms give an indication of the type of bonding that can exist between them.

Figure 6-15 on the next page gives the electronegativity values of the elements. A study of this chart shows that

1. Low electronegativity is characteristic of metals. The lower the electronegativity, the more active the metal. Thus, the lowest electronegativities are found at the lower left of the periodic table.

2. High electronegativity is characteristic of nonmetals. Thus, the highest electronegativities are found at the upper right of the periodic table. Fluorine is the most electronegative element. Oxygen is second.

3. Electronegativity generally decreases within the numbered groups or families with increasing atomic number. In the transition element groups, there is usually only a slight variation in electronegativity.

4. Electronegativity increases within a period or series through the middle of the periodic table. It decreases slightly in the remaining metals and then increases usually to a maximum in Group VII or VIII.

6.20 Electronegativity difference and chemical bonding

The electronegativity difference between two elements is related to the percentage of ionic character of a single bond be-

PERIODIC TABLE OF ELECTRONEGATIVITIES

I	II											III	IV	V	VI	VII	VIII
2.1 **H** 1																	**He** 2
1.0 **Li** 3	1.5 **Be** 4											2.0 **B** 5	2.5 **C** 6	3.0 **N** 7	3.5 **O** 8	4.0 **F** 9	**Ne** 10
0.9 **Na** 11	1.2 **Mg** 12											1.5 **Al** 13	1.8 **Si** 14	2.1 **P** 15	2.5 **S** 16	3.0 **Cl** 17	**Ar** 18
0.8 **K** 19	1.0 **Ca** 20	1.3 **Sc** 21	1.5 **Ti** 22	1.6 **V** 23	1.6 **Cr** 24	1.5 **Mn** 25	1.8 **Fe** 26	1.8 **Co** 27	1.8 **Ni** 28	1.9 **Cu** 29	1.6 **Zn** 30	1.6 **Ga** 31	1.8 **Ge** 32	2.0 **As** 33	2.4 **Se** 34	2.8 **Br** 35	3.0 **Kr** 36
0.8 **Rb** 37	1.0 **Sr** 38	1.2 **Y** 39	1.4 **Zr** 40	1.6 **Nb** 41	1.8 **Mo** 42	1.9 **Tc** 43	2.2 **Ru** 44	2.2 **Rh** 45	2.2 **Pd** 46	1.9 **Ag** 47	1.7 **Cd** 48	1.7 **In** 49	1.8 **Sn** 50	1.9 **Sb** 51	2.1 **Te** 52	2.5 **I** 53	2.6 **Xe** 54
0.7 **Cs** 55	0.9 **Ba** 56	1.2 **Lu** 71	1.3 **Hf** 72	1.5 **Ta** 73	1.7 **W** 74	1.9 **Re** 75	2.2 **Os** 76	2.2 **Ir** 77	2.2 **Pt** 78	2.4 **Au** 79	1.9 **Hg** 80	1.8 **Tl** 81	1.8 **Pb** 82	1.9 **Bi** 83	2.0 **Po** 84	2.2 **At** 85	2.4 **Rn** 86
0.7 **Fr** 87	0.9 **Ra** 88	**Lr** 103	104	105	106	107											

1.1 **La** 57	1.1 **Ce** 58	1.1 **Pr** 59	1.1 **Nd** 60	1.1 **Pm** 61	1.1 **Sm** 62	1.1 **Eu** 63	1.1 **Gd** 64	1.1 **Tb** 65	1.1 **Dy** 66	1.1 **Ho** 67	1.1 **Er** 68	1.1 **Tm** 69	1.1 **Yb** 70
1.1 **Ac** 89	1.3 **Th** 90	1.5 **Pa** 91	1.7 **U** 92	1.3 **Np** 93	1.3 **Pu** 94	1.3 **Am** 95	1.3 **Cm** 96	1.3 **Bk** 97	1.3 **Cf** 98	1.3 **Es** 99	1.3 **Fm** 100	1.3 **Md** 101	1.3 **No** 102

Fig. 6-15. Periodic table showing the electronegativities of the elements on an arbitrary scale.

tween atoms of the two elements. Table 6-6 gives values for this useful approximate relationship.

Bonds with more than 50% ionic character are considered to be largely ionic. Thus, the bonds between metallic elements and the distinctly nonmetallic elements are largely ionic. Sodium chloride, NaCl, electronegativity difference $3.0 - 0.9 = 2.1$, is a compound with ionic bonds. Similarly, $CaBr_2$ and BaO are examples of compounds with ionic bonds. ($CaBr_2$: $2.8 - 1.0 = 1.8$; BaO: $3.5 - 0.9 = 2.6$)

Bonds with less than 50% ionic character are considered to be largely covalent. Below 5% ionic character, a bond is considered nonpolar covalent. Between 5% and 50% ionic character, a bond is considered polar covalent. The nonmetallic elements have rather similar electronegativity values. So the bonding between nonmetallic elements is largely covalent. The hydrogen-oxygen bonds in water, electronegativity difference $3.5 - 2.1 = 1.4$, are 39% ionic. Thus these are polar covalent bonds, with the oxygen being somewhat negative and the hydrogen being somewhat positive.

Bonds between like atoms are found in molecules of elements such as oxygen or chlorine. These bonds have no ionic character since the electronegativity difference is zero. (O_2: $3.5 - 3.5 = 0$; Cl_2: $3.0 - 3.0 = 0$)

We have classed chemical bonds as ionic bonds or covalent bonds. But it is apparent that these classifications are not clear and distinct. On the periodic table, the type of bonding gradually changes. Bonds are essentially ionic between the active metals of Groups I and II and oxygen or the halogens. But they are essentially covalent between metalloids and nonmetals as well as between two nonmetals. A third type of bonding, metallic bonding, occurs between atoms of metals. It will be described in Chapter 12.

The noble gases have electron configurations that are chemically very stable. It is possible, however, to produce compounds in which xenon is bonded to fluorine, chlorine, oxygen, or nitrogen. Compounds of krypton or radon with fluorine are also known.

We are now ready to introduce the sixth rule for assigning oxidation numbers.

Rule 6: *In combinations involving nonmetals, the oxidation number of the less electronegative element is positive, and that of the more electronegative element is negative.*

Rule 6 leads us to two further exceptions to the rules as already stated. First, hydrogen forms some ionic compounds with very active metals, such as lithium and sodium. In these compounds, the hydrogen atom gains an electron from the metal and forms a *hydride* ion, $\mathbf{H^-}$. In hydrides, the oxidation number of hydrogen is −1. Second, in compounds with fluorine, oxygen is the less electronegative element. In such compounds, oxygen, therefore, must have a positive oxidation number +2.

Table 6-6

RELATIONSHIP BETWEEN ELECTRONEGATIVITY DIFFERENCE AND IONIC CHARACTER

Electronegativity Difference		Percentage of Ionic Character
0.2	nonpolar	1
0.4	covalent bond	4
0.6		9
0.8		15
1.0	polar	22
1.2	covalent	30
1.4	bond	39
1.6		47
1.8		55
2.0		63
2.2		70
2.4	ionic	76
2.6	bond	82
2.8		86
3.0		89
3.2		92

6.21 Molecular polarity

If all the bonds in a molecule are nonpolar, the valence electrons are equally shared by the bonding atoms. Thus, there is a uniform distribution of electrons on the exterior of the molecule. This uniform distribution occurs regardless of the number of bonds and their direction in space. A molecule with such characteristics is a *nonpolar molecule*. Molecules such as H_2, Cl_2, O_2, N_2, CH_4, and C_2H_6 are nonpolar because all of the bonds in such molecules are nonpolar.

Diatomic molecules like HCl and HBr have only one bond and it is a polar bond. These molecules have one somewhat more negative end and a somewhat less negative end. On the more negative end, the electron density (probability of finding electrons) is greater than on the less negative end. Molecules with such unbalanced electron distributions are *polar molecules*. Because polar molecules have two regions of different electric charge, they are sometimes also called *dipolar molecules*, or simply *dipoles*.

If a molecule has more than one polar bond, the molecule as

A model of a carbon dioxide molecule is shown in Figure 17-8.

a whole may be nonpolar or polar depending on the arrangement in space of the bonds in the molecule. If the polar bonds in a molecule are all alike, the polarity of the molecule as a whole depends only on the arrangement in space of the bonds. Thus, water molecules are polar owing to a bent structure.

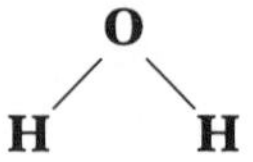

But carbon dioxide is nonpolar due to a linear structure.

$$O{=}C{=}O$$

Triangular boron trifluoride molecules

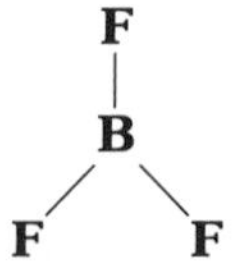

are nonpolar, but pyramidal ammonia molecules are polar.

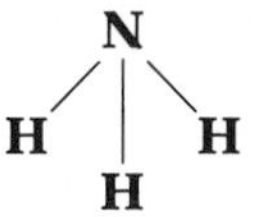

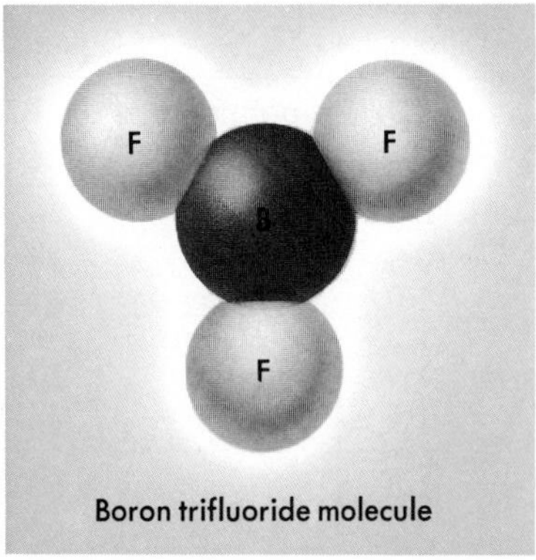

Fig. 6-16. Even though the boron-fluorine bonds are polar bonds, their symmetrical arrangement in the molecule explains why boron trifluoride molecules are nonpolar.

6.22 Resonance

If we attempt to draw an electron-dot formula for the molecular compound sulfur dioxide, we find that two formulas may be written. Each formula gives all three atoms in the molecule an octet. These are shown in the left margin.

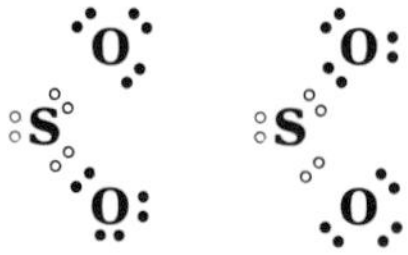

From these formulas, we might suspect that the two sulfur-oxygen bonds in the molecule are different. Experimental evidence, however, indicates that these bonds are identical. Hence, neither of the formulas we have written can be correct. Unfortunately, *we cannot satisfactorily represent this bond identity by any single formula using the electron-dot notation system and keeping the octet rule.* To describe such situations we make use of a concept called ***resonance.***

Sulfur dioxide molecules may be considered to have a structure intermediate between the two electron-dot structures given. In this sense, the electron arrangement in the molecule is a *resonance hybrid* of the written structures. The term "resonance" is not really very accurate in this connection. It encourages the wrong idea that the structure of the molecule switches from one electron-dot formula to the other and that a pair of electrons is sometimes part of one bond and sometimes part of the other.

Sulfur dioxide molecules have only one real structure. The properties of a resonance hybrid do not switch from those of one electron-dot structure to those of the other. The properties

Fig. 6-17. A model that shows the arrangement of atoms in sulfur dioxide molecules.

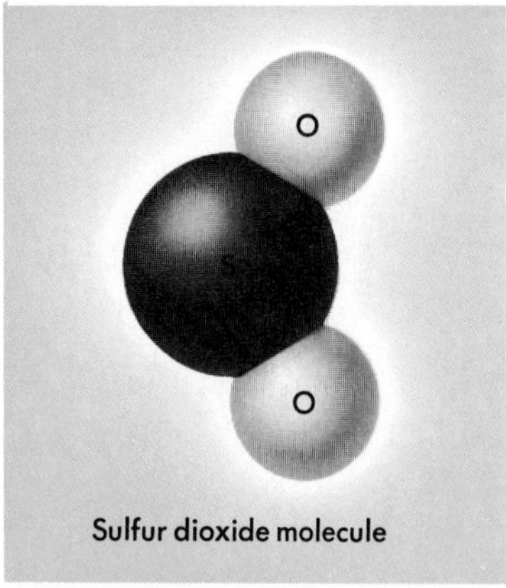

are definite and are characteristic of the hybrid structure. The concept of resonance is an attempt to make up for deficiencies in the electron-dot structures of certain molecules. Difficulties occur when the electron-pair and electron-octet rules are used to write the structures of these molecules.

The difficulties lie in our method of writing formulas, not in the molecules that we are trying to represent.

6.23 Polyatomic ions

Some covalently bonded groups of atoms act like single atoms in forming ions. These charged groups of covalently bonded atoms are called *polyatomic* (many-atomed) *ions*. Some common polyatomic ions are the sulfate ion, $\mathbf{SO_4^{--}}$, the nitrate ion, $\mathbf{NO_3^{-}}$, and the phosphate ion, $\mathbf{PO_4^{---}}$. The bonds within these polyatomic ions are largely covalent. But the groups of atoms have an excess of electrons when combined and thus are negative ions. There is only one common positive polyatomic ion, the ammonium ion, $\mathbf{NH_4^{+}}$. It is produced when a molecule of ammonia, $\mathbf{NH_3}$, acquires a proton. Electron-dot representations of these polyatomic ions are shown in the margin at the right.

There are some covalent bonds in which both electrons that form the bond between two atoms come from only one of the bonded atoms. Each of the electron-dot formulas shown here has at least one such bond. Let us use the ammonium ion as an example. In this ion, three of the covalent nitrogen-hydrogen bonds consist of one shared electron from nitrogen and one shared electron from hydrogen. The other covalent nitrogen-hydrogen bond consists of two electrons, both of which are supplied by a nitrogen atom. A hydrogen ion (proton) can thus bond at this position and produce the single net positive charge of the NH_4^+ ion.

Looking at the structure another way, there are eleven protons (seven in the nitrogen nucleus and one in each of four hydrogen nuclei) in the ammonium ion. There are only ten electrons (two 1*s* electrons of the nitrogen atom, and eight valence electrons shown). With eleven protons and only ten electrons, an ammonium ion has a net charge of +1.

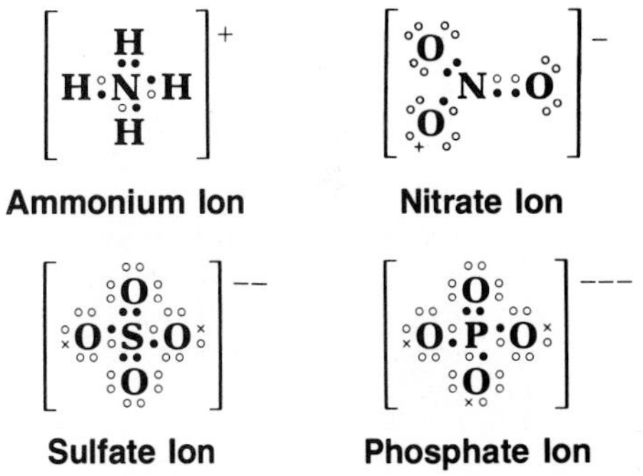

Fig. 6-18. Models showing the arrangement of atoms in four common polyatomic ions.

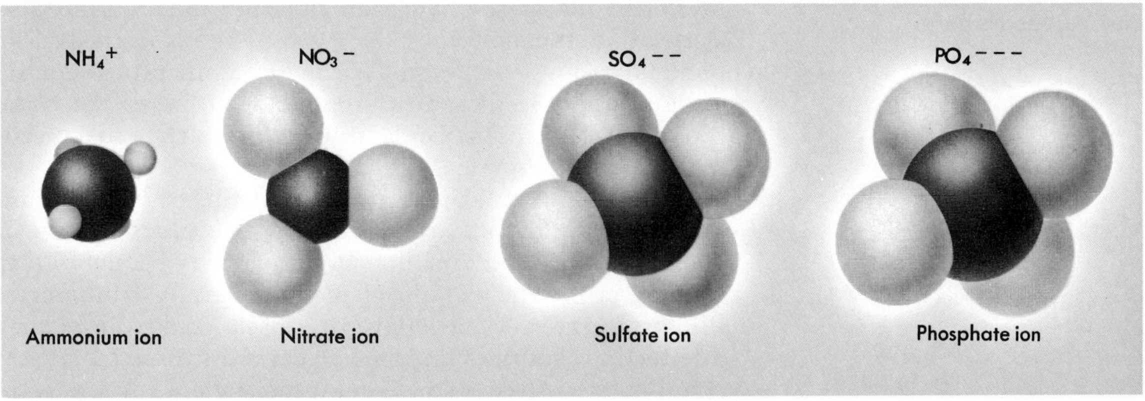

Rule 7: *The algebraic sum of the oxidation numbers of the atoms in the formula of a polyatomic ion is equal to its charge.*

In an ammonium ion, the oxidation number of hydrogen is +1 (Rules 4 and 6). But the algebraic sum of the oxidation numbers must equal +1 (Rule 7). Using x as the oxidation number of nitrogen:

$$\overset{x}{\mathbf{[N}}\overset{+1}{\mathbf{H}}_4\mathbf{]}^+$$

$$x + 4(+1) = +1 \quad \text{and} \quad x = -3$$

The bonding, charges, and oxidation numbers of the elements in the other polyatomic ions can be examined in similar fashion. The electrons represented by small crosses are acquired by the ion from other elements through electron transfer.

The electron-dot formula shown for the nitrate ion is only one of several possible formulas that can be written. Nitrate ions have a resonance-hybrid structure.

6.24 More about particles of matter

Free and isolated atoms are rarely found in nature. Instead, atoms of most elements combine with one another at ordinary temperatures and form larger structural particles. Notable exceptions are the noble elements: helium, neon, argon, krypton, xenon, and radon. The atoms of these noble gases do not combine with each other and form larger particles. There is no distinction, therefore, between the atoms and molecules of these gases. We may say that a molecule of helium is monatomic (one-atomed) and is written as **He.**

Fig. 6-19. Helium, which has monatomic molecules, is less dense than air. Therefore, it is used to fill "lighter-than-air" craft, such as this blimp.

We have already mentioned that the atoms of some elements combine naturally and form pairs that exist as simple diatomic molecules. Atmospheric oxygen and nitrogen are two examples. Their molecules are represented respectively as $\mathbf{O_2}$ and $\mathbf{N_2}$. Observe that $\mathbf{O_2}$ means two atoms of oxygen are bonded together and form one oxygen molecule. On the other hand, **2O** means two separate unbonded oxygen atoms. The expression $\mathbf{3O_2}$ means three molecules of oxygen, each of which consists of two oxygen atoms bonded together. The other elemental gases, hydrogen, fluorine, and chlorine, also exist as diatomic molecules, $\mathbf{H_2}$, $\mathbf{F_2}$, and $\mathbf{Cl_2}$, respectively. The nonmetal bromine, a liquid at ordinary temperatures, exists as diatomic molecules, $\mathbf{Br_2}$. Another element in the same group, iodine, forms molecular crystals in which each molecular particle is diatomic, $\mathbf{I_2}$.

Other elements may form groups consisting of a larger number of atoms . Phosphorus may form molecules consisting of four atoms, written $\mathbf{P_4}$. Sulfur molecules may be eight-atom particles, or $\mathbf{S_8}$. The metallic elements generally exhibit crystalline structures. Their atoms are closely packed in regular patterns that show no simple molecular units. Each individual crystal is considered a single giant molecule.

Some compounds have distinct unit structures composed of simple molecules. Water is a familiar example. Water molecules consist of two hydrogen atoms and one oxygen atom represented as **H_2O**. The expression **$2H_2O$** represents two molecules of water, each containing two atoms of hydrogen and one atom of oxygen. Similarly, **$5H_2O$** signifies five molecules of water. When no other coefficient (the number before the formula) is used, it is understood that the coefficient is 1. Molecules of compounds range from a minimum of two atoms to large numbers of atoms.

Some substances show complex unit structures formed by groups of molecules or molecular aggregates. Still others have no molecular organization at all. Ordinary table salt, sodium chloride, consists of sodium and chloride ions distributed in a regular crystalline lattice pattern that is continuous to each face of the salt crystal. Simple molecules of sodium chloride do not exist except in the vapor state at very high temperatures. In general, *a coefficient of a symbol or formula gives the number of particles whose composition is given by the symbol or formula; a subscript gives the number of atoms of a particular kind in the particle.*

Fig. 6-20. Chemical bonds in the drop of cyano acrylate glue between this workman's helmet and the steel beam are strong enough to support his weight.

6.25 Summary of oxidation-number rules

1. The oxidation number of an atom of a free element is zero.

2. The oxidation number of a monatomic ion is equal to its charge.

3. The algebraic sum of the oxidation numbers of the atoms in the formula of a compound is zero.

4. In compounds, the oxidation number of hydrogen is $+1$, *except* in metallic hydrides where its oxidation number is -1.

5. In compounds, the oxidation number of oxygen is -2, *except* in peroxides, where its oxidation number is -1. In compounds with fluorine, oxygen is the less electronegative element and has a positive oxidation number, $+2$.

6. In combinations involving nonmetals, the oxidation number of the less electronegative element is positive, and that of the more electronegative element is negative.

7. The algebraic sum of the oxidation numbers of the atoms in the formula of a polyatomic ion is equal to its charge.

SUMMARY

There is a relationship between the structure of an atom and the number of other atoms that combine with it. The electrons in an incomplete outer shell of an atom are known as valence electrons. In forming chemical compounds from the elements, valence electrons are usually either transferred from the outer shell of one atom to the outer shell of another atom or shared among the outer shells of the combining atoms. This transfer or sharing of electrons produces chemical bonds. Electron transfer results in ionic bonding while electron sharing produces covalent bonding. The process of electron transfer is always exothermic and that of electron sharing is usually exothermic. Bond energy is the energy required to break chemical bonds.

A chemical formula is a shorthand method of using chemical symbols to represent the composition of a substance. An empirical formula indicates the simplest whole-number ratio of the kinds of atoms in a compound. A molecule is the smallest chemical unit of a substance that is capable of stable independent existence. A molecule is also the neutral particle that results from the covalent bonding of atoms. A formula that indicates the actual composition of a molecule is called a molecular formula.

Any chemical reaction that involves the loss of one or more electrons by an atom or ion is called oxidation. A chemical reaction that involves the gain of one or more electrons by an atom or ion is called reduction. The substance that is oxidized is also the reducing agent. The substance that is reduced is the oxidizing agent. The oxidation state of an element is represented by a positive or negative number called an oxidation number.

Positive ions are called cations; they are smaller than the atoms from which they are formed. Negative ions are called anions; they are larger than the atoms from which they are formed.

Hybridization is the combining of two or more orbitals of nearly the same energy into new orbitals of equal energy. Some molecular shapes can be explained by the hybridization of orbitals.

A covalent bond in which there is an equal attraction for the shared electrons and a resulting balanced distribution of charge is called a pure, or nonpolar, covalent bond. A covalent bond in which there is an unequal attraction for the shared electrons and a resulting unbalanced distribution of charge is called a polar covalent bond. The attraction of an atom for the shared electrons forming a bond between it and another atom is called electronegativity. Electronegativity difference between atoms accounts for the different kinds of bonds.

Molecules with a uniform exterior electron distribution are nonpolar molecules. Molecules with unbalanced exterior electron distributions are polar molecules or dipoles.

The concept of resonance is used to explain the structure of a molecule whose bond characteristics cannot be described adequately by a single electron-dot formula.

Some covalently bonded groups of atoms act like single atoms in forming ions. These are called polyatomic ions.

QUESTIONS

Group A

1. (*a*) What part of the atom is involved in the production of a chemical bond? (*b*) How are such bonds formed?
2. (*a*) What are the types of chemical bonding? (*b*) What particles result from each type of bonding?
3. (*a*) What kind of outer electron shell does an atom usually attain when it combines with other atoms? (*b*) Why is this electron structure chemically stable?
4. Which type of energy changes may occur (*a*) in electron transfer? (*b*) in electron sharing?
5. (*a*) What is a chemical formula? (*b*) Distinguish between an empirical formula and a molecular formula.
6. Which type of formula is used to represent the composition of (*a*) an ionic compound? (*b*) a covalent compound?
7. Draw an electron-dot symbol for (*a*) a potassium atom; (*b*) a potassium ion.
8. Draw an electron-dot symbol for (*a*) a sulfur atom; (*b*) a sulfide ion.

9. Using electron-dot symbols, represent a compound of potassium and sulfur.
10. (*a*) State the general definition for oxidation; (*b*) for reduction.
11. (*a*) Why is a substance that undergoes oxidation a reducing agent? (*b*) Why may a substance that undergoes reduction be considered an oxidizing agent?
12. Explain: A barium atom is larger than a calcium atom.
13. Explain: A bromide ion is larger than a chloride ion.
14. For a fluorine molecule, draw: (*a*) its orbital notation; (*b*) its electron-dot formula; (*c*) its molecular formula.
15. Distinguish between an atom and a molecule.
16. What is the difference between a symbol and a formula?
17. (*a*) From a comparison of the bond energies of H_2, N_2, O_2, and Cl_2, which is the most stable molecule? (*b*) Which is the least stable molecule?
18. What is electronegativity?
19. What electronegativity difference is there between atoms that form (*a*) ionic bonds; (*b*) polar covalent bonds; (*c*) bonds with no ionic character?
20. Assuming chemical union between the following pairs, indicate in each case which element would have the positive oxidation number: (*a*) hydrogen-sodium; (*b*) chlorine-fluorine; (*c*) chlorine-oxygen; (*d*) hydrogen-lithium; (*e*) bromine-hydrogen.
21. What is the oxidation number of each element in the following compounds: (*a*) MnO_2, a dioxide; (*b*) H_3PO_4; (*c*) HNO_3; (*d*) P_4O_{10}; (*e*) Na^+OH^-?
22. (*a*) What gaseous elements have diatomic molecules? (*b*) By what symbol or formula is each represented?
23. (*a*) What gaseous elements have monatomic molecules? (*b*) By what symbol or formula is each represented?
24. How many atoms of each element are represented by the following formulas: sugar, $C_{12}H_{22}O_{11}$; sand, SiO_2; salt, NaCl; hydrogen peroxide, H_2O_2; soap, $C_{17}H_{35}$-COONa?
25. What does each of the following represent? (*a*) Ar; (*b*) $4N_2$; (*c*) HI; (*d*) $6H_2SO_4$; (*e*) 3Cu; (*f*) $2K^+Br^-$; (*g*) CO; (*h*) Co.

Group B

26. Draw the orbital notation for (*a*) a calcium atom; (*b*) a calcium ion.
27. Draw the orbital notation for (*a*) a fluorine atom; (*b*) a fluoride ion.
28. Using orbital notation, show how an ionic compound of calcium and fluorine is formed.
29. Explain why a calcium atom is smaller than a potassium atom.
30. Explain why a sulfide ion is larger than a chloride ion.
31. For a hydrogen bromide molecule, HBr, draw: (*a*) its orbital notation; (*b*) its electron-dot formula.
32. Hydrogen and sulfur form a simple molecular compound. Using both orbital notation and electron-dot notation, show how such a compound may be represented. Then determine its probable molecular formula.
33. (*a*) From a consideration of the electron-dot notation of phosphorus, what is the shape of a PH_3 molecule? (*b*) Consider sulfur and H_2S in similar fashion.
34. For each of the following bonds give the percent ionic character and indicate whether the bond is largely ionic, polar covalent, or pure covalent. (*a*) K—Br; (*b*) C—O; (*c*) Na—O; (*d*) C—H; (*e*) Br—Br.
35. What is the oxidation number of manganese in (*a*) potassium permanganate, $K^+MnO_4^-$; (*b*) manganese(II) sulfate, $Mn^{++}SO_4^{--}$? (*c*) If manganese(II) sulfate is one of the products of a reaction in which potassium permanganate was one of the reactants, what kind of change has manganese undergone? (*d*) What name is given to manganese in this change?
36. What is the oxidation number of (*a*) iron in $Fe^{++}SO_4^{--}$ and in $Fe^{+++}Cl_3^-$? (*b*) chromium in Cr_2O_3, $K_2^+CrO_4^{--}$, and $K_2^+Cr_2O_7^{--}$?

37. The four oxygen acids of chlorine are hypochlorous acid, $HClO$; chlorous acid, $HClO_2$; chloric acid, $HClO_3$; and perchloric acid, $HClO_4$. What is the oxidation number of chlorine in each acid of the series?

38. What is the oxidation number of each element in the following polyatomic ions? (*a*) SO_4^{--}; (*b*) SO_3^{--}; (*c*) NO_2^{-}; (*d*) CO_3^{--}; (*e*) CrO_4^{--}.

39. Oxygen atoms form a triatomic molecule, O_3, called ozone. (*a*) Draw an electron-dot formula for this molecule that satisfies the octet rule. (*b*) Is this the only formula you can draw for this molecule that satisfies the octet rule? (*c*) What is the explanation of the actual structure of an ozone molecule?

40. Classify each of the following as ionic crystal, polar covalent molecule, or nonpolar covalent molecule. (*a*) $MgCl_2$; (*b*) CF_4, consisting of a central carbon atom and four symmetrically arranged fluorine atoms; (*c*) HBr; (*d*) SO_2, consisting of an oxygen atom, a sulfur atom, and a second oxygen atom arranged in a bent molecule; (*e*) P_4.

41. Explain what the caption of the illustration on page 93 means in terms of chemical bonds.

PROBLEMS

Group A

1. From bond-energy data, determine whether the energy change in this reaction is exothermic or endothermic. What is the amount of the energy change?

$$\tfrac{1}{2}\text{ mole } H_2 + \tfrac{1}{2}\text{ mole } Br_2 \rightarrow 1\text{ mole } HBr$$

2. From bond-energy data, determine the kind and amount of energy change for the reaction

$$1\text{ mole } H_2 + \tfrac{1}{2}\text{ mole } O_2 \rightarrow 1\text{ mole } H_2O$$

Group B

3. Calculate the energy change for the reaction

$$1\text{ mole Mg} + 2\text{ moles Br} \rightarrow 1\text{ mole } Mg^{++}Br^{-}_2$$

As described in Section 6.6, this reaction may be assumed to consist of three separate reactions.

$$1\text{ mole Mg} + \text{energy} \rightarrow 1\text{ mole } Mg^{++} + 2\text{ moles } e^{-}$$

The energy required for this reaction is the sum of the ionization energies for removing the first and second electrons from a magnesium atom. Obtain energy data from Chapter 5.

$$2\text{ moles Br} + 2\text{ moles } e^{-} \rightarrow 2\text{ moles } Br^{-} + \text{energy}$$

The energy released is the electron affinity of *two* moles of bromine atoms. Obtain energy data from Chapter 5.

$$1\text{ mole } Mg^{++} + 2\text{ moles } Br^{-} \rightarrow 1\text{ mole } Mg^{++}Br^{-}_2 + 587\text{ kcal}$$

Set up these three equations in suitable form and do the required calculations. Is the overall reaction exothermic or endothermic?

4. From bond-energy data, determine the kind and amount of energy change for the reaction:

$$1\text{ mole } H_2 + 1\text{ mole } O_2 \rightarrow 1\text{ mole } H_2O_2$$

Assume four reaction steps: (1) breaking bonds in H_2 molecules; (2) breaking bonds in O_2 molecules; (3) combining of H atoms and O atoms into H—O groups; (4) combining of H—O groups into H_2O_2 molecules by forming O—O bonds between them.

5. From bond-energy data, determine the kind and amount of the energy change for the reaction

$$1\text{ mole } N_2 + 2\text{ moles } H_2 \rightarrow 1\text{ mole } N_2H_4 \text{ (hydrazine)}$$

chapter 7

CHEMICAL COMPOSITION

A few chemical symbols from the time of the ancient Greeks to Dalton's day. (See Question 21 on page 142.)

7.1 Common ions and their charges

The formula of a compound represents the relative number of atoms of each element present.

The formula of a compound is useful only if it correctly represents the composition of the substance. The composition of a compound is determined by chemical analysis. Its formula is then derived from the analysis data using concepts from atomic theory and chemical bonding. You will see how this is done in this chapter.

It is possible to write the formulas for many common compounds without using composition data from chemical analyses. This is done by using the positively and negatively charged ions that compose ionic compounds. A list of common ions and their charges is presented in Table 7-1. Knowing these will help you become proficient in writing the formulas of compounds correctly. You should *memorize* the ions and their charges listed in this table.

As you study Table 7-1 on the next page, note that positive ions, except for the ammonium ion, have the same names as the elements from which they are derived. The atoms of some metallic elements form ions in more than one oxidation state. For example, copper forms Cu^{+} and Cu^{++} ions. The *name* of each copper ion includes its oxidation number as a Roman numeral in parentheses. The copper(I) ion is called simply the "copper-one" ion and is represented by Cu^{+}. The copper(II) ion is called the "copper-two" ion and is represented by Cu^{++}. This Roman numeral notation is not used with metals that form ions in only a single oxidation state.

Many of the common negative ions in Table 7-1 are poly-

Table 7-1

COMMON IONS AND THEIR CHARGES

+1	+2	+3
ammonium, NH_4^+	barium, Ba^{++}	aluminum, Al^{+++}
copper(I), Cu^+	calcium, Ca^{++}	chromium(III), Cr^{+++}
potassium, K^+	copper(II), Cu^{++}	iron(III), Fe^{+++}
silver, Ag^+	iron(II), Fe^{++}	
sodium, Na^+	lead(II), Pb^{++}	
	magnesium, Mg^{++}	
	mercury(I), Hg_2^{++}	
	mercury(II), Hg^{++}	
	nickel(II), Ni^{++}	
	zinc, Zn^{++}	
−1	**−2**	**−3**
acetate, $C_2H_3O_2^-$	carbonate, CO_3^{--}	phosphate, PO_4^{---}
bromide, Br^-	chromate, CrO_4^{--}	
chlorate, ClO_3^-	dichromate, $Cr_2O_7^{--}$	
chloride, Cl^-	oxide, O^{--}	
fluoride, F^-	peroxide, O_2^{--}	
hydrogen carbonate, HCO_3^-	sulfate, SO_4^{--}	
hydrogen sulfate, HSO_4^-	sulfide, S^{--}	
hydroxide, OH^-	sulfite, SO_3^{--}	
iodide, I^-		
nitrate, NO_3^-		
nitrite, NO_2^-		

Table 7-2

METALLIC ION NAME EQUIVALENTS

Old System		New System	
chromic	Cr^{+++}	chromium(III)	Cr^{+++}
ferrous	Fe^{++}	iron(II)	Fe^{++}
ferric	Fe^{+++}	iron(III)	Fe^{+++}
cuprous	Cu^+	copper(I)	Cu^+
cupric	Cu^{++}	copper(II)	Cu^{++}
mercurous	Hg^+	mercury(I)	Hg_2^{++}
mercuric	Hg^{++}	mercury(II)	Hg^{++}

atomic (as is the positive ammonium ion). They are covalently bonded groups of atoms that form ions just as single atoms do. You will find it helpful to review polyatomic ions and their electron-dot configurations in Section 6.23. See also the table inside the front cover or Table 6, Appendix B, for a more extensive list of common ions and their charges.

7.2 Writing chemical formulas

The first step in writing a formula is to recognize the positive and negative ions named in the compound. With this information you can write the ion notations (including their charges) in the order named. Then adjust the number of each kind of ion as needed to provide *total* positive and negative ionic charges of equal magnitudes. This procedure is called the *ion-charge* method of writing formulas. Its use depends on a compound having been named systematically on the basis of its composition. Several examples to illustrate the ion-charge procedure follow.

Let us use *sodium chloride* as the first example. The sodium ion is represented by Na^+, while the chloride ion is represented by Cl^-. In writing formulas for ionic compounds, *the total charge of the first (positive) part of the compound must be equal and opposite to the total charge of the second (negative) part of the compound.* The total charge of an ion is found by multiplying the charge of the ion by the number of that ion taken. The charge of one sodium ion is equal and opposite to the charge of one chloride ion. The formula for sodium chloride is *NaCl.* It says that there is one of each kind of ion.

Using the same method, you can derive the formula for *calcium chloride.* Calcium ion is represented by Ca^{++}. Chloride ion is represented by Cl^-. The total charge of the negative part of the compound must be equal and opposite to that of the positive part of the compound. So two chloride ions will be needed with one calcium ion. One calcium ion has a charge of +2 and the total charge of two chloride ions is −2. The formula is written $CaCl_2$. The subscript $_2$ indicates that two chloride ions per calcium ion is the composition of calcium chloride. No subscript is used with Ca since only one calcium ion is needed in the formula. When no subscript is written, a subscript $_1$ is always understood.

What is the formula for *aluminum bromide?* Aluminum ion is Al^{+++}. Bromide ion is Br^-. Three bromide ions are needed to balance the positive charge of one Al^{+++} ion. The formula is $AlBr_3$.

Note that this ion-charge method of formula writing yields only an empirical formula. Recall that an empirical formula shows the simplest whole-number ratio of atoms in a compound.

Fig. 7-1. The layers of these geological formations weather differently because of differences in their chemical composition.

7.3 Writing the formulas for other compounds

The formula for *lead(II) sulfate* is easy to write. Lead(II) ion is Pb^{++}. Sulfate ion is SO_4^{--}. The charges are already equal and opposite. So the simplest formula for lead(II) sulfate includes just one lead ion and one sulfate ion, $PbSO_4$.

In the formula for *magnesium hydroxide,* a polyatomic ion must be used more than once. Magnesium ion is Mg^{++}. Hydroxide ion, a polyatomic ion, is written OH^-. Two hydroxide ions are needed for a negative charge equal and opposite to the positive charge of one magnesium ion. In writing the formula for magnesium hydroxide, parentheses are used to enclose the formula for the hydroxide ion, (OH). Then the subscript $_2$ is written outside the parentheses, $(OH)_2$. This way of representing the composition shows that the *entire* OH^- ion is taken twice. The complete formula for *magnesium hydroxide* is $Mg(OH)_2$. This formula must ***not*** be written

Cu + O	S + 30	$CuO + SO^3$	$2SO^3 + PoO^2$
Copper oxide	Sulfur trioxide	Copper sulfate	Potassium sulfate (K, from kalium, was used later)

1814 J. J. BERZELIUS

Fig. 7-2. Berzelius introduced letter symbols for elements and also represented the composition of compounds with letter symbols for the constituent elements.

$MgOH_2$. The incorrect formula $MgOH_2$ represents two hydrogen atoms and one oxygen atom instead of two hydroxide ions. Chemists put the subscript number outside the parentheses to indicate that the polyatomic ion inside the parentheses is taken that number of times in the formula. *Parentheses are not used when a polyatomic ion is taken only once in a formula.* For example, the formula for potassium hydroxide represents one K^+ ion and one OH^- ion. The formula is written KOH. No parentheses are used.

Polyatomic ions are covalent structures with an electric charge. Review Section 6.23.

Let us work out another similar formula, that for *lead(II) acetate.* Lead(II) ion is Pb^{++}. The acetate ion is $C_2H_3O_2^-$. For each lead ion, two acetate ions must be represented by the formula. Following the same system used in writing the formula for magnesium hydroxide, the formula for lead(II) acetate becomes $Pb(C_2H_3O_2)_2$. Note that in order to represent two acetate ions in the formula, $C_2H_3O_2$ is enclosed in parentheses, and the subscript $_2$ is placed outside.

If a metallic atom forms more than one ion, a Roman numeral is used in the name of the ion to identify its oxidation state.

Ammonium sulfate has two polyatomic ions in its formula. Ammonium ion is NH_4^+ and sulfate ion is SO_4^{--}. In order to make the total charges equal and opposite, two ammonium ions must be used with one sulfate ion. To represent these in the formula, the NH_4 is enclosed in parentheses with the subscript $_2$ outside. The formula is then written $(NH_4)_2SO_4$.

Finally, let us write the formula for *iron(III) carbonate.* Iron(III) ion is Fe^{+++} and the carbonate ion is CO_3^{--}. Again the total charge of the positive part of the formula must be equal and opposite to that of the negative part of the formula. So for every two Fe^{+++} ions, three CO_3^{--} ions must be used. Six charges of each sign are involved—six positive charges on the two Fe^{+++} ions and six negative charges on the three CO_3^{--} ions. The formula is $Fe_2(CO_3)_3$.

You must recognize that the ion-charge method has limitations. A formula can give no more information than that required to write it. It is possible to write the formula for a compound and then learn that such a compound does not exist! On the other hand, there are many covalent compounds that *do* exist but whose formulas cannot be written using the ion-charge method.

7.4 Naming compounds from their formulas

A Roman numeral used in the name of a metallic ion does not appear in the formula of a compound containing the ion.

The names of many chemical compounds consist of two words: the name of the first part of the formula and the name of the second part. $BaSO_4$ is called barium sulfate (Ba^{++} represents the barium ion; SO_4^{--} represents the sulfate ion). $FeCl_3$ is the formula for iron(III) chloride. Notice that there are two possible oxidation states for iron. One is iron(II), with an oxidation number of +2; the other is iron(III), with an oxidation number of +3. There are 3 chloride ions associated with one iron ion in the formula, $FeCl_3$. Therefore, the iron ion has a charge of +++, and the compound is *iron(III) chloride.* $FeCl_2$ is *iron(II) chloride.*

The use of Roman numerals to indicate oxidation states does not always provide simple and useful names for compounds. The system is commonly used with ionic compounds in which the metallic ion has different possible oxidation states. Another system, using Greek numeral prefixes, is used for certain binary covalent compounds. ***Binary compounds** are those that consist of only two elements.* Some elements form more than one covalent compound with another element. For example, there are two covalent compounds of sulfur and oxygen, SO_2 and SO_3. Nitrogen forms a series of five different compounds with oxygen. The formulas and corresponding names of this series are given in Table 7-3. The names of these compounds must provide a way of distinguishing between them. Covalent binary compounds are named by the following steps.

Table 7-3

NITROGEN-OXYGEN SERIES OF BINARY COMPOUNDS

Formula	Name
N_2O	dinitrogen monoxide
NO	nitrogen monoxide
N_2O_3	dinitrogen trioxide
NO_2	nitrogen dioxide
N_2O_5	dinitrogen pentoxide

Names of binary compounds have -ide endings.

1. The first word of the name is made up of (*a*) a prefix indicating the number of atoms of the first element appearing in the formula, if more than one; and (*b*) the name of the first element in the formula.

2. The second word of the name is made up of (*a*) a prefix indicating the number of atoms of the second element appearing in the formula, if there exists more than one compound of these two elements; (*b*) the root of the name of the second element; and (*c*) the suffix *-ide,* which means that *only* the two elements named are present.

Carbon monoxide is written CO. Only one atom of the first element appears in the formula, so no prefix is used with the first word. It consists only of the name of the first element, *carbon.* The prefix *mon-* is used in the second word of the name because only one atom of oxygen appears in this formula, but more than one compound of carbon and oxygen exists. *Ox-* is the root of the name of the element oxygen. Then comes the suffix *-ide.*

In like manner, CO_2 is *carbon dioxide.* The prefix indicating three is *tri-;* for four it is *tetra-;* and for five it is *pent-* or *penta-.* These prefixes can be used with both the first and second words in the name. Some examples of the use of Greek numerical prefixes are: $SbCl_3$, *antimony trichloride;* CCl_4, *carbon tetrachloride;* and As_2S_5, *diarsenic pentasulfide.*

A few negative polyatomic ions have names with an *-ide* suffix. The hydroxide ion, OH^-, and cyanide ion, CN^-, are examples. Compounds formed with either of these polyatomic ions obviously are not binary. All binary compounds end in *-ide,* but not all compounds with *-ide* endings are binary. For example, NaOH, $Ca(CN)_2$, and NH_4Cl have names that end in *-ide,* but they are not binary compounds.

7.5 Significance of chemical formulas

We have learned to write formulas for many chemical compounds, using our knowledge of the charges of the ions composing them. When it is known that a substance exists as simple molecules, its formula represents one molecule of the substance. Such a formula is known as a ***molecular formula.***

The molecular structure of some substances is not known. Other substances have no simple molecular structure. For these substances, the formula represents (*1*) the elements in the substances and (*2*) the simplest whole-number ratio of the atoms of these elements. In these cases, the formula is called an ***empirical,*** or simplest, ***formula.***

An empirical formula gives the simplest whole-number ratio of the atoms of constituent elements in a compound.

From Section 6.20, you learned that the character of the chemical bonds between elements in a compound is related to the electronegativity difference between these elements. Table 6-6 shows that the ionic character of the bond increases with electronegativity difference, and that the change-over region from covalent to ionic bond is indistinct and somewhat arbitrary. From these observations, you can reasonably assume that nonmetal-nonmetal compounds are molecular, and their formulas are molecular formulas. Similarly, metal-nonmetal compounds are essentially ionic and their formulas are empirical. When no specific information about the structure of a compound is available, you can use this loose guideline to decide whether its formula is a molecular formula.

Fig. 7-3. The material that makes up both synthetic and natural sapphires (top) and rubies (bottom) is aluminum oxide and has the formula Al_2O_3. Trace amounts of a chromium impurity give the ruby its red color.

Let us examine some chemical formulas to learn what information they contain. Hydrogen sulfide has the molecular formula H_2S. It has a nonmetal-nonmetal composition. The formula shows that each molecule of hydrogen sulfide is composed of *two atoms of hydrogen* and *one atom of sulfur.*

The atomic weight of hydrogen is 1.0 and the atomic weight of sulfur is 32.1. Hence this molecular formula signifies that the *formula weight of hydrogen sulfide* is 34.1.

$$\begin{array}{r} \text{2 atoms H} \times \text{atomic weight } 1.0 = 2.0 \\ \text{1 atom S} \times \text{atomic weight } 32.1 = 32.1 \\ \hline \text{formula weight } H_2S = 34.1 \end{array}$$

*The **formula weight** of any compound is the sum of the atomic weights of all of the atoms represented in the formula.*

The compound sodium chloride, table salt, has the empirical formula **NaCl.** It is a crystalline solid that has no molecular structure. It is composed of an orderly arrangement of sodium and chloride ions. This empirical formula tells us the relative number of atoms of each element present in the compound, sodium chloride. It shows that for each sodium atom there is one chlorine atom. The atomic weight of sodium is 23.0 and that of chlorine is 35.5. So the empirical formula signifies that the formula weight of sodium chloride is 23.0 + 35.5, or 58.5.

A molecular formula may also be empirical.

7.6 Molecular weight

We have seen that a molecular formula represents one molecule of a substance. The formula H_2S is a molecular formula. It represents one molecule of hydrogen sulfide. The formula weight, 34.1, is then the relative weight of *one molecule* of hydrogen sulfide. *The formula weight of a molecular substance is its* ***molecular weight.***

In the strictest sense it is not correct to use the "molecular weight" for a nonmolecular substance. Sodium chloride, for example, is represented by an empirical formula. Empirical formulas have "formula weights." The term *formula weight* is a more general term than *molecular weight* and therefore is preferred. In elementary chemical calculations the distinction is not important.

7.7 Formula weight of a compound

To find the total weight of all the members of your chemistry class, you must add the weights of the individual members of the class. Similarly, to find the formula weight of any substance for which a formula is given, you must add the atomic weights of all the atoms represented in the formula. Let us use the formula for cane sugar, $C_{12}H_{22}O_{11}$, as an example. The approximate atomic weights found inside the front cover and in Table 5, Appendix B can be used.

Formula weight is the sum of the atomic weights of all the atoms represented in a formula.

Number of Atoms	Atomic Weight	Total Weight
12 of C	12.0	$12 \times 12.0 = 144.0$
22 of H	1.0	$22 \times 1.0 = 22.0$
11 of O	16.0	$11 \times 16.0 = 176.0$
	formula weight (molecular weight)	= 342.0

Molecular weights are formula weights of molecular substances.

The formula for calcium hydroxide is $Ca(OH)_2$. The subscript $_2$ following the parentheses indicates that there are two polyatomic hydroxide ions per calcium ion in calcium hydroxide. Thus, the formula $Ca(OH)_2$ indicates that we need the atomic weights of one calcium atom, two oxygen atoms, and two hydrogen atoms.

Atomic weights apply to monatomic ions and atoms alike.

Number of Atoms	Atomic Weight	Total Weight
1 of Ca	40.1	$1 \times 40.1 = 40.1$
2 of O	16.0	$2 \times 16.0 = 32.0$
2 of H	1.0	$2 \times 1.0 = 2.0$
		formula weight = 74.1

The atomic weights of the elements are relative weights. They are based on the fact that an atom of carbon-12 has been assigned a value of exactly 12. In the quantitative study of chemical reactions, the atomic weights and formula weights are very useful. They tell us the relative weights of elements or compounds that combine or react. We can convert these relative weights to any desired units. Thus, atomic weights, formulas, and formula weights play a very important part in chemical calculations.

7.8 Percentage composition of a compound

Frequently it is important to know the composition of a compound in terms of the *mass percentage* of each element of which it is made. We may want to know the percentage of iron in the compound, iron(III) oxide. Or, we may want to know the percentage of oxygen in potassium chlorate. This knowledge enables us to determine the amount of potassium chlorate needed to supply enough oxygen for a laboratory experiment.

The chemical formula for a compound can be used directly to determine its formula weight. This is done simply by adding the atomic weights of all the atoms represented. The formula weight represents *all*, or 100 percent, of the composition of the substance as indicated by the formula. The part of the formula weight contributed by each element represented in the formula is the *total atomic weight* of that element (atomic weight × number of atoms). The *fractional part* due to each element is

$$\frac{\textbf{total atomic weight of the element}}{\textbf{formula weight of the compound}}$$

or

$$\frac{\textbf{(atomic weight} \times \textbf{number of atoms) of the element}}{\textbf{formula weight of the compound}}$$

The percentage of each element present in the compound is therefore a fractional part of 100 percent of the compound.

$$\frac{\textbf{(atomic weight} \times \textbf{number of atoms) of the element}}{\textbf{formula weight of the compound}} \times \textbf{100\% of the compound}$$

Remember that atomic weights and formula weights are relative weights. They are expressed by numbers without dimensions, that is, numbers without units of measure. The relationship for the mass percentage of an element in a compound is dimensionally correct when expressed as follows:

$$\frac{\text{(atomic weight} \times \text{number of atoms) element}}{\text{formula weight of compound}} \times 100\% \text{ compound}$$

$$= \%\text{ element by mass}$$

Let us consider the compound iron(III) oxide, mentioned earlier. The formula is Fe_2O_3. What is the percentage of each of the elements in this compound?

1. *Formula weight of Fe_2O_3*

$$\begin{aligned} \text{total atomic weight Fe} &= 2 \times 55.8 = 111.6 \\ \text{total atomic weight O} &= 3 \times 16.0 = 48.0 \\ \hline \text{formula weight } Fe_2O_3 &= 159.6 \end{aligned}$$

2. *Percentage of Fe*

$$\frac{\text{total atomic weight Fe}}{\text{formula weight } Fe_2O_3} \times 100\%\ Fe_2O_3 = \%\text{ Fe by mass}$$

Using three significant figures,

$$\frac{112\text{ Fe}}{160\ Fe_2O_3} \times 100\%\ Fe_2O_3 = 70.0\%\text{ Fe}$$

3. *Percentage of O*

$$\frac{\text{total atomic weight O}}{\text{formula weight } Fe_2O_3} \times 100\%\ Fe_2O_3 = \%\text{ O by mass}$$

$$\frac{48.0\text{ O}}{16\bar{0}\ Fe_2O_3} \times 100\%\ Fe_2O_3 = 30.0\%\text{ O}$$

Of course, since there is no third element present, the percentage of oxygen is 100.0% − 70.0% = 30.0%.

Observe that the formulas Fe_2O_3 in step 2 cancel leaving the symbol Fe in the result. In step 3, the formulas Fe_2O_3 cancel leaving the symbol O in the result. The symbols remaining are the ones we expect for each of these answers. Many errors in the solutions to problems in chemistry can be avoided by consistently labeling each quantity properly. You must also remember to solve the expression for both the numerical value and the unit or label of the result.

As a second example, let us use a crystallized form of sodium carbonate: $Na_2CO_3 \cdot 10H_2O$. (The raised period indicates that these crystals contain 10 molecules of water for each 2 sodium ions or for each carbonate ion. The formula does not tell us how the water molecules are placed with respect to the sodium and carbonate ions in the crystal.) To find the percentage composition of this crystalline material (to 3 significant figures), we proceed as before:

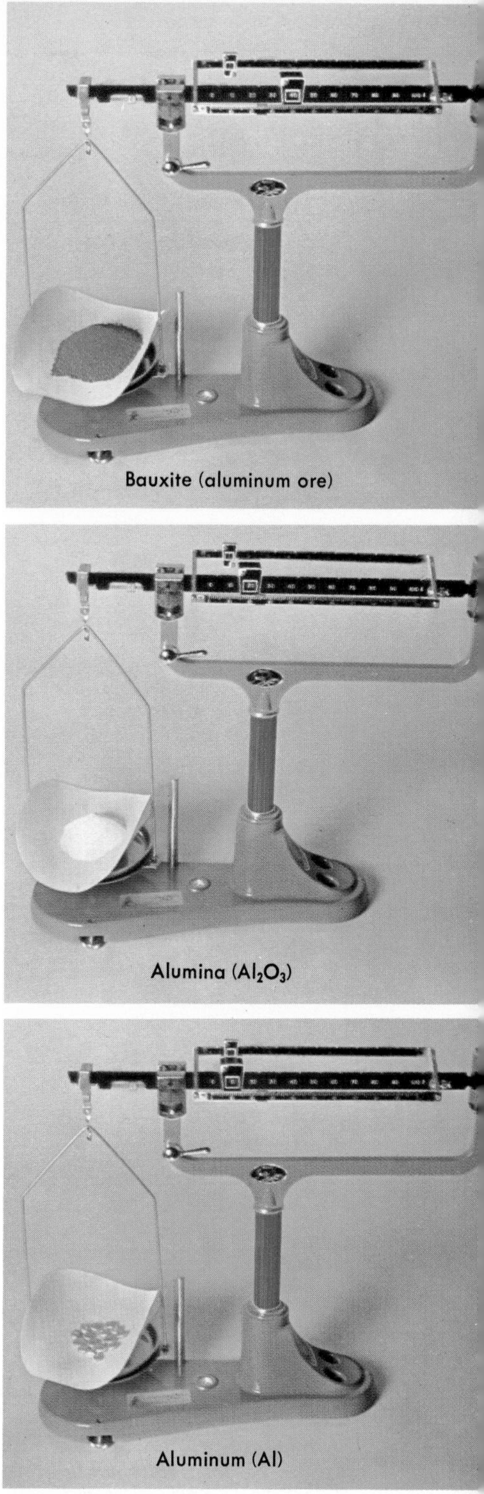

Fig. 7-4. If 40 g of bauxite (aluminum ore) produce 20 g of alumina (Al_2O_3), which produce 10 g of aluminum (Al), what is the mass percentage of aluminum in alumina?

1. Formula weight $Na_2CO_3 \cdot 10H_2O$

	2 Na	$2 \times 23.0 =$	46.0	
	1 C	$1 \times 12.0 =$	12.0	
	3 O	$3 \times 16.0 =$	48.0	
$10H_2O$	20 H	$20 \times 1.0 =$	$2\bar{0}$	$18\bar{0}$
	10 O	$10 \times 16.0 =$	$16\bar{0}$	
		formula weight =	286	

2. Percentage of Na

$$\frac{46.0 \text{Na}}{286 \text{Na}_2\text{CO}_3 \cdot 10\text{H}_2\text{O}} \times 100\% \ \text{Na}_2\text{CO}_3 \cdot 10\text{H}_2\text{O} = 16.1\% \ \text{Na}$$

3. Percentage of C

$$\frac{12.0 \ \text{C}}{286 \text{Na}_2\text{CO}_3 \cdot 10\text{H}_2\text{O}} \times 100\% \ \text{Na}_2\text{CO}_3 \cdot 10\text{H}_2\text{O} = 4.2\% \ \text{C}$$

4. Percentage of O (in CO_3^{--} ion)

$$\frac{48.0 \ \text{O}}{286 \text{Na}_2\text{CO}_3 \cdot 10\text{H}_2\text{O}} \times 100\% \ \text{Na}_2\text{CO}_3 \cdot 10\text{H}_2\text{O} = 16.8\% \ \text{O}$$

5. Percentage of H_2O

$$\frac{18\bar{0} \text{H}_2\text{O}}{286 \text{Na}_2\text{CO}_3 \cdot 10\text{H}_2\text{O}} \times 100\% \ \text{Na}_2\text{CO}_3 \cdot 10\text{H}_2\text{O} = 62.9\% \ \text{H}_2\text{O}$$

Approximate atomic weights usually have no more than two or three significant figures. The accuracy of a result cannot be improved by carrying out the computations beyond the accuracy of the data used. The sum of the mass percentages, therefore, may only approximate 100 percent. Such results do not make us doubt the chemistry involved. Rather, they properly reflect the approximations employed in the computations.

7.9 Law of definite composition and the atomic theory

The law of definite composition (Section 2.10) states, in effect, that the percentage composition of a chemical compound is constant. This characteristic of constant composition of chemical compounds depends upon two facts: (*1*) The relative mass of the atoms of an element is constant, and (*2*) the proportion in which atoms are present in a compound is constant. The idea that, under most conditions, atomic weights are constant is basic to the atomic theory. For practical purposes, the atomic weight we use for an element is the average relative mass of the naturally occurring mixture of its isotopes.

The law of definite composition in its present form may not hold rigorously for certain metallic sulfides and oxides under all reaction conditions.

(This fact was discussed in Section 3.14.) For example, the average relative mass (atomic weight) of a hydrogen atom is 1.0080. That of a chlorine atom is 35.453.

The atomic theory explains how atoms combine in a constant proportion by mass. Individual atoms can lose, gain, or share only a definite number of electrons. Therefore, the mass of one element that can combine with a given mass of another element is limited. In forming hydrogen chloride, for example, only one hydrogen atom can combine with one chlorine atom. One hydrogen atom can share only 1 electron. One chlorine atom has room for only 1 electron to complete its octet of 3rd energy level electrons. So the ratio of these two atoms that combine can be only 1 to 1. It cannot be 1 to 2, or 3 to 2, or any other ratio. Consequently, a molecule of hydrogen chloride always consists of one atom of hydrogen, atomic weight 1.0080, and one atom of chlorine, atomic weight 35.453. The molecule has a molecular weight of 36.461. Furthermore, hydrogen chloride always contains $\frac{1.0080}{36.461}$ parts by weight of hydrogen or 2.765% hydrogen, and $\frac{35.453}{36.461}$ parts by weight of chlorine, or 97.235% chlorine.

Elements in compounds are combined in simple whole-number ratios.

7.10 Law of multiple proportions

Hydrogen and oxygen are present in an unvarying ratio in all samples of water. This ratio is approximately 1 to 8, *by mass*. There is also another compound of hydrogen and oxygen, hydrogen peroxide. The composition of hydrogen peroxide is 1 part of hydrogen to 16 parts of oxygen by mass. Note that for the same mass of hydrogen in the two compounds, 8 is to 16 just as 1 is to 2. In other words, the relative masses of the second element (oxygen) in the two compounds can be expressed as a ratio of small whole numbers. It is not uncommon in chemistry for two or more compounds to be composed of the same two elements. For example,

H_2O	**1 g of H**	**and**	**8 g of O**
H_2O_2	**1 g of H**	**and**	**16 g of O**
$FeCl_2$	**56 g of Fe**	**and**	**71 g of Cl**
$FeCl_3$	**56 g of Fe**	**and**	**106.5 g of Cl**

The mass of the hydrogen in the first pair of compounds is fixed or constant. The mass of iron in the second pair of compounds is also constant. The masses of oxygen, 8 and 16, in the first case are in the simple ratio of 1 to 2. The masses of chlorine, 71 and 106.5, in the second case are in the simple ratio of 2 to 3. It would be possible to give other examples, but in every case the ***law of multiple proportions*** is found to describe such pairs of compounds. *If two or more different com-*

pounds composed of the same two elements are analyzed, the masses of the second element combined with a fixed mass of the first element can be expressed as a ratio of small whole numbers.

Fig. 7-5. The compounds formed from two elements combined in different proportions frequently have strikingly different chemical properties. The H_2O (top beaker) has no reaction with the green felt. The H_2O_2 (bottom beaker) readily bleaches the green dye of the felt.

This law was first proposed by John Dalton, in connection with his atomic theory. He recognized the possibility that two kinds of atoms could combine in more than one way and in more than one proportion. But only whole atoms could be involved in such combinations. Therefore, Dalton reasoned, the masses of the second atom combined with fixed masses of the first atom would have to be in the ratio of small whole numbers. This ratio is the same as the ratio of the actual numbers of atoms of the second element combined with a fixed number of atoms of the first element. The information summarized in the law of multiple proportions is one of the strongest supports for the atomic theory.

Today scientists recognize two reasons for the truth of the law of multiple proportions. (1) Some elements exist in more than one oxidation state. (2) Some elements combine in more than one way with another element. Iron can exist in compounds as iron(II) ions with an oxidation number of +2 or as iron(III) ions with an oxidation number of +3. The elements iron and chlorine can be found combined in two different compounds: $FeCl_2$, iron(II) chloride, and $FeCl_3$, iron(III) chloride. The ratio of the numbers of atoms of chlorine combined with a single atom of iron is 2 to 3. As recognized by Dalton, the relative numbers of atoms that combine is proportional to the masses that combine. Therefore, the ratio of the masses of chlorine combined with a fixed mass of iron in these two compounds is also 2 to 3.

Analysis of the composition and molecular structure of water and hydrogen peroxide lead to these electron-dot formulas:

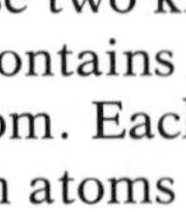

Water

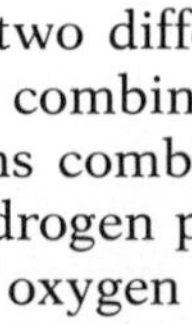

Hydrogen Peroxide

These two formulas represent the two different patterns in which these two kinds of atoms can combine. Each molecule of water contains 2 hydrogen atoms combined with only 1 oxygen atom. Each molecule of hydrogen peroxide contains 2 hydrogen atoms combined with 2 oxygen atoms. The numbers of atoms combined are proportional to the masses combined. So the ratio of the masses of oxygen combined with the same mass of hydrogen in these two compounds is 1 to 2, a ratio of small whole numbers.

Fig. 7-6. These students are determining the composition of a substance in the laboratory.

7.11 Mole concept

Imagine that all the people on the earth were assigned the task of counting the molecules in a tablespoon of water. If each person counted at the rate of one molecule each second, it would take approximately 8×10^6 years to complete the project. The number of molecules involved is so large that it staggers the imagination!

Fortunately, chemists are not ordinarily faced with the problem of weighing out a certain number of molecules of a compound or atoms of an element. They do frequently need to weigh out equal numbers of atoms or molecules of different substances. A knowledge of the atomic weights of the elements allows this to be done very simply.

In Sections 3.13 and 3.14, we recognized four important quantitative definitions.

1. The number of carbon-12 atoms in the defined quantity of exactly 12 grams of this nuclide is the *Avogadro number*, approximately 6.02×10^{23}.

The Avogadro number is 6.02×10^{23}.

2. The amount of substance containing the Avogadro number of any kind of chemical unit is called a *mole* of that substance.

The Avogadro number of any kind of particles is one mole of those particles.

3. The mass in grams of one mole of naturally occurring atoms of an element is the *gram-atomic weight* of the element.

4. The numerical portion of the gram-atomic weight of an element is the *atomic weight* of the element.

From these definitions, we see that if we wish to weigh out an Avogadro number (one mole) of carbon atoms, we must take one gram-atomic weight of carbon, 12 g. If we wish to weigh out an Avogadro number (one mole) of hydrogen atoms,

Fig. 7-7. In the front row (left) are one gram-formula weight (58.5 g) of sodium chloride, (center) one gram-atomic weight (63.55 g) of copper, and (right) one gram-atomic weight (26.98 g) of aluminum. One gram-molecular weight (18.0 g) of water is in the graduated cylinder. The beaker (center) contains one gram-molecular weight (32.0 g) of methanol. If the beaker (upper left) contains 72 g of water, how many gram-molecular weights of water does it contain?

we must take one gram-atomic weight of hydrogen, 1.0 g. These two quantities, 12 g of carbon and 1.0 g of hydrogen, contain the same number of atoms. Thus, any given masses of carbon and hydrogen that are in the ratio of 12:1 (the ratio of their atomic weights) must also have the same number of atoms.

To obtain 5.0 moles of oxygen atoms, we must weigh out $5.0 \times 16\ g = 8\bar{0}$ g of oxygen. To obtain 5.0 moles of sulfur atoms, we must take $5.0 \times 32\ g = 160$ g of sulfur. The $8\bar{0}$ g of oxygen and 160 g of sulfur contain the same number of atoms. Note that the ratio of these masses equals the ratio of the atomic weights of the elements:

$$\frac{\mathbf{8\bar{0}\ g}}{\mathbf{160\ g}} = \frac{\mathbf{16}}{\mathbf{32}} = \frac{\mathbf{1}}{\mathbf{2}}$$

By similar reasoning, using the atomic weights of other elements, we can recognize the following important generalization: *If the mass quantities of two elements are in the same ratio as their atomic weights, they contain the same number of atoms.*

Chemists measure quantities of substances in gram (mass) units. They sometimes refer to these masses of substances as "weights" because "weighing" methods are used to determine them. However, it should be recognized that quantities measured in gram units are, in fact, mass quantities. Atomic weights are most useful when expressed in gram units. *The*

Table 7-4

MASS-MOLE RELATIONSHIPS	
1 gross = 144 objects	
If we compare 144 erasers @ 10.0 g each = 1440 g 144 pencils @ 5.0 g each = 720 g 144 tablets @ $30\bar{0}$ g each = 43200 g	The masses of the gross-quantity packages are different because the mass of each kind of object is different. However, the ratios between the masses of the packages, 1440 g: 720 g: 43200 g, are the same as the ratios between the masses of the individual objects, 10.0 g: 5.0 g: $30\bar{0}$ g, since each package contains the same number of objects.
1 mole = 6.02×10^{23} particles	
If we compare 6.02×10^{23} helium atoms = 4.0 g 6.02×10^{23} hydrogen molecules = 2.0 g 6.02×10^{23} water molecules = 18.0 g 6.02×10^{23} NaCl formula units = 58.5 g	The mass of the mole varies just as the mass of the gross varies. It depends upon what the particles are. However, the ratios between the masses of the moles are the same as the ratios between the masses of the individual particles since each mole contains the same number of particles.

gram-atomic weight of an element is the mass of one mole of atoms of the element. Thus, the mass of one mole of O atoms is 16 g of oxygen, of one mole of S atoms is 32 g of sulfur, and of one mole of Fe atoms is 56 g of iron.

Let us extend our concept of a mole of atoms of an element to a mole of diatomic molecules of an element. One mole of O_2 molecules contains two moles of O atoms. We know that two moles of O atoms has a mass of 2×16 g = 32 g. Hence a mole of O_2 molecules must have this same mass, 32 g. But we recognize that this is the molecular weight of O_2, 32, expressed in gram units. *The mass of a molecular substance in grams equal to its molecular weight is its* ***gram-molecular weight.*** Similar reasoning leads us to see that a mole of H_2 molecules has a mass of 2.0 g, and a mole of Cl_2 molecules has a mass of 71.0 g. *Thus the gram-molecular weight of a diatomic molecular element is the mass of one mole of molecules of the element.* Note that one mole of O atoms has a mass of 16 g, but one mole of O_2 molecules has a mass of 32 g, and so on. Also note that 16 g of O atoms, 32 g of O_2 molecules, 1.0 g of H atoms, 2.0 g of H_2 molecules, 35.5 g of Cl atoms, and 71.0 g of Cl_2 molecules all contain the same number of *particles*—atoms or molecules as the case may be.

Gram-molecular weight is the gram-formula weight of a molecular substance.

One mole of H_2O molecules contains two moles of H atoms and one mole of O atoms. Two moles of H atoms has a mass of 2.0 g; one mole of O atoms has a mass of 16 g. Thus, by addition, one mole of H_2O molecules has a mass of 18 g. This mass is the gram-molecular weight of water. One mole of methane, CH_4, contains one mole of C atoms and four moles of H atoms. One mole of C atoms has a mass of 12 g; four moles of H atoms has a mass of 4 g. One mole of CH_4 molecules has a mass, then, of 16 g, its gram-molecular weight. From these examples, we see that the *gram-molecular weight of a molecular substance is the mass of one mole of molecules of the substance.* There are the same number of molecules in 32 g of O_2, 18 g of H_2O, and 16 g of CH_4. One-mole quantities of all molecular substances contain the same number of molecules, the Avogadro number, 6.02×10^{23} molecules. It follows that *any mass quantities of oxygen, water, and methane that are in the ratio 32 : 18 : 16 contain equal numbers of molecules.*

The mole concept can also be extended to substances that do not have molecules but are expressed by empirical formulas. For example, the ***gram-formula weight*** (the formula weight in grams) of sodium chloride is 58.5 g of sodium chloride. One mole of sodium atoms (as Na^+ ions) has a mass of 23.0 g; one mole of chlorine atoms (as Cl^- ions) has a mass of 35.5 g. Thus, 58.5 g is the mass of one mole of sodium chloride. One mole of sodium chloride then contains one mole of Na^+ ions *and* one mole of Cl^- ions.

Gram-formula weights are formula weights expressed in gram units.

Not only does the symbol for an element stand for one atom

Table 7-5

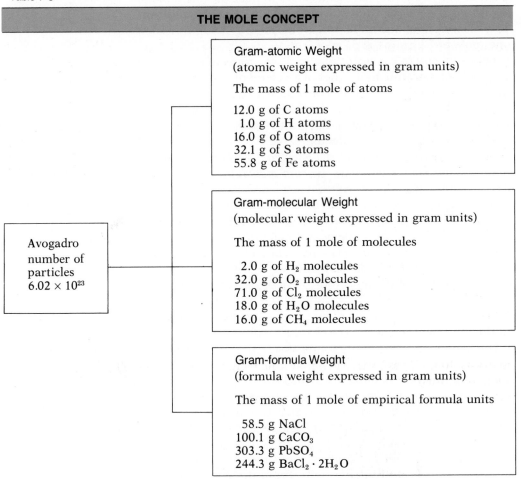

THE MOLE CONCEPT

Avogadro number of particles 6.02×10^{23}	**Gram-atomic Weight** (atomic weight expressed in gram units) The mass of 1 mole of atoms 12.0 g of C atoms 1.0 g of H atoms 16.0 g of O atoms 32.1 g of S atoms 55.8 g of Fe atoms
	Gram-molecular Weight (molecular weight expressed in gram units) The mass of 1 mole of molecules 2.0 g of H_2 molecules 32.0 g of O_2 molecules 71.0 g of Cl_2 molecules 18.0 g of H_2O molecules 16.0 g of CH_4 molecules
	Gram-formula Weight (formula weight expressed in gram units) The mass of 1 mole of empirical formula units 58.5 g NaCl 100.1 g $CaCO_3$ 303.3 g $PbSO_4$ 244.3 g $BaCl_2 \cdot 2H_2O$

of that element, but *in quantitative relationships,* it stands for the mass of one mole of atoms of that element. A formula for a diatomic molecule may represent one molecule of the element. But it also may represent the mass of one mole of such molecules. Similarly, the formula for a compound may represent the composition of the compound and the mass of one mole of that compound. These mole relationships are summarized in Table 7-5.

7.12 Determining the empirical formula of a compound

We have learned (Section 7.8) how to determine the percentage composition of a compound if we are given its formula. Now let us calculate the ratio of the number of atoms of the elements combined in a compound from its percentage composition. The elements of a compound and their smallest whole-number ratio are used to write the empirical formula for the compound.

The simplest whole-number ratio of elements in a compound provides its empirical formula.

This is the method by which most formulas are originally determined. A compound is analyzed to identify the elements present and to determine their mass ratios or the percentage composition. The empirical formula is then calculated from this information. The mass per mole of atoms (gram-atomic weight) of each element is used to reduce the mass ratios to atom ratios.

Edward W. Morley (1838–1923) of Western Reserve University found that 1.0000 part by weight of hydrogen combines with 7.9396 parts by weight of oxygen and forms 8.9396 parts by weight of water vapor. Every 8.9396 parts of water formed requires 1.0000 part of hydrogen and 7.9396 parts of oxygen. Thus, water consists of

$$\frac{\textbf{1.0000 part H}}{\textbf{8.9396 parts water}} \times \textbf{100\% water} = \textbf{11.186\% hydrogen}$$

and

$$\frac{\textbf{7.9396 parts O}}{\textbf{8.9396 parts water}} \times \textbf{100\% water} = \textbf{88.814\% oxygen}$$

Fig. 7-8. This chemist is using an instrument to analyze various petroleum samples for carbon, hydrogen, and nitrogen.

We can easily determine the relative number of atoms of hydrogen and oxygen in water. This is done by comparing the mass percentages of the elements, or their actual masses by analysis, to their respective gram-atomic weights (masses per mole of atoms).

$$\textbf{moles of atoms of an element} = \frac{\textbf{mass of the element}}{\textbf{mass of 1 mole of atoms of the element}}$$

1. From percentage composition data. The simplest way to think of percentage composition is in terms of *parts per hundred.* Morley's experiments show that (rounding to 3 significant figures) 11.2% of water is hydrogen and 88.8% is oxygen. In other words, 100.0 parts of water consists of 11.2 parts hydrogen and 88.8 parts oxygen. Similarly, there are 11.2 g of hydrogen and 88.8 g of oxygen per 100.0 g of water. How many moles of hydrogen and oxygen atoms are present in 100.0 g of water?

$$\textbf{H:} \quad \frac{\textbf{11.2 g H}}{\textbf{1.01 g/mole}} = \textbf{11.1 moles H}$$

$$\textbf{O:} \quad \frac{\textbf{88.8 g O}}{\textbf{16.0 g/mole}} = \textbf{5.55 moles O}$$

You will remember that 1 mole of atoms of one element is the same number of atoms as 1 mole of atoms of any other element (the Avogadro number). Therefore, the relative number of atoms is

$$\textbf{H : O = 11.1:5.55}$$

2. *From relative mass data.* Since the table of approximate atomic weights is used, we may round off the relative masses given. We then have 1.00 part hydrogen and 7.94 parts oxygen in 8.94 parts of water. Accordingly, each 8.94-g quantity of water produced requires 1.00 g of hydrogen and 7.94 g of oxygen. We can determine the number of moles of hydrogen and oxygen atoms in 8.94 g of water and reduce this to the relative number of atoms of each as before.

$$\mathbf{H:}\quad \frac{1.00 \text{ g H}}{1.01 \text{ g/mole}} = 0.990 \text{ mole H}$$

$$\mathbf{O:}\quad \frac{7.94 \text{ g O}}{16.0 \text{ g/mole}} = 0.496 \text{ mole O}$$

The relative number of atoms is

$$\mathbf{H : O = 0.990 : 0.496}$$

From these calculations, we can write the empirical formula of water as

$$\mathbf{H_{11.1}O_{5.55}} \quad \text{or} \quad \mathbf{H_{0.990}O_{0.496}}$$

To find an empirical formula, (1) Convert gram ratio to mole ratio; and (2) Adjust mole ratio to simplest whole-number ratio.

Both formulas show the correct ratio of hydrogen atoms to oxygen atoms in the compound water. However, according to the atomic theory, only whole atoms combine chemically. We need to convert these atom ratios to their simplest whole-number values. This is accomplished by dividing each ratio by its smaller term, shown as

$$\mathbf{H} : \mathbf{O}$$

$$\frac{11.1}{5.55} : \frac{5.55}{5.55}$$

$$\mathbf{2.00 : 1.00}$$

and

$$\mathbf{H} : \mathbf{O}$$

$$\frac{0.990}{0.496} : \frac{0.496}{0.496}$$

$$\mathbf{2.00 : 1.00}$$

The empirical formula for water is therefore H_2O.

Sometimes the operation just performed does not yield a simple whole-number ratio. In such instances the simplest whole-number ratio can be found by expressing the result as fractions and clearing. **CAUTION:** In some problems, dividing by the smallest term may result in such ratios as 1:2.01, 1:2.98, or 1:3.99. Remember that results obtained by using approximate atomic weights can be no more accurate than these values. You should not attempt to clear the fractions in such instances; simply round off to 2, 3, or 4 respectively. These operations are illustrated further in the Sample Problems which follow.

SAMPLE PROBLEM

A compound is found by analysis to contain 75.0% carbon and 25.0% hydrogen. What is the empirical formula?

SOLUTION

Since the compound is 75.0% carbon (75.0 parts per 100.0), 75.0 g per 100.0 g is carbon. Similarly 25.0 g per 100.0 g of the compound is hydrogen. The number of moles of atoms of each element in 100.0 g of the compound is determined by the following relation:

$$\textbf{Moles of atoms of an element} = \frac{\textbf{mass of the element}}{\textbf{mass of 1 mole of atoms of the element}}$$

$$\text{C:} \quad \frac{75.0 \text{ g C}}{12.0 \text{ g/mole}} = 6.25 \text{ moles C}$$

$$\text{H:} \quad \frac{25.0 \text{ g H}}{1.01 \text{ g/mole}} = 24.8 \text{ moles H}$$

Relative number of atoms, C:H = 6.25:24.8

$$\textbf{Smallest ratio of atoms} = \frac{6.25}{6.25} : \frac{24.8}{6.25} = 1:4$$

Empirical formula = CH_4

SAMPLE PROBLEM

A compound contains carbon, 81.7%, and hydrogen, 18.3%. Find the empirical formula.

SOLUTION

Each 100.0-g quantity of the compound contains 81.7 g of carbon and 18.3 g of hydrogen as shown by the percentage composition.

$$\textbf{Moles of atoms of an element} = \frac{\textbf{mass of the element}}{\textbf{mass of 1 mole of atoms of the element}}$$

$$\text{C:} \quad \frac{81.7 \text{ g C}}{12.0 \text{ g/mole}} = 6.81 \text{ moles C}$$

$$\text{H:} \quad \frac{18.3 \text{ g H}}{1.01 \text{ g/mole}} = 18.1 \text{ moles H}$$

Relative number of atoms, C:H = 6.81:18.1

$$\textbf{Smallest ratio of atoms} = \frac{6.81}{6.81} : \frac{18.1}{6.81} = 1:2.66$$

$$\textbf{Simplest whole number ratio} = 1:2.66 = 1:2\tfrac{2}{3} = \tfrac{3}{3}:\tfrac{8}{3} = 3:8$$

Empirical formula = C_3H_8

SAMPLE PROBLEM

The decomposition of 11.47 g of a compound of copper and oxygen yields 9.16 g of copper. What is the empirical formula for the compound?

SOLUTION

Since the compound is composed of only copper and oxygen, the mass of oxygen removed in the decomposition process must be

$$\mathbf{11.47\ g - 9.16\ g = 2.31\ g\ oxygen}$$

$$\textbf{Moles of atoms of an element} = \frac{\textbf{mass of the element}}{\textbf{mass of 1 mole of atoms of the element}}$$

$$\mathbf{Cu:}\quad \frac{\mathbf{9.16\ g\ Cu}}{\mathbf{63.5\ g/mole}} = \mathbf{0.144\ mole\ Cu}$$

$$\mathbf{O:}\quad \frac{\mathbf{2.31\ g\ O}}{\mathbf{16.0\ g/mole}} = \mathbf{0.144\ mole\ O}$$

Relative number of atoms, Cu:O = 0.144:0.144

Smallest ratio of atoms = 1:1

Empirical formula = CuO

7.13 Finding the molecular formula

The analysis of a substance enables us to determine its empirical formula. This simplest formula may or may not be the molecular formula. We calculated the empirical formula for the gas, methane, and found it to be CH_4. Any multiple of CH_4, such as C_2H_8, C_3H_{12}, or C_nH_{4n}, represents the same ratio of carbon and hydrogen atoms. How then can we know which is the correct molecular formula?

It is not possible to decide which is the true formula unless the molecular weight of the substance has been determined. Some substances lend themselves to known methods of determining molecular weights and some do not. These methods will be discussed in Chapters 11 and 13. But, if the molecular weight is known, it is a simple matter to decide which multiple of the empirical formula is the molecular formula.

Molecular weight must be known for a molecular formula to be determined.

Let us represent the correct multiple of the empirical formula by the subscript $_x$. Then

$$\textbf{(empirical formula)}_x = \textbf{molecular formula}$$

and (empirical formula weight)$_x$ can then be equated to the known molecular weight.

$$\textbf{(empirical formula weight)}_x = \textbf{molecular weight}$$

In the case of methane, the molecular weight is known to be 16.0. The equation is

Molecular weight is a whole-number multiple of the empirical formula weight.

$$(\mathbf{CH_4\ weight})_x = 16.0$$
$$[12.0 + 4(1.0)]_x = 16.0$$
$$x = 1$$
$$\text{molecular formula} = (CH_4)_1 \text{ or } CH_4$$

Hence the empirical formula for methane is also the molecular formula. We have seen that this is true also in the case of water. For another example, see the Sample Problem that follows.

SAMPLE PROBLEM

Hydrogen peroxide is found by analysis to consist of 5.9% hydrogen and 94.1% oxygen. Its molecular weight is determined to be 34.0. What is the correct formula?

SOLUTION

1. The empirical formula, determined from the analysis by the method described in Section 7.12, is

HO

2. The molecular formula determined from the empirical formula and molecular weight is

$$(\mathbf{HO\ weight})_x = 34.0$$
$$(1.0 + 16.0)_x = 34.0$$
$$x = 2$$
$$\text{molecular formula} = (HO)_2 \text{ or } H_2O_2$$

SUMMARY

The formulas for common ionic compounds can be written using the ion-charge method. The ion notations are written in the order used in the name of the compound. The number of each kind of ion is then adjusted to make the total positive and negative ionic charges equal.

The names of ionic compounds include the names of the constituent ions. If the metallic ion present has different possible oxidation states, Roman numerals are added to the name of the ion to indicate the oxidation state. A system of prefixes is used in the names of covalent compounds when an element forms more than one compound with another element. For binary compounds, the *-ide* ending means that only two elements are present.

The gram-atomic weights of elements and the gram-formula weights of compounds represent the mass of a mole of these substances.

The percentage composition of a compound can be calculated if the formula is known. Conversely, the empirical formula can be calculated if the composition of a compound is known. Furthermore, if the compound is molecular and its molecular weight is known, the molecular formula can be determined.

QUESTIONS

Group A

1. What is the full significance of the molecular formula for ammonia, NH_3?
2. Why is *formula weight* a more general term than *molecular weight?*
3. What is the symbol and charge of (*a*) sodium ion; (*b*) copper(I) ion; (*c*) iron(III) ion; (*d*) nickel(II) ion; (*e*) lead(II) ion; (*f*) iron(II) ion; (*g*) chloride ion; (*h*) oxide ion; (*e*) sulfide ion; (*j*) iodide ion; (*k*) copper(II) ion; (*l*) potassium ion; (*m*) silver ion; (*n*) mercury(I) ion.
4. What are the names and charges of these polyatomic ions: (*a*) NH_4; (*b*) SO_4; (*c*) NO_3; (*d*) CO_3; (*e*) $C_2H_3O_2$; (*f*) Cr_2O_7; (*g*) ClO_3; (*h*) HSO_4; (*i*) OH; (*j*) NO_2.
5. What is the symbol or formula and charge of (*a*) hydrogen carbonate ion; (*b*) bromide ion; (*c*) chromate ion; (*d*) sulfite ion; (*e*) phosphate ion; (*f*) peroxide ion; (*g*) magnesium ion; (*h*) zinc ion; (*e*) barium ion; (*j*) fluoride ion.
6. Write formulas for these compounds: (*a*) barium chloride; (*b*) calcium oxide; (*c*) magnesium sulfate; (*d*) silver bromide; (*e*) zinc carbonate.
7. Name these compounds: (*a*) $NaHCO_3$; (*b*) K_2O_2; (*c*) $HgCl_2$; (*d*) $Fe(OH)_3$; (*e*) $Ni(C_2H_3O_2)_2$.
8. Write the formulas for these compounds: (*a*) ammonium nitrate; (*b*) aluminum sulfide; (*c*) copper(II) hydroxide; (*d*) lead(II) phosphate; (*e*) iron(III) sulfate.
9. Name these compounds: (*a*) $CuCl_2$; (*b*) CaS; (*c*) $KHSO_4$; (*d*) $NaNO_2$; (*e*) $Ni_3(PO_4)_2$.
10. Write the formulas for these compounds: (*a*) chromium(III) fluoride; (*b*) nickel(II) chlorate; (*c*) potassium hydrogen carbonate; (*d*) calcium chromate; (*e*) mercury(II) iodide.
11. Name these compounds: (*a*) Na_2O_2; (*b*) NH_4NO_2; (*c*) $Mg_3(PO_4)_2$; (*d*) $FeSO_4$; (*e*) Ag_2CO_3; (*f*) Na_2O; (*g*) Hg_2Cl_2; (*h*) $HgCl_2$; (*i*) H_2O_2.
12. Write the formulas for (*a*) sodium hydrogen sulfate; (*b*) lead(II) chromate; (*c*) copper(I) chloride; (*d*) mercury(I) nitrate; (*e*) iron(II) oxide.
13. Name the following: (*a*) K_2SO_4; (*b*) $BaCr_2O_7$; (*c*) $Cr(OH)_3$; (*d*) $PbBr_2$; (*e*) HgI_2.
14. What is the formula for: (*a*) aluminum hydroxide; (*b*) copper(I) oxide; (*c*) ammonium sulfide; (*d*) lead(II) acetate; (*e*) iron(III) bromide?
15. Write the formulas for (*a*) magnesium hydrogen carbonate; (*b*) silver sulfide; (*c*) potassium sulfite; (*d*) chromium(III) sulfate; (*e*) sodium phosphate.

Group B

16. How are percentage composition, the law of definite composition, and the atomic theory related?
17. How is the law of multiple proportions related to the atomic theory?
18. Write the names for these compounds according to the system for naming binary compounds: (*a*) SO_3; (*b*) $SiCl_4$; (*c*) PBr_3; (*d*) As_2O_5; (*e*) PbO.
19. Write the formulas for these compounds: (*a*) sulfur dioxide; (*b*) bismuth trichloride; (*c*) manganese dioxide; (*d*) arsenic pentiodide; (*e*) carbon tetraiodide.
20. Name these compounds: (*a*) CO; (*b*) CO_2; (*c*) CBr_4; (*d*) N_2O_3; (*e*) N_2O_5.
21. How many of the symbols shown in the illustration at the top of page 121 can you identify?

Group A

1. What is the formula weight of hydrazine, N_2H_4?
2. Find the formula weight of sulfuric acid, H_2SO_4.
3. Dextrose, or grape sugar, has the formula $C_6H_{12}O_6$. Determine its formula weight.
4. Find the formula weight of ethyl alcohol, C_2H_5OH.
5. Calcium phosphate has the formula $Ca_3(PO_4)_2$. Determine the formula weight.
6. Crystallized magnesium sulfate, or Epsom salts, has the formula $MgSO_4 \cdot 7H_2O$. What is its formula weight?
7. Determine the formula weight for each of these compounds: (*a*) HNO_3; (*b*) NaOH; (*c*) HgO; (*d*) $CuSO_4 \cdot 5H_2O$; (*e*) $HC_2H_3O_2$; (*f*) $MgBr_2$; (*g*) Al_2S_3; (*h*) $Ca(NO_3)_2$; (*i*) $Fe_2(Cr_2O_7)_3$; (*j*) $KMnO_4$.
8. Vinegar contains acetic acid, $HC_2H_3O_2$. Find its percentage composition.
9. All baking powders contain sodium hydrogen carbonate, $NaHCO_3$. Calculate its percentage composition.
10. What is the percentage composition of a soap having the formula $C_{17}H_{35}COONa$?
11. What is the percentage composition of each of these compounds: (*a*) SO_2; (*b*) $Ca(OH)_2$; (*c*) $Ca(H_2PO_4)_2 \cdot H_2O$; (*d*) $MgSO_4 \cdot 7H_2O$?
12. Which of these compounds contains the highest percentage of nitrogen: (*a*) $Ca(NO_3)_2$; (*b*) $CaCN_2$; or (*c*) $(NH_4)_2SO_4$?
13. A strip of pure copper, mass 6.356 g, is heated with oxygen until it is completely converted to a compound of copper and oxygen, mass 7.956 g. What is the percentage composition of the compound?
14. Calculate the mass of (*a*) 1.00 mole of chlorine atoms; (*b*) 5.00 moles of nitrogen atoms; (*c*) 3.00 moles of bromine molecules; (*d*) 6.00 moles of hydrogen chloride; (*e*) 10.0 moles of magnesium sulfate; (*f*) 2.50 moles of potassium iodide; (*g*) 0.500 mole of silver nitrate; (*h*) 0.100 mole of sodium chloride.
15. You are given 25.0 g of each of these compounds: (*a*) CaO; (*b*) $Na_2CO_3 \cdot 10H_2O$; (*c*) $BaCl_2 \cdot 2H_2O$; (*d*) $(NH_4)_2SO_4$; (*e*) $Fe(NO_3)_3 \cdot 6H_2O$; (*f*) $Al_2(SO_4)_3 \cdot 18H_2O$; (*g*) K_2CrO_4. How many moles of each do you have?
16. How many moles of iron may be recovered from 1.000 metric ton ($100\bar{0}$ kg) of Fe_3O_4?
17. Cinnabar, an ore of mercury, has the formula HgS. Calculate the number of moles of mercury recovered from 1.00 kg of cinnabar.
18. Calculate the percentage of copper in each of these minerals: cuprite, Cu_2O; malachite, $CuCO_3 \cdot Cu(OH)_2$; and cubanite, $CuFe_2S_4$.
19. Calculate the percentage of CaO in $CaCO_3$.
20. Calculate the percentage of H_2O in $CuSO_4 \cdot 5H_2O$.

Group B

21. One compound of platinum and chloride is known to consist of 42.1% chlorine. Another consists of 26.7% chlorine. What are the two empirical formulas?
22. What is the empirical formula for silver fluoride, which is 85% silver?
23. What is the percentage composition of the drug Chloromycetin, $C_{11}H_{12}N_2O_5Cl_2$?
24. Analysis: phosphorus, 43.67%; oxygen, 56.33%. What is the empirical formula?
25. Analysis: potassium, 24.58%; manganese, 34.81%; oxygen, 40.50%. What is the empirical formula?
26. Calculate the empirical formula for a compound having 37.70% sodium, 22.95% silicon, and 39.34% oxygen.
27. A compound has the following compo-

sition: sodium, 28.05%; carbon, 29.26%; hydrogen, 3.66%; oxygen, 39.02%. What is the empirical formula?

28. The analysis of a compound shows the following: nitrogen, 21.20%; hydrogen, 6.06%; sulfur, 24.30%; oxygen, 48.45%. Find the simplest formula.
29. A compound has this composition: potassium, 44.82%; sulfur, 18.39%; oxygen, 36.79%. Determine its empirical formula.
30. A compound has the following composition: calcium, 24.7%; hydrogen, 1.2%; carbon, 14.8%; oxygen, 59.3%. What is its empirical formula?
31. An oxide of iron has the following composition: Fe = 72.4%, O = 27.6%. Determine its empirical formula.
32. The analysis of a gas reveals this composition: carbon, 92.3%; hydrogen, 7.7%. Its molecular weight is 26.0. What is the molecular formula?
33. Analysis of a compound reveals this composition: $8\bar{0}\%$ carbon and $2\bar{0}\%$ hydrogen. Its molecular weight is 30.0. What is its molecular formula?
34. By analysis, a compound is found to be 76.0% iodine and 24.0% oxygen. Its molecular weight is 334. (*a*) Determine the molecular formula. (*b*) What is the oxidation state of iodine in this iodine-oxygen compound.
35. The percentages by weight of carbon in its two oxides are 42.8% and 27.3%. Use these data to illustrate the law of multiple proportions.

chapter 8

EQUATIONS AND MASS RELATIONSHIPS

This Calder sculpture suggests a principle important in art that also applies to a chemical equation. After studying this chapter, you should be able to determine what this principle is.

Chemical Equations

8.1 Writing equations

1. Word equations. Balanced chemical equations are concise symbolized expressions of chemical reactions. A simple way to describe chemical reactions is by means of *word equations.* Using this verbal equation form, a brief statement of the basic facts about a particular reaction is possible. The word equation simply states the names of the substances that react (reactants) and the names of the substances formed (products). It does not state the *quantities* of reactants and products of the reaction. Thus, a word equation has only *qualitative,* or descriptive, significance.

Chemical equations represent chemical reactions.

Qualitative information about a reaction system relates to the kind of reaction but gives no details about the amounts of reactants and products.

Experiments show that water is formed by the combustion of hydrogen in oxygen. The word equation for this reaction is

hydrogen + oxygen → water

It reads, "Hydrogen *and* oxygen *yields* water." The arrow (→) is the reaction symbol, or a "yields" sign. It means that a chemical reaction occurs. The word equation signifies that as hydrogen and oxygen react chemically, water is formed as the only product. Thus, it briefly states an experimental fact. It does not tell the conditions under which the reaction occurs, or the quantities of hydrogen and oxygen used, or the quantity of water formed.

2. Formula equations. The law of conservation of matter and energy is fundamental to science. From this law a very useful generalization is possible: *In ordinary chemical reactions,*

Fig. 8-1. The elements, zinc (top) and iodine (middle), mixed at room temperature do not react until a drop of water is added to the mixture (bottom). The equation for the reaction is $Zn + I_2 \rightarrow ZnI_2$.

Fig. 8-2. The balanced equation for a known chemical reaction shows the substances that react, the products that are formed, and the relative mass quantities of the reactants and products.

$$2H_2 + O_2 \rightarrow 2H_2O$$

2 molecules hydrogen	+	1 molecule oxygen	→	2 molecules water
2 moles hydrogen	+	1 mole oxygen	→	2 moles water
4 grams hydrogen	+	32 grams oxygen	→	36 grams water
any mass quantity of hydrogen	+	mass of oxygen in ratio 8:1 with mass of hydrogen	→	mass of water in ratio 9:1 with mass of hydrogen

the total mass of the reacting substances is equal to the total mass of the products formed. This statement may be referred to as the ***law of conservation of atoms.***

Suppose you replace the names of the reactants, hydrogen and oxygen, and the name of the product, water, with their respective formulas. By adjusting for the relative quantities of reactants and product as found by experiment, the equation can be written as a *balanced formula equation.* This equation agrees with the law of conservation of atoms.

$$\mathbf{2H_2 + O_2 \rightarrow 2H_2O}$$

This agreement is verified by comparing the total number of atoms of hydrogen and oxygen on the left side of the reaction sign (→) to their respective totals on the right. Two molecules of hydrogen contain 4 atoms of hydrogen; two molecules of water also contain 4 hydrogen atoms. One molecule of oxygen contains 2 atoms of oxygen; two molecules of water also contain 2 oxygen atoms. Thus, a chemical equation is similar to an algebraic equation. They both express equalities. *Until it is balanced, a chemical equation cannot express a chemical equality and is not a valid equation.* The yields sign (→) has the meaning of an equals sign (=). In addition, the yields sign indicates the direction in which the reaction proceeds.

3. *Significance of equations.* This formula equation now signifies much more than a word equation.

(*a*) It tells us the relative proportions of the reactants, hydrogen and oxygen, and the product, water.

(*b*) It tells us that *2 molecules* of hydrogen react with *1 molecule* of oxygen, and *2 molecules* of water are formed.

And since there is an Avogadro number of molecules in each mole of a molecular substance, most important,

(*c*) *it tells us that 2 moles of hydrogen molecules react with 1 mole of oxygen molecules, and 2 moles of water are formed.*

The mass of a mole of a molecular substance is its gram-molecular weight.

(*d*) It tells us that *4 g* of hydrogen react with *32 g* of oxygen, and *36 g* of water are formed.

Furthermore, these masses are only relative masses. Hence,

(*e*) *it tells us that any masses of hydrogen and oxygen which are in the ratio of 1:8, respectively, and which react and form only water will yield a mass of water that is related to the masses of hydrogen and oxygen as 1:8:9.*

Finally, in any equation, the equality exists in both directions. If $x + y = z$, then $z = x + y$. So our formula equation

(*f*) tells us that *2 moles* of water, if decomposed, would yield *2 moles* of hydrogen molecules and *1 mole* of oxygen molecules.

From these six statements, it is clear that formula equations have *quantitative* significance. Formula equations represent facts concerning reactions that have been established by experiments or other means. They indicate the nature and relative masses of reactants and products. But equations reveal nothing about the mechanism by which the reactants are converted into the products.

Quantitative information relates to the measured quantities of reactants and products in a reaction system.

It is possible to write an equation for a reaction that does not occur. Gold and oxygen do not combine directly to form gold(III) oxide, Au_2O_3. But we can write a word equation that says gold and oxygen react and yield gold(III) oxide. The corresponding formula equation can even be balanced to conform to the law of conservation of atoms. However, these would be false equations, since they are contrary to known facts.

8.2 Factors in equation writing

A chemical equation has no value unless it is correct in every detail. Three factors must be considered in writing a balanced equation.

1. The equation must represent the facts. If you are to write the equation for a reaction, you must know the facts concerning the reaction. You must know all the reactants and all the products. The chemist relies upon analysis for facts.

2. The equation must include the symbols and formulas of all elements and compounds that are used as reactants or formed as products. You must know these symbols and formulas and must be sure that they are correctly written. The elements that exist as diatomic molecules are oxygen, hydrogen, nitrogen, fluorine, chlorine, bromine, and iodine. These elements are listed in Table 8-1 for review purposes. Other elements are usually considered to be monatomic (one-atomed) structures when writing equations. Your knowledge of the oxidation states of the elements and the ion-charge method of

Table 8-1

ELEMENTS WITH DIATOMIC MOLECULES

Element	Symbol	Atomic Number	Molecular Formula	Structural Formula
hydrogen	H	1	H_2	H—H
nitrogen	N	7	N_2	N≡N
oxygen	O	8	O_2	O=O
fluorine	F	9	F_2	F—F
chlorine	Cl	17	Cl_2	Cl—Cl
bromine	Br	35	Br_2	Br—Br
iodine	I	53	I_2	I—I

writing correct formulas will enable you to satisfy this requirement for correct symbols and formulas.

3. *The law of conservation of atoms must be satisfied.* There must be the same number of atoms of each kind represented on each side of the equation. A new species of atom cannot be represented on the product side and no species of atom can disappear from the reactant side. These are the *balancing requirements.* They are met by adjusting the *coefficients* of the formulas of reactants and products. You must adjust these coefficients to the *smallest possible whole numbers* that satisfy the law of conservation of atoms.

Balanced equations have (1) the chemical facts, (2) correct formulas, and (3) atoms conserved.

8.3 Procedure in writing equations

Let us consider some simple chemical reactions and write the chemical equations that represent them. We must proceed in steps that satisfy the three factors in equation writing.

1. *Represent the facts.*
2. *Write correct formulas of compounds balanced as to oxidation number or ion charge.* (Formulas for elemental gases with diatomic molecules also must be correctly written.)
3. *Balance the equation according to the law of conservation of atoms.*

Passing an electric current through a slightly acid solution of water produces the elements hydrogen and oxygen. Let us write the word equation and write and balance the formula equation for this reaction.

Fig. 8-3. The decomposition of water to hydrogen and oxygen by an electric current.

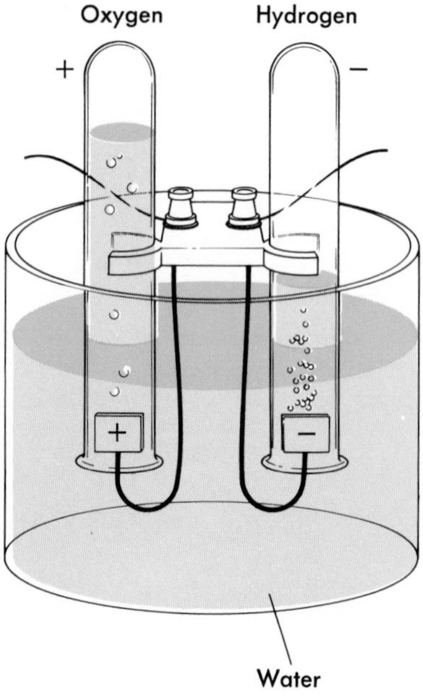

Step 1: What are the facts? The only reactant is water and the only products are hydrogen and oxygen. We can represent these facts by the word equation

water → hydrogen + oxygen

Now let us substitute the formulas for these substances.

$$H_2O \rightarrow H_2 + O_2 \quad \textbf{(not balanced)}$$

Step 2: Are the formulas correctly written? The oxidation number of hydrogen is +1 and of oxygen −2. So the formula for water is correctly written as H_2O. Both hydrogen and oxygen exist in the free state as diatomic molecules. So the formulas of molecular hydrogen and molecular oxygen are correctly written as H_2 and O_2.

Step 3: Is the equation balanced as to atoms? On the left, 1 molecule of water is represented. It consists of 2 hydrogen atoms and 1 oxygen atom. To the right of the yields sign (→), 1 molecule of hydrogen consisting of 2 atoms and 1 molecule of oxygen made up of 2 atoms are represented. *But there is only 1 atom of oxygen on the left.* How may we adjust this difference? A subscript $_2$ may *not* be added to the oxygen of the water formula, for this subscript would change a formula that we know is correctly written. Once you write the formulas of the substances correctly, do not change the subscripts. This rule applies because *the number of atoms in a molecule* is an established experimental fact. However, *the number of molecules* of a substance in an equation may be changed by changing its coefficient.

Change coefficients, not subscripts, to balance atoms in an equation.

Suppose the number of water molecules is increased to 2. This change can be made by placing the coefficient 2 ahead of the formula H_2O, making it $2H_2O$. Now the equation shows 2 molecules of water, each having 1 oxygen atom. This change gives the necessary 2 atoms of oxygen on the left.

$$\mathbf{2H_2O \rightarrow H_2 + O_2 \quad (not\ balanced)}$$

Two molecules of water have a total of 4 atoms of hydrogen. We must now move to the right side of the equation and adjust the number of hydrogen atoms represented to 4. We can do this by placing the coefficient 2 ahead of the hydrogen molecule, making it $2H_2$. There is now a total of 4 atoms of hydrogen represented on the right. (Why would it be incorrect to get the 4-atom balance for hydrogen by changing the subscript $_2$ to subscript $_4$ in the hydrogen molecule?) The equation now reads

$$\mathbf{2H_2O \rightarrow 2H_2 + O_2}$$

Phase symbols in an equation:
(s) = solid
(l) = liquid
(g) = gas
(aq) = water solution

We have represented the same number of atoms of each element on both sides of the equation. Furthermore, we have used the lowest whole-number ratio of coefficients possible. Thus, the equation is balanced.

If we wish to indicate the physical phases of the reactant and products, we may write the balanced equation

$$\mathbf{2H_2O(l) \rightarrow 2H_2(g) + O_2(g)}$$

The abbreviations commonly used in this way are (s), solid; (l), liquid; (g), gas; and (aq), water solution. In this text, these abbreviations are used *only* when they contribute to a better understanding of the reaction represented by the equation. Frequently they are used only to designate solid or gaseous products.

When sulfur burns, oxygen gas combines with solid sulfur and forms sulfur dioxide gas. These are the facts, so we may write

sulfur + oxygen → sulfur dioxide

$$\mathbf{S(s) + O_2(g) \rightarrow SO_2(g)}$$

Fig. 8-4. Sulfur burns in oxygen and forms sulfur dioxide gas.

Molecular oxygen is diatomic, O_2, and the binary name "sulfur dioxide" indicates that its formula is SO_2. All formulas are correctly written. The numbers of atoms of sulfur and oxygen are the same on both sides of the equation. No further adjustments are required; the equation is balanced.

Oxygen can be prepared in the laboratory by heating solid mercury(II) oxide. The facts are heating mercury(II) oxide yields liquid metallic mercury and oxygen gas.

mercury(II) oxide → mercury + oxygen

Substituting the proper symbols and formulas, we write

$$\mathbf{HgO \rightarrow Hg + O_2} \quad \textbf{(not balanced)}$$

Mercury(II) has an oxidation number of +2 and oxygen has an oxidation number of −2. So the formula of mercury(II) oxide is correctly written. However, the equation is not balanced. We must have two molecules of HgO decomposing and yielding the 2 atoms of the diatomic oxygen molecule. After making this adjustment, 2 additional atoms of mercury must also appear on the right. The balanced equation is

$$\mathbf{2HgO(s) \rightarrow 2Hg(l) + O_2(g)}$$

Zinc reacts with hydrochloric acid (a water solution of hydrogen chloride gas). This reaction produces hydrogen gas and a solution of zinc chloride. These facts may be represented by the word equation

zinc + hydrochloric acid → zinc chloride + hydrogen

With proper consideration for oxidation numbers and ion charges, we can write

$$\mathbf{Zn + HCl \rightarrow ZnCl_2 + H_2} \quad \textbf{(not balanced)}$$

The equation shows 1 hydrogen atom on the left and 2 on the right. Hydrogen atoms are balanced by representing 2 molecules of hydrogen chloride as 2HCl. Note that 2 chlorine atoms now show on the left, which balance the 2 on the right. The balanced equation is

$$\mathbf{Zn(s) + 2HCl(aq) \rightarrow ZnCl_2(aq) + H_2(g)}$$

Do not become discouraged if equations cause you some difficulty. One of the most common mistakes that beginners make in balancing equations is that of destroying the ion-charge balance or oxidation-number balance of a formula while trying to get the required number of atoms for balance.

Keep in mind that once a formula is correctly written, *subscripts cannot be added, deleted, or changed.* Formulas must be written correctly *before* proceeding with the final atom-balancing step. As you continue your study of chemistry and gain experience in the laboratory, the equations that now seem difficult will become simple.

Let us try an equation for a reaction that occurs in a process of water purification. Aluminum sulfate and calcium hydroxide are added to water containing unwanted suspended matter. These two substances react in water and produce two insoluble products, aluminum hydroxide and calcium sulfate. These products settle out, taking the suspended matter with them. The reaction may be represented by the word equation

aluminum sulfate + calcium hydroxide → aluminum hydroxide + calcium sulfate

By ion-charge balancing to assure correct formulas, we may write

$$\mathbf{Al_2(SO_4)_3 + Ca(OH)_2 \rightarrow Al(OH)_3 + CaSO_4} \quad \textbf{(not balanced)}$$

Now begin at the left, with $Al_2(SO_4)_3$, to balance atoms. Two Al atoms are indicated. To represent 2 Al atoms on the right, place the coefficient 2 ahead of $Al(OH)_3$. The equation now reads

$$\mathbf{Al_2(SO_4)_3 + Ca(OH)_2 \rightarrow 2Al(OH)_3 + CaSO_4} \quad \textbf{(not balanced)}$$

Three (SO_4) groups are indicated on the left. Therefore, place a coefficient 3 in front of $CaSO_4$. The equation now reads

$$\mathbf{Al_2(SO_4)_3 + Ca(OH)_2 \rightarrow 2Al(OH)_3 + 3CaSO_4} \quad \textbf{(not balanced)}$$

Next, observe that there must be 3 Ca atoms on the left to equal the 3 Ca atoms now on the right. Place the coefficient 3 in front of $Ca(OH)_2$. This gives 6 OH groups on the left and 6 OH groups on the right. The equation is now balanced.

$$\mathbf{Al_2(SO_4)_3 + 3Ca(OH)_2 \rightarrow 2Al(OH)_3(s) + 3CaSO_4(s)}$$

(The (s) indicates those products that are insoluble and leave the reaction environment as *precipitates*. A precipitate is an insoluble solid that separates from a solution.)

To write chemical equations correctly,

1. You must know the symbols of the common elements.

2. You must know the usual oxidation numbers or ionic charges of the common elements and polyatomic (many-atomed) ions.

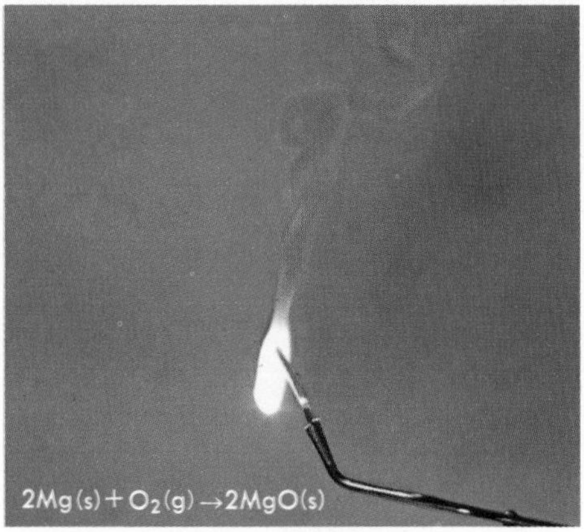

Fig. 8-5. A composition reaction.

3. You must know the facts relating to the reaction for which an equation is to be written.

4. You must be sure that all formulas are correctly written before attempting to balance the equation.

5. You must balance the equation for atoms of all elements represented. You must do this using the lowest ratio of whole-number coefficients possible.

8.4 General types of chemical reactions

There are several different ways of classifying chemical reactions. No single scheme is entirely satisfactory. In elementary chemistry, it is helpful to recognize reactions that fall into the main categories given below. Later you will learn other ways in which chemical reactions can be classified. The main types of reactions are

1. *Composition reactions,* in which two or more substances combine and form a more complex substance. Composition reactions have the general form

$$A + X \rightarrow AX$$

Examples:
Iron and sulfur combine and form iron(II) sulfide.

$$Fe + S \rightarrow FeS$$

Magnesium burns in air (combines with oxygen) and forms magnesium oxide. This combustion is shown in Figure 8-5.

Reactants in composition reactions are not necessarily elements.

Products of decomposition reactions are not necessarily elements.

$$2Mg + O_2 \rightarrow 2MgO$$

Water and sulfur trioxide combine and form hydrogen sulfate (sulfuric acid).

$$H_2O + SO_3 \rightarrow H_2SO_4$$

2. *Decomposition reactions,* the reverse of the first type. Here one substance breaks down and forms two or more simpler substances. Decomposition reactions have the general form

$$AX \rightarrow A + X$$

Examples:
Water is decomposed, yielding hydrogen and oxygen.

$$2H_2O \rightarrow 2H_2(g) + O_2(g)$$

When heated, potassium chlorate decomposes, yielding potassium chloride and oxygen.

$$2KClO_3 \rightarrow 2KCl + 3O_2(g)$$

Mercury(II) oxide decomposes when heated. The products are metallic mercury and oxygen. See Figure 8-6.

$$2HgO \rightarrow 2Hg + O_2(g)$$

Fig. 8-6. A decomposition reaction.

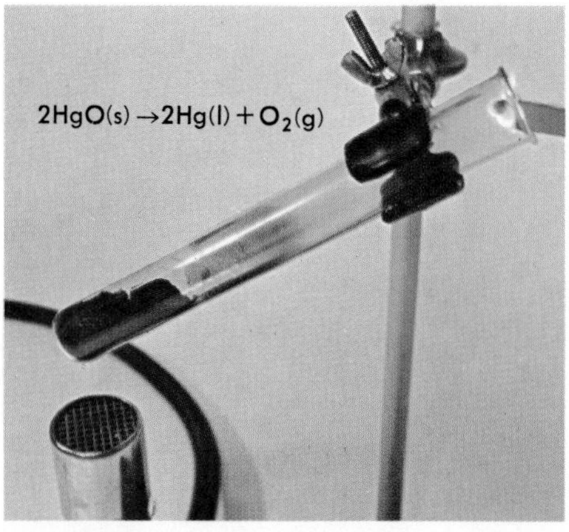

3. *Replacement reactions,* in which one substance is replaced in its compound by another substance. Replacement reactions have the general form

$$\mathbf{A + BX \rightarrow AX + B}$$

or

$$\mathbf{Y + BX \rightarrow BY + X}$$

Examples:
Iron replaces copper in a solution of copper(II) sulfate, yielding iron(II) sulfate and copper.

$$\mathbf{Fe + CuSO_4 \rightarrow FeSO_4 + Cu(s)}$$

Copper replaces silver in a solution of silver nitrate, and copper(II) nitrate and silver are the products.

$$\mathbf{Cu + 2AgNO_3 \rightarrow Cu(NO_3)_2 + 2Ag(s)}$$

This reaction is shown in Figure 8-7. Silver nitrate solutions are colorless; copper(II) nitrate solutions are blue. Observe the color of the solution and the spongy deposit of silver on the copper strip in the beaker on the right. Chlorine replaces iodine in a solution of potassium iodide, yielding potassium chloride and iodine.

$$\mathbf{Cl_2 + 2KI \rightarrow 2KCl + I_2}$$

In this replacement reaction, the iodide ion, I^-, loses an electron to a chlorine atom. The I^- ion becomes an I atom, and the Cl atom becomes a chloride ion, Cl^-. Potassium ions, K^+, do not participate in the replacement reaction.

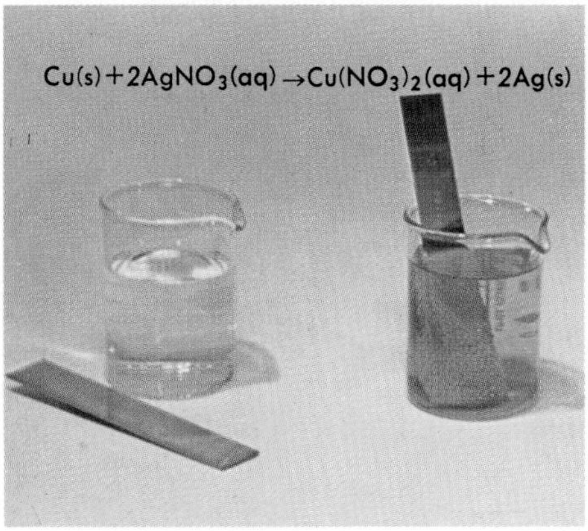

Fig. 8-7. A replacement reaction.

In these first three types of reactions (composition, decomposition, and replacement), some change in the sharing of electrons occurs, or there is a transfer of electrons from one atom to another. Usually, but not always, there are changes in oxidation states.

4. *Ionic reactions* involve no transfer of electrons. Instead, ions in solution combine and form a product that leaves the reaction environment. Ionic reactions may have the general form

$$\mathbf{A^+(aq) + B^-(aq) \rightarrow AB}$$

Examples:
A solution of sodium chloride, containing sodium ions and chloride ions, is added to a solution of silver nitrate, containing silver ions and nitrate ions. A reaction occurs between the silver ions and chloride ions. A white precipitate of silver chloride is formed.

$$\mathbf{Ag^+(aq) + Cl^-(aq) \rightarrow Ag^+Cl^-(s)}$$

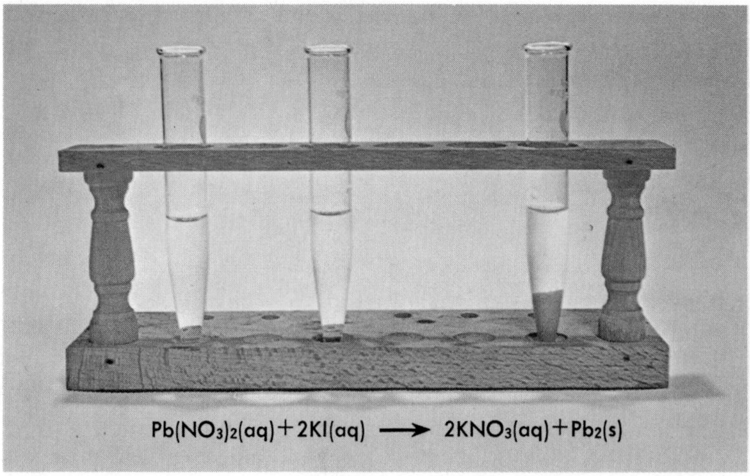

Fig. 8-8. An ionic reaction.

The sodium ions and nitrate ions remain uncombined in solution. But they can be recovered as sodium nitrate by evaporating the water. The sodium ions and silver ions may be regarded as having exchanged places. For this reason, ionic reactions are sometimes called *exchange* reactions.

When we wish to show what substances are used to bring about ionic reactions, we may write formula equations. The equations have the general form

$$\mathbf{AX + BY \rightarrow AY + BX}$$

In this sense, the ionic reaction just described may be written

$$\mathbf{NaCl + AgNO_3 \rightarrow NaNO_3 + AgCl(s)}$$

When a solution of lead(II) nitrate is added to a solution of potassium iodide, insoluble lead(II) iodide separates as a yellow precipitate. See Figure 8-8. The potassium ions and nitrate ions remain in solution and do not participate in the ionic reaction. The net equation is

$$\mathbf{Pb^{++}(aq) + 2I^-(aq) \rightarrow PbI_2(s)}$$

Use the solubility table, Table 12 in the Appendix, to help determine whether a proposed ionic reaction occurs.

In order for an ionic reaction to occur, a product must be formed that separates ions from the reaction environment (the solution). The product may be a solid precipitate, an insoluble gas, or a new molecular species.

8.5 Six kinds of decomposition reactions

You have learned that the first step in writing a balanced equation is to represent the facts about the reaction. You must know what substances react and what products are formed. In this connection, it can be very helpful to recognize general reaction patterns among chemically similar substances.

For example, many metallic carbonates have a similar reaction pattern when heated. They decompose into the corresponding metallic oxide and carbon dioxide gas. Knowing this particular reaction pattern, you have facts and can write equations for the decomposition of several different metallic carbonates. Other helpful patterns are evident in decomposition and replacement reactions.

Decomposition reactions are promoted by heat or electricity. The kinds generally recognized are as follows:

1. Metallic carbonates, when heated, form metallic oxides and carbon dioxide. Calcium carbonate, $CaCO_3$, on being heated, forms calcium oxide, CaO. Carbon dioxide, CO_2, is given off as a gas.

$$\mathbf{CaCO_3 \rightarrow CaO + CO_2(g)}$$

Ammonium carbonate, $(NH_4)_2CO_3$, because of the nonmetallic nature of the ammonium ion, decomposes in a special manner. The equation for this reaction is

$$\mathbf{(NH_4)_2CO_3 \rightarrow 2NH_3(g) + H_2O(g) + CO_2(g)}$$

Ammonia, steam, and carbon dioxide are produced.

2. Many metallic hydroxides, when heated, decompose into metallic oxides and water. If we strongly heat calcium hydroxide, $Ca(OH)_2$, steam is given off and calcium oxide, CaO, remains.

$$\mathbf{Ca(OH)_2 \rightarrow CaO + H_2O(g)}$$

Sodium hydroxide and potassium hydroxide are common exceptions to this rule.

3. Metallic chlorates, when heated, decompose into metallic chlorides and oxygen. This is the type of reaction used to prepare oxygen from potassium chlorate.

Knowing these general decomposition reaction patterns helps you predict the decomposition products of other similar reactants.

$$\mathbf{2KClO_3 \rightarrow 2KCl + 3O_2(g)}$$

4. Some acids, when heated, decompose into nonmetallic oxides and water. Acids may be formed by the reaction of certain nonmetallic oxides and water. The reactions described below involve the reverse process—the decomposition of the acid. Examples are as follows: Carbonic acid yields water and carbon dioxide gas.

$$\mathbf{H_2CO_3 \rightarrow H_2O + CO_2(g)}$$

Sulfurous acid yields water and sulfur dioxide gas.

$$\mathbf{H_2SO_3 \rightarrow H_2O + SO_2(g)}$$

The two reactions above take place quite readily at room temperature. The following reaction occurs at elevated temperatures.

$$\mathbf{H_2SO_4 \rightarrow H_2O + SO_3(g)}$$

5. *Some oxides, when heated, decompose.* Most oxides are very stable compounds. There are only a few of them that decompose on heating. Two of these oxides and the reactions for their decomposition are

$$2HgO \rightarrow 2Hg + O_2(g)$$

$$2PbO_2 \rightarrow 2PbO + O_2(g)$$

6. *Some decomposition reactions are produced by an electric current.* The reactions represented by the following equations are typical.

Important reaction conditions are sometimes written above or below the "yields" sign.

$$2H_2O \xrightarrow{\text{(electricity)}} 2H_2(g) + O_2(g)$$

$$2NaCl \xrightarrow{\text{(electricity)}} 2Na + Cl_2(g)$$

Electrolysis *is the separation of a compound into simpler substances by an electric current.*

8.6 Four kinds of replacement reactions

The quantities of energy involved in replacement reactions are generally smaller than in composition and decomposition reactions. The possibility of reaction depends on the relative activities of the elements involved. We generally use an experimentally derived *activity series* much like the one discussed in Section 8.8 in writing replacement equations. We will consider four kinds of replacement reactions.

Fig. 8-9. Zinc is a more active metal than copper and replaces copper in the $CuSO_4$ solution.

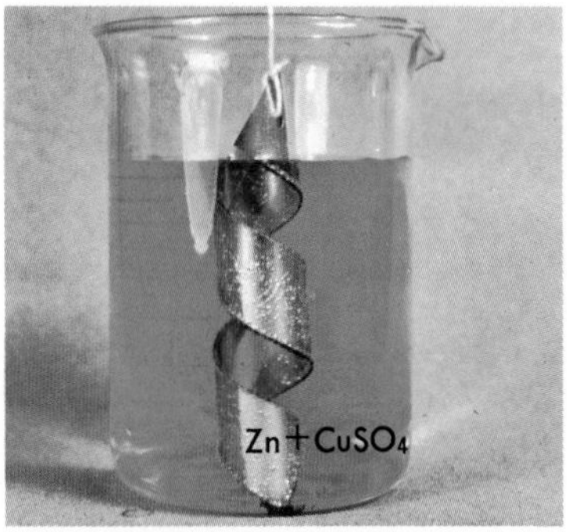

1. *Replacement of a metal in a compound by a more active metal.* One reaction of this type involves zinc and a solution of copper(II) sulfate, $CuSO_4$. Zinc replaces the copper in the solution. From this reaction we conclude that zinc is a more active metal than copper.

$$Zn + CuSO_4 \rightarrow ZnSO_4 + Cu(s)$$

2. *Replacement of hydrogen in water by metals.* The very active metals, such as potassium, calcium, and sodium, react vigorously with water. They replace half the hydrogen and form metallic hydroxides. The reaction represented by the following equation is typical.

$$Ca + 2H_2O \rightarrow Ca(OH)_2 + H_2(g)$$

Less active metals, such as magnesium, zinc, and iron, react at elevated temperatures with water (steam) and replace hydrogen. Because of the high temperature involved, oxides rather than hydroxides are formed. Metals less active than iron do not react measurably with water.

Refer to the activity series when determining whether a proposed replacement reaction occurs.

3. *Replacement of hydrogen in acids by metals.* Many metals react with certain acids, such as hydrochloric acid and dilute sulfuric acid. These metals replace hydrogen in the acids and form the corresponding metallic compounds. You may have used this method for the laboratory preparation of hydrogen by reacting sulfuric acid with zinc.

$$\mathbf{Zn + H_2SO_4 \rightarrow ZnSO_4 + H_2(g)}$$

4. *Replacement of halogens.* The halogens are the elements in Group VII of the periodic table. They have somewhat similar properties. These elements are fluorine, chlorine, bromine, and iodine. Experiments show that fluorine is the most active halogen; it replaces the other three halogens in their compounds. Chlorine replaces bromine and iodine in their compounds. Bromine replaces only iodine. An example of a halogen replacement reaction is chlorine replacing bromide ions in a potassium bromide solution.

$$\mathbf{Cl_2 + 2KBr \rightarrow 2KCl + Br_2}$$

Chlorine replaces iodide ions, forming the corresponding chloride.

$$\mathbf{Cl_2 + 2NaI \rightarrow 2NaCl + I_2}$$

Bromine replaces iodide ions, but not so vigorously as does chlorine.

$$\mathbf{Br_2 + 2KI \rightarrow 2KBr + I_2}$$

8.7 Many reactions are reversible

Frequently, the products of a chemical reaction can react and produce the original reactants. Hydrogen can be used as a reducing agent to separate certain metals from their oxides. If dry hydrogen gas is passed over hot magnetic iron oxide, iron and steam are produced.

$$\mathbf{4H_2 + Fe_3O_4 \rightarrow 3Fe + 4H_2O(g)}$$

If the procedure is reversed and steam is passed over hot iron, magnetic iron oxide and hydrogen are formed.

$$\mathbf{3Fe + 4H_2O \rightarrow Fe_3O_4 + 4H_2(g)}$$

Such reactions are said to be reversible. They may be indicated by two yields signs pointing in opposite directions ($\leftrightarrows$)

$$\mathbf{3Fe + 4H_2O \leftrightarrows Fe_3O_4 + 4H_2}$$

Conditions may be such as to allow both reactions to occur at the same time. That is, if none of the products leaves the field of action, they may react and form the original reactants. Under such circumstances, an equilibrium (state of balance) may develop between the two reactions. After equilibrium is

Table 8-2

ACTIVITY SERIES OF THE ELEMENTS

Metals	Nonmetals
lithium	fluorine
potassium	chlorine
calcium	bromine
sodium	iodine
magnesium	
aluminum	
zinc	
chromium	
iron	Decreasing activity ↓
nickel	
tin	
lead	
HYDROGEN	
copper	
mercury	
silver	
platinum	
gold	

reached, the quantities of all the reactants remain constant. The subject of equilibrium reactions will be discussed in Chapter 21.

8.8 The activity series of the elements

In general, the ease with which the atoms of a metal lose electrons determines the ease with which the metal forms compounds. In the replacement reaction

$$\mathbf{A + BX \rightarrow AX + B}$$

metal **A** gives up electrons to **B** and replaces it. Thus we know that **A** is more active than **B.** If metal **B** is immersed in a solution of the compound **AX, B** does not replace **A.** Atoms of a more active metal lose electrons to positively charged ions of a less active metal under proper reaction conditions. Similarly, atoms of more active nonmetals acquire electrons from negatively charged ions of less active nonmetals.

Zinc, being a more active metal than copper, replaces copper from a copper(II) sulfate solution. This replacement reaction was described in Section 8.6 and is shown in Figure 8-9.

$$\mathbf{Zn + Cu^{++}SO_4^{--} \rightarrow Zn^{++}SO_4^{--} + Cu}$$

Each Zn atom loses two electrons to a Cu^{++} ion and forms a Zn^{++} ion.

$$\mathbf{Zn \rightarrow Zn^{++} + 2e^-}$$

Each Cu^{++} that gains two electrons forms a Cu atom.

$$\mathbf{Cu^{++} + 2e^- \rightarrow Cu}$$

Observe that SO_4^{--} ions do not participate in this replacement reaction. The net equation is

$$\mathbf{Zn(s) + Cu^{++}(aq) \rightarrow Zn^{++}(aq) + Cu(s)}$$

When copper is placed in a solution of zinc sulfate, no reaction is observed. Copper is a less active metal than zinc and does not replace zinc from a solution of a zinc compound.

Many exothermic chemical reactions can be carried out in such a way that electric energy is given off. From a study of such reactions, chemists are able to devise an activity series of elements to help predict the course of replacement reactions. Some composition and decomposition reactions can likewise be predicted with the aid of an activity series. The series presented in Table 8-2 lists important common elements in descending order of their metallic and nonmetallic activities.

The relative positions of the elements in the activity series enable us to apply some of the following generalizations to appropriate composition, decomposition, and replacement reactions.

1. Each element in the list displaces from a compound any of the elements below it. The larger the interval between elements in the series, the more vigorous the action.
2. All metals above hydrogen displace hydrogen from hydrochloric acid or dilute sulfuric acid.
3. Metals above magnesium vigorously displace hydrogen from water. Magnesium displaces hydrogen from steam.
4. Metals above silver combine directly with oxygen; those near the top do so rapidly.
5. Metals below mercury form oxides only indirectly.
6. Oxides of metals below mercury decompose with mild heating.
7. Oxides of metals below chromium easily undergo reduction to metals by heating with hydrogen.
8. Oxides of metals above iron resist reduction by heating with hydrogen.
9. Elements near the top of the series are never found free in nature.
10. Elements near the bottom of the series are often found free in nature.

Mass Relationships

8.9 Stoichiometry

The determination of empirical formulas of compounds is always the result of experimentation. Empirical formulas are derived from the relative numbers of moles of atoms of the elements present in compounds. Therefore, they indicate the relative numbers of atoms present. An empirical formula tells us nothing about the nature of the association of the atoms or the make-up of the molecular structure. It does not even tell us whether a substance actually exists in simple molecular units. Nevertheless, empirical formulas are very useful in calculations involving the combining and reacting relationships among substances.

The branch of chemistry that deals with the numerical relationships of elements and compounds and the mathematical proportions of reactants and products in chemical reactions is known as ***stoichiometry*** (stoy-key-*om*-eh-tree). The determinations of percentage composition of compounds and of empirical formulas were discussed in Chapter 7. The calculations for these determinations are based upon *stoichiometric relations.* We are now ready to learn to solve stoichiometric problems involving the mass relations of reactants and products in chemical reactions. To do this, you will need an understanding of the mole concept and some skill in writing and balancing chemical equations. The concept of mole volumes of gases is introduced in Chapter 11. This concept will enable you to solve a great number of problems involving mass and volume relations of gaseous reactants and products by means of very simple computations. Simple mass and volume relations exist only for gases.

8.10 Mole relations of reactants and products

When carbon burns in the oxygen of the air, carbon dioxide, a covalent molecular gas, is produced.

$$\mathbf{C = O_2 \rightarrow CO_2(g)}$$

The balanced equation indicates the mole proportions of the reactants and products. It also gives the composition of each substance in terms of the kinds of elements and the relative number of each kind of atom present. Thus, the equation signifies that 1 mole of carbon combines with 1 mole of oxygen molecules and yields 1 mole of carbon dioxide. This may be indicated as follows:

C	+	**O_2**	**→ $CO_2(g)$**
1 mole		**1 mole**	**1 mole**
= 12.0 g		**= 32.0 g**	**= 44.0 g**

The mole proportions of reacting substances and products convert readily to equivalent mass quantities as shown above. An equation is used in this way when we wish to determine the mass of one substance that reacts with, or is produced from, a definite mass of another. This is one of the common problems chemists are called upon to solve.

8.11 Mole method of solving mass-mass problems

The mole concept is both important and practical in chemistry. Here is an example of its use in solving a typical mass-mass problem.

Suppose you want to determine the mass of calcium oxide produced by heating 50.0 g of calcium carbonate. Observe that the mass of the reactant is given and the mass of a product is required. From the data given in the problem and the facts known concerning this reaction, you can *set up the problem.* This can be done in four steps.

A balanced equation is required for a correct problem solution.

Step 1. Write the balanced equation.

Step 2. Show the problem specifications: what is given and what is required. To do this, write the mass of calcium carbonate, 50.0 g, above the formula $CaCO_3$. Letting X represent the unknown mass of calcium oxide produced, we write X above the formula CaO.

Step 3. Show the mole proportions established by the balanced equation. We do this by writing under each substance in the problem the number of *moles* indicated by the equation.

Step 4. Determine the mass of 1 mole of each substance involved in the problem. These masses should be written below the equation set up. The problem is now ready to be solved.

Step 2: 50.0 g $\quad\quad X$
Step 1: $\mathbf{CaCO_3 \rightarrow CaO + CO_2(g)}$
Step 3: 1 mole $\quad$ 1 mole

Step 4: 1 mole $CaCO_3$ = 100.1 g
1 mole CaO = 56.1 g

The number of moles of $CaCO_3$ *given in the problem* is found by multiplying the given mass of $CaCO_3$, 50.0 g, by the fraction $\frac{\text{mole}}{100.1\text{ g}}$, or

$$\mathbf{50.0\ g\ CaCO_3 \times \frac{mole}{100.1\ \mathit{g}} = number\ moles\ CaCO_3}$$

The balanced equation indicates that for each mole of $CaCO_3$ decomposed, 1 mole of CaO is produced. So from the given mass of $CaCO_3$ you can produce

$$\mathbf{50.0\ g\ CaCO_3 \times \frac{mole}{100.1\ g} \times \frac{1\ mole\ CaO}{1\ mole\ CaCO_3} = number\ moles\ CaO}$$

To determine the mass of CaO produced, we next multiply by the mass of 1 mole of CaO.

$$\mathbf{50.0\ g\ CaCO_3 \times \frac{mole}{100.1\ g} \times \frac{1\ mole\ CaO}{1\ mole\ CaCO_3} \times \frac{56.1\ g}{mole} = g\ CaO}$$

It is always wise to make a preliminary estimate of the answer to a problem before starting your computations. Thus you may avoid accepting an answer as correct that actually is quite absurd because of errors in computation or in operations with units. In this problem, a check of the units indicates that they are correct. The numerical result of the first multiplication is $\frac{1}{2}$, the numerical value of the second fraction is 1, and that of the third fraction is about 60. So you estimate the numerical answer to be $\frac{1}{2} \times 1 \times 60 = 30$. You are now ready to perform the arithmetic calculations.

$$\mathbf{X = 50.0\ \cancel{g}\ \cancel{CaCO_3} \times \frac{\cancel{mole}}{100.1\ g} \times \frac{1\ \cancel{mole}\ CaO}{1\ \cancel{mole}\ \cancel{CaCO_3}} \times \frac{56.1\ g}{\cancel{mole}}}$$

$$\mathbf{X = 28.0\ g\ CaO}$$

This calculated answer is in good agreement with our estimate.

Note that solving a mass-mass problem by the mole method involves four operations following the problem set-up.

1. Determine the number of moles of the substance whose mass is given in the problem by multiplying its mass by the fraction $\frac{\text{mole}}{\text{mass of one mole}}$ of the substance.

2. Determine the number of moles of substance whose mass is required. To do this, multiply the expression from operation 1 by the ratio of the number of moles of substance whose mass is required and the number of moles of substance whose mass is given. This ratio is indicated by the balanced equation.

3. Determine the mass of the substance required. To do this, multiply the expression from operation 2 by the number of grams per mole of the substance required.

4. Check the units assigned to make sure they yield the proper units for the answer, and estimate the answer. Perform the arithmetic operations. Compare the calculated result with your estimated one.

See the Sample Problems.

SAMPLE PROBLEM

How many grams of potassium chlorate must be decomposed to yield 30.0 g of oxygen?

SOLUTION

First, set up the problem by writing the balanced equation. *Second,* write the specifications of the problem above the equation. *Third,* write the number of moles of each specified substance under its formula. And *fourth,* calculate the mass/mole of each of the specified substances. Let *X* represent the mass of potassium chlorate decomposed.

Step 2:	**X**		**30.0 g**
Step 1:	$\mathbf{2KClO_3 \rightarrow 2KCl +}$		$\mathbf{3O_2(g)}$
Step 3:	**2 moles**		**3 moles**
Step 4:	$\mathbf{1\ mole\ KClO_3 = 122.6\ g}$		
	$\mathbf{1\ mole\ O_2 = 32.0\ g}$		

$$\mathbf{X = \underbrace{30.0\ \cancel{g}\ \cancel{O_2} \times \frac{\cancel{mole}}{32.0\ \cancel{g}}}_{\text{Operation 1}} \times \underbrace{\frac{2\ \cancel{moles}\ KClO_3}{3\ \cancel{moles}\ \cancel{O_2}}}_{\text{Operation 2}} \times \underbrace{\frac{122.6\ g}{\cancel{mole}}}_{\text{Operation 3}} = \underbrace{76.6\ g\ KClO_3}_{\text{Operation 4}}}$$

Operation 1	Operation 2	Operation 3	Operation 4
gives expression for moles O_2 given	**gives expression for moles $KClO_3$ required**	**gives expression for grams $KClO_3$ required**	**involves unit check, estimate of answer, and arithmetic operations**

SAMPLE PROBLEM

(*a*) How many grams of oxygen are required to oxidize $14\bar{0}$ g of iron to iron(III) oxide?
(*b*) How many moles of iron(III) oxide are produced?

SOLUTION

The problem set-up for Parts (*a*) and (*b*) is

Step 2:	**$14\bar{0}$ g**	***X***	***Y***
Step 1:	**4Fe**	**+ $3O_2(g)$ →**	**$2Fe_2O_3$**
Step 3:	**4 moles**	**3 moles**	**2 moles**
Step 4:	**1 mole Fe = 55.8 g**		
	1 mole O_2 = 32.0 g		

The solution set-up for Part (*a*) is

$$\mathbf{X = 14\bar{0}\ \cancel{g\ Fe} \times \frac{\cancel{mole}}{55.8\ \cancel{g}} \times \frac{3\ \cancel{moles}\ O_2}{4\ \cancel{moles\ Fe}} \times \frac{32.0\ g}{\cancel{mole}} = 60.2\ g\ O_2}$$

The solution set-up for Part (*b*) is

$$\mathbf{Y = 14\bar{0}\ \cancel{g\ Fe} \times \frac{\cancel{mole}}{55.8\ \cancel{g}} \times \frac{2\ moles\ Fe_2O_3}{4\ \cancel{moles\ Fe}} = 1.25\ moles\ Fe_2O_3}$$

SUMMARY

A chemical equation is a concise symbolized statement of a chemical reaction. Useful quantitative information about a reaction is provided by a balanced formula equation.

Three conditions must be met in a balanced equation. (*1*) The equation must represent the facts of the reaction, the substances that react and the products formed; (*2*) The symbols or formulas of all reactants and products must be written correctly; and (*3*) The law of conservation of atoms must be satisfied.

In some chemical reactions, changes occur in the sharing of electrons or electrons are transferred from one reactant to another. In other reactions, aqueous ions combine and form a product that separates from the reaction environment. Chemical reactions may be separated into four main types: (*1*) composition; (*2*) decomposition; (*3*) replacement; and (*4*) ionic.

The numerical relationships of elements and compounds, and the proportions of reactants and products in chemical reactions are called stoichiometry. Problems dealing with mass relations of the reactants and products in chemical reactions are stoichiometric problems. Solutions of stoichiometric problems are based on the fact that balanced equations establish the quantitative relations among reactants and products. The quantities in these equations are expressed in moles.

Group A

Write balanced formula equations for these reactions and identify the type of reaction. *Do not write in this book.*

1. zinc + sulfur → zinc sulfide.
2. potassium chloride + silver nitrate → silver chloride(s) + potassium nitrate.
3. calcium oxide + water → calcium hydroxide.
4. sodium hydroxide + hydrochloric acid (HCl) → sodium chloride + water.
5. magnesium bromide + chlorine → magnesium chloride + bromine.
6. sodium chloride + sulfuric acid (H_2SO_4) → sodium sulfate + hydrogen chloride(g).
7. aluminum + iron(III) oxide → aluminum oxide + iron.
8. ammonium nitrite → nitrogen(g) + water.
9. silver nitrate + nickel → nickel(II) nitrate + silver(s).
10. hydrogen + nitrogen → ammonia (NH_3)(g).

Complete the word equation and write the balanced formula equation. Give a reason for the product(s) in each case. Consult the activity series, Table 8-2, and solubilities, Table 12, Appendix B, as necessary.

Composition reactions:

11. sodium + iodine →
12. calcium + oxygen →
13. hydrogen + chlorine →

Decomposition reactions:

14. nickel(II) chlorate →
15. barium carbonate →
16. zinc hydroxide →

Replacement reactions:

17. aluminum + sulfuric acid →
18. potassium iodide + chlorine →
19. iron + copper(II) nitrate → iron(II) nitrate +

Ionic reactions:

20. silver nitrate + zinc chloride →
21. copper(II) hydroxide + acetic acid ($HC_2H_3O_2$) →
21. iron(II) sulfate + ammonium sulfide →

Group B

Where the word equation is complete, write and balance the formula equation. Where the word equation is incomplete, complete it, write and balance the formula equation, tell the type of reaction, and give a reason for the product(s).

23. barium chloride + sodium sulfate →
24. calcium + hydrochloric acid →
25. iron(II) sulfide + hydrochloric acid → hydrogen sulfide(g) +
26. zinc chloride + ammonium sulfide →
27. ammonia + oxygen → nitric acid (HNO_3) + water.
28. magnesium + nitric acid →
29. potassium + water →
30. sodium iodide + bromine →
31. silver + sulfur →
32. sodium chlorate →
33. carbon + steam (H_2O) → carbon monoxide(g) + hydrogen(g).
34. zinc + lead(II) acetate →
35. iron(III) hydroxide →
36. iron(III) oxide + carbon monoxide → iron + carbon dioxide(g).
37. lead(II) acetate + hydrogen sulfide →
38. aluminum bromide + chlorine →
39. magnesium carbonate →
40. iron(III) chloride + sodium hydroxide →
41. calcium oxide + diphosphorus pentoxide → calcium phosphate.
42. chromium + oxygen →
43. sodium + water →
44. calcium carbonate + hydrochloric acid →

45. calcium hydroxide + phosphoric acid (H_3PO_4) →
46. sodium carbonate + nitric acid →
47. aluminum hydroxide + sulfuric acid →
48. sodium sulfite + sulfuric acid →
49. copper + sulfuric acid → copper(II) sulfate + water + sulfur dioxide(g).
50. calcium hydroxide + ammonium sulfate → calcium sulfate + water + ammonia(g).

PROBLEMS

Group A

1. Mercury(II) oxide (25.0 g) is to be decomposed by heating. (*a*) How many moles of mercury(II) oxide are given? (*b*) How many moles of oxygen can be prepared? (*c*) How many grams of oxygen can be prepared?
2. Potassium chlorate (25.0 g) is to be decomposed by heating. (*a*) How many moles of potassium chlorate are given? (*b*) How many moles of oxygen can be prepared? (*c*) How many grams of oxygen can be prepared?
3. A quantity of zinc reacts with sulfuric acid and produces 0.10 g of hydrogen. (*a*) How many moles of hydrogen are produced? (*b*) How many moles of zinc are required? *c*) How many grams of zinc are required?
4. Sodium chloride reacts with 10.0 g of silver nitrate in water solution. (*a*) How many moles of silver nitrate react? (*b*) How many moles of sodium chloride are required? (*c*) How many grams of sodium chloride are required?
5. (*a*) How many moles of silver chloride are precipitated in the reaction of Problem 4? (*b*) How many grams of silver chloride is this?
6. In a reaction between sulfur and oxygen, 80.0 g of sulfur dioxide are formed. How many grams of sulfur were burned?
7. How many grams of hydrogen are required to completely convert 25 g of hot magnetic iron oxide (Fe_3O_4) to elemental iron? Steam is the other product of the reaction.
8. What mass of copper(II) oxide in grams is formed by oxidizing 1.00 kg of copper?
9. What mass of silver in grams is precipitated when 40.0 g of copper react with silver nitrate in solution?
10. Suppose 10.0 g of iron(II) sulfide are treated with enough hydrochloric acid so that the iron(II) sulfide completely reacts. How many grams of hydrogen sulfide gas will be given off?

Group B

11. An excess of sulfuric acid reacts with $15\bar{0}$ g of barium peroxide. (*a*) How many moles of hydrogen peroxide are produced? (*b*) How many moles of barium sulfate are formed?
12. Approximately 130 g of zinc were added to a solution containing $10\bar{0}$ g of HCl. After the action ceased, 41 g of zinc remained. How many moles of hydrogen were produced?
13. A mixture of 10.0 g of powdered iron and 10.0 g of sulfur is heated to its reaction temperature in an open crucible. (*a*) How many grams of iron(II) sulfide are formed? (*b*) The reactant in excess is oxidized. How many grams of its oxide are formed?
14. What mass of calcium hydroxide in grams can be produced from 1.00 kg of limestone, calcium carbonate? (Decomposition of calcium carbonate by heating produces calcium oxide and carbon dioxide. Calcium hydroxide is formed by the reaction of calcium oxide and water.)

15. How many grams of air are required to complete the combustion of 93 g of phosphorus to diphosphorus pentoxide, assuming the air to be 23% oxygen by mass?
16. How many metric tons of carbon dioxide can be produced from the combustion of 1.00 metric ton ($10\bar{0}0$ kg) of coke that is $9\bar{0}$% carbon?
17. (*a*) What mass of H_2SO_4 in grams is required in a reaction with an excess of aluminum to produce 0.50 mole of aluminum sulfate? (*b*) How many moles of hydrogen are also produced?
18. A certain rocket uses butane, C_4H_{10}, as fuel. How many kilograms of liquid oxygen should be carried for the complete combustion of each 1.00 kg of butane to carbon dioxide and water vapor?
19. When 45 g of ethane gas, C_2H_6, are burned completely in air, carbon dioxide and water vapor are formed. (*a*) How many moles of carbon dioxide are produced? (*b*) How many moles of water are produced?
20. (*a*) How many grams of sodium sulfate are produced in the reaction between $15\bar{0}$ g of sulfuric acid and an excess of sodium chloride? (*b*) How many grams of sodium chloride are used? (*c*) How many grams of hydrogen chloride are also produced?

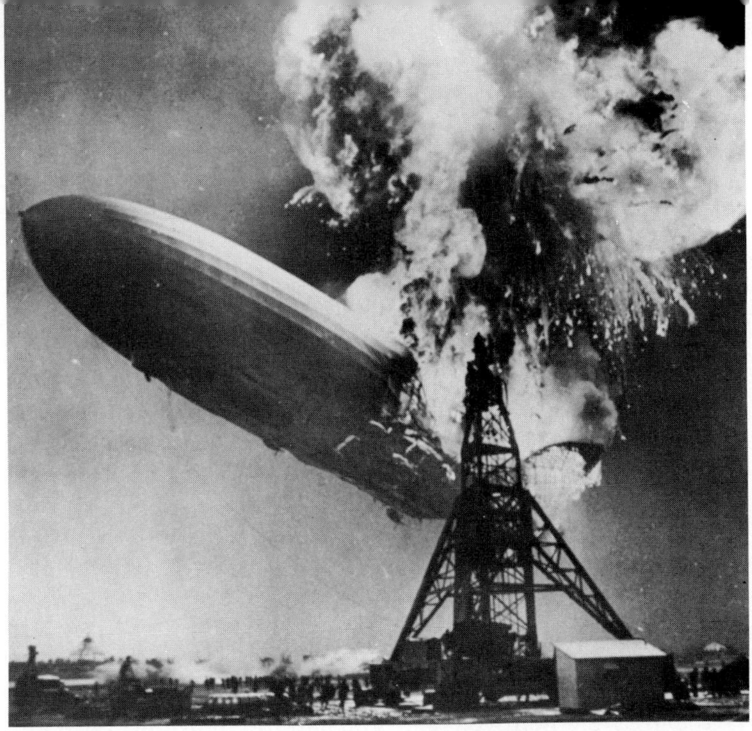

chapter 9

TWO IMPORTANT GASES: OXYGEN AND HYDROGEN

Two properties of hydrogen gas are apparent in the disaster scene that occurred in 1937. (See Question 41 on page 186.)

Oxygen

9.1 Introduction

So far in your study of chemistry, you have been concerned mostly with the theory of atomic structure and its explanation of the nature of elements and compounds. You have also learned about common types of chemical reactions. The writing of chemical formulas and equations has been explained. Some calculations involving formulas and equations have been described, and you have had problems for practice. Now we are ready for a more detailed description of gases, liquids, and solids than was given in Chapter 1. But before we consider gases generally, we are going to study two important gaseous elements, oxygen and hydrogen.

9.2 The occurrence of oxygen

Oxygen, atomic number 8, has several characteristics that make it an important element, worthy of special attention. It is the most abundant element in the earth's crust. In fact, it is estimated that even if the composition of the entire earth is considered, there are more oxygen atoms in the earth, the waters on the earth, and in the atmosphere surrounding the earth, than atoms of any other single element. After hydrogen and helium, oxygen atoms rank third in abundance in the known universe.

About one fifth of the earth's atmosphere by volume is oxygen. Animals living in water get their oxygen from the small amount that is dissolved in water. Oxygen in the air and oxygen that is dissolved in water are examples of *free oxygen.*

Fig. 9-1. After removing the oxygen from a measured volume of air, this student is measuring the volume of the gas that remains. He is adjusting the level of the eudiometer so the pressure on the gas in the tube is the same as atmospheric pressure.

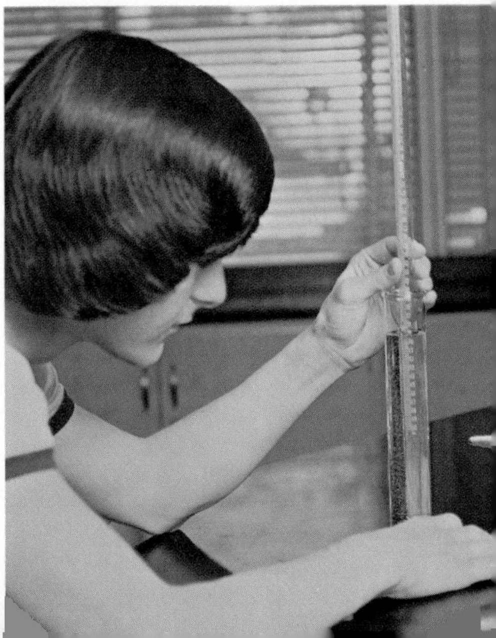

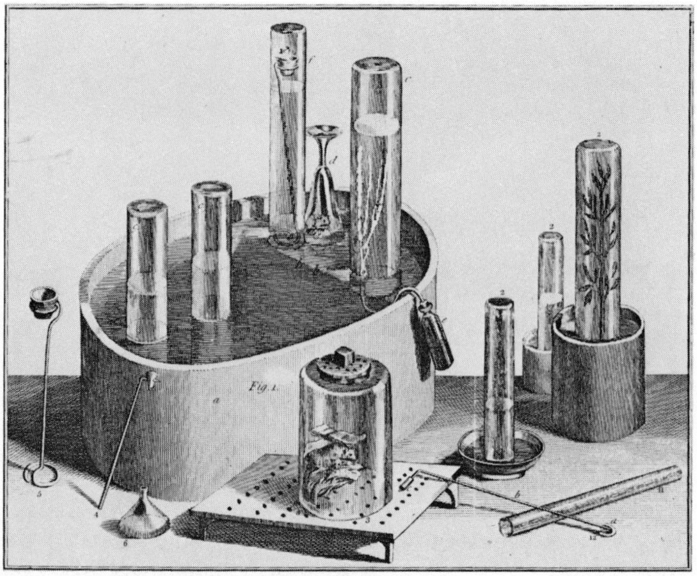

Fig. 9-2. Some of the laboratory apparatus used by Priestley in his experiments on the properties of gases. The pneumatic trough *a* is fitted with a shelf *bb*. The trough is filled with water. Two collecting jars *c* and *c* stand in the water. A gas is being produced by a chemical reaction in the generator bottle *e* and delivered through tubing into a jar *c* on the shelf of the trough. An inverted glass *d* contains a mouse breathing a confined gas. Jar *f* contains a cup mounted on a wire stand, also shown as *5*. A growing plant is surrounded by a gas in jar *2*. Compare this equipment with that which you use for collecting and testing gases.

As the free element, oxygen consists of diatomic covalent molecules, O_2.

Oxygen that has united with other elements in compounds is called *combined oxygen* and is much more plentiful than free oxygen. Water contains almost 89% oxygen by weight in combination with hydrogen. Such minerals as clay, sand, and limestone contain a large percentage of combined oxygen. Oxygen is one of the elements present in most of the rocks and minerals of the earth's crust.

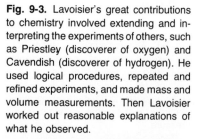

Fig. 9-3. Lavoisier's great contributions to chemistry involved extending and interpreting the experiments of others, such as Priestley (discoverer of oxygen) and Cavendish (discoverer of hydrogen). He used logical procedures, repeated and refined experiments, and made mass and volume measurements. Then Lavoisier worked out reasonable explanations of what he observed.

9.3 The discovery of oxygen

Joseph Priestley was an English clergyman and scientist. His greatest discovery came in 1774 when he used a lens to focus the sun's rays on mercury(II) oxide, a red powder. When this oxide is heated strongly, it decomposes. Oxygen gas is evolved, and liquid mercury remains. The equation for this chemical change is

$$2HgO(s) \rightarrow 2Hg(l) + O_2(g)$$

Priestley did not use the name *oxygen* for the gas that he discovered. He described it as "dephlogisticated air." He was delighted to find that a candle would flare up and continue to burn brightly in the gas. Priestley inhaled some of the gas and said that he felt peculiarly light and easy for some time. The gas was later given the name *oxygen* by the French chemist Antoine-Laurent Lavoisier.

Between 1772 and 1786, Lavoisier carried out many combustion experiments with careful mass measurements. From these experiments his conclusion was that oxygen is an element, and that it is a component of the atmosphere. He further found that when substances burn in air or oxygen, they gain weight because of the oxygen they combine with. These observations brought about a re-evaluation of the phlogiston theory and its eventual abandonment.

Karl Wilhelm Scheele (*shay*-luh) (1742–1786), a Swedish pharmacist, also discovered oxygen at about the same time. His results were not published until several years after his discovery. By that time Priestley had been generally acknowledged as the discoverer of oxygen. Scheele should be given equal credit as its codiscoverer.

9.4 The preparation of oxygen

There are several ways of preparing oxygen.

1. By the decomposition of hydrogen peroxide. This is a safe and convenient laboratory method of preparing oxygen. A dilute (3%) solution of hydrogen peroxide in water decomposes very slowly at room temperature. But manganese dioxide may be used as a catalyst to increase the rate of decomposition. If hydrogen peroxide solution is allowed to react drop by drop with manganese dioxide powder at room temperature, the hydrogen peroxide decomposes rapidly and smoothly. (See Figure 9-4.) In this process, oxygen gas is given off and water is formed. The equation for this decomposition reaction is

A catalyst is a substance or combination of substances that increases the rate of a chemical reaction without itself being permanently changed. The purpose and use of catalysts are described in Section 2.14(5).

$$2H_2O_2 \rightarrow 2H_2O(l) + O_2(g)$$

The oxygen gas produced in the flask passes through the delivery tube into a water-filled inverted bottle. As the oxygen rises in the bottle, it displaces the water. This method of collecting gases, known as *water displacement,* is used for gases that are not very soluble in water.

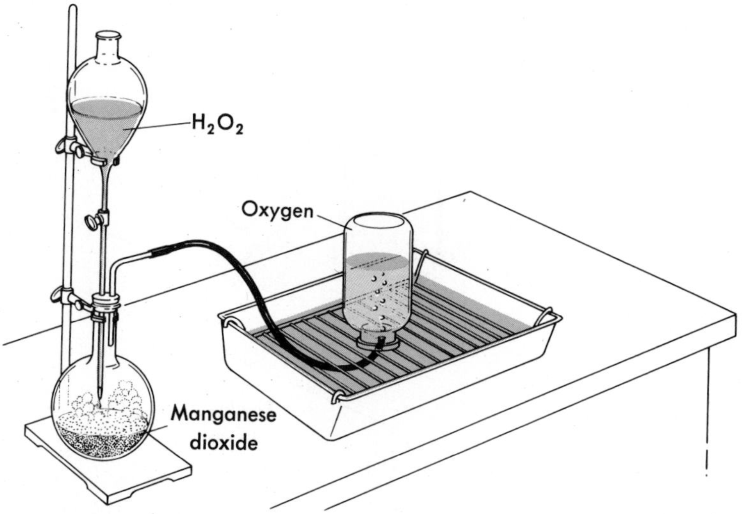

Fig. 9-4. Oxygen may be prepared in the laboratory by the catalytic decomposition of hydrogen peroxide. Manganese dioxide is used as the catalyst. Oxygen is collected by water displacement. This same generator setup may be used for preparing oxygen by the action of water (placed in the dropping funnel) on sodium peroxide (placed in the flask).

2. *By adding water to sodium peroxide.* Sodium peroxide, Na_2O_2, is prepared by burning sodium in air. If water is allowed to drop onto sodium peroxide in a generator like that shown in Figure 9-4, oxygen is liberated.

$$2Na_2O_2 + 2H_2O \rightarrow 4NaOH + O_2(g)$$

This is another convenient laboratory method for preparing small quantities of oxygen since it does not require heat. ***CAUTION:*** The sodium hydroxide solution that is formed must be disposed of carefully. It can burn the skin and destroy certain textile fibers.

Decomposition of metallic chlorates, as a type of decomposition reaction, was explained in Section 8.5(3).

3. *By heating potassium chlorate.* Potassium chlorate is a white, crystalline solid. When this compound is heated, it decomposes. Oxygen is given off and potassium chloride is left as a residue.

$$2KClO_3 \rightarrow 2KCl + 3O_2(g)$$

Manganese dioxide is usually mixed with the potassium chlorate in this laboratory preparation. It acts as a catalyst by lowering the decomposition temperature of potassium chlorate.

Figure 9-5 shows the laboratory set-up for the generation of oxygen from potassium chlorate and the collection of oxygen by water displacement. ***CAUTION:*** The decomposition of potassium chlorate is dangerous. It should be carried out only with small quantities of reagent-grade chemicals using well-shielded equipment and under close supervision. Potassium chlorate is extremely dangerous when mixed with combustible materials.

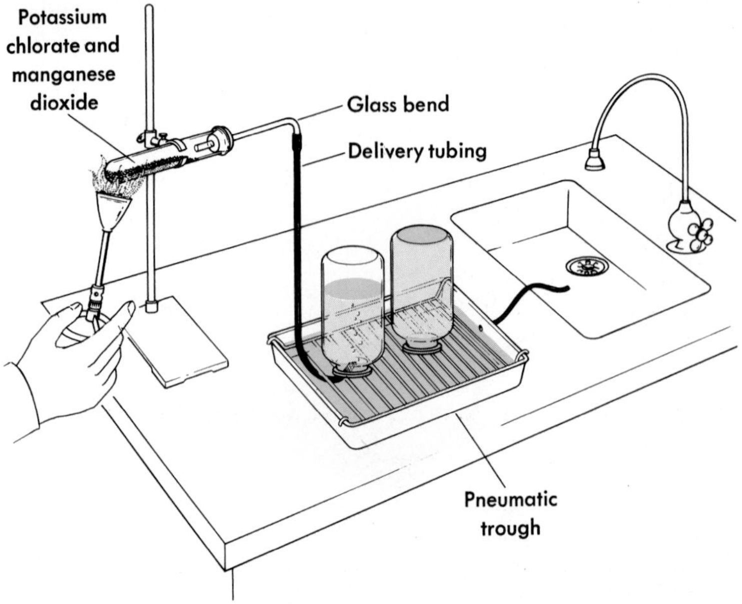

Fig. 9-5. An alternate, though very hazardous, method for preparing oxygen in the laboratory is the decomposition of potassium chlorate. Manganese dioxide is used as a catalyst to lower the decomposition temperature.

4. *By the electrolysis of water.* Figure 9-6 represents a laboratory apparatus in which water may be decomposed by an electric current. During the electrolysis of water, a direct current is passed through the water. Oxygen gas collects at the positive terminal and hydrogen gas at the negative terminal. Sulfuric acid is added to make the water a better conductor of electricity.

Electrolysis is the producing of a chemical change by electricity. Decomposition by electrolysis was explained in Section 8.5(6).

$$\mathbf{2H_2O \rightarrow 2H_2(g) + O_2(g)}$$

Large quantities of electric energy are needed to decompose the water. Industrially, this method yields oxygen of the highest purity. The hydrogen, which is produced along with it, is sold as a by-product.

5. *From liquid air.* This is the common industrial method for preparing oxygen. Air liquefies when compressed greatly while being cooled to a very low temperature (−200°C). The liquid air that results consists largely of oxygen and nitrogen. In order to separate oxygen from nitrogen, we make use of boiling point differences between them. Liquid nitrogen boils at −195.8°C, or about thirteen degrees lower than liquid oxygen at −183.0°C. If liquid air is permitted to stand, the nitrogen soon boils away and leaves nearly pure liquid oxygen. The oxygen which then boils away is pure enough for industrial purposes. The raw material for this method of preparing oxygen costs nothing, but the machinery used is very expensive.

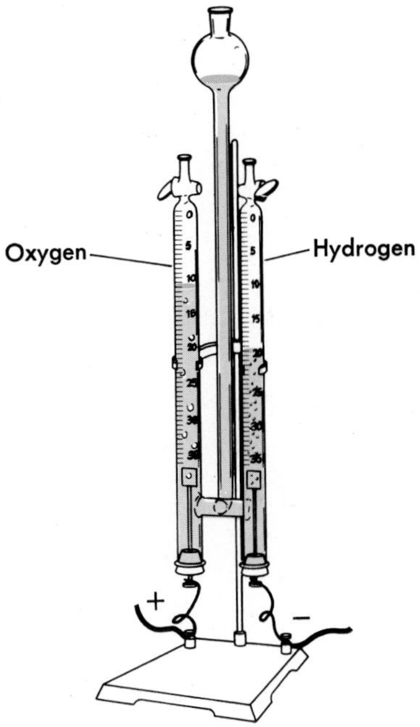

Fig. 9-6. Water may be decomposed by electrolysis into its constituent elements oxygen and hydrogen.

9.5 The physical properties of oxygen

Pure oxygen is a colorless, odorless, tasteless gas. It is slightly denser than air. At 0°C and one atmosphere pressure, one liter of oxygen has a mass of 1.43 g. Under the same conditions, one liter of air has a mass of 1.29 g. Oxygen is slightly soluble in water. The colder the water, the more oxygen can be dissolved in it. About five liters of oxygen can be dissolved in 100 liters of water at 0°C, but only three liters at 20°C.

Any gas may be converted into a liquid if it is compressed under a high enough pressure and cooled sufficiently at the same time. Liquid oxygen is pale-blue in color. It is attracted by a magnet, which leads chemists to believe that there are unpaired electrons in an oxygen molecule. That is why

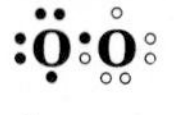

is sometimes written as the electron-dot formula for an oxygen molecule rather than

Further cooling of liquid oxygen results in its freezing to a pale-blue crystalline solid at −218.4°C.

Table 9-1

PROPERTIES OF OXYGEN	
atomic number	8
atomic weight	15.9994
electron configuration	2, 6
oxidation numbers	−2, −1, +2
melting point	−218.4°C
boiling point	−183.0°C
density, 0°C, 1 atm	1.429 g/liter
atom radius	0.73 Å
ion radius, O^{--}	1.40 Å

9.6 Chemical properties of oxygen

Oxygen is one of the most active elements. Oxygen combines with other elements and forms compounds called *oxides. An* **oxide** *is a compound consisting of oxygen and usually one other element; in oxides, the oxidation number of oxygen is −2.* When oxides are formed by direct combination of the elements, the reaction is exothermic. Generally, oxides are very stable compounds. Pure oxygen is much more active than air.

Oxygen reacts with the metals of Groups I and II. High temperatures are required to start reactions with the lower-atomic-weight metals lithium, sodium, potassium, magnesium, and calcium. The higher-atomic-weight metals rubidium, cesium, strontium, and barium, on the other hand, react spontaneously at room temperature. The electronegativity difference between oxygen and each of these metals is large. The oxygen compounds formed are ionic compounds.

Lithium reacts with oxygen and forms lithium oxide.

$$\mathbf{4Li + O_2 \rightarrow 2Li^+{}_2O^{--}(s)}$$

Depending on conditions, sodium reacts with oxygen and forms sodium oxide or sodium peroxide. Heating sodium with dry oxygen at 180°C yields sodium oxide.

$$\mathbf{4Na + O_2 \xrightarrow{180°C} 2Na^+{}_2O^{--}(s)}$$

Combustion of sodium in oxygen yields sodium peroxide.

$$\mathbf{2Na + O_2 \rightarrow Na^+{}_2O_2{}^{--}(s)}$$

The combustion of potassium, rubidium, and cesium in oxygen yields the peroxides.

The composition reaction of magnesium burning in the oxygen of the air is shown in Figure 8-5.

The Group II metals react with oxygen under the temperature conditions stated above and yield oxides. The reaction with barium is typical.

$$\mathbf{2Ba + O_2 \rightarrow 2Ba^{++}O^{--}(s)}$$

The reactions of nonmetals and oxygen generally occur at the high temperatures of combustion. The electronegativity difference between oxygen and the nonmetals is small. The resulting oxides contain covalent bonds and exist as molecules. These reactions are examples of this type of oxide formation.

The burning of sulfur in oxygen is shown in Figure 8-4.

$$\mathbf{S + O_2 \rightarrow SO_2(g)}$$
$$\mathbf{C + O_2 \rightarrow CO_2(g)}$$
$$\mathbf{2H_2 + O_2 \rightarrow 2H_2O(l)}$$

Reactions between oxygen and the metals other than those of Groups I and II may occur slowly at room temperature. They will occur, sometimes quite rapidly, if the temperature is raised. The electronegativity difference between oxygen and these metals is of intermediate value, about 0.8 – 1.8.

Iron at room temperature and in the presence of moisture unites slowly with oxygen. The resulting product is iron(III) oxide, commonly called rust.

$$4Fe + 3O_2 \rightarrow 2Fe_2O_3(s)$$

A strand of steel picture wire or a small bundle of steel wool, heated red hot and plunged into pure oxygen, burns brilliantly and gives off bright sparks. Molten drops of Fe_3O_4, another oxide of iron, are formed in this reaction but quickly solidify as they cool.

$$3Fe + 2O_2 \rightarrow Fe_3O_4(s)$$

Fig. 9-7. Iron burns brilliantly in pure oxygen and forms the iron oxide, Fe_3O_4.

Such metals as tin, lead, copper, and zinc unite with oxygen and form oxides. These reactions occur slowly when the elements are cold, but more rapidly when they are heated. The oxides of metals of intermediate electronegativity difference usually have structures that are more complex than those of ionic compounds or simple molecular compounds.

The detailed explanation of the structures of solids is given in Chapter 12.

9.7 The test for oxygen

A blazing splint continues to burn in air, but it burns more vigorously in pure oxygen. A glowing splint, lowered into a bottle of pure oxygen, bursts into flame immediately. If a glowing splint, lowered into a bottle of colorless, odorless gas, bursts into flame, the gas *is* oxygen. This test is commonly used to identify oxygen.

9.8 The uses of oxygen

1. As an essential for life. In higher order animals, oxygen enters the lungs with the inhaled air. It diffuses through thin membranes of the lungs into the bloodstream from which it passes into the tissues and fluids of the body.

Fish and other animals that breathe by gills get their oxygen from air that is dissolved in the water.

All plants, except some of the simplest bacteria, also require oxygen.

The need for oxygen, for burning fuels to produce heat energy, is well known.

2. In the iron and steel industry. This is the most important industrial use for oxygen. Oxygen is used in large quantities in the basic-oxygen method of making steel. It is also used for removing surface impurities from steel slabs, for welding and cutting steel. Welding and cutting iron and steel are done using oxygen-acetylene torches.

The basic-oxygen method of steel production is described in Chapter 25.

The operation of oxyacetylene torches is explained in Chapters 18 and 19.

3. For producing chemical compounds. Depending on the proportion of oxygen used, the temperature, and selection of catalyst, different products are formed when pure oxygen

Fig. 9-8. The "oxygen blow" stage of the basic oxygen method for making steel.

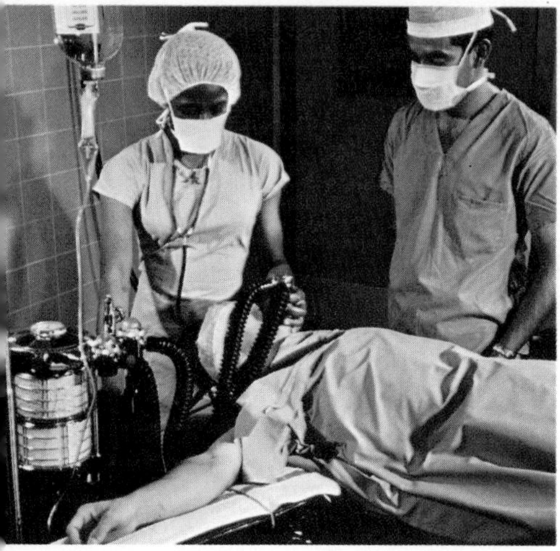

Fig. 9-9. Oxygen equipment used in resuscitation.

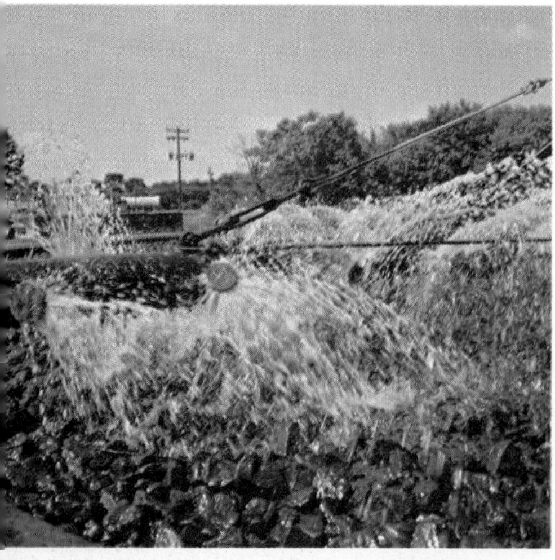

Fig. 9-10. The liquid effluent from a sewage processing plant is treated with oxygen by sprinkling it into the air over rocks.

reacts with coal, natural gas, or other fuels. Sometimes a mixture of hydrogen and carbon monoxide results. This mixture can be used to make synthetic gasoline, methanol, or ammonia. Under other conditions, partially oxygenated carbon and hydrogen compounds are formed. These can be used to make compounds like antifreeze, or for making synthetic rubber, or detergents.

4. *For medical treatment.* Pure oxygen, or air to which more oxygen has been added, is sometimes given to persons suffering from pneumonia or other diseases. It is also administered to persons who may be too weak to inhale a normal quantity of air because of heart attacks. For these purposes the patient is placed in an oxygen tent. A pump keeps the tent supplied with air mixed with oxygen in any desired proportion. Small portable oxygen tanks are used as the oxygen supply for active persons with chronic lung disease.

In cases of asphyxiation from inhaling smoke or suffocating gases, from apparent drowning, or from electric shock, oxygen may be administered by using a resuscitator.

5. *For water and sewage treatment.* Sunlight and oxygen are excellent agents for destroying harmful bacteria. Fountains, cascades, and other aerating devices are used to purify water supplies. By exposing water to air, disease bacteria are destroyed, and the water also becomes tastier for drinking.

In sewage disposal plants, sewage is exposed to air in order to increase the amount of dissolved oxygen and thus speed up the purification process. Sometimes oxygen is added to sewage to purify it even faster.

6. *For rocket propulsion.* Liquid oxygen is used in many rockets and missiles. The fuel may be a kerosene-like liquid or liquid hydrogen. For the very rapid burning needed to propel rockets, oxygen must be supplied in large quantities. Oxygen is needed whether the rocket is moving through the earth's atmosphere or in interplanetary space.

Ozone

9.9 The occurrence of ozone

A peculiar odor is often noticed where static electricity machines are operating. This odor is due to the presence of ozone, another form of elemental oxygen. Electric discharges through the air, such as sparks from a static electricity machine or a lightning flash, convert some of the oxygen of the air into ozone.

The ultraviolet rays from the sun change some of the oxygen in the upper atmosphere into ozone. In the stratosphere, between 15 km and 50 km above the earth, ozone occurs to the extent of 5 to 10 parts per million. The greatest concentration of ozone is found at an altitude of about 25 km.

The absorption of ultraviolet rays by this upper-atmosphere layer of ozone protects the earth's surface from most of the sun's ultraviolet radiation. The sun's ultraviolet radiation is one cause of human skin cancer. Too much ultraviolet radiation can cause increased sunburning, skin aging, and eye damage. It can also damage crops, cause cancer in livestock, produce changes in the climate, and bring about changes in the balance between both the water and land systems of plants and animals. You may now have a greater appreciation of the ozone layer's protective action. This is the reason why we are now greatly concerned about the breakdown of this layer by man-made products.

Fig. 9-11. The Atmosphere Explorer (AE-E) is a maneuverable, unmanned spacecraft launched to study the upper atmosphere, including the Earth's protective ozone layer.

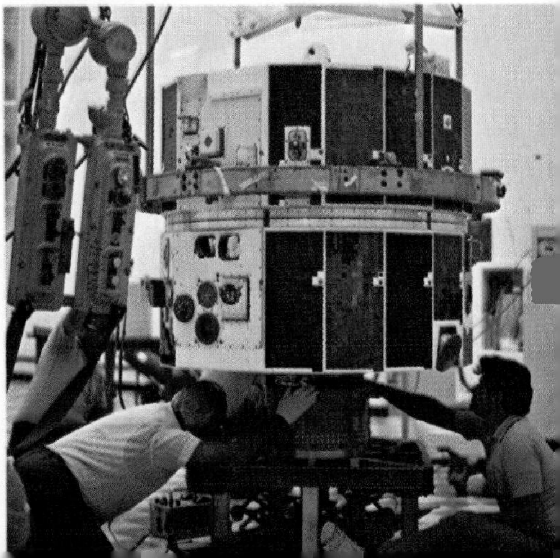

9.10 The preparation of ozone

Ozone is commonly produced by passing oxygen through an ozone generator like that shown in Figure 9-12. This device consists of glass tubes that are partially covered with layers of metal foil. The inner layers of metal foil are connected to one terminal of an induction coil or static electricity machine. The outer layers are connected to the other terminal. The discharge of electricity from one layer to the other provides the energy that converts some of the oxygen passing through the generator to ozone.

In converting oxygen to ozone, energy is absorbed. The preparation of ozone from oxygen is an endothermic reaction. Ozone, therefore, has a higher energy content than oxygen.

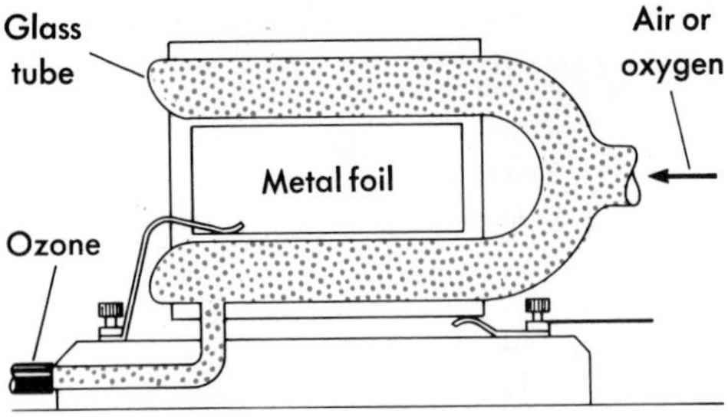

Fig. 9-12. An ozone generator. Some of the oxygen passing through the generator is converted to ozone by the electric discharge from one metal foil layer to the other.

Consequently, ozone is less stable and more active than oxygen. Three molecules of oxygen form two molecules of ozone, because oxygen, O_2, has 2 atoms per molecule, while ozone, O_3, has 3 atoms per molecule.

$$\mathbf{3O_2 + energy \rightarrow 2O_3(g)}$$

9.11 The difference between oxygen and ozone

Several chemical elements exist in two or more different forms. Oxygen is one of these elements. We shall learn later that other elements such as carbon, sulfur, and phosphorus also occur in different forms. *The existence of an element in two or more forms in the same physical phase is known as* ***allotropy.*** The different forms of such elements are called *allotropes.*

Another reason for allotropy is described in Section 17.3.

Ordinary oxygen and ozone are allotropes of the element oxygen. Allotropes are generally given different names; in this case, oxygen and ozone. One reason for allotropy is that an element has two or more kinds of molecules, each with different numbers of atoms. Thus, oxygen's allotropy is due to the existence of oxygen molecules $\mathbf{O_2}$ and ozone molecules $\mathbf{O_3}$.

9.12 The structure of ozone molecules

You may wish to review how resonance explains the structure of sulfur dioxide molecules, Section 6.22.

Ozone molecules are bent molecules with electron-dot formulas similar to those of sulfur dioxide. The angle between the two oxygen-oxygen bonds is about 117°.

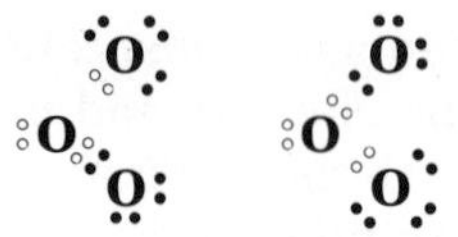

Experimental evidence shows that there is no difference between the two oxygen-oxygen bonds in the ozone molecule. Each bond has a length of 1.28 Å. Thus, we must resort to the concept of resonance to describe ozone's molecular structure. The electron arrangement in the ozone molecule is a resonance hybrid of the electron-dot formulas written above. Each oxygen-oxygen bond in the molecule is intermediate in properties between single and double covalent bonds.

The oxygen-oxygen bond energy in the ozone molecule is 72 kcal/mole compared to 119 kcal/mole in the oxygen molecule. This bond energy difference means that the oxygen-oxygen bonds in the ozone molecule are weaker than the oxygen-oxygen bond in the oxygen molecule. This bond energy difference is expected because, even though the bonded atoms are the same kind, the bonds in the ozone molecule are longer, 1.28 Å, than those in the oxygen molecule, 1.21 Å.

Fig. 9-13. Oxygen molecules consist of two atoms of oxygen. Ozone molecules consist of three atoms of oxygen. Oxygen and ozone are allotropes.

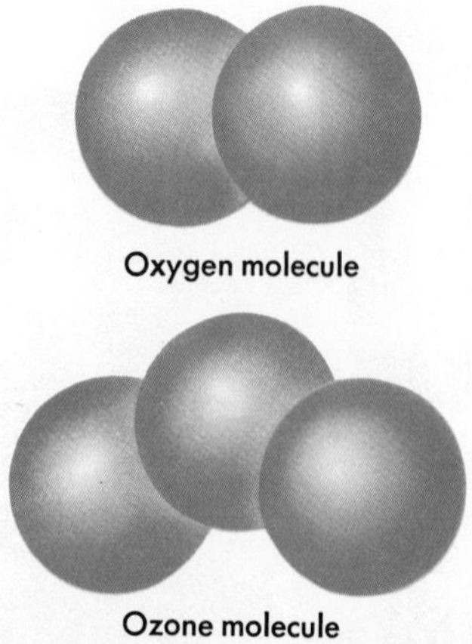

Table 9-2

PHYSICAL PROPERTIES OF OXYGEN AND OZONE

Allotrope	Molecular Formula	Color	Odor	Density, 0°C, 1 atm (g/liter)	Melting Point (°C)	Boiling Point (°C)	Solubility in Water, 0°C ($cm^3/100\ cm^3\ H_2O$)
oxygen	O_2	colorless	odorless	1.429	−218.4	−183.0	4.89
ozone	O_3	blue	pungent, irritating	2.144	−192.7	−111.9	49

9.13 The properties of ozone

Ozone is a poisonous blue gas with an irritating and pungent odor. It is denser than oxygen and much more soluble in water. Some physical properties of oxygen and ozone are compared in Table 9-2. Because ozone molecules have more energy than oxygen molecules, ozone is one of the most vigorous oxidizing agents known. It destroys bacteria and it causes many colors to fade rapidly.

9.14 Ozone has several important uses

The uses of ozone are applications of its oxidizing properties. Ozone destroys bacteria, fungi, and algae. Ozone has been used for many years as an excellent water purifying agent. In concentrations of less than one part per million, it completely sterilizes the water, deodorizes it, and removes certain objectionable impurities such as iron and manganese compounds. Ozone may be used to disinfect sewage. Ozone is also used in producing metal oxides, in bleaching wet paper pulp and wet textile fibers, and in preparing some complex compounds containing carbon, hydrogen, and oxygen.

Hydrogen

9.15 The occurrence of hydrogen

Hydrogen is a gas at ordinary temperatures. It ranks ninth in abundance by weight among the chemical elements in the earth's surface environment. In the known universe, however, there are more atoms of hydrogen than of any other chemical element. On the earth, hydrogen is usually combined with other elements in a variety of compounds. There are more compounds of hydrogen than of any other element. Free, or elemental hydrogen, which exists as covalent diatomic molecules, H_2, is not common on earth because of its flammability.

Very small traces of elemental hydrogen, probably derived from volcanoes and coal mines, do exist in the air. However, these amounts are so small that hydrogen is not listed as one of the important gases of the atmosphere. Tremendous quantities of elemental hydrogen occur in the sun and the stars. One ninth of water by weight is combined hydrogen, and all acids contain this element. Hydrogen is a constituent of nearly all plant and animal tissues. Fuels such as natural gas, wood, coal, and oil contain hydrogen compounds.

9.16 The early history of hydrogen

In the seventeenth century it was observed that a combustible gas was produced when sulfuric acid reacted with iron. Henry Cavendish (1731–1810), an English scientist, is usually credited as the discoverer of hydrogen, because in 1766 he prepared a quantity of the gas and observed its properties. Cavendish observed that hydrogen burns. He called the gas "inflammable air." In 1783, he showed that water is the only product formed when hydrogen burns in air. That same year Lavoisier suggested the name *hydrogen,* a word derived from two Greek words meaning "water producer."

9.17 The preparation of hydrogen

Replacement reactions of this type were explained in Section 8.6(3). The activity series appears in Table 8-2.

1. From acids by replacement. This is the usual laboratory way of preparing hydrogen. All acids contain hydrogen, which may be displaced by reaction with metals that are above hydrogen in the activity series. Several different acids and several different metals can be used. For example, iron, zinc, or magnesium will react with either hydrochloric acid or sulfuric acid and produce hydrogen. The rate at which hydrogen is given off in such reactions depends upon several factors: the amount of metal surface exposed to the acid; the temperature; the strength and kind of acid used; the kind of metal used; and the purity of the metal.

Fig. 9-14. Laboratory setup for the preparation of hydrogen. Any metal more active than hydrogen can be used to replace the hydrogen from any one of many acids. The metal is put in the wide-mouth generator bottle and the acid is added through the funnel tube. Hydrogen is collected by water displacement.

Figure 9-14 shows one type of apparatus commonly used for the laboratory preparation of hydrogen. Zinc is put into the generator bottle and either dilute sulfuric or hydrochloric acid is then added through the funnel tube. The hydrogen is collected by water displacement. The equations for the chemical reactions of zinc with sulfuric acid, H_2SO_4, and hydrochloric acid, HCl, are

$$\mathbf{Zn + H_2SO_4 \rightarrow ZnSO_4 + H_2(g)}$$
$$\mathbf{Zn + 2HCl \rightarrow ZnCl_2 + H_2(g)}$$

If the formulas of the acids are compared with the formulas of the zinc compounds produced, we can easily see that an atom of zinc has replaced two atoms of hydrogen. The zinc sulfate or zinc chloride products are dissolved in the excess water in the generator. Either may be recovered as a white solid by evaporating the water.

2. *From water by replacement.* Hydrogen may also be prepared by the reaction of sodium with water. Sodium is a silvery metal, soft enough to be easily cut with a knife, and of low enough density to float on water. It reacts vigorously with water and displaces hydrogen from it. Each sodium atom replaces one of the hydrogen atoms in a molecule of water. To show this reaction more clearly, the formula for water is written as HOH, instead of the usual H_2O.

Replacement of hydrogen in water by metals is described in Section 8.6(2).

$$\mathbf{2Na + 2HOH \rightarrow 2NaOH + H_2(g)}$$

This equation shows that each water molecule has had *one* of its hydrogen atoms replaced by a sodium atom. The sodium hydroxide produced may be recovered as a white, crystalline solid if the excess water is evaporated.

Potassium, a metal similar to sodium can be used instead of sodium in this method of hydrogen preparation. It is below sodium in Group I in the periodic table and is more active. It displaces hydrogen from water so vigorously, however, that the heat of the reaction ignites the hydrogen. The equation for the reaction of potassium and water is

Figure 1-10 is a photo showing the reaction of potassium and water.

$$\mathbf{2K + 2HOH \rightarrow 2KOH + H_2(g)}$$

Magnesium and calcium are two other metals that react with water to release hydrogen. Magnesium reacts slowly with *boiling* water. Calcium, in the same family as magnesium but more reactive, replaces hydrogen from cold water. At a high temperature, iron displaces hydrogen from steam. This iron-steam reaction is the only one of the water-replacement methods of preparing hydrogen we have described that is used commercially. All the other methods are laboratory methods.

3. *From water by electrolysis.* In the electrolysis of water, hydrogen as well as oxygen is produced. Commercially, if oxygen is the main product, hydrogen becomes a useful by-

product. This method is used in the United States for producing pure hydrogen wherever cheap electricity is available. It is also a laboratory method of preparing hydrogen.

4. *From hydrocarbons.* Hydrocarbons are compounds of hydrogen and carbon, commonly derived from petroleum or natural gas. If a hydrocarbon, such as methane, CH_4, reacts with steam in the presence of a nickel catalyst at a temperature of about 850°C, hydrogen and carbon monoxide are produced.

$$\mathbf{CH_4 + H_2O \rightarrow CO(g) + 3H_2(g)}$$

When this mixture of gaseous products is cooled and compressed, the carbon monoxide liquefies. The remaining hydrogen gas is then compressed into steel cylinders. This is the principal commercial method for producing hydrogen.

5. *From water by hot carbon.* This is another commercial method for producing hydrogen. When steam is passed over red-hot coal or coke, a mixture of gases called *water gas* is formed. It consists mainly of hydrogen and carbon monoxide. The equation for the reaction is

$$\mathbf{C + H_2O \rightarrow CO(g) + H_2(g)}$$

Frequently, the carbon monoxide is converted to carbon dioxide by passing the water gas with additional steam over a catalyst, such as iron oxide, at a temperature below 500°C.

$$\mathbf{CO + H_2O \rightarrow CO_2(g) + H_2(g)}$$

Additional hydrogen is produced from the steam in this way, and the resulting carbon dioxide is separated by dissolving it in water under moderate pressure.

Table 9-3

PROPERTIES OF HYDROGEN

atomic number	1
atomic weight	1.0080
electron configuration	1
oxidation numbers	+1, −1
melting point	−259.1°C
boiling point	−252.5°C
density, 0°C, 1 atm	0.0899 g/liter
atom radius	0.32 Å
ion radius, H^-	1.53 Å

9.18 The physical properties of hydrogen

Hydrogen gas is colorless, odorless, and tasteless. It is the gas of lowest density. Its density is only one fourteenth that of air. One liter of hydrogen at 0°C under one atmosphere pressure has a mass of 0.0899 gram. It is less soluble than oxygen in water.

In 1898, James Dewar succeeded in converting hydrogen into a liquid by cooling the gas to a very low temperature and at the same time applying very high pressure. Liquid hydrogen is clear and colorless, and only one fourteenth as dense as water. Thus, liquid hydrogen is the liquid of lowest density, with a mass of only about 70 grams per liter. Under atmospheric pressure, liquid hydrogen boils at −252.5°C. When a part of the liquid is evaporated, the remainder freezes to an icelike solid. Its melting point is −259.1°C. Solid hydrogen is also the solid of lowest density, having a mass of about 80 grams per liter.

Hydrogen is *adsorbed* on certain metals, such as platinum and palladium. ***Adsorption*** *is an acquisition of one substance*

Do not confuse ad*sorption with* ab*sorption. Absorption is the soaking up of one substance through the entire mass of another.*

by the surface of another. Heat is evolved when adsorption occurs. During adsorption, widely separated gas molecules are brought much closer together. This process causes the molecules to give up energy, which appears as heat. Finely divided platinum can adsorb hydrogen so rapidly that the heat given off may ignite the hydrogen.

Hydrogen, as a gas, a liquid, or a solid, is a nonconductor of electricity under usual conditions. The elements, other than hydrogen, that have a single valence electron are metals. Metals have the general property of being conductors of electricity. Scientists believe that it is possible, under very high pressure, to convert hydrogen into a solid having metallic properties.

In 1976, a group of Russian physicists reported that very pure solid hydrogen at about −269°C is a good electric conductor when under a pressure of about 3 million atmospheres. This evidence suggests that solid hydrogen had been converted to a metal under these low temperature-high pressure conditions.

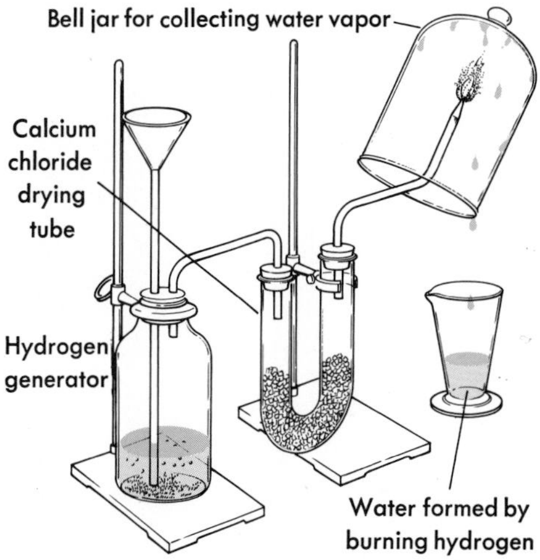

Fig. 9-15. When hydrogen is burned in air, water is the only product.

9.19 The chemical properties of hydrogen

1. Reactions with nonmetals. The electronegativity of hydrogen, 2.1, equals or is less than the electronegativity of other nonmetals. Consequently, hydrogen reacts with nonmetals and forms molecular compounds. The polarity of the covalent bonds in these compounds depends on the electronegativity of the nonmetal. The bonds range in polarity from the almost nonpolar H—C bond to the highly polar H—F bond.

Electronegativity information is given in Figure 6-15 and Table 6-6.

Hydrogen burns in air or oxygen with a very hot, pale blue, and nearly invisible flame. Water is the only product. See Figure 9-15.

$$2H_2 + O_2 \rightarrow 2H_2O(g)$$

Hydrogen does not support combustion. If a bottle of hydrogen is held mouth downward while a blazing splint is thrust slowly upward into the bottle, the hydrogen ignites and burns at the mouth of the bottle. But the splint does not burn inside the bottle in an atmosphere of hydrogen. See Figure 9-16.

Fig. 9-16. When a blazing splint is thrust upward into a bottle of hydrogen, the hydrogen is ignited and burns at the mouth of the bottle. The splint does not burn inside the bottle in an atmosphere of hydrogen. Hydrogen does not support combustion.

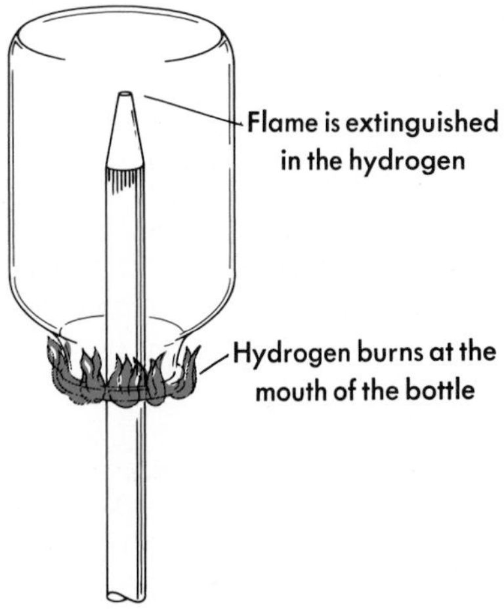

Hydrogen is not a very active element at ordinary temperatures. A mixture of hydrogen and oxygen must be heated to 800°C or ignited at a lower temperature by an electric spark to make the gases combine. Then they combine explosively and form water.

Hydrogen and chlorine do not combine when they are mixed in the dark. But in the presence of direct sunlight, they unite explosively and form hydrogen chloride. A jet of hydrogen will burn in chlorine. The equation for these chemical changes is the same:

$$H_2 + Cl_2 \rightarrow 2HCl(g)$$

Under suitable conditions, hydrogen may be made to unite with nitrogen and form ammonia, NH_3, a very important compound, as we shall see later.

$$3H_2 + N_2 \rightarrow 2NH_3(g)$$

2. *Reactions with metals.* Hydrogen reacts with many nontransition metals and forms binary compounds called *hydrides.* In these compounds, hydrogen is the more electronegative element. The hydrides of Group I metals and of the Group II metals, calcium, strontium, and barium, are ionic compounds which at room temperature are white crystalline solids. In these compounds, hydrogen is present as the H^-, hydride ion, and has an oxidation number of -1. Metallic hydrides may be produced by heating the metal in an atmosphere of hydrogen.

$$2Na + H_2 \rightarrow 2Na^+H^-(s)$$
$$Ba + H_2 \rightarrow Ba^{++}H^-{}_2(s)$$

9.20 The test for hydrogen

Suppose you are given a colorless gas to identify. You suspect it might be hydrogen. If the gas burns in air and forms water, you know that hydrogen is present. If the gas burns in air or oxygen with a nearly colorless flame, and water is the *only* product, then the gas *is* hydrogen.

9.21 The uses of hydrogen

1. *For making hydrogen compounds.* Ninety percent of elemental hydrogen produced today is used for preparing two useful hydrogen compounds, ammonia and methanol. Ammonia, NH_3, is made by direct union of nitrogen and hydrogen. Ammonia is then used as the starting point for making fertilizers, explosives, dyestuffs, and many other valuable and useful compounds. Methanol, CH_3OH, which is used as a solvent and for preparing other compounds, is made from hydrogen and carbon monoxide.

Increasing quantities of hydrogen chloride, HCl, are being prepared by direct combination of hydrogen and chlorine. Hydrogen chloride is then dissolved in water to produce hydrochloric acid.

2. *For solidifying oils.* Millions of pounds of cottonseed oil are changed each year from liquid oil to solid or semisolid fat by hydrogenation. Finely divided nickel is the catalyst used in this reaction. Some of the molecules in the liquid oil combine with hydrogen atoms and produce a substance that is solid at room temperature but is still a liquid at body temperature. Most vegetable shortenings found on the market today are examples of such hydrogenated oil.

Hydrogenation is the chemical addition of hydrogen to a material.

Peanut, corn, soybean, and coconut oil are also hardened by hydrogenation to make margarine. Some fish oils lose their offensive odor when hydrogenated and thus become suitable for making soap. Lard is sometimes hydrogenated to produce a whiter, firmer product.

3. *As a reducing agent.* Hydrogen can remove oxygen from the oxides of some metals, such as copper, tin, lead, zinc, and iron. Hydrogen is then used as a reducing agent to separate certain metals from their oxide ores. More often, however, carbon in the form of coke is used as the reducing agent because it is usually less expensive and more convenient.

Some metals must be worked in an atmosphere free of oxygen, called a *reducing atmosphere.* A reducing atmosphere prevents the unwanted reaction of the metal with oxygen at the high temperatures needed for the processes. Tungsten, a metal that is used for making the filaments of electric lamps, is worked in a reducing atmosphere. By surrounding the tungsten with hydrogen in a closed furnace, the oxidation of the metal is prevented.

4. *As a fuel.* Nearly all our fuels contain hydrogen, either free or combined with other elements. Coal gas and oil gas contain hydrogen in quantity. Methane, CH_4, is a major component of natural gas. Hydrogen is used as a fuel for the oxyhydrogen torch. Pure hydrogen makes an excellent fuel but is somewhat more expensive than other available gaseous fuels.

Liquid hydrogen and the liquid oxygen needed to burn it were used in the second- and third-stage engines of the launch vehicles in the Apollo mission flights.

Fig. 9-17. The second and third stage engines of the launch vehicles used for the Apollo mission flights were powered by liquid hydrogen burned with liquid oxygen.

9.22 Deuterium

Deuterium, described in Section 3.6, was discovered and named in 1931 by a research team at Columbia University headed by Harold C. Urey. Besides its occurrence on the earth, deuterium exists in the atmosphere of Jupiter, in our sun, in distant stars and nebulae, and in interstellar space. The discoveries of deuterium in space were made by ultraviolet spectroscopes and radio telescopes from the earth's surface or from aboard earth satellites.

Protium (hydrogen-1) atoms consist of a proton nucleus and an orbital electron. Deuterium atoms have a proton and a neutron in the nucleus, and an orbital electron. Consequently, deuterium atoms have a mass about double that of protium atoms. This mass difference between hydrogen isotopes is proportionally larger than between isotopes of any other element. The mass difference is related to differences in physical properties. See Table 9-4 on the next page.

Differences in chemical properties of most isotopes are so slight that they are not usually considered. But because of the significant mass difference between its isotopes, this is not true for hydrogen. Protium and deuterium react the same way and form similar compounds. But the rates of their reactions

Fig. 9-18. Artist's concept of the NASA Orbiting Astronomical Observatory, designed to conduct studies of the chemical composition of interstellar space.

Table 9-4

PHYSICAL PROPERTIES OF PROTIUM AND DEUTERIUM						
Isotope	Symbol	Atomic Mass	Molecular Formula	Melting Point (°C)	Boiling Point (°C)	Density of Liquid (g/liter)
protium	H	1.007825	H_2	−259.1	−252.5	0.0709 (−252.7°C)
deuterium	D	2.01410	D_2	−254.6	−249.7	0.169 (−250.9°C)

are different. Reactions of deuterium and deuterium compounds are generally much slower than those of protium and protium compounds. This rate difference makes possible the electrolytic separation of deuterium oxide from water.

The separation of deuterium oxide from water by electrolysis is described in Section 12.21.

Deuterium is being used in experiments that attempt to produce helium nuclei by combining two deuterium nuclei. Light from a laser beam is being used to provide the energy to start this reaction. If successful, this method may provide another method of generating electricity.

SUMMARY

Oxygen, the earth's most abundant element, is found in the air, in water, and in the earth's crust. Priestley and Scheele are codiscoverers of oxygen. Oxygen was shown by Lavoisier to be an element, and was named by him. Oxygen can be prepared in the laboratory by decomposing hydrogen peroxide, adding water to sodium peroxide, heating potassium chlorate, and electrolyzing water. Commercially, oxygen is produced from liquid air or by electrolyzing water.

Oxygen is a colorless, odorless, tasteless gas, which is slightly denser than air, and slightly soluble in water. Liquid oxygen is slightly attracted by a magnet. Oxygen is an active element which combines with other elements and forms oxides. An oxide is a compound consisting of oxygen and usually one other element; in oxides the oxidation number of oxygen is −2.

Oxygen is necessary for life. It is used extensively in the iron and steel industry and for producing many chemical compounds. Patients who have difficulty breathing are sometimes administered oxygen. Oxygen aids in the purification of water and sewage. It is used to support the combustion of fuels in rockets and missiles.

Ozone is a more active form of oxygen that is produced by electric discharge. It exists naturally in the stratosphere where it shields the earth from much of the sun's ultraviolet radiation.

The existence of an element in two or more forms in the same physical phase is known as allotropy. The different forms of such elements are allotropes. Oxygen, O_2, and ozone, O_3, are allotropes of the element oxygen. The structure of the ozone molecule is a resonance hybrid of two different structures. Ozone is a vigorous oxidizing agent. It is used in water and sewage purification, for producing metal oxides, for bleaching, and in preparing chemical compounds.

Hydrogen is the most abundant element in the universe. It is found in water, acids, living tissues, and many fuels. It was discovered by Cavendish and named by Lavoisier. In the laboratory, hydrogen is prepared from acids by replacement, from water by replacement, and from water by electrolysis. Industrially, hydrogen is prepared from hydrocarbons, from water by hot carbon, and from water by electrolysis.

Hydrogen is a colorless, odorless, tasteless gas that has the lowest density of any material known. It is very slightly soluble in water. Platinum and palladium adsorb hydrogen. Adsorption is an acquisition of one substance by the surface of another. It is believed that at very low temperatures and extremely high pressures, solid hydrogen can acquire metallic properties.

Hydrogen burns with a very hot flame that is nearly invisible. Hydrogen is not active at ordinary temperatures. A mixture of hydrogen and oxygen, when ignited, produces an explosion and water vapor is the only product. Hydrogen and chlorine react and form hydrogen chloride. Hydrogen and nitrogen can be made to react; ammonia is the product. Hydrogen reacts with many nontransition metals and forms hydrides.

Hydrogen is used for making hydrogen compounds, principally ammonia and methanol. It is used for solidifying oils, as a reducing agent, and as a fuel.

Deuterium, the hydrogen isotope with mass number 2, has different physical properties and chemically reacts more slowly than protium, hydrogen-1. This is the result of the proportionally great mass difference between the two isotopes.

QUESTIONS

Group A

1. (*a*) Distinguish between *free* oxygen and *combined* oxygen. (*b*) What are the most abundant sources of each on the earth?
2. Describe Priestley's discovery of oxygen.
3. (*a*) What is a catalyst? (*b*) What is its purpose in the preparation of oxygen from hydrogen peroxide? (*c*) What is its purpose in the preparation of oxygen from potassium chlorate?
4. Why is it possible to collect oxygen by water displacement?
5. (*a*) When liquid air is permitted to stand, which gas boils away first? (*b*) Why?
6. What are the physical properties of oxygen gas?
7. What is an *oxide*?
8. How do you test a colorless, odorless, and tasteless gas to determine whether it is oxygen or not?
9. How is oxygen used in the iron and steel industry?
10. What chemical property of oxygen makes it useful in water and sewage purification?
11. (*a*) Where does ozone occur naturally? (*b*) How does this affect life on the earth's surface?
12. (*a*) What is allotropy? (*b*) In what way does the element oxygen exhibit allotropy?
13. What chemical property of ozone determines its uses?
14. Describe the abundance of free and combined hydrogen on the earth.
15. In the universe we are able to explore, which is more abundant, oxygen or hydrogen?
16. (*a*) What substances are used for the usual laboratory preparation of hydrogen? (*b*) What products are formed?
17. Give five physical properties of hydrogen.
18. Distinguish between *adsorption* and *absorption*.
19. (*a*) Does hydrogen support combustion? (*b*) What simple laboratory test can you use to demonstrate this?
20. How do you test a colorless, odorless, and tasteless gas to determine whether it is hydrogen or not?
21. For what purpose is most elemental hydrogen used commercially?

22. (*a*) What is a reducing atmosphere? (*b*) Why is it useful?

Group B

23. Lavoisier did not discover any new substances. He did not design any new laboratory apparatus. He did not develop any better preparation methods. Yet Lavoisier is recognized as one of the greatest eighteenth-century chemists. Why?
24. (*a*) Write balanced formula equations for each of the four laboratory methods of preparing oxygen. (*b*) Assign oxidation numbers to each oxygen atom in these equations. (*c*) For each equation, determine whether the oxygen was oxidized, reduced, or both.
25. Why do chemists believe there are unpaired electrons in an oxygen molecule?
26. Write balanced formula equations for the following reactions: (*a*) Potassium burns in oxygen and yields the ionic compound potassium peroxide. (*b*) Calcium reacts with oxygen and yields the ionic compound calcium oxide. (*c*) Nitrogen reacts with oxygen and forms the covalent compound nitrogen monoxide.
27. Oxygen and fluorine combine indirectly and form OF_2. Is this compound an oxide? Give a reason for your answer.
28. Why is air enriched with oxygen helpful to persons with lung or heart disease?
29. Compare the energy content and activity of oxygen molecules and ozone molecules.
30. Describe the bonding in the ozone molecule.
31. Why is Cavendish credited with the discovery of hydrogen, even though the gas had been known much earlier?
32. What factors determine the rate at which hydrogen is evolved from hydrochloric acid by reaction with coarse iron filings?
33. (*a*) From its position in the periodic table, would you expect cesium to react with water more or less vigorously than potassium? (*b*) Why?
34. Write the balanced chemical equation for the principal commercial method for producing hydrogen.
35. In the reaction of steam on hot coke for producing water gas, which substance is (*a*) the oxidizing agent; (*b*) the reducing agent; (*c*) the substance oxidized; (*d*) the substance reduced?
36. What physical property change of hydrogen can be used to determine the conditions under which hydrogen can be changed from its usual nonmetallic properties to those of metals?
37. (*a*) What product is formed when hydrogen combines with chlorine? (*b*) with nitrogen? (*c*) What type of bond does hydrogen form with these two elements? (*d*) Of what type of particle do these compounds consist?
38. (*a*) What product is formed when hydrogen combines with potassium? (*b*) with strontium? (*c*) What type of bond does hydrogen form with these two elements? (*d*) Of what type of particle do these compounds consist?
39. Tin(II) oxide reacts with hydrogen and forms tin and water vapor. In this reaction, which substance is (*a*) the oxidizing agent; (*b*) the reducing agent; (*c*) oxidized; (*d*) reduced?
40. (*a*) Protium atoms and deuterium atoms are both classed as hydrogen atoms, yet they have different physical properties. Why? (*b*) In what way are their chemical properties different?
41. What properties of hydrogen gas are referred to in the caption of the photograph of the Hindenburg disaster shown on page 167? Explain.

chapter 10

THE GAS LAWS

Gas volumes are related to the temperature and pressure of the gas. (See Question 22 on page 203.)

10.1 Kinetic theory

In Chapter 1, matter was described as existing in three physical phases—gas, liquid, and solid. In later chapters, it was explained that the particles that make up various substances are atoms, molecules, or ions. Now we are going to learn about the *kinetic theory*. The kinetic theory is a useful physical model that helps us understand the properties of gases, liquids, and solids. It does this by explaining these properties in terms of (1) the forces between the particles of matter, and (2) the energy these particles possess.

Most of the data in support of the kinetic theory comes from indirect observation. It is almost impossible to observe the behavior of individual particles of matter. Scientists, however, can observe the behavior of large groups of particles. From the results of these observations, they can then describe the average behavior of the particles under study.

The three basic assumptions of the *kinetic theory* are

1. Matter is composed of very tiny particles. The chemical properties of the particles of matter depend on their composition. Their physical properties depend on the forces they exert on each other and the distance separating them.

2. The particles of matter are in continual motion. Their average kinetic energy (energy of motion) depends on temperature.

3. The total kinetic energy of colliding particles remains constant. When individual particles collide, some lose energy while others gain energy. But there is no overall energy loss. Collisions of this type are said to be *elastic* collisions.

Fig. 10-1. The behavior of a radiometer can be explained in terms of the kinetic molecular theory. A radiometer has vanes that reflect light (white) on one side and absorb light (black) on the other. The black side is heated by light more than the white side. Gas molecules near the vane are heated on the black side. Therefore, they strike the black side more frequently and with greater force than those on the white side. The vane moves toward the white side.

10.2 Observed properties of gases

A study of gases reveals four characteristic properties:

1. Expansion. A gas does not have a definite shape or a definite volume. It completely fills any container into which it is confined. For example, the container determines the shape and volume of the air in balloons of various sizes and shapes, in automobile tires, and in air mattresses.

2. Pressure. When we inflate a toy balloon, it becomes larger because we increase the pressure on its inside surface. If we let air escape, the balloon becomes smaller because the pressure is decreased. If we raise the temperature of the air in the balloon by warming it, the balloon becomes larger. This observation indicates that pressure increases with an increase in temperature. If we cool the balloon, its size decreases as the pressure decreases.

3. Low density. The density of a gas is about $\frac{1}{1000}$ of the density of the same substance in the liquid or solid phase. The densities of gaseous, liquid, and solid oxygen and hydrogen are typical data. Oxygen gas has a density of 1.429 g/liter (0.001429 g/ml) at 0°C and 1 atmosphere pressure. Liquid oxygen has a density of 1.149 g/ml at −183°C and solid oxygen has a density of 1.426 g/ml at −252.5°C. Hydrogen gas has a density of 0.0899 g/liter (0.0000899 g/ml) at 0°C and 1 atmosphere pressure. Liquid hydrogen has a density of 0.0708 g/ml at −253°C. Solid hydrogen has a density of 0.0807 g/ml at −262°C. See Figure 10-2.

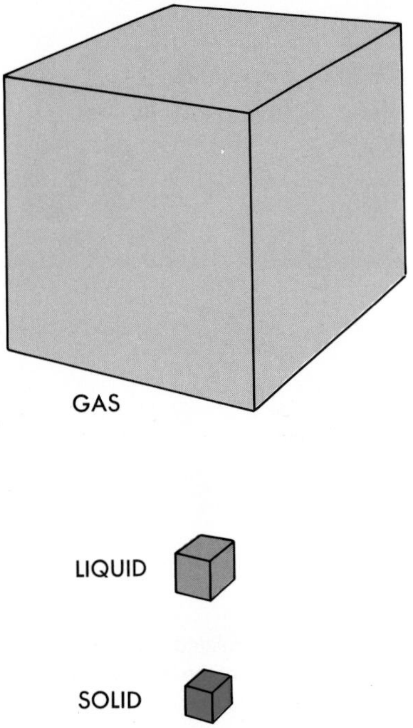

Fig. 10-2. The density of many substances in the gaseous phase is about 1/1000 of their density in the liquid and solid phases. This diagram shows the relative volumes of 1.5 g of oxygen as a gas, a liquid, and a solid. The oxygen gas occupies 1050 ml, while liquid oxygen occupies 1.3 ml and solid oxygen occupies 1.0 ml.

4. Diffusion. If the stopper is removed from a container of ammonia, the irritating effects of this gas on the eyes, nose, and throat soon become evident throughout the room. When the chemistry class makes the foul-odored hydrogen sulfide gas in the laboratory, objections may come from other students and teachers in all parts of the building. This process of spreading out spontaneously (without additional help) to occupy a space uniformly, is characteristic of all gases. It is known as *diffusion*. See Figure 10-3.

Fig. 10-3. The rate of diffusion of bromine vapor in air. Diffusion has occurred for 2 minutes in the left cylinder. Diffusion has occurred for 20 minutes in the right cylinder.

10.3 Kinetic-theory description of a gas

According to the kinetic theory, a gas consists of very small independent particles. These particles move at random in space and experience elastic collisions. This theoretical description is of an imaginary gas called the ***ideal gas.***

The particles of substances that are gases at room temperature are molecules. Some of these molecules consist of a single atom (He, Ne, Ar). Many consist of two atoms (O_2, H_2, HCl, etc.). Others consist of several atoms (NH_3, CH_4, C_2H_2, etc.). Matter in the gaseous phase occupies a volume of the order of 1000 times that which it occupies in the liquid or solid phases. Thus, molecules of gases are much farther apart than those of liquids or solids. This difference accounts for the much lower density of gases as compared to solids or liquids. Even so, 1 ml of a gas at 0°C and 1 atmosphere pressure contains about 3×10^{19} molecules. Many ordinary molecules have diameters of the order of 4 Å, or 4×10^{-10} m. In gases, these molecules are widely separated. They are, on an average, about 4×10^{-9} m (or about 10 diameters) apart at 0°C and 1 atmosphere pressure. The kinetic energy of the molecules of a gas (except near its condensing temperature) overcomes the attractive forces between them. The molecules of a gas are on the average essentially independent particles. These molecules travel in random directions at high speed. This speed is of the order of 10^3 m/sec at 0°C and 1 atmosphere pressure. At this speed, molecules of a gas travel about 10^{-7} m before colliding with other gas molecules or with the walls of the container. Because gas molecules collide and exchange energy, their speeds will vary. They undergo about 5×10^9 collisions per second.

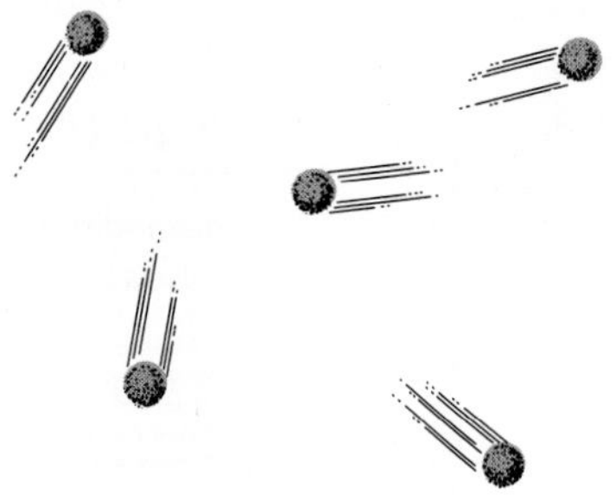

Fig. 10-4. Molecules of a gas are widely separated and move rapidly.

The expansion and diffusion of gases are both explained by the fact that gas molecules are essentially independent particles. They move through space until they strike other gas molecules or the walls of the container. A gas moves very rapidly into an evacuated container. Gaseous diffusion is slowed down, but not prevented, by the presence of other gases. The rate of diffusion of one gas through another depends on three properties of the intermingling gas molecules:

1. Speed,
2. Diameter,
3. Attractive force.

Hydrogen diffuses rapidly because hydrogen molecules are smaller and move about with greater speed than the larger, heavier molecules of other gases at the same temperature. The diffusion of hydrogen can be demonstrated by placing a bottle filled with hydrogen above another bottle filled with air, as shown in Figure 10-5. After a few minutes, the mouth of each bottle is held in the flame of a laboratory burner. The resulting explosions show that the hydrogen molecules moved so that there were some in both bottles.

Fig. 10-5. Even though hydrogen is less dense than air, hydrogen diffuses downward and air upward.

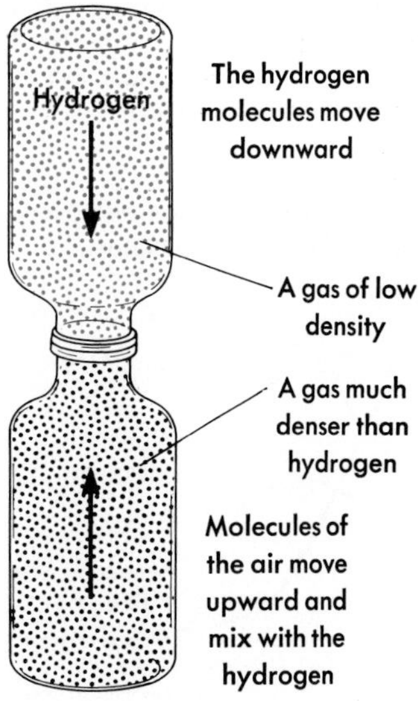

Even if two gases are separated by a porous barrier, such as a membrane or an unglazed porcelain cup, diffusion takes place through the pores, as shown in Figure 10-6. An unglazed porcelain cup is closed by a rubber stopper through which a piece of glass tubing has been inserted. When a large beaker filled with hydrogen is placed over the porcelain cup, hydrogen molecules diffuse into the cup faster than the molecules of the gases in air diffuse into the beaker. This creates a pressure in the cup which forces gas out the end of the tube.

Gas pressure results from many billions of moving molecules continuously hitting the walls of the container. If we increase the number of molecules within the container, the num-

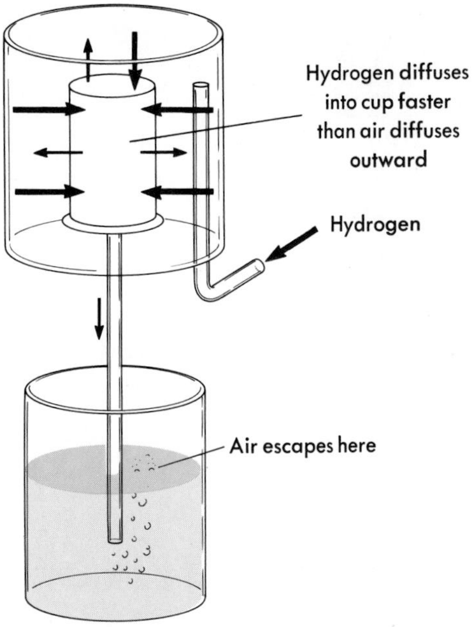

Fig. 10-6. Since hydrogen diffuses into the cup faster than air diffuses outward, the net pressure in the cup increases, forcing gas bubbles out of the tube.

Fig. 10-7. Molecular speed distribution in a gas at different temperatures.

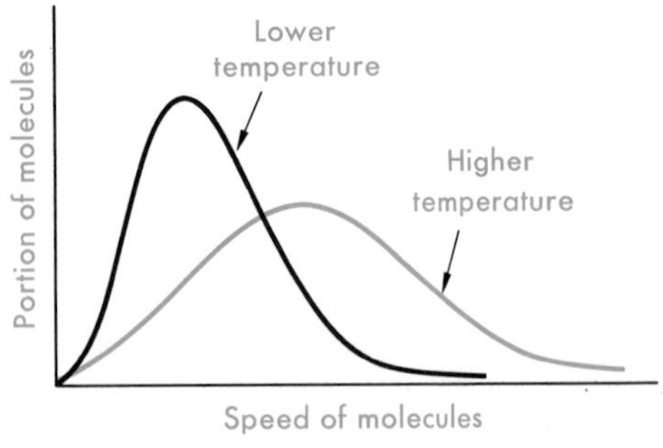

ber that strike any area of the inside surface increases. Therefore, the pressure on the inside surface increases. If the temperature of the gas is raised, the molecules on an average have more kinetic energy. They move more rapidly and collide more energetically with the walls of the container. These more frequent and more energetic collisions with the container walls increase the pressure. The pressure drops when the number of molecules is decreased or the temperature is lowered.

Figure 10-7 shows the distribution of molecular speeds in a gas at two different temperatures. From these graphs we draw two conclusions:

1. Molecules of a gas do not all have the same speed.

2. An increase in temperature increases the average rate at which gas molecules move.

The kinetic energy of a molecule is related to its speed by the equation.

$$E_k = \frac{1}{2}mv^2$$

in which E_k is the kinetic energy of the molecule, m is its mass, and v is its speed. Since the molecules of a gas do not all have the same speed, they will not all have the same kinetic energy. Since the average molecular speed varies with the temperature, the average kinetic energy of the molecules of a gas varies with the temperature. Thus, the temperature of a gas provides an indication of the average kinetic energy of the molecules. The higher the temperature, the higher the average kinetic energy. The lower the temperature, the lower the average kinetic energy.

10.4 Attractive forces between gas molecules

The lowest temperature at which a substance can exist as a gas at atmospheric pressure is the *condensation temperature* of the gas. At this temperature, the kinetic energy of the gas particles is not sufficient to overcome the forces of attraction between them. The gas condenses to a liquid. The kinetic theory tells us that the temperature of a substance is a measure of the kinetic energy of its particles. So a study of condensation temperatures of various substances should give us an idea of the magnitude (size) of the forces of attraction between particles of matter. Table 10-1 gives selected condensation temperatures.

Substances such as H_2, O_2, and CH_4 (methane) consist of low-molecular-weight nonpolar covalent molecules. They can exist as gases at very low temperatures. Evidently the attractive forces between such molecules in the gaseous phase are very small. More complex substances such as CCl_4 and C_6H_6 (benzene) have condensation temperatures somewhat above room temperature. They have higher-molecular-weight nonpolar molecules. The forces of attraction between such molecules must be greater than those between similar molecules that are less complex.

Ammonia (NH_3) and H_2O consist of polar covalent molecules. Notice that their molecular weights are low and their molecular structures are simple. Even so, their condensation temperatures are considerably above those of nonpolar molecules of the same molecular weight.

The condensation temperatures of ionic compounds such as sodium chloride, covalent network substances such as diamond, and metals are all very high. Evidently the forces between particles of such substances are very strong. The nature of these forces will be described in Chapter 12.

The attractive forces between molecules are called *van der Waals forces.* These forces are important only when molecules are very close together. Hence van der Waals forces are not important in gases unless the gas molecules are under very high pressure or are at a temperature near their condensation temperature. Van der Waals forces are of two types. One type, called *dispersion interaction,* exists between all molecules. The other type, called *dipole-dipole attraction,* exists between polar molecules only.

The strength of dispersion interaction depends on the number of electrons in a molecule and the tightness with which the electrons are held. The greater the number of electrons and the less tightly they are bound, the more powerful is the attractive force of dispersion interaction. We can observe this effect most easily between nonpolar molecules, where dispersion interaction is the only type of attractive force. Thus, for nonpolar molecules in general, the higher the molecular weight, the higher the condensation temperature. This generalization can be observed in Table 10-1. Compare the condensation temperatures of oxygen, hydrogen, and methane with those of carbon tetrachloride and benzene. The energy associated with dispersion interaction is only a few tenths of a kilocalorie per mole.

Dipole-dipole attraction is the attraction between the oppositely charged portions of neighboring polar molecules. Remember from Section 6.21 that polar molecules are sometimes called dipoles. Dipole-dipole attractive forces as well as dispersion interaction forces act between polar molecules. This combination of forces accounts for the much higher condensation temperatures of polar molecules as compared to nonpolar molecules of similar complexity. For example, methane, ammonia, and water have comparable molecular weights. Yet the condensation temperature of ammonia is about 130C° higher than that of methane. The condensation temperature of water is over 130C° higher than that of ammonia. The energy associated with dipole-dipole attraction may be as high as 6 kilocalories per mole.

Table 10-1

CONDENSATION TEMPERATURES OF VARIOUS SUBSTANCES

Type of Substance	Substance	Condensation Temperature (1 atm, °C)
nonpolar covalent molecular	H_2	−253
	O_2	−183
	CH_4	−161
	CCl_4	77
	C_6H_6	80
polar covalent molecular	NH_3	−33
	H_2O	100
ionic	NaCl	1413
	MgF_2	2239
covalent network	$(SiO_2)_x$	2230
	C_x (diamond)	4827
metallic	Hg	357
	Cu	2595
	Fe	3000
	W	5927

Johannes Diderik van der Waals (1837–1923) was a Dutch scientist who helped explain the differences in physical properties between real gases and the ideal gas.

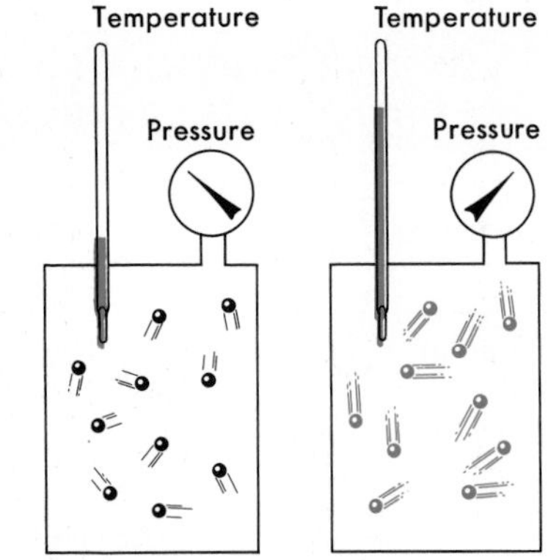

Fig. 10-8. At constant volume, as the temperature of a gas increases, the pressure it exerts increases.

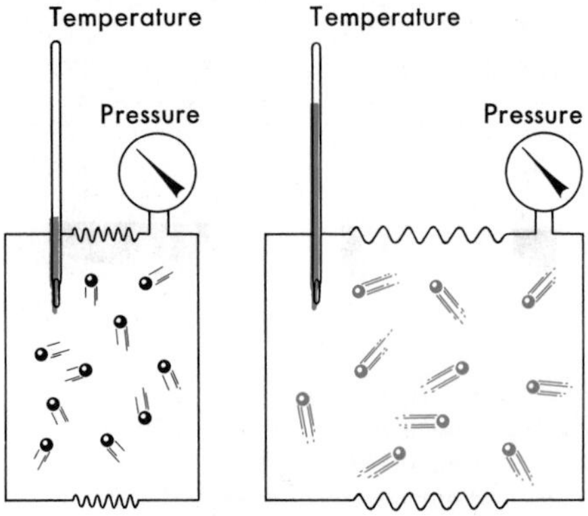

Fig. 10-9. At constant pressure, as the temperature of a gas increases, the volume it occupies increases.

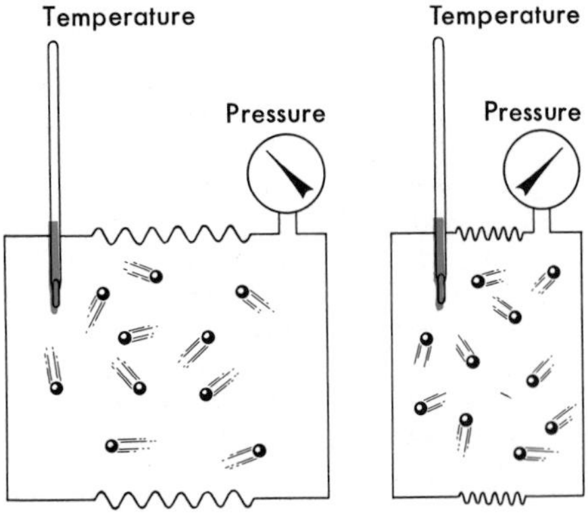

Fig. 10-10. At constant temperature, as the volume of a gas decreases, the pressure it exerts increases.

10.5 Dependence of gas volume on temperature and pressure

A given number of molecules can occupy widely different volumes. The expression "a liter of air" means little unless the temperature and pressure at which it is measured are known. A liter of air can be compressed to a few milliliters in volume. It can also expand to fill an auditorium. Steel cylinders containing oxygen and hydrogen are widely used in industry. They have an internal volume of about 55 liters. When such cylinders are returned "empty," they still contain about 55 liters of gas, although when they were delivered "full" they may have had 100 times as many molecules of the gas compressed within the cylinder.

We have stated that the temperature of a gas is an indication of the average kinetic energy of its molecules. The higher the temperature of a gas, the more kinetic energy its molecules have, and the more rapidly they move about. The pressure that a gas exerts on the walls of its container is the result of the collisions of gas molecules with the walls. If the volume of one mole of gas molecules remains constant, the pressure exerted by the gas increases as its temperature is raised. It follows that the pressure exerted by one mole of gas molecules decreases as the temperature is lowered (Figure 10-8).

Furthermore, if the pressure exerted by one mole of gas molecules is to remain the same as the temperature increases, the volume that the gas occupies must increase. Since the molecules move faster at higher temperatures, they strike the walls of the container more frequently and with more force. Suppose the area of the wall is increased. Then the force of collisions on a unit area of the wall can remain the same as at the lower temperature, and the pressure will remain the same. The area that the molecules strike can be enlarged by enlarging the volume of the container. On the other hand, if pressure remains constant and the temperature decreases, the volume that one mole of gas molecules occupies must decrease (Figure 10-9).

Finally, suppose the temperature of one mole of gas molecules remains constant. Then the pressure exerted by the gas becomes greater as the volume that the gas occupies becomes smaller. And similarly, the pressure exerted by one mole of gas molecules is less if the volume available to the gas is larger (Figure 10-10). In light of these consequences, the kinetic theory explains satisfactorily how gas volumes are related to the temperature and pressure of the gas. Accordingly, we must consider both temperature and pressure when measuring the volume of a gas.

10.6 Standard temperature and pressure

As explained in Section 10.5, the volume of a gas depends greatly on temperature and pressure. For this reason, it is very helpful to have a standard temperature and a standard pressure for use in measuring or comparing gas volumes. ***Standard temperature*** *is defined as exactly zero degrees Celsius.* It is the temperature of melting ice. This temperature was selected because pure water is widely available and the melting temperature of ice is not much affected by pressure changes. ***Standard pressure*** *is defined as the pressure exerted by a column of mercury exactly 760 millimeters high.* We use 760 millimeters of mercury as the standard pressure because that is the average atmospheric pressure at sea level. Temperatures are easily measured with an accurate thermometer. The pressure of a gas in simple gas experiments may be determined from a properly corrected barometer reading. Standard temperature and pressure are commonly abbreviated as STP.

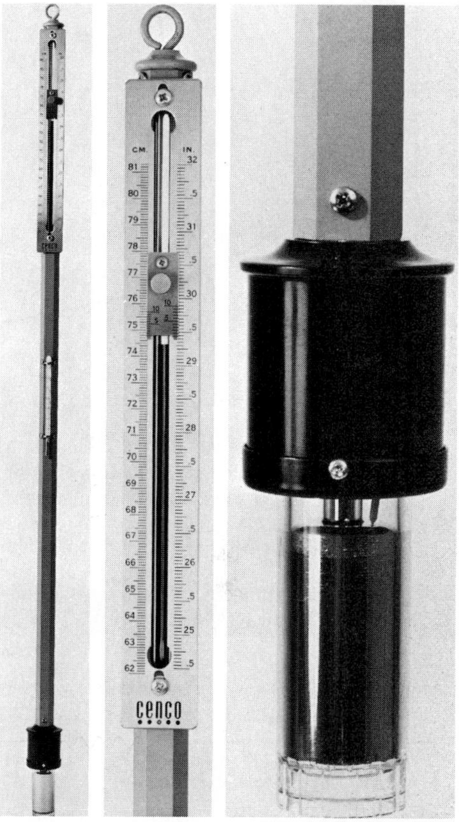

Fig. 10-11. A barometer is used to measure atmospheric pressure. Left, a laboratory mercurial barometer. Center, a close-up of the top of the mercury column showing the height-measuring scales. Right, the adjustable reservoir with indicator pin for setting the height of the mercury level exposed to the atmosphere.

Robert Boyle is considered to be the founder of modern chemistry because (1) he recognized that chemistry is a worthwhile field of learning and not just a branch of medicine or alchemy; (2) he introduced careful experimentation into chemistry; and (3) he defined an element as something that could not be decomposed—a definition that held for over 200 years.

If you need to review inverse proportion, see Section MR9 in the Appendix.

10.7 Variation of gas volume with pressure: Boyle's law

If a rubber ball filled with air is squeezed, the volume of the gas inside is decreased. But the gas expands again when the pressure is released. Robert Boyle (1627–1691) was the first scientist to make careful measurements showing the relationship between pressures and volumes of gases. He found that doubling the pressure on a gas reduces its volume by one half. Boyle formulated the results of his experiments into a law that bears his name. ***Boyle's law*** is stated: *The volume of a definite quantity of dry gas is inversely proportional to the pressure, provided the temperature remains constant.*

This law is expressed mathematically as

$$\frac{V}{V'} = \frac{p'}{p}$$

V is the original volume, V' the new volume, p the original pressure, and p' the new pressure. Solving the expression for V', we get a useful mathematical form of Boyle's law:

$$V' = V\,\frac{p}{p'}$$

10.8 Using Boyle's law

Suppose 40.0 ml of hydrogen gas, collected when the barometer reading is $74\bar{0}$ mm, stands until the barometric pressure has risen to $75\bar{0}$ mm. If the temperature is unchanged, the volume of gas becomes smaller because of the increased pressure. If we measure the new gas volume, we find it to be 39.5 ml.

Using Boyle's law, we can calculate the new volume resulting from the pressure change without actually experiencing the pressure change. The new volume V' is p/p' or $74\bar{0}$ mm/

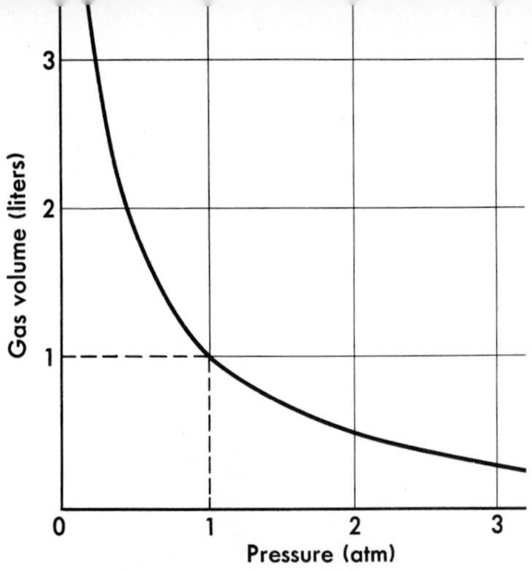

Fig. 10-12. The variation of volume with pressure at constant temperature of 1 liter of an ideal gas measured at 1 atmosphere pressure. *pV = constant.*

$75\bar{0}$ mm of the original volume *V*, 40.0 ml. Substituting in the Boyle's law formula and solving, we obtain

$$V' = Vp/p'$$
$$V' = 40.0 \text{ ml} \times 74\bar{0} \text{ mm}/75\bar{0} \text{ mm}$$
$$V' = 39.5 \text{ ml}$$

Later, if the pressure has fallen to $72\bar{0}$ mm, the new gas volume V' is calculated as

$$V' = 40.0 \text{ ml} \times 74\bar{0} \text{ mm}/72\bar{0} \text{ mm}$$
$$V' = 41.1 \text{ ml}$$

The following Sample Problem gives another example of Boyle's law in use.

SAMPLE PROBLEM

A $20\bar{0}$-ml sample of hydrogen is collected when the pressure is $80\bar{0}$ mm of mercury. What volume will the gas occupy at $76\bar{0}$ mm pressure?

SOLUTION

$$V' = Vp/p'$$
$$V'_{76\bar{0}\text{ mm}} = 20\bar{0} \text{ ml} \times 80\bar{0} \text{ mm}/76\bar{0} \text{ mm}$$
$$V'_{76\bar{0}\text{ mm}} = 211 \text{ ml}$$

10.9 Variation of gas volume with temperature

Bread dough rises when put in a hot oven. The increase in temperature causes the bubbles of carbon dioxide gas within the dough to expand. The rather large increase in the volume of the dough during baking shows that the gas must expand considerably as the temperature increases. In fact, gases expand many times as much per degree rise in temperature as do liquids and solids.

Jacques Charles (1746–1823) was the first to make careful measurements of the changes in volume of gases with changes in temperature. His experiments revealed that

1. All gases expand or contract at the same rate with changes in temperature, provided the pressure is unchanged.

2. The change in volume amounts to $\frac{1}{273}$ of the original volume at 0°C for each Celsius degree the temperature is changed.

We may start with a definite volume of a gas at 0°C and experiment by heating it. Just as the whole of anything may be considered as made up of two halves, $\frac{2}{2}$, or three thirds, $\frac{3}{3}$, so we can consider this volume as $\frac{273}{273}$. If we warm the gas one

Celsius degree, it expands $\frac{1}{273}$ of its original volume. Its new volume is $\frac{274}{273}$. In the same manner, the gas expands $\frac{100}{273}$ when it is heated 100C°. Such expansion, added to the original volume, makes the new volume $\frac{373}{273}$. Any gas warmed 273 Celsius degrees expands $\frac{273}{273}$. That is, its volume is just doubled, as represented by the fraction $\frac{546}{273}$.

A gas whose volume is measured at 0°C contracts by $\frac{1}{273}$ of this volume if it is cooled 1 C°. Its new volume is $\frac{272}{273}$ of its original volume. Cooling the gas to −100°C reduces the volume by $\frac{100}{273}$. In other words, the gas shrinks to $\frac{173}{273}$ of its original volume. At this rate, if we cooled the gas to −273°C, it would lose $\frac{273}{273}$ of its volume, and its volume would become zero. Such a situation cannot occur, however, because all gases become liquids before such a low temperature is reached. This rate of contraction with cooling applies only to gases.

10.10 Kelvin temperature scale

In Section 1.7, the Celsius temperature scale was described. This scale is based on the *triple point* of water. *The* ***triple point*** *of pure water is that single temperature and pressure condition at which water exists in all three phases at the same time.* On the Celsius scale, the triple point of water has a temperature of 0.01°C.

From measuring the variation of gas volume with temperature at low pressures, scientists believe that −273.15°C is the lowest possible temperature. At this temperature a body would have lost all the heat that it is possible for it to lose. Scientists have come very close to this lowest possible temperature, but theoretically it is impossible to reach. The interval between the lowest possible temperature, −273.15°C, and the triple point temperature of water, 0.01°C, is 273.16 C°.

The physicist Sir William Thomson (1824–1907), better known by his title, Lord Kelvin, invented the Kelvin temperature scale. A Kelvin degree is the same temperature interval as a Celsius degree. But 0°K is the lowest possible temperature, −273.15°C. The temperature of the triple point of water is 273.16°K. The lowest possible temperature, 0°K, is frequently called *absolute zero.* Temperatures measured on the Kelvin scale are often called *absolute temperatures.*

The normal freezing point of water is 0.01 C° lower than the triple point temperature of water. On the Celsius scale the normal freezing point of water is 0.00°C. Recall that a Kelvin degree is the same temperature interval as a Celsius degree. So the normal freezing point of water is also 0.01 K° lower than the triple point temperature of water, 273.16°K, or 273.15°K. Thus, 0.00°C = 273.15°K. In many calculations, 273.15°K is rounded off to 273°K. Table 10-2 will help you compare Kelvin and Celsius temperatures.

Kelvin temperature = Celsius temperature + 273°

Table 10-2

COMPARISON OF TEMPERATURES ON THE KELVIN AND CELSIUS SCALES

Celsius Scale (°C)	Kelvin Scale (°K)
100°	373°
50°	323°
20°	293°
5°	278°
4°	277°
3°	276°
2°	275°
1°	274°
0°	273°
−100°	173°
−273°	0°

In Section 10.3, you learned that the temperature of a gas provides an indication of the average kinetic energy of the molecules. Since the Kelvin scale starts at what is believed to be the lowest possible temperature, the average kinetic energy of the molecules of a gas is directly proportional to the Kelvin temperature of the gas.

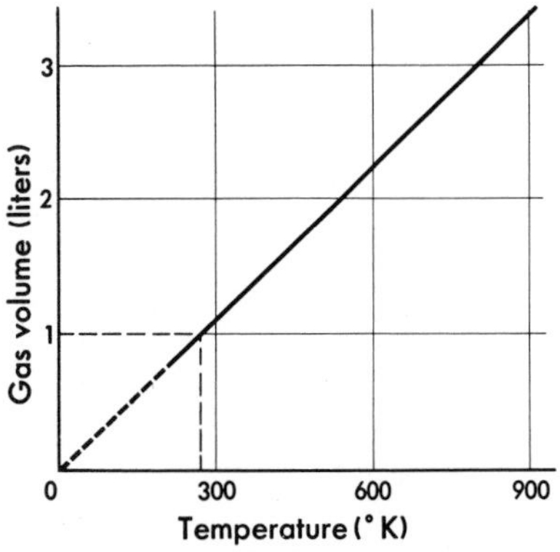

Fig. 10-13. The variation in volume with Kelvin temperature at constant pressure of 1 liter of an ideal gas measured at 273°K. *V/T = constant.*

10.11 Charles' law

Thermometers are not graduated (marked) to give Kelvin-scale readings. But use of the Kelvin scale does give results that correspond with actual volume changes observed in gases. In problems dealing with changes in gas volumes as temperatures vary, the Kelvin scale eliminates the use of zero and of negative numbers. Using the Kelvin temperature scale, ***Charles' law*** can be stated: *The volume of a definite quantity of dry gas varies directly with the Kelvin temperature, provided the pressure remains constant.*

Charles' law may be expressed mathematically as

$$\frac{V}{V'} = \frac{T}{T'}$$

where V is the original volume, V' the new volume, T the original *Kelvin* temperature, and T' the new *Kelvin* temperature. Solving the expression for V'

If you need to review direct proportion, see Section MR9 in the Appendix.

$$V' = V\frac{T'}{T}$$

The Sample Problem below illustrates the use of this formula.

SAMPLE PROBLEM

A 50.0-ml volume of gas is measured at $2\bar{0}$°C. If the pressure remains unchanged, what will be the volume of the gas at $\bar{0}$°C?

SOLUTION

Change the Celsius temperatures to Kelvin temperatures:

$$2\bar{0}°\mathrm{C} + 273° = 293°\mathrm{K} \qquad \bar{0}°\mathrm{C} + 273° = 273°\mathrm{K}$$

$$V' = VT'/T$$

$$V'_{\bar{0}°\mathrm{C}} = 50.0 \text{ ml} \times 273°\mathrm{K}/293°\mathrm{K}$$

$$V'_{\bar{0}°\mathrm{C}} = 46.6 \text{ ml}$$

10.12 Use of Boyle's and Charles' laws combined

Calculation of the new volume of a gas when both temperature and pressure are changed involves no new principles. The new volume is the same whether the changes in temperature and pressure are done together or in either order. We multiply the original volume first by a ratio of the pressures. In this way, we determine the new volume corrected for pressure alone. Then we multiply this answer by a ratio of the Kelvin temperatures. This gives us the new volume corrected for both pressure and temperature.

Expressed mathematically, $V' = V \times \frac{p}{p'} \times \frac{T'}{T}$

The Sample Problem below illustrates the use of this formula. You will find it much easier to solve gas-law problems if you use logarithms, a slide rule, or a calculator in making your calculations.

SAMPLE PROBLEM

A gas measures 25.0 ml at $2\bar{0}$°C and 735 mm pressure. What will be its volume at 15°C and $75\bar{0}$ mm pressure?

SOLUTION

$$2\bar{0}°\mathrm{C} = 293°\mathrm{K};\ 15°\mathrm{C} = 288°\mathrm{K}$$

$$V' = V \times p/p' \times T'/T$$

$$V'_{15°\mathrm{C},\,75\bar{0}\,\mathrm{mm}} = 25.0\ \mathrm{ml} \times 735\ \mathrm{mm}/75\bar{0}\ \mathrm{mm} \times 288°\mathrm{K}/293°\mathrm{K}$$

$$V'_{15°\mathrm{C},\,75\bar{0}\,\mathrm{mm}} = 24.1\ \mathrm{ml}$$

10.13 Pressure of a gas collected by displacement of mercury We have discussed how gas volume varies with pressure and temperature changes. But we have not considered any practical laboratory methods of making the necessary measurements. We must now explain these laboratory operations. In the laboratory, a gas may be collected and its volume measured by using a long graduated tube closed at one end. This tube is called a *eudiometer* (you-dee-*om*-eh-ter), Figure 10-14.

Suppose some hydrogen is delivered into a eudiometer that was previously filled with mercury. As hydrogen enters the tube, it bubbles to the top, and pushes the mercury down. Suppose enough hydrogen is added to make the level of the mercury inside the tube the same as the level of the mercury in the bowl, as in (1), Figure 10-14. *When these two levels are the same, the pressure of the hydrogen is the same as that of the atmosphere.* This pressure can be found by reading a barometer. The volume of hydrogen is read from the graduations (markings) on the eudiometer.

Suppose, however, that not enough hydrogen is delivered into the eudiometer to make the mercury levels the same even when the eudiometer rests on the bottom of the bowl of mercury. Then the mercury level inside the tube is above the level

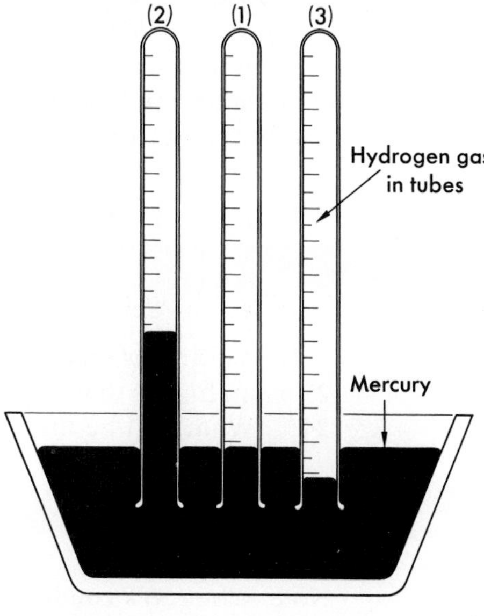

Fig. 10-14. In (1), $p = 1$ atm. In (2), $p < 1$ atm. In (3), $p > 1$ atm.

outside the tube, as in (2), Figure 10-14. The pressure of the gas inside the tube is less than the pressure of the air outside. Otherwise, the enclosed gas would push the mercury down to the same level as that outside the tube. To determine the pressure of the hydrogen, the difference between the levels of the mercury inside and outside the tube must be *subtracted* from the barometer reading. The gas volume is read, as before, from the eudiometer graduations.

Suppose enough hydrogen is delivered into the eudiometer to force the mercury level inside the tube below the outside level. Then the gas inside the tube is under a greater pressure than the air outside, as in (3), Figure 10-14. To determine the pressure of the gas in this case, the difference between the levels of the mercury inside and outside the tube must be *added* to the barometer reading. To make this measurement and that of the gas volume directly would not be practical, since mercury is not transparent. It is easier to raise the eudiometer in the bowl of mercury until the mercury levels inside and outside the tube are the same. Then the gas pressure inside will be the same as that read on the barometer. See the following Sample Problem.

SAMPLE PROBLEM

What is the pressure of the gas in a eudiometer (gas-measuring tube) when the mercury level in the tube is 14 mm higher than that outside? The barometer reads 735 mm.

SOLUTION

Since the mercury level inside is higher than that outside, the pressure on the gas in the eudiometer must be less than atmospheric pressure. Accordingly, the difference in levels is subtracted from the barometric pressure to obtain the pressure of the gas,

735 mm − 14 mm = 721 mm, the pressure of the gas

SAMPLE PROBLEM

The volume of oxygen in a eudiometer is 37.0 ml. The mercury level inside the tube is 25.0 mm higher than that outside. The barometer reading is 742.0 mm. The temperature is 24°C. What will be the volume of the oxygen at STP?

SOLUTION

Note: When STP conditions are involved, 0°C and 760 mm are considered exact quantities. No bars are required over the zeros. These terms have no effect on the number of significant figures in the calculated result.

1. Correction for difference in levels:

$$742.0 \text{ mm} - 25.0 \text{ mm} = 717.0 \text{ mm}$$

2. Conversion of Celsius temperatures to Kelvin temperatures:

$$24°C + 273° = 297°K;\ 0°C + 273° = 273°K$$

3. Correction for change in pressure and temperature:

$$V' = V \times p/p' \times T'/T$$
$$V'_{STP} = 37.0 \text{ ml} \times 717.0 \text{ mm}/760 \text{ mm} \times 273°K/297°K$$
$$V'_{STP} = 32.1 \text{ ml}$$

10.14 Pressure of a gas collected by water displacement
In elementary work, gases are usually collected by water displacement rather than by mercury displacement. (Mercury is very expensive and poisonous.) Water is $\frac{1}{13.6}$ as dense as mercury. Therefore, a given gas pressure will support a column of water 13.6 times as high as an equivalent column of mercury (Figure 10-15). When a gas is collected by water displacement, pressure corrections are made just as with mercury displacement. *But a difference in water levels must first be divided by 13.6 to convert it to its equivalent height in terms of a column of mercury.*

In advanced work, gases are often collected by mercury displacement. The advantage of this method is that mercury does not evaporate measurably at room temperatures. When a gas is bubbled through water, however, the collected gas always has some water vapor mixed with it. Water vapor, like other gases, exerts pressure. Since the gas pressure is the result of the collision of the various gas molecules with the walls of the container, *the total pressure of the mixture of gases* (the collected gas and the water vapor) *is the sum of their partial pressures.* This is a statement of ***Dalton's law of partial pressures.*** The partial pressure is the pressure each gas would exert if it alone were present. The partial pressure of the water vapor, called *water vapor pressure,* depends only on the temperature of the water. Table 8 in the Appendix, gives the pressure of water vapor at different water temperatures. *To determine the partial pressure of the dry gas* (unmixed with water vapor), *the vapor pressure of water at the given temperature is subtracted from the total pressure of the gas within the tube.*

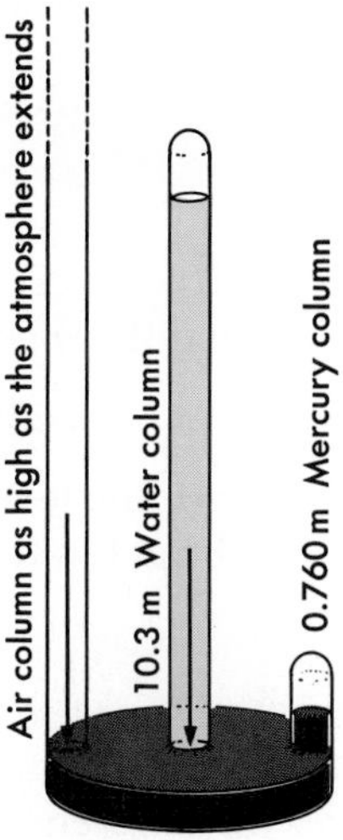

Fig. 10-15. The pressure of the atmosphere supports a column of water 13.6 times as high as the column of mercury it supports.

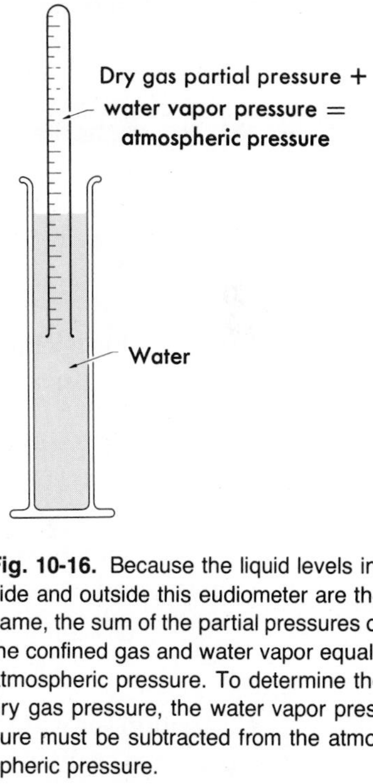

Fig. 10-16. Because the liquid levels inside and outside this eudiometer are the same, the sum of the partial pressures of the confined gas and water vapor equals atmospheric pressure. To determine the dry gas pressure, the water vapor pressure must be subtracted from the atmospheric pressure.

SAMPLE PROBLEM

Oxygen is collected in a eudiometer by water displacement. The water level inside the tube is 27.2 mm higher than that outside. The temperature is 25.0°C. The barometric pressure is 741.0 mm. What is the partial pressure of the dry oxygen in the eudiometer?

SOLUTION

To convert the difference in water levels to an equivalent difference in mercury levels, the difference in water levels is divided by 13.6.

27.2 mm ÷ 13.6 = 2.0 mm, the equivalent difference in mercury levels

Since the level inside the tube is higher than that outside, the difference in levels must be subtracted from the barometric pressure.

741.0 mm − 2.0 mm = 739.0 mm

To correct for the water vapor pressure, Table 8 in the Appendix, indicates that the water vapor pressure at 25.0°C is 23.8 mm. This must be subtracted from the pressure corrected for difference in levels.

739.0 mm − 23.8 mm = 715.2 mm, the partial pressure of the dry oxygen

SAMPLE PROBLEM

A gas-measuring tube contains 38.4 ml of air, collected by water displacement at a temperature of 20.0°C. The water level inside the eudiometer is $14\bar{0}$ mm higher than that outside. The barometer reading is 740.0 mm. Calculate the volume of dry air at STP. (See Figure 10-17 at the top of the next page.)

SOLUTION

Note that in this problem we were able to measure the barometric pressure to the nearest 0.1 mm, while we measured the water level difference to the nearest unit millimeter.

1. Correction for difference in levels:

$14\bar{0}$ mm ÷ 13.6 = 10.3 mm

Since the water level inside is higher than that outside, the air is under pressure less than atmospheric, and the correction is subtracted:

740.0 mm − 10.3 mm = 729.7 mm

2. Correction for water vapor pressure: Table 8 in the Appendix, indicates that the water vapor pressure at 20.0°C is 17.5 mm. This correction is subtracted:

729.7 mm − 17.5 mm = 712.2 mm

3. Correction for pressure and temperature changes:

$$V' = V \times p/p' \times T'/T$$
$$V'_{STP} = 38.4 \text{ ml} \times 712.2 \text{ mm}/760 \text{ mm} \times 273°\text{K}/293°\text{K}$$
$$V'_{STP} = 33.5 \text{ ml}$$

10.15 Behavior of real gases

Boyle's and Charles' laws describe the behavior of the *ideal gas.* Real gases consist of molecules of finite size which do exert forces on each other. These forces affect the behavior of the molecules. But at temperatures near room temperature and at pressures of less than a few atmospheres, real gases conform closely to the behavior of an ideal gas. Under these conditions of temperature and pressure, the spaces separating the molecules are large enough so that the size of the molecules and forces between them have little effect.

Boyle's law applies to real gases with a fairly high degree of accuracy. But it does not apply to gases under very high pressure. Under such pressures the molecules are close enough together to attract each other, and the gas is almost at its condensation point.

Charles' law holds for real gases with considerable accuracy, except at low temperature. Under this condition, gas molecules move more slowly and molecular attraction exerts a greater influence. Thus, Charles' law does not apply at temperatures near the point at which a gas condenses into a liquid.

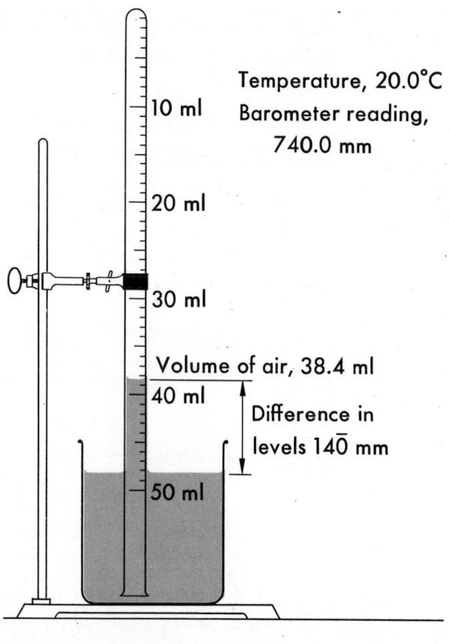

Fig. 10-17. A typical laboratory setup for a gas-volume conversion problem.

SUMMARY

The kinetic theory helps explain the properties of gases, liquids, and solids in terms of the forces between the particles of matter and the energy these particles possess. The three basic assumptions of the kinetic theory are: (*1*) matter is composed of very tiny particles; (*2*) the particles of matter are in continual motion; and (*3*) the total kinetic energy of colliding particles remains constant.

Gases have four characteristic properties: expansion, pressure, low density, and diffusion. These may be explained by describing the motion of the widely spaced particles in a gas.

The attractive forces between molecules are van der Waals forces. These are of two types: dispersion interaction, which exists between all molecules; and dipole-dipole interaction, which exists between polar molecules only.

If the volume that a certain number of gas molecules occupies remains constant, the pressure exerted by the gas increases as its temperature increases. If the pressure exerted by this number of gas molecules remains the same as the temperature is increased, the volume that the gas occupies increases. If the temperature of these gas molecules remains constant, the pressure exerted by the gas increases if its volume becomes smaller. Gas volumes are related to the temperature and pressure of the gas.

Standard temperature is zero degrees Celsius. Standard pressure is the pressure exerted by a column of mercury exactly 760 millimeters high. The temperature of a gas is measured by means of a thermometer, and its pressure is measured using a barometer. When a gas is collected over water, some water vapor becomes mixed with the gas. The amount of pressure due to water vapor varies according to the temperature.

Boyle's law: The volume of a definite quantity of dry gas is inversely proportional to the pressure, provided the temperature remains constant. Jacques Charles found that all gases expand or contract at the same rate. Gases expand $\frac{1}{273}$ of the volume at 0°C for each Celsius degree the temperature is raised. The lowest possible temperature is −273°C. The Kelvin temperature scale has its 0°K reading at −273°C. The readings on the Kelvin scale are 273 degrees higher than on the Celsius scale. Charles' law: The volume of a definite quantity of dry gas varies directly with the Kelvin temperature, provided the pressure remains constant. Boyle's law and Charles' law may be combined in the formula $V' = V \times p/p' \times T'/T$.

QUESTIONS

Group A

1. What are the three basic assumptions of the kinetic theory?
2. Why does the pressure of a gas in a closed vessel remain constant indefinitely under constant conditions?
3. (*a*) What is the relationship between the temperature of a gas and the kinetic energy of its molecules? (*b*) Do gas molecules all have exactly the same kinetic energy at the same temperature? Explain.
4. (*a*) What is the condensation temperature of a gas? (*b*) What occurs at this temperature? (*c*) Explain in terms of the kinetic theory.
5. What two types of attractive forces may exist between the molecules of molecular substances? Explain each.
6. Why is the term "a cubic meter of air" unsatisfactory?
7. (*a*) What is standard temperature? (*b*) What is standard pressure?
8. State Boyle's law (*a*) in words; (*b*) mathematically.
9. (*a*) What is the Celsius temperature corresponding to 0°K? (*b*) How does any Celsius temperature compare with the corresponding Kelvin temperature?
10. State Charles' law (*a*) in words; (*b*) mathematically.
11. If some hydrogen gas is enclosed in a eudiometer, what are three possibilities concerning its pressure compared with that of the air in the room?

Group B

12. In terms of the kinetic theory explain (*a*) expansion; (*b*) pressure; (*c*) low density; (*d*) diffusion; of a gas.
13. If we assume that the molecules of a solid or a liquid are in contact with each other but those of a gas are about 10 diameters apart, why is the volume occupied by a gas about 1000 times that of the solid or liquid?
14. Compare the strength of the attractive forces between the particles of nonpolar covalent molecular substances and polar covalent molecular substances as indicated by their condensation temperatures.
15. Compare the strength of the attractive forces between the particles of molecular substances and the particles of ionic, covalent network, and metallic substances, as indicated by their condensation temperatures.
16. At constant volume, how is the pressure exerted by a gas related to the Kelvin temperature?
17. At constant pressure, how is the volume occupied by a gas related to the Kelvin temperature?
18. At constant temperature, how is the volume occupied by a gas related to its pressure?
19. (*a*) What is meant by the vapor pressure of water? (*b*) What effect does it have on the observed pressure of a gas collected by water displacement? (*c*) How is the

observed pressure corrected to obtain the partial pressure of the dry gas?

20. What corrections are applied to the barometer reading: (*a*) gas collected by displacement of mercury, level inside the eudiometer the same as that outside; (*b*) gas collected by displacement of mercury, level inside eudiometer higher than that outside; (*c*) gas collected by displacement of water, level inside eudiometer same as that outside; (*d*) gas collected by displacement of water, level inside eudiometer higher than that outside?
21. Boyle's and Charles' laws describe the behavior of the ideal gas. Under what conditions do they describe the behavior of real gases?
22. Explain what makes the hot air balloon that is shown on page 187 rise? (*Hint:* Your answer should include the concept of density.)

PROBLEMS

Group A

Use cancellation whenever possible.

1. Some oxygen occupies $25\bar{0}$ ml when its pressure is $72\bar{0}$ mm. How many milliliters will it occupy when its pressure is $75\bar{0}$ mm?
2. A gas collected when the pressure is $80\bar{0}$ mm has a volume of $38\bar{0}$ ml. What volume, in milliliters, will the gas occupy at standard pressure?
3. A gas has a volume of $10\bar{0}$ ml when the pressure is 735 mm. How many milliliters will the gas occupy at $70\bar{0}$ mm pressure?
4. A gas has a volume of 240.0 ml at 70.0 cm pressure. What pressure, in centimeters of mercury, is needed to reduce the volume to 60.0 ml?
5. Convert the following temperatures to Kelvin scale: (*a*) $2\bar{0}$°C; (*b*) 85°C; (*c*) −15°C; (*d*) $-19\bar{0}$°C.
6. Given 90.0 ml of hydrogen gas collected when the temperature is 27°C, how many milliliters will the hydrogen occupy at 42°C?
7. A gas has a volume of $18\bar{0}$ ml when its temperature is 43°C. What change in Celsius temperature reduces its volume to 135 ml?
8. A gas measures $50\bar{0}$ ml at a temperature of −23°C. What will be its volume in milliliters at 23°C?
9. A sample of gas occupies 50.0 liters at 27°C. What will be the volume of the gas in liters at standard temperature?
10. Convert to standard conditions: 2280 ml of gas measured at $3\bar{0}$°C and 808 mm pressure.
11. Convert to standard conditions: $10\bar{0}0$ ml of gas at −23°C and $70\bar{0}$ mm pressure.
12. Convert to standard conditions: 1520 ml of gas at −33°C and $72\bar{0}$ mm pressure.
13. A gas collected when the temperature is 27°C and the pressure is 80.0 cm measures $50\bar{0}$ ml. Calculate the volume in milliliters at −3°C and 75.0 cm pressure.
14. Given $10\bar{0}$ ml of gas measured at 17°C and $38\bar{0}$ mm pressure, what volume, in milliliters, will the gas occupy at 307°C and $50\bar{0}$ mm pressure?

Use logarithms, a slide rule, or a calculator, as directed by your instructor.

Group B

15. Hydrogen, 35.0 ml, was collected in a eudiometer by displacement of mer-

cury. The mercury level inside the eudiometer was $4\bar{0}$ mm higher than that outside. The temperature was 25°C and the barometric pressure was 740.0 mm. Convert the volume of hydrogen to STP.

16. A gas collected by displacement of mercury in an inverted graduated cylinder occupies 60.0 ml. The mercury level inside the cylinder is 25 mm higher than that outside; temperature, $2\bar{0}$°C; barometer reading, 715 mm. Convert the volume of gas to STP.
17. Hydrogen is collected by water displacement in a eudiometer. Gas volume, 25.0 ml; liquid levels inside and outside the eudiometer are the same; temperature, 17°C; barometer reading, 720.0 mm. Convert the volume to that of dry gas at STP.
18. Some nitrogen is collected by displacement of water in a gas-measuring tube. Gas volume, 45.0 ml; liquid levels inside and outside the gas-measuring tube are the same; temperature, 23°C; barometer reading, 732.0 mm. Convert the volume to that of dry gas at STP.
19. A volume of 50.0 ml of oxygen is collected by water displacement. The water level inside the eudiometer is 65 mm higher than that outside. Temperature, 25°C; barometer reading, 727.0 mm. Convert the volume to that of dry gas at STP.
20. At 18°C and 745.0 mm barometric pressure, 12.0 ml of hydrogen is collected by water displacement. The liquid level inside the gas-measuring tube is 95 mm higher than that outside. Convert the volume to that of dry gas at STP.
21. The density of carbon dioxide at STP is 1.98 g/liter. What is the mass of exactly one liter of the gas, if the pressure increases by $4\bar{0}$ mm of mercury?
22. The density of oxygen at STP is 1.43 g/liter. Find the mass of exactly one liter of oxygen at a temperature of 39°C, if the pressure remains unchanged.
23. The density of nitrogen is 1.25 g/liter at STP. Find the mass of exactly one liter of nitrogen at a temperature of 27°C and at a pressure of 90.0 cm of mercury.
24. A gas measures $40\bar{0}$ ml at a temperature of 25°C, under a pressure of $80\bar{0}$ mm. To what Celsius temperature must the gas be cooled, if its volume is to be reduced to $35\bar{0}$ ml when the pressure falls to $74\bar{0}$ mm?

chapter 11

MOLECULAR COMPOSITION OF GASES

Avogadro's number is an important constant in chemistry. (See Problem 44 on page 244.)

11.1 Law of combining volumes of gases

In Chapter 2, you read that the observations made by Proust led to the law of definite composition. Dalton worked with masses of combining substances, and by using the law of definite composition, developed his atomic theory. Meanwhile, the Swedish chemist Berzelius was improving methods of chemical analysis. At this same time, the French chemist Joseph Louis Gay-Lussac experimented with gaseous substances. He was particularly interested in measuring and comparing the volumes of gases that react with each other. He also measured and compared the volumes of any gaseous products.

Gay-Lussac investigated the reaction between hydrogen and oxygen. He observed that 2 liters of hydrogen reacted with 1 liter of oxygen and formed 2 liters of water vapor, when the volumes of reactants and products were measured at the same temperature and pressure.

2 liters hydrogen + 1 liter oxygen → 2 liters water vapor

We can write this equation in a more general form to show the simple relationship between the volumes of the reactants and the volume of the product.

2 volumes hydrogen + 1 volume oxygen → 2 volumes water vapor

Gay-Lussac also found that 1 liter of hydrogen combined with 1 liter of chlorine and formed 2 liters of hydrogen chloride gas.

1 volume hydrogen + 1 volume chlorine → 2 volumes hydrogen chloride

From a third experiment, Gay-Lussac discovered that 1 liter of hydrogen chloride combined with 1 liter of ammonia and produced a white powder. No hydrogen chloride or ammonia remained.

1 volume hydrogen chloride + 1 volume ammonia → ammonium chloride(s)

Another French chemist, Claude Louis Berthollet (1748–1822), recognized a similar relationship in experiments with hydrogen and nitrogen. He found that 3 liters of hydrogen always combined with 1 liter of nitrogen and formed 2 liters of ammonia.

3 volumes hydrogen + 1 volume nitrogen → 2 volumes ammonia

In 1808, Gay-Lussac summarized the results of these experiments and stated the principle that bears his name. ***Gay-Lussac's law of combining volumes of gases*** *states: Under the same conditions of temperature and pressure, the volumes of reacting gases and of their gaseous products are expressed in ratios of small whole numbers.*

Proust had demonstrated the definite proportion of elements in a compound. Dalton's atomic theory had explained this regularity in the composition of substances. However, Dalton pictured an atom of one element combining with an atom of another element and forming a single particle of the product. He could not explain why *one* volume of hydrogen reacted with *one* volume of chlorine and formed *two* volumes of hydrogen chloride gas. To explain this volume relationship according to Dalton's theory would require that atoms be subdivided. Dalton had described the atoms of elements as "ultimate particles" and not capable of subdivision. Here was a disagreement between Dalton's theory and Gay-Lussac's observations. Was there an explanation to resolve the difficulty?

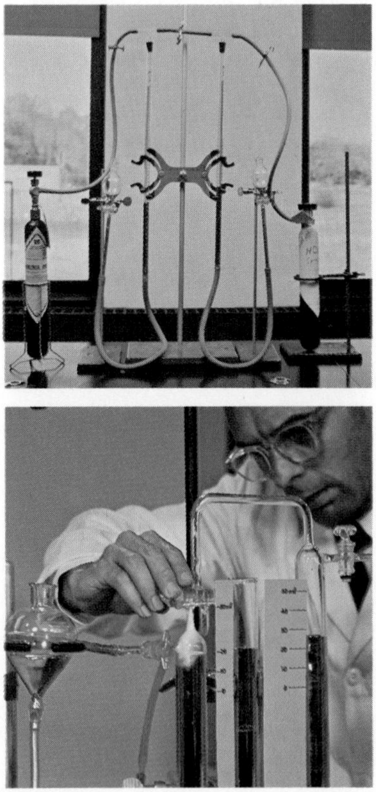

Fig. 11-1. (Top) Measured volumes of gases can be combined in an apparatus such as this. One volume of hydrogen chloride gas combines completely with one volume of ammonia gas, confirming Gay-Lussac's law. Ammonium chloride is the white cloud visible in the measuring tube (bottom).

11.2 Avogadro's principle

Avogadro proposed a possible explanation for Gay-Lussac's simple ratios of combining gases in 1811. This explanation was to become one of the basic principles of chemistry, although its importance was not understood until after Avogadro's death.

Avogadro's explanation was that *equal volumes of all gases, under the same conditions of temperature and pressure, contain the same number of molecules.* Avogadro decided upon this believable explanation after studying the behavior of gases. He immediately saw its application to Gay-Lussac's volume ratios.

Avogadro further reasoned that the numbers of molecules of all gases, as reactants and products, *must be in the same ratio as their respective gas volumes.* Thus the composition of water vapor

2 volumes hydrogen + 1 volume oxygen → 2 volumes water vapor

could be represented as 2 molecules of hydrogen combining with 1 molecule of oxygen and producing 2 molecules of water vapor.

2 molecules hydrogen + 1 molecule oxygen → 2 molecules water vapor
(Equation 1)

Avogadro saw that the oxygen molecules must somehow be equally divided between the two molecules of water vapor formed. *Thus, each molecule of oxygen must consist of* ***at least*** *two identical parts (atoms).* Avogadro did not reject the atoms of Dalton. He merely stated that they did not exist as independent basic particles. Instead, he said, they were grouped into molecules that consisted of two identical parts. The simplest such molecule would, of course, contain two atoms.

Avogadro's reasoning applied equally well to the combining volumes in the composition of hydrogen chloride gas.

1 volume hydrogen + 1 volume chlorine → 2 volumes hydrogen chloride

1 molecule hydrogen + 1 molecule chlorine → 2 molecules hydrogen chloride
(Equation 2)

Each molecule of hydrogen must consist of two identical parts. One of these parts is found after the reaction in each of the two molecules of hydrogen chloride. Likewise, each chlorine molecule must consist of two identical parts. One of these parts is found in each of the two molecules of hydrogen chloride.

By Avogadro's explanation, the simplest molecules of hydrogen, oxygen, and chlorine each contain two atoms. The simplest possible molecule of water contains two atoms of hydrogen and one atom of oxygen. The simplest molecule of hydrogen chloride contains one atom of hydrogen and one atom of chlorine.

The correctness of Avogadro's explanation is so well recognized today that it has become known as ***Avogadro's principle.*** It is supported by the kinetic theory of gases. Chemists use it widely in determining molecular weights and molecular formulas.

11.3 Molecules of active gaseous elements are diatomic

By applying Avogadro's principle to Gay-Lussac's law of combining volumes of gases, we can find out the simplest possible makeup of elemental gases. But we also need to know whether the simplest structure of an elemental gas is the correct one. To do this, we must determine the molecular formula for the product of each composition reaction described so far. In Sections 7.12 and 7.13, we discussed empirical and molecular formulas. You will recall that an empirical formula can be determined from percentage composition data obtained by chemical analysis. The molecular formula can then be calculated if the molecular weight is known. We can determine the molecular weights of gases from their densities. We can find the molecular weights of solids and liquids that exist as molecules by measuring the freezing or boiling temperatures of their solutions.

Chemists have analyzed hydrogen chloride gas and, with the aid of atomic weights, have determined its empirical formula to be HCl. The molecular formula could be the same as the empirical formula or it could be any multiple of the empirical formula such as H_2Cl_2, H_3Cl_3, etc. To decide which formula is correct, chemists must experimentally determine the molecular weight. By measuring the density of hydrogen chloride, they have found its molecular weight to be 36.5. So the molecular formula must be HCl. The weight of one atom of hydrogen is 1.0 and the weight of one atom of chlorine is 35.5, giving a calculated molecular weight of 36.5. Any other multiple of the empirical formula gives a calculated molecular weight that is too high compared to the molecular weight determined experimentally. Thus, a molecule of hydrogen chloride contains *only one* atom of hydrogen and *only one* atom of chlorine.

Equation 2 in Section 11-2 indicates that two molecules of hydrogen chloride (2HCl) are formed from one molecule of hydrogen and one molecule of chlorine. But 2HCl contains two atoms of hydrogen. These must have been provided by the one molecule of hydrogen reactant. Therefore this molecule must be a two-atomed, or *diatomic*, molecule, H_2. Similarly, 2HCl contains two atoms of chlorine which must have been provided by the one molecule of chlorine reactant. This chlorine molecule must therefore be a diatomic molecule, Cl_2. We may write the equation correctly as

$$\mathbf{H_2 + Cl_2 \rightarrow 2HCl}$$

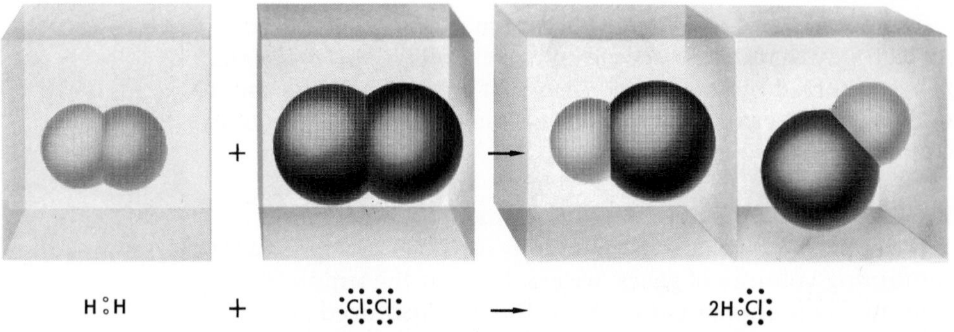

Fig. 11-2. As HCl is known to be the correct molecular formula for hydrogen chloride gas, the molecules of hydrogen and chlorine are proved to be diatomic.

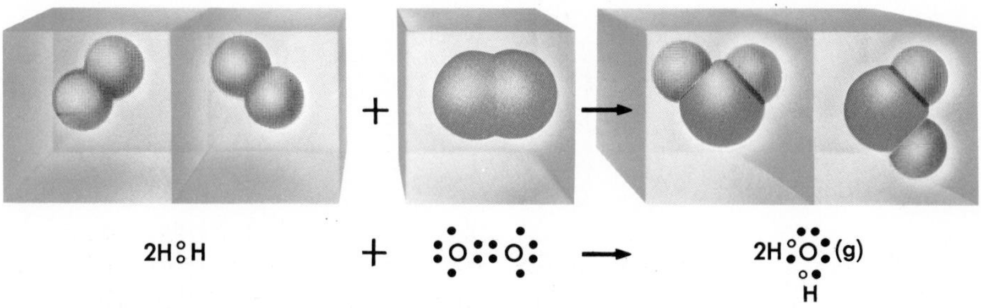

Fig. 11-3. The correct molecular formula for water vapor is H_2O. Applying Avogadro's principle to the gas volumes observed by Gay-Lussac shows that hydrogen and oxygen molecules are diatomic.

Similarly, oxygen molecules are proved to be diatomic because H_2O is the known molecular formula of water vapor.

$$2H_2 + O_2 \rightarrow 2H_2O$$

Let us examine one additional gaseous reaction. Berthollet found that *3 volumes* of hydrogen combined with *1 volume* of nitrogen and formed *2 volumes* of ammonia. By Avogadro's principle we conclude that *3 molecules* of hydrogen combine with *1 molecule* of nitrogen and form *2 molecules* of ammonia. Analysis of ammonia reveals that it is composed of 82% nitrogen and 18% hydrogen. The atomic weights of nitrogen and hydrogen are 14 and 1.0, respectively. The molecular weight of ammonia is known from gas density measurements to be 17.0. Therefore, the molecular formula is determined as follows:

At this point, you may wish to review the calculations explained in Sections 7.12 and 7.13.

$$\text{N}: \frac{82 \text{ g N}}{14 \text{ g/mole}} = 5.9 \text{ moles N}$$

$$\text{H}: \frac{18 \text{ g H}}{1.0 \text{ g/mole}} = 18 \text{ moles H}$$

$$\text{N}:\text{H} = \frac{5.9}{5.9} : \frac{18}{5.9} = 1.0 : 3.0$$

$$\begin{aligned} \text{Empirical formula} &= NH_3 \\ \text{Molecular formula} &= (NH_3)_x \\ \text{and } (NH_3 \text{ weight})_x &= 17.0 \\ \text{thus } \quad x &= 1 \\ \text{Molecular formula} &= NH_3 \end{aligned}$$

Since each molecule of NH_3 contains 1 nitrogen atom, the 2 molecules of NH_3 produced must contain a total of 2 nitrogen atoms. Therefore, 2 nitrogen atoms must come from the 1 molecule of nitrogen reactant. Again the 2 molecules of NH_3 produced must contain a total of 6 hydrogen atoms. Therefore, these 6 atoms must come from the 3 molecules of hydrogen reactant. We may summarize these relations as follows:

$$\text{3 volumes hydrogen} + \text{1 volume nitrogen} \rightarrow \text{2 volumes ammonia}$$

$$\text{3 molecules hydrogen} + \text{1 molecule nitrogen} \rightarrow \text{2 molecules ammonia}$$

$$3H_2 + N_2 \rightarrow 2NH_3$$

Both nitrogen and hydrogen molecules are diatomic.

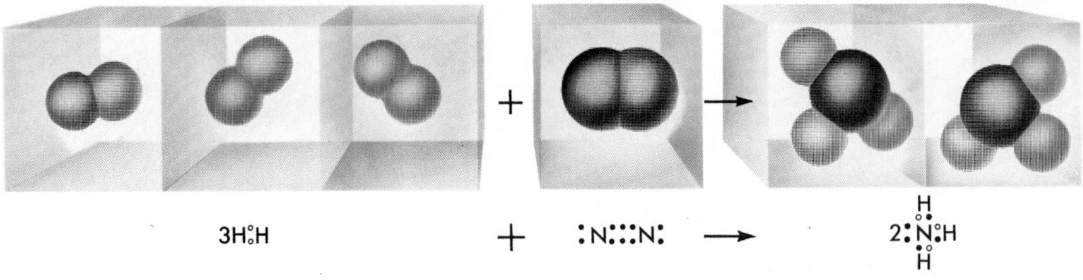

Fig. 11-4. Application of Avogadro's principle to Gay-Lussac's combining volumes shows that molecules of elemental gas reactants are diatomic.

11.4 Molecules of the noble gases are monatomic

Particles of matter were described in Section 6.24.

By using the methods described in the preceding sections, we can show that the molecules of all *ordinary* gaseous elements contain *two* atoms. Other methods have shown that the *noble* gaseous elements, such as helium and neon, have only *one* atom to each molecule. None of these methods applies to solids and may not even apply to the vapors of certain elements that are liquid or solid at room temperature. For example, at high temperatures the molecules of mercury and iodine vapors are known to consist of only one atom each.

11.5 Molar volume of a gas

The Avogadro number and the mole were explained in Section 3.13.

Oxygen gas consists of diatomic molecules. One mole of $\mathbf{O_2}$ contains the Avogadro number of molecules (6.02×10^{23}) and has a mass of 31.9988 g. One mole of $\mathbf{H_2}$ contains the same number of molecules and has a mass of 2.016 g. Helium is a monatomic gas. One mole of **He** contains the Avogadro number of monatomic molecules and has a mass of 4.003 g. One-mole quantities of all molecular substances contain the Avogadro number of molecules.

Recall from Section 10.6 that STP means standard temperature and pressure.

The volume occupied by one mole (or by one gram-molecular weight) of a gas at STP is called its ***molar volume.*** Since moles of gases all have the same numbers of molecules, Avogadro's principle tells us that they must occupy equal volumes under the same conditions of temperature and pressure. *The molar volumes of all gases are equal under the same conditions.* This has great practical significance in chemistry. Let us see how the molar volume of gases may be determined.

The densities of gases represent the masses of *equal numbers* of their respective molecules measured at STP. Since different gases have different densities, the mass of an *individual molecule* of one gas must be different from the mass of an individual molecule of a different gas.

Density was defined in Section 1.10 as mass per unit volume.

The density of hydrogen is 0.0899 gram/liter, measured at STP. A mole of hydrogen, or 1 g-mol wt of hydrogen, has a mass of 2.016 g. (G-mol wt is an abbreviation for gram-molecular weight.) Since 0.0899 g of H_2 occupies 1 liter volume at STP, what volume will 2.016 g of H_2 occupy under the same conditions? The molar volume expressed in liters bears the same relation to 1 liter as 2.016 g bears to 0.0899 g. This proportionality may be expressed as follows:

$$\frac{\textbf{molar volume of } \mathbf{H_2}}{\textbf{1 liter}} = \frac{\textbf{2.016 g}}{\textbf{0.0899 g}}$$

Solving for molar volume,

$$\textbf{molar volume of } \mathbf{H_2} = \frac{\textbf{2.016 g} \times \textbf{1 liter}}{\textbf{0.0899 g}}$$

$$\textbf{molar volume of } \mathbf{H_2} = \textbf{22.4 liters}$$

The density of oxygen is 1.43 grams/liter. A mole of oxygen has a mass of 31.9988 g. Following our reasoning in the case of hydrogen, we may compute the molar volume of O_2.

$$\frac{\textbf{molar volume of } \mathbf{O_2}}{\textbf{1 liter}} = \frac{\textbf{32.0 g}}{\textbf{1.43 g}}$$

$$\textbf{molar volume of } \mathbf{O_2} = \frac{\textbf{32.0 g} \times \textbf{1 liter}}{\textbf{1.43 g}}$$

$$\textbf{molar volume of } \mathbf{O_2} = \textbf{22.4 liters}$$

Fig. 11-5. Hydrogen is used to fill this stratosphere balloon because it is less dense than air. Such balloons carry instruments to altitudes of 100,000 feet or higher for astronomical observations, cosmic-ray measurements, and chemical sampling of the ozone layer.

Computations with other gases would yield similar results. However, it is clear from Avogadro's principle that this is unnecessary. We may generalize the proportion used above to read as follows:

$$\frac{\textbf{1 molar volume}}{\textbf{1 liter}} = \frac{\textbf{g-mol wt}}{\textbf{mass of 1 liter}}$$

Transposing terms,

$$\frac{\textbf{mass of 1 liter}}{\textbf{1 liter}} = \frac{\textbf{g-mol wt}}{\textbf{1 molar volume}}$$

But

$$\frac{\textbf{mass of 1 liter}}{\textbf{1 liter}} = \textbf{density } (\boldsymbol{D}) \textbf{ of a gas}$$

and

$$\textbf{1 molar volume} = \textbf{22.4 liters}$$

So

$$\boldsymbol{D} \textbf{ (of a gas)} = \frac{\textbf{g-mol wt}}{\textbf{22.4 liters}}$$

and

$$\textbf{g-mol wt} = \boldsymbol{D} \times \textbf{22.4 liters}$$

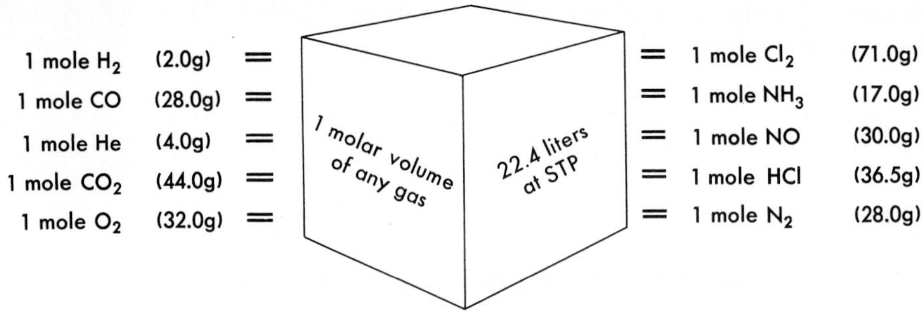

Fig. 11-6. At STP, 22.4 liters of all gases have the same number of molecules, and the mass of each volume in grams is numerically equal to its molecular weight.

Thus, the *gram-molecular weight* (mass in grams of one mole) *of a gaseous substance is the mass, in grams, of 22.4 liters of the gas measured at STP.* In other words, it is simply the density of the gas multiplied by the constant, 22.4 liters. Similarly, the density of a gas can be found by dividing its gram-molecular weight by the constant, 22.4 liters.

If we know the molecular formula for a gas, we can determine its density directly from the formula. Let us use sulfur dioxide, SO_2, as an example. The mass of one mole of SO_2 is 64.1 g. Thus

$$D_{SO_2} = \frac{\textbf{64.1 grams}}{\textbf{22.4 liters}} = \textbf{2.86 grams/liter at STP}$$

11.6 Molecular weight of gases determined experimentally The molecular weights of gases, or of the vapors of substances that vaporize without decomposition, can be determined by the *molar-volume method.*

Conversion of a gas volume at given conditions to STP was explained in Section 10.14.

It is generally impractical in the laboratory to weigh directly a molar volume (22.4 liters) of a gas or vapor at STP. Indeed, some substances, otherwise suitable for this method, are liquids or even solids under STP conditions. Fortunately, we need not weigh a full molar volume of a gas or vapor to find its molecular weight. Any quantity of a gas or vapor that can be weighed to determine its mass precisely may be used. Its volume may be measured under any suitable conditions of temperature and pressure. This volume is then converted to STP and the mass of 22.4 liters is calculated. The Sample Problem shows how this experimental method is used to determine molecular weight.

SAMPLE PROBLEM

A gas sample, mass 0.350 g, is collected by water displacement at $2\bar{0}$°C and $75\bar{0}$ mm pressure. Its volume is $15\bar{0}$ ml. What is the molecular weight of the gas?

SOLUTION

Correction for water vapor pressure: From Table 8 in the Appendix, the water vapor pressure at $2\bar{0}$°C is 17.5 mm. This water vapor pressure is subtracted from the barometric pressure to obtain the pressure of the dry gas.

$$\mathbf{7\bar{5}0\ mm - 17.5\ mm = 732\ mm}$$

Conversion of Celsius temperatures to Kelvin temperatures:

$$\mathbf{2\bar{0}°C + 273° = 293°K;\ 0°C + 273° = 273°K}$$

Correction for pressure and temperature changes:

$$V' = V \times p/p' \times T'/T$$

$$V'_{\text{STP}} = 15\bar{0}\ \text{ml} \times \frac{732\ \text{mm}}{760\ \text{mm}} \times \frac{273°\text{K}}{293°\text{K}}$$

$$V'_{\text{STP}} = 135\ \text{ml, or } 0.135\ \text{liter}$$

The quantity of 0.350 g per 0.135 liter at STP is an expression of the density of the gas and may be substituted for it. Thus

$$\text{g-mol wt} = D \times 22.4\ \text{liters}$$

$$\text{g-mol wt} = \frac{0.350\ \text{gram}}{0.135\ \text{liter}} \times 22.4\ \text{liters}$$

$$\text{g-mol wt} = 58.1\ \text{g}$$

$$\text{mol wt} = 58.1$$

We can also calculate the volume occupied by a known mass of a gas under any conditions of temperature and pressure, if we know the molecular formula of the gas. The molecular formula provides the mass of 1 mole of the gas. We know that one mole of any gas occupies the molar volume, 22.4 liters, at STP. By proportion, we can determine the volume of the known mass of the gas at STP. Then by applying the gas laws, we can compute the volume at any temperature and pressure. See the following Sample Problem.

SAMPLE PROBLEM

What is the volume of $1\bar{0}$ g of carbon dioxide gas, CO_2, at $2\bar{0}$°C and 740 mm?

SOLUTION

The formula CO_2 indicates that the molecular weight is 44. Now 44 g (1 mole) of CO_2 occupies 22.4 liters (1 molar volume) at STP. The volume occupied by 10 g will be represented as X.

$$\frac{44\ \text{g}}{22.4\ \text{liters}} = \frac{1\bar{0}\ \text{g}}{\text{X}}$$

Solving for X,

$$\text{X} = 1\bar{0}\ \text{g} \times \frac{22.4\ \text{liters}}{44\ \text{g}} = 5.1\ \text{liters, at STP}$$

Correction for pressure and temperature changes:

$$V' = V \times p/p' \times T'/T$$

$$V'_{2\bar{0}^\circ\text{C},\,740\,\text{mm}} = 5.1\ \text{liters} \times \frac{760\ \text{mm}}{740\ \text{mm}} \times \frac{293^\circ\text{K}}{273^\circ\text{K}}$$

$$V'_{2\bar{0}^\circ\text{C},\,740\,\text{mm}} = 5.6\ \text{liters}$$

11.7 Chemical problems involving gases

As shown in Section 8.1, the equation for a chemical reaction expresses quantities of reactants and products in *moles*. The numerical coefficients in the balanced equation tell us the number of moles of each substance.

Frequently, a reactant or a product of a reaction is a gas. Indeed in certain reactions, *all* reactants and products may be gaseous. Avogadro's principle indicates that single moles of all such gases have the same volume under the same conditions of temperature and pressure. At STP, a mole of any gas occupies 1 molar volume, 22.4 liters. *Consequently, the mole relationships in the equation are also the volume relationships of gases.*

Remember that the behavior of real gases is not described exactly by the ideal gas laws. Calculations that involve the molar volume as 22.4 liters can give only approximately correct answers.

There are two general types of problems that involve chemical equations and the volumes of gases.

1. ***Gas volume–gas volume problems.*** In these problems, a certain *volume of a gas* reactant or product is given. The *volume of another gas* reactant or product is required.

2. ***Mass–gas volume problems.*** Here a certain *mass* of a reactant or product is given and the *volume of a gas* reactant or product is required, or vice versa.

11.8 Gas volume–gas volume problems

The *volume* of one *gaseous substance* is given in gas volume-gas volume problems. In this type of problem, we are asked to determine the *volume* of another *gaseous substance* involved in the chemical action. We recall that single moles of all gases at the same temperature and pressure occupy the same volume. Thus, in a balanced equation, the volumes of gases are proportional to the number of moles shown by the numerical coefficients. To illustrate,

$2CO(g)$	+	$O_2(g)$	→	$2CO_2(g)$
2 moles		**1 mole**		**2 moles**
2 volumes		**1 volume**		**2 volumes**

The balanced equation signifies that 2 moles of CO reacts with 1 mole of O_2 and produces 2 moles of CO_2. From Avogadro's principle, 2 volumes (liters, milliliters, etc.) of carbon monoxide reacts with 1 volume (liter, milliliter, etc.) of oxygen and produces 2 volumes (liters, milliliters, etc.) of carbon dioxide. (In this relationship we assume, of course, that the temperature and pressure of all three gases are the same.) Thus, 10 liters of CO would require 5 liters of O_2 for complete combustion and would produce 10 liters of CO_2. The volume relationship is 2:1:2 under the same conditions of temperature and pressure.

Since the above reaction is exothermic, the gas that is produced expands because of the rise in temperature. The volume relations apply only after the temperature of the gaseous product has been lowered to that of the reactants at the beginning of the reaction.

We must know the conditions of temperature and pressure in order to determine which substances exist as gases. Whenever the conditions are not stated, they are assumed to be standard. Let us consider the complete combustion of methane.

$CH_4(g)$	+	$2O_2(g)$	→	$CO_2(g)$	+	$2H_2O(l)$
1 mole		**2 moles**		**1 mole**		**2 moles**
1 volume		**2 volumes**		**1 volume**		

The formula for water is followed by the symbol (l) because water is a liquid at temperatures under 100°C. Let us assume that the volumes of the gaseous reactants are measured under ordinary room conditions. If so, water cannot be included in the volume ratio. But the reactants, methane and oxygen, and the product, carbon dioxide, are gases. Their volume relationship is seen to be 1:2:1.

Gas volume-gas volume problems are very simple to solve. The problem setup is similar to that of mass-mass problems (see Section 8.11). However, it is not necessary to use atomic weights to convert moles of the specified gases to their respective masses as represented in the equation. Once set up, most gas volume-gas volume problems can be solved by inspection. The following example shows how these problems are commonly solved.

Suppose we wish to know the volume of hydrogen that combines with 4.0 liters of nitrogen and forms ammonia gas. We set up the problem this way:

$$\begin{array}{ccc} X & 4.0 \text{ liters} & \\ 3H_2(g) + & N_2(g) & \rightarrow 2NH_3(g) \\ 3 \text{ moles} & 1 \text{ mole} & \end{array}$$

The equation shows that H_2 and N_2 combine in the ratio of 3 moles to 1 mole. From Avogadro's principle, these gases must combine in the ratio of 3 volumes to 1 volume. Thus, 4.0 liters of nitrogen requires 12 liters of hydrogen for complete reaction. Since 2 moles of NH_3 is shown, 8.0 liters of this gas is produced.

Mathematically, the problem may be set up

$$X = 4.0 \text{ liters } \cancel{N_2} \times \frac{3 \cancel{\text{ moles}} H_2}{1 \cancel{\text{ mole}} N_2}$$

Solving,

$$X = 12 \text{ liters } H_2$$

See the following Sample Problem.

SAMPLE PROBLEM

Assuming air to be 21.0% oxygen by volume: (*a*) How many liters of air must enter a carburetor to complete the combustion of 60.0 liters of octane vapor? (*b*) How many liters of carbon dioxide are formed? (All gases are measured at the same temperature and pressure.)

SOLUTION

Octane has the formula C_8H_{18}. Its complete combustion produces carbon dioxide and water. Note that it is only the *oxygen* of the air that reacts with octane. Therefore we must determine first the volume of oxygen required. Let X be this volume and Y the volume of CO_2 formed. The problem setup is

$$\begin{array}{cccc} 60.0 \text{ liters} & X & Y & \\ 2C_8H_{18}(g) + & 25O_2(g) & \rightarrow 16\,CO_2(g) & + 18H_2O(l) \\ 2 \text{ moles} & 25 \text{ moles} & 16 \text{ moles} & \end{array}$$

(*a*) Solving

$$X = 60.0 \text{ liters } \cancel{C_8H_{18}} \times \frac{25 \cancel{\text{ moles}} O_2}{2 \cancel{\text{ moles}} \cancel{C_8H_{18}}}$$

$$X = 7\bar{5}0 \text{ liters } O_2$$

Now $7\bar{5}0$ liters of O_2 is 21.0% of the air required. So

$$\text{air required} = 7\bar{5}0 \text{ liters} \times \frac{100\%}{21.0\%} = 3570 \text{ liters}$$

(*b*) Solving as before,

$$\mathbf{Y = 60.0\ liters\ \cancel{C_8H_{18}} \times \frac{16\ \cancel{moles}\ CO_2}{2\ \cancel{moles\ C_8H_{18}}}}$$

$$\mathbf{Y = 48\bar{0}\ liters\ CO_2}$$

Reminder: The volumes of air and CO_2 computed are those that would be measured at the temperature and pressure of the octane vapor prior to its combustion. Under such conditions, the water formed as water vapor at the reaction temperature would have condensed. Thus, it could not enter the problem as a gas.

11.9 Mass–gas volume problems

This type of problem involves the relation between the *volume of gas* and the *mass* of another substance in a reaction. In some cases, the mass of the substance is given and the volume of the gas is required. In others, the volume of the gas is given and the mass of the substance is required.

As an illustration, let us determine how many grams of calcium carbonate, $CaCO_3$, must be decomposed to produce 4.00 liters of carbon dioxide, CO_2, at STP. The problem setup is

$$\mathbf{\underset{1\ mole}{\overset{X}{CaCO_3(s)}} \rightarrow CaO(s) + \underset{1\ mole}{\overset{4.00\ liters}{CO_2(g)}}}$$

$$\mathbf{1\ mole\ CaCO_3 = 10\bar{0}\ g}$$
$$\mathbf{1\ mole\ CO_2 = 22.4\ liters}$$

Observe that the molar volume (22.4 liters) is used in place of the mass/mole (44 g/mole) of CO_2. This is possible since each mole of gas occupies 22.4 liters at STP (*and only at STP*). The problem may now be solved by the method used for mass-mass problems.

The volume of CO_2 multiplied by the fraction $\frac{\text{mole}}{22.4\text{ liters}}$ will indicate the number of moles of CO_2 given (operation 1):

$$\mathbf{4.00\ liters\ CO_2 \times \frac{mole}{22.4\ liters} = number\ of\ moles\ CO_2}$$

Then, after operations 2, 3, and 4 of the solution of a mass-mass problem,

The four operations in solving mass-mass problems are explained in Section 8.11.
1. Determine the number of moles of the substance given.
2. Determine the number of moles of the substance whose mass is required.
3. Determine the mass of the substance required.
4. Check the units; estimate the answer. Perform the arithmetic operations and compare the calculated result with the estimated one.

$$\mathbf{X = 4.00\ \cancel{liters}\ \cancel{CO_2} \times \frac{\cancel{mole}}{22.4\ \cancel{liters}} \times \frac{1\ \cancel{mole}\ CaCO_3}{1\ \cancel{mole}\ CO_2} \times \frac{10\bar{0}\ g}{\cancel{mole}} = 17.9\ g\ CaCO_3}$$

11.10 Gases not measured at STP

Gases are seldom measured under standard conditions of temperature and pressure. But *only* gas volumes under standard conditions can be placed in a proportion with the molar volume of 22.4 liters. Therefore, *gas reactants measured under conditions other than STP must first be corrected to STP before proceeding with mass-gas volume calculations.* These corrections are performed in agreement with the gas laws in Chapter 10.

For example, suppose that the gas in question is a *product* whose volume is to be measured under conditions other than STP. *We first must calculate the volume at STP from the chemical equation.* We then convert this volume at STP to the required conditions of temperature and pressure by proper application of the gas laws.

Gas volume-gas volume calculations do not require STP corrections since volumes of gases are related to moles rather than to molar volumes. Thus, in gas volume-gas volume problems, it is necessary only that all measurements of gas volumes be made at the same temperature and pressure.

11.11 Gases collected by water displacement

The volume of any gas in a mass-gas volume problem is calculated under STP conditions and must be corrected for any other specified conditions of temperature and pressure. If this gas is collected by water displacement, the vapor pressure of the water must be taken into account. The partial pressure of the gas is the difference between the measured pressure and the partial pressure exerted by water vapor at the specified temperature.

This type of calculation was explained in Section 10.14.

Let us suppose that a gaseous product is collected by water displacement. The volume of this product is to be determined at 29°C and 752 mm pressure by a mass-gas volume calculation. The volume at STP is computed from an appropriate chemical equation. The vapor pressure of water at 29°C is found in the tables to be $3\bar{0}$ mm. Thus

$$V_{29°\text{C}, 752\,\text{mm}} = V_{\text{STP}} \times \frac{760\ \text{mm}}{(752 - 3\bar{0})\ \text{mm}} \times \frac{302°\text{K}}{273°\text{K}}$$

See the Sample Problem that follows.

SAMPLE PROBLEM

What volume of oxygen, collected by water displacement at $2\bar{0}$°C and 750.0 mm pressure, can be obtained by the decomposition of 175 g of potassium chlorate?

SOLUTION

A mass is given and a gas volume is required. The volume of the gas at STP may first be found from the chemical equation. The problem setup is as follows:

This type of problem setup was described in Section 11.9.

$$\begin{array}{lcl} \textbf{175 g} & & \textbf{X} \\ 2KClO_3(s) \rightarrow 2KCl(s) + & & 3O_2(g) \\ \textbf{2 moles} & & \textbf{3 moles} \end{array}$$

$$1\ \text{mole}\ KClO_3 = 122.6\ \text{g}$$
$$1\ \text{mole}\ O_2 = 22.4\ \text{liters}$$

Solution by moles

$$\mathbf{X} = 175\ \text{g KClO}_3 \times \frac{\text{mole}}{122.6\ \text{g}} \times \frac{3\ \text{moles O}_2}{2\ \text{moles KClO}_3} \times \frac{22.4\ \text{liters}}{\text{mole}}$$

$$\mathbf{X} = 48.0\ \text{liters O}_2\ \text{at STP}$$

The vapor pressure of water at $2\bar{0}$°C is found to be 17.5 mm.

Correction for change in pressure and temperature:

$$V' = V \times p/p' \times T'/T$$

$$V'_{2\bar{0}°\text{C}, 750.0\ \text{mm}} = 48.0\ \text{liters} \times \frac{760\ \text{mm}}{750.0 - 17.5\ \text{mm}} \times \frac{293°\text{K}}{273°\text{K}}$$

$$V'_{2\bar{0}°\text{C}, 750.0\ \text{mm}} = 53.5\ \text{liters}$$

11.12 The gas constant

From Avogadro's principle, we know that the volume of a mole is the same for all gases under the same conditions of temperature and pressure. The volume of any gas is directly proportional to the number of moles (n) of the gas, if pressure and temperature are constant. The $\propto$ means "varies directly as."

Direct and inverse proportion are explained in Section MR9 in the Mathematics Refresher.

$$V \propto n \quad (p \text{ and } T \text{ constant})$$

From Boyle's law we know that the volume of a gas is inversely proportional to the pressure applied to it, if the quantity of gas (number of moles of gas) and temperature are constant. The inverse relationship is shown by placing the pressure in the denominator.

$$V \propto \frac{1}{p} \quad (n \text{ and } T \text{ constant})$$

Similarly, from Charles' law, we know that the volume of a gas is directly proportional to the Kelvin temperature, if the pressure and quantity of gas remain constant.

$$V \propto T \quad (p \text{ and } n \text{ constant})$$

Thus,

$$V \propto n \times \frac{1}{p} \times T$$

By inserting a proportionality constant R of suitable dimensions, this proportion may be restated as an equation.

$$V = nR\left(\frac{1}{p}\right)T$$

or

$$pV = nRT$$

The proportionality constant R is known as the *gas constant.* When the quantity of gas is expressed in moles, R has the same value for all gases. Usually the gas volume V is expressed in *liters*, the quantity n in *moles*, the temperature T in *degrees Kelvin*, and the pressure p in *atmospheres* (abbreviated atm). Of course, the standard pressure of 760 mm is *1 atmosphere*. So

$$\frac{\text{pressure in mm Hg}}{\text{760 mm Hg/atm}} = \text{pressure in atm}$$

Let us determine the dimensional units of the gas constant R from the ideal-gas equation.

$$pV = nRT$$

Solving for R,

$$R = \frac{pV}{nT}$$

Using the units stated,

$$R = \frac{\text{atm} \times \text{liters}}{\text{moles} \times {}^\circ\text{K}}$$

Thus, R must have the dimensions *liter · atm per mole · °K.*

Careful measurements of the density of oxygen at low pressures yield the molar volume of 22.414 liters. This is accepted as the accurate molar volume of an ideal gas. It represents the volume occupied by exactly 1 mole of ideal gas under conditions of exactly 1 atm and 273.15°K. Substituting in the ideal gas equation and solving the expression for R,

$$R = \frac{pV}{nT} = \frac{1 \text{ atm} \times 22.414 \text{ liters}}{1 \text{ mole} \times 273.15^\circ\text{K}}$$

$$R = 0.082057 \text{ liter} \cdot \text{atm/mole} \cdot {}^\circ\text{K}$$

Suppose the properties of an unknown gas are examined at a temperature of 28°C and $74\bar{0}$ mm pressure. It is found that the mass of 1 liter is 4.62 g under these conditions. We wish to determine the molecular weight of the gas. This calculation can be made directly by using the gas constant R, 0.0821 liter · atm per mole · °K, and the ideal-gas equation, $pV = nRT$. The use of R in the ideal-gas equation enables moles per liter of gas to be computed.

$$T = 273^\circ + 28^\circ\text{C} = 301^\circ\text{K}$$

$$V = 1 \text{ liter}$$

$$p = \frac{74\bar{0} \text{ mm}}{760 \text{ mm/atm}} = 0.974 \text{ atm}$$

$$pV = nRT$$

Solving for n moles,

$$n = \frac{pV}{RT}$$

$$n = \frac{0.974 \text{ atm} \times 1 \text{ liter}}{\frac{0.0821 \text{ liter} \cdot \text{atm}}{\text{mole} \cdot °\text{K}} \times 301°\text{K}}$$

$$n = \frac{0.974 \text{ mole}}{0.0821 \times 301} = 0.0394 \text{ mole}$$

This calculation shows that the experimental mass of 1 liter of the gas, 4.62 g, is 0.0394 mole.

Since 0.0394 mole has a mass of 4.62 g, the mass of 1 mole is

$$1 \text{ mole} \times \frac{4.62 \text{ g}}{0.0394 \text{ mole}} = 117 \text{ g}$$

Therefore, the molecular weight of the gas is 117.

The ideal-gas equation simplifies the solution of mass-gas volume problems under nonstandard conditions. The number of moles of gas required is calculated by the mole method. This result may then be substituted in the ideal-gas equation, together with the pressure and temperature conditions. The gas volume is then calculated directly. On the other hand, suppose we know the volume of a gas under nonstandard temperature and pressure conditions. We can then use the ideal-gas equation to calculate the *number of moles* of the gas. This quantity may then be used to complete the solution of a gas volume-mass problem by the mole method.

11.13 Real gases and the ideal gas

Precise experiments involving molar volumes of gases show that all gases vary slightly from the ideal-gas characteristics assigned to them by the gas laws and Avogadro's principle. This does not mean that the laws are only approximately true. Rather, it indicates that real gases do not behave as ideal gases over wide ranges of temperature and pressure. They act most like ideal gases at low pressures and high temperatures.

Two factors contribute to the difference between the behavior of real gases and our equations for an ideal gas:

1. Compression of a gas is *limited* by the fact that the molecules themselves occupy space, even though the volume of the molecules is extremely small.

The behavior of real gases was described earlier in Section 10.15.

2. Compression of a gas is *aided* by the fact that van der Waals (attractive) forces, however weak, do exist between the molecules. Only when these two opposing tendencies within the gas exactly balance, will it respond as an ideal gas.

When expressed to five significant figures, the molar volume of an ideal gas is 22.414 liters. Gases such as ammonia and chlorine, which at ordinary temperatures are not far above their condensation points, show rather marked deviations from 22.4 liters as the molar volume. The molar volumes of ammonia and chlorine, measured at standard conditions, are 22.09 liters and 22.06 liters, respectively. Gases such as oxygen and nitrogen, which have low condensation points, behave more nearly as ideal gases under ordinary conditions. The molar volumes of oxygen and nitrogen at standard conditions are 22.39 liters and 22.40 liters, respectively. For most gases, deviations from ideal-gas performance through ordinary ranges of temperature and pressure do not exceed two percent.

SUMMARY

According to Gay-Lussac's law, under the same conditions of temperature and pressure, the volumes of reacting gases may be expressed in a ratio of small whole numbers. If a product is a gas, its volume under the same conditions has a simple whole-number relationship to the volumes of the reacting gases.

Avogadro suggested that equal volumes of all gases, under similar conditions of temperature and pressure, contain the same number of molecules. He applied this idea to Gay-Lussac's volume ratios and obtained the ratios of the numbers of reacting molecules. Avogadro's principle, together with Gay-Lussac's law and molecular-weight data, can be used to show that molecules of the active elemental gases are diatomic.

The volume occupied by one mole of a gas at STP is called the molar volume of the gas. Molar volumes of all gases are equal and are found experimentally to be 22.4 liters at STP. This relationship provides a simple experimental method for determining the molecular weights of gases and of other molecular substances that can be vaporized without undergoing decomposition.

There are two general types of problems involving gas volumes. In one, gas volumes are given and gas volumes are required. In the other, masses are given and gas volumes are required, or vice versa. Both types of problems are based on application of Avogadro's principle.

When gas volumes are measured under conditions other than standard temperature and pressure, they must be adjusted to STP before being placed in a calculation with the molar volume, 22.4 liters. Only gas volumes measured at standard conditions can be used in problems involving volumes and masses in chemical reactions. Calculations from chemical equations yield gas volumes at standard temperature and pressure. If gas volumes at other temperatures and pressures are required, conversion is made using the gas laws.

The gas laws can be developed into a useful equation involving a gas constant. This equation enables certain calculations with gas measurements to be made easily.

An ideal gas conforms exactly to the gas laws and Avogadro's principle. Real gases deviate slightly from the behavior of the ideal gas except where the responsible molecular characteristics just balance out.

PROBLEMS

In the absence of stated conditions of temperature and pressure, assume gases at STP.

Group A

1. Calculate the density of hydrogen chloride gas, HCl, at STP to three significant figures.
2. What is the density of hydrogen sulfide, H_2S, at STP, calculated to three significant figures?
3. What is the mass in grams of 1.00 liter of methane gas, CH_4, at STP?
4. The mass of 1.00 liter of gas at STP is 2.75 g. What is its molecular weight?

5. The mass of 1.00 liter of nitrogen at STP is 1.25 g. (*a*) Calculate the molecular weight of nitrogen from these data. (*b*) From this calculated molecular weight, determine the number of atoms in a molecule of nitrogen.
6. Hydrogen is the gas of lowest density. What is the mass in grams of $30\bar{0}$ ml of hydrogen at STP?
7. At standard conditions, 225 ml of a gas has a mass of 0.6428 g. Calculate the molecular weight of the gas from these data.
8. What is the mass in grams of $75\bar{0}$ ml of CO_2 at STP?
9. If the mass of $25\bar{0}$ ml of methane is 0.179 g at STP, what is its molecular weight?
10. The compounds HBr, PH_3, and N_2O are all gaseous at room temperature. (*a*) Calculate their molecular weights to 3 significant figures. (*b*) What is the density of each?
11. Find the mass in grams of 4.00 liters of N_2, NH_3, and C_2H_2.
12. How many liters of hydrogen and of nitrogen are required to produce $2\bar{0}$ liters of ammonia gas?
13. Carbon monoxide burns in oxygen and forms carbon dioxide. (*a*) How many liters of carbon dioxide are produced when 15 liters of carbon monoxide burn? (*b*) How many liters of oxygen are required?
14. Acetylene gas, C_2H_2, burns in oxygen and forms carbon dioxide and water vapor. (*a*) How many liters of oxygen are needed to burn 25.0 liters of acetylene? (*b*) How many liters of carbon dioxide are formed?
15. Ethane gas, C_2H_6, burns in air and produces carbon dioxide and water vapor. (*a*) How many liters of carbon dioxide are formed when 12 liters of ethane are burned? (*b*) How many moles of water are formed?
16. How many liters of air are required to furnish the oxygen to complete the reaction in Problem 15? (Assume the air to be 21% oxygen by volume.)
17. If $40\bar{0}$ ml of hydrogen and $40\bar{0}$ ml of oxygen are mixed and ignited, (*a*) what volume of oxygen remains uncombined? (*b*) What volume of water vapor is formed if all gases are measured at $15\bar{0}$°C?
18. How many grams of sodium are needed to release 4.0 liters of hydrogen from water?
19. (*a*) How many liters of hydrogen are required to convert 25.0 g of hot copper(II) oxide to metallic copper? (*b*) How many moles of water are formed?
20. When $13\bar{0}$ g of zinc reacts with $15\bar{0}$ g of HCl, how many liters of hydrogen are formed? (Note: first determine which reactant is in excess.)
21. (*a*) How many liters of oxygen can be produced by the decomposition of 90.0 g of water? (*b*) How many liters of hydrogen are produced in the same reaction?
22. (*a*) How many grams of copper will be produced when hydrogen is passed over 39.75 g of hot copper(II) oxide? (*b*) How many liters of hydrogen are required?
23. How many liters of hydrogen will be produced by the action of 25 g of calcium metal and an excess of hydrochloric acid? Calcium chloride is the other product of the reaction.

Group B

24. A compound contains nitrogen, 30.51%; oxygen, 69.49%. The density of the gas is 4.085 grams/liter. Find (*a*) its empirical formula; (*b*) its molecular weight; (*c*) its molecular formula.
25. It is found that 1.00 liter of a certain gas, collected at a pressure of $72\bar{0}$ mm of mercury and a temperature of 27°C, has a mass of 1.30 g. Calculate its molecular weight.
26. It is found that 1.00 liter of nitrogen combines with 1.00 liter of oxygen in an electric arc and forms 2.00 liters of a gas. By analysis, this gas contains 46.7%

nitrogen and 53.3% oxygen. Its density is determined to be 1.34 grams/liter. (*a*) Find the empirical formula of the product. (*b*) What is the molecular formula? (*c*) Using the information of this problem and the arguments of Avogadro, determine the number of atoms per molecule of nitrogen and oxygen.

27. How many liters will 2.0 g of CS_2 vapor occupy at 756 mm pressure and $5\bar{0}$°C?
28. A 1.00-liter flask filled with a gas at STP is attached to a high vacuum pump and evacuated until the pressure is only 1.00×10^{-4} mm. Assuming no temperature change, how many molecules remain in the flask?
29. A sample of a vapor having a mass of 0.865 g measures 174 ml at $10\bar{0}$°C and 745 mm. What is the molecular weight?
30. (*a*) How many liters of sulfur dioxide gas at STP are formed when $5\bar{0}$ g of sulfur burns? (*b*) What volume will this gas occupy at 25°C and 745 mm pressure?
31. Hydrogen ($40\bar{0}$ ml) measured at $2\bar{0}$°C and $74\bar{0}$ mm pressure is to be prepared by reacting magnesium with hydrochloric acid. What mass in grams of magnesium is required?
32. How many liters of hydrogen, collected by water displacement at 25°C and 755.0 mm pressure, can be obtained from 6.0 g of magnesium and an excess of sulfuric acid?
33. What is the mass in grams of 12.0 liters of oxygen collected by water displacement at 23°C and 745.0 mm pressure?
34. A reaction between 5.0 g of aluminum and an excess of dilute sulfuric acid is used as a source of hydrogen gas. What volume of hydrogen is collected by water displacement at $2\bar{0}$°C and 765 mm pressure? Aluminum sulfate is the other product of the reaction.
35. How many liters of dry air, measured at 29°C and 744 mm pressure, are required to complete the combustion of 1.00 mole of carbon disulfide, CS_2, to carbon dioxide, CO_2, and sulfur dioxide, SO_2?
36. What is the volume of the mixture of CO_2 and SO_2 produced in the reacton of Problem 35, if measured under the same conditions as the air used in the reaction?
37. Chlorine gas may be generated in the laboratory by a reaction between manganese dioxide and hydrogen chloride. The equation is

$$\mathbf{MnO_2(s) + 4HCl(aq) \rightarrow MnCl_2(aq) + 2H_2O(l) + Cl_2(g)}$$

(*a*) How many grams of MnO_2 are required to produce 1.00 liter of Cl_2 gas at STP? (*b*) How many grams of HCl are required?

38. In Problem 37, the HCl is available as a water solution which is 37.4% hydrogen chloride by mass. The solution has a density of 1.189 g/ml. What volume of HCl solution (hydrochloric acid) must be supplied to the reaction?
39. How many grams of charcoal, 90.0% carbon, must be burned to produce $10\bar{0}$ liters of CO_2 measured at $2\bar{0}$°C and 747 mm pressure?
40. How many grams of chlorine gas are contained in a 5.00-liter flask at $2\bar{0}$°C and $60\bar{0}$ mm pressure?
41. What temperature must be maintained to insure that a 2.50-liter flask containing 0.100 mole of a certain gas will show a continuous pressure of 745 mm?
42. From the ideal-gas equation, $pV = nRT$, and the density of a gas defined as the mass per unit volume, $D = m/V$, prove that the density of a gas at STP is directly proportional to its molecular weight.
43. At 12.0°C and $74\bar{0}$ mm, 1.07 liters of a gas has a mass of 1.98 g. Calculate the molecular weight of the gas from the ideal-gas equation.
44. The student in the cartoon on page 205 is concerned about fitting a twenty-three digit number on an eight digit calculator. Using significant figures, and exponential notation, how would you resolve this dilemma?

chapter 12

LIQUIDS—SOLIDS—WATER

"Water, water, everywhere, nor any drop to drink." (From *The Rime of the Ancient Mariner* by Coleridge. See Question 41 on page 248.)

Liquids

12.1 Properties of liquids

The phases of matter were first described in Section 1.5.

All liquids have several easily observed properties in common.

1. Definite volume. A liquid occupies a definite volume; it does not expand and completely fill its container as does a gas. A liquid may have one free surface; its other surfaces must be supported by the container walls.

2. Fluidity. A liquid can be made to flow or can be poured from one container to another. A liquid takes the shape of its container.

3. Noncompressibility. If water at 20°C is subjected to a pressure of 1000 atmospheres, its volume decreases by only 4%. This behavior of water is typical of all liquids. Even under very high pressure, liquids are compressed only slightly.

4. Diffusion. Suppose we slowly pour some ethanol (ethyl alcohol) down the side of a graduated cylinder already half full of water. If we pour carefully, the alcohol can be made to float on the water. At first, a fairly definite boundary exists between the liquids. However, if we let this system stand, the boundary becomes less and less distinct. Some of the water diffuses into the alcohol while at the same time some of the alcohol diffuses into the water. If the cylinder stands undisturbed for some time, the alcohol and water completely mix.

5. Evaporation. If a liquid is left in an open container, it may gradually disappear. Spontaneously, many liquids slowly change into vapors at room temperature.

12.2 Kinetic-theory description of a liquid

The basic assumptions of the kinetic theory were listed in Section 10.1.

Densities of gases and liquids were compared in Section 10.2(3).

Liquids are denser than gases. This fact indicates that the particles of liquids are much closer together than those of gases. Further, we know that liquids are practically noncompressible. Therefore, the particles of a liquid must be almost as close together as it is possible for them to be. A liquid has a definite volume and can have one free surface. This observation shows that a body of liquid holds together. Consequently, the attractive forces among the particles of a liquid must be much stronger than those among the particles of a gas.

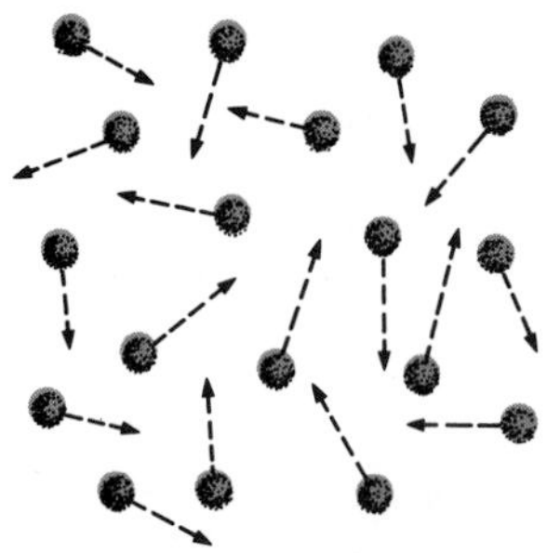

Fig. 12-1. The attractive forces between the particles of a liquid are strong enough so that a liquid has a definite volume, but are weak enough so that the particles can move with respect to one another.

Liquids are fluid and take the shape of their containers. These observations show that single particles or groups of particles in a liquid move with respect to one another. The kinetic energy of the liquid particles must be large enough to make this motion possible despite the attractive forces among them. (See Figure 12-1.)

Substances composed of low-molecular-weight nonpolar molecules are liquids only at temperatures below room temperature. Higher-molecular-weight nonpolar molecular substances may be liquids at room temperature. Hence, the forces of attraction among nonpolar molecules are the relatively weak dispersion interaction forces.

Substances composed of polar molecules may be liquids at room temperature. Thus, the attractive forces among polar molecules are the stronger combination of dispersion interaction and dipole-dipole attraction forces.

Van der Waals forces—dispersion interaction and dipole-dipole attraction—were explained in Section 10.4.

Most metals, ionic compounds, and covalent network substances are liquids only at temperatures well above room temperature. Therefore, we believe that the attractive forces among the particles of these substances are much stronger than van der Waals forces. Table 12-1 gives the range of temperatures over which examples of each of these kinds of substances exist as liquids.

There is abundant evidence that the particles of liquids are in motion. Very small particles of a solid suspended in water or some other liquid can be viewed through a microscope. They are observed to move about in a random manner. The motion is increased by using smaller particles and higher temperatures. We may conclude that the observed random motion is caused by collisions with molecules of the liquid. (See Figure 12-2.)

Fig. 12-2. This enlarged diagram shows the movement of particles of paint as they are bombarded by invisible molecules of the liquid in which they are suspended.

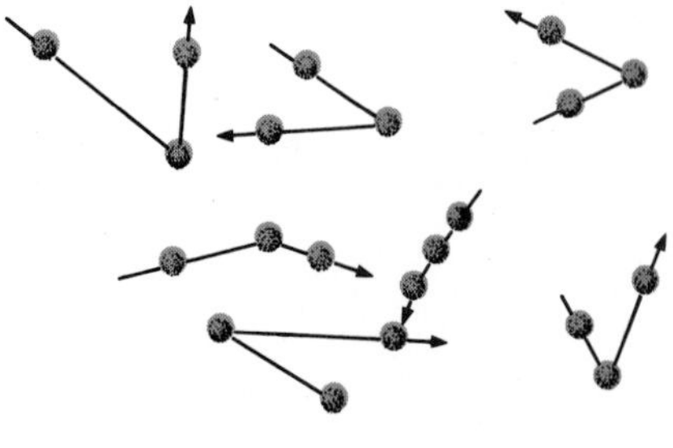

The diffusion of liquid molecules results from the intermingling of such molecules owing to their motion. The diffusion of liquids is slower than that of gases because the molecules of liquids move more slowly and are closer together. Their movement in a given direction is thereby hindered.

Water and some other liquids, such as perfume, evaporate fairly rapidly. Evaporation occurs when some molecules acquire enough kinetic energy to escape from the surface into the vapor phase. See Figure 12-3. The vapor molecules of liquids in closed containers exert pressure, as do the molecules of all confined gases. This vapor pressure reaches some maximum value depending on the temperature and nature of the substance.

The molecules of the vapors of liquids and solids have properties similar to those of gases. *Vapor is the term used for the gaseous phase of materials which normally exist as liquids or solids.* On cooling, gases may condense and become liquids. With further cooling, they may ultimately become solids.

Table 12-1

LIQUID-PHASE TEMPERATURE RANGES OF REPRESENTATIVE SUBSTANCES

Type of Substance	Substance	Temperature Range of Liquid Phase (1 atm, °C)
nonpolar covalent molecular	H_2	−259 – −252
	O_2	−218 – −183
	CH_4	−182 – −161
	CCl_4	−23 – 77
	C_6H_6	6 – 80
polar covalent molecular	NH_3	−78 – −33
	H_2O	0 – 100
ionic	NaCl	801 – 1413
	MgF_2	1266 – 2239
covalent network	$(SiO_2)_x$	1610 – 2230
	C_x (diamond)	3500 – 4827
metallic	Hg	−39 – 357
	Cu	1083 – 2595
	Fe	1535 – 3000
	W	3410 – 5927

12.3 Dynamic equilibrium

Suppose we place a cover over a container partially filled with a liquid. It appears that evaporation of the liquid continues for a while and then ceases. Let us examine this apparent situation in terms of the kinetic theory. The temperature of the liquid is proportional to the average kinetic energy of all the molecules of the liquid. Most of these molecules have energies very close to the average. However, as a result of collisions with other molecules, some have very high energies and a few have very low energies at any given time. The motions of all are random.

Some high-energy molecules near the surface are moving toward the surface. These molecules may overcome the attractive forces of the surface molecules completely and escape, or evaporate. But some of them then collide with molecules of gases in the air or other vapor molecules and rebound into the liquid. As the evaporation continues, the concentration of vapor molecules continues to increase. This causes the chance of collisions of escaping molecules with vapor molecules to increase. Consequently, the number of vapor molecules rebounding into the liquid increases.

Eventually, the number of vapor molecules returning to the liquid equals the number of liquid molecules evaporating. Beyond this point, there will be no *net* increase in the *concentration* of vapor molecules. That is, there will be no change in the number of vapor molecules per unit volume of air above the liquid. But the motions of the molecules do not cease. The two actions, evaporation and condensation, do not cease either. They merely continue at equal rates. We may conclude that an *equilibrium* is reached between the rate of liquid molecules evaporating and the rate of vapor molecules condensing. This equilibrium is a dynamic condition in which *opposing* changes occur at *equal* rates. Since this dynamic equilibrium involves only physical changes, it is referred to as ***physical equilibrium:*** *a dynamic state in which two opposing physical changes occur at equal rates in the same system.*

Fig. 12-3. Water evaporates because some molecules acquire sufficient kinetic energy to escape from the surface into the vapor phase. Some molecules rebound into the surface after colliding with molecules of gases in the air or with other water vapor molecules.

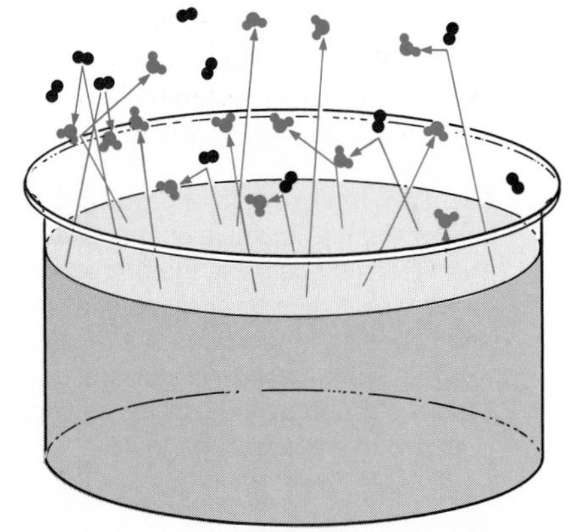

We may represent the evaporation process:

$$\textbf{liquid} + \textbf{energy} \rightarrow \textbf{vapor}$$

Then the condensation process will be

$$\textbf{vapor} \rightarrow \textbf{liquid} + \textbf{energy}$$

We can represent the state of dynamic equilibrium occurring in a confined space as

$$\textbf{liquid} + \textbf{energy} \rightleftarrows \textbf{vapor}$$

Because of the double "yields" sign in an equation representing an equilibrium reaction, the equation may be read in either direction. The *forward* reaction is represented when the equation is read from *left to right:* liquid + energy → vapor. The *reverse* reaction is represented when the equation is read from *right to left:* vapor → liquid + energy.

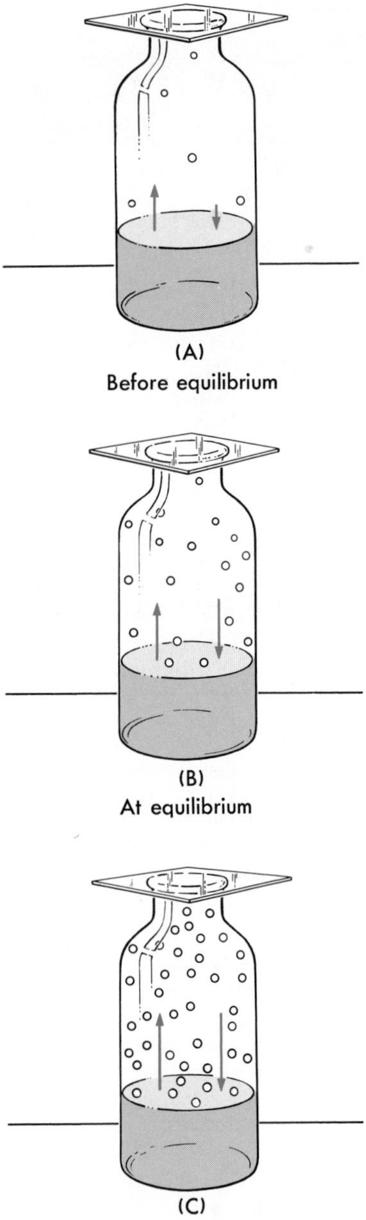

Fig. 12-4. An example of physical equilibrium and the influence of temperature. The different lengths of the arrows indicate the relative rates of evaporation (up) and condensation (down). The pressure exerted by the vapor molecules at equilibrium is known as the equilibrium vapor pressure of that particular liquid.

12.4 Equilibrium vapor pressure

We have stated that the vapor molecules of liquids in closed containers exert pressure, as do the molecules of all confined gases. But when equilibrium is reached, there is no further net change in the system. The concentration of vapor molecules in the space above the liquid surface remains constant. Thus, at equilibrium, there is a vapor pressure characteristic of the liquid present in the system. It is known as the *equilibrium vapor pressure* of the liquid. ***Equilibrium vapor pressure*** *is the pressure exerted by a vapor in equilibrium with its liquid.*

What is the effect on a liquid-vapor equilibrium system if the temperature of the liquid is raised? Again, let us examine this situation in terms of the kinetic theory. The rise in temperature means that the average kinetic energy of the liquid molecules has been increased. A relatively larger number of liquid molecules now possess enough energy to escape through the liquid surface. Thus, the rate of evaporation is increased. In this way, the liquid-vapor equilibrium is *disturbed.* The concentration of vapor molecules above the liquid surface is increased. More vapor molecules, in turn, increase the chances of collision with escaping molecules and cause an increase in the rate of condensation. Soon the equilibrium is reestablished but at a *higher equilibrium vapor pressure.* See Figure 12-4.

All liquids have characteristic forces of attraction between their molecules. If the attractive forces are strong, there is less tendency for the liquid to evaporate. The equilibrium vapor pressure of such a liquid is correspondingly low. Glycerol is an example of a liquid with a low equilibrium vapor pressure. On the other hand, the attractive forces between liquid molecules may be relatively weak. Then the liquid tends to evaporate readily, with a resulting high equilibrium vapor pressure. Ether is such a liquid. The amount of equilibrium vapor pressure of a liquid depends on the *nature of the liquid and its temperature.*

12.5 Le Chatelier's principle

In systems that have attained equilibrium, opposing actions occur at equal rates. Any change that alters the rate of either the forward or the reverse action disturbs the equilibrium. It is often possible to displace an equilibrium in a desired direction by changing the equilibrium conditions.

In 1888, the French chemist Henri Louis Le Chatelier (luh-*shah*-teh-lee-ay) (1850–1936) published an important principle. This principle is the basis for much of our knowledge of equilibrium. ***Le Chatelier's principle*** may be stated as follows: *If a system at equilibrium is subjected to a stress, the equilibrium will be displaced in such direction as to relieve the stress.* This principle is a general law that applies to all kinds of dynamic equilibria. Let us apply it to the

Fig. 12-5. Henri Louis Le Chatelier, a French mining engineer and chemist, was a brilliant scientist, teacher, writer, and editor. He did work in the science and technology of metals, high temperature measurement, microscopy, ceramics, cements, chemical mechanics, and the theory of combustion of gases. His important contribution to the understanding of the direction in which a physical or chemical change will occur is now known as Le Chatelier's principle.

$$\textbf{liquid} + \textbf{energy} \rightleftarrows \textbf{vapor}$$

system we have been considering.

We have already learned something about how the kinetic theory applies to this system. We know that the system may reach equilibrium at a given temperature. If the temperature is then raised, equilibrium can be reestablished, but at a greater vapor concentration. *The rise in temperature is a stress on the system.* According to Le Chatelier's principle, the equilibrium is displaced in the direction that relieves this stress. In this case, the forward (left-to-right) reaction is endothermic. The forward reaction absorbs heat energy and displaces the equilibrium to the right. This displacement means that the vapor concentration is higher when equilibrium is reestablished. Similarly, we can apply Le Chatelier's principle to a lowering of the temperature of the system at equilibrium. Here, the reverse (right-to-left) reaction is favored. Equilibrium is reestablished at the lower temperature with a reduced vapor concentration. Thus, Le Chatelier's principle enables us to predict the dependence of equilibrium vapor pressure on temperature.

Suppose we keep the temperature of the system constant but alter the volume that the system occupies. This constant-temperature condition means that the vapor pressure at equilibrium remains constant. It also means that the concentration of vapor molecules (density of the vapor) at equilibrium remains constant.

First, let us increase the volume that the system occupies. The volume of the liquid cannot change measurably, but the volume of the vapor can. When the volume of the vapor increases at constant temperature, its pressure must drop (Boyle's law). In order to restore the vapor to its equilibrium concentration, more vapor molecules must be produced. Le Chatelier's principle indicates that the equilibrium must shift to the right, and more liquid must evaporate. Equilibrium is then restored with the same vapor pressure and the same concentration of vapor molecules as before. But with a larger volume of vapor, the actual number of vapor molecules must be greater. The number of liquid molecules is therefore necessarily reduced.

If we reduce the volume that the system occupies, the pressure of the vapor increases. To restore equilibrium, this increased pressure must be reduced to the equilibrium vapor pressure at the same temperature. Le Chatelier's principle indicates that some vapor molecules must condense to liquid molecules. The reverse reaction, condensation, is favored. Equilibrium is once again established. This time there are fewer vapor molecules and a greater number of liquid molecules. But the same *concentration* of vapor molecules exists as before.

12.6 Boiling of liquids

We now have some understanding of equilibrium and of the way in which equiiibrium vapor pressures arise. Let us apply this knowledge to the phenomenon of *boiling*.

We know that pressure exerted uniformly on the surface of a confined liquid is transmitted undiminished in every direction throughout the liquid (Pascal's law). Consider a beaker of water being heated over a Bunsen flame (Figure 12-6). Vapor bubbles first appear at the bottom of the beaker, where the water is hottest. They diminish in size and disappear completely as they rise into cooler water. Atmospheric pressure presses from all directions perpendicular to the surface of the vapor bubble, according to Pascal's law, collapsing it. Only when the equilibrium vapor pressure exerted by the vapor molecules on the liquid at the surface of the bubbles is equal to the atmospheric pressure can the vapor bubble be maintained as it rises through the liquid.

Fig. 12-6. A liquid boils when its equilibrium vapor pressure becomes equal to the prevailing atmospheric pressure.

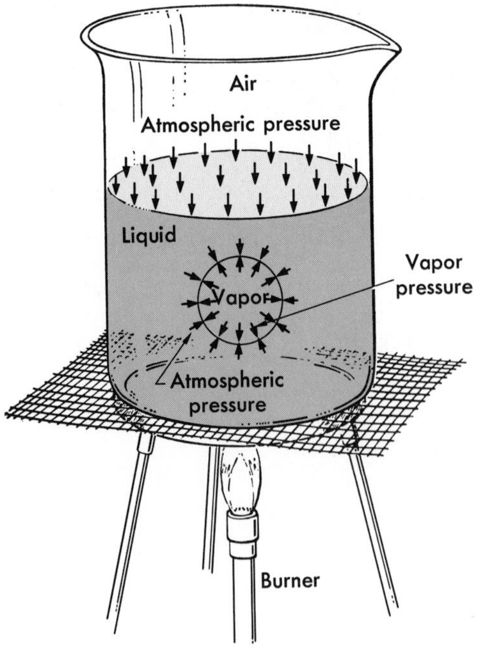

As the temperature of the water increases, the vapor pressure also increases. *Ultimately a temperature is reached at which the equilibrium vapor pressure is equal to the pressure of the atmosphere acting on the surface of the liquid.* At this temperature, the vapor bubbles maintain themselves in the liquid. They present to the liquid a greatly increased liquid-vapor surface. This allows evaporation (a surface phenomenon) to occur at a greatly increased rate. We say that the liquid *boils. The* ***boiling point*** *of a liquid is the temperature at which the equilibrium vapor pressure of the liquid is equal to the prevailing atmospheric pressure.* If the pressure on the surface of a liquid is increased, the boiling point of the liquid is raised. If the pressure is decreased, the boiling point of the liquid is lowered.

The boiling point of water is exactly 100°C at *standard atmospheric pressure.* This temperature is known as the *standard* (or *normal*) *boiling point of water.* When the boiling points of liquids are given, standard pressure conditions are understood. Ether, which has a high equilibrium vapor pressure, boils at 34.6°C. The boiling point of glycerol, mentioned earlier (Section 12.4) for its low equilibrium vapor pressure, is 290°C. See Figure 12-7.

During boiling, the temperature of a liquid remains constant. The temperature of the vapor is the same as that of the liquid. Hence, the kinetic energies of linear motion of liquid and vapor molecules must be the same. But energy must be supplied for boiling to continue. This energy is absorbed by the liquid as it becomes a vapor. The energy separates the molecules in the liquid to the much wider spacing of molecules in the gas. It effects this separation by overcoming the attractive forces between the molecules. Thus, this supplied energy increases the potential energy of the molecules.

The heat energy required to vaporize one mole of liquid at its standard boiling point is its *standard molar heat of vaporization.* Its magnitude is a measure of the degree of attraction between liquid molecules.

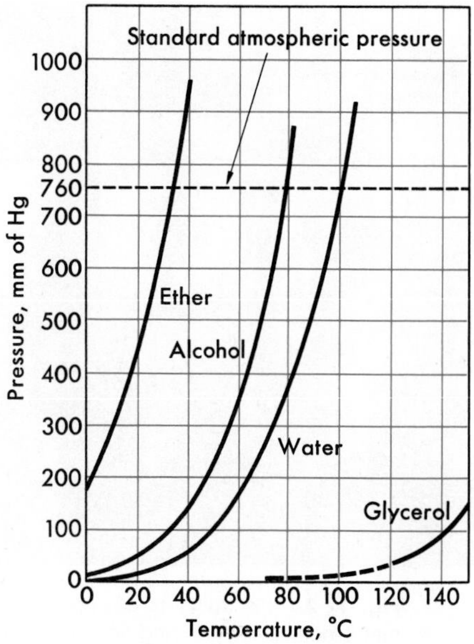

Fig. 12-7. The equilibrium vapor pressures of some common liquids as a function of temperature.

It will be helpful at this point to refer to Figure 2-13.

12.7 Liquefying gases

Michael Faraday (1791–1867) discovered that it is possible to liquefy certain gases by cooling and compressing them at the same time. He used a thick-walled sealed tube of the type shown in Figure 12-8. With this apparatus, Faraday liquefied chlorine, sulfur dioxide, and some other gases. One end of the glass tube containing the chlorine gas was strongly heated. That caused the gas in the heated end of the tube to expand. The expanding gas exerted pressure on the gas in the other end of the tube, which was cooled in a freezing mixture. Cooling and compression in this manner converted the gaseous chlorine into liquid chlorine.

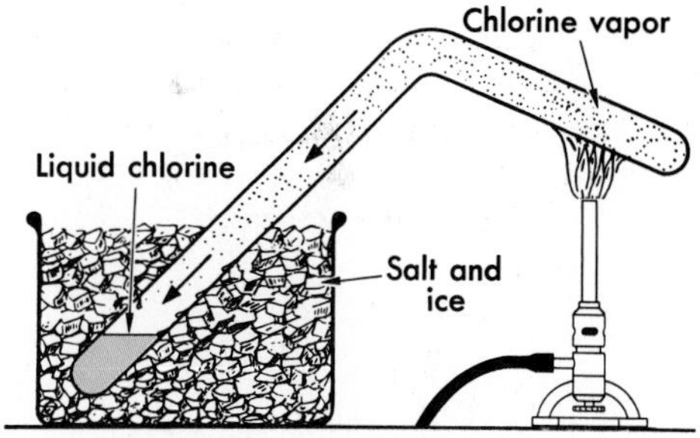

Fig. 12-8. By using a tube like the one shown above, Faraday succeeded in liquefying chlorine, sulfur dioxide, and several other gases that have high critical temperatures.

The modern method of liquefying a gas is more complicated. The first step involves compressing the gas and then removing the heat of compression. Compressing a gas always raises its temperature since energy is acquired by the molecules of a gas when work is done to push them closer together. In liquefying gases the heat of compression is absorbed by a suitable coolant. The gas molecules thereby lose the energy acquired during compression. The compressed gas is cooled to the same temperature that it had before compression. The molecules possess the same kinetic energy they had before compression but are now closer together.

This is the method used to produce liquid air, Section 9.4(5).

The second step in liquefying a gas is to permit the cool compressed gas to expand without absorbing external energy. When a compressed gas expands, the molecules lose energy as

Fig. 12-9. This trailer is equipped with metal bottles for carrying liquefied propane.

they do work in spreading apart against the force of molecular attraction. This energy loss by the molecules is observed as a decrease in the temperature of the gas. Remember that the temperature of the compressed gas was that which it had *before* compression. So the *expanded* gas is now at a much lower temperature than originally. By repeating this compression, cooling, and expansion cycle, the temperature of the gas is lowered still further.

Liquefying a gas is the result of a combination of lowered temperature and increased pressure. The increased pressure crowds the gas molecules together. The lowered temperature slows their movement. Ultimately, they are slowed down greatly and crowded together very closely. At this point, the attractive forces between the molecules cause them to condense to a liquid.

Scientists have found that above a certain characteristic temperature it is impossible to liquefy a gas by pressure alone. Above this temperature, the kinetic energy of the molecules is great enough to overcome the attractive forces between them. Thus the gas does not liquefy no matter how great the pressure applied. *The highest temperature at which it is possible to liquefy a gas with any amount of pressure is called its* ***critical temperature.*** *The pressure required to liquefy a gas at its critical temperature is called its* ***critical pressure.*** *The volume occupied by one mole of a gas under these conditions is called its* ***critical volume.*** The critical temperature and critical pressure of several common gases are given in Table 12-2.

From these data, we see that two conditions are necessary to liquefy a gas:

1. Its temperature must be lowered to or below its critical temperature.

2. Its pressure must be raised to or above the vapor pressure of the liquefied gas at this temperature.

This combination of conditions enables the attractive forces between the molecules to effect condensation. All gases can be liquefied.

Table 12-2

CRITICAL TEMPERATURES AND PRESSURES

Gas	Critical Temperature (°C)	Critical Pressure (atm)
water	374.0	217.7
sulfur dioxide	157.2	77.7
chlorine	144.0	76.1
carbon dioxide	31.1	73.0
oxygen	−118.8	49.7
nitrogen	−147.1	33.5
hydrogen	−239.9	12.8

12.8 Critical temperature and molecular attraction

We have defined the critical temperature of a gas as the temperature above which it cannot be liquefied no matter how great the pressure. Thus, the magnitude of the critical temperature of a gas serves as a measure of the attractive forces between its molecules. The higher the critical temperature of a gas, the larger is the attractive force between its molecules. The lower the critical temperature of a gas, the smaller is the attractive force between its molecules.

The high critical temperature of water is shown in Table 12-2. This high critical temperature indicates that the forces of attraction between polar water molecules are very great.

In fact, they can cause water vapor to liquefy even at 374°C. The critical temperature of sulfur dioxide is less than that of water. Thus, the attractive forces between sulfur dioxide molecules must be less than those between water molecules. This difference is expected because sulfur dioxide molecules are less polar than water molecules. Consequently, sulfur dioxide can be condensed to a liquid only below 157°C.

Attractive forces also exist between nonpolar covalent molecules such as chlorine, carbon dioxide, oxygen, nitrogen, and hydrogen. These attractive forces are dispersion interaction forces. Such forces generally increase with an increase in the complexity of a nonpolar molecule. Thus, the higher the molecular weight of such a molecule, the higher its critical temperature. This phenomenon is clearly illustrated in Table 12-2. Notice the descending order of the critical temperatures of chlorine, carbon dioxide, oxygen, nitrogen, and hydrogen.

Solids

12.9 Properties of solids

Some of the general properties of solids that we can easily see are

1. *Definite shape.* A solid maintains its shape. Unlike liquids and gases, it does not flow under ordinary circumstances. The shape of a solid is independent of its container.
2. *Definite volume.* All of the surfaces of a solid are free surfaces. Hence, the volume of a solid is also independent of its container.
3. *Noncompressibility.* The pressures required to decrease the volumes of solids are even greater than those required for liquids. For all practical purposes, solids are noncompressible. Solids such as wood, cork, sponge, etc. may *seem* to be compressible. But we must remember that these materials are very porous. Compression does not reduce the volume of the solid portion of such substances significantly. It merely reduces the volume of the pores of the solid.
4. *Very slow diffusion.* Suppose a lead plate and a gold plate are placed in close contact. After several months, particles of gold can be detected in the lead and vice versa. This observation is evidence that diffusion occurs even in solids, although at a *very slow rate.*
5. *Crystal formation.* Solids may be described as either *crystalline* or *amorphous.* Crystalline solids have a regular arrangement of particles. Amorphous solids have a completely random particle arrangement.

12.10 Kinetic-theory description of a solid

Particles of solids are held close together in fixed positions by forces that are stronger than those between particles of liquids. This is how scientists explain the definite shape and volume of a solid as well as its noncompressibility. Whether

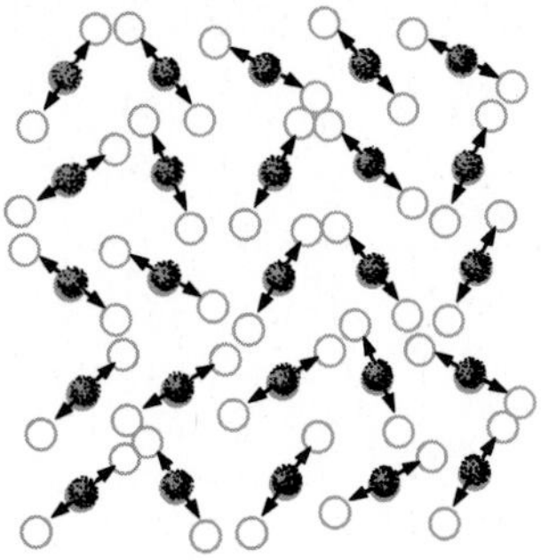

Fig. 12-10. The particles of a solid vibrate about fixed equilibrium positions.

the particle arrangement is orderly or not determines whether the solid is crystalline or amorphous. The particles of a solid vibrate weakly back and forth about fixed equilibrium positions. Their kinetic energy is related to the extent of this vibratory motion. Their kinetic energy is proportional to the temperature of the solid. At low temperatures, the kinetic energy is small. At higher temperatures, it is larger. Crystal particles vibrate extensively at high temperatures. But there is relatively little diffusion in any solid because the vibration is about fixed positions.

12.11 Changes of phase involving solids

As you study this section, it will be helpful to refer again to Figure 2-13.

The physical change of a liquid to a solid is called *freezing*, and involves a loss of energy by the liquid.

$$\textbf{liquid} \rightarrow \textbf{solid} + \textbf{energy}$$

Since this change occurs at constant temperature, the liquid and solid particles must have the same kinetic energy. The energy loss is a loss of *potential* energy. The particles lose potential energy as the forces of attraction do work on them.

The reverse physical change, *melting*, also occurs at constant temperature.

$$\textbf{solid} + \textbf{energy} \rightarrow \textbf{liquid}$$

It involves a gain of potential energy by the particles of the solid as they do work against the attractive forces in becoming liquid particles.

For pure crystalline solids, the temperatures at which these two processes occur coincide. That is, the freezing point and the melting point are the same. For pure water, both processes occur at 0°C. Ice melts at 0°C and forms liquid water; water freezes at 0°C and forms ice. The heat energy required to melt one mole of solid at its melting point is its *molar heat of fusion*.

Fig. 12-11. The liquid and solid phases of water make artistic patterns on this window.

If ice gradually disappears in a mixture of ice and water, the melting process clearly is proceeding faster than the freezing process. Suppose, however, that the relative amounts of ice and water remain unchanged in the mixture. Then both processes must be proceeding at equal rates and a state of physical equilibrium is indicated.

$$\textbf{solid} + \textbf{energy} \rightleftarrows \textbf{liquid}$$

Not all particles of a solid have the same energy. A surface particle of a solid may acquire sufficient energy to overcome the attractive forces holding it to the body of the solid. Such a particle may escape from the solid and become a vapor particle.

$$\textbf{solid} + \textbf{energy} \rightarrow \textbf{vapor}$$

If a solid is placed in a closed container, vapor particles cannot escape from the system. Eventually they come in contact with the solid and are held by its attractive forces.

vapor → solid + energy

Thus a solid in contact with its vapor can reach an equilibrium.

solid + energy ⇄ vapor

In such a case, the solid exhibits a characteristic equilibrium vapor pressure. Like that of a liquid, the equilibrium vapor pressure of a solid depends only on the temperature and the substance involved. Some solids like camphor and naphthalene (moth crystals) have fairly high equilibrium vapor pressures. They evaporate noticeably when exposed to air. Solids like carbon dioxide (Dry Ice) and iodine have equilibrium vapor pressures that rise very rapidly as the temperature is raised. The equilibrium vapor pressures of these solids equal atmospheric pressure before the solids melt. In such cases the solid vaporizes directly, without passing through the liquid phase. The change of phase from a solid to a vapor is known as *sublimation.*

Fig. 12-12. X-ray diffraction photograph of ice. Chemists use X-ray diffraction in their study of crystal structure.

12.12 Amorphous solids

The term *amorphous solids* refers to those that appear to have random particle arrangement. But truly amorphous solids are rare. Many solids that scientists once thought were amorphous have been found to have a partially crystalline structure. Charcoal is such a solid. However, materials like glass and paraffin may be considered amorphous. These materials have the properties of solids. That is, they have definite shape and volume and diffuse slowly. But they do not have the orderly arrangement of particles characteristic of crystals. They also lack sharply defined melting points. In many respects, they resemble liquids that flow very slowly at room temperature.

12.13 Nature of crystals

Homogeneous materials, such as crystals, have similar properties throughout.

Most substances exist as solids in some characteristic crystalline form. *A* ***crystal*** *is a homogeneous portion of a substance bounded by plane surfaces making definite angles with each other, giving a regular geometric form.*

Scientists determine the arrangement of particles composing a crystal by mathematical analysis of its diffraction patterns. These patterns appear clearly on photographs produced when the crystal is illuminated by X rays. An example of an X-ray diffraction photograph is shown in Figure 12-12. Every crystal structure shows a pattern of points that describes the arrangement of its particles. This pattern of points is known as the *crystal lattice*. The smallest portion of the crystal lattice that exhibits the pattern of the lattice structure is called the *unit cell*. The unit cell defines the kind of symmetry to be found throughout a crystalline substance. The kinds of unit cells are shown in Figure 12-13.

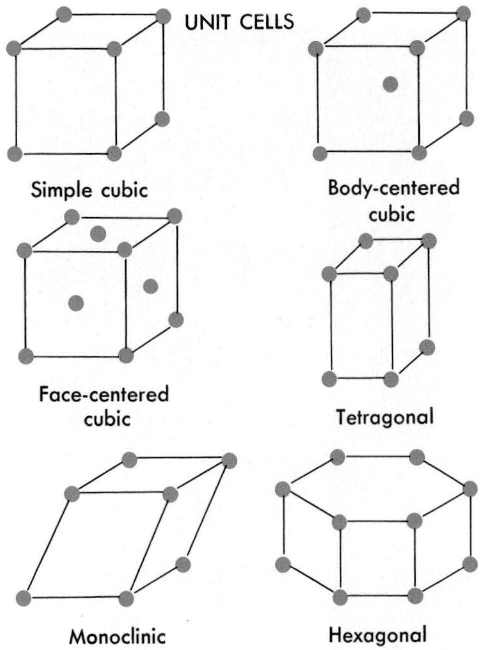

Fig. 12-13. The kind of symmetry found throughout a crystalline substance is determined by the type of unit cell that generates the lattice structure.

Fig. 12-14. Schematic diagram of the six basic crystal systems.

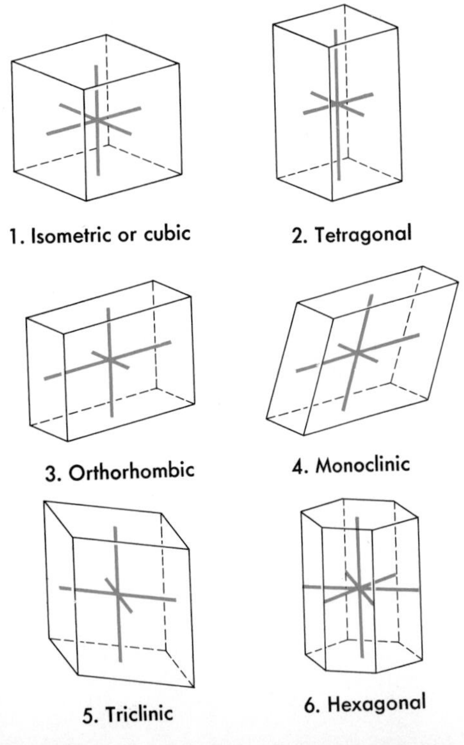

The classification of crystals by shape is a part of the science of *crystallography*. Shape classification helps chemists to identify crystals. Any crystal can be placed in one of six crystalline systems:

1. *Isometric* (or *cubic*). The three axes are at right angles as in a cube, and are of equal length.
2. *Tetragonal.* The three axes are at right angles to each other, but only the two lateral axes are of equal length.
3. *Orthorhombic.* Three unequal axes are at right angles to each other.
4. *Monoclinic.* There are three unequal axes, with one oblique (not a right angle) intersection.
5. *Triclinic.* There are three unequal axes and three oblique intersections.
6. *Hexagonal.* Three equilateral axes intersect at angles of 60°. A vertical axis of variable length is at right angles to the equilateral axes. (See Figure 12-14.)

Crystals of common salt, NaCl, are isometric (cubic). This cubic nature can be seen by sprinkling a little table salt on a black surface and examining it with a magnifying lens. Alum crystals, $K_2SO_4 \cdot Al_2(SO_4)_3 \cdot 24H_2O$, are also isometric, being formed as *octahedrons* (regular eight-sided solids). An example of a tetragonal crystal is $NiSO_4 \cdot 6H_2O$. Both KNO_3 and $AgNO_3$ form orthorhombic crystals. The compounds $KClO_3$ and $BaCl_2 \cdot 2H_2O$ crystallize as monoclinic crystals. Copper(II) sulfate pentahydrate, $CuSO_4 \cdot 5H_2O$, forms blue triclinic crystals. Hexagonal crystals are formed by $NaNO_3$ and $CaCO_3$.

Crystals of many chemical compounds are formed when their solutions evaporate or when their hot, saturated solutions cool. Crystals also form when certain substances change from the liquid to the solid phase and when others change from the gaseous to the solid phase. Most of us are familiar with snowflake crystals. These are formed when water vapor changes directly to the solid phase. Melted sugar, sulfur, and iron form crystals in a similar manner when they change from the liquid to the solid phase. In some cases, crystals grow from the solid phase.

12.14 Binding forces in crystals

The regularity of crystal structures is their most fascinating feature. When possible, ions or atoms or molecules arrange themselves in positions of least energy. The more opportunity there is for particles to do this during the formation of crystals, the more symmetrical and regular the crystals will be. Thus, the more slowly crystals form, the more closely their shapes approach perfect regularity. Crystal-growing experiments have been carried out in the near-zero gravity environment of the Skylab. These experiments have shown that crystals of metalloids grow more rapidly and more perfectly from the vapor phase under such conditions than they do on earth.

We describe the six crystalline systems in terms related to symmetry. But it is frequently more useful to classify crystals according to the types of lattice structure. Is the crystal lattice *ionic, covalent network, metallic,* or *covalent molecular?* Ionic and covalent molecular crystal lattices represent the two extremes of bonding. Covalent network and metallic crystal lattices are intermediate types. (See Table 12-3.)

1. Ionic crystals. The ionic crystal lattice consists of positive and negative ions arranged in a characteristic regular pattern. No molecular units are evident within the crystal. The strong bonding forces result from the attraction of positive and negative charges. Consequently, ionic crystals are hard and brittle, have rather high melting points, and are good insulators. Generally, ionic crystals result from Group I or Group II metals combining with Group VI or Group VII nonmetals, or the nonmetallic polyatomic ions.

2. Covalent network crystals. The covalent network crystal lattice consists of an array of atoms. Each of the atoms shares electrons with neighboring atoms. The binding forces are

Fig. 12-15. A garnet crystal (top) and a group of quartz crystals (bottom) show how crystal structure follows a characteristic pattern.

Table 12-3

MELTING POINTS AND BOILING POINTS OF REPRESENTATIVE TYPES OF SUBSTANCES

Type of Substance	Substance	Melting Point (°C)	Boiling Point (1 atm, °C)
nonpolar covalent molecular	H_2	−259	−252
	O_2	−218	−183
	CH_4	−182	−161
	CCl_4	−23	77
	C_6H_6	6	$8\overline{0}$
polar covalent molecular	NH_3	−78	−33
	H_2O	$\overline{0}$	$10\overline{0}$
ionic	NaCl	801	1413
	MgF_2	1266	2239
covalent network	$(SiO_2)_x$	1610	2230
	C_x (diamond)	3500	4827
metallic	Hg	−39	357
	Cu	1083	2595
	Fe	1535	3000
	W	3410	5927

strong covalent bonds which extend in fixed directions. The resulting crystals are compact, interlocking, covalent network structures. They may be considered to be giant molecules. They are very hard and brittle, have rather high melting points, and are nonconductors. Diamond, silicon carbide, silicon dioxide, and oxides of transition metals are of this type.

3. *Metallic crystals.* The metallic crystal lattice consists of positive ions surrounded by a cloud of valence electrons. This cloud is commonly referred to as the *electron "gas."* The binding force is the attraction between the positive ions of the metal and the electron "gas." The valence electrons are donated by the atoms of the metal and belong to the crystal as a whole. These electrons are free to migrate throughout the crystal lattice. This electron mobility explains the high electric conductivity associated with metals. The hardness (resistance to wear) and melting points of metallic crystals vary greatly for different metals. Sodium, iron, tungsten, copper, and silver are typical examples of metallic crystals that have good electric conductivity. But they are quite different in terms of other characteristics, such as hardness and melting point.

4. *Covalent molecular crystals.* The covalent molecular crystal lattice consists of an orderly arrangement of individually distinct molecules. If the molecules are nonpolar, the binding force is the relatively weak dispersion interaction force. If the molecules are polar, both types of van der Waals attractions make up the binding force. The covalent chemical bonds that bind the atoms within the molecules are much stronger than the forces which form the crystal lattice. Thus, molecular crystals have low melting points, are relatively soft, volatile (easily vaporized), and good insulators. Iodine, carbon dioxide, water, and hydrogen form crystals of this type. See Section 12-16 for the discussion of ice crystals.

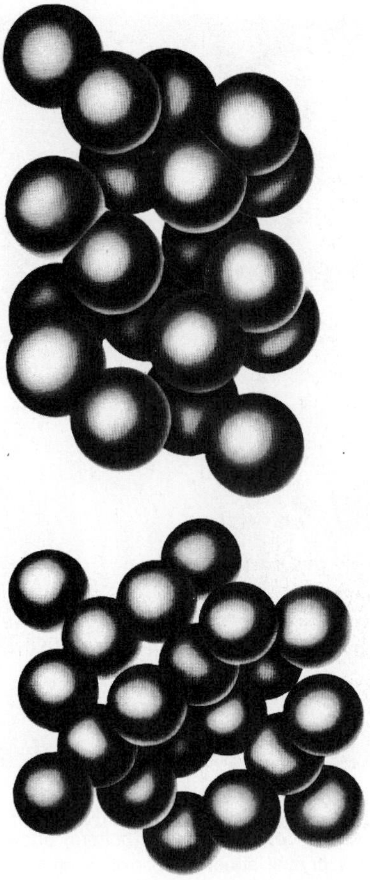

Fig. 12-16. Solid iodine (top) forms molecular crystals. Compare its molecular structure with that of diamond (bottom), which forms covalent crystals that may be considered to be giant molecules.

Water

12.15 Occurrence of water

On the earth, water is the most abundant and essential liquid. The oceans, rivers, and lakes cover about 75% of the surface of the earth. Significant quantities of water are frozen in glaciers, which cover almost 10% of the land surface. Water vapor is always present in the air, and there are large quantities of underground water.

Water is essential to human, animal, and vegetable life. From 70% to 90% of the weight of living things is water. The chemical reactions of life processes take place in water; water is frequently also a reactant or product of such reactions.

The Viking mission has produced evidence that leads scientists to believe that the planet Mars has an underground layer of ice. The northern polar region of Mars is covered with a layer consisting mostly of ice. Studies have revealed that water vapor is also present in Jupiter's atmosphere.

In early 1977, it was announced that astronomers using a radio telescope had found water molecules on the edge of a nebula 2.2 million light years away. (A light year is the distance light travels in one year. It is 9.46×10^{12} kilometers.) The distance 2.2 million light years is about 10^{12} times the distance from the earth to the sun. One astronomer said of this discovery, "What is decisive is that we find the same conditions of physical matter one billion light years away from earth as on earth. That means that this matter exists in the same way as here and behaves in the same way."

Fig. 12-17. Photomosaic of the Viking mission's pictures of Mars' north polar ice cap. The translucent streaks that lie over both ice and layered material are seen here for the first time.

12.16 Physical properties of water

Pure water is a transparent, odorless, tasteless, and almost colorless liquid. The faint blue or blue-green color of water is apparent only in deep layers.

Any odor or taste in water is caused by impurities such as dissolved mineral matter, dissolved liquids, or dissolved gases. The strong odor and taste of water from some mineral springs are caused by the presence of such substances in detectable quantity.

Depending on temperature and pressure, water may exist as a vapor, liquid, or solid. Liquid water changes to ice at 0°C under standard pressure, 760 mm of mercury. As water solidifies, it gives off heat and expands one ninth in volume. Consequently, ice has a density of about 0.9 g/cm^3. The density of ice increases slightly as ice is cooled below 0°C. The molar heat of fusion of ice at 0°C is 1.44 kcal.

When water at 0°C is warmed, it contracts until its temperature reaches 4°C. Then water gradually expands as its temperature is raised further. *At its temperature of maximum density, 4°C, one milliliter of water has a mass of one gram.*

When the pressure on the surface of water is *one atmosphere* (760 mm of mercury), water boils at a temperature of 100°C. The molar heat of vaporization of water at 100°C is 9.70 kcal. The steam that is formed by boiling water occupies a much greater volume than the water from which it was formed. When one liter of water at 100°C is completely boiled away, the steam occupies about 1700 liters at 100°C and 1 atmosphere pressure.

When water is heated in a closed vessel so that the steam cannot escape, the pressure on the water's surface increases. As a result, the boiling temperature of the water is raised above 100°C. But suppose that the air and water vapor above the liquid in a closed vessel are partially removed by means of a vacuum pump. Then the pressure is decreased and the water boils at a lower temperature than 100°C. Pressure cookers are used for cooking food because the higher temperature of the water cooks the food in a shorter time. Vacuum evaporators are used to concentrate milk and sugar solutions. Under reduced pressure, the water boils away at a temperature low enough so that the sugar or milk is not scorched.

12.17 Structure and properties of water molecules

Water molecules are composed of two atoms of hydrogen and one atom of oxygen joined by polar covalent bonds. Studies of the crystal structure of ice indicate that these atoms are not joined in a straight line. Instead, the molecule is bent, with a structure that may be represented as shown at the left.

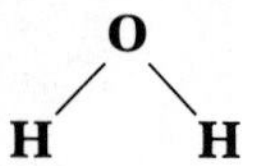

The angle between the two hydrogen-oxygen bonds is about 105°. This was explained in Section 6.17 as evidence of considerable sp^3 hybridization of the oxygen-atom orbitals.

Since oxygen is more strongly electronegative than hydrogen, the bonds in a water molecule are polar. The electronegativity difference indicates that H—O bonds have about 39% ionic character. Thus, the electrons are not distributed perfectly uniformly about the molecule. On the average, they are clustered slightly about the oxygen nucleus. This gives the oxygen part of the molecule a partial negative charge and leaves the hydrogen parts with a partial positive charge. Since the polar covalent bonds in this molecule do not lie on the same straight line, the molecule as a whole is polar. Water molecules, being polar, are sometimes called water dipoles.

The polarity of water molecules enables them to be attracted to one another. This mutual attraction causes water molecules to *associate,* or join together into groups of molecules. One slightly positive hydrogen atom of a water molecule may weakly, but effectively, attract the slightly negative oxygen of a second water molecule. In this way, one hydrogen serves as a link between the oxygen atoms of two water molecules by sharing electrons with them. This situation is an example of a *hydrogen bond. A* ***hydrogen bond*** *is a weak chemical bond between a hydrogen atom in one polar molecule and a very electronegative atom in a second polar molecule.* A hydrogen of the second water molecule may be attracted to the oxygen of a third water molecule, and so on. In this way, a group of molecules is formed. The number of molecules in such a group decreases with an increase in temperature. But there are usually from four to eight molecules per group in liquid water. The formation of molecular groups by hydrogen bonding causes water to be liquid at room temperature. Other substances, such as methane, CH_4, have nonpolar molecules similar in size and mass to water molecules. But these substances do not undergo hydrogen bonding and are gases at room temperature. Hydrogen bonding seems to occur only between hydrogen and highly electronegative small nonmetallic atoms such as oxygen, fluorine, and nitrogen.

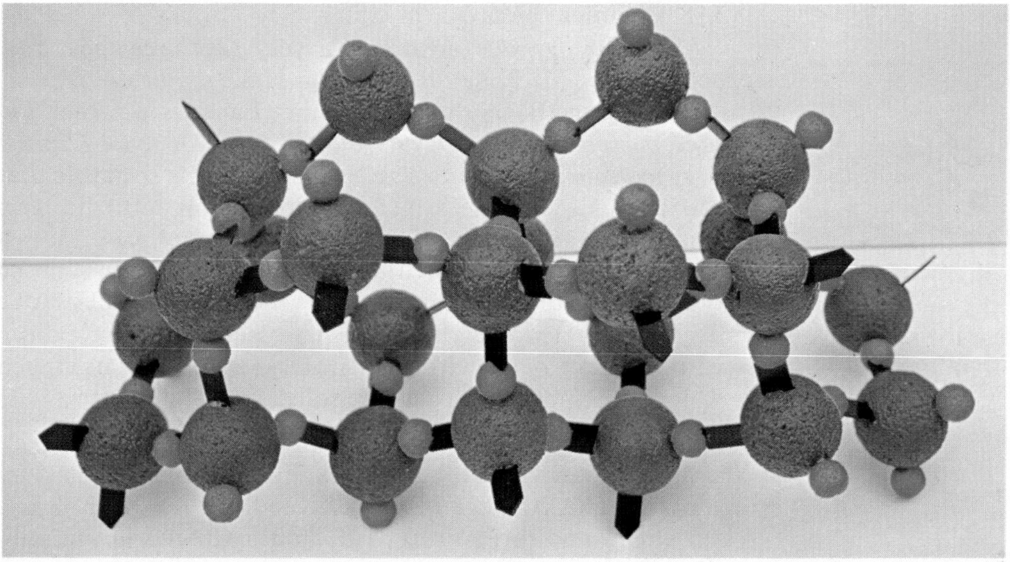

Fig. 12-18. Model of the crystal structure of ice.

Ice consists of H_2O molecules arranged in a definite hexagonal structure. They are held together by hydrogen bonds in a rather open hexagonal pattern (Figure 12-18). As heat is applied to ice, the increased energy of the atoms and molecules causes them to vibrate more vigorously. This stretches the hydrogen bonds, and the ice expands as it is heated.

When the melting point of ice is reached, the energy of the atoms and molecules is so great that the rigid open lattice structure of the ice crystals breaks down. The ice turns into water. The hydrogen bonds in water at 0°C are longer than those in ice. But they are more flexible. Thus, the groups of liquid molecules can crowd together more compactly than those in ice. As a result, H_2O molecules occupy less volume as water than they do as ice. Water is denser than ice.

As water is warmed from 0°C, two phenomena having opposite effects occur:

1. The breaking down of some hydrogen bonds enables water molecules to crowd closer together.

2. The increased energy of the water molecules causes them to overcome molecular attractions more effectively and spread apart.

Up to 4°C, the first effect wins out and water increases in density. Above 4°C, the first phenomenon continues to occur, but the effect of the second becomes much greater. Thus, above 4°C, the density of water decreases.

Groups of water molecules must absorb enough energy to break up into single molecules before water boils. This energy requirement makes the boiling point of water relatively high. It also makes it necessary to use a large amount of heat to vaporize water at its normal boiling point.

Table 12-4

DENSITY OF WATER

°C	g/ml
0	0.99987
1	0.99993
2	0.99997
3	0.99999
4	1.00000
5	0.99999
6	0.99997
7	0.99993
8	0.99988
9	0.99981
10	0.99973
15	0.99913
20	0.99823
25	0.99707
30	0.99567
40	0.99224
50	0.98807
60	0.98324
70	0.97781
80	0.97183
90	0.96534
100	0.95838

12.18 Chemical behavior of water

1. Stability of water. Water is a very ***stable compound.*** *A stable compound is one that does not break up, or decompose, easily.* Mercury(II) oxide, on the other hand, is a rather ***unstable compound.*** *This means that it does not require much energy to decompose it into its elements.* Water is so stable that it does not decompose a measurable amount until its temperature reaches about 2700°C. The stability of water is evidence of the strength of the covalent bonds between the oxygen and hydrogen atoms.

The type of replacement reaction, replacement of hydrogen in water by metals, was described in Section 8.6(2).

2. Behavior with metals. Very active metals such as sodium and potassium react with cold water, setting free hydrogen and forming metallic hydroxide solutions.

$$2Na(s) + 2HOH(l) \rightarrow 2NaOH(aq) + H_2(g)$$

Magnesium reacts with boiling water and forms magnesium hydroxide and hydrogen. When heated red hot, iron reacts with steam and forms iron oxide and hydrogen. Aluminum and zinc also react with water at high temperatures.

The reactions of water with metallic oxides are composition reactions. See Section 8.4(1).

3. Behavior with metallic oxides. The oxides of many metals are insoluble, and water has little or no effect upon them. But water does react with the ionic oxides of the very active metals. The oxides of sodium, potassium, calcium, and barium unite with water and form soluble hydroxides. Soluble metallic hydroxides are compounds whose water solutions have *basic* properties. Some basic properties of a solution are a slippery feeling, a bitter taste, and the ability to change red litmus to blue. Calcium hydroxide is formed when water is added to calcium oxide, CaO.

$$CaO(s) + H_2O(l) \rightarrow Ca(OH)_2(s)$$

Compounds such as calcium oxide, CaO, are known as *anhydrides.* The word anhydride means "without water." Since it forms a solution with basic properties when water is added to it, calcium oxide is called a *basic anhydride. A* ***basic anhydride*** *is the oxide of a metal that unites with water and forms a solution having basic properties.*

The reactions of water with the oxides of nonmetals are also composition reactions, Section 8.4(1).

4. Behavior with oxides of nonmetals. The oxides of such nonmetals as carbon, sulfur, and phosphorus are molecular compounds with polar covalent bonds. They unite with water and form a solution with *acidic* properties. Two acidic properties are a sour taste and the ability to turn blue litmus to red. For example, water unites with carbon dioxide and forms carbonic acid, H_2CO_3.

$$CO_2(g) + H_2O(l) \rightarrow H_2CO_3(aq)$$

Carbon dioxide is an anhydride which, with water, forms a solution having acidic properties. Therefore, it is called an *acid anhydride. An* ***acid anhydride*** *is the oxide of a nonmetal which unites with water and forms a solution having acidic properties.*

5. *Water of crystallization.* In some crystals, many positive ions and a few negative ions are surrounded by a definite number of water molecules. These crystals are formed by evaporating the water from their solutions. This water is called *water of crystallization or water of hydration. A crystallized substance that contains water of crystallization is a* ***hydrate.*** Each hydrate holds a definite proportion of water that is necessary for the formation of its crystal structure. For example, blue crystals of copper(II) sulfate consist of copper(II) ions, sulfate ions, and water molecules. Each copper(II) ion is surrounded by four water molecules. Each sulfate ion is associated with one water molecule. The formula of this substance is written as

$$CuSO_4 \cdot 5H_2O$$

This formula is empirical in two ways:

1. The empirical formula $CuSO_4$ shows the composition of the crystal with respect to copper(II) and sulfate ions.

2. The water of crystallization is shown as the *total* per formula unit of copper(II) sulfate. This total is expressed as $\cdot 5H_2O$. If $CuSO_4 \cdot 5H_2O$ is heated to a temperature slightly above the boiling point of water, the water of crystallization is driven off.

$$CuSO_4 \cdot 5H_2O(s) \rightarrow CuSO_4(s) + 5H_2O(g)$$

The substance that then remains is called an ***anhydrous compound.*** Anhydrous copper(II) sulfate, $CuSO_4$, is a white powder. It can be prepared by heating the blue $CuSO_4 \cdot 5H_2O$ crystals gently in a test tube. The fact that water turns anhydrous copper(II) sulfate blue may be used as a *test for water.*

Other examples of hydrates are the compounds $ZnSO_4 \cdot 7H_2O$, $CoCl_2 \cdot 6H_2O$, and $Na_2CO_3 \cdot 10H_2O$. Some hydrates have two or more forms that are stable over different temperature ranges. Many other compounds form crystals that do not require water of crystallization. Examples are NaCl, KNO_3, and $KClO_3$.

6. *Water promotes many chemical changes.* One good example of these changes is the reaction of an effervescent (fizzing) alkalizing tablet, which is a dry mixture. As long as the tablet is kept dry, no chemical action occurs. When the tablet is dropped in water, the substances in the mixture dissolve and react immediately. Bubbles of gas are given off (see Figure 12-19). Mixtures of many other dry substances do not react until water is added. The way water promotes chemical changes will be more fully explained in Unit 5.

Fig. 12-19. Water acts to promote some reactions, as shown when effervescent alkalizing tablets are added to water.

12.19 Efflorescence

Suppose we put ten grams of sodium carbonate crystals, $Na_2CO_3 \cdot 10H_2O$, on a watch glass on one pan of a balance. We add weights to the other pan until the pans are balanced.

Fig. 12-20. Calcium chloride removes water vapor from the air to control the dust on an unpaved road.

In a few minutes, the crystals begin to show a loss of mass. At the same time, the crystals lose their glassy luster (shine) and become powdery. By the end of the laboratory period, the loss in mass may amount to a gram or more. This loss in mass results from the loss of some of the molecules of water of crystallization.

$$\mathbf{Na_2CO_3 \cdot 10H_2O(s) \rightarrow Na_2CO_3 \cdot H_2O(s) + 9H_2O(g)}$$

The loss of some or all molecules of water of crystallization when a hydrate is exposed to the air is called ***efflorescence.***

Efflorescence occurs when the water vapor pressure of the hydrate is greater than the partial pressure of the water vapor in the air surrounding it. Consequently, efflorescence occurs much more rapidly in a warm, dry atmosphere than in one that is cool and moist. The water vapor pressure of hydrates varies greatly. $Na_2CO_3 \cdot 10H_2O$ has a high water vapor pressure and effloresces quite rapidly. $CuSO_4 \cdot 5H_2O$, on the other hand, has a low water vapor pressure. It can be exposed to the air at room temperature without efflorescence.

12.20 Deliquescence

Suppose we now put ten grams of calcium chloride granules on a watch glass on one pan of a balance. We add weights to the other pan until the pans are just balanced. After the calcium chloride has been exposed to moist air for half an hour, it shows a decided gain in mass. The granules have become moist; they may even have formed a solution with water from the air. *Certain substances take up water from the air and form solutions. This property is called* ***deliquescence.*** Deliquescent substances are very soluble in water. Their concentrated solutions have water vapor pressures lower than the normal range of partial pressures of water vapor in the air. Consequently, such substances and their solutions absorb water vapor from the air more rapidly than they give it off. The absorption of water results in a gradual dilution of the solution involved. Absorption and dilution continue until the water vapor pressure of the solution and the partial pressure of water vapor in the surrounding air are equal.

Many insoluble materials such as silk, wool, hair, and tobacco take up water vapor from the air. The water molecules may be held in pores and imperfections of the solid. All such materials, along with deliquescent substances, are classed as *hygroscopic.*

12.21 Deuterium oxide

Most water molecules are composed of hydrogen atoms with mass number 1 and oxygen atoms with mass number 16. But there are other possible types of water molecules. There are two natural isotopes of hydrogen with mass numbers 1 and 2.

There are three natural isotopes of oxygen, with mass numbers 16, 17, and 18. The possible combinations of these five nuclides give nine types of water molecules. In liquid water, these molecules are associated most commonly in chains of from four to eight units. In water, there is also a very small proportion of hydronium (H_3O^+) ions, hydroxide ions, and oxide ions. These ions are formed from the various isotopes of hydrogen and oxygen. Thus, water is a complex mixture of many kinds of molecules and ions.

Particles other than ordinary water molecules exist in only small traces in a water sample. But one such type of water molecule has been studied rather extensively. This is the *deuterium oxide* molecule, D_2O. The symbol D is used to represent an atom of the isotope of hydrogen with mass number 2. Electrolysis separates D_2O from H_2O. The D_2O molecules are not as readily decomposed by the passage of electric current as are H_2O molecules. Thus, the concentration of D_2O molecules increases as H_2O molecules are decomposed. From 2400 liters of water, 83 ml of D_2O that is 99% pure can be obtained.

Deuterium oxide is about 10% denser than ordinary water. It boils at 101.42°C, freezes at 3.82°C, and has its maximum density at 11.6°C. Delicate tests have been devised for detecting deuterium oxide. It has been used as a "tracer" in research work on living organisms. By tracing the course of deuterium oxide molecules through such organisms, scientists have gained new information about certain life processes. Deuterium oxide usually produces harmful effects on living things, particularly when present in high concentrations. The most important use of deuterium oxide is in nuclear reactors. You will learn more about this use of deuterium oxide in Chapter 30.

SUMMARY

All liquids have the properties of definite volume, fluidity, noncompressibility, diffusion, and evaporation. These properties can be explained by the spacing, motion, and attractive forces of molecules of liquids.

Physical equilibrium is a dynamic state in which two opposing physical changes occur at equal rates in the same system. Equilibrium vapor pressure is the pressure exerted by a vapor in equilibrium with its liquid. The amount of equilibrium vapor pressure depends on the nature of the liquid and its temperature. The principle of Le Chatelier is as follows: If a system at equilibrium is subjected to a stress, the equilibrium will be displaced in such a direction as to relieve the stress. Stresses on a physical equilibrium system may be changes in pressure, temperature, and volume. The boiling point of a liquid is the temperature at which the equilibrium vapor pressure of the liquid equals the prevailing atmospheric pressure.

Liquefying a gas requires two steps: (*1*) compressing the gas and then removing the heat of compression; (*2*) permitting the cool compressed gas to expand without absorbing external energy. The highest temperature at which it is possible to liquefy a gas with any amount of pressure is called its critical temperature. The pressure required to liquefy a gas at its critical temperature is called its critical pressure. The volume occupied by one mole of a gas under these conditions is called its critical volume. Critical temperature is related to the strength of the attractive forces between molecules.

General properties of solids are definite shape, definite volume, noncompressibility, very slow diffusion, and crystal formation. These properties can also be explained by the spacing, motion, and attractive forces between particles of solids.

Freezing is the physical change of a liquid to a solid. The reverse physical change is melting. The change of phase from a solid to a vapor is known as sublimation.

Amorphous solids are those that appear to have random particle arrangement. A crystal is a homogeneous portion of a substance bounded by plane surfaces making definite angles with each other, giving a regular geometric form. There are six crystal systems. Crystalline materials may have ionic, covalent-network, metallic, or covalent-molecular lattice structures.

Water is the most abundant and essential liquid on earth, and water molecules are widespread in the known universe. Pure water is transparent, odorless, tasteless, and almost colorless. Impurities may affect its odor and taste. Water freezes at 0°C and boils at 100°C under standard pressure. Water molecules are polar molecules. They are linked by hydrogen bonds into groups of from four to eight molecules in liquid water. A hydrogen bond is a weak chemical bond between a hydrogen atom in one polar molecule and a very electronegative atom in a second polar molecule.

Water is a very stable compound. It reacts with active metals such as sodium and potassium. Steam reacts with red-hot iron. The ionic oxides of very active metals are basic anhydrides, and the covalent oxides of nonmetals are acid anhydrides. Many crystals contain water of crystallization which may be driven off by heat, forming anhydrous compounds. Water promotes many chemical changes.

The loss of some or all molecules of water of crystallization when a hydrate is exposed to the air is called efflorescence. The property of certain substances of taking up water from the air and forming solutions is deliquescence. Insoluble materials that take up water vapor from the air, as well as deliquescent substances, are hygroscopic.

Deuterium oxide is used in research work on living organisms and in nuclear reactors.

QUESTIONS

Group A

1. How does the kinetic theory explain these properties of liquids: (*a*) definite volume; (*b*) fluidity; (*c*) noncompressibility; (*d*) diffusion; (*e*) evaporation?
2. What evidence is there that the particles of a liquid are in constant motion?
3. Describe the conditions prevailing in a system in equilibrium.
4. Would you expect an equilibrium vapor pressure to be reached in the space above a liquid in an open container? Why?
5. Water standing in a covered flask experiences a drop in temperature of $\bar{10}$ C°. How is the liquid-vapor equilibrium disturbed? Explain.
6. What effect does the pressure on a water surface have on the boiling temperature of the water?
7. Define (*a*) critical temperature; (*b*) critical pressure; (*c*) critical volume.
8. What conditions must be met in order for a gas to be liquefied?
9. How does the kinetic theory explain these properties of solids: (*a*) definite

shape; (*b*) definite volume; (*c*) noncompressibility; (*d*) very slow diffusion; (*e*) crystal formation?

10. What are the general properties of solids composed of (*a*) ions; (*b*) molecules; (*c*) atoms in a covalent network structure; (*d*) metal ions in an electron "gas"?
11. Where does water occur?
12. List six physical properties of water.
13. How does the volume of steam compare with the volume of water from which it was produced?
14. (*a*) Write a formula equation for the melting of one mole of ice at 0°C to water at 0°C, including the quantity of energy involved. (*b*) Similarly, write an equation for the boiling of one mole of water at 100°C to steam at 100°C.
15. Describe the structure of the water molecule, and tell why it is a polar molecule.
16. (*a*) What is a hydrogen bond? (*b*) What effect do the hydrogen bonds in water have on its boiling point?
17. (*a*) What is a stable compound? Give an example. (*b*) What is an unstable compound? Give an example.
18. (*a*) List five metals that react with water. (*b*) Give the conditions under which they react.
19. (*a*) What is an anhydride? (*b*) Distinguish between a basic anhydride and an acid anhydride. (*c*) What type of compound may be an acid anhydride? (*d*) What type of compound may be a basic anhydride?
20. What is the significance of the raised dot in $BaCl_2 \cdot 2H_2O$?
21. Give an example of a chemical change promoted by the presence of water.
22. A package of washing soda, $Na_2CO_3 \cdot 10H_2O$, labeled "one pound" was found to weigh only 14 ounces. Was the packer necessarily dishonest? Explain.
23. (*a*) Explain why anhydrous calcium chloride may be used to keep the air in a basement dry. (*b*) Suggest a suitable method of accomplishing this.
24. How is deuterium oxide separated from ordinary water?
25. Give some uses for deuterium oxide.

Group B

26. What kinds of particles compose substances that are liquids (*a*) well below room temperature; (*b*) at room temperature; (*c*) well above room temperature?
27. (*a*) Using the curves of Fig. 12-7, determine the temperature at which water in an open vessel will boil when the atmospheric pressure is reduced to $60\bar{0}$ mm. (*b*) What is the boiling point of alcohol at this pressure? (*c*) of ether?
28. The system **alcohol(l) + energy $\leftrightarrows$ alcohol(g)** is at equilibrium in a closed container at $5\bar{0}$°C. What will be the effect of each of the following stresses on the equilibrium? (*a*) Temperature is raised to $6\bar{0}$°C. (*b*) Volume of container is doubled. (*c*) Barometer rises from $72\bar{0}$ mm to $74\bar{0}$ mm.
29. (*a*) Why does compressing a gas raise its temperature? (*b*) Why does a gas become colder when it is allowed to expand?
30. (*a*) Can carbon dioxide be liquefied at $10\bar{0}$°C? (*b*) Can chlorine be liquefied at $10\bar{0}$°C? Explain.
31. (*a*) How does the addition of the molar heat of vaporization affect the energy of the particles of one mole of liquid at its standard boiling point? (*b*) How does the addition of the molar heat of fusion affect the energy of the particles of one mole of a solid at its standard melting point?
32. A bottle of alum crystals was erroneously labeled "sodium chloride." How could the error be detected at once by an alert chemistry student?
33. Camphor crystals are soft and volatile. Explain.
34. Why is water essential on earth?
35. Explain why ice occupies a greater volume than the water from which it is formed.

36. The system **ice + energy ⇄ water** is at equilibrium at 0°C in an open vessel. What will be the effect on the system if (*a*) heat is supplied to the system; (*b*) heat is removed from the system; (*c*) the pressure on the system is increased?
37. Explain why water has a point of maximum density at 4°C.
38. What does the extreme stability of H_2O molecules indicate about the strength of the covalent bonds between the oxygen and hydrogen atoms?
39. Tobacco growers prefer to handle dried tobacco leaves during damp weather. Explain.
40. What particles are present in pure water besides ordinary H_2O molecules?
41. The quotation from Coleridge's "*The Rime of the Ancient Mariner*" in the caption of the illustration on page 225 is a good reminder of water's abundance and necessity. Discuss the meaning of this quotation in terms of the properties of sea water.

PROBLEMS

Group A

1. A mixture of 50.0 ml of hydrogen and 30.0 ml of oxygen is ignited by an electric spark. What gas remains? What is its volume in milliliters?
2. A mixture of 40.0 ml of oxygen and 120.0 ml of hydrogen is ignited. What gas remains and how many milliliters does it occupy?
3. (*a*) How many milliliters of hydrogen are needed for complete reaction with 37.5 ml of oxygen? (*b*) What fraction of a mole of water is produced?
4. A mixture of equal volumes of oxygen and hydrogen has a volume of 100.0 ml. (*a*) After the mixture is ignited, what gas remains, and what is its volume in milliliters? (*b*) How many millimoles of water are formed?
5. How many grams of hydrogen and oxygen are required in order to produce 15.0 moles of water?
6. (*a*) The volume of a water molecule is 15 Å³. From this information, calculate the volume in milliliters one mole of water should occupy. (*b*) From the gram-molecular weight of water and its density at 4°C, calculate the volume in milliliters actually occupied by one mole of water. (*c*) What is the meaning of the difference between these two results?

Group B

7. How many grams of anhydrous sodium carbonate can be obtained by heating $1\bar{0}0$ g of $Na_2CO_3 \cdot 10H_2O$?
8. Calculate the percentage of cobalt, chlorine, and water in $CoCl_2 \cdot 6H_2O$.
9. What is the empirical formula of hydrated crystals composed of 56.14% $ZnSO_4$ and 43.86% water?
10. If 124.8 g of copper(II) sulfate crystals is heated to drive off the water of crystallization, the loss of mass is 45.0 g. What is the percentage of water in hydrated copper(II) sulfate?
11. The anhydrous copper(II) sulfate in Problem 10 was found to contain copper, 31.8 g; sulfur, 16.0 g; and oxygen, 32.0 g. What is the empirical formula of hydrated copper(II) sulfate crystals?
12. The density of carbon tetrachloride at 0°C is 1.600 g/ml. (*a*) Calculate the volume in milliliters occupied by a molecule of CCl_4. (*b*) Assuming the CCl_4 molecule to be spherical, calculate its approximate diameter in angstroms.
13. Obtain from Figure 5-6 the radius of an atom of mercury. (*a*) Assuming this atom to be spherical, what is its volume in Å³? (*b*) If liquid mercury atoms are packed in a cubic array with six nearest neighbors, what is the volume in milliliters of 1.00 mole of liquid mercury?

chapter 13

THE SOLUTION PROCESS

Certain kinds of crystals separating from solution may rival the artistic constructions of humans. (See Question 26 on page 274.)

13.1 Solutions and suspensions

If a lump of sugar is dropped into a cup of water, it gradually disappears. The sugar is said to *dissolve* in the water. If you examined a drop of this water with a microscope, you would not see the dissolved sugar. By tasting the liquid, however, you can tell that the sugar is there. What happens is that molecules of sugar become uniformly distributed among the molecules of water. For this reason, the same degree of sweetness is detected in all parts of the liquid. Such a mixture of sugar and water is homogeneous throughout. It is an example of a *solution*.

By definition, then, *a* ***solution*** *is a homogeneous mixture of two or more substances, whose composition may vary within characteristic limits.* The dissolving medium is called the *solvent*. The substance that dissolves is called the *solute*. The simplest solution is made up of molecules of a single solute distributed throughout a single solvent. In the example of the sugar-water solution given above, sugar is the solute and water is the solvent.

Water is the most common solvent.

Not all substances form true solutions in water. If clay is mixed with water, for example, very little actually dissolves. Particles of clay are huge compared to molecules of water. The result is a muddy, heterogeneous mixture called a *suspension*. Because the components of the mixture have different densities, they readily separate into two distinct phases. However, some very small particles, though still much larger than water molecules, are kept permanently suspended. They are bombarded from all sides by water molecules and this bombard-

Fig. 13-1. A beam of light can be used to distinguish a colloidal suspension from a true solution. The jar at the left contains a water solution of sodium chloride. The jar at the right contains a suspension of gelatin in water.

The colloidal state has been called the world of neglected dimensions. It lies between true solutions and coarse suspensions that separate on standing. Colloidal size ranges between ordinary molecular size and a size great enough to be seen through a microscope. Colloidal particles have dimensions ranging from approximately 10 Å to 10,000 Å. Ordinary simple molecules are only a few angstroms in diameter.

Solutions are homogeneous mixtures.

Colloidal suspensions are heterogeneous mixtures.

Fig. 13-2. A colloidal suspension is held back by the parchment membrane, permitting it to be separated from substances in solution.

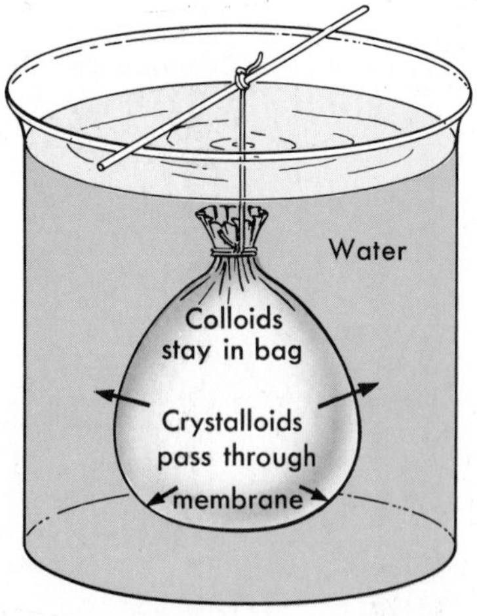

ment keeps them from settling out. Such mixtures may appear to be homogeneous, but careful examination shows that they are not true solutions. Mixtures of this type are called *colloidal suspensions.* See Figure 13-1.

The term *colloid* was originally applied to sticky substances such as starch and glue. *Colloids* are substances that, when mixed with water, do not pass through parchment membranes. In contrast, substances such as sugar and salt form true solutions with water and do pass through parchment membranes. These substances were called *crystalloids.*

Under certain conditions, some substances are nondiffusing and colloidal. Under different conditions, they are crystalloidal in behavior. We now know that *the state of subdivision,* rather than the chemical nature of a substance, determines whether it forms a suspension or a true solution when dispersed (scattered) in a second medium. For example, a colloidal suspension may be formed if sodium ions and chloride ions are brought together in a medium in which sodium chloride is not soluble. Colloidal-sized crystals, each consisting of many sodium ions and chloride ions, may form in the medium.

A true solution is formed when a solute, as molecules or ions, is dispersed throughout a solvent and forms a homogeneous mixture. It consists of a *single phase.* The solute is said to be *soluble* in the solvent. A colloidal suspension, on the other hand, is a *two-phase system.* It has dispersed particles rather than a solute, and a dispersing medium rather than a solvent. The dispersed substance (*internal phase*) is not soluble in the dispersing medium (*external phase*). The system consists of finely divided particles that remain suspended in the medium.

We stated in Section 6.3 that electrovalent solids do not exist as molecules. Instead, each has a crystal lattice composed of ions bound together by the strong electrostatic force of attraction between positive and negative charges. Such substances are called ***electrolytes*** because their water solutions conduct electricity.

Generally, covalent substances that dissolve in water are present in the solution as neutral molecules. Neutral molecules do not conduct electricity. Such substances are called ***nonelectrolytes.*** Many acids are exceptions. When undissolved, they are molecular and do not conduct an electric current. However, their water solutions do conduct electricity. These acids are electrolytes.

Solutions of electrolytes have physical properties that are different from solutions of nonelectrolytes. Electrolytes will be considered in detail in Chapters 14 and 15. The remainder of our present discussion of the properties of solutions will deal primarily with solutions of nonelectrolytes.

skin deep

1

2

3

4

Vinegar is mostly water. When it's shaken with oil in a salad dressing, the oil and vinegar separate quickly into two layers (1). However, the oil and water in mayonnaise, hand cream, or kitchen cleaner stay mixed indefinitely (2). All three are emulsions. They are colloidal suspensions of two liquids that ordinarily are not soluble in each other.

Emulsions are often stabilized with an emulsifying agent. In the case of mayonnaise, the emulsifying agent is a mixture of egg yolk and spices that acts on the surface of the oil giving each droplet the same electric charge. Since electric charges that are alike repel each other, these charges keep each droplet separated from the others. The droplets cannot join together and form particles large enough to float to the surface.

Foam is a mixture of a gas in a liquid. The gas particles are of colloidal size. Whipped egg white and foamy shave cream are examples of foams (3).

Some colloids flow so slowly that they are nearly solids. These colloids are called gels. Examples are jelly, gelatin dessert, or stick deodorant (4).

Colloids are very important to life. Many foods we eat are colloids. In addition, biocolloids—particles of carbohydrates, proteins, and fats of colloidal size, make up the protoplasm of cells. As a cell carries on the processes of life, these biocolloids form gels in some places while in other places they flow freely. This "streaming" of the protoplasm nourishes all parts of the cell while the biocolloid gels give the cell its shape.

Table 13-1

TYPES OF SOLUTION		
Solute	Solvent	Example
gas	gas	air
gas	liquid	soda water
gas	solid	hydrogen on platinum
liquid	gas	water vapor in air
liquid	liquid	alcohol in water
liquid	solid	mercury in copper
solid	gas	sulfur vapor in air
solid	liquid	sugar in water
solid	solid	copper in nickel

Adsorption is a surface phenomenon. See Section 9.18.

Fig. 13-3. Models of solutions.

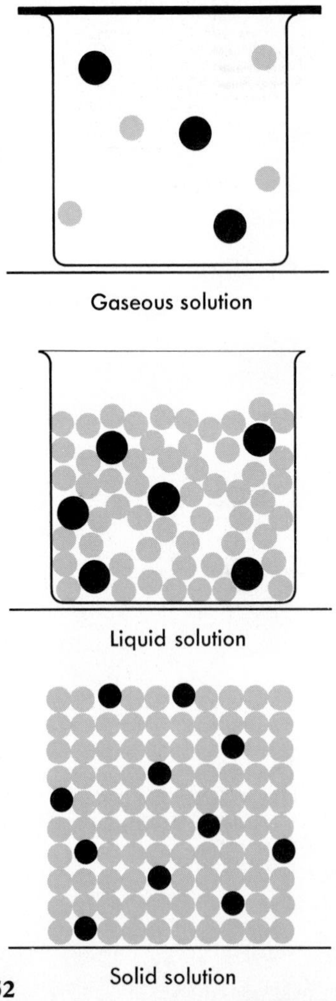

13.2 Types of solutions

Matter may exist as a solid, liquid, or gas, depending upon temperature and pressure. Therefore, nine different types of solutions are possible. These types of solutions are listed in Table 13-1.

All mixtures of gases are solutions, since they consist of homogeneous systems of different kinds of molecules. Solutions of solids in liquids are very common. Since water is a liquid at ordinary temperatures, we may think of water vapor in air as a liquid-in-gas solution. Solutions of gases in solids are rare. An example is the *condensation* of hydrogen on the surface of palladium and platinum. This phenomenon, called *adsorption,* approaches the nature of a solution.

Perhaps a more familiar example of adsorption is illustrated in the use of a charcoal gas mask to remove toxic gases from air before it is inhaled. A porous wafer of charcoal presents an unusually large surface area of carbon atoms. These surface carbon atoms attract gas molecules, especially of the polar type. When a mixture of toxic gases and air is passed over the surface of the charcoal, the toxic gas molecules are selectively adsorbed and air passes on through for respiration. Toxic gases are usually complex polar molecules. The air gases, mainly nitrogen and oxygen, are simple nonpolar molecules. Layers of other materials can be added to the charcoal wafer to remove smokes, dusts, mists, carbon monoxide, etc.

In general, substances that are alike in their chemical makeup are apt to form solutions. Silver and gold, or alcohol and water, are examples. *Two liquids that are mutually soluble in each other are said to be* ***miscible.*** Ethanol (ethyl alcohol) and water are miscible in all proportions. Similarly, ether and ethanol are completely miscible. Ether and water, on the other hand, are only slightly miscible. Acetone is completely miscible with water, alcohol, and ether.

13.3 Solvents are selective

High solubility occurs when solutes and solvents are alike structurally. In a very general sense, the *possibility* of solvent action is increased by a similarity in the composition and structure of substances. Chemists believe that the distribution of electronic forces helps to explain why solvents are *selective.* That is, it may explain why solvents dissolve some substances readily and others only to an insignificant extent.

The water molecule is a polar structure with a distinct negative region (the oxygen atom) and a distinct positive region (the hydrogen atoms). It is frequently referred to as the *water dipole.* The two polar covalent O—H bonds in water form an angle of about 105°. Thus, the molecule as a whole is polar and behaves as a dipole (has a negative region and a positive region).

The carbon tetrachloride molecule, CCl_4, contains four polar covalent bonds. Each C—Cl bond is formed by electron sharing between an sp^3 hybrid orbital of the carbon atom and a p orbital of a chlorine atom. The set of four sp^3 orbitals of carbon (see Section 6.17) leads to the regular tetrahedral shape of the CCl_4 molecules (Figure 13-4). Because of the symmetrical arrangement of the four polar bonds, the molecule is nonpolar. On the other hand, gasoline-type compounds, while unsymmetrical in bond arrangement, are practically nonpolar. They are practically nonpolar because the electronegativity difference between the hydrogen and carbon atoms of which they are composed is small.

Suppose we apply the rough rule that *like dissolves like* to these solvents. According to this rule, we would expect water to dissolve polar substances and carbon tetrachloride to dissolve nonpolar substances. Solute crystals composed of polar molecules or ions are held together by strong attractive forces. They are more likely to be attracted away from their solid structures by polar water molecules than by nonpolar solvents. Thus, many crystalline salts like table salt and molecular solids like sugar readily dissolve in water. Compounds that are insoluble in water, such as oils and greases, readily dissolve in nonpolar carbon tetrachloride.

Ethanol, C_2H_5OH, is typical of a group of solvents that dissolve both polar and nonpolar substances.

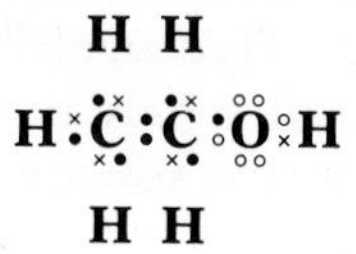

There are five essentially nonpolar carbon-hydrogen bonds. Also, there is one carbon-carbon bond that is completely nonpolar. The carbon-oxygen bond and the hydrogen-oxygen bond are polar. As in water, the oxygen region of an ethanol molecule is more negative than the other regions. Thus, an ethanol molecule has some polar character. This may account for the fact that ethanol is a good solvent for some polar and some nonpolar substances. As a solvent, it is in an intermediate position between the strongly polar water molecule and the nonpolar carbon tetrachloride molecule.

13.4 Hydrogen bonds and properties of solvents

Electronegativity is the measure of the tendency of an atom in a molecule to attract shared electrons (Section 6.9). Hydrogen atoms form distinctly polar covalent bonds with atoms of such highly electronegative elements as fluorine, oxygen, chlorine, and nitrogen. The hydrogen end of these polar bonds is unique. It consists of an essentially exposed proton. Shared electrons are more strongly attracted by the highly electro-

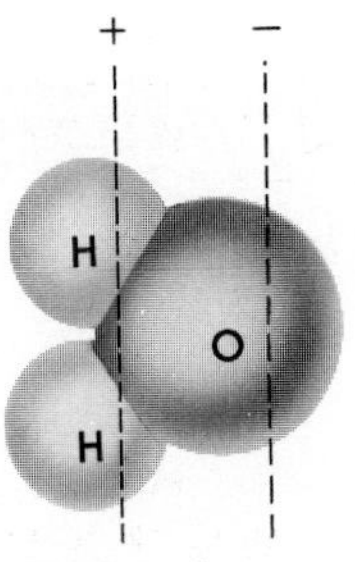

H_2O (polar)

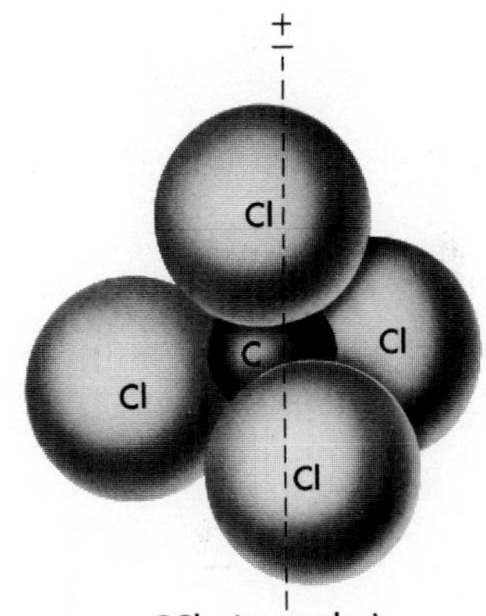

CCl_4 (nonpolar)

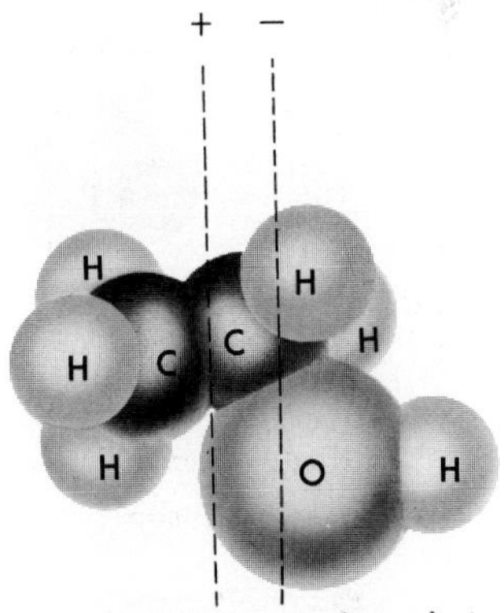

C_2H_5OH (nonpolar-polar)

Fig. 13-4. Molecular models of three common solvents. Differences in molecular structure may help to explain why they are selective.

negative atom than by hydrogen. The effect of this unequal sharing is to leave the hydrogen nucleus (a proton) without an electron shield to isolate its positive charge.

Hydrogen bonds are loose chemical bonds.

Because of the unique character of the hydrogen end of the bond, the polar molecules formed may experience relatively strong intermolecular forces. The positive hydrogen end of one molecule may attract the highly electronegative atom of another molecule strongly enough to think of it as a loose chemical bond. This bond between such molecules is called the *hydrogen bond* (Section 12.17). Although hydrogen bonds between hydrogen and fluorine are stronger, those with oxygen are by far the most common. See Figure 13-5.

We have learned that it is the uniqueness of the polar bonds between atoms of hydrogen atoms and those of highly electronegative elements that explains hydrogen bonding between their molecules. Apart from hydrogen, all elements that share electrons with highly electronegative elements differ with hydrogen in one significant way. Their atoms have inner-shell electrons that continue to isolate or shield their nuclear charges when the polar bonds are formed. The positive ends of their bonds do not have the unique character of hydrogen in such polar bonds. Their molecules, however polar, do not exhibit hydrogen-bond behavior. The abnormally high boiling and melting points of water may be attributed in part to hydrogen bonds among water molecules. Also, the formation of hydrogen bonds between a solvent and a solute increases the solubility of the solute. Hydrogen bond formation between water and ethanol molecules may partially explain the complete miscibility of these two substances.

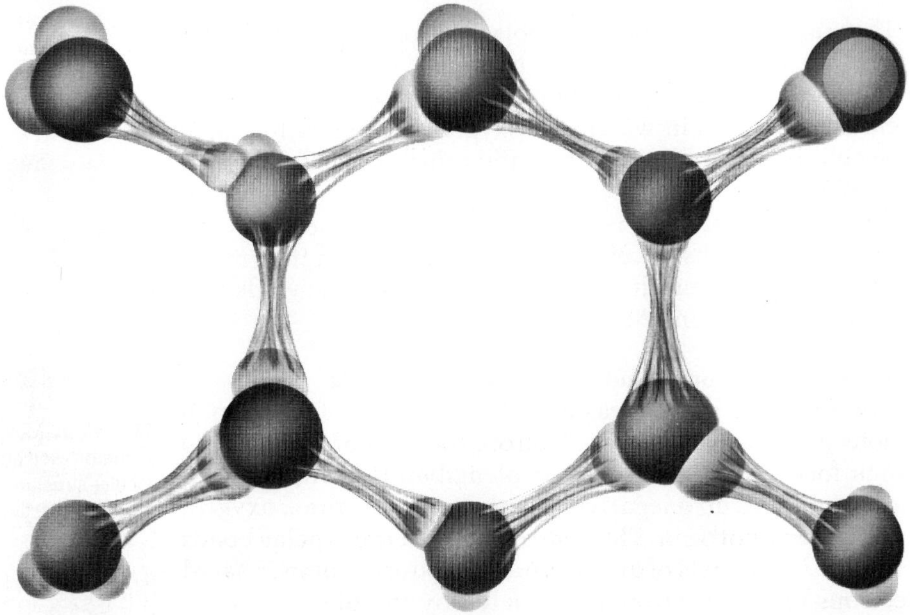

Fig. 13-5. Hydrogen bond formation in an ice crystal.

13.5 Solution equilibrium

We may think of the solution process as being *reversible.* Suppose we again consider the lump of sugar dropped into a beaker of water. The sugar molecules that break away from the crystals and enter the water have completely random motions. Some of these molecules that have broken away come in contact with the undissolved sugar. Here they are attracted by the sugar molecules in the crystal and become part of the crystal structure once more. Thus, the solution process includes both the act of dissolving and the act of crystallizing.

At first, there are no sugar molecules in solutions. The solution process occurs only in the direction of dissolving. Molecules leave the crystal structure and diffuse throughout the water. *As the solution concentration (number of sugar molecules per unit volume of solution) increases, the reverse process begins.* The rate at which the sugar crystals rebuild increases as the concentration of the sugar solution increases. Eventually, if undissolved sugar remains, sugar crystals rebuild as fast as they dissolve.

The solution process involves two actions: (1) *dissolving and* (2) *crystallizing.*

At this point, the concentration of the solution is the maximum possible under existing conditions. Such a solution is said to be *saturated.* An *equilibrium* is reached between undissolved sugar and sugar dissolved in water. ***Solution equilibrium*** *is the physical state in which the opposing processes of dissolving and crystallizing of a solute occur at equal rates. A* ***saturated solution*** *is one in which the dissolved and undissolved solutes are in equilibrium.* (In Figure 13-6, what visible evidence is there that this solution is saturated?)

Equilibrium is a dynamic state; two opposing actions go on at equal rates.

If more water is added to the sugar solution, it is no longer saturated; the concentration of solute molecules has been decreased. In the language of the Le Chatelier principle, the decrease in concentration of solute particles places a *stress* on the equilibrium. This stress is relieved by an increase in the dissolving rate. More sugar dissolves and restores *the same equilibrium concentration* of solute molecules. Solution equilibrium exists when no more solute can dissolve in a given quantity of solvent. *The* ***solubility*** *of a substance is defined as the maximum amount of that substance that can dissolve in a given amount of a certain solvent under specified conditions.*

Fig. 13-6. A saturated solution contains the equilibrium concentration of solute under existing conditions.

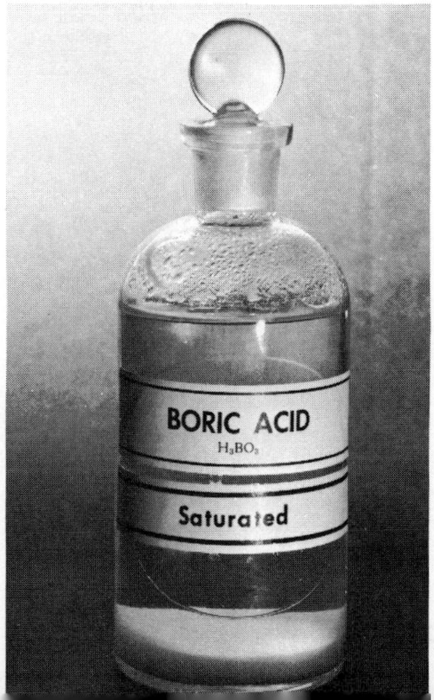

13.6 Influence of pressure on solubility

Ordinary changes in pressure affect the solubility of solids and liquids so slightly that we may ignore them altogether. Because all mixtures of gases are homogeneous, the solubility of one gas in another is independent of pressure. The gas laws describe the behavior of mixtures of gases just as they do of individual gases.

Fig. 13-7. A comparison of the masses of three common solutes that can be dissolved in $10\bar{0}$ g of water at 0°C. Convert these quantities to moles of solute per $10\bar{0}$ g of water and compare them.

The "fizz" of an opened bottle of any carbonated soft drink is an example of effervescence.

The solubility of gases in liquids and solids, on the other hand, is measurably affected by changes in pressure. Carbonated beverages *fizz* or *effervesce* when poured into an open glass tumbler. At the bottling plant, carbon dioxide gas is forced into solution in the flavored water under a pressure of from 5 to 10 atmospheres. While under such pressure, the gas-in-liquid solution is sealed in the bottles. When the cap is removed, the pressure is reduced to 1 atmosphere and some of the carbon dioxide escapes from solution as gas bubbles. *This rapid escape of a gas from a liquid in which it is dissolved is known as* ***effervescence.***

Solutions of gases in liquids reach equilibrium in about the same way that solids in liquids do. The attractive forces between gas molecules are insignificant on the average and their motions are relatively free. If a gas is in contact with the surface of a liquid, gas molecules can easily enter the liquid surface. As the concentration of dissolved gas molecules increases, some begin to escape from the liquid. The escaping molecules reenter the gaseous phase above the liquid. An equilibrium is eventually reached between the rates at which gas molecules are dissolving and escaping from solution. After the equilibrium is attained, there is no increase in the concentration of the gaseous solute. Thus, the solubility of the gas is limited to its equilibrium concentration in the liquid under existing conditions.

Suppose the pressure of the gas above the liquid is increased. The equilibrium is then disturbed in accordance with Le Chatelier's principle, and more gas dissolves. This action, of course, increases the concentration of the dissolved gas. The increased concentration, in turn, causes gas molecules to escape from the liquid surface at a faster rate. When equilibrium is restored, there is a higher concentration of solute at the higher external pressure. The increase in gas pressure also increases the concentration of undissolved gas in contact with the solvent. Thus, the solubility of the gas in the liquid is increased. *The solubility of a gas in a liquid is directly proportional to the pressure of the gas above the liquid.* This statement is known as ***Henry's law.*** It is named after William Henry, an English chemist (1775–1836).

Henry's law relates gas solubility and pressure.

Some gases react chemically with their liquid solvents. Such gases are generally more soluble than those that do not form compounds with the solvent molecules. Oxygen, hydrogen, and nitrogen are only slightly soluble in water. Ammonia, carbon dioxide, and sulfur dioxide are more soluble probably because they form the weak monohydrates $NH_3 \cdot H_2O$, $CO_2 \cdot H_2O$, and $SO_2 \cdot H_2O$ with the water solvent. Such gases do not follow Henry's law as stated above.

If different gases are mixed in a confined space of constant volume and at a definite temperature, *each gas exerts the same pressure as if it alone occupied the space.* The pressure of the mixture as a whole is the *total* of the individual or *partial* pressures of the gases composing the mixture. You will recognize this statement as *Dalton's law of partial pressures,* discussed in Section 10.14. The partial pressure of each gas is proportional to the number of molecules of that gas in the mixture.

If a mixture of gases is in contact with a liquid, the solubility of each gas is proportional to its partial pressure. Let us assume that the gases present in the mixture do not react in any way when in solution. Then each gas dissolves to the same extent that it would if the other gases were not present.

Air is about 20 percent oxygen. When air is bubbled through water, only about 20 percent as much oxygen dissolves as would dissolve if pure oxygen were used instead of air, at the same pressure. Oxygen remains dissolved in the water because it is in equilibrium with the oxygen in the air above the water. If the oxygen were removed from the air above the water, this equilibrium would be disturbed. By Le Chatelier's principle, the dissolved oxygen must eventually escape from the water. This fact is important when we consider the abundance of life that exists in water.

*Chemistry students should **know** Le Chatelier's principle.*

13.7 Temperature and solubility

1. Gases in liquids. A glass of water drawn from the hot water tap often appears milky. Tiny bubbles of air suspended throughout the water cause this cloudiness. The suspended air originally was *dissolved* in cold water. It was driven out of solution as the water was heated.

Raising the temperature of a solution increases the average speed of its molecules. Molecules of dissolved gas leave the solvent at a faster rate than gas molecules enter the solvent. This lowers the equilibrium concentration of the solute. Thus, the solubility of a gas decreases as the temperature of the solvent is increased. Table 11 of the Appendix shows how the solubility of gases varies with the kind of gas and the temperature.

2. *Solids in liquids.* An excess of sugar added to water results in an equilibrium between the sugar solute and the undissolved crystals. This equilibrium is characteristic of a saturated solution.

If the solution is warmed, the equilibrium is disturbed and solid sugar dissolves as the temperature of the solution rises. It is evident that the solubility of the sugar in water has increased with the rise in temperature. A new solution equilibrium is eventually reached at the higher solution temperature. At this temperature, the solution has a higher equilibrium concentration of solute sugar.

Solubility of a solute depends on the temperature of the solvent.

Cooling the solution causes dissolved sugar to separate as crystals. The separation of solute from the solution indicates that solubility diminishes as the temperature falls. No more than the equilibrium concentration of the solute can normally remain in solution. Thus, lowering the temperature disturbs the equilibrium, and sugar crystallizes from solution faster than solid crystals dissolve.

When hot saturated solutions are allowed to cool, the excess solutes usually but not always separate as expected. If, on cooling, crystallization of the excess solute does not occur, the solution is said to be *supersaturated.* The solution contains a higher concentration of solute than does the saturated solution at the lower temperature. Supersaturation can easily be demonstrated using a solute that is much more soluble in hot water than in cold water (sodium thiosulfate or sodium acetate for example). The hot saturated solution is filtered and left undisturbed to cool slowly.

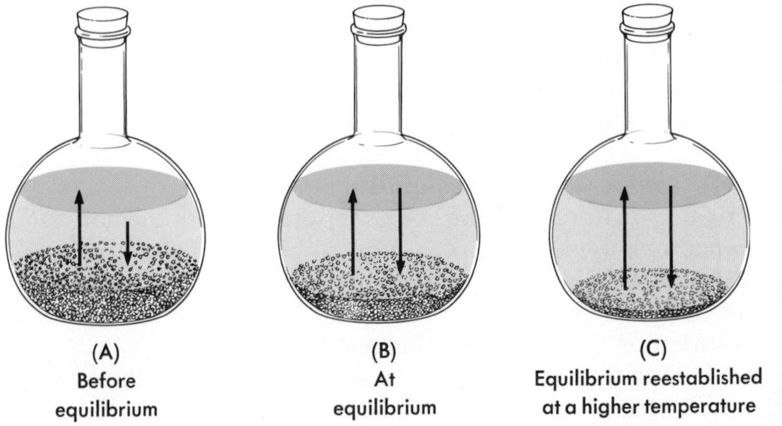

Fig. 13-8. An example of solution equilibrium in which the solubility of solute increases with temperature. The different lengths of arrows indicate the relative rates of dissolving (up) and crystallizing (down).

A supersaturated solution is unstable and usually has a strong tendency to reestablish normal equilibrium. A sudden shock or disturbance may cause the excess solute to separate. A small crystal fragment of the solute dropped into the solution (called seeding) starts the crystallizing process instantly.

Many pure liquids can be cooled below their normal freezing points with similar treatment. They are called *supercooled* liquids. As expected, this condition is unstable and the solutes usually show a strong tendency to solidify.

Increasing the temperature usually increases the solubility of solids in liquids. Sometimes, however, the reverse effect is observed. A certain rise in temperature may result in a large increase in solubility in one case, a slight increase in another case, and a definite decrease in still another. For example, the solubility of potassium nitrate in $1\bar{0}0$ g of water at 0°C is 13 g. Solubility increases to nearly 140 g when the temperature is raised to 70°C. Under similar circumstances, the solubility of sodium chloride increases only about 2 g. The solubility of cerium sulfate, on the other hand, decreases nearly 14 g. Typical solubility curves are shown in Figure 13-10. If the solubility curve for cane sugar in water were included, the graph would have to be extended considerably. At 0°C, 179 g of sugar dissolves in $1\bar{0}0$ g of water. The solubility increases to 487 g at 100°C. The solubility of solids depends upon the nature of the solid, the nature of the solvent, and the temperature. Solubility data for various substances in water are given in Table 13-2.

Fig. 13-9. Crystals of sugar growing on a string from a supersaturated solution of sugar in water.

The most common solutions are solids dissolved in liquids.

When a solid dissolves in a liquid, we may think of the solid as changing in phase to something resembling a liquid. Such a change is endothermic, and heat is absorbed. Thus, we expect

Table 13-2

SOLUBILITY OF SOLUTES AS A FUNCTION OF TEMPERATURE
(Grams of solute per 100 grams of H_2O)

Substance	0°	20°	40°	60°	80°	100°
$AgNO_3$	122	222	376	525	669	952
$Ba(OH)_2$	1.67	3.89	8.22	20.94	101.4	—
$C_{12}H_{22}O_{11}$	179	204	238	287	362	487
$Ca(OH)_2$	0.185	0.165	0.141	0.116	0.094	0.077
$Ce_2(SO_4)_3$	20.8	10.1	—	3.87	—	—
KCl	27.6	34.0	40.0	45.5	51.1	56.7
KI	128	144	$16\bar{0}$	176	192	208
KNO_3	13.3	31.6	63.9	$11\bar{0}$	169	246
Li_2CO_3	1.54	1.33	1.17	1.01	0.85	0.72
NaCl	35.7	36.0	36.6	37.3	38.4	39.8
$NaNO_3$	73	88	104	124	148	$18\bar{0}$
$Yb_2(SO_4)_3$	44.2	$38.4^{10°}$	$21.0^{30°}$	10.4	6.92	4.67
CO_2 (gas at SP)	0.335	0.169	0.097	0.058	—	—
O_2 (gas at SP)	0.0069	0.0043	0.0031	0.0023	0.0014	0.0000

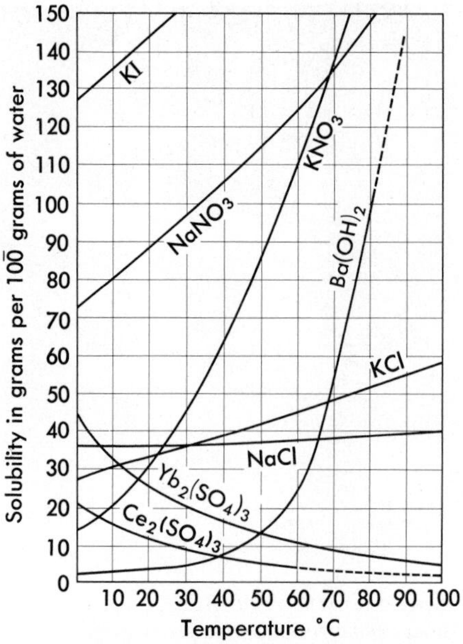

Fig. 13-10. Solubility curves. The solubility of a solute is expressed in grams per 10$\bar{0}$ grams of solvent, at a stated temperature.

Fig. 13-11. Solubility plotted in moles of solute per 10$\bar{0}$ g of water as a function of temperature. Compare the relative positions of the curves with those of Fig. 13-10.

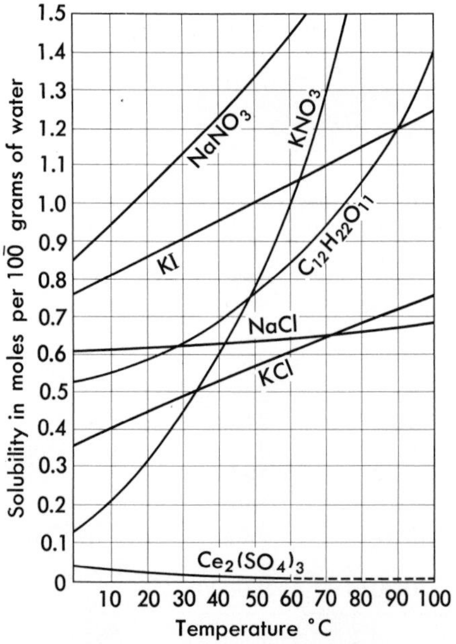

the temperature of the solution to be lowered as a solid dissolves. We also expect the solubility of a solid to increase as the temperature is raised. Deviations from this normal pattern may indicate some kind of chemical reaction between solute and solvent.

3. *Liquids in liquids.* Similar logic applies to solutions of liquids in liquids. As no change in phase occurs when such solutions are prepared, we expect little change in temperature.

A great change in temperature, as in the case of sulfuric acid in water, suggests some type of chemical reaction between solute and solvent. When water is the solvent, this reaction may involve *hydration*, a clustering of water dipoles about the solute particles.

13.8 Increasing the rate of dissolving

The rate at which a solid dissolves in a liquid depends on the solid and liquid involved. As a rule, the more nearly the solute and solvent are alike in structure, the more readily solution occurs. We may, however, increase the rate of solution of a solid in a liquid in three ways.

1. *By stirring.* The diffusion of solute molecules throughout the solvent occurs rather slowly. Stirring or shaking the mixture aids in the dispersion of the solute particles. It does so by bringing fresh portions of the solvent in contact with the undissolved solid.

2. *By powdering the solid.* Solution action occurs only at the surface of the solid. By grinding the solid into a fine powder, we greatly increase the surface area. Hence, finely powdered solids dissolve much more rapidly than large lumps or crystals of the same substance.

3. *By heating the solvent.* The rate of dissolving increases with temperature. If we apply heat to a solvent, the molecular activity increases. As a result, the dissolving action is speeded up. At the same time, the solubility of the substance increases if the dissolving process is endothermic.

The first two actions influence the rate of dissolving by increasing the effective contact area between solid and liquid. The third does so by producing a more favorable energy distribution among the particles of the solid. As temperature is raised, the average kinetic energy of the solute particles is also raised. A larger portion of the particles has enough kinetic energy to overcome the binding forces and leave the surface of the solid.

13.9 Dissolving mechanisms

Chemists do not fully understand the actual manner in which substances enter into solution. However, some aspects of the solution process are fairly well understood. Let us examine possible mechanisms by which a solid dissolves in a liquid.

Why is this process *spontaneous,* or self-acting? We may assume that at least three important actions occur in the dissolving process:

1. Solute particles must be separated from the solid mass (as a solid changing phase to a liquid). *This action takes up energy.*

2. Solvent particles must be moved apart to allow solute particles to enter the liquid environment. *This action also takes up energy.*

3. Solute particles are attracted to solvent particles. *This action gives up energy.*

The first two of these actions are endothermic and the last one is exothermic. If this exothermic action is less than the combined effect of the first two, the net change is endothermic. Consequently, the temperature of the solution *decreases* as the solid dissolves. This is the usual pattern for solid-in-liquid solutions. In such cases, heating the solution results in an increase in the solubility of the solid. If the net change is exothermic, the temperature of the solution *increases* as the solid dissolves. Heating such solutions results in a decrease in the solubility of the solid. Refer to Figure 13-10 for examples of dissolving processes that are endothermic and those that are exothermic. The reasons for these effects will be discussed in the next section.

We may think of dissolving as being aided by the attraction between solute and solvent particles. Solvent molecules move at random. Some may be attracted to surface molecules of undissolved crystals. As they cluster about the surface molecules, enough energy may be released to enable the solvent

Fig. 13-12. Gasoline, acetone, or paint thinners must be kept out of plastic containers because these solvents dissolve some plastics.

If dissolving is endothermic, solubility increases with temperature.

If dissolving is exothermic, solubility decreases with rise in temperature.

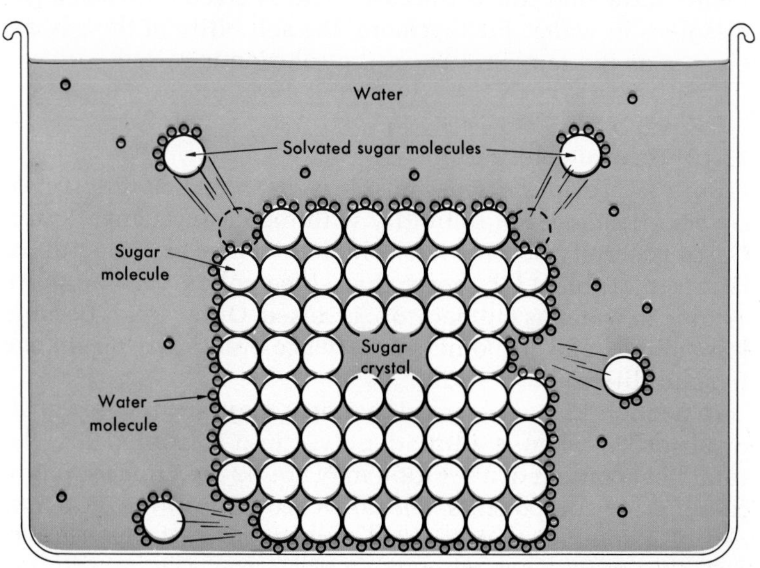

Fig. 13-13. A possible mechanism of the solution process.

molecules to carry off solute molecules. This process arises from the attraction between unlike molecules of solute and solvent. It is known as *solvation.* If water is the solvent, the solvation process is known more specifically as *hydration.* The solute molecule that leaves the crystal, along with its cluster of solvent molecules, is said to be *solvated.* If water molecules compose the solvent cluster, the solute molecule is said to be *hydrated.*

Solvation aids dissolving.

Hydration is solvation in which water is the solvent.

We have seen that natural processes generally lead to lower energy states (see Section 2.15). Thus, an endothermic energy change cannot account for the fact that the dissolving process occurs spontaneously. Perhaps the entropy change in such instances can account for it.

The mixture of solute and solvent particles in a solution is in a more disordered state (higher entropy) than that of the unmixed solid and liquid. Thus, the mixture is more probable than the unmixed state because of this higher entropy. The favorable entropy change of the dissolving process may cause solution to occur even though the energy change is not toward a lower state.

How well does this logic hold up when it is applied to solutions of gases in liquids? The solute is in a more random state as a gas than when dissolved in the liquid. Thus, the higher entropy of the gaseous state opposes the dissolving process. For dissolving to occur, the energy change must be favorable (to a lower state). It also must be great enough to overcome the unfavorable entropy change.

Accordingly, the dissolving process for a gas-in-liquid solution should be exothermic. If the temperature of the solution is raised, the solubility of the gas should be lowered. Experiments show that this is the case. Heat is given off when a gas dissolves in water. Furthermore, the solubility of the gas decreases as the temperature of the solution is raised.

13.10 Heat of solution

From the previous discussions, it is clear that no single rule covers all changes of solubility with increasing temperature. Gases generally become less soluble in water as temperature is raised. Table 13-2 shows that some solids become more soluble in water as temperature is raised. Other solids become less soluble, and still others experience practically no change in solubility.

In Section 13.9, we learned that heat may be either given off or absorbed when a solute dissolves in a solvent. Thus, the total heat content of a solution may not be the same as that of its separate components. *The difference between the heat content of a solution and the heat contents of its components is called the* ***heat of solution.***

solute + solvent → solution + heat (exothermic)

or

solute + solvent + heat → solution (endothermic)

When the dissolving process is exothermic, the total heat content of the solution is less than that of its separate components. The solution warms as dissolving proceeds. The heat of solution is said to be *negative*. When the process is endothermic, the heat content of the solution is *greater* than that of its components. The solution cools as dissolving proceeds and the heat of solution is said to be *positive*.

Negative heat of solution: solute solubility decreases with rising temperature.

Positive heat of solution: solute solubility increases with temperature.

The dilution of a concentrated solution may cause the release or absorption of heat. Thus, the heat of solution of any system depends upon the concentration of the final solution. For this reason, heat of solution is measured in kilocalories per mole of solute dissolved in a specific number of moles of solvent. Heats of solution for some common substances are given in Table 13-3. How do these data relate to the solubility information of Table 13-2?

Observe that the change in solubility of a substance with temperature is closely related to its heat of solution. The heat of solution of sodium chloride, for example, is nearly zero. The solubility change of sodium chloride with temperature is also very small.

In a saturated solution with undissolved solute, an equilibrium exists between the dissolving and crystallizing processes. Let us consider such a solution of KCl. The symbols (s) and (l) indicate solid and liquid, respectively.

$$\mathbf{KCl(s) + H_2O(l) + heat \rightleftarrows solution}$$

The heat of solution is +4.20 kcal/mole. The dissolving process is endothermic. The crystallizing process must then be exothermic. At equilibrium, the tendency toward lower energy (release of heat) as solute crystallizes just balances the tendency toward higher entropy (greater disorder) as crystals dissolve. Consequently, there is no net driving force in the system.

Suppose we now add heat to the solution. The rise in temperature produces a stress on the equilibrium. From Le Chatelier's principle, the system relieves this stress by increasing the rate of the *endothermic* process. Thus, dissolving proceeds faster than crystallizing until the concentration of KCl in solution is increased and the stress is relieved. Solutes with *positive* heats of solution become more soluble as the temperature of their solution is raised.

The effect of temperature on saturated solutions of solutes having *negative* heats of solutions is the reverse of the process just described. Here, the dissolving process is exothermic and the crystallizing process is endothermic. A rise in solution temperature disturbs the equilibrium and the rate of the en-

Table 13-3

HEATS OF SOLUTION
(kcal/mole solute in 200 moles H_2O)
[(s) = solid, (1) = liquid, (g) = gas at SP]

Substance	Heat of Solution
$AgNO_3(s)$	+5.44
$CO_2(g)$	−4.76
$CuSO_4(s)$	−16.20
$CuSO_4 \cdot 5H_2O(s)$	+2.75
$HC_2H_3O_2(l)$	−0.38
$HCl(g)$	−17.74
$HI(g)$	−7.02
$H_2SO_4(l)$	−17.75
$KCl(s)$	+4.20
$KClO_3(s)$	+10.04
$KI(s)$	+5.11
$KNO_3(s)$	+8.52
$KOH(s)$	−13.04
$LiCl(s)$	−8.37
$Li_2CO_3(s)$	−3.06
$MgSO_4 \cdot 7H_2O(s)$	+3.80
$NaCl(s)$	+1.02
$NaNO_3(s)$	+5.03
$NaOH(s)$	−9.94
$Na_2SO_4 \cdot 10H_2O(s)$	+18.76
$NH_3(g)$	−8.28
$NH_4Cl(s)$	+3.88
$NH_4NO_3(s)$	+6.08

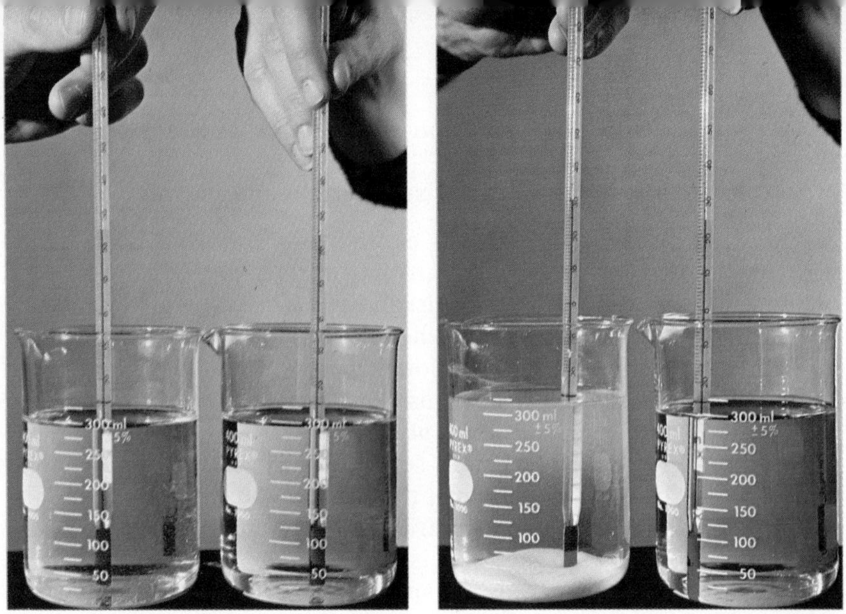

Fig. 13-14. Two beakers of water are at the same temperature (left). The temperature of the water in the beaker at the left (right) has been increased by dissolving sodium sulfite.

dothermic process (crystallizing) increases. Solute separates from the solution. Solutes with *negative* heats of solution become less soluble as the temperature of their solution is raised.

13.11 Concentration of solutions

The *concentration* of a solution depends upon the relative proportions of solute and solvent. The more solute that is dissolved in a solvent, the more *concentrated* the solution becomes. On the other hand, the more solvent that is added, the more *dilute* the solution becomes.

The terms *dilute* and *concentrated* are qualitative. They are useful in a general sense only. In order to be of value to the chemist, the concentrations of solutions must be known quantitatively. Chemists have developed several methods of expressing concentrations to suit various problems that arise in the laboratory.

We shall use only three methods for expressing the concentrations of solutions quantitatively. One method expresses the *ratio of solute to solvent.* We shall discuss this method immediately. Two other methods will be introduced later, as they are needed. They both express the *ratio of solute to solution,* but in different ways.

If it is important to know the ratio of solute molecules to solvent molecules in a solution, we will state the concentration in terms of *molality. The **molality** of a solution is the number of moles of solute per kilogram of solvent.* The symbol for molality is the small letter *m*.

A 0.1-molal solution contains 0.1 mole of solute per kilogram of solvent.

A one-molal (1-*m*) solution contains *1 mole of solute per kilogram of solvent.* You will recognize that 0.5 mole of solute dissolved in 0.5 kg of solvent, or 0.25 mole of solute in 0.25 kg of solvent, also gives a 1-*m* solution. A *half-molal* (0.5-*m*) solution contains *one-half mole* of solute per kilogram of solvent.

Table 13-4

CONCENTRATION OF SOLUTIONS IN MOLALITY						
Quantity of Solute	Quantity of Solvent	Mass Solute per Mole	Conversion to Moles Solute	Conversion to kg Solvent	Moles Solute per kg Solvent	Molality
18.2 g HCl	$25\bar{0}$ g H_2O	$\frac{36.5\ g}{mole}$	$18.2\ \text{g}\ HCl \times \frac{mole}{36.5\ g}$	$25\bar{0}\ g\ H_2O \times \frac{kg}{10^3\ g}$	$\frac{0.499\ mole\ HCl}{0.250\ kg\ H_2O}$	$= 1.99\ m$
2.50 g NH_3	175 g H_2O	$\frac{17.0\ g}{mole}$	$2.50\ g\ NH_3 \times \frac{mole}{17.0\ g}$	$175\ g\ H_2O \times \frac{kg}{10^3\ g}$	$\frac{0.147\ mole\ NH_3}{0.175\ kg\ H_2O}$	$= 0.840\ m$
15.6 g NaCl	$50\bar{0}$ g H_2O	$\frac{58.5\ g}{mole}$	$15.6\ g\ NaCl \times \frac{mole}{58.5\ g}$	$50\bar{0}\ g\ H_2O \times \frac{kg}{10^3\ g}$	$\frac{0.267\ mole\ NaCl}{0.500\ kg\ H_2O}$	$= 0.533\ m$
12.2 g I_2	$10\bar{0}$ g CCl_4	$\frac{254\ g}{mole}$	$12.2\ g\ I_2 \times \frac{mole}{254\ g}$	$10\bar{0}\ g\ CCl_4 \times \frac{kg}{10^3\ g}$	$\frac{0.0480\ mole\ I_2}{0.100\ kg\ CCl_4}$	$= 0.480\ m$

A *two-molal* (2-m) solution has *two moles* of solute in 1 kilogram of solvent. Several exercises for expressing the concentration of solutions in terms of molality are given in Table 13-4.

Molal solutions are important to chemists because (for a given solvent) *two solutions of equal molality have the same ratio of solute to solvent molecules.* (A kilogram, 1000 g, of solvent can be expressed in terms of moles since 1000 g ÷ number of grams/mole of solvent = number of moles of solvent.) Molality is preferred for expressing the concentration of solutions in procedures in which temperature changes may occur. The following Sample Problems illustrate calculations involving solution concentrations in molalities.

SAMPLE PROBLEM

How many grams $AgNO_3$ are needed to prepare a 0.125-m solution in $25\bar{0}$ ml of water?

SOLUTION

Molality expresses solution concentration in moles of solute per kilogram of solvent.

$$\mathbf{25\bar{0}\ ml\ H_2O = 25\bar{0}\ g\ H_2O}$$

The gram-formula weight of $AgNO_3$ = $17\bar{0}$ g = mass of 1 mole $AgNO_3$. Our 0.125-m $AgNO_3$ solution = 0.125 mole $AgNO_3$/kg H_2O. We wish to determine the mass of $AgNO_3$ required for $25\bar{0}$ g of H_2O to give the 0.125-m concentration. So we must convert moles of $AgNO_3$ to grams and grams of H_2O to kilograms. This is done by unit cancellations as follows:

$$\frac{\mathbf{0.125\ mole\ AgNO_3}}{\mathbf{kg\ H_2O}} \times \frac{\mathbf{17\bar{0}\ g}}{\mathbf{mole}} \times \mathbf{25\bar{0}\ g\ H_2O} \times \frac{\mathbf{kg}}{\mathbf{10^3\ g}} = \mathbf{5.31\ g\ AgNO_3}$$

SAMPLE PROBLEM

A solution contains 17.1 g of sucrose, $C_{12}H_{22}O_{11}$, dissolved in 125 g of water. Determine the molal concentration.

SOLUTION

The formula weight $C_{12}H_{22}O_{11} = 342$. Thus, 1 mole has a mass of 342 g. The concentration is 17.1 g sucrose/125 g H_2O. To express in terms of molality, we must convert grams of sucrose to moles, and grams of H_2O to kilograms, giving moles of sucrose per kilogram of water. This is accomplished by unit cancellations as follows:

$$\frac{\mathbf{17.1\ g\ C_{12}H_{22}O_{11}}}{\mathbf{125\ g\ H_2O}} \times \frac{\mathbf{mole}}{\mathbf{342\ g}} \times \frac{\mathbf{10^3\ g}}{\mathbf{kg}} = \frac{\mathbf{0.400\ mole\ C_{12}H_{22}O_{11}}}{\mathbf{kg\ H_2O}} = \mathbf{0.400}\ m$$

13.12 Freezing-point depression of solvents

In the preceding sections, we have examined in some detail the nature of the solution process. Now let us see how the addition of a solute affects the properties of the solvent.

A solute always lowers the vapor pressure of a solvent.

An important effect is known from experiments involving vapor pressure. *At any temperature, the vapor pressure of a pure solvent is higher than that of the same solvent when it contains dissolved solute.* We can think of the vapor pressure of a liquid as a measure of the *escaping tendency* of the liquid molecules. Thus, the presence of solute particles in solution lowers the escaping tendency of the solvent molecules. This effect is reasonable if we think of the solute particles in solution as *decreasing the concentration* of solvent molecules.

Figure 13-15 shows plots of vapor pressure of a solvent as a function of temperature. Curves are given for a pure solvent, a dilute solution of molal concentration X, and a dilute solution of molal concentration 2X. Observe that, at any given temperature, the vapor pressure of the solvent decreases in proportion to the concentration of *solute particles.* This decrease in solvent vapor pressure has the effect of extending the liquid range of the solution. That is, the solution can exist in the liquid phase at both higher and lower temperatures than can the pure solvent. What can we conclude from this observation concerning the boiling and freezing points of solutions?

Salt water freezes at a lower temperature than fresh water. Sea water is a dilute solution of common salt, NaCl, and many other minerals. Suppose a sample of sea water is cooled enough for freezing to occur. The crystals produced are those of the *pure solvent* itself (in this case, water), not of the solution. This phenomenon occurs when any dilute solution is cooled enough for freezing to occur. We may conclude that *solutes lower the freezing point of the solvent in which they are*

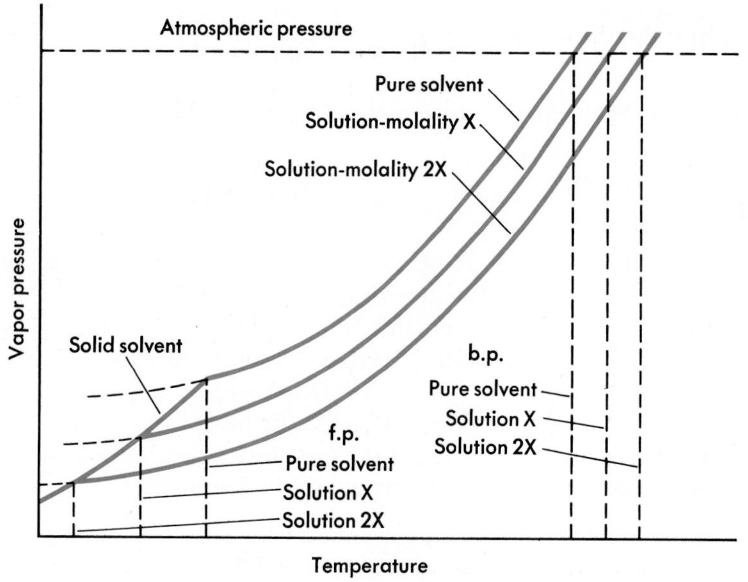

Fig. 13-15. Vapor pressure of solvent as a function of temperature plotted for a pure solvent and dilute solutions of molalities X and 2X. Freezing-point depressions and boiling-point elevations are shown to be proportional to the molal concentrations of the solutions.

dissolved. We make use of this fact when we add alcohol or ethylene glycol (permanent antifreeze) to the water in an automobile radiator during the winter months.

Solutes depress the freezing points of solvents.

Chemists have investigated many dilute solutions of nonelectrolytes in water. They have found that the *freezing-point depression* of the water is determined by the *number* of solute particles in a given quantity of water, not by their identity. Dilute solutions of equal molality, but which contain different solutes, yield the same freezing-point depression for water. Dilute solutions of different molality give different freezing-point depressions. These facts suggest that the *lowering of the freezing point of the solvent is directly proportional to the molecular concentration of the solute.*

Freezing-point depressions of solvents are represented by the symbol ΔT_f. They are expressed in Celsius degrees, C°. The Greek letter Δ (delta) signifies "change in." Suppose the freezing point of a quantity of water is lowered from 0.00°C to −0.36°C by the addition of a small amount of some molecular solute. The freezing-point depression of the water is indicated to be 0.36 C°.

$$\Delta T_f = 0.36\ \mathrm{C}^\circ$$

The depression of the freezing point has been calculated for a 1-molal solution of any molecular solute in water. It has been found to have the constant value of 1.86 C°. *This freezing-point depression for a 1-molal water solution is called the* ***molal freezing-point constant,*** K_f, *for water.* It is expressed as 1.86 C°/molal. Since

Freezing-point changes are observed for solvents containing volatile solutes as well as nonvolatile solutes.

$$\text{molality} = \frac{\text{moles solute}}{\text{kg solvent}}$$

K_f has the dimensions $\frac{\text{C}°}{\text{mole solute/kg solvent}}$.

The molal freezing-point constant for water is

$$\mathbf{K_f = \frac{1.86\ C°}{molal} = \frac{1.86\ C°}{mole\ solute/kg\ H_2O}}$$

Using this value of K_f, a molecular solute added to 1 kg of water should lower the freezing point 1.86 C° per mole of solute dissolved. However, this relation holds experimentally only for dilute solutions. Even a 1-molal solution is concentrated enough so that the freezing-point depression is somewhat less than 1.86 C°. All solvents have their own characteristic molal freezing-point constants. The values of K_f for some common solvents are given in Table 13-5.

Table 13-5

MOLAL FREEZING-POINT AND BOILING-POINT CONSTANTS

Solvent	Normal f.p. (°C)	Molal f.p. Constant, K_f (C°/molal)	Normal b.p. (°C)	Molal b.p. Constant, K_b (°C/molal)
acetic acid	16.6	3.90	118.5	3.07
acetone	−94.8	—	56.00	1.71
aniline	−6.1	5.87	184.4	3.22
benzene	5.48	5.12	80.15	2.53
carbon disulfide	−111.5	3.80	46.3	2.34
carbon tetrachloride	−22.96	—	76.50	5.03
ethanol	−114.5	—	78.26	1.22
ether	−116.3	1.79	34.42	2.02
naphthalene	80.2	6.9	218.0	5.65
phenol	40.9	7.27	181.8	3.56
water	0.00	1.86	100.0	0.51

The depression of the freezing point of the solvent in a dilute solution of a molecular solute is directly proportional to the molal concentration of the solution. The freezing-point depression *is equal to the product of the molal freezing-point constant of the solvent and the molality of the solution.*

The molal f.p. constant (K_f) for water is 1.86 C°.

$$\Delta T_f = K_f m$$

Here K_f is the molal freezing-point constant of the solvent expressed in C°/(mole solute/kg solvent). The quantity m is the molality of the solution expressed in moles of solute/kg of solvent. The freezing-point depression in C° is ΔT_f. The following Sample Problems illustrate the use of the equation.

SAMPLE PROBLEM

A solution is prepared in which 17.1 g of sucrose, $C_{12}H_{22}O_{11}$, is dissolved in $20\bar{0}$ g of water. What is the freezing-point depression of the solvent?

SOLUTION

The gram-molecular weight of $C_{12}H_{22}O_{11}$ = 342 g. Thus, for sucrose 342 g = 1 mole. The mass, 17.1 g of sucrose, must be converted to moles. The mass, $20\bar{0}$ g of water, must be converted to kilograms. These conversions are accomplished by familiar unit-cancellation methods.

$$K_f \text{ for water} = \frac{1.86\ C°}{\text{molal}} = \frac{1.86\ C°}{\text{mole solute/kg } H_2O}$$

Solving for ΔT_f:

$$\Delta T_f = K_f m$$

$$\Delta T_f = \frac{1.86\ C°}{\text{mole } C_{12}H_{22}O_{11}/\text{kg } H_2O} \times \frac{17.1\ \text{g } C_{12}H_{22}O_{11}}{20\bar{0}\ \text{g } H_2O} \times \frac{\text{mole}}{342\ \text{g}} \times \frac{10^3\ \text{g}}{\text{kg}}$$

$$\Delta T_f = 0.465\ C°$$

Observe that the unit-cancellation operations yield the answer unit C°.

$$\Delta T_f = \frac{C°}{\cancel{\text{mole } C_{12}H_{22}O_{11}}/\cancel{\text{kg } H_2O}} \times \frac{\cancel{\text{g } C_{12}H_{22}O_{11}}}{\cancel{\text{g } H_2O}} \times \frac{\cancel{\text{mole}}}{\cancel{\text{g}}} \times \frac{\cancel{\text{g}}}{\cancel{\text{kg}}}$$

$$\Delta T_f = C°$$

SAMPLE PROBLEM

A water solution of a nonelectrolyte is found to have a freezing point of −0.23°C. What is the molal concentration of the solution?

SOLUTION

The normal freezing point of water is 0.00°C, so the freezing-point depression, ΔT_f, = 0.23 C°.

$$K_f\ (\text{water}) = 1.86\ C°/\text{molal}$$
$$\Delta T_f = K_f m$$

Solving for m:

$$m = \frac{\Delta T_f}{K_f} = \frac{0.23\ \cancel{C°}}{1.86\ \cancel{C°}/\text{molal}} = 0.12\ \text{molal}$$

13.13 Boiling-point elevation of solvents

The boiling point of the solvent in a solution is higher than that of the pure solvent alone, provided the solute present is not *volatile*. (A volatile solute is one easily vaporized.) Experiments with dilute solutions of nonvolatile nonelectrolytes have shown that the rise in boiling point of the solvent is directly proportional to the molecular concentration of the solute. This rise in boiling point is called the *boiling-point elevation*, ΔT_b, of the solvent.

Nonvolatile solutes elevate the boiling points of solvents.

The boiling-point elevation for a 1-molal water solution of any molecular solute is determined indirectly. It is derived from the properties of dilute water solutions at standard pressure. This boiling-point elevation has the constant value of 0.51 C°. That is, based on the behavior of dilute water solutions, the boiling point at 1-molal concentration should be raised to 100.51°C at 760 mm pressure. *The boiling-point elevation for a 1-molal water solution is called the* ***molal boiling-point constant,*** K_b, *for water.* It is expressed as 0.51 C°/molal. Thus, the molal boiling-point constant for water is

Alcohol and ammonia are examples of volatile solutes in water solutions.

$$K_b = \frac{\mathbf{0.51\ C°}}{\mathbf{molal}} = \frac{\mathbf{0.51\ C°}}{\mathbf{mole\ solute/kg\ H_2O}}$$

The actual elevation of the boiling point in concentrated solutions deviates somewhat from that indicated by K_b. Thus, the proportionality between boiling-point elevation and solution molality is limited to dilute solutions. All solvents have their own characteristic molal boiling-point constants. The values of K_b for some common solvents are given in Table 13-5.

Sugar is a nonvolatile solute in water solution.

The elevation of the boiling point of a dilute solution of a nonvolatile molecular solute is directly proportional to the molal concentration of the solution. It is equal to the product of the molal boiling-point constant and the molality of the solution.

$$\Delta T_b = K_b m$$

The molal boiling-point constant, K_b, is expressed in the units C°/(mole solute/kg solvent). The molality of the solution, m, is expressed in moles of solute/kg of solvent. Thus, ΔT_b is the boiling-point elevation in C°.

The molal b.p. constant (K_b) for water is 0.51 C°.

The freezing points and boiling points of solutions of electrolytes are also depressed or elevated. However, they do not follow the simple relationships just described. Such solutes are not molecular and our generalizations about molecular substances do not hold for them.

13.14 Molecular weights of solutes

We have applied the Avogadro principle to determine the molecular weights of gases and volatile liquids by the molar-volume method. The molecular weights of substances that decompose when heated instead of vaporizing cannot be determined by this vapor-density method. We have learned that the freezing-point depression and the boiling-point elevation of solvents are determined by the number of solute molecules in solution. Using this fact, we can now determine molecular weights of substances that are soluble in water or some other common solvent. Of course, such solutes must not react with their solvents. There are substances, such as starch, that decompose when heated and form colloidal suspensions instead of solutions. Chemists do not know their molecular weights.

In previous sections we discussed the freezing-point depression and the boiling-point elevation of solvents. We found that both phenomena depend on the relative number of solute molecules mixed with a definite number of solvent molecules. They do *not* depend upon the nature of the solute.

The molal freezing-point constants, K_f, and molal boiling-point constants, K_b, are known for many common solvents. Suppose we know the concentration of a molecular solution in terms of the mass of solute and mass of solvent (for which K_f or K_b is known). The freezing-point depression or boiling-point elevation can be determined experimentally. The molecular weight can then be calculated. The freezing-point method is favored in these molecular-weight determinations.

From Section 13.12, we have the expression

$$\Delta T_f = K_f m$$

$$\text{Molality } m = \frac{\text{moles solute}}{\text{kg solvent}} = \frac{\text{g solute/g-mol wt}}{\text{kg solvent}}$$

Thus,

$$\Delta T_f = K_f \times \frac{\text{g solute/g-mol wt}}{\text{kg solvent}}$$

Solving for gram-molecular weight:

$$\text{g-mol wt} = \frac{K_f \times \text{g solute}}{T_f \times \text{kg solvent}}$$

The following Sample Problem illustrates this method of determining the molecular weight of a solute.

SAMPLE PROBLEM

It is found experimentally that 1.8 g of sulfur dissolved in $10\bar{0}$ g of naphthalene, $C_{10}H_8$, decreases the freezing point of the solvent 0.48C°. What is the molecular weight of the solute?

SOLUTION

The molal freezing-point constant for naphthalene is 6.9 C°/molal (Table 13-5). Molality is expressed in terms of kilograms of solvent. Therefore, the quantity of naphthalene used must be converted from grams to kilograms, using the factor 10^3 g/kg.

$$\Delta T_f = K_f m$$

$$\text{where } m = \frac{\text{moles solute}}{\text{kg solvent}} = \frac{\text{g solute/g-mol wt}}{\text{kg solvent}}$$

$$\Delta T_f = K_f \times \frac{\text{g solute/g-mol wt}}{\text{kg solvent}}$$

$$\text{g-mol wt} = \frac{K_f \times \text{g solute}}{\Delta T_f \times \text{kg solvent}}$$

$$\text{g-mol wt} = \frac{6.9\ \text{C}^\circ \times 1.8\ \text{g S}}{\text{mole S/kg } C_{10}H_8 \times 0.48\ \text{C}^\circ \times 10\bar{0}\ \text{g } C_{10}H_8 \times \text{kg}/10^3\ \text{g}}$$

$$\text{g-mol wt} = 260\ \text{g/mole}$$

$$\text{mol wt} = 260$$

What does this result suggest about the composition of the sulfur molecule?

SUMMARY

A solution is a homogeneous mixture made up of two parts, a solute that dissolves and a solvent in which the solute dissolves. Solutes whose water solutions conduct electricity are called electrolytes. Solutes whose water solutions do not conduct are nonelectrolytes. Solutions are single-phase systems.

The particles of substances that are too large to form solutions but are small enough to form permanent suspensions are called colloids. A colloidal suspension is a two-phase system. In colloids, dispersed particles correspond to the solute of a solution, and a dispersing medium corresponds to the solvent of a solution.

The possibility of solubility is increased when substances are alike in composition and structure. The solubility of a solute is increased by hydrogen bonds between solute and solvent particles.

When a solution is in equilibrium, the opposing processes of dissolving and crystallizing occur at equal rates. Solution equilibrium limits the quantity of solute that can dissolve in a given quantity of solvent. Equilibrium is affected by temperature. The solubility of a solute is determined by the equilibrium concentration of solute.

The solubility of a gas in a liquid is affected by pressure in accordance with Henry's law. Gases that react chemically with their liquid solvents are generally more soluble than those that do not. The solubility of a gas decreases as temperature increases. The solubility of most but not all solids in liquids increases with temperature.

When the dissolving process is endothermic, the solution cools as dissolving proceeds, and the heat of solution is positive. When the dissolving process is exothermic, the solution warms, and the heat of solution is negative. Heats of solution are expressed in kilocalories per mole of solute dissolved in 200 moles of water.

The concentration of a solution can be expressed in molality as moles of solute per kilogram of solvent. Molecular solutes lower the freezing points of their solvents characteristic amounts. If nonvolatile, molecular solutes raise the boiling points characteristic amounts also. Each solvent has a specific molal-freezing point depression and molal-boiling point elevation. Specific molal-freezing point depression and molal-boiling point elevation are used to determine molecular weights of soluble substances that cannot be vaporized.

Group A

1. Define: (*a*) solution; (*b*) solvent; (*c*) solute.
2. Why are the terms *dilute* and *concentrated* not entirely satisfactory as applied to solutions?
3. (*a*) Name the nine different types of solutions possible. (*b*) Which type is the most common?
4. Why does carbonated water effervesce when drawn from the soda fountain?
5. What action limits the amount of a solute that can dissolve in a given quantity of solvent under fixed conditions?
6. Explain the difference between *dissolve* and *melt*.
7. What is the influence of pressure on the solubility of: (*a*) a gas in a liquid; (*b*) a solid in a liquid?
8. What is the influence of temperature on the solubility of: (*a*) a gas in a liquid; (*b*) a solid in a liquid?
9. (*a*) What is the difference between *miscible* and *immiscible?* (*b*) Give an example of each.
10. What is the distinguishing characteristic of *polar* molecules?
11. State three methods of increasing the rate of solution of a solid in a liquid.
12. Explain the expression *saturated solution* in terms of solution equilibrium.
13. Referring to Figure 13-9, what is the solubility of potassium nitrate in water (*a*) at 15°C? (*b*) at 65°C?
14. How would you prepare a supersaturated solution of potassium chloride in water?
15. Explain why ethanol (alcohol) is miscible with both ether and water.

Group B

16. Ice cubes made with cold water are usually cloudy while ice cubes made with hot water may be clear. Explain.
17. Alcohol is a nonelectrolyte and is soluble in water, yet a molal solution of alcohol in water does not give the molal boiling-point elevation of water. Explain.
18. (*a*) What determines the amount of oxygen that remains dissolved in water that is at constant temperature and in contact with the atmosphere? (*b*) Explain what would happen if the oxygen were removed from the air above the water.
19. Suppose you wished to make a concentrated solution of copper(II) sulfate in water, using the crystalline hydrate as the solute. How would you hasten the solution process?
20. The carbon tetrachloride molecule contains four polar covalent bonds yet the molecule as a whole is nonpolar. Explain.
21. How can you explain the fact that alcohol is a solvent for both water and carbon tetrachloride?
22. Why do caps sometimes blow off the tops of ginger ale bottles when they are exposed to direct sunlight for some time?
23. Why is cold water more appropriate than hot water for making a saturated solution of calcium hydroxide?
24. How are the solubility curves like those in Figure 13-10 constructed?
25. Liquid methanol, CH_3OH, and water are miscible in all proportions. When 1 mole of CH_3OH (solute) is mixed with 10 moles of H_2O (solvent), the heat of solution is found to be -1.43 kcal. (*a*) Is the formation of solution accompanied by an increase or decrease in entropy? (State the argument upon which your answer is based.) (*b*) Does the change in entropy favor the separate components or the solution? (*c*) Is the dissolving process endothermic or exothermic?

Justify your answer. (*d*) Does the energy change as indicated by the sign of the heat of solution favor the separate components or the solution? (*e*) Are your previous answers consistent with the fact that methanol and water are freely miscible? Explain.

26. What phenomenon of solutes is responsible for the formation of the crystal garden shown on page 249?

PROBLEMS

Group A

1. How many grams of ethanol, C_2H_5OH, are required to prepare a 0.175-*m* solution in 40$\bar{0}$ g of water?
2. Calculate the mass in grams of sucrose, $C_{12}H_{22}O_{11}$, which must be dissolved in 250$\bar{0}$ g of water to make up a 0.100-*m* solution.
3. A solution of glucose, $C_6H_{12}O_6$, is prepared by dissolving 6.75 g of the glucose in 326 g of water. What is the molality of this solution?
4. What is the molality of a solution containing 46.0 g of glycerol, $C_3H_5(OH)_3$, in 75$\bar{0}$ g of water?
5. A solution contains 96.0 g of methanol, CH_3OH, in 350$\bar{0}$ g of water. Calculate the molality of the solution.
6. How many grams of water must be added to 90.0 g of glucose, $C_6H_{12}O_6$, to make a 0.250-*m* solution?
7. A 0.400-*m* solution of naphthalene, $C_{10}H_8$, in benzene, C_6H_6, is needed. If 32.0 g of naphthalene are available, how many grams of the benzene must be used?
8. A solution contains 31.0 g of ethylene glycol, $C_2H_4(OH)_2$, in 10$\bar{0}$ g of water. What is the molality of the solution?
9. Calculate the molality of a solution containing 0.762 g of I_2 (solute) in 45$\bar{0}$ g of CCl_4 (solvent).
10. A solution consists of 15.0 g sucrose, $C_{12}H_{22}O_{11}$, in 150.0 g of water. What is the freezing point of the water?
11. What is the boiling point of the solution described in Problem 10?
12. What is the freezing point of 250 g of water containing 11.25 g of a nonelectrolyte that has a molecular weight of 180?
13. A solution of iodine in benzene is found to have a freezing point of 4.3°C. What is the molality of the solution?
14. A sucrose-in-water solution raises the boiling point of the solvent to 100.11°C at standard pressure. Determine the molality of the solution.

Group B

15. The analysis of a compound yields: carbon, 32.0%; hydrogen, 4.0%; oxygen, 64.0%. It is found that 15.0 g of the compound added to 1.00 kg of water lowers the freezing point of the water 0.186 C°. (*a*) Find the empirical formula. (*b*) What is its molecular weight? (*c*) What is its molecular formula?
16. A compound contains: carbon, 40.00%; hydrogen, 6.6%; oxygen, 53.33%. Tests show that 9.0 g of the compound dissolved in 50$\bar{0}$ g of water raises the boiling point of the water 0.051 C°. (*a*) Find its empirical formula. (*b*) Find its molecular weight. (*c*) What is its molecular formula?
17. The analysis of a compound shows: carbon, 30.3%; hydrogen, 1.7%; bromine, 68%. The substance is soluble in benzene and 10.0 g of it lowers the freezing point of 10$\bar{0}$ g of benzene 2.1 C°. (*a*) Find the empirical formula of the solute. (*b*) Determine its molecular weight. (*c*) What is its molecular formula?

chapter 14

IONIZATION

The earth's most abundant conducting solution—the seven seas that cover three fourths of its surface. (See Question 31 on page 292.)

14.1 Conductivity of solutions

We have seen that solutions of electrovalent compounds may have properties that are quite different from those of covalent compounds. These differences in behavior and properties result from differences in the chemical structures of electrovalent and covalent solutes. Electrovalent compounds are ionic, and their water solutions conduct electric currents.

The conductivity of a solution can be tested by the use of the apparatus shown in Figure 14-1. A lamp is connected as in the

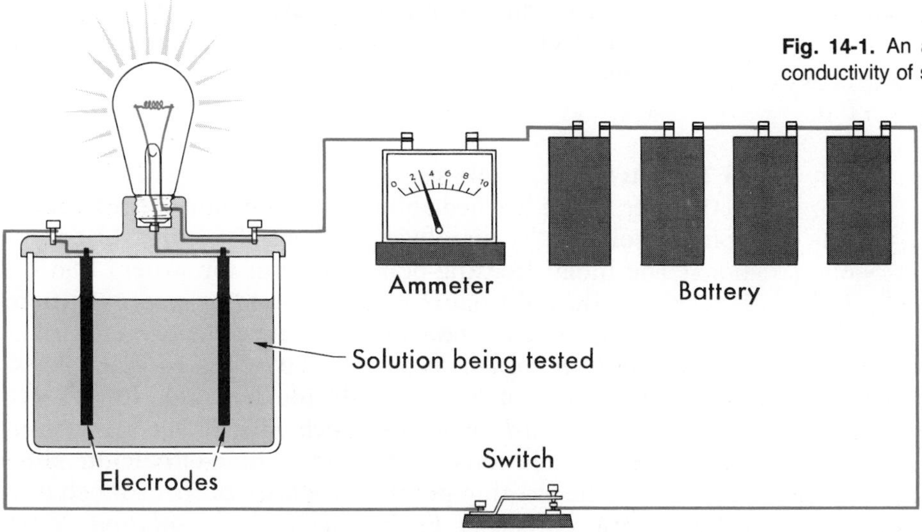

Fig. 14-1. An apparatus for testing the conductivity of solutions.

Figure with an ammeter (a meter that measures electric currents), a switch, and a pair of electrodes. The electrodes are conductors used to make electric contact with the test solution. A battery or other suitable electric energy supply is used as the source of current.

If the liquid tested is a good *conductor* of electricity, the lamp filament glows brightly when the switch is closed. The meter registers the current in the circuit. For a liquid that is a poorer conductor, the lamp is not as bright and the meter shows a smaller current. If a liquid is a very poor conductor, the lamp does not glow at all and the meter registers only a feeble current.

The term "pure water" means water that contains no other kind of matter.

When pure water is tested, the lamp does not glow and the meter (depending on its sensitivity) may not register a current. Pure water is such a poor conductor that, except in special situations, it may be regarded as a *nonconductor.* Similarly, water solutions of such covalent substances as sugar, alcohol, and glycerol (glycerin) are nonconductors of electricity. These solutes are *nonelectrolytes.*

In general, all solutes whose water solutions conduct an electric current are *electrolytes.* Solutions of electrovalent substances such as sodium chloride, copper(II) sulfate, and potassium nitrate are conductors. These solutes are electrolytes. Hydrogen chloride is one of several covalent compounds whose water solution conducts an electric current. These compounds are also electrolytes.

For an electric current to be conducted through a solution, there must be charged particles (ions) in the solution. These ions must be free to move or migrate through the solution. Chemical reactions must take place at the two electrodes by which electric charges enter and leave the solution environment. Consequently, an oxidation reaction must occur at one electrode and a reduction reaction must occur simultaneously at the other electrode. (Review Section 6.5.) These electrode reactions will be treated in greater detail in Chapter 22.

Oxidation: loss of electrons.
Reduction: gain of electrons.

14.2 Electrolytes as solutes

In Chapter 13, we learned about the depression of the freezing point of solvents by dissolved nonelectrolytes in dilute solutions. The molal freezing-point constant for water, 1.86 C°, is related to the influence of nonelectrolytes in water solution. *Solutes that are electrolytes have a greater influence on the freezing point of their solvents than solutes that are not electrolytes.* A 0.1-*m* solution of sodium chloride in water lowers the freezing point *nearly twice* as much as a 0.1-*m* solution of sugar. A 0.1-*m* solution of potassium sulfate or calcium chloride lowers the freezing point *nearly three times* as much as a 0.1-*m* solution of sugar. *Electrolytes in water solutions lower the freezing point nearly two, or three, or more times as much as nonelectrolytes in water solutions of the same molality.*

The molal boiling-point constant for water is 0.51 C°. Nonvolatile electrolytes in solution have a greater effect on the boiling point of the solvent than do nonelectrolytes. Dilute sodium chloride solutions have boiling-point elevations *almost twice* those of sugar solutions of equal molality. A 0.1-*m* solution of potassium sulfate shows *almost three times* the rise in boiling point as a 0.1-*m* solution of sugar. *Electrolytes in water solutions raise the boiling point nearly two, or three, or more times as much as nonelectrolytes in water solutions of the same molality.*

Fig. 14-2. Svante August Arrhenius investigated the nature of solutions that conduct an electric current when he was a graduate student in chemistry at the University of Stockholm. He decided to solve this problem for his doctor's thesis in spite of opposition from his professors. In 1883, at the age of 24, he presented his thesis on "electrolytic dissociation," and his professors gave him a barely passing mark. Twenty years later, he received the Nobel prize in chemistry in recognition of this outstanding contribution to chemistry.

14.3 Behavior of electrolytes explained

Michael Faraday first used the terms *electrolyte* and *nonelectrolyte* in describing his experiments on the conductivity of solutions. He assumed that ions were formed from molecules in solution by the electric potential difference (voltage) between the electrodes. He concluded that the formation of these ions was what enabled the solution to conduct an electric current. Later experiments showed that electrolytic solutions contained ions regardless of the presence of the charged electrodes.

In 1887, the Swedish chemist Svante Arrhenius (1859–1927) published a report on his study of solutions of electrolytes. In this report (written in 1883), he introduced the original *theory of ionization.* Arrhenius began with a different assumption as to the origin of ions in electrolytic solutions from that of Faraday. He assumed that charged electrodes were not necessary for ionization. He then described many kinds of properties of electrolytes to show that this assumption was correct. Arrhenius concluded that ions were produced by the *ionization* of molecules of electrolytes in water solution. He considered the ions to be electrically charged. When molecules ionized, they produced both positive ions and negative ions. The solution as a whole contained equal numbers of positive and negative charges. He considered the ionization to be complete only in very dilute solutions. In more concentrated solutions, the ions were in equilibrium with *un-ionized* molecules of the solute.

These assumptions formed the basis of the theory of solutions of electrolytes. As chemists gained a better understanding of crystals and water molecules, some of the original concepts were modified or replaced. It is a great tribute to Arrhenius that his original theory served for so long. Our present knowledge of the crystalline structure of electrovalent compounds was not available to him when, at the age of 24, he wrote his thesis on ionization.

According to the modern theory of ionization, the solvent plays an important part in the solution process. Water is by far the most important solvent. Knowledge of the polar nature of water molecules helps us understand the solution process. The theory of ionization assumes

1. that electrolytes in solution exist in the form of ions;

2. that an ion is an atom or a group of atoms that carries an electric charge;

3. that in the water solution of an electrolyte, the total positive ionic charge equals the total negative ionic charge.

14.4 Structure of electrovalent compounds

A review of Section 6.3 will be helpful at this point.

Electrovalent compounds result from the transfer of electrons from one kind of atom to another. Consequently, electrovalent compounds are not made up of neutral atoms. They consist of atoms that have lost or gained electrons. Atoms that *gained* electrons in forming the compound have a *negative charge.* Those that *lost* electrons have a *positive charge.* Such atoms or groups of atoms that have an electric charge are called *ions.* In forming ions, atoms lose electric neutrality and gain chemical stability by associating with other ions of opposite charge.

The properties of ions are very different from those of the atoms from which they were produced. Such differences accompany changes in electronic structure and the acquisition of charge resulting from the formation of ions. For example, a neutral sodium atom with a single 3*s* electron in the third energy level is different from a sodium ion. The sodium ion does not have the 3*s* electron and thus has one excess positive charge. There is an octet in the second energy level consisting of two 2*s* and six 2*p* electrons.

It is useful to remember that chemical properties are determined chiefly by the outer electron arrangement of an atom or an ion. If the outer electron structure changes, the properties change. The loss of the 3*s* electron gives sodium the stable

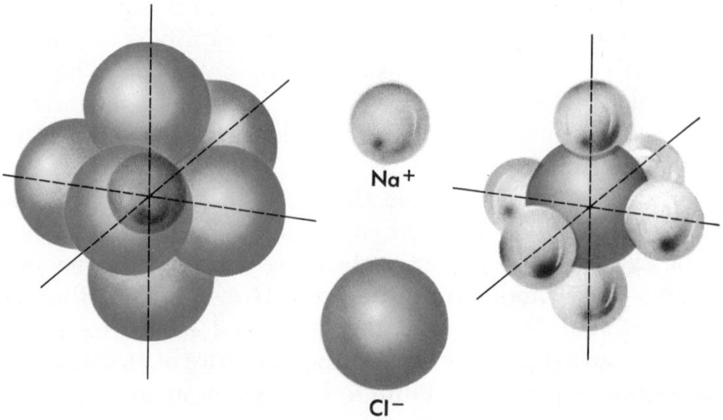

Fig. 14-3. The packing of Na^+ and Cl^- ions in the NaCl crystal. In the model on the left, the six Cl^- ions are clustered about one Na^+ ion, which cannot be seen here but can be seen in Figure 14-4.

electron configuration of neon. *The charge of a monatomic ion and its oxidation number are the same.* In fact, the charge of the ion determines its oxidation state.

Electrovalent compounds usually exist as crystals made up of positive and negative ions arranged in a very orderly fashion. For example, the cubic structure of crystalline sodium chloride is shown in Figures 14-3, 14-4, and 14-5. X-ray analysis show that these crystals are composed of ions. Other electrovalent compounds crystallize in different patterns. Each has a characteristic lattice structure that depends on the relative size and charge of the ions.

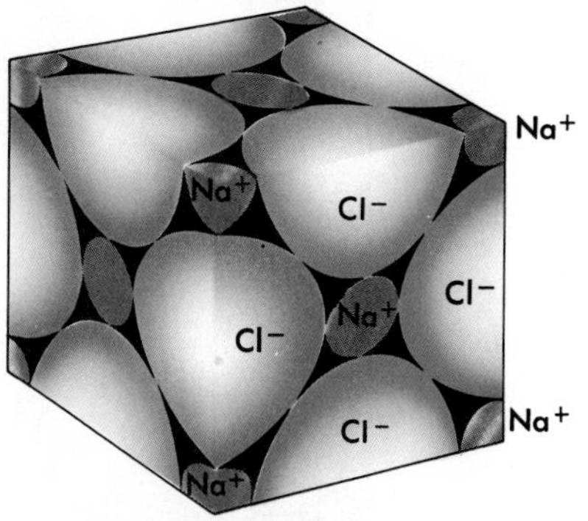

Fig. 14-4. The sodium chloride unit cell showing the lattice arrangement of ions in the crystal.

14.5 Hydration of ions

Suppose a few crystals of sodium chloride are dropped into a beaker of water. The water dipoles exert an attractive force on the ions forming the surfaces of the crystals. The negative oxygen ends of several water dipoles exert an attractive force on a positive sodium ion. Similarly, the positive hydrogen ends of other water dipoles exert an attractive force on a negative chloride ion. These forces weaken the bond by which the sodium and chloride ions are held together in the crystal lattice. The sodium and chloride ions then break away from the crystal lattice. They diffuse throughout the solution, loosely bonded to the solvent water molecules. See Figure 14-6.

Other sodium and chloride ions are similarly attracted by solvent molecules and diffuse in the solution. In this way, the salt crystal is gradually dissolved and the ions are dispersed throughout the solution. *The separation of ions from the crystals of ionic compounds during the solution process is called* ***dissociation.*** We may represent the dissociation of sodium chloride crystals in water by use of an ionic equation:

$$Na^+Cl^- \text{ (solid)} \rightarrow Na^+ \text{ (in water)} + Cl^- \text{ (in water)}$$

Sodium chloride is said to *dissociate* when it is dissolved in water.

We have already used the symbol (s) for "solid." Solutions in water are commonly referred to as "aqueous solutions." In this sense, (aq) means "in water." Thus, the dissociation of an ionic salt in water is usually written as

$$Na^+Cl^-(s) \rightarrow Na^+(aq) + Cl^-(aq)$$

The number of water dipoles that attach themselves to the ions of the crystal depends largely upon the size and charge of the ion. *This attachment of water molecules to ions of the solute is called* ***hydration.*** The ions are said to be *hydrated.* The degree of hydration of these ions is somewhat indefinite. Water molecules are interchanged continuously from ion to ion. They are also interchanged between ions and solvent.

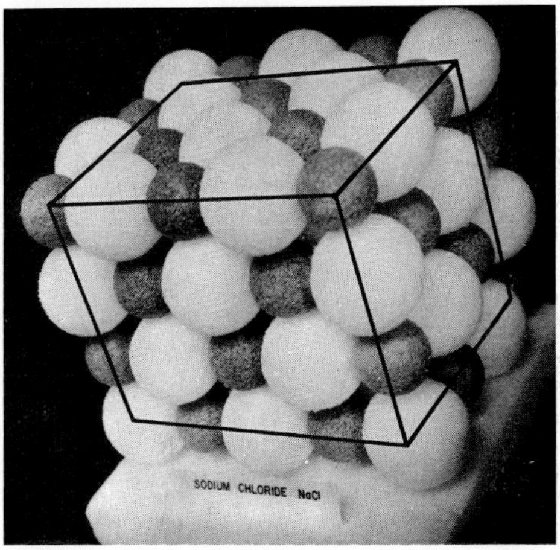

Fig. 14-5. Model of a portion of a cubic sodium chloride crystal. The lattice structure is composed of sodium ions and chloride ions. Each ion has six neighbors of opposite charge, the arrangement being repeated in each direction to the edge of the crystal.

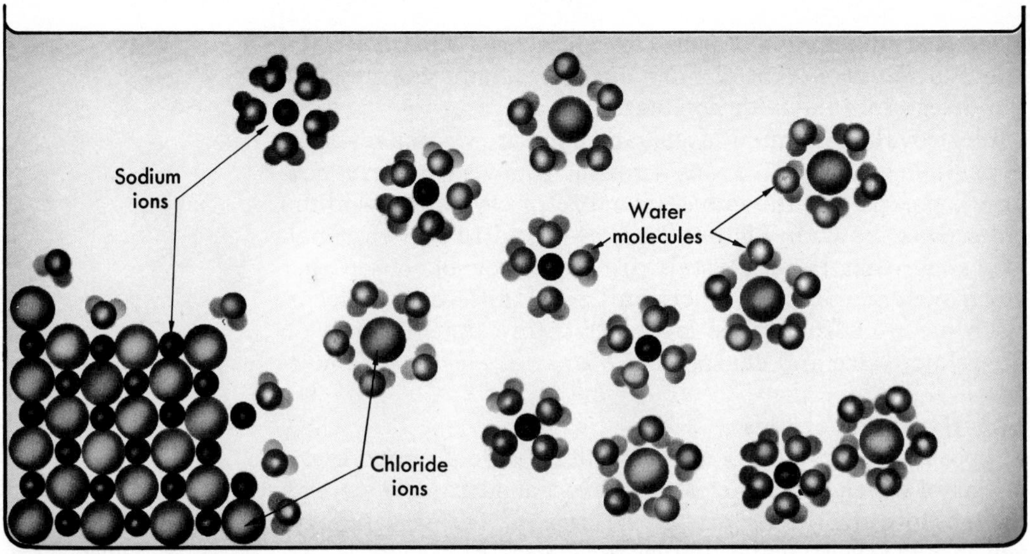

Fig. 14-6. When sodium chloride crystals are dissolved in water, the polar water molecules exert attracting forces that weaken the ionic bonds. The process of solution occurs as the ions of sodium and chloride become hydrated.

In certain cases, the water dipoles are not involved in re-forming the crystal structure during the evaporation of the solvent. This situation occurs with sodium chloride, whose crystals do not contain water of crystallization. On the other hand, some ions retain a characteristic number of water molecules in re-forming the crystal lattice of their salt in the hydrated form. An example is crystalline copper(II) sulfate, $CuSO_4 \cdot 5H_2O$. Four of the five water molecules are associated with the Cu^{++} ion. The fifth water molecule is associated with the SO_4^{--} ion.

Extensive hydration of the solute ions ties up a large portion of the solvent molecules. This reduces the number of *free* water molecules in the spaces separating hydrated ions of opposite charge. Attraction between ions then becomes stronger and the crystal begins to form again. Eventually, the tendency for ions to reform the crystal lattice reaches an *equilibrium* with the tendency for ions to be hydrated. At this point, the practical limit of solubility is reached. The solution is saturated under existing conditions.

$$\mathbf{Na^+Cl^-(s) \rightleftarrows Na^+(aq) + Cl^-(aq)}$$

Here, the tendency toward minimum energy (crystallizing) equals the tendency toward maximum entropy (dissolving).

Many ionic compounds that exist as crystalline solids are very soluble in water. They dissolve and produce solutions with high concentrations of hydrated ions. The following examples are typical.

When a formula of the type $CaCl_2$ is written ionically, the form $Ca^{++}Cl^-{}_2$ is used. The subscript $_2$ is spaced out to mean two Cl^- ions as in $Ca^{++}(Cl^-)_2$.

$$\mathbf{Ca^{++}Cl^-{}_2(s) \rightarrow Ca^{++}(aq) + 2Cl^-(aq)}$$
$$\mathbf{K^+Cl^-(s) \rightarrow K^+(aq) + Cl^-(aq)}$$
$$\mathbf{K^+ClO_3^-(s) \rightarrow K^+(aq) + ClO_3^-(aq)}$$
$$\mathbf{Ag^+NO_3^-(s) \rightarrow Ag^+(aq) + NO_3^-(aq)}$$

Even ionic compounds of very slight solubility in water show measurable dissociation tendencies. Low concentrations of ions are present in water solutions of slightly soluble salts. Silver chloride, AgCl, is so slightly soluble that it is ordinarily described as being insoluble. However, "insoluble" salts precipitate from solutions saturated with respect to their ions, regardless of how low their concentration may be. The dissociation equation for AgCl in aqueous solution is

$$\mathbf{Ag^+Cl^-(s) \rightarrow Ag^+(aq) + Cl^-(aq)}$$

Both KCl and $AgNO_3$ have been described as very soluble ionic compounds. Their aqueous solutions contain hydrated ions which can be present in very high concentrations. These hydrated particles are K^+(aq) and Cl^-(aq) ions for the KCl solute. They are Ag^+(aq) and NO_3^-(aq) ions for the $AgNO_3$ solute. On the other hand, AgCl is only very slightly soluble in water. Its solubility at 20°C is 1×10^{-5} mole/liter. This number means that only very low concentrations of both Ag^+ ions and Cl^- ions can be present in the same water solution.

Solubility of KCl in water at 20°C is 4.5 moles/liter.

Solubility of $AgNO_3$ in water at 20°C is 13 moles/liter.

Suppose we mix fairly concentrated solutions of KCl and $AgNO_3$. In a single solution environment we have the four ionic species: K^+(aq), Cl^-(aq), Ag^+(aq), and NO_3^-(aq). However, the concentrations of Ag^+ and Cl^- ions greatly exceed the solubility of AgCl. Excess Ag^+ and Cl^- ions separate from the solution as a *precipitate* of solid AgCl. *The separation of a solid from a solution is called* ***precipitation.***

The term species *is used whenever reference is made to atomic particles that may be atoms, molecules, or ions.*

The empirical equation for this reaction can be written as

$$\mathbf{KCl + AgNO_3 \rightarrow KNO_3 + AgCl(s)}$$

The salts KCl, $AgNO_3$, and KNO_2 are all very soluble in water. Only their aqueous ions are present in the solution environment. A more useful representation is the *ionic equation,*

$$\mathbf{K^+(aq) + Cl^-(aq) + Ag^+(aq) + NO_3^-(aq) \rightarrow K^+(aq) + NO_3^-(aq) + Ag^+Cl^-(s)}$$

In this form, the equation shows clearly that the K^+(aq) and NO_3^-(aq) ions take no part in the action. We will refer to ions that take no part in a chemical reaction as ***"spectator ions."*** Suppose we ignore these spectator ions and retain only the reacting species. The chemical action is then shown most simply by the following *net ionic equation:*

$$\mathbf{Ag^+(aq) + Cl^-(aq) \rightarrow Ag^+Cl^-(s)}$$

Sometimes there is no reason to write the complete empirical equation or the complete ionic equation for such a reaction. The net ionic equation, which includes only the participating chemical species, may be the most useful way to represent the reaction.

Ionic compounds can act as conductors of electric charge in another way. Any effect that overcomes the attraction between the ions allows them the mobility to conduct an electric current. We have seen how water as a solvent provides ion mobility through the dissociation process. Heating produces the same effect. If an ionic compound is heated until it melts, or *fuses,* the ions become mobile and can conduct an electric current through the melted substance. Some solid ionic compounds, such as silver nitrate and potassium chlorate, melt at fairly low temperatures. The electric conductivity of such fused salts can be demonstrated easily in the laboratory. Other ionic compounds, such as sodium chloride and potassium fluoride, must be heated to relatively high temperatures before they melt. When melted, they too conduct an electric current.

14.6 Some covalent compounds ionize

Covalent bonds are formed when two atoms share electrons. The shared electrons move about the nuclei of both atoms joined by the covalent bond. If the two atoms differ in electronegativity, the shared electrons are drawn toward the more highly electronegative atom. The covalent bond is polar to some degree. The molecule formed by these two atoms is polar covalent with a negative region and a positive region.

When a polar molecule is dissolved in water, the water dipoles exert attractive forces on the oppositely charged regions of the solute molecule. These attractive forces oppose the bonding force within the molecule. If they exceed the bonding force, the covalent bond breaks and the molecule is separated into simpler (charged) fragments. The charged fragments disperse in the solvent as hydrated ions. *The formation of ions from solute molecules by the action of the solvent is called* ***ionization.***

The smaller an ion and the higher its charge, the stronger the hydration tendency is likely to be.

Factors that favor the ionization of solute molecules are the weakness of their covalent bonds and the ability of the ions formed to associate with the solvent. The tendency for solute molecules to ionize in a suitable solvent is determined by the relative stabilities of the molecules and the separated ions in the solution.

The extent to which covalent solutes ionize varies over a wide range. Some substances may be almost completely ionized in aqueous solutions. Others may be only slightly ionized. This difference among covalent solutes is related to their relative bond strengths and their entropy changes on ionization.

Let us consider an example of ionization. Hydrogen chloride is one of a series of compounds of hydrogen and a member of the Halogen Family of elements. These elements are fluorine, chlorine, bromine, and iodine. (Refer to Section 5.4.) The compounds, collectively called *hydrogen halides,* are molecular and have single covalent bonds. All are gases and are very soluble in water. Hydrogen chloride, HCl, is the most important hydrogen halide.

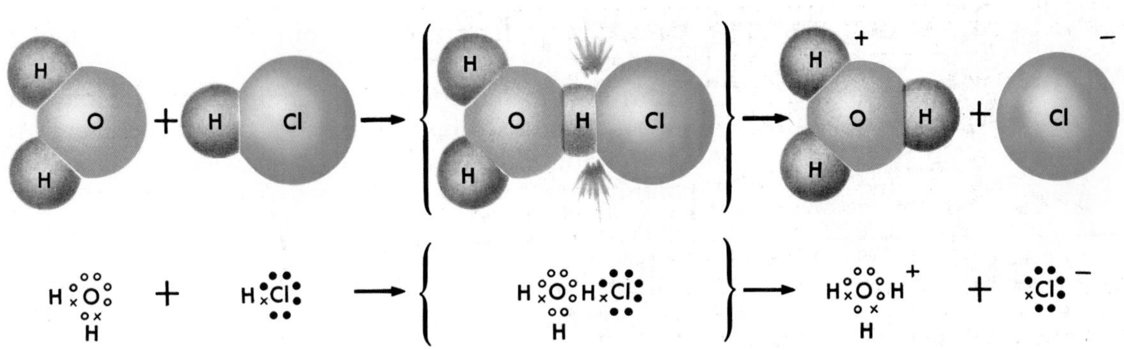

Fig. 14-7. Water molecules react with hydrogen chloride molecules and form hydronium ions and chloride ions, an ionization process.

As a pure liquid, hydrogen chloride *does not* conduct an electric current. When dissolved in water, the hydrogen chloride solution *does* conduct. Ions are present in the aqueous solution. A solution of hydrogen chloride in a nonpolar solvent such as benzene *does not* conduct. We may conclude that the ions in the aqueous solution result from a chemical reaction between hydrogen chloride molecules and water molecules. The solvent water dipoles are able to overcome the H—Cl bonds and separate the solute molecules into hydrogen ions, H^+, and chloride ions, Cl^-.

Arrhenius believed that the ionization of HCl involved simply the dissociation of solute molecules into H^+ ions and Cl^- ions on entering the solution. Today chemists recognize that single H^+ ions do not exist as free particles in water solutions. They do, however, show a strong tendency to become hydrated.

The H^+ is a bare hydrogen nucleus and approaches very close to a water molecule. This fact may account for the strong hydrating effect of water molecules on H^+ ions, which increases the tendency for ionization. Most covalent compounds are nonelectrolytes and do not ionize in solution. Those that do ionize are most often hydrogen-containing compounds that can form H^+ ions.

Fig. 14-8. A model of the hydronium ion, H_3O^+.

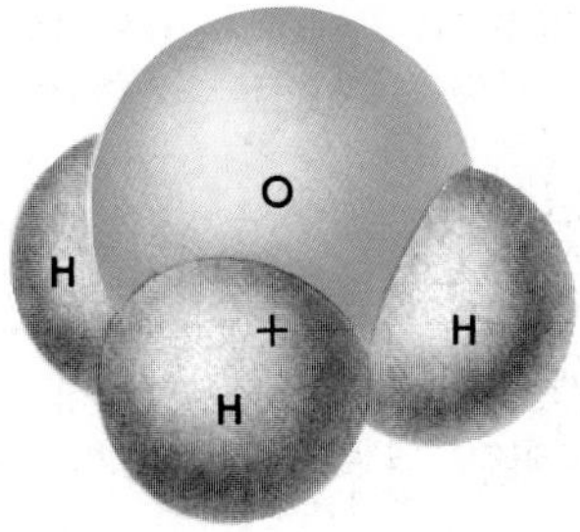

The ionization of HCl in aqueous solution is illustrated with models in Figure 14-7. The ionization reaction is given by the following equation.

$$\mathbf{HCl(g) + H_2O(l) \rightarrow H_3O^+(aq) + Cl^-(aq)}$$

Omitting the phase notations for reactants and products, we can write the equation more simply as

$$\mathbf{HCl + H_2O \rightarrow H_3O^+ + Cl^-}$$

The H_3O^+ *ion is a hydrated proton* ($H^+ \cdot H_2O$) *and is known as the hydronium ion.* A model of this ion is shown in Figure 14-8. Because of ionization, a solution of hydrogen chloride in water has distinctly different properties from those of the

"Proton" as used here refers to the H^+ *ion, not to a proton from the nucleus of any of the atoms.*

hydrogen chloride gas. The aqueous solution is given the name *hydrochloric acid.* The properties of acids will be studied in greater detail in Chapter 15.

The aluminum halides, binary compounds of aluminum with a halogen of Group VII, are molecular. The energy required to remove the two 3*s* and one 3*p* electrons from each aluminum atom exceeds the energy available when the elements combine. The bonds are covalent with a partial ionic character.

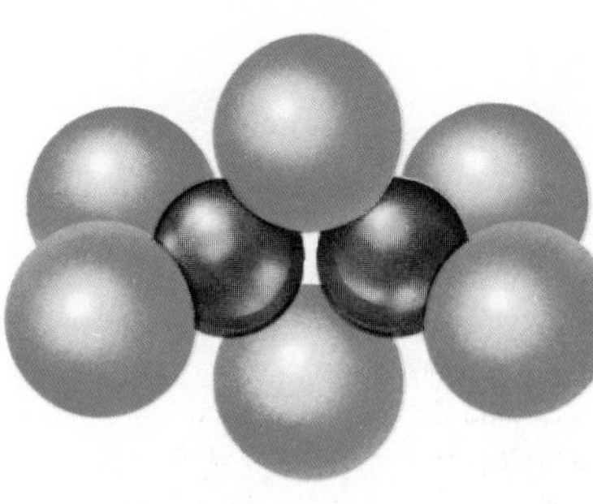

Fig. 14-9. A model of the aluminum chloride molecule, Al_2Cl_6.

Aluminum chloride has the structure Al_2Cl_6 in both liquid and vapor phases. A model of this molecule is shown in Figure 14-9. The structure of the solid is less certain but is thought to consist of $AlCl_3$ units. Thus, the empirical formula $AlCl_3$ is generally used for this halide.

Aluminum chloride in the liquid phase is a very poor conductor of electricity. In water solution, however, it is a good conductor. This change indicates that ionization occurs during the solution process. The aluminum ion has a strong tendency for hydration. The hydration process provides the energy needed to complete the transfer of three electrons from each aluminum atom to three chlorine atoms. The ionization can be represented as follows:

$$\mathbf{Al_2Cl_6 + 12H_2O \rightarrow 2Al(H_2O)_6^{+++} + 6Cl^-}$$

or, more simply, using the empirical formula

$$\mathbf{AlCl_3 + 6H_2O \rightarrow Al(H_2O)_6^{+++} + 3Cl^-}$$

Other hydrated aluminum ions are probably formed at the same time.

14.7 Strength of electrolytes

The strength of an electrolyte is determined by the concentration of its ions in solution. Electrovalent compounds in the solid phase are crystals composed of ions. Their solutions contain the solute only in the form of dispersed hydrated ions. The solutions are said to be completely ionized. Electrovalent substances, if very soluble in water, can form solutions with high concentrations of ions. Their water solutions are good conductors of electricity. We call these substances *strong electrolytes.*

The single covalent bonds of the hydrogen halide molecules range from the very strong and very polar H—F bond, through the H—Cl and H—Br bonds, to the very weak and slightly polar H—I bond. Even moderately dilute solutions of HCl, HBr, and HI are essentially completely ionized. They are strong electrolytes. Of these halides, HI has the weakest bonds and is the strongest electrolyte.

Aqueous solutions of hydrogen fluoride, HF, are only slightly ionized. The very strong H—F bond prevents an extensive

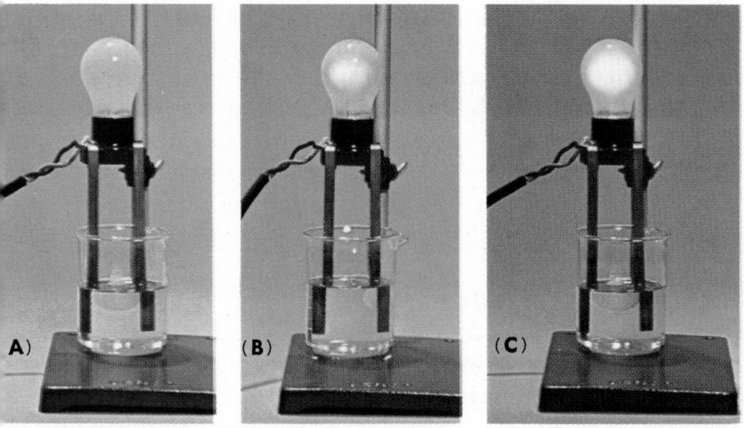

Fig. 14-10. The brightness of the lamp filament indicates the conductivity of the tested material. (A) Distilled water, pure solvent, a nonconductor; (B) dilute acetic acid, a poor conductor—contains a weak electrolyte; (C) dilute hydrochloric acid, a good conductor—contains a strong electrolyte.

onization reaction with the solvent molecules. The concen-rations of H_3O^+ ions and F^- ions remain low and the con-entration of HF molecules remains high. Hydrogen fluoride s a *weak electrolyte.* Solutions of weak electrolytes contain ow concentrations of ionic species and high concentrations of nolecular species.

A water solution of hydrogen acetate, $HC_2H_3O_2$, is a poor onductor. Its relative merit as a conductor is shown in Figure 4-10. The fact that the solution does conduct slightly tells us hat some ionization has occurred. This ionization is shown n the reversible reaction

$$HC_2H_3O_2 + H_2O \rightleftarrows H_3O^+ + C_2H_3O_2^-$$

Ve must assume that the ion concentration is low. A 0.1-*m* olution of $HC_2H_3O_2$ is approximately 1% ionized; a 0.001-*m* olution is approximately 15% ionized. Of course, if 1% of the $IC_2H_3O_2$ molecules in solution is present in the form of ions, hen 99% is present in the form of covalent molecules. Hydro-gen acetate is a weak electrolyte.

Ammonia, NH_3, is a covalent compound and is a gas at ordi-ary temperatures. It is extremely soluble in water and its vater solution is a poor conductor. Ammonia ionizes slightly n water solution giving a low concentration of ammonium ons, NH_4^+, and hydroxide ions, OH^-. It is a weak electrolyte. The reaction with water is

$$NH_3(g) + H_2O(l) \rightleftarrows NH_4^+(aq) + OH^-(aq)$$

Ammonia-water solutions are sometimes called *ammonium ydroxide.* This is a traditional name and it may be justified by he fact that many useful properties of aqueous ammonia are hose of the few NH_4^+ and OH^- ions present. (A more plausible eason that it is still used might be that all the reagent bottles re now labeled "**AMMONIUM HYDROXIDE**" and no one vants to change the labels.)

We must avoid confusing the terms *strong* and *weak* with the terms *dilute* and *concentrated. Strong* and *weak* refer to the *degree of ionization. Dilute* and *concentrated* refer to the *amount of solute dissolved in a solvent.* These terms, *strong* and *weak,* are not precise descriptions of electrolytes. There are all degrees of strongness and of weakness and the dividing lines are not clear-cut. We can qualify the terms *dilute* and *concentrated* in a similar way.

14.8 Ionization of water

The ordinary electric conductivity test of solutions described in Section 14.1 shows water to be a nonconductor. More sensitive electric conductivity tests show that pure water has a slight but measurable conductivity. It ionizes to the extent of about two molecules in a billion. Even though this concentration of ions is very low, it is important. We neglect the slight ionization of water when dealing with solutes such as hydrogen chloride, which may ionize completely in aqueous solutions. Ionization of water is discussed further in Chapter 16.

The ionization of water probably begins with the formation of a hydrogen bond between two water molecules as shown in Figure 14-11. The ionization products are hydronium ions and hydroxide ions. They are formed by the following reaction:

Chemists do not have experimental evidence that H_3O^+ ions exist in water solution in precisely this form. Some evidence suggests a more aqueous structure such as $H_9O_4^+$ because of hydrogen bonding. When the ion is written H_3O^+, it is with the understanding that additional water molecules might be associated with it.

$$\mathbf{H_2O + H_2O \rightleftharpoons H_3O^+ + OH^-}$$

In any reaction involving the hydronium ion, the water of hydration is always left behind. This water of hydration often is of little significance in the reaction process. If this is the case, the ion may be written as $\mathbf{H^+}$ or $\mathbf{H^+}$ **(aq)** in the interest of simplicity. *In all such cases, it is understood that this ion exists in hydrated form in aqueous solution.*

14.9 Electrolytes and the freezing and boiling points of solvents

Molal solutions have a definite ratio of solute particles to solvent molecules (see Section 13.11). The depression of the freez-

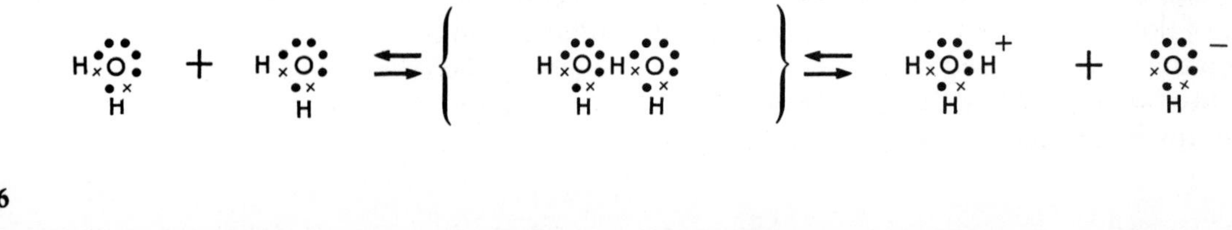

Fig. 14-11. The formation of a hydrogen bond between two water dipoles may be an intermediate step in the ionization of water.

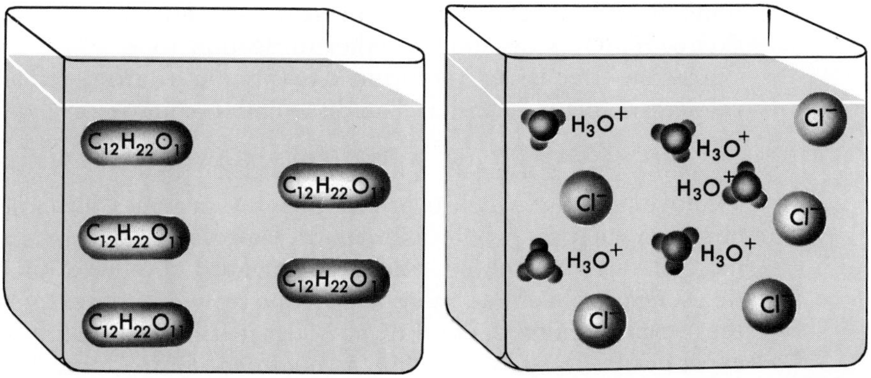

Fig. 14-12. Five sugar molecules produce only five particles in solution. Five hydrogen chloride molecules, on the other hand, produce ten particles when dissolved in water.

ing point of a solvent by a solute is directly proportional to the number of particles of solute present. The same reasoning applies to the elevation of the boiling point of a solvent by a nonvolatile solute. Why, then, does one mole of hydrogen chloride dissolved in 1 kg of water lower the freezing point more than one mole of sugar does? The greater freezing-point depression is caused by the separation into *two* particles of each molecule of hydrogen chloride that ionizes. This comparison is illustrated in Figure 14-12.

Suppose that, in a concentrated solution, 90 out of every 100 molecules ionize. Then, for every 100 molecules in solution, 190 particles are formed (180 ions and 10 un-ionized molecules). Such a solute therefore lowers the freezing point of its solvent 1.9 (190 ÷ 100) times as much as would a solute which does not ionize.

Suppose 100% of the hydrogen chloride molecules were ionized, as in a more dilute solution. The lowering of the freezing point should be double that caused by the solute in a solution of a nonelectrolyte having the same molality.

The following equation assumes the complete ionization of hydrogen sulfate in very dilute solutions.

$$\mathbf{H_2SO_4 + 2H_2O \rightarrow 2H_3O^+ + SO_4^{--}}$$

Each molecule of hydrogen sulfate that ionizes completely forms *three ions*. Two are hydronium ions, each with one positive charge. One is a sulfate ion with two negative charges. A very dilute solution of a given molality should, if completely ionized, lower the freezing point of its solvent *three times as much* as a solution of a nonelectrolyte having the same molality. Nonvolatile electrolytes in solution raise the boiling points of solvents in a similar way because of their ionization.

Actually, hydrogen sulfate ionizes in aqueous solutions in two steps. The two hydrogen atoms in each molecule are ionized one at a time. In the first step, H_3O^+ ions and HSO_4^- ions are formed. In the second step, the HSO_4^- ions are further ionized to H_3O^+ ions and SO_4^{--} ions. Except in *very* dilute solutions, the second step may be far from complete. The ionization of H_2SO_4 is discussed further in Section 15.3.

Now let us consider a solution of an ionic substance such as calcium chloride in water. The dissociation equation is

$$\mathbf{Ca^{++}Cl^{-}_2(s) \rightarrow Ca^{++}(aq) + 2Cl^{-}(aq)}$$

We have seen that a mole of a nonelectrolyte provides one mole of solute particles when dissolved in water. An example is a mole of sugar, which provides the Avogadro number of particles. One mole of $CaCl_2$ dissociates and provides three times the Avogadro number of solute particles in solution. We might expect a $CaCl_2$ solution of a given molality to lower the freezing-point of its solvent three times as much as a nonelectrolyte having the same molality. However, experiments do not confirm this effect except for very dilute solutions. At ordinary dilutions, the freezing-point depressions of ionic solutes are less than those expected from ideal solutions. Table 14-1 gives observed values of freezing-point depressions in Celsius degrees for several ionic solutes at different dilutions of their aqueous solutions. Note the trend *toward* a whole number multiple of K_f (1.86 C° for water) as the concentrations decrease. This problem is dealt with in Section 14.10.

Table 14-1

FREEZING-POINT DEPRESSIONS FOR AQUEOUS SOLUTIONS OF IONIC SOLUTES

Solute	Concentration (in moles solute/kg H_2O) 0.1	0.05	0.01	0.005	0.001
	Table values are observed molal freezing-point depressions in C° for concentrations indicated				
$2K_f = 2 \times 1.86C° = 3.72C°$					
$AgNO_3$	3.32	3.42	3.60	—	—
KCl	3.45	3.50	3.61	3.65	3.66
KNO_3	3.31	2.43	3.59	3.64	—
LiCl	3.52	3.55	3.60	3.61	—
$MgSO_4$	2.25	2.42	2.85	3.02	3.38
NH_4Cl	3.40	3.49	3.58	3.62	—
NH_4NO_3	3.40	3.47	3.57	—	—
$3K_f = 3 \times 1.86C° = 5.58C°$					
$BaCl_2$	4.70	4.80	5.03	5.12	5.30
$Ba(NO_3)_2$	4.25	—	5.01	—	5.39
$CaCl_2$	4.83	4.89	5.11	—	—
$Cd(NO_3)_2$	5.08	—	5.20	5.28	—
$CoCl_2$	4.88	4.92	5.11	5.21	—
K_2SO_4	5.32	4.60	5.01	5.15	5.28
$ZnCl_2$	4.94	—	5.15	5.28	—
$4K_f = 4 \times 1.86C° = 7.44C°$					
$K_3Fe(CN)_6$	5.30	5.60	6.26	6.53	7.10

Fig. 14-13. The first multicell lithium metal battery is prepared for performance testing at Argonne National Laboratory. This high-temperature battery promises to provide six times the electric energy of a comparable lead-acid battery. These batteries would be useful in electric vehicles.

14.10 Apparent degree of ionization

The larger the number of ions in a given volume of a solution, the better it conducts electricity. This fact suggests one way of determining the concentration of ions in a solution. Another way is to measure the lowering of the freezing point caused by an ionized solute in a measured amount of solvent. Suppose a 0.1-*m* solution of sodium chloride were to freeze at $-0.372°C$ $[0° - (2 \times 0.186\ C°)]$. If so, we could assume the solute to be 100% ionized.

Actual measurements, however, give only an *apparent degree of ionization*. We have seen that electrovalent compounds, by the nature of their structure, must be 100% ionic in solution. Experimental results give an apparent degree of ionization somewhat less than 100%. For example, consider the 0.1-*m* solution of sodium chloride referred to above. This solution actually freezes at $-0.346°C$, yielding a freezing-point depression of 0.346 C° instead of the predicted value of 0.372 C°. For many years, such differences prevented chemists from deciding whether or not a compound was completely ionized in water solution.

Today we recognize that attractive forces exist between ions in aqueous solutions. These forces are small compared with those in the crystalline salt. However, they do interfere with the movements of the aqueous ions, even in dilute solutions.

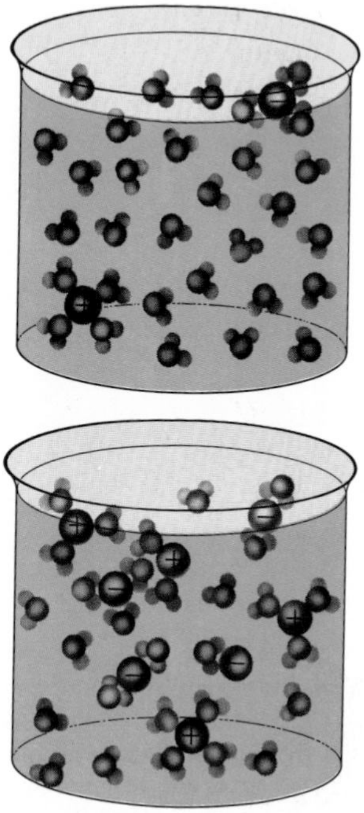

Fig. 14-14. The ions in the dilute solution on the top are far apart and act independently. The activity of the ions in the solution on the bottom is somewhat restricted because of the concentration. Thus, the apparent number of ions present may be less than the actual number.

Only in very dilute solutions is the average distance between ions great enough, and the attraction between ions small enough, for the aqueous solute ions to move freely. Therefore, the more dilute the sodium chloride solution, the more nearly the freezing-point depression approaches twice the value for a molecular solute.

These observations are consistent with the Debye-Hückel theory of inter-ionic attraction which accounts quantitatively for the attraction between dissociated ions of ionic solids in dilute water solutions. According to the Debye-Hückel theory, each ion is surrounded on the average by more ions of opposite charge than of like charge. See Figure 14-14. The effect is to hinder the movements of an ion. Thus, the "ion activity" is less than that expected on the basis of the number of ions known to be present. Table 14-2 gives the observed freezing-point depressions of aqueous solutions of sodium chloride at various concentrations. The table also shows freezing-point depressions per mole of NaCl calculated from the observed values.

In concentrated solutions, an additional effect on the freezing-point depression may arise from a shortage of solvent molecules. There may not be enough water molecules to hydrate completely all solute ions. In such a case, clusters of ions may act as a single solute unit.

Table 14-2

INFLUENCE OF CONCENTRATION ON FREEZING POINT OF AQUEOUS SOLUTIONS OF NaCl

Concentration of NaCl (m)	Freezing-point Depression (C°)	Freezing-point Depression/mole NaCl (C°)
0.100	0.346	3.46
0.0100	0.0361	3.61
0.00100	0.00366	3.66
0.000100	0.000372	3.72

SUMMARY

Ions that have mobility and are free to move through a liquid medium are able to conduct electricity. Two electrodes connected to a source of electric current must be in contact with the liquid for conduction to occur through it.

Electrovalent compounds are ionic substances. In crystal form they are composed of ions. When melted, their liquid phase consists of ions. They are soluble only in highly polar solvents like water and form solutions that contain ions. Electrovalent compounds conduct electricity only when melted or when dissolved in water. Their ions have mobility in either situation.

The process by which electrovalent substances are dissolved in water is called dissociation. In dissociation, ions that compose the electrovalent compounds are pulled apart by the action of the solvent. They dissolve in the solvent as hydrated ions.

Some covalent compounds form solutions that contain ions. As pure liquids covalent compounds do not conduct. The ions are produced by chemical reaction between the solute molecules and the solvent, a process called ionization. Water is the best, but not the only, ionizing agent.

Substances whose water solutions conduct electricity are called electrolytes. Those whose water solutions do not conduct electricity are nonelectrolytes. Electrolytes are strong or weak depending on how well their solutions conduct an electric current. Solutions of strong electrolytes have high concentrations of ions. Those of weak electrolytes have low concentrations of ions. Water ionizes to a very small extent forming hydronium ions and hydroxide ions in very low concentrations.

Electrolytes affect the freezing and boiling points of solvents to a greater extent than nonelectrolytes. Freezing-point depressions and boiling-point elevations of solvents vary with the number of solute particles in solution. The apparent degree of ionization increases with dilution of an electrolyte in solution. Electrovalent solutes are composed of ions and consequently their solutions are completely ionic. An apparent degree of ionization less than the actual ion concentration can be explained on the basis of the theory of inter-ionic attraction.

QUESTIONS

Group A

1. What is the distinction between an electrolyte and a nonelectrolyte?
2. What effect does the addition of electrolytes have on the boiling points and freezing points of solvents such as water?
3. What theory helps to explain the behavior of electrolytes?
4. What are the important assumptions of this theory?
5. What is an ion?
6. Write the equation for the ionization of water.
7. Explain why the water molecule is a polar molecule.
8. What is the nature of the crystal structure of an electrovalent compound?
9. How does an atom differ from an ion?
10. How may we account for the stability of an ion?
11. (*a*) How do water molecules cause an electrovalent compound to dissociate? (*b*) How may the process be reversed?
12. Why is the dissociation of electrovalent compounds 100%?
13. Melted potassium chloride conducts an electric current. Explain.
14. Predict the approximate freezing-point depressions for 0.01-*m* aqueous solutions of the following substances: (*a*) KI, (*b*) C_2H_5OH, (*c*) $Al_2(SO_4)_3$.
15. (*a*) Explain how the action of water on a polar compound like hydrogen chloride produces ionization. (*b*) Write the equation for the ionization of hydrogen chloride in water solution showing the part played by the water.
16. What is the distinction between dissociation and ionization?
17. Describe the solution equilibrium in a saturated solution of sodium nitrate containing an excess of the crystals.
18. (*a*) What are symmetrical covalent molecules? (*b*) Why don't they ionize?

19. Explain the abnormal freezing-point lowering and boiling-point elevation of solvents produced by electrolytes in terms of the theory of ionization.
20. (*a*) Write an equation for the dissociation of calcium chloride. (*b*) What is the theoretical freezing point of a one-molal solution of calcium chloride in water?
21. Describe two ways of measuring the apparent degree of ionization.
22. Why does the measurement of the apparent degree of ionization not coincide with the evidence that electrovalent compounds are 100% dissociated in solution?
23. How does a concentrated solution of a weak electrolyte differ from a dilute solution of a strong electrolyte?
24. When potassium nitrate is dissolved in water, the dissolving process is endothermic. (*a*) What temperature change does the solution undergo? (*b*) Which is greater, the hydration energy or the lattice energy? (*c*) To what do you attribute the driving force that causes the dissolving process to proceed?
25. (*a*) How is the solubility of potassium nitrate affected by warming the solution of Question 24? (*b*) Apply the principle of Le Chatelier to account for this change in solubility.
26. Suppose 0.1 mole of a substance dissolved in 1 kg of water lowers the freezing point of the water 0.360 C°. (*a*) What can you predict about the nature of the solution? (*b*) What can you conclude about the oxidation numbers of the particles of solute? Questions 27–30: For each reaction, (*1*) write the complete ionic equation; (*2*) identify the spectator ions; (*3*) write the net ionic equation.
27. Barium bromide + ammonium sulfate →
28. Silver nitrate + magnesium chloride →
29. Manganese(II) sulfate + ammonium sulfide →
30. Zinc iodide + calcium hydroxide →
31. What makes ocean water a conductor of electricity? How is the freezing point of the water affected?

PROBLEMS

Group B

1. In a certain experiment it was found that 185 drops of water were required to give a volume of 10.0 ml. (*a*) How many molecules of water are in each drop? (*b*) How many hydronium ions are in each drop? (*c*) How many hydroxide ions are in each drop?
2. How many grams of copper(II) sulfate pentahydrate must be added to 125 g of water to give a 0.0156-*m* solution?
3. Calculate the freezing point of $60\bar{0}$ g of water to which 12.0 g of ethyl alcohol, C_2H_5OH, has been added.
4. The composition of a substance was determined by analysis to be 10.1% carbon, 0.846% hydrogen, and 89.1% chlorine. It was found to be soluble in benzene and when 2.50 g was dissolved in 100 g of benzene, the freezing point of the benzene was 4.41°C. Determine the molecular formula of the substance.
5. A chemistry student collected 15.0 ml of dry HCl gas at 21.0°C and 748 mm pressure and then dissolved the gas in 1.00 kg of water. Assuming complete ionization and no interionic attraction, calculate the freezing-point depression of the water.

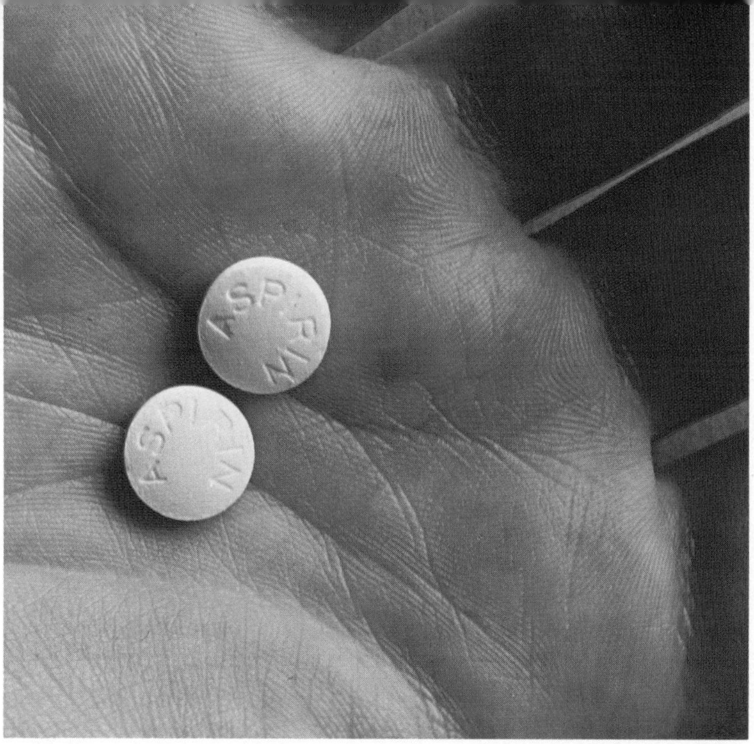

chapter 15

ACIDS, BASES, AND SALTS

The twentieth century's number one wonder drug is an acid. (See Question 28 on page 320.)

Acids

15.1 The nature of acids

Electrolytes are substances whose water solutions conduct an electric current. Their solutions contain ions. They are historically classified as *acids, bases,* or *salts*. In this sense, ***acids** are substances that react with water and form hydronium ions,* H_3O^+. Acids are limited by this definition to aqueous solutions. *Bases* are electrolytes that provide hydroxide ions, OH^-, in water solutions. *Salts* are electrovalent compounds of metal-nonmetal composition. They are ionic structures as crystalline solids, and in water solution they are dissociated as separate metallic and nonmetallic ions. Bases and salts will be treated in detail beginning with Sections 15.8 and 15.13, respectively.

Acids as a group share a common structural characteristic. Their molecules contribute one or more hydrogen ions to the solution when they are ionized in water. As we might expect, acids share a common set of properties to varying degrees. All acids have a sour taste. **CAUTION: Never use a "taste test" to identify an acid.** Some acids are very corrosive and some are poisonous. You are already familiar with the sour taste of lemon juice (citric acid) and cider vinegar (acetic acid). Acids react with metals that stand above hydrogen in the replacement series (Table 8-2) and liberate hydrogen. They affect the color of indicators and neutralize bases. You will learn about these last two properties of acids and will make use of them in Chapter 16.

Indicators are organic dyes that have one color in acidic solutions and another color in basic solutions.

Nearly all fruits contain acids, and so do many common

foods. Lemons, oranges, and grapefruit contain citric acid. Apples contain malic acid. The souring of milk produces lactic acid. Rancid butter contains butyric acid. The fermentation of hard cider forms the acetic acid of vinegar. These acids, because of their origin and nature, are called *organic* acids.

The carboxyl group in organic acids:

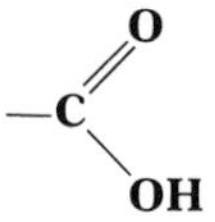

All organic acids are covalent (molecular) structures and contain a specific configuration (COOH) called the carboxyl group. They are weak acids, being slightly ionized in water solution. To the extent that ionization occurs, the hydrogen atom of the carboxyl group becomes hydrated as an H_3O^+ ion. Organic acids are discussed in Chapter 19.

Acids manufactured from minerals are known as *inorganic* acids, or simply as *mineral* acids. These substances have been known for centuries because their properties are very distinctive. When the term "acid" is used in a very general sense, the reference is usually to these compounds. They are the substances known historically as acids; their water solutions are called *aqueous acids.* For many years, mineral acids have occupied major roles in the chemical industry. Four mineral acids are among the largest-volume industrial chemicals produced in the United States. Modern definitions of acids give the name "acid" to many substances that are not acids in this traditional sense.

15.2 Industrial acids

If a manufacturing chemist were asked to name the most important acid, he or she would probably mention *sulfuric acid.* It is a very versatile industrial product. It is used in so many technical and manufacturing processes that the consumption of sulfuric acid is an index to a country's industrialization and prosperity. More sulfuric acid is manufactured in the United States than any other chemical—approximately 70 billion pounds each year.

The second ranking industrial acid is *phosphoric acid* and the third is *nitric acid.* The dominant use of these three acids is in agriculture. More specifically, the production of fertilizers consumes 60% of the sulfuric acid, 80% of the phosphoric acid, and 70% of the nitric acid produced in the United States.

Ranking fourth in importance is *hydrochloric acid.* The gastric secretion in the human stomach is about 0.4% hydrochloric acid. Its industrial uses have little in common with the three acids just mentioned.

Phosphoric acid, H_3PO_4, is a weak acid. It is made by reacting sulfuric acid with phosphate rock, and by burning phosphorus and reacting the oxide with water. Its major uses are in making fertilizers and detergents. It is not as commonly used in the chemistry laboratory as are sulfuric, nitric, and hydrochloric acids. A brief description of each of these three common laboratory acids follows.

1. Sulfuric acid. H_2SO_4 is the formula used for this acid. It is a dense, oily liquid with a high boiling point. *Concentrated* sulfuric acid contains 95% to 98% sulfuric acid (by weight), and the balance is water. Its density is 1.84 g/ml. Common dilute sulfuric acid is made by adding 1 volume of concentrated acid to 6 volumes of water. Its major industrial uses are in producing phosphoric acid, other chemicals, cellulose products, and in refining petroleum.

CAUTION: Add sulfuric acid to water slowly while stirring. Never add water to acid.

2. Nitric acid. HNO_3 is the formula used to represent this volatile liquid. Pure nitric acid is too unstable for commercial use. Concentrated nitric acid, a 70% solution in water, is fairly stable. It has a density of 1.42 g/ml. Common dilute nitric acid is made by adding 1 volume of concentrated acid to 5 volumes of water. A pure solution of nitric acid is colorless, but it gradually becomes yellow on standing because of slight decomposition that forms brown nitrogen dioxide gas.

$$\mathbf{4HNO_3 \rightarrow 4NO_2 + O_2 + 2H_2O}$$

Its major industrial uses are in producing fertilizers, explosives, and other chemicals.

3. Hydrochloric acid. HCl is the formula for hydrogen chloride gas. This gas is extremely soluble in water. It forms the colorless solution known as hydrochloric acid. Concentrated hydrochloric acid is a water solution containing about 36% hydrogen chloride. Its density is 1.19 g/ml. Common dilute hydrochloric acid is prepared by adding 1 volume of concentrated acid to 4 volumes of water. Such a solution contains approximately 7% hydrogen chloride. Its industrial uses include pickling steel and recovery of magnesium.

Pickling: Immersion of iron or steel in an acid solution to remove surface oxides.

15.3 Aqueous acids

Arrhenius gave us a clue to the chemical nature of acids in his *Theory of Ionization.* He believed that acids ionize in water solutions and form hydrogen ions.

The acids we have just described are essentially covalently bonded structures. They have one element in common, *hydrogen.* Concentrated sulfuric and nitric acids are very poor conductors, since they are only very slightly ionized. Liquid hydrogen chloride is a nonconductor of electricity. In dilute water solution, however, each of these substances is highly ionized because of the hydrating action of the water dipoles. We can represent their ionization in water solutions by the following equations:

$$\mathbf{H_2SO_4 + H_2O \rightarrow H_3O^+ + HSO_4^-}$$
$$\mathbf{HNO_3 + H_2O \rightarrow H_3O^+ + NO_3^-}$$
$$\mathbf{HCl + H_2O \rightarrow H_3O^+ + Cl^-}$$

Hydronium ions, H_3O^+, are present in all of these solutions. We can assume that the acid properties of the solutions are due to these H_3O^+ ions.

Table 15-1

COMMON AQUEOUS ACIDS

Strong Acids	
$HClO_4$	$\rightleftarrows H^+ + ClO_4^-$
HCl	$\rightleftarrows H^+ + Cl^-$
HNO_3	$\rightleftarrows H^+ + NO_3^-$
H_2SO_4	$\rightleftarrows H^+ + HSO_4^-$
Weak Acids	
HSO_4^-	$\rightleftarrows H^+ + SO_4^{--}$
H_3PO_4	$\rightleftarrows H^+ + H_2PO_4^-$
HF	$\rightleftarrows H^+ + F^-$
$HC_2H_3O_2$	$\rightleftarrows H^+ + C_2H_3O_2^-$
H_2CO_3	$\rightleftarrows H^+ + HCO_3^-$
H_2S	$\rightleftarrows H^+ + HS^-$
HCN	$\rightleftarrows H^+ + CN^-$
HCO_3^-	$\rightleftarrows H^+ + CO_3^{--}$

When a sulfuric acid solution is diluted enough, the ionization of HSO_4^- ions may become appreciable.

$$\mathbf{HSO_4^- + H_2O \rightarrow H_3O^- + SO_4^{--}}$$

The ionization of HSO_4^- ions may be complete in very dilute solutions of sulfuric acid. If so, the equation is written

$$\mathbf{H_2SO_4 + 2H_2O \rightarrow 2H_3O^+ + SO_4^{--}}$$

Observe that this equation merely summarizes the two partial ionizations that occur with increasing dilution of the sulfuric acid solution.

$$\begin{array}{ll} \textbf{(1st stage)} & \mathbf{H_2SO_4 + H_2O \rightarrow H_3O^+ + HSO_4^-} \\ \textbf{(2nd stage)} & \mathbf{HSO_4^- + H_2O \rightarrow H_3O^+ + SO_4^{--}} \\ \hline \textbf{(summary)} & \mathbf{H_2SO_4 + 2H_2O \rightarrow 2H_3O^+ + SO_4^{--}} \end{array}$$

Acids that ionize completely, or nearly so, in water solution provide high concentrations of hydronium ions. Such concentrations characterize strong acids. Sulfuric, nitric, and hydrochloric acids are strong mineral acids. Substances that produce few hydronium ions in water solution, such as acetic acid and carbonic acid, are weak acids. They ionize slightly in water.

15.4 Modern definitions of acids

The hydronium ion is a hydrated proton. In water solution, it is considered to be in the hydrated form, $H^+ \cdot H_2O$, and is usually represented as H_3O^+. The proton is vigorously hydrated in water because of its small size and high positive charge density.

Chemists have found conclusive evidence that H_3O^+ ions exist in hydrated crystals of percholoric acid (a very strong acid) and in concentrated solutions of strong acids. In dilute aqueous solutions of acids, however, the proton hydration may be more extensive. Physical evidence, such as electric and thermal conductivities, suggests the formula $H^+ \cdot 4H_2O$. This formula corresponds to the ionic species $H_9O_4^+$. A model of the $H_9O_4^+$ ion having the spatial structure of a triagonal pyramid is shown in Figure 15-1.

Fig. 15-1. A possible model of the $H^+ \cdot 4H_2O$ or $H_9O_4^+$ ion that suggests an H_3O^+ ion with three H_2O molecules attached through hydrogen bonds.

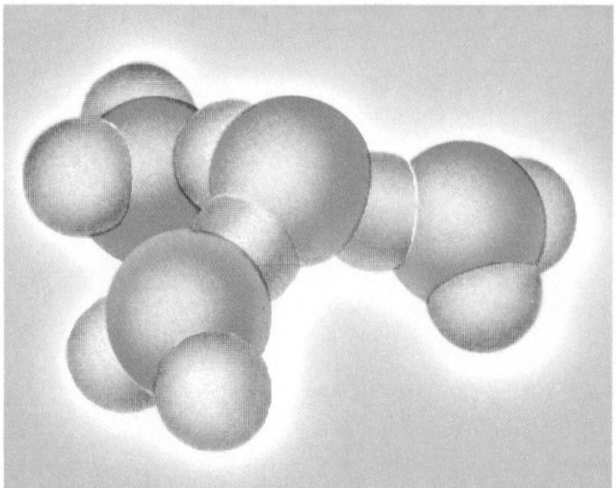

Other species of the hydrated proton have been suggested for dilute aqueous acid solutions. These species are $H^+ \cdot 2H_2O$ and $H^+ \cdot 3H_2O$, corresponding respectively to the species $H_5O_2^+$ and $H_7O_3^+$. Chemists write formulas of this kind only when the degree of hydration is itself the subject of discussion. Otherwise, for simplicity, the hydrated proton in aqueous solutions is written as $H^+(aq)$ or as the hydronium ion, H_3O^+.

When hydrogen chloride is dissolved in a nonpolar solvent, the solution remains a nonconductor. *We conclude that protons*

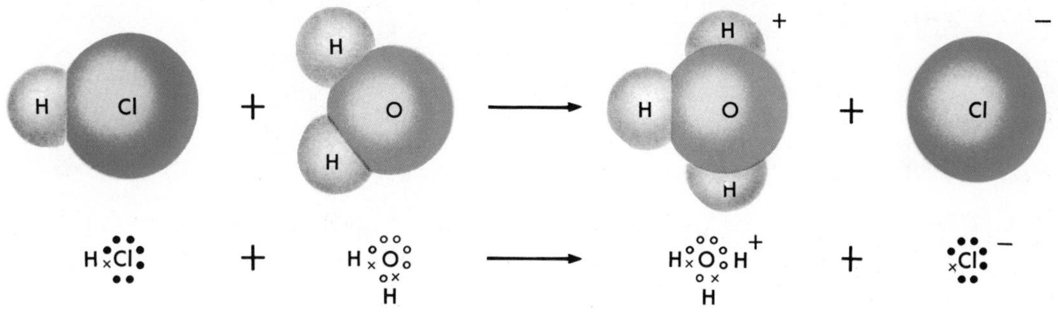

Fig. 15-2. When HCl is dissolved in water, a proton is donated by the polar HCl molecule forming the hydronium ion, H_3O^+, and the chloride ion, Cl^-.

(hydrogen ions) are not released by molecules such as HCl unless there are molecules or ions present that can accept them.

Hydrogen chloride dissolved in ammonia transfers protons to the solvent much as it does in water.

$$\mathbf{HCl + H_2O \rightarrow H_3O^+ + Cl^-}$$
$$\mathbf{HCl + NH_3 \rightarrow NH_4^+ + Cl^-}$$

The similarity of these reactions is very clear when we use electron-dot formulas.

$$\mathbf{H{:}\overset{\cdot\cdot}{\underset{\cdot\cdot}{Cl}}{:} + H{:}\overset{\circ\circ}{\underset{\underset{\displaystyle H}{\circ\times}}{O}}{:} \rightarrow H{:}\overset{\circ\circ}{\underset{\underset{\displaystyle H}{\circ\times}}{O}}{:}H^+ + {:}\overset{\cdot\cdot}{\underset{\cdot\cdot}{Cl}}{:}^-}$$

$$\mathbf{H{:}\overset{\cdot\cdot}{\underset{\cdot\cdot}{Cl}}{:} + H{:}\overset{\circ\circ}{\underset{\underset{\displaystyle H}{\circ\times}}{N}}{:}H \rightarrow H{:}\overset{\overset{\displaystyle H^+}{\circ\circ}}{\underset{\underset{\displaystyle H}{\circ\times}}{N}}{:}H + {:}\overset{\cdot\cdot}{\underset{\cdot\cdot}{Cl}}{:}^-}$$

A proton is transferred to the ammonia molecule, forming the *ammonium ion,* just as one is transferred to the water molecule, forming the hydronium ion. See Figures 15-2 and 15-3. In each case, the proton is given up by the hydrogen chloride molecule. This molecule is said to be a *proton donor.* In 1923, J. N. Brønsted, a Danish chemist, defined all proton donors as acids. According to Brønsted's definition, *an* ***acid*** *is any species (molecule or ion) that gives up protons to another substance.* For example, hydrogen chloride is an acid in this sense

Fig. 15-3. When hydrogen chloride is dissolved in ammonia, a proton is donated by the polar HCl molecule to the NH_3 molecule forming the ammonium ion, NH_4^+, and the chloride ion, Cl^-.

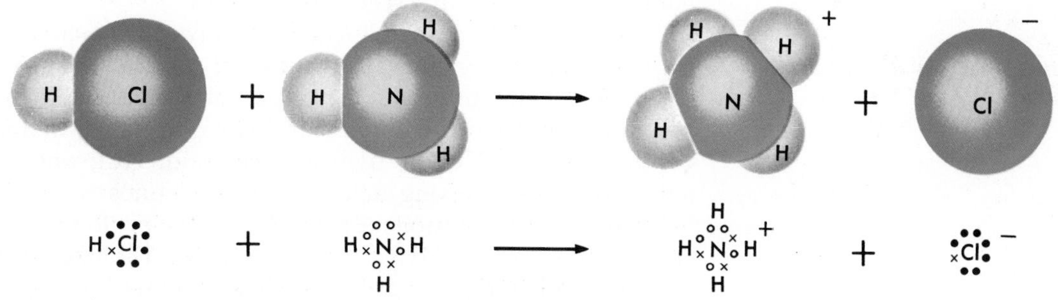

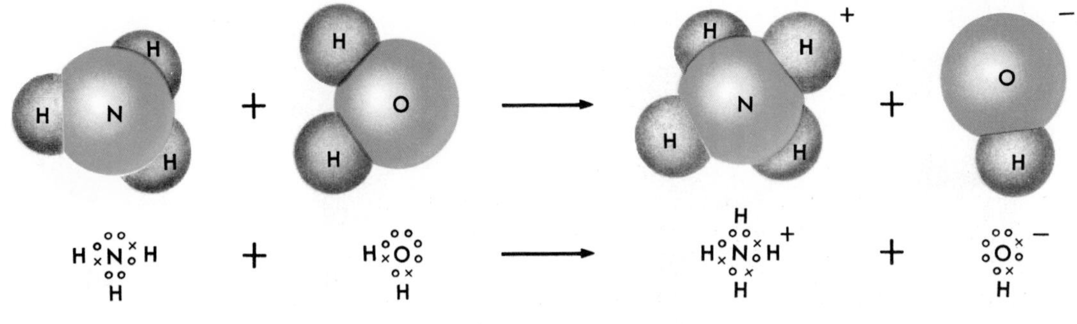

Fig. 15-4. When ammonia is dissolved in water, water molecules are the proton donors and ammonia molecules are the proton acceptors.

even though it does not contain hydrogen ions as a pure substance.

Water is an acid when ammonia is dissolved in it because water molecules donate protons to ammonia molecules.

$$\begin{array}{c}\mathrm{H{:}\underset{H}{\ddot{N}}{:}H + H{:}\underset{H}{\ddot{O}}{:} \rightleftarrows H{:}\overset{H^{+}}{\underset{H}{\ddot{N}}}{:}H + {:}\underset{H}{\ddot{O}}{:}^{-}}\end{array}$$

$$NH_3 + H_2O \rightleftarrows NH_4^+ + OH^-$$

Furthermore, in water solutions of the strong mineral acids described in Section 15.3, the hydronium ion, H_3O^+, is an acid. The ion is the actual proton donor in reactions involving these solutions. This modern definition of acids can be applied to any molecule or ion capable of donating a proton to another molecule or ion.

15.5 Properties of aqueous acids

Acids such as hydrochloric, nitric, and sulfuric are quite soluble in water. Their other physical properties differ widely. However, they have many *chemical* properties in common.

1. Acids donate protons when they react with bases. The many common properties of acids depend on this characteristic behavior. Acids that donate only one proton per molecule are called *monoprotic acids.* Examples are HCl, HNO_3, and $HC_2H_3O_2$. Sulfuric acid, H_2SO_4, and carbonic acid, H_2CO_3, are *diprotic,* being capable of donating two protons per molecule. Phosphoric acid, H_3PO_4, is *triprotic.*

Relative strengths of aqueous acids are listed in Table 15-5.

2. Acids contain ionizable hydrogen in covalent combination with a nonmetallic element or polyatomic species. The strength of an acid depends upon the *degree* of ionization in water solution, not upon the *amount* of hydrogen in the molecule. Perchloric acid, $HClO_4$, hydrochloric acid, HCl, and nitric acid, HNO_3, are strong acids. They are almost completely ionized in water solutions. Each donates one proton per molecule. Acetic acid, $HC_2H_3O_2$, is a weak acid. It ionizes slightly in water and yields one proton and one acetate ion, $C_2H_3O_2^-$, per ionized molecule.

In Section 15.3, we stated that sulfuric acid ionizes in two stages depending on the amount of dilution:

$$H_2SO_4 + H_2O \rightleftarrows H_3O^+ + HSO_4^-$$
$$HSO_4^- + H_2O \rightleftarrows H_3O^+ + SO_4^{--}$$

The first stage is completed in fairly concentrated solutions. The second stage may be appreciable in more dilute solutions. All stages in the ionization of diprotic and triprotic acids occur in the same solution. Therefore, solutions of H_2SO_4 may contain H_3O^+, HSO_4^-, and SO_4^{--} ions. The concentration of ions formed in the first stage is very much greater than the concentration of ions formed in the second stage.

The rather weak phosphoric acid ionizes in three stages:

$$H_3PO_4 + H_2O \rightleftarrows H_3O^+ + H_2PO_4^-$$
$$H_2PO_4^- + H_2O \rightleftarrows H_3O^+ + HPO_4^{--}$$
$$HPO_4^{--} + H_2O \rightleftarrows H_3O^+ + PO_4^{---}$$

Thus a solution of H_3PO_4 may contain each of the following species: H_3PO_4, H_3O^+, $H_2PO_4^-$, HPO_4^{--}, and PO_4^{---}. As with diprotic acids, the concentration of ions formed in the first stage is very much greater than in the second stage. Similarly, the concentration of ions formed in the second stage is very much greater than the concentration of ions formed in the third stage.

3. *Acids have a sour taste.* Lemons, grapefruit, and limes are sour. These fruits contain weak acids in solution. A solid acid tastes sour as it dissolves in the saliva and forms a water solution. Most laboratory acids are very corrosive (they destroy the skin) and they are powerful poisons.

CAUTION: Never use the "taste test" in the laboratory.

4. *Acids affect indicators.* If a drop of an acid solution is placed on a test strip of blue *litmus,* the *blue* color changes to *red.* Litmus is a dye extracted from certain lichens. Some other substances may be used as indicators. *Phenolphthalein* (fee-nole-*thall*-een) is colorless in the presence of acids. *Methyl orange* turns red in acid solutions.

Fig. 15-5. Blue litmus indicator changes to red in an aqueous acid.

5. *Acids neutralize hydroxides.* Solutions of an acid and a metallic hydroxide may be mixed in chemically equivalent quantities. If so, each cancels the properties of the other. This process is called *neutralization* and is an example of an ionic reaction. The products are a salt and water. The salt is recovered in crystalline form by evaporating the water. The acid and the hydroxide neutralize each other.

Suppose a solution containing 1 mole of NaOH is added to a dilute solution containing 1 mole of HCl. The reaction is represented empirically by the following equation:

$$HCl + NaOH \rightarrow NaCl + H_2O$$

Molecular HCl is ionized in dilute solution. The reactants present are H_3O^+ and Cl^- ions.

$$HCl + H_2O \rightarrow H_3O^+ + Cl$$

Electrovalent NaOH is dissociated in water solution. The reactants in this solution are Na^+ and OH^- ions.

$$Na^+OH^- \rightarrow Na^+ + OH^-$$

Thus, the reactants in the separate solutions are present as aqueous ions. The Na^+ and Cl^- ions remain dissociated in the combined solution. They are spectator ions. The ionic species that actually participate in the neutralization reaction are H_3O^+ and OH^- ions. They form essentially un-ionized water. The net ionic equation is

$$H_3O^+ + OH^- \rightarrow 2H_2O$$

The neutralization reaction between an acid and a base is illustrated with space-filling models in Figure 15-6.

The neutralization reaction is entirely between hydronium ions from the acid and hydroxide ions from the soluble metallic hydroxide. In all neutralizations of very soluble hydroxides by strong acids, the reaction is the same. The nonmetallic ions of the acid and metallic ions of the hydroxide undergo no chemical change. However, we still may prefer to write the complete equation because it shows what pure substances were the original reactants and what salt can be recovered by evaporating the water solvent.

6. *Acids react with many metals.* The reaction products are hydrogen gas and a salt. The equation for the reaction between zinc and aqueous sulfuric acid is typical. The species involved in the reaction are included in the net ionic equation.

$$Zn(s) + 2H^+(aq) \rightarrow Zn^{++}(aq) + H_2(g)$$

Metallic zinc replaces hydrogen from the aqueous acid as aqueous Zn^{++} ions. On evaporation of the water solvent, the aqueous Zn^{++} ions and SO_4^{--} ions separate from solution as

Fig. 15-6. In neutralization reactions, hydronium ions and hydroxide ions combine and form essentially un-ionized water molecules.

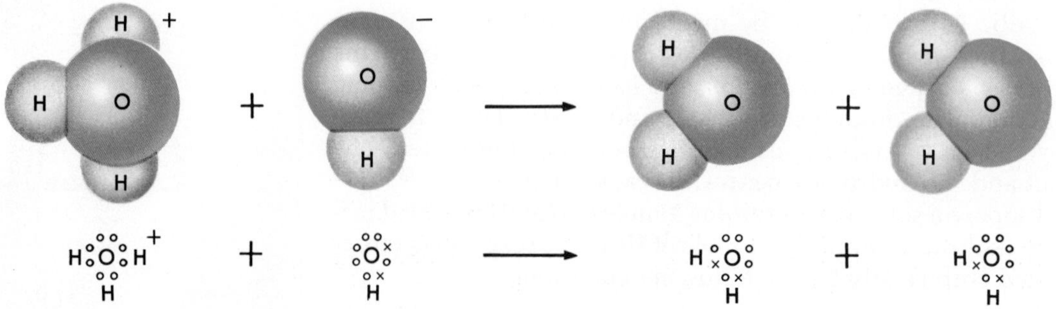

crystals of $ZnSO_4$. Recall that such *salts* are simply dissociated ions in aqueous solution.

7. *Acids react with oxides of metals.* They form salts and water. As an example, consider the reaction of copper(II) oxide and sulfuric acid.

$$\mathbf{CuO + H_2SO_4 \rightarrow CuSO_4 + H_2O}$$

Written ionically,

$$\mathbf{CuO + 2H^+(aq) + SO_4^{--} \rightarrow CU^{++} + SO_4^{--} + H_2O}$$

The net reaction is

$$\mathbf{CuO + 2H^+(aq) \rightarrow Cu^{++} + H_2O}$$

Crystalline $CuSO_4$ is recovered only by evaporating the solvent water.

8. *Acids react with carbonates.* These reactions give off carbon dioxide and produce a salt and water.

$$\mathbf{CaCO_3 + 2HCl \rightarrow CaCl_2 + H_2O + CO_2(g)}$$

Of course, $CaCl_2$ is recovered as a product of the reaction upon evaporation of the solvent water.

This reaction of an acid and a carbonate provides a simple test for carbonates as in calcium carbonate. Being insoluble in water, calcium carbonate is found in such forms as limestone, marble, and sea shells. A sea shell placed in an acid solution gives the "fizzy" production of CO_2 gas.

Fig. 15-7. This statue is the victim of air pollution. Coal, oil, or gasoline are fossil fuels that contain carbon and may contain sulfur as an impurity. When these fuels are burned, oxides of carbon and sulfur are released to the air. These oxides combine with moisture and form acids which dissolve marble.

15.6 Naming aqueous acids

Some acids are *binary* compounds. They contain only *two* elements, hydrogen and another nonmetal. Other acids contain oxygen as a third element. They are often referred to as *oxyacids*.

1. *Binary acids.* The name of an acid having only two elements begins with the prefix *hydro*. The root of the name of the nonmetal in combination with hydrogen follows this prefix. The name has the ending *-ic*. This scheme is illustrated by the examples given in Table 15-2. Water solutions of the binary compounds listed are acids known by the names given in the right column.

Table 15-2

NAMES OF BINARY ACIDS

Formula	Name of Pure Substance	Name of Acid
HF	hydrogen fluoride	hydrofluoric acid
HCl	hydrogen chloride	hydrochloric acid
HBr	hydrogen bromide	hydrobromic acid
HI	hydrogen iodide	hydroiodic acid
H_2S	hydrogen sulfide	hydrosulfuric acid

Table 15-3

NAMES OF OXYACIDS	
Formula	Name of Acid
$HC_2H_3O_2$	acetic acid
H_2CO_3	carbonic acid
$HClO$	hypochlorous acid
$HClO_2$	chlorous acid
$HClO_3$	chloric acid
$HClO_4$	perchloric acid
HNO_2	nitrous acid
HNO_3	nitric acid
H_3PO_3	phosphorous acid
H_3PO_4	phosphoric acid
H_2SO_3	sulfurous acid
H_2SO_4	sulfuric acid

2. *Oxyacids.* These acids contain hydrogen, oxygen, and a third element. The formulas and names of the series of oxyacids of chlorine illustrate the general method of naming such acids. The acid name for the water solution of each oxychlorine is shown at the right in the following series.

$HClO$ .... hypo-chlor-ous acid
$HClO_2$ .... chlor-ous acid
$HClO_3$ .... chlor-ic acid
$HClO_4$ .... per-chlor-ic acid

In all of these oxyacids, chlorine is the central element. For this reason the root *-chlor-* is used in each case. $HClO_3$ is named *chlor-ic acid.* It contains the chlorate group and no prefix is used. The oxyacid of chlorine that contains *more* oxygen per molecule than chloric acid is called *per-chlor-ic acid.* The prefix *per-* is a contraction of *hyper,* which means *above.* The acid containing *less* oxygen per molecule than chloric acid is called *chlor-ous acid.* The oxyacid of chlorine that contains *still less* oxygen than chlorous acid has the prefix *hypo-*, the root *-chlor-*, and the suffix *-ous.* The prefix *hypo-* means *below.*

To use this scheme, it is only necessary to know the formula and name of one oxyacid in any series. The formula and name of the member of each series that you should memorize are listed below.

$HClO_3$ .... chloric acid
HNO_3 .... nitric acid
$HBrO_3$ .... bromic acid
H_2SO_4 .... sulfuric acid
H_3PO_4 .... phosphoric acid

The names of common oxyacids are given in Table 15-3.

15.7 Acid anhydrides

Only fluorine is more electronegative than oxygen. Its compound with oxygen, OF_2, is a fluoride rather than an oxide. Other elements form oxides with oxygen. The oxidation number of oxygen in these compounds is −2. Oxides range structurally from ionic to covalent. The more ionic oxides involve the highly electropositive metals on the left side of the periodic table. The oxides formed with nonmetals on the right side of the periodic table are covalent molecular structures.

Many of the molecular (nonmetallic) oxides are gases at ordinary temperatures. Examples are carbon monoxide, CO, carbon dioxide, CO_2, and sulfur dioxide, SO_2. Diphosphorus pentoxide, on the other hand, is a solid. The name "diphosphorus pentoxide" is that of the empirical formula P_2O_5. (The molecular formula is now known to be P_4O_{10}.) Most nonmetallic oxides react with water and form *oxyacids.*

All oxyacids contain one or more oxygen-hydrogen (O—H) groups in the covalent structure. They are called *hydroxyl* groups. They are not to be confused with O—H groups existing as OH^- ions whose compounds are called *hydroxides*. The hydroxyl group is arranged in the molecule in such a manner that it may donate a proton. This arrangement gives the molecule its acid character.

Figure 15-8 shows the electron-dot formulas of the four oxyacids of chlorine. Each formula contains the O—H group, not as an ion but as a group covalently bonded to the central Cl atom. Aqueous solutions of these solutes are acidic because the O—H bond is broken during ionization. The O—H group provides the proton donated by the oxychlorine acid molecule.

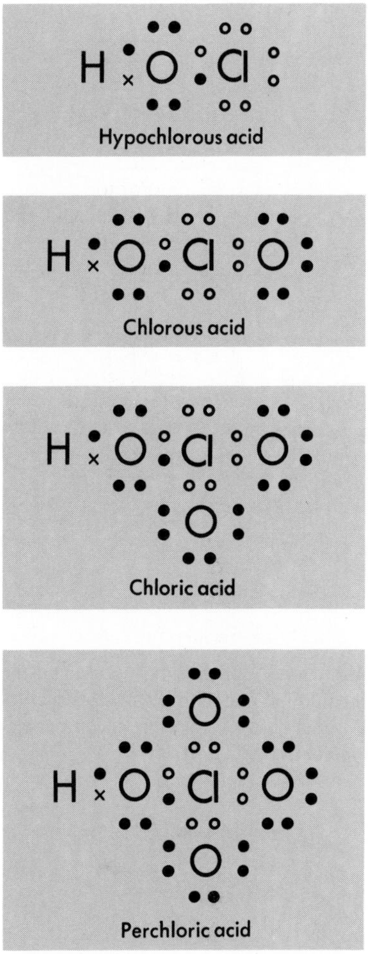

Fig. 15-8. Electron-dot formulas of the four oxyacids of chlorine.

When carbon dioxide dissolves in water, a very small amount of it reacts chemically with the solvent and forms carbonic acid:

$$\mathbf{CO_2 + H_2O \rightleftarrows H_2CO_3}$$

These H_2CO_3 molecules can ionize and give the aqueous solution a very low concentration of H_3O^+ ions.

$$\mathbf{H_2CO_3 + H_2O \rightleftarrows H_3O + HCO_3}$$

The net equation that shows the acid-producing behavior of CO_2 in aqueous solution is

$$\mathbf{CO_2 + 2H_2O \rightleftarrows H_3O^+ + HCO_3^-}$$

Carbonic acid and carbon dioxide differ in composition from each other just by a molecule of water. For this reason, carbon dioxide is called the *acid anhydride* of carbonic acid. The name *anhydride* means "without water." *Oxides that react with water and form acids, or that are formed by the removal of water from acids, are known as* ***acid anhydrides.***

Acid anhydride: *See Section 12.18(4).*

Binary acids do not contain oxygen and do not have an anhydride form. Thus, the reaction between an acid anhydride and water cannot be used to prepare such acids. However, it is an important method of preparing some oxyacids.

Sulfur dioxide is the acid anhydride of sulfurous acid.

$$\mathbf{SO_2 + H_2O \rightleftarrows H_2SO_3}$$

Sulfur trioxide is the acid anhydride of sulfuric acid.

$$\mathbf{SO_3 + H_2O \rightleftarrows H_2SO_4}$$

Acid anhydrides form oxyacids.

These anhydrides are important in the manufacture of sulfuric acid. Sulfuric acid, because it is cheap and has a high boiling point, can be used in the laboratory to produce several other acids. Although most hydrochloric acid is now produced commercially by other methods, the reaction for producing hydrogen chloride gas is an example.

$$\mathbf{H_2SO_4 + 2NaCl \rightarrow Na_2SO_4 + 2HCl(g)}$$

Nitric acid can be produced by the reaction of sulfuric acid with a nitrate. However, this process is not used commercially for preparing HNO_3 because it is more expensive than other processes.

Bases

15.8 The nature of bases

Several substances long known as bases are commonly found in homes. Household ammonia, an ammonia-water solution, is a familiar cleaning agent. Lye is a commercial grade of sodium hydroxide, NaOH, used for cleaning clogged sink drains. Limewater is a solution of calcium hydroxide, $Ca(OH)_2$. Milk of magnesia is a suspension of magnesium hydroxide, $Mg(OH)_2$, in water; it is used as an antacid, a laxative, and an antidote for strong acids. All of these hydroxides are *aqueous bases.*

Arrhenius considered a base to be any soluble hydroxide that neutralized an acid when their solutions were mixed. We now know that the only reaction occurring in such a neutralization is between hydronium ions and hydroxide ions. The nonmetal of the acid and the metal of the hydroxide remain in solution as hydrated ions. Hydronium ions combine with hydroxide ions and form water.

$$H_3O^+(aq) + OH^-(aq) \rightarrow 2H_2O(l)$$

Ammonia-water solutions and water solutions of soluble metallic hydroxides are commonly referred to as *aqueous bases.* They are our most useful basic solutions. Aqueous ammonia solutions are traditionally called *ammonium hydroxide,* NH_4OH. This molecular species probably does not exist in water solutions except possibly through the formation of hydrogen bonds between some NH_3 and H_2O molecules. These solutions are more appropriately called ammonia-water solutions, or simply $NH_3(aq)$ (aqueous ammonia). The most common basic solutions used in the laboratory are those of NaOH, KOH, $Ca(OH)_2$, and $NH_3(aq)$. Chemists refer to these solutions as being *alkaline* in their behavior.

In the Brønsted definition, an acid is a *proton donor.* Accordingly, *a* ***base*** *is a proton acceptor.* In this sense, the hydroxide ion, OH^-, is the most common base. However, many other species also combine with protons. The Brønsted use of the term *base* includes all species that accept protons in solution.

We have stated that hydrogen chloride ionizes in water solution as a result of the hydrating action of the solvent dipoles.

		weaker		weaker
$HCl + H_2O \rightarrow$		H_3O^+	+	CL^-
acid	base	acid		base

Fig. 15-9. A space-filling model of the hydroxide ion and its electron-dot formula. When it accepts a proton, a water molecule is formed.

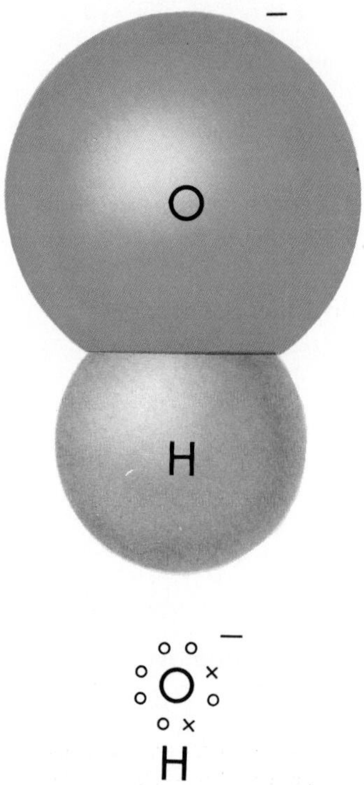

Here, the water molecule is the base. It accepts a proton from the HCl molecule, the acid. This reaction forms the H_3O^+ ion, which is a weaker acid than HCl, and the Cl^- ion, which is a weaker base than H_2O. The relative strengths of acids and bases are discussed further in Section 15.12.

Earlier, we described the neutralization reaction between aqueous solutions of HCl and NaOH. Here, the H_3O^+ ion acts as the acid since it, and not the HCl molecule, is the proton donor. The OH^- ion is, of course, the proton acceptor or base.

$$\underset{\text{acid}}{H_3O^+} + \underset{\text{base}}{OH^-} \rightarrow \underset{\text{acid}}{H_2O} + \underset{\text{base}}{H_2O}$$

When HCl gas is dissolved in liquid ammonia, the ammonia acts as the base.

$$\underset{\text{acid}}{HCl} + \underset{\text{base}}{NH_3} \rightarrow \underset{\text{acid}}{NH_4^+} + \underset{\text{base}}{Cl^-}$$

When NH_3 gas is dissolved in water, the water donates protons and therefore acts as an acid. Ammonia accepts protons and therefore is the base. A low concentration of NH_4^+ ions and OH^- ions is produced in the reversible reaction.

$$\underset{\text{base}}{NH_3} + \underset{\text{acid}}{H_2O} \rightleftarrows \underset{\text{acid}}{NH_4^+} + \underset{\text{base}}{OH^-}$$

Suppose we place open vessels of a saturated aqueous NH_3 solution (concentrated ammonium hydroxide) and a saturated aqueous HCl solution (concentrated hydrochloric acid) near each other. A dense white cloud of NH_4Cl forms above the vessels. This result demonstrates that HCl (the acid) and NH_3 (the base) can react without the intervention of water. See Figure 15-10.

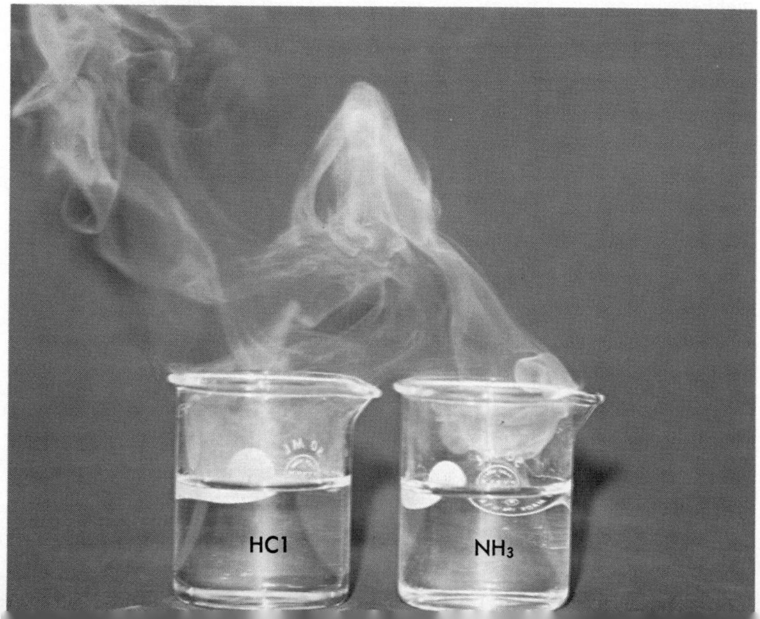

Fig. 15-10. The acid, HCl, and the base, NH_3, react and form the white cloud of NH_4Cl.

The Brønsted proton-transfer system of acids and bases is more general in scope than the aqueous system of acids and bases. It extends the acid-base concept to reactions in non-aqueous solutions. Here we are concerned mainly with aqueous acids and aqueous bases, water solutions of H_3O^+ ions, and water solutions of OH^- ions.

An even more general concept of acids and bases was defined in 1938 by G. N. Lewis, an American chemist. According to the Lewis acid-base system, any species that acts as an *electron-pair acceptor* in a chemical reaction is an acid. An *electron-pair donor* is a base. The Brønsted system extends the proton transfer concept of acid-base reactions beyond the aqueous system to nonaqueous solutions. The Lewis acid-base system extends the concept of acid-base reactions to some that do not involve proton transfers.

15.9 Properties of hydroxides

1. Hydroxides of the active metals supply OH^- *ions in solution.* Sodium and potassium hydroxides are very soluble in water. They are electrovalent (ionic) compounds and are, therefore, completely ionized in water solution. Their solutions are *strongly alkaline* because of the high concentration of strongly basic OH^- ions. In speaking of such solutions, chemists often attach the property of the ions to the solution itself. Thus, they may speak of "strongly basic solutions."

$$\mathbf{Na^+OH^- \rightarrow Na^+(aq) + OH^-(aq)}$$
$$\mathbf{K^+OH^- \rightarrow K^+(aq) + OH^-(aq)}$$

Calcium and strontium hydroxides also are ionic compounds. Thus, their water solutions are completely ionized. However, they are only slightly soluble in water. Therefore, they are only *moderately basic.*

$$\mathbf{Ca^{++}(OH^-)_2 \rightarrow Ca^{++}(aq) + 2OH^-(aq)}$$
$$\mathbf{Sr^{++}(OH^-)_2 \rightarrow Sr^{++}(aq) + 2OH^-(aq)}$$

The strength of the base depends on the *concentration* of OH^- ions *in solution.* It does not depend on the number of hydroxide ions per mole of the compound.

Ammonia-water solutions are *weakly basic* because they have a low concentration of OH^- ions. Ammonia, NH_3, is not a strong base and so does not acquire very many protons from water molecules when in solution. Relatively few NH_4^+ ions and OH^- ions are present.

$$\mathbf{NH_3(aq) + H_2O \rightleftarrows NH_4^+(aq) + OH^-(aq)}$$

2. Soluble hydroxides have a bitter taste. Possibly you have tasted limewater and know that it is bitter. Soapsuds also taste bitter because of the presence of hydroxide ions. **CAUTION: Never use the "taste test" in the laboratory.** Strongly basic solutions are very caustic (they chemically burn the skin) and the metallic ions in them are sometimes poisonous.

3. *Solutions of hydroxides feel slippery.* The very soluble hydroxides, such as sodium hydroxide, attack the skin and may produce severe caustic burns. Dilute solutions have a soapy, slippery feel when rubbed between the thumb and fingers.

4. *Soluble hydroxides affect indicators.* The basic OH^- ions in solutions of the soluble hydroxides cause *litmus* to turn from *red* to *blue*. This is just the opposite of the color change caused by H_3O^+ ions of acid solutions. In a basic solution, *phenolphthalein* turns *red* and *methyl orange* changes to *yellow*. Many insoluble hydroxides, on the other hand, produce too few hydroxide ions to affect indicators.

Fig. 15-11. Red litmus indicator changes to blue in an aqueous hydroxide.

5. *Hydroxides neutralize acids.* The neutralization of HNO_3 by KOH may be represented empirically by the equation

$$\mathbf{KOH + HNO_3 \rightarrow KNO_3 + H_2O}$$

Of course, ionic KOH dissociates in water solution and exists as hydrated K^+ ions and OH^- ions.

$$\mathbf{K^+OH^- \rightarrow K^+ + OH^-}$$

In water solution, the covalent HNO_3 is ionized and exists as hydrated protons and nitrate ions.

$$\mathbf{HNO_3 + H_2O \rightarrow H_3O^+ + NO_3^-}$$

The complete ionic equation for this neutralization reaction is

$$\mathbf{H_3O^+ + NO_3^- + K^+ + OH^- \rightarrow K^+ + NO_3^- + 2H_2O}$$

Removing the spectator ions, we have

$$\mathbf{H_3O^+ + OH^- \rightarrow 2H_2O}$$

This represents the only chemical reaction that takes place in the neutralization process. The hydrated K^+ and NO_3^- ions join as ionic crystals of the salt, KNO_3, only when the water is evaporated.

6. *Hydroxides react with the oxides of nonmetals.* Such reactions form salts and sometimes water. For example, sodium hydroxide reacts with carbon dioxide in different ways. The products may be either carbonate *or* hydrogen carbonate ions, depending on the relative quantities of reactants. Two moles of NaOH per mole of CO_2 forms sodium carbonate, Na_2CO_3, and H_2O.

$$\mathbf{CO_2 + 2NaOH \rightarrow Na_2CO_3 + H_2O}$$

One mole of NaOH per mole of CO_2 forms only sodium hydrogen carbonate, $NaHCO_3$.

$$\mathbf{CO_2 + NaOH \rightarrow NaHCO_3}$$

Table 15-4

SOLUBILITY OF METALLIC HYDROXIDES	
Hydroxide	Solubility ($g/100\ g\ H_2O$ at 20°C)
soluble (>1 $g/100\ g\ H_2O$)	
KOH	112
NaOH	109
LiOH	12.8
$Ba(OH)_2$	3.89
slightly soluble (>0.1 $g/100\ g\ H_2O$)	
$Ca(OH)_2$	0.165
insoluble (<0.1 $g/100\ g\ H_2O$)	
$Pb(OH)_2$	0.016
$Mg(OH)_2$	0.0009
$Sn(OH)_2$	0.0002
$Zn(OH)_2$	negligible
$Cu(OH)_2$	negligible
$Al(OH)_3$	negligible
$Cr(OH)_3$	negligible
$Fe(OH)_3$	negligible

Amphoteric species can be either acidic or basic.

The net reactions are

$$\mathbf{CO_2 + 2OH^- \rightarrow CO_3^{--} + H_2O}$$

and

$$\mathbf{CO_2 + OH^- \rightarrow HCO_3^-}$$

Carbon dioxide is the acid anhydride of carbonic acid. Therefore, these reactions are essentially neutralization reactions between carbonic acid and sodium hydroxide.

7. *Certain hydroxides are amphoteric.* The metallic hydroxides, except those of the active metals, are practically insoluble in water. They are weakly basic in the presence of strong acids. They are weakly acidic in the presence of strong bases. *Substances that have acidic or basic properties under appropriate conditions are said to be* ***amphoteric.*** Amphoteric hydroxides, while insoluble in water, are soluble in bases and acids. Aluminum is a metal whose ions form an amphoteric hydroxide. The amphoteric nature of such metallic hydroxides is related to reactions involving hydrated ions.

Aluminum hydroxide separates as a white jelly-like precipitate when hydroxide ions (as NaOH, for example) are added to a solution of a soluble aluminum salt.

$$\mathbf{Al(H_2O)_6^{+++}(aq) + 3OH^-(aq) \rightarrow Al(H_2O)_3(OH)_3(s) + 3H_2O(l)}$$

The OH^- ions are strongly basic. They accept protons from three water molecules of each hydrated aluminum ion and form the insoluble hydrated aluminum hydroxide, $Al(H_2O)_3(OH)_3$.

When an excess of the base is added, the high concentration of hydroxide ions causes the aluminum hydroxide precipitate to dissolve. The negative aluminate ions are formed.

$$\mathbf{Al(H_2O)_3(OH)_3(s) + OH^-(aq) \rightarrow Al(H_2O)_2(OH)_4^-(aq) + H_2O(l)}$$

The OH^- ion removes a proton from one of the three water molecules in the hydrated aluminum hydroxide structure. Observe the soluble aluminate ion formed has two molecules of water of hydration. In this reaction, the hydrated aluminum hydroxide *acts as an acid in the presence of the strong base.*

The amphoteric aluminum hydroxide also dissolves in an excess of hydronium ions. Hydrated aluminum ions and water are the products.

$$\mathbf{Al(H_2O)_3(OH)_3(s) + 3H_3O^+ \rightarrow Al(H_2O)_6^{+++}(aq) + 3H_2O(l)}$$

This reaction is the reverse of the reaction above in which the hydrated aluminum hydroxide is precipitated. The three hydroxide ions accept protons from the three hydronium ions and form the three water molecules. In this reaction, the hy-

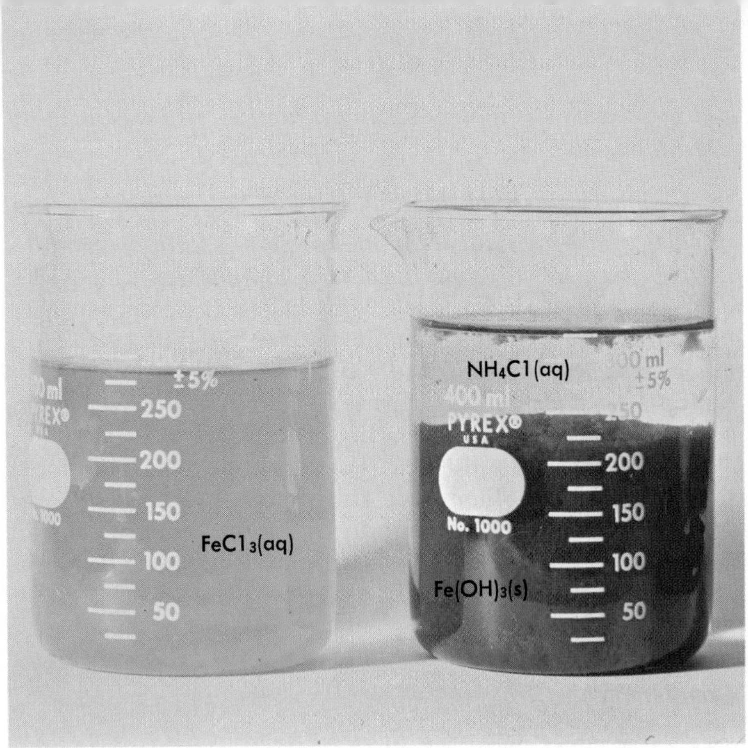

Fig. 15-12. The hydroxides of heavy metals are practically insoluble.

drated aluminum hydroxide *acts as a base in the presence of the strong acid.* It illustrates proton-transfer reactions, or protolysis, in which protons are transferred from an acid to a base.

The hydroxides of zinc, lead(II), chromium(III), and antimony(III) are other common amphoteric hydroxides. Iron(III) hydroxide is not amphoteric. It is not soluble in an excess of OH^- ions.

In the Brønsted system of acids and bases, water is an amphoteric substance. When a water molecule accepts a proton from hydrogen chloride, it acts as a base. On the other hand, when a water molecule donates a proton to ammonia, it acts as an acid. Indeed, in the slight ionization of water, one water molecule donates a proton to another water molecule. Thus, some of the water molecules behave as an acid while others behave as a base.

$$\mathbf{H_2O + H_2O \rightleftarrows H_3O^+ + OH^-}$$

Liquid ammonia undergoes a similar ionization, but to a lesser extent than water. Ammonium ions and amide ions, NH_2^-, are formed.

$$\mathbf{NH_3 + NH_3 \rightleftarrows NH_4^+ + NH_2^-}$$

Ammonia is therefore amphoteric.

15.10 Basic anhydrides

Oxides of sodium, potassium, calcium, strontium, and barium react vigorously with water. You may have seen a plasterer

slaking quicklime, CaO, by adding water to it. He was forming *slaked lime,* $Ca(OH)_2$.

$$CaO + H_2O \rightarrow Ca(OH)_2$$

Oxides that react with water and produce solutions containing the basic OH^- ions are called ***basic anhydrides.*** The oxides of the active metals are basic anhydrides. (In contrast, acid anhydrides are oxides of nonmetals. See Section 15-7. They are covalent compounds and have molecular structures. In reactions with water they form oxyacids with one or more O—H groups capable of donating protons.)

Basic anhydrides are oxides of active metals. See Section 12.18(3).

We have stated that the oxides of the active metals are ionic in structure. Like other ionic substances, they are solid at room temperature. They contain O^{--} ions. When placed in water, O^{--} ions react with the water and form basic OH^- ions.

$$O^{--} + H_2O \rightarrow 2OH^-$$

If the metallic hydroxide is soluble in water, the solution is basic because of the presence of OH^- ions.

15.11 Hydroxides and periodic trends

In general, the hydroxides of the active metals are strongly basic. The O—H groups are present as ions and the compounds are usually quite soluble. Other hydroxide compounds may be weakly basic, amphoteric, or acidic. The higher the oxidation state of the atom combined with the O—H group, the more covalent is the bond between this atom and the O—H group. Further, the more covalent the bond, the more difficult it is to remove the OH^- ion. For example, chromium(II) hydroxide is basic, chromium(III) hydroxide is amphoteric, and chromium(VI) forms an oxyacid.

With amphoteric hydroxides, it appears that the O—H bond is as easily broken as the bond between the metal and the O—H group. A strong base acquires a proton by breaking the O—H bond. An acid, on the other hand, donates a proton to the O—H group. In doing so, it breaks the bond between the O—H group and the metal atom.

Hydroxides of atoms having high electronegativity and high oxidation states are acidic. The O—H bond is more easily broken than the bond between the O—H group and the central atom. For example, O_3ClOH is strongly acidic. The chlorine atom is in the +7 oxidation state. It is also the central atom to which three oxygen atoms and one O—H group are bonded. In water solution, the molecule donates a proton from its O—H group and forms the negative O_3ClO^- ion.

$$O_3ClOH + H_2O \rightarrow H_3O^+ + O_3ClO^-$$

If we rewrite the formula in the conventional form of acids, O_3ClOH becomes $HClO_4$. We can recognize this formula as

perchloric acid, an oxyacid. The equation now has a more familiar appearance.

$$HClO_4 + H_2O \rightarrow H_3O^+ + ClO_4^-$$

Figure 15-8 shows the electron-dot configuration from which the formula O_3ClOH is easily recognized.

It may not be apparent from the formula of a substance whether it has acidic or basic properties. We have observed that oxides that react with water form oxygen-hydrogen groups. In general, the oxygen-hydrogen groups formed by ionic oxides (metal oxides) are OH^- ions. Their compounds are hydroxides and their solutions are basic.

Oxygen-hydrogen groups formed by molecular oxides (nonmetal oxides) are not ionic. Instead, they are bonded covalently to another atom in the product molecule. Such groups were identified as hydroxyl groups in Section 15.7. Hydroxyl groups donate protons in aqueous solution. The compounds have acid properties and are oxyacids.

Figure 15-13 shows electron-dot formulas for several molecular substances that contain hydroxyl groups. Considering their structures alone, their molecular formulas could be written $SO_2(OH)_2$, CH_3COOH, $PO(OH)_3$, and C_2H_5OH. However, none has the basic properties characteristic of the OH^- ion in water solution. The first three are oxyacids. This acidic character is recognized by writing their formulas as H_2SO_4, $HC_2H_3O_2$, and H_3PO_4. Experimental evidence must establish the acidic or basic character of a substance.

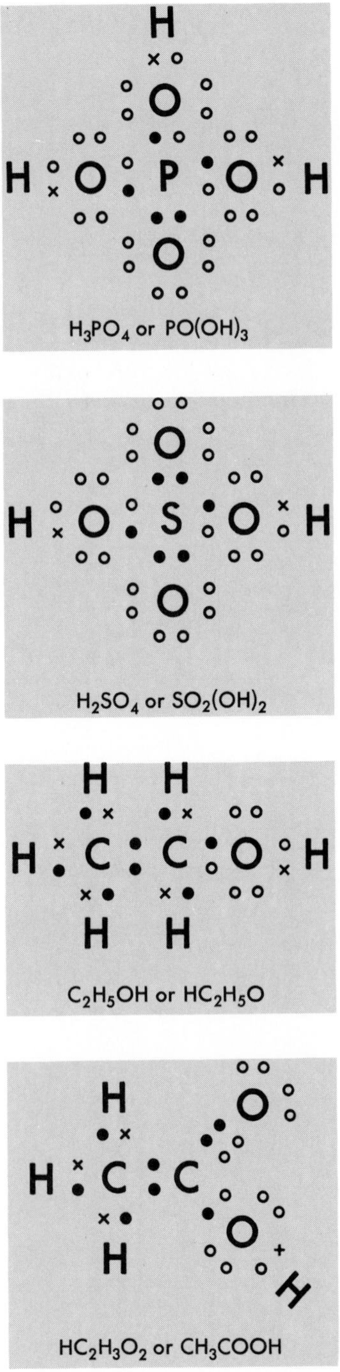

Fig. 15-13. Molecular formulas alone will not identify acidic or basic properties.

15.12 Relative strengths of acids and bases

The Brønsted definition of acids and bases provides a basis for the study of protolysis, or proton-transfer reactions. Any molecule or ion capable of donating a proton is considered to be an acid. Any molecule or ion that can accept the proton is a base.

Suppose that an acid (in the Brønsted sense) gives up a proton. The remainder of the acid particle itself is then capable of accepting a proton. Therefore, we may consider this remaining particle to be a base; it is called a *conjugate base*. ***A conjugate base** is the species that remains after an acid has given up a proton.*

Acids have conjugate bases.

An aqueous solution of sulfuric acid contains H_3O^+ ions and HSO_4^- ions. With further dilution, the HSO_4^- ions may give up protons to H_2O molecules.

$$HSO_4^- + H_2O \rightarrow H_3O^+ + SO_4^{--}$$

acid **base** **acid** **base**

The SO_4^{--} ion is what is left of the HSO_4^- after its proton has been removed. It is the conjugate base of the acid HSO_4^-.

The SO_4^{--} ion, as a base, can accept a proton from H_3O^+. When this occurs, the acid HSO_4^- ion is formed.

$$\mathbf{H_3O^+ + SO_4^{--} \rightarrow HSO_4^- + H_2O}$$

acid **base** **acid** **base**

The HSO_4^- ion can be called the *conjugate acid* of the base SO_4^{--}. *A* ***conjugate acid*** *is the species formed when a base takes on a proton.* Thus, in the example given, the HSO_4^- ion and the SO_4^{--} ion are a *conjugate acid-base pair.*

Bases have conjugate acids.

The H_2O molecule also acts as a base in this reaction. It receives the proton given up by the HSO_4^- ion and forms the H_3O^+ ion. Thus, the H_3O^+ ion is the conjugate acid of the base H_2O.

Similarly, the acidic H_3O^+ ion gives up a proton to the basic SO_4^{--} ion and forms the H_2O molecule. Thus, the H_2O molecule is the conjugate base of the H_3O^+ ion. The H_2O molecule and the H_3O^+ ion make up the second conjugate acid-base pair in the reaction.

In the above reaction, each reactant and product is labeled either as an acid or a base. There are two conjugate acid-base pairs.

Conjugate acid-base pair	$\mathbf{HSO_4^-}$	$\mathbf{SO_4^{--}}$
	acid	**base**
Conjugate acid-base pair	$\mathbf{H_2O}$	$\mathbf{H_3O^+}$
	base	**acid**

Each acid has one more proton than its conjugate base.

We can apply similar reasoning to the equation for the initial ionization of H_2SO_4. Here, the HSO_4^- ion is the *conjugate* base of H_2SO_4.

$$\mathbf{H_2SO_4 + H_2O \rightarrow H_3O^+ + HSO_4^-}$$

acid **base** **acid** **base**

The HSO_4^- ion is *both* the conjugate acid of the base SO_4^{--} and the conjugate base of the acid H_2SO_4. Thus, the HSO_4^- ion is amphoteric.

We know that HCl is highly ionized even in concentrated aqueous solutions. The hydrogen chloride molecule gives up protons readily and is therefore a strong acid. It follows that the Cl^- ion, the conjugate base of this acid, has little tendency to retain the proton. It is, consequently, a weak base.

This observation suggests an important statement that follows naturally from the Brønsted definition of acids and bases:

the stronger an acid, the weaker its conjugate base; and the stronger a base, the weaker its conjugate acid.

The stronger the acid, the weaker its conjugate base.

An aqueous solution of the strong acid $HClO_4$ is highly ionized. The reaction to the right is practically complete even in concentrated solutions.

stronger		stronger		weaker		weaker
$HClO_4$	+	H_2O	$\rightleftarrows$	H_3O^+	+	ClO_4^-
acid		base		acid		base

The ClO_4^- ion is the conjugate base of $HClO_4$. It is too weak a base to compete successfully with the base H_2O in acquiring a proton. The H_3O^+ ion is the conjugate acid of H_2O. It is too weak an acid to compete successfully with the acid $HClO_4$ in donating a proton. Thus, there is little tendency for the reaction to proceed to the left and re-form the $HClO_4$ and H_2O molecules.

Now let us examine the situation in an aqueous solution of acetic acid.

weaker		weaker		stronger		stronger
$HC_2H_3O_2$	+	H_2O	$\rightleftarrows$	H_3O^+	+	$C_2H_3O_2^-$
acid		base		acid		base

The H_3O^+ ion concentration is quite low even in dilute solutions. This fact indicates that $HC_2H_3O_2$ is indeed a weak acid. It does not compete very successfully with H_3O^+ ions in donating protons to a base. The H_2O molecules do not compete very successfully with $C_2H_3O_2^-$ ions in accepting protons. The H_3O^+ ion is the stronger acid and the $C_2H_3O_2^-$ ion is the stronger base. Thus, the reaction tends to proceed to the left.

The stronger the base, the weaker its conjugate acid.

Observe that in each example the stronger acid had the weaker conjugate base and the stronger base had the weaker conjugate acid. Also note that, in each reversible situation, the reaction tended to proceed toward the weaker acid and base.

These observations suggest a second important statement that follows naturally from the Brønsted definition: *protolysis reactions favor the production of the weaker acid and the weaker base.*

We have stated that protolysis occurs when a proton donor and a proton acceptor are brought together in a solution. The extent of this protolysis depends on the relative strengths of the acids and bases involved. For a proton-transfer reaction to approach completeness, the reactants must be much stronger as an acid and a base than the products.

Table 15-5 on the next page shows the relative strengths of several Brønsted acids and of their conjugate bases. Observe that the strongest acid listed, $HClO_4$, has the weakest conjugate base listed, ClO_4^-. The weakest acid, H_2, has the strongest conjugate base, the hydride ion, H^-. A violent protolysis could

Table 15-5

RELATIVE STRENGTHS OF ACIDS AND BASES

Acid	Formula	Conjugate Base	Formula
perchloric	$HClO_4$	perchlorate ion	ClO_4^-
hydrogen chloride	HCl	chloride ion	Cl^-
nitric	HNO_3	nitrate ion	NO_3^-
sulfuric	H_2SO_4	hydrogen sulfate ion	HSO_4^-
hydronium ion	H_3O^+	water	H_2O
hydrogen sulfate ion	HSO_4^-	sulfate ion	SO_4^{--}
phosphoric	H_3PO_4	dihydrogen phosphate ion	$H_2PO_4^-$
acetic	$HC_2H_3O_2$	acetate ion	$C_2H_3O_2^-$
carbonic	H_2CO_3	hydrogen carbonate ion	HCO_3^-
hydrogen sulfide	H_2S	hydrosulfide ion	HS^-
ammonium ion	NH_4^+	ammonia	NH_3
hydrogen carbonate ion	HCO_3^-	carbonate ion	CO_3^{--}
water	H_2O	hydroxide ion	OH^-
ammonia	NH_3	amide ion	NH_2^-
hydrogen	H_2	hydride ion	H^-

Decreasing Acid Strength ↓ *Decreasing Base Strength* ↑

result from bringing together the strongest acid and the strongest base in certain proportions. Such a reaction would be highly exothermic and very dangerous.

Salts

15.13 Nature of salts

Common table salt, NaCl, is only one of a large class of compounds that chemists refer to as *salts*. The solution of an aqueous acid contains H_3O^+ ions and negatively charged nonmetal ions (anions). These particles result from ionization of the acid in water. On the other hand, the solution of an aqueous base contains positively charged metal ions (cations) and OH^- ions. These particles result from dissociation of the ionic metallic hydroxide in water. A neutralization reaction between two such solutions removes almost all of the H_3O^+ and OH^- ions. They unite and form water, which is only very slightly ionized. The cations of the hydroxide and the anions of the acid are spectator ions. They have no part in the neutralization reaction.

As an example, let us consider the neutralization reaction between aqueous solutions of HCl and KOH. Aqueous ions are present in the acid solution because of ionization.

$$\mathbf{HCl(g) + H_2O \rightarrow H_3O^+(aq) + Cl^-(aq)}$$

Aqueous ions are present in the hydroxide solution because of dissociation.

$$\mathbf{K^+OH^-(s) \rightarrow K^+(aq) + OH^-(aq)}$$

Neutralization occurs when the proper quantities of the two solutions are mixed.

$$H_3O^+(aq) + Cl^-(aq) + K^+(aq) + OH^-(aq) \rightarrow K^+(aq) + Cl^-(aq) + 2H_2O$$

Removing all spectator ions, the net equation for the neutralization reaction becomes

$$H_3O^+(aq) + OH^-(aq) \rightarrow 2H_2O$$

As solvent water is evaporated, K^+ cations and Cl^- anions no longer remain separated from each other by water dipoles. They form a characteristic ionic crystalline structure and separate from solution as the *salt* KCl. *A compound composed of the positive ions of an aqueous base and the negative ions of an aqueous acid is called a* ***salt.*** All salts, by this definition, are electrovalent substances. They vary in solubility in water, but their aqueous solutions are solutions of hydrated ions. Some useful solubility information regarding salts is summarized in Table 15-6.

ROUGH RULES OF SOLUBILITY

soluble:	>1 g/100 g H_2O
slightly soluble:	>0.1 g/100 g H_2O
insoluble:	<0.1 g/100 g H_2O

15.14 Salt-producing reactions

There are several ways of forming salts, but not all of these ways apply to the formation of every salt.

1. *Direct union of the elements.* Some metals react directly with certain nonmetals and form a salt. For example, burning sodium in an atmosphere of chlorine gas produces sodium chloride.

$$2Na + Cl_2 \rightarrow 2NaCl$$

2. *Reaction of a metal with an acid.* Many metals replace hydrogen in an aqueous acid and form the corresponding salt. Zinc reacts with hydrochloric acid and forms zinc chloride and hydrogen.

$$Zn + 2HCl \rightarrow ZnCl_2 + H_2(g)$$

3. *Reaction of a metallic oxide with an aqueous acid.* The oxides of some metals react with an acid and form a salt. Magnesium oxide, when treated with hydrochloric acid, forms magnesium chloride and water.

$$MgO + 2HCl \rightarrow MgCl_2 + H_2O$$

Table 15-6

SOLUBILITY OF SALTS

1. Common sodium, potassium, and ammonium compounds are soluble in water.
2. Common nitrates, acetates, and chlorates are soluble.
3. Common chlorides are soluble except silver, mercury(I), and lead. (Lead(II) chloride is soluble in hot water.)
4. Common sulfates are soluble except calcium, barium, strontium, and lead.
5. Common carbonates, phosphates, and silicates are insoluble except sodium, potassium, and ammonium.
6. Common sulfides are insoluble except calcium, barium, strontium, magnesium, sodium, potassium, and ammonium.

If calcium oxide is substituted for magnesium oxide in this reaction, the salt formed is calcium chloride.

$$CaO + 2HCl \rightarrow CaCl_2 + H_2O$$

4. *Reaction of a nonmetallic oxide with a base.* The oxides of some nonmetals react with a soluble hydroxide and form a salt. Carbon dioxide gas passed into limewater (saturated calcium hydroxide solution) forms insoluble calcium carbonate and water.

$$CO_2 + Ca(OH)_2 \rightarrow CaCO_3(s) + H_2O$$

Additional carbon dioxide converts the calcium carbonate to soluble calcium hydrogen carbonate.

$$CO_2 + H_2O + CaCO_3 \rightarrow Ca(HCO_3)_2$$

The reactions of sulfur dioxide in limewater are similar. Insoluble calcium sulfite, $CaSO_3$, is first formed.

$$SO_2 + Ca(OH)_2 \rightarrow CaSO_3(s) + H_2O$$

When excess sulfur dioxide gas is bubbled through limewater, however, soluble calcium hydrogen sulfite is formed.

$$SO_2 + H_2O + CaSO_3 \rightarrow Ca(HSO_3)_2$$

5. *Acid-base neutralization.* When an acid neutralizes a soluble hydroxide, a salt may be recovered from the water solvent. This salt corresponds to the metallic ion of the base and the nonmetallic ion of the acid. Many different salts can be prepared by neutralization. An example is the reaction between hydrochloric acid and sodium hydroxide mixed in chemically equivalent quantities. When the solvent water is evaporated, sodium chloride remains.

$$NaOH + HCl \rightarrow NaCl + H_2O$$

6. *Ionic reaction.* Two salts may be prepared in ionic reactions if one of them is practically insoluble. The equation for the reaction between solutions of sodium sulfate and barium chloride is

$$BaCl_2 + Na_2SO_4 \rightarrow 2NaCl + BaSO_4(s)$$

Since both reactants are dissociated in water solution, the ionic equation is more useful.

$$Ba^{++}(aq) + SO_4^{--}(aq) \rightarrow Ba^{++}SO_4^{--}(s)$$

In this reaction, barium sulfate is only very slightly soluble. It precipitates readily and can be filtered from the solution. The sodium chloride can be obtained by evaporating the solvent water. Sodium chloride thus recovered contains some barium sulfate since precipitates always separate from saturated solutions.

7. *Reaction of an acid with a carbonate.* A salt can be obtained from this reaction because the other products are water and carbon dioxide gas. If hydrochloric acid is added to a solution of sodium carbonate, the following reaction occurs:

$$\mathbf{2HCl + Na_2CO_3 \rightarrow 2NaCl + H_2O + CO_2(g)}$$

Carbon dioxide bubbles out of the solution as a gas. Sodium chloride can be recovered by evaporation.

8. *Reaction of a metallic oxide with a nonmetallic oxide.* An oxygen-containing salt may be formed by the reaction between a basic oxide and an acidic oxide. Water is not involved in this process. Instead, the dry oxides are mixed and heated. Metallic carbonates and phosphates are typical of the salts produced.

$$\mathbf{MgO + CO_2 \rightarrow MgCO_3}$$
$$\mathbf{CaO + CO_2 \rightarrow CaCO_3}$$
$$\mathbf{3CaO + P_2O_5 \rightarrow Ca_3(PO_4)_2}$$

15.15 Naming salts

Salts are generally named by combining the names of the ions of which they are composed. For example, the name of $Ba(NO_3)_2$ is *barium nitrate.* By agreement the positive ion, in this case the Ba^{++} ion, is named first. The name of the negative ion, in this case the NO_3^- ion, follows.

Over the years, many difficulties have arisen in the naming of salts. For example, many outdated names of salts have carried over into our present naming system. These old names do not provide for a simple translation from name to formula or from formula to name. In 1940, the International Union of Pure and Applied Chemistry recommended a more logical system for naming inorganic compounds. It is known as the *Stock system,* and it provides the uniformity needed for chemical names.

This text uses the Stock system for naming salts that contain metals *with variable oxidation states.* Several examples of Stock names for salts are given in Table 15-7. Observe that the more electropositive cation is named first in *double salts. A* ***double salt*** *is one in which two different kinds of metallic ions are present.*

The names of anions (negative ions) take the same root and prefix as the acid in which they occur. However, the acid ending *-ic* is changed to *-ate,* and the ending *-ous* is changed to *-ite.* Salts derived from binary acids take the ending *-ide.* Table 15-8 on the next page shows the names of the anions of salts produced by the reactions of various acids.

Salt anions that are polyatomic and include metallic atoms with variable oxidation states may have rather complex names in the Stock system. For example, polyatomic MnO_4^-

Table 15-7

SALT NOMENCLATURE

Formula	Stock Name
$CuCl$	copper(I) chloride
$CuCl_2$	copper(II) chloride
FeO	iron(II) oxide
Fe_2O_3	iron(III) oxide
Fe_3O_4	iron(II, III) oxide
$MnCl_2$	manganese(II) chloride
$MnCl_4$	manganese(IV) chloride
PtO_2	platinum(IV) oxide
$Cr_2(SO_3)_3$	chromium(III) sulfite
$CoCO_3$	cobalt(II) carbonate
$Co_2(SO_4)_3$	cobalt(III) sulfate
Cu_2SO_4	copper(I) sulfate
$CuSO_4$	copper(II) sulfate
$Fe_3(PO_4)_2$	iron(II) phosphate
$Hg(NO_3)_2$	mercury(II) nitrate
$KCaPO_4$	potassium calcium phosphate
$NaHCO_3$	sodium hydrogen carbonate

Table 15-8

ACID-SALT NOMENCLATURE		
Formula	Name of Acid	Name of Salt Anion
HF	hydrofluoric	fluoride
HBr	hydrobromic	bromide
HI	hydriodic	iodide
HCl	hydrochloric	chloride
$HClO$	hypochlorous	hypochlorite
$HClO_2$	chlorous	chlorite
$HClO_3$	chloric	chlorate
$HClO_4$	perchloric	perchlorate
HIO_3	iodic	iodate
H_2MnO_4	manganic	manganate
$HMnO_4$	permanganic	permanganate
H_2S	hydrosulfuric	sulfide
H_2SO_3	sulfurous	sulfite
H_2SO_4	sulfuric	sulfate
HNO_2	nitrous	nitrite
HNO_3	nitric	nitrate
H_2CO_3	carbonic	carbonate
H_3PO_3	phosphorous	phosphite
H_3PO_4	phosphoric	phosphate

anion is the *tetraoxomanganate(VII) ion* in this system. However, its potassium salt, $KMnO_4$, is well known as *potassium permanganate;* it will not likely become *potassium tetraoxomanganate(VII)*.

SUMMARY

Acids and bases are described historically in terms of their water solutions. In this aqueous acid-base system, a substance is an acid if it produces hydronium ions in water solution. Similarly, a substance is a base if it contributes hydroxide ions to its water solution. The properties of acids and bases, their reactions with other substances, and the neutralization reaction between them are the properties of these traditional acids and bases in aqueous solutions.

In the aqueous acid-base system, an acid contains hydrogen which, through ionization in water solution, is transferred as a proton (hydrogen ion) to a water molecule to form the hydronium ion. This aqueous system has been broadened by the Brønsted definition of acids and bases. By this definition, all proton donors are acids and proton acceptors are bases. The Brønsted proton-transfer system extends the acid-base concept of reactions to nonaqueous solutions. Hydrogen chloride gas is a Brønsted acid when dissolved in ammonia. An HCl molecule donates a proton to an NH_3 molecule. Ammonia is a Brønsted base. It accepts a proton from the HCl molecule.

Other acid-base systems have been defined. The Lewis acid-base system defines an acid as an electron-pair donor. A proton-transfer may not necessarily be involved in a Lewis acid-base reaction.

The hydroxides of certain metals in the middle region of the Periodic Table are amphoteric. They are insoluble in water but dissolve in acidic and basic solutions. Amphoteric hydroxides behave as acids in the presence of strong bases. They behave as bases in the presence of strong acids.

In a proton-transfer reaction, the acid gives up a proton to the base. The species that remains is a base, the conjugate base of the acid donor. The base that accepts the proton in the reaction becomes an acid. It is the conjugate acid of the base. Together they constitute an acid-base pair. The stronger the acid, the weaker is its conjugate acid. Proton-transfer reactions tend to produce weaker acids and weaker bases.

Some nonmetallic oxides combine with water and form oxyacids. These oxides are called acid anhydrides. Oxides of active metals react with water and form hydroxides. These oxides are called basic anhydrides.

Salts are compounds composed of the positive ion of an aqueous base and the negative ion of an aqueous acid. They are electrovalent compounds. Salts vary in their solubility in water; their aqueous solutions are solutions of hydrated ions. Generally, the names of salts follow the Stock system for naming inorganic compounds.

QUESTIONS

Group A

1. Name the four most important industrial acids and tell why each is important.
2. What ion is responsible for the acidic properties of aqueous acid solutions?
3. List eight properties that characterize aqueous acids.
4. Why is an acid thought of as a proton donor?
5. (*a*) What is an acid anhydride? (*b*) a basic anhydride? (*c*) Give an example of each.
6. (*a*) State the rules for naming binary acids. (*b*) for naming oxyacids.
7. A base is defined as a proton acceptor. How do you interpret this definition?
8. Write the net ionic equation for the neutralization reaction between an acid and a base.
9. List seven properties that characterize hydroxides of active metals.
10. Aluminum hydroxide has basic properties in the presence of a strong acid, and acidic properties in the presence of a solution that is strongly basic. What term is used to describe such substances?
11. What composition and structure characterize salts?
12. How are salts named?
13. What method would you use to prepare a small quantity of calcium sulfate quickly and safely in the laboratory? Explain why you chose the method you did and write the equation.
14. Would barium sulfate be a suitable source of the sulfate ion for an ionic reaction with another salt? Explain.

Group B

15. Explain why a water solution of hydrogen chloride has acidic properties but pure hydrogen chloride does not, in the usual sense.
16. (*a*) How can you justify calling hydrogen chloride an acid when it is dissolved in ammonia? (*b*) Write the equation for this reaction.
17. (*a*) Explain how the structure and behavior of water can be interpreted as water behaving like an acid. (*b*) Write an equation that illustrates this behavior using electron-dot formulas.
18. (*a*) What basic solution would you use for cleaning a greasy sink trap? Ex-

plain. (*b*) for removing grease spots from clothing? Explain.

19. What basic solutions would you use for neutralizing acid stains on clothing? Explain.
20. Predict the relative solubilities of the following salts in water (as *soluble*, *slightly soluble*, or *insoluble*): NaCl, $CaCO_3$, $BaSO_4$, $(NH_4)_2S$, $Al(C_2H_3O_2)_3$, Ag_2SO_4, $Pb(NO_3)_2$, Hg_2Cl_2, $Mg_3(PO_4)_2$, CuS.
21. Name the following compounds: (*a*) H_2Se, (*b*) HIO_3, (*c*) $Ga(OH)_3$, (*d*) CsOH, (*e*) $RaBr_2$, (*f*) K_2MnO_4, (*g*) $MgSO_4$, (*h*) $Fe(ClO_4)_2$, (*i*) $KMnO_4$, (*j*) $Cu(IO_3)_2$, (*k*) CaI_2, (*l*) $BaSO_3$, (*m*) NH_4F, (*n*) $AlPO_4$, (*o*) $NaClO_3$.
22. (*a*) When H_2O molecules act as a base, what is the conjugate acid? (*b*) When H_2O molecules act as an acid, what is the conjugate base?
23. (*a*) When NH_3 molecules act as a base, what is the conjugate acid? (*b*) When NH_3 molecules act as an acid, what is the conjugate base?
24. Write the equations that show the amphoteric character of HSO_4^- ions.
25. Balance the following equation:

$$\mathbf{Zn(H_2O)_4^{++}(aq) + OH^-(aq) \rightarrow Zn(OH)_2(H_2O)_2(s) + H_2O}$$

26. Hydrated zinc hydroxide is insoluble in water but dissolves in an excess of $OH^-(aq)$ ions and forms the soluble zincate ion, $Zn(OH)_4^{--}$, and water. Write the balanced net ionic equation.
27. Hydrated zinc hydroxide also dissolves in an excess of H_3O^+ ions and forms hydrated zinc ions and water. Write the balanced net ionic equation.
28. Aspirin is a form of salicylic acid which you may have used from time to time as medicine. Why can it be referred to as a genuine wonder drug?

PROBLEMS

Group A

1. Nitric acid can be prepared in the laboratory by the reaction of sodium nitrate with sulfuric acid. Sodium hydrogen sulfate is also formed. (*a*) How many grams of sulfuric acid are required to produce 50.0 g of nitric acid? (*b*) How many grams of sodium hydrogen sulfate are formed?
2. How many liters of carbon dioxide can be collected at 20°C and 745 mm pressure from a reaction between 25.0 g of calcium carbonate and an excess of hydrochloric acid?
3. How much calcium silicate, $CaSiO_3$, can be prepared by heating a mixture of 75.0 g of calcium oxide and 90.0 g of silicon dioxide?
4. Suppose 75.0 liters of dry carbon dioxide gas, measured at 25.0°C and 755 mm pressure, are available to convert hot calcium oxide to calcium carbonate. (*a*) What quantity of calcium oxide is required? (*b*) What quantity of calcium carbonate is produced?

chapter 16

ACID-BASE TITRATION AND pH

One more drop and the color of the solution changes. (See Question 21 on page 347.)

Solution Concentrations

16.1 Molar solutions

In Chapter 13, we learned to express the concentration of solutions of molecular solutes in terms of *molality (m)*. Solutions of known molality are prepared when the ratio of solute to solvent molecules is important to know. Recall that the molality of a solution expresses the quantity of solute in *moles* and the quantity of solvent in *kilograms*. For example, a 1-molal (l-*m*) solution contains 1 mole of solute per kilogram of solvent. For any given solvent, two solutions of equal molalities have the same ratios of solute to solvent molecules. We use solutions of known molalities for studying the effects of solutes on the freezing and boiling points of solvents. These studies provide chemists with one way to determine molecular weights of soluble substances (Section 13.14).

In our present studies with solutions, we use a solvent merely as a medium that contains a solute. The interest is in the quantity of solute needed to perform a chemical reaction. We have no real interest in the amount of solvent that is present. The volume of a solution is easily measured. Thus, we use concentration units and a way of preparing solutions so that measured volumes give us known quantities of solutes. Using this scheme, we express solution concentration in terms of a *known quantity of solute in a given volume of solution.* When a solution is prepared in this way, any required quantity of solute can be selected by simply measuring out the volume of solution that contains that amount of solute.

If we state the quantity of solute in *moles* and the volume of

Fig. 16-1. A volumetric flask. When filled to the mark with liquid at 20°C, it contains 500 ml ± 0.15 ml.

Molarity: moles solute/liter solution.
Molality: moles solute/kilogram solvent.

solution in *liters,* the concentration of a solution is expressed in *molarity*. The symbol for molarity is *M*. *The* ***molarity*** *of a solution is an expression of the number of moles of solute per liter of solution. A one-molar* (1-*M*) solution contains *1 mole of solute per liter of solution.* Solutions of the same molarity have the same mole concentration of solutes.

A mole of sodium chloride, NaCl, has a mass of 58.5 g, its gram-formula weight. This quantity of NaCl dissolved in enough water to make exactly 1 liter of solution gives a 1-*M* solution. Half this quantity of NaCl in 1 liter of solution forms a 0.5-*M* solution. Twice this quantity of NaCl per liter of solution yields a 2-*M* solution.

A *volumetric flask* like the one shown in Figure 16-1 is commonly used in preparing solutions of known molarity. A measured quantity of solute is dissolved in a portion of solvent in the flask. Then more solvent is added to fill the flask to the mark on the neck. Thus, the quantity of solute and the volume of solution are known. The molarity of the solution is easily calculated.

As an example, suppose we wish to prepare a 1-*M* solution of potassium chromate. The formula weight of K_2CrO_4 is 194. Thus, a mole of K_2CrO_4 has a mass of 194 g. To prepare 1 liter of the 1-M solution, we must use 194 g of K_2CrO_4 solute. To make 100 ml of the 1-*M* solution, we must use 19.4 g of K_2CrO_4 solute. Similarly, a 0.5-*M* solution requires 0.5 mole (97.0 g) of K_2CrO_4 per liter of solution. A 0.05-*M* solution requires 0.05 mole (9.70 g) of K_2CrO_4 per liter of solution.

Note that solution *molarity* is based on the *volume of solution.* (Solution *molality,* on the other hand, is based on the *mass of solvent.*) Equal volumes of solutions of the same molarity have equal mole quantities of solutes. Molarity is preferred when volumes of solutions are to be measured. For very dilute solutions, the distinction between the molality and molarity of solutions is not significant.

16.2 Chemical equivalents of acids and bases

Solution concentrations can be expressed in a way that allows *chemically equivalent quantities* of different solutes to be measured very simply. These quantities of solutes are called *equivalents* (equiv). ***Equivalents*** *are the quantities of substances that have the same combining capacity in chemical reactions.*

Consider the following equations. They show that 36.5 g (1 mole) of HCl and 49 g (1/2 mole) of H_2SO_4 are chemically equivalent in neutralization reactions with basic KOH.

$$\begin{array}{ccccccc} \mathbf{HCl} & + & \mathbf{KOH} & \rightarrow & \mathbf{KCl} & + & \mathbf{H_2O} \\ \textbf{1 mole} & & \textbf{1 mole} & \rightarrow & \textbf{1 mole} & & \textbf{1 mole} \\ \textbf{36.5 g} & & \textbf{56 g} & & & & \end{array}$$

$$\mathbf{H_2SO_4 + 2KOH \rightarrow K_2SO_4 + 2H_2O}$$

or,

$$\begin{array}{cccc} 1/2\ H_2SO_4 + & KOH & \rightarrow 1/2\ K_2SO_4 + & H_2O \\ 1/2 \text{ mole} & 1 \text{ mole} & 1/2 \text{ mole} & 1 \text{ mole} \\ 49 \text{ g} & 56 \text{ g} & & \end{array}$$

The equations also reveal that both 36.5 g of HCl and 49 g of H_2SO_4 are chemically equivalent to 56 g (1 mole) of KOH in these neutralization reactions.

Suppose we replace KOH with $Ca(OH)_2$ in one of the above reactions. The new equation shows that 37 g (1/2 mole) of $Ca(OH)_2$ is equivalent to 56 g (1 mole) of KOH.

$$2HCl + Ca(OH)_2 \rightarrow CaCl_2 + 2H_2O$$

or,

$$\begin{array}{cccc} HCl & + 1/2\ Ca(OH)_2 \rightarrow & 1/2\ CaCl_2 + & H_2O \\ 1 \text{ mole} & 1/2 \text{ mole} & 1/2 \text{ mole} & 1 \text{ mole} \\ 36.5 \text{ g} & 37 \text{ g} & & \end{array}$$

In proton-transfer reactions, *one equivalent of an acid is the quantity, in grams, which supplies one mole of protons.* HCl and H_2SO_4 are the acids in the neutralization reactions we have just considered. We can determine the quantity representing *one equivalent* of each acid in these reactions as follows:

An acid equivalent donates 1 mole of protons.

$$1 \text{ equiv HCl} = \frac{1 \text{ mole HCl}}{1 \text{ mole } H_3O^+} \times \frac{36.5 \text{ g}}{\text{mole}} = \frac{36.5 \text{ g HCl}}{\text{mole } H_3O^+}$$

$$1 \text{ equiv } H_2SO_4 = \frac{1 \text{ mole } H_2SO_4}{2 \text{ moles } H_3O^+} \times \frac{98 \text{ g}}{\text{mole}} = \frac{49 \text{ g } H_2SO_4}{\text{mole } H_3O^+}$$

One equivalent of a base is the quantity, in grams, which accepts one mole of protons, or supplies one mole of OH^- ions. For KOH and $Ca(OH)_2$ in the above reactions,

A base equivalent accepts 1 mole of protons or supplies 1 mole of OH^- ions.

$$1 \text{ equiv KOH} = \frac{1 \text{ mole KOH}}{1 \text{ mole } OH^-} \times \frac{56 \text{ g}}{\text{mole}} = \frac{56 \text{ g KOH}}{\text{mole } OH^-}$$

$$1 \text{ equiv } Ca(OH)_2 = \frac{1 \text{ mole } Ca(OH)_2}{2 \text{ moles } OH^-} \times \frac{74 \text{ g}}{\text{mole}} = \frac{37 \text{ g } Ca(OH)_2}{\text{mole } OH^-}$$

A diprotic acid has 2 atoms of ionizable hydrogen per molecule.

HCl, HNO_3, and $HC_2H_3O_2$ are monoprotic acids. One mole of each can supply 1 mole of H_3O^+ ions. Therefore, *1 equivalent of a monoprotic acid is the same as 1 mole of the acid.* One mole of a diprotic acid such as H_2SO_4 can supply 2 moles of H_3O^+ ions. Thus, *for complete neutralization, 1 equivalent of a diprotic acid is the same as 1/2 mole of the acid.* H_3PO_4 is triprotic and can furnish 3 moles of H_3O^+ ions per mole of acid. *When completely neutralized, 1 equivalent of a triprotic acid is the same as 1/3 mole of the acid.*

A similar relationship exists between chemical equivalents and moles of bases. One mole of KOH supplies 1 equivalent of OH^- ions. One mole of $Ca(OH)_2$ supplies 2 equivalents of OH^-

ions. Therefore, 1 equivalent of KOH is the same as 1 mole of KOH, and 1 equivalent of $Ca(OH)_2$ is the same as 1/2 mole of $Ca(OH)_2$.

A triprotic acid has 3 atoms of ionizable hydrogen per molecule.

In many chemical reactions, a diprotic or triprotic acid is not completely neutralized. In such a case, we determine the number of moles of protons supplied per mole of acid by the reaction it undergoes. For example, suppose we add a solution containing 1 mole of H_2SO_4 to a solution containing 1 mole of NaOH. The salt, sodium hydrogen sulfate, is then recovered by evaporating the water solvent. Observe that the neutralization of H_2SO_4 is *not* complete.

$$\begin{array}{cccc} \mathbf{H_2SO_4} + & \mathbf{NaOH} \rightarrow & \mathbf{NaHSO_4} + & \mathbf{H_2O} \\ \textbf{1 mole} & \textbf{1 mole} & \textbf{1 mole} & \textbf{1 mole} \\ \textbf{98 g} & \textbf{40 g} & & \end{array}$$

One mole of H_2SO_4 supplies 1 mole of protons to the base and forms an "acid salt" containing HSO_4^- ions. Therefore, 1 equivalent of H_2SO_4 is the same as 1 mole of the acid, 98 g, *in this reaction.*

$$\textbf{1 equiv } \mathbf{H_2SO_4} = \frac{\textbf{1 mole } \mathbf{H_2SO_4}}{\textbf{1 mole } \mathbf{H_3O^+}} \times \frac{\textbf{98 g}}{\textbf{mole}} = \frac{\textbf{98 g } \mathbf{H_2SO_4}}{\textbf{mole } \mathbf{H_3O^+}}$$

Now, suppose we add a solution containing 1 mole of H_3PO_4 to one containing 1 mole of NaOH. The reaction is

$$\begin{array}{cccc} \mathbf{H_3PO_4} + & \mathbf{NaOH} \rightarrow & \mathbf{NaH_2PO_4} + & \mathbf{H_2O} \\ \textbf{1 mole} & \textbf{1 mole} & \textbf{1 mole} & \textbf{1 mole} \\ \textbf{98.0 g} & \textbf{40.0 g} & & \end{array}$$

An equivalent of H_3PO_4 depends on the reaction.

The salt, sodium dihydrogen phosphate, can be recovered by evaporation. One mole of H_3PO_4 supplies 1 mole of protons to the base and forms a salt containing $H_2PO_4^-$ ions. Thus, one equivalent of H_3PO_4 is the same as 1 mole of the acid, 98.0 g, *in this reaction.*

$$\textbf{1 equiv } \mathbf{H_3PO_4} = \frac{\textbf{1 mole } \mathbf{H_3PO_4}}{\textbf{1 mole } \mathbf{H_3O^+}} \times \frac{\textbf{98.0 g}}{\textbf{mole}} = \frac{\textbf{98.0 g } \mathbf{H_3PO_4}}{\textbf{mole } \mathbf{H_3O^+}}$$

Suppose the basic solution in the reaction above contained 2 moles of NaOH. The salt recovered by evaporation would then be Na_2HPO_4. One equivalent of H_3PO_4 in this reaction is the same as 1/2 mole of the acid, 49.0 g. Of course, in another reaction, if the neutralization of the triprotic acid is complete, 1 equivalent of H_3PO_4 is the same as 1/3 mole of the acid, 32.7 g.

16.3 Chemical equivalents of elements

Now let us consider a reactant in an electron-transfer reaction. A chemical equivalent of such a reactant is *that quantity, in grams, which supplies or acquires 1 mole of electrons in a chemical reaction.* In the following reaction, a mole of sodium atoms (23 g) loses 1 mole of electrons and forms 1 mole of Na^+ ions.

$$\begin{array}{cccc} \textbf{Na} & \rightarrow \textbf{Na}^+ & + & \textbf{e}^- \\ \textbf{1 mole} & \textbf{1 mole} & & \textbf{1 mole} \\ \textbf{23 g} & \textbf{23 g} & & \end{array}$$

Therefore, 1 equivalent of sodium is the same as 1 mole of sodium atoms, 23 g.

A mole of calcium atoms ($4\bar{0}$ g) supplies 2 moles of electrons when Ca^{++} ions are formed. A mole of aluminum atoms (27 g) supplies 3 moles of electrons when Al^{+++} ions are formed. Thus, 1 equivalent of calcium is the mass of 1/2 mole of calcium atoms, $2\bar{0}$ g. One equivalent of aluminum is the mass of 1/3 mole of aluminum atoms, 9.0 g.

$$\begin{array}{cccc} \textbf{1/2 Ca} & \rightarrow \textbf{1/2 Ca}^{++} & + & \textbf{e}^- \\ \textbf{1/2 mole} & \textbf{1/2 mole} & & \textbf{1 mole} \\ \mathbf{2\bar{0}}\textbf{ g} & \mathbf{2\bar{0}}\textbf{ g} & & \end{array}$$

and

$$\begin{array}{cccc} \textbf{1/3 Al} & \rightarrow \textbf{1/3 Al}^{+++} & + & \textbf{e}^- \\ \textbf{1/3 mole} & \textbf{1/3 mole} & & \textbf{1 mole} \\ \textbf{9.0 g} & \textbf{9.0 g} & & \end{array}$$

These relationships can be summarized as follows:

$$\textbf{1 equiv Na} = \frac{\textbf{1 mole Na}}{\textbf{1 mole e}^-} \times \frac{\textbf{23 g}}{\textbf{mole}} = \frac{\textbf{23 g Na}}{\textbf{mole e}^-}$$

$$\textbf{1 equiv Ca} = \frac{\textbf{1 mole Ca}}{\textbf{2 moles e}^-} \times \frac{\mathbf{4\bar{0}}\textbf{ g}}{\textbf{mole}} = \frac{\mathbf{2\bar{0}}\textbf{ g Ca}}{\textbf{mole e}^-}$$

$$\textbf{1 equiv Al} = \frac{\textbf{1 mole Al}}{\textbf{3 moles e}^-} \times \frac{\textbf{27 g}}{\textbf{mole}} = \frac{\textbf{9.0 g Al}}{\textbf{mole e}^-}$$

Observe that when its ions are formed, the numerical *change* in oxidation state for sodium atoms is 1. This change for calcium atoms is 2. For aluminum atoms it is 3. We can ordinarily use such numbers to determine one equivalent of an element for a given reaction. We simply divide the mass of 1 mole of atoms of the element (1 g-at wt) by the *change in oxidation state* these atoms undergo in a chemical reaction.

Oxidizing and reducing agents with several common oxidation states are given special attention in Chapter 22.

$$\textbf{1 equiv Na} = \frac{\textbf{23 g}}{\textbf{1}} = \textbf{23 g}$$

$$\textbf{1 equiv Ca} = \frac{\mathbf{4\bar{0}}\textbf{ g}}{\textbf{2}} = \mathbf{2\bar{0}}\textbf{ g}$$

$$\textbf{1 equiv Al} = \frac{\textbf{27 g}}{\textbf{3}} = \textbf{9.0 g}$$

16.4 Chemical equivalents of salts

A somewhat similar method can ordinarily be used to find the mass of 1 equivalent of a salt. The mass of 1 mole of the salt is divided by the *total* positive (or negative) ionic charge indicated by its formula. This total positive charge is determined by multiplying the number of cations (shown in the formula of the salt) by the charge on each cation.

$$\textbf{1 equiv (salt)} = \frac{\textbf{mass of 1 mole of salt}}{\textbf{total positive charge}}$$

The formula of sodium sulfate is Na_2SO_4 and the mass of 1 mole is 142 g. Each of the two Na^+ ions has a +1 charge. The total positive charge = 2. (Notice that the total negative charge also = 2.)

$$\textbf{1 equiv } Na_2SO_4 = \frac{142 \text{ g}}{2} = 71.0 \text{ g}$$

One mole of calcium phosphate, $Ca_3(PO_4)_2$, has a mass of $31\bar{0}$ g. Each of the three Ca^{++} ions has a +2 charge. The total positive charge = 6. (Note that the total negative charge also = 6.)

$$\textbf{1 equiv } Ca_3(PO_4)_2 = \frac{31\bar{0} \text{ g}}{6} = 51.7 \text{ g}$$

16.5 Normal solutions

Normality: equivalents solute/liter solution.

We can now express solution concentration based on the volume of solution in a second way. This method involves stating the quantity of solute in equivalents and is called *normality*. The symbol for normality is *N*. *The* ***normality*** *of a solution expresses the number of equivalents of solute per liter of solution.*

A one-normal (1-*N*) solution contains 1 equivalent of solute per *liter of solution.* Equal volumes of solutions of the same normality are chemically equivalent.

Knowing solution concentrations in molarity or normality can be very helpful. Using these expressions, we can take any desired mass of *solute* in the form of its solution. We simply measure out a certain volume of the solution. A disadvantage is that the mass or volume of *solvent* present is not known precisely. The expressions for solution concentration are summarized in Table 16-1.

Table 16-1

METHODS OF EXPRESSING CONCENTRATION OF SOLUTIONS

Name	Symbol	Solute Unit	Solvent Unit	Dimensions
molality	*m*	mole	kilogram solvent	$\frac{\text{mole solute}}{\text{kg solvent}}$
molarity	*M*	mole	liter solution	$\frac{\text{mole solute}}{\text{liter solution}}$
normality	*N*	equivalent	liter solution	$\frac{\text{equiv solute}}{\text{liter solution}}$

A mole of the monoprotic hydrogen chloride has a mass of 36.5 g. As a reactant, it can furnish 1 mole of protons. Thus, 1 mole of HCl in 1 liter of aqueous solution provides 1 mole of protons as H_3O^+ ions. This solution has a 1-*N* concentration.

Suppose we require a solution of HCl which furnishes 0.100 mole of H_3O^+ ions per liter. This is a 0.100-*N* HCl solution. It is evident that the solute must be 3.65 g of HCl dissolved in water and diluted to a 1.00-liter volume. However, *this solute is 3.65 g of anhydrous hydrogen chloride in one liter of solution.* It is not 3.65 g of the concentrated hydrochloric acid found in the laboratory.

How can we determine the volume of concentrated hydrochloric acid which contains 3.65 g of hydrogen chloride? First we must know the mass percentage of HCl in the concentrated solution and the density of the concentrated solution. This information is printed on the label of the concentrated hydrochloric acid container. See Figure 16-2. Representative values are

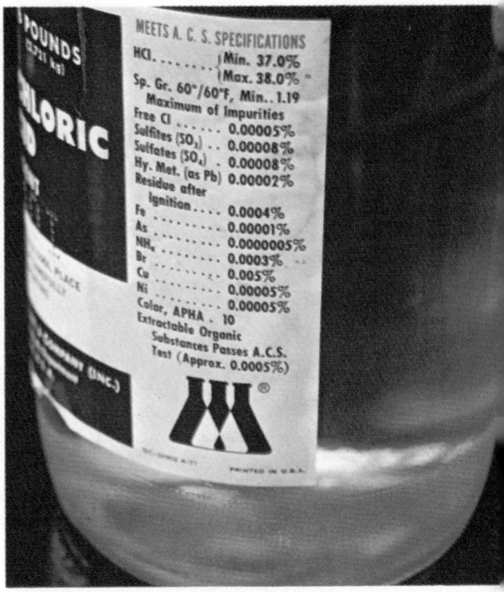

Fig. 16-2. The manufacturer's label on a reagent bottle provides important information to the chemist.

$$\textbf{percent HCl} = \textbf{37.23\%}$$
$$\textbf{density} = \textbf{1.19 g/ml}$$

Thus, we have 37.23 g HCl per $10\bar{0}$ g of concentrated solution. The density of this solution is 1.19 g/ml. From these data we can determine the mass of HCl in each milliliter of concentrated solution.

$$\frac{37.23\text{ g HCl}}{10\bar{0}\text{ g conc soln}} \times \frac{1.19\text{ g}}{\text{ml}} = \frac{0.443\text{ g HCl}}{\text{ml conc soln}}$$

For 1.00 liter of 0.100-*N* solution, 3.65 g of HCl is required, since

$$\frac{0.100\text{ equiv HCl}}{\text{liter}} \times \frac{36.5\text{ g}}{\text{equiv}} \times 1.00\text{ liter} = 3.65\text{ g HCl}$$

We now know the mass of HCl per milliliter of concentrated solution and the mass of HCl required. From these data we can calculate the volume of concentrated hydrochloric acid solution required.

$$3.65\text{ g HCl} \times \frac{\text{ml conc soln}}{0.443\text{ g HCl}} = 8.24\text{ ml conc soln}$$

Thus, 8.24 ml of concentrated HCl solution diluted to 1.00 liter with distilled water gives a 0.100-*N* solution of HCl.

We have already seen that 1 mole of H_2SO_4 contains 2 equivalents of that substance. A 1-*M* solution contains 98 g of H_2SO_4 per liter of solution. However, a 1-*N* solution contains 49 g (98 g ÷ 2) of H_2SO_4 per liter of solution. A 5-*N* solution contains 245 g (49 g × 5) of H_2SO_4 per liter. Similarly, 0.01-*N* H_2SO_4 contains 0.49 g (49 g ÷ 100) of H_2SO_4 per liter of solution. Concentrated sulfuric acid is usually 95%–98% H_2SO_4

Table 16-2

CONCENTRATIONS OF COMMON ACIDS

(Average values for freshly opened bottles)

	Acetic	Hydrochloric	Nitric	Sulfuric
formula	$HC_2H_3O_2$	HCl	HNO_3	H_2SO_4
molecular weight	60.03	36.46	63.02	98.08
density of concentrated reagent, g/cm³	1.06	1.19	1.42	1.84
percentage assay concentrated reagent	99.5	36.0	69.5	96.0
grams active ingredient/ml	1.055	0.426	0.985	1.76
normality of concentrated reagent	17.6	11.7	15.6	35.9
ml concentrated reagent/liter *N* solution	56.9	85.5	64.0	27.9
molarity of concentrated reagent	17.6	11.7	15.6	17.95
ml concentrated reagent/liter *M* solution	56.9	85.5	64.0	55.8

and has a density of about 1.84 g/ml. Dilutions to desired normalities are calculated as shown above for HCl.

Compounds containing water of crystallization present special problems in preparing solutions. For example, crystalline copper(II) sulfate has the empirical formula

$$\mathbf{CuSO_4 \cdot 5H_2O}$$

The formula weight is 249.5. One mole of this hydrate, 249.5 g, contains 1 mole of $CuSO_4$, 159.5 g. This fact must be recognized when moles or equivalents of crystalline hydrates are measured.

A 1-*M* $CuSO_4$ solution contains 159.5 g of $CuSO_4$ per liter of solution. This 1-*M* solution is also a 2-*N* solution because 1 mole of $CuSO_4$ contains 2 equivalents. A 1-*N* solution requires 79.75 g of $CuSO_4$ per liter. Of course, this solution is 0.5 *M*.

If a mole of a solute is also 1 equivalent, the molarity and normality of the solution *are the same.* A 1-*M* HCl solution is also a 1-*N* solution. If a mole of solute is two equivalents, a 1-*M* solution is 2 *N*. A 0.01-*M* H_2SO_4 solution is therefore 0.02 *N*. Similarly, a 0.01-*M* H_3PO_4 solution is 0.03 *N* if it is completely neutralized. *Solutions of equal normality are chemically equivalent, volume for volume.*

16.6 Ion concentration in water

Water is very weakly ionized by self-ionization. This process is sometimes referred to as *autoprotolysis.* The very poor conductivity of pure water results from the slight ionization of water itself. This fact can be demonstrated by testing water that has been highly purified by several different techniques.

Electric conductivity measurements of pure water show that, at 25°C, it is very slightly ionized to H_3O^+ and OH^- ions. Concentrations of these ions in pure water are only

$$\frac{\textbf{1 mole } \mathbf{H_3O^+}}{\mathbf{10^7} \textbf{ liters } \mathbf{H_2O}} \quad \textbf{and} \quad \frac{\textbf{1 mole } \mathbf{OH^-}}{\mathbf{10^7} \textbf{ liters } \mathbf{H_2O}}$$

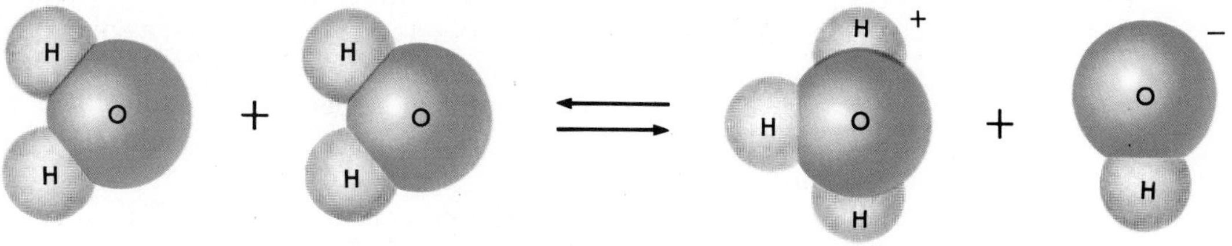

Fig. 16-3. Water is weakly ionized by a process of self-ionization.

One liter of water has a mass of 997 g at 25°C (1 liter = 1000 g at 4°C). The mass of 1 mole of water is 18.0 g. Using these quantities, 1 liter contains 55.4 moles of water at 25°C.

Pure water is very slightly ionized.

$$\frac{\mathbf{997\ g}}{\mathbf{liter}} \times \frac{\mathbf{1\ mole}}{\mathbf{18.0\ g}} = \mathbf{55.4\ moles/liter}$$

The extent of the ionization can be stated as a percentage if the concentration of H_3O^+ ions (and also OH^- ions) is expressed in moles of ions per mole of water.

$$\frac{\mathbf{1\ mole\ H_3O}}{\mathbf{10^7\ liters\ H_2O}} \times \frac{\mathbf{1\ liter}}{\mathbf{55.4\ moles}} = \frac{\mathbf{2 \times 10^{-9}\ mole\ H_3O^+}}{\mathbf{mole\ H_2O}}$$

This result shows that water is about 0.0000002% ionized at 25°C.

It is more useful to express ion concentration as *moles per liter* than as moles per 10,000,000 liters. This change is accomplished by dividing both terms in the expression moles per 10^7 liters by 10^7.

$$\frac{\mathbf{1\ mole\ H_3O^+ \div 10^7}}{\mathbf{10^7\ liters\ H_2O \div 10^7}} = \frac{\mathbf{10^{-7}\ mole\ H_3O^+}}{\mathbf{liter\ H_2O}}$$

Thus, the concentration of H_3O^+ ions (and OH^- ions) in water at 25°C is 10^{-7} mole per liter of H_2O.

Chemists use a standard notation to represent concentration in terms of *moles/liter*. The symbol or formula of the particular ion or molecule is enclosed in brackets, [ ]. *For example,* $[H_3O^+]$ means *hydronium ion concentration in moles per liter.* For the ionic concentrations in water at 25°C, we may write

$$\mathbf{[H_3O^+] = 10^{-7}\ mole/liter}$$

and

$$\mathbf{[OH^-] = 10^{-7}\ mole/liter}$$

or

$$\mathbf{[H_3O^+] = [OH^-] = 10^{-7}\ mole/liter}$$

Because the H_3O^+ ion concentration and the OH^- ion concentration are equal, water is neutral. It is neither acidic nor basic. This neutrality prevails in any solution in which $[H_3O^+] = [OH^-]$.

Pure water is neutral because $[H_3O^+] = [OH^-]$.

If the H_3O^+ ion concentration in a solution exceeds 10^{-7} mole/liter, the solution is acidic. For example, a solution containing 10^{-5} mole H_3O^+ ion per liter is acidic. If the OH^- ion concentration exceeds 10^{-7} mole per liter, the solution is basic or alkaline. Thus, a solution containing 10^{-4} mole OH^- ion per liter is basic.

In water and dilute solutions ($[H_3O^+] \times [OH^-] = 10^{-14}$) is a constant.

It is also true that the *product* of the $[H_3O^+]$ and $[OH^-]$ remains constant in water and dilute aqueous solutions as long as the temperature does not change. Recall that Le Chatelier's principle tells us that an increase in concentration of either of these ionic species in an aqueous mixture at equilibrium causes a decrease in concentration of the other species. In water and dilute aqueous solutions at 25°C,

$$[H_3O^+] \times [OH^-] = \text{a constant}$$

$$[H_3O^+][OH^-] = (1 \times 10^{-7} \text{ mole/liter})^2$$

$$[H_3O^+][OH^-] = 1 \times 10^{-14} \text{ mole}^2\text{/liter}^2$$

The ionization of water increases as its temperature rises. At 0°C the product $[H_3O^+][OH^-]$ is 0.11×10^{-14} mole^2 per liter^2. At 60°C it is 9.6×10^{-14} mole^2 per liter^2.

16.7 The pH of a solution

The range of solution concentrations encountered by chemists is great. It varies from about 10 *M* to perhaps 10^{-15} *M*. However, concentrations of less than 1 *M* are most commonly used.

We have stated that the product of $[H_3O^+]$ and $[OH^-]$ is a constant. Therefore, if we know the concentration of either ionic species, we can determine the concentration of the other. For example, the OH^- ion concentration of a 0.01-*M* NaOH solution is 0.01 or 10^{-2} mole/liter. The H_3O^+ ion concentration of this solution is calculated as follows:

$$[H_3O^+][OH^-] = 1 \times 10^{-14} \text{ mole}^2\text{/liter}^2$$

$$[H_3O^+] = \frac{1 \times 10^{-14} \text{ mole}^2\text{/liter}^2}{[OH^-]}$$

$$[H_3O^+] = \frac{1 \times 10^{-14} \text{ mole}^2\text{/liter}^2}{1 \times 10^{-2} \text{ mole/liter}}$$

$$[H_3O^+] = 1 \times 10^{-12} \text{ mole/liter}$$

See the Sample Problem that follows.

SAMPLE PROBLEM

Nitric acid, HNO_3, is completely ionized in a 0.001-*M* aqueous solution. (*a*) What is the H_3O^+ ion concentration in this solution? (*b*) What is the OH^- concentration?

(*a*) HNO_3 is a monoprotic acid giving 1 mole of H_3O^+ ions per mole of HNO_3 when completely ionized in water solution.

For 0.001-*M* aqueous HNO_3

$$[H_3O^+] = 0.001 \text{ mole/liter} = 10^{-3} \text{ mole/liter}$$

(*b*) $[H_3O^+][OH^-] = 10^{-14}$ mole²/liter²

$$[OH^-] = \frac{10^{-14} \text{ mole}^2/\text{liter}^2}{[H_3O^+]} = \frac{10^{-14} \text{ mole}^2/\text{liter}^2}{10^{-3} \text{ mole/liter}}$$

$$[OH^-] = 10^{-11} \text{ mole/liter}$$

pH is called the H_3O^+ ion index.

We can express the acidity or alkalinity of a solution in terms of its hydronium ion concentration. An $[H_3O^+]$ *larger* than 10^{-7} mole/liter (a *smaller* negative exponent) indicates an acid solution. An $[H_3O^+]$ *smaller* than 10^{-7} mole/liter (a *larger* negative exponent) indicates an alkaline solution.

Expressing acidity or alkalinity in this way can become cumbersome, especially in dilute solutions, whether decimal or exponential notations are used. Because it is more convenient, chemists use a quantity called pH to indicate the hydronium ion concentration of a solution.

Numerically, the pH of a solution is the common logarithm of the number of liters of solution that contains one mole of H_3O^+ ions. This number of liters of solution is equal to the *reciprocal* of the H_3O^+ ion concentration. This concentration is given in moles of H_3O^+ ions per liter of solution. The reciprocal expression is

$$\frac{1}{[H_3O^+]}$$

*Thus, the **pH of a solution** is defined as the common logarithm of the reciprocal of the hydronium ion concentration. The pH is expressed by the equation*

$$pH = \log \frac{1}{[H_3O^+]}$$

The common logarithm of a number is the power to which 10 must be raised to give the number. Thus 0.0000001 is 10^{-7} and its reciprocal is 10,000,000, or 10^7. The logarithm of 10^7 is 7.

pH of neutral solutions = 7

Pure water is slightly ionized, and at 25°C contains 0.0000001 or 10^{-7} mole of H_3O^+ per liter. The pH of water is therefore *pH of acidic solutions <7*

$$pH = \log \frac{1}{0.0000001}$$

$$pH = \log \frac{1}{10^{-7}}$$

$$pH = \log 10^7$$

$$pH = 7$$

Suppose the H_3O^+ ion concentration in a solution is *greater* than that in pure water. Then the number of liters required to provide 1 mole of H_3O^+ ions is *smaller*. Consequently, the pH is a *smaller* number than 7. Such a solution is *acidic*. On the other hand, suppose the H_3O^+ ion concentration is *less than* that in pure water. The pH is then a larger number than 7. Such a solution is *basic*.

pH of basic solutions >7

The range of pH values usually falls between 0 and 14. The pH system is particularly useful in describing the acidity or alkalinity of solutions that are not far from neutral. This includes many food substances and fluids encountered in physiology. The pH of some common substances is given in Table 16-3.

Table 16-3

APPROXIMATE pH OF SOME COMMON SUBSTANCES

Substance	pH
1.0-*N* HCl	0.1
1.0-*N* H_2SO_4	0.3
0.1-*N* HCl	1.1
0.1-*N* H_2SO_4	1.2
gastric juice	2.0
0.01-*N* H_2SO_4	2.1
lemons	2.3
vinegar	2.8
0.1-*N* $HC_2H_3O_2$	2.9
soft drinks	3.0
apples	3.1
grapefruit	3.1
oranges	3.5
cherries	3.6
tomatoes	4.2
bananas	4.6
bread	5.5
potatoes	5.8
rainwater	6.2
milk	6.5
pure water	7.0
eggs	7.8
0.1-*N* $NaHCO_3$	8.4
seawater	8.5
milk of magnesia	10.5
0.1-*N* NH_3	11.1
0.1-*N* Na_2CO_3	11.6
0.1-*N* NaOH	13.0
1.0-*N* NaOH	14.0
1.0-*N* KOH	14.0

There are two basic types of pH problems that concern us. These are

1. The calculation of pH when the $[H_3O^+]$ of a solution is known.

2. The calculation of $[H_3O^+]$ when the pH of a solution is known.

We will examine these two calculation methods in Sections 16.8 and 16.9.

16.8 Calculation of pH

In the simplest pH problems, the $[H_3O^+]$ of the solution is an integral power of 10, such as1 *M*, or 0.01 *M*. These problems can be solved *by inspection*. The pH equation based on the definition stated in Section 16.7 is

$$pH = \log \frac{1}{[H_3O^+]}$$

Since

$$\log \frac{1}{[H_3O^+]} = -\log [H_3O^+]$$

we can write the first equation in a more useful form to solve for pH.

$$pH = -\log [H_3O^+]$$

In an aqueous solution in which $[H_3O^+] = 10^{-6}$ mole/liter, the pH = 6.

Chemical solutions with pH values below 0 and above 14 can be prepared. For example, the pH of 6-*M* H_2SO_4 is between 0 and -1. The pH of 3-*M* KOH is near 14.5. However, we will deal only with pH values in the 0-14 range. Observe that the *pH of a solution is the exponent of the hydronium ion concentration with the sign changed.* The following Sample Problems further illustrate this fact.

$pH = -log\ [H_3O^+]$

SAMPLE PROBLEM

What is the pH of a 0.001-*M* HCl solution?

SOLUTION

$$\mathbf{pH = -log[H_3O^+]}$$

$$\mathbf{[H_3O^+] = 0.001\ mole/liter = 10^{-3}\ mole/liter}$$

$$\mathbf{pH = -log\ 10^{-3} = -(-3)}$$

$$\mathbf{pH = 3}$$

(Notice that if the $[H_3O^+] = 10^{-3}$, the pH = 3)

SAMPLE PROBLEM

What is the pH of a 0.001-*M* NaOH solution?

SOLUTION

$$\mathbf{pH = -log[H_3O^+]}$$

$$\mathbf{[H_3O^+][OH^-] = 10^{-14}\ mole^2/liter^2}$$

$$\mathbf{[H_3O^+] = \frac{10^{-14}\ mole^2/liter^2}{[OH^-]}}$$

$$\mathbf{[OH^-] = 0.001\ mole/liter = 10^{-3}\ mole/liter}$$

$$\mathbf{[H_3O^+] = \frac{10^{-14}\ mole^2/liter^2}{10^{-3}\ mole/liter} = 10^{-11}\ mole/liter}$$

$$\mathbf{pH = -log\ 10^{-11} = -(-11)}$$

$$\mathbf{pH = 11}$$

Fig. 16-4. The relationship between the numerical expression for the pH of a solution and its corresponding hydronium ion concentration, $[H_3O^+]$, may be easily compared in this chart.

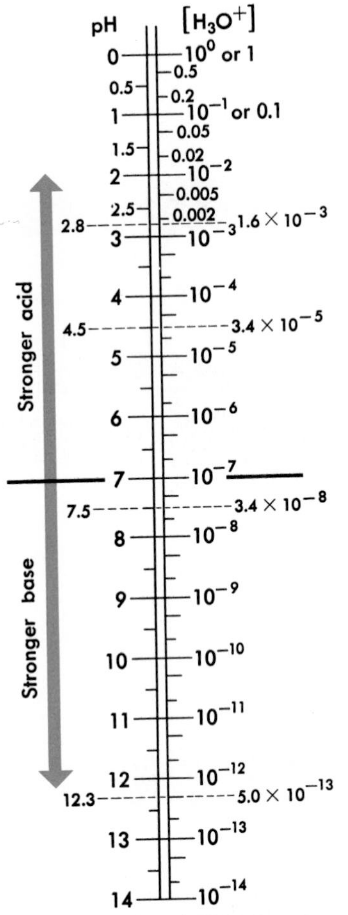

The preceding problems have hydronium ion concentrations that are integral powers of ten. They are easily solved by inspection. However, many problems involve hydrogen ion concentrations that are not integral powers of ten. Solving such problems requires some basic knowledge of logarithms and exponents. Reviews of exponents, logarithms, and the use of the table of logarithms are in Appendix A. A table of the logarithms of numbers is in Table 17 in the Appendix.

Suppose the $[H_3O^+]$ of a solution is 3.4×10^{-5} mole/liter. Observe that 3.4×10^{-5} lies between 1×10^{-4} and 1×10^{-5}. Thus, the pH of the solution must be between 4 and 5. Calculations are required to determine a more precise pH value. However, this simple estimate of pH helps prevent errors that otherwise occur quite commonly.

The relationship between the pH and $[H_3O^+]$ is shown on the scale of Figure 16-4. This scale can be used to estimate the pH value described in the preceding paragraph. Calculations for this pH value and for $[H_3O^+]$ from a known pH value are shown in the following Sample Problem.

SAMPLE PROBLEM

What is the pH of a solution if $[H_3O^+]$ is 3.4×10^{-5} mole/liter?

SOLUTION

$$\mathbf{pH = -\log [H_3O^+]}$$
$$\mathbf{pH = -\log (3.4 \times 10^{-5})}$$

The logarithm of a product is equal to the sum of the logarithms of each of the factors. Thus,

$$\mathbf{pH = -(\log 3.4 + \log 10^{-5})}$$

The log of $10^{-5} = -5$ and, from the table of logarithms (Table 17 in the Appendix), the log of 3.4 is found to be 0.53.

$$\mathbf{pH = -(0.53 - 5)}$$

Therefore,

$$\mathbf{pH = 4.47}$$

16.9 Calculation of $[H_3O^+]$

We have calculated the pH of a solution knowing its hydronium ion concentration. Now, suppose the pH of a solution is known. How can we determine its hydronium ion concentration?

The equation for the pH in terms of the $[H_3O^+]$ was used in Section 16.8. It is

$$\mathbf{pH = -\log [H_3O^+]}$$

Remember that the base of common logarithms is 10. This equation can be restated in terms of H_3O^+ as follows:

$$\log [H_3O^+] = -pH$$

$$[H_3O^+] = \text{antilog } (-pH)$$

$$[H_3O^+] = 10^{-pH}$$

For an aqueous solution in which the pH = 2, the $[H_3O^+] = 10^{-2}$ mole/liter (by inspection). When the pH = 0, the $[H_3O^+] =$ 1 mole/liter. Recall that 10^0 (ten to the zero power) = 1. The following Sample Problem has a pH value that is a positive whole number.

$[H_3O^+] = \text{antilog } (-pH)$

SAMPLE PROBLEM

What is the hydronium ion concentration of a sulfuric acid solution that has a pH of 4?

SOLUTION

$$pH = -\log [H_3O^+]$$

$$\log [H_3O^+] = -pH$$

$$[H_3O^+] = \text{antilog } (-pH) = \text{antilog } (-4)$$

$$\text{antilog } (-4) = 10^{-4}$$

$$[H_3O^+] = 10^{-4} \text{ mole/liter}$$

(Notice that if the pH = 4, the $[H_3O^+] = 10^{-4}$)

The pH value in the next Sample Problem is not a whole number.

SAMPLE PROBLEM

The pH of a solution is found to be 7.52. What is the hydronium ion concentration?

SOLUTION

The $[H_3O^+]$ is the number whose logarithm is −7.52. Therefore the antilog of −7.52 will give the hydronium ion concentration.

$$pH = -\log [H_3O^+]$$

Solving for $[H_3O^+]$

$$\log [H_3O^+] = -pH$$
$$[H_3O^+] = \text{antilog } (-pH)$$
$$[H_3O^+] = \text{antilog } (-7.52)$$

But

$$\text{antilog}\,(-7.52) = \text{antilog}\,(0.48 - 8)$$

Thus

$$[H_3O^+] = \text{antilog}\,(0.48 - 8)$$
$$[H_3O^+] = \text{antilog}\,(0.48) \times \text{antilog}\,(-8)$$

The antilog of $(-8) = 10^{-8}$. The antilog of (0.48) is found from the table of logarithms to be 3.0. Therefore,

$$[H_3O^+] = 3.0 \times 10^{-8} \text{ mole/liter}$$

Table 16-4

RELATIONSHIP OF $[H_3O^+]$ TO $[OH^-]$ AND pH

Solution	$[H_3O^+]$	$[OH^-]$	$[H_3O^+][OH^-]$	pH
0.02-*M* KOH	5.0×10^{-13}	2.0×10^{-2}	1.0×10^{-14}	12.3
0.01-*M* KOH	1.0×10^{-12}	1.0×10^{-2}	1.0×10^{-14}	12.0
pure H_2O	1.0×10^{-7}	1.0×10^{-7}	1.0×10^{-14}	7.0
0.001-*M* HCl	1.0×10^{-3}	1.0×10^{-11}	1.0×10^{-14}	3.0
0.1-*M* $HC_2H_3O_2$	1.3×10^{-3}	7.7×10^{-12}	1.0×10^{-14}	2.9

Table 16-4 shows the relationship between the hydronium ion and hydroxide ion concentrations, the product of these concentrations, and the pH for several solutions of typical molarities. Since KOH is a soluble ionic compound, its aqueous solutions are completely ionized. The molarity of each KOH solution indicates directly the $[OH^-]$. Note that the product $[H_3O^+][OH^-]$ is constant, 10^{-14} mole² per liter² at 25°C. Therefore, the $[H_3O^+]$ can be calculated. If we know the $[H_3O^+]$, we can then determine the pH as $-\log\,[H_3O^+]$.

In aqueous solutions: if $[H_3O^+]$ increases, $[OH^-]$ decreases.

Any aqueous solution of HCl that has a concentration below 1-*M* can be considered to be completely ionized. Thus, the molarity of the 0.001-*M* HCl solution indicates directly the $[H_3O^+]$.

In aqueous solutions: if $[OH^-]$ increases, $[H_3O^+]$ decreases.

The weakly ionized $HC_2H_3O_2$ solution presents a different problem. We may lack information about the concentrations of $HC_2H_3O_2$ molecules, H_3O^+ ions, and $C_2H_3O_2^-$ ions in the equilibrium mixture in the aqueous solution. However, we can determine the hydronium ion concentration by measuring the pH of the solution experimentally. The $[H_3O^+]$ is determined then as the antilog (−pH).

$$[H_3O^+] = \text{antilog}\,(-\text{pH})$$

16.10 The neutralization reaction

In a neutralization reaction, the basic OH^- ion acquires a proton from the H_3O^+ ion and forms a molecule of water.

$$H_3O^+ + OH^- \rightarrow 2H_2O$$

One mole of H_3O^+ ions (19 g) and 1 mole of OH^- ions (17 g) are chemically equivalent. Neutralization occurs when H_3O^+ ions and OH^- ions are supplied in equal numbers. We know that a liter of water at room temperature has an $[H_3O^+]$ and $[OH^-]$ of 10^{-7} *M* each. Furthermore, we know that the product $[H_3O^+][OH^-]$ of 10^{-14} mole²/liter² is a constant for water and all dilute aqueous solutions.

If 0.1 mole of gaseous HCl is dissolved in the liter of water, the H_3O^+ ion concentration rises to 0.1 or 10^{-1} *M*. Since the product $[H_3O^+][OH^-]$ remains at 10^{-14}, the $[OH^-]$ obviously must decrease from 10^{-7} to 10^{-13} *M*.

In the neutralization reaction, OH^- ions are removed from the solution when they combine with H_3O^+ ions and form H_2O molecules. Almost 10^{-7} mole of H_3O^+ ions is also removed in this way. However, this quantity is only a small portion (0.0001%) of the 0.1 mole of H_3O^+ ions present in the liter of solution.

Neutralization:
$H^+(aq) + OH^-(aq) \rightarrow H_2O(l)$

Now suppose we add 0.1 mole (4 g) of solid NaOH to the liter of 0.1-*M* HCl solution. Imagine, also, that the hydroxide and hydronium ions are somehow temporarily prevented from reacting with each other. The NaOH dissolves and supplies 0.1 mole of OH^- ions to the solution. Both $[H_3O^+]$ and $[OH^-]$ are now high and their product is much greater than the constant value 10^{-14} for the dilute aqueous solution.

Now, suppose the chemical reaction is allowed to begin. The ion-removal reaction will be as before except that this time there are as many OH^- ions as H_3O^+ ions to be removed. H_3O^+ and OH^- ions combine until the product $[H_3O^+][OH^-]$ returns to the constant value 10^{-14} and

$$[H_3O^+] = [OH^-] = 10^{-7}\ M$$

The solution is now neither acidic nor basic but is neutral. The process was one in which chemically equivalent quantities of H_3O^+ ions and OH^- ions combined, a neutralization reaction.

16.11 Acid-base titration

Titration

The above examples should help you understand the nature of the chemical reaction that occurs between acids and bases as a solution of one is added progressively to a solution of the

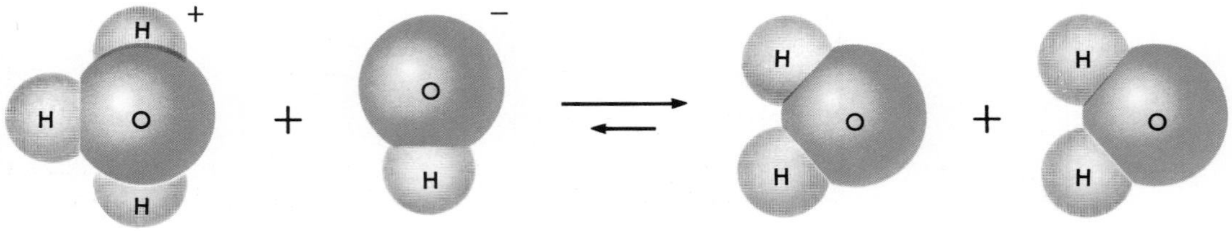

Fig. 16-5. The neutralization reaction. Hydronium ions and hydroxide ions form very slightly ionized water molecules.

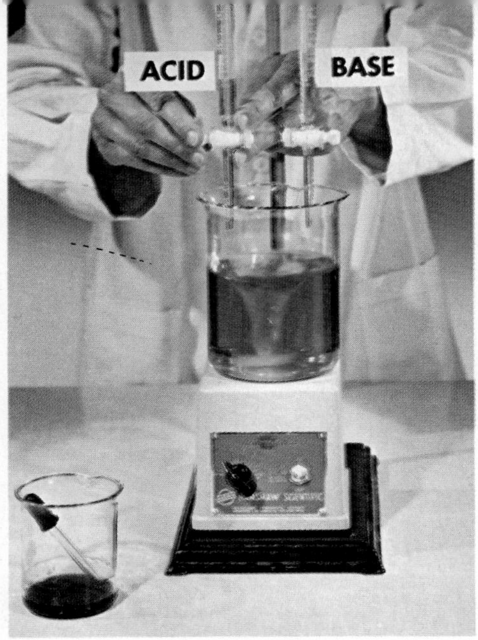

Fig. 16-6. An acid-base titration using an indicator.

other. This progressive addition of an acid to a base (or a base to an acid) in order to compare their concentrations is called *titration*. ***Titration*** *is the controlled addition of the measured amount of a solution of known concentration required to react completely with a measured amount of a solution of unknown concentration.*

Titration provides a sensitive means of determining the relative volumes of acidic and basic solutions that are chemically equivalent. If we know the concentration of one solution, we can calculate the concentration of the other solution. Titration is an important laboratory procedure and is much used in analytical chemistry. See Figure 16-6.

Suppose we make successive additions of an aqueous base to a measured volume of an aqueous acid. Eventually, the acid is neutralized. With continued addition of base, the solution becomes distinctly basic. The pH has now changed from a low to a high numerical value. The change in pH occurs slowly at first, then rapidly through the neutral point, and slowly again as the solution becomes basic. Typical pH curves for strong acid-strong base and weak acid-strong base titrations are shown in Figure 16-7.

Equivalence point: just enough of one reactant has been added to a second reactant.

Indicators "indicate" pH by color changes.

The very rapid change in pH occurs in the region where equivalent quantities of H_3O^+ and OH^- ions are present. Any method that shows this abrupt change in pH can be used to detect the *equivalence point* of the titration.

Many dyes have colors that are sensitive to pH changes. Some change color within the pH range in which an equivalence point occurs. Such dyes may serve as *indicators* in the titration process. Several indicators are listed in Table 16-5.

In order to actually know the concentration of a "known" solution, it is compared to a *standard solution* whose concentration is well established. The known solution is first prepared and its volume is adjusted to the desired concentration.

Fig. 16-7. Acid-base titration curves: (A) strong acid-strong base; (B) weak acid-strong base.

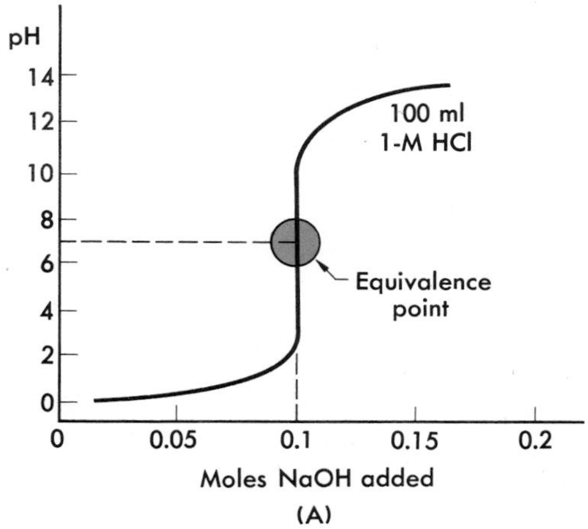

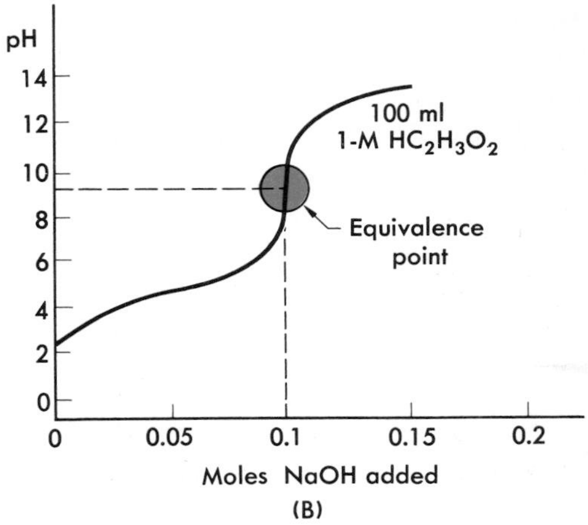

This concentration information is then refined by titrating the solution against a carefully measured quantity of a highly purified compound known as a *primary standard*. The actual concentration of the known solution becomes that established by this standardizing procedure.

Fig. 16-8. An acid-base titration stand.

16.12 Titration with molar solutions

Burets like those shown in Figure 16-8 are used in titration to measure solution volumes with good precision. Suppose we have an aqueous solution of NaOH of unknown concentration. We add successive small amounts of this solution to 10.0 ml of 0.01-*M* aqueous solution of HCl containing a few drops of a suitable indicator until the equivalence point is reached. Reading the base buret, we find that 20.0 ml of the basic solution has been used. How can these titration data indicate the *molarity* of the basic solution?

The empirical equation for the neutralization reaction is

$$\mathbf{HCl + NaOH \rightarrow NaCl + H_2O}$$

We know the volume and molarity of the solution of HCl used. From these data, we can determine the quantity, in moles, of HCl used:

$$\frac{\text{10.0 ml}}{\text{1000 ml/liter}} \times \frac{\text{0.01 mole HCl}}{\text{liter}} = \text{0.0001 mole HCl used}$$

The balanced equation shows that *1 mole* of NaOH is used for *1 mole* of HCl. In other words, NaOH and HCl show chemical equivalence in the reaction, mole for mole. Therefore, the quantity of NaOH used in the titration is also 0.0001 mole. This quantity was furnished by 20.0 ml of NaOH solution. The molarity of the NaOH solution is obtained as follows:

$$\frac{\text{0.0001 mole NaOH}}{\text{20.0 ml}} \times \frac{\text{1000 ml}}{\text{liter}} = \text{0.005 mole NaOH/liter}$$

or

$$\textbf{0.005-}\boldsymbol{M}\textbf{ NaOH}$$

Let us repeat the titration with the same "unknown" NaOH solution as the base. But this time we will use 10.0 ml of a 0.01-*M* solution of the diprotic acid H_2SO_4 (instead of HCl) as the "known" acid solution. When we have titrated to the equivalence point, the base buret shows that 40.0 ml of the NaOH solution has been used. The empirical equation for this reaction is

$$\mathbf{H_2SO_4 + 2NaOH \rightarrow Na_2SO_4 + 2H_2O}$$

$$\frac{\text{10.0 ml}}{\text{1000 ml/liter}} \times \frac{\text{0.01 mole } H_2SO_4}{\text{liter}} = \text{0.0001 mole } H_2SO_4 \text{ used}$$

The equation shows that *2 moles* of NaOH are required for *1 mole* of H_2SO_4. Therefore, 0.0002 mole NaOH is used in the titration as the chemical equivalent of 0.0001 mole H_2SO_4. The molarity of the NaOH solution is obtained as follows:

$$\frac{\textbf{0.0002 mole NaOH}}{\textbf{40.0 ml}} \times \frac{\textbf{1000 ml}}{\textbf{liter}} = \textbf{0.005 mole NaOH/liter}$$

or

$$\textbf{0.005-}M\textbf{ NaOH}$$

To summarize, we can determine the molarity of an aqueous base (or acid) of unknown concentration by titrating against an aqueous acid (or base) of known concentration. The following steps are involved:

1. Determine moles solute of known solution used in the titration.

2. Determine ratio—moles unknown solute/moles known solute—from balanced equation.

3. Determine moles solute of unknown solution used in the titration.

4. Determine molarity of unknown solution.

The accompanying Sample Problem illustrates the titration process.

SAMPLE PROBLEM

In a titration, 27.4 ml of a standard solution of $Ba(OH)_2$ is added to a 20.0 ml-sample of an HCl solution. The concentration of the standard solution is 0.0154 *M*. What is the molarity of the acid solution?

SOLUTION

The equation for this reaction is

$$\mathbf{2HCl + Ba(OH)_2 \rightarrow BaCl_2 + 2H_2O}$$

The quantity, in moles, of $Ba(OH)_2$ used in the reaction can be found from the molarity of the standard solution and the volume used.

$$\frac{\textbf{27.4 ml}}{\textbf{1000 ml/liter}} \times \frac{\textbf{0.0154 mole Ba(OH)}_2}{\textbf{liter}} = \textbf{0.000422 mole Ba(OH)}_2\textbf{ used}$$

The equation shows that *2 moles* of HCl are used for *1 mole* of $Ba(OH)_2$. Therefore, 0.000844 mole of HCl is used since this is the chemical equivalent of 0.000422 mole of $Ba(OH)_2$.

20.0 ml of the unknown solution contains 0.000844 mole of HCl. The concentration is

$$\frac{\textbf{0.000844 mole HCl}}{\textbf{20.0 ml}} \times \frac{\textbf{1000 ml}}{\textbf{liter}} = \textbf{0.0422 mole/liter}$$

or

$$\textbf{0.0422-}M\textbf{ HCl}$$

16.13 Titration with normal solutions

Chemists sometimes prefer to express solution concentrations in terms of *normality*. The advantage in doing so is that concentrations are expressed directly in terms of equivalents of solute. Solutions of the same normality are always chemically equivalent, milliliter for milliliter. We have seen that the normality of a given solution is a whole number times its molarity. The relationship between the two depends upon the substance and the reaction in which it is involved.

A very simple relationship exists between volumes and normalities of solutions used in titration. For example, a titration required 50.0 ml of a 0.100-N solution of NaOH to reach an equivalence point with 10.0 ml of vinegar, a water solution of acetic acid ($HC_2H_3O_2$). The chemical equivalent of $HC_2H_3O_2$ used is the product of the volume of acid solution, V_a, used and its normality, N_a.

$$V_a \times N_a = \mathbf{equiv}_a$$

Similarly, the chemical equivalent of NaOH used is the product of the volume of base solution, V_b, used and its normality, N_b.

$$V_b \times N_b = \mathbf{equiv}_b$$

At the equivalence point in the titration,

$$\mathbf{equiv}_a = \mathbf{equiv}_b$$

Therefore,

$$V_a N_a = V_b N_b$$

We are seeking the normality of the vinegar, N_a. Solving the above equation for N_a

$$N_a = \frac{V_b N_b}{V_a} = \frac{\textbf{50.0 ml} \times \textbf{0.100 } N}{\textbf{10.0 ml}}$$

$$N_a = \textbf{0.500 } N$$

In this simple numerical example, we see that 5 times as much base solution was used in the titration as vinegar. Clearly, the vinegar is 5 times more concentrated than the base.

The acidity of vinegar is due to the presence of acetic acid. A 1.0-N acetic acid solution contains 1.0 equivalent per liter of solution. In this case, 1.0 equivalent equals 1.0 mole or $6\overline{0}$ g of $HC_2H_3O_2$ per liter of solution. The 0.50-*N* solution must contain $3\overline{0}$ g of $HC_2H_3O_2$ per liter. A liter of vinegar has a mass of about 1000 g. Thus, the sample of vinegar used contains 3.0% acetic acid.

Aqueous solutions of some salts may be acidic or basic, depending on the composition of the salt. If the anions are sufficiently basic, some protons are removed from water and the [OH^-] increases. Or, if the cations are slightly acidic, some protons are donated to water and the [H_3O^+] increases.

NaOH is a strong base and $HC_2H_3O_2$ is a weak acid. The pH curve for this titration, Figure 16-7(B), differs from the curve for a strong acid-strong base titration. The equivalence point occurs at a higher pH because the sodium acetate solution formed in the titration is slightly basic.

16.14 Indicators in titration

Chemists have a wide choice of indicators for use in titration. They are able to choose one that changes color over the correct pH range for any particular reaction. Let us see why it is not always suitable to have an indicator that changes color at a pH of 7.

Solutions of soluble hydroxides and acids mixed in chemically equivalent quantities may not be exactly neutral. They are neutral only if both solutes are ionized to the same degree. The purpose of the indicator is to show that the equivalence point has been reached. That is, it shows when equivalent quantities of the two solutes are together. Table 16-5 gives the color changes of several common indicators used in acid-base titrations. In this table, the pH range over which an indicator color change occurs is referred to as its *transition interval.* Notice the variations in the transition intervals for the different indicators. These variations enable a chemist to choose the best indicator for a given acid-base reaction.

There are four possible types of acid-base combinations. In titration, these combinations may have equivalence points occurring in different pH ranges as follows:

Table 16-5

INDICATOR COLORS

Indicator	Color			Transition Interval (pH)
	Acid	Transition	Base	
methyl violet	yellow	aqua	blue	0.0– 1.6
methyl yellow	red	orange	yellow	2.9– 4.0
bromphenol blue	yellow	green	blue	3.0– 4.6
methyl orange	red	orange	yellow	3.2– 4.4
methyl red	red	buff	yellow	4.8– 6.0
litmus	red	pink	blue	5.5– 8.0
bromthymol blue	yellow	green	blue	6.0– 7.6
phenol red	yellow	orange	red	6.6– 8.0
phenolphthalein	colorless	pink	red	8.2–10.6
thymolphthalein	colorless	pale blue	blue	9.4–10.6
alizarin yellow	yellow	orange	red	10.0–12.0

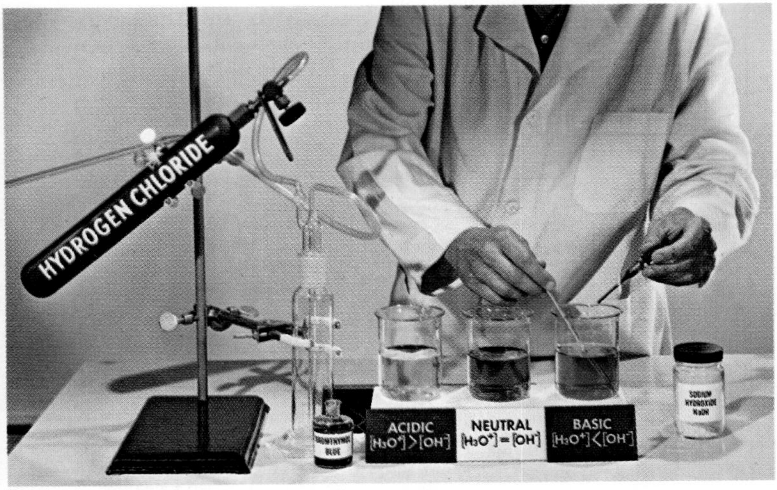

Fig. 16-9. The acid, base, and transition colors of bromthymol blue.

1. *Strong acid—strong base:* pH is about 7. Litmus is a suitable indicator, but the color change is not sharply defined. Bromthymol blue performs more satisfactorily. See Figure 16-9.

2. *Strong acid—weak base:* pH is less than 7. Methyl orange is a suitable indicator.

3. *Weak acid—strong base:* pH is greater than 7. Phenolphthalein is a suitable indicator.

4. *Weak acid—weak base:* pH may be either greater than or less than 7, depending on which solution is stronger. None of the indicators performs very well.

16.15 pH measurements

Indicators used to detect equivalence points in neutralization reactions are organic compounds. They have the characteristics of weak acids. When added to a solution in suitable form and concentration, an indicator gives the solution a characteristic color. If the pH of the solution is changed enough, as in titration, the indicator changes color over a definite pH range. We have called this pH range the *transition interval.*

Because indicators are color sensitive to the pH, we use them to give information about the $[H_3O^+]$ of a solution. The color of un-ionized indicator molecules is different from that of indicator ions. In solutions of high hydronium ion concentration, the color of the molecular species prevails. Solutions of low hydronium ion concentrations have the color of the ionic species. The acid, base, and transition colors of several indicators are shown in Figure 16-10 on the next page.

An indicator added to different solutions may show the same *transition color.* If so, the solutions are considered to have the

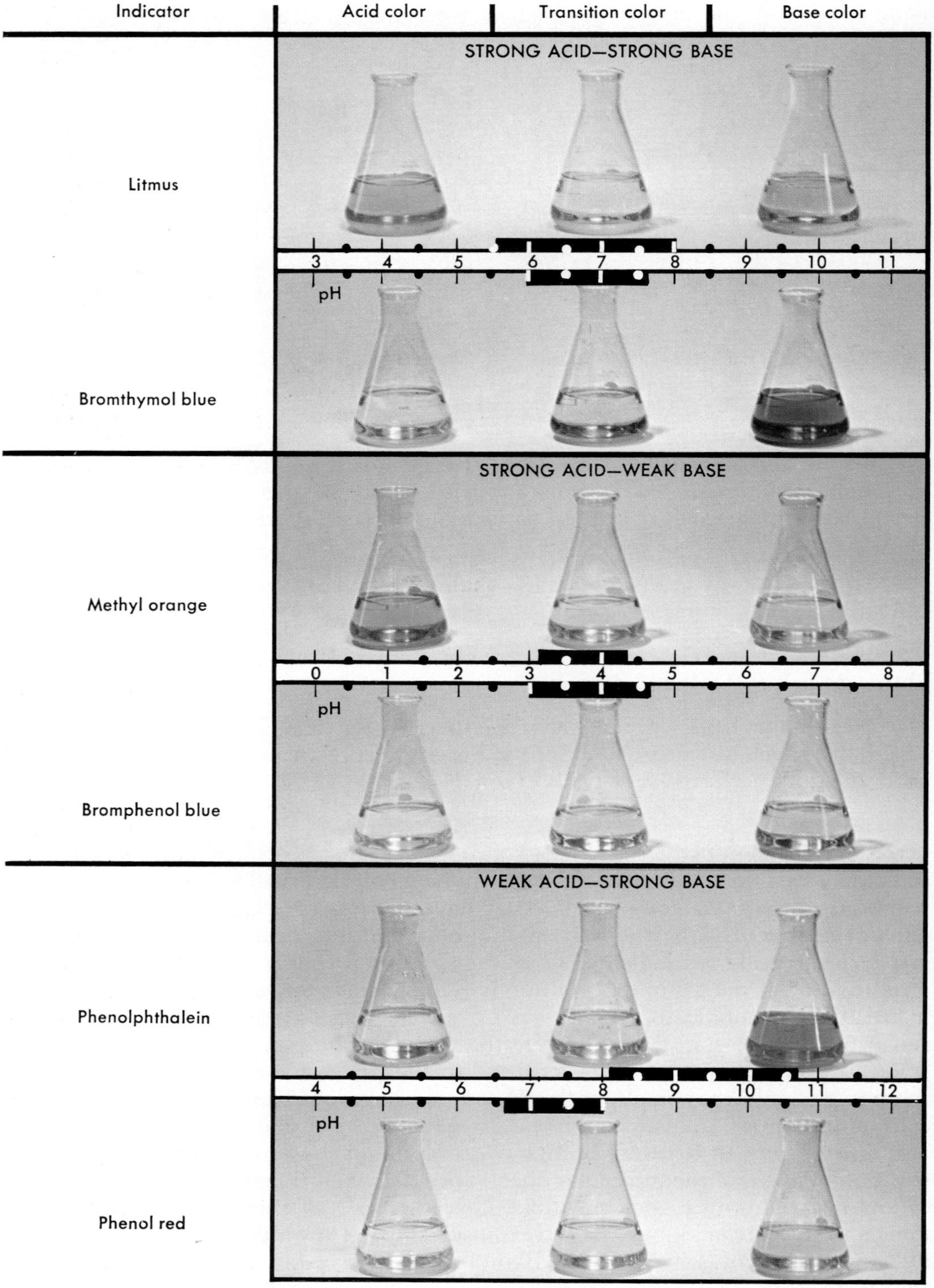

Fig. 16-10. Indicator colors in titration.

same pH. This is the basis for the common colorimetric determination of pH. A measured volume of a suitable indicator is added to each solution whose pH is to be determined. The color is then compared with that of the same indicator in solutions of known pH. By careful color comparison, the pH of a solution can be estimated with a precision of about 0.1 pH interval.

Determining equivalence points in titrations and the pH of solutions can be done in ways other than by the use of indicators. Instrumented methods are also used by chemists to make rapid titrations and pH determinations. A pH meter provides a convenient method of measuring the pH of a solution. See Figure 16-11. The pH meter measures the voltage difference between a special electrode and a reference (standard) electrode placed in the solution. The special electrode is usually a thin-walled glass electrode. The voltage changes as the H_3O^+ ion concentration of the solution changes. In an acid-base titration, a large change in the voltage occurs at the equivalence point. This change is related to the sharp color change of an indicator near the equivalence point.

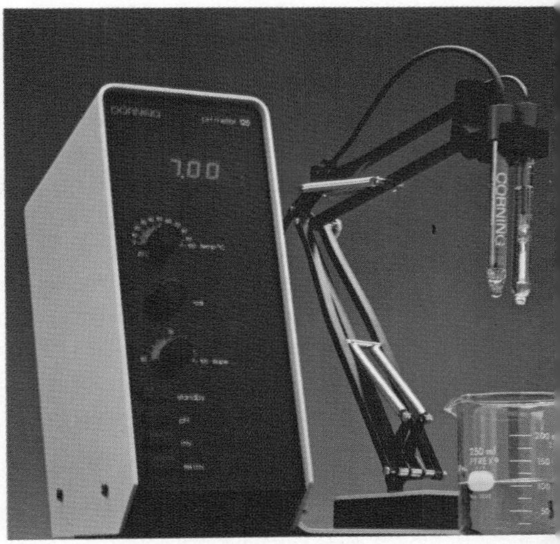

Fig. 16-11. A modern pH meter.

SUMMARY

Solution concentrations are expressed in terms of molality, molarity, or normality. When we are interested in the ratio of solute to solvent molecules in the solution, we use molality. When we are interested in the amount of solute present and have no interest in the amount of solvent in the solution, we use molarity or normality. These solutions have known quantities of solutes dissolved in given volumes of solution. Any required quantity of solute can be selected by measuring out the proper volume of the solution. Molar solutions are prepared using moles of solute per liter of solution. Normal solutions are prepared using chemical equivalents of solute per liter of solution.

Chemical equivalents of substances have the same combining capacities in reactions. One equivalent of an acid supplies one mole of protons. One equivalent of a base supplies one mole of OH^- ions or accepts one mole of protons. For diprotic and triprotic acids, the reactions they undergo determine their chemical equivalencies.

Water is weakly ionized by autoprotolysis. At 25°C, the hydronium ion concentration and hydroxide ion concentration are each 10^{-7} mole/liter. The product of these ion concentrations remains constant at 10^{-14} mole²/liter² for water and aqueous solutions as long as temperature remains at 25°C. The ionization of water increases slightly with rise in temperature.

The pH scale is used to indicate the hydronium ion concentration in aqueous solutions. Numerically, the pH of a solution is the common logarithm of the number of liters that contain one mole of H_3O^+ ions. Since this number of liters is the reciprocal of the H_3O^+ ion concentration of the solution, the pH is also the common logarithm of the reciprocal of the hydronium ion concentration. If the hydronium ion concentration of a solution is known, the pH can be calculated. Conversely, the hydronium ion concentration can be calculated if the pH of a solution is known. The pH of pure water and neutral aqueous solutions is 7. Acidic solutions have pH values smaller than 7. Basic solutions have pH values larger than 7.

The concentrations of acids and bases are compared by a technique called titration. A solution of a base (or acid) of unknown concentration is added to a solution of an acid (or base) of known concentration until equal chemical equivalents of acid and base are present in the solution. An acid-base indicator is used to show when the equivalence point in the titration is reached. Knowing the concentration of one solution and the volumes of both solutions used to reach the equivalence point, the concentration of the other solution can be calculated.

Indicators change color over characteristic short pH ranges called their transition intervals. The equivalence point is reached at a pH of about 7 for titrations of strong acids and strong bases. Indicators with transition intervals around a pH of 7 are used. Indicators with transition intervals below a pH of 7 are used in titration of strong acids and weak bases. Weak acid-strong base titrations require indicators with transition intervals above a pH of 7.

QUESTIONS

Group A

1. Distinguish between solution concentrations expressed in terms of molality and molarity.
2. (*a*) What determines the mass of 1 equivalent of an acid? (*b*) of a base?
3. How many grams are in 1 equivalent of each of the following? (*a*) $Ca(NO_3)_2$ (*b*) Zn (*c*) HCO_3^- (*d*) KCl (*e*) Li (*f*) H_3O^+ (*g*) $ZnSO_4$ (*h*) OH^- (*i*) $HC_2H_3O_2$ (*j*) $Al_2(SO_4)_3$.
4. Determine the number of equivalents per mole of each of the following: (*a*) H_2O (*b*) $HClO_4$ (*c*) $Sr(NO_3)_2$ (*d*) $AuCl_3$ (*e*) $Mg(OH)_2$ (*f*) HF (*g*) $NaC_2H_3O_2$ (*h*) K_2SO_4 (*i*) $CaCl_2$ (*j*) Bi.
5. Write the equations that show the partial and complete ionization of sulfuric acid.
6. What is the conjugate base for the HCO_3^- ion?
7. Explain the meaning of the notation $[NH_4^+]$.
8. (*a*) Explain the meaning of pH. (*b*) What is the usual range of the pH scale?
9. In a certain aqueous solution, the hydronium ion concentration is 1×10^{-3} mole per liter. (*a*) What is the pH of the solution? (*b*) What is the hydroxide ion concentration?
10. (*a*) Explain why neither bromphenol blue nor methyl orange is a suitable indicator for the titration of 0.02-*N* acetic acid with sodium hydroxide. (*b*) Name two indicators that are suitable for this titration.

Group B

11. Hydrogen chloride, HCl, has 1 equivalent of hydrogen per mole and hydrogen phosphate, H_3PO_4, has 3 equivalents of hydrogen per mole. Yet hydrochloric acid is described as a *strong* acid and phosphoric acid as a *weak* acid. Explain.
12. (*a*) How would you test the soil in your lawn or garden to find out whether it is acidic or basic? (*b*) If you find it to be acidic, what can be added to it to remedy the condition?
13. Test your saliva with litmus paper. (*a*) Is the saliva acidic or alkaline? (*b*) Do you think that a tooth paste is likely to be acidic or basic? Test some of them.
14. In a neutralization reaction between hydrochloric acid and potassium hydroxide, the K^+ ion and the Cl^- ion are called *spectator ions*. (*a*) Explain. (*b*) How could the potassium chloride be recovered?

15. What indicator would you use to show the end-point of the neutralization reaction described in Question 14? Explain why you selected this particular indicator for the neutralization reaction.
16. How many moles of sodium hydroxide are needed for the complete neutralization of (*a*) 1 mole of hydrochloric acid? (*b*) 1 mole of sulfuric acid? (*c*) 1 mole of phosphoric acid? (*d*) Write the equation for each reaction.
17. (*a*) What mass of calcium hydroxide is required to prepare 1.0 liter of 0.010-*N* solution? (*b*) to prepare 1.0 liter of 0.010-*M* solution?
18. (*a*) What volume of water contains a mole of H_3O^+ ions? (*b*) How many equivalents of hydronium ions is this? (*c*) How many grams of H_3O^+ ion? (*d*) What is the mole-concentration of OH^- ion in this volume of water? (*e*) How many equivalents of hydroxide ions is this? (*f*) How many grams of OH^- ion?
19. What is the normality of (*a*) a 0.0040-*M* solution of copper(II) chloride? (*b*) a 0.15-*M* solution of potassium hydroxide? (*c*) a 2-*M* solution of sulfuric acid?
20. What is the molarity of (*a*) a 0.006-*N* solution of hydroiodic acid? (*b*) a 0.0036-*N* solution of aluminum sulfate? (*c*) a 0.030-*N* solution of barium hydroxide?
21. The titration experiment on page 321 suggests a good magic show act. How would you prepare two colorless solutions that would instantly change bright red when one is poured into the other?

PROBLEMS

Group A

1. (*a*) How many grams of sodium hydroxide are required to neutralize 54.75 g of hydrogen chloride in water solution? (*b*) How many moles of each reactant are involved in the reaction?
2. What quantity of potassium nitrate would you add to $50\bar{0}$ g of water to prepare a 0.250-*M* solution?
3. How many grams of sugar, $C_{12}H_{22}O_{11}$, are contained in 50.0 ml of an 0.800-*M* solution?
4. What is the molarity of a solution containing 49.0 g of H_2SO_4 in 3.00 liters of solution?
5. What is the molarity of a $CuBr_2$ solution that contains 446 g of solute in 5.00 liters of solution?
6. How many grams of NaCl are required to make $25\bar{0}$ ml of 0.500-*M* solution?
7. How many grams of $Al_2(SO_4)_3 \cdot 18\ H_2O$ are required to make $80\bar{0}$ ml of 0.300-*M* solution?
8. Calculate the mass of one equivalent of (*a*) K; (*b*) Ca; (*c*) NaCl; (*d*) $CuSO_4$; (*e*) $Na_2CO_3 \cdot 10H_2O$; (*f*) $FeCl_3 \cdot 6H_2O$.
9. What is the normality of a solution that contains 4.0 g of Na_2SO_4 per liter of solution?
10. Calculate the normality of a solution containing $71\bar{0}$ g of $Al(NO_3)_3$ in 15.0 liters of solution?
11. How many grams of $CuSO_4 \cdot 5\ H_2O$ are needed to make up $50\bar{0}$ ml of 0.100-*N* solution?
12. How many grams of $FeCl_3 \cdot 6H_2O$ are needed to prepare $20\bar{0}$ ml of 0.500-*N* solution?
13. (*a*) What is the pH of a 0.01-*M* solution of HCl, assuming complete ionization? (*b*) What is the $[OH^-]$ of a 0.01-*M* solution of sodium hydroxide? (*c*) What is the pH of this solution?
14. How many milliliters of a 0.150-*N* solution of a metallic hydroxide are required to neutralize 30.0 ml of a 0.500-*N* solution of an acid?

15. A chemistry student finds that it takes 34 ml of a 0.50-*N* acid solution to neutralize $1\bar{0}$ ml of a sample of household ammonia. What is the normality of the ammonia-water solution?

Group B

16. How many solute molecules are contained in each milliliter of a 0.1-*M* solution of a nonelectrolyte?
17. An excess of zinc reacts with $40\bar{0}$ ml of hydrochloric acid, and 2.55 liters of H_2 gas is collected over water at $2\bar{0}$°C and 745.0 mm. What is the molarity of the acid?
18. Concentrated hydrochloric acid has a density of 1.19 g/ml and contains 37.2% HCl by weight. How many milliliters of concentrated hydrochloric acid are required to prepare (*a*) 1.00 liter of 1.00-*M* HCl solution; (*b*) 2.00 liters of 3.00-*M* HCl solution; (*c*) 5.00 liters of 0.100-*N* HCl solution; (*d*) $25\bar{0}$ ml of 0.200-*N* HCl solution?
19. The stockroom supply of concentrated sulfuric acid is 95.0% H_2SO_4 by weight and has a density of 1.84 g/ml. How many milliliters of concentrated sulfuric acid are needed to prepare (*a*) 2.50 liters of 0.500-*M* H_2SO_4 solution; (*b*) $10\bar{0}$ ml of 0.250-*M* H_2SO_4 solution; (*c*) 1.00 liter of 1.00-*N* H_2SO_4 solution; (*d*) 3.00 liters of 0.200-*N* H_2SO_4 solution?
20. In a laboratory titration, 15.0 ml of 0.275-*M* H_2SO_4 solution neutralizes 20.0 ml of NaOH solution. What is the molarity of the NaOH solution?
21. Suppose a 10.0 ml sample of vinegar is diluted to $10\bar{0}$ ml with distilled water and titrated against 0.100-*M* sodium hydroxide solution. From the burets, 30.0 ml of the diluted vinegar and 25.0 ml of the solution of the base were withdrawn. What percentage of acetic acid, $HC_2H_3O_2$, does the vinegar contain?
22. A solution is determined experimentally to have a pH of 2.9. (*a*) Find the $[H_3O^+]$. (*b*) What is the $[OH^-]$?
23. Find the pH of a 0.02-*M* LiOH solution.
24. What is the pH of a 0.054-*M* solution of HCl?
25. Suppose 25.0 ml of 0.150-*M* NaOH and 50.0 ml of 0.100-*M* HCl solutions are mixed. What is the pH of the resulting solution?

chapter 17

CARBON AND ITS OXIDES

Diamond has something in common with a chunk of coal. (See Question 56 on page 368.)

Carbon

17.1 Abundance and importance of carbon

Charcoal and soot are forms of carbon that have been known from earliest times. But the elemental nature of carbon, its occurrence in charcoal, and its existence as diamond and graphite were not discovered until the late eighteenth century.

Carbon ranks seventeenth in abundance by weight among the elements in the earth's crust. In importance, carbon ranks far higher. Carbon is present in body tissue and in the foods we eat. It is found in coal, petroleum, natural gas, limestone, and in all living things. In addition to its natural occurrence, chemists have synthesized hundreds of thousands of carbon compounds in the laboratory.

The study of carbon compounds is so important that it forms a separate branch of chemistry called *organic chemistry*. Originally, organic chemistry was defined as the study of materials derived from living organisms. Inorganic chemistry was the study of materials derived from mineral sources. We have known for over a century that this is not a clear distinction. Many substances identical to those produced in living things can also be made from mineral materials. As a result, ***organic chemistry*** *today includes the study of carbon compounds whether or not these are produced by living organisms.*

In most substances containing carbon, the carbon is present in the *combined* form. It is usually united with hydrogen, or with hydrogen and oxygen. In this chapter, we shall first describe carbon in its *free* or *uncombined* forms. Then we shall consider carbon dioxide and carbon monoxide.

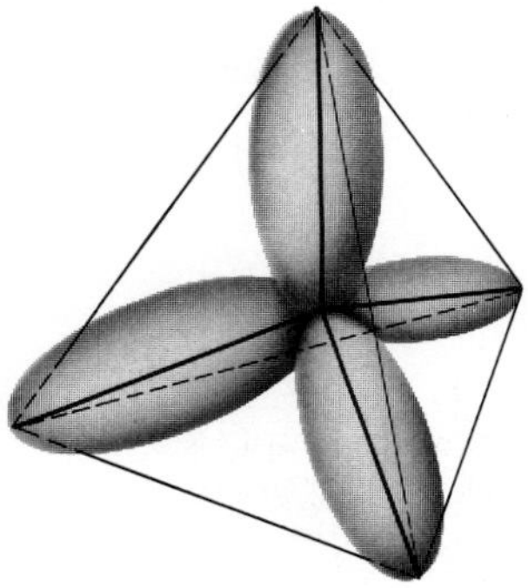

Fig. 17-1. In sp^3 hybridization, the four covalent bonds of a carbon atom are directed in space toward the four vertices of a regular tetrahedron. The nucleus of the atom is at the center of the tetrahedron.

Hybridization was explained in Section 6.17.

17.2 Characteristics of carbon atoms

Carbon is the element with atomic number 6 and electron configuration $1s^2 2s^2 2p^2$. On the periodic table, it is in the second period, midway between the active metal lithium and the active nonmetal fluorine. The two 1*s* electrons are tightly bound to the nucleus. The two 2*s* electrons and the two 2*p* electrons are the valence electrons. Carbon atoms show a very strong tendency to share electrons and form covalent bonds. This electron sharing usually has the effect of producing a stable outer-shell octet about a carbon atom. Having four valence electrons makes it possible for a carbon atom to form four covalent bonds. These bonds are directed in space toward the four vertices of a regular tetrahedron. This arrangement of carbon valence bonds is explained by sp^3 hybridization. The nucleus of the atom is at the center of the tetrahedron. See Figure 17-1.

The property of forming covalent bonds is so strong in carbon atoms that they join readily with other elements. They also link together with other carbon atoms in chains, rings, plates, and networks. The variety of ways in which carbon atoms can be linked explains why there are several times as many carbon compounds as noncarbon compounds.

17.3 Allotropic forms of carbon

Allotropy occurs for either of two reasons: (1) An element has two or more kinds of molecules, each with different numbers of atoms, which exist in the same phase; or (2) an element has two or more different arrangements of atoms or molecules in a crystal.

In Section 9.11, the allotropic forms of the element oxygen, oxygen molecules, O_2, and ozone molecules, O_3, were described. Allotropy was defined as the existence of an element in two or more forms in the same physical phase. The reason for oxygen's allotropy is the existence of two kinds of molecules, each with different numbers of atoms.

Carbon occurs in two solid allotropic forms. *Diamond* is a hard crystalline form. *Graphite* is a soft, grayish-black crystalline form. The reason for carbon's allotropy is the existence of two different arrangements of atoms in a crystal.

When substances that contain combined carbon are decomposed by heat, they leave black residues. These residues are sometimes collectively called *amorphous carbon* because they seem to have no definite crystalline shape. Examples of amorphous carbon are *coke, charcoal, boneblack,* and *carbon black.* Studies of the structures of these substances have been made by X-ray scattering. These studies reveal that the various forms of so-called amorphous carbon actually contain regions in which the carbon atoms are arranged in an orderly way. In carbon black, for example, the carbon atoms are arranged somewhat as they are in a layer of graphite.

17.4 Diamond

The most famous diamond mines in the world are located in South Africa. Diamonds in this region usually occur in the shafts of extinct volcanoes. It is believed that they were formed slowly under extreme heat and pressure. Diamonds, as they are mined, do not have the shape or sparkle of gem stones. The art of cutting and polishing gives them their brilliant appearance.

Synthetic diamonds are chemically identical to natural diamonds but are produced in the laboratory. They are prepared by subjecting graphite and a metal that acts as solvent and catalyst to extremely high pressure (55,000 atm) and high temperature (2,000°C) for nearly a day.

A solvent is a dissolving medium; a catalyst is a substance that increases the rate of a chemical reaction without itself being permanently changed.

Diamond is the hardest material. It is the densest form of carbon, about 3.5 times as dense as water. Both the hardness (resistance to wear) and density are explained by its structure. Figure 17-2 shows that carbon atoms in diamond are covalently bonded in a strong, compact fashion. The distances between the carbon nuclei are 1.54 Å. Note that each carbon atom is tetrahedrally oriented to its four nearest neighbors. This type of structure gives the crystal a great deal of strength in all three dimensions.

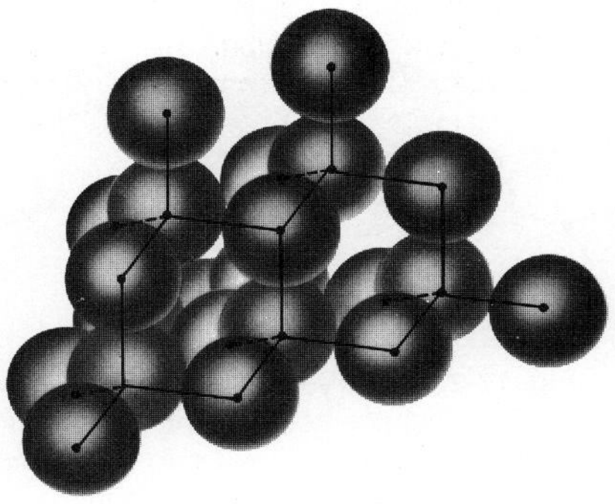

Fig. 17-2. The crystal structure of diamond.

The rigidity of its structure gives diamond its hardness. The compactness, resulting from the small distances between nuclei, gives diamond its high density. The covalent network structure of diamond accounts for its extremely high melting point, above 3500°C. Since all the valence electrons are used in forming covalent bonds, none can migrate. This explains why diamond is a nonconductor of electricity. Besides its use as a gem, diamond is used for cutting, drilling, and grinding because of its extreme hardness. A diamond is used as a long-lasting phonograph needle.

Diamond is the best conductor of heat. A perfect single diamond crystal conducts heat more than five times better than silver or copper. Silver and copper are the best metallic conductors. In diamond, heat is conducted by the transfer of energy of vibration from one carbon atom to the next. In a perfect single diamond crystal, this process is very efficient. The carbon atoms have a small mass. The forces binding the atoms together are strong and can easily transfer vibratory motion from one atom to another. The combination of nonconduction of electricity and excellent heat conduction may make diamond useful in semiconductor devices.

Diamond is insoluble in ordinary solvents. In 1772, the French chemist Lavoisier burned a clear diamond in pure oxygen and obtained carbon dioxide as a product. This experiment proved to him that diamond contains carbon. The English chemist Smithson Tennant repeated the experiment in 1797. He found that the mass of carbon dioxide produced was the same as that which would be produced if diamond were pure carbon. Both of these experiments provided conclusive evidence that diamond is pure carbon.

Smithson Tennant was the discoverer of the transition elements osmium, atomic number 76, and iridium, atomic number 77. He discovered these in impure platinum.

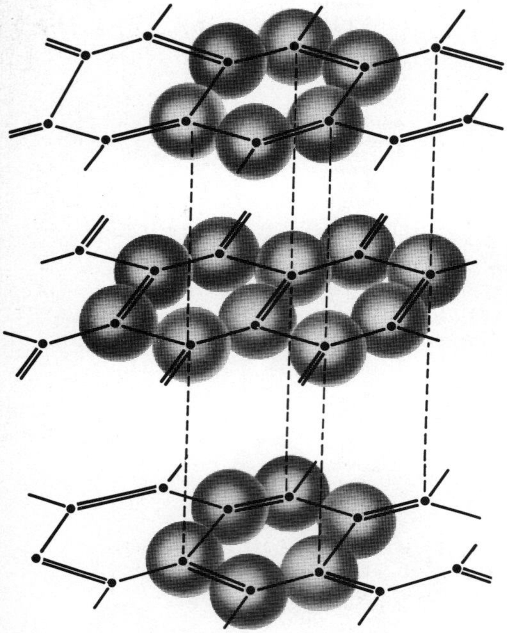

Fig. 17-3. The crystal structure of graphite. The distance between the layers has been exaggerated in order to show the structure of each layer more clearly.

Resonance was explained in Section 6.22.

17.5 Graphite

Natural graphite deposits are found throughout the world. The major producers are the Republic of Korea, Austria, North Korea, and the Soviet Union.

More than 70% of the graphite used in the United States is synthetic graphite. Most of this synthetic graphite is produced from petroleum coke. The process involves heating petroleum coke to about 2800°C in special furnaces.

Graphite is nearly as remarkable for its softness as diamond is for its hardness. It is easily crumbled and has a greasy feel. Graphite crystals are hexagonal (six-sided) in cross-section, with a density of about 2.25 g/cm^3. Although graphite is a nonmetal, it is a fairly good conductor of electricity.

The structure of graphite readily explains these properties. The carbon atoms in graphite are arranged in layers of thin hexagonal plates (Figure 17-3). The distance between the centers of adjacent carbon atoms within a layer is 1.42 Å. This distance is less than the distance between adjacent carbon atoms in diamond. However, the distance between the centers of atoms in adjacent layers is 3.35 Å.

Figure 17-3 shows the bonding within a layer of graphite. Each carbon atom in a layer is bonded to only three other carbon atoms in that layer. This bonding consists of single and double covalent bonds between carbon atoms. When represented in this fashion, three *different* equivalent patterns appear. In each of these, some carbon-carbon bonds are single and others are double. There is, however, no experimental evidence that the bonds in a layer of graphite are of these two distinct types. On the contrary, the evidence indicates that the bonds are all the same. The layers of graphite have a resonance structure in which the carbon-carbon bonds are intermediate in character between single and double bonds. Each layer in graphite is a strongly bonded covalent network structure. As with diamond, this structure gives graphite a very high melting point, about 3500°C. The strong bonds between the carbon atoms within a layer make graphite difficult to pull apart in the direction of the layer. Carbon fibers, in which the carbon is in the form of graphite, are very strong.

The layers of carbon atoms in graphite are too far apart for the formation of covalent bonds between them. They are held together by weak dispersion interaction forces. These forces result from electron motion within the layers. The weak attraction between layers accounts for the softness of graphite and its greasy feel as one layer slides over another.

On the average, the carbon atoms in graphite are farther apart than they are in diamond, so graphite has a lower density. The mobile electrons in each carbon-atom layer make graphite a fairly good conductor of electricity. Like diamond, graphite does not dissolve in any ordinary solvent. Similarly, it forms carbon dioxide when burned in oxygen.

17.6 Uses of graphite

The largest single use of natural graphite is for coating the molds used in metal casting. It is also used to increase the carbon content of steel and to make clay-graphite crucibles in which steel and other metals are melted. All of these applications take advantage of the very high melting point of graphite. Graphite is a very good lubricant. It is sometimes mixed with petroleum jelly to form a graphite grease. It can be used for lubricating machine parts that operate at temperatures too high for the usual petroleum lubricants. Graphite leaves a gray streak or mark when it is drawn across a sheet of paper. In making "lead" pencils, graphite is powdered, mixed with clay, and then formed into sticks. The hardness of a pencil depends upon the relative amount of clay that is used.

The most important use of synthetic graphite is in electrodes for electric-arc steelmaking furnaces. Synthetic graphite electrodes are also used in the electrolysis of salt water for making chlorine and sodium hydroxide. Graphite does not react with acids, bases, and organic and inorganic solvents. These properties make it useful for equipment for a variety of processes in the food, chemical, and petroleum industries. Graphite is also used in nuclear reactors.

If certain synthetic fibers are combined with plastic resins and heated under pressure, they become carbon fibers. As mentioned in Section 17.5, the form of carbon in these fibers is graphite. Carbon fibers are less dense than steel but are stronger and stiffer. They are being used in aircraft floor decking and wing flaps, and in weather and communication satellites. In sporting goods, carbon fibers are used to make golf club shafts, tennis rackets, fishing rods, and bicycle frames.

Fig. 17-4. Graphite fibers in this tennis racquet give it stiffness and light weight.

17.7 Destructive distillation

Suppose a complex material containing compounds of carbon such as wood or bituminous coal is *heated in a closed container without access to air or oxygen. The complex material decomposes into simpler substances.* This process is known as ***destructive distillation.*** Coke, charcoal, and boneblack are prepared by destructive distillation of coal, wood, and bones, respectively.

17.8 Coke

When bituminous coal is heated in a hard-glass test tube, a gas escapes that is flammable. It burns readily if mixed with air and ignited. Also, a tar-like liquid condenses on the upper walls of the tube. If the heating is continued until all the volatile material is driven off, coke is left as a residue.

Commercially, coke is prepared by destructive distillation of bituminous coal in by-product coke ovens. The volatile (easily vaporized) products are separated into *coal gas, am-*

monia, and *coal tar*. Coal gas can be used as a fuel. Ammonia is used in making fertilizers. Coal tar can be separated by distillation into many useful materials. These materials are used to make drugs, dyes, and explosives. The black pitch that remains after distillation of coal tar is used to surface roads.

Nearly 70,000,000 tons of coke are produced each year in the United States. Coke is a gray, porous solid that is harder and denser than charcoal. It burns with little flame, has a high heat content, and is a valuable fuel.

Coke is an excellent reducing agent. It is widely used in obtaining the metals from the ores of iron, tin, copper, and zinc. These ores are either oxides or are converted into oxides. Coke readily reduces the metals in these oxides. It also has great structural strength and is free from volatile impurities.

Fig. 17-5. Coke is produced by the destructive distillation of bituminous coal in by-product coke ovens. Here the red-hot coke is being discharged from an oven into a waiting railroad car.

17.9 Charcoal

Destructive distillation of wood yields several gases that can be burned. It also produces methanol (wood alcohol), acetic acid, and other volatile products. The solid part, or *residue*, that remains is charcoal. Charcoal is prepared commercially by heating wood in *retorts*. These are closed containers in which substances are distilled or decomposed by heat. The burnable gases that result provide supplementary fuel. The other volatile products may be condensed and sold as by-products.

Adsorption was defined in Section 9.18 and further explained in Section 13.2.

Charcoal is a porous, black, brittle solid. It is odorless and tasteless. It is denser than water, but it often adsorbs enough gas to make it float on water. This ability to *adsorb* a large quantity of gas is the most remarkable physical property of charcoal. One cubic centimeter of freshly prepared willow charcoal adsorbs about 90 cubic centimeters of ammonia gas. Charcoal has also been used to adsorb toxic waste products from the blood of persons suffering from liver failure.

At ordinary temperatures, charcoal is inactive and insoluble in all ordinary solvents. It is a good reducing agent because it unites with oxygen at a high temperature. Charcoal is also a good fuel, but it is more expensive than other common fuels.

17.10 Boneblack

Animal charcoal, or *boneblack*, is produced by the destructive distillation of bones. The by-products of the process include bone oil and pyridine. These products are used for *denaturing* alcohol (making it unfit for humans to drink). Boneblack usually contains calcium phosphate as an impurity. This can be removed by treating the boneblack with an acid.

17.11 Activated carbon

Activated carbon is a form of carbon that is prepared in a way that gives it a very large internal surface area. This large surface area makes activated carbon useful for the adsorption of liquid or gaseous substances. Activated carbon can be made from a variety of carbon-containing materials. Such a material is first destructively distilled. The carbon produced is treated with steam or carbon dioxide at about 100°C. These two processes produce a very porous form of carbon. This porosity creates a very large internal surface area. The surface area of a portion of activated carbon may be as high as 2000 m^2/g, most of the area being internal.

Activated carbon used for adsorption of gases must have a small pore structure. Coconut and other nut shells are the best sources of this type of activated carbon. Gas-adsorbent activated carbon is used in gas masks. It is also used for the recovery of volatile solvent vapors and the removal of impurities from gases in industrial processes. This form of activated carbon can remove odors from the air circulated by large air conditioning systems in offices, restaurants, and theaters.

Activated carbon used for adsorption from the liquid phase comes from both animal and vegetable sources. Boneblack was first used for this purpose, but now such activated carbon is also made from coal, peat, and wood. Inorganic impurities are removed from activated carbon that is to be used in processing food or chemical products. Acids such as dilute hydrochloric or sulfuric react with these impurities to form soluble products that are washed away with water. Liquid-adsorbent activated carbon is used in the refining of cane sugar, beet sugar, and corn syrup. It is also used in municipal and industrial water treatment to adsorb impurities that would give the water an objectionable odor and taste.

Fig. 17-6. Activated charcoal is used in some cigarette filters. Even though it adsorbs impurities from gases and liquids efficiently, some tar and nicotine pass through.

17.12 Other forms of amorphous carbon

Finely divided particles of carbon are set free when liquid or gaseous fuels composed of carbon and hydrogen are burned in an insufficient supply of air. We commonly call these particles *soot.* Soot is an example of the form of amorphous carbon called *carbon black.* Commercially, the production of carbon black involves making soot under carefully controlled conditions.

The most important method of making carbon black is called the *furnace process.* The furnace is made of materials that have high melting points, such as fire brick. In making carbon black, three materials are introduced into the furnace:

1. A spray of liquid fuel or the gaseous fuel vapor.

2. An additional fuel, such as natural gas. Petroleum-refinery gas, the fuel gas produced when petroleum is refined, may also be used. So may coal gas, the fuel gas produced by destructive distillation of bituminous coal in by-product ovens.

3. Air, as a source of oxygen.

The supply of oxygen is so low that the fuels are only partially burned in the furnace. But enough fuel burns to provide the energy needed for decomposing the rest of the fuel. The carbon black is collected from the combustion products.

Over 95% of all carbon black produced is used in natural and synthetic rubber. It adds bulk to the rubber and acts as a reinforcing agent. Most of this rubber is used in tires. Carbon black helps to preserve the rubber and makes the tire wear longer. The second largest use of carbon black is in printer's ink. Other uses are in paints, phonograph records, carbon paper, and in coloring plastics and synthetic fibers.

An oil residue remains after the refining of crude petroleum. When destructively distilled, this residue produces a form of amorphous carbon called *petroleum coke.* Rods of petroleum coke are converted to synthetic graphite for use as electrodes. Such electrodes are used as the positive electrodes in dry cells. They also are used in the production of aluminum by electrolysis.

Carbon Dioxide

17.13 Occurrence

Carbon dioxide comprises only about 0.03% of the earth's atmosphere by volume. But it is a very important component of the air. The water of rivers, lakes, and oceans contains about 60 times as much dissolved carbon dioxide as the atmosphere. The decay of organic matter and the burning of fossil fuels both produce carbon dioxide. So do the respiration processes of living things. Carbon dioxide is somewhat denser than air. So it sometimes gathers in relatively high amounts in low-lying areas such as bogs, swamps, and marshes. It may also collect in mines, caves, and caverns. Some natural gases contain significant amounts of carbon dioxide.

The atmosphere of the planet Venus is 97% carbon dioxide by volume, with an atmospheric pressure 90 times that on the earth. On Mars, carbon dioxide is also the most abundant component of the atmosphere. It is 95% by volume of the Martian atmosphere. But the atmospheric pressure on Mars is only about $\frac{1}{200}$ of that on the earth.

17.14 Preparation of carbon dioxide

1. By burning material that contains the element carbon. Carbon dioxide is one of the products of the complete combustion in oxygen or air of any material that contains carbon. If air is used, the carbon dioxide prepared in this way is mixed with other gases. But if these gases do not interfere with the intended use of the carbon dioxide, this method is by far the cheapest and easiest.

$$\textbf{C (combined)} + \mathbf{O_2} \rightarrow \mathbf{CO_2}$$

2. By reaction of steam and natural gas. Natural gas is usually a mixture of several gaseous compounds of carbon and hydrogen. The principal component of natural gas is methane, CH_4. Methane undergoes a series of reactions with steam in the presence of metallic oxide catalysts at temperatures between 500°C and 1000°C. The end products of these reactions are carbon dioxide and hydrogen. The equation for the overall reaction is

$$\mathbf{CH_4 + 2H_2O \rightarrow 4H_2 + CO_2}$$

The primary purpose of this reaction is the preparation of hydrogen for making synthetic ammonia. The carbon dioxide is a by-product. The carbon dioxide is separated from the hydrogen by dissolving the carbon dioxide in cold water under high pressure.

3. *By fermentation of molasses.* The enzymes of *zymase* are produced by yeast. They catalyze the fermentation of the sugar, $C_6H_{12}O_6$, in molasses. This fermentation produces ethanol (ethyl alcohol) and carbon dioxide. While the process is complex, the overall reaction is

$$\mathbf{C_6H_{12}O_6(aq) \rightarrow 2C_2H_5OH(aq) + 2CO_2(g)}$$

This equation represents a method by which some industrial alcohol is produced. The process is also an important source of carbon dioxide.

4. *By heating a carbonate.* When calcium carbonate (as limestone, marble, or shells) is heated strongly, calcium oxide and carbon dioxide are the products.

$$\mathbf{CaCO_3 \rightarrow CaO + CO_2}$$

Calcium oxide, known as *quicklime,* is used for making plaster and mortar. The carbon dioxide is a by-product.

5. *By the action of an acid on a carbonate.* This is the usual laboratory method for preparing carbon dioxide. The gas-generating bottle in Figure 17-7 contains a few pieces of marble, $CaCO_3$. If dilute hydrochloric acid is poured through the funnel tube, carbon dioxide is given off rapidly. Calcium chloride may be recovered from the solution in the bottle.

This reaction proceeds in two stages. *First,* the marble and hydrochloric acid undergo an exchange reaction:

$$\mathbf{CaCO_3(s) + 2HCl(aq) \rightarrow CaCl_2(aq) + H_2CO_3(aq)}$$

Second, carbonic acid is unstable and decomposes:

$$\mathbf{H_2CO_3(aq) \rightarrow H_2O(l) + CO_2(g)}$$

The equation that summarizes these two reactions is

$$\mathbf{CaCO_3(s) + 2HCl(aq) \rightarrow CaCl_2(aq) + H_2O(l) + CO_2(g)}$$

Even though carbon dioxide is soluble in water, it may be collected by water displacement if it is generated rapidly. It may also be collected by displacement of air. In this case, the receiver must be kept *mouth upward* because carbon dioxide is denser than air.

Fig. 17-7. Carbon dioxide is prepared in the laboratory by the reaction of dilute hydrochloric acid on marble chips, calcium carbonate. Carbon dioxide is collected by water displacement.

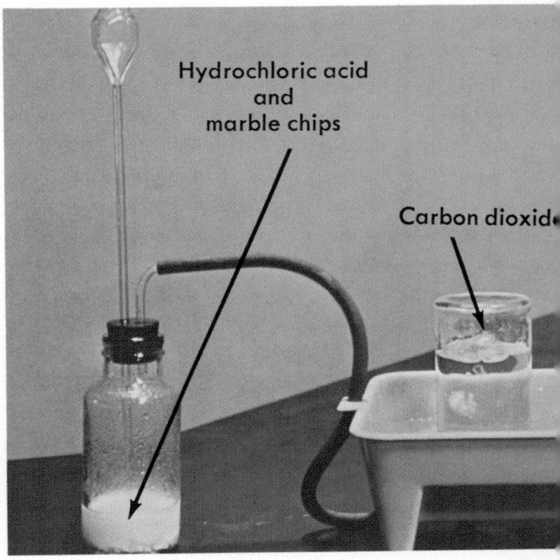

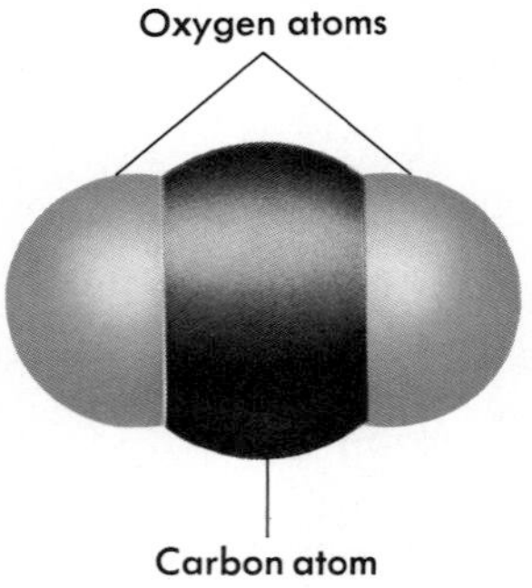

Fig. 17-8. A carbon dioxide molecule is linear and consists of one carbon atom and two oxygen atoms.

This reaction is an example of the general reaction of an acid and carbonate. Almost any acid may be used, even a weak one such as the acetic acid in vinegar. Almost any carbonate may also be used, provided its cation does not have an interfering reaction with the anion of the acid. The ionic equation for the reaction is

$$CO_3^{--} + 2H_3O^+ \rightarrow 3H_2O + CO_2(g)$$

6. *By respiration and decay.* This process is a natural method of preparing carbon dioxide. The foods we eat contain compounds of carbon. Oxygen from the air we inhale is used in oxidizing this food. This oxidation supplies us with energy to maintain body temperature, move muscles, synthesize new compounds in the body, and transmit nerve impulses. Carbon dioxide, which we exhale into the air, is one of the products of this oxidation. All living things give off carbon dioxide during respiration.

When plants and animals die, decay begins and carbon dioxide is produced. This gas eventually finds its way into the surrounding air, or becomes dissolved in surface or underground streams.

17.15 Structure of carbon dioxide molecules

Carbon dioxide molecules are linear, with two oxygen atoms bonded on opposite sides of the carbon atom. See Figure 17-8. The carbon-oxygen bonds in the molecule are somewhat polar. This polarity is explained by the electronegativity difference between carbon and oxygen. However, the arrangement of these bonds, exactly opposite one another, causes the molecule to be nonpolar.

Considering the electron-dot symbols for carbon and oxygen, we might assign carbon dioxide molecules the electron-dot formula

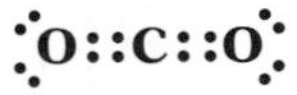

However, this formula is not strictly accurate. The carbon-oxygen bond distance predicted by it is larger than that actually found in carbon dioxide molecules. Carbon dioxide molecules are believed to be *resonance hybrids of four electron-dot structures*. Each of these structures shown at the left contributes about equally to the actual structure.

Such a resonance hybrid has the carbon-oxygen bond distance and energy actually observed for carbon dioxide molecules.

17.16 Physical properties of carbon dioxide

Carbon dioxide is a gas at room temperature. This fact supports our theory that it has a simple nonpolar molecular structure. Carbon dioxide is colorless with a faintly irritating odor and a slightly sour taste. The molecular weight of carbon dioxide is 44. Thus, its density is about 1.5 times that of air at the same temperature and pressure. The large, heavy molecules of carbon dioxide gas move more slowly than the smaller, lighter molecules of gaseous oxygen or hydrogen. Because of its high density and slow rate of diffusion, carbon dioxide can be poured from one vessel to another.

At high pressures, the molecules of a gas are much closer together than they are at a pressure of one atmosphere. At a pressure of about 70 atmospheres and room temperature, molecules of carbon dioxide attract each other strongly enough to condense to a liquid. If this liquid is permitted to evaporate rapidly under atmospheric pressure, part of it changes into a gas. This process absorbs heat from the remaining liquid, which is thus cooled until it solidifies in the form called *Dry Ice*.

Solid carbon dioxide has a high vapor pressure. Many molecules of solid carbon dioxide possess enough energy to escape from the surface of the solid into the air. The vapor pressure of solid carbon dioxide equals atmospheric pressure at −78.5°C. As a result, solid carbon dioxide under atmospheric pressure sublimes (changes directly from a solid to a gas) at this temperature. Liquid carbon dioxide does not exist at atmospheric pressure. It can exist only at low temperatures with pressures higher than 5 atmospheres.

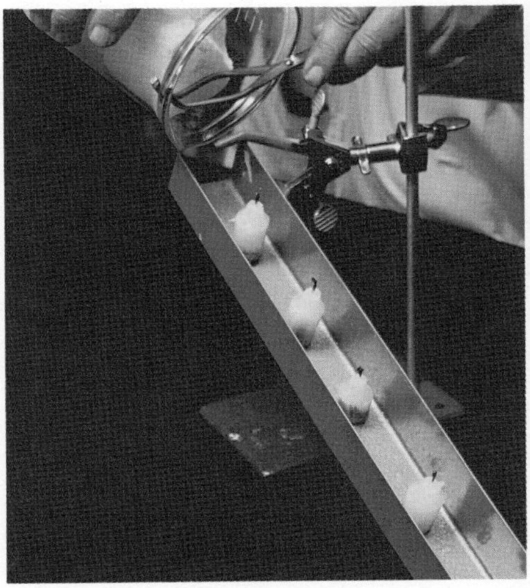

Fig. 17-9. Carbon dioxide can be poured down this stair of candles because of its high density and slow rate of diffusion. The candles are extinguished because carbon dioxide does not support combustion.

17.17 Chemical properties of carbon dioxide

Carbon dioxide has a critical temperature of 31.1°C and a critical pressure of 73.0 atm (Section 12.7). The liquid carbon dioxide in a fire extinguisher is under a pressure of 60 atm.

Carbon dioxide is a stable gas. It neither burns nor supports combustion. However, burning magnesium is hot enough to decompose carbon dioxide. A piece of burning magnesium ribbon continues to burn in a bottle of the gas. The magnesium unites vigorously with the oxygen set free by the decomposition. Carbon is produced, as shown by a coating of soot on the inside of the bottle.

$$\mathbf{2Mg(s) + CO_2(g) \rightarrow 2MgO(s) + C(s)}$$

Carbon dioxide dissolves readily in cold water. A few of the dissolved molecules also unite with the water and form carbonic acid. Carbon dioxide is therefore the acid anhydride of carbonic acid.

An acid anhydride is the compound formed by removal of water from an acid.

$$\mathbf{H_2O + CO_2 \rightleftarrows H_2CO_3}$$

Almost all of the H_2CO_3 molecules ionize. Carbonic acid exists in water solution principally as ions.

$$\mathbf{H_2O + H_2CO_3 \rightleftarrows H_3O^+ + HCO_3^-}$$

$$\mathbf{H_2O + HCO_3^- \rightleftarrows H_3O^+ + CO_3^{--}}$$

Carbonic acid is a weak acid because of the slight reaction between CO_2 and H_2O, even though the few H_2CO_3 molecules formed ionize extensively. Carbonic acid is easily decomposed by heat since CO_2 is less soluble at higher temperatures. The reduction of the concentration of CO_2 in the water causes all the equilibria to shift to the left. This shift further decreases the H_2CO_3 and H_3O^+ concentrations.

When carbon dioxide is passed into a water solution of a hydroxide, it reacts and forms a carbonate.

$$\mathbf{CO_2 + 2OH^- \rightarrow CO_3^{--} + H_2O}$$

If the positive ion of the hydroxide forms an insoluble carbonate, it is precipitated when carbon dioxide passes through the hydroxide solution.

A *test for carbon dioxide* is to bubble the gas through a saturated solution of $Ca(OH)_2$, called limewater. A precipitate of white calcium carbonate indicates the presence of carbon dioxide.

$$\mathbf{Ca^{++} + 2OH^- + CO_2 \rightarrow Ca^{++}CO_3^{--}(s) + H_2O}$$

If excess carbon dioxide gas is bubbled through the solution, the precipitate disappears. It does so because the excess carbon dioxide reacts with the precipitate and water and forms soluble calcium hydrogen carbonate.

$$\mathbf{Ca^{++}CO_3^{--} + H_2O + CO_2 \rightarrow Ca^{++} + 2HCO_3^-}$$

As stated earlier (Section 17.13), normal air contains about 0.03% carbon dioxide by volume. The air in a crowded, poorly ventilated room may contain as much as 1% carbon dioxide by volume. A concentration of from about 0.1% to 1% brings on a feeling of drowsiness and a headache. Concentrations of 8% to 10% or more cause death from lack of oxygen.

17.18 Uses of carbon dioxide

1. It is necessary for photosynthesis. ***Photosynthesis*** *means "putting together by means of light."* It is a complex process by which green plants manufacture carbohydrates with the aid of sunlight. *Chlorophyll,* the green coloring matter of plants, acts as a catalyst. Carbon dioxide from the air and water from the soil are the raw materials. Glucose, a simple sugar, $C_6H_{12}O_6$, is one of the products. The following simplified equation gives only the *reactants* and the *final products.*

$$\mathbf{6CO_2 + 12H_2O \rightarrow C_6H_{12}O_6 + 6O_2 + 6H_2O}$$

The sugar may then be converted into a great variety of other plant products. The oxygen is given off to the atmosphere. Photosynthesis and the various other natural and artificial methods of producing atmospheric carbon dioxide comprise the *oxygen-carbon dioxide cycle.*

2. Carbon dioxide is used in fire extinguishers. When the *soda-acid type* of fire extinguisher is inverted, sulfuric acid reacts with sodium hydrogen carbonate solution.

$$\mathbf{2NaHCO_3(aq) + H_2SO_4(aq) \rightarrow Na_2SO_4(aq) + 2H_2O(l) + 2CO_2(g}$$

The pressure of the gas forces a stream of liquid a considerable distance. The carbon dioxide dissolved in the liquid helps put out the fire, but water is the main extinguishing agent.

The *foam type* of fire extinguisher contains a solution of aluminum sulfate, $Al_2(SO_4)_3$. This solution contains hydronium ions because of the reaction of aluminum sulfate with the water in which it is dissolved.

$$2Al^{+++} + 3SO_4^{--} + 4H_2O \rightleftarrows 2Al(OH)^{++} + 2H_3O^{+} + 3SO_4^{--}$$

The hydronium ions of the aluminum sulfate solution react with sodium hydrogen carbonate solution and carbon dioxide is given off.

$$Na^{+} + HCO_3^{-} + H_3O^{+} \rightarrow Na^{+} + 2H_2O + CO_2(g)$$

A sticky substance is dissolved in the sodium hydrogen carbonate solution. This substance strengthens the foam bubbles so that the gas does not escape from them. The sprayed foam forms a thick, frothy blanket where it falls. It shuts off the air, smothering the fire. Foam fire extinguishers are particularly effective for putting out oil and gasoline fires.

Liquid carbon dioxide fire extinguishers are widely used and very efficient. When the valve is opened, the nozzle directs a stream of carbon dioxide "snow" against the flame. Such an extinguisher is effective against oil fires. Also, it may be used around electric switchboards where water would be hazardous.

Fig. 17-10. A liquid carbon dioxide fire extinguisher is effective in putting out oil fires.

3. *Carbonated beverages contain carbon dioxide in solution.* Soft drinks are carbonated by forcing the gas into the beverages under pressure. When the bottles are opened, the excess pressure is released. Bubbles of carbon dioxide then escape rapidly from the liquid.

4. *Leavening agents produce carbon dioxide.* Yeast is a common leavening agent. It is mixed with the flour and other ingredients used in making dough for bread. The living yeast plants produce enzymes which ferment the starches and sugars in the dough. This fermentation reaction produces ethanol and carbon dioxide. The carbon dioxide forms bubbles in the soft dough, causing it to "rise," or decrease in density. The ethanol is vaporized and driven off during the baking process.

Baking powder differs from baking soda, which is the compound sodium hydrogen carbonate. Baking powder is not a compound. Instead, it is a dry mixture of compounds. It contains baking soda, which can yield the carbon dioxide. It also contains some powder that forms an acid when water is added. The acid compound varies with the kind of baking powder used. Cornstarch is used in baking powders to keep them dry until they are used.

5. *Carbon dioxide is used as a refrigerant.* Dry Ice costs more

than ice for refrigeration. But it is superior to ice in two respects. First, it leaves no liquid because it changes directly from a solid to a gas. Also, because of its low temperature, Dry Ice produces a greater cooling effect than an equal weight of ice. The temperature of Dry Ice is so low that it *must never be handled with bare hands,* because serious frostbite may result.

Carbon Monoxide

17.19 The occurrence of carbon monoxide

Carbon monoxide is found in samples of the atmosphere all over the world. The amounts vary from 0.04 ppm over the South Pacific Ocean to 360 ppm at street level in a crowded city on a calm day. (Ppm means parts per million. 1 ppm = 0.0001%.) A safe amount of carbon monoxide is somewhat under 50 ppm.

In congested areas, the carbon monoxide in the air comes mainly from poorly burned fuels. The sources range from the chimney gases of improperly fired coal-burning furnaces to the exhaust gases from automobile engines. In the United States, as much as 90% of the people-caused carbon monoxide in the air may come from gasoline engines. Decaying plants and live algae add significant amounts of carbon monoxide to the air. It has been estimated that the oceans may release up to 85% as much carbon monoxide to the air as poorly burned fuels do.

Specialists estimate that the carbon monoxide produced on a given day remains in the air for about one to three months. Research is being carried out to determine what happens to carbon monoxide in the air, since no world-wide increase in its concentration has yet been detected. One explanation under study is that certain soil fungi convert carbon monoxide in the air to carbon dioxide. Another possible explanation is that carbon monoxide reacts with OH groups in the lower stratosphere and forms carbon dioxide and hydrogen.

Traces of carbon monoxide have been found in the atmospheres of Venus, Mars, and Jupiter. Carbon monoxide is widespread in the interstellar gas clouds of our galaxy, especially in regions where stars are being formed. Carbon monoxide has also been detected in galaxies outside our own.

17.20 Preparation of carbon monoxide

1. By reducing carbon dioxide. If carbon dioxide comes into contact with white-hot carbon or coke, it is reduced to carbon monoxide.

$$\mathbf{CO_2(g) + C(s) \rightarrow 2CO(g)}$$

2. By action of steam on hot coke. Passing steam over white-hot coke produces a mixture called *water gas.* This mixture consists mainly of carbon monoxide and hydrogen. This industrial method produces both carbon monoxide and hydrogen for use as fuel gases.

$$C(s) + H_2O(g) \rightarrow CO(g) + H_2(g)$$

The two gases may be separated by cooling and compression. This process liquefies the carbon monoxide but not the hydrogen.

3. *By decomposing formic acid.* This decomposition reaction is the usual laboratory method for preparing carbon monoxide. Formic acid, HCOOH, is introduced one drop at a time into hot, concentrated sulfuric acid. Carbon monoxide is produced as each drop strikes the hot acid (see Figure 17-11). Concentrated sulfuric acid is an excellent dehydrating agent. It removes a molecule of water from each molecule of the formic acid, leaving only carbon monoxide, CO.

$$HCOOH(l) \xrightarrow{H_2SO_4} H_2O(l) + CO(g)$$

CAUTION: *When using this method, be sure the connections are tight so that the carbon monoxide does not escape.* It is preferable to prepare carbon monoxide in a hood.

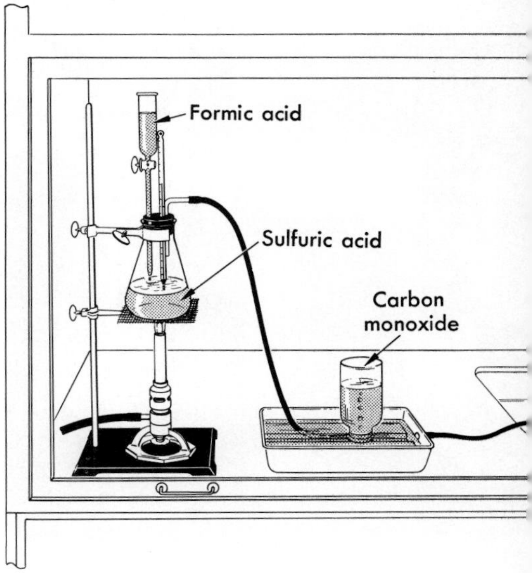

Fig. 17-11. Carbon monoxide can be prepared in the laboratory by decomposing formic acid with hot, concentrated sulfuric acid.

17.21 Structure of the carbon monoxide molecule

Carbon monoxide molecules consist of one carbon atom and one oxygen atom covalently bonded. See Figure 17-12. The distance between the nuclei is 1.13 Å. The molecule is slightly polar, with *the carbon atom somewhat negative.* In order to account for these properties, the carbon monoxide molecule is believed to be a resonance hybrid of four structures:

$$\left\{ \begin{matrix} {}^{+}\text{:C:}\ddot{\underset{\cdot\cdot}{\text{O}}}\text{:}^{-} & \text{:C::}\ddot{\text{O}}\text{:} \\ \text{:C::}\underset{\cdot\cdot}{\text{O}}\text{:} & {}^{-}\text{:C:::O:}^{+} \end{matrix} \right\}$$

Unlike carbon dioxide, however, these four structures do not contribute equally. The hybrid is estimated to be 10 percent $^{+}\text{:C:}\ddot{\underset{\cdot\cdot}{\text{O}}}\text{:}^{-}$, 20 percent each $\text{:C::}\ddot{\text{O}}\text{:}$ and $\text{:C::}\underset{\cdot\cdot}{\text{O}}\text{:}$, and 50 per cent $^{-}\text{:C:::O:}^{+}$. The electronegativity difference discussed in Chapter 6 indicates that the oxygen in carbon monoxide would be negative. However, you must remember that those data apply only to *single* bonds between elements. The structure of carbon monoxide is complicated. Carbon monoxide's stability at ordinary temperatures is explained by the effect of the high percentage of triple-bonded structure. It also gives the carbon atom the slight negative charge in the polar molecule.

Fig. 17-12. A carbon monoxide molecule is a slightly polar molecule consisting of one carbon atom and one oxygen atom.

17.22 Physical properties of carbon monoxide

Carbon monoxide is a colorless, odorless, tasteless gas. It is slightly less dense than air and is only slightly soluble in water. Carbon monoxide has a low critical temperature, −138.7°C, and a high critical pressure, 34.6 atm (atmospheres). These

Fig. 17-13. A firefighter wearing a self-contained breathing apparatus. This equipment furnishes air from the cylinder worn on the back through a hose to the face mask. With this equipment a fire-fighter can work safely in an atmosphere containing carbon monoxide.

data indicate that the attractive forces between carbon monoxide molecules are low. Consequently, carbon monoxide is not easily liquefied. Neither is it readily adsorbed by charcoal. However, charcoal can be treated with certain metallic oxides that oxidize carbon monoxide to carbon dioxide. Gas masks containing treated charcoal protect wearers against carbon monoxide concentrations up to 2%. In atmospheres containing more than 2% carbon monoxide, a self-contained breathing apparatus is needed. This equipment, often used by fire fighters, furnishes air from a cylinder of compressed air.

17.23 Chemical properties and uses of carbon monoxide

1. As a reducing agent. Carbon monoxide is used in the production of iron, copper, and other metals from their oxides.

$$Fe_2O_3(s) + 3CO(g) \rightarrow 2Fe(s) + 3CO_2(g)$$

2. As a fuel. Carbon monoxide burns with a blue flame. Many fuel gases contain carbon monoxide mixed with other gases that can be burned. Coal gas and water gas always contain some carbon monoxide.

3. For synthesizing organic compounds. Methanol, CH_3OH, is made from carbon monoxide and hydrogen under pressure. A mixture of oxides of copper, zinc, and chromium is used as a catalyst.

$$CO + 2H_2 \rightarrow CH_3OH$$

Carbon monoxide is also used in the synthesis of many other organic compounds.

17.24 The action of carbon monoxide on the human body

Carbon monoxide is poisonous because it unites very readily with *hemoglobin* molecules. Hemoglobin molecules in red blood cells serve as an oxygen carrier in the body's circulatory system. The attraction of hemoglobin for carbon monoxide is about 300 times greater than for oxygen. If carbon monoxide unites with hemoglobin, the hemoglobin is not available for carrying oxygen. When this happens, cells that need a lot of oxygen function less efficiently. Such cells are found in the heart, the skeletal muscles, and the central nervous system. Low levels of carbon monoxide thus impair a person's vision and reflexes. When persons breathe a large enough amount of carbon monoxide, they collapse because of oxygen starvation.

As stated earlier, Section 17.19, the safe level of carbon monoxide in the air is less than 50 ppm (parts per million). A person breathing air with as little as one part of carbon monoxide per thousand parts of air (1000 ppm) experiences nausea and headache in less than one hour. One part of carbon monoxide in one hundred parts of air (10,000 ppm) may kill people in ten minutes.

To repeat: Carbon monoxide is colorless, odorless, tasteless, and induces drowsiness before actual collapse and death. Therefore, *extreme care must be taken to see that it does not contaminate the air in closed areas.* If a coal-burning furnace is not properly operated, carbon monoxide may escape and mix with the air in living or sleeping rooms. An unvented gas heater, one without a chimney to the outside, is also a potential source of carbon monoxide in a home. Carbon monoxide is a component of some fuel gases. Leaking gas lines are dangerous because of the poisonous nature of the gas as well as the fire hazard. Carbon monoxide is present in the exhaust of internal combustion engines. Therefore, the engine of an automobile should never be left running in a closed garage. Similarly, an automobile should not be kept running to provide heat in a car parked with the windows closed. The smoke from burning tobacco contains up to 200 ppm of carbon monoxide. The blood of those who smoke contains several times the amount of hemoglobin-carbon monoxide found in the blood of nonsmokers.

SUMMARY

In combined form, carbon occurs in all living things. Foods, fuels, and carbonates contain combined carbon. In addition, hundreds of thousands of carbon compounds have been synthesized. Organic chemistry is the study of carbon compounds.

A carbon atom, with four valence electrons, forms covalent bonds with atoms of other elements or with other carbon atoms. Carbon atoms can link together in chains, rings, plates, and networks. The variety of ways in which carbon atoms can be linked accounts for the tremendous number of carbon compounds.

Uncombined carbon occurs in the crystalline allotropic forms, graphite and diamond. Amorphous carbon includes coke, charcoal, boneblack, carbon black, and petroleum coke. The forms of amorphous carbon seem to have no definite shape, but contain regions in which the carbon atoms are arranged in an orderly way nonetheless.

Diamond is the hardest substance known. Diamonds are used as gems, and for cutting, drilling, and grinding very hard substances. Graphite is a soft solid that is a conductor of electricity. It is used in metallurgy, in electrodes, as a lubricant, and for making "lead" pencils.

Coke, charcoal, and boneblack are prepared by the destructive distillation of coal, wood, and bones, respectively. Coke is used as a metallurgical reducing agent, while charcoal and boneblack are excellent adsorbents.

Activated carbon is a form of carbon having a very large internal surface area. The large surface area makes activated carbon useful for the adsorption of liquids and gases. It is used as a deodorizer, a decolorizer, and in gas masks.

Carbon black is produced by the incomplete combustion of fuels composed of carbon and hydrogen. It is used in automobile tires, printer's ink, paints, and plastics. Petroleum coke is used to make synthetic graphite electrodes.

At ordinary temperatures, all forms of carbon are inactive; but at higher temperatures they react with oxygen and form carbon dioxide.

Carbon dioxide is present in the air, although only in small amounts, as a result of decay, combustion, and the respiration of living things. Carbon dioxide can be prepared by burning carbon or carbon compounds, by reaction of steam and natural gas, by fermentation of molasses, by heating a carbonate, by the action of an acid on a carbonate, or by respiration and decay.

Carbon dioxide is a dense, colorless gas that is moderately soluble in water. Its water solution is carbonic acid. Carbon dioxide does not burn.

Carbon dioxide is used by plants during photosynthesis, in fire extinguishers, in carbonated beverages, as a leavening agent, and as Dry Ice in refrigeration.

Carbon monoxide can be prepared by reducing carbon dioxide, by the action of steam on hot coke, and by decomposing formic acid. Carbon monoxide is a colorless, odorless, tasteless gas that is exceedingly poisonous. It burns with a blue flame.

Carbon monoxide is used as a reducing agent in the production of iron, copper, and other metals from their ores. It is also a fuel. Large quantities of carbon monoxide are used for synthesizing organic compounds.

The exhaust gases from internal combustion engines always contain some carbon monoxide. So does tobacco smoke. Carbon monoxide unites with the hemoglobin of the blood and reduces its oxygen-carrying capacity. The presence in the blood of small amounts of carbon monoxide impairs the function of body cells. In large amounts, it can cause death by oxygen starvation.

QUESTIONS

Group A

1. (*a*) Why is the study of carbon compounds a separate branch of chemistry? (*b*) What is this branch of chemistry called?
2. What is the orientation of the four covalent bonds of a carbon atom in sp^3 hybridization?
3. What property of carbon atoms makes possible the large number of carbon compounds?
4. (*a*) What is *allotropy?* (*b*) What are the allotropic forms of carbon? (*c*) Why is amorphous carbon not considered to be a third allotropic form of carbon?
5. Why are diamonds useful in industry?
6. Explain why diamond is an excellent conductor of heat but a nonconductor of electricity.
7. Graphite is soft, yet carbon fibers in which the carbon is in the form of graphite are very strong. Explain.
8. Using valence-bond structures for graphite layers, show how the structure of graphite illustrates resonance.
9. Give several reasons why graphite is used as a lubricant.
10. (*a*) What is *destructive distillation?* (*b*) Is it really destructive? Explain.
11. Why does a form of carbon such as charcoal or coke remain after the destructive distillation of bituminous coal or wood?
12. What is *adsorption?*
13. Why is boneblack a relatively impure form of carbon?
14. What physical characteristic of activated carbon makes it a useful adsorbent?
15. What are the two successive steps in the preparation of activated carbon?
16. What is the most important use of carbon black?
17. What use is made of petroleum coke?
18. Why is carbon dioxide an important component of the atmosphere even though it occurs to only 0.03% by volume?
19. (*a*) Name the four commercial methods for preparing carbon dioxide. (*b*) What is the usual laboratory method? (*c*) Write balanced chemical equations for these methods.
20. What is the function of an enzyme?
21. What difficulties are experienced when

collecting carbon dioxide (*a*) by water displacement; (*b*) by air displacement?

22. What are the chemical properties of carbon dioxide?
23. (*a*) How is carbonic acid produced? (*b*) Is it a strong or a weak acid? Explain.
24. What is the test for carbon dioxide?
25. What are the two parts of the oxygen-carbon dioxide cycle?
26. How does a liquid carbon-dioxide fire extinguisher put out fires?
27. (*a*) Write a balanced formula equation for the reaction that occurs in the discharging of a soda-acid fire extinguisher. (*b*) Write the ionic and net ionic equations.
28. (*a*) What is the source of carbon dioxide in most leavening agents? (*b*) How is it released?
29. What are the sources of carbon monoxide contamination in the atmosphere?
30. What is the function of sulfuric acid in the preparation of carbon monoxide from formic acid?
31. By comparing their molecular weights, arrange oxygen, hydrogen, carbon dioxide, and carbon monoxide in order of increasing density.
32. What are three uses of carbon monoxide?

Group B

33. Explain why carbon atoms usually do not form ionic bonds with other elements.
34. Show how the carbon atom illustrates hybridization in the formation of sp^3 orbitals.
35. (*a*) What are the two reasons for allotropy? (*b*) Which of these reasons is illustrated by the allotropic forms of carbon?
36. What proof is there that diamond is pure carbon?
37. Diamond is very hard and is a nonconductor of electricity. Graphite is soft and is a conductor of electricity. Diamond is more dense than graphite. Both diamond and graphite withstand very high temperatures without melting. Explain how these properties are related to the similarities and differences in the structures of diamond and graphite.
38. (*a*) What uses does natural graphite find in metallurgy? (*b*) What property of graphite makes these uses possible?
39. (*a*) What is the most important use for synthetic graphite? (*b*) What property of graphite makes this use possible?
40. When coke is used as a reducing agent, what is oxidized?
41. Powdered charcoal, copper(II) oxide, and manganese dioxide are all black substances. How could you identify each?
42. For what purposes might activated carbon be used in a large dry cleaning plant?
43. (*a*) What materials are used in producing carbon black? (*b*) What is the function of each?
44. Why is it so difficult to remove stains made by printer's ink?
45. Write a net ionic equation for the reaction between calcium carbonate and hydrochloric acid that produces carbon dioxide.
46. Write a net ionic equation for the reaction between sodium carbonate and sulfuric acid.
47. What property of a solid determines whether it will sublime or melt when heated?
48. Does magnesium ribbon actually burn in carbon dioxide? Explain.
49. Show by means of ionic equations that the reaction between carbon dioxide and aqueous sodium hydroxide may be considered to be a hydronium ion-hydroxide ion neutralization reaction.
50. Show by means of ionic equations that the reaction that serves as a test for carbon dioxide may be considered to be a neutralization reaction combined with a precipitation.
51. When a bottle of limewater is left unstoppered, a white ring is formed on the

inside of the bottle at the surface of the liquid. Explain its cause, and tell how it can be removed.
52. Distinguish between baking soda and baking powder.
53. Explain why carbon dioxide molecules are nonpolar, while carbon monoxide molecules are polar.
54. Why are both carbon dioxide and carbon monoxide gases at room temperature when water, with a lower molecular weight, exists as a liquid?
55. Both carbon dioxide and carbon monoxide will produce asphyxiation. Explain the difference in their action on the body.
56. After studying this chapter, you know a lot more about the diamond sparkling in the photograph on page 349. How many uses of carbon in this hard crystalline form can you think of that are not mentioned in the text?

PROBLEMS

Group A

1. What is the percentage composition of formic acid, HCOOH?
2. (*a*) How many moles of iron(III) oxide can be reduced by the carbon in 2.00 moles of carbon monoxide, according to the equation: $Fe_2O_3 + 3CO \rightarrow 2Fe + 3CO_2$? (*b*) How many moles of iron are produced? (*c*) How many moles of carbon dioxide are produced?
3. How many grams of carbon monoxide are needed to react with 12.2 g of zinc oxide and produce elemental zinc? $ZnO + CO \rightarrow Zn + CO_2$
4. In Problem 3 (*a*), how many grams of zinc are produced? (*b*) What is the volume in liters at STP of the carbon dioxide produced?
5. How many grams of H_2SO_4 are required for the reaction with 1.00 kg of sodium hydrogen carbonate in a soda-acid fire extinguisher?

$$\mathbf{2NaHCO_3 + H_2SO_4 \rightarrow Na_2SO_4 + 2H_2O + 2CO_2}$$

6. Calculate the number of liters of carbon dioxide at STP given off during the discharge of the fire extinguisher of Problem 5.

Group B

7. How many grams of carbon monoxide can be obtained by the dehydration of $23\bar{0}$ g of formic acid by sulfuric acid?
8. How many liters of dry carbon monoxide will be produced in Problem 7 if the temperature is 27°C and the barometer reading is $75\bar{0}$ mm?
9. How many liters of carbon dioxide result from the combustion of carbon monoxide in Problem 8 if the product is restored to 27°C and $75\bar{0}$ mm pressure?
10. How many grams of calcium carbonate are needed to prepare 2.50 liters of dry carbon dioxide at 17°C and $74\bar{0}$ mm pressure by the reaction between calcium carbonate and hydrochloric acid?
11. How many milliliters of concentrated hydrochloric acid must be diluted with water to provide the HCl needed for the reaction of Problem 10? Concentrated hydrochloric acid is 38.0% HCl by weight and has a density of 1.20 g/ml.
12. A gaseous compound contains 52.9% carbon and 47.1% oxygen. One volume of this gas reacts with two volumes of oxygen and yields three volumes of carbon dioxide. Knowing that oxygen molecules are diatomic, determine the molecular formula of this compound.

chapter 18

HYDROCARBONS

The endless quest for "black gold." (See Question 47 on page 394.)

An Introduction to Organic Compounds

18.1 Abundance of carbon compounds

The number of possible carbon compounds is almost unlimited. Over 3,000,000 are known and about 100,000 new ones are isolated or synthesized each year. Why are there so many carbon compounds and how do they differ from noncarbon compounds? These questions will be answered in this section and in Section 18.4. Then we will learn about natural gas and petroleum, the current sources of simple organic compounds. Most of these simple organic compounds are ***hydrocarbons,*** *compounds composed only of carbon and hydrogen.* We will next find out what specific hydrocarbons occur in natural gas and petroleum and how these compounds may be changed into other fundamental hydrocarbon compounds. Since the known supply of petroleum in the earth is rapidly being used up, we must consider some possible substitutes for petroleum as a source of organic compounds. In Chapter 19, we will describe a variety of organic compounds derived from hydrocarbons which are important in everyday life.

There are two reasons why there are so many carbon compounds:

1. Carbon atoms link together with covalent bonds. In Section 17.2, we described how carbon atoms readily form covalent bonds with other carbon atoms. This makes possible the existence of molecules in which thousands of carbon atoms are bonded one to another. The molecules of some organic compounds are principally long carbon-atom chains with carbon-atom groups attached. Other carbon-compound molecules

Fig. 18-1. Models of the molecules of four isomers of octane. Can you tell if any of the isomers pictured are the same as the electron dot formulas given as examples in the text?

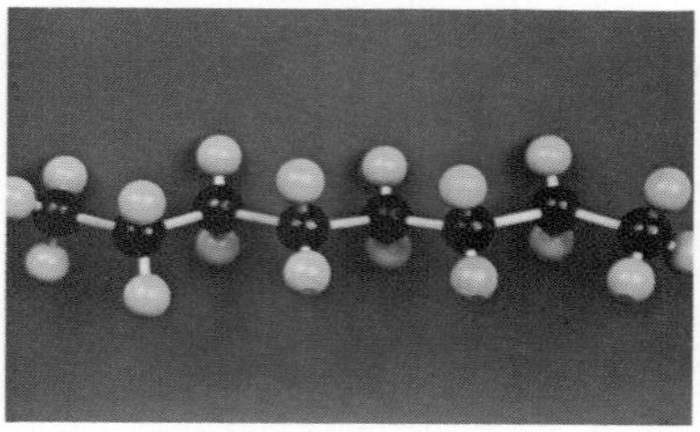

have carbon atoms linked together in rings. Still others may consist of several such rings joined together. Not only are carbon atoms linked by single covalent bonds, but they are sometimes linked by double or triple covalent bonds.

2. *The same atoms may be arranged in several different ways.* One of the substances in petroleum is a hydrocarbon called *octane.* Its molecular formula is C_8H_{18}. A molecule of octane consists of 8 carbon atoms and 18 hydrogen atoms. A carbon atom may form four single covalent bonds while a hydrogen atom forms only one single covalent bond. The straight-chain electron-dot structure for an octane molecule is written like this:

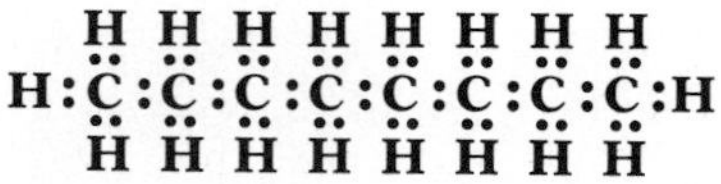

But there are other ways in which these same atoms can be arranged. For instance, here are three branched-chain formulas:

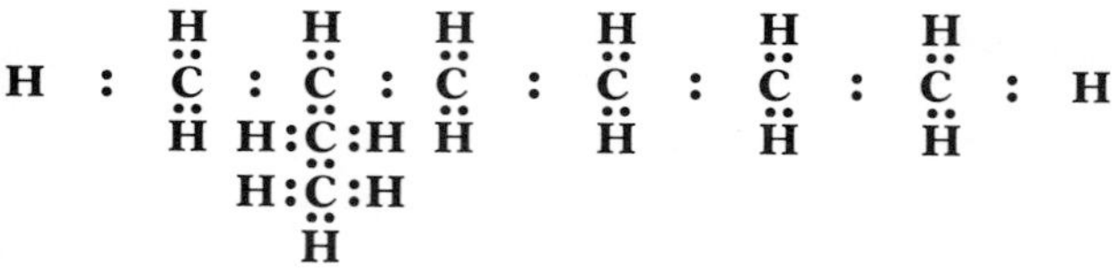

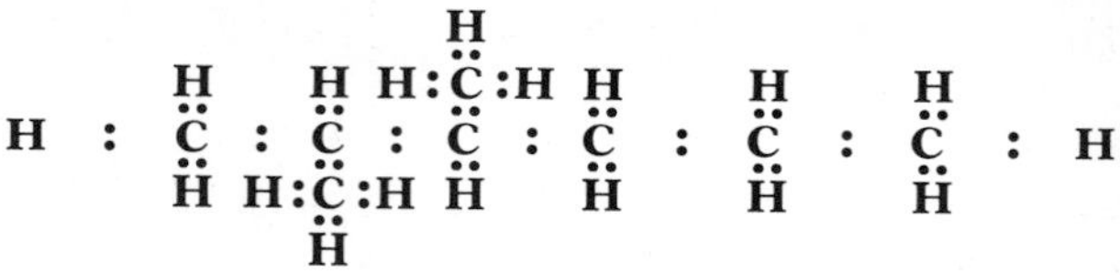

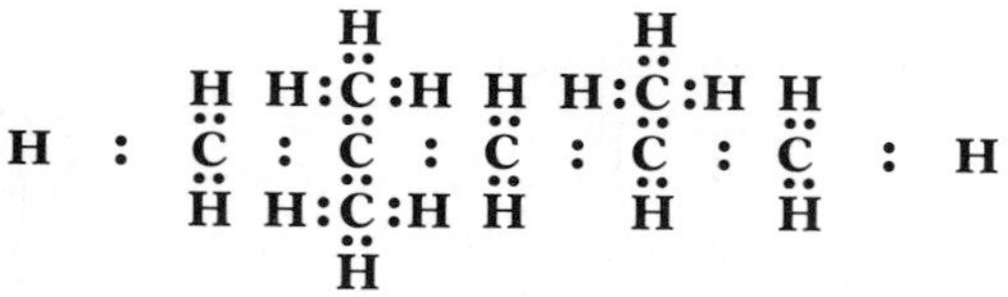

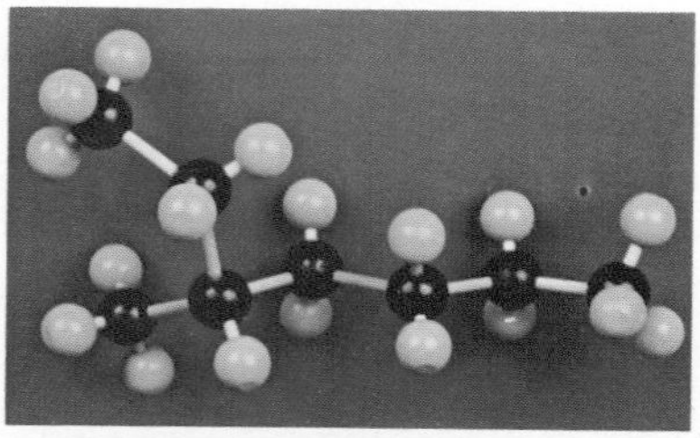

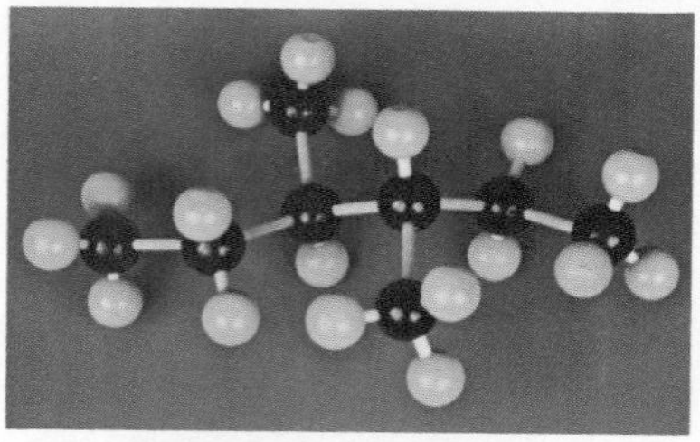

All of these formulas represent arrangements of 8 carbon atoms and 18 hydrogen atoms. Each carbon atom shares four electrons and each hydrogen atom shares one electron. In addition to these four structures for octane, there are 14 others, making a total of 18 possible structures for octane. Each of these 18 structures has the same molecular formula. However, the different arrangements of the atoms in the molecules give each molecule slightly different properties. Thus, each of these molecular arrangements represents a separate chemical compound. *Compounds having the same molecular formula but different structures are called* ***isomers.***

18.2 Structural formulas for organic compounds

The formula H_2SO_4 for sulfuric acid gives enough information for most purposes in inorganic chemistry. But a molecular formula such as C_8H_{18} is not at all satisfactory in organic chemistry. We have already noted that there are 18 different isomers of this compound. In order to indicate clearly a particular isomer, the organic chemist uses a ***structural formula.*** *Such a* *formula not only indicates what kinds of atoms and how many of each but also shows how they are arranged in the molecule.* Electron-dot formulas have been used to illustrate the isomers of octane. However, such formulas are tedious to draw for routine equation work. Organic chemists often substitute a dash (—) for the pair of shared electrons forming a covalent bond. Using the dash, the straight-chain structural formula for octane can be represented

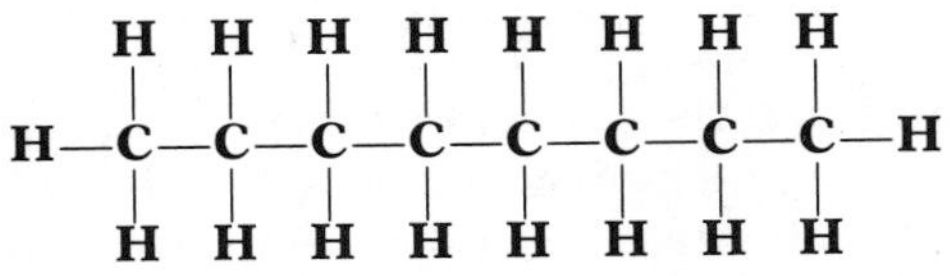

When structural formulas are written, there must be no dangling bonds. Each dash must represent an electron pair that forms the covalent bond linking two atoms.

For practice, on a separate sheet of paper, write the structural formulas for the three branched-chain isomers of octane given in Section 18.1.

18.3 Determination of an organic structural formula

There are two different organic compounds that consist of carbon, 52.2%, hydrogen, 13.0%, and oxygen, 34.8%. They have the same molecular weight, 46, and thus are isomers. One compound is a colorless liquid which boils at 78°C. The other is a colorless gas which condenses to a liquid at −25°C under one atmosphere pressure. Each has its own distinctive odor. How can we determine their structural formulas?

From the percentage composition, we can calculate the empirical formula by the method described in Section 7.12. We find the empirical formula to be C_2H_6O. Since this empirical formula has a formula weight of 46, it must also be the molecular formula of each compound. From what we have already learned about bonding, there are only two ways in which two carbon atoms, six hydrogen atoms, and a single oxygen atom can combine:

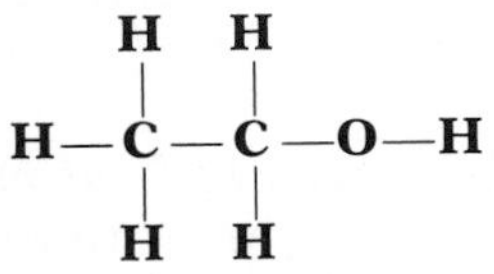

Structure A

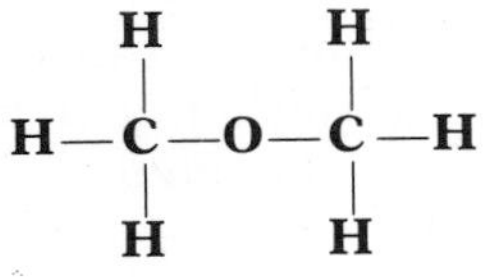

Structure B

Now our problem is to match these structures to the two compounds. If we test each compound for reaction with metallic sodium, only the liquid reacts. In the reaction, hydrogen is given off. The amount of hydrogen given off is equal to one-sixth of the hydrogen that the compound contains. This evidence indicates that in the molecules of the liquid, one of the six hydrogen atoms is bonded differently from the others. Structure *A* is indicated.

Next we discover that the liquid reacts with phosphorus trichloride and gives a product with the molecular formula C_2H_5Cl. In this reaction, chlorine has replaced both a hydrogen atom and an oxygen atom. We can write only one structural formula for C_2H_5Cl:

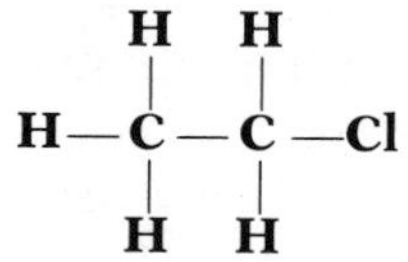

We may assume that the chlorine atom occupies the same position as the oxygen and hydrogen atoms that it replaced. Structure *A* is again indicated. We might continue further, because much more evidence can be found to indicate that the liquid does indeed have Structure *A*. This liquid substance is ethanol or ethyl alcohol. The gaseous substance has the other structural formula and is called dimethyl ether.

We can use methods similar to those just described to determine the structural formulas of other simple organic compounds. Complicated molecules are generally broken down into simpler molecules. From the structures of these simpler molecules, we can reason out the structure of the complex molecule. Sometimes simple molecules of known structure are combined to produce a complex molecule. A comparison of chemical and physical properties of compounds of unknown structure with those of known structure is sometimes helpful.

18.4 Differences between organic and inorganic compounds The basic laws of chemistry are the same for organic and inorganic chemistry. However, the behavior of organic compounds is somewhat different from that of inorganic compounds. Some of the most important differences are:

1. Most organic compounds do not dissolve in water. The majority of inorganic compounds do dissolve more or less readily in water. Organic compounds generally dissolve in such organic liquids as alcohol, chloroform, ether, carbon disulfide, or carbon tetrachloride.

2. Organic compounds are decomposed by heat more easily than most inorganic compounds. The decomposition (charring) of sugar when it is heated moderately is familiar. Such charring on heating is often a test for organic substances. But many inorganic compounds, such as common salt (sodium chloride), can be vaporized at a red heat without decomposition.

3. Organic reactions generally proceed at much slower rates. Such reactions often require hours or even days for completion. However, organic reactions in living cells may take place with great speed. Most inorganic reactions occur almost as soon as solutions of the reactants are brought together.

4. Organic compounds exist as molecules consisting of atoms joined by covalent bonds. Many inorganic compounds have ionic bonds.

CAUTION: *Many organic compounds are* ***flammable*** *and* ***poisonous.*** *Some organic reactions are rapid and highly exothermic. A student should not perform any experiments with organic compounds without detailed laboratory directions, and then only with adequate ventilation and other safety precautions, and under the supervision of an experienced instructor.*

18.5 Natural gas and petroleum

Natural gas is a mixture of hydrocarbon gases and vapors found in porous formations in the earth's crust. Natural gas is mostly methane, CH_4. Frequently natural gas occurs with petroleum, or crude oil. Petroleum is a complex mixture of hydrocarbons. This hydrocarbon mixture varies greatly in composition from place to place. The hydrocarbon molecules in petroleum contain from one to more than 50 carbon atoms.

Natural gas and petroleum were probably formed by the decay of plants and animals living millions of years ago. Because of changes in the earth's surface, these plant and animal residues were trapped in rock formations where they slowly decomposed in the absence of atmospheric oxygen.

Natural gas and petroleum are the most common sources of fuels. But, more importantly, they are a source of hydrocarbon chemical raw materials that is rapidly being used up. Discoveries of new sources of natural gas and petroleum are not keeping up with the amounts being used. This disturbing fact will surely affect our standard of living in the very near future.

Fig. 18-2. The United States can increase its supply of natural gas by importing this valuable chemical raw material. It will be brought in liquid form from foreign sources in tanker ships such as the one shown in the photograph. Each tank is 35 meters in diameter and holds over 20,000 m^3 of liquefied natural gas.

18.6 The processing of natural gas

About 97% of natural gas is methane, CH_4. Mixed with the methane are other hydrocarbons whose molecules contain between two and seven carbon atoms. These different hydrocarbons have different boiling points and can be separated on this basis. This method of separation is called *fractional distillation.* The separation of nitrogen from oxygen in liquid air was an example of this method.

The separation of nitrogen from oxygen in liquid air was described in Section 9.4(5).

The hydrocarbons having 3 or 4 carbon atoms per molecule are sometimes separated and used as "bottled gas" for fuel. The hydrocarbons having 5 to 7 carbon atoms per molecule are liquids at ordinary temperature. Their vapors can be condensed and used as a solvent or in gasoline.

18.7 The refining of petroleum

Fractional distillation is a method of separating the components of a mixture on the basis of differences in their boiling points.

Petroleum is refined by separating crude oil into portions with properties suitable for certain uses. The method used is fractional distillation. No attempt is made to separate the petroleum into individual hydrocarbons. Instead, portions that

Table 18-1

SUMMARY OF FRACTIONAL DISTILLATION OF PETROLEUM			
Portion	No. of C Atoms per Molecule	Boiling Point Range (°C)	Uses
gas	C_1 to C_5	−161–30	fuel; making carbon black, hydrogen, gasoline by alkylation
petroleum ether	C_5 to C_7	20–100	solvent ; dry cleaning
gasoline	C_5 to C_{12}	30–200	motor fuel
kerosene	C_{12} to C_{16}	175–275	fuel
fuel oil Diesel oil	C_{15} to C_{18}	250–400	furnace fuel; Diesel engine fuel; cracking
lubricating oils greases petroleum jelly	C_{16}	350	lubrication
paraffin wax	C_{20}	melts 52–57	candles; waterproofing; home canning
pitch tar		residue	road construction
petroleum coke		residue	electrodes

distill between certain temperature ranges are collected in separate receivers. Table 18-1 summarizes the characteristics of the portions obtained from the fractional distillation of petroleum.

Petroleum refining is carried out in a *pipe still* and a *fractionating tower.* See Figure 18-3. The crude oil is heated to

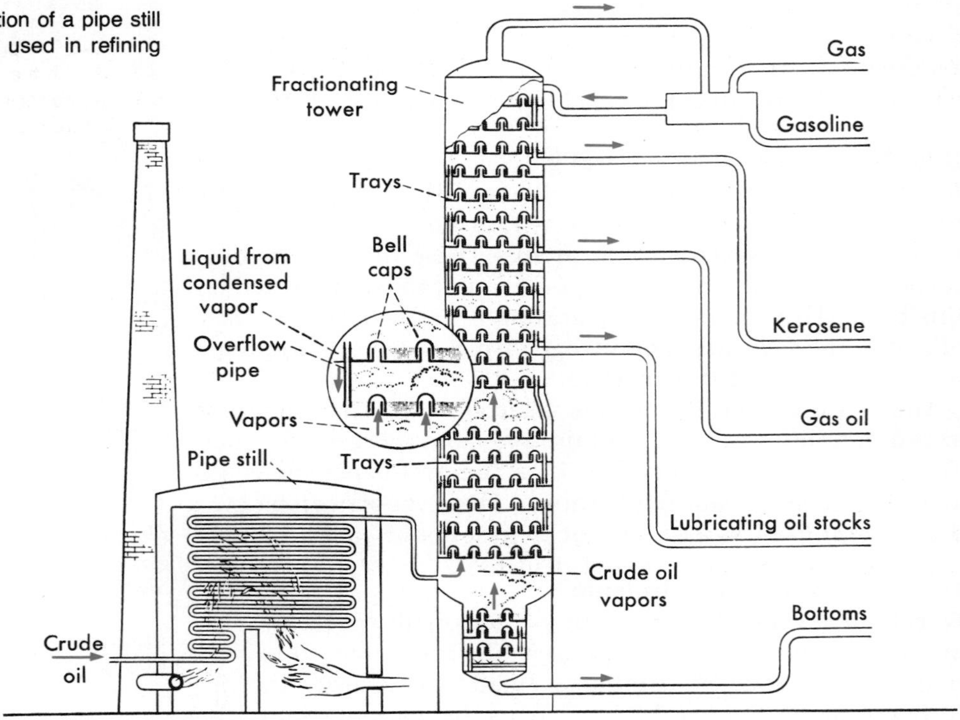

Fig. 18-3. A cross section of a pipe still and fractionating tower used in refining petroleum.

about 370°C in the pipe still. At this temperature, nearly all the components of the crude oil are vaporized. The hot vapors are then discharged into the fractionating tower at a point near its base. Here, the portions with the highest condensation temperatures condense and are drawn off to collecting vessels. Portions with lower condensation temperatures continue to rise in the tower. As they rise, they are gradually cooled. In this way, the various portions reach their condensation temperatures at different levels. As they condense, the liquids collect in shallow troughs that line the inside of the tower. Pipes lead off the overflow of condensed liquids from the troughs. The gasoline fraction, together with the more volatile portions of the petroleum, passes as a gas from the top of the tower. It is then liquefied in separate condensers. The uncondensed gases may be piped to where they are to be used in the refinery. The liquid and gaseous fractions are subjected to other reactions or processes depending on what products are required.

Fig. 18-4. A petroleum refinery. The building with the tall chimney is the pipe still. The tower-like structure is a fractionating tower.

18.8 Classification of hydrocarbons

Compounds composed of only the two elements—hydrogen and carbon—are called *hydrocarbons*. We study the hydrocarbons first because they are the basic structures from which other organic compounds are derived. Hydrocarbons are grouped into several different series of compounds. These groupings are based mainly on the type of bonding between carbon atoms.

1. The *alkanes* (al-*kaynes*) are straight-chain or branched-chain hydrocarbons. Their carbon atoms are connected by only *single* covalent bonds:

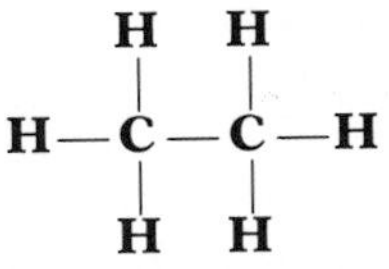

Alkanes are the most abundant hydrocarbons in natural gas and petroleum.

2. The *alkenes* (al-*keens*) are straight- or branched-chain hydrocarbons in which two carbon atoms in each molecule are connected by a *double* covalent bond:

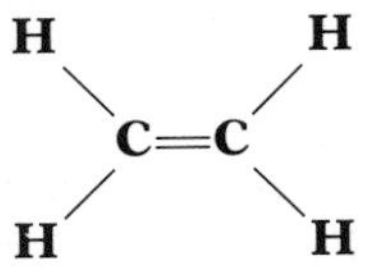

3. The *alkynes* (al-*kynes*) are straight- or branched-chain hydrocarbons in which two carbon atoms in each molecule are connected by a *triple* covalent bond:

$$H—C\equiv C—H$$

4. The *alkadienes* (al-kah-*dy*-eens) are straight- or branched-chain hydrocarbons that have *two double* covalent bonds between carbon atoms in each molecule:

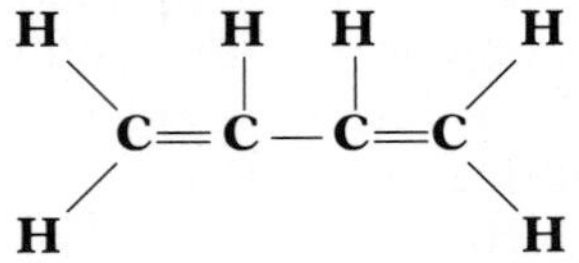

5. The *aromatic hydrocarbons* have resonance structures. These structures sometimes are represented by alternate single and double covalent bonds in six-membered carbon *rings:*

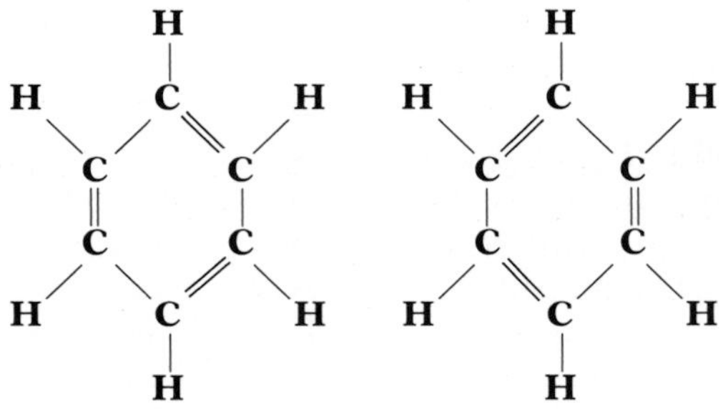

Petroleum from most sources contains some aromatic hydrocarbons. The amount varies from a few percent to as high as 40%.

18.9 The alkane series

This series of organic compounds is sometimes called the *paraffin series* because paraffin wax is a mixture of hydrocarbons of this series. The word *paraffin* means *little attraction.* Compared with the other hydrocarbon series, the alkanes have low chemical reactivity. This stability results from their single covalent bonds. Because they have only single covalent bonds in each molecule, the alkanes are known as *saturated hydrocarbons*. Saturated bonding occurs when each carbon atom in the molecule forms four single covalent bonds to other atoms.

Table 18-2 lists a few members of the alkane series. The names of the first four members of this series follow no system. However, beginning with pentane, the first part of each name is a Greek or Latin numerical prefix. This prefix indicates the number of carbon atoms. The name of each member ends in *-ane,* the same as the name of the series. The letter prefix "*n*" for "normal" indicates the straight-chain isomer.

Table 18-2

SOME MEMBERS OF THE ALKANE SERIES

Name	Formula	Melting Point (°C)	Boiling Point (°C)
methane	CH_4	−182	−161
ethane	C_2H_6	−183	−89
propane	C_3H_8	−190	−44
n-butane	C_4H_{10}	−138	0
isobutane	C_4H_{10}	−160	−12
n-pentane	C_5H_{12}	−130	36
isopentane	C_5H_{12}	−160	28
neopentane	C_5H_{12}	−20	10
n-hexane	C_6H_{14}	−95	68
n-heptane	C_7H_{16}	−91	98
n-octane	C_8H_{18}	−56	126
n-nonane	C_9H_{20}	−51	151
n-decane	$C_{10}H_{22}$	−30	174
***			
n-eicosane	$C_{20}H_{42}$	37	343
***			
n-hexacontane	$C_{60}H_{122}$	99	

If you examine the formulas for successive alkanes, you will see a clear pattern. Each member of the series differs from the preceding one by the group $\mathbf{CH_2}$,

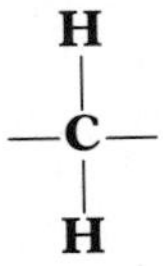

Compounds that differ in this fashion belong to a *homologous series*. It is not necessary to remember the formulas for all members of a homologous series. A general formula, such as C_nH_{2n+2} for the alkanes, can be derived. Suppose a member of this series has 30 carbon atoms in its molecules. To find the number of hydrogen atoms, multiply 30 by 2, then add 2. The formula is $C_{30}H_{62}$.

18.10 Structures of the lower alkanes

Each of the first three alkanes can have only *one* molecular structure. The formulas for these structures are

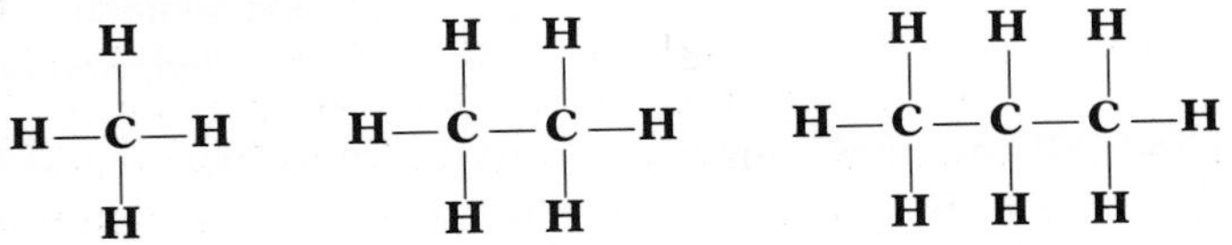

Methane **Ethane** **Propane**

Butane, the alkane with four carbon atoms and ten hydrogen atoms, has *two* isomers. The straight-chain molecule is

Fig. 18-5. Models of molecules of the first three members of the alkane series of hydrocarbons.

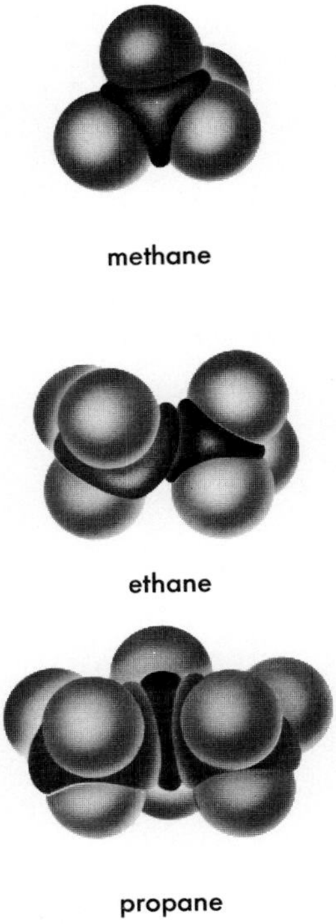

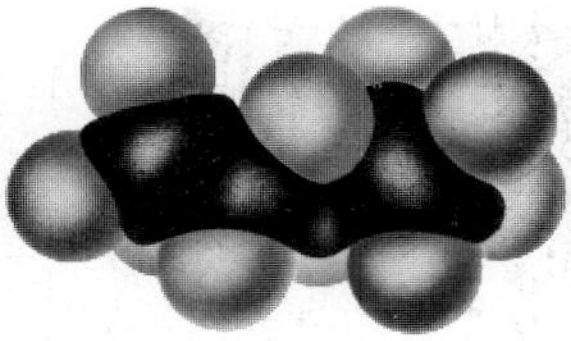

n-butane

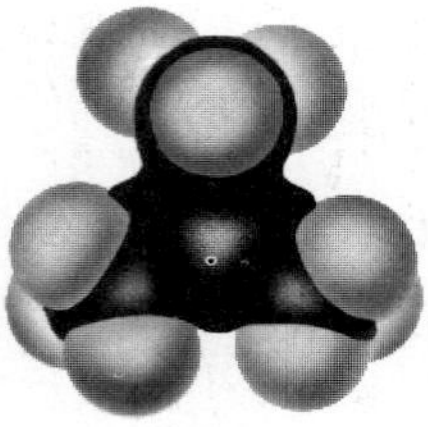

isobutane

Fig. 18-6. Models of molecules of the two isomers of butane.

named *n*-butane (*n* for *normal*). The branched-chain molecule is named isobutane or 2-methylpropane. Their melting and boiling points are given in Table 18-2.

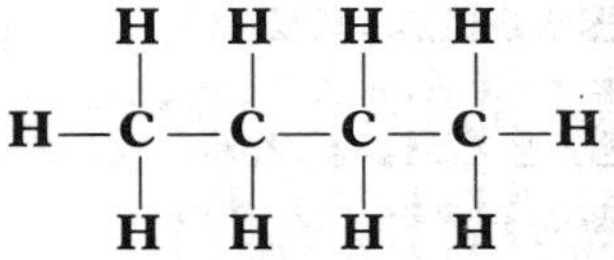

***n*-butane**

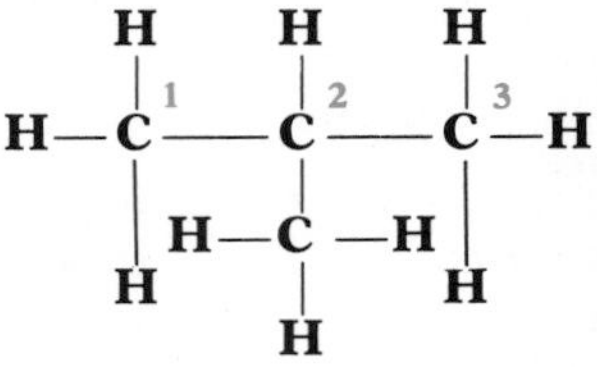

Isobutane or 2-methylpropane

The name 2-methylpropane is derived from the structure of the molecule. The longest continuous carbon chain in the molecule is three carbon atoms long, as in propane. One hydrogen atom attached to the second carbon atom in propane is replaced by the $\mathbf{CH_3}$— group. This is a *substitution group*. It is called the *methyl group*. 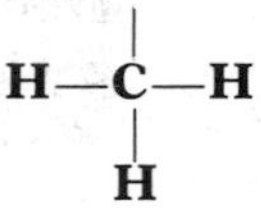 is methane with one of the hydrogen atoms removed. The carbon atoms in the main chain of the molecule are numbered. This numbering begins at the end of the molecule that gives the carbon atoms with substitution groups the smallest numbers.

Thus in the name **2-methylpropane,** the *2* refers to the number of the carbon atom on which there is a substitution. *Methyl* is the substituting group. *Propane* is the parent hydrocarbon.

There are *three* possible pentanes (C_5H_{12}): *n*-pentane, isopentane, and neopentane. Their melting and boiling points are given in Table 18-2. Their structural formulas are

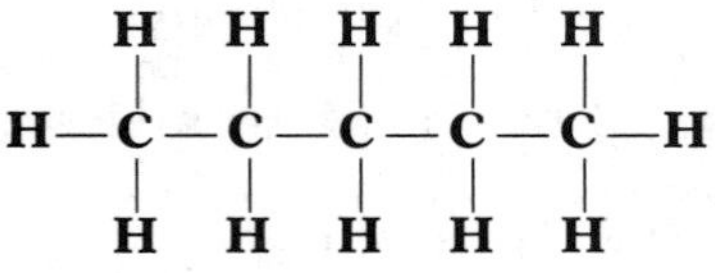

***n*-pentane**

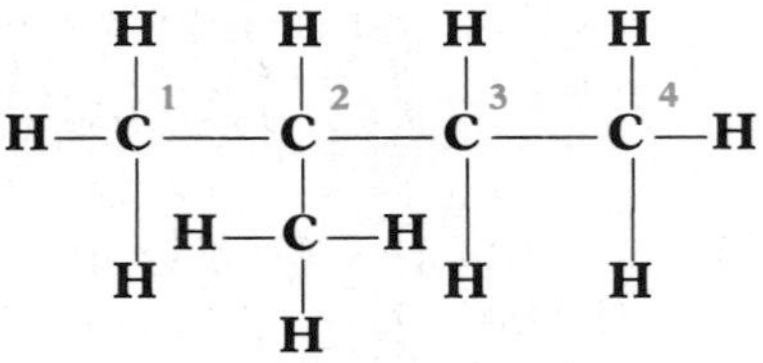

Isopentane
2-methylbutane

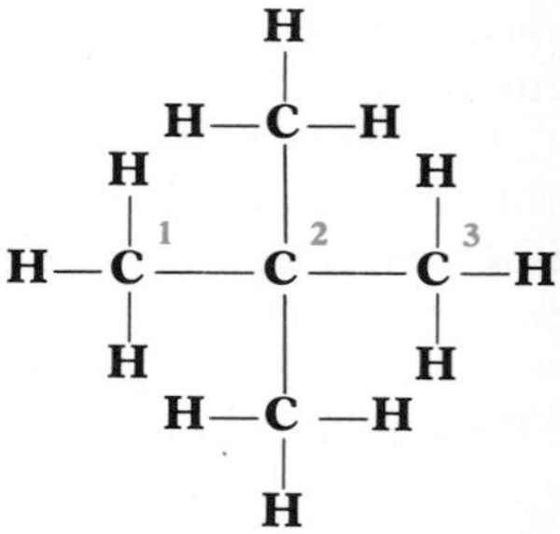

Neopentane
2,2-dimethylpropane

Isopentane is also called 2-methylbutane. Why would 3-methylbutane be incorrect? Another name for neopentane is **2,2-dimethylpropane.** The *2,2* refers to the position of both substitutions. The prefix *dimethyl* shows that the *two* substitutions are both *methyl* groups. *Propane* is the parent hydrocarbon.

Just as the CH_3— group derived from methane is the *methyl* group, C_2H_5— derived from ethane is the *ethyl* group. C_3H_7— derived from propane is the *propyl* group. C_4H_9—derived from butane is the *butyl* group. C_5H_{11}—is usually called the *amyl* group rather than the pentyl group. Other groups are given names following the general rule of dropping the *-ane* suffix and adding *-yl.* Any such group derived from an *alkane* is an *alkyl* group. The symbol **R**— is frequently used to represent an *alkyl* group in a formula.

Fig. 18-7. A small quantity of methane can be prepared in the laboratory by heating a mixture of sodium acetate and soda lime. Methane is collected by water displacement.

18.11 Preparation of the alkanes

We have already noted that alkanes are generally found in petroleum and natural gas. It is fairly easy to separate the lower members of the alkane series individually from petroleum and natural gas by fractional distillation. However, the alkanes with higher boiling points are usually separated into mixtures with similar boiling points.

Methane is a colorless, nearly odorless gas that forms about 90% of natural gas. Pure methane can be separated from the other components of natural gas. Chemists sometimes prepare small amounts of methane in the laboratory by heating soda lime (which contains sodium hydroxide) with sodium acetate.

$$NaC_2H_3O_2(s) + NaOH(s) \rightarrow CH_4(g) + Na_2CO_3(s)$$

Ethane is a colorless gas which occurs in natural gas and is a product of petroleum refining. It has a higher melting point and boiling point than methane. These properties are related to ethane's higher molecular weight.

Methane and ethane are minor components of the atmosphere of the planet Jupiter. Some gaseous methane is present around Saturn, and it is abundant about Uranus and Neptune. Solid methane has been detected on the surface of Pluto.

18.12 Reactions of the alkanes

1. Combustion. The most important reaction of the alkanes is combustion, since they make up a large proportion of our gaseous and liquid fuels. Methane burns with a bluish flame.

$$CH_4 + 2O_2 \rightarrow CO_2 + 2H_2O$$

Ethane and other alkanes also burn in air and form carbon dioxide and water vapor.

$$2C_2H_6 + 7O_2 \rightarrow 4CO_2 + 6H_2O$$

2. Substitution. The alkanes react with halogens such as chlorine or bromine. In such reactions, one or more atoms of a halogen are substituted for one or more atoms of hydrogen. Therefore, the products are called *substitution products.*

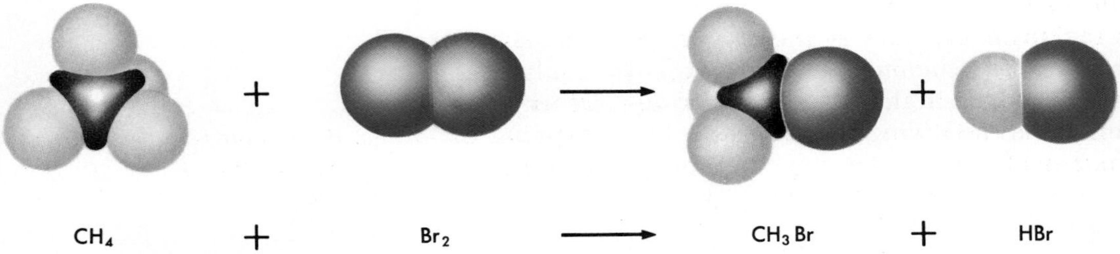

Fig. 18-8. Methane and bromine undergo a substitution reaction.

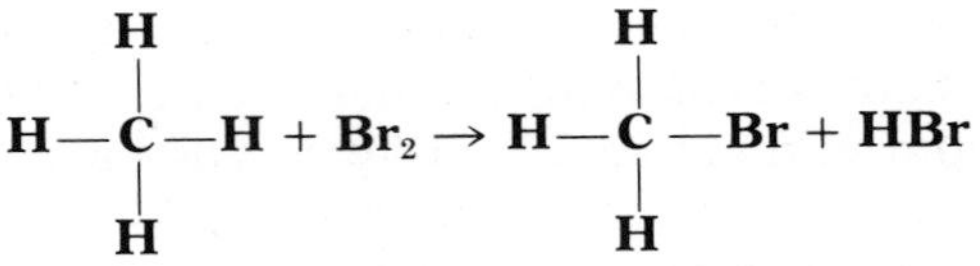

By supplying additional molecules of the halogen, a halogen atom can be substituted for each of the hydrogen atoms. Carbon tetrachloride, chloroform, and Teflon are examples of halogen-substituted alkanes.

Compare this reaction with the ones in Sections 9.17(4) and 17.14(2).

3. *Preparation of hydrogen.* Propane reacts with steam in the presence of a nickel catalyst at a temperature of about 850°C.

$$C_3H_8 + 6H_2O \rightarrow 3CO_2 + 10H_2$$

To separate the carbon dioxide from the hydrogen, the carbon dioxide under pressure may be dissolved in water.

18.13 Alkene series

The alkenes, sometimes called the *olefin series,* are distinguished by a double covalent bond between two carbon atoms. Thus, the simplest alkene must have two carbon atoms. Its structural formula is

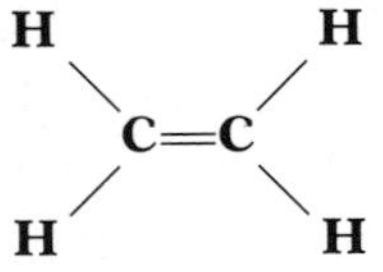

Its name is ethene. The name of an alkene comes from the name of the alkane with the same number of carbon atoms. We simply substitute the suffix *-ene* for the suffix *-ane*. Since eth*ane* is the alk*ane* with two carbon atoms, the alk*ene* with two carbon atoms is named eth*ene*. (This substance is also commonly called *ethylene*.) The general formula for the alkenes is $\mathbf{C_nH_{2n}}$.

18.14 Preparations of alkenes

1. *Cracking alkanes.* The commercial method of producing alkenes is by *cracking* petroleum. ***Cracking*** *is a process by which complex organic molecules are broken up into simpler*

molecules. This process involves the action of heat, or the action of heat and a catalyst.

Cracking which uses heat alone is known as *thermal cracking.* Alkanes decompose during cracking in several ways which produce a variety of unsaturated products. A simple example is the thermal cracking of propane, which proceeds in either of two ways in nearly equal proportions.

Important reaction conditions are sometimes written near the yields sign.

$$C_3H_8 \xrightarrow{460°C} C_3H_6 + H_2$$

$$C_3H_8 \xrightarrow{460°C} C_2H_4 + CH_4$$

Alkenes (especially ethene), smaller alkanes, and hydrogen are typical products of the thermal cracking of alkanes. They can be separated and purified and used as starting materials for making other organic compounds.

The cracking process that involves heat and a catalyst is *catalytic cracking.* The high-boiling fractions from petroleum distillation are catalytically cracked to produce smaller, lower boiling, hydrocarbons useful in gasoline. The catalysts used are mostly oxides of silicon and aluminum. The cracking reactions produce smaller alkanes and alkenes with highly branched structures. Aromatic hydrocarbons are also formed.

2. *Dehydration of alcohols.* Ethene can be prepared in the laboratory by dehydrating (removing water from) ethyl alcohol. Hot concentrated sulfuric acid is used as the dehydrating agent.

$$C_2H_5OH \xrightarrow[170°C]{H_2SO_4} C_2H_4 + H_2O$$

18.15 Reactions of alkenes

1. Addition. An organic compound that has one or more double or triple covalent bonds in each molecule is said to be *unsaturated.* It is chemically possible to add other atoms directly to such molecules and form molecules of a new compound. For example, hydrogen atoms may be added to an alkene in the presence of a finely divided nickel catalyst. This reaction produces the corresponding alkane.

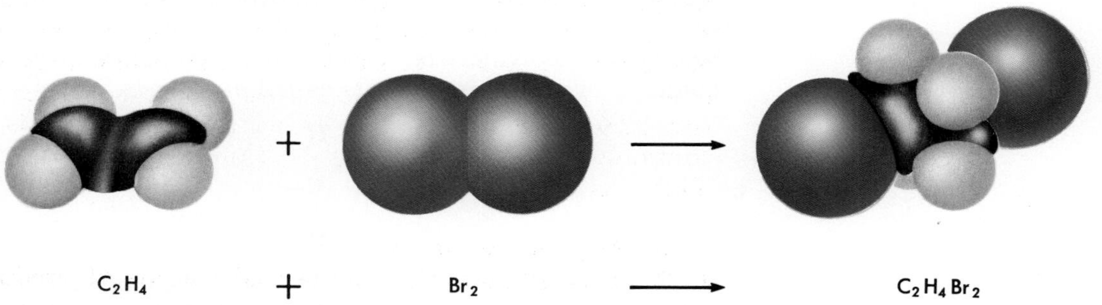

Fig. 18-9. Ethene and bromine undergo an addition reaction.

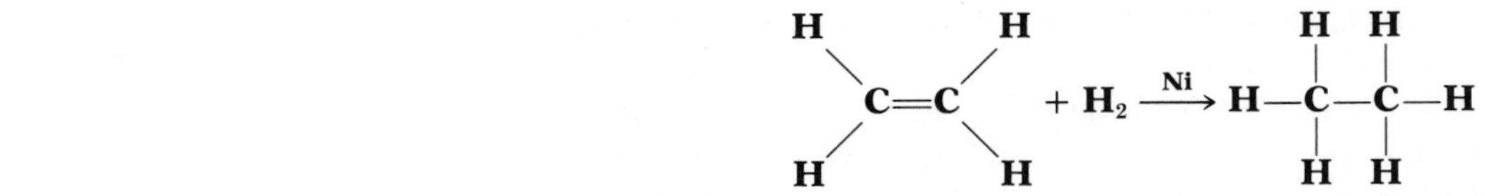

Halogen atoms can be added readily to alkene molecules. For example, two bromine atoms added directly to ethene form 1,2-dibromoethane.

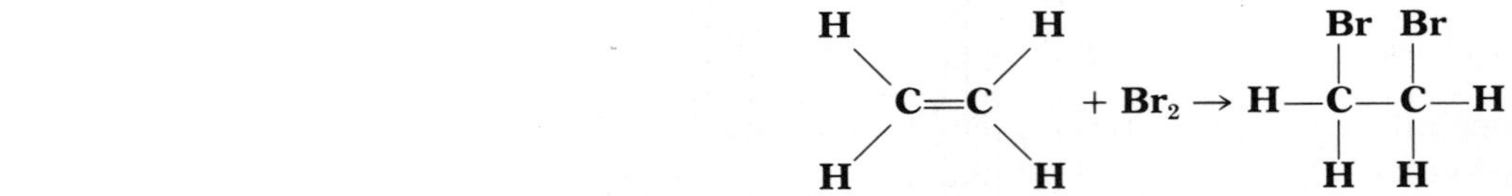

As the double bond between the carbon atoms breaks, there is one bond position available for each bromine atom.

The name of the product is 1,2-dibromoethane. The basic part of the name, *ethane,* is that of the related alkane with two carbon atoms. *Dibromo-* refers to the two bromine atoms that have been substituted for hydrogen atoms in ethane. *1,2-* means that one bromine atom is bonded to the first carbon atom and the other is bonded to the second carbon atom. An isomer, 1,1-dibromoethane has the formula

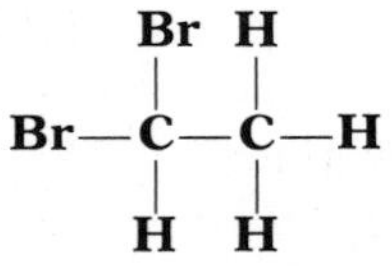

A molecule of a hydrogen halide, such as hydrogen bromide, can be added to an alkene molecule.

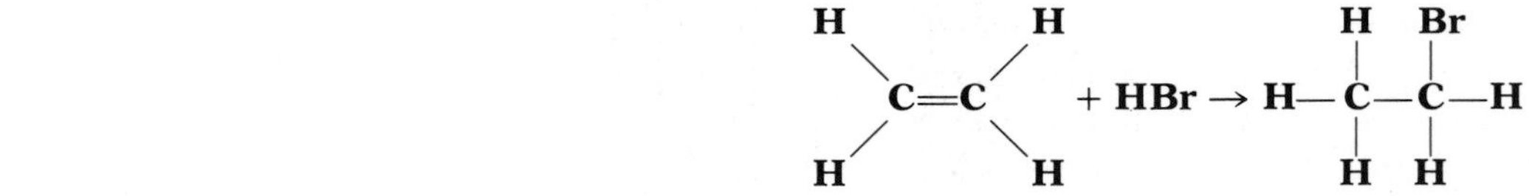

2. *Polymerization.* Molecules of ethene join together, or *polymerize,* at 250°C and 1000 atmospheres pressure. The resulting large molecules have molecular weights of about 30,000. This polymerized material is called *polyethylene.* It is made up of many single units called *monomers.*

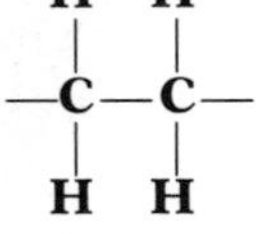

Many monomers join together to make the ***polymer*** (many units). Polyethylene is used in electric insulation, transparent wrappings, and a variety of containers.

3. Alkylation. In alkylation, gaseous alkanes and alkenes are combined. For example, isobutene and isobutane combine in the presence of a sulfuric acid or anhydrous hydrogen fluoride catalyst. The result is a highly branched octane, 2,2,4-trimethylpentane, an important component of gasoline.

4. Combustion. The alkenes burn in oxygen. For example,

$$C_2H_4 + 3O_2 \rightarrow 2CO_2 + 2H_2O$$

18.16 Alkyne series

The alkynes are distinguished by a triple covalent bond between two carbon atoms. This series is sometimes called the *acetylene series* because the simplest alkyne has the common name *acetylene*. It has two carbon atoms, with the formula

$$H—C{\equiv}C—H$$

The names of the alk*ynes* are derived from the names of the alk*anes* that have the same number of carbon atoms. The suffix *-yne* is substituted for *-ane*. Hence the chemical name for acetylene, the simplest alkyne, is *ethyne*. The general formula for the alkynes is C_nH_{2n-2}.

Ethyne, C_2H_2, is a minor component of the atmosphere of Jupiter. Ethyne molecules have also been detected in interstellar space.

18.17 Preparations of ethyne

1. From calcium carbide. Ethyne, a colorless gas, can be prepared by the action of water on calcium carbide, CaC_2. Calcium carbide is made from limestone, $CaCO_3$, in a series of operations. First, the limestone is heated in a kiln (oven). CaO is produced.

$$CaCO_3(s) \rightarrow CaO(s) + CO_2(g)$$

The calcium oxide is then heated with coke at 2000°C in an electric resistance furnace.

$$CaO(s) + 3C(s) \rightarrow CaC_2(s) + CO(g)$$

Calcium carbide is an ionic compound with the electron-dot structure

$$Ca^{++}$$
$$^{-}\overset{\times}{\underset{\times}{\cdot}}C\,\overset{\cdot\cdot\cdot}{\underset{\circ\circ\circ}{}}\,C\overset{\circ}{\underset{\times}{\cdot}}{}^{-}$$

When it reacts with water, hydrogen replaces the calcium in the calcium carbide structure. The bonding of hydrogen and carbon in ethyne is covalent.

$$CaC_2(s) + 2H_2O(l) \rightarrow C_2H_2(g) + Ca(OH)_2(aq)$$

The preparation of ethyne from calcium carbide is both a commercial and laboratory method.

Fig. 18-10. A convenient method of preparing a small quantity of ethyne (acetylene) in the laboratory by the action of water on calcium carbide.

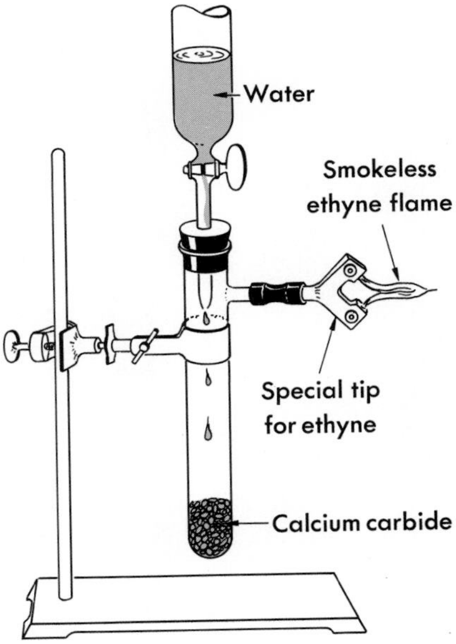

2. By partial oxidation of methane. This is an alternate commercial preparation of ethyne. Methane can be partially oxidized under controlled conditions and yields ethyne, carbon monoxide, and hydrogen.

$$6CH_4 + O_2 \xrightarrow{1500°C} 2C_2H_2 + 2CO + 10H_2$$

The preparation of methanol from carbon monoxide and hydrogen was described in Section 17.23(3).

The source of the methane is petroleum refining. The carbon monoxide and some of the hydrogen can be used to produce methanol. The balance of the hydrogen can be used to produce methanol. The balance of the hydrogen can be used as a fuel to maintain the temperature required for the reaction.

18.18 Reactions of ethyne

1. Combustion. Ethyne burns in air with a very smoky flame. Carbon, carbon dioxide, and water vapor are the products of combustion. With special burners, the combustion to carbon dioxide and water vapor is complete.

$$2C_2H_2 + 5O_2 \rightarrow 4CO_2 + 2H_2O$$

The oxyacetylene welding torch burns ethyne in the presence of oxygen.

2. Halogen addition. Ethyne is more unsaturated than ethene because of the triple bond. It is chemically possible to add to an ethyne molecule two molecules of bromine and form 1,1,2,2-tetrabromoethane.

$$H-C\equiv C-H + 2Br_2 \rightarrow H-\underset{\underset{Br}{|}}{\overset{\overset{Br}{|}}{C}}-\underset{\underset{Br}{|}}{\overset{\overset{Br}{|}}{C}}-H$$

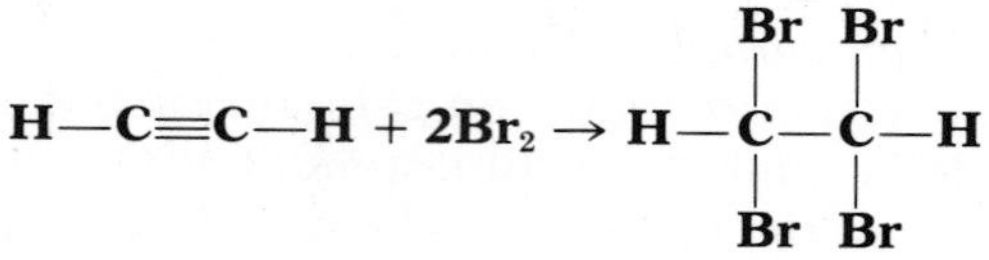

3. Dimerization. Two molecules of ethyne may combine and form the *dimer* (two units), vinylacetylene. This dimerization is brought about by passing ethyne through a water solution of copper(I) chloride and ammonium chloride. This solution acts as a catalyst.

$$2H-C\equiv C-H \xrightarrow[NH_4Cl]{Cu_2Cl_2} \underset{H}{\overset{H}{\underset{|}{C}}}=\overset{H}{\underset{|}{C}}-C\equiv C-H$$

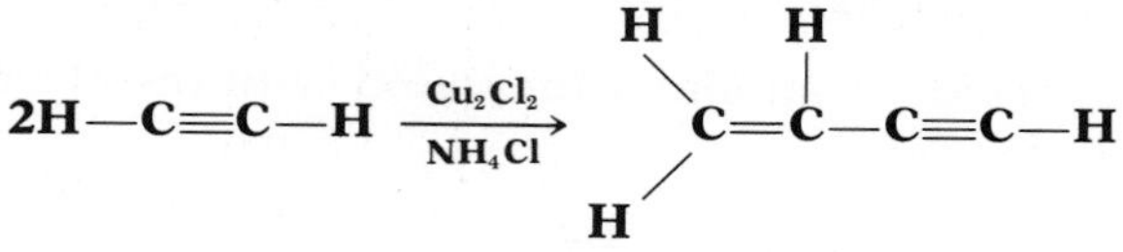

Vinylacetylene

The $CH_2=CH-$ group is the *vinyl* group. Vinylacetylene is the basic raw material for producing Neoprene, a synthetic rubber.

18.19 Butadiene: an important alkadiene

Alkadienes have two double covalent bonds in each molecule. The *-ene* suffix indicates a double bond. The *-diene* suffix indicates two double bonds. The names of the alkadienes are derived in much the same way as those of the other hydrocarbon series. Butadiene must, therefore, have four carbon atoms and contain two double bonds in each molecule.

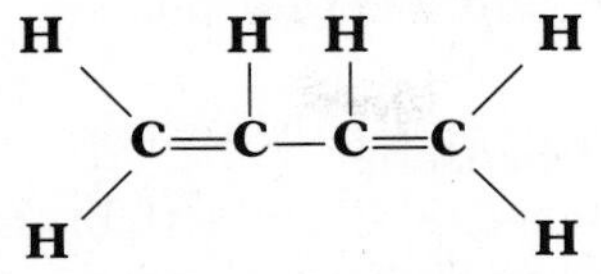

Actually, this structure is 1,3-butadiene, since the double bonds follow the first and third carbon atoms. However, 1,2-butadiene, its isomer, is so uncommon that 1,3-butadiene is usually called simply butadiene.

Butadiene is prepared by cracking petroleum fractions containing butane. It is used in the manufacture of *SBR* rubber, the most common type of synthetic rubber.

18.20 The aromatic hydrocarbons

The aromatic hydrocarbons are generally obtained from coal tar and petroleum. Benzene, the best known aromatic hydrocarbon, has the molecular formula C_6H_6. It may be represented by the following resonance formula, in which the two structures contribute equally.

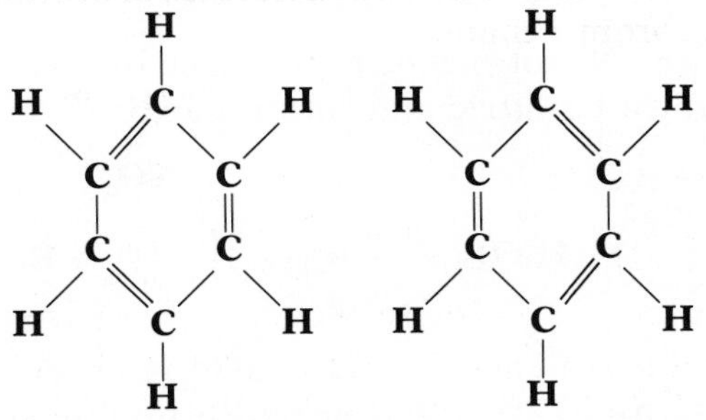

The bonds in benzene are neither single bonds nor double bonds. Instead, each bond is a *resonance hybrid bond.* All the carbon-carbon bonds in the molecule are the same. As a result, benzene and other aromatic hydrocarbons are not as unsaturated as the alkenes.

Because of the resonance structure of benzene, the benzene ring is sometimes abbreviated:

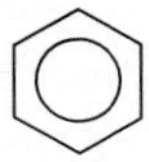

The $\mathbf{C_6H_5}$— group derived from benzene is called the *phenyl* group.

Benzene is produced commercially from petroleum. It is a flammable liquid that is used as a solvent. Benzene is used in manufacturing many other chemicals, including dyes, drugs, and explosives. Benzene has a strong, yet fairly pleasant, aromatic odor. It is less dense than water and only very slightly soluble in water. *Benzene is poisonous.* The vapors are harmful to breathe and are very flammable. It should be used only where there is adequate ventilation.

18.21 Reactions of benzene

1. *Halogenation.* Benzene reacts with bromine in the presence of iron and forms the substitution product, bromobenzene, or phenyl bromide.

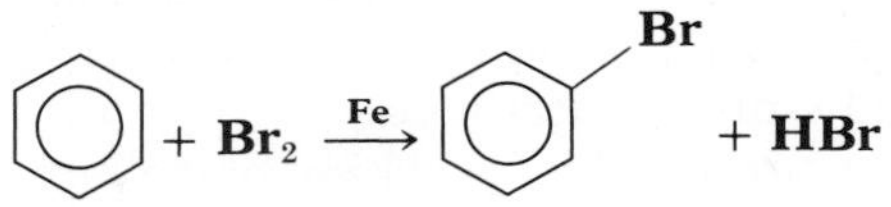

Further treatment causes the successive substitution of other bromine atoms for hydrogen atoms. With complete substitution, hexabromobenzene is produced.

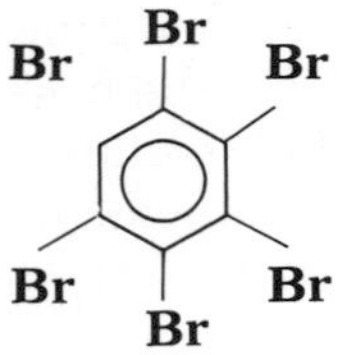

2. *Nitration.* Nitrobenzene is produced by treating benzene with concentrated nitric and sulfuric acids.

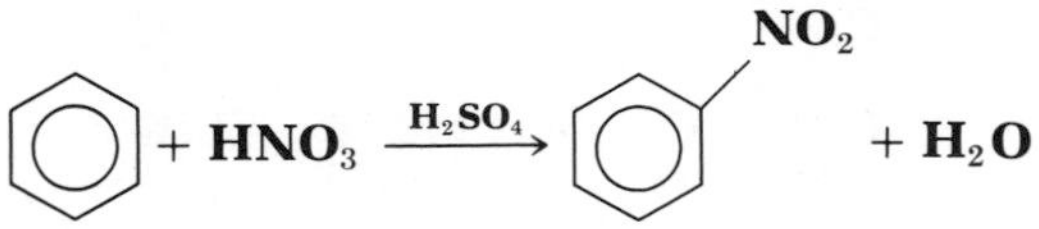

3. *Sulfonation.* Benzenesulfonic acid is produced at room temperature by treating benzene with fuming sulfuric acid. (Fuming sulfuric acid contains an excess of sulfur trioxide.)

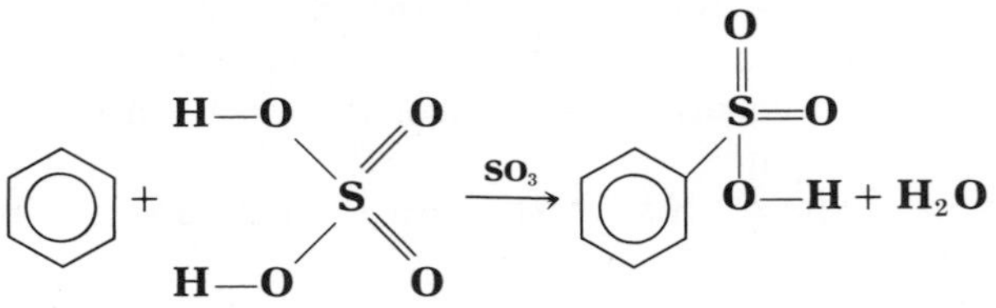

4. *Friedel-Crafts reaction.* An alkyl group may be introduced into the benzene ring by using an alkyl halide in the presence of anhydrous aluminum chloride.

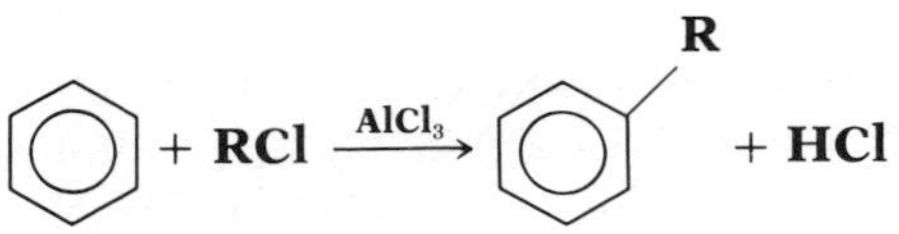

Fig. 18-11. Molecular models of common aromatic hydrocarbons.

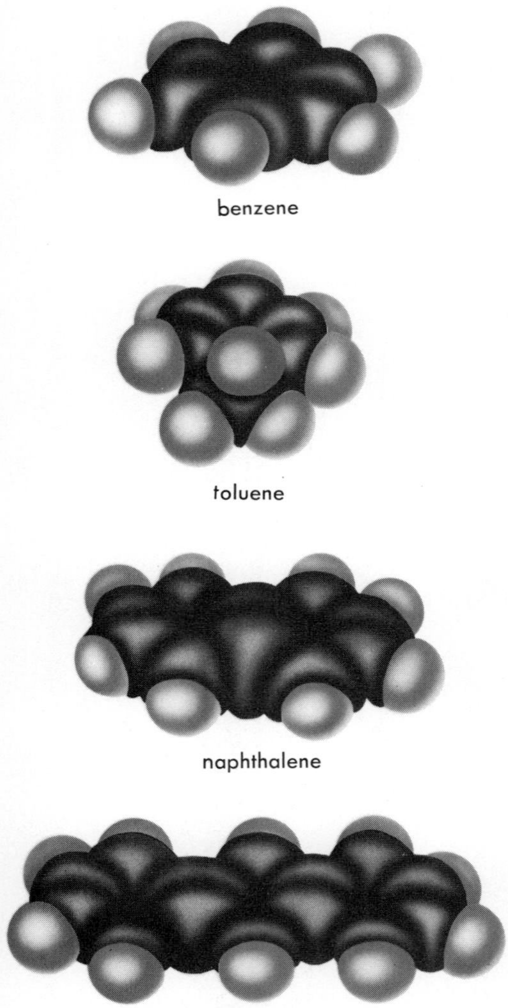

18.22 Other aromatic hydrocarbons

Toluene, or methyl benzene, is obtained from petroleum.

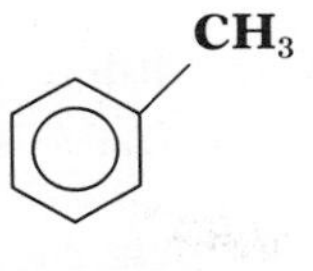

Toluene is used to make benzene.

The xylenes or dimethylbenzenes, $C_6H_4(CH_3)_2$, are a mixture of three liquid isomers. The xylenes are used as starting materials for the production of polyester fibers, plasticizers, and resins (raw materials for plastics).

Ethylbenzene is produced by the Friedel-Crafts reaction of benzene and ethene in the presence of hydrogen chloride.

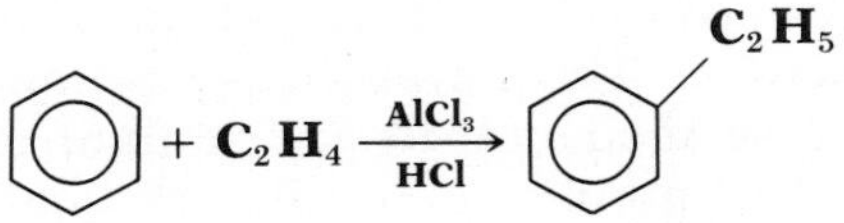

What is the original raw material from which both the benzene and ethene needed for this reaction are derived?

Ethylbenzene is treated with a catalyst of mixed metallic oxides to eliminate hydrogen and produce styrene, used along with butadiene in making *SBR* synthetic rubber.

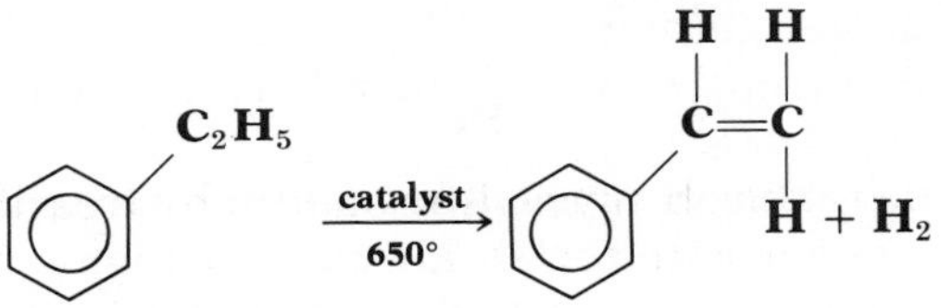

Styrene may be polymerized to polystyrene, a tough, transparent plastic. Polystyrene molecules in this form have molecular weights of about 500,000. Styrofoam, a porous form of polystyrene, is used as a packaging and insulating material.

Naphthalene, $C_{10}H_8$, is a coal-tar or petroleum product that crystallizes in white shining scales. Naphthalene molecules have a structure made up of two benzene rings joined by a common side.

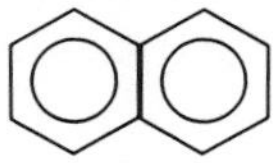

Naphthalene is used as a raw material for the manufacture of some resins and dyes.

Anthracene, $C_{14}H_{10}$, has a structure made up of three benzene rings joined together.

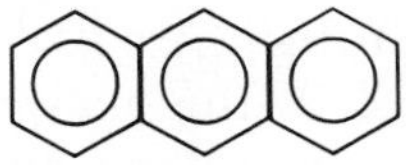

Like naphthalene, anthracene forms a whole series of hydrocarbons. They differ from the compounds related to benzene in that there is more than one ring. Anthracene is obtained

Fig. 18-12. Testing a catalyst for the octane rating of the gasoline produced.

commercially from coal tar. It is used in the production of synthetic dyes.

18.23 Octane number of gasoline

Knocking occurs in an automobile engine when the mixture of gasoline vapor and air in the cylinders explodes spontaneously rather than burning at a uniform rate. Knocking causes a loss of power and may harm the engine. It can be prevented by using a gasoline that resists this tendency to explode spontaneously as the temperature and pressure increase within the cylinder.

Air mixtures of gasoline that consist mostly of straight-chain hydrocarbons tend to knock badly in automobiles. Air mixtures of hydrocarbons with branched-chains and rings resist exploding spontaneously as the temperature and pressure in the cylinder increase. Thus, branched-chain and ring hydrocarbons have less tendency to knock than straight-chain hydrocarbons. To improve the antiknock qualities, refiners produce a gasoline mixture that contains a large proportion of branched-chain and ring hydrocarbon molecules.

Certain compounds, when added to gasoline in small amounts, improve the antiknock properties. The best known of these is lead tetraethyl, $Pb(C_2H_5)_4$. The use of lead tetraethyl in gasoline is currently being reduced because it contributes to air pollution.

The octane rating of a gasoline is a number that indicates the tendency of a gasoline to knock in a high-compression engine. The higher the number, the less the tendency of the gasoline to knock. To determine the octane rating, the gasoline is burned in a standard test engine. Its performance in the test engine is compared with a fuel of known octane rating. The fuels used as standards are *n*-heptane and 2,2,4-trimethylpentane, which is also named iso-octane. Iso-octane has excellent antiknock properties. It has an arbitrary octane rating of 100. Normal heptane knocks very badly and has a rating of zero. A gasoline with the characteristics of a mixture of 90% iso-octane and 10% *n*-heptane has an octane rating of 90.

Straight-chain alkanes have low octane ratings. Saturated ring-type hydrocarbons have intermediate octane ratings. Highly branched alkanes and aromatic (benzene ring-shaped) hydrocarbons have high octane ratings.

18.24 Petroleum substitutes

It is estimated that 75% of the energy needs of the United States are being met by natural gas and petroleum. It is now clearly evident that we are only a few decades away from exhausting the known supplies of these important chemical raw materials. Continued wasteful use of natural gas and petroleum as fuels threatens the future supply of these raw materials for other important products. Alternate fuels or sources of energy need to be developed. Energy will have to be used more efficiently as the sources become scarcer. These are problems that greatly concern governments of all industrial nations today.

Coal is by far the most widespread and plentiful fuel remaining in the United States. It is used to supply 21% of our energy needs. At the present rate of consumption, the amount of recoverable coal in the United States will last at least 2000 years. The mining of coal and the burning of coal both present environmental problems that will have to be resolved. Research is currently underway on developing large-scale systems of producing fuel gases and petroleum-like liquids from coal.

Oil shales, found in some western states, are another source of a petroleum-like liquid. More research is needed in order to develop economical production methods. Here, too, environmental problems must be resolved.

Nuclear fission, described in Chapter 30, is already accounting for the production of 11% of the electricity in the United States. This, however, is only 3% of our total energy use. Nuclear fission is a promising source of energy for the next several decades if the environmental and safety problems associated with the location and operation of nuclear power plants can be quickly resolved.

Obtaining energy in the large quantities needed from underground steam, from the sun, and from nuclear fusion is currently being researched. Practical results, however, may be many years away.

Rubber

18.25 Nature of rubber

Rubber is an elastic hydrocarbon material obtained from rubber trees. Each tree yields, daily, about one ounce of a milky fluid called *latex*. Latex contains about 35% rubber in colloidal suspension. When formic acid is added to latex, the rubber separates out as a curd-like mass. After being washed and dried, it is shipped to market as large sheets of crude rubber.

The simplest formula for rubber is $(C_5H_8)_x$. The structural formula for a single C_5H_8 unit is thought to be

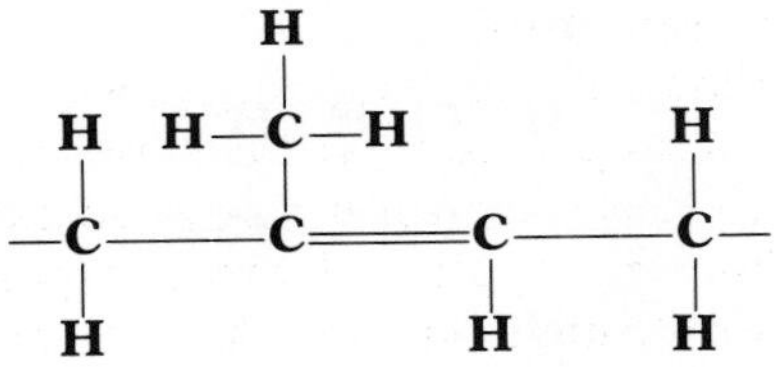

The C_5H_8 unit is a monomer of rubber. The "*x*" is believed to be a large number. Thus, rubber is a polymer made up of a large number of C_5H_8 units. The units are joined in a zigzag chain. This arrangement accounts for the elasticity of rubber.

18.26 Compounding of rubber

For commercial processing, raw rubber is mixed with a number of other materials in large batches. The ingredients in these batches vary according to the products to be made. Sulfur, however, is always one of the ingredients. Automobile tires contain considerable amounts of carbon black. This substance adds to the bulk and increases the wearing qualities of the tires.

After mixing, the product is shaped either in a mold or from thin sheets. The whole mass is then vulcanized. ***Vulcanization*** *involves heating the rubber mixture to a definite temperature for a definite time.* It gives the article a permanent shape, makes the rubber more elastic, and causes it to lose its sticky qualities. The changes that occur during vulcanization are many and complex. It is believed, however, that the sulfur atoms form bonds between adjacent rubber molecules. Organic catalysts are added to speed the process. Other organic chemicals are added to reduce the effect of oxygen from the air. This treatment slows the aging process that makes the rubber become hard and brittle.

18.27 Neoprene, a synthetic rubber

About the year 1910, scientists first produced hydrocarbon synthetic rubber by polymerizing isoprene, C_5H_8. This synthetic product cost too much and was inferior to natural rubber from plantations in the East Indies. In 1931, a successful synthetic rubber called *neoprene* appeared on the market.

Hydrogen chloride adds to vinylacetylene and yields chloroprene:

The dimerization of ethyne to form vinylacetylene was described in Section 18.18(3). From what materials can ethyne be prepared?

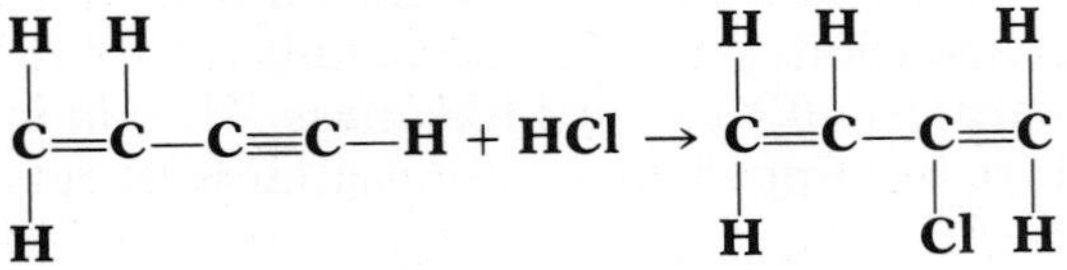

Vinylacetylene   Chloroprene

The catalytic polymerization of chloroprene yields the neoprene unit:

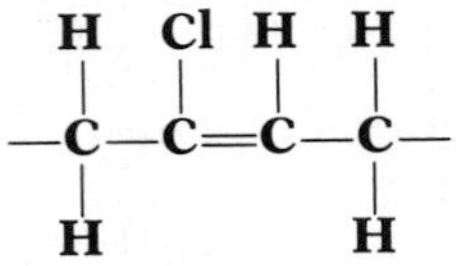

Oils and greases cause natural rubber to swell and rot. They have little effect on neoprene. Hence, neoprene is used in gasoline delivery hoses and in other objects that must be flexible while resisting the action of hydrocarbons.

18.28 *SBR,* a synthetic rubber for tires

SBR, Styrene Butadiene Rubber, is a good all-purpose synthetic rubber. It can replace natural rubber for most purposes. It is used for automobile tire treads because it resists wear better than other synthetic rubbers. It is made by churning *butadiene* (Section 18.19) and *styrene* (Section 18.22) together in soapy water. The churning is carried out at 5°C, using a catalyst. This causes the chemicals to polymerize and form *SBR* rubber. The addition of an acid causes the rubber to separate in curd-like masses, which are washed and dried. A possible structural unit is shown in the following structural formula:

What is the original raw material from which SBR *rubber is derived?*

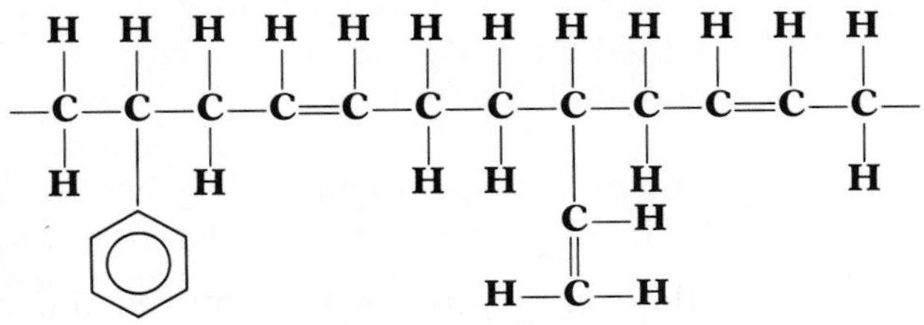

***SBR* Structural Unit**

SUMMARY

The number of possible carbon compounds is almost unlimited. There are many carbon compounds because (*1*) carbon atoms link together with covalent bonds, and (*2*) the same atoms may be arranged in several different ways. Isomers are compounds having the same molecular formula but different structures. Structural formulas indicate what kinds of atoms, how many of each, and how they are arranged in the molecule.

Most organic compounds do not dissolve in water. Organic compounds are decomposed by heat more easily than most inorganic compounds. Organic reactions generally proceed at much slower rates than inorganic reactions. Organic compounds exist as molecules consisting of atoms joined by covalent bonds.

Hydrocarbons are compounds composed only of carbon and hydrogen. Their sources are natural gas and petroleum. Some pure hydrocarbons, but more commonly mixtures of hydrocarbons, are separated from natural gas and petroleum by fractional distillation. Fractional distillation is a method of separating the components of a mixture on the basis of differences in their boiling points.

Hydrocarbons are grouped into different series based mainly on the type of bonding between carbon atoms. (*1*) Alkanes —straight-chain or branched-chain hydrocarbons with carbon atoms connected by only single covalent bonds. (*2*) Alkenes—straight- or branched-chain hydrocarbons in which two carbon atoms in each molecule are connected by a double covalent bond. (*3*) Alkynes—straight- or branched-chain hydrocarbons in which two carbon atoms in each molecule are connected by a triple covalent bond. (*4*) Alkadienes—straight- or branched-chain hydrocarbons having two double covalent bonds between carbon atoms in each molecule. (*5*) Aromatic hydrocarbons—resonance structures represented by alternate single and double covalent bonds in six-membered carbon rings.

Alkanes are found in natural gas and petroleum. Alkenes are produced from petroleum by cracking. Cracking is a process by which complex organic molecules are broken up into simpler molecules by the action of heat, and sometimes a catalyst. Ethyne, the simplest alkyne, is prepared from calcium carbide or by the partial oxidation of methane from petroleum refining. Butadiene, an alkadiene, is prepared by cracking butane separated from petroleum. Simple aromatic hydrocarbons are obtained from petroleum; more complex aromatic hydrocarbons come from coal tar.

Important types of hydrocarbon reactions: Alkanes—combustion, substitution, and cracking. Alkenes—addition, polymerization, alkylation, and combustion. Alkynes—combustion, addition, dimerization. Benzene—halogenation, nitration, sulfonation, and addition of alkyl groups.

The octane rating of a gasoline is a number that indicates the tendency of a gasoline to knock in a high-compression engine. Straight-chain alkanes have low octane ratings. Saturated ring-type hydrocarbons have intermediate octane ratings. Highly branched alkanes and aromatic hydrocarbons have high octane ratings. Gasoline is a mixture of all these types of hydrocarbons blended in the proportions needed to give the desired octane rating.

Natural rubber is an elastic hydrocarbon material obtained from rubber trees. It is a polymer of a large number of C_5H_8 units joined in a zigzag chain. Rubber is compounded by mixing it with sulfur, sometimes carbon black, and other ingredients. The mixture is vulcanized by heating it to a definite temperature for a definite time. This gives the rubber article a permanent shape, makes it more elastic, and causes it to lose its sticky qualities. Neoprene and styrene butadiene rubber are two kinds of synthetic rubber.

QUESTIONS

Group A

1. Give two reasons for the existence of so many carbon compounds.
2. What does a dash(—) represent in a structural formula?
3. What information do you obtain from a properly written structural formula?
4. Give four important differences between organic and inorganic compounds.
5. Describe the composition of (*a*) natural gas; (*b*) petroleum.
6. (*a*) What is *fractional distillation*? (*b*) How effective is it in separating the components of petroleum?
7. (*a*) What use is made of the petroleum fraction having 5 to 7 carbon atoms per molecule? (*b*) What use is made of the petroleum fraction that has a boiling point range of 250°C to 400°C?
8. What are the general formulas for (*a*) the alkane series; (*b*) the alkene series; (*c*) the alkyne series?
9. A hydrocarbon contains six carbon atoms. Give its empirical formula if it is (*a*) an alkane; (*b*) an alkene; (*c*) an alkyne.
10. Beyond the first four members of the alkane series, how are the hydrocarbons of this series named?
11. What does the formula RH represent?

12. How is methane produced in the laboratory?
13. Write a balanced formula equation for the complete combustion of (*a*) methane; (*b*) ethene; (*c*) ethyne (*d*) butadiene.
14. Write equations for the step-by-step substitution of each of the hydrogen atoms in methane by bromine.
15. (*a*) What is *cracking*? (*b*) Distinguish between thermal and catalytic cracking.
16. Butene reacts with hydrogen in the presence of a nickel catalyst. Write a structural-formula equation for the reaction.
17. (*a*) What is a monomer? (*b*) a dimer? (*c*) a polymer? (*d*) polymerization?
18. What are two uses for ethyne?
19. What do the terms *saturated* and *unsaturated* mean when applied to hydrocarbons?
20. Why is calcium carbide sold in air-tight metal cans?
21. How are naphthalene and anthracene related structurally to benzene?
22. (*a*) What causes knocking in an automobile engine? (*b*) How is gasoline formulated to prevent knocking?
23. If a gasoline has an octane rating of 96, what does this mean?
24. How is rubber separated out from latex?
25. What probably accounts for the elasticity of rubber?
26. How is rubber compounded?
27. Why are additives used in making rubber goods?
28. What is vulcanization?
29. What advantage does neoprene have over natural rubber?

Group B

30. Why would you expect organic compounds with covalent bonds to be less stable to heat than inorganic compounds with ionic bonds?
31. Compare the action shown in Figure 12-6 with that on a single trough in Figure 18-3.
32. Draw structural formulas for the five isomers of hexane.
33. When burned completely, decane, $C_{10}H_{22}$, forms carbon dioxide and water vapor. Write the chemical equation.
34. Draw the structural formula for 2,2-dichloropropane.
35. Draw structural formulas for three isomers of trichloropentane.
36. The element that appears in the greatest number of compounds is hydrogen. The element forming the second greatest number of compounds is carbon. Why are there more hydrogen compounds than carbon compounds?
37. Write a structural formula equation for the reaction of isobutane and isobutene which produces 2,2,4-trimethylpentane.
38. Write the structural formula equation for the preparation of vinylacetylene from ethyne.
39. (*a*) Is it geometrically possible for the four hydrogen atoms attached to the end carbon atoms in the 1,3-butadiene molecule to lie in the same plane? (*b*) If carbon-hydrogen bonds on adjacent singly bonded carbon atoms tend to repel each other, would it be likely that all six hydrogen atoms lie in the same plane? (*c*) If they do, what is their relation to the plane of the carbon atoms?
40. For the compound propadiene (*a*) draw the structural formula; (*b*) write the electron-dot formula; (*c*) using tetrahedral carbon atoms, draw the molecule, showing the orientation of the valence bonds; (*d*) from your drawing, decide whether all the hydrogen atoms lie in the same plane or not.
41. The formulas for the first four members of the benzene series are C_6H_6, C_7H_8, C_8H_{10}, C_9H_{12}. What is the general formula for the benzene series?
42. (*a*) What is *resonance?* (*b*) Using structural valence-bond formulas, explain resonance in the benzene molecule.

(*c*) Is a double bond in a benzene molecule the same as a double bond in an ethene molecule?

43. Write equations for the step-by-step substitution of each of the hydrogen atoms in benzene by bromine.
44. Write a structural-formula equation for the preparation of methyl benzene from benzene and methyl chloride by the Friedel-Crafts reaction.
45. Draw (*a*) the three possible valence-bond structural formulas for naphthalene; (*b*) the four possible valence-bond structural formulas for anthracene.
46. (*a*) What materials are polymerized to produce *SBR* rubber? (*b*) What is an important use for *SBR* rubber? (*c*) Why is it used for this purpose?
47. The off-shore drilling rig shown on page 369 will tap an underwater source of petroleum. Why is petroleum sometimes referred to as "black gold"?

PROBLEMS

Group A

1. What is the mass in kilograms of 15.0 gallons of gasoline? Assume the gasoline is iso-octane which has a density of 0.692 g/ml.
2. Calculate the percentage composition of butane.
3. What volume of carbon dioxide is produced by the complete combustion of 25.0 liters of propane? The volumes of carbon dioxide and of propane are measured under the same conditions.
4. How many grams of calcium carbide are required for the production of 2.0 liters of ethyne at STP?

Group B

5. A compound consists of 60.0% carbon, 26.7% oxygen, and 13.3% hydrogen. Its molecular weight is $6\bar{0}$. What are the possible structures for molecules of this compound?
6. Calculate the energy change of the substitution reaction between one mole of methane and one mole of bromine molecules. Use the bond energies given in Table 6-4.
7. A volume of ethene (135 ml) is collected by water displacement at 22°C and 738 mm pressure. What is the volume of the dry ethene at STP?
8. A compound consists of 93.75% carbon and 6.25% hydrogen. The substance dissolves in benzene and 6.40 g of it lowers the freezing point of $10\bar{0}$ g of benzene 2.55 C°. (*a*) What is the empirical formula of the compound? (*b*) What is its molecular weight? (*c*) What is its molecular formula? See Table 13-5 for necessary data.

chapter 19

HYDROCARBON SUBSTITUTION PRODUCTS

Apple cider in the making. (The chemistry involved here is discussed in Section 19-10.)

Halogen Substitution Products

19.1 Preparation of alkyl halides

*An **alkyl halide** is an alkane in which a halogen atom*—fluorine, chlorine, bromine, or iodine—*is substituted for a hydrogen atom.* Since **R** often is used to represent an alkyl group and **X** may represent any halogen, we may represent an alkyl halide as **RX.**

1. Direct halogenation. In Section 18.12, we noted that the halogens react with alkanes and form substitution products. Under suitable conditions, for example, halogen atoms can be substituted for each of the four hydrogen atoms in methane. This reaction occurs in four stages.

$$CH_4 + X_2 \rightarrow CH_3X + HX$$
$$CH_3X + X_2 \rightarrow CH_2X_2 + HX$$
$$CH_2X_2 + X_2 \rightarrow CHX_3 + HX$$
$$CHX_3 + X_2 \rightarrow CX_4 + HX$$

2. From alkenes and alkynes. We recognized in Sections 18.15 and 18.18 that alkenes and alkynes react with halogens or hydrogen halides and form alkyl halides.

3. From alcohols. Alcohols are alkanes in which the hydroxyl group, **—OH,** has been substituted for hydrogen. Hence, an alcohol has the type formula **ROH.** The reaction of an alcohol with a hydrogen halide, HCl, HBr, or HI, yields the corresponding alkyl halide.

$$ROH + HX \rightarrow RX + H_2O$$

19.2 Reactions of the alkyl halides

Alkyl halides react with many molecules and ions. One result of these changes is the substitution of another atom or group of atoms for the halogen atom.

For example, alkyl halides react with water solutions of strong hydroxides and yield alcohols and the halide ion. The hydroxyl group is substituted for the halogen atom in the alkyl halide.

$$\mathbf{RX + OH^- \rightarrow ROH + X^-}$$

The Friedel-Crafts reaction [Section 18.21(4)] is an alkyl halide substitution reaction. Here the phenyl group, $C_6H_5^-$, is substituted for the halogen atom in the alkyl halide.

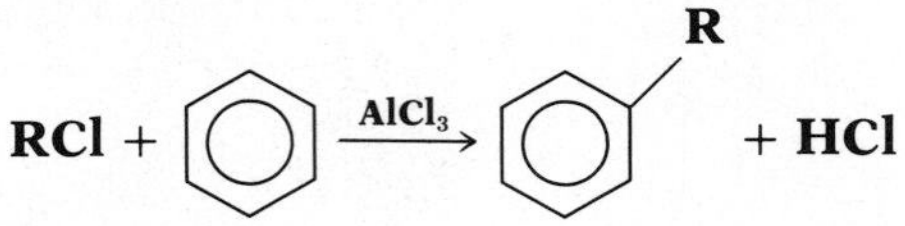

19.3 Specific alkyl halides

Tetrachloromethane, CCl_4, is commonly called carbon tetrachloride. It is a colorless, volatile, nonflammable liquid. It is an excellent solvent. Carbon tetrachloride is sometimes used for dry cleaning fabrics, removing grease from metals, and extracting oils from seeds. Its vapors are poisonous. Therefore, *there must be good ventilation when carbon tetrachloride is used.* Its most important use is in the preparation of Freon-type compounds. Carbon tetrachloride is prepared commercially by the direct chlorination of methane.

$$\mathbf{CH_4 + 4Cl_2 \rightarrow CCl_4 + 4HCl}$$

Trichloromethane, $CHCl_3$, commonly named chloroform, is a sweet-smelling, colorless liquid. It is used as a solvent. Its use in medicinal preparations has been restricted because it can possibly cause cancer. Chloroform is manufactured by reducing carbon tetrachloride with moist iron.

Dichlorodifluoromethane, CCl_2F_2, is the most important member of a family of compounds named Freon. It is used as a refrigerant in mechanical refrigerators and air conditioners. This particular Freon is an odorless, nontoxic, nonflammable, easily liquefied gas. It is prepared from carbon tetrachloride and hydrofluoric acid with antimony compounds as catalysts.

$$\mathbf{CCl_4 + 2HF \xrightarrow{catalyst} CCl_2F_2 + 2HCl}$$

The presence of ozone in the stratosphere and its role in protecting the earth's surface from an excess of ultraviolet radiation from the sun were described in Section 9.9.

Freon-type compounds, released into the air, do rise into the stratosphere. There it is believed ultraviolet radiation from the sun decomposes these compounds, releasing free halogen atoms. The free halogen atoms then react with the ozone molecules. By a series of reactions it is believed the ozone molecules become oxygen molecules. What happens to the halogen atoms after these reactions is unclear. One theory is that the halogen atoms start the decomposition of more ozone. In this way, a small number of halogen atoms can decompose a large number of ozone molecules. Another theory is that the halogen atoms become combined in a compound with nitrogen and oxygen and do not react with more ozone. A decrease in the concentration of ozone in the stratosphere will allow more potentially harmful ultraviolet radiation to reach the earth. As a consequence, the use of Freons as propellants in aerosol cans is being discontinued in the United States.

Tetrafluoroethene, C_2F_4, can be polymerized. The product has a structure in which the following unit occurs again and again:

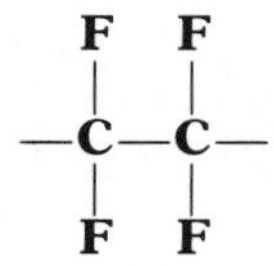

This material is called Teflon. Teflon is a very inactive, flexible substance that is stable up to about 325°C. It is made into fibers for weaving chemical-resistant fabrics, or into rods from which small parts may be formed. Teflon has a very low coefficient of friction. It is useful where heat-resistant, nonlubricated moving parts are needed. It is also used to coat metals and give them a "nonsticking" surface.

Alcohols

19.4 Preparations of alcohols

Alcohols are alkanes in which one or more *hydroxyl* groups, —OH, have been substituted for a like number of hydrogen atoms. (The covalent bonded hydroxyl group must not be confused with the ionic bonded hydroxide ion.)

1. Hydration of alkenes. Ethene reacts exothermically with concentrated sulfuric acid at room temperature. The sulfuric acid molecule adds to the double bond. One hydrogen atom of the sulfuric acid molecule adds to one carbon. The remainder of the sulfuric acid molecule adds to the other carbon.

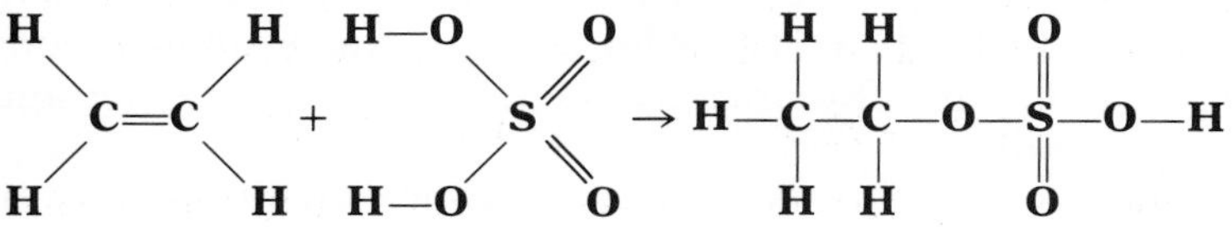

If this mixture is diluted with water, the ethene-sulfuric acid-addition compound reacts and produces C_2H_5OH, called ethanol or ethyl alcohol.

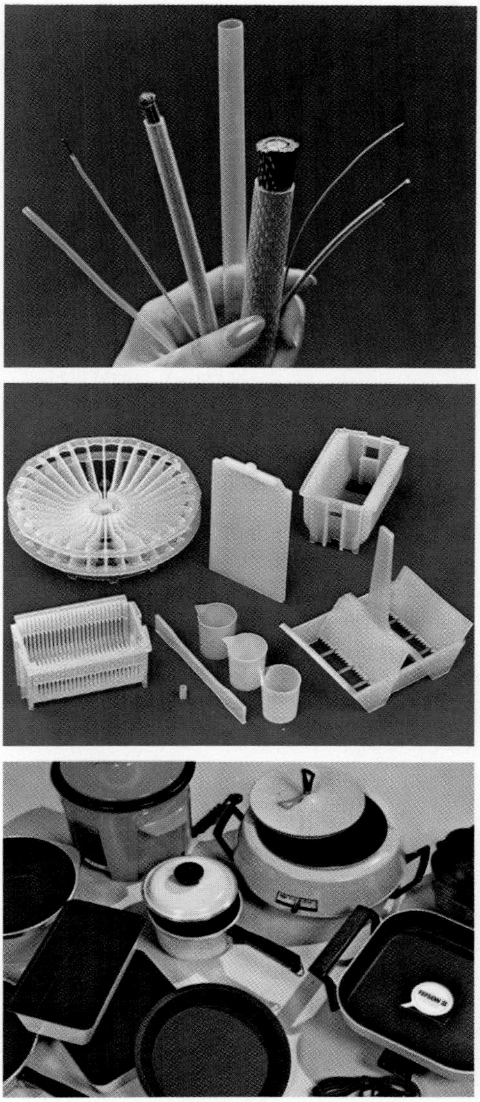

Fig. 19-1. Teflon is used to make tubing, wire insulation, a variety of molded containers, and a nonstick coating on cooking utensils.

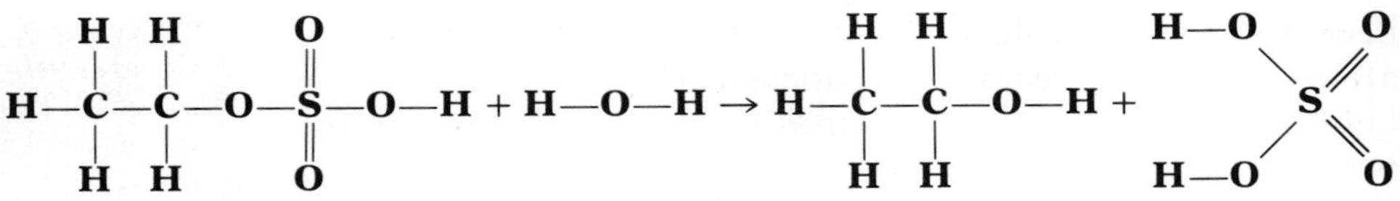

The overall effect of these two reactions is the addition of water across the ethene double bond.

2. From alkyl halides. We mentioned in Section 19.2 that alkyl halides react with water solutions of strong hydroxides and yield alcohols.

3. Methanol. Methanol is prepared from carbon monoxide and hydrogen under pressure, using a catalyst. See Section 17.23. Methanol is a colorless liquid with a rather pleasant odor. It has a low density and boils at 64.7°C. *It is very poisonous, even when used externally.* If taken internally in small quantities, it causes blindness by destroying the cells of the nerve that connects the eyes to the brain. Larger quantities may cause death. Methanol is a good fuel, burning with a hot, smokeless flame. It is used as a solvent and in denaturing alcohol. It serves as a starting material for preparing other organic compounds such as formaldehyde. Methanol is also used in automobile gas-tank de-icers. The methanol in these products prevents water which has condensed in the tank from freezing there as well as in the gas line and carburetor.

The depression of the freezing point of solvents by molecular solutes was explained in Section 13.12.

4. Ethanol. Large quantities of ethanol are produced by hydrating ethene. Another method is by fermentation. If we add yeast to a dilute solution of sugar or molasses at room temperature, chemical action soon occurs. The yeast plants secrete the enzymes sucrase and zymase. These enzymes act as catalysts in changing the sugar into alcohol and carbon dioxide.

$$C_{12}H_{22}O_{11} + H_2O \rightarrow 4CO_2 + 4C_2H_5OH$$

Both processes are used in producing industrial ethanol. However, hydration of ethene is a less expensive method and is replacing the fermentation process.

Ethanol is a colorless liquid. It has a characteristic odor and a sharp, biting taste. It boils at 78°C, freezes at −115°C, and burns with a nearly colorless blue flame. Ethanol is a good solvent for many organic compounds that are insoluble in water. Accordingly, it is used for making a variety of solutions for medicinal use. Ethanol is also used for making ether and acetaldehyde.

Denatured alcohol is a mixture composed principally of ethanol. But it contains added poisonous and nauseating materials that make it unfit for beverage purposes.

Molecules of methanol and ethanol have been detected in interstellar space.

5. Ethylene glycol. The compound ethylene glycol, $C_2H_4(OH)_2$, has the structural formula

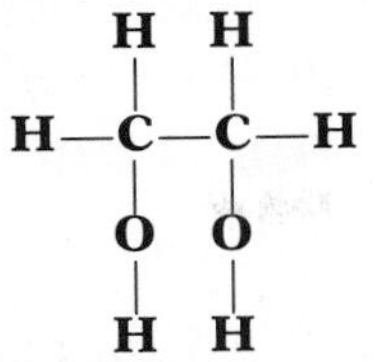

In ethylene glycol and other alcohols with more than one hydroxyl group, the hydroxyl groups are usually bonded to different carbon atoms. Two hydroxyl groups attached to the same carbon atom are mostly unstable. They may produce a formyl group (Section 19.7), or a carbonyl group (Section 19.9), and water.

Ethylene glycol is an alcohol containing two hydroxyl groups. It is used extensively as a "permanent" antifreeze in automobile radiators. Its boiling point is so much higher than that of water that it does not readily evaporate or boil away. Ethylene glycol is poisonous.

6. Glycerol. Glycerol, or glycerin, $C_3H_5(OH)_3$, has the structural·formula

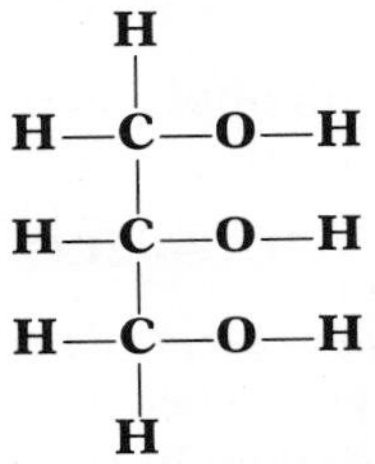

It is a colorless, odorless, slow-flowing liquid with a sweet taste. It has a low vapor pressure and is hygroscopic. It is used in making synthetic resins for paints and in cigarettes to keep the tobacco moist. It is also used in the manufacture of cellophane, in making nitroglycerin, and in some toilet soaps. Glycerol is an ingredient of cosmetics and drugs and is used in many foods and beverages. It is a by-product of soap manufacture. Large quantities of glycerol are synthesized from propene, a product of petroleum cracking.

Hygroscopic materials are described in Section 12.20.

Alcohols with several hydroxyl groups have a sweet taste and are used as sugar substitutes. Xylitol, $CH_2OH(CHOH)_3CH_2OH$, is used in sugarless chewing gum. Mannitol and sorbitol, isomers of $CH_2OH(CHOH)_4CH_2OH$, are used as sweeteners in foods for diabetics.

If the molecular formula for glycerol were written like the formulas given here, it would be $CH_2OH(CHOH)CH_2OH$.

19.5 Reactions of alcohols

1. With sodium. Sodium reacts vigorously with ethanol, releasing hydrogen. A second product of the reaction is sodium ethoxide, C_2H_5ONa. This compound is recovered as a white solid after the excess ethanol is evaporated. This reaction is similar to the reaction of sodium with water.

$$2C_2H_5OH + 2Na \rightarrow 2C_2H_5ONa + H_2$$

2. *With HX.* Alcohols react with concentrated water solutions of hydrogen halides, particularly hydrobromic, HBr, and hydriodic, HI, acids. These reactions produce alkyl halides. Sulfuric acid is used as a dehydrating agent.

$$\mathbf{ROH + HBr \rightarrow RBr + H_2O}$$

3. *Dehydration.* Depending on reaction conditions, ethanol dehydrated by hot concentrated sulfuric acid yields either diethyl ether, $C_2H_5OC_2H_5$, or ethene, C_2H_4.

$$\mathbf{2C_2H_5OH \rightarrow C_2H_5OC_2H_5 + H_2O}$$

$$\mathbf{C_2H_5OH \rightarrow C_2H_4 + H_2O}$$

4. *Oxidation.* Alcohols that have the hydroxyl group attached to the end carbon may be oxidized by hot copper(II) oxide. The product of such an oxidation is an aldehyde, RCHO.

$$\mathbf{RCH_2OH + CuO \rightarrow RCHO + H_2O + Cu}$$

Low-molecular-weight alcohols are flammable, and burn readily in air.

$$\mathbf{2CH_3OH + 3O_2 \rightarrow 2CO_2 + 4H_2O}$$

5. *Sulfation of long-chain alcohols.* 1-dodecanol, $C_{12}H_{25}OH$, is commonly called lauryl alcohol. It is obtained from coconut oil by hydrogenation and partial decomposition. Lauryl alcohol may be *sulfated* by treatment with sulfuric acid and then neutralized with sodium hydroxide. This process yields sodium lauryl sulfate, $C_{12}H_{25}OSO_2ONa$, a very effective cleaning agent.

$$\mathbf{C_{12}H_{25}OH + H_2SO_4 \rightarrow C_{12}H_{25}OSO_2OH + H_2O}$$

$$\mathbf{C_{12}H_{25}OSO_2OH + NaOH \rightarrow C_{12}H_{25}OSO_2ONa + H_2O}$$

Ethers

19.6 Ethers: organic oxides

Ethers have the general formula **ROR′**. **R** and **R′** represent the same or different alkyl groups. Ethers may be thought of as being structurally similar to water. But both hydrogen atoms have been replaced by alkyl groups. Ethers can be prepared by dehydrating alcohols as described in Section 19.5. Diethyl ether is commonly known as *ether*. It is a volatile, very flammable, colorless liquid of characteristic odor. It can be made by heating ethanol and sulfuric acid to 140°C.

$$\mathbf{2C_2H_5OH \xrightarrow{H_2SO_4} C_2H_5OC_2H_5 + H_2O}$$

Ether is used as a solvent for fats and oils. Ether molecules have been found in outer space.

Ethers may be synthesized by the action of a sodium alkoxide, such as sodium ethoxide, on an alkyl halide, such as methyl bromide. The ether and a sodium halide are products.

This is another example of a substitution reaction of an alkyl halide (Section 19.2). The alkoxide group is substituted for the halogen.

$$\mathbf{RONa + R'X \rightarrow ROR' + NaX}$$

$$\mathbf{C_2H_5ONa + CH_3Br \rightarrow C_2H_5OCH_3 + NaBr}$$

Depending on the alkyl group in the alkoxide and in the alkyl halide, ethers with different alkyl groups attached to the oxygen may be produced. The equation above shows the preparation of methyl ethyl ether.

Aldehydes

19.7 Preparations of aldehydes

An aldehyde is a compound that has a hydrocarbon group and one or more *formyl* groups, 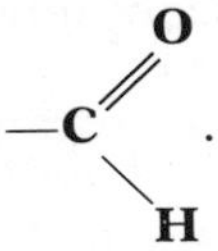. The general formula for an *aldehyde* is **RCHO.**

The general method of preparing aldehydes was mentioned in Section 19.5. A common process of this type involves passing methanol vapor and a regulated amount of air over heated copper. Formaldehyde, HCHO, is produced.

$$\mathbf{2Cu + O_2 \rightarrow 2CuO}$$

$$\mathbf{CH_3OH + CuO \rightarrow HCHO + H_2O + Cu}$$

The commercial preparation of formaldehyde involves a silver or an iron-molybdenum oxide catalyst. At room temperature, formaldehyde is a gas with a strangling odor. Dissolved in water, it makes an excellent disinfectant. It is also used to preserve biological or medical specimens. By far the largest use of formaldehyde is in making certain types of adhesives for plywood and particle board and resins for plastics.

Acetaldehyde, CH_3CHO may be made by the oxidation of ethanol. It is a stable liquid used in preparing other organic compounds. Both formaldehyde and acetaldehyde molecules are found in space.

Fig. 19-2. A brick-red precipitate of copper(I) oxide is evidence of a positive Fehling's test.

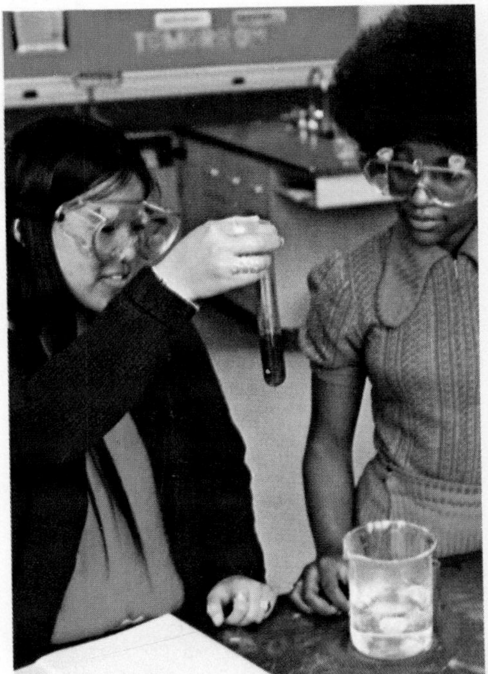

19.8 Reactions of aldehydes

1. Oxidation. The mild oxidation of an aldehyde produces the organic acid having the same number of carbon atoms. The oxidation of acetaldehyde to acetic acid is typical.

$$\mathbf{CH_3CHO + O\ (from\ oxidizing\ agent) \rightarrow CH_3COOH}$$

2. Fehling's test. Fehling's solution A is copper(II) sulfate solution. Fehling's solution B is sodium hydroxide and sodium tartrate solution. If these are mixed with an aldehyde and heated, the aldehyde is oxidized. The copper(II) ion is reduced to copper(I) and precipitated as brick-red copper(I) oxide.

$$RCHO + 2CuSO_4 + 5NaOH \rightarrow RCOONa + Cu_2O + 2Na_2SO_4 + 3H_2O$$

3. *Hydrogen addition.* Adding hydrogen to aldehydes in the presence of finely divided nickel or platinum produces alcohols.

$$RCHO + H_2 \xrightarrow{Ni} RCH_2OH$$

This reaction is the reverse of the oxidation of alcohols to aldehydes.

Ketones

19.9 Preparation and properties of acetone

Organic compounds containing the carbonyl group $\rangle C{=}O$ and having the general formula **RCOR′** are *ketones.*

Ketones may be prepared from alcohols that do *not* have the hydroxyl group attached to an end-carbon atom. For example, acetone, CH_3COCH_3, is prepared by the mild oxidation of 2-propanol, $CH_3CHOHCH_3$. Potassium dichromate, $K_2Cr_2O_7$, in water solution is the oxidizing agent.

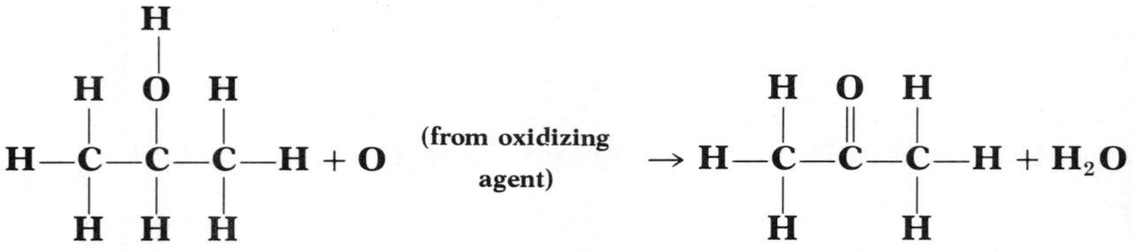

2-propanol **Acetone**

Acetone is a colorless, volatile liquid. It is widely used as a solvent in the manufacture of acetate rayon. Storage tanks for ethyne gas are loosely filled with asbestos saturated with acetone. The ethyne dissolves in the acetone and by doing so occupies less volume. This procedure increases the amount of ethyne that can safely be compressed into the tank. Acetone and other ketones are used for cleaning metals, removing stains, and for preparing synthetic organic chemicals. Acetone is a digestive product of untreated diabetics.

Carboxylic Acids and Esters

19.10 Preparations of carboxylic acids

Many organic acids and their salts occur naturally. They are found in sour milk, unripe fruits, rhubarb, sorrel, and other plants. All organic acids contain the *carboxyl* group,

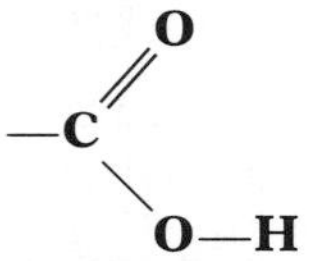

The general formula for a *carboxylic acid* is **RCOOH.**

1. Oxidation of alcohols or aldehydes. The oxidation of alcohols to aldehydes and of aldehydes to carboxylic acids was described in Sections 19.5 and 19.8. Pure acetic acid is produced by the catalytic oxidation of acetaldehyde. Concentrated acetic acid is a colorless liquid that is a good solvent for some organic chemicals. It is used for making cellulose acetate, a basic material of many fibers and films.

Cider vinegar is made from apple cider that has fermented to hard cider. The ethanol in hard cider is slowly oxidized by the oxygen of the air. This oxidation produces acetic acid. The reaction is catalyzed by enzymes from certain bacteria.

$$\mathbf{C_2H_5OH + O_2 \rightarrow CH_3COOH + H_2O}$$

Vinegar contains from 4% to 6% acetic acid.

2. Formic acid. Formic acid, HCOOH, is prepared from sodium hydroxide solution and carbon monoxide under pressure. This reaction yields sodium formate, HCOONa.

$$\mathbf{NaOH + CO \rightarrow HCOONa}$$

If sodium formate is carefully heated with sulfuric acid, formic acid distills off.

$$\mathbf{HCOONa + H_2SO_4 \rightarrow HCOOH + NaHSO_4}$$

Formic acid is found in nature in stinging nettle plants, in the sting of bees, wasps, and hornets, and in red ants. It is also one of the molecules found in outer space. Formic acid is used as an acidifying agent in the textile industry.

Formic acid molecules

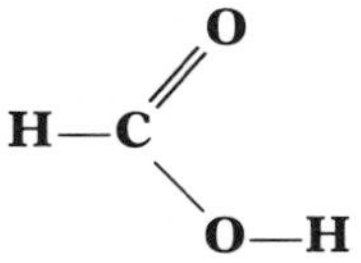

contain two carbon-oxygen bonds. One of them, the double bond, is 1.23 Å long. The other, the single bond, is 1.36 Å long. This evidence supports our idea that these bonds are different. In sodium formate, an ionic compound, the formate ion also has two carbon-oxygen bonds. But these bonds have the same length, 1.27 Å. What explanation is there for this difference? Because the carbon-oxygen bonds in the formate ion are the same length, they should be similar. The formate ion must be a resonance hybrid of two structures

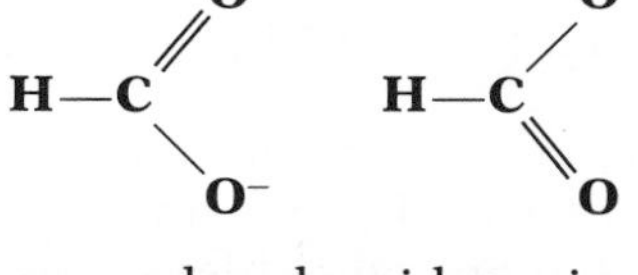

and have carbon-oxygen bonds midway in character between single and double covalent bonds. Similar resonance hybrid

Fig. 19-3. Welding, using ethyne (acetylene) gas. The tank in which the ethyne is stored is loosely filled with asbestos saturated with acetone. The ethyne dissolves in the acetone. The amount of ethyne that may be safely stored in the tank under pressure is increased.

Resonance was first described in Section 6.22.

structures are characteristic of the anions of other carboxylic acids.

19.11 Reactions of carboxylic acids

1. Ionization. This reaction involves the one hydrogen atom bonded to an oxygen atom in the carboxyl group. This hydrogen atom ionizes in water solution, giving carboxylic acids their acid properties. The hydrogen atoms bonded to carbon atoms in these acids *never* ionize in water solution.

$$HCOOH + H_2O \rightleftarrows H_3O^+ + HCOO^-$$

$$CH_3COOH + H_2O \rightleftarrows H_3O^+ + CH_3COO^-$$

These equilibria yield low H_3O^+ ion concentrations. Therefore, carboxylic acids are generally weak acids.

2. Neutralization. An organic acid may be neutralized by a hydroxide. A salt is formed in a reaction similar to those of inorganic acids.

$$CH_3COOH + NaOH \rightarrow CH_3COONa + H_2O$$

3. Esterification. An **ester** *is produced when an acid reacts with an alcohol.* Such reactions are called *esterification reactions.* For example, ethyl acetate is the ester formed when ethanol and acetic acid react.

$$CH_3COOH + C_2H_5OH \xrightarrow{H_2SO_4} CH_3COOC_2H_5 + H_2O$$

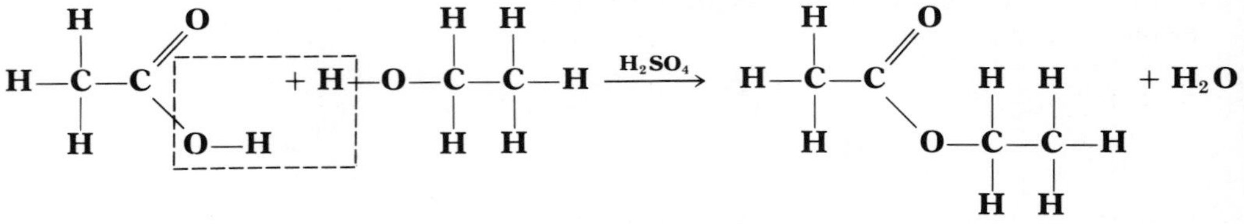

All such reactions between acids and alcohols are reversible. Achievement of equilibrium is slow and a small amount of sulfuric acid is used as a catalyst. Experiments with alcohols containing oxygen-18 show that the oxygen of the water product comes from the acid.

19.12 Esters

It is also possible to prepare esters by the reaction of alcohols with inorganic acids. Glyceryl trinitrate, known as nitroglycerin, is an example.

$$C_3H_5(OH)_3 + 3HNO_3 \xrightarrow{H_2SO_4} C_3H_5(NO_3)_3 + 3H_2O$$

Esters give fruits their characteristic flavors and odors. Amyl acetate, $CH_3COOC_5H_{11}$, has an odor somewhat resembling bananas. As "banana oil," this ester is used as the carrier for some aluminum paints. Ethyl butyrate has an odor and flavor that resemble pineapples. Ripe pineapples contain some of this ester and smaller amounts of other esters.

Esters can be decomposed by hydrolysis into the alcohol and acid from which they were derived. This hydrolysis may occur in the presence of dilute acid or metallic hydroxide solutions.

Fig. 19-4. In the *kettle method* of soap making, fats and oils are boiled with sodium hydroxide.

19.13 Saponification

Fats and oils are esters of glycerol and long-carbon-chain acids. The carbon chains of the acids usually contain from 12 to 20 carbon atoms. The structure of a fat or oil may be represented as

$$\begin{array}{c} \mathbf{RCOOCH_2} \\ | \\ \mathbf{R'COOCH} \\ | \\ \mathbf{R''COOCH_2} \end{array}$$

R, **R′**, and **R″** are saturated or unsaturated long-chain-hydrocarbon groups.

The only difference between a fat and an oil is the physical phase of each at room temperature. Oils are liquids at room temperature, while fats are solids. Long-carbon-chain acids with double bonds produce esters having lower melting points. Hence, oils usually contain more unsaturated hydrocarbon chains than those found in fats.

Saponification *is the hydrolysis of a fat using a solution of a strong hydroxide.* Alkaline hydrolysis produces the sodium salt of the long-chain carboxylic acid instead of the acid itself.

$$\begin{array}{l} \mathbf{RCOOCH_2} \\ \quad\quad | \\ \mathbf{R'COOCH} + \mathbf{3NaOH} \rightarrow \mathbf{RCOONa} + \mathbf{R'COONa} + \mathbf{R''COONa} + \mathbf{C_3H_5(OH)_3} \\ \quad\quad | \\ \mathbf{R''COOCH_2} \end{array}$$

Soaps are generally made by hydrolyzing fats and oils with water heated to about 250°C in a closed container. The water is under a pressure of about 50 atmospheres. At this pressure, it does not boil despite the temperature which is well above its boiling point. The long-chain carboxylic acids thus produced are neutralized with sodium hydroxide. This neutralization yields a mixture of sodium salts that makes up soap.

If the acid chains are unsaturated, a soft soap results. Soaps with hydrocarbon chains of 10 to 12 carbon atoms are soluble in water and produce a large-bubble lather. Soaps containing hydrocarbon chains of 16 to 18 carbon atoms are less soluble in water and give a longer-lasting small-bubble lather. Soap that is a mixture of potassium salts, rather than of sodium salts, is generally more soluble in water.

stronger and stronger

For centuries, fabrics were made from natural fibers — cotton, wool, flax, and hemp. The first synthetic fiber was rayon, made from wood, a natural product. Nylon was the first entirely synthetic fiber made from the elements in coal, air, and water. "Kevlar" aramid fiber, the most recently discovered synthetic, is more than five times stronger than steel. Kevlar is used in tires and astronauts' suits because of its strength and puncture resistance.

At left: Walter H. Carothers, an organic chemist, is shown stretching a piece of neoprene, the first successful synthetic rubber. Dr. Carothers also directed the research team that produced nylon.

Below: Liquefied cellulose, squirted into an acid solution, forms viscose rayon.

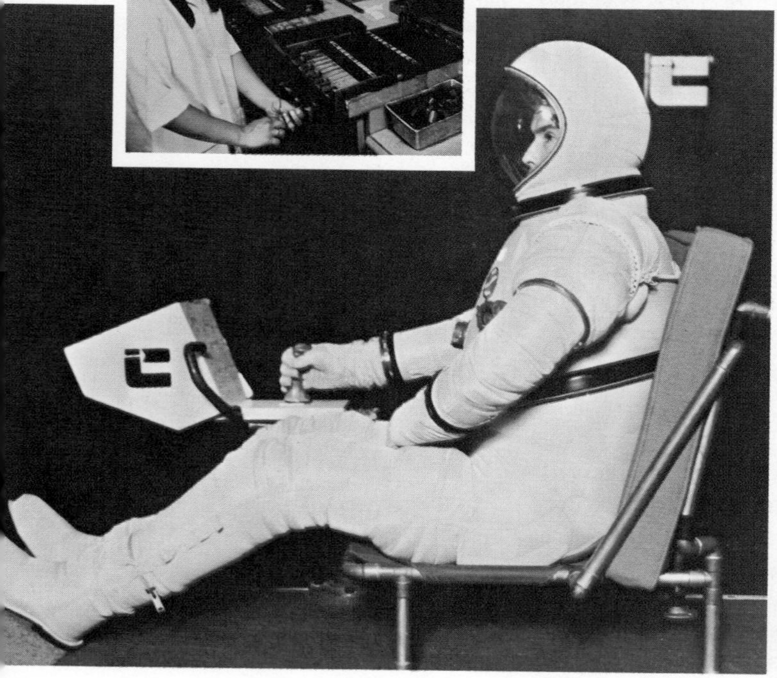

Above: Fatigue tests on "Kevlar" aramid fiber determine its strength under differing conditions (inset). The entire outer layer of this astronaut's suit is woven of "Kevlar" aramid because it must resist punctures and hold an atmosphere around the astronaut's body against the vacuum of space.

At right: Nylon, formed at the layer between these two chemicals, is pulled out as a rope (inset). Nylon is used for parachutes because it exceeds the strength of natural fibers.

SUMMARY

Hydrocarbon substitution products are those in which an atom such as chlorine or a group such as hydroxyl is substituted for one or more of the hydrogen atoms in a hydrocarbon.

An alkyl halide is an alkane in which a halogen atom is substituted for a hydrogen atom. Alkyl halides are prepared by the reaction of halogens with alkanes, alkenes, and alkynes and by the reaction of hydrogen halides with alkenes, alkynes, and alcohols. Many reactions of alkyl halides are substitution reactions. Examples of alkyl halides are carbon tetrachloride, chloroform, the Freons, and Teflon.

Alcohols are alkanes in which one or more hydroxyl groups have been substituted for a like number of hydrogen atoms. They are prepared by the hydration of alkenes and from alkyl halides by substitution. Important alcohols are methanol, ethanol, ethylene glycol, and glycerol. Alcohols react with sodium and with hydrogen halides. They also undergo dehydration, oxidation, and sulfation reactions.

Ethers are organic oxides with the general formula ROR′. They may be prepared by dehydrating alcohols or by the reaction of a sodium alkoxide and an alkyl halide. Diethyl ether is an important example.

Aldehydes have a hydrocarbon group and one or more formyl groups. The general formula is RCHO. They are prepared by the controlled oxidation of alcohols having an hydroxyl group on an end carbon. Formaldehyde and acetaldehyde are examples. Aldehydes undergo oxidation to acids and reduction with hydrogen to alcohols. They give positive Fehling's tests.

Ketones are organic compounds containing the carbonyl group and have the general formula RCOR′. They are prepared by oxidizing alcohols that do not have the hydroxyl group attached to the end-carbon atom. Acetone is an important ketone.

The general formula for carboxylic acids is RCOOH. They may be prepared by the oxidation of alcohols and aldehydes. Formic acid and acetic acid are familiar examples. Organic acids undergo ionization, neutralization, and esterification reactions. An ester is produced when an acid reacts with an alcohol. Esters give fruits their characteristic flavors and odors. Saponification is the hydrolysis of a fat using a solution of a strong hydroxide, such as sodium hydroxide. The sodium salts produced make up soap.

QUESTIONS

Group A

1. What are the type formulas for (*a*) alkyl halides; (*b*) alcohols; (*c*) ethers; (*d*) aldehydes; (*e*) ketones; (*f*) carboxylic acids; (*g*) esters?
2. (*a*) What are the uses of carbon tetrachloride? (*b*) What precautions must be exercised in its use?
3. How do alcohols differ from inorganic hydroxides?
4. What is the effect of methanol on the human body?
5. What property of glycerol makes it useful for keeping tobacco moist?
6. Compare the action of sodium with water and with methanol.
7. How many molecules of oxygen are required for the complete combustion of one molecule of butanol?
8. How is formaldehyde used in a biology laboratory?
9. (*a*) What is Fehling's test? (*b*) What organic group gives a positive Fehling's test?
10. For what purposes is acetone used?
11. (*a*) What is cider vinegar? (*b*) How may it be prepared?

12. (*a*) Oxalic acid is a dicarboxylic acid with the structural formula

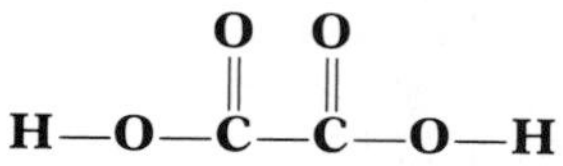

Write equations for the step-by-step complete ionization of oxalic acid. (*b*) How many moles of potassium hydroxide are required for the complete neutralization of four moles of oxalic acid?
13. What is the source of the hydrogen and oxygen atoms of the water eliminated during an esterification reaction?
14. In what types of reactions mentioned in this chapter is sulfuric acid used as a dehydrating agent?
15. (*a*) How are fats and oils alike? (*b*) How do they differ? (*c*) Why do they differ?
16. What is *saponification?*

Group B

17. Draw structural formulas for (*a*) dichloromethane; (*b*) 1,2,3-trihydroxypropane; (*c*) diethyl ether; (*d*) formaldehyde; (*e*) diethylketone; (*f*) acetic acid; (*g*) methyl formate.
18. Write the equations for the preparation of ethyl chloride starting with (*a*) ethane; (*b*) ethene; (*c*) ethanol.
19. Describe the types of alkyl halide substitution reactions given in this chapter.
20. Starting with methane, chlorine, and hydrogen fluoride, show how dichlorodifluoromethane is prepared.
21. What is believed to be the effect of Freon-type compounds in the stratosphere?
22. Using structural formula equations, show how ethanol may be prepared from (*a*) ethene; (*b*) ethyl chloride; (*c*) sugar ($C_{12}H_{22}O_{11}$).
23. On the basis of molecular weight and boiling point, compare the advantages of methanol, ethanol, and ethylene glycol as automobile antifreezes?
24. Write an equation for preparing propyl iodide starting with propyl alcohol.
25. Describe two methods by which dipropyl ether may be prepared.
26. What ketone is prepared by the mild oxidation of 2-butanol?
27. (*a*) How do the two carbon-oxygen bonds in formic acid compare? (*b*) How do the two carbon-oxygen bonds in sodium formate compare? (*c*) Account for the difference.
28. Write an equation showing the formation of the ester *n*-butyl acetate.
29. A fat has the formula $(C_{17}H_{35}COO)_3C_3H_5$. Write a balanced formula equation for its saponification with NaOH.

PROBLEMS

Group A

1. Calculate the molecular weight of dichlorodifluoromethane.
2. Sodium hydroxide solution (40.0 ml) exactly neutralizes 35.0 ml of 0.150-*N* formic acid solution. What is the normality of the sodium hydroxide solution?
3. Calculate the number of grams of glycerol that must be dissolved in 0.300 kg of water in order to prepare a 0.400-*m* solution.
4. How many grams of diprotic oxalic acid, $(COOH)_2$, are required in order to prepare 1.50 liters of 0.200-*N* acid?

Group B

5. What is the percentage composition of sodium lauryl sulfate, $C_{12}H_{25}OSO_2ONa$?
6. A compound is found to contain 54.5% carbon, 9.1% hydrogen and 36.4% oxygen. (*a*) Determine the empirical formula. (*b*) If the molecular weight is 88, what is the molecular formula?
7. The hydronium ion concentration in 0.05-*M* acetic acid is 9.4×10^{-4} mole/liter. What is the pH of this solution?
8. What volume of ethanol must be diluted with water to prepare $50\overline{0}$ ml of 0.750-*M* solution? The density of ethanol is 0.789 g/ml.

chapter 20

REACTION ENERGY AND REACTION KINETICS

Every substance has a characteristic internal energy because of its structure and physical state. (See Question 26 on page 437.)

20.1 Introduction

Chemical equations are often written to represent reactions between different molecular species. These equations show the initial reactants and the final products. They do not show how reactant molecules become product molecules during the reaction process. For example, gaseous iodine and hydrogen may react chemically and form gaseous hydrogen iodide. The equation for this reaction is written as follows:

$$H_2(g) + I_2(g) \rightarrow 2HI(g)$$

This equation makes it easy to picture molecules of hydrogen and iodine colliding in just the right way and separating as hydrogen iodide molecules. For this to happen, H—H and I—I bonds must be broken and H—I bonds must be formed during the extremely brief encounter.

Chemists are very interested in learning how reacting molecules change as a reaction proceeds. New techniques have been developed for studying molecular changes even in fast reaction systems. These methods explore the rates of chemical reactions and the pathways along which they occur. The branch of chemistry that is concerned with *reaction rates* and *reaction pathways* is called *chemical kinetics*. The pathway from reactants to products may be a sequence of simple steps called the *reaction mechanism.*

When chemists investigate reaction systems they look for the role of energy in these processes. Every substance has a characteristic internal energy because of its structure and physical state. Definite amounts of energy are released or absorbed when new substances are formed from reacting substances. These energy changes occur even when products and reactants are both at the same temperature. The energy change is related directly to the change in the number of bonds breaking and forming, and to the strengths of these bonds as the reactants form products.

The first part of this chapter will deal with changes in heat energy that accompany chemical reactions. This is *thermochemistry*. Later in the chapter, we will study the modern theories of reaction pathways and reaction rates.

Energy of Reaction

20.2 Heat of reaction

Heat is thermal energy in the process of being added to or removed from a substance.

Chemical reactions are either exothermic or endothermic processes. During a reaction, a certain amount of chemical binding energy is changed into thermal (internal) energy, or vice versa. Usually the energy change can be measured as heat released or absorbed during the reaction. That is, the energy change can be measured as the *change in heat content* of the substances reacting.

Chemical reactions are usually carried out in open vessels. Volumes may change in such vessels, but pressures remain constant. The heat content of a substance under constant pressure is often called *enthalpy* of the substance. The symbol for enthalph (and for heat content at constant pressure) is H. If a process is exothermic, the total heat content of the products is *lower* than that of the reactants. The products of an endothermic reaction must have a *higher* heat content than the reactants.

One mole of a substance has a characteristic heat content just as it has a characteristic mass. The heat content is a measure of the internal energy stored in the substance during its formation. This stored heat content cannot be measured directly. However, the *change* in heat content that occurs during chemical reaction *can* be measured. This quantity is the heat released during an exothermic change or the heat absorbed during an endothermic change. It is called *heat of reaction. The* ***heat of reaction*** *is the quantity of heat released or absorbed during a chemical reaction.*

The heat of reaction is measured when the final state of a system is brought to the same temperature as that of the initial state. Unless otherwise stated, the reaction is assumed to be at 25°C under standard atmospheric pressure. Further, each substance is assumed to be in its usual (standard) state at these conditions. For this reason, the phases of reactants and products should be shown along with their formulas in thermochemical equations.

A thermochemical equation includes heat of reaction information.

If a mixture of hydrogen and oxygen is ignited, water is formed and heat energy is released. This reaction is measured in a device called a *calorimeter* (Figure 20-1). Because the reaction is an explosion, the calorimeter used is commonly called a "bomb" calorimeter. Known quantities of reactants are sealed in the reaction chamber. This chamber (the bomb) is immersed in a known quantity of water in an insulated vessel. The heat given off (or absorbed) during the reaction is determined from the temperature change in the water.

1 kcal of heat is required to change the temperature of 1 kg of water 1 C°.

The quantity of heat given up is proportional to the quantity of water formed in the reaction. No heat is supplied externally, except to ignite the mixture. For this reason, the heat content of the product water must be less than the heat content of the reactants before ignition. The equation for this reaction is ordinarily written as follows:

$$2H_2 + O_2 \rightarrow 2H_2O$$

From this equation we may state the following: when 2 moles of hydrogen gas at room temperature are burned, 1 mole of oxygen gas is used and 2 moles of water vapor are formed.

Suppose the product water is brought back to room temperature (the temperature of the initial state). The reaction heat given up by the system is found to be 136.64 kcal. The thermochemical equation is then written

The symbols (g), (l), and (s) indicate gas, liquid, and solid phases, respectively.

$$2H_2(g) + O_2(g) \rightarrow 2H_2O(l) + 136.64 \text{ kcal}$$

Here, (g) and (l) indicate gas and liquid phases, respectively. When a solid phase is indicated, (s) is used.

Heats of reaction are usually expressed in terms of *kilocalories per mole* of substance. From the previous equation, the following equality can be stated:

$$\begin{matrix}\text{heat content} & & \text{heat content} & & \text{heat content} & \\ \text{of 1 mole of} & + & \text{of } \tfrac{1}{2} \text{ mole of} & = & \text{of 1 mole of} & + 68.32 \text{ kcal} \\ \text{hydrogen gas} & & \text{oxygen gas} & & \text{liquid water} & \end{matrix}$$

We can now write the thermochemical equation to indicate the heat of reaction in kcal/mole of product:

$$H_2(g) + \tfrac{1}{2}O_2(g) \rightarrow H_2O(l) + 68.32 \text{ kcal}$$

This equation tells us that one mole of the product (liquid) water has a heat content 68.32 kcal *lower* than that of the gaseous reactants. To decompose one mole of water and produce hydrogen and oxygen, this much energy must be supplied from an external source. The reaction is written

$$H_2O(l) + 68.32 \text{ kcal} \rightarrow H_2(g) + \tfrac{1}{2}O_2(g)$$

Here the products are 1 mole of hydrogen plus ½ mole of oxygen. Together, they have a heat content *higher* by 68.32 kcal than the 1 mole of water that is decomposed. The two reactions can be shown by a reversible equation:

$$H_2(g) + \tfrac{1}{2}O_2(g) \rightleftarrows H_2O(l) + 68.32 \text{ kcal}$$

Fig. 20-1. Schematic diagram of a bomb-type calorimeter. Compare this apparatus with the student calorimeter pictured in Fig. 1-22. If asked to determine the heat of combustion of a potato chip, why should a calorimeter similar to this give more accurate results?

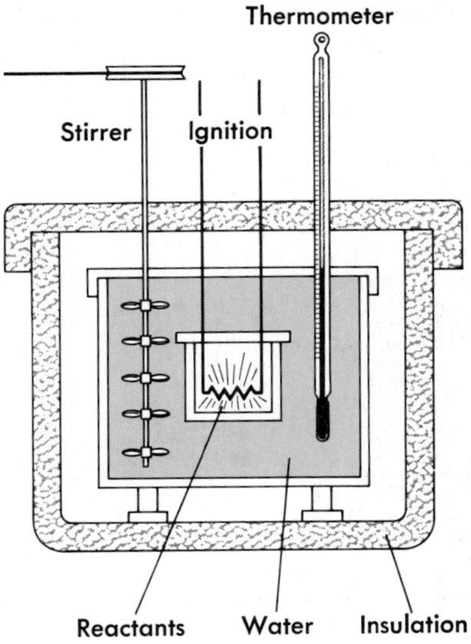

As stated, we symbolize the heat content of a substance by the letter H. We can represent a *change* in heat content by ΔH. The Greek letter Δ (delta) signifies "change in." The change in heat content, ΔH, during a reaction is the difference between the heat content of the products and the heat content of the reactants.

$$\Delta H = \text{heat content of products} - \text{heat content of reactants}$$

Exothermic processes: ΔH is negative.

Endothermic processes: ΔH is positive.

In this notation scheme, the ΔH for an exothermic reaction has a *negative* sign. Thus, in the above reaction

$$\Delta H = -68.32 \text{ kcal/mole}$$

The thermochemical equation

$$H_2(g) + \tfrac{1}{2}O_2(g) \rightarrow H_2O(l) + 68.32 \text{ kcal}$$

means the same as

$$H_2(g) + \tfrac{1}{2}O_2(g) \rightarrow H_2O(l) \qquad \Delta H = -68.32 \text{ kcal}$$

The ΔH for an endothermic reaction is signified by using a *positive* sign. This sign convention is an arbitrary one, but it is logical since the heat of reaction is said to be *negative* when the heat content of the system is *decreasing* (exothermic reaction). It is said to be *positive* when the heat content of the system is *increasing* (endothermic reaction). See Figure 20-2.

Fig. 20-2. Change in heat content during chemical action.

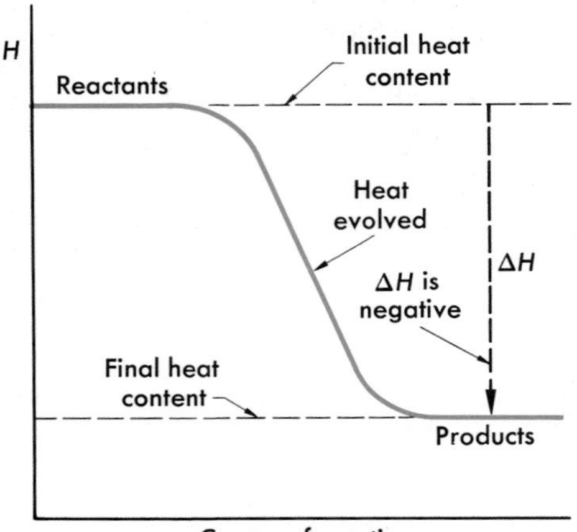

(A) Exothermic change

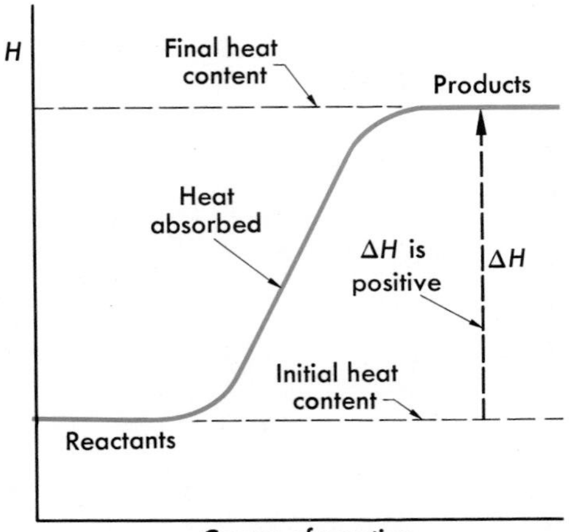

(B) Endothermic change

20.3 Heat of formation

Chemical reactions in which elements combine and form compounds are generally exothermic. In these composition reactions the product compounds have lower heat contents than their separate elements, the reactants. The products are also more stable than the uncombined reactants. The formation of water from hydrogen and oxygen illustrates this change in stability.

Elementary hydrogen and oxygen exist as nonpolar diatomic molecules. Water molecules are covalent structures. They are polar because they are bent molecules with an electronegativity difference between the hydrogen and oxygen atoms.

Energy was given up when the single covalent bonds of the diatomic hydrogen and oxygen molecules were formed originally. Therefore, energy is required to break these bonds if the hydrogen and oxygen atoms are to combine. On the other hand, more energy is released when the two polar bonds of the water molecule are formed. Consequently, heat is given off during the composition reaction. The heat of reaction is quite high ($\Delta H = -68.3$ kcal/mole of water formed). This high heat of reaction suggests that water molecules are more stable than hydrogen and oxygen molecules.

The heat released or absorbed in a composition reaction is

a useful indicator of product stability. It is referred to as the *heat of formation* of the compound. *The heat of reaction released or absorbed when 1 mole of a compound is formed from its elements is called the* ***molar heat of formation*** *of the compound.* By convention, each element in its standard state is said to have a heat content of zero. Then the ΔH during the formation of one mole of a compound from its elements (all in their standard states) is its standard heat of formation. Table 20-1 gives the heats of formation of some common compounds. A more complete list is given in Table 14 of Appendix B.

The sign convention and ΔH notation we adopted for heat of reaction apply to heat of formation as well. Heat of formation is merely one category of reaction heats. To distinguish a particular reaction heat as a heat of formation, we may use the more specific notation ΔH_f. Heats of formation have negative values for exothermic composition reactions. They have positive values for endothermic composition reactions.

Observe that most of the heats of formation given in Table 14, Appendix B, are negative. Only a few compounds, such as hydrogen iodide and carbon disulfide, have positive heats of formation.

Table 20-1

HEAT OF FORMATION

ΔH_f = heat of formation of the substance from its elements. All values of ΔH_f are expressed as kcal/mole at 25°C. Negative values of ΔH_f indicate exothermic reactions. (s) = solid, (l) = liquid, (g) = gas.

Substance	Formula	ΔH_f
ammonia (g)	NH_3	−11.04
barium nitrate (s)	$Ba(NO_3)_2$	−237.06
benzene (l)	C_6H_6	+11.72
calcium chloride (s)	$CaCl_2$	−190.00
carbon (diamond) (s)	C	+0.45
carbon (graphite) (s)	C	0.00
carbon dioxide (g)	CO_2	−94.05
copper(II) sulfate (s)	$CuSO_4$	−184.00
ethyne (acetylene) (g)	C_2H_2	+54.19
hydrogen chloride (g)	HCl	−22.06
water(l)	H_2O	−68.32
nitrogen dioxide (g)	NO_2	+8.09
ozone (g)	O_3	+34.00
sodium chloride (s)	NaCl	−98.23
sulfur dioxide (g)	SO_2	−70.96
zinc sulfate (s)	$ZnSO_4$	−233.88

20.4 Stability and heat of formation

A large amount of energy is released when a compound with a high negative heat of formation is formed. The same amount of energy is required to decompose such a compound into its separate elements. This energy must be supplied to the reaction from an external source. *Such compounds are very stable.* The reactions forming them proceed spontaneously, once they start, and are usually vigorous. Carbon dioxide has a high heat of formation. The ΔH_f of carbon dioxide is −94.05 kcal per mole of gas produced.

The stability of a compound is related to its ΔH_f.

Compounds with low positive and negative values of heats of formation are generally unstable. Hydrogen sulfide, H_2S has a heat of formation of −4.82 kcal per mole. It is not very stable and decomposes when heated. Hydrogen iodide, HI, has a low positive heat of formation, +6.20 kcal/mole. It is a colorless gas that decomposes somewhat when stored at room temperature. As it does, violet iodine vapor becomes visible throughout the container of the gas.

A compound with a high positive heat of formation may react or decompose explosively. For example, ethyne reacts explosively with oxygen. Nitrogen tri-iodide and mercury fulminate decompose explosively. The formation reactions of such compounds store a great deal of energy within them. Mercury fulminate, $HgC_2N_2O_3$, has a heat of formation of +64 kcal/mole. It is used as a detonator for explosives because of its instability.

Table 20-2

HEAT OF COMBUSTION		

ΔH_c = heat of combustion of the given substance. All values of ΔH_c are expressed as kcal/mole of substance oxidized to H_2O (l) and/or CO_2 (g) at constant pressure and 25°C. (s) = solid, (l) = liquid, (g) = gas.

Substance	Formula	ΔH_c
hydrogen (g)	H_2	−68.32
carbon (graphite) (s)	C	−94.05
carbon monoxide (g)	CO	−67.64
methane (g)	CH_4	−212.80
ethane (g)	C_2H_6	−372.82
propane (g)	C_3H_8	−530.60
butane (g)	C_4H_{10}	−687.98
pentane (g)	C_5H_{12}	−845.16
hexane (l)	C_6H_{14}	−995.01
heptane (l)	C_7H_{16}	−1151.27
octane (l)	C_8H_{18}	−1307.53
ethene (ethylene) (g)	C_2H_4	−337.23
propane (propylene) (g)	C_3H_6	−491.99
ethyne (acetylene) (g)	C_2H_2	−310.62
benzene (l)	C_6H_6	−780.98
toluene (l)	C_7H_8	−934.50

20.5 The heat of combustion

Fuels, whether for the furnace, automobile, or rocket, are energy-rich substances. The products of their combustion are energy-poor substances. In these combustion reactions the energy yield may be very high. The products of the chemical action may be of little importance compared to the quantity of heat energy given off.

The combustion of 1 mole of pure carbon (graphite) yields 94.05 kcal of heat energy.

$$\mathbf{C(s) + O_2(g) \rightarrow CO_2(g) \qquad \Delta H = -94.05 \text{ kcal}}$$

The heat of reaction released by the complete combustion of 1 mole of a substance is called the ***heat of combustion*** *of the substance.* Observe that we define the heat of combustion in terms of *1 mole of reactant.* The heat of formation, on the other hand, is defined in terms of *1 mole of product.* The general heat of reaction notation, ΔH, applies to heats of combustion as well. However, the ΔH_c notation may be used to refer specifically to heat of combustion. See Table 20-2.

In some cases, a substance cannot be formed in a rapid composition reaction directly from its elements. The heat of formation of such a compound can be found by using the heats of reaction of a series of related reactions. Heats of combustion are sometimes useful in these calculations when used according to the following equation:

heat of formation of compound X = sum of heats of formation of products of combustion of compound X − heat of combustion of compound X

ΔH_f can be determined indirectly.

CO_2 and H_2O are the products of complete combustion of many organic compounds. Their heats of formation are known. The heats of formation of these organic compounds can be calculated according to the above equation. Methane, CH_4, can be used as an example. Its heat of combustion, ΔH_c, is determined to be −212.80 kcal/mole from the following reaction.

$$\mathbf{CH_4 + 2O_2 \rightarrow CO_2 + 2H_2O + 212.80 \text{ kcal}}$$

The combustion of 1 mole of CH_4 forms 1 mole of CO_2 and 2 moles of H_2O. From Table 20-1, ΔH_f for CO_2 is −94.05 kcal/mole and for H_2O is −68.32 kcal/mole. We can calculate the heat of formation for methane from these data as follows:

$$\Delta H_f(CH_4) = \Delta H_f(CO_2) + 2\Delta H_f(H_2O) - \Delta H_c(CH_4)$$

$$\Delta H_f(CH_4) = -94.05\frac{\text{kcal}}{\text{mole}} + 2\left(-68.32\frac{\text{kcal}}{\text{mole}}\right) - \left(-212.80\frac{\text{kcal}}{\text{mole}}\right)$$

$$\Delta H_f(CH_4) = -17.89 \text{ kcal/mole}$$

CO is formed indirectly.

When carbon is burned in a limited supply of oxygen, carbon monoxide is produced. In this reaction carbon is probably first oxidized to CO_2. Some of the CO_2 may be reduced in turn to CO by hot carbon. The result is an uncertain mixture of the two gases.

$$C(s) + O_2(g) \rightarrow CO_2(g)$$

$$C(s) + CO_2(g) \rightarrow 2CO(g)$$

Because of this uncertainty, we cannot determine the heat of formation of CO by measuring directly the heat given off during the reaction. However, both carbon and carbon monoxide can be burned completely to carbon dioxide. The heat of formation of CO_2 and the heat of combustion of CO are then known (Tables 20-1 and 20-2). From these reaction heats, we can find the heat of formation of CO by using the equality stated above.

For the combustion of carbon,

$$C(s) + O_2(g) \rightarrow CO_2(g) + 94.05 \text{ kcal}$$

Thus

$$\Delta H_f \text{ of } CO_2 = -94.05 \text{ kcal/mole}$$

For the combustion of carbon monoxide,

$$2CO(g) + O_2(g) \rightarrow 2CO_2(g) + 135.28 \text{ kcal}$$

Rewriting this equation in the form that yields 1 mole of CO_2,

$$CO(g) + \tfrac{1}{2}O_2(g) \rightarrow CO_2(g) + 67.64 \text{ kcal}$$

Thus

$$\Delta H_c \text{ of } CO = -67.64 \text{ kcal/mole}$$

But

$$\Delta H_f(CO) = \Delta H_f(CO_2) - \Delta H_c(CO)$$

Then, by substitution,

$$\Delta H_f(CO) = -94.05 \text{ kcal/mole} - (-67.64 \text{ kcal/mole})$$

$$\Delta H_f(CO) = -26.41 \text{ kcal/mole}$$

Now we know the heat of formation of CO. We can add this to the heat of combustion of CO and find the heat of formation of CO_2 as follows:

$$C(s) + \tfrac{1}{2}O_2(g) \rightarrow \cancel{CO(g)} \qquad \Delta H_f = -26.41 \text{ kcal}$$

$$\cancel{CO(g)} + \tfrac{1}{2}O_2(g) \rightarrow CO_2(g) \qquad \Delta H_c = -67.64 \text{ kcal}$$

$$C(s) + O_2(g) \rightarrow CO_2(g) \qquad \Delta H_f = -94.05 \text{ kcal}$$

We can now derive a thermochemical equation for the formation of CO directly from its elements. To do so, we employ

Fig. 20-3. Heat of formation diagram for carbon dioxide and carbon monoxide.

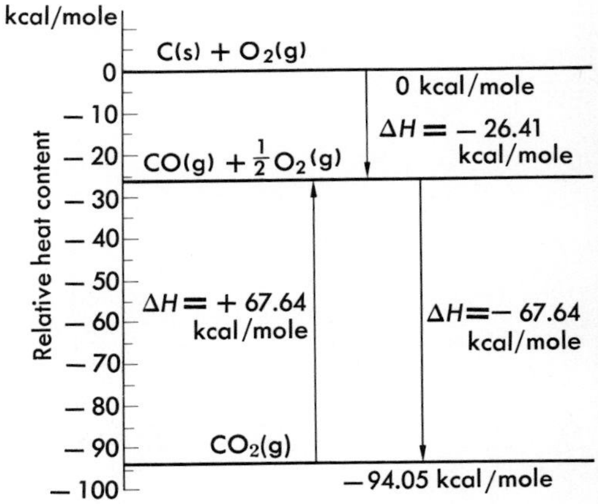

the equations for the oxidation of carbon and the reduction of carbon dioxide as follows:

$$\begin{array}{ll} C(s) + O_2(g) \rightarrow \cancel{CO_2(g)} & \text{(oxidation of C)} \\ C(s) + \cancel{CO_2(g)} \rightarrow 2CO(g) & \text{(reduction of } CO_2\text{)} \\ \hline 2C(s) + O_2(g) \rightarrow 2CO(g) & \text{(net reaction)} \end{array}$$

Energy is conserved during a chemical reaction; the heat absorbed in decomposing a compound must be equal to the heat released in its formation under the same conditions. Thus, if we have reason to write the equation for a reaction in reverse form, we must reverse the sign of ΔH for the reaction.

Let us apply these principles to the thermochemical equation for the combustion of carbon monoxide:

$$CO(g) + \tfrac{1}{2}O_2(g) \rightarrow CO_2(g) \qquad \Delta H_c = -67.64 \text{ kcal}$$

Writing the reverse of this reaction:

$$CO_2(g) \rightarrow CO(g) + \tfrac{1}{2}O_2(g) \qquad \Delta H_c = +67.64 \text{ kcal}$$

ΔH for a given overall reaction is independent of the reaction pathway.

Here we have applied the principle of reversing the sign of ΔH to express the change in heat content for a reverse action. This principle is actually part of a more general one: *The heat of a given overall reaction is the same regardless of the intermediate steps involved.* The heat of formation of CO calculated from the following equations illustrates this additivity principle.

$$\begin{array}{ll} C(s) + O_2(g) \rightarrow CO_2(g) & \Delta H_f = -94.05 \text{ kcal} \\ CO_2(g) \rightarrow CO(g) + \tfrac{1}{2}O_2(g) & \Delta H_c = +67.64 \text{ kcal} \\ \hline C(s) + \tfrac{1}{2}O_2(g) \rightarrow CO(g) & \Delta H_f = -26.41 \text{ kcal} \end{array}$$

In Section 2.15, we mentioned an endothermic reaction between carbon and steam. This "water-gas" reaction occurs spontaneously at the temperature of white-hot carbon. It produces a mixture of CO and H_2 that can be used as a gaseous fuel. What is the thermochemistry of this fuel?

The heat of formation of water is normally expressed in terms of the change in heat content between liquid water at 25°C and its separate elements at the same temperature. Water vapor must give up 10.52 kcal/mole in order to condense to its liquid phase at 25°C. This condensation is a physical change.

$$H_2O(g) \rightarrow H_2O(l) + 10.52 \text{ kcal}$$

Thus, the steam in the reaction has a higher heat content (and a lower heat of formation) by 10.52 kcal than liquid water.

The following thermochemical equation shows the heat of formation of the product water as a gas from its composition reaction.

$$H_2(g) + \tfrac{1}{2}O_2(g) \rightarrow H_2O(g) + 57.80 \text{ kcal}$$

The complete relationship is shown by the following series of equations.

$$H_2(g) + \tfrac{1}{2}O_2(g) \rightarrow H_2O(g) \qquad \Delta H = -57.80 \text{ kcal}$$

$$H_2O(g) \rightarrow H_2O(l) \qquad \Delta H = -10.52 \text{ kcal}$$

$$H_2(g) + \tfrac{1}{2}O_2(g) \rightarrow H_2O(l) \qquad \Delta H = -68.32 \text{ kcal}$$

The water-gas reaction is endothermic and spontaneous.

Experiments have established the quantity of heat absorbed in the water-gas reaction as 31.39 kcal per mole of carbon used. The thermochemical equation is

$$H_2O(g) + C(s) + 31.39 \text{ kcal} \rightarrow CO(g) + H_2(g)$$

The heat of reaction is absorbed; the heat content of the products CO and H_2 is greater than the heat content of the reactants C and H_2O.

When the product gases are burned as fuel, two combustion reactions occur. Carbon dioxide is the product of one and water vapor is the product of the other. Both are familiar reactions shown earlier in this section.

$$CO(g) + \tfrac{1}{2}O_2(g) \rightarrow CO_2(g) + 67.64 \text{ kcal}$$

$$H_2(g) + \tfrac{1}{2}O_2(g) \rightarrow H_2O(g) + 57.80 \text{ kcal}$$

These reactions are exothermic and the heats of combustion have negative values.

We now have three thermochemical equations representing the formation of the water gas and its combustion as a fuel. Suppose we arrange these equations in a series. The net additive result is shown below.

$$H_2O(g) + C(s) \rightarrow CO(g) + H_2(g) \qquad \Delta H = +31.39 \text{ kcal}$$

$$CO(g) + \tfrac{1}{2}O_2(g) \rightarrow CO_2(g) \qquad \Delta H = -67.64 \text{ kcal}$$

$$H_2(g) + \tfrac{1}{2}O_2(g) \rightarrow H_2O(g) \qquad \Delta H = -57.80 \text{ kcal}$$

$$C(s) + O_2(g) \rightarrow CO_2(g) \qquad \Delta H = -94.05 \text{ kcal}$$

The combined heat of combustion of CO and H_2 is −125.44 kcal. Observe that this value is higher than that of carbon (−94.05 kcal). However, it is higher only by the amount of heat energy put into the first reaction (+31.39 kcal).

20.6 Bond energy and reaction heat

In Section 20.1 we saw that the change in heat content of a reaction system is related to (*1*) the change in the number of bonds breaking and forming, and (*2*) the strengths of these bonds as the reactants form products. We can use the reaction for the formation of water gas to test this relationship.

The two oxygen-to-hydrogen bonds of each steam molecule must be broken. So must the carbon-to-carbon bonds of the graphite. Carbon-to-oxygen and hydrogen-to-hydrogen bonds

$$C(s) + H_2O(g) + 31.4\ \text{kcal} \longrightarrow CO(g) + H_2(g)$$

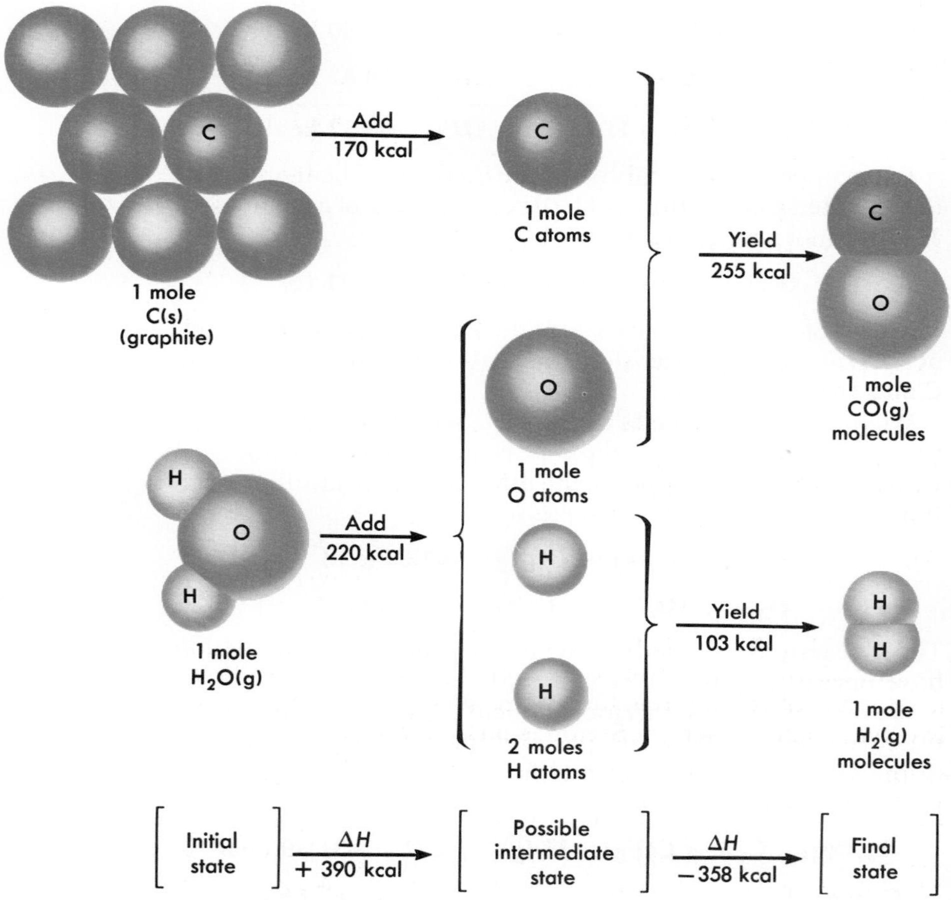

Fig. 20-4. A possible mechanism for the water-gas reaction.

must be formed. Energy is absorbed when bonds are broken and energy is released when bonds are formed.

Let us assume a possible reaction mechanism in which there is an intermediate stage of free atoms. This reaction mechanism is illustrated in Figure 20-4. Notice that a heat input of 390 kcal is required to break the bonds of 1 mole of graphite and 1 mole of steam. The formation of bonds in the final state releases 358 kcal of heat energy. The net effect is that 32 kcal of heat must be supplied to the system from an external source. This quantity agrees closely with the experimental value of 31.39 kcal of heat input per mole of carbon used.

20.7 The driving force of reactions

"Whether a reaction will occur" and "how a reaction does occur" are questions that have always concerned chemists. We can find complete answers to these questions only through a thorough quantitative study of reaction mechanisms and reaction kinetics. This study must be conducted within the framework of the laws of thermodynamics. Such work is in the realm of *physical chemistry*. What we can do here is examine the concepts that chemists label collectively as the "driving force" of chemical reactions. Some of these ideas were discussed briefly in Section 2.15.

By observation, we have come to recognize that most reactions that occur spontaneously in nature are exothermic. These exothermic processes give off energy and lead to lower energy states and more stable configurations. The quantity H, the energy content of a system, is a function of the state of the system. The drive toward a favorable change in energy content, ΔH, is responsible for this *tendency for processes to go toward the lowest possible energy state.*

If the driving force depended on this energy-change tendency alone, no chemical reaction could take place spontaneously with absorption of energy. We could predict that only exothermic reactions are spontaneous. A great deal of evidence shows that most reactions do release energy. In fact, the greater the quantity of energy given up, the more vigorous the reactions tend to be.

The disturbing fact is that chemical reactions *do* take place spontaneously with absorption of energy. They occur simply as a result of mixing reactants. The production of water gas involves such a reaction. Steam is passed into white-hot coke (impure carbon) and the reaction proceeds spontaneously. It is not driven by any activity outside the reacting system. The absorption of heat has a cooling effect. Therefore, more heat must be supplied by blowing air into the coke periodically to cause some combustion. We know from Section 20.5 that the product gases, carbon monoxide and hydrogen, have collectively a higher heat content than the reactants, steam and carbon. The energy change is positive, so this unfavorable energy change cannot be the driving force of the reaction.

$$\mathbf{H_2O(g) + C(s) \rightarrow CO(g) + H_2(g) \qquad \Delta \mathit{H} = +31.39\ kcal}$$

To see how an endothermic reaction can occur spontaneously, consider this a simple physical process that proceeds by and of itself with no energy change. Figure 20-5 shows two identical flasks connected by a valve. One flask is filled with ideal gas **A** and the other with ideal gas **B.** The entire system is at room temperature.

When the valve is opened, the two gases mix until they are distributed evenly throughout the two containers. The gases will remain in this state indefinitely, with no tendency to separate or become unmixed. The temperature remains constant throughout the process. Thus the total heat content cannot have changed to a lower level. Clearly, the self-mixing process

Fig. 20-5. The mixing of the gases may occur without an energy change.

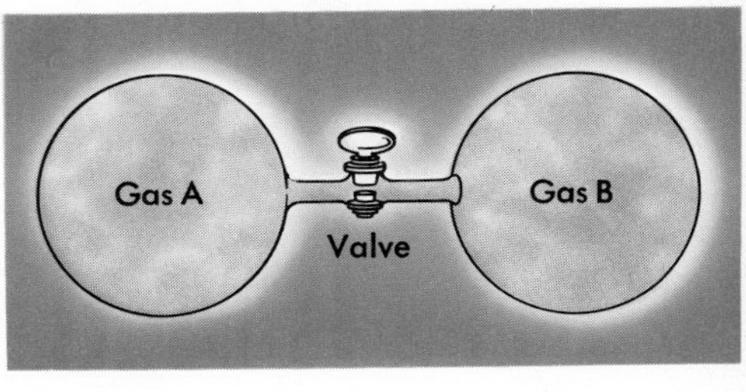

must be caused by a driving force other than the energy-change tendency. What, then, is the driving force for this process?

In Section 2.15, we identified *a tendency for processes to occur that lead to the highest possible state of disorder*. In general, a system that can go from one state to another without an energy change will go to the more disordered state. There is a quantity S, called *entropy,* which is a function of the state of a system. Entropy describes the state of disorder of a system. In the above example, the final mixed system of gases is a more disordered state than the initial pure-gas system. In other words, a favorable entropy change has occurred. The entropy of the mixed-gas system is higher than the entropy of the pure-gas system. The driving force is the tendency for the entropy of the system to *increase.*

Entropy describes the state of disorder.

Natural processes tend toward (1) minimum energy, and (2) maximum disorder.

Thus, the property of a system that drives the reaction depends on two tendencies. One tendency is toward the *lowest* energy; the other tendency is toward the *highest* entropy. For convenience, a new function of the state of a system to relate the energy and entropy functions at a given temperature is defined. It is the *free energy, G,* of the system. Free energy is the function that assesses both the energy-change and entropy-change tendencies at the same time. A system tends to change spontaneously in a way that *lowers* its free energy.

A process is spontaneous in the direction of lower free energy.

The net driving force is called the *free-energy change,* ΔG, of the system. Where the energy change and the entropy change oppose each other, the direction of the net driving force is determined by the one having the larger influence.

At a constant pressure and temperature, the free energy-change, ΔG, is a property of the reaction system. ΔG is the difference between the change in heat content, ΔH, and the product of temperature and the entropy change, $T\Delta S$. In abbreviated form, this is stated in the equation

$$\mathbf{\Delta G = \Delta H - T\Delta S}$$

Here ΔG is the change in free energy of the system, ΔH is the change in the heat content, T is the temperature in °K, and ΔS is the change in entropy. (ΔG, ΔH, and the product $T\Delta S$ all have the same dimensions, usually kilocalories per mole. What are the dimensions of ΔS?)

A chemical reaction proceeds spontaneously if it is accompanied by a decrease in free energy. That is, it proceeds spontaneously if the free energy of the products is lower than that of the reactants. In such a case, the *free energy change,* ΔG, in the system is *negative.*

In exothermic reactions ΔH has a negative value. In endothermic reactions its value is positive. From the expression for ΔG note that the more negative ΔH is, the more negative ΔG is likely to be. Reaction systems that change from a high- to a low-energy state tend to proceed spontaneously. Also note that the more positive ΔS is, the more negative ΔG is likely to be. Thus, systems that change from well ordered states to highly disordered states also tend to proceed spontaneously. Both of these tendencies in a given reaction system are assessed simultaneously in terms of the free-energy change, ΔG.

In some processes ΔH is negative and ΔS is positive. Here, the process should proceed spontaneously because ΔG is negative regardless of the relative magnitudes of ΔG and ΔS. Processes in which ΔH and ΔS have the same signs are more common. Note that the sign of ΔG can be either positive or negative depending on the temperature T. The temperature of the system is the dominant factor that determines the relative importance of the tendency toward lower energy and the tendency toward higher entropy.

Spontaneous reaction: ΔG is negative.

Looking back at the water-gas reaction,

$$\mathbf{H_2O(g) + C(s) \rightarrow CO_2(g) + H_2(g) \qquad \Delta H = +31.39\ kcal}$$

Here, a negative free-energy change would require that $T\,\Delta S$ be positive and greater than 31.39 kcal. This can be so if T is large, or if ΔS is large and positive, or both. Let us first look at the sign and size of ΔS.

Recall that the solid phase is well ordered and the gaseous phase is random. One of the reactants, carbon, is a solid and the other, steam, is a gas. However, both products are gases. The change from the orderly solid phase to the random gaseous phase involves an *increase* in entropy.
In general, a change from a solid to a gas will proceed with an increase in entropy. If all reactants and products are gases, an increase in the number of product particles increases entropy.

At low temperatures, whether ΔS is positive or negative, the product $T\,\Delta S$ may be small compared to ΔH. In such cases, the reaction proceeds as the energy change predicts.

Careful measurements show that ΔS for the water-gas reaction is +0.0320 kcal/mole °K at 25°C (298°K). Thus

$$T\Delta S = 298°\text{K} \times 0.0320\ \frac{\text{kcal}}{\text{mole°K}} = 9.54\ \frac{\text{kcal}}{\text{mole}}$$

$$\Delta G = \Delta H - T\Delta S = +31.39\ \frac{\text{kcal}}{\text{mole}} - 9.54\ \frac{\text{kcal}}{\text{mole}}$$

and

$$\Delta G = +\,21.85\ \frac{\text{kcal}}{\text{mole}}$$

Since ΔG has a positive value, the reaction is not spontaneous at 25°C.

Increases in temperature tend to favor increases in entropy.

When ΔS is positive, a high temperature gives $T\Delta S$ a large positive value. We can expect that at a high enough temperature $T\Delta S$ will be larger than ΔH and ΔG will be negative.

Higher temperature–higher entropy.

The water-gas reaction occurs at the temperature of white hot carbon, approximately 900°C. The values of ΔH and S are different at different temperatures. However, if we assume they remain about the same at the reaction temperature of 900°C, we can calculate an approximate value of ΔG for this temperature. Retaining the value of ΔH as +31.39 kcal/mole, we must determine $T\Delta S$ at 1173°K (900°C).

$$\mathbf{T\Delta S = 1173°K \times 0.0320\ \frac{kcal}{mole°K} = 37.5\ \frac{kcal}{mole}}$$

$$\mathbf{\Delta G = \Delta H - T\Delta S = +31.39\ \frac{kcal}{mole} - 37.5\ \frac{kcal}{mole}}$$

$$\mathbf{\Delta G = -6.2\ kcal/mole}$$

The free-energy change for the water-gas reaction is negative at 900°C and the reaction is spontaneous at this temperature.

Reaction Mechanisms

20.8 Reaction pathways

Chemical reactions involve breaking existing chemical bonds and forming new ones. The relationships and arrangements of atoms in the products of a reaction are different from those in the reactants. Colorless hydrogen gas consists of pairs of hydrogen atoms bonded together as diatomic molecules, H_2. Violet-colored iodine vapor is also diatomic, consisting of pairs of iodine atoms bonded together as I_2 molecules. A chemical reaction between these two gases produces hydrogen iodide, HI, a colorless gas. Hydrogen iodide molecules, in turn, tend to decompose, reforming hydrogen and iodine molecules. We may write the equations for the reactions as follows:

$$\mathbf{H_2(g) + I_2(g) \rightarrow 2HI(g)}$$

and

$$\mathbf{2HI(g) \rightarrow H_2(g) + I_2(g)}$$

These equations indicate only what molecular species disappear as a result of the reactions and what species are produced. They do not show the pathway along which either reaction proceeds. That is, they do not show the step-by-step sequence of reactions by which the over-all chemical change may occur. Such a sequence, when known, is called the *reaction pathway* or *reaction mechanism.*

We usually can examine a chemical system before reaction occurs or after the reaction is over. However, such an examination reveals nothing about the pathway along which the action proceeded. See Figure 20-6. For most chemical reactions, only the reactants that disappear and the final products that appear are known. In other words, only the net chemical change is directly observable.

Sometimes chemists are able to devise experiments that reveal a sequence of steps in a reaction pathway. They attempt to learn how the speed of a reaction is affected by various factors. Such factors may include temperature, concentrations of reactants and products, and the effects of catalysts. Radioactive tracer techniques are sometimes helpful.

A chemical reaction might occur in a single step or in a sequence of steps. Each reaction step is usually a relatively simple process. Complicated chemical reactions take place in a sequence of simple steps. Even a reaction that appears from its balanced equation to be a simple process may actually occur in a sequence of steps.

An overall chemical reaction may proceed in a sequence of simple steps.

The reaction between hydrogen gas and bromine vapor which produces hydrogen bromide gas is an example of a *homogeneous reaction*. The chemical change takes place in one phase—the gas phase. This reaction system is also an example of a *homogeneous chemical system*. In such a system, all reactants and products are in the same phase. The overall chemical equation for this reaction is

$$\mathbf{H_2(g) + Br_2(g) \rightleftarrows 2HBr(g)}$$

It might appear that one hydrogen molecule reacts with one bromine molecule and forms the product in a simple, one-step process. However, chemists have found through kinetic studies that the reaction follows a more complex pathway. The initial forward reaction (and the terminating reverse reaction) is

$$\mathbf{Br_2 \rightleftarrows 2Br} \qquad (1)$$

This initial step provides bromine atoms. These atoms initiate a sequence of two steps which can repeat themselves.

$$\mathbf{Br + H_2 \rightleftarrows HBr + H} \qquad (2)$$

$$\mathbf{H + Br_2 \rightleftarrows HBr + Br} \qquad (3)$$

Observe that the sum of steps 2 and 3 gives the net reaction as shown in the overall equation above.

The equation

$$\mathbf{H_2(g) + I_2(g) \rightleftarrows 2HI(g)}$$

represents another homogeneous chemical system. For many years chemists thought that this reaction was a simple, one-step process. They assumed it involved two molecules, $H_2 + I_2$, in the forward direction and two molecules, HI + HI, in the reverse reaction.

Recent experiments have disproved this assumption. The reaction, $H_2 + I_2$, does not take place. Instead, two possible

Fig. 20-6. The initial and final states of a mixture of hydrogen gas and iodine vapor which react and form hydrogen iodide gas.

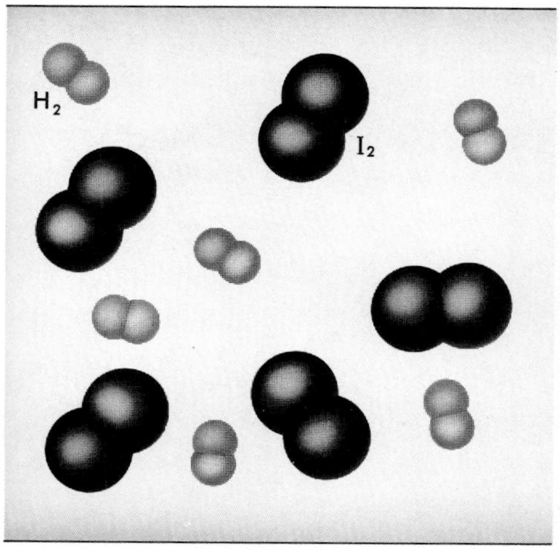

Initial state

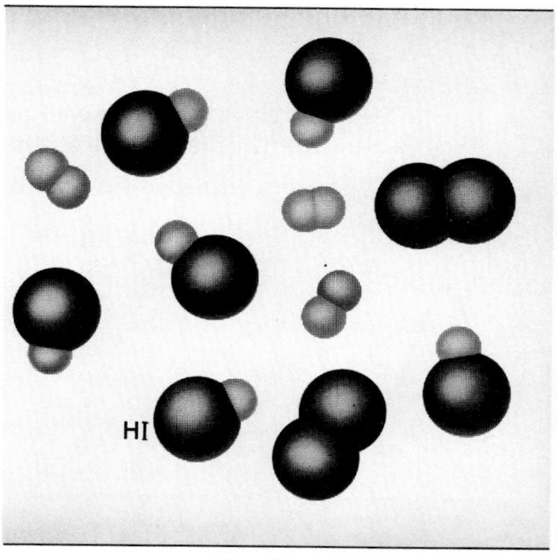

Final state

mechanisms have been proposed. The first has a two-step pathway:

$$I_2 \rightleftarrows 2I \quad (1)$$

$$2I + H_2 \rightleftarrows 2HI \quad (2)$$

The second possible mechanism has a three-step pathway:

$$I_2 \rightleftarrows 2I \quad (1)$$

$$I + H_2 \rightleftarrows H_2I \quad (2)$$

$$H_2I + I \rightleftarrows 2HI \quad (3)$$

It appears that, no matter how simple the balanced equation, the reaction pathway may be complicated and difficult to determine. Some chemists feel that simple, one-step reaction mechanisms are unlikely. They suggest that the only simple reactions are those that have not been thoroughly studied.

20.9 Collision theory

In order for reactions to occur between substances, their particles (molecules, atoms, or ions) must collide. Further, these collisions must result in interactions. Chemists use this *collision theory* to interpret many facts they observe about chemical reactions.

From the kinetic theory we know that the molecules of gases are continuously in random motion. The molecules have kinetic energies ranging from very low to very high values. The energies of the greatest portion are near the average for all the molecules in the system. When the temperature of a gas is raised, the average kinetic energy of the molecules is increased. Therefore, their speed is increased. This relationship is shown in Figure 20-7.

Let us consider what happens on a molecular scale in one step of a homogeneous reaction system. A good example is the decomposition of hydrogen iodide. The reaction for the first step in the decomposition pathway is

$$HI + HI \rightarrow H_2 + 2I$$

Fig. 20-7. Energy distribution among gas molecules at two different temperatures.

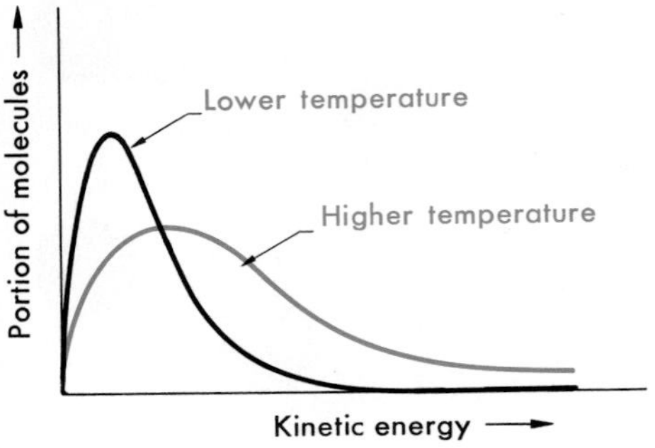

According to the collision theory, for the two gas molecules to react, they must collide. Further, they must collide while favorably oriented and with enough energy to disrupt the bonds of the molecules. If they do so, a reshuffling of bonds leads to the formation of the new particle species of the products.

A collision may be too gentle. Here, the distance between the colliding molecules is never small enough to disrupt old bonds or form new ones. The two molecules simply rebound from each other unchanged. This effect is illustrated in Figure 20-8(A).

Similarly, a collision in which the reactant molecules are

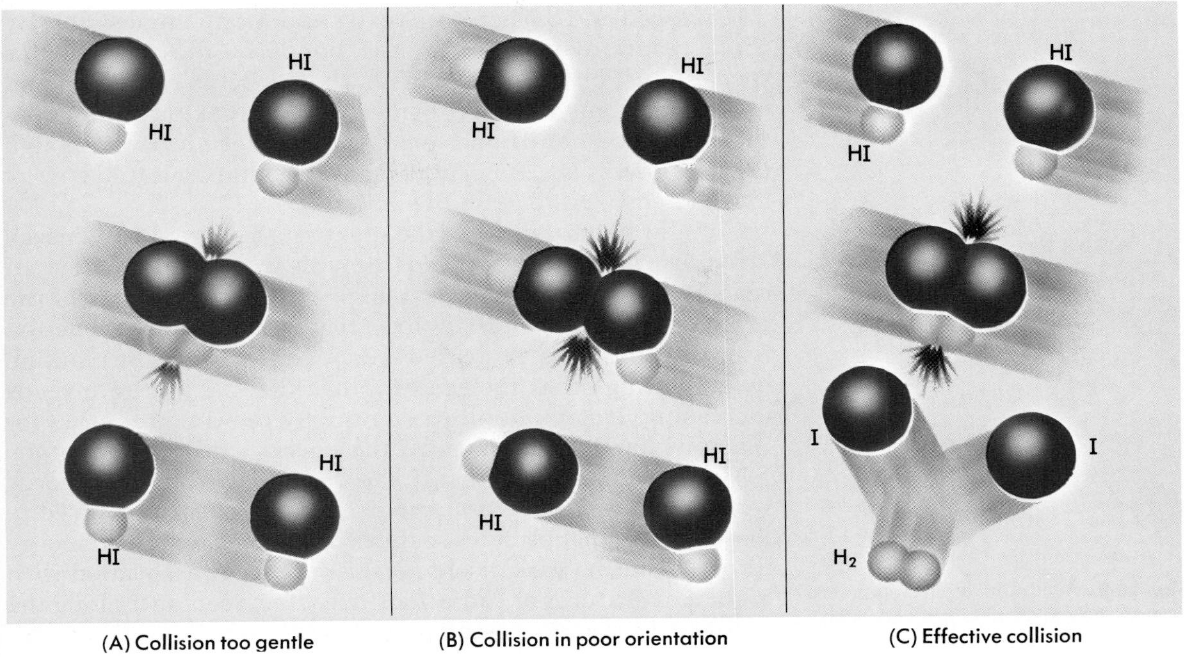

Fig. 20-8. Possible collision patterns for HI molecules.

poorly oriented has little effect. The distance between certain of the atoms is never small enough for new bonds to form. The colliding molecules rebound without changing. A poorly oriented collision is shown in Figure 20-8(B).

However, a collision may be suitably oriented and violent enough to cause an interpenetration of the electron clouds of the colliding molecules. Then the distance between the reactant particles *does* become small enough for new bonds to form. See Figure 20-8(C). The minimum energy required to produce this effective collision is called the *activation energy* for the reaction.

Thus, collision theory provides two reasons why a collision between reactant molecules may fail to produce a new chemical species. (1) *The collision is not energetic enough to supply the required activation energy.* (2) *The colliding molecules are not oriented in a way that enables them to react with each other.* What then is the reaction pathway of an effective collision that produces a new chemical species?

20.10 Activation energy

Let us consider the reaction for the formation of water from the diatomic gases, oxygen and hydrogen. The heat of formation is quite high; $\Delta H = -68.3$ kcal/mole at 25°C. The free energy change is also large, ΔG_f being -56.7 kcal/mole. Why then, when hydrogen and oxygen are mixed at room temperature, do they not combine spontaneously and form water?

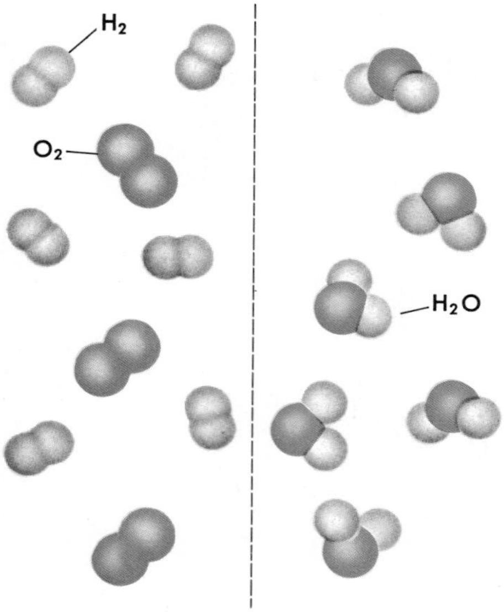

Fig. 20-9. A mixture of hydrogen and oxygen molecules will form very stable water molecules when properly activated.

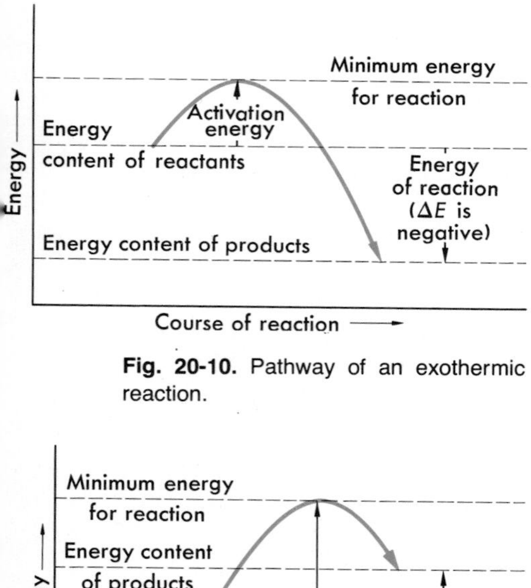

Fig. 20-10. Pathway of an exothermic reaction.

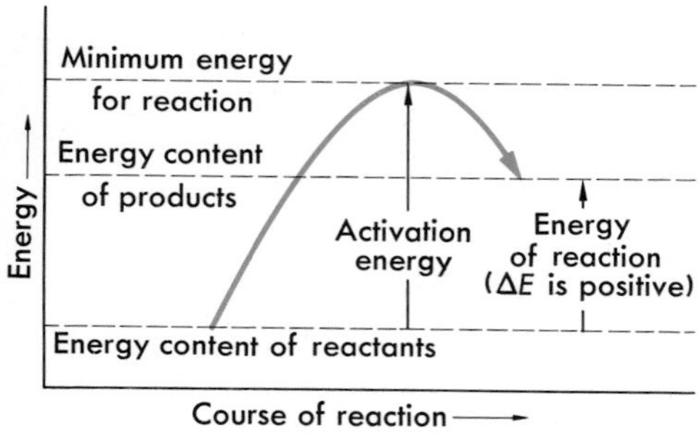

Fig. 20-11. Pathway of an endothermic reaction.

Hydrogen and oxygen gases exist as diatomic molecules. By some reaction mechanism, the bonds of these molecular species must be broken. Then new bonds between oxygen and hydrogen atoms must be formed. Bond-breaking is an endothermic process and bond-forming is exothermic. Even though the net process is exothermic, it appears that an initial energy "kick" is needed to start the action.

It might help to think of the reactants as lying in an energy "trough." They must be lifted from this trough before they can react and form water, even though the energy content of the product is lower than that of the reactants. Once the reaction is started, the energy released is enough to sustain the reaction by activating other molecules. Thus, the reaction rate keeps increasing. It is finally limited only by the time required for reactant particles to acquire the energy and make contact.

The energy needed to lift the reactants from the energy trough is called *activation energy*. It is the energy required to loosen bonds in molecules so they can become reactive. Energy from a flame, a spark discharge, or the energy associated with high temperatures or radiations may start reactants along the pathway of reaction. See Figure 20-10.

The reverse reaction is the decomposition of water molecules. The product water lies in an energy trough deeper than the one from which the reactants were lifted. The water molecules must be lifted from this deeper energy trough before they can decompose and form oxygen and hydrogen. The activation energy needed to start this endothermic reaction is greater than that required for the original exothermic change. The difference equals the amount of energy of reaction ΔE released in the original reaction. See Figure 20-11.

We could compare this situation to two mountain valleys separated by a high mountain pass. One valley is lower than the other. Still, to get to it from the upper valley, one must climb over the high pass. The return trip to the upper valley can be made only by climbing over the same high pass again. However, for this trip, one must climb up a greater height since the starting point is lower.

In Figure 20-12, we can compare the difference in height of the two valley floors with the energy of reaction, ΔE. Energies E_a and E_a' represent the activation energies of the forward and reverse reactions respectively. We can compare these quantities to the heights of the pass above the high and low valleys.

20.11 The activated complex

The possession of high motion (kinetic) energy does not make molecules unstable. However, when molecules collide, some of this energy is converted into internal (potential) energy within the colliding molecules. If enough energy is converted, the molecules may be activated.

Effective collisions produce transitional complexes.

When particles collide with energy at least equal to the activation energy for the species involved, their interpenetration disrupts existing bonds. New bonds can then form. In the brief interval of bond disruption and bond formation, the *collision complex* is said to be in a *transition state.* Some sort of partial bonding exists in this state. *A transitional structure results from an effective collision. This structure persists while old bonds are breaking and new bonds are forming. It is called the* ***activated complex.***

An activated complex is formed when an effective collision raises the internal energies of the reactants to their *minimum-energy-for-reaction level.* See Figure 20-12. Both forward and reverse reactions go through the same activated complex. Suppose a bond is in the process of being broken in the activated complex for the forward reaction. The same bond is in the process of being formed in the activated complex for the reverse reaction. Observe that the activated complex occurs at the maximum energy position along the reaction pathway. In this sense the activated complex defines the activation energy for the system. ***Activation energy*** *is the energy required to transform the reactants into the activated complex.*

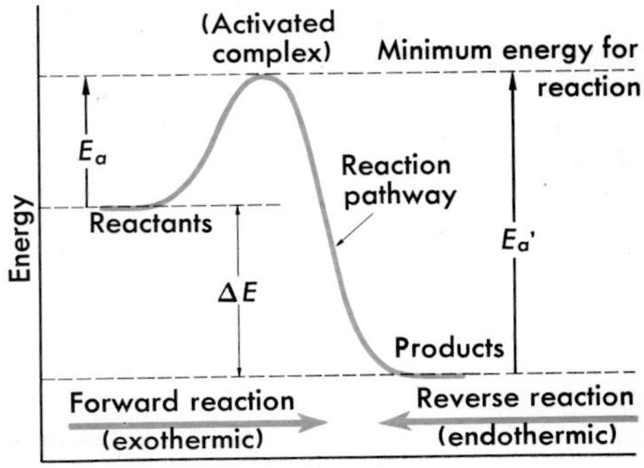

Fig. 20-12. Activation energies for the forward reaction E_a and the reverse reaction E'_a, and the change in internal energy ΔE in a reversible reaction.

In its brief existence, the activated complex has partial bonding of both reactant and product. In this state, it may respond to either of two possibilities. (1) It may re-form the original bonds and separate into the reactant particles. (2) It may form new bonds and separate into product particles. Usually the formation of products is just as likely as the formation of reactants. Do not confuse the activated complex with the intermediate compounds produced at different steps of a reaction mechanism. It is a molecular complex in which bonds are in the process of being broken or formed.

A possible configuration of the activated complex in the hydrogen iodide reaction is shown in Figure 20-13. The broken lines represent some sort of partial bonding in the particle. This transitional structure may produce two HI molecules or an H_2 molecule and two I atoms.

Fig. 20-13. Possible activated complex configuration which could form either 2HI or H_2 + 2I.

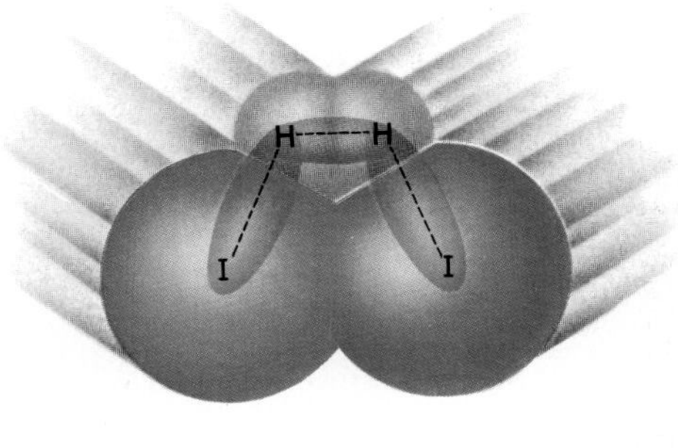

Figure 20-14 shows the energy profile for the HI decomposition. Of the 43.8 kcal activation energy, 40.8 kcal is available for excitation of the H_2 and I_2 molecules. Of this amount, 35.5 kcal is used in producing I atoms.

Reaction Rates

20.12 Rate influencing factors

The rates of chemical reactions vary widely. Some reactions are over in an instant, while others take months or years to complete. *The rate of reaction is measured by the amount of reactants converted to products in a unit of time.* We have seen that two conditions are necessary for reactions (other than simple

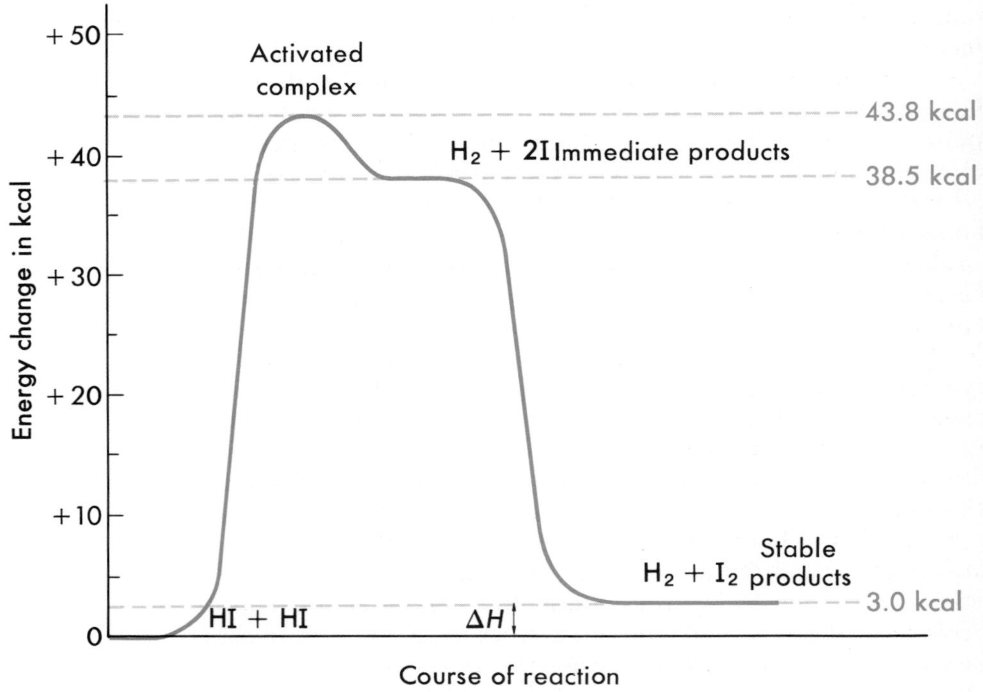

Fig. 20-14. An energy profile—experimental results of kinetic studies of hydrogen iodide decomposition.

Reaction rates depend on (1) collision frequency, and (2) collision efficiency.

decompositions) to occur at all. First, particles must come in contact. Second, this contact must result in interaction. Thus, the *rate* of a reaction depends on the *collision frequency* of the reactants and on the *collision efficiency*. (An efficient collision is one with enough energy for activation and in which the reactant molecules are favorably oriented.)

Changing conditions may affect either the frequency of collisions or the collision efficiency. Any such change influences the reaction rate. Let us consider five important factors that influence the rate of chemical reaction.

1. Nature of the reactants. Hydrogen combines vigorously with chlorine under certain conditions. Under the same conditions it may react only feebly with nitrogen. Sodium and oxygen combine much more rapidly than iron and oxygen under similar conditions. Platinum and oxygen do not combine directly. Atoms, ions, and molecules are the particles of substances that react. Bonds are broken and other bonds are formed in chemical reactions. The rate of reaction depends on the particular bonds involved.

2. Amount of surface. We know that the solution rate for a crystalline solid in water is increased if the crystals are first broken down into small pieces. A cube of solute measuring 1 cm on each edge presents only 6 cm^2 of contact area to the solvent. This same cube when ground to a fine powder might provide a contact area 10^4 times the original area. Consequently, the solution rate of the powdered solid is greatly increased.

A lump of coal burns slowly when kindled in air. The rate of burning can be increased by breaking the lump into smaller pieces, exposing new surfaces. If the piece of coal is powdered and ignited while suspended in air, it burns explosively. Nickel in large pieces shows no noticeable oxidation in air, but finely powdered nickel reacts vigorously and spectacularly.

Heterogeneous: not uniform throughout.

These reactions between solids and gases are examples of *heterogeneous reactions. Heterogeneous reactions involve reactants in two different phases or states.* Such reactions can occur only where the two phases are in contact. Thus, the amount of surface of a solid (or liquid) reactant is an important *rate* consideration. *Gases* and *dissolved* particles do not have surfaces in the sense just described. *In heterogeneous reactions the reaction rate is proportional to the area of contact of the reacting substances.*

Some chemical reactions between gases actually take place at the walls of the container. Others occur at the surface of a solid or liquid catalyst. If the products are also gases, such a reaction system presents a problem of language. It is a *heterogeneous* reaction because it takes place between two phases. On the other hand, it is a *homogeneous* chemical system because all of the reactants and all of the products are in one phase.

3. *Effect of concentration.* Suppose a small lump of charcoal is heated in air until combustion begins. If it is then lowered into a bottle of pure oxygen, the reaction proceeds at a much faster rate. A substance that oxidizes in air reacts more vigorously in pure oxygen. See Figure 20-15. The partial pressure of oxygen in air is approximately one-fifth of the total pressure. Pure oxygen at the same pressure as the air has five times the *concentration* of oxygen molecules.

This charcoal oxidation is a heterogeneous reaction system in which one reactant is a gas. Not only does the reaction rate depend on the amount of exposed charcoal surface; *it depends on the concentration of the gas as well.*

Homogeneous reactions may involve reactants in liquid or gaseous solutions. The concentration of gases changes with pressure according to Boyle's law. In liquid solutions, the concentration of reactants changes if either the quantity of solute or the quantity of solvent is changed. Solids and liquids are practically incompressible. Thus, it is not possible to change the concentration of pure solids and pure liquids to any measurable extent.

Reaction rate: effect of concentration of reactants is determined experimentally.

In homogeneous reaction systems, reaction rates depend on the concentration of the reactants. From collision theory, we might expect a rate increase if the concentration of one or more of the reactants is increased. Lowering the concentration

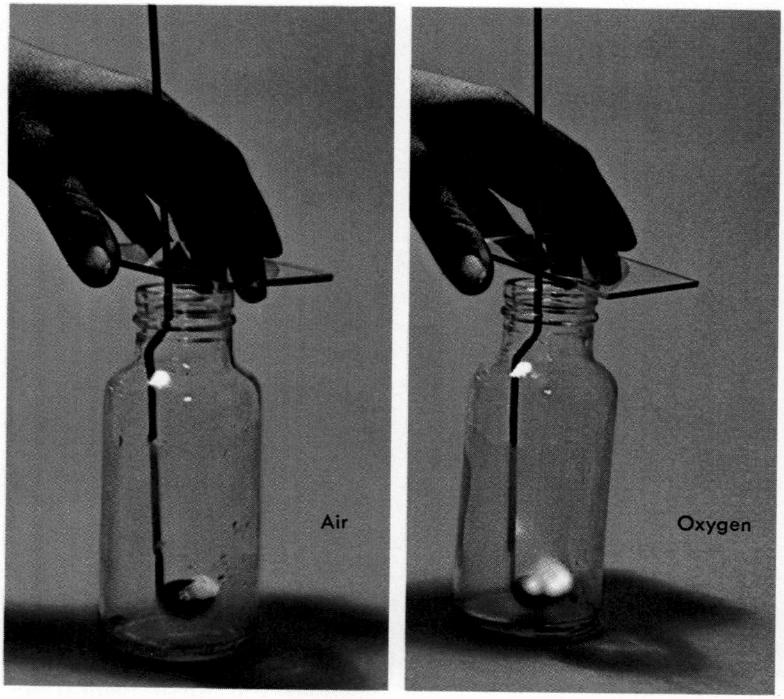

Fig. 20-15. Carbon burns faster in oxygen than in air because of the higher concentration of oxygen molecules.

should have the opposite effect. However, the specific effect of concentration changes in a reaction system *must be determined experimentally*.

Increasing the concentration of substance **A** in reaction with substance **B** could increase the reaction rate, decrease it, or have no effect on it. The effect depends on the particular reaction. *One cannot tell from the balanced equation for the net reaction how the reaction rate is affected by a change in concentration of reactants.* Chemists account for these differences in behavior in terms of the reaction mechanisms.

Reaction rate: slowest step is the rate determining step.

Complex chemical reactions may take place in a *series* of simple steps. Instead of a single activated complex, there may be several activated complexes in sequence along the reaction pathway. Of these steps, the one that proceeds at the slowest rate will determine the overall reaction rate. When this slowest-rate step can be identified, it is called the *rate-determining step* for the reaction.

4. *Effect of temperature.* The average kinetic energy of the particles of a substance is proportional to the temperature of the substance. Collision theory explains why a rise in temperature increases the rate of chemical reaction. According to this theory, a decrease in temperature lowers the reaction rate for both exothermic and endothermic reactions.

At room temperature, the rates of many reactions roughly double or triple with a 10 C° rise in temperature. However, this rule must be used with caution. The actual increase in reaction rate with a given rise in temperature must be determined experimentally.

Large increases in reaction rate are caused partly by the increase in collision frequency of reactant particles. However, for chemical reaction to occur, the particles must also collide with enough energy to cause them to react. At higher temperatures more particles possess enough energy to form the activated complex when collisions occur. In other words, more particles have the necessary activation energy. Thus, a rise in temperature produces an increase in collision energy as well as collision frequency.

5. *Action of catalysts.* Some reactions proceed quite slowly. Frequently, the rate of such reactions can be increased greatly by the presence of *catalysts.* Catalysts are foreign substances, sometimes present in trace quantities. They do not themselves appear in the final products of the reaction.

Catalysts may provide alternate reaction pathways.

A catalyst that is in the same phase as all the reactants and products in a reaction system is called a *homogeneous catalyst.* When the phase is different from that of the reactants, it is called a *heterogeneous catalyst.* Metals are often used in this category.

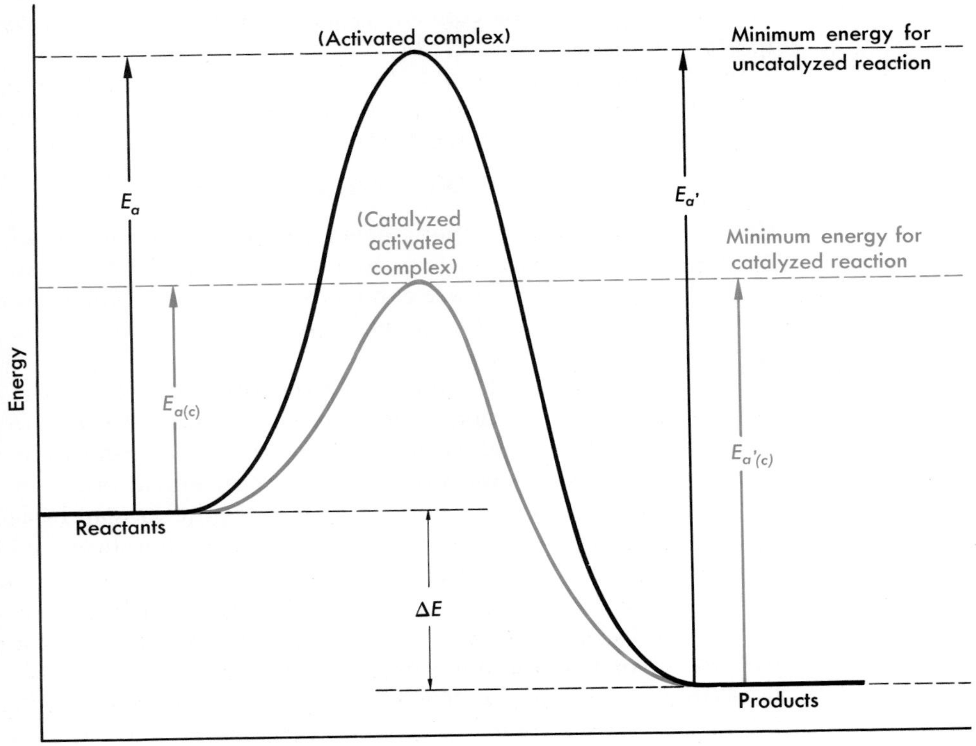

Fig. 20-16. Possible difference in potential-energy change along alternate reaction pathways, one catalyzed and the other uncatalyzed.

Catalytic action may be hindered by the presence of substances called *inhibitors*. Trace quantities of certain other substances may increase the activity of catalysts. These substances are called *promotors*. A catalyst that promotes one reaction may be worthless in another reaction. Catalysis plays an important role in many modern chemical processes. Nonetheless the catalytic mechanism is little understood and remains one of the challenging problems in chemistry.

It is believed that a catalyst somehow provides an alternate pathway or reaction mechanism. On this pathway, the potential energy barrier between reactants and products is lowered. It is thought that the catalyst may help to form an alternate activated complex requiring a lower activation energy. See Figure 20-16 on the preceding page.

20.13 Reaction rate law

We have mentioned the influence of reactant concentrations on reaction rate in a given chemical system. Measuring this influence is a challenging part of kinetics. How do chemists determine the relationship between the rate of a reaction and the concentration of one reactant? First, the concentrations of other reactants and the temperature of the system are kept constant. Then the reaction rate is measured for various concentrations of the reactant in question. A series of such experiments reveals how the concentration of each reactant affects the reaction rate.

We will use the following homogeneous reaction as an illustration. It is carried out in a vessel of constant volume and at an elevated *constant* temperature.

$$\mathbf{2H_2(g) + 2NO(g) \rightarrow N_2(g) + 2H_2O(g)}$$

Here, four moles of reactant gases produce three moles of product gases. Thus, the pressure of the system will diminish as the reaction proceeds. We can measure the rate of the reaction by measuring the change with time of the pressure in the vessel.

Suppose we conduct a series of experiments. We use the same initial concentration of nitrogen monoxide but vary the initial concentrations of hydrogen. The initial reaction rate is found to vary directly with the hydrogen concentration. That is, doubling the concentration of H_2 doubles the rate and tripling the concentration of H_2 triples the rate. Therefore,

$$\mathbf{R \propto [H_2]}$$

Here, R is the reaction rate and $[H_2]$ is the molecular concentration of hydrogen in moles per liter. The $\propto$ is a proportionality symbol meaning "is proportional to" or "varies directly with."

Suppose we now use the same initial concentration of hydrogen but vary the initial concentrations of nitrogen monoxide. We find that the initial reaction rate increases four times when the NO concentration is doubled. It increases *nine* times when the concentration of NO is tripled. Thus, the reaction rate varies directly with the *square* of the nitrogen monoxide concentration.

$$R \propto [\mathrm{NO}]^2$$

Since R is proportional to $[H_2]$ and to $[NO]^2$, it is proportional to their product.

$$R \propto [\mathrm{H_2}][\mathrm{NO}]^2$$

By introducing an appropriate proportionality constant, k, the expression becomes an equality.

$$R = k[\mathrm{H_2}][\mathrm{NO}]^2$$

This equation relating the reaction rate and concentrations of reactants is called the *rate law* for the reaction. It is constant for a specific reaction at a given temperature. A rise in temperature causes an increase in the rate of nearly all reactions. Thus, the value of k usually increases as the temperature increases.

Collision theory indicates that the number of collisions between particles increases as the concentration of these particles is raised. The reaction rate for any step in a reaction pathway is directly proportional to the frequency of collisions between the particles involved. It is also directly proportional to the collision efficiency.

Let us consider a single step in a reaction pathway. Suppose one molecule of gas **A** collides with one molecule of gas **B** and forms two molecules of substance **C.** The equation for the step is

$$\mathbf{A + B \rightarrow 2C}$$

One particle of each reactant is involved in each collision. Thus, doubling the concentration of either reactant will double the collision frequency. It also will double the reaction rate *for this step*. Therefore, the rate is directly proportional to the concentration of **A** and of **B.** The rate law for the step becomes

$$R = k[\mathrm{A}][\mathrm{B}]$$

Now, suppose the reaction is reversible. In this reverse step, two molecules of **C** must collide and form one molecule of **A** and one of **B.**

$$\mathbf{2C \rightarrow A + B}$$

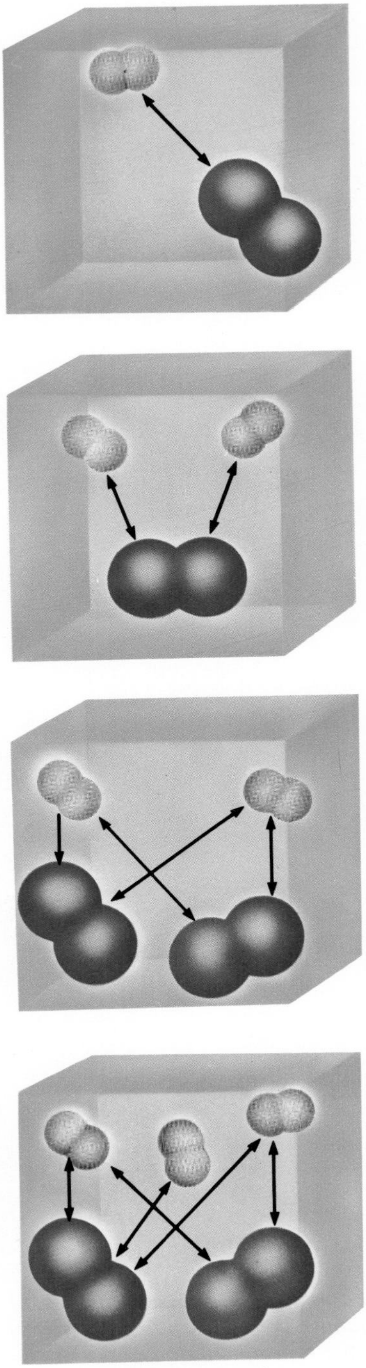

Fig. 20-17. Under constant condition, the collision frequency increases with the concentration of each reactant.

Thus, the reaction rate *for this reverse step* is directly proportional to [C] × [C]. The rate law for the step becomes

$$R = k[\mathrm{C}]^2$$

A simple relationship *may* exist between the chemical equation *for a step in a reaction pathway* and *the rate law for that step*. Notice the *power* to which the molar concentration of each reactant or product is raised in the rate laws above. This exponent is the same as the coefficient for the reactant or product in the balanced equation.

This relationship *does not always hold*. It holds if the reaction follows a simple one-step pathway. A reaction may proceed in a series of steps. In such reactions, the rate law is simply that for the slowest (rate determining) step. Thus, the rate law for a reaction must be determined experimentally. *It cannot be written from the balanced equation for the net reaction.*

Let us return to the hydrogen-nitrogen monoxide reaction. The balanced equation for the net reaction is

$$2H_2(g) + 2NO(g) \rightarrow N_2(g) + 2H_2O(g)$$

Suppose we assume that this reaction occurs in a single step involving a collision between two H_2 molecules and two NO molecules. Doubling the concentration of either reactant would quadruple the collision frequency and the rate. The rate law would be proportional to $[H_2]^2$ as well as $[NO]^2$. It would take the form

$$R = k[H_2]^2[NO]^2$$

This equation is not in agreement with experimental results. Thus, our assumed reaction mechanism cannot be correct.

The experimental rate law for the net reaction is actually

$$R = k[H_2][NO]^2$$

Therefore, the reaction pathway must consist of more than one step. The slowest step is rate-determining. The rate law found experimentally for the net reaction is the rate expression of this step.

The general form for a rate law is

$$R = k[\mathrm{A}]^n[\mathrm{B}]^m\text{-----}$$

In a rate law, the exponents of reactant concentrations are determined experimentally.

Here R is the reaction rate, k is the rate constant, and [**A**] and [**B**]----- represent the molar concentrations of reactants. The n and m are the respective powers to which the concentrations must be raised, *based on experimental data*. Again it should be emphasized: one *cannot* assume that the coefficients in the balanced equation for a net reaction are the exponents in the rate law for the reaction.

The dependence of reaction rate on concentration of reactants was first recognized as a general principle by two Norweigian chemists, Guldberg and Waage, in 1867. It was stated as the ***law of mass action:*** *the rate of a chemical reaction is directly proportional to the product of the concentrations of reacting substances, each raised to the appropriate power.* This principle is interpreted in terms of the rate law for a chemical system in modern reaction kinetics.

SUMMARY

Heat energy is released or absorbed during chemical reactions as the heat of reaction. An exothermic reaction has products with a total heat content lower than that of the reactants. An endothermic reaction has products with a heat content higher than that of the reactants. Inclusion of the heat of reaction information in the chemical equation for a reaction is customary when the energy change is important. Such an equation is called a thermochemical equation.

The heat content of a substance is represented by the letter H and is usually expressed in kilocalories per mole. The change in heat content, the difference between the heat content of products and reactants, is represented as ΔH. For endothermic reactions, ΔH is a positive quantity. Changes in heat content in reaction systems are related to changes in the number of bonds breaking and forming, and the strengths of these bonds as reactants form products.

The heat of reaction released or absorbed during the formation of one mole of a compound from its elements is called its heat of formation. The stability of a compound is related to its heat of formation. The heat of reaction released during the complete combustion of one mole of a substance is called its heat of combustion. The heat of formation of a compound not formed directly from its elements may be determined from its heat of combustion and the heats of formation of its combustion products.

The driving force of reaction systems consists of tendencies for processes to occur that lead to lower energy and to higher entropy. The assessment of these two tendencies in a reaction system is expressed in terms of a change in the free energy of the system. If the reaction process results in lower free energy, it tends to proceed spontaneously. At low temperatures, the change in heat content toward a lower energy state is the driving force that dominates reaction systems. At high temperatures, the change in entropy toward a higher entropy state dominates reaction systems. Processes that do not proceed spontaneously at low temperatures may become spontaneous at some higher temperature.

A chemical reaction may occur in a sequence of simple steps called the reaction pathway or reaction mechanism. Chemists use the collision theory to help them interpret their observations of reaction processes. According to the collision theory, for reactions to occur, particles must collide and these collisions must result in interactions between the particles. The minimum energy required to produce effective collisions is the activation energy for the reaction. If a collision is energetic enough and the colliding molecules are suitably oriented, an activated complex is formed for a brief interval. It is a molecular complex in which bonds are being broken or formed.

Factors that influence the rate of a chemical reaction are (*1*) the nature of the reactants, (*2*) amount of contact area, (*3*) concentration of reactants, (*4*) temperature, and (*5*) catalysis. The rate of a reaction is determined by the amount of reactants converted to products per unit of time. An equation that relates the reaction rate and the concentration of reactants is called the rate law for the reaction. The rate law for a reaction is the rate law for the slowest step in the reaction pathway. This slowest step is the rate-determining step for the reaction. The rate law for a reaction must be determined experimentally. It cannot be written from the balanced equation for the overall reaction.

QUESTIONS

Group A

1. What evidence can be cited to show that a substance has a characteristic internal energy?
2. How does the heat content of the products of a reaction system compare with the heat content of the reactants when the reaction is (*a*) exothermic? (*b*) endothermic?
3. Define the molar heat of formation of a compound.
4. Name two factors that can be identified in the driving force of chemical reactions.
5. What is the basis for assigning a negative value to the change in heat content, ΔH, in an exothermic system?
6. Changes of state in the direction of the solid state favor what kind of an entropy change?
7. What is the effect on the entropy of a system when temperature is raised?
8. Define activation energy in terms of the activated complex.
9. In a reversible reaction, how does the activation energy required for the exothermic change compare with the activation energy for the endothermic change?
10. Give two reasons why a collision between reactant molecules may not be effective in producing new chemical species.
11. To what does the term "activated complex" refer?

Group B

12. Considering the structure and physical phase of substances in a reacting system, to what is the energy change in the reaction related?
13. Using the energy profile of Figure 20-14, what is the activation energy for the reaction that produces hydrogen iodide?
14. A compound is found to have a heat of formation H_f of −87.3 kcal/mole. What is the implication regarding its stability? Explain.
15. Suppose flasks containing two different gases at room temperature are connected so that the gases mix. What kind of evidence would show that they experienced no change in energy content during the mixing?
16. How can the mixing tendency of Question 15 be explained?
17. Explain the circumstances under which an exothermic reaction does not proceed spontaneously.
18. Explain the circumstances under which an endothermic reaction is spontaneous.
19. Referring to Figure 20-12, (*a*) how could you justify calling the reaction pathway the minimum energy pathway for reaction? (*b*) What significance is associated with the maximum energy region of this minimum energy pathway?
20. The balanced equation for a homogeneous reaction between two gases shows

that 4 molecules of A react with 1 molecule of B and form 2 molecules of C and 2 molecules of D. $4A + B \rightarrow 2C + 2D$. The simultaneous collision of 4 molecules of one reactant with 1 molecule of the other reactant is extremely improbable. Recognizing this, what would you assume about the nature of the reaction mechanism for this reaction system?

21. Suppose 2 moles of hydrogen gas and 1 mole of iodine vapor are passed simultaneously into a 1-liter flask. The rate law for the forward reaction is $R = k[I_2][H_2]$. What is the effect on the rate of the forward reaction if (*a*) the temperature is increased; (*b*) 1 mole of iodine vapor is added; (*c*) 1 mole of hydrogen is removed; (*d*) the volume of the flask is reduced (assume this is possible); (*e*) a catalyst is introduced into the flask?

22. The decomposition of nitrogen dioxide

$$2NO_2 \rightarrow 2NO + O_2$$

occurs in a two-step sequence at elevated temperatures. The first step is

$$NO_2 \rightarrow NO + O$$

Predict a possible second step which, when combined with the first step, gives the complete reaction.

23. For each of the following reactions, predict whether the reaction, once started, is likely to proceed rapidly or slowly. State the reason for each prediction.

(*a*) $H_2(g) + Cl_2(g) \rightarrow 2HCl(g)$

(*b*) $Ag^+(aq) + Cl^-(aq) \rightarrow AgCl(s)$

(*c*) $Fe(chunk) + S(l) \rightarrow FeS(s)$

24. What property would you measure in order to determine the reaction rate for the following reaction? Justify your choice.

$$2NO_2(g) \rightarrow N_2O_4(g)$$

25. Ozone decomposes according to the following equation.

$$2O_3 \rightarrow 3O_2$$

The reaction proceeds in two steps. Propose a possible 2-step mechanism.

26. The caption for the photograph at the top of page 409 is a direct quote from Section 20-1. Explain how it applies to this fireplace scene.

PROBLEMS

Group A

(Consult Appendix B tables for essential thermochemical data.)

1. Write the thermochemical equation for the complete combustion of 1 mole of ethane gas. Then calculate its heat of formation from the heat of reaction and product heats of formation data.
2. Write the thermochemical equation for the complete combustion of 1 mole of ethyne (acetylene) and calculate its heat of formation.
3. Write the thermochemical equation for the complete combustion of 1 mole of benzene and calculate its heat of formation.
4. Using heats of formation data, calculate the heat of combustion of 1 mole of hydrogen gas.
5. The concentration of reactant A changes from 0.0375 M to 0.0268 M in the reaction time interval 0.0 min–18.0 min. What is the reaction rate during this time interval (*a*) per minute? (*b*) per second?

Group B

6. Calculate the heat of formation of $H_2SO_4(l)$ from the ΔH for the combustion of sulfur to $SO_2(g)$, the oxidation of SO_2 to $SO_3(g)$, and the solution of SO_3 in $H_2O(l)$ to give $H_2SO_4(l)$ at 25°C.
7. Suppose the following reactants could be used to provide thrust for a rocket engine:

$$\textbf{(1)}\ H_2(g) + \tfrac{1}{2}O_2(g) \rightarrow H_2O(g)$$

$$\textbf{(2)}\ H_2(g) + F_2(g) \rightarrow 2HF(g)$$

(*a*) Calculate the heat of reaction ΔH at 25°C for each reaction per kilogram of reactants carried aloft.
(*b*) Since the thrust is greater when the molecular weight of the exhaust gas is lower, which reaction would be preferred on the basis of thrust?

8. A chemical reaction is expressed by the balanced chemical equation

$$A + B \rightarrow C$$

and three reaction rate experiments yielded the following data:

Experiment Number	Initial [A]	Initial [B]	Initial rate of Formation of C
1	0.20 *M*	0.20 *M*	2.0×10^{-4} *M*/min
2	0.20 *M*	0.40 *M*	8.0×10^{-4} *M*/min
3	0.40 *M*	0.40 *M*	1.6×10^{-3} *M*/min

(*a*) Determine the rate law for the reaction.
(*b*) Calculate the value of the specific rate constant.
(*c*) If the initial concentrations of both A and B are 0.30 *M*, at what initial rate is C formed?

chapter 21

CHEMICAL EQUILIBRIUM

If a system at equilibrium is subjected to a stress, the equilibrium is displaced in the direction that relieves the stress. (See Question 26 on page 468.)

21.1 Reversible reactions

The products formed in a chemical reaction may, in turn, react and re-form the original reactants. The chemical reaction is said to be reversible. Most chemical reactions may be reversible under suitable conditions. Some reverse reactions occur less easily than others. For example, a temperature near 3000°C is required to decompose water vapor into hydrogen and oxygen in measurable amounts. In some cases, the conditions for the reverse reactions are not known. An example is the reaction in which potassium chlorate decomposes to oxygen and potassium chloride. Chemists do not know how to reverse this reaction in a single process.

Reversible reactions may eventually reach equilibrium.

Mercury(II) oxide decomposes when heated strongly.

$$2HgO(s) \rightarrow 2Hg(l) + O_2(g)$$

Mercury and oxygen combine and form mercury(II) oxide when heated gently.

$$2Hg(l) + O_2(g) \rightarrow 2HgO(s)$$

Suppose mercury(II) oxide is heated in a closed container from which neither the mercury nor the oxygen can escape. Once decomposition has begun, the mercury and oxygen released can recombine, forming mercury(II) oxide again. Thus both reactions proceed at the same time. Under these conditions, the rate of the composition reaction will eventually equal that of the decomposition reaction. Mercury and oxygen combine and form mercury(II) oxide just as fast as mercury(II)

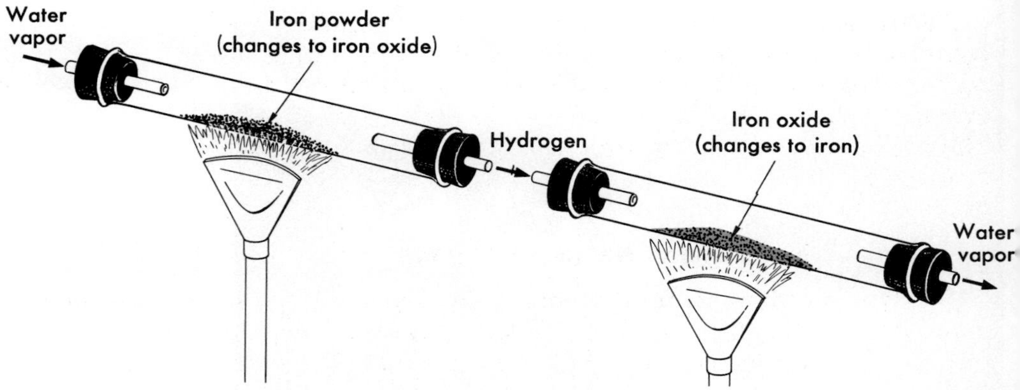

Fig. 21-1. A reversible reaction. Water vapor passed over the hot iron is reduced to hydrogen while the iron is oxidized to iron(II, III) oxide. Hydrogen passed over the hot iron oxide is oxidized to water vapor and the iron oxide is reduced to iron.

oxide decomposes to mercury and oxygen. We can expect the amount of mercury(II) oxide, mercury, and oxygen to remain constant as long as these conditions persist. A state of *equilibrium* has been reached between the two chemical reactions. *Both reactions continue, but there is no net change in the composition of the system.* The equilibrium may be written as

Equilibrium: *opposing processes proceeding at the same rate.*

$$2HgO(s) \rightleftarrows 2Hg(l) + O_2(g)$$

Chemical equilibrium *is a state of balance in which the rates of opposing reactions are exactly equal.*

A reaction system in equilibrium shows equal tendencies to proceed in the forward and reverse directions. In Section 20.7, we distinguished two factors that make up the driving force for reactions. These factors were the tendency toward lower energy and the tendency toward higher entropy. *At equilibrium, the driving force of the energy change is balanced by the driving force of the entropy change.*

21.2 Equilibrium, a dynamic state

Equilibrium systems consist of opposing processes occurring simultaneously and at the same rate. The evaporation of a liquid in a closed vessel and the condensation of its saturated vapor proceed at equal rates. The resulting equilibrium vapor pressure is a characteristic of the liquid at the prevailing temperature.

If an excess of sugar is placed in water, sugar molecules go into solution. Some of these molecules in turn separate from solution and rejoin the crystals. At saturation, molecules of sugar are crystallizing at the same rate that crystal molecules are dissolving. See Section 12.3.

Solution equilibrium is an example of physical equilibrium.

The above are examples of *physical equilibria*. The opposing physical processes occur at exactly the same rate. *Equilibrium is a dynamic state in which two opposing processes proceed simultaneously at the same rate.*

Electrovalent compounds, such as sodium chloride, are completely ionized in water solution. When an excess of sodium chloride is placed in water, a saturated solution eventually results. The saturated solution is at equilibrium. The rate of association of ions re-forming the crystal equals the rate of dissociation of ions from the crystal. This equilibrium is shown in the ionic equation

$$\mathbf{Na^+Cl^-(s) \rightleftarrows Na^+(aq) + Cl^-(aq)}$$

Equilibrium is a dynamic state.

The dynamic character of this equilibrium system is easily demonstrated. Suppose we place an irregularly shaped crystal of sodium chloride in a saturated solution of the salt. The *shape* of the crystal gradually changes, becoming more regular as time passes. However, the *mass* of the crystal does not change.

Polar compounds, such as acetic acid, are very soluble in water. Molecules of acetic acid in water solution ionize, forming H_3O^+ and $C_2H_3O_2^-$ ions. Pairs of these ions tend to rejoin, forming acetic acid molecules in the solution. This tendency is very strong. Even in fairly dilute solutions, equilibrium is quickly established between un-ionized molecules in solution and their hydrated ions. This system is an example of *ionic equilibrium*. The ionic equilibrium of acetic acid in water solution is represented by the equation

$$\mathbf{HC_2H_3O_2(aq) + H_2O(l) \rightleftarrows H_3O^+(aq) + C_2H_3O_2^-(aq)}$$

An equilibrium established late in the reaction process favors the products of the forward reaction.

Many chemical reactions are reversible under ordinary conditions of temperature and concentration. They may reach a state of equilibrium unless at least one of the substances involved escapes or is removed. In some cases, however, the forward reaction is nearly completed before the reverse reaction rate becomes high enough to establish equilibrium. *Here the products of the forward reaction* (→) *are favored.* This kind of reaction is referred to as the *reaction to the right* because the convention for writing chemical reactions is that *left-to-right* is forward and *right-to-left* is reverse. In other cases, the forward reaction is barely under way when the rate of the reverse reaction becomes equal to that of the forward reaction and equilibrium is established. *In these cases, the products of the reverse reaction* (←), *the original reactants, are favored.* This kind of reaction is referred to as the *reaction to the left*. In still other cases, both the forward and reverse reactions occur to nearly the same extent before chemical equilibrium is established. *Neither reaction is favored; considerable concentrations of both reactants and products are present at equilibrium.*

An equilibrium established early in the reaction process favors the reactants of the forward reaction.

Chemical reactions are employed ordinarily to convert available reactants into more desirable products. Chemists try to produce as much of these products as possible from the reactants used. Chemical equilibrium may seriously limit the possibilities of a seemingly useful reaction. In dealing with equilibrium systems, it is important to recognize the conditions that influence reaction rates. Factors that determine the rate of chemical action were discussed in Section 20.12. These are *(1) the nature of the reactants, (2) the temperature, (3) the presence of a catalyst, (4) the surface area, and (5) the concentration of reactants.*

Heterogeneous reactions involve two or more phases.

In heterogeneous reactions, the chemical reaction takes place at the surfaces where the reactants in different phases meet. Thus, the surface area presented by solid and liquid reactants is important in rate considerations. Homogeneous reactions occur between gases and between substances dissolved in liquid solvents. Here, the concentration of each reactant is an important rate factor.

In homogeneous reactions, reactants and products are in the same phase.

21.3 The equilibrium constant

Many chemical reactions seem likely to yield useful products. After they are started, however, they *appear* to slow down and finally stop without having run to completion. Such reactions are reversible and happen to *reach a state of equilibrium* before the reactants are completely changed into products. Both forward and reverse processes continue at the same rate. However, the concentrations of products and reactants remain constant.

The time required for reaction systems to reach equilibrium varies widely. It may be a fraction of a second or a great many years, depending on the system and the conditions. Ionic reactions in solution usually reach equilibrium very quickly.

Suppose two substances, **A** and **B,** react and form products **C** and **D.** In turn, **C** and **D** react and produce **A** and **B.** Under certain conditions, equilibrium occurs in this reversible reaction. See Figure 21.2. This hypothetical equilibrium reaction is represented by the equation

$$\mathbf{A + B \rightleftarrows C + D}$$

Initially, the concentrations of **C** and **D** are zero and those of **A** and **B** are maximum. With time, the rate of the forward reaction *decreases* as **A** and **B** are used up. Meanwhile, the rate of the reverse reaction increases as **C** and **D** are formed. As these two reaction rates become equal, equilibrium is established. The individual concentrations of **A, B, C,** and **D** undergo no further change if conditions remain the same.

At equilibrium, the ratio of the product [**C**] × [**D**] *to the product* [**A**] × [**B**] *has a definite numerical value at a given temperature.* It is known as the ***equilibrium constant*** of the reaction and is designated by the letter ***K***. Thus,

$$\frac{[\mathbf{C}] \times [\mathbf{D}]}{[\mathbf{A}] \times [\mathbf{B}]} = K$$

Fig. 21-2. Reaction rates for the hypothetical reaction system **A + B ⇄ C + D.** The rate of the forward reaction is represented by curve **A + B.** Curve **C + D** represents the rate of the reverse reaction. At equilibrium, the two rates are equal.

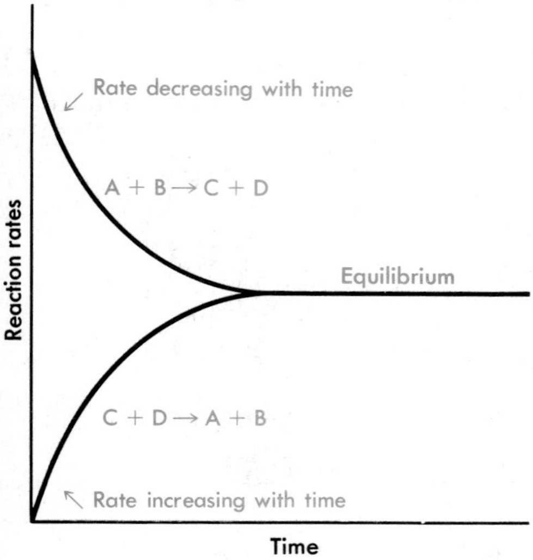

Notice that the concentrations of substances on the right side of the chemical equation are given in the numerator. These substances are the *products* of the forward reaction. The concentrations of substances on the left side of the chemical equation are in the denominator. These substances are the *reactants* of the forward reaction. Concentrations of reactants and products are given in *moles per liter*. The constant, ***K***, is independent of the initial concentrations. It is, however, dependent on the fixed temperature of the system.

Equilibrium constant: K *has a unique value for each equilibrium system at a specific temperature.*

The value of ***K*** for a given equilibrium reaction is important to chemists. It shows them the extent to which the reactants are converted into the products of the reaction. If ***K*** is equal to 1, the products of the concentrations in the numerator and denominator have the same value. If the value of ***K*** is very small, the forward reaction occurs only very slightly before equilibrium is established. A large value of ***K*** indicates an equilibrium in which the original reactants are largely converted to products. The numerical value of ***K*** for a particular equilibrium system is obtained experimentally. The chemist must analyze the equilibrium mixture and determine the concentrations of all substances present.

If $K < 1$, *reactants are favored.*

If $K > 1$, *products are favored.*

Suppose the balanced equation for an equilibrium system has the general form

$$nA + mB + \text{-----} \rightleftarrows xC + yD + \text{-----}$$

The constant relationship at equilibrium (for this generalized reaction system) becomes

$$K = \frac{[C]^x[D]^y\text{-----}}{[A]^n[B]^m\text{-----}}$$

The ***equilibrium constant, K,*** *is the ratio of the product of the concentrations of substances formed at equilibrium to the product of the concentrations of reacting substances, each concentration being raised to the power that is the coefficient of that substance in the chemical equation.* This equation for ***K*** is sometimes referred to as the *chemical equilibrium law* or as the *mass action expression.*

To illustrate, suppose a reaction system at equilibrium is shown by the equation

$$3A + B \rightleftarrows 2C + 3D$$

The equilibrium constant ***K*** is given by the expression

$$K = \frac{[C]^2[D]^3}{[A]^3[B]}$$

The reaction between H_2 and I_2 in a closed flask at an elevated temperature is easy to follow. We simply observe the rate at which the violet color of the iodine vapor diminishes.

Suppose this reaction runs to completion with respect to iodine. If so, the color must disappear entirely since the product, hydrogen iodide, is a colorless gas.

The color does not disappear entirely because the reaction is reversible. Hydrogen iodide decomposes and re-forms hydrogen and iodine. The rate of this reverse reaction increases as the concentration of hydrogen iodide builds up. Meanwhile, the concentrations of hydrogen and iodine decrease as they are used up. The rate of the forward reaction decreases accordingly.

As the rates of the opposing reactions become equal, an equilibrium is reached. A constant intensity of the violet color indicates that equilibrium exists among hydrogen, iodine, and hydrogen iodide. The net chemical equation for the reaction system at equilibrium is

$$\mathbf{H_2(g) + I_2(g) \rightleftarrows 2HI(g)}$$

Thus,

$$K = \frac{[\mathrm{HI}]^2}{[\mathrm{H_2}][\mathrm{I_2}]}$$

Concentrations of substances in an equilibrium system are determined experimentally.

Chemists have carefully measured the concentrations of H_2, I_2, and HI in equilibrium mixtures at various temperatures. In some experiments, the flasks were filled with hydrogen iodide at known pressure. The flasks were held at fixed temperatures until equilibrium was established. In other experiments, hydrogen and iodine were the substances introduced.

Experimental data together with the calculated values for K are listed in Table 21-1. Experiments 1 and 2 began with hydrogen iodide. Experiments 3 and 4 began with hydrogen and iodine. Note the close agreement obtained for numerical values of the equilibrium constant.

Equilibrium constants are computed from experimental data.

The equilibrium constant K for this equilibrium system at 425°C has the average value of 54.34. This value for K should hold for any system of H_2, I_2, and HI at equilibrium *at this temperature*. If the calculation for K yields a different result,

Table 21-1

TYPICAL EQUILIBRIUM CONCENTRATIONS OF H_2, I_2, AND HI IN MOLE/LITER AT 425°C

Exp.	$[H_2]$	$[I_2]$	[HI]	$K = \frac{[HI]^2}{[H_2][I_2]}$
(1)	0.4953×10^{-3}	0.4953×10^{-3}	3.655×10^{-3}	54.56
(2)	1.141×10^{-3}	1.141×10^{-3}	8.410×10^{-3}	54.33
(3)	3.560×10^{-3}	1.250×10^{-3}	15.59×10^{-3}	54.62
(4)	2.252×10^{-3}	2.336×10^{-3}	16.85×10^{-3}	53.97
			Average	54.34

there must be a reason. Either the H_2, I_2, and HI system has not reached equilibrium or the temperature of the system is not 425°C. The following Sample Problem is a typical example.

SAMPLE PROBLEM

An equilibrium mixture of H_2, I_2, and HI gases at 425°C is determined to consist of 4.5647×10^{-3} mole/liter of H_2, 0.7378×10^{-3} mole/liter of I_2, and 13.544×10^{-3} mole/liter of HI. What is the equilibrium constant for the system at this temperature?

SOLUTION

The balanced equation for the equilibrium system is

$$\mathbf{H_2(g) + I_2(g) \rightleftarrows 2HI(g)}$$

$$K = \frac{[\mathrm{HI}]^2}{[\mathrm{H_2}][\mathrm{I_2}]}$$

$$K = \frac{[13.544 \times 10^{-3}]^2}{[4.5647 \times 10^{-3}][0.7378 \times 10^{-3}]} = 54.46$$

This value is in close agreement with the average of the four experimental values given in Table 21-1.

The balanced chemical equation for the equilibrium system yields the expression for the equilibrium constant. The data in Table 21-1 show that this expression is an experimental fact. The equilibrium concentrations of reactants and product are determined experimentally. The values of K are calculated from these concentrations. No information concerning the kinetics of the reacting systems is required.

However, we know that an equilibrium system involves forward and reverse reactions proceeding at equal rates. Thus, the rate laws for the forward and reverse reactions should yield the same equilibrium constant as does the balanced chemical equation.

Suppose we have an equilibrium system expressed by the chemical equation

$$\mathbf{A_2 + B_2 \rightleftarrows 2C}$$

We will assume that both forward and reverse reactions are simple, one-step processes. The rate law for the forward reaction becomes

$$R_f = k_f[\mathrm{A_2}][\mathrm{B_2}]$$

The rate law for the reverse reaction becomes

$$R_r = k_r[\mathrm{C}]^2$$

At equilibrium,

$$R_f = R_r$$

Therefore,

$$k_f[A_2][B_2] = k_r[C]^2$$

Rearranging terms,

$$\frac{k_f}{k_r} = \frac{[C]^2}{[A_2][B_2]} = K$$

The expression is the same as the mass action equation derived from the balanced chemical equation (Section 21.3).

Most reaction mechanisms are complex and proceed by way of a sequence of simple steps. We know that the exponents in the *rate equation* for such a reaction cannot be taken from the balanced equation. They must be determined experimentally.

21.4 Factors that disturb equilibrium

In systems that have attained chemical equilibrium, opposing reactions are proceeding at equal rates. Any change that alters the rate of either reaction *disturbs the original equilibrium.* The system then seeks a new equilibrium state. By displacing an equilibrium in the desired direction, chemists can often increase production of important industrial chemicals.

Le Chatelier's principle is a "must know."

Le Chatelier's principle (Section 12.5) provides a means of predicting the influence of disturbing factors on equilibrium systems. We have already made use of this important principle on several occasions. It may be helpful at this point to restate Le Chatelier's principle: *If a system at equilibrium is subjected to a stress, the equilibrium is displaced in the direction that relieves the stress.* This principle holds for all kinds of dynamic equilibria, physical and ionic as well as chemical. In applying Le Chatelier's principle to chemical equilibrium, we will consider three important stresses.

1. Change in concentration. From collision theory, we know that an increase in the concentration of a reactant causes an increase in collision frequency. We also know that a reaction resulting from these collisions should then proceed at a faster rate. Consider the hypothetical reaction

$$\mathbf{A + B \rightleftarrows C + D}$$

A change in concentration of a reactant places a stress on an equilibrium system.

An increase in the concentration of **A** will displace the equilibrium to the *right.* Both **A** and **B** will be used up faster and more of **C** and **D** will be formed. The equilibrium will be reestablished with a lower concentration of **B.** *The equilibrium has shifted in such direction as to reduce the stress caused by the increase in concentration.*

Similarly, an increase in the concentration of **B** drives the reaction to the *right*. An increase in either **C** or **D** displaces the equilibrium to the *left*. A *decrease* in the concentration of either **C** or **D** has the same effect as an *increase* in the concentration of **A** or **B**. That is, it will displace the equilibrium to the *right*.

Changes in concentration have no effect on the value of the equilibrium constant. All concentrations still give the same numerical ratio for the equilibrium constant when equilibrium is reestablished. Thus, Le Chatelier's principle leads us to the same predictions for changes in concentration as does the equilibrium constant.

Pressure changes alter the concentration of gases.

2. *Change in pressure.* A change in pressure can affect only equilibrium systems in which *gases* are involved. According to Le Chatelier's principle, *if the pressure on an equilibrium system is increased, the reaction is driven in the direction that relieves the pressure.*

The Haber process for catalytic synthesis of ammonia from its elements illustrates the influence of pressure on an equilibrium system.

$$\mathbf{N_2(g) + 3H_2(g) \rightleftarrows 2NH_3(g)}$$

The equation indicates that 4 molecules of the reactant gases form 2 molecules of ammonia gas. Suppose the equilibrium mixture is subjected to an increase in pressure. This pressure can be relieved by the reaction that produces fewer gas molecules and therefore a smaller volume. Thus, the stress is *lessened* by the formation of ammonia. Equilibrium is displaced toward the right. *High* pressure is desirable in this industrial process. Figure 21-3 shows the effect of pressure on this equilibrium system.

Fig. 21-3. Increased pressure results in a higher yield of ammonia since the equilibrium shifts in the direction that produces fewer molecules.

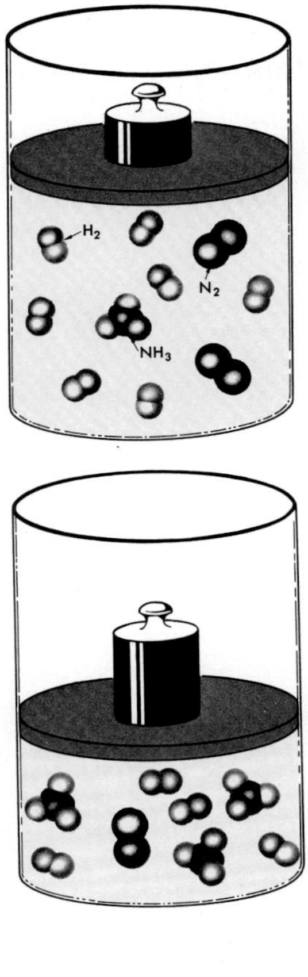

In the Haber process, the ammonia produced is continuously removed by condensation to a liquid. This condensation removes most of the product from the phase in which the reaction occurs. This change in concentration also tends to displace the equilibrium to the right.

Many chemical processes involve heterogeneous reactions in which the reactants and products are in different phases. The *concentrations* in equilibrium systems of pure substances in solid and liquid phases are not changed by adding or removing quantities of such substances. The equilibrium constant expresses a relationship between *relative* concentrations of reactants and products. Therefore, a pure substance in a condensed phase can be removed from the expression for the equilibrium constant; we simply substitute the number "1" for its concentration (which remains at unity value in the equilibrium system).

Consider the equilibrium system represented by the equation

$$CaCO_3(s) \rightleftarrows CaO(s) + CO_2(g)$$

Carbon dioxide is the only substance in the system subject to changes in concentration. Since it is a gas, the forward (decomposition) reaction is favored by a *low* pressure.

The expression for the equilibrium constant is

$$K = \frac{[CaO][CO_2]}{[CaCO_3]} = \frac{[1][CO_2]}{[1]} = [CO_2]$$

In the reaction,

$$CO(g) + H_2O(g) \rightleftarrows CO_2(g) + H_2(g)$$

there are equal numbers of molecules of gaseous reactants and gaseous products. Pressure change could not produce a shift in equilibrium. Thus, *pressure change has no effect* on this equilibrium reaction.

Obviously, an increase in pressure on confined gases has the same effect as an increase in the concentrations of these gases. We stated earlier that changes in concentration have no effect on the value of the equilibrium constant. Thus, *changes in pressure do not affect the value of the equilibrium constant.*

In an equilibrium system, one reaction is exothermic and the other is endothermic.

3. *Change in temperature.* Chemical reactions are either exothermic or endothermic. Reversible reactions are exothermic in one direction and endothermic in the other. The effect of changing the temperature of an equilibrium mixture depends on which of the opposing reactions is endothermic.

According to Le Chatelier's principle, *addition* of heat displaces the equilibrium so that heat is absorbed. This favors the *endothermic* reaction. The *removal* of heat favors the *exothermic* reaction. A rise in temperature increases the rate of any reaction. In an equilibrium, the rates of the opposing reactions are raised *unequally*. Thus, *the value of the equilibrium constant for a given system is affected by the temperature.*

The synthesis of ammonia is *exothermic.*

$$N_2(g) + 3H_2(g) \rightleftarrows 2NH_3(g) + 22\ \text{kcal}$$

K changes if temperature is changed.

A high temperature is not desirable as it favors the decomposition of ammonia, the *endothermic* reaction. However, at ordinary temperatures, the forward reaction is too slow to be commercially useful. The temperature used represents a compromise between kinetic and equilibrium requirements. It is high enough that equilibrium is established rapidly but low enough that the equilibrium concentration of ammonia is significant. The reactions of the system are also accelerated by the use of a suitable catalyst. Moderate temperature (about 500°C) and very high pressure (700–1000 atmospheres) produce a satisfactory yield of ammonia.

The numerical values of equilibrium constants range from very large to very small numbers. We have found that they are independent of changes in concentrations but not of changes in temperature. The addition of a catalyst accelerates both forward and reverse reactions equally. Therefore, it does not affect the value of ***K***. The time required for a system to reach equilibrium may be reduced dramatically when the system is catalyzed.

Several equilibrium systems are listed in Table 21-2. The table also gives numerical values of the equilibrium constants at various temperatures. A very small ***K*** value means that the equilibrium mixture consists mainly of the substances on the left of the equation. If the value of ***K*** is large, the equilibrium mixture consists mainly of the substances on the right of the equation.

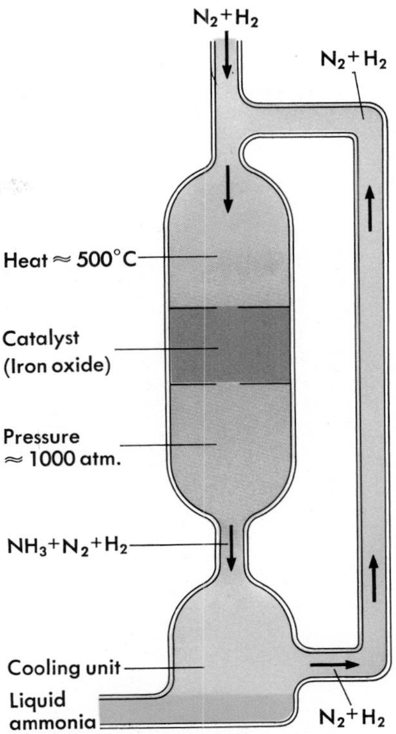

Fig. 21-4. The Haber process for the production of ammonia. Application of the Le Chatelier principle to the equilibrium system, $N_2(g) + 3H_2(g) \rightarrow 2NH_3(g) + 22$ kcal, suggests that high pressure and low temperature favor the yield of ammonia. Why, then, is a moderately high temperature used in this process?

21.5 Reactions that run to completion

Many reactions are easily reversible under suitable conditions. A state of equilibrium may be established unless one or more of the products escapes or is removed. An equilibrium reaction may be driven in the preferred direction by applying Le Chatelier's principle.

Some reactions appear to go to completion in the forward direction. No one has found a method of recombining potassium chloride and oxygen directly once potassium chlorate decomposes. Sugar is decomposed into carbon and water by the application of heat. Yet no single-step method of recombining these products is known.

Table 21-2

EQUILIBRIUM CONSTANTS

Equilibrium system	Value of ***K***	Temp. (°C)
$N_2(g) + 3H_2(g) \rightleftharpoons 2NH_3(g)$	2.66×10^{-2}	350°
$N_2(g) + 3H_2(g) \rightleftharpoons 2NH_3(g)$	6.59×10^{-3}	450°
$N_2(g) + 3H_2(g) \rightleftharpoons 2NH_3(g)$	2.37×10^{-3}	727°
$2H_2(g) + S_2(g) \rightleftharpoons 2H_2S(g)$	9.39×10^{-5}	477°
$H_2(g) + CO_2(g) \rightleftharpoons H_2O(g) + CO(g)$	4.40	1727°
$2H_2O(g) \rightleftharpoons 2H_2(g) + O_2(g)$	5.31×10^{-10}	1727°
$2CO(g) + O_2(g) \rightleftharpoons 2CO_2(g)$	2.24×10^{22}	727°
$H_2(g) + I_2(g) \rightleftharpoons 2HI(g)$	66.9	350°
$H_2(g) + I_2(g) \rightleftharpoons 2HI(g)$	54.4	425°
$H_2(g) + I_2(g) \rightleftharpoons 2HI(g)$	45.9	490°
$C(s) + CO_2(g) \rightleftharpoons 2CO(g)$	14.1	1123°
$Cu(s) + 2Ag^+(aq) \rightleftharpoons Cu^{++}(aq) + 2Ag(s)$	2×10^{15}	25°
$I_2(g) \rightleftharpoons 2I(g)$	3.76×10^{-5}	727°
$2O_3(g) \rightleftharpoons 3O_2(g)$	2.54×10^{12}	1727°
$N_2(g) \rightleftharpoons 2N(g)$	1.31×10^{-31}	1000°

Ionic reactions do not involve electron-transfer mechanisms.

Many compounds are formed by the interaction of ions in solutions. If solutions of two electrolytes are mixed, two pairings of ions are possible. These pairings may or may not occur. If dilute solutions of sodium chloride and potassium bromide are mixed, no reaction occurs. The resulting solution merely contains a mixture of Na^+, K^+, Cl^-, and Br^- ions. Association of ions occurs only if enough water is evaporated to cause crystals to separate from solution. The yield is then a mixture of NaCl, KCl, NaBr, and KBr.

With some combinations of ions, reactions do occur. *Such reactions may run to completion in the sense that the ions are almost completely removed from solution.* Chemists can predict that certain ion reactions will run to completion. The extent to which the reacting ions are removed from solution depends on *(1) the solubility of the compound formed and (2) the degree of ionization, if the compound is soluble.* Thus, a product that *escapes as a gas or is precipitated as a solid, or is only slightly ionized,* effectively removes the reacting ions from solution. Let us consider some specific examples of the different types of reactions that run to completion.

1. Formation of a gas. Unstable substances formed as products of ionic reactions decompose spontaneously. An example is carbonic acid, which yields a gas as a decomposition product.

$$\mathbf{H_2CO_3 \rightarrow H_2O + CO_2(g)}$$

Carbonic acid is produced in the reaction between sodium hydrogen carbonate and hydrochloric acid as shown by the equation

$$\mathbf{NaHCO_3 + HCl \rightarrow NaCl + H_2CO_3}$$

Carbonic acid: *Aqueous solutions called "carbonic acid" are mostly solutions of CO_2 in water. The relatively few H_2CO_3 molecules formed are ionized making the solution weakly acidic. H_2CO_3 has never been isolated.*

The water solution of HCl contains H_3O^+ and Cl^- ions. Thus, a closer examination of the reaction mechanism suggests that the HCO_3^- ion acts as a base and acquires a proton from the H_3O^+ acid. The Na^+ and Cl^- ions are merely spectator ions in the water solution. Thus, the following equations may be more appropriate for this reaction.

$$\mathbf{H_3O^+ + HCO_3^- \rightarrow H_2O + \cancel{H_2CO_3}}$$

$$\mathbf{\cancel{H_2CO_3} \rightarrow H_2O + CO_2(g)}$$

or, simply,

$$\mathbf{H_3O^+ + HCO_3^- \rightarrow 2H_2O + CO_2(g)}$$

The reaction runs to completion because one of the products escapes as a gas. Of course, the sodium ions and chloride ions produce sodium chloride crystals when the water is evaporated.

The reaction between iron(II) sulfide and hydrochloric acid goes to completion because a gaseous product escapes. The reaction equation is

$$\mathbf{FeS + 2HCl \rightarrow FeCl_2 + H_2S(g)}$$

The net ionic equation is

$$\mathbf{FeS(s) + 2H_3O^+(aq) \rightarrow Fe^{++}(aq) + H_2S(g) + 2H_2O(l)}$$

The hydrogen sulfide formed is only moderately soluble and is given off as a gas. The iron(II) chloride is formed on evaporation of the water.

2. *Formation of a precipitate.* When solutions of sodium chloride and silver nitrate are mixed, a white precipitate of silver chloride immediately forms.

$$\mathbf{Na^+ + Cl^- + Ag^+ + NO_3^- \rightarrow Na^+ + NO_3^- + Ag^+Cl^-(s)}$$

If chemically equivalent amounts of the two solutes are used, only sodium ions and nitrate ions remain in solution in appreciable amounts. The silver ions and chloride ions combine quantitatively and form a precipitate of that salt. Silver chloride is only very slightly soluble. *The reaction runs to completion because an insoluble product is formed.*

The only reaction that occurs is between the silver ions and chloride ions. Omitting the spectator ions, Na^+ and NO_3^-, the equation is rewritten simply as

$$\mathbf{Ag^+(aq) + Cl^-(aq) \rightarrow Ag^+Cl^-(s)}$$

Crystalline sodium nitrate is recovered by evaporation of the water.

3. *Formation of a slightly ionized product.* Neutralization reactions between H_3O^+ ions from aqueous acids and OH^- ions from aqueous bases result in the formation of water molecules. A reaction between HCl and NaOH illustrates this process. The water solution of HCl provides H_3O^+ ions and Cl^- ions. The water solution of NaOH supplies Na^+ ions and OH^- ions. The ionic equation is

$$\mathbf{H_3O^+ + Cl^- + Na^+ + OH^- \rightarrow Na^+ + Cl^- + 2H_2O}$$

Neglecting the spectator ions, the net ionic equation is simply

$$\mathbf{H_3O^+(aq) + OH^-(aq) \rightarrow 2H_2O(l)}$$

Water is only slightly ionized and exists almost entirely as covalent molecules. Thus, hydronium ions and hydroxide ions are effectively removed from the solution. *The reaction runs to completion because the product is only slightly ionized.* Sodium chloride crystallizes on evaporation of the water.

In the proton-transfer system of acids and bases, the H_3O^+ ion is the acid and the OH^- ion is the base.

21.6 Common ion effect

***Common ion effect:** Add a common ion species to a saturated solution of a salt and solute precipitates.*

Suppose hydrogen chloride gas is bubbled into a saturated solution of sodium chloride. As the hydrogen chloride dissolves, sodium chloride separates as a precipitate. The mass action principle applies to this example, since chloride ions are *common* to both solutes. The concentration of chloride ions is increased, while that of sodium ions is not. As sodium chloride crystals form, the concentration of sodium ions in the solution is lowered. Thus, increasing the concentration of chloride ions has the effect of decreasing the concentration of sodium ions. This phenomenon is known as the *common ion effect.*

Eventually, the rate of dissociation of sodium chloride crystals equals the rate of association of sodium and chloride ions. An equilibrium then exists.

$$\mathbf{Na^+ Cl^-(s) \rightleftarrows Na^+(aq) + Cl^-(aq)}$$

Further additions of hydrogen chloride disturb this equilibrium and drive the reaction to the *left. By forcing the reaction to the left,* more sodium chloride separates. This further reduces the concentration of the sodium ions in solution.

The common ion effect is also observed when *one* ion species of a weak electrolyte is added in excess to a solution. Acetic acid is such an electrolyte. A 0.1-*M* $HC_2H_3O_2$ solution is about 1.4% ionized. The ionic equilibrium is shown by the equation

$$\mathbf{HC_2H_3O_2 + H_2O \rightleftarrows H_3O^+ + C_2H_3O_2^-}$$

***Common ion effect:** Add a salt of a weak acid to a solution of the weak acid and the $[H_3O^+]$ decreases.*

***Common ion effect:** Add a salt of a weak base to a solution of the weak base and the $[OH^-]$ decreases.*

Sodium acetate, an ionic salt, is completely dissociated in water solution. Small additions of sodium acetate to a solution containing acetic acid greatly increase the acetate ion concentration. The equilibrium shifts in the direction that uses acetate ions. More molecules of acetic acid are formed and the concentration of hydronium ions is reduced. In general, *the addition of a salt with an ion common to the solution of a weak electrolyte reduces the ionization of the electrolyte.* A 0.1-*M* $HC_2H_3O_2$ solution has a pH of 2.9. A solution containing 0.1-*M* concentrations of both acetic acid and sodium acetate has a pH of 4.6.

21.7 Ionization constant of a weak acid

About 1.4% of the solute molecules in a 0.1-*M* acetic acid solution are ionized at room temperature. The remaining 98.6% of the $HC_2H_3O_2$ molecules are un-ionized. Thus, the water solution contains three species of particles in equilibrium. These species are $HC_2H_3O_2$ molecules, H_3O^+ ions, and $C_2H_3O_2^-$ ions.

At equilibrium, the *rate* of the forward reaction

$$\mathbf{HC_2H_3O_2 + H_2O \rightarrow H_3O^+ + C_2H_3O_2^-}$$

is equal to the *rate* of the reverse reaction

$$HC_2H_3O_2 + H_2O \leftarrow H_3O^+ + C_2H_3O_2^-$$

The equilibrium equation is

$$HC_2H_3O_2 + H_2O \rightleftarrows H_3O^+ + C_2H_3O_2^-$$

The equilibrium constant for this system expresses the *equilibrium ratio of ions to molecules.*

From the equilibrium equation for the ionization of acetic acid,

$$K = \frac{[H_3O^+][C_2H_3O_2^-]}{[HC_2H_3O_2][H_2O]}$$

Water molecules are greatly in excess of acetic acid molecules at the 0.1-*M* concentration. Without introducing a measurable error, we can assume that the mole concentration of H_2O molecules remains constant in such a solution. Thus, the product $K[H_2O]$ is constant.

Weak acids are slightly ionized in aqueous solution.

$$K[H_2O] = \frac{[H_3O^+][C_2H_3O_2^-]}{[HC_2H_3O_2]}$$

By setting $K[H_2O] = K_a$,

$$K_a = \frac{[H_3O^+][C_2H_3O_2^-]}{[HC_2H_3O_2]}$$

In this expression, K_a is called the *ionization constant* of the weak acid. The concentration of water molecules in pure water and in dilute solutions is about 55 moles per liter. (At 25°C it is 55.4 moles/liter.) Therefore, the ionization constant of a weak acid, K_a, is about 55 times larger than the equilibrium constant K.

The equilibrium equation for the typical weak acid **HB** is

Ionization constant:
$K_a = K[H_2O] = 55.4K$.

$$HB(aq) + H_2O(l) \rightleftarrows H_3O^+(aq) + B^-(aq)$$

From this equation, we can write the expression for K_a in the general form

$$K_a = \frac{[H_3O^+][B^-]}{[HB]}$$

How can we determine the numerical value of the ionization constant K_a for acetic acid at a specific temperature? First we must know the equilibrium concentrations of H_3O^+ ions, $C_2H_3O_2^-$ ions, and $HC_2H_3O_2$ molecules. The ionization of a molecule of $HC_2H_3O_2$ in water yields one H_3O^+ ion and one $C_2H_3O_2^-$ ion. Therefore, these concentrations can be found experimentally by measuring the pH of the solution.

Suppose that precise measurements in an experiment show the pH of a 0.1000-*M* solution of acetic acid to be 2.876 at 25°C.

$[H_3O^+] = 10^{-pH}$

We can determine the numerical value of K_a for $HC_2H_3O_2$ at 25°C as follows:

$$[H_3O^+] = [C_2H_3O_2^-] = 10^{-2.876}\ \frac{\text{mole}}{\text{liter}}$$

$$\text{antilog}\ (-2.876) = \text{antilog}\ (0.124 - 3) = 1.33 \times 10^{-3}$$

$$[H_3O^+] = [C_2H_3O_2^-] = 1.33 \times 10^{-3}$$

$$[HC_2H_3O_2] = 0.1000 - 0.00133 = 0.0987$$

$$K_a = \frac{[H_3O^+][C_2H_3O_2^-]}{[HC_2H_3O_2]}$$

$$K_a = \frac{(1.33 \times 10^{-3})^2}{9.87 \times 10^{-2}} = 1.79 \times 10^{-5}$$

Ionization data and constants for some dilute acetic acid solutions at room temperature are given in Table 21-3.

K_a changes value with temperature change.

An increase in temperature causes the equilibrium to shift according to Le Chatelier's principle. Thus, K_a has a new value for each temperature. An increase in the concentration of $C_2H_3O_2^-$ ions, through the addition of $NaC_2H_3O_2$, also disturbs the equilibrium. This disturbance causes a decrease in $[H_3O^+]$ and an increase in $[HC_2H_3O_2]$. Eventually the equilibrium is reestablished with the same value of K_a. However, there is a higher concentration of un-ionized acetic acid molecules and a lower concentration of H_3O^+ ions. Changes in the hydronium ion concentration and changes in pH go together. In this example, the reduction in $[H_3O^+]$ means an increase in the pH of the solution.

A solution containing both a weak acid and a salt of the acid can react with either an acid or a base. The pH of the solution remains nearly constant even when small additions of acids or bases are present. Suppose we add an acid to a solution of acetic acid and sodium acetate. Acetate ions react with the added hydronium ions and form un-ionized acetic acid molecules.

$$C_2H_3O_2^-(aq) + H^+(aq) \rightarrow HC_2H_3O_2(aq)$$

Table 21-3

IONIZATION CONSTANT OF ACETIC ACID

Molarity	% ionized	$[H_3O^+]$	$[HC_2H_3O_2]$	K_a
0.1000	1.35	0.00135	0.09865	1.85×10^{-5}
0.0500	1.90	0.000950	0.04905	1.84×10^{-5}
0.0100	4.16	0.000416	0.009584	1.81×10^{-5}
0.0050	5.84	0.000292	0.004708	1.81×10^{-5}
0.0010	12.48	0.000125	0.000875	1.78×10^{-5}

The hydronium concentration and the pH of the solution remain practically unchanged.

Suppose we add a small amount of a base to the solution. The OH^- ions of the base remove hydronium ions as un-ionized water molecules. However, acetic acid molecules ionize and restore the equilibrium concentration of hydronium ions.

$$HC_2H_3O_2(aq) \rightarrow H^+(aq) + C_2H_3O_2^-(aq)$$

The pH of the solution again remains practically unchanged.

A solution of a weak base containing a salt of the base behaves in a similar manner. The hydroxide-ion concentration (and the pH) of the solution remain essentially constant with small additions of acids or bases. Suppose a base is added to an aqueous solution of ammonia that also contains ammonium chloride. Ammonium ions remove the added hydroxide ions as un-ionized water molecules.

$$NH_4^+(aq) + OH^-(aq) \rightarrow NH_3(aq) + H_2O$$

Suppose we add a small amount of an acid to the solution. Hydroxide ions from the solution remove the added hydronium ions as un-ionized water molecules. Ammonia molecules in the solution ionize and restore the equilibrium concentration of hydronium ions and the pH of the solution.

$$NH_3(aq) + H_2O \rightarrow NH_4^+(aq) + OH^-(aq)$$

The common ion salt in each of these solutions acts as a "buffer" against significant changes in pH in the solution. The solutions are referred to as *buffered* solutions. They are buffered against changes in pH.

Buffer action has many important applications in chemistry and physiology. Human blood is naturally buffered to maintain a pH of about 7.3. Certain physiological functions require slight variations in pH. However, large changes would lead to serious disturbances of normal body functions, or even death.

21.8 Ionization constant of water

Pure water is a very poor conductor of electricity because it is very slightly ionized. According to the proton-transfer system of acids and bases, some water molecules donate protons, acting as an acid. Other water molecules, which accept these protons, act as a base.

$$H_2O + H_2O \rightleftarrows H_3O^+ + OH^-$$

The degree of ionization is slight. Equilibrium is quickly established with a very low concentration of H_3O^+ and OH^- ions.

Conductivity experiments with very pure water at 25°C show that the concentrations of H_3O^+ and OH^- ions are both

10^{-7} mole per liter. The expression for the equilibrium constant is

$$K = \frac{[H_3O^+][OH^-]}{[H_2O]^2}$$

A liter of water at 25°C (see Table 12-4) contains

$$\frac{998 \text{ g}}{18.0 \text{ g/mole}} = 55.4 \text{ moles}$$

This concentration of water molecules remains practically the same in all dilute solutions.

In water and water solutions, $[H_3O^+][OH^-] = 10^{-14}$.

Thus, both $[H_2O]^2$ and K in the above equilibrium expression are constants. Their product is the constant K_w, *the ion-product constant for water.* It is equal to the product of the molar concentrations of the H_3O^+ and OH^- ions.

$$K_w = [H_3O^+][OH^-]$$

At 25°C,

$$K_w = 10^{-7} \times 10^{-7} = 10^{-14}$$

$10^{-7} \times 10^{-7} = 10^{-14}$
$10^{-4} \times 10^{-10} = 10^{-14}$
$10^{-8} \times 10^{-6} = 10^{-14}$

The product (K_w) of the molar concentrations of H_3O^+ and OH^- has this constant value not only in pure water but in all water solutions at 25°C. An acid solution with a pH of 4 has a $[H_3O^+]$ of 10^{-4} mole per liter and a $[OH^-]$ of 10^{-10} mole per liter. An alkaline solution with a pH of 8 has a $[H_3O^+]$ of 10^{-8} mole per liter and a $[OH^-]$ of 10^{-6} mole per liter.

21.9 Hydrolysis of salts

When a salt is dissolved in water, we might expect the solution to be neutral. The aqueous solutions of many salts, such as NaCl and KNO_3, are neutral. *These salts are formed from strong acids and strong hydroxides;* their solutions have a pH of 7.

Some ions that do not hydrolyze in aqueous solution: Ba^{++}, Ca^{++}, K^+, Na^+, Cl^-, HSO_4^-, NO_3^-

When other salts are dissolved in water, solutions may be produced that are not neutral; they may be either acidic or alkaline. Such salts are said to *hydrolyze* in water solution. ***Hydrolysis*** *is a reaction between water and ions of a dissolved salt.*

There are two general types of hydrolysis reactions:

1. *Reactions between an anion (negative ion) base and water.* Some anions, such as CO_3^{--} and $C_2H_3O_2^-$ ions, are the conjugate bases of weak acids. These anions may act as proton acceptors in water solution. Water molecules are the proton donors. The net effect is an increase in the hydroxide-ion concentration of the solution.

2. *Reactions between a cation (positive ion) acid and water.* Some cations contain hydrogen. Examples are the NH_4^+ ion and hydrated cations like the $Cu(H_2O)_4^{++}$ ion. Such cations

may act as proton donors in water solution. Water molecules are the proton acceptors. The net effect is an increase in the hydronium-ion concentration of the solution.

21.10 Basic anion hydrolysis

This type of hydrolysis involves a salt whose cation is not an acid but whose anion is a base. Such salts form basic solutions in water. The net reaction pattern for the basic anion B^- in water is

Salts of weak acids and strong bases form basic solutions.

$$B^-(aq) + H_2O(l) \rightleftarrows HB(aq) + OH^-(aq)$$

A basic B^- ion accepts a proton from a water molecule and forms the weak acid HB and the basic OH^- ion. This *anion hydrolysis* increases the hydroxide ion concentration $[OH^-]$ of the solution.

The equilibrium constant of a hydrolysis reaction is called the *hydrolysis constant* (K_h). From the general hydrolysis equation above, we can write the expression for K_h as

$$K_h = \frac{[HB][OH^-]}{[B^-]}$$

This hydrolysis constant K_h may be expressed in terms of the ion-product constant K_w for water and the ionization constant K_a for the weak acid.

Some anions that hydrolyze in aqueous solution:
$C_2H_3O_2^-$, CO_3^{--}, CN^-, PO_4^{---}, S^{--}

$$K_h = \frac{K_w}{K_a}$$

We can demonstrate the validity of this expression in the following way. From Sections 21.7 and 21.8,

$$K_w = [H_3O^+][OH^-] \quad \text{and} \quad K_a = \frac{[H_3O^+][B^-]}{[HB]}$$

Thus,

$$K_h = \frac{K_w}{K_a} = \frac{[H_3O^+][OH^-]}{\frac{[H_3O^+][B^-]}{[HB]}} = \frac{[HB][OH^-]}{[B^-]}$$

Suppose we dissolve sodium carbonate in water and test the solution with litmus papers. We find that the solution turns red litmus blue. The solution contains more OH^- ions than pure water and is alkaline or basic.

Sodium ions do not react noticeably with water. Carbonate ions, CO_3^{--}, react as a base. Each accepts a proton from a water molecule and forms the slightly ionized hydrogen carbonate ion, HCO_3^-, and the OH^- ion.

Anion hydrolysis:
$pH > 7$

$$CO_3^{--} + H_2O \rightleftarrows HCO_3^- + OH^-$$

The OH^- ion concentration builds up until equilibrium is reached. The H_3O^+ ion concentration decreases since the product $[H_3O^+][OH^-]$ remains equal to the ionization constant of water, 10^{-14}. Thus the pH is *greater* than 7 and the solution is *alkaline*. In general, *salts formed from weak acids and strong hydroxides hydrolyze in water and form alkaline solutions.*

21.11 Acid cation hydrolysis

A water solution of ammonium chloride, NH_4Cl, turns blue litmus paper red. This shows that hydrolysis occurs and the solution contains more H_3O^+ ions than does pure water. Chloride ions show no noticeable tendency to react with water in solution. The ammonium ions donate protons to water molecules.

$$\mathbf{NH_4^+ + H_2O \rightleftarrows H_3O^+ + NH_3}$$

Salts of strong acids and weak bases form acidic solutions.

Equilibrium is established with an increased H_3O^+ concentration. The pH is *less* than 7 and the solution is thus *acidic*.

The metallic ions of many salts are hydrated in water solution. Such hydrated ions may donate protons to water molecules. The solution then becomes acidic. For example, aluminum chloride produces the hydrated cations

$$\mathbf{Al(H_2O)_6^{+++}}$$

Some cations that hydrolyze in water: Al^{+++}, NH_4^+, Cr^{+++}, Cu^{++}, Fe^{+++}, Sn^{++++}

Copper(II) sulfate in water solution yields the light blue hydrated cations

$$\mathbf{Cu(H_2O)_4^{++}}$$

These ions react with water and produce hydronium ions as follows:

$$\mathbf{Al(H_2O)_6^{+++} + H_2O \rightleftarrows Al(H_2O)_5OH^{++} + H_3O^+}$$

$$\mathbf{Cu(H_2O)_4^{++} + H_2O \rightleftarrows Cu(H_2O)_3OH^+ + H_3O^+}$$

Cations such as $Cu(H_2O)_3OH^+$ ions may experience a secondary hydrolysis to a slight extent:

$$\mathbf{Cu(H_2O)_3OH^+ + H_2O \rightleftarrows Cu(H_2O)_2(OH)_2 + H_3O^+}$$

Hydrated copper(II) hydroxide is not very soluble. The scummy appearance of reagent bottles in which copper(II) salt solutions are stored for a long period of time is caused by the slight secondary hydrolysis of $CU(H_2O)_3OH^+$ cations. This hydrolysis is aided by the formation of a slightly soluble product.

Expressions for the hydrolysis constant K_h for cation acids are similar to those for anion bases. In general, *salts formed from strong acids and weak hydroxides hydrolyze in water and form acidic solutions.*

Both ions of a salt formed from a *weak acid* and a *weak base* hydrolyze extensively in water. If both ions hydrolyze equally, the solution remains neutral. Ammonium acetate is such a salt. In extreme cases, both the acid and the base are very weak indeed. In these cases, the salt may undergo complete decomposition to hydrolysis products.

When aluminum sulfide is placed in water, both a precipitate and a gas form as hydrolysis products. The reaction is

$$\mathbf{Al_2S_3 + 6H_2O \rightarrow 2Al(OH)_3(s) + 3H_2S(g)}$$

Both products are removed from the solution and the hydrolysis therefore runs to completion.

Salts of weak acids and weak bases form solutions that may be neutral.

Hydrolysis often has important effects on the properties of solutions. Sodium carbonate, washing soda, is widely used as a cleaning agent because of the alkaline properties of its water solution. Sodium hydrogen carbonate, baking soda, forms a mildly alkaline solution in water and has many practical uses. Through the study of hydrolysis we can understand why the equivalence point of a neutralization reaction (Section 16.14) may occur at a pH other than 7.

21.12 Solubility product

A *saturated* solution contains the maximum amount of solute possible at a given temperature. This solute usually exists in equilibrium with an undissolved excess of the substance. A saturated solution is *not necessarily* a concentrated solution. The concentration may be large or small, depending on solubility of the solute.

A rough rule is often used to express solubilities qualitatively. By this rule, a substance is said to be *soluble* if the solubility is greater than 1 g per 100 g of water. It is said to be *insoluble* if the solubility is less than 0.1 g per 100 g of water. Solubilities that fall between these limits are described as *slightly soluble.*

Solubility guide:
soluble: > 1 g/100 g H_2O
slightly soluble: > 0.1 g/100 g H_2O
insoluble: < 0.1 g/100 g H_2O

Substances usually referred to as insoluble are, in fact, very *sparingly soluble.* An extremely small quantity of such a solute saturates the solution. Equilibrium is established with the undissolved excess remaining in contact with the solution. Equilibria between sparingly soluble solids and their saturated solutions are especially important in analytical chemistry.

"Insoluble" salts are actually very sparingly soluble in water.

We have observed that silver chloride precipitates when Ag^+ and Cl^- ions are placed in the same solution. Silver chloride is so sparingly soluble in water that it is described as insoluble. The solution reaches saturation at a very small concentration of its ions. All Ag^+ and Cl^- ions in excess of this concentration eventually separate as solid AgCl.

The equilibrium principles developed in this chapter apply to all saturated solutions of sparingly soluble salts. Suppose we consider the equilibrium system in a saturated solution of silver chloride. The system contains an excess of the solid salt. The equilibrium equation is

$$\mathbf{AgCl(s) \rightleftarrows Ag^+(aq) + Cl^-(aq)}$$

The equilibrium constant is expressed as follows:

$$K = \frac{[\mathrm{Ag^+}][\mathrm{Cl^-}]}{[\mathrm{AgCl}]}$$

In Section 21.4, we stated that the concentration of a *pure* substance in the solid or liquid phase remains constant. In

Here, [AgCl] refers to concentration of undissolved AgCl.

this equilibrium system, adding more solid AgCl would not change the *concentration* of the undissolved AgCl present. Thus, [AgCl] in the above equation is a constant. By combining the two constants we can write

$$\boldsymbol{K[\mathrm{AgCl}] = [\mathrm{Ag}^+][\mathrm{Cl}^-]}$$

The product, $\boldsymbol{K}$**[AgCl]**, is also a constant. It is called the *solubility-product constant* $\boldsymbol{K_{sp}}$.

$$\boldsymbol{K_{sp} = K[\mathrm{AgCl}]}$$

Therefore,

$$\boldsymbol{K_{sp} = [\mathrm{Ag}^+][\mathrm{Cl}^-]}$$

Thus, the solubility-product constant $\boldsymbol{K_{sp}}$ of AgCl *is the product of the molar concentrations of its ions in a saturated solution.*

Calcium fluoride is another sparingly soluble salt. The equilibrium system in a saturated CaF_2 solution is given by the equation

$$\mathbf{CaF_2(s) \rightleftarrows Ca^{++}(aq) + 2F^-(aq)}$$

The solubility-product constant is given by

$$\boldsymbol{K_{sp} = [\mathrm{Ca}^{++}][\mathrm{F}^-]^2}$$

Notice how this constant differs from the solubility-product constant for AgCl. For CaF_2, $\boldsymbol{K_{sp}}$ is the product of the molar concentration of Ca^{++} ions and the molar concentration *squared* of F^- ions.

Similar equations apply to any sparingly soluble salt having the general formula M_aX_b. The equilibrium system in a saturated solution is shown by

$$\mathbf{M_aX_b \rightleftarrows aM^{+b} + bX^{-a}}$$

The solubility-product constant is expressed by

$$\boldsymbol{K_{sp} = [\mathrm{M}^{+b}]^a[\mathrm{X}^{-a}]^b}$$

The ***solubility-product constant*** *of a substance is the product of the molar concentrations of its ions in a saturated solution, each raised to the appropriate power.*

From solubility data, Table 13 of Appendix B, we find that 1.5×10^{-4} g of AgCl saturates 100 g of water at 20°C. We know that 1 mole of AgCl has a mass of 143.4 g. Thus, we can express the saturation concentration (solubility) of AgCl in moles per liter:

$$\mathbf{\frac{1.5 \times 10^{-4}\ g}{10^2\ g} \times \frac{10^3\ g}{liter} \times \frac{mole}{1.434 \times 10^2\ g} = 1.0 \times 10^{-5}\ mole/liter}$$

The equilibrium equation is

$$\mathbf{AgCl \rightleftarrows Ag^+ + Cl^-}$$

Fig. 21-5. The heterogeneous equilibrium in a saturated solution is not disturbed by the addition of more of the solid phase.

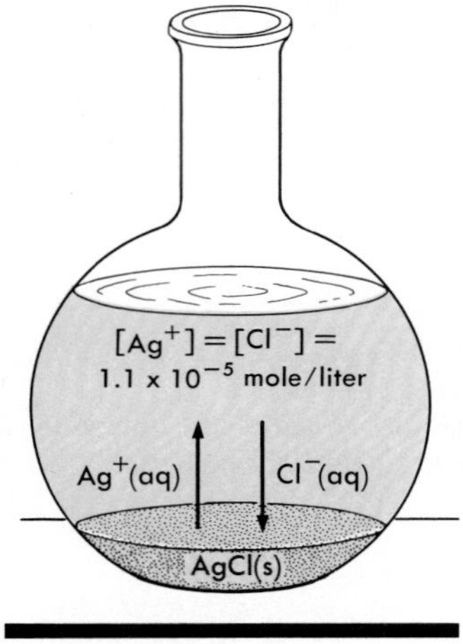

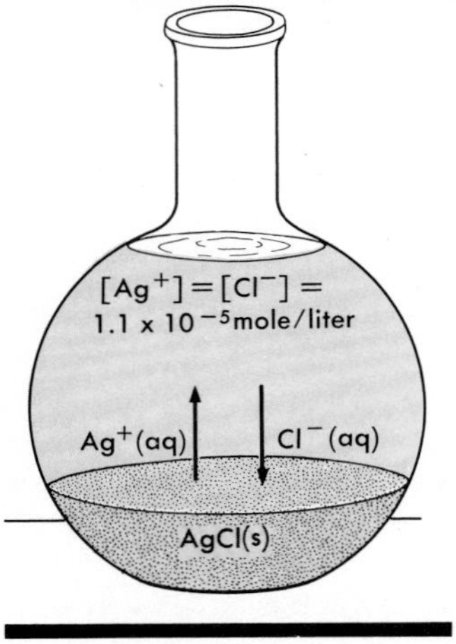

Silver chloride dissociates in solution and yields equal numbers of Ag^+ ions and Cl^- ions. Therefore, the ion concentrations in the saturated solution are

$$[Ag^+] = 1.0 \times 10^{-5}$$

$$[Cl^-] = 1.0 \times 10^{-5}$$

and

$$K_{sp} = [Ag^+][Cl^-]$$

$$K_{sp} = (1.0 \times 10^{-5})(1.0 \times 10^{-5})$$

$$K_{sp} = (1.0 \times 10^{-5})^2 = 1.0 \times 10^{-10}$$

This result is the solubility-product constant of AgCl at 20°C.

The solubility of CaF_2 at 25°C is 1.7×10^{-3} g/100 g H_2O (see Table 13, Appendix B). Expressed in moles per liter as above, this concentration becomes 2.2×10^{-4} mole/liter.

The equilibrium equation for a saturated solution of CaF_2 is

$$CaF_2 \rightleftarrows Ca^{++} + 2F^-$$

Thus, CaF_2 dissociates in solution and yields *twice as many* F^- ions as Ca^{++} ions. The ion concentrations in the saturated solution are

The conversion of solubility in terms of g solute/100 g solvent to mole/liter is a "factor-label" exercise.

$$[Ca^{++}] = 2.2 \times 10^{-4}$$

$$[F^-] = 2(2.2 \times 10^{-4})$$

and

$$K_{sp} = [Ca^{++}][F^-]^2$$

$$K_{sp} = (2.2 \times 10^{-4})(4.4 \times 10^{-4})^2$$

$$K_{sp} = (2.2 \times 10^{-4})(1.9 \times 10^{-7})$$

$$K_{sp} = 4.2 \times 10^{-11}$$

Thus, the solubility-product constant of CaF_2 is 4.2×10^{-11} at 25°C.

If the ion product $[Ca^{+++}][F^-]^2$ is *less* than the value for K_{sp}, the solution is *unsaturated*. If the ion product is *greater* than the value for K_{sp}, CaF_2 precipitates. This precipitation reduces the concentrations of Ca^{++} and F^- ions until equilibrium is established. The solubility equilibrium is then

Salts precipitate from their saturated solutions.

$$CaF_2(s) \rightleftarrows Ca^{++}(aq) + 2F^-(aq)$$

It is difficult to measure very small concentrations of a solute with precision. For this reason, solubility data from different sources may result in slightly different values of K_{sp} for a substance. Thus, calculations of K_{sp} ordinarily should be limited to two significant figures. The values of K_{sp} at 25°C for some sparingly soluble compounds are listed in Table 21-4.

21.13 Calculating solubilities

Solubility-product constants are computed from very careful measurements of solubilities and other solution properties. Once known, the solubility product is very helpful in determining the solubility of a sparingly soluble salt.

Suppose we wish to know how much barium carbonate, $BaCO_3$, can be dissolved in one liter of water at 25°C. From Table 21-4 we find that K_{sp} for $BaCO_3$ has the numerical value 4.9×10^{-9}. The solubility equation is written as follows:

$$\mathbf{BaCO_3(s) \rightleftarrows Ba^{++}(aq) + CO_3^{--}(aq)}$$

Table 21-4

SOLUBILITY-PRODUCT CONSTANTS K_{sp} at 25°C

Salt	Ion Product	K_{sp}
$AgC_2H_3O_2$	$[Ag^+][C_2H_3O_2^-]$	2.5×10^{-3}
$AgBr$	$[Ag^+][Br^-]$	4.8×10^{-13}
Ag_2CO_3	$[Ag^+]^2[CO_3^{--}]$	8.2×10^{-12}
$AgCl$	$[Ag^+][Cl^-]$	1.2×10^{-10}
AgI	$[Ag^+][I^-]$	1.5×10^{-16}
Ag_2S	$[Ag^+]^2[S^{--}]$	1.1×10^{-49}
$Al(OH)_3$	$[Al^{+3}][OH^-]^3$	5×10^{-33}
$BaCO_3$	$[Ba^{++}][CO_3^{--}]$	4.9×10^{-9}
$BaSO_4$	$[Ba^{++}][SO_4^{--}]$	1.1×10^{-10}
Bi_2S_3	$[Bi^{+++}]^2[S^{--}]^3$	6.8×10^{-97}
CdS	$[Cd^{++}][S^{--}]$	7.8×10^{-27}
$CaCO_3$	$[Ca^{++}][CO_3^{--}]$	4.8×10^{-9}
CaF_2	$[Ca^{++}][F^-]^2$	4.2×10^{-11}
$Ca(OH)_2$	$[Ca^{++}][OH^-]^2$	1.2×10^{-6}
$CaSO_4$	$[Ca^{++}][SO_4^{--}]$	6.1×10^{-5}
CoS	$[Co^{++}][S^{--}]$	8.7×10^{-23}
Co_2S_3	$[Co^{+++}]^2[S^{--}]^3$	2.6×10^{-124}
$CuCl$	$[Cu^+][Cl^-]$	3.2×10^{7}
Cu_2S	$[Cu^+]^2[S^{--}]$	1.6×10^{-48}
CuS	$[Cu^{++}][S^{--}]$	8.7×10^{-36}
FeS	$[Fe^{++}][S^{--}]$	4.9×10^{-18}
Fe_2S_3	$[Fe^{+++}]^2[S^{--}]^3$	1.4×10^{-85}
$Fe(OH)_3$	$[Fe^{+3}][OH^-]^3$	1.5×10^{-36}
HgS	$[Hg^{++}][S^{--}]$	3×10^{-52}
$MgCO_3$	$[Mg^{++}][CO_3^{--}]$	2.5×10^{-5}
$Mg(OH)_2$	$[Mg^{++}][OH^-]^2$	1.2×10^{-11}
MnS	$[Mn^{++}][S^{--}]$	5.1×10^{-15}
NiS	$[Ni^{++}][S^{--}]$	1.8×10^{-21}
$PbCl_2$	$[Pb^{++}][Cl^-]^2$	1.0×10^{-4}
$PbCrO_4$	$[Pb^{++}][CrO_4^{--}]$	1.8×10^{-14}
$PbSO_4$	$[Pb^{++}][SO_4^{--}]$	1.9×10^{-8}
PbS	$[Pb^{++}][S^{--}]$	8.4×10^{-28}
SnS	$[Sn^{++}][S^{--}]$	1.2×10^{-25}
$SrSO_4$	$[Sr^{++}][SO_4^{--}]$	1.8×10^{-7}
ZnS	$[Zn^{++}][S^{--}]$	1.1×10^{-21}

Knowing the value for K_{sp}, we can write

$$K_{sp} = [Ba^{++}][CO_3^{--}] = 4.9 \times 10^{-9}$$

We see that $BaCO_3$ dissolves until the product of the molar concentrations of Ba^{++} and CO_3^{--} equals 4.9×10^{-9}.

$K_{sp} = [Ba^{++}][CO_3^{--}]$

The solubility equilibrium equation shows that Ba^{++} ions and CO_3^{--} ions enter the solution in equal numbers as the salt dissolves. Thus,

$$[Ba^{++}] = [CO_3^{--}] = [BaCO_3] \text{ dissolved}$$

$$K_{sp} = 4.9 \times 10^{-9} = [BaCO_3]^2$$

$$[BaCO_3] = \sqrt{4.9 \times 10^{-9}} = \sqrt{49 \times 10^{-10}}$$

$$[BaCO_3] = 7.0 \times 10^{-5} \text{ mole/liter}$$

The solubility of $BaCO_3$ is 7.0×10^{-5} mole/liter. Thus, the solution concentration is 7.0×10^{-5} *M* for Ba^{++} ions and 7.0×10^{-5} *M* for CO_3^{--} ions.

21.14 Precipitation calculations

In the example used in Section 21.13, the $BaCO_3$ served as the source of both Ba^{++} and CO_3^{--} ions. Thus, the concentrations of the two ions were equal. However, the equilibrium condition does not require the two ion concentrations to be equal. It requires only that the *ion product* $[Ba^{++}][CO_3^{--}]$ *not* exceed the value of K_{sp} for the system.

Suppose unequal amounts of $BaCl_2$ and $CaCO_3$ are added to water. A large concentration of Ba^{++} ions and a small concentration of CO_3^{--} ions might result. If the ion product $[Ba^{++}]$ $[CO_3^{--}]$ exceeded the K_{sp} of $BaCO_3$, a precipitate of $BaCO_3$ forms. Precipitation would continue until the ion concentrations decreased to equilibrium values.

We can use the solubility product to predict whether a precipitate forms or not when two solutions are mixed. An illustration of the calculations involved in such a prediction is given in the following Sample Problem.

SAMPLE PROBLEM

Will a precipitate form if 20.0 ml of 0.010-*M* $BaCl_2$ solution are mixed with 20.0 ml of 0.0050-*M* Na_2SO_4 solution?

SOLUTION

The two possible new pairings of ions are NaCl and $BaSO_4$. Of these, $BaSO_4$ is a sparingly soluble salt. It will then precipitate from the resulting solution if the ion product $[Ba^{++}]$ $[SO_4^{--}]$ exceeds the value of the solubility-product constant K_{sp} for $BaSO_4$. From the table of solubility products (Table 20-4), the K_{sp} is found to be 1.1×10^{-10}.

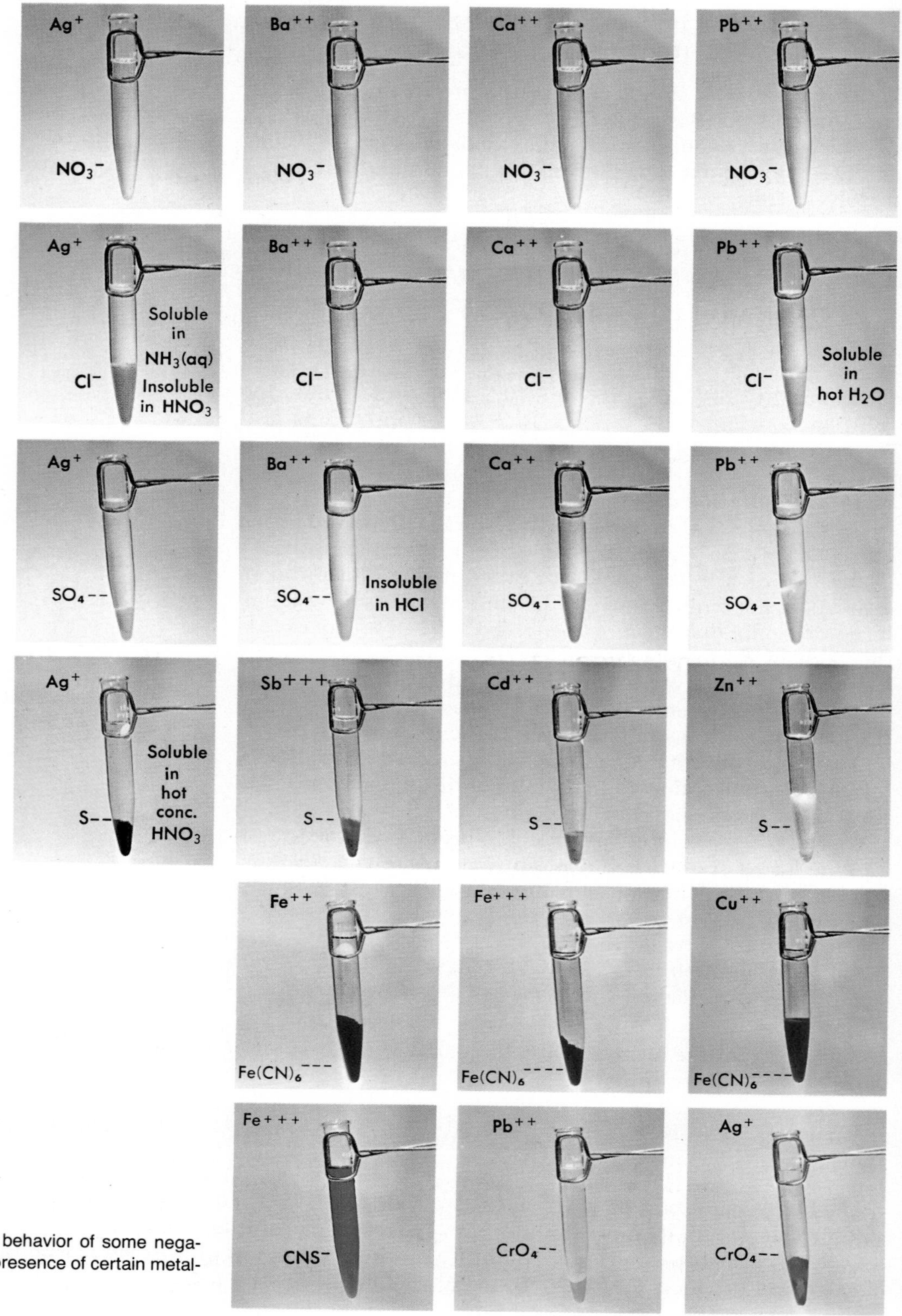

Fig. 21-6. The behavior of some negative ions in the presence of certain metallic ions.

The solubility equilibrium equation is

$$\mathbf{BaSO_4(s) \rightleftarrows Ba^{++}(aq) + SO_4^{--}(aq)}$$

and the equilibrium condition is

$$K_{sp} = [\mathbf{Ba^{++}}][\mathbf{SO_4^{--}}] = \mathbf{1.1 \times 10^{-10}}$$

If the ion product $[Ba^{++}][SO_4^{--}]$ exceeds 1.1×10^{-10}, precipitation of $BaSO_4$ is predicted.
Mole quantities of Ba^{++} *and* SO_4^{--} *ions:*

$$\mathbf{0.020\ liter \times \frac{0.010\ mole\ Ba^{++}}{liter} = 0.00020\ mole\ Ba^{++}}$$

$$\mathbf{0.020\ liter \times \frac{0.0050\ mole\ SO_4^{--}}{liter} = 0.00010\ mole\ SO_4^{--}}$$

Total volume of solution containing Ba^{++} *and* SO_4^{--} *ions:*

$$\mathbf{0.020\ liter + 0.020\ liter = 0.040\ liter}$$

Ba^{++} *and* SO_4^{--} *ion concentrations:*

$$\mathbf{\frac{0.00020\ mole\ Ba^{++}}{0.040\ liter} = 5.0 \times 10^{-3}\ mole\ Ba^{++}/liter}$$

$$\mathbf{\frac{0.00010\ mole\ SO_4^{--}}{0.040\ liter} = 2.5 \times 10^{-3}\ mole\ SO_4^{--}/liter}$$

Trial value of ion product:

$$\mathbf{[Ba^{++}][SO_4^{--}] = (5.0 \times 10^{-3})(2.5 \times 10^{-3}) = 1.2 \times 10^{-5}}$$

The ion product is much greater than K_{sp} ($K_{sp} = 1.1 \times 10^{-10}$), so precipitation occurs.

The solubility-product principle can be very useful when applied to solutions of sparingly soluble substances. It *cannot* be applied to solutions of moderately soluble or very soluble substances. Many solubility-product constants are known only roughly because of difficulties involved in solubility measurements. Sometimes, as with the hydrolysis of an ion in solution, it is necessary to consider two equilibria simultaneously. Finally, the solubility product is sensitive to changes in solution temperature to the extent that the solubility of the dissolved substance is affected by such changes.

SUMMARY

Many chemical reactions are reversible. A reaction system in which the forward and reverse reactions occur simultaneously at the same rate is said to be in equilibrium. Both reactions continue, but there is no net change in the composition of the system.

Equilibrium is a dynamic state involving physical as well as chemical processes. At equilibrium, the energy-change and the entropy-change influences are equal. The relative concentrations of reactants and products in a reaction system at equilibrium are expressed in terms of an equilibrium constant. At equilibrium, the ratio of the product of the mole concentrations of substances formed to the product of the mole concentrations of reactants has a definite numerical value at a given temperature. This numerical ratio is the equilibrium constant, $\boldsymbol{K}$. For values of K greater than 1, the products of the forward reaction are favored. For values of K less than 1, the reactants of the forward reaction are favored. The equilibrium constant for an equilibrium system varies only with the system's temperature.

Any change that alters the rate of either the forward or reverse reaction disturbs the equilibrium of the system. The equilibrium is subjected to a stress. According to the Le Chatelier principle, the equilibrium is displaced in the direction that relieves the stress. Only when change in temperature causes the stress is the numerical value of K changed when equilibrium is reestablished. Reactions for which the conditions that encourage the reverse reactions are very different show little tendency to reach an equilibrium state. These reactions are said to run to completion.

The common ion effect is recognized when a solute containing ions like those of a reactant in an equilibrium system are added to the system. The Le Chatelier principle explains the response of the system to the stress caused by the increase in concentration of common ions.

The equilibrium expressions of weak acids can be modified to give an expression for the ionization constant of the acid. This ionization constant is derived from the fact that the equation for the equilibrium constant includes $[H_2O]$, which is also a constant. The ionization constant then is set equal to the product of these two constants, $\boldsymbol{K_a = K[H_2O]}$. When the equilibrium expression for the slight ionization of water is considered, the ionization constant for water becomes $\boldsymbol{K_w = K[H_2O] = [H_3O^+][OH^-]}$. At 25°C, $K_w = 1 \times 10^{-14}$ for water and all aqueous solutions.

When salts are dissolved in water, the resulting solutions are not always neutral. Salts formed from strong bases and weak acids have aqueous solutions that are basic. The anions of the salt act as a base. They acquire protons from water molecules and increase the $[OH^-]$ of the solution. The process is called anion hydrolysis.

Salts formed from strong acids and weak bases have aqueous solutions that are acidic. The cations of the salt act as an acid. They donate protons to water molecules and increase the $[H_3O^+]$ of the solution. This process is called cation hydrolysis.

Salts formed from strong acids and strong bases do not hydrolyze in water and their solutions are neutral. Salts formed from weak acids and weak bases may hydrolyze completely in water solution.

Salts that are usually described as being insoluble in water are, in fact, very sparingly soluble. Their ions form saturated aqueous solutions at extremely low concentrations. Equilibrium is quickly established between undissolved solute and dissolved solute ions. Because the concentration of undissolved salt is constant, the equilibrium expression yields a useful constant, K_{sp}, called the solubility-product constant. The numerical value of K_{sp} is determined by the product of the mole concentrations of solute ions in the saturated solution. Solubility-product constants are very useful in analytical chemistry.

QUESTIONS

Group A

1. State three examples of physical equilibrium.
2. Write the ionic equations for three examples of ionic equilibrium.
3. What is wrong with this statement? When equilibrium is reached, the opposing reactions stop.
4. State the law of mass action.
5. A combustion reaction proceeding in air

under standard pressure is transferred to an atmosphere of pure oxygen under the same pressure. (*a*) What effect would you observe? (*b*) How can you account for this effect?

6. (*a*) State the principle of Le Chatelier. (*b*) To what kinds of equilibria does it apply?
7. (*a*) Name three factors that may disturb, or shift, an equilibrium. (*b*) Which of these affects the value of the equilibrium constant?
8. What are the three conditions under which ionic reactions involving ionic substances may run to completion? Write an equation for each.
9. What are the solubility characteristics of substances involved in solubility equilibrium systems?
10. Define the solubility-product constant.

Group B

11. The reaction between steam and iron is reversible. Steam passed over hot iron produces magnetic iron oxide (Fe_3O_4) and hydrogen. Hydrogen passed over hot magnetic iron oxide reduces it to iron and forms steam. Suggest a method by which this reversible reaction may be brought to a state of equilibrium.
12. What is the meaning of the term *dynamic* as applied to an equilibrium state?
13. Methanol is produced synthetically as a gas by the reaction between carbon monoxide and hydrogen, in the presence of a catalyst, according to the equilibrium reaction: $CO + 2H_2 \rightleftarrows CH_3OH + 24$ kcal. Write the expression for the equilibrium constant of this reaction.
14. How would you propose to regulate the temperature of the equilibrium mixture of CO, H_2, and CH_3OH of Question 13 in order to increase the yield of methanol? Explain.
15. How would you propose to regulate the pressure on the equilibrium mixture of Question 13 in order to increase the yield of methanol? Explain.
16. In the reaction, $\mathbf{A} + \mathbf{B} \rightleftarrows \mathbf{C}$, the concentration of **A**, **B**, and **C** in the equilibrium mixture were found to be 2.0, 3.0, and 1.0 moles per liter respectively. What is the equilibrium constant of this reaction?
17. Write the balanced ionic equations for the following reactions in water solution. If no visible reaction takes place, write NO REACTION. Omit all *spectator* ions. Show precipitates by (s) and gases by (g). Use solubility data in Appendix B as needed. Use a separate sheet of paper. *Do not write in this book.*

    (*a*) $\mathbf{BaCO_3 + HNO_3 \rightarrow}$
    (*b*) $\mathbf{Pb(NO_3)_2 + NaCl \rightarrow}$
    (*c*) $\mathbf{CuSO_4 + HCl \rightarrow}$
    (*d*) $\mathbf{Ca_3(PO_4)_2 + NaNO_3 \rightarrow}$
    (*e*) $\mathbf{Ba(NO_3)_2 + H_2SO_4 \rightarrow}$
    (*f*) $\mathbf{FeS + NaCl \rightarrow}$
    (*g*) $\mathbf{AgC_2H_3O_2 + HCl \rightarrow}$
    (*h*) $\mathbf{Na_3PO_4 + CuSO_4 \rightarrow}$
    (*i*) $\mathbf{BaCl_2 + Na_2SO_4 \rightarrow}$
    (*j*) $\mathbf{CuO + H_2SO_4 \rightarrow}$

18. Explain why the pH of a solution containing both acetic acid and sodium acetate is higher than that of a solution containing the same concentration of acetic acid alone.
19. Referring to Table 21-2, write the expression for the equilibrium constant for each equilibrium system listed.
20. Referring to Table 21-1, explain why $[H_2] = [I_2]$ in the first two experiments.
21. What is the effect of changes in pressure on the $H_2 + I_2 \rightleftarrows 2HI$ equilibrium? Explain.
22. (*a*) From the development of K_a in Section 21-7, show how you would express an ionization constant K_b for the weak base NH_3. (*b*) In this case $K_b = 1.8 \times 10^{-5}$. What is the meaning of this numerical value?
23. Given a hydrolysis reaction $B^- + H_2O \rightleftarrows HB + OH^-$, demonstrate that $K_h = K_w/K_a$.

24. Complete the table shown below, using a separate sheet of paper.
25. The ionization constant K_a for acetic acid is 1.8×10^{-5} at 25°C. Explain the meaning of this value.
26. Whose principle is quoted under the football photograph on page 439? Can you explain the analogy intended in terms of the motion of the players once the ball has been snapped?

pH	$[H_3O^+]$ (mole/liter)	$[OH^-]$ (mole/liter)	$[H_3O^+][OH^-]$	Property
0				
1				
3				
5				
7	$10^{-7} = 0.0000001$	$10^{7} = 0.0000001$	10^{-14}	Neutral
9				
11				
13				
14				

PROBLEMS

Group A

1. The H_3O^+ ion concentration of a solution is 0.00040 mole per liter. This may be expressed as $H_3O^+ = 4.0 \times 10^{-4}$ mole per liter. What is the pH of the solution?
2. What is the pH of a 0.002-*M* solution of HCl? (At this concentration HCl is completely ionized.)
3. Find the pH of a 0.02-*M* solution of KOH.
4. Given a 250 ml volumetric flask, distilled water, and NaOH, (*a*) state how you would prepare 250 ml of 0.50-*M* NaOH solution. (*b*) What is the normality of the solution?
5. What quantity of copper(II) sulfate pentahydrate is required to prepare 750 ml of 2.00-*M* solution?

Group B

6. A 0.01000-*N* solution of acetic acid is found to have a pH of 3.3799 at 18°C. What is the ionization constant of this weak acid?
7. Ammonia is a weak base and its water solution is slightly basic. The ionization constant for the equilibrium reaction $NH_3 + H_2O \rightleftarrows NH_4 + OH^-$ is $K_b = 1.8 \times 10^{-5}$. What is the pH of a 0.50-*M* NH_3 solution? (Note: Assume that the change in mole concentration of NH_3 at equilibrium is insignificant.)
8. It is found by experiment that 1.3×10^{-4} g AgBr dissolves in 1 liter of water and forms a saturated solution. Find K_{sp} for AgBr.
9. How many grams of $AgC_2H_3O_2$ can be dissolved in 10.0 liters of water at 25°C? (Note: The value of K_{sp} for $AgC_2H_3O_2$ can be found in Table 21-4.)
10. If 0.0015 mole of solid $Pb(NO_3)_2$ is added to one liter of 0.0015-*M* H_2SO_4, (*a*) what substance might precipitate? (*b*) will the precipitate form?

chapter 22

OXIDATION-REDUCTION REACTIONS

An electrochemical cell for every purpose. They come in a great variety of shapes and sizes. (See Question 21 on page 494.)

22.1 Oxidation and reduction processes

In Section 6.5, we defined reactions that involve the loss of electrons by atoms or ions as oxidation processes. The element species that lose electrons are said to be *oxidized.* We also defined reactions that involve the gain of electrons by atoms or ions as reduction processes. The element species that gain electrons are said to be *reduced.*

The combustion of sodium in chlorine illustrates an electron-transfer process. The empirical equation is

$$\mathbf{2Na + Cl_2 \rightarrow 2NaCl}$$

In this reaction, a sodium atom loses an electron to a chlorine atom and becomes a sodium ion. The sodium atom is oxidized to the sodium ion.

$$\mathbf{Na \rightarrow Na^+ + e^-}$$

The oxidation state of sodium has changed from the 0 state of the atom to the +1 state of the ion. This change in oxidation state is indicated by the oxidation numbers assigned to the atom and the ion.

$$\overset{0}{\mathbf{Na}} \rightarrow \overset{+1}{\mathbf{Na}}{}^{+} + \mathbf{e^-}$$

A less obvious oxidation process occurs when hydrogen burns in chlorine and forms hydrogen chloride. The hydrogen-chlorine bond is covalent. We may think of this reaction as a process in which the hydrogen atom *merely changes the way*

Table 22-1

RULES FOR ASSIGNING OXIDATION NUMBERS

1. The oxidation number of an atom of a free element is zero.
2. The oxidation number of a monatomic ion is equal to its charge.
3. The algebraic sum of the oxidation numbers of the atoms in the formula of a compound is zero.
4. The oxidation number of hydrogen is +1, except in metallic hydrides where it is −1.
5. The oxidation number of oxygen is −2. A common exception is in peroxides where it is −1. (In compounds with fluorine, the oxidation number of oxygen is +2.)
6. In combinations of nonmetals, the oxidation number of the less electronegative element is positive and of the more electronegative element is negative.
7. The algebraic sum of the oxidation numbers of the atoms in the formula of a polyatomic ion is equal to its charge.

it shares electrons with another atom. Originally, it shared electrons with another hydrogen atom in the hydrogen molecule. Now it shares electrons with a chlorine atom in a molecule of the hydrogen chloride product.

Detailed rules for assigning oxidation numbers were presented in Chapter 6. By these rules, the oxidation state of the hydrogen atom in the hydrogen molecule is zero. This zero oxidation state is true for both hydrogen atoms in the molecule. In the hydrogen chloride product, a hydrogen atom shares a pair of electrons with a chlorine atom. Chlorine atoms are more electronegative than hydrogen atoms. Thus, the electron pair in this molecule is less attracted to the hydrogen atom than to the chlorine atom. This unequal sharing amounts to a partial transfer of electrons; it constitutes a polar covalent bond. The hydrogen atom is considered to have changed from the 0 to the +1 oxidation state. This change is an oxidation process.

How shall we regard the behavior of chlorine in these reactions with sodium and hydrogen? With sodium, the result is clear. Each chlorine atom acquires an electron from a sodium atom and becomes a chloride ion. The chlorine atom is reduced to the chloride ion. The oxidation state of chlorine changes from the 0 state of the chlorine atom to the −1 state of the chloride ion. For the chlorine molecule

$$\overset{0}{\mathbf{Cl}}_2 + \mathbf{2e^-} \rightarrow \mathbf{2}\overset{-1}{\mathbf{Cl}}{}^-$$

The hydrogen-chlorine reaction is more obscure. The pair of electrons shared by the hydrogen and chlorine atoms is not shared equally. The electrons are more strongly attracted to the chlorine atom because of its higher electronegativity. In this sense, the chlorine atom changes from the 0 to the −1 oxidation state, a reduction process.

Oxidation numbers are assigned to the atoms of covalent molecular species in this way to indicate their oxidation states. For the hydrogen chloride molecule, the oxidation number of the hydrogen atom is +1 and that of the chlorine atom is −1.

$$\overset{0}{\mathbf{H}}_2 + \overset{0}{\mathbf{Cl}}_2 \rightarrow \mathbf{2}\overset{+1}{\mathbf{H}}\overset{-1}{\mathbf{Cl}}$$

The rules for assigning oxidation numbers are restated in summary form in Table 22-1.

22.2 Oxidation and reduction occur simultaneously

Clearly, one particle cannot gain electrons unless another particle loses electrons. If *oxidation* occurs during a chemical reaction, then *reduction* must occur simultaneously. Furthermore, the *amount of oxidation* that occurs must match the *amount of reduction* that occurs. *Any chemical process in which*

Oxidation-reduction reactions are called "redox" reactions.

elements undergo a change in oxidation number is an ***oxidation-reduction reaction.*** The name is often shortened to *"redox" reaction.* The processes of oxidation and reduction are *equivalent* in every oxidation-reduction reaction.

As sodium burns in chlorine gas, electrons are transferred directly from sodium atoms to chlorine atoms as the chlorine molecules (Cl_2) strike the metallic sodium.

$$\begin{array}{rcl} 2Na & \rightarrow & 2Na^+ + \cancel{2e^-} \\ Cl_2 + \cancel{2e^-} & \rightarrow & 2Cl^- \\ \hline 2Na + Cl_2 & \rightarrow & 2Na^+Cl^- \end{array}$$

Note that *two* sodium atoms are oxidized to Na^+ ions as one diatomic chlorine molecule is reduced to two Cl^- ions.

A scheme can be devised to recover metallic aluminum from an aluminum salt. In this scheme, sodium atoms are oxidized to Na^+ ions and Al^{+++} ions are reduced to aluminum atoms. The oxidation and reduction processes must be equivalent. Therefore, three Na^+ ions are formed for each Al^{+++} ion reduced.

$$\begin{array}{rcll} 3Na & \rightarrow & 3Na^+ + \cancel{3e^-} & \text{(oxidation)} \\ Al^{+++} + \cancel{3e^-} & \rightarrow & Al & \text{(reduction)} \\ \hline 3Na + Al^{+++} & \rightarrow & 3Na^+ + Al & \end{array}$$

In each example the number of electrons in the oxidation and reduction equations are equal. This equality shows that the oxidation and reduction processes in the reaction are indeed equivalent.

Many of the reactions studied in elementary chemistry involve oxidation-reduction processes. Of the three examples of oxidation-reduction just considered, the first and second are composition reactions. The third example is a replacement reaction. Not all composition reactions are oxidation-reduction reactions, however. Sulfur dioxide gas, SO_2, dissolves in water and gives an acid solution containing a low concentration of sulfurous acid, H_2SO_3.

$$\overset{+4}{S}\overset{-2}{O_2} + \overset{+1}{H_2}\overset{-2}{O} \rightarrow \overset{+1}{H_2}\overset{+4}{S}\overset{-2}{O_3}$$

Observe that the oxidation states of all elements species remain unchanged in this composition reaction.

Suppose we add sodium chloride to a solution of silver nitrate. An ion-exchange reaction occurs and a white precipitate forms.

$$Na^+ + Cl^- + Ag^+ + NO_3^- \rightarrow Na^+ + NO_3^- + Ag^+Cl^-(s)$$

Or more simply,

$$Ag^+(aq) + Cl^-(aq) \rightarrow Ag^+Cl^-(s)$$

Fig. 22-1. The combustion of antimony in chlorine is an oxidation-reduction reaction.

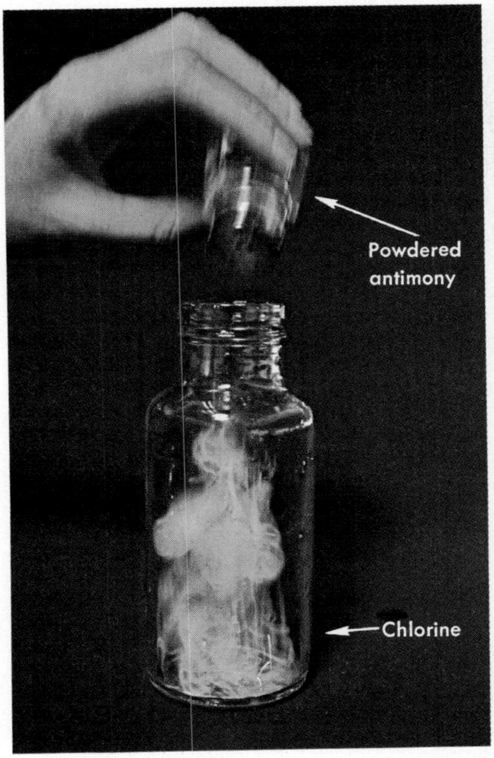

Silver chloride is the insoluble ionic compound that precipitates. The charge on each species of monatomic ion remains unchanged, as does its oxidation state. It is *not* an oxidation-reduction reaction.

Oxidation-reduction reactions sometimes involve polyatomic ions. An example is the *permanganate ion* in a solution of potassium permanganate. It is a polyatomic ion with an ionic charge of -1, MnO_4^-. Under proper conditions this ion can be reduced to the *manganese(II) ion,* Mn^{++}. Under other conditions, the MnO_4^- ion can be reduced to the *manganate ion,* MnO_4^{--}.

In writing the equation for either of these reactions, we must know the number of electrons transferred. The ionic charge alone is of little help if the ion consists of two or more different elements. Assigning the proper oxidation number to each atom present simplifies the task of balancing oxidation-reduction equations. Suppose we review the assignment of oxidation numbers and their implications in the oxidation-reduction process.

Loss of electrons produces a more *positive* oxidation state, and gain of electrons produces a more *negative* oxidation state. The oxidation state of an atom of an element is 0. This statement holds true whether the atom exists as a free single atom or as one of several in a molecule of the element. We have already seen that the oxidation state is 0 for hydrogen in the molecule H_2. It is also 0 for hydrogen in the gaseous atom H. In the same way, the oxidation state of sulfur is 0 in S, S_2, S_4, S_6, and S_8, all of which exist. All atoms in their elemental form have oxidation numbers of 0. These may be written as $\overset{0}{Na}$, $\overset{0}{K}$, $\overset{0}{Cu}$, $\overset{0}{H_2}$, and $\overset{0}{N_2}$.

In the following electronic equations, the substances on the left are oxidized.

$$\overset{0}{\mathbf{Na}} \rightarrow \overset{+1}{\mathbf{Na}^+} + \mathbf{e}^-$$

$$\overset{0}{\mathbf{Fe}} \rightarrow \overset{+2}{\mathbf{Fe}^{++}} + \mathbf{2e}^-$$

$$\overset{+2}{\mathbf{Fe}^{++}} \rightarrow \overset{+3}{\mathbf{Fe}^{+++}} + \mathbf{e}^-$$

$$\mathbf{2}\overset{-1}{\mathbf{Cl}^-} \rightarrow \overset{0}{\mathbf{Cl}_2} + \mathbf{2e}^-$$

The number above each symbol is the oxidation number of that particle. (Ionic charges are shown as right superscripts where appropriate.) The difference between oxidation numbers indicates the number of electrons lost by each atom or ion. The chloride ion has the oxidation number—1, a *negative* oxidation state. Recall that oxidation results in an algebraic increase in the oxidation number of a substance. A change from −1 to 0 is an algebraic increase in oxidation number; so is a change from 0 to +1, or +1 to +2. Each of these changes accompanies the loss of 1 electron.

In the electronic equations that follow, the substances on the left are reduced.

$$\overset{+1}{\mathbf{Na^+}} + e^- \rightarrow \overset{0}{\mathbf{Na}}$$

$$\overset{0}{\mathbf{Cl_2}} + 2e^- \rightarrow 2\overset{-1}{\mathbf{Cl^-}}$$

$$\overset{+3}{\mathbf{Fe^{+++}}} + e^- \rightarrow \overset{+2}{\mathbf{Fe^{++}}}$$

$$\overset{+2}{\mathbf{Cu^{++}}} + 2e^- \rightarrow \overset{0}{\mathbf{Cu}}$$

$$\overset{0}{\mathbf{Br_2}} + 2e^- \rightarrow 2\overset{-1}{\mathbf{Br^-}}$$

The third equation represents the reduction of the iron(III) ion, oxidation number +3. It is reduced to the iron(II) state, oxidation number +2. Two more electrons would be needed to complete the reduction of the iron(II) ion to the iron atom with oxidation number 0. Recall that reduction results in algebraic decrease in the oxidation number of a substance.

The oxidation state of each monatomic ion in a binary salt is the same as the ionic charge. In binary covalent compounds, shared electrons are arbitrarily assigned to the more electronegative element.

In the two compounds, H_2SO_4 and H_2SO_3, oxygen is given the oxidation number −2 and hydrogen +1. In the H_2SO_4 molecule, the total contribution of the 4 atoms of oxygen is 4 times −2, or −8. The total contribution of the 2 atoms of hydrogen is 2(+1) = +2. The H_2SO_4 molecule is neutral. Therefore, the oxidation number of the single sulfur atom is +6. We can now write the proper oxidation number near each symbol in the formula. (The numbers are usually placed *above* the symbols. In this way, they are not mistaken for ionic charges. This practice also prevents undue spreading of the formula in a long equation.)

$$\overset{+1}{\mathbf{H_2}}\overset{+6}{\mathbf{S}}\overset{-2}{\mathbf{O_4}}$$

$$2(+1) + 1(+6) + 4(-2) = 0$$

In the sulfurous acid molecule, H_2SO_3, the total contribution of oxygen is 3(−2) = −6. For the hydrogen, it is 2(+1) = +2. Thus, the oxidation number of the single atom of sulfur must be +4.

$$\overset{+1}{\mathbf{H_2}}\overset{+4}{\mathbf{S}}\overset{-2}{\mathbf{O_3}}$$

$$2(+1) + 1(+4) + 3(-2) = 0$$

Fig. 22-2. The displacement of the copper(II) ion by zinc, which happens when a clean strip of zinc is placed in a solution of copper(II) sulfate, is a good example of a spontaneous oxidation-reduction reaction.

This assignment of oxidation numbers is consistent with the electron structures of these two molecules. The electron-dot formula for sulfuric acid is

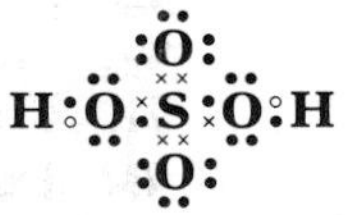

Electron-dot formulas are useful in assigning oxidation numbers.

Oxygen is the most electronegative element present. Therefore, *we assign to oxygen all electrons shared with oxygen.* The sulfur atom must contribute all of its electrons. Hence, the oxidation number of sulfur is +6.

The electron-dot formula for sulfurous acid is

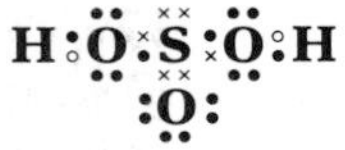

Observe that one pair of electrons belonging to sulfur is unshared. The atom of sulfur contributes *four* electrons, hence the oxidation number is +4.

Suppose these rules are applied to a salt containing a polyatomic ion. Potassium permanganate is made up of potassium ions, K^+, and polyatomic permanganate ions, MnO_4^-. The empirical formula is $KMnO_4$. Oxygen has the oxidation number −2 as before. The total contribution of the 4 oxygen atoms is 4(−2) = −8. The K^+ ion is assigned the oxidation number that equals its ionic charge, +1. The oxidation number of the manganese atom in the polyatomic ion must then be +7. The formula showing these oxidation states of the elements can be written

$$\overset{+1}{\mathbf{K}}{}^{+}[\overset{+7}{\mathbf{Mn}}(\overset{-2}{\mathbf{O}})_4]^-$$

or more simply,

$$\overset{+1}{\mathbf{K}}\overset{+7}{\mathbf{Mn}}\overset{-2}{\mathbf{O}}_4$$

Manganese has several important oxidation states. This oxidation number, +7, represents its highest oxidation state.

Fig. 22-3. As $KMnO_4$ solution is added to an acidic solution of $FeSO_4$, Fe^{++} ions are oxidized to Fe^{+++} ions and the red MnO_4^- ions are reduced to colorless Mn^{++} ions.

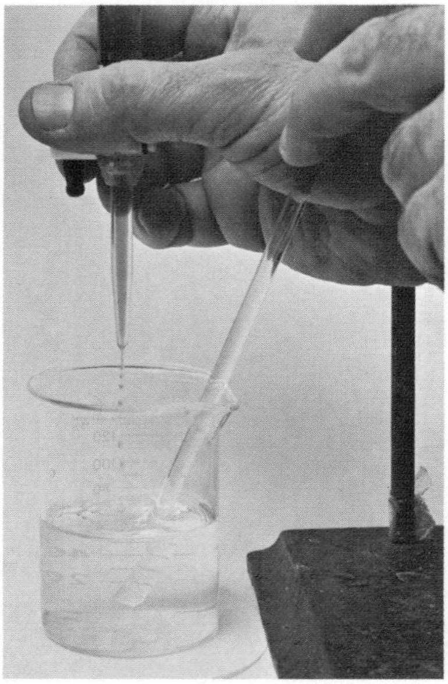

22.3 Balancing oxidation-reduction equations

The principle use of oxidation numbers is in balancing equations for oxidation-reduction reactions. It is very important to follow an orderly procedure in equation writing. First, we must know the *facts:* what the reactants are and what the products are. Then, represent the reactants and products by their *correct formulas.* Finally, adjust the coefficients of all reactants and products to agree with the *conservation of atoms.*

Oxidation-reduction (redox) reactions are those in which changes in oxidation numbers occur. In writing redox equations, provide for *conservation of electrons* as well as for conservation of atoms. In all but the simplest equations, first *balance the electron shift* between the particles oxidized and the particles reduced. Then *adjust the coefficients* for the rest of the equation. The procedure for writing oxidation-reduction equations includes the following steps:

Step 1: Write the skeleton equation for the reaction. To do this, the reactants and products must be known and each represented by the correct formula.
Step 2: Assign oxidation numbers to all elements and determine what is oxidized and what is reduced.
Step 3: Write the electronic equation for the oxidation process and the electronic equation for the reduction process.
Step 4: Adjust the coefficients in both electronic equations so that the number of electrons lost equals the number gained.
Step 5: Place these coefficients in the skeleton equation.
Step 6: Supply the proper coefficients for the rest of the equation to satisfy the conservation of atoms.

Some redox equations are simple enough to balance easily by inspection.

Let us apply these steps to a very simple oxidation-reduction reaction. Hydrogen sulfide gas burns in air and forms sulfur dioxide and water. These facts enable us to write the skeleton equation.

Step 1:

$$\mathbf{H_2S + O_2 \rightarrow SO_2 + H_2O}$$

We now assign oxidation numbers. Changes in oxidation numbers indicate that sulfur is oxidized from the −2 state to the +4 state; oxygen is reduced from the 0 state to the −2 state. The oxidation number of hydrogen remains the same; it plays no part in the primary action of oxidation-reduction.

Step 2:

$$\mathbf{\overset{+1}{H_2}\overset{-2}{S} + \overset{0}{O_2} \rightarrow \overset{+4}{S}\overset{-2}{O_2} + \overset{+1}{H_2}\overset{-2}{O}}$$

The change in oxidation state of sulfur requires the loss of 6 electrons: (−2) − (+4) = −6. The change in oxidation state of oxygen requires the gain of 2 electrons: (0) − (−2) = +2. The electronic equations for these two reactions are

Step 3:

$$\mathbf{\overset{-2}{S} \rightarrow \overset{+4}{S} + 6e^- \qquad (oxidation)}$$

$$\mathbf{\overset{0}{O} + 2e^- \rightarrow \overset{-2}{O} \qquad (reduction)}$$

Free oxygen is diatomic. Thus, 4 electrons must be gained during the reduction of a molecule of free oxygen.

$$\mathbf{\overset{0}{O_2} + 4e^- \rightarrow 2\overset{-2}{O}}$$

We now adjust the coefficients of the two electronic equations. The number of electrons lost in the oxidation of sulfur must equal the number gained in the reduction of oxygen. The smallest number of electrons common to both equations is 12. To show the gain and loss of 12 electrons in the two equations, multiply the oxidation equation by 2, and multiply the reduction equation by 3.

Step 4:

$$2\overset{-2}{S} \rightarrow 2\overset{+4}{S} + 12e^-$$

$$3\overset{0}{O}_2 + 12e^- \rightarrow 6\overset{-2}{O}$$

Hence, the coefficients of H_2S and SO_2 are both 2, and the coefficient of O_2 is 3. Notice that the $6\overset{-2}{O}$ is divided between the two products SO_2 and H_2O. The coefficient 6 is accounted for by the coefficient 2 in front of each formula. These coefficients are transferred to the skeleton equation.

Step 5:

$$2H_2S + 3O_2 \rightarrow 2SO_2 + 2H_2O$$

When a redox equation is complex enough that balancing by inspection would be tedious, the redox sequence should be used.

We can now adjust the coefficients of the equation in the usual way to satisfy the law of conservation of atoms. In this case, no further adjustments are needed; the equation is balanced.

Step 6:

$$2H_2S + 3O_2 \rightarrow 2SO_2 + 2H_2O$$

As a second example, we will use an oxidation-reduction equation that is slightly more difficult to balance. This reaction occurs between manganese dioxide and hydrochloric acid. Water, manganese(II) chloride, and chlorine gas are formed. The skeleton equation is

$$\overset{+4}{Mn}\overset{-2}{O}_2 + \overset{+1}{H}\overset{-1}{Cl} \rightarrow \overset{+1}{H}_2\overset{-2}{O} + \overset{+2}{Mn}\overset{-1}{Cl}_2 + \overset{0}{Cl}_2$$

We assign oxidation numbers to the elements in the reaction and see that $\overset{+4}{Mn}$ is reduced to $\overset{+2}{Mn}{}^{++}$. Also, some of the $\overset{-1}{Cl}{}^-$ is oxidized to $\overset{0}{Cl}$. Hydrogen and oxygen do not take part in the oxidation-reduction reaction. The electronic equations are

$$2\overset{-1}{Cl}{}^- \rightarrow \overset{0}{Cl}_2 + 2e^-$$

$$\overset{+4}{Mn} + 2e^- \rightarrow \overset{+2}{Mn}{}^{++}$$

The number of electrons lost and gained is the same. We now transfer the coefficients to the skeleton equation, which becomes

$$MnO_2 + 2HCl \rightarrow H_2O + MnCl_2 + Cl_2$$

The complete equation can now be balanced by inspection. Two additional molecules of HCl are needed to supply the two Cl^- ions of the $MnCl_2$. This balancing requires 2 molecules of water. These water molecules also account for the 2 oxygen atoms of the MnO_2. The final equation reads

$$MnO_2 + 4HCl \rightarrow 2H_2O + MnCl_2 + Cl_2$$

The equations for both of these examples can be balanced easily without using electronic equations to balance electron shifts. Let us now apply the step process to a more complicated oxidation-reduction reaction. See the following Sample Problem.

SAMPLE PROBLEM

The oxidation-reduction reaction between hydrochloric acid and potassium permanganate yields water, potassium chloride, manganese(II) chloride, and chlorine gas. Write the balanced equation.

SOLUTION

First, write the skeleton equation. Be careful to show the correct formula of each reactant and each product. Appropriate oxidation numbers are placed above the symbols of the elements.

$$\overset{+1}{H}\overset{-1}{Cl} + \overset{+1}{K}\overset{+7}{Mn}\overset{-2}{O_4} \rightarrow \overset{+1}{H_2}\overset{-2}{O} + \overset{+1}{K}\overset{-1}{Cl} + \overset{+2}{Mn}\overset{-1}{Cl_2} + \overset{0}{Cl_2}$$

Some chloride ions are oxidized to chlorine atoms. The manganese of the permanganate ions is reduced to manganese(II) ions. Electronic equations for these two reactions are

$$2\overset{-1}{Cl^-} \rightarrow \overset{0}{Cl_2} + 2e^-$$

$$\overset{+7}{Mn} + 5e^- \rightarrow \overset{+2}{Mn^{++}}$$

The electron shift must involve an equal number of electrons in these two equations. This number is 10. The first equation is multiplied by 5 and the second by 2. We now have

$$10\overset{-1}{Cl^-} \rightarrow 5\overset{0}{Cl_2} + 10e^-$$

$$2\overset{+7}{Mn} + 10e^- \rightarrow 2\overset{+2}{Mn^{++}}$$

These coefficients are transferred to the skeleton equation, which becomes

$$10HCl + 2KMnO_4 \rightarrow H_2O + KCl + 2MnCl_2 + 5Cl_2$$

By inspection, $2KMnO_4$ produces 2KCl and $8H_2O$. Now 2KCl and $2MnCl_2$ call for 6 additional molecules of HCl. The balanced equation then becomes

$$\mathbf{16HCl + 2KMnO_4 \rightarrow 8H_2O + 2KCl + 2MnCl_2 + 5Cl_2}$$

The method used to balance oxidation-reduction reactions has several names. It is called the *electron-shift, electron-transfer,* and *oxidation number method.* The use of oxidation numbers to represent the oxidation state of an element does not necessarily imply that the element exists as ions. In different compounds, the transfer of electrons may be partial, as in polar covalent bonds, or complete, as in ionic bonds. Oxidation numbers are assigned in either case.

22.4 Oxidizing and reducing agents

A strong oxidizing agent easily accepts electrons and becomes a weak reducing agent that does not easily give up electrons.

An ***oxidizing agent*** *acquires* electrons during an oxidation-reduction reaction. A ***reducing agent*** *loses* the electrons. These terms are defined in Section 6.5. It follows that the substance oxidized is also the reducing agent, and the substance reduced is the oxidizing agent. An oxidized substance becomes a potential oxidizing agent. Similarly, a reduced substance is a potential reducing agent. Study the oxidation-reduction terms presented in Table 22-2.

A weak oxidizing agent reluctantly accepts electrons and becomes a strong reducing agent that easily gives up electrons.

The relatively large atoms of the Sodium Family of metals make up Group I of the periodic table. These atoms have weak attraction for their valence electrons and form positive ions readily. They are *very active reducing agents.* According to electrochemical measurements, the lithium atom is the most active reducing agent of all the common elements. The lithium ion, on the other hand, is the weakest oxidizing agent of the common ions. The electronegativity scale suggests that Group I metals starting with lithium should become progressively more active reducing agents. With the exception of lithium, this is the case. A possible basis for the unusual activity of lithium is discussed in Chapter 23.

Atoms of the Halogen Family, Group VII of the periodic table, have a strong attraction for electrons. They form nega-

Table 22-2

OXIDATION-REDUCTION TERMINOLOGY

Term	Change in Oxidation Number	Change in Electron Population
oxidation	increase	loss of electrons
reduction	decrease	gain of electrons
oxidizing agent	decrease	acquires electrons
reducing agent	increase	supplies electrons
substance oxidized	increase	loses electrons
substance reduced	decrease	gains electrons

tive ions readily and are *very active oxidizing agents.* The fluorine atom is the most highly electronegative atom. It is also the most active oxidizing agent among the elements. Because of its strong attraction for electrons, the fluoride ion is the weakest reducing agent.

A strong reducing agent easily gives up electrons and becomes a weak oxidizing agent that does not easily accept electrons.

It is possible to arrange the elements according to their activity as oxidizing and reducing agents. See Table 22-3. The left column shows the relative abilities of some metals to displace other metals from their compounds. Such displacement is an oxidation-reduction process. Zinc, for example, appears above copper. Thus, zinc is the more active reducing agent and displaces copper ions from solutions of copper compounds.

A weak reducing agent reluctantly gives up electrons and becomes a strong oxidizing agent that easily accepts electrons.

$$\mathbf{Zn(s) + Cu^{++}(aq) \rightarrow Zn^{++}(aq) + Cu(s)}$$

$$\overset{0}{\mathbf{Zn}} \rightarrow \overset{+2}{\mathbf{Zn}}{}^{++} + 2e^- \qquad \textbf{(oxidation)}$$

$$\overset{+2}{\mathbf{Cu}}{}^{++} + 2e^- \rightarrow \overset{0}{\mathbf{Cu}} \qquad \textbf{(reduction)}$$

The copper(II) ion, on the other hand, is a more active oxidizing agent than the zinc ion.

Nonmetals and some important ions are included in the series. Any reducing agent is oxidized by the oxidizing agents below it. Observe that F_2 displaces Cl^-, Br^-, and I^- ions from their solutions. Cl_2 displaces Br^- and I^- ions and Br_2 displaces I^- ions.

$$\mathbf{Cl_2 + 2Br^-(aq) \rightarrow 2Cl^-(aq) + Br_2}$$

$$2\overset{-1}{\mathbf{Br}}{}^- \rightarrow \overset{0}{\mathbf{Br}}{}_2 + 2e^- \qquad \textbf{(oxidation)}$$

$$\overset{0}{\mathbf{Cl}}{}_2 + 2e^- \rightarrow 2\overset{-1}{\mathbf{Cl}}{}^- \qquad \textbf{(reduction)}$$

Permanganate ions, MnO_4^-, and dichromate ions, $Cr_2O_7^{--}$, are very useful oxidizing agents. They are used mainly in the form of their potassium salts. In neutral or mildly basic solutions, permanganate ions are reduced to MnO_2. If a solution is strongly basic, manganate ions, MnO_4^{--} are formed. In acid solutions, permanganate ions are reduced to manganese(II) ions, Mn^{++}. Dichromate ions, in acid solution, are reduced to chromium(III) ions, Cr^{+++}.

Peroxide ions, O_2^{--}, have a single covalent bond between the two oxygen atoms. The electron-dot formula is

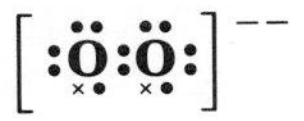

This structure represents an intermediate state of oxidation between free oxygen and oxides. The oxidation number of oxygen in the peroxide form is −1.

Table 22-3

RELATIVE STRENGTH OF OXIDIZING AND REDUCING AGENTS

	Reducing Agents	Oxidizing Agents	
Strong	Li	Li^+	Weak
↓	K	K^+	↑
	Ca	Ca^{++}	
	Na	Na^+	
	Mg	Mg^{++}	
	Al	Al^{+++}	
	Zn	Zn^{++}	
	Cr	Cr^{+++}	
	Fe	Fe^{++}	
	Ni	Ni^{++}	
	Sn	Sn^{++}	
	Pb	Pb^{++}	
	H_2	H_3O^+	
	H_2S	S	
	Cu	Cu^{++}	
	I^-	I_2	
	MnO_4^{--}	MnO_4^-	
	Fe^{++}	Fe^{+++}	
	Hg	Hg_2^{++}	
	Ag	Ag^+	
	NO_2^-	NO_3^-	
	Br^-	Br_2	
	Mn^{++}	MnO_2	
	SO_2	H_2SO_4 (conc)	
	Cr^{+++}	$Cr_2O_7^{--}$	
	Cl^-	Cl_2	
	Mn^{++}	MnO_4^-	
Weak	F^-	F_2	Strong

Hydrogen peroxide, H_2O_2, decomposes by oxidizing and reducing itself. The products are water and molecular oxygen.

$$\mathbf{H_2\overset{-1}{O}_2 + H_2\overset{-1}{O}_2 \rightarrow H_2\overset{-2}{O} + \overset{0}{O}_2(g)}$$

In this decomposition, half of the oxygen in the peroxide is *reduced* to the oxide, forming water. Half is *oxidized* to gaseous oxygen. The process is called *auto-oxidation*. Impurities in a water solution of hydrogen peroxide act as catalysts and speed up this process.

Oxygen in H_2O_2 is *oxidized* from the -1 to the 0 oxidation state when oxygen is formed. It is *reduced* from the -1 to the -2 state when water is formed. Thus, H_2O_2 can be either an oxidizing agent or a reducing agent.

22.5 Chemical equivalents of oxidizing and reducing agents In Section 16.2, we recognized the chemical equivalent (equiv) of a reactant as the *mass of the reactant that loses or acquires the Avogadro number of electrons* in a chemical reaction. If a reactant is oxidized, the mass that loses the Avogadro number of electrons is one equivalent (1 equiv) of that reactant. If a reactant is reduced, the mass that acquires the Avogadro number of electrons is one equivalent of the reactant. Thus, 1 equiv of any reducing agent will always react with 1 equiv of any oxidizing agent.

We often express the quantities of reactants in terms of chemical equivalents. To do so for oxidizing and reducing agents, *the particular oxidation-reduction reaction must be known.* For example, one atom of iron loses 2 electrons when oxidized to iron(II), Fe^{++}.

$$\mathbf{Fe \rightarrow Fe^{++} + 2e^-}$$

One mole of iron, 55.8 g, gives up 2 times the Avogadro number of electrons when oxidized to the +2 oxidation state. Thus, the mass of iron that releases the Avogadro number of electrons in such a reaction is one-half mole. It follows that one equivalent is 55.8 g Fe ÷ 2 = 27.9 g Fe.

One atom of iron loses 3 electrons when oxidized to iron(III), Fe^{+++}. One mole of iron oxidized to the +3 oxidation state gives up 3 times the Avogadro number of electrons. Therefore, one equivalent of iron oxidized to the +3 oxidation state is 55.8 g Fe ÷ 3 = 18.6 g Fe.

Fe^{+++} ions in an iron(III) chloride solution are reduced to the +2 oxidation state by the addition of a tin(II) chloride solution. The Sn^{++} ions are the reducing agent. Here, one mole of Fe^{+++} ions acquires one Avogadro number of electrons and is reduced to Fe^{++} ions. One equivalent of iron in this reaction is 55.8 g ÷ 1 = 55.8 g. One mole of the reducing agent, Sn^{++} ions, loses 2 times the Avogadro number of electrons. One equivalent of tin in this reaction is 118.7 g ÷ 2 = 59.35 g. These relationships are shown clearly in the electronic equations for this oxidation-reduction reaction:

$$2Fe^{+++} + 2e^- \rightarrow 2Fe^{++}$$

$$Sn^{++} \rightarrow Sn^{++++} + 2e^-$$

$$1 \text{ equiv } Fe^{+++} = \frac{2Fe^{+++}}{e^- \text{ gained}} = \frac{2 \times 55.8 \text{ g}}{2} = 55.8 \text{ g}$$

$$1 \text{ equiv } Sn^{++} = \frac{Sn^{++}}{e^- \text{ lost}} = \frac{118.7 \text{ g}}{2} = 59.35 \text{ g}$$

22.6 Electrochemical reactions

1. Electrochemical cells. Oxidation-reduction reactions involve a transfer of electrons from the substance oxidized to the substance reduced. If such reactions occur *spontaneously,* they can be used as sources of electric energy. If the reactants are in contact, the energy released during the electron transfer is in the form of heat. However, suppose we place the reactants separately in an electrolytic solution with a conducting wire joining them externally. The transfer of electrons then takes place through the wire. Such an arrangement is known as an *electrochemical cell.* The flow of electrons through the wire is an electric current. Under these conditions, only part of the energy released during the electron transfer appears as heat; the rest is available as electric energy.

The cathode is the electron-rich electrode.

The anode is the electron-poor electrode.

In electrochemical cells, oxidation occurs at the cathode; reduction occurs at the anode.

The dry cell is a common source of electric energy in the laboratory. Small dry cells are familiar as flashlight batteries. A zinc container serves as the negative electrode or *cathode.* A carbon rod serves as the positive electrode or *anode.* The carbon rod is surrounded by a mixture of manganese dioxide and powdered carbon. The electrolyte is a moist paste of ammonium chloride containing some zinc chloride. Figure 22-4 shows these parts of the dry cell in a schematic diagram.

When the external circuit is closed, *zinc atoms are oxidized at the cathode.*

$$Zn \rightarrow Zn^{++} + 2e^-$$

Electrons flow through the external circuit to the carbon anode. There, if manganese dioxide were not present, hydrogen gas would be formed by the reduction shown in the following equation.

$$2NH_4^+ + 2e^- \rightarrow 2NH_3 + H_2(g)$$

However, hydrogen gas is oxidized to water by the manganese dioxide. This explains why *manganese* rather than hydrogen *is actually reduced at the anode.*

$$2MnO_2 + 2NH_4^+ + 2e^- \rightarrow Mn_2O_3 + 2NH_3 + H_2O$$

The ammonia is taken up by Zn^{++} ions, forming complex $Zn(NH_3)_4^{++}$ ions.

Fig. 22-4. In dry cells, zinc is oxidized at the cathode and manganese(IV) is reduced to manganese(III) at the anode.

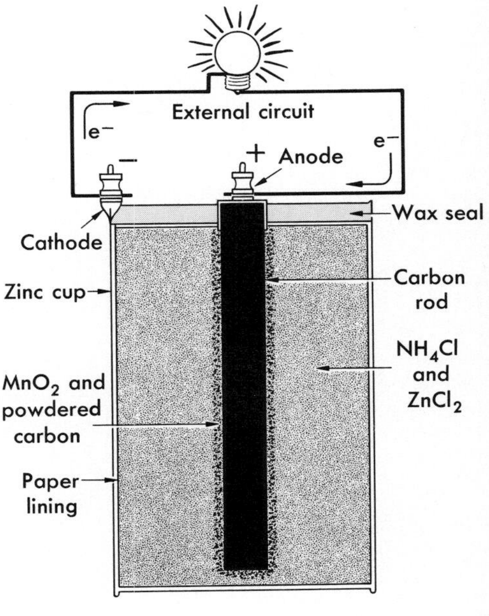

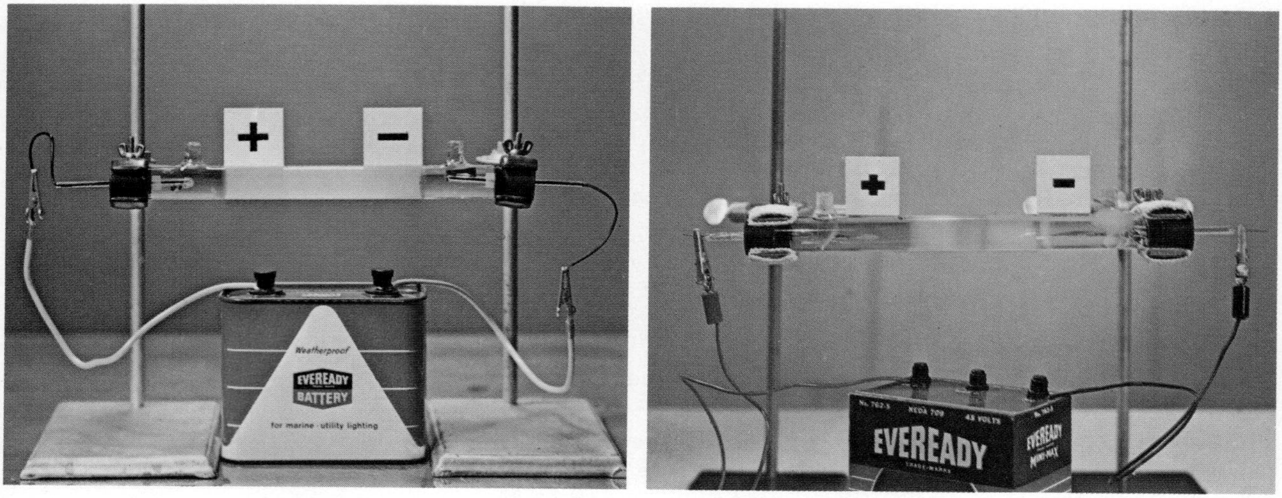

(A) (B)

Fig. 22-5. Positively charged copper ions (blue) and negatively charged chromate ions (yellow) in (A) are shown migrating through a gel toward oppositely charged electrodes in (B).

In electrolytic cells, reduction occurs at the cathode; oxidation occurs at the anode.

2. *Electrolytic cells.* Some oxidation-reduction reactions *are not spontaneous.* However, such reactions can be forced to occur by means of electric energy. *The process whereby an electric current is used to bring about oxidation-reduction reactions is called* ***electrolysis.*** Basically, the *electrolytic cell* consists of a pair of electrodes and an electrolyte solution in a suitable container. An electric current supplied by a battery or other direct-current source is connected across the cell. One electrode (the cathode) then becomes negatively charged and the other (the anode) becomes positively charged.

Ion *migration* in the cell is responsible for the transfer of electric charge. Positively charged ions *migrate* toward the cathode. Negatively charged ions migrate toward the anode. This + and − ion migration is shown in Figure 22-5.

In an electrolytic cell, reduction occurs at the cathode. Electrons are removed from the cathode in this process. Oxidation takes place at the anode, which acquires electrons in the process. The chemical reactions at the electrodes complete the electric circuit between the battery and the cell. The closed-loop path for electric current allows energy to be transferred from the battery to the electrolytic cell. This energy drives the electrode reactions in the cell.

22.7 Electrolysis of water

In the decomposition of water by electrolysis, energy is transferred from the energy source to the decomposition products. The reaction is endothermic and the energy required is 68.32 cal/mole of water decomposed. (See Section 20.2) The overall reaction is

$$\mathbf{2H_2O(l) + 136.64\ kcal \rightarrow 2H_2(g) + O_2(g)}$$

Hydrogen gas is given up at the cathode and oxygen gas is given up at the anode.

A suitable electrolysis cell is shown in Figure 22-6. It consists of two inert electrodes made of platinum immersed in water. A very small amount of an electrolyte, such as H_2SO_4, is added to provide adequate conductivity. The electrodes are connected to a battery which supplies the electric energy that drives the decomposition reaction forward.

The electric current provided by the battery consists of a flow of electrons. The electrode connected to the negative electrode of the battery acquires an excess of electrons. This electrode becomes the *cathode* of the electrolytic cell. The other electrode is connected to the positive electrode of the battery. It loses electrons to the battery and becomes the *anode* of the electrolytic cell. In a sense, the battery acts as an electron pump by forcing electrons into the cathode of the electrolytic cell and pumping them back from the anode of the cell.

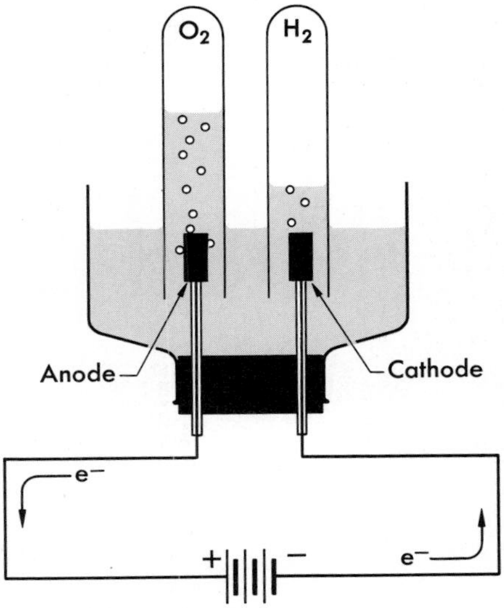

Fig. 22-6. The electrolysis of water. In electrolytic cells, reduction occurs at the cathode and oxidation occurs at the anode.

Reduction occurs at the *cathode;* hydrogen gas is the product. If the amount of H_2SO_4 added to improve conductivity is small, its contribution of hydronium ions to the water is also small. At very low hydronium ion concentrations, it is believed that water molecules are reduced by acquiring electrons directly from the cathode.

cathode reaction: (reduction)

$$2H_2O + 2e^- \rightarrow 2OH^- + H_2(g)$$

The OH^- ion concentration in the solution around the cathode rises.

Oxidation occurs at the *anode,* and oxygen gas is the product. There are SO_4^{--} ions, OH^- ions, and water molecules in the region about the anode. The OH^- ion concentration is quite low and they are not likely to appear in the anode reaction. The SO_4^{--} ions, also at low concentration, are more difficult to oxidize than water molecules. For these reasons, chemists believe that water molecules are oxidized by giving up electrons directly to the anode.

anode reaction: (oxidation)

$$6H_2O \rightarrow 4H_3O^+ + O_2(g) + 4e^-$$

The H_3O^+ ion concentration in the solution around the anode rises.

The overall cell reaction is the sum of the net cathode and anode reactions. We will double the equation for the cathode reaction because we know that the oxidation and reduction processes are equivalent.

$$\text{cathode:}\quad 4H_2O + 4e^- \rightarrow 4OH^- + 2H_2(g)$$

$$\text{anode:}\quad 6H_2O \rightarrow 4H_3O^+ + O_2(g) + 4e^-$$

$$\text{cell:}\quad 10H_2O \rightarrow 2H_2(g)\ O_2(g) + 4H_3O^+ + 4OH^-$$

The solution around the cathode becomes basic because of the production of OH^- ions. The solution around the anode becomes acidic because of the production of H_3O^+ ions. We can expect these ions to eventually diffuse together and form water because of the ordinary mixing tendency in the solution. If this neutralization is complete, the net electrolysis reaction is

$$10H_2O \rightarrow 2H_2(g) + O_2(g) + 4H_3O^+ + 4OH^-$$

$$4H_3O^+ + 4OH^- \rightarrow 8H_2O$$

$$\text{net:}\quad 2H_2O \rightarrow 2H_2(g) + O_2(g)$$

Reduction at the cathode lowers the oxidation state of hydrogen from +1 to 0; the oxidation state of oxygen at the cathode remains −2. At the anode, oxidation raises the oxidation state of oxygen from −2 to 0; the oxidation state of hydrogen at the anode remains +1.

22.8 Electrolysis of aqueous salt solutions

The electrode products from the electrolysis of aqueous salt solutions are determined by the relative ease with which the different particles present can be oxidized or reduced. In the case of aqueous NaCl, for example, Na^+ ions are more difficult to reduce at the cathode than H_2O molecules or H_3O^+ ions. Since the solution of NaCl is neutral, the H_3O^+ ion concentration remains very low (10^{-7} mole/liter). Therefore, H_2O molecules are the particles reduced at the cathode.

cathode reaction: (reduction)

$$2H_2O + 2e^- \rightarrow 2OH^- + H_2(g)$$

Thus, Na^+ ions remain in solution and hydrogen gas is released.

In general, metals that are easily oxidized form ions that are difficult to reduce. That is why hydrogen gas, not sodium metal, is the cathode product above. On the other hand, metals such as copper, silver, and gold are difficult to oxidize and form ions which are easily reduced. Aqueous solutions of their salts give up the metal at the cathode.

Electrolysis of concentrated NaCl solutions yields Cl_2 at the anode.

The choice for anode reaction in the aqueous NaCl electrolysis lies between Cl^- ions and H_2O molecules. The Cl^- ions are more easily oxidized, so Cl_2 gas is produced at the anode.

anode reaction: (oxidation)

$$2Cl^- \rightarrow Cl_2(g) + 2e^-$$

Adding the cathode and anode equations gives the net reaction for the cell.

Dilute NaCl solutions may yield both Cl_2 and O_2 at the anode.

$$\textbf{net:}\quad 2H_2O + 2Cl^- \rightarrow 2OH^- + H_2(g) + Cl_2(g)$$

The electrolytic solution gradually changes from aqueous NaCl to aqueous NaOH as the electrolysis continues, providing the Cl_2 gas is continuously removed from the cell.

Very dilute NaCl solutions yield O_2 at the anode.

Aqueous Br^- ions and I^- ions are oxidized electrolytically in the same way as Cl^- ions. Their solutions give the free halogen at the anode. On the other hand, aqueous solutions of negative ions that do not participate in the oxidation reaction (NO_3^- ions, for example) give O_2 gas at the anode.

22.9 Electroplating

Note that inactive metals form ions that are more easily reduced than hydrogen. This fact makes possible an electrolytic process called *electroplating.*

An electroplating cell contains a solution of a salt of the plating metal. It has an object to be plated (the cathode) and a piece of the plating metal (the anode). A silverplating cell, for example, contains a solution of a soluble silver salt and a silver anode. The cathode is the object to be plated. See Figure 22-7. The silver anode is connected to the positive electrode of a battery or other source of direct current. The object to be plated is connected to the negative electrode. *Silver ions are reduced at the cathode* of the cell when electrons flow through the circuit.

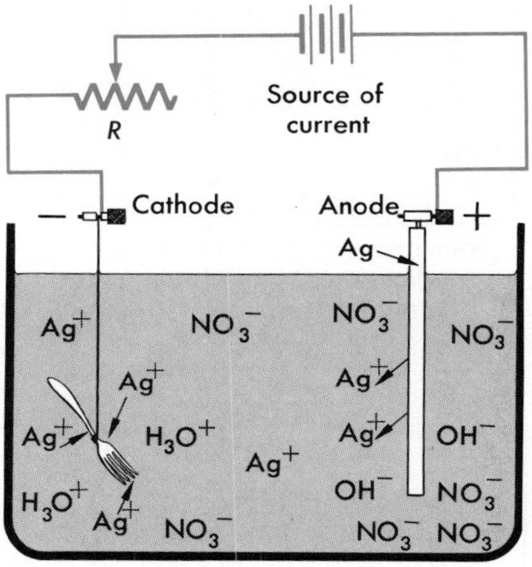

Fig. 22-7. An electrolytic cell used for silver plating.

$$Ag^+ + e^- \rightarrow Ag$$

Silver atoms are oxidized at the anode.

$$Ag \rightarrow Ag^+ + e^-$$

Silver ions are removed from the solution at the cathode and deposited as metallic silver. Meanwhile, metallic silver is removed from the anode as ions. This action maintains the Ag^+ ion concentration of the solution. Thus, in effect, silver is transferred from the anode to the cathode of the cell.

In discussing electrochemical and electrolytic cells we have identified electrodes according to their *state of charge.* We refer to the negative electrode as the cathode and the positive electrode as the anode. These terms agree with modern definitions of such electrodes in physics and electronics. The *electron-rich electrode is the* ***cathode*** and the *electron-poor electrode is the* ***anode*** in any system of which they are part.

An older scheme for naming electrodes still is used widely in electrochemistry. This scheme defines the electrode at which oxidation occurs as the anode; the electrode at which reduction occurs is the cathode. In this system, we must reverse the names of the electrodes, with respect to their electric

Fig. 22-8. A comparison of electrochemical and electrolytic cells.

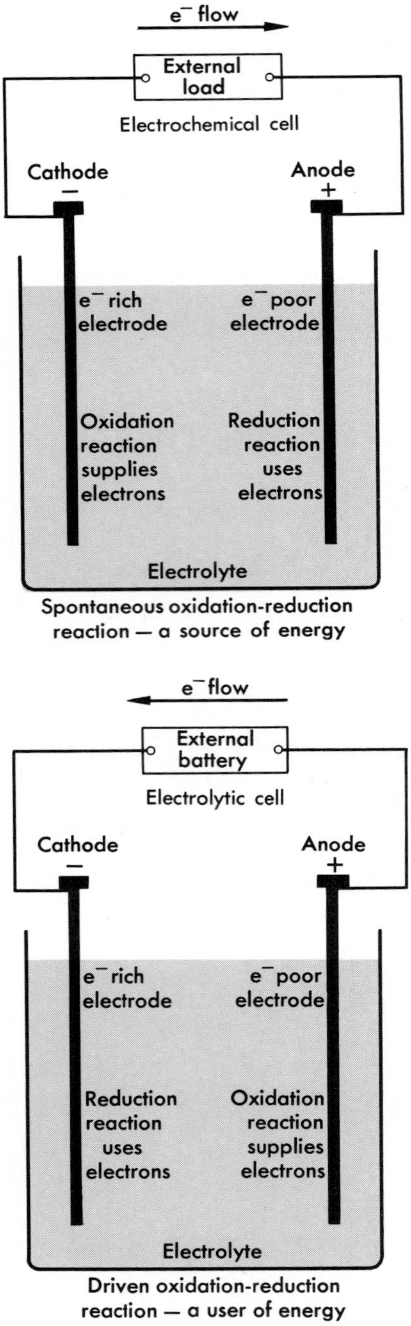

charge for electrochemical and electrolytic cell reactions. Electrochemical and electrolytic cells are compared in Figure 22-8.

22.10 Lead storage battery

The basic unit of the lead storage battery is a lead(IV) oxide-lead-sulfuric acid cell. The standard twelve-volt automobile battery consists of six of these cells connected in series. As the name implies, the *storage* battery is a *storehouse* of energy. The battery is charged by electric energy from an external source. This electric energy is converted to chemical energy by an oxidation-reduction reaction in which each cell acts as an *electrolytic* cell. While the battery is being discharged, the reverse oxidation-reduction reaction occurs. Chemical energy in the battery is converted to electric energy and the cells act as *electrochemical* cells.

A fully charged lead storage cell contains an anode of lead(IV) oxide and a cathode of spongy lead. The electrolyte is moderately dilute sulfuric acid. During the *discharging cycle*, the lead at the cathode is oxidized to Pb^{++} ions. Lead(II) sulfate, $PbSO_4$, is formed as a precipitate on the cathode. This oxidation can be summarized as follows:

cathode reaction: (on discharge)

$$\mathbf{Pb(s) + H_2O + HSO_4^- \rightarrow PbSO_4(s) + H_3O^+ + 2e^-}$$

At the anode, H_3O^+ ions may be reduced. In turn, they may reduce the PbO_2 to PbO, forming water in the process. Reaction with sulfuric acid then produces lead(II) sulfate and water. Lead(II) sulfate precipitates on the anode. The anode reduction is not fully understood, and the above reactions may oversimplify the actual reaction mechanism. However, we can summarize this reduction as follows:

anode reaction: (on discharge)

$$\mathbf{PbO_2(s) + HSO_4^- + 3H_3O^+ + 2e^- \rightarrow PbSO_4(s) + 5H_2O}$$

The net oxidation-reduction reaction of the cell during discharge is the sum of the two electrode reactions.

cell reaction: (on discharge)

$$\mathbf{Pb(s) + PbO_2(s) + 2HSO_4^- + 2H_3O^+ \rightarrow 2PbSO_4(s) + 4H_2O}$$

Observe that sulfuric acid is used up and water is formed at both electrodes as the discharging action proceeds. Electrons released by oxidation at the cathode flow through the external circuit to the anode. There, the reduction occurs. This flow of electrons is the electric current. It is capable of delivering energy to devices in the external circuit.

When the battery is completely discharged, both electrodes consist of lead(II) sulfate. The electrolyte is diluted because some sulfuric acid has been used up and water has been produced. The cell can be made electrochemically active again by reversing the reaction at each electrode. To recharge the cell, a direct current is supplied from an external source. This current is in the opposite direction to the discharging current. During the *charging cycle,* the cell is in the role of an electrolytic cell. The net reaction is the reverse of the net reaction for the discharge cycle.

During charging, sulfuric acid is formed and water is decomposed. The density of the acid solution increases to about 1.300 g/ml for a fully charged cell. The density decreases

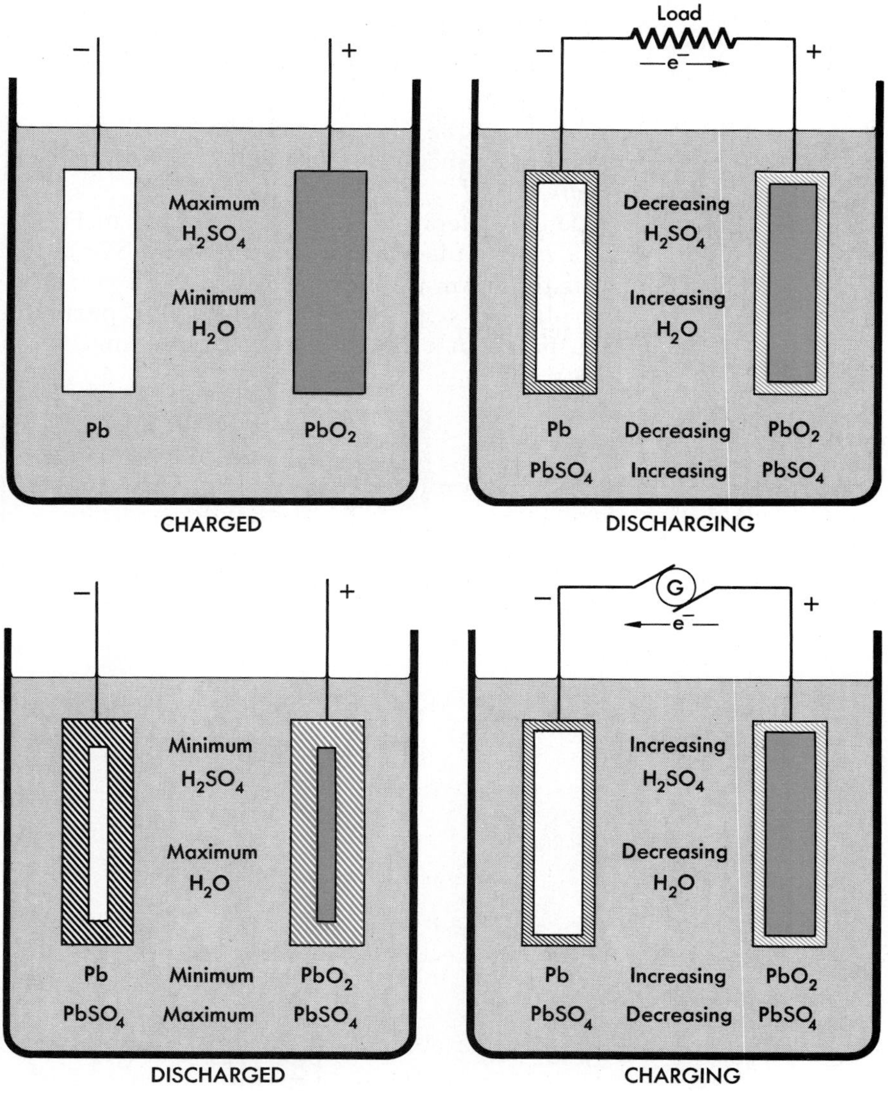

Fig. 22-9. Diagrams illustrating the essential action in a storage cell.

during discharge. In a completely discharged cell, it is lowered to about 1.100 g/ml. Thus, a measurement of the density of the battery electrolyte indicates the condition of charge.

22.11 Electrode potentials

Oxidation-reduction systems are the result of two distinct reactions: *1. oxidation,* in which electrons are supplied to the system, and *2. reduction,* in which electrons are acquired from the system. In electrochemical cells, these reactions take place at the separate electrodes. The oxidation-reduction reaction is the sum of these two separate reactions. As stated in Section 22.6, oxidation occurs at the negative electrode in an electrochemical cell; reduction occurs at the positive electrode.

As the cell reaction begins, a difference in *electric potential* develops between the electrodes. This potential difference can be measured by a voltmeter connected across the two electrodes. It is a measure of the energy required to move a certain electric charge between the electrodes. Potential difference is measured in *volts.*

Let us consider the electrochemical cell shown in Figure 22-10. A strip of zinc is placed in a solution of $ZnSO_4$ and a strip of copper is placed in a solution of $CuSO_4$. The two solutions are separated by a porous partition. This partition permits ions to pass but otherwise prevents mixing of the

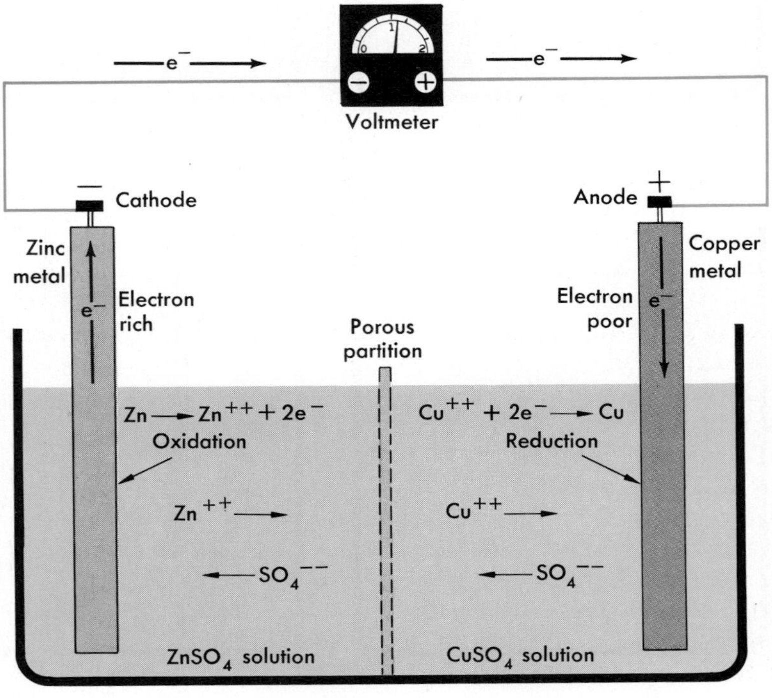

Fig. 22-10. A Zn–Cu voltaic cell.

solutions. Such an arrangement is called a *voltaic cell.* It is capable of generating a small electron current in an external circuit connected between the electrodes.

In the two electrode reactions, the zinc electrode acquires a negative charge relative to the copper. The copper electrode becomes positively charged relative to the zinc. This reaction shows that zinc atoms have a stronger tendency to enter the solution as ions than do copper atoms. Zinc is said to be more active, or more easily oxidized, than copper.

The reaction at the surface of the zinc electrode is an oxidation. It is shown by the following equation:

$$\mathbf{Zn(s) \rightarrow Zn^{++}(aq) + 2e^-}$$

The reaction at the surface of the copper electrode is a reduction:

$$\mathbf{Cu^{++}(aq) + 2e^- \rightarrow Cu(s)}$$

As Zn^{++} ions form, electrons accumulate on the zinc electrode giving it a negative charge. As Cu atoms form, electrons are removed from the copper electrode giving it a positive charge. Electrons also flow through the external circuit from the zinc electrode to the copper electrode. Here they replace the electrons removed as Cu^{++} ions undergo reduction to Cu atoms. Thus, in effect, electrons are transferred from Zn atoms through the external circuit to Cu^{++} ions. The overall reaction can be written as

$$\mathbf{Zn + Cu^{++} \rightarrow Zn^{++} + Cu}$$

A voltmeter connected across the Cu-Zn voltaic cell measures the potential difference. This difference is about 1.1 volts when the solution concentrations of Zn^{++} and Cu^{++} are each 1 *m.*

A voltaic cell consists of two metal electrodes, each in contact with a solution of its ions. Each of these portions is called a *half-cell.* The reaction taking place at each electrode is called a *half-reaction.*

The potential difference between an electrode and its solution in a half-reaction is known as its ***electrode potential.*** The sum of the electrode potentials for the two half-reactions roughly equals the potential difference measured across the complete voltaic cell.

The potential difference across a voltaic cell is easily measured. However, there is no way to measure an individual electrode potential. The electrode potential of a half-reaction can be determined by using a *standard half-cell* along with it as a reference electrode. An arbitrary potential is assigned to the standard reference electrode. Relative to this potential, a specific potential can be determined for the other electrode of the complete cell. Electrode potentials are expressed as

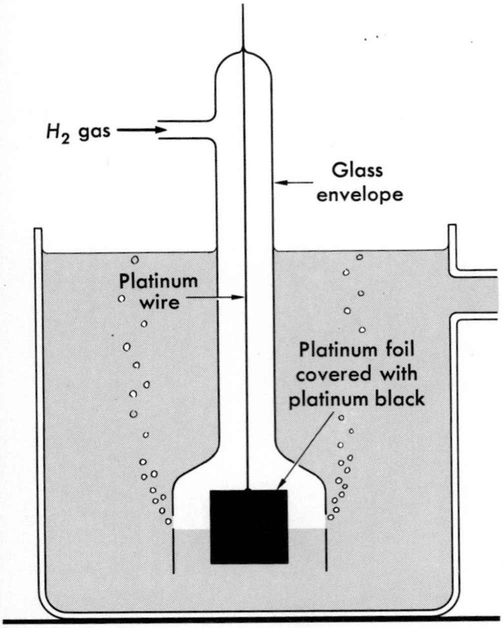

Fig. 22-11. Hydrogen electrode, the standard reference electrode for measuring standard electrode potentials.

reduction (or oxidation) potentials. They provide a reliable indication of the tendency of a substance to undergo reduction (or oxidation).

Chemists use a *hydrogen electrode* immersed in a molal solution of $H^+(aq)$ ions as a standard reference electrode. This practice provides a convenient way to examine the relative tendencies of metals to react with aqueous hydrogen ions (H_3O^+). It is responsible for the activity series of metals listed in Table 8-2. A hydrogen electrode is shown in Figure 22-11. It consists of a platinum electrode dipping into an acid solution of 1-*m* concentration and surrounded by hydrogen gas at 1 atmosphere pressure. This *standard hydrogen electrode is assigned a potential of zero volt.* The half-cell reaction is

$$H_2(g) \rightleftarrows 2H^+(aq) + 2e^-$$

To repeat, the potential of the hydrogen electrode is arbitrarily set at zero volt. Therefore, the potential difference across the complete cell is attributed entirely to the electrode of the other half-cell.

Suppose we construct a complete cell consisting of a zinc half-cell and a standard hydrogen half-cell. See Figure 22-12. The potential difference across the cell measures the electrode potential of the zinc electrode relative to the hydrogen electrode (the zero reference electrode). It is found to be −0.76

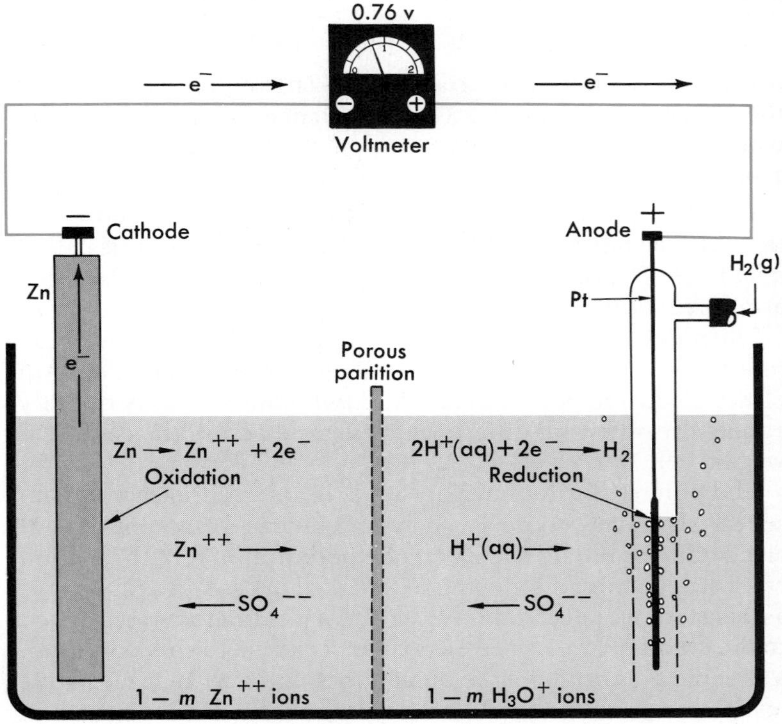

Fig. 22-12. The electrode potential of the zinc half-cell is measured by coupling it with a standard hydrogen electrode.

volt. *The standard electrode potential, E^0, of an electrode is given a negative value if this electrode has a negative charge relative to the standard hydrogen electrode.* Electrons flow through the external circuit from the zinc electrode to the hydrogen electrode. There, $H^+(aq)$ ions are reduced to H_2 gas.

This reaction means that the tendency for Zn^{++} ions to be reduced to Zn atoms is 0.76 volt less than the tendency for $H^+(aq)$ ions to be reduced to H_2. The half-reaction (as a reduction) is

$$\mathbf{Zn^{++} + 2e^- \rightarrow Zn \qquad E^0 = -0.76\ v}$$

This reaction has less tendency to occur than

$$\mathbf{2H^+(aq) + 2e^- \rightarrow H_2(g)}$$

by 0.76 volt. This statement also means that the half-reaction (as an oxidation)

$$\mathbf{Zn \rightarrow Zn^{++} + 2e^- \qquad E^0 = +0.76\ v}$$

has a greater tendency to occur by 0.76 volt than

$$\mathbf{H_2(g) \rightarrow 2H^+(aq) + 2e^-}$$

Observe that the sign of the electrode potential is reversed when the Zn half-cell reaction is written as an oxidation.

A copper half-cell coupled with the standard hydrogen electrode gives a potential difference measurement of +0.34 volt. This measurement indicates that $Cu^{++}(aq)$ ions are more readily reduced than $H^+(aq)$ ions. *The standard electrode potential, E^0, of an electrode is given a positive value if this electrode has a positive charge relative to the standard hydrogen electrode.* The half-reaction for copper (as a reduction) is

$$\mathbf{Cu^{++} + 2e^- \rightarrow Cu \qquad E^0 = +0.34\ v}$$

This reaction has a greater tendency to occur than

$$\mathbf{2H^+(aq) + 2e^- \rightarrow H_2(g)}$$

by 0.34 volt.

From these measurements, we make two observations. *1.* Zinc has a greater tendency to yield electrons than hydrogen by 0.76 volt. *2.* Hydrogen has a greater tendency to yield electrons than copper by 0.34 volt. Taken together, these potentials indicate that zinc has a greater tendency toward oxidation than copper by 1.10 volts (0.76 v + 0.34 v).

How do these electrode potentials apply to the Zn/Cu voltaic cell of Figure 22-10? First, we obtain the potential difference across the complete cell. This is done by adding the electrode potentials of the two half-reactions, writing the Zn half-reaction as an oxidation and the Cu half-reaction as a reduction.

$$Zn \rightarrow Zn^{++} + 2e^- \qquad E^0 = +0.76 \text{ v}$$

$$Cu^{++} + 2e^- \rightarrow Cu \qquad E^0 = +0.34 \text{ v}$$

$$Zn + Cu^{++} \rightarrow Zn^{++} + Cu \qquad E^0 = +1.10 \text{ v}$$

The positive sign of the potential difference shows that the reaction proceeds spontaneously to the right.

Half-reactions for some common electrodes and their standard electrode potentials are listed in Table 22-4. These reactions are arranged according to their standard electrode potentials, E^0, relative to a standard hydrogen reference electrode. All electrode reactions are written as *reduction reactions* to the right. Electrode potentials are given as *reduction potentials*. Half-reactions with *positive* reduction potentials occur spontaneously to the right as *reduction reactions*. Half-reactions with *negative* reduction potentials occur spontaneously to the left as *oxidation reactions*. When a half-reaction is written as an oxidation reaction, the sign of the electrode potential is changed. The potential then becomes an *oxidation potential.*

The magnitude of the electrode potential measures the tendency of the *reduction half-reaction* to occur as written in the table. The half-reaction at the top of the column has the *least* tendency toward reduction (adding electrons). Stated in another way, it has the *greatest* tendency to occur as an oxidation (yielding electrons). The half-reaction at the bottom of the column has the *greatest* tendency to occur as a reduction. Thus, it has the *least* tendency to occur as an oxidation.

The *lower* a half-reaction is in the column, the *greater* is the tendency for its *reduction reaction* to occur. The *higher* a half-reaction is in the column, the *greater* is the tendency for the *oxidation reaction* to occur. For example, potassium has a large negative electrode potential and a strong tendency to form K^+ ions. Thus, potassium is a strong reducing agent. Fluorine has a large positive electrode potential and a strong tendency to form F^- ions. Fluorine, then, is a strong oxidizing agent. Compare the listings in Table 22-3 with those in Table 22-4.

Table 22-4

STANDARD ELECTRODE POTENTIALS (as reduction potentials)

Half-reaction	Electrode Potential (E°)
$Li^+ + e^- \rightleftharpoons Li$	−3.04 v
$K^+ + e^- \rightleftharpoons K$	−2.92 v
$Ba^{++} + 2e^- \rightleftharpoons Ba$	−2.90 v
$Ca^{++} + 2e^- \rightleftharpoons Ca$	−2.76 v
$Na^+ + e^- \rightleftharpoons Na$	−2.71 v
$Mg^{++} + 2e^- \rightleftharpoons Mg$	−2.38 v
$Al^{+++} + 3e^- \rightleftharpoons Al$	−1.71 v
$Zn^{++} + 2e^- \rightleftharpoons Zn$	−0.76 v
$Cr^{+++} + 3e^- \rightleftharpoons Cr$	−0.74 v
$S + 2e^- \rightleftharpoons S^{--}$	−0.51 v
$Fe^{++} + 2e^- \rightleftharpoons Fe$	−0.41 v
$Cd^{++} + 2e^- \rightleftharpoons Cd$	−0.40 v
$Co^{++} + 2e^- \rightleftharpoons Co$	−0.28 v
$Ni^{++} + 2e^- \rightleftharpoons Ni$	−0.23 v
$Sn^{++} + 2e^- \rightleftharpoons Sn$	−0.14 v
$Pb^{++} + 2e^- \rightleftharpoons Pb$	−0.13 v
$Fe^{+++} + 3e^- \rightleftharpoons Fe$	−0.04 v
$2H^+(aq) + 2e^- \rightleftharpoons H_2$	0.00 v
$S + 2H^+(aq) + 2e^- \rightleftharpoons H_2S(aq)$	+0.14 v
$Cu^{++} + e^- \rightleftharpoons Cu^+$	+0.16 v
$Cu^{++} + 2e^- \rightleftharpoons Cu$	+0.34 v
$I_2 + 2e^- \rightleftharpoons 2I^-$	+0.54 v
$MnO_4^- + e^- \rightleftharpoons MnO_4^{--}$	+0.56 v
$Fe^{+++} + e^- \rightleftharpoons Fe^{++}$	+0.77 v
$Hg_2^{++} + 2e^- \rightleftharpoons 2Hg$	+0.80 v
$Ag^+ + e^- \rightleftharpoons Ag$	+0.80 v
$Hg^{++} + 2e^- \rightleftharpoons Hg$	+0.85 v
$Br_2 + 2e^- \rightleftharpoons 2Br^-$	+1.06 v
$MnO_2 + 4H^+(aq) + 2e^- \rightleftharpoons Mn^{++} + 2H_2O$	+1.21 v
$Cr_2O_7^{--} + 14H^+(aq) + 6e^- \rightleftharpoons 2Cr^{+++} + 7H_2O$	+1.33 v
$Cl_2 + 2e^- \rightleftharpoons 2Cl^-$	+1.36 v
$Au^{+++} + 3e^- \rightleftharpoons Au$	+1.42 v
$MnO_4^- + 8H^+(aq) + 5e^- \rightleftharpoons Mn^{++} + 4H_2O$	+1.49 v
$F_2 + 2e^- \rightleftharpoons 2F^-$	+2.87 v

SUMMARY

The atoms or ions of an element that lose electrons in a chemical reaction are oxidized. Those particles that gain electrons are reduced. The oxidation state of an element is indicated by an oxidation number. Oxidation results in an algebraic increase in the oxidation number. Reduction results in an algebraic decrease in the oxidation number. Both processes of oxidation and reduction occur simultaneously and in equivalent amounts in redox reactions.

The equations for simple oxidation-reduction reactions can be balanced by inspection. Equations for more complicated oxidation-reduction reactions are more easily balanced if the electrons gained and lost by particles that change oxidation numbers are first made equivalent. These equations can be successfully balanced by following a sequence of steps.

In redox reactions, the substance reduced acts as an oxidizing agent because it acquires electrons from the substance oxidized. The substance oxidized becomes a reducing agent because it supplies the electrons to the substance reduced. A strong oxidizing agent easily accepts electrons and becomes a weak reducing agent reluctant to give up electrons. A strong reducing agent easily gives up electrons and becomes a weak oxidizing agent reluctant to accept electrons.

One equivalent of a reactant oxidized or reduced is the quantity that loses or gains one mole (the Avogadro number) of electrons. For a chemical equivalent of a substance involved in a redox reaction to be determined, the particular oxidation-reduction process must be known.

Some oxidation-reduction reactions occur spontaneously and may be used as sources of electric energy when arranged in electrochemical cells. Oxidation-reduction reactions that are not spontaneous can be forced to react by an electric current. These redox reactions are called electrolysis processes.

The oxidation or reduction action between one electrode and its electrolyte in an electrochemical cell is called a half-reaction. The potential difference between the electrode and its solution is called the electrode potential. The electrode potentials of the two half-reactions of a cell indicate roughly the potential difference across the cell.

When measured under standard conditions using a standard half-cell as a reference, the measured value is the standard electrode potential of that electrode. These standard electrode potentials indicate the relative strengths of electrode substances as oxidizing and reducing agents.

QUESTIONS

Group A

1. Describe the differences between the processes of oxidation and reduction.
2. Why do oxidation and reduction occur simultaneously?
3. What change in oxidation state do particles undergo that acquire electrons during a chemical action?
4. Which of the following are oxidation-reduction reactions?

(*a*) $2Na + Cl_2 \rightarrow 2NaCl$
(*b*) $C + O_2 \rightarrow CO_2$
(*c*) $2H_2O \rightleftarrows 2H_2 + O_2$
(*d*) $NaCl + AgNO_3 \rightarrow AgCl + NaNO_3$
(*e*) $NH_3 + HCl \rightarrow NH_4^+ + Cl^-$
(*f*) $2KClO_3 \rightarrow 2KCl + 3O_2$
(*g*) $H_2 + Cl_2 \rightarrow 2HCl$
(*h*) $2H_2 + O_2 + 2H_2O$
(*i*) $H_2SO_4 + 2KOH \rightarrow K_2SO_4 + 2H_2O$
(*j*) $Zn + CuSO_4 \rightarrow ZnSO_4 + Cu$

5. For each oxidation-reduction reaction in Question 4 identify: (*a*) the substance oxidized; (*b*) the substance reduced; (*c*) the oxidizing agent; and (*d*) the reducing agent.
6. What is the oxidation number of each element in the following compounds? (*a*) $Ca(ClO_3)_2$; (*b*) Na_2HPO_4; (*c*) K_2SO_3; (*d*) H_3PO_3; (*e*) $Fe(OH)_3$.
7. Assign oxidation numbers to each element in the following compounds: (*a*) $PbSO_4$; (*b*) H_2O_2; (*c*) $K_2Cr_2O_7$; (*d*) H_2SO_3; (*e*) $HClO_4$.
8. What constitutes the anode, cathode, and electrolyte of a fully charged lead storage cell?
9. Define (*a*) electrode potential; (*b*) half-reaction; (*c*) half-cell.
10. Why is the standard hydrogen electrode assigned an electrode potential of 0.00 volt?

Group B

11. What are the six steps involved in balancing oxidation-reduction equations? List them in the proper sequence.
12. Carry out the first four steps called for in Question 11 for the following:
(*a*) zinc + hydrochloric acid → zinc chloride + hydrogen.
(*b*) iron + copper(II) sulfate → iron(II) sulfate + copper.
(*c*) copper + sulfuric acid → copper(II) sulfate + sulfur dioxide + water.
(*d*) potassium dichromate + sulfur + water → sulfur dioxide + potassium hydroxide + chromium(III) oxide.
(*e*) bromine + water → hydrobromic acid + hypobromous acid.
13. The oxidation-reduction reaction between copper and *concentrated* nitric acid yields the following products: copper(II) nitrate, water, and nitrogen dioxide. Write the balanced equation.
14. The reaction between copper and *dilute* nitric acid yields the following products: copper(II) nitrate, water, and nitrogen monoxide. Write the balanced equation.
15. Referring to Table 22-3, the active metals down to magnesium replace hydrogen from water. Magnesium and succeeding metals replace hydrogen from steam. Metals near the bottom of the list will not replace hydrogen from steam. How does this table help to explain this behavior?
16. Balance the oxidation-reduction equation:
$K_2Cr_2O_7 + HCl \rightarrow KCl + CrCl_3 + H_2O + Cl_2$.
17. Using information from Table 22-4, write the equations for the half-reactions of a voltaic cell having Cu and Ag electrodes.
18. (*a*) Determine the potential difference across the voltaic cell of Question 17. (*b*) Write the equation for the overall reaction of the cell in the direction that it proceeds spontaneously.
19. Potassium carbonate and bromine react and form potassium bromide, potassium bromate, and carbon dioxide. Write and balance the equation.
20. Potassium permanganate, sodium sulfite, and sulfuric acid react and form potassium sulfate, manganese(II) sulfate, sodium sulfate, and water. Write and balance the equation for this oxidation-reduction reaction.
21. Refer to the photograph on page 469 and make as extensive a list as you can of all the possible uses for these electrochemical cells of different sizes and shapes.

chapter 23

THE METALS OF GROUP I

The horsehead nebula in Orion surrounded by luminous clouds of cosmic dust. (See Question 27 on page 508.)

23.1 Structure and properties

The group of elements at the left of the periodic table includes lithium, sodium, potassium, rubidium, cesium, and francium. These elements are all chemically active metals. They are known as the *alkali metals* and also as the Sodium Family of elements. None exists in nature in the elemental state because of their great chemical reactivity. They are found only in natural compounds as monatomic ions with a +1 charge. Sodium and potassium are plentiful, lithium is fairly rare, and rubidium and cesium are rarer still. Francium does not exist as a stable element. Only trace quantities have been produced in certain nuclear reactions.

The Group I elements form hydroxides that are strongly basic. Their aqueous hydroxide solutions are extremely alkaline, giving rise to the name "alkali" metals. They possess certain metallic characteristics to a high degree. Each has a silvery luster, is a good conductor of electricity and heat, and is ductile and malleable. These metals are relatively soft and can be cut with a knife. The properties of the Group I metals are related to their characteristic crystalline lattice structures.

The crystal lattice is made up of metallic ions with a +1 (monopositive) charge. The lattice is built around a body-centered cubic unit cell. In this body centered structure, each metallic ion is surrounded by eight nearest neighbors at the corners of the cube. A model of the body-centered cubic unit cell is shown in Figure 23-1. Valence electrons form an "electron gas" that permeates the lattice structure. These "free"

Fig. 23-1. Body-centered cubic unit cell.

The electron gas is also called an electron cloud.

electrons belong to the solid as a whole. The mobility of the free electrons gives Group I metals their high thermal and electric conductivity. These electrons are responsible for the characteristic silvery luster as well.

Ductile: *capable of being drawn into a wire.*

Malleable: *capable of being rolled or pounded into a sheet.*

The softness, ductility, and malleability of the alkali metals are explained by the binding force in the metallic crystal lattice. See Section 12.14. Their low melting points and densities, together with their softness, distinguishes these elements from the more familiar common metals. Table 23-1 lists some representative physical properties of the alkali metals.

The atoms of each element in Group I have a single electron in their outermost shell. Lithium atoms have the electron configuration $1s^2 2s^1$. All other Group I elements have next-to-outermost shells consisting of eight electrons. An outer octet is easily attained by removing a single electron. Thus, an ion formed in this way has the stable electron configuration of the preceding noble gas. For example, the sodium ion has the electron configuration $1s^2 2s^2 2p^6$. This matches the configuration of the neon atom. The electron configuration of the potassium ion, $1s^2 2s^2 2p^6 3s^3 3p^6$, matches that of the argon atom.

23.2 Chemical activity

The very active free metals of the Sodium Family are obtained by the reduction of the monopositive ions from their compounds occurring in nature. The metals are vigorous reducing agents. They have a weak attraction for their valence electrons. Ionization energy decreases as the atom size increases going down the group. See Table 23.2. This decreasing energy with increasing size shows that it is easier to remove electrons physically from the outer shells of the heavier atoms. However, if you examine the net energy of reactions in which electrons are given up to other elements, you find that the lithium atom is the strongest reducing agent. Although it may be harder to remove an electron from the lithium atom, more energy is given back by the subsequent interaction of the

Ionization energy measures the tendency of an atom to hold a valence electron.

Table 23-1

PROPERTIES OF GROUP I ELEMENTS

Element	Atomic Number	Atomic Weight	Electron Configuration	Oxidation Number	Melting Point (°C)	Boiling Point (°C)	Density (g/cm³)	Metallic Radius (Å)	Ionic Radius (Å)
lithium	3	6.939	2,1	+1	179	1317	0.53	1.55	0.68
sodium	11	22.9898	2,8,1	+1	97.8	892	0.97	1.90	0.97
potassium	19	39.102	2,8,8,1	+1	63.6	774	0.86	2.35	1.33
rubidium	37	85.47	2,8,18,8,1	+1	38.8	701	1.53	2.48	1.47
cesium	55	132.905	2,8,18,18,8,1	+1	28.7	685	1.87	2.67	1.67
francium	87	[223]	2,8,18,32,18,8,1	+1	(27)	(677)	—	—	1.80

lithium ion and its surroundings than by the larger ions with their surroundings.

Handling and storing the alkali metals is difficult because of their chemical activity. They usually are stored submerged in kerosene or some other liquid hydrocarbon because they react vigorously with water. See Figure 23.2. In reaction with water, they release hydrogen and form strongly basic hydroxide solutions.

$$2K(s) + 2H_2O(l) \rightarrow 2K^+(aq) + 2OH^-(aq) + H_2(g)$$

The metals do not exist free in nature, but are found only in combined form.

All of the ordinary compounds of the alkali metals are ionic, including their hydrides. Only lithium forms the oxide directly with oxygen. Sodium forms the peroxide instead, and the higher metals tend to form superoxides of the form $M^+O_2^-$. However, the ordinary oxides can be prepared indirectly. These oxides are basic anhydrides. They react with water and form the hydroxides.

Nearly all of the compounds of the alkali metals are quite soluble in water. The alkali-metal ions are colorless. They have little tendency to hydrolyze in water solution or to form polyatomic ions.

Compounds of the more important alkali metals are easily identified by *flame tests*. Their compounds impart characteristic colors to a Bunsen flame. Sodium compounds color the flame yellow. Lithium compounds give a flame a red (carmine) color. Potassium colors a flame violet, rubidium and cesium give reddish violet (magenta) flames.

Table 23-2

IONIZATION ENERGY AND THE SIZE OF ATOMS

Element	Relative Size of Atoms	Ionization Energy (kcal/mole)
Li		124
Na		119
K		100
Rb		96.3
Cs		89.8
Fr	—	—

Sodium

23.3 Occurrence of sodium

Metallic sodium is never found free in nature. However, compounds containing the Na^+ ion and sodium complexes exist in soil, natural waters, and in plants and animals. Sodium is such a widely distributed element because of the solubility of its compounds that it is almost impossible to find a sodium-free material. Vast quantities of sodium chloride are present in sea water and rock salt deposits. There are important deposits of sodium nitrate in Chile and Peru. The carbonates, sulfates, and borates of sodium are found in dry lake beds.

23.4 The preparation of sodium

Sir Humphry Davy first prepared metallic sodium in 1807, by the electrolysis of fused sodium hydroxide. Today, sodium is prepared by the electrolysis of fused sodium chloride. An apparatus called the *Downs cell* (see Figure 23-3) is used in this process. Sodium chloride has a high melting point (801°C). Calcium chloride is mixed with it to lower the melting point to 580°C. Liquid sodium is collected under oil. Chlorine

Fig. 23-2. Potassium, a Group I metal, like other members of this group, reacts vigorously with water. The light for this photograph was produced by dropping a small amount of potassium into a beaker of water.

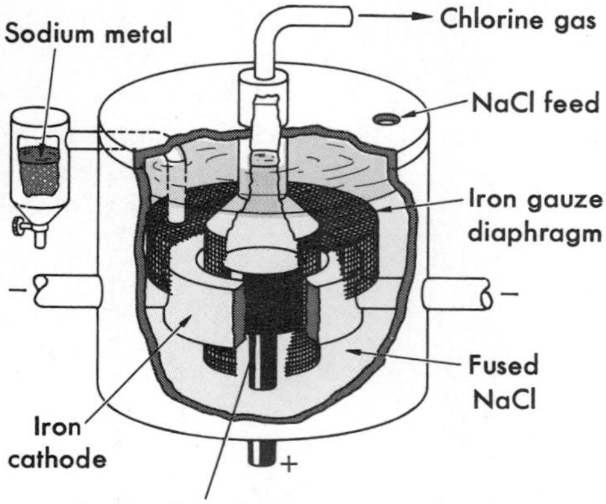

Fig. 23-3. The element sodium is produced by the electrolysis of melted sodium chloride in a Downs cell. Chlorine is a valuable by-product.

gas is produced simultaneously. This gas is kept separate from the metallic sodium by an iron-gauze diaphragm.

The sodium is recovered by reducing Na^+ ions. This occurs at the cathode of the Downs cell. Each sodium ion acquires an electron from the cathode and forms a neutral sodium atom.

$$\mathbf{Na^+ + e^- \rightarrow Na(l)}$$

Chloride ions are oxidized at the anode. Each chloride ion loses an electron to the anode and forms a neutral chlorine atom.

$$\mathbf{Cl^- \rightarrow Cl + e^-}$$

Two chlorine atoms, however, form the diatomic molecule of elemental chlorine gas. The net anode reaction is

$$\mathbf{2Cl^- \rightarrow Cl_2(g) + 2e^-}$$

In the overall cell reaction, electron-transfer balance is maintained between the electrodes. Two Na^+ ions are reduced for each Cl_2 molecule formed. The cell reaction can be written

$$\begin{array}{ll} \textbf{cathode:} & \mathbf{2Na^+ + 2e^- \rightarrow 2Na(l)} \\ \textbf{anode:} & \mathbf{2Cl^- \rightarrow Cl_2(g) + 2e^-} \\ \hline \textbf{cell:} & \mathbf{2Na^+ + 2Cl^- \rightarrow 2Na(l) + Cl_2(g)} \end{array}$$

23.5 Properties and uses of sodium

Sodium is a silvery-white, lustrous metal that tarnishes rapidly when exposed to air. It is very soft, has a lower density than water, and a low melting point. A pellet of sodium dropped into water melts from the heat of the vigorous exothermic reaction that occurs. This reaction yields hydrogen gas and a strongly basic solution.

$$\mathbf{2Na(s) + 2H_2O \rightarrow 2Na^+(aq) + 2OH^-(aq) + H_2(g)}$$

When exposed to air, sodium unites with oxygen and forms sodium peroxide, Na_2O_2. By supplying sodium in excess, some sodium oxide, Na_2O, can be produced along with the bulk product, Na_2O_2. The Na_2O production results from the strong reducing character of the sodium atoms. Lithium forms primarily the normal oxide, Li_2O, with oxygen. Sodium oxide can be formed by heating NaOH with sodium.

$$\mathbf{2NaOH + 2Na \rightarrow 2Na_2O + H_2(g)}$$

Oxide ion: O^{--}
Peroxide ion: O_2^{--}
Superoxide ion: O_2^-

The remaining alkali metals react directly with oxygen and form superoxides of the type M^+O_2. The superoxide of sodium, NaO_2, can be prepared indirectly. Superoxides contain the O_2^- ion that has one unpaired electron. The oxides and peroxides of potassium, rubidium, and cesium are formed in reactions with oxygen and an excess of the metals.

Sodium reacts with all aqueous acids. It burns in an atmosphere of chlorine gas, uniting directly with the chlorine and forming sodium chloride.

A flame test of sodium compounds reveals a strong yellow color characteristic of vaporized sodium atoms. This yellow flame is a common identification test for sodium. See Figure 23-4.

Most of the sodium produced in the United States is used in making tetraethyl lead, an antiknock additive for gasoline. Sodium is used as a heat-transfer agent and in making dyes and other organic compounds. Another use is in sodium vapor lamps.

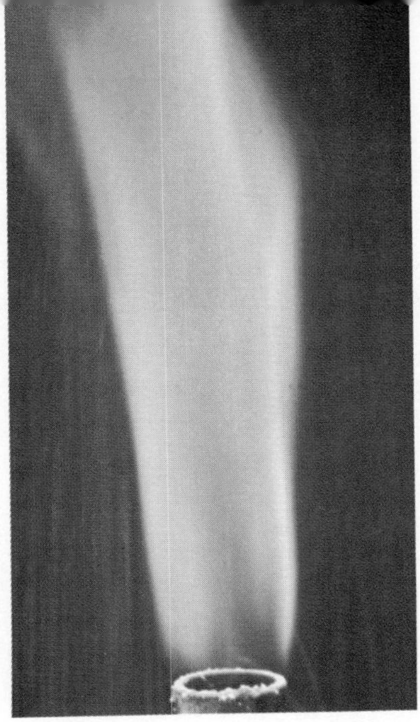

Fig. 23-4. Sodium salts impart a strong yellow color to the Bunsen flame. The sodium flame is obscured by cobalt-blue glass.

23.6 Sodium chloride

Sodium chloride is found in sea water, in salt wells, and in deposits of rock salt. Rock salt is mined in many places in the world.

Pure sodium chloride is not deliquescent. Magnesium chloride is very deliquescent, however, and is usually present in sodium salt as an impurity. This explains why table salt becomes wet and sticky in damp weather. Sodium chloride crystallizes in a cubic pattern. See Figure 23-5.

Sodium chloride is essential in the diets of humans and animals and is present in certain body fluids. Perspiration contains considerable amounts of it. People who perspire freely in hot weather often need to increase their salt intake by the use of salt tablets.

Since sodium chloride is the cheapest compound of sodium, it is used as a starting material in making many other sodium compounds. Some sodium compounds are most easily prepared directly from metallic sodium, however. Practically all sodium metal production utilizes sodium chloride as the raw material.

Fig. 23-5. Native crystals of sodium chloride, known as halite, recovered from the Mojave Desert in California.

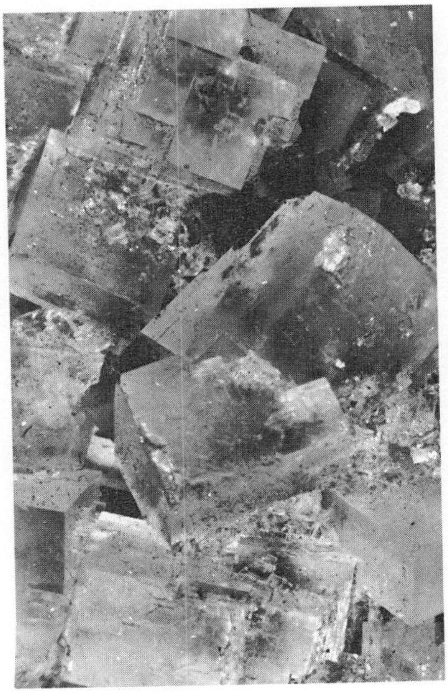

23.7 Sodium hydroxide

Most commercial sodium hydroxide is produced by electrolysis of an aqueous sodium chloride solution. This electrolysis of aqueous NaCl is somewhat different from that of fused NaCl in the Downs cell. Chlorine gas is produced at the anode, but hydrogen gas (instead of metallic sodium) is produced at the cathode. The solution, meanwhile, becomes aqueous NaOH. Evidence indicates that water molecules acquire electrons from the cathode and are reduced to H_2 gas and OH^- ions.

The cell reaction for the electrolysis of an aqueous NaCl solution is

cathode: $$2H_2O + 2e^- \rightarrow H_2(g) + 2OH^-(aq)$$

anode: $$2Cl^- \rightarrow Cl_2(g) + 2e^-$$

cell: $$2H_2O + 2Cl^- \rightarrow H_2(g) + Cl_2(g) + 2OH^-(aq)$$

As the Cl^- ion concentration diminishes, the OH^- ion concentration increases. The Na^+ ion concentration remains unchanged during electrolysis. Thus, the solution is converted from aqueous NaCl to aqueous NaOH.

Commercial NaOH is called lye or caustic soda.

Sodium hydroxide converts some types of animal and vegetable matter into soluble materials by chemical action. It is a very *caustic* substance and has destructive effects on skin, hair, and wool.

Sodium hydroxide is a white crystalline solid. It is marketed in the form of flakes, pellets, and sticks. It is very deliquescent and dissolves in the water that it removes from the air. It reacts with carbon dioxide from the air, producing sodium carbonate. Its water solution is strongly basic.

Sodium hydroxide reacts with fats, forming soap and glycerol. One of its important uses, therefore, is in making soap. It is also used in the production of rayon, cellulose film, paper pulp, and in petroleum refining. A commercial grade of sodium hydroxide is sold as lye, or caustic soda.

23.8 The Solvay process

Solvay process: *raw materials are salt, limestone, and coal.*

Almost all of the sodium carbonate and sodium hydrogen carbonate produced in the world is manufactured by the Solvay process. It was developed in 1864 by Ernest Solvay (1838–1922), a Belgian. The process is a classic example of efficiency in chemical production.

The raw materials for the Solvay process are common salt, limestone, and coal. The salt is pumped as brine from salt wells. The thermal decomposition of limestone yields the carbon dioxide and calcium oxide needed in the process.

$$\mathbf{CaCO_3(s) \rightarrow CaO(s) + CO_2(g)}$$

Coal is converted into coke, gas, coal tar, and ammonia by destructive distillation. The coke and gas are used as fuel in the plant. The ammonia is also used in the process, while the coal tar is sold as a useful by-product.

To begin the process, a cold saturated solution of sodium chloride is further saturated with ammonia and carbon dioxide. The following reactions occur:

$$\mathbf{CO_2(g) + H_2O \rightarrow H_2CO_3}$$

$$\mathbf{H_2CO_3 + NH_3(g) \rightarrow NH_4^+(aq) + HCO_3^-(aq)}$$

$$\textbf{Net:} \quad \mathbf{CO_2(g) + NH_3(g) + H_2O \rightarrow NH_4^+(aq) + HCO_3^-(aq)}$$

The HCO_3^- ions form in a solution that has a high concentration of Na^+ ions. Since sodium hydrogen carbonate is only slightly soluble in this cold solution, it precipitates.

$$\mathbf{Na^+(aq) + HCO_3^-(aq) \rightarrow NaHCO_3(s)}$$

The solution that remains contains NH_4^+ ions and Cl^- ions. The precipitated sodium hydrogen carbonate is filtered and dried. It is either sold as *baking soda* or converted into sodium carbonate by thermal decomposition.

$$2NaHCO_3(s) \rightarrow Na_2CO_3(s) + H_2O(g) + CO_2(g)$$

The dried sodium carbonate is an important industrial chemical called soda ash.

The ammonia used in the process is more valuable than the sodium carbonate or sodium hydrogen carbonate. Hence, it must be recovered and used over again if the process is to be profitable. The calcium oxide from the first reaction is slaked by adding water. Calcium hydroxide is formed in this reaction.

$$CaO(s) + H_2O(l) \rightarrow Ca(OH)_2(s)$$

The calcium hydroxide is added to the solution to release the ammonia from the ammonium ion.

$$NH_4^+(aq) + OH^-(aq) \rightarrow NH_3(g) + H_2O$$

The solution now contains mainly Ca^{++} ions and Cl^- ions. Neither of these ions is recycled into the process. As a by-product, calcium chloride has some use as an inexpensive dehydrating agent. The supply generally exceeds the demand, however.

Sodium hydrogen carbonate, as baking soda, is the main ingredient of baking powders. One important industrial use of sodium carbonate is in the production of glass.

The water solution of sodium carbonate is mildly basic because of hydrolysis of CO_3^{--} ions.

$$CO_3^{--} + H_2O \rightleftarrows HCO_3^- + OH^-$$

Fig. 23-6. A flow diagram of the Solvay process.

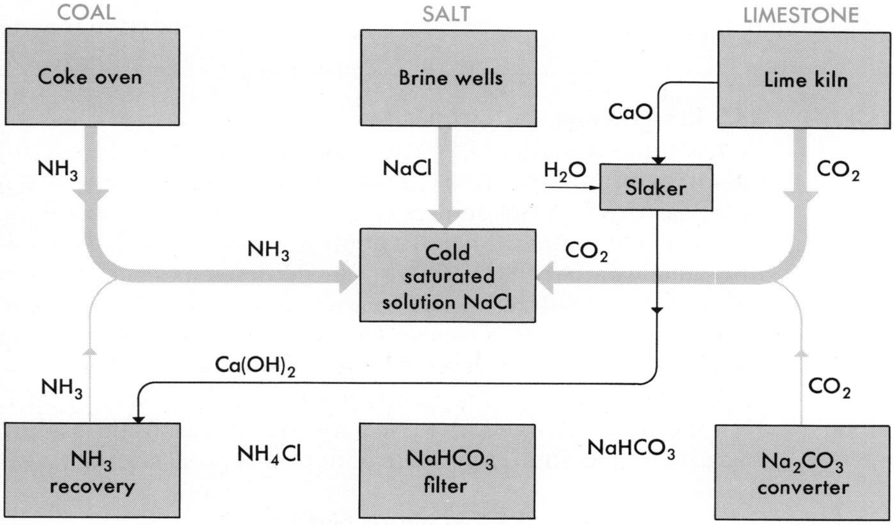

Table 23-3

REPRESENTATIVE SODIUM COMPOUNDS				
Chemical Name	Common Name	Formula	Color	Uses
sodium tetraborate, decahydrate	borax	$Na_2B_4O_7 \cdot 10H_2O$	white	as a water softener; in making glass; as a flux
sodium carbonate, decahydrate	washing soda	$Na_2CO_3 \cdot 10H_2O$	white	as a water softener; in glassmaking
sodium hydrogen carbonate	baking soda	$NaHCO_3$	white	as a leavening agent in baking
sodium cyanide	prussiate of soda	$NaCN$	white	to destroy vermin; to extract gold from ores; in silver and gold plating; in case-hardening steel
sodium hydride	(none)	NaH	white	in cleaning scale and rust from steel forgings and castings
sodium nitrate	Chile saltpeter	$NaNO_3$	white, or colorless	as a fertilizer
sodium peroxide	(none)	Na_2O_2	yellowish white	as an oxidizing and bleaching agent; as a source of oxygen
sodium phosphate, decahydrate	TSP	$Na_3PO_4 \cdot 10H_2O$	white	as a cleaning agent; as a water softener
sodium sulfate, decahydrate	Glauber's salt	$Na_2SO_4 \cdot 10H_2O$	white, or colorless	in making glass; as a cathartic in medicine
sodium thiosulfate, pentahydrate	hypo	$Na_2S_2O_3 \cdot 5H_2O$	white, or colorless	as a fixer in photography; as an antichlor
sodium sulfide	(none)	Na_2S	colorless	in the preparation of sulfur dyes; for dyeing cotton; to remove hair from hides

Potassium

23.9 Preparation and properties

Potassium is abundant in nature and is widely distributed but only in combined form. Great deposits of combined potassium occur in the form of feldspar, a potassium aluminosilicate mineral. This mineral is part of all granitic rocks. It is insoluble and weathers very slowly. Large deposits of potassium chloride, crystallized with magnesium and calcium compounds, are found in Texas and New Mexico. Some potassium compounds are taken from Searles Lake in California.

Potassium was first prepared by Sir Humphry Davy in 1807. His method involved the electrolysis of fused potassium hydroxide. The small annual production of potassium today is by the reaction

$$\mathbf{KCL + Na \rightarrow NaCl + K}$$

The reaction proceeds to the right and equilibrium is prevented by removing the potassium.

Potassium metal is soft and of low density. It has a silvery luster that quickly tarnishes bluish-gray when exposed to air. Potassium is more active than sodium. It floats on water and reacts with the water so rapidly that the hydrogen gas given off usually ignites.

Potassium imparts a fleeting violet color to a Bunsen flame. The color comes from vaporizing potassium atoms. The presence of sodium, however, masks the violet color of potassium in the flame. Potassium is detected in a mixture of sodium and potassium compounds by observing the colored flame through cobalt-blue glass. This glass filters out the yellow sodium flame color. The violet potassium flame color then shows clearly. A typical potassium flame is shown in Figure 23-8.

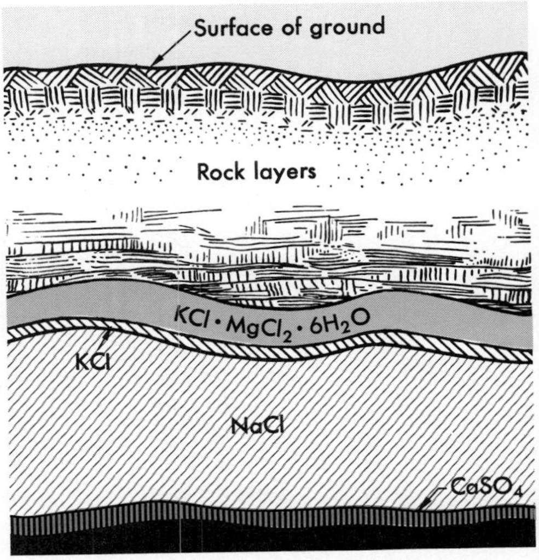

Fig. 23-7. A cross section of a salt deposit, showing how the different minerals were deposited as the sea water evaporated.

23.10 Compounds of potassium

All common potassium compounds are soluble in water. Potassium hydroxide is prepared by the electrolysis of a solution of potassium chloride. It has the typical properties of a strong alkali. Potassium nitrate is made by mixing hot, concentrated solutions of potassium chloride and sodium nitrate.

$$\mathbf{KCl + NaNO_3 \rightarrow KNO_3 + NaCl(s)}$$

The solubility curves of Figure 13-10 can be helpful in understanding how potassium nitrate is recovered in this process. Examine the solubility curves of the four possible pairs of ions in the mixed solution. Sodium chloride is the least soluble. It has almost the same solubility over the liquid temperature range of water. Potassium nitrate is much less soluble at low temperature than at high temperature.

The solution is evaporated at high temperature and sodium chloride first crystallizes. As evaporation continues, sodium chloride continues to separate and the concentration of potassium and nitrate ions increases. The crystallized sodium chloride is removed and the solution is allowed to cool. Very little sodium chloride separates as the solubility remains about the same. Potassium nitrate crystallizes very rapidly as the solution cools. It can be purified by recrystallization.

Sodium compounds are often used instead of potassium compounds because they usually are less expensive. Most glass is made with sodium carbonate, but potassium carbonate yields a more lustrous glass that is preferred for optical uses. Potassium nitrate is not hygroscopic. For this reason, it is used instead of sodium nitrate in making black gunpowder.

There is one very important use for potassium compounds for which there is no substitution. Green plants must have these compounds to grow properly. Therefore, complete chemical fertilizers always contain an appropriate amount of potassium.

Fig. 23-8. Potassium salts color the Bunsen flame violet. The potassium flame is masked by the presence of sodium salts and is purple through cobalt-blue glass.

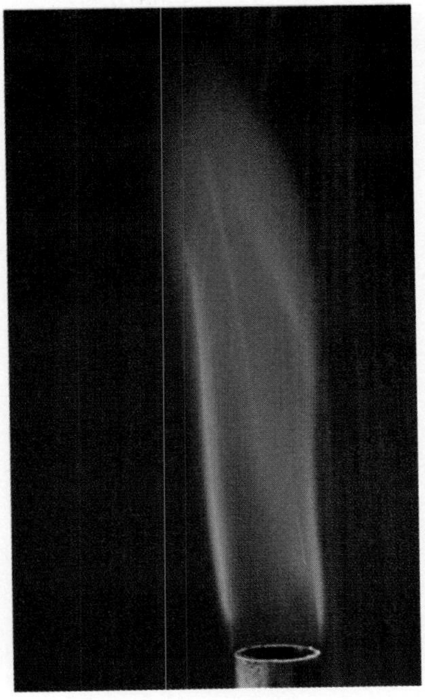

Table 23-4

REPRESENTATIVE POTASSIUM COMPOUNDS				
Chemical Name	Common Name	Formula	Color	Uses
potassium bromide	(none)	KBr	white	as a sedative; in photography
potassium carbonate	potash	K_2CO_3	white	in making glass; in making soap
potassium chlorate	(none)	$KClO_3$	white	as an oxidizing agent; in fireworks; in explosives
potassium chloride	(none)	KCl	white	as a source of potassium; as a fertilizer
potassium hydroxide	caustic potash	KOH	white	in making soft soap; as a battery electrolyte
potassium iodide	(none)	KI	white	in medicine; in iodized salt; in photography
potassium nitrate	saltpeter	KNO_3	white	in black gunpowder; in fireworks; in curing meats
potassium permanganate	(none)	$KMnO_4$	purple	as a germicide; as an oxidizing agent

Spectroscopy

23.11 Use of a spectroscope

One type of ***spectroscope*** consists of a glass prism and a *collimator tube* to focus a narrow beam of light rays upon the prism. It also has a small telescope for examining the light which passes through the prism. When white light passes through a triangular prism, a band of colors called a *continuous spectrum* appears. This effect is caused by the unequal bending of light of different wavelengths as it enters the prism and as it emerges from it.

Examination of a sodium flame by spectroscope reveals a characteristic bright-yellow line. Since this yellow line is always in the same relative place in the spectrum, it identifies sodium. Potassium produces both red and violet spectral lines. The spectrum chart, Figure 23-9, shows the characteristic color lines of several chemical elements. It also shows the continuous spectrum of white light produced by an *incandescent* (white hot) solid.

23.12 Origin of spectral lines

A platinum wire held in a Bunsen flame becomes incandescent and emits (gives off) white light. When the incandescent wire is viewed through a spectroscope, a continuous spectrum of colors is observed. The energy of the white light is distributed over a continuous range of light frequencies. This range includes the entire visible spectrum. White light is spread out forming a spectrum as it passes through the prism of the spectroscope. Here the light rays of different frequencies are bent different amounts. Light energy of the shortest wave-

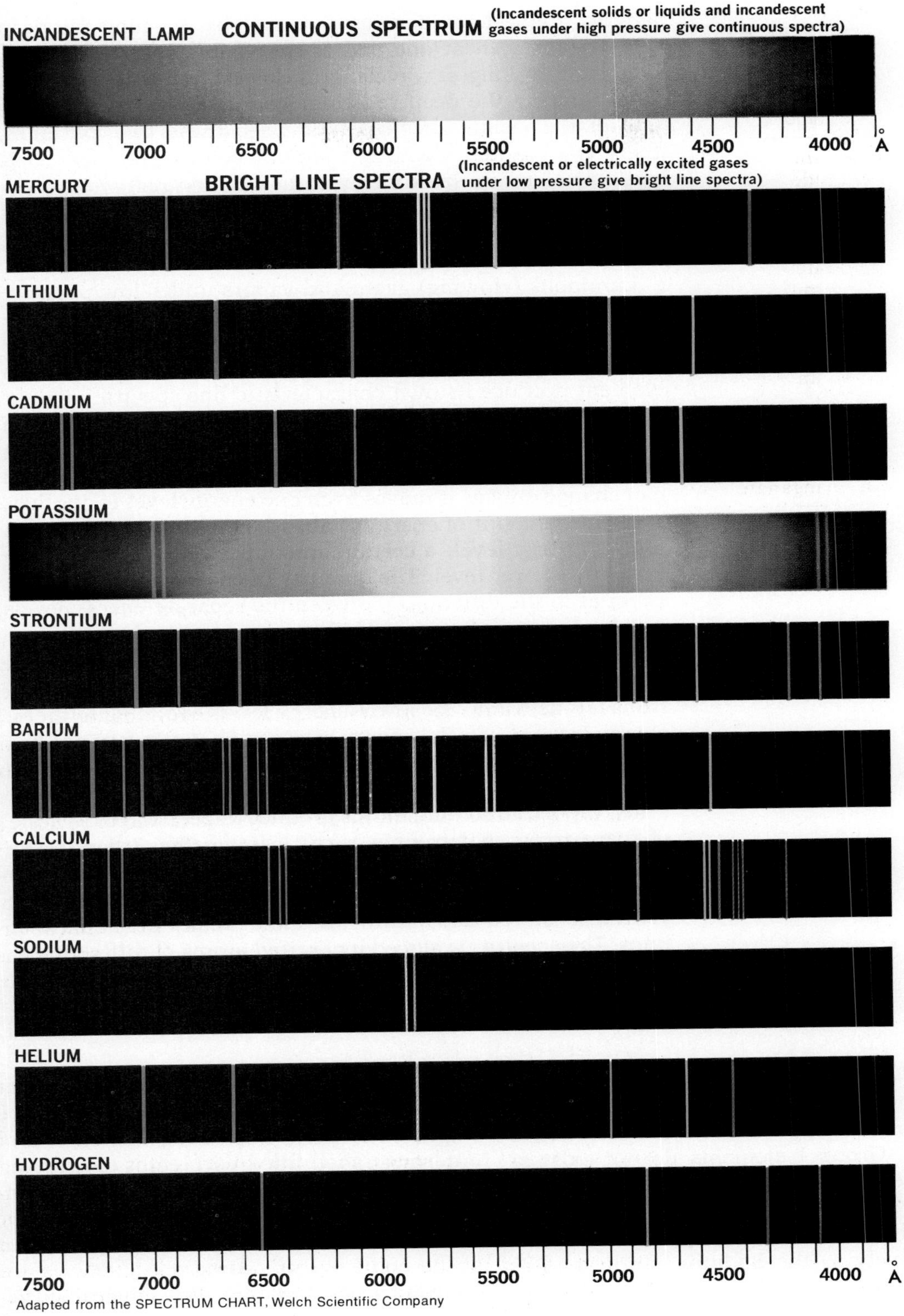

Fig. 23-9. Emission spectra.

lengths (highest frequencies) is bent most forming the deep violet color seen at one end of the visible spectrum. Light energy of the longest wavelengths (lowest frequencies) is bent least forming the deep red color characteristic of the other end of the visible spectrum. Between these two extremes, there is a gradual blending from one color to the next. It is possible to recognize six elementary colors: *red, orange, yellow, green, blue,* and *violet*. In general, incandescent solids and gases under high pressure give continuous spectra. The first spectrum in Figure 23-9 is a continuous spectrum.

Luminous (glowing) gases and vapors under low pressure give discontinuous spectra called *bright-line spectra*. These spectra consist of narrow lines of color which correspond to the light energy of certain wavelengths. The atoms of each element produce its own characteristic line spectra.

Electrons in atoms are restricted to energies of only certain values. In unexcited atoms, electrons occupy the lowest energy levels available to them. The energy of an electron can change only as it moves from one energy level to another. A certain amount of energy is absorbed with each jump to a higher energy level; a certain amount is released with each jump to a lower level. The quantity of energy in each change is equal to the difference between the separate energy levels involved.

When substances are vaporized in a flame, electrons are raised to higher energy levels by heat energy. When these electrons fall back into the lower energy levels available to them, energy is released. The energy released by any substance has wavelengths characteristic of that substance. Different wavelengths produce different spectral lines in the spectroscope. Thus, vaporized sodium atoms produce a spectrum consisting of two narrow yellow lines very close together (seen in the ordinary spectroscope as a single yellow line). Potassium atoms produce two red lines and a violet line. Lithium atoms yield intense red and yellow lines and weak blue and violet lines. The spectra produced by excited atoms of different elements are as distinct as fingerprints.

SUMMARY

The elements of Group I in the periodic table are among the most chemically active metals. Group I elements do not exist as free elements in nature—they are found only in natural compounds as monopositive ions. The elements of Group I are referred to collectively as the Sodium Family and as the alkali metals.

Group I elements are characterized by a single outer-shell electron and a next-to-outermost shell filled with eight electrons. They have relatively low ionization energies. When the outer *s* electron is removed, each has the stable electron configuration of the noble gas preceding it.

Group I elements are soft, silvery-white

metals and are good conductors of heat and electricity. Their structure is a lattice of metallic ions built around a body-centered cubic unit cell. The valence electrons form an electron gas that permeates the lattice structure.

The alkali metals form electrovalent compounds. When combined, they are in the +1 oxidation state. Because of their activity, they must be stored in oil or kerosene. They react with water releasing hydrogen and forming metallic hydroxides that are strongly basic.

Sodium is used in making antiknock gasoline, dyes, and other organic compounds. It is an important reducing agent. Sodium is a heat-transfer agent in certain nuclear reactors. It is prepared by the electrolysis of fused sodium chloride in a special cell called a Downs cell. Important compounds of sodium are found in nature in great abundance.

The Solvay process is a classic example of efficiency in chemical production. It is used to produce sodium carbonate and sodium hydrogen carbonate commercially. The raw materials used are sodium chloride, limestone, and coal.

Potassium is abundant in nature in combined forms. The metal is recovered from potassium chloride by reduction with sodium. Potassium compounds are essential in plant fertilizers. A flame test is used to identify the element. Its common compounds are soluble in water. Sodium and potassium ions are essential reactants in the electrochemical processes that move nerve impulses along a nerve axon.

QUESTIONS

Group A

1. Describe the electron configuration of the atoms and ions of the elements in Group I.
2. Compare the methods of preparing lithium, sodium, and potassium.
3. List three uses for metallic sodium.
4. Distinguish between the terms *caustic* and *corrosive*.
5. (*a*) What are the raw materials for the Solvay process? (*b*) What are the products and by-products?
6. (*a*) What is caustic soda? (*b*) washing soda? (*c*) baking soda?
7. Why do molasses and baking soda have a leavening action in cookies?
8. What are the sources of potassium compounds in the United States?
9. (*a*) How are sodium and potassium stored in the laboratory stockroom? (*b*) Why must they be stored in this fashion?
10. Write the ionic equation for the reaction of potassium and water.
11. Describe the flame tests for sodium and potassium.
12. Write three equations to show how sodium carbonate can be produced in the Solvay process.
13. Write three equations for the recovery of ammonia in the Solvay process.
14. (*a*) Describe the metallic crystal lattice of the alkali metals. (*b*) Describe the unit cell upon which this lattice is built.

Group B

15. Why are the members of the Sodium Family soft, malleable metals with low melting points and low boiling points?
16. Why is NaCl necessary in the diet of many animals and people?
17. Why is sodium chloride used as a starting material for preparing metallic sodium and other compounds of sodium?
18. (*a*) Why are sodium compounds more frequently used than potassium com-

pounds? (*b*) What are the purposes for which sodium compounds cannot be substituted for potassium compounds?

19. What by-product of the Solvay process has such limited use and yet is produced in such quantity that disposal of it is actually a problem to the manufacturers?
20. Why does table salt become sticky in damp weather, although pure sodium chloride is not deliquescent?
21. Explain why potassium has a lower density than sodium, although it consists of heavier atoms.
22. Write the equation for the net reaction that occurs when sodium hydroxide is exposed to the air.
23. In the Solvay process, why does the reaction between sodium chloride and ammonium hydrogen carbonate run to completion?
24. Why does a solution of sodium carbonate in water turn red litmus paper blue?
25. Suppose you had a tremendous quantity of acid that had to be neutralized, and that NaOH, KOH, and LiOH were all available at the same price per pound. Which of these three would you use? Why?
26. A 0.1-*M* solution of $HC_2H_3O_2$ is found to have a pH of 2.9. A solution of 0.1-*M* $NaC_2H_3O_2$ is added to the acetic acid solution and the pH rises. Explain.
27. What experimental technique is used by astronomers to determine the composition of nebulae like the one shown on page 495? What element is predominant in these clouds of cosmic dust?

PROBLEMS

Group A

1. (*a*) How many grams of sulfuric acid in water solution can be neutralized by 10.0 g of sodium hydroxide? (*b*) 10.0 g of potassium hydroxide?

2. If you have 1.00 kg of sodium nitrate and 1.00 kg of potassium chloride, how many kilograms of potassium nitrate can you make by reacting these two substances, assuming that all the potassium nitrate can be recovered?

3. If crystallized sodium carbonate, $Na_2CO_3 \cdot 10H_2O$, sells for 12.5 cents per kilogram, what is anhydrous sodium carbonate worth per kilogram?

4. How many liters of carbon dioxide can be liberated from 50.0 g of each of the following? (*a*) Na_2CO_3; (*b*) $NaHCO_3$; (*c*) K_2CO_3; (*d*) $KHCO_3$

Group B

5. How many kilograms of sodium chloride are required to produce 1.00 metric ton of anhydrous sodium carbonate?
6. How many cubic meters of carbon dioxide (at STP) are needed in Problem 5?
7. How many cubic meters of carbon dioxide gas must be produced at $15\overline{0}$°C and 745 mm pressure to supply that needed in Problem 6?
8. A load of limestone, analyzed as 92.0% $CaCO_3$, measured 2.72 metric tons. When decomposed by heat in a lime kiln, how many kilograms of calcium oxide are produced?
9. From the reaction of Problem 8, how many liters of carbon dioxide can be stored at 25°C and 855 mm pressure?
10. A solution is prepared by dissolving 1.1 g NaOH in water and diluting to $50\overline{0}$ ml. What is the pH of the solution?

chapter 24

THE METALS OF GROUP II

The fantastic world of caves and caverns is a phenomenon resulting from the formation of a common compound of a Group II metal. (See Question 28 on page 521.)

24.1 The Calcium Family

The elements of Group II of the periodic table are members of the Calcium Family. They are the metals beryllium, magnesium, calcium, strontium, barium, and radium. These elements are also called the alkaline-earth metals. Like the alkali metals, they are never found as the free element in nature. The metals must be recovered from their natural compounds. Many of their compounds are insoluble or slightly soluble and are found in the earth's crust. Their carbonates, phosphates, silicates, and sulfates are the most important deposits.

Beryllium and magnesium are commercially important light metals. In their chemical behavior, they resemble the corresponding alkali metals, lithium and sodium. Radium is important because it is radioactive. Radioactivity and other properties of radium are discussed in Chapter 30. The remaining three elements of Group II—calcium, strontium, and barium—have similar properties. They are considered to be typical members of the Calcium Family.

Each alkaline-earth element has two outer-shell electrons beyond the stable configuration of the preceding noble gas. All form doubly charged ions of the M^{++} type. Thus, ions of the alkaline-earth metals have the stable noble gas structures. Their chemistry, like that of the alkali metals of Group I, is generally uncomplicated.

Almost all of the metals that occupy the transition region of the periodic table (to the right of Group II) also have two outer-shell electrons. However these transition metals have *incomplete* inner shells, which give variety to their chemistry. The transition metals are the subject of Chapter 25.

Group II metals are harder and stronger than Group I metals.

The attraction between the metal ions and the electron gas of the metallic crystals is stronger than in the alkali metals. Therefore, these metals are denser, harder, and have higher melting and boiling points than the corresponding Sodium Family metals.

The atoms and ions of the alkaline-earth metals are smaller than those of the corresponding alkali metals because of their higher nuclear charge. For example, the magnesium ion, Mg^{++}, has the same electron configuration as the sodium ion, Na^{+}. This configuration is $1s^2 2s^2 2p^6$. However, Mg^{++} has a nuclear charge of +12, while Na^{+} has a nuclear charge of +11. The higher nuclear charge of the Mg^{++} ion attracts electrons more strongly and results in smaller K and L shells. Some properties of Group II metals are listed in Table 24-1.

Metallic character increases down the group.

We found that ionization energies of the Group I metals decreased down the group as atomic size increased. See Section 23.2. This same relationship is seen in Group II. The smaller atoms hold their outer electrons more securely than do larger atoms.

Recall that ionization energy measures the tendency of an isolated atom to hold a valence electron. The *first* ionization energy relates to the removal of an electron from the neutral atom. The *second* ionization energy is that required to remove an electron from the ion with a +1 charge (the atom that has already had 1 valence electron removed). This second ionization energy is always higher than the first because the particle now has a positive charge.

If a third electron were to be removed from a Group II atom, it would come from the stable inner electron configuration (the noble gas structure) of the +2 ion. We would expect the energy requirement to increase much more. In fact, the energies required for a third level of ionization of alkaline-earth elements are very high. They exceed the energies usually

Table 24-1

PROPERTIES OF GROUP II ELEMENTS

Element	Atomic Number	Atomic Weight	Electron Configuration	Oxidation Number	Melting Point (°C)	Boiling Point (°C)	Density (g/cm³)	Metallic Radius (Å)	Ionic Radius (Å)
beryllium	4	9.0128	2,2	+2	1278	2970	1.85	1.12	0.35
magnesium	12	24.305	2,8,2	+2	651	1107	1.74	1.60	0.66
calcium	20	40.08	2,8,8,2	+2	842	1487	1.54	1.97	0.99
strontium	38	87.62	2,8,18,8,2	+2	769	1384	2.60	2.15	1.12
barium	56	137.34	2,8,18,18,8,2	+2	725	1140	3.50	2.22	1.34
radium	88	226.0254	2,8,18,32,18,8,2	+2	700	<1737	5(?)	—	1.43

available in chemical reactions. Thus, +2 ions of these elements are the only ones we observe. The first, second, and third ionization energies of the Group II elements are listed in Table 24-2.

The alkaline-earth metals form hydrides, oxides or peroxides, and halides similar to those of the alkali metals. Almost all hydrides are ionic and contain H^- ions. An exception is BeH_2. Binary compounds of beryllium have fairly strong covalent bond character. They react with water, releasing hydrogen gas and forming basic hydroxide solutions. Calcium hydride is often used as a laboratory source of hydrogen.

The oxides of beryllium, magnesium, and calcium have very high melting points. CaO and MgO are used as heat-resistant (refractory) materials. Beryllium oxide is amphoteric and both BeO and MgO are polymeric. All alkaline-earth oxides are more covalent than alkali-metal oxides. Strontium and barium form peroxides with oxygen, probably because of the large size of their ions.

The hydroxides are formed by adding water to the oxides. Except for $Be(OH)_2$, which is amphoteric, the hydroxides dissociate in water solution and yield OH^- ions. Hydroxides above barium are only slightly soluble in water, the solubility increasing with size of the metallic ions. Solutions of these hydroxides have low concentrations of OH^- ions; they are weakly basic because of the slight solubility in water.

Table 24-2

IONIZATION ENERGIES OF GROUP II ATOMS

Element	Ionization Energy (kcal/mole) First	Second	Third
Be	215	418	3532
Mg	176	345	1839
Ca	141	273	1176
Sr	$13\underline{1}$	$25\underline{3}$	(992)?
Ba	$12\overline{0}$	$23\overline{0}$	(831)?
Ra	122	233	—

Amphoteric: *acts either as an acid or a base.*

Polymeric: *capable of repeating structural units.*

24.2 Occurrence of magnesium

Magnesium compounds are widely distributed on land and in the sea. Magnesium sulfate is found in the earth's crust in many places. Important deposits occur in the state of Washington and in British Columbia, Canada. A double chloride of potassium and magnesium is mined from the potash deposits of Texas and New Mexico. Sea water contains significant amounts of magnesium compounds. Talc and asbestos are silicates of magnesium. Their properties are related to their silicate structures.

Dolomite, $CaCO_3 \cdot MgCO_3$, is a double carbonate of magnesium and calcium that is found throughout the United States and Europe. It is an excellent building stone and is used for lining steel furnaces. Pulverized dolomite neutralizes soil acids and also supplies magnesium for plant growth.

Elemental magnesium, shown in Figure 24-2, was first prepared by Davy in 1807. This same series of experiments resulted in the isolation of sodium, calcium, and similar active metals.

Magnesium

Fig. 24-1. Fused pellets of beryllium. This metal produces alloys that are extremely elastic.

24.3 Extraction of magnesium

Most commercial magnesium is produced by electrolytic reduction of molten magnesium chloride. The Mg^{++} ions may be

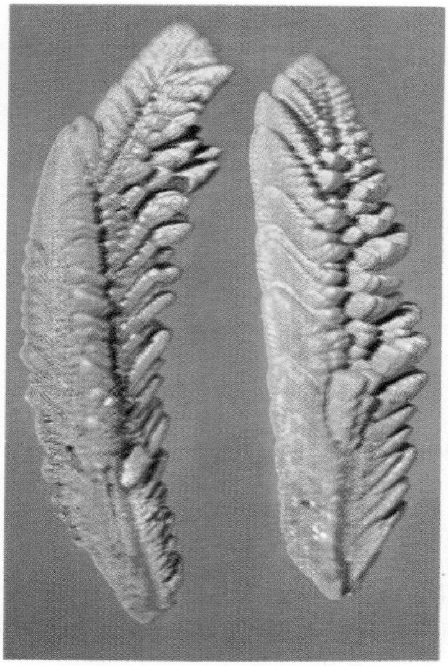

Fig. 24-2. Feathery crystals shown here are composed of magnesium, the eighth most abundant element.

Fig. 24-3. A baseball bat made of magnesium.

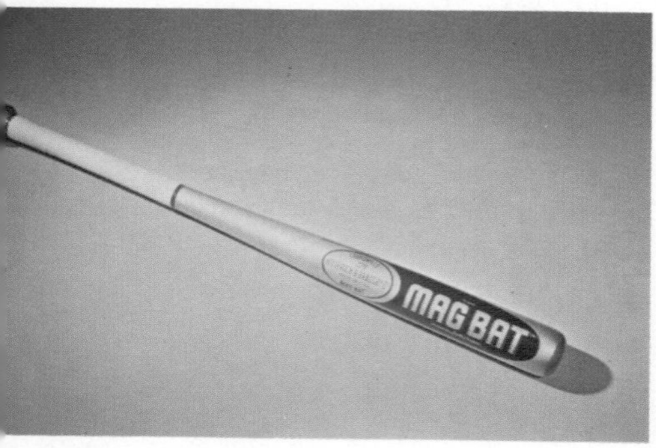

obtained from sea water, brine, or minerals. Sea water is the most economical source.

About three kilograms of magnesium are recovered from each metric ton of sea water processed. The water is first treated with lime made from oyster shells, which are cheap and readily available. This treatment causes magnesium ions to precipitate as magnesium hydroxide. The reactions are shown by the following equations.

$$\mathbf{CaO(s) + H_2O(l) \rightarrow Ca(OH)_2(s)}$$

$$\mathbf{Ca(OH)_2(s) \rightleftarrows Ca^{++}(aq) + 2OH^-(aq) \qquad K_{sp} = 1.3 \times 10^{-6}}$$

$$\mathbf{Mg^{++}(aq) + 2OH^-(aq) \rightleftarrows Mg(OH)_2(s) \qquad K_{sp} = 1.2 \times 10^{-11}}$$

The two values for K_{sp} show that $Mg(OH)_2$ is less soluble than $Ca(OH)_2$. The precipitation of $Mg(OH)_2$ lowers the concentration of OH^- ions in equilibrium with $Ca(OH)_2$ and more $Ca(OH)_2$ dissolves.

Magnesium hydroxide is separated from the water by filtration. The addition of hydrochloric acid converts the magnesium hydroxide to magnesium chloride.

$$\mathbf{Mg(OH)_2 + 2HCl \rightarrow MgCl_2 + 2H_2O}$$

Calcium chloride and sodium chloride are added to increase the conductivity and lower the melting point of the magnesium chloride. Magnesium metal is then recovered from the fused $MgCl_2$ by electrolysis.

$$\mathbf{Mg^{++} + 2Cl^- \rightarrow Mg(l) + Cl_2(g)}$$

Chlorine gas collected at the anode is used to produce the hydrochloric acid required in the process.

24.4 Properties of magnesium

Magnesium is a silver-white metal with a density of 1.74 g/cm^3. When heated, it becomes ductile and malleable. Its tensile strength (resistance to being pulled apart) is not quite as great as that of aluminum.

Dry air does not affect magnesium. In moist air, however, a coating of basic magnesium carbonate forms on its surface. Because this coating is not porous, it protects the metal underneath from tarnishing. *A metal that forms a nonporous, nonscaling coat of tarnish is said to be a* ***self-protective metal.***

When heated in air to the kindling point, magnesium burns with an intensely hot flame and gives off a dazzling white light. (See Figure 8-5.) The combustion produces magnesium oxide, MgO, and magnesium nitride, Mg_3N_2. Magnesium is one of the few metals that combines directly with nitrogen. Boiling water reacts slowly with magnesium and forms the hydroxide and hydrogen. Common acids react with magnesium.

Table 24-3

COMMON MAGNESIUM COMPOUNDS				
Chemical Name	Common Name	Formula	Appearance	Uses
magnesium carbonate	(none)	$MgCO_3$	white, usually fluffy	for lining furnaces; in making the oxide
basic magnesium carbonate	magnesia alba	$Mg_4(OH)_2(CO_3)_3 \cdot 3H_2O$	soft, white powder	in tooth cleansers; for pipe coverings
magnesium chloride	(none)	$MgCl_2$	white, crystalline solid	with asbestos for stone flooring
magnesium hydroxide	milk of magnesia	$Mg(OH)_2$	white, milky suspension	as antacid; in laxatives
magnesium oxide	magnesia	MgO	white powder	as refractory; for lining furnaces
magnesium sulfate, heptahydrate	Epsom salts	$MgSO_4 \cdot 7H_2O$	white, crystalline solid	in laxatives, cathartics; in dye industry

Once ignited, magnesium burns in steam, in carbon dioxide, and in nitrogen.

24.5 Uses of magnesium

The brilliant white light of burning magnesium makes it useful for flares and fireworks. Magnesium forms light, strong alloys with aluminum. Examples are *magnalium* and *Dowmetal.* Other alloying metals are lithium, thorium, zinc, and manganese. Magnesium alloys are used for making tools and fixtures, for the beams of chemical balances, and for automobile and airplane parts.

***Caution:** looking directly at burning magnesium can seriously damage the eyes.*

Calcium

24.6 Preparation of calcium

Calcium ranks fifth in abundance by weight among the elements in the earth's crust, atmosphere, and surface waters. It is widely distributed in many rock and mineral forms. The best known of these mineral forms are the carbonate and the sulfate.

Since calcium occurs as combined Ca^{++} ions, the metal must be recovered by reduction. Electrolytic reduction involves fused calcium chloride.

$$Ca^{++} + 2Cl^- \rightarrow Ca + Cl_2(g)$$

Chemical reduction is generally employed today for recovering calcium. Calcium oxide is heated with aluminum in a vacuum retort.

$$3CaO + 2Al \rightarrow Al_2O_3 + 3Ca(g)$$

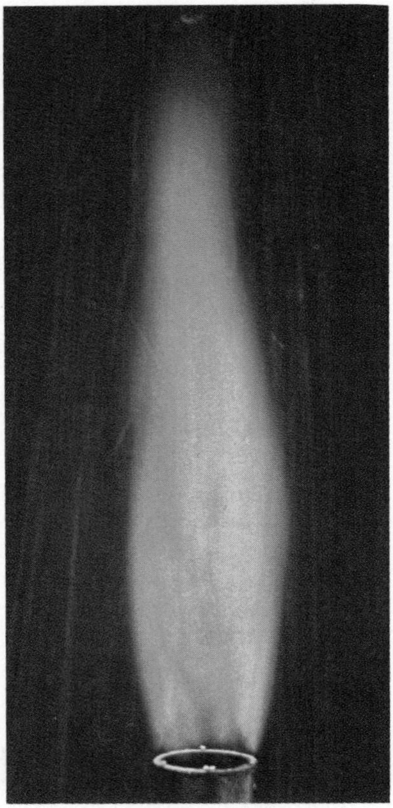

Fig. 24-4. Calcium salts impart a yellowish-red color to the Bunsen flame. The calcium flame is masked by the presence of barium salts.

The reaction proceeds because the calcium metal is distilled off as a gas at the reaction temperature.

24.7 Properties of calcium

Metallic calcium is silver-white in color, but a freshly cut piece tarnishes to bluish-gray within a few hours. Calcium is somewhat harder than lead, but it is only about one-eighth as dense. If a piece of calcium is added to water, it reacts with the water and gives off hydrogen gas slowly.

$$Ca + 2H_2O \rightarrow Ca(OH)_2 + H_2(g)$$

The calcium hydroxide produced is only slightly soluble and coats the surface of the calcium. This coating protects the metal from rapid interaction with the water.

Calcium is a good reducing agent. It burns with a bright, yellowish-red flame in oxygen. It also unites directly with chlorine. Calcium salts yield a yellowish-red color in flame tests. See Figure 24-4.

Calcium is used in small amounts to reduce uranium tetrafluoride to uranium, and thorium dioxide to thorium.

$$UF_4 + 2Ca \rightarrow 2CaF_2 + U$$

$$ThO_2 + 2Ca \rightarrow 2CaO + Th$$

Calcium is an effective deoxidizer for iron, steel, and copper. Some alloy steels contain it in small quantities. Lead-calcium alloys are used for bearings in machines. Calcium is also used to harden lead for cables and storage-battery plates.

24.8 Calcium carbonate

Calcium carbonate, $CaCO_3$, is an abundant mineral found in many different forms.

1. Limestone. This is the most common form of calcium carbonate. It was formed in past geologic ages by great pressures on layers of seashells. Limestone is found in layers, as a *sedimentary rock*. It is quarried in varying amounts in almost every state in the country. Pure calcium carbonate is white or colorless when crystalline. Most deposits, however, are gray because of impurities.

Limestone is used for making glass, iron, and steel, and as a source of carbon dioxide. It is a building stone, and large quantities are used for building roads. Powdered or pulverized limestone is used to neutralize acid soils. It is heated to produce calcium oxide, CaO. Calcium oxide, called *quicklime*, is one of the largest tonnage chemicals in industry.

A mixture of limestone and clay is converted to *cement* by heating strongly in a rotary kiln. Some limestone deposits contain clay and calcium carbonate naturally mixed in about the right proportions for making cement. Such deposits are called *natural cement*.

2. *Calcite.* The clear, crystalline form of calcium carbonate is known as calcite. Transparent, colorless specimens are called *Iceland spar.*

3. *Marble.* This rock was originally limestone. Later heat and pressure changed it into marble with a resulting increase in the size of the calcium carbonate crystals. Hence it is classed as a *metamorphic* (changed) *rock.*

4. *Shells.* The shells of such animals as snails, clams, and oysters consist largely of calcium carbonate. In some places, large masses of such shells have become cemented together and formed rock called *coquina* (koh-*kee*-nuh). It is used as a building stone in the southern states. Tiny marine animals, called *polyps,* deposit limestone as they build *coral* reefs. *Chalk,* such as that of the chalk cliffs of England, consists of the microscopic shells of small marine animals. Blackboard "chalk" is made of claylike material mixed with calcium carbonate; it should not be confused with natural chalk.

5. *Precipitated chalk.* This form of calcium carbonate is made by the reaction of sodium carbonate and calcium chloride.

$$\mathbf{Na_2CO_3 + CaCl_2 \rightarrow CaCO_3(s) + 2NaCl}$$

It is soft and finely divided. Thus, it forms a nongritty scouring powder suitable for toothpastes and tooth powders. Under the name of *whiting* it is used in paints to fill the pores in the wood. When it is ground with linseed oil, it forms putty.

Fig. 24-5. Calcite, a crystalline form of calcium carbonate.

Fig. 24-6. Marble is an excellent stone for the construction of buildings and monuments. Here it is shown being quarried in Vermont.

24.9 Hardness in water

Rainwater falling on the earth usually contains carbon dioxide in solution. As it soaks through the ground, it reaches deposits of limestone or dolomite. Some of the calcium carbonate and magnesium carbonate in these rocks react with the Co_2 solution. This reaction produces the soluble hydrogen carbonates of these metals.

$$\mathbf{CaCO_3(s) + CO_2(aq) + H_2O(l) \rightarrow Ca^{++}(aq) + 2HCO_3^-(aq)}$$

$$\mathbf{MgCO_3(s) + CO_2(aq) + H_2O(l) \rightarrow Mg^{++}(aq) + 2HCO_3^-(aq)}$$

The ground water now contains Ca^{++}, Mg^{++}, and HCO_3^- ions in solution. It is said to be *"hard"* water. This term indicates that it is "hard" to get a lather when soap is added to the water. Water that lathers readily with soap is called *"soft"* water. The terms are not precise, but they are in common use. Deposits of iron and other heavy metals in the ground may also produce hard water.

Water hardness is of two types. *Temporary hardness* results from the presence of HCO_3^- ions along with the metal ions. *Permanent hardness* results when other negative ions (usually SO_4^{--}) more stable than the HCO_3^- ion are present along with the metal ions.

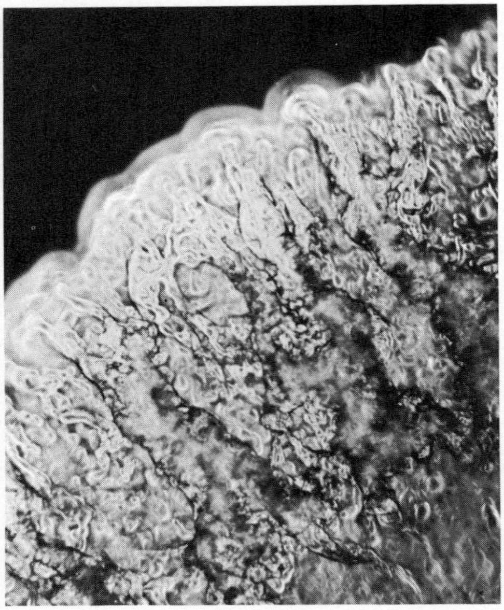

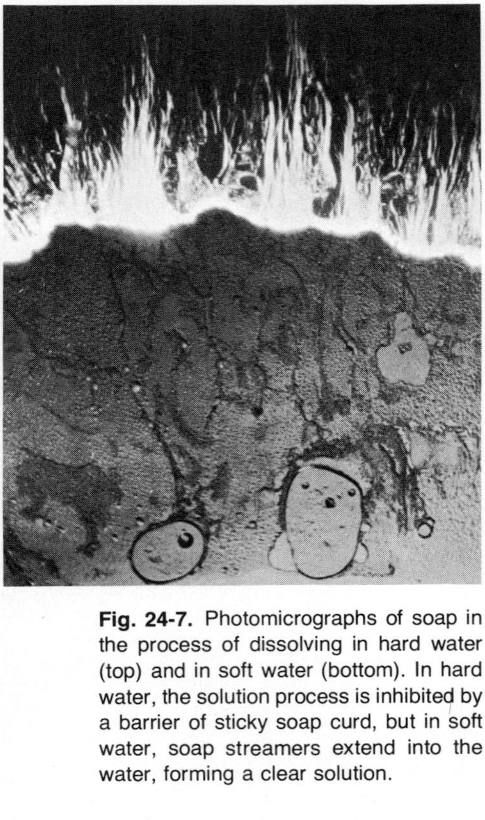

Fig. 24-7. Photomicrographs of soap in the process of dissolving in hard water (top) and in soft water (bottom). In hard water, the solution process is inhibited by a barrier of sticky soap curd, but in soft water, soap streamers extend into the water, forming a clear solution.

The main ingredient of ordinary soap is water-soluble sodium stearate, $NaC_{18}H_{35}O_2$. When soap is added to water containing Ca^{++} ions, the large $C_{18}H_{35}O_2^-$ ions react with the Ca^{++} ions. The reaction produces the insoluble stearate, $Ca(C_{18}H_{35}O_2)_2$, which deposits as a gray scum.

$$\mathbf{Ca^{++} + 2C_{18}H_{35}O_2^- \rightarrow Ca(C_{18}H_{35}O_2)_2(s)}$$

The metal ions in hard water react with the soap and form precipitates until all of these ions are removed. Until this occurs, no lasting lather is produced. Soft water does not contain these ions and therefore lathers easily when soap is added.

24.10 Softening of hard water

Hard water is a nuisance in laundering. The sticky precipitate wastes soap and collects on the fibers of the garments being laundered. In bathing, the hard water does not lather freely, and the precipitate forms a scum on the bathtub. In steam boilers, temporary hard water containing HCO_3^- ions has a still more serious fault. When this water is boiled, calcium carbonate collects as a hard scale inside the boiler and the steam pipes. It may form a thick crust, acting as a heat insulator and preventing efficient transfer of heat. Thus, for most purposes, hard water should be softened before it is used.

There are several practical methods of softening water. Generally, the nature of the hardness and the quantity of soft water required determine the best method.

1. Boiling (for temporary hardness). Hard water containing HCO_3^- ions can be softened by boiling. The metal ions precipitate as carbonates according to the following equation:

$$\mathbf{Ca^{++} + 2HCO_3^- \rightarrow CaCO_3(s) + H_2O + CO_2(g)}$$

This reaction is reversible except for the fact that boiling drives off the CO_2.

2. Precipitation. When sodium carbonate, Na_2CO_3, is added to hard water, Ca^{++} and Mg^{++} ions precipitate as insoluble carbonates. The Na^+ ions added to the water cause no difficulties with soap.

$$\mathbf{Ca^{++} + CO_3^{--} \rightarrow CaCO_3(s)}$$

$$\mathbf{Mg^{++} + CO_3^{--} \rightarrow MgCO_3(s)}$$

The addition of a basic solution such as $NH_3(aq)$ or limewater to temporary hard water supplies OH^- ions. These ions neutralize the HCO_3^- ions and precipitate the "hard" metal ions as carbonates.

$$\mathbf{Ca^{++} + HCO_3^- + OH^- \rightarrow CaCO_3(s) + H_2O}$$

$$\mathbf{Mg^{++} + HCO_3^- + OH^- \rightarrow MgCO_3(s) + H_2O}$$

Other precipitating agents such as borax and sodium phosphate are sometimes used. Both produce basic solutions by hydrolysis, and the phosphate salts of calcium and magnesium are insoluble.

3. Ion exchange. Certain natural minerals called *zeolites* have porous, three-dimensional networks of silicate-aluminate groups. These networks are negatively charged. Mobile Na^+ ions are distributed throughout the porous network. If hard water is allowed to stand in contact with sodium zeolite, Na^+ ions are exchanged for the aqueous Ca^{++} and Mg^{++} ions. The process is an *ion exchange.* The zeolite is the *ion exchanger.*

$$\mathbf{Ca^{++}(aq) + 2Na\ zeolite \rightleftarrows Ca(zeolite)_2 + 2Na^+(aq)}$$

The reaction can be reversed and the Na zeolite regenerated by adding a concentrated sodium chloride solution to the $Ca(zeolite)_2$. The solution has a high concentration of Na^+ ions. The Ca^{++} ions are replaced by Na^+ ions according to the mass-action principle.

A synthetic zeolite, known as *permutit,* reacts more rapidly than natural zeolites. Permutit is used today in many household water softeners. Sodium chloride, the cheapest source of Na^+ ions, is used to renew the exchanger in these softeners.

Household water softeners use permutit.

Chemists have developed *ion-exchange resins* far superior to the zeolites. One type of resin is called an *acid-exchange resin* or a *cation exchanger.* This type has large negatively charged organic units whose neutralizing ions in water are H_3O^+ ions. A second type of resin is the *base-exchange resin*

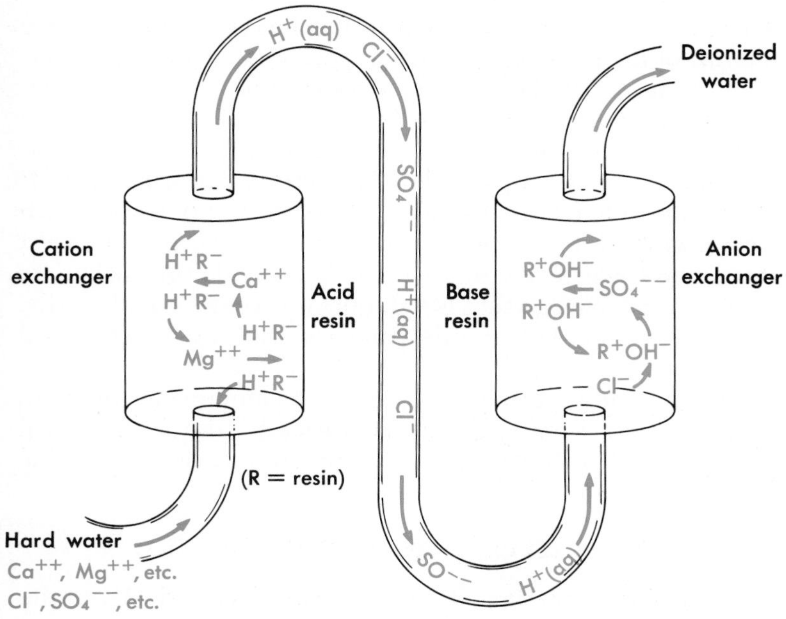

Fig. 24-8. An ion-exchange system. All positive ions in the water are exchanged for hydronium ions in the acid resin. All negative ions are exchanged for hydroxide ions in the base resin. Water leaving the system is completely deionized.

or *anion exchanger*. These resins have large positively charged organic units whose neutralizing ions in water are OH^- ions.

Used together, the two types of ion-exchange resins can remove all positive and negative ions from water. The cation exchanger removes metallic ions (cations) and replaces them with H_3O^+ ions. The water is then passed through the anion exchanger. Here, negative ions (anions) are removed and replaced by OH^- ions. The H_3O^+ and OH^- ions form water by neutralization.

Natural water or a water solution of salts treated by combinations of ion-exchange resins is made *ion-free*. (Only the small equilibrium quantities of H_3O^+ and OH^- ions remain.) This treated water is called *deionized* or *demineralized* water. Deionized water is now used in many processes that once required distilled water. Deionized water is as free of ions as the most carefully distilled water, although it may contain some dissolved carbon dioxide.

An acid-exchange resin can be renewed by running a strong acid through it. Similarly, a base-exchange resin can be renewed by using a basic solution.

Lime heated to incandescence gives off a brilliant white light—"lime-light"—that once served as a theater spotlight.

24.11 Calcium oxide

Calcium oxide is a white, ionic solid commonly called *lime* or *quicklime*. It is *refractory* since it does not melt or vaporize below the temperature of the electric arc. It unites chemically with water and forms calcium hydroxide.

$$\mathbf{CaO(s) + H_2O \rightarrow Ca(OH)_2(s) \qquad \Delta \mathit{H} = -16\ kcal}$$

During this process, called *slaking*, the mass swells and a large amount of heat is released. The reaction is strongly exothermic. Because $Ca(OH)_2$ is prepared by this *slaking* process, its common name is *slaked lime*.

A lump of quicklime exposed to air gradually absorbs water. It swells, then cracks, and finally crumbles to a powder. It first forms calcium hydroxide, and then slowly unites with carbon dioxide from the air and forms calcium carbonate. Thus, a mixture of calcium hydroxide and calcium carbonate is formed. Such a mixture is valuable for treating acidic soils. However, air slaking ruins lime for making mortar and plaster.

Calcium oxide is produced by heating calcium carbonate to a high temperature in a kiln. Historically, the decomposed $CaCO_3$ is said to have been *calcined*, the process being one of *calcination*.

$$\mathbf{CaCO_3(s) \rightarrow CaO(s) + CO_2(g)}$$

A high concentration of carbon dioxide would drive the

reaction in the reverse direction according to Le Chatelier's principle. Such an equilibrium is avoided by removing the carbon dioxide from the kiln as it forms.

24.12 Calcium hydroxide

Calcium hydroxide, or *slaked lime,* is a white solid that is sparingly soluble in water. Its water solution, called *limewater,* has basic properties. A suspension of calcium hydroxide in water is known as milk of lime. Mixed with flour paste or glue, it makes whitewash.

Calcium hydroxide is the cheapest of the hydroxides. It is used to remove hair from hides before they are tanned or made into leather. It is useful for treating soils, for freeing ammonia from ammonium compounds, and for softening temporary hard water. Large quantities are used for making mortar and plaster.

Lime mortar consists of slaked lime, sand, and water. Mortar of this type has been used for many centuries. The mortar first hardens as water evaporates. Crystals of $Ca(OH)_2$ form and cement the grains of sand together. On exposure to air, the mortar continues to get harder. The calcium hydroxide is slowly converted to the carbonate by action of atmospheric carbon dioxide.

$$\mathbf{Ca(OH)_2 + CO_2 \rightarrow CaCO_3 + H_2O}$$

This conversion process may continue for many years.

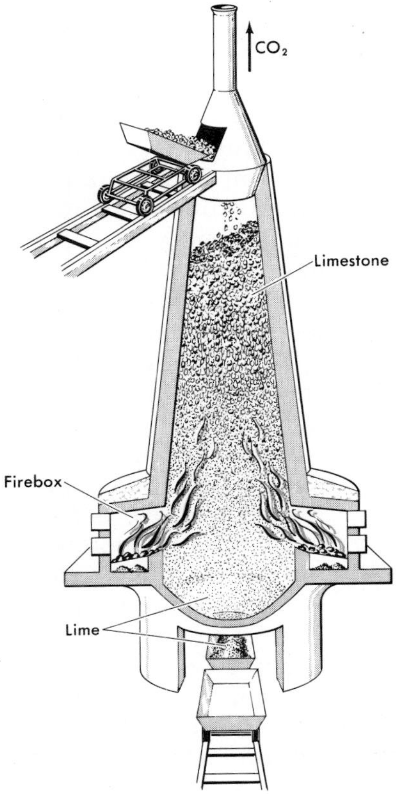

Fig. 24-9. Calcination: an ancient process used by alchemists and still used today to convert limestone to lime.

24.13 Calcium sulfate

Calcium sulfate occurs as the mineral *gypsum,* a dihydrate $CaSO_4 \cdot 2H_2O$. When gypsum is heated gently, it partially dehydrates and forms a white powder known as *plaster of paris*. The equation is

$$\mathbf{2CaSO_4 \cdot 2H_2O(s) \rightarrow (CaSO_4)_2 \cdot H_2O(s) + 3H_2O(g)}$$

gypsum **plaster of paris**

The formula for plaster of paris, $(CaSO_4)_2 \cdot H_2O$, is equivalent to $CaSO_4 \cdot \frac{1}{2}H_2O$ as it is sometimes written.

When plaster of paris is mixed with water, it hydrates back to the gypsum structure. The reaction is the reverse of the equation given above.

$$\mathbf{(CaSO_4)_2 \cdot H_2O + 3H_2O \rightarrow 2CaSO_4 \cdot 2H_2O}$$

A thin paste (or slurry) of plaster of paris and water sets quickly and expands slightly. It forms a solid mass of interlacing crystals of gypsum. Because of the slight expansion, it gives remarkably faithful reproductions when cast in molds. The plaster of paris slurries are suited for making wallboard and rocklath, surgical casts, pottery molds, statuary, and numerous other uses.

SUMMARY

The elements of Group II are the metals beryllium, magnesium, calcium, strontium, barium, and radium. They are known as the alkaline-earth metals and as the Calcium Family of elements. They are not found as the free elements in nature. The metals of Group II are recovered from their natural compounds.

The alkaline-earth metals are characterized by two outer shell electrons and next-to-outermost shells with a stable octet of electrons. Their ions have the electron configurations of their preceding noble gases. The metals are denser, harder, and have higher melting points than the corresponding members of the alkali metals of Group I. Bonding shows some covalency. The chemistry of the elements of Group II, like the Group I elements, is uncomplicated.

Magnesium is recovered mainly by electrolysis of its chloride. Sea water is the most economical source of magnesium. It is a light, self-protective metal. Magnesium is used structurally when alloyed with other metals. Soluble magnesium compounds contribute to the "hardness" of water.

Calcium is a low density and relatively hard metal. It is a good reducing agent. It reacts with water slowly and burns in oxygen with a yellow-red flame. Calcium is widely distributed in the earth's crust as insoluble compounds, mainly as carbonates and sulfates. It is recovered by electrolytic reduction from its chloride and by chemical reduction with aluminum.

Ground water usually contains Ca^{++} ions contributed by soluble and slightly soluble calcium compounds. Water containing minerals in solution, mainly the hydrogen carbonates and sulfates of calcium and magnesium, is called hard water. The presence of these substances interferes with the use of water in laundering and in steam boilers and steam pipes. Water may be softened by the removal of the hardening agents. Hard water is softened by boiling, precipitation, and ion-exchange methods.

The oxide, hydroxide, carbonate, and sulfate of calcium are important industrial substances. Calcium oxide is reduced by heating calcium carbonate. Calcium hydroxide is formed by reacting calcium oxide and water. Calcium sulfate is mined mainly as the mineral gypsum.

QUESTIONS

Group A

1. (*a*) Write the equation for the production of quick lime from limestone. (*b*) How is an equilibrium avoided in this process?
2. (*a*) What is dolomite? (*b*) For what purposes is it used?
3. Since magnesium is an active metal, why do objects made from it not corrode rapidly as iron does?
4. Compare the preparation of elementary calcium with that of elementary sodium.
5. What are the important uses for metallic calcium?
6. In what forms is calcium carbonate found in nature?
7. (*a*) What does the term *hard water* mean? (*b*) What does the term *soft water* mean? (*c*) What is the difference between temporary and permanent hardness of water?
8. What principle is employed to regenerate a zeolite water softener?
9. Distinguish (*a*) limestone; (*b*) quicklime; (*c*) slaked lime; (*d*) lime; (*e*) hydrated lime.

10. For what gas is limewater used as a test solution?
11. How could you demonstrate that a piece of coral is a carbonate?
12. Write an empirical equation to show the action of water containing dissolved carbon dioxide on limestone.
13. How is cement manufactured from clay and limestone?

Group B

14. Write three balanced equations to show the steps in the preparation of magnesium from sea water.
15. Why must the reduction of magnesium oxide by ferrosilicon be carried out in a vacuum?
16. How do beryllium compounds differ from those of the other Group II elements?
17. Why are the members of the Calcium Family denser and harder then the corresponding members of the Sodium Family?
18. (*a*) Write the equation for the slaking of lime. (*b*) Give a reason for the reaction going to completion.
19. Give two reasons why the reaction of calcium with water is not as vigorous as that of potassium and water.
20. (*a*) What metallic ions cause water to be hard? (*b*) What negative ion causes temporary hardness? (*c*) What negative ion causes permanent hardness?
21. What type of chemical reaction occurs between soap and hard water?
22. Write an empirical equation to show the softening action of sodium carbonate on hard water containing (*a*) calcium sulfate; (*b*) magnesium hydrogen carbonate.
23. What are some uses for calcium chloride produced in large quantities as a by-product of the manufacture of Solvay soda?
24. (*a*) How is plaster of paris made? (*b*) Why does it harden?
25. (*a*) What impurity may still remain in water that has been passed through both an acid exchange resin and a base exchange resin? (*b*) For what kind of solutions would such water be unsuited?
26. How can you account for the fact that temporary hard water, containing Ca^{++} ions, is softened by the addition of limewater, a solution containing Ca^{++} ions and OH^- ions?
27. Iron has two outer-shell electrons. Why is its chemistry more varied than that of the alkaline-earth metals?
28. As a research assignment, look up an encyclopedia account of caves and caverns. Briefly report on the chemistry of the limestone formations such as the ones shown in the photograph on page 509 taken in the Carlsbad caverns of New Mexico.

PROBLEMS

Group A

1. How many kilograms of calcium oxide can be produced from 1.000 metric ton of limestone that contains 12.5% of impurities?
2. How much mass will 86.0 kg of gypsum lose when it is converted into plaster of paris?
3. Calculate the percentage of beryllium in beryl, $Be_3Al_2Si_6O_{18}$.
4. What quantity of magnesium can be prepared from a metric ton of magnesium oxide, MgO?
5. A cubic kilometer of sea water contains in solution enough minerals to form about 4.0×10^6 kg of magnesium chloride. How much metallic magnesium

could be obtained from this volume of sea water?

Group B

6. If dolomite is 95.0% a double carbonate of calcium and magnesium, together with 5.0% of impurities such as iron and silica, what is the percentage of magnesium in the sample? (Compute to 3 significant figures.)
7. How many kilograms of carbon dioxide can be obtained from a metric ton of oyster shells that are 81.0% calcium carbonate?
8. How many liters will the carbon dioxide produced in Problem 7 occupy at STP?
9. If the carbon dioxide of Problem 8 is measured at $72\bar{0}$ mm pressure and $2\bar{0}$°C, what volume does it occupy?
10. The thermal decomposition of a charge of limestone produced $50\bar{0}$ m^3 of carbon dioxide when stored at 28°C and $95\bar{0}$ mm pressure. How many moles of the gas was this?

chapter 25

THE TRANSITION METALS

The copper ware displayed here illustrates a use of copper far more ancient than its present principal use as a conductor of electricity. (See Question 11 on page 545.)

25.1 General properties

Periodic table: periods are horizontal rows; groups are vertical columns.

The periodic table as arranged in Chapter 5 has short periods (or series) through the third row of elements. The fourth and succeeding rows are long periods. Beginning with Period 4, ten subgroups of elements intervene between Group II and Group III. These elements occupy the *transition region* of the periodic table. They are called the *transition elements* because, with increasing atomic number, they involve an electron population buildup in the next-to-outermost shell. This inner building of electronic structure may be looked upon as an interruption, between Group II and Group III, of the regular buildup of outer-shell electrons from Group I to Group VIII across a period. See Figure 25-1.

We have observed that properties of the elements remain similar going down each main group. Properties change steadily from metallic to nonmetallic going horizontally across a short period from Group I to Group VII. In the transition region, horizontal similarities may be as great, or in some cases even greater, than similarities going down a subgroup.

All transition elements are metals. The metallic character is related to the presence of no more than one or two electrons in the outermost shells of their atoms. These metals are generally harder and more brittle than the Group I and Group II metals. Their melting points are higher. Mercury (at. no. 80) is a familiar exception. It is the only metal that is liquid at room temperature. (In very hot weather, mercury may lose this distinction since gallium (at. no. 31) and cesium (at. no.

24.305 Mg 12 (2, 8, 2)	TRANSITION ELEMENTS										26.9815 Al 13
40.08 Ca 20 (2, 8, 8, 2)	44.9559 Sc 21 (2, 8, 9, 2)	47.90 Ti 22 (2, 8, 10, 2)	50.9414 V 23 (2, 8, 11, 2)	51.996 Cr 24 (2, 8, 13, 1)	54.9380 Mn 25 (2, 8, 13, 2)	55.847 Fe 26 (2, 8, 14, 2)	58.9332 Co 27 (2, 8, 15, 2)	58.71 Ni 28 (2, 8, 16, 2)	63.546 Cu 29 (2, 8, 18, 1)	65.37 Zn 30 (2, 8, 18, 2)	69.72 Ga 31
87.62 Sr 38 (2, 8, 18, 8, 2)	88.9059 Y 39 (2, 8, 18, 9, 2)	91.22 Zr 40 (2, 8, 18, 10, 2)	92.9064 Nb 41 (2, 8, 18, 12, 1)	95.94 Mo 42 (2, 8, 18, 13, 1)	98.9062 Tc 43 (2, 8, 18, 13, 2)	101.07 Ru 44 (2, 8, 18, 15, 1)	102.9055 Rh 45 (2, 8, 18, 16, 1)	106.4 Pd 46 (2, 8, 18, 18, 0)	107.868 Ag 47 (2, 8, 18, 18, 1)	112.40 Cd 48 (2, 8, 18, 18, 2)	114.82 In 49
137.34 Ba 56 (2, 8, 18, 18, 8, 2)	Lanthanide Series; 174.97 Lu 71 (2, 8, 18, 32, 9, 2)	178.49 Hf 72 (2, 8, 18, 32, 10, 2)	180.9479 Ta 73 (2, 8, 18, 32, 11, 2)	183.85 W 74 (2, 8, 18, 32, 12, 2)	186.2 Re 75 (2, 8, 18, 32, 13, 2)	190.2 Os 76 (2, 8, 18, 32, 14, 2)	192.22 Ir 77 (2, 8, 18, 32, 15, 2)	195.09 Pt 78 (2, 8, 18, 32, 17, 1)	196.9665 Au 79 (2, 8, 18, 32, 18, 1)	200.59 Hg 80 (2, 8, 18, 32, 18, 2)	204.37 Tl 81
226.0254 Ra 88 (2, 8, 18, 32, 18, 8, 2)	Actinide Series; [257] Lr 103 (2, 8, 18, 32, 32, 9, 2)	[261] 104 (2, 8, 18, 32, 32, 10, 2)	[260] 105 (2, 8, 18, 32, 32, 11, 2)	[263] 106 (2, 8, 18, 32, 32, 12, 2)	[261] 107 (2, 8, 18, 32, 32, 13, 2)						

Fig. 25-1. Transition metals are characterized by the buildup of the *d* sublevel in the next-to-outermost shell.

55) have melting points of 29.8°C and 28.7°C, respectively.) The transition metals are good conductors of heat and electricity. Such conduction is characteristic of a metallic crystal lattice permeated by an electron gas.

The chemical properties of transition elements are varied. Electrons of the next-to-outermost *d* sublevel as well as those of the outer shell may become involved in the formation of some compounds. Most transition metals exhibit variable oxidation states in forming compounds, and most of their compounds have color. They have a pronounced tendency to form complex ions. Many of their compounds are attracted into a magnetic field (a property called paramagnetism).

25.2 Transition subgroups

The electron population of each transition element is shown in Figure 25-1. Compare the electron populations of the Group II metals with the corresponding metals of the first transition subgroup, the scandium (Sc) subgroup. What differences do you observe? Now compare the electron populations across the first-row transition metals. Note the generally regular pattern of change in electron population with increasing atomic number. Notice also whether irregularities appear in the pattern.

The stepwise buildup of the electron population across the first-row transition metals results in the 3*d* sublevel being filled with 10 electrons. Following this 3*d* filling, the regular buildup of 4*p* electrons occurs in Group III through Group VIII.

There are minor irregularities in the 3*d* electron buildup at Cr (at. no. 24) and at Cu (at. no. 29). The electron configuration for chromium is -----$3d^5 4s^1$ instead of -----$3d^4 4s^2$ as we might have predicted. That for copper is -----$3d^{10} 4s^1$ instead of the -----$3d^9 4s^2$ we might have expected. These apparent

Special stability of half-filled and filled sublevels: see Section 4.7.

irregularities are attributed to the extra stability associated with half-filled and completely filled sublevels.

In the fifth period, there is a similar filling of the 4*d* sublevel following strontium (-----$4s^2 4p^6 5s^2$) before the buildup of the 5*p* sublevel occurs to complete the period. In the sixth period, the filling of the 5*d* sublevel following barium -----$4s^2 4p^6 5s^2 5p^6 6s^2$) is interrupted by the buildup of the 4*f* sublevel. These two expansions greatly complicate this period. There are seven 4*f* orbitals that can accommodate 14 electrons. In the *Lanthanide Series* of elements, the 4*f* electron population increases with atomic number.

In the seventh period, the 6*d* sublevel filling is similarly interrupted by the buildup of the 5*f* sublevel characteristic of the *Actinide Series* of elements. The placement of lawrencium (at. no. 103) in the scandium subgroup marks the resumption of the 6*d* buildup. Elements 104, 105, 106, and 107 in the titanium, vanadium, chromium, and manganese subgroups, respectively, indicate a continuation of this 6*d* buildup of electrons.

The transition elements occupy the long periods in the periodic table. The choice of the first and last elements in the series depends somewhat on the definition used. Based on *d* and *s* electron populations, the transition elements are considered to consist of the ten subgroups between Group II and Group III. The first-row transition elements are the most important and they are the most abundant. Their electron configurations are shown in Table 25-1.

25.3 Oxidation states

Variable oxidation states are common among the transition metals. Some form different compounds in which they exhibit several oxidation states. The energies of the outermost *d* and *s* electrons do not differ greatly. The energies to remove these electrons are relatively low.

Table 25-1

ELECTRONIC CONFIGURATIONS OF FIRST-ROW TRANSITION ELEMENTS

Name	Symbol	Atomic Number	Number of Electrons in Sublevels						
			1*s*	2*s*	2*p*	3*s*	3*p*	3*d*	4*s*
scandium	Sc	21	2	2	6	2	6	1	2
titanium	Ti	22	2	2	6	2	6	2	2
vanadium	V	23	2	2	6	2	6	3	2
chromium	Cr	24	2	2	6	2	6	5	1
manganese	Mn	25	2	2	6	2	6	5	2
iron	Fe	26	2	2	6	2	6	6	2
cobalt	Co	27	2	2	6	2	6	7	2
nickel	Ni	28	2	2	6	2	6	8	2
copper	Cu	29	2	2	6	2	6	10	1
zinc	Zn	30	2	2	6	2	6	10	2

The d sublevel has five available orbitals that can hold ten electrons when all are filled. The s sublevel has one orbital and it can hold two electrons. Electrons occupy the d orbitals singly as long as unoccupied orbitals of similar energy exist. The s electrons and one or more d electrons can be used in chemical bonding.

In the first-row transition metals, several $4s$ and $3d$ electrons may be transferred to or shared with other substances. Thus, several oxidation states become possible. Remember that the maximum oxidation state is limited by the total number of $4s$ and $3d$ electrons present.

Table 25-2 gives the common oxidation states and $3d$ and $4s$ electron populations of these metals. This table uses orbital notations introduced in Chapter 4. In these notations ○ represents an unoccupied orbital. The symbol ⦸ represents an orbital occupied by one electron, and ⊗ represents an orbital with an electron pair.

Observe that the maximum oxidation state increases to +7 for manganese and then decreases abruptly beyond manganese. The difficulty of forming the higher oxidation states increases toward the end of the row. This increase in difficulty is caused by the general increase in ionization energy with atomic number. The higher oxidation states generally involve covalent bonding.

Manganese atoms lose two $4s$ electrons and become Mn^{++} ions. Higher oxidation states involve one or more of the $3d$ electrons. In the permanganate ion, MnO_4^-, manganese is in the +7 oxidation state. It is covalently bonded with the oxygen atoms.

When the electron configuration includes both $3d$ and $4s$ valence electrons, the $3d$ electrons are lower in energy than the $4s$ electrons. Thus, the first electron removed in an ionizing reaction is the one most loosely held, a $4s$ electron. This

Table 25-2

OXIDATION STATES OF FIRST-ROW TRANSITION ELEMENTS

Element	Electron Populations			Common Oxidation States
	$1s^2 2s^2 2p^6 3s^2 3p^6$	$3d$	$4s$	
scandium	Each transition	⦸○○○○	⊗	+3
titanium	element has all	⦸⦸○○○	⊗	+2 +3 +4
vanadium	of these	⦸⦸⦸○○	⊗	+2 +3 +4 +5
chromium	sublevels filled	⦸⦸⦸⦸⦸	⦸	+2 +3 +6
manganese		⦸⦸⦸⦸⦸	⊗	+2 +3 +4 +6 +7
iron		⊗⦸⦸⦸⦸	⊗	+2 +3
cobalt		⊗⊗⦸⦸⦸	⊗	+2 +3
nickel		⊗⊗⊗⦸⦸	⊗	+2 +3
copper		⊗⊗⊗⊗⊗	⦸	+1 +2
zinc		⊗⊗⊗⊗⊗	⊗	+2

fact is illustrated by the step-by-step ionization of titanium. The ground-state configurations of the valence electrons are as follows:

Ti	$3d^2 4s^2$
Ti^+	$3d^2 4s^1$
Ti^{++}	$3d^2 4s^0$
Ti^{+3}	$3d^1$
Ti^{+4}	$3d^0$

25.4 Color

A striking property of many compounds of transition metals is their color. Not all compounds formed with transition metals are colored. On the other hand, most colored inorganic compounds involve elements of the transition region of the periodic table. See Figure 25-2. The color of the compounds and their solutions may vary depending on what other ions or polyatomic groups are associated with the transition element. The colors of compounds of several first-row transition metals are listed in Table 25-3. In general, these colored compounds are thought to have some electrons that are easily excited by selectively absorbing part of the energy of white light.

The continuous spectrum of Figure 23-9 shows that white light is composed of red, orange, yellow, green, blue, and violet colors of light. If light energy of a discrete band of wavelengths corresponding to a color region is absorbed by a substance, the remaining light reflected or transmitted is no longer white. It is the *complement* of the color removed. The color of the substance that we recognize is the complement of the color of light absorbed. *The energies of the wavelengths of white light that are absorbed giving these compounds color are the energies required to raise* **d** *electrons to higher energy states.*

Mixing colored lights is an additive process. Mixing colored pigments is a subtractive process. Results are not the same.

Copper(II) sulfate pentahydrate crystals are blue when viewed in white light. Their aqueous solutions are also blue.

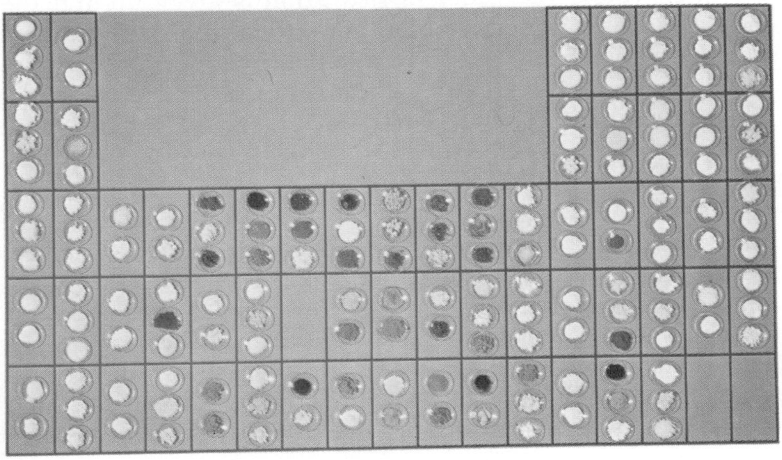

Fig. 25-2. Most compounds of transition metals are colored. The color depends on the metal, its oxidation state, and the anion with which it is combined.

Table 25-3

COLORS OF COMPOUNDS OF TRANSITION METALS

Compound	Formula	Color
titanium(III) chloride	$TiCl_3$	violet
titanium(III) sulfate	$Ti_2(SO_4)_3$	green
titanium(IV) chloride	$TiCl_4$	yellow
vanadium(II) chloride	VCl_2	green
vanadium(II) sulfate, heptahydrate	$VSO_4 \cdot 7H_2O$	violet
vanadium(III) chloride	VCl_3	pink
vanadium(IV) chloride	VCl_4	violet
chromium(II) acetate	$Cr(C_2H_3O_2)_2$	red
chromium(II) sulfate, heptahydrate	$CrSO_4 \cdot 7H_2O$	blue
chromium(III) chloride	$CrCl_3$	violet
manganese(II) chloride	$MnCl_2$	pink
manganese(III) sulfate	$Mn_2(SO_4)_3$	green
manganese(IV) oxide	MnO_2	black
iron(II) chloride, dihydrate	$FeCl_2 \cdot 2H_2O$	green
iron(II) sulfate, heptahydrate	$FeSO_4 \cdot 7H_2O$	blue-green
iron(III) chloride, hexahydrate	$FeCl_3 \cdot 6H_2O$	brown-yellow
iron(III) sulfate,	$Fe_2(SO_4)_3$	yellow
iron(III) thiosulfate	$Fe(CNS)_3$	red
cobalt(II) chloride, hexahydrate	$CoCl_2 \cdot 6H_2O$	red
cobalt(II) nitrate, hexahydrate	$Co(NO_3)_2 \cdot 6H_2O$	red
cobalt(II) sulfate, heptahydrate	$CoSO_4 \cdot 7H_2O$	pink
cobalt(III) sulfate	$Co_2(SO_4)_3$	blue-green
nickel(II) hydroxide	$Ni(OH)_2$	green
nickel(II) nitrate, hexahydrate	$Ni(NO_3)_2 \cdot 6H_2O$	green
nickel(II) sulfate	$NiSO_4$	yellow
copper(I) carbonate	Cu_2CO_3	yellow
copper(I) oxide	Cu_2O	red
copper(II) oxide	CuO	black
copper(II) nitrate, hexahydrate	$Cu(NO_3)_2 \cdot 6H_2O$	blue
copper(II) sulfate, pentahydrate	$CuSO_4 \cdot 5H_2O$	blue

They are blue because energy of wavelengths corresponding to *yellow light* is absorbed. The light reflected (or transmitted) is *blue light,* the complement of yellow light. When these crystals are heated, the water of hydration is given up and the anhydrous salt is neither blue nor crystalline. It is a white powder. If water is added to the anhydrous powder, it turns blue. We know that many sulfate compounds are colorless. Thus, it is the *hydrated* copper(II) ion, $Cu(H_2O)_4^{++}$, that is blue.

25.5 The formation of complex ions

The NO_3^- ion, SO_4^{--} ion, and the NH_4^+ ion are examples of *polyatomic* ions. They are charged particles made up of more than a single atom. These familiar ions are covalent structures. Their net ionic charge is the algebraic sum of the oxidation numbers of all the atoms present. Because of their small size and their stability, they behave just like single-atom ions. They go through many chemical reactions unchanged. Such ions, even though polyatomic, are not called *complex ions.*

The name *complex ion* is ordinarily restricted to an ionic species composed of a central metal ion combined with a specific number of polar molecules or ions. The charge on the complex ion is the sum of the charge on the central ion and that of all the attached units. Complex ions vary in stability, but none is as stable as the common polyatomic ions mentioned above.

The most common complex ions are formed by ions of the transition metals with chemical species such as chloride ions (Cl), ammonia molecules (NH_3), water molecules (H_2O), and cyanide ions (CN^-). The transition cation is always the central ion upon which the complex is formed. The number of units covalently bonded to, or *coordinated* with, the central ion is its *coordination number* for that complex ion. The Fe^{++} ion in the $[Fe(CN)_6]^{----}$ complex shown in Figure 25-3 has a coordination number of 6.

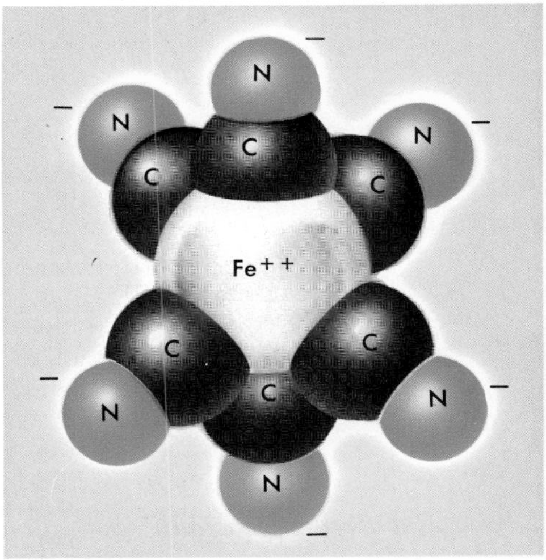

Fig. 25-3. A possible space model of a complex ion, the hexacyanoferrate(II) ion $Fe(CN)_6^{----}$. It is sometimes called the ferrocyanide ion.

The hydrated Cu^{++} ion, $Cu(H_2O)_4^{++}$, discussed in Section 25.4, is a complex ion. The Cu^{++} ion is coordinated with 4 molecules of water of hydration. It is the ionic species that crystallizes from an aqueous sulfate solution as the compound $CuSO_4 \cdot 5H_2O$.

In the $CuSO_4 \cdot 5H_2O$ crystal four water molecules are close to the copper(II) ion, the fifth is more distant.

When an excess of concentrated ammonia-water solution is added to an aqueous solution of Cu^{++} ions (a $CuSO_4$ solution, for example), the light blue color of the solution changes to a deep blue color. The soluble $[Cu(NH_3)_4]^{++}$ complex has been formed.

$$\underset{\text{light blue}}{[Cu(H_2O)_4]^{++}} + 4NH_3(aq) \rightarrow \underset{\text{deep blue}}{[Cu(NH_3)_4]^{++}} + 4H_2O$$

Zinc and cadmium form similar complex ions with ammonia. Table 25-4 gives some typical complex ions formed by transition metals.

Table 25-4

SOME COMMON COMPLEX IONS

Coordinating Atom	Coordinating Group	Complex Ions	Color
N	$H:\ddot{N}:H$ with H (ammonia, NH_3)	$Ag(NH_3)_2^+$ $Ni(NH_3)_4^{++}$ $Co(NH_3)_6^{+++}$	— blue blue
C	$:C:::N:^-$	$Fe(CN)_6^{----}$ $Fe(CN)_6^{---}$	yellow red
S	$:\ddot{S}:\ddot{S}:\ddot{O}:^{--}$ with $:\ddot{O}:$ above and below (thiosulfate)	$Ag(S_2O_3)_2^{---}$	—
N	$:\ddot{N}::C::\ddot{S}:^-$	$FeNCS^{++}$	red

If the ammonia-water solution is added to a solution of silver nitrate, the complex $[Ag(NH_3)_2]^+$ ion is formed.

$$Ag^+ + 2NH_3 \rightarrow [Ag(NH_3)_2]^+$$

$$Ag^+ + 2 \begin{matrix} H \\ \cdot\cdot \\ :N:H \\ \cdot\cdot \\ H \end{matrix} \rightarrow \left[\begin{matrix} H & & H \\ \cdot\cdot & & \cdot\cdot \\ H:N:Ag:N:H \\ \cdot\cdot & & \cdot\cdot \\ H & & H \end{matrix} \right]^+$$

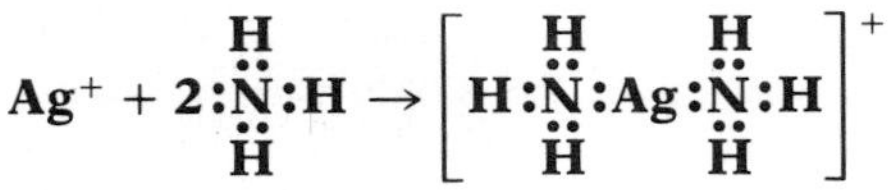

Because complex ions are unstable to some extent, the reaction is reversible. The more stable the complex ion, the more quickly equilibrium is established between the reactions involving the formation and dissociation of the complex ions. At equilibrium, the equation is

$$[Ag(NH_3)_2]^+ \rightleftarrows Ag^+ + 2NH_3$$

Equilibrium constant: see Section 21.3. The equilibrium constant has the usual form.

$$K = \frac{[Ag^+][NH_3]^2}{[Ag(NH_3)_2{}^+]} = 6 \times 10^{-8}$$

In the case of complex-ion equilibria, the equilibrium constant is called an *instability* constant. The *larger* the value of K, the more unstable is the complex ion.

When metallic ions in solution form complexes, they are, in effect, removed from the solution as simple ions. Thus, the formation of complex ions increases the solubility of metallic ions. The solubility of a precipitate may also be increased if cations of the substance form complex ions. For example, the formation of chloride complexes may *increase* solubility *Common ion effect: see Section 21.6.* where, by common ion effect, a *decrease* would be expected.

Let us consider the equilibrium of sparingly soluble AgCl.

$$AgCl(s) \rightleftarrows Ag^+(aq) + Cl^-(aq)$$

A small addition of Cl^- ions *does* shift the equilibrium to the left and lower the solubility as expected. However, if a large concentration of Cl^- ions is added, *the solid AgCl dissolves.* This apparent contradiction is explained by the formation of $[AgCl_2]^-$ complex ions.

The stability of complex ions is indicated by the small values of the equilibrium constants, K. See Table 25-5. The smaller the value of K, the more stable is the complex ion and the more effectively it holds the central metallic ion as part of the soluble complex.

25.6 Paramagnetism

*Substances that are weakly attracted into a magnetic field are said to be **paramagnetic**.* Paramagnetism among elements and their compounds indicates that there are unpaired electrons in the structure. Some transition metals have unpaired *d* electrons.

Table 25-5

STABILITY OF COMPLEX IONS		
Complex Ion	Equilibrium Reaction	K
$Ag(NH_3)_2^+$	$Ag(NH_3)_2^+ \rightleftharpoons Ag^+ + 2NH_3$	6×10^{-8}
$Co(NH_3)_6^{++}$	$Co(NH_3)_6^{++} \rightleftharpoons Co^{++} + 6NH_3$	1×10^{-5}
$Co(NH_3)_6^{+++}$	$Co(NH_3)_6^{+++} \rightleftharpoons Co^{+++} + 6NH_3$	2×10^{-34}
$Cu(NH_3)_4^{++}$	$Cu(NH_3)_4^{++} \rightleftharpoons Cu^{++} + 4NH_3$	5×10^{-14}
$Ag(CN)_2^-$	$Ag(CN)_2^- \rightleftharpoons Ag^+ + 2CN^-$	2×10^{-19}
$Au(CN)_2^-$	$Au(CN)_2^- \rightleftharpoons Au^+ + 2CN^-$	5×10^{-39}
$Cu(CN)_3^{--}$	$Cu(CN)_3^{--} \rightleftharpoons Cu^+ + 3CN^-$	1×10^{-35}
$Fe(CN)_6^{----}$	$Fe(CN)_6^{----} \rightleftharpoons Fe^{++} + 6CN^-$	1×10^{-35}
$Fe(CN)_6^{---}$	$Fe(CN)_6^{---} \rightleftharpoons Fe^{+++} + 6CN^-$	1×10^{-42}
$FeNCS^{++}$	$FeNCS^{++} \rightleftharpoons Fe^{+++} + NCS^-$	8×10^{-3}
$Ag(S_2O_3)_2^{---}$	$Ag(S_2O_3)_2^{---} \rightleftharpoons Ag^+ + 2S_2O_3^{--}$	6×10^{-14}

Manganese atoms, for example, have 5 unpaired $3d$ electrons as do Mn^{++} ions. Electron sharing in covalent complexes may reduce the number of unpaired electrons to the point where the substance is not paramagnetic. Most compounds of transition metals are paramagnetic in all but the highest oxidation states.

25.7 Transition metal similarities

The electron population in the outermost shell of the transition elements remains fairly constant. It never exceeds two electrons as the *d* sublevel buildup proceeds across a period. Similarities often appear in a horizontal sequence of transition elements as well as vertically through a subgroup. In some cases, horizontal similarity may exceed vertical similarity. The first five subgroups are those headed by Sc, Ti, V, Cr, and Mn. Generally, similarites among these elements are recognized within each subgroup. The 6th, 7th, and 8th subgroups are headed by Fe, Co, and Ni. Here, the similarities across each period are greater than those down each subgroup. Iron, cobalt, and nickel resemble each other more than do iron, ruthenium, and osmium, the members of the iron subgroup.

The 9th and 10th subgroups are headed by Cu and Zn. Here we again find the greatest similarity within each subgroup. We will now examine some common and important transition metals within the framework of their similarities.

The Iron Family

25.8 Members of the Iron Family

The Iron Family consists of the heavy metals *iron, cobalt,* and *nickel.* These metals are all in the fourth period. Each is the first member of a subgroup of transition metals that bears its name. These subgroups and their members are shown in Figure 25-1.

As stated in Section 25.7, the similarities betweeen iron, cobalt, and nickel are greater than those within each of the

Table 25-6

THE IRON FAMILY							
Element	Atomic Number	Atomic Weight	Electron Configuration	Oxidation Number	Melting Point (°C)	Boiling Point (°C)	Density (g/cm³)
iron	26	55.874	2,8,14,2	+2, +3	1535	3000	7.87
cobalt	27	58.9332	2,8,15,2	+2, +3	1495	2900	8.9
nickel	28	58.71	2,8,16,2	+2, +3	1453	2732	8.90

three subgroups they head. The remaining six members of these three subgroups have properties similar to platinum. Thus, they are considered to be members of the *Platinum Family*. They are called *noble metals* because they show little chemical activity. They are rare and expensive.

Iron is by far the most important member of the Iron Family. Alloys of iron, cobalt, and nickel are important structural metals. Some properties of the Iron Family are listed in Table 25.6.

The Iron Family is located in the middle of the transition elements. The next-to-outermost shell is incomplete. The 3*d* sublevels of iron, cobalt, and nickel contain only 6, 7, and 8 electrons instead of the full population of 10. Each member exhibits the +2 and +3 oxidation states. The Fe^{++} ion is easily oxidized to the Fe^{+++} ion by air and other oxidizing agents. The +3 oxidation state occurs only rarely in cobalt and nickel. The electron populations of iron, cobalt, and nickel sublevels are shown in Table 25-7. In this table paired and unpaired electrons of the 3*d* and 4*s* sublevels are represented by paired and unpaired dots.

The two 4*s* electrons are removed easily, as is usually the case with metals. This removal forms the Fe^{++}, Co^{++}, or Ni^{++} ion. In the case of iron, one 3*d* electron is also easily removed since the five remaining 3*d* electrons make a half-filled sublevel. (Recall that filled and half-filled sublevels have extra stability.) When two 4*s* and one 3*d* electrons are removed, the Fe^{+++} ion is formed. It becomes increasingly more difficult to remove a 3*d* electron from cobalt and nickel. This increasing difficulty is partly explained by the higher nuclear charges. Another factor is that neither 3*d* sublevel would be left at the filled or half-filled stage. Neither Co^{+++} nor Ni^{+++} ions are common. However, cobalt atoms in the +3 oxidation state occur in complexes.

All three metals of the Iron Family have a strong magnetic property. This property is commonly known as *ferromagnetism* because of the unusual extent to which it is possessed by iron. Cobalt is strongly magnetic, while nickel is the least magnetic of the three. The ferromagnetic nature of these

Table 25-7

ELECTRON POPULATION OF THE IRON FAMILY							
Sublevel	1*s*	2*s*	2*p*	3*s*	3*p*	3*d*	4*s*
Maximum population	2	2	6	2	6	10	2
iron	2	2	6	2	6	:....	:
cobalt	2	2	6	2	6	::...	:
nickel	2	2	6	2	6	:::..	:

metals is thought to be related to the similar spin orientations of their unpaired $3d$ electrons. From Table 25-7 we see that atoms of iron have 4, cobalt 3, and nickel 2 unpaired $3d$ electrons.

Each spinning electron acts like a tiny magnet. Electron pairs are formed by two electrons spinning in opposite directions. The electron magnetisms of such a pair of electrons neutralize each other. In Iron Family metals, groups of atoms may be aligned and form small magnetized regions called *domains*. Ordinarily, magnetic domains within the metallic crystals point in random directions. In this way, they cancel one another so that the net magnetism is zero. A piece of iron becomes magnetized when an outside force aligns the domains in the same direction. Figure 25-4 illustrates the mechanism of electron spin for paired and unpaired electrons.

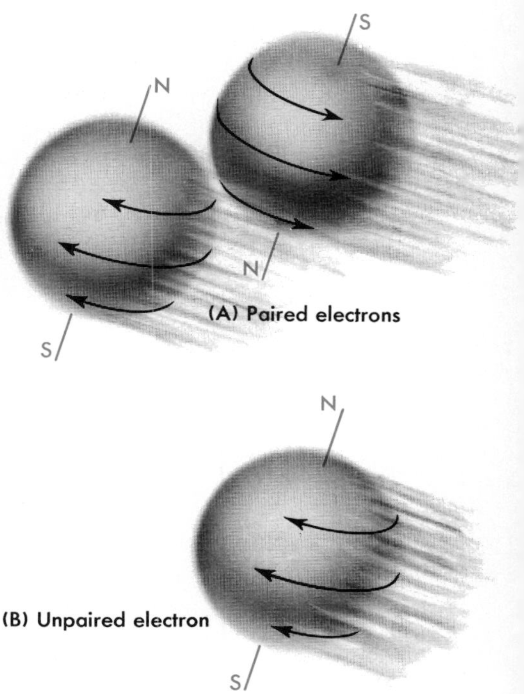

Fig. 25-4. Magnetism in matter stems basically from the spin of electrons.

25.9 Occurrence of iron

Iron is the fourth element in abundance by weight in the earth's crust. Nearly 5% of the earth's crust is iron. It is the second most abundant metal, following only aluminum. Meteors are known to contain iron. This fact and the known magnetic nature of the earth itself suggest that the earth's core may consist mainly of iron.

Unfortunately, much of the iron in the crust of the earth cannot be removed profitably. Only minerals from which iron can be profitably recovered by practical methods are considered iron ores.

Great deposits of *hematite*, Fe_2O_3, once existed in the Lake Superior region of the United States. They were the major sources of iron in this country for many years. These rich ores are now used up. Today the iron industry depends on medium- and low-grade ores, the most abundant of which is *taconite*.

Taconite has an iron content of roughly 25% to 50% in mixtures of chemically complex ores. The main iron minerals present are hematite, Fe_2O_3, and magnetite, Fe_3O_4. The rest of the ore is rock. Modern blast furnaces for reducing iron ore to iron require ores containing well above 60% iron. Thus, the raw ores must be concentrated by removing much of the

Fig. 25-5. Enrichment of low-grade iron ores. Today nearly all iron ore mined in the United States is concentrated before shipment to the blast furnace.

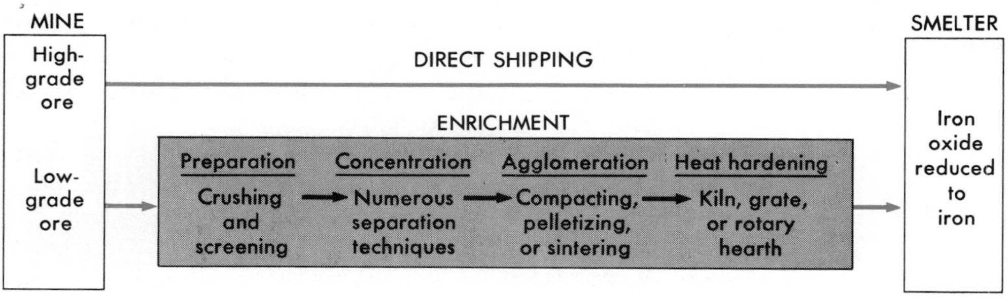

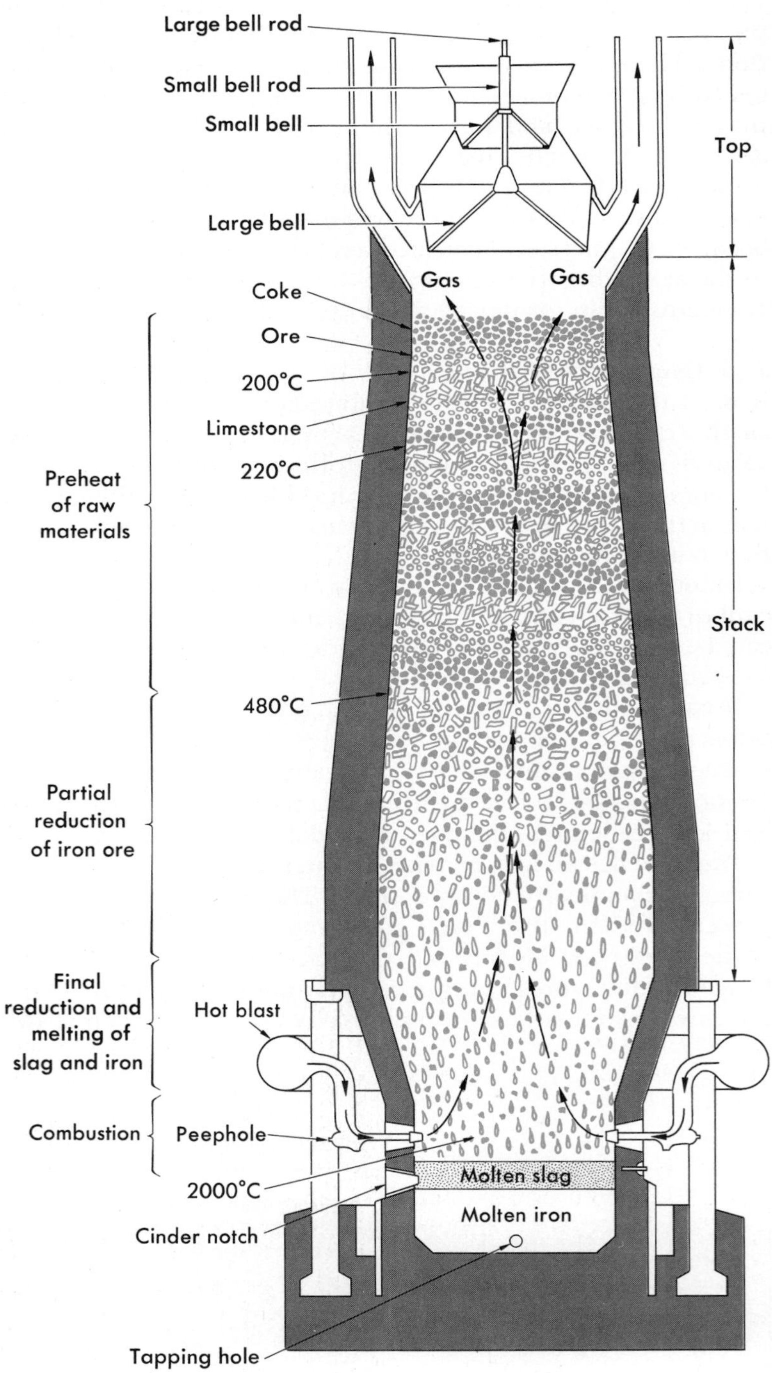

Fig. 25-6. A sectional view of a blast furnace.

waste materials. This process is performed at the mines before the ores are transported to the blast furnaces.

Taconite ores are first crushed and pulverized. They are then concentrated by a variety of complex methods. The concentrated ores are hardened into pellets for shipment to the smelters. Ore concentrates containing 90% iron are produced by the chemical removal of oxygen during the pelletizing treatment.

25.10 The blast furnace

Iron oxide is reduced to iron in a giant structure called a blast furnace. The charge placed in the blast furnace consists of iron oxide, coke, and a flux (which causes mineral impurities in the ore to melt more readily). The proper proportions for the charge are calculated by analyzing the raw materials. Usually the flux is limestone, because silica or sand is the most common impurity in the iron ore. Some iron ores contain limestone as an impurity and, in such cases, the flux added is sand. See Figure 25-6. A blast of hot air, sometimes enriched with oxygen, is forced into the base of the furnace.

Iron ore is reduced in the blast furnace to iron. The earthy impurities are removed as slag. Coke is required for the first function and limestone for the second. The products of the blast furnace are *pig iron, slag,* and *flue gas.*

The actual chemical changes that occur are complex and somewhat unclear. The coke is ignited by the blast of hot air and some of it burns, forming carbon dioxide.

$$C(s) + O_2(g) \rightarrow CO_2(g)$$

The carbon dioxide comes in contact with other pieces of hot coke when the oxygen is blown in and is reduced to carbon monoxide.

$$CO_2(g) + C(s) \rightarrow 2CO(g)$$

The carbon monoxide thus formed is actually the reducing agent that reduces the iron oxide to metallic iron.

$$Fe_2O_3 + 3CO \rightarrow 2Fe(l) + 3CO_2(g)$$

This reduction probably occurs in steps as the temperature increases toward the bottom of the furnace. Possible steps are

$$Fe_2O_3 \rightarrow Fe_3O_4 \rightarrow FeO \rightarrow Fe$$

The white-hot liquid iron collects in the bottom of the furnace. Every four or five hours it is tapped off. It may be cast in molds as *pig iron,* or converted directly to steel. See Figure 25-7.

In the middle region of the furnace, the limestone decomposes to calcium oxide and carbon dioxide.

$$CaCO_3(s) \rightarrow CaO(s) + CO_2(g)$$

Fig. 25-7. A basic-oxygen furnace receives a charge of molten iron directly from the blast furnace.

The calcium oxide combines with silica and forms a calcium silicate slag. This slag melts more readily than silica.

$$CaO + SiO_2 \rightarrow CaSiO_3(l)$$

Note the acid-base character of the reaction between the basic metallic oxide CaO and the acidic nonmetallic oxide SiO_2.

This glassy slag also collects at the bottom of the furnace. Since it has a much lower density than liquid iron, it floats on top of the iron. It prevents the reoxidation of the iron. The melted slag is tapped off every few hours. Uusually it is thrown away, although it is sometimes used for making Portland cement.

25.11 Steel production

The relatively high carbon content of iron recovered from the blast furnace makes it very hard and brittle. Two other impurities are phosphorus and sulfur. The phosphorus makes pig iron brittle at low temperatures. The sulfur makes it brittle at high temperatures.

The conversion of iron to steel *is essentially a purification process in which impurities are removed by oxidation.* This purification process is carried out in a furnace at a high temperature. Scrap steel that is being recycled is added to the charge of iron. Iron ore may be added to supply oxygen for oxidizing the impurities. Often, oxygen gas is added directly for very rapid oxidation. Limestone or lime is included in the charge for forming a slag with nongaseous oxides. Near the end of the process, selected alloying substances are added. By using different kinds and quantities of these alloys, the steel is given different desired properties.

Fig. 25-8. Steel cans being reclaimed as scrap for recycling in steelmaking furnaces.

The impurities in the pig iron are oxidized in the following way:

$$3C + Fe_2O_3 \rightarrow 3CO(g) + 2Fe$$

$$3Mn + Fe_2O_3 \rightarrow 3MnO + 2Fe$$

$$12P + 10Fe_2O_3 \rightarrow 3P_4O_{10} + 20Fe$$

$$3Si + 2Fe_2O_3 \rightarrow 3SiO_2 + 4Fe$$

$$3S + 2Fe_2O_3 \rightarrow 3SO_2(g) + 4Fe$$

The limestone flux decomposes as in the blast furnace.

$$CaCO_3 \rightarrow CaO + CO_2(g)$$

Carbon and sulfur escape as gases. Calcium oxide and the oxides of other impurities react and form slag.

These three reactions are between acidic nonmetallic oxides and basic metallic oxides.

$$P_4O_{10} + 6CaO \rightarrow 2Ca_3(PO_4)_2$$

$$SiO_2 + CaO \rightarrow CaSiO_3$$

$$MnO + SiO_2 \rightarrow MnSiO_3$$

Despite large imports from Japan and Western Europe, steel production in the United States exceeds 100 million tons each year. Present technological developments deal mainly with improving steel quality and production efficiency, rather than with increasing output. Examples of these improvements are

1. *Continuous casting,* in which freshly made liquid steel is cast directly into slabs ready for the rolling mills.
2. *Vacuum degassing,* in which steel is melted in a high vacuum and gases are removed.

Most steel produced in the United States is made by the *basic-oxygen process,* or *BOP*. This process is steadily replacing the older *open-hearth process*. Special steels are made in an *electric-furnace.*

The basic-oxygen furnace is an open-top vessel lined with heat-resistant bricks. It can be rotated through 360° for charging, tapping, and relining. The furnace is charged with scrap steel, molten iron, and lime as required.

A water-cooled lance is inserted over the charge from above and oxygen is blown in at about twice the speed of sound. A tremendous turbulence is produced by the oxygen crashing into the molten metal at this speed. The oxygen is delivered for 20 minutes. It combines with carbon and other unwanted elements, eliminating these impurities from the charge. During the oxygen "blow," lime is added to remove the oxidized impurities as a floating slag. The operation takes about 45 minutes to produce as much as 300 tons of steel. The steel is poured into a ladle and alloying substances are added according to precise specifications. It is then cast into ingots or delivered directly to a continuous casting unit for immediate working.

An improved version of the basic-oxygen process, called *Q-BOP,* has been developed. In this process, oxygen is blown in from the bottom of the furnace instead of the top. The time required for refining a "heat" (batch) of steel is reduced by 10%. Also, 20% more scrap steel can be used with each charge of pig iron.

There are several advantages to using the electric-furnace process: (*1*) The steel can be tested at various stages before it is finished. (*2*) High quality raw materials are used. (*3*) A reducing atmosphere can be maintained to prevent oxidation of the steel.

25.12 Pure iron

Pure iron is a metal that is seldom seen. It is silver-white, soft, ductile, tough, and does not tarnish readily. It melts at 1535°C. Commercial iron contains carbon and other impurities that alter its properties. Cast iron melts at about 1150°C. All forms of iron corrode, or rust, in moist air, so it is not a self-protective

Fig. 25-9. A tiny "whisker" of pure iron, free of the structural imperfections of the ordinary metal, provides scientists with a means of studying the nature of the enormous forces that bind atoms tightly together.

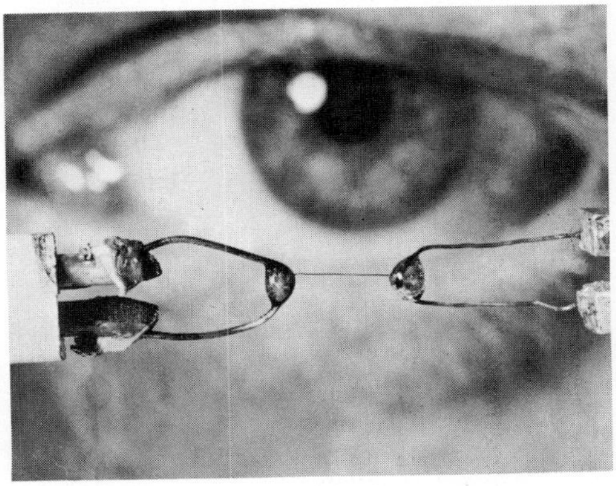

metal. The rust that forms is brittle and scales off, exposing the metal underneath to further corrosion. Iron does not rust in dry air or in water that is free of dissolved oxygen.

Iron is only moderately active chemically. Even so, it corrodes more extensively than more active metals such as zinc and aluminum. These metals form oxide coatings that adhere to the metal surface and protect it from further corrosion. The rusting of iron is a complicated (and not completely understood) electrochemical process that involves water, air, and carbon dioxide.

Water containing CO_2 in solution is acidic. It reacts with iron and forms Fe^{++} ions. The iron(II) ions are oxidized to the iron(III) state as hydrated Fe_2O_3 (rust) by oxygen. Iron is made rust-resistant in several ways: (*1*) By alloying it with chromium, copper, or nickel; (*2*) by treating it to form a coating of Fe_3O_4 which adheres and protects the surface; (*3*) by painting it. Paint protects the surface as long as it adheres and is not chipped or scratched; (*4*) by dip-coating it with a self-protective metal (galvanizing with zinc); (*5*) by plating it with nickel or chromium; and (*6*) by coating it with a material like porcelain.

Dilute acids generally act readily on iron. Alkalies do not react with it. Concentrated nitric acid does not react with iron. In fact, dipping iron into concentrated nitric acid makes the iron *passive,* or *inactive,* with other chemicals. Concentrated sulfuric acid has little effect on iron.

25.13 Three oxides of iron

Of the three oxides of iron, *iron(II) oxide,* FeO, is of little importance. It oxidizes rapidly when exposed to air and forms *iron(III) oxide,* Fe_2O_3. This oxide is the important ore of iron. It is used as a cheap red paint pigment (coloring material) known as red ocher, Venetian red, or Indian red. It is also used for grinding and polishing glass lenses and mirrors. When used for this purpose it is referred to as rouge.

Limonite is a natural *hydrated iron(III) oxide* that is powdered to make pigment called yellow ocher. When heated or roasted, it forms pigments known as *siennas* and *umbers. Magnetic iron oxide,* Fe_3O_4, is an important ore. It is composed of Fe_2O_3 and FeO. Thus, it may be considered to be iron(II,III) oxide, and can be written $FeO \cdot Fe_2O_3$.

25.14 Reactions of the Fe^{++} ion

Hydrated iron(II) sulfate, $FeSO_4 \cdot 7H_2O$, is the most useful compound of iron in the +2 oxidation state. It is used as a reducing agent and in medicine for iron tonics. Iron(II) sulfate can be prepared by the action of dilute sulfuric acid on iron. The crystalline hydrate loses water of hydration when exposed to air and turns brown because of oxidation. Iron(II) sulfate in solution is gradually oxidized to the iron(III) state by dissolved oxygen. The brown precipitate of basic iron(III) sulfate that forms is evidence of this change:

$$4FeSO_4 + O_2 + 2H_2O \rightarrow 4Fe(OH)SO_4(s)$$

The Fe^{++} ions can be kept in the reduced state by making the solution acidic with sulfuric acid and adding pieces of iron. Hydrated iron(II) ammonium sulfate, $Fe(NH_4)_2(SO_4)_2 \cdot 6H_2O$, is a better source of Fe^{++} ions in the laboratory because it is stable in contact with air.

Iron(II) salts are readily oxidized to iron(III) salts by the corresponding acid and an oxidizing agent. In the case of the nitrate, nitric acid meets both requirements:

$$3Fe(NO_3)_2 + 4HNO_3 \rightarrow 3Fe(NO)_3)_3 + NO(g) + 2H_2O$$

25.15 Reactions of the Fe^{+++} ion

Hydrated iron(III) chloride, $FeCl_3 \cdot 6H_2O$, is the most useful compound of iron in the +3 oxidation state. It is used as a mordant for dyeing cloth and as an oxidizing agent. The yellow crystalline hydrate is deliquescent. It is recovered from solutions in which iron(II) chloride was oxidized to the iron(III) state with chlorine. The anhydrous salt can be recovered as black crystals by passing chlorine gas over heated iron.

A mordant is used to "fix" or lock a dye color into a fabric.

Deliquescence: *takes up water from the air.*

$$2Fe + 3Cl_2 \rightarrow 2FeCl_3$$

The hydrated Fe^{+++} ion, $Fe(H_2O)_6^{+++}$, is pale violet in color. This color usually is not seen, however, because of hydrolysis, which yields hydroxide complexes that are yellow-brown in color. The hydrolysis of Fe^{+++} ions in water solutions of its salts gives solutions that are acidic.

$$Fe^{+++} + 2H_2O \rightleftarrows FeOH^{++} + H_3O^+$$

$$FeOH^{++} + 2H_2O \rightleftarrows Fe(OH)_2^+ + H_3O^+$$

$$Fe(OH)_2^+ + 2H_2O \rightleftarrows Fe(OH)_3 + H_3O^+$$

The hydrolysis is extensive when it occurs in boiling water. A blood-red colloidal suspension of iron(III) hydroxide is formed. This colloidal suspension can be produced by adding a few drops of $FeCl_3$ solution to a flask of boiling water.

Iron(III) ions are removed from solution by adding a solution containing hydroxide ions. A red-brown jelly-like precipitate of iron(III) hydroxide is formed.

$$Fe^{+++} + 3OH^- \rightarrow Fe(OH)_3(s)$$

By evaporating the water, red Fe_2O_3 remains. This is the Venetian red pigment, or the rouge polishing powder referred to in Section 25.13.

25.16 Tests for iron ions

Potassium hexacyanoferrate(II), $K_4Fe(CN)_6$ (also called potassium ferrocyanide), is a light yellow crystalline salt. It contains the complex hexacyanoferrate(II) ion (ferrocyanide ion), $Fe(CN)_6^{----}$. The iron is in the +2 oxidation state. It forms when an excess of cyanide ions is added to a solution of an iron(II) salt.

$$6CN^- + Fe^{++} \rightarrow Fe(CN)_6^{----}$$

Suppose KCN is used as the source of CN^- ions and $FeCl_2$ as the source of Fe^{++} ions. The empirical equation for the reaction then becomes

CAUTION: Solutions containing cyanide ions are deadly poisons and should never be handled by inexperienced chemistry students.

$$6KCN + FeCl_2 \rightarrow K_4Fe(CN)_6 + 2KCl$$

The iron of the $Fe(CN)_6^{----}$ ion can be oxidized by chlorine to the +3 state. This reaction forms the hexacyanoferrate(III) ion (ferricyanide ion) $Fe(CN)_6^{---}$.

$$2Fe(CN)_6^{----} + Cl_2 \rightarrow 2Fe(CN)_6^{---} + 2Cl^-$$

As the iron is oxidized from the +2 oxidation state to the +3 state, the chlorine is reduced from the 0 state to the −1 state.

Using the potassium salt as the source of the $Fe(CN)_6^{----}$ ions, the empirical equation is

$$2K_4Fe(CN)_6 + Cl_2 \rightarrow 2K_3Fe(CN)_6 + 2KCl$$

(II) following hexacyanoferrate tells you it is the Fe^{++} ion in the complex. (III) tells you it is the Fe^{+++} ion.

$K_3Fe(CN)_6$, potassium hexacyanoferrate(III) (known also as potassium ferricyanide), is a dark red crystalline salt.

Intense colors are observed in most compounds that have an element present in *two different oxidation states.* When iron(II) ions and hexacyanoferrate(III) ions are mixed, and when iron(III) ions and hexacyanoferrate(II) ions are mixed, *the same intense blue substance is formed.*

Before chemists learned that both blue hexacyanoferrate precipitates were the same substances, the one formed with Fe^{++} ions was called Turnbull's blue. That formed with Fe^{+++} ions was called Prussian blue.

$$Fe^{++} + K^+ + Fe(CN)_6^{---} + H_2O \rightarrow K\overset{+2}{Fe}\overset{+3}{Fe}(CN)_6 \cdot H_2O(s)$$

and

$$Fe^{+++} + K^+ + Fe(CN)_6^{----} + H_2O \rightarrow K\overset{+3}{Fe}\overset{+2}{Fe}(CN)_6 \cdot H_2O(s)$$

In both reactions, the precipitate contains iron in each of the +2 and +3 oxidation states and we observe the same intense blue color.

Iron(II) ions, Fe^{++}, and hexacyanoferrate(II) ions, $Fe(CN)_6^{----}$, both form a white precipitate of $K_2FeFe(CN)_6$. Note that both Fe ions are in the same +2 oxidation state. This precipitate remains white if measures are taken to prevent the oxidation of any Fe^{++} ions. Of course, on exposure to air, it begins to turn blue. Iron(III) ions, Fe^{+++}, and hexacyanoferrate(III) ions, $Fe(CN)_6^{---}$, give only a brown solution. Here, both Fe ions are in the same +3 oxidation state. The reactions given in the two equations above provide us with ways to detect the presence of iron in each of its two oxidation states.

1. Test for the Fe^{++} ion. Suppose a few drops of $K_3Fe(CN)_6$ solution are added to a solution of iron(II) sulfate. The characteristic intense blue precipitate, $KFeFe(CN)_6 \cdot H_2O$ forms. Two-thirds of the potassium ions and the sulfate ions are merely spectator ions. The net ionic reaction is

$$\mathbf{Fe^{++} + K^+ + Fe(CN)_6^{---} + H_2O \rightarrow KFeFe(CN)_6 \cdot H_2O(s)}$$

The formation of a blue precipitate when $K_3Fe(CN)_6$ is added to an unknown solution serves to identify the Fe^{++} ion.

2. Test for the Fe^{+++} ion. Suppose a few drops of $K_4Fe(CN)_6$ solution are added to a solution of iron(III) chloride. The characteristic blue precipitate, $KFeFe(CN)_6 \cdot H_2O$, is formed. The net reaction is

$$\mathbf{Fe^{+++} + K^+ + Fe(CN)_6^{----} + H_2O \rightarrow KFeFe(CN)_6 \cdot H_2O(s)}$$

The formation of a blue precipitate when $K_4Fe(CN)_6$ is added to an unknown solution serves to identify the Fe^{+++} ion.

Potassium thiocyanate, KSCN, provides another good test for the Fe^{+++} ion. It is often used to confirm the $K_4Fe(CN)_6$ test. A blood-red solution results from the formation of the complex $FeNCS^{++}$ ion.

***Blueprints:** The basis for the blueprinting process is a photochemical reaction that reduces Fe^{+++} ions to Fe^{++} ions which react with hexacyanoferrate(III) ions and form the blue color in the paper. Blueprint paper is first treated with a solution of iron(III) ammonium citrate and potassium hexacyanoferrate(III) and allowed to dry in the dark. A drawing on tracing paper is laid over the blueprint paper and exposed to light. Where light strikes the paper Fe^{+++} ions are reduced to Fe^{++} ions. The paper is dipped in water and the Fe^{++} ions react with the hexacyanoferrate(III) ions forming the blue color in the paper. Where drawing lines covered the paper, no reduction of Fe^{+++} ions occurred. This part of the paper rinses out white. Thus, a blueprint has white lines on blue paper.*

The Copper Family

25.17 Members of the Copper Family

The Copper Family consists of *copper, silver,* and *gold,* the copper subgroup of transition metals. All three metals appear below hydrogen in the electrochemical series. They are not easily oxidized and often occur in nature in the free, or *native,* state. Because of their pleasing appearance, durability, and relative scarcity, these metals have been highly valued since the time of their discovery. All have been used in ornamental objects and coins throughout history.

The atoms of copper, silver, and gold have a single electron in their outermost energy levels. Thus, they often form compounds in which they exhibit the +1 oxidation state. To this extent, they resemble the Group I metals of the Sodium Family.

Each metal of the Copper Family has 18 electrons in the next-to-outermost shell. The *d* electrons in this next-to-

Table 25-8

THE COPPER FAMILY

Element	Atomic Number	Atomic Weight	Electron Configuration	Oxidation Numbers	Melting Point (°C)	Boiling Point (°C)	Density (g/cm³)
copper	29	63.546	2,8,18,1	+1, +2	1083.0	2595	8.96
silver	47	107.868	2,8,18,18,1	+1	960.8	2212	10.50
gold	79	196.9665	2,8,18,32,18,1	+1, +3	1063.0	2966	19.32

outermost shell have energies that differ only slightly from the energy of the outer *s* electron. Thus, one or two of these *d* electrons can be removed with relative ease. For this reason, copper and gold often form compounds in which they respectively exhibit the +2 and +3 oxidation states. In the case of silver, the +2 oxidation state is reached only under extreme oxidizing conditions.

Copper, silver, and gold are very dense, ductile, and malleable. They are classed as heavy metals along with other transition metals in the central region of the periodic table. Some important properties of each metal are shown in Table 25-8.

25.18 Copper and its recovery

Copper, alloyed with tin in the form of bronze, has been in use for over 5000 years. Native copper deposits lie deep underground and are difficult to mine.

Sulfide ores of copper yield most of the supply of this metal. *Chalcocite,* Cu_2S, *chalcopyrite,* $CuFeS_2$, and *bornite,* Cu_3FeS_3, are the major sulfide ores. The minerals *malachite,* $Cu_2(OH)_2CO_3$, and *azurite,* $Cu_3(OH)_2(CO_3)_2$, are basic carbonates of copper. Malachite is a rich green, and azurite is a deep blue. Besides serving as ores of copper, fine specimens of these minerals are sometimes polished for use as ornaments or in making jewelry.

The carbonate ores of copper are washed with dilute sulfuric acid, forming a solution of copper(II) sulfate. The copper is then recovered by electrolysis. High-grade carbonate ores are heated in air to convert them to copper(II) oxide. The oxide is then reduced with coke, yielding metallic copper.

The sulfide ores are usually low-grade and require concen-

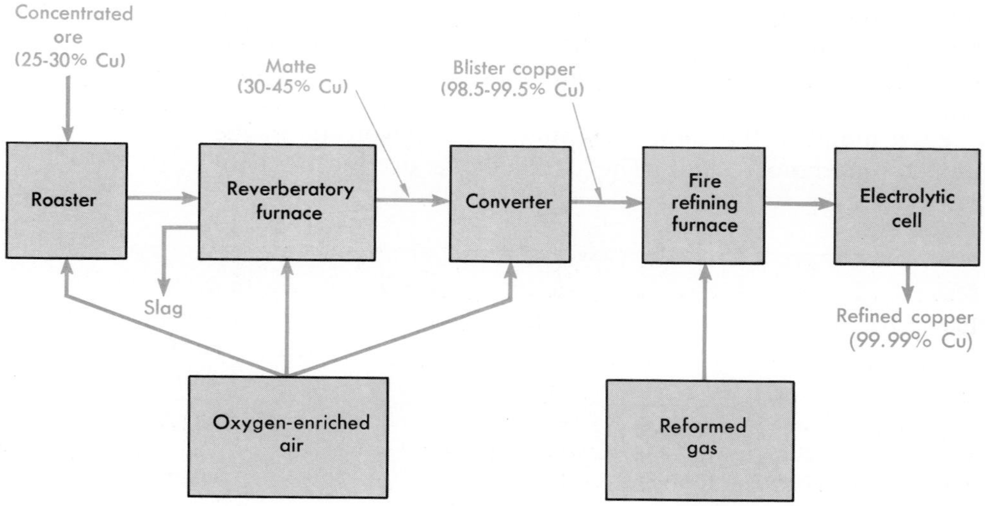

Fig. 25-10. The copper refining process.

Fig. 25-11. Copper anodes being cast using smeltered copper, 99.7% pure, for electrolytic refining to 99.99% purity.

trating before they can be refined profitably. The concentration is accomplished by *oil-flotation*. Earthy impurities are wetted by water and the ore is wetted by oil. Air is blown into the mixture to form a froth. The oil-wetted ore floats to the surface in the froth. This treatment changes the concentration of the ore from about 2% copper to as high as 30% copper.

25.19 Properties of copper

Copper is a soft, ductile, malleable, red metal with a density of 8.96 g/cm³. Next to silver, it is the best conductor of electricity.

Heated in air, copper forms a black coating of copper(II) oxide, CuO. Metallic copper and most copper compounds color a Bunsen flame green.

Copper forms copper(II) salts which dissociate in water and give blue solutions. The color is characteristic of the hydrated copper(II) ion, $Cu(H_2O)_4^{++}$. Adding an excess of ammonia to solutions containing this ion produces the deeper blue complex ion, $Cu(NH_3)_4^{++}$. Aqueous solutions of copper(II) salts are weakly acidic because of the mild hydrolysis of the Cu^{++} ion.

$$\mathbf{Cu(H_2O)_4^{++} + H_2O \rightarrow Cu(H_2O)_3OH^+ + H_3O^+}$$

An excess of sulfur vapor forms a blue-black coating of copper(I) sulfide on hot copper. In moist air, copper tarnishes and forms a protective coating. This coating is a green basic carbonate, $Cu_2(OH)_2CO_3$. Sulfur dioxide in the air may also combine with copper. If so, a green basic sulfate, $Cu_4(OH)_6SO_4$, is produced. The green color seen on copper roofs is caused by the formation of these compounds.

Fig. 25-12. The roof of the *Palace of the One Hundred Suns* in Mexico City is made of copper.

Both copper(I) and copper(II) compounds are known. The copper(II) compounds are much more common. Copper(II) oxide is used to change alternating current to direct current. It is also used as an oxidizing agent in chemical laboratories.

Hydrated copper(II) sulfate, $CuSO_4 \cdot 5H_2O$, called *blue vitriol,* is an important copper compound. It is used to kill algae in reservoirs and to make certain pesticides. It is also used in electroplating and in preparing other copper compounds.

Because copper stands below hydrogen in the activity series (see Section 8.8), it does not replace hydrogen from acids. Thus, it is not acted on by nonoxidizing acids such as hydrochloric and dilute sulfuric except very slowly when oxygen is present. The oxidizing acids, nitric and hot concentrated sulfuric, react vigorously with copper. Such reactions produce the corresponding copper(II) salts. These chemical changes are typical oxidation-reduction reactions.

25.20 Tests for the Cu^{++} ion

A dilute solution of a copper(II) salt changes to a very deep blue color when an excess of ammonia is added. This color change is caused by the formation of complex $Cu(NH_3)_4^{++}$ ions.

$$\mathbf{Cu^{++} + 4NH_3 \rightarrow Cu(NH_3)_4^{++}}$$

The addition of $K_4Fe(CN)_6$ to a solution containing Cu^{++} ions produces a red precipitate of $Cu_2Fe(CN)_6$. This precipitate is copper(II) hexacyanoferrate(II), also known as copper(II) ferrocyanide. If copper is present in a borax bead formed in an *oxidizing flame,* a clear blue color appears on cooling. The hot bead is green. A bead formed in a *reducing* flame is colorless while hot, and an opaque red when cool.

SUMMARY

The transition metals consist of ten subgroups interposed between main Group II and main Group III in the periodic table. They are in this position because they represent an interruption of the regular buildup of outer-shell electrons from Group I to Group VIII in the long periods.

Chemical properties of transition metals are varied. Electrons of the next-to-outermost *d* sublevel as well as those of the outer shell may become involved in the formation of compounds. Most of the transition metals show different oxidation states in their reactions. They have strong tendencies to form complex ions. Many of their compounds are paramagnetic and are colored.

With minor apparent irregularities, the transition metals have two outer-shell electrons. In the first row of transition elements, chromium and copper have one 4*s* electron. The availability of 3*d* electrons tends to increase the number of oxidation states up to manganese in the middle of the row. Following manganese, the number of common oxidation states for each element decreases.

The color of the compounds of transition

elements depends to some extent on the ions or polyatomic groups associated with the element. The colors result from the ease with which *d* electrons can be excited by absorption of discrete quantities of light energy.

Transition metals form many complex ions. A transition element cation is the central ion in the complex. Certain ionic or molecular species coordinate with the central ion to form the complex ion. The coordinating atom of the species must have unshared electron pairs that the central ion can share. Formation of complex ions in a solution has the effect of increasing the solubility of the metallic ions that form the complex.

The Iron Family consists of iron, cobalt, and nickel. These transition metals are ferromagnetic. All are present in nature in combined form. Purified iron is used as a construction on metal in the form of steel. By alloying other metals with steel, a variety of structural characteristics can be obtained. The metals of the Iron Family are recovered from their ores by reduction methods.

Iron forms compounds in two oxidation states, +2 and +3. Iron(II) ions are easily oxidized to the iron(III) state. Iron(II) compounds are used as reducing agents. Iron(III) compounds are used as oxidizing agents. The iron(III) ion hydrolyzes in water solutions of its salts. Its hydroxide is very sparingly soluble and is precipitated by the addition of aqueous ammonia to solutions of iron(III) salts. Both the Fe^{++} ion and the Fe^{+++} ion can be identified by precipitation reactions with potassium hexacyanoferrate(III) and potassium hexacyanoferrate(II), respectively. The color of the intense blue precipitate results from iron being present in both the +2 and +3 oxidation states.

The Copper Family consists of copper, silver, and gold. All are found as the native metals in nature. Most copper used in commerce and industry is recovered from its sulfide ores by reduction and electrolytic refining. All soluble compounds of copper, silver, and gold are very toxic. The copper(II) ions can be identified by the formation of colored complex ions.

QUESTIONS

Group A

1. What structural similarity determines the metallic character of transition elements?
2. Which process is most used for making steel in this country?
3. Copper(II) sulfate crystals are blue. To what color does the light energy absorbed by the crystals correspond?
4. List five points of similarity between copper, silver, and gold.
5. Why does the copper trim on roofs frequently acquire a green surface?

Group B

6. When potassium hexacyanoferrate(II) is added to a solution of iron(II) sulfate, a white precipitate forms which gradually turns blue. Explain the color change.
7. How can you detect an iron(II) and an iron(III) compound, if both are present in the same solution?
8. Identify three factors that make the basic oxygen process attractive in steel production.
9. Why were some metals used in very early times, while many other metals were obtained only within the last century?
10. Why does it usually pay to refine copper by electrolysis?
11. The gleaming copper ware shown on page 523 makes an attractive display for any kitchen. What properties of copper make it suitable for use as cooking utensils?

PROBLEMS

Group A

1. How much iron(II) chloride can be produced by adding 165 g of iron to an excess of hydrochloric acid? Compute to three significant figures.
2. How much iron(III) chloride can be prepared from the iron(II) chloride in the preceding problem if more hydrochloric acid is added and air is blown through the solution?
3. What is the percentage of iron in a sample of limonite, $2Fe_2O_3 \cdot 3H_2O$?
4. How many grams of silver nitrate can be obtained by adding $10\bar{0}$ g of pure silver to an excess of nitric acid?
5. A sample of hematite ore contains Fe_2O_3 87.0%, silica 8.0%, moisture 4.0%, other impurities 1.0%. What is the percentage of iron in the ore?
6. What will be the loss in mass when 1.0×10^6 metric tons of the ore in the preceding problem are heated to $20\bar{0}$°C?

Group B

7. How much limestone will be needed to combine with the silica in 1.0×10^6 metric tons of the ore of Problem 5?
8. (*a*) How much carbon monoxide is required to reduce 1.0×10^6 metric tons of the ore of Problem 5? (*b*) How much coke must be supplied to meet this requirement? (Assume the coke to be $10\bar{0}$% carbon.)
9. Iron(II) sulfate is oxidized to iron(III) sulfate in the presence of sulfuric acid using nitric acid as the oxidizing agent. Nitrogen monoxide and water are also formed. Balance the equation.
10. Silver reacts with dilute nitric acid and forms silver nitrate, water, and nitrogen monoxide. Balance the equation.
11. Copper reacts with hot concentrated sulfuric acid and forms copper(II) sulfate, sulfur dioxide, and water. Balance the equation.

chapter 26

ALUMINUM AND THE METALLOIDS

Oxides of aluminum and boron are used in the manufacture of art and decorative glass. (See Question 18 page 560.)

26.1 Nature of metalloids

Some elements are neither distinctly metallic nor distinctly nonmetallic. Their properties are intermediate between those of metals and nonmetals. As a group, these elements are called *metalloids* or *semimetals*. They appear along the diagonal region from upper center and descending toward the lower right of the periodic table shown in Figure 26-1.

Fig. 26-1. The metalloids are the elements *boron, silicon, germanium, arsenic, antimony, tellurium, and polonium.*

METALS				NONMETALS					
				III	IV	V	VI	VII	VIII
									4.00260 He 2 (2)
				10.81 B 5 (2, 3)	12.011 C 6 (2, 4)	14.0067 N 7 (2, 5)	15.9994 O 8 (2, 6)	18.9984 F 9 (2, 7)	20.179 Ne 10 (2, 8)
				26.9815 Al 13 (2, 8, 3)	28.086 Si 14 (2, 8, 4)	30.9738 P 15 (2, 8, 5)	32.06 S 16 (2, 8, 6)	35.453 Cl 17 (2, 8, 7)	39.948 Ar 18 (2, 8, 8)
58.9332 Co 27 (2, 8, 15, 2)	58.71 Ni 28 (2, 8, 16, 2)	63.546 Cu 29 (2, 8, 18, 1)	65.37 Zn 30 (2, 8, 18, 2)	69.72 Ga 31 (2, 8, 18, 3)	72.59 Ge 32 (2, 8, 18, 4)	74.9216 As 33 (2, 8, 18, 5)	78.96 Se 34 (2, 8, 18, 6)	79.904 Br 35 (2, 8, 18, 7)	83.8 Kr 36 (2, 8, 18, 8)
102.9055 Rh 45 (2, 8, 18, 16, 1)	106.4 Pd 46 (2, 8, 18, 18, 0)	107.868 Ag 47 (2, 8, 18, 18, 1)	112.40 Cd 48 (2, 8, 18, 18, 2)	114.82 In 49 (2, 8, 18, 18, 3)	118.69 Sn 50 (2, 8, 18, 18, 4)	121.75 Sb 51 (2, 8, 18, 18, 5)	127.60 Te 52 (2, 8, 18, 18, 6)	126.9045 I 53 (2, 8, 18, 18, 7)	131.30 Xe 54 (2, 8, 18, 18, 8)
192.22 Ir 77 (2, 8, 18, 32, 15, 2)	195.09 Pt 78 (2, 8, 18, 32, 17, 1)	196.9665 Au 79 (2, 8, 18, 32, 18, 1)	200.59 Hg 80 (2, 8, 18, 32, 18, 2)	204.37 Tl 81 (2, 8, 18, 32, 18, 3)	207.2 Pb 82 (2, 8, 18, 32, 18, 4)	208.9806 Bi 83 (2, 8, 18, 32, 18, 5)	[210] Po 84 (2, 8, 18, 32, 18, 6)	[211] At 85 (2, 8, 18, 32, 18, 7)	222 Rn 86 (2, 8, 18, 32, 18, 8)

The metalloids are the elements *boron, silicon, germanium, arsenic, antimony, tellurium,* and *polonium.* Although aluminum is not included in the metalloids listed here, it is studied in this chapter because of its unique position in the periodic table relative to the metalloids.

The amphoterism of aluminum hydroxide is discussed in detail in Section 15.9.

Aluminum is distinctly metallic and is recognized by the familiar properties of metals. On the other hand, aluminum forms the negative aluminate ion, $Al(OH)_4^-$. Its hydroxide, $Al(OH)_3$, is amphoteric. The oxide of aluminum is ionic, yet the hydride is polymeric. As a metal, aluminum is so resistant to oxidation that it can be used as cooking ware on hot stove burners. It is so easily oxidized in sodium hydroxide solutions that it is added to "Drano" to generate the bubbles of hydrogen gas that stir things up in clogged sink drains. These are the characteristics that relate aluminum to the metalloids.

Boron, silicon, arsenic, and antimony are the typical metalloids. Table 26-1 lists some of their important properties, together with those of aluminum and the other metalloids.

Semiconductor: *a substance with an electric conductivity between that of a metal and an insulator.*

Germanium is a moderately rare element. Its compounds until recently had little importance. With the development of the transistor, germanium became important as a semiconductor material. It is chemically similar to silicon, the element above it in Group IV. Germanium is more metallic than arsenic just to its right in Period Four. The major oxidation state of germanium is +4.

Group VI elements are shown in Figure 26-1.

Tellurium is a member of Group VI in the periodic table. As expected, the metal-like characteristics of Group VI elements increase as you go down the group. Tellurium is more metallic (or less nonmetallic) than selenium above it. It is less metallic (or more nonmetallic) than polonium below it. This gradation in properties down the group is illustrated by the change in the odor of their hydrogen compounds. Hydrogen

Table 26-1

PROPERTIES OF ALUMINUM AND METALLOIDS

Element	Atomic Number	Electron Configuration	Oxidation States	Melting Point (°C)	Boiling Point (°C)	Density (g/cm³)	Atomic Radius (Å)	First Ionization Energy (kcal/mole)
boron	5	2,3	+3	2300	2550	2.34	0.82	191
aluminum	13	2,8,3	+3	660	2467	2.70	1.18	138
silicon	14	2,8,4	+2,+4,−4	1410	2355	2.33	1.11	188
germanium	32	2,8,18,4	+2,+4,−4	938	2825	5.36	1.22	182
arsenic	33	2,8,18,5	+3,+5,−3	sublimes		5.73	1.20	226
antimony	51	2,8,18,18,5	+3,+5,−3	631	1380	6.69	1.40	199
tellurium	52	2,8,18,18,6	+2,+4,+6,−2	450	987	6.24	1.36	208
polonium	84	2,8,18,32,18,6	+4,+6	254	962	9.32	1.46	196

oxide (water) is odorless. Hydrogen sulfide has the offensive odor of rotten eggs. The odor of hydrogen selenide is even more offensive, and that of hydrogen telluride is the foulest of them all.

Although it can be amorphous, tellurium is more commonly a brittle, silvery, metal-like crystalline substance. It is classed as a semiconductor and its chemistry is typically metalloidal. It appears with oxygen in both tellurite (TeO_3^{--}) and tellurate (TeO_4^{--}) ions. In these ions, tellurium shows, respectively, the +4 and +6 oxidation states. Tellurium combines covalently with oxygen and the halogens in which the +2, +4, and +6 oxidation states are observed. It forms tellurides (−2 oxidation state) with such elements as gold, hydrogen, and lead. In fact, tellurium is the only element combined with gold in nature.

Amorphous: *without form; noncrystalline.*

The foul-smelling nature of tellurium compounds is well known to chemists. When taken up by the body, these odors are given off again with perspiration and breath. The stench of "tellurium breath" may persist for several weeks.

Tellurium (at. no. 52) appears just before iodine (at. no. 53) in the periodic table. Notice that its atomic weight (127.60) is higher than that of iodine (126.90). The periodic placement of elements in the table depends only on their number of protons. However, different isotopes of an element have different numbers of neutrons. *The atomic weight of an element depends on the atomic masses and natural abundance of its isotopes.* While iodine has one naturally occurring isotope (I-127), tellurium has several, the two most abundant being Te-128 and Te-130. (Review Sections 3.12, 3.13, and 3.14.) This apparent irregularity of atomic weights occurs several times in the periodic table.

See Problem 7 at the end of this chapter.

Polonium is a radioactive element. It was discovered by Pierre and Marie Curie in 1898 just prior to their discovery of radium. Polonium is so rare in nature that little is known of its chemistry. It appears to be more metallic than tellurium.

Aluminum

26.2 Aluminum as a light metal

Aluminum, atomic number 13, is the second member of Group III. This group is headed by boron and includes gallium, indium, and thallium. All are typically metallic except boron, which is classed as a metalloid. The chemistry of boron differs from that of aluminum and the other Group III elements mainly because of the small size of the boron atom. Its chemistry resembles that of silicon and germanium more than it does that of aluminum. Much of the chemistry of aluminum is similar to that of its corresponding Group II metal, magnesium.

Except in the United States, aluminum is spelled ***aluminium*** *and pronounced al-yuh-*min*-ee-um.*

Aluminum is a low-density metal, being about one-third the density of steel. The pure metal is used in chemical processes,

Fig. 26-2. Aluminum-sheathed transit cars operating over the San Francisco Bay Area Rapid Transit System.

in electronics, for forming jewelry, and as foil wrapping. Aluminum alloys are used in structural and industrial applications. Each alloying substance improves certain properties of the aluminum to which it is added. For example, approximately 1% manganese yields aluminum alloys that are 20% stronger and more resistant to corrosion than pure aluminum. The common alloying elements are copper, magnesium, manganese, silicon, and zinc. Other elements may be added for special effects.

Historically, anhydrous aluminum oxide is called ***alumina.***

Aluminum is the most abundant metal in the earth's crust. It is found in many clays, rocks, and other minerals. The aluminum industry is working on processes for profitably separating aluminum from clay. Such processes would make the United States less dependent on foreign sources of aluminum ore.

Bauxite, a hydrated aluminum oxide ore, is the source of aluminum today. It has been found in every continent except Antarctica. Major deposits are located throughout the tropical and semitropical regions of the earth. Bauxite containing 40–60% aluminum oxide is required for our present aluminum recovery technology. Major foreign sources are Australia, Jamaica, Surinam, and Guyana. Bauxite is also mined in Georgia, Alabama, Tennessee, and Arkansas.

Fig. 26-3. Bauxite being placed in storage at Pinjarra on the southwestern coast of Australia.

26.3 Discovery of aluminum

Pottery has been made from clays consisting largely of a hydrated aluminum silicate, $AlSi_2O_5(OH)_4$, for several thousand years. It was long suspected that the clay contained a metal, referred to as the "metal of clay." However, known reduction methods were unsuccessful in separating this elusive metal.

Chemical historians believe that Hans Christian Oersted, a

Danish chemist, may have first isolated aluminum in impure form in 1825. However, a German chemist, Friedrich Wöhler, repeated his experiment without success. With Oersted's encouragement, Wöhler continued his efforts and in 1827 succeeded in isolating impure aluminum by reducing aluminum chloride with potassium. The reaction for this reduction is

$$AlCl_3 + 3K \rightarrow 3KCl + Al$$

Wöhler was the first to describe the properties of metallic aluminum and is usually credited with its discovery.

The French chemist, Henri Sainte-Claire Deville, improved Wöhler's method and substituted cheaper sodium for potassium as the reducing agent. Deville's advances in isolating aluminum made its commercial production feasible. Aluminum plants using his process were operating in France by 1855.

Bars of aluminum were exhibited next to the crown jewels at the Paris Exposition of 1855. Emperor Napoleon III served his most distinguished guests with aluminum dinnerware. Lesser guests had to be satisfied with silver and gold. Aluminum was a rare and priceless metal prior to its commercial production. In 1852, aluminum cost $545 per pound. By 1886, the price had dropped to about $8 per pound. At this price, the metal was still too expensive for structural and household uses.

Today, kitchenware is usually made of aluminum.

In 1886, a young American, Charles Martin Hall, developed a cheap practical method for producing aluminum. While a student at Oberlin College, Hall discovered a way that aluminum could be separated from its oxide by electrolysis. His process, first used commercially in 1889, lowered the price of aluminum to about $2 per pound, and eventually to about 20¢ per pound. A similar process was developed independently in France at about this same time by Paul Héroult. Today aluminum is one of the most widely used metals.

26.4 Recovery of aluminum

Fused-salt electrolysis has great commercial value. It is used to produce alkali and alkaline-earth metals as well as aluminum and related metals. Review Sections 22.6, 23.4, and 24.6. Aluminum is extracted by electrolyzing anhydrous aluminum oxide (refined bauxite) dissolved in molten cryolite, Na_3AlF_6. The process requires a temperature slightly below 1000°C. It is basically the process developed by Hall in 1886.

In the electrolytic cell, an iron box lined with graphite serves as the cathode. Graphite rods serve as the anode, and molten cryolite-aluminum oxide is the electrolyte. The cryolite is melted in the cell and the aluminum oxide dissolves as it is added to the molten cryolite. The operating temperature of the

Fig. 26-4. Batteries of electrolytic cells used for the recovery of aluminum from aluminum oxide. In the foreground, molten aluminum is being poured into a transfer ladle.

cell is above the melting point of aluminum (660°C). Thus the aluminum metal in the bottom of the cell is in the liquid phase and is easily drawn off. See Figure 26-4.

The electrode reactions are complex and are not understood completely. Aluminum is reduced at the cathode. The anode is gradually converted to carbon dioxide. This fact suggests that oxygen is formed at the anode by oxidation of the O^{--} ion. The following equations for the reaction mechanism may be overly simple. However, they serve to summarize the oxidation-reduction processes in the cell.

cathode: $4Al^{+++} + 12e^- \rightarrow 4Al$

anode: $6O^{--} \rightarrow 3O_2 + 12e^-$

$3C + 3O_2 \rightarrow 3CO_2(g)$

Efforts to replace the Hall process for recovering aluminum and to improve the efficiency of existing reduction cells have been in progress for many years. Wastes from the bauxite-to-aluminum oxide process and from the electrolysis process create serious pollution problems. The huge quantity of electric energy consumed during electrolysis may require production cutbacks during an energy shortage. For example, the average amount of energy required to produce 1 kg of aluminum will operate an ordinary 100-watt lamp 6 hours a day for about a month. Recycling aluminum scrap such as beverage cans uses only 5% of the energy required to recover an equal amount of the metal from its ore.

26.5 Properties of aluminum

Ductile: *drawn into wire.*
Malleable: *rolled into sheets.*
Tenacious: *resists being pulled apart.*

Aluminum has a density of 2.7 g/cm^3. It is ductile and malleable but is not as tenacious as brass, copper, or steel. Only silver, copper, and gold are better conductors of electricity. Aluminum can be welded, cast, or spun but can be soldered only by using a special solder.

Aluminum is a very active metal. The surface is always covered with a thin layer of aluminum oxide. This oxide layer is not affected by air or moisture, hence aluminum is a self-protective metal. At high temperatures, the metal combines vigorously with oxygen, releasing intense light and heat. Photoflash lamps contain aluminum foil or fine wire in an atmosphere of oxygen.

Aluminum is a very good reducing agent but is not as active as the Group I and Group II metals.

$$Al \rightarrow Al^{+++} + 3e^-$$

The Al^{+++} ion is quite small and carries a large positive charge. The ion hydrates vigorously in water solution and is usually written as the hydrated ion, $Al(H_2O)_6^{+++}$. Water solutions of aluminum salts are generally acidic because of the hydrolysis of $Al(H_2O)_6^{+++}$ ions.

$$Al(H_2O)_6^{+++} + H_2O \rightarrow Al(H_2O)_5OH^{++} + H_3O^+$$

Water molecules are amphoteric but are very weak proton donors or acceptors. However, water molecules that hydrate the Al^{+++} ion give up protons more readily. This increased activity results from the repulsion effect of the highly positive Al^{+++} ion. In the hydrolysis shown above, a water molecule does succeed in removing one proton from the $Al(H_2O)_6^{+++}$ ion.

Hydrochloric acid reacts readily with aluminum, forming aluminum chloride and releasing hydrogen.

$$2Al(s) + 6H_3O^+ + 6H_2O \rightarrow 2Al(H_2O)_6^{+++} + 3H_2(g)$$

Nitric acid does not react readily with aluminum because of aluminum's protective oxide layer.

In basic solutions, aluminum forms aluminate ions, $Al(OH)_4^-$, and releases hydrogen. The reaction equation is

$$2Al(s) + 2OH^- + 6H_2O \rightarrow 2Al(OH)_4^- + 3H_2(g)$$

If the base is sodium hydroxide, sodium aluminate, $NaAl(OH)_4$, is the soluble product and hydrogen is given up as a gas. The equation for the reaction now becomes

$$2Al(s) + 2NaOH + 6H_2O \rightarrow 2NaAl(OH)_4 + 3H_2(g)$$

This reaction of aluminum and sodium hydroxide is used in some household products for opening plugged sink drains. A mixture of granulated aluminum and solid sodium hydroxide is added to the water in a stopped-up drain. The vigorous release of H_2 gas agitates the water and raises pressure in the drain. Excess sodium hydroxide converts grease in the pipe to a water-soluble soap. The combined actions unplug the drain in most cases.

The oxide surface coating protects aluminum under normal atmospheric conditions. It must be removed before the metal underneath can react with hydronium ions as in the reaction with hydrochloric acid above, and with the hydroxide ions in the reaction with the base. The hydroxide ions dissolve this oxide layer more readily than hydronium ions. This explains why aluminum reacts so vigorously in the household drain-opener reaction.

Fig. 26-5. This top-charging aluminum melting furnace receives a charge of 30,000 pounds of metal in less than 2 minutes.

26.6 The thermite reaction

When a mixture of powdered aluminum and an oxidizing agent such as iron oxide is ignited, the aluminum reduces the oxide to the free metal. This reduction is rapid and violent, and yields a tremendous amount of heat. The sudden release of this heat energy produces temperatures from 3000 to

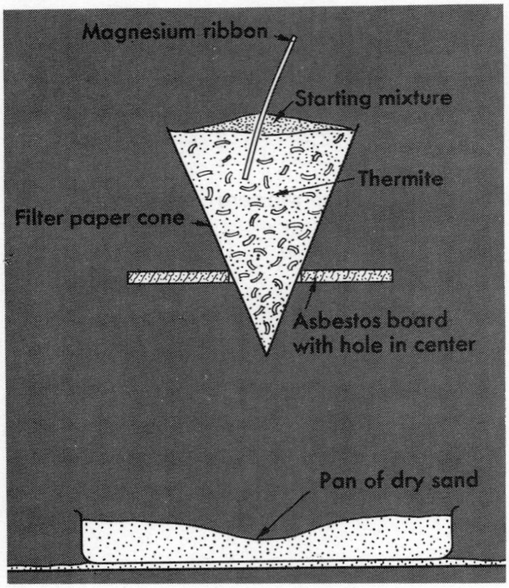

Fig. 26-6. The thermite reaction. Dry sand protects the table top. Spectators must stand at a safe distance. Sharp black and white contrast shows the brilliance of the molten iron.

3500°C, enough to melt the iron. Such a reaction between aluminum and the oxide of a less active metal is called the *thermite reaction*. See Figure 26.6.

The formation of aluminum oxide is strongly exothermic. The reaction releases 399 kilocalories of heat per mole of aluminum oxide formed. The heat of formation of iron(III) oxide is 196 kilocalories per mole. In the thermite reaction, the amount of heat released per mole of aluminum oxide formed equals the difference between these values. The net thermite reaction is considered to be the sum of these two separate reactions.

$$\mathbf{2Al + \tfrac{3}{2}O_2 \rightarrow Al_2O_3} \qquad \Delta H = -399 \text{ kcal}$$

$$\mathbf{Fe_2O_3 \rightarrow 2Fe + \tfrac{3}{2}O_2} \qquad \Delta H = +196 \text{ kcal}$$

$$\mathbf{2Al + Fe_2O_3 \rightarrow 2Fe + Al_2O_3} \qquad \Delta H = -203 \text{ kcal}$$

It is not practical to use aluminum to reduce cheaper metals. However, the thermite reaction is often used to produce small quantities of carbon-free metal. A more important use of this reaction is to reduce metallic oxides which are not readily reduced with carbon. Chromium, manganese, titanium, tungsten, and molybdenum can be recovered from their oxides by the thermite reaction. All of these metals are used in making alloy steels. Uranium, used to produce nuclear energy, can also be reduced by the thermite reaction.

The very high temperature produced by the thermite reaction makes it useful in welding. Large steel parts, such as propeller shafts and rudder posts on a ship or the crankshafts of heavy machinery, are repaired by thermite welding. A mold is formed around the metals to be welded. A mixture of powdered aluminum and either Fe_2O_3 or Fe_3O_4 is placed in a cone-shaped crucible above this mold. A starting mixture of barium peroxide and powdered magnesium is placed on top of the aluminum-iron oxide mixture. Seconds after the starting mixture is ignited, white-hot iron flows out through the bottom of the crucible. The liquid iron fills the preheated mold and welds the broken ends of the steel.

26.7 Uses of aluminum oxide

Bauxite, the chief ore of aluminum, is an oxide. *Corundum* and *emery* are also natural oxides of this metal, and are used as abrasives. Emery is used in emery paper, emery cloth, or emery grinding wheels.

Rubies and sapphires are aluminum oxide colored by traces of other metallic oxides. Synthetic rubies and sapphires are made by fusing pure aluminum oxide in the flame of an oxy-hydrogen blowtorch. In making clear sapphires, no coloring matter is added. Synthetic rubies are colored by adding a very small amount of chromium. Synthetic rubies and sapphires are used as gem stones in jewelry. Because of the hardness of Al_2O_3, these synthetic stones are also used as bearings (jewels) in watches and other precision instruments, and as dies for drawing wires.

Scientists are finding new ways to strengthen and stiffen structural materials. One important development involves monocrystalline strands or fibers of one substance embedded in and held in place by some other material. An aluminum rod containing very hard, strong sapphire "whiskers" is quite unlike ordinary soft, ductile aluminum. Such a structure is six times stronger than aluminum and twice as stiff. These *fiber composites* enable engineers to improve the strength-to-weight ratio of structural materials greatly. See Figure 26-8.

Alundum is an oxide of aluminum made by fusing bauxite. It is used for making grinding wheels and other abrasives. It is also found in crucibles, funnels, tubing, and other pieces of laboratory equipment.

Fig. 26-7. Verneuil flame fusion furnace for synthetic sapphire.

26.8 The alums

Alums are common compounds that usually contain aluminum. They have the type formula $M^+M^{+++}(SO_4)_2 \cdot 12H_2O$. The M^+ can be any one of several monopositive ions but is usually Na^+, K^+, or NH_4^+. The M^{+++} can be any one of a number of tripositive ions such as Al^{+++}, Cr^{+++}, Co^{+++}, Fe^{+++}, or Mn^{+++}. Potassium aluminum sulfate, $KAl(SO_4)_2 \cdot 12H_2O$, is the most common alum. We can see from this formula why alums are sometimes called double sulfates.

Alums are hydrated double sulfates.

All alums have the same crystal structure. This crystal-structure requirement may explain why some monopositive and tripositive ions do not form alums. The alum crystals are hydrated structures in which six water molecules are coordinated to each metallic ion. This coordination number of six for both the monopositive and tripositive ions may restrict the kinds of metallic ions that can form alums.

Fig. 26-8. Cross section of a fiber composite magnified 245 times. The experimental composite shown here consists of sapphire whiskers in a silver matrix.

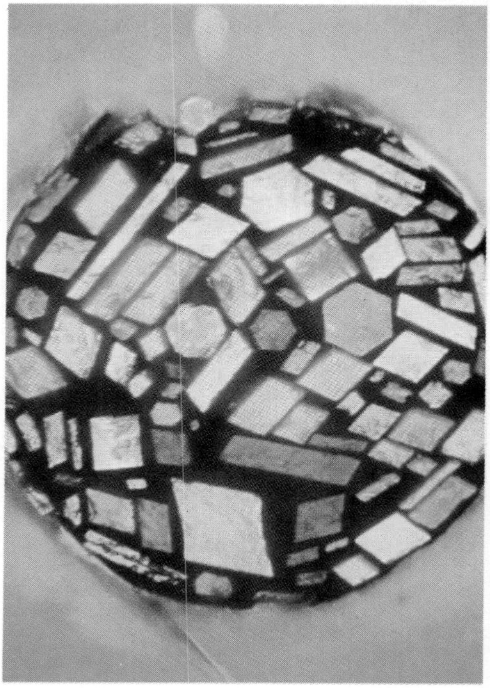

Metalloids

26.9 Boron as a metalloid

The first member of a periodic group often has properties somewhat different from those of the rest of the group. This is true because the outer electrons of its atoms are shielded from the nucleus only by the K shell. The first member of Group III, boron, is a metalloid while all other Group III elements are metals. Boron also has the highest electronegativity of any element in Group III. Boron atoms are small, with an atomic radius of only 0.82 Å. Their valence electrons are quite tightly bound. Thus, boron has a relatively high ionization energy for a Group III element. The properties of boron indicate that it forms only covalent bonds with other atoms. At low temperatures boron is a poor conductor of electricity. As the temperature is raised, its electrons have more kinetic energy and

Fig. 26-9. Boron, a metalloid, is best known as a constituent of borax.

Fig. 26-10. Boron filaments being produced in a research laboratory.

its conductivity increases. This behavior is typical of a *semiconductor*.

26.10 Occurrence of boron

Boron is not found as the free element. It can be isolated in fairly pure form by reducing boron trichloride with hydrogen at a high temperature. Elemental boron is important in monocrystalline fiber research (see Section 26.7), but at present it has little commercial value. Hence, it is seldom seen except in compounds.

Boron filaments, embedded in and held in place by an epoxy plastic, form a very strong and stiff structural material. Such materials are much lighter than structural metals. They are called "advanced fiber composite materials." These composite materials are of great interest to aircraft and aerospace engineers.

Colemanite is a hydrated borate of calcium with the formula $Ca_2B_6O_{11} \cdot 5H_2O$. It is found in the desert regions of California and Nevada. Sodium tetraborate, $Na_2B_4O_7 \cdot 4H_2O$, is found as the mineral *kernite,* also in California. The salt brines of Searles Lake, California, yield most of the commercial supply of boron compounds today. Some hot springs contain small amounts of boric acid, H_3BO_3, in solution.

26.11 Useful compounds of boron

Boron carbide, B_4C, known as *Norbide,* is an extremely hard abrasive. It is made by combining boron with carbon in an electric furnace. Boron nitride, BN, has a soft, slippery structure similar to graphite. Under very high pressure, it acquires a tetrahedral structure similar to diamond. This form of boron nitride, called *Borazon,* has a hardness second only to diamond. It is used industrially for cutting, grinding, and polishing. Alloys of boron with iron or manganese are used to increase the hardness of steel.

Boric acid, H_3BO_3, can be prepared by adding sulfuric acid to a concentrated solution of sodium tetraborate in water.

$$\mathbf{B_4O_7^{--} + 2H_3O^+ \rightarrow H_2B_4O_7 + 2H_2O}$$

$$\mathbf{H_2B_4O_7 + 5H_2O \rightarrow 4H_3BO_3}$$

$$\mathbf{B_4O_7^{--} + 2H_3O^+ + 3H_2O \rightarrow 4H_3BO_3}$$

The acid is only moderately soluble and separates as colorless, lustrous scales. It is a weak acid and is used as a mild antiseptic.

Esters: *see Section 19.11.*

Recall that an acid and an alcohol react and form an ester. Sulfuric acid catalyzes the reaction. Suppose we add a small quantity of methanol and a few drops of dilute sulfuric acid to a sample of boric acid. The solution is warmed and the methanol vapors ignited. The flame has green edges as shown in Figure 26-11. The alcohol vapor contains the volatile ester $(CH_3)_3BO_3$ which is responsible for the green flame color.

$$3CH_3OH + H_3BO_3 \xrightarrow{H_2SO_4} (CH_3)_3BO_3(g) + 3H_2O$$

If the alcohol is ethanol, the ester formed is ethyl borate, $(C_2H_5)_3BO_3$. This green-flame test indicates the presence of boric acid, or more specifically, the borate ion.

Borax is sodium tetraborate with the formula $Na_2B_4O_7 \cdot 10H_2O$. It is used alone and in washing powders as a water softener. Because it dissolves metallic oxides, leaving a clean metallic surface, it is also used in welding metals.

$$B_4O_7^{--} + 5O^{--} \rightarrow 4BO_3^{---}$$

The borates of certain metals are used in making glazes and enamels. Large amounts of boron compounds are used to make borosilicate glass, Pyrex being a familiar example.

When borax is heated, the water of hydration is driven off and the anhydrous salt melts (fuses) as a clear glass. The oxides of some metals impart colors to the borax glass when fused with it. This is the basis for *borax bead tests* for some metals.

Boron combines with hydrogen and forms several boron hydrides, such as diborane, B_2H_6, and tetraborane, B_4H_{10}. Methyl and ethyl groups can be substituted for the hydrogen atoms. These boron compounds have positive heats of formation. When they are oxidized, unusually large amounts of energy are released.

Fig. 26-11. An alcohol flame has green edges when boric acid is present. This serves as a qualitative test for boric acid.

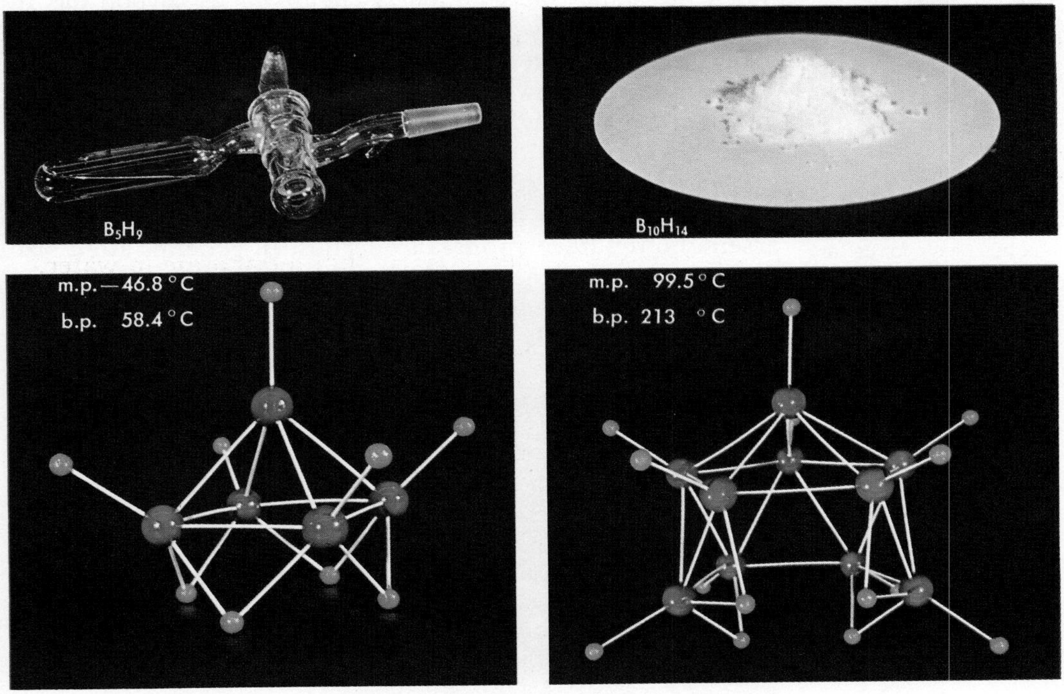

Fig. 26-12. The melting and boiling points of the boranes rise with increasing molecular weight. (left) Pentaborane, B_5H_9. (right) Decaborane, $B_{10}H_{14}$.

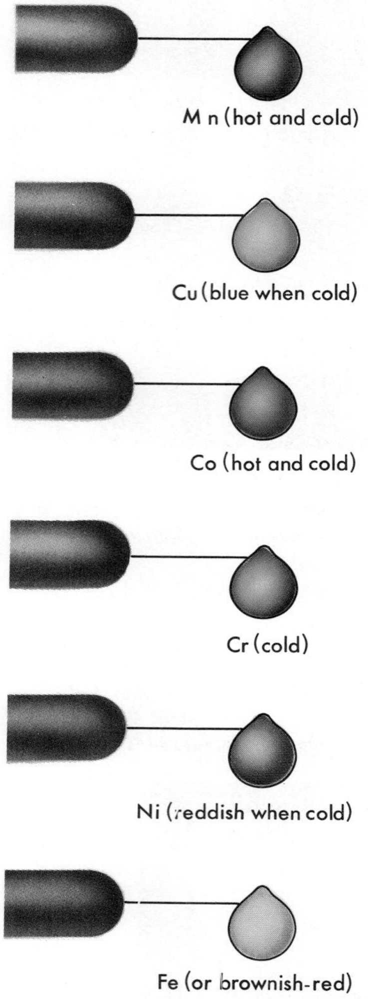

Fig. 26-13. Borax bead tests for certain metals. Color is due to a minute trace of a certain metal.

26.12 Borax bead tests

Powdered borax held in a burner flame on a platinum wire loop swells and then fuses into a clear, glass-like bead. This bead can be used to identify certain metals. The bead is contaminated with a tiny speck of metal or metallic compound and heated again in the oxidizing flame. The metallic oxide formed fuses with the bead. Certain metals give characteristic transparent colors to the borax bead. Such colors serve to identify the metal involved. For example, cobalt colors the bead *blue;* chromium produces a *green* bead; and nickel yields a *brown* bead. Other metals that can be identified by means of the borax bead test are manganese, copper, and iron. The borax bead colors are shown in Figure 26-13.

26.13 Silicon as a metalloid

Silicon atoms have four valence electrons. Silicon crystallizes with a tetrahedral bond arrangement similar to that of carbon atoms in diamond. Atoms of silicon also have small atomic radii and tightly held electrons. Thus, their ionization energy and electronegativity are fairly high. Silicon is a metalloid. It forms bonds with other elements that are essentially covalent. The electric conductivity of silicon is similar to that of boron; it, too, is a semiconductor. Unlike carbon, silicon forms only single bonds. It forms silicon-oxygen bonds more readily than silicon-silicon or silicon-hydrogen bonds. However, much of its chemistry is similar to that of carbon. Silicon has much the same role in mineral chemistry as carbon has in organic chemistry.

Boron and silicon atoms have roughly similar small radii. This similarity allows them to be substituted for one another in glass, even though boron is a member of Group III and silicon of Group IV.

Where relative size of atoms defines properties, elements in diagonal positions in the periodic table (as boron-silicon-arsenic) often have similar properties. In general, atom size decreases to the right from Groups I to VIII. It increases down each group. This balancing effect results in atoms of similar size along diagonals in the periodic table.

Fig. 26-14. Silicon, the second most abundant element.

SUMMARY

Metalloids have properties intermediate between those of metals and nonmetals. They occupy a diagonal region of the periodic table from upper center toward lower right. Metalloids include boron, silicon, germanium, arsenic, antimony, tellurium, and polonium.

Aluminum is distinctly metallic in many of its properties. It is always covered with an oxide surface coating that protects it from corrosion by air and moisture. Aluminum is a self-protective metal. Certain properties tend to place aluminum among the metalloids. It forms negative aluminate ions and some covalent halides, and its hydroxide is amphoteric. Its oxide is ionic, its hydride polymeric.

Aluminum is recovered by electrolysis of the oxide dissolved in molten cryolite. It is a good reducing agent. Aluminum is a low-density structural metal when alloyed with selected elements. Powdered aluminum mixed with iron oxide and ignited reduces the oxide to the free metal in a rapid, violent combustion reaction. This reaction is the thermite process. The aluminum-oxygen bond is a very strong bond. Some natural synthetic oxides of aluminum are very hard and are used as abrasives. Alums are double sulfates with the general formula $M^{+}M^{+++}(SO_4)_2 \cdot 12H_2O$. The most common alum is $KAl(SO_4)_2 \cdot 12H_2O$.

Boron has typical metalloidal properties. It is a semiconductor. The element can be recovered from its trichloride by reduction with hydrogen. Boron carbide (Norbide) is an extremely hard abrasive with a tetrahedral structure similar to diamond. Borax, sodium tetraborate, is the most common boron compound. It is used as a cleaning agent and a welding flux. Boric acid is prepared by reacting borax and aqueous sulfuric acid. When present in an alcohol, boric acid imparts a green color to the alcohol flame. Boron hydrides (boranes) are potentially useful high-energy fuels. Borax bead tests are used to identify cobalt, chromium, nickel, manganese, copper, and iron.

Silicon forms strong bonds with oxygen. Silicon-oxygen lattice chains are similar to carbon-carbon chains. Much of the chemistry of the element silicon is similar to that of carbon.

QUESTIONS

Group A

1. In what materials does aluminum occur in nature?
2. What are the important physical properties of aluminum?
3. (*a*) What is the chemical composition of corundum and emery? (*b*) Write the formulas for these substances. (*c*) What is their important use?
4. Why must aluminum oxide be dissolved in molten cryolite before it can be decomposed by electricity?
5. Why are certain metallic oxides reduced with aluminum rather than with carbon?
6. Write the chemical formulas for four different alums.
7. What is the main source of boron compounds in the United States?
8. Why can borax be used to prepare metals for welding?

Group B

9. What reaction occurs when aluminum is placed in: (*a*) hydrochloric acid solution, (*b*) sodium hydroxide solution?

(*c*) Why is there no reaction when aluminum is placed in neutral water?

10. Write equations to show the net anode and cathode reactions during the electrolysis of aluminum oxide.
11. Why do we import bauxite from the West Indies and South America when almost any clay bank in the United States contains aluminum?
12. What geographic conditions affect the location of plants for the production of aluminum from purified bauxite?
13. Describe the properties characteristic of metalloids such as boron and silicon in terms of (*a*) atomic radius; (*b*) ionization energy; (*c*) electronegativity; (*d*) type of bonds formed; (*e*) electric conductivity.
14. Explain the test for boric acid.
15. When a red crystalline compound was tested by means of a borax bead, the bead turned blue. What metal was probably present in the compound?
16. Borazon, a form of boron nitride, and diamond have similar crystal structures. Is there any relationship between this fact and the similarity of their hardness?
17. (*a*) What is the principal form of boric acid in water solution: molecular or ionic? (*b*) What evidence supports your answer?
18. How does the glass used to make the glass bowl shown on page 547 differ from ordinary window glass? Refer to an encyclopedia for this information.

PROBLEMS

Group A

1. How much aluminum and how much iron(III) oxide must be used in a thermite mixture to produce 10.0 kg of iron for a welding job?
2. What is the percentage of aluminum in sodium alum which crystallizes with 12 molecules of water of hydration?
3. How many liters of hydrogen can be prepared by the reaction of 50.0 g of aluminum and $10\bar{0}$ g of sodium hydroxide in solution?
4. Calculate the percentage of boron in colemanite, $Ca_2B_6O_{11} \cdot 5H_2O$.

Group B

5. A compound contains 96.2% arsenic and 3.85% hydrogen. Its vapor is found to have a density of 3.48 g/liter. What is the molecular formula of the compound?
6. Boric acid, H_3BO_3, is produced when sulfuric acid is added to a water solution of borax, $Na_2B_4O_7$. How much boric acid can be prepared from 5.00 g of borax?
7. Using the following data, show that the atomic weight of tellurium is higher than that of iodine.

Isotope	Atomic Mass	Distribution
Te-122	121.903	2.46%
Te-123	122.904	0.87%
Te-124	123.903	4.61%
Te-125	124.904	6.99%
Te-126	125.903	18.71%
Te-128	127.905	31.79%
Te-130	129.907	34.48%
I-127	126.904	100.00%

chapter 27

NITROGEN AND ITS COMPOUNDS

Having good things to eat depends on nature's bounty—with a generous assist from chemistry. (See Question 18 on page 570.)

Nitrogen

27.1 Occurrence of nitrogen

About four-fifths of the volume of the earth's atmosphere is elemental nitrogen. The earth is the only planet of the solar system where nitrogen is a significant component of the atmosphere. Its presence on earth is directly related to the action of bacteria.

Combined nitrogen is widely distributed on the earth. It is found in the proteins of both plants and animals. Natural deposits of potassium nitrate and sodium nitrate are used as raw materials for producing other nitrogen compounds.

27.2 Preparation of nitrogen

By fractional distillation of liquid air. Air condenses to a liquid if it is cooled enough. Small amounts of liquid air were first produced in France in 1877. Today it is made in large amounts as a first step in separating the various gases of the atmosphere. The physical principles involved in liquefying gases were discussed in Section 12.7.

Liquefying a gas involves compressing the gas and removing the heat of compression. Then the cool compressed gas is allowed to expand without absorbing external energy.

Liquid air resembles water in appearance. Under ordinary atmospheric pressure, liquid air boils at a temperature of about −190°C. Its boiling temperature is not constant, because liquid air is mainly a mixture of liquid nitrogen and liquid oxygen. Liquid nitrogen boils at −195.8°C, while liquid oxygen boils at −183.0°C. The lower boiling point of the nitrogen causes it to separate in the first portions evaporated. Fractional distillation of liquid air is the commercial method for producing nitrogen, oxygen, and the noble gases (except helium.)

27.3 Physical properties of nitrogen

Nitrogen is a colorless, odorless, and tasteless gas. It is slightly less dense than air, and is only slightly soluble in water. Its density shows that its molecules are diatomic, N_2. Nitrogen condenses to a colorless liquid at −195.8°C and freezes to a white solid at −209.9°C.

27.4 Chemical properties of nitrogen

Nitrogen atoms have the electron configuration $1s^2 2s^2 2p^3$. Nitrogen atoms share $2p$ electrons and form nonpolar diatomic molecules having a triple covalent bond.

$$:N:::N:$$

This triple covalent bond is very strong. Even at 3000°C, nitrogen molecules do not decompose measurably. The nitrogen molecule bond energy is very large, 227 kcal/mole. This explains why elemental nitrogen is rather inactive. It combines with other elements only with difficulty. Many nitrogen compounds have positive heats of formation.

At a high temperature, nitrogen combines directly with such metals as magnesium, titanium, and aluminum. Nitrides are formed in these reactions.

The electron-dot symbol for a nitride ion is

$$:\ddot{\underset{..}{N}}:^{---}$$

Nitrogen does not burn in oxygen. However, when nitrogen and oxygen are passed through an electric arc, nitrogen monoxide, NO, is formed. Similarly, NO is formed when lightning passes through the air.

By use of a catalyst, nitrogen can be made to combine with hydrogen at a practical rate. Ammonia, NH_3, is formed in this reaction.

27.5 Uses of elemental nitrogen

An important use of pure nitrogen is in the commercial preparation of ammonia. Other uses of pure nitrogen are based upon its inactivity.

Substances burn rapidly in pure oxygen, but nitrogen does not support combustion. In the air, therefore, nitrogen serves as a diluting agent and lowers the rate of combustion. Its inactivity makes pure nitrogen useful in food processing, metallurgical operations, chemical production, and the manufacture of electronic devices. As a "blanket" atmosphere, it prevents unwanted oxidation in these processes. It is used similarly in the chemical, petroleum, and paint industries to prevent fires or explosions. Electric lamps are filled with a mixture of nitrogen and argon.

Liquid nitrogen is used for freezing and cooling foods to about −100°C for preservation during storage and transportation.

27.6 Nitrogen fixation

All living things contain nitrogen compounds. The nitrogen in these compounds is called *combined* or *fixed* nitrogen. *Any process that converts free nitrogen to nitrogen compounds is called* ***nitrogen fixation.*** Such processes are important because nitrogen compounds in the soil are necessary for plant growth. There are both *natural* and *artificial* nitrogen fixation methods.

1. One natural method is to grow crops that restore nitrogen compounds to the soil. Most crops rapidly remove such compounds from the soil. On the other hand, certain plants called legumes actually restore large amounts of nitrogen compounds. These plants include beans and peas. They have small swellings or *nodules* on their roots. Organisms known as ***nitrogen-fixing bacteria*** grow in these nodules.

In alkaline soil, the nitrogen-fixing bacteria take free nitrogen from the air and convert it to nitrogen compounds. Despite current research, chemists do not yet fully understand how this is done. If these plants are plowed under or if their roots are left to decay, the soil is enriched by nitrogen compounds.

Certain blue-green algae have nitrogen-fixing ability, also.

2. Another *natural method* of nitrogen fixation occurs during electric storms. Lightning supplies energy, which enables some of the nitrogen and oxygen of the air to combine. An oxide of nitrogen is formed. After a series of changes, nitrogen compounds are washed down into the soil in rain.

3. The most important *artificial method* of nitrogen fixation involves making ammonia from a mixture of nitrogen and hydrogen. This ammonia is then oxidized to nitric acid. The nitric acid, in turn, is converted to nitrates suitable for fertilizer.

Fig. 27-1. These black-eyed pea roots have nodules containing nitrogen-fixing bacteria.

Ammonia and Ammonium Compounds

27.7 Preparation of ammonia

1. By decomposing ammonium compounds. In the laboratory, ammonia is prepared by heating a mixture of a moderately strong hydroxide and an ammonium compound. Usually, calcium hydroxide and ammonium chloride are used.

$$Ca(OH)_2(s) + 2NH_4Cl(s) \rightarrow CaCl_2(s) + 2NH_3(g) + 2H_2O(g)$$

The mixture is heated in a test tube fitted with an L-shaped delivery tube, as shown in Figure 27-2. Ammonia is so soluble in water that it cannot be collected by water displacement. Instead, it is collected by downward displacement of air in an inverted container. In what way would moist red litmus paper show when the test tube is full?

2. By destructive distillation of bituminous coal. When bituminous coal is heated in a closed container without air, ammonia is one of the gaseous products.

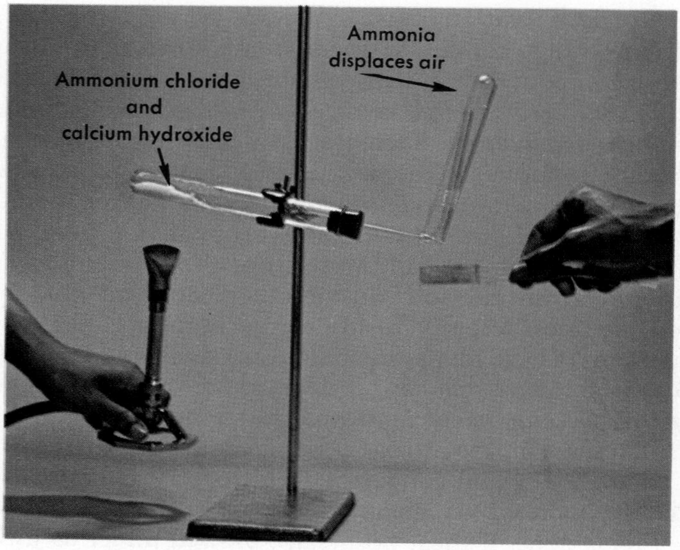

Fig. 27-2. When the mixture of ammonium chloride and calcium hydroxide in the test tube is heated, ammonia is given off. Ammonia is collected by downward displacement of air because it is less dense than air and very soluble in water.

3. *By the Haber process.* Chemists long ago discovered that ammonia is formed when an electric spark passes through a mixture of nitrogen and hydrogen. But the reaction is reversible:

$$N_2(g) + 3H_2(g) \rightleftarrows 2NH_3(g) + 22 \text{ kcal}$$

Only a very small percentage of ammonia is produced at equilibrium. The problem of increasing that percentage was solved in 1913 by Fritz Haber (1868–1934), a German chemist.

Fig. 27-3. A flow diagram of the Haber process. Ammonia gas produced in the catalyst chamber is condensed into a liquid in the cooler. The uncombined nitrogen and hydrogen are recirculated through the catalyst chamber.

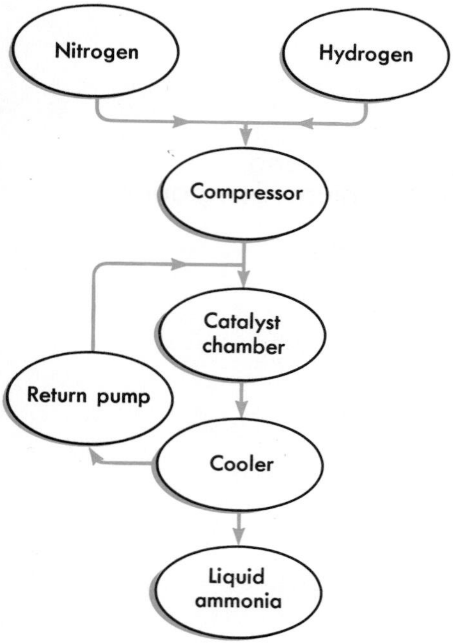

27.8 Physical properties of ammonia

Ammonia is a colorless gas with a characteristic, strong odor. It is less dense than air and is easily liquefied when cooled to the proper temperature. Liquid ammonia, which boils at −33°C at atmospheric pressure, is sold in steel cylinders. The melting point of ammonia is −78°C.

An important property of ammonia is its great solubility in water. One liter of water at 20°C dissolves about 700 liters of ammonia. At 0°C nearly 1200 volumes of ammonia can be dissolved in one volume of water.

27.9 Chemical properties of ammonia

Gaseous ammonia does not support combustion. It does burn in air or oxygen.

$$4NH_3 + 3O_2 \rightarrow 2N_2 + 6H_2O$$

At ordinary temperatures it is a stable compound. However, it decomposes into nitrogen and hydrogen at high temperatures. When ammonia is dissolved in water, most of the ammonia forms a simple solution. A very small part of the ammonia, however, reacts with water and ionizes.

Fig. 27-4. (Left) This farmer is applying liquid ammonia directly to the soil as a fertilizer. (Right) Using household ammonia to clean windows. Household ammonia is a colorless ammonia-water solution to which a dye is sometimes added to make the commercial product more visible and more attractive.

27.10 Uses of ammonia and ammonium compounds

1. As fertilizers. Ammonium compounds have long been used to supply nitrogen to the soil for growing plants. Recently, methods have been worked out for using ammonia directly as a fertilizer.

2. As a cleaning agent. Ammonia-water solution makes a good cleaning agent. It is weakly basic, emulsifies grease, and leaves no residue to be wiped up.

3. As a refrigerant. Ammonia is used as a refrigerant in frozen food production and storage plants.

4. For making other compounds. Great quantities of ammonia are oxidized to make nitric acid, as explained in Section 27.11. It is also used in producing nylon and one type of rayon, and as a catalyst in making several types of plastic. Ammonia is used to make sulfa drugs, vitamins, and drugs for treating the tropical disease malaria. It is also used as a neutralizing agent in the petroleum industry. In the rubber industry, it prevents the rubber in latex from separating out during shipment.

Nitric Acid

27.11 Preparation of nitric acid

Two methods are commonly used to prepare this important acid.

1. From nitrates. Small amounts of nitric acid are prepared in the laboratory by heating a nitrate with concentrated sulfuric acid. The reaction is carried out in a glass-stoppered retort because nitric acid oxidizes rubber stoppers or rubber connectors.

$$NaNO_3(s) + H_2SO_4(aq) \rightarrow NaHSO_4(aq) + HNO_3(g)$$

The nitric acid vapor is condensed in the side arm of the retort and collected in the receiver. The reddish-brown gas nitrogen dioxide, NO_2, is produced because some of the HNO_3 formed

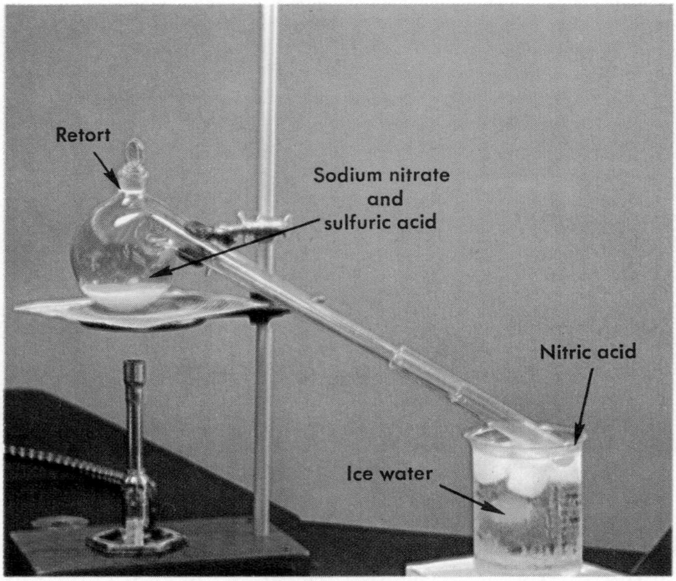

Fig. 27-5. Nitric acid may be prepared in the laboratory by the action of sulfuric acid on sodium nitrate. Some reddish-brown nitrogen dioxide is also formed because of decomposition of some nitric acid. It fills the retort and colors the nitric acid product. Pure nitric acid is colorless.

does decompose. Nitrogen dioxide appears in the retort and contaminates the nitric acid.

2. *From ammonia.* Wilhelm Ostwald (1853–1933), a German chemist, discovered how to oxidize ammonia to nitric acid with a catalyst.

In the Ostwald process, a mixture of ammonia and air is heated to a temperature of 600°C. It is then passed through a tube containing platinum gauze, which serves as the catalyst. On the surface of the platinum, the ammonia is oxidized to nitrogen monoxide, NO.

$$4NH_3 + 5O_2 \rightarrow 4NO + 6H_2O$$

This reaction is exothermic and raises the temperature of the mixture of gases to about 1000°C. Then more air is mixed with colorless nitrogen monoxide to oxidize it to reddish-brown nitrogen dioxide, NO_2.

$$2NO + O_2 \rightarrow 2NO_2$$

The nitrogen dioxide is cooled and absorbed in water, forming nitric acid.

$$3NO_2(g) + H_2O(l) \rightarrow 2HNO_3(aq) + NO(g)$$

The nitrogen monoxide produced is recycled to oxidize it to nitrogen dioxide and absorb it in water.

Fig. 27-6. Flow diagram of the Ostwald process for the oxidation of ammonia into nitric acid.

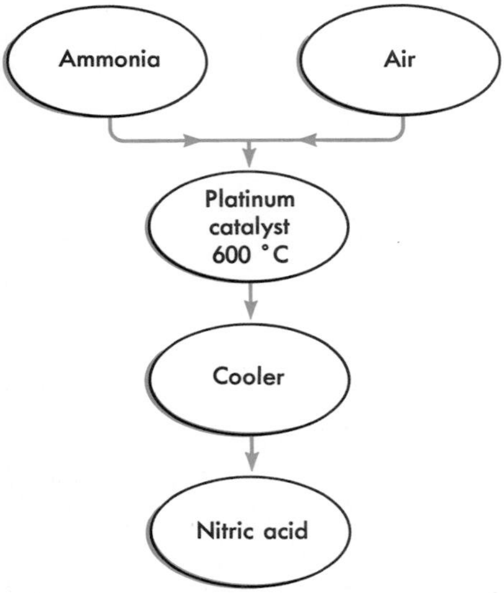

27.12 Physical properties of nitric acid

Pure HNO_3 is a colorless liquid, about 1.5 times as dense as water. It fumes in moist air and boils at 86°C. Pure HNO_3 is unstable. For this reason, commercial concentrated nitric acid is a 68% solution of HNO_3 in water. The solution boils at 120°C.

27.13 Chemical properties of nitric acid

1. Stability. Concentrated nitric acid is not very stable. When boiled, or even when exposed to sunlight, it decomposes to some extent. Water, nitrogen dioxide, and oxygen are the decomposition products.

$$4HNO_3 \rightarrow 4NO_2 + 2H_2O + O_2$$

2. Acid properties. Dilute nitric acid has the usual properties of acids. It reacts with metals, metallic oxides, and metallic hydroxides, forming salts known as *nitrates.*

3. As an oxidizing agent. Nitric acid is a powerful oxidizing agent. It may react as an oxidizing agent in a variety of ways. The concentration of the acid, the acitivity of the reducing agent mixed with it, and the reaction temperature determine what products are formed. Under ordinary conditions, moderately dilute nitric acid is reduced to nitrogen monoxide. If concentrated nitric acid is reduced, nitrogen dioxide is the product.

4. Action with metals. Nitric acid is such a vigorous oxidizing agent that hydrogen gas is *not* produced in significant amounts when the acid is added to common metals. *Very dilute nitric acid* reacts with the active metal magnesium. The reaction forms a nitrate and produces hydrogen.

$$Mg(s) + 2HNO_3(aq) \rightarrow Mg(NO_3)_2(aq) + H_2(g)$$

In reactions with less active metals such as zinc and copper, the hydrogen appears in the water product. In these reactions, the nitrogen of the nitric acid is reduced. Copper reacts with cold, dilute nitric acid as shown by this equation:

$$3Cu(s) + 8HNO_3(aq) \rightarrow 3Cu(NO_3)_2(aq) + 2NO(g) + 4H_2O(l)$$

With concentrated nitric acid, copper reacts as follows:

$$Cu(s) + 4HNO_3(aq) \rightarrow Cu(NO_3)_2(aq) + 2NO_2(g) + 2H_2O(l)$$

Nitric acid does not react with gold or platinum because of the stability of these metals. Very concentrated nitric acid reacts with aluminum and iron very slowly.

27.14 Uses of nitric acid

1. For making fertilizers. About 75% of the nitric acid produced in the United States is used in the manufacture of fertilizers. Ammonium nitrate is the most important nitrate so used.

2. For making explosives. Many explosives are made directly or indirectly from nitric acid. The acid itself is not an explosive. However, some of its compounds form the most

Fig. 27-7. The reactions of concentrated nitric acid with copper and zinc. What is the reddish-brown gas? What salt is in solution in each beaker? The gaseous products are being drawn off to the right by an exhaust system not shown in the photograph. These reactions should be carried out in a hood or where there is similar provision for removing the product gases, since they are poisonous.

Fig. 27-8. An explosion set off in the Gulf of Mexico helps in the search for oil. Shock waves from this explosion, reflected from different geological formations, are detected at different points using seismological instruments. Interpreting the graphs from these instruments reveals formations that could possibly contain oil.

violent explosives known. Among these are nitroglycerin, smokeless powders, and TNT (trinitrotoluene).

3. *For making dyes.* Nitric acid reacts with several products obtained from coal tar, forming *nitro compounds.* One of these coal tar products is benzene. Benzene reacts with nitric acid and forms nitrobenzene, $C_6H_5NO_2$. (See Section 18.21.) Aniline, $C_6H_5NH_2$, is used in making many different dyes. It is made by reducing nitrobenzene with hydrogen.

4. *For making plastics.* Cotton consists mainly of cellulose, $(C_6H_{10}O_5)_n$. When treated with a mixture of nitric acid and sulfuric acid, cellulose forms nitrocellulose plastics. Celluloid, pyroxylins, and many other products are made from nitrocellulose plastics.

SUMMARY

About four-fifths by volume of the earth's atmosphere is free nitrogen. Nitrogen is obtained commercially from the air by fractional distillation. Nitrogen is colorless, odorless, tasteless, slightly less dense than air, and only slightly soluble in water. Elemental nitrogen is rather inactive. Because of this inactivity, nitrogen is used as a blanketing atmosphere to prevent unwanted oxidation. Nitrogen does not readily combine with other elements. The compounds that do form are usually unstable. Nitrogen does not burn, but nitrogen and oxygen do combine and form several oxides of nitrogen. Nitrogen and hydrogen combine and form ammonia under proper conditions. The conversion of free nitrogen to nitrogen compounds is called nitrogen fixation.

In the laboratory, ammonia is prepared by heating calcium hydroxide and an ammonium compound. Using the Haber process, ammonia is made industrially from nitrogen of the air and hydrogen prepared from natural gas. Ammonia is a colorless gas with a distinctly strong odor. It is less dense than air, easily liquefied, and very soluble in water. Ammonium ions act like metallic ions; they combine with negative ions and form salts. Ammonia and ammonium compounds are used as fertilizers. Ammonia-water solution is a good cleaning agent. Ammonia is also used as a refrigerant and for making medicinal drugs such as sulfa drugs and vitamins.

Nitric acid is prepared in the laboratory by heating a mixture of sodium nitrate and concentrated sulfuric acid. Commercially, nitric acid is prepared by the catalytic oxidation of ammonia, using the Ostwald process. Nitric acid is a dense, colorless liquid. Pure nitric acid is not very stable. Concentrated nitric acid is a powerful oxidizing agent. Nitric acid reacts with metals, metallic oxides, and metallic hydroxides. Its salts are called nitrates. Nitric acid is used for making fertilizers, explosives, dyes, and plastics.

QUESTIONS

Group A

1. (*a*) Where can you find elemental nitrogen in large quantities? (*b*) In what kinds of compounds does combined nitrogen occur naturally?
2. (*a*) Which has the higher boiling point, liquid nitrogen or liquid oxygen? (*b*) What practical use is made of this difference in boiling points?
3. What is meant by *nitrogen fixation?*
4. (*a*) What are two natural methods of nitrogen fixation? (*b*) Name an artificial method.
5. Give two reasons why ammonia-water solution makes an excellent window cleaner.
6. Why is a completely glass apparatus used for the laboratory preparation of nitric acid?
7. What condition must be met for the reaction between sodium nitrate and sulfuric acid to run to completion?
8. Write three equations to show the steps in the production of nitric acid from ammonia.

Group B

9. (*a*) Why does compressing a gas raise its temperature? (*b*) Why does a gas become colder when it is allowed to expand?
10. What structural feature of nitrogen molecules accounts for the stability of this element?
11. (*a*) Name three uses for nitrogen. (*b*) For each use, give the related physical or chemical property of nitrogen that makes the use possible.
12. What must be the condition of the soil for nitrogen-fixing bacteria to be most effective?
13. Why might farmers alternate crops of corn and lima beans on one of their fields in successive years?
14. (*a*) Write the balanced equation for the reaction between calcium hydroxide and ammonium nitrate for producing ammonia. (*b*) Write the net ionic equation for this reaction. (*c*) How does the net ionic equation for this reaction compare with the net ionic equation for the

reaction between calcium hydroxide and ammonium chloride? Between sodium hydroxide and ammonium sulfate?

15. Why can zinc be used with either dilute hydrochloric or sulfuric acids for producing hydrogen but not with dilute nitric acid?
16. The equation for the reaction of copper and dilute nitric acid indicates that colorless nitrogen monoxide gas is one of the products. Yet when we carry out this reaction in an evaporating dish, dense reddish-brown nitrogen dioxide gas flows over the rim of the dish. Explain.
17. What is the oxidation number of nitrogen in (*a*) NH_3, (*b*) N_2H_4, (*c*) N_2, (*d*) NO, (*e*) HNO_2, (*f*) NO_2, (*g*) HNO_3?
18. The food display shown on page 561 suggests something about the chemistry involved in the production of these edibles. Write a brief commentary relating chemistry and food production for future generations, and include energy conservation in your discussion.

PROBLEMS

Group A

1. How many grams of ammonia can be produced by the reaction of calcium hydroxide and 15.0 g of ammonium chloride?
2. How many liters of nitrogen and hydrogen are required for the preparation of $2\bar{0}0$ liters of ammonia?
3. If 15 g of HNO_3 is needed for a laboratory experiment, what mass of sodium nitrate is required for its preparation?

Group B

4. What volume, in liters, of nitrogen at STP can be prepared from a mixture of $1\bar{0}$ g of NH_4Cl and $1\bar{0}$ g of $NaNO_2$?
5. How many grams of nitric acid can be prepared from 50.0 g of potassium nitrate of 80.0% purity?
6. (*a*) What mass of copper(II) nitrate can be prepared from 254 g of copper by reaction with nitric acid? (*b*) How many liters of nitrogen monoxide at STP are also produced?

chapter 28

SULFUR AND ITS COMPOUNDS

The industrial progress of America depends heavily upon an abundant supply of bright yellow elemental sulfur. (See Question 20 on page 578.)

Sulfur

28.1 Occurrence of sulfur

Sulfur is one of the elements known since ancient times. It occurs in nature as the free element or combined with other elements in sulfides and sulfates.

The United States is the greatest producer of sulfur. Huge deposits of nearly pure sulfur occur between 500 and 2000 feet underground in Texas and Louisiana, near the Gulf of Mexico.

28.2 The production of sulfur

The sulfur beds in Texas and Louisiana are as much as 200 feet thick. Between the surface of the ground and the sulfur there is usually a layer of quicksand. This makes it difficult to sink a shaft and mine the sulfur by ordinary methods.

The American chemist, Herman Frasch (1852–1914), developed a method for obtaining the sulfur without sinking a shaft. This method uses a complex system of pipes. Superheated water (170°C, under pressure) is pumped into the sulfur deposit. The hot water melts the sulfur, which is then forced to the surface by compressed air. See Figure 28-1.

Fig. 28-1. The system of concentric pipes used in the Frasch process of mining sulfur.

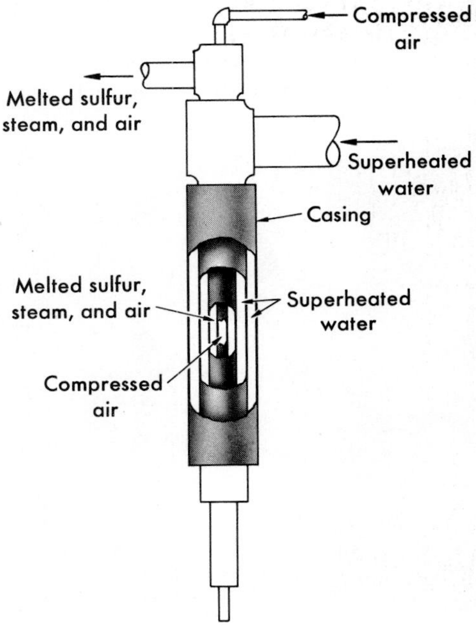

28.3 Physical properties of sulfur

Common sulfur is a yellow, *odorless* solid. It is practically insoluble in water and is twice as dense as water. It dissolves readily in carbon disulfide and less readily in carbon tetrachloride.

Sulfur melts at a temperature of 114.5°C, forming a pale-yellow easily flowing liquid. When heated to a higher temperature, instead of flowing more easily as liquids usually do, it becomes thicker (more *viscous*). At a temperature above about 160°C, melted sulfur becomes so thick that it hardly flows at all. As the temperature rises, the color changes from a light yellow to a reddish-brown, and then almost to black. Near the boiling point the liquid again flows freely. Sulfur boils at 455°C. This unusual behavior is caused by the properties of different allotropes of liquid sulfur. These allotropes are formed at different temperatures.

Allotropy is explained in Sections 9.11 and 17.3.

28.4 Allotropes of sulfur

Sulfur exists in several different solid and liquid allotropic forms. These forms are produced by different arrangements of groups of sulfur atoms.

1. Rhombic sulfur. Solid rhombic sulfur is stable at ordinary temperatures. Crystals of rhombic sulfur are prepared by dissolving sulfur in carbon disulfide and then allowing the solvent to evaporate slowly.

2. Monoclinic sulfur. Sulfur can also be crystallized in the form of long needle-like monoclinic crystals. This allotropic form is prepared by first melting some sulfur in a crucible at as low a temperature as possible. It is next allowed to cool slowly until a crust begins to form. The crust is broken and the liquid sulfur remaining is poured off. A mass of monoclinic crystals is then found lining the walls of the crucible.

3. λ-sulfur. (Lambda-sulfur.) This is the liquid allotropic form of sulfur produced at temperatures just above the melting point of sulfur. It flows easily and has a straw-yellow color.

4. μ-sulfur. (Mu-sulfur.) If λ-sulfur is heated to about 160°C, it darkens to a reddish and then almost black liquid. The melted sulfur becomes so viscous that it does not flow. As the temperature is raised, however, the sulfur begins to flow more easily. The color becomes still darker. Sulfur vapor is produced when sulfur boils at 445°C.

5. Amorphous sulfur. Amorphous sulfur is a rubbery, plastic mass made by pouring boiling sulfur into cold water. It is dark-brown or even black in color, and is elastic, like rubber. A mass of amorphous sulfur soon loses its elasticity and becomes hard and brittle. In room-temperature amorphous sulfur, the changes into successive allotropic forms occur in reverse order. Finally, it once again becomes stable rhombic sulfur. Amorphous sulfur is insoluble in carbon disulfide.

Fig. 28-2. Elemental sulfur is a yellow nonmetallic solid. What other physical property of sulfur is shown by this photograph?

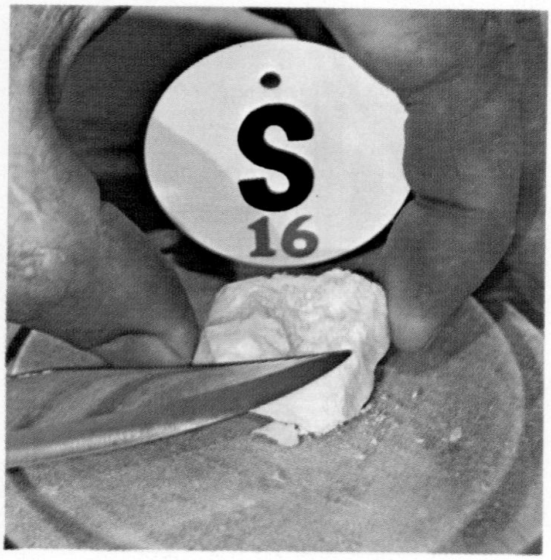

28.5 Chemical properties of sulfur

At room temperature, sulfur is not very active chemically. When heated, sulfur combines with oxygen and produces sulfur dioxide.

$$\mathbf{S(s) + O_2(g) \rightarrow SO_2(g)}$$

Traces of sulfur trioxide, SO_3, also form when sulfur burns in the air. Sulfur can be made to combine with nonmetals, such as hydrogen, carbon, and chlorine. However, such compounds are formed with difficulty and are not very stable.

The formulas SO_3, SO_2, and H_2S indicate that sulfur can have oxidation numbers of +6 or +4 when combined with oxygen, and of −2 when combined with hydrogen. Electron-dot formulas for these compounds are shown below.

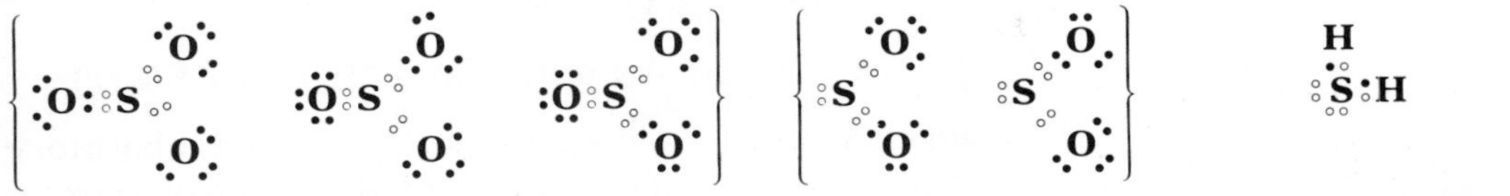

Sulfur Trioxide **Sulfur Dioxide** **Hydrogen Sulfide**

The actual molecules of sulfur trioxide and sulfur dioxide are resonance hybrids of the possible structures given.

Sulfur combines directly with all metals except gold and platinum. Powdered zinc and sulfur combine vigorously. The heat produced when iron filings and sulfur unite causes the whole mass to glow red hot. Copper unites with the vapor of boiling sulfur and forms copper(I) sulfide.

Fig. 28-3. The sudden cooling of mu-sulfur produces amorphous sulfur.

28.6 Uses of sulfur

Sulfur is used in making sulfur dioxide, carbon disulfide, sulfuric acid, and other sulfur compounds. Several million tons are used annually to make sulfuric acid. Matches, fireworks, and black gunpowder all contain either sulfur or sulfur compounds. Sulfur is also used in the preparation of certain dyes, medicines, and fungicides. It is also used in the vulcanization of rubber. (See Section 18.26.)

Oxides of Sulfur

28.7 Occurrence of sulfur dioxide

Traces of sulfur dioxide get into the air from several sources. Sulfur dioxide occurs in some volcanic gases and in some mineral waters. Coal and fuel oil may contain sulfur as an impurity. As these fuels are burned, the sulfur burns to sulfur dioxide. Coal and fuel oil of low sulfur content produce less sulfur dioxide air pollution than similar fuels having high sulfur content.

The roasting of sulfide ores converts the sulfur in the ore to sulfur dioxide. In modern smelting plants, this sulfur dioxide is converted to sulfuric acid.

28.8 Preparation of sulfur dioxide

1. By burning sulfur. The simplest way to prepare sulfur dioxide is to burn sulfur in air or in pure oxygen.

$$S(s) + O_2(g) \rightarrow SO_2(g)$$

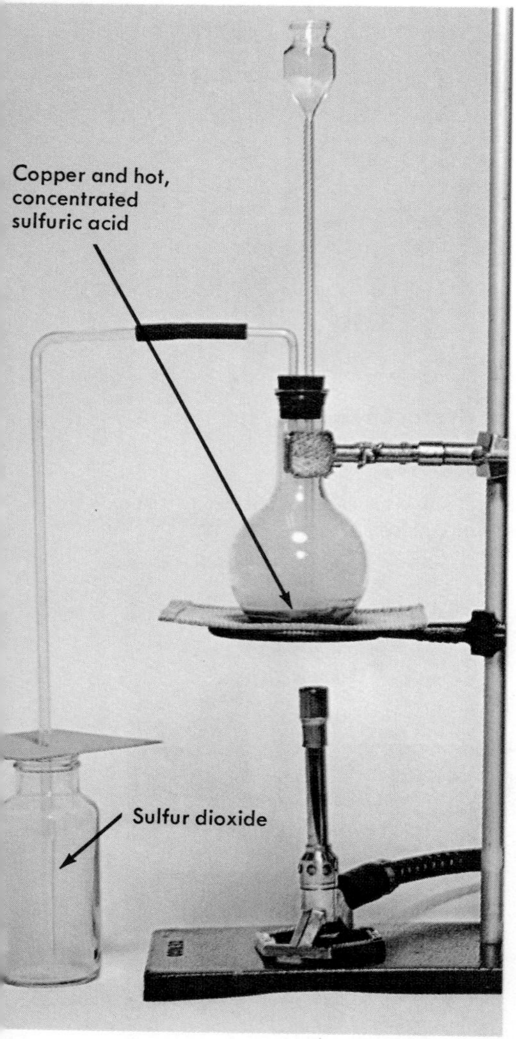

Fig. 28-4. Sulfur dioxide can be prepared in the laboratory by reducing hot, concentrated sulfuric acid with copper. This preparation should be performed in a hood to prevent the escape of sulfur dioxide with its suffocating, choking odor.

2. *By roasting sulfides.* Huge quantities of sulfur dioxide are produced by roasting sulfide ores. The roasting of zinc sulfide ore is typical.

$$2ZnS(s) + 3O_2(g) \rightarrow 2ZnO(s) + 2SO_2(g)$$

Sulfur dioxide is a by-product in this operation.

3. *By the reduction of sulfuric acid.* In one laboratory method of preparing this gas, copper is heated with concentrated sulfuric acid (see Figure 28-4).

$$Cu(s) + 2H_2SO_4(aq) \rightarrow CuSO_4(aq) + 2H_2O(l) + SO_2(g)$$

4. *By the decomposition of sulfites.* In this second laboratory method, pure sulfur dioxide is formed by the action of a strong acid on a sulfite.

$$Na_2SO_3(aq) + H_2SO_4(aq) \rightarrow Na_2SO_4(aq) + H_2O(l) + SO_2(g)$$

Sulfurous acid, H_2SO_3, is first formed. It then decomposes into water and sulfur dioxide (see Figure 28-5).

28.9 Physical properties of sulfur dioxide

Pure sulfur dioxide is a colorless gas with a suffocating, choking odor. It is more than twice as dense as air and is very soluble in water. It is one of the easiest gases to liquefy, becoming liquid at room temperature under a pressure of about three atmospheres.

28.10 Chemical properties of sulfur dioxide

1. *It is an acid anhydride.* Sulfur dioxide is the anhydride of sulfurous acid. As it dissolves in water, it also reacts with the water:

$$SO_2(aq) + H_2O(l) \rightleftarrows H_2SO_3(aq)$$

This reaction partly accounts for the high solubility of sulfur dioxide in water. Sulfurous acid is a weak acid. It turns litmus paper red, neutralizes hydroxides, and forms hydrogen sulfites and sulfites. If exposed to the air, a solution of sulfurous acid reacts slowly with oxygen and forms sulfuric acid.

2. *It is a stable gas.* Sulfur dioxide does not burn. With a suitable catalyst and at a high temperature, it can be oxidized to sulfur trioxide.

$$2SO_2(g) + O_2(g) \rightleftarrows 2SO_3(g)$$

28.11 Uses for sulfur dioxide and sulfurous acid

1. *For making sulfuric acid.* In the chemical industry, great quantities of sulfur dioxide are oxidized to sulfur trioxide. The sulfur trioxide is then combined with water, forming sulfuric acid. (See Section 28.12.)

2. *As a preservative.* Dried fruits such as apricots and prunes are treated with sulfur dioxide, which acts as a preservative.

3. *For bleaching.* Sulfurous acid does not harm the fibers of wool, silk, straw, or paper. Thus, it can be used to bleach these materials. It is believed that sulfurous acid converts the colored compounds in these materials to colorless sulfites.

4. *In preparing paper pulp.* Sulfurous acid reacts with limestone and forms calcium hydrogen sulfite, $Ca(HSO_3)_2$. Wood chips are heated in calcium hydrogen sulfite solution as a first step in paper-making. The hot solution dissolves the lignin, which binds the cellulose fibers of wood together. The cellulose fibers are left unchanged and are processed to form paper.

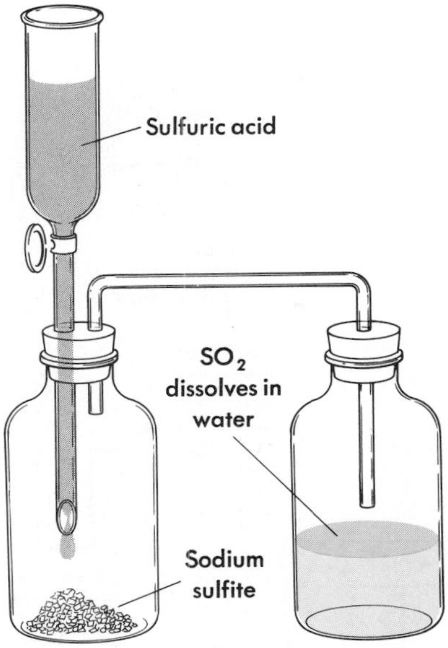

Sulfuric Acid

28.12 Preparation of sulfuric acid

Most of the sulfuric acid produced in the United States today is made by the contact process. In this process, sulfur dioxide is prepared by burning sulfur or by roasting iron pyrite, FeS_2. Impurities that later might combine with the catalyst and ruin it are removed from the gas. The purified sulfur dioxide is mixed with air and passed through heated iron pipes. These pipes contain the catalyst, usually divanadium pentoxide, V_2O_5. This close "contact" of the sulfur dioxide and the catalyst gives the *contact process* its name. Sulfur dioxide and oxygen of the air are both adsorbed on the surface of the catalyst. There, they react and form sulfur trioxide. See Figure 28-6.

The sulfur trioxide is then dissolved in approximately 98% sulfuric acid. Sulfur trioxide combines readily and smoothly with sulfuric acid, forming pyrosulfuric acid, $H_2S_2O_7$.

$$\mathbf{SO_3(g) + H_2SO_4(l) \rightarrow H_2S_2O_7(l)}$$

Pyrosulfuric acid, when diluted with water, yields sulfuric acid.

$$\mathbf{H_2S_2O_7(l) + H_2O(l) \rightarrow 2H_2SO_4(l)}$$

Very pure, highly concentrated sulfuric acid is produced by the contact process.

Fig. 28-5. An acid added to a sulfite forms unstable sulfurous acid, which decomposes into sulfur dioxide and water. This preparation should also be performed in a hood.

28.13 Physical properties of sulfuric acid

Concentrated sulfuric acid is a dense, oily liquid. It contains about 2% water, has a density of about 1.84 g/ml, and a boiling point of 338°C.

When sulfuric acid is added to water much heat is released as the hydrates $H_2SO_4 \cdot H_2O$ and $H_2SO_4 \cdot 2H_2O$ are formed. ***CAUTION:*** *Never add water to sulfuric acid.*

28.14 Chemical properties of sulfuric acid

1. *Its acid properties.* Sulfuric acid is a diprotic acid. It ionizes in dilute water solution in two stages:

$$\mathbf{H_2SO_4 + H_2O \rightleftarrows H_3O^+ + HSO_4^-}$$

$$\mathbf{HSO_4^- + H_2O \rightleftarrows H_3O^+ + SO_4^{--}} \qquad K_i = \mathbf{1.26 \times 10^{-2}}$$

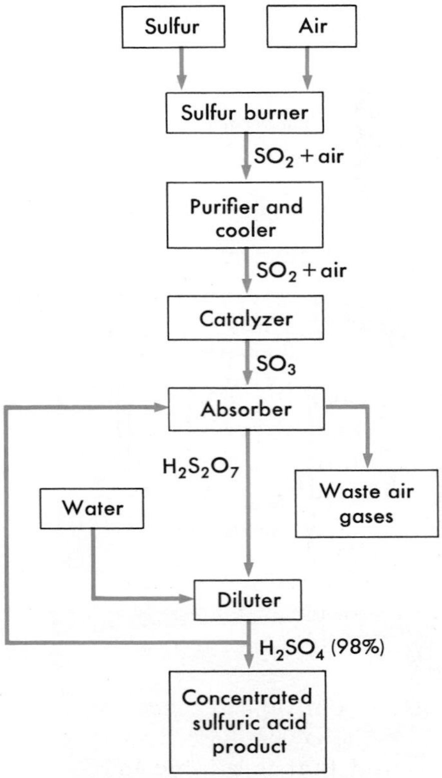

Fig. 28-6. A flow diagram of the contact process for manufacturing sulfuric acid.

At 25°C, 0.1-M H_2SO_4 is completely ionized in the first stage and about 10% ionized in the second stage. Sulfuric acid reacts with hydroxides and forms hydrogen sulfates and sulfates. It reacts with metals and with the oxides of metals. Dilute sulfuric acid is more highly ionized than cold, concentrated sulfuric acid. Thus, the dilute acid reacts more vigorously than the cold, concentrated acid with metals above hydrogen in the oxidizing and reducing agents series. See Table 22-3 for this series.

2. *Its oxidizing properties.* Hot, concentrated sulfuric acid is a vigorous oxidizing agent. The sulfur is reduced from the +6 oxidation state to the +4 or −2 oxidation state. The extent of the reduction depends on the strength of the acid and on the reducing agent used.

3. *Its dehydrating properties.* The strong attraction of sulfuric acid for water makes it a very good *dehydrating* agent. Gases that do not react with sulfuric acid can be dried by bubbling them through the concentrated acid. Sulfuric acid is such an active dehydrating agent that it takes hydrogen and oxygen *directly and in the proportion found in water* from certain substances. It does so, for example, with sucrose, $C_{12}H_{22}O_{11}$, and cellulose, $(C_6H_{10}O_5)_n$, leaving the carbon uncombined. The equation for this process with sucrose is

$$C_{12}H_{22}O_{11} + 11H_2SO_4 \rightarrow 12C + 11H_2SO_4 \cdot H_2O$$

In some commercial chemical processes, water is formed as a by-product. The reaction for making nitroglycerin, $C_3H_5(NO_3)_3$, is such a process.

$$C_3H_5(OH)_3 + 3HNO_3 \rightarrow C_3H_5(NO_3)_3 + 3H_2O$$

The sulfuric acid acts as a dehydrating agent. It absorbs the water as fast as it is formed and thus maintains the rate of the reaction.

***CAUTION:** Sulfuric acid burns the flesh severely.* Sulfuric acid burns are the result of its dehydrating action on the skin. Handling sulfuric acid requires constant care to prevent its contact with the skin.

28.15 Uses of sulfuric acid

Calcium phosphate, $Ca_3(PO_4)_2$, is found in great amounts especially in Florida and Tennessee. This rock phosphate is treated with sulfuric acid (about 4 million tons/year) to make it more soluble. The soluble form is used as *superphosphate* fertilizer.

Sulfuric acid is used also in making other acids, various sulfates, and many other chemicals.

The iron and steel industries consume large quantities of sulfuric acid. The acid removes oxides from the surface of iron or steel before the metal is plated or coated with an enamel.

In petroleum refining, sulfuric acid is used to remove certain organic impurities. The electrolyte in lead storage batteries is dilute sulfuric acid.

Sulfuric acid serves as a dehydrating agent in the production of smokeless powder and nitroglycerin. It is used in making photographic film, nitrocellulose plastics, and rayon. It is useful in producing paints and pigments, cellophane, and thousands of other commercial articles.

SUMMARY

Sulfur occurs in nature as the free element from or combined with other elements in sulfides and sulfates. The Frasch process is used to mine sulfur in Texas and Louisiana.

Ordinary sulfur is a yellow, odorless solid that is practically insoluble in water. It is soluble in carbon disulfide and in carbon tetrachloride. Sulfur exists in several allotropic forms. The solid allotropes are rhombic, monoclinic, and amorphous sulfur. The liquid allotropes are lambda- and mu-sulfur. Sulfur is not very active chemically at room temperature. When heated, sulfur combines with oxygen and forms sulfur dioxide. Zinc, iron, and copper unite with sulfur at elevated temperatures and form sulfides of the metals. Sulfur is used for making sulfur dioxide, carbon disulfide, sulfuric acid, and other sulfur compounds.

Sulfur dioxide is produced by (*1*) burning sulfur, (*2*) by roasting sulfides, (*3*) by the reduction of sulfuric acid, and (*4*) by the decomposition of sulfites. It is a dense, suffocating gas that is easily liquefied and extremely soluble in water. Sulfur dioxide is the anhydride of sulfurous acid. It does not burn and is a fairly stable compound. With a suitable catalyst, sulfur dioxide can be oxidized to sulfur trioxide.

Sulfur dioxide is used for making sulfuric acid and sulfites. It is also used as a preservative, for bleaching, and in preparing paper pulp.

Sulfuric acid is made from sulfur dioxide, oxygen, and water by the contact process. It is a dense, oily liquid that is soluble in water in all proportions. In dilute form, it acts as an acid. When hot and concentrated, it is a vigorous oxidizing agent. It is also a good dehydrating agent. Sulfuric acid is one of the most important chemicals used in industry. Some of its uses are (*1*) in making fertilizer, (*2*) in cleaning metals, (*3*) in petroleum refining, (*4*) as the electrolyte in lead storage batteries, and (*5*) in producing explosives.

QUESTIONS

Group A

1. Where are sulfur deposits located in the United States?
2. (*a*) What is the function of the superheated water in the Frasch process? (*b*) the function of the compressed air? (*c*) Why is this process used instead of more common mining methods?
3. (*a*) What is the odor of sulfur? (*b*) of sulfur dioxide?
4. A pupil prepared some nearly black amorphous sulfur in the laboratory. When it was examined the following week, it had become brittle and much lighter in color. Explain.
5. What are the uses of elemental sulfur?

6. Sulfur dioxide may be found as an impurity in the air. From what sources does it come?
7. Write balanced formula equations for (*a*) a commercial preparation of sulfur dioxide; (*b*) a laboratory preparation of sulfur dioxide.
8. (*a*) What method of gas collection is used in a laboratory preparation of sulfur dioxide? (*b*) What properties of sulfur dioxide determine this choice?
9. What is the principal use for sulfur dioxide?
10. Write balanced chemical equations to show the formation from sulfurous acid and sodium hydroxide of (*a*) sodium hydrogen sulfite; (*b*) sodium sulfite.
11. Why is the contact process for producing sulfuric acid so named?
12. What is the proper method of diluting sulfuric acid?
13. Why are large quantities of sulfuric acid used in the iron and steel industries?
14. Why is a mixture of nitric acid and sulfuric acid used in making nitroglycerin?

Group B

15. Draw electron-dot formulas to show the resonance structure of sulfur dioxide.
16. Is sulfur dioxide easy or difficult to liquefy? Explain.
17. Why is sulfur dioxide so soluble in water?
18. Balance the following oxidation-reduction equations:

    (*a*) $Hg + H_2SO_4 \rightarrow HgSO_4 + SO_2(g) + H_2O$
    (*b*) $Cu_2S + O_2 \rightarrow Cu_2O + SO_2(g)$

19. Give two reasons why boiling concentrated sulfuric acid burns the flesh so badly.
20. It has been said that the industrial stature of a nation can be measured by the amount of sulfuric acid it uses. Explain how this relates to the caption of the photograph on page 571.

PROBLEMS

Group A

1. How many kilograms of sulfur dioxide can be produced by burning 1.0 kg of pure sulfur?
2. What is the percentage composition of H_2SO_4?
3. How many grams of sodium sulfite are needed to produce 1.00 liter of sulfur dioxide at STP by reaction with sulfuric acid?
4. A lead smelter processes $50\bar{0}$ metric tons of zinc sulfide, ZnS, each day. If no sulfur dioxide is lost, how many kilograms of sulfuric acid could be made in the plant daily?

Group B

5. How many kilograms of sulfuric acid can be prepared from 5.00 kg of sulfur that is 99.5% pure?
6. How many liters of sulfur dioxide at 25°C and $74\bar{0}$ mm pressure can be produced by roasting $120\bar{0}$ kg of iron pyrite, FeS_2?
7. (*a*) If $14\bar{0}$ kg of scrap iron is added to a large vat of dilute sulfuric acid, how many kilograms of iron(II) sulfate can be produced? (*b*) How many kilograms of 95% sulfuric acid are required?
8. How many liters of sulfur dioxide at STP can be prepared from a mixture of $10\bar{0}$ g of copper and $10\bar{0}$ g of H_2SO_4?

chapter 29

THE HALOGEN FAMILY

A member of the halogen family works as a lifeguard in all public and private swimming pools. (See Question 25 on page 590.)

29.1 The Halogen Family: Group VII of the Periodic Table The members of the Halogen Family are the colorful, active elements fluorine, chlorine, bromine, iodine, and astatine. Figure 29-1 shows samples of the first four of these elements. Table 29-1 gives some data about them. The Table shows that the atoms of each of these elements have seven electrons in the outer shell. The addition of one electron to a halogen atom converts it to a halide ion having an outer octet of electrons.

Table 29-1

THE HALOGEN FAMILY

Element	Atomic Number	Atomic Weight	Electron Configuration	Principal Oxidation Number	Melting Point (°C)	Boiling Point (°C)	Color	Density, 0°C	Atomic Radius (Å)	Ionic Radius (Å)
fluorine	9	18.9984	2,7	−1	−219.6	−188.1	pale-yellow gas	1.695 g/liter	0.72	1.33
chlorine	17	35.453	2,8,7	−1	−101.0	−34.6	greenish-yellow gas	3.214 g/liter	0.99	1.81
bromine	35	79.904	2,8,18,7	−1	−7.2	58.78	reddish-brown liquid	3.12 g/ml	1.14	1.96
iodine	53	126.9045	2,8,18,18,7	−1	113.5	184.35	grayish-black crystals	4.93 g/ml	1.33	2.20
astatine	85	$21\overline{0}$	2,8,18,32,18,7						1.45	

Using a chlorine atom as an example,

$$:\ddot{\underset{\cdot}{Cl}}: + e^- \rightarrow :\ddot{\underset{\cdot\circ}{Cl}}:^-$$

The halogens are all active elements having a high electronegativity. They are very rarely found free in nature. In the elemental state they exist as covalent diatomic molecules.

Fluorine has the smallest atoms in the Halogen Family and has a strong attraction for electrons. It is both the most highly electronegative element and the most active nonmetal. Because of these properties, fluorine cannot be prepared from its compounds by chemical reduction. It must be prepared by electrolysis.

The other halogens, with increasingly larger atoms, are less electronegative than fluorine. As a result, the smaller, lighter halogens can replace and oxidize the larger, heavier halogens from their compounds. Astatine is a synthetic radioactive halogen.

Table 29-1 shows clearly the regular change in properties that occurs in this family. This change in properties proceeds from the smallest and lightest to the largest and heaviest. You should refer to Figure 5-8, Figure 5-11, and Figure 6-15 while studying Table 29-1. These tables provide ionization energy, electron affinity, and electronegativity data for members of the Halogen Family.

Each of the halogens combines with hydrogen. The great electronegativity difference between hydrogen and fluorine explains why hydrogen fluoride molecules are so polar that they associate by hydrogen bonding. The remaining hydrogen halides have smaller electronegativity differences and do not show this property. All hydrogen halides are colorless gases that ionize in water solution. Except for hydrofluoric acid, these acids are highly ionized in water and are strong acids.

Each of the halogens forms ionic salts with metals. Hence the name *halogen,* which means "salt producer."

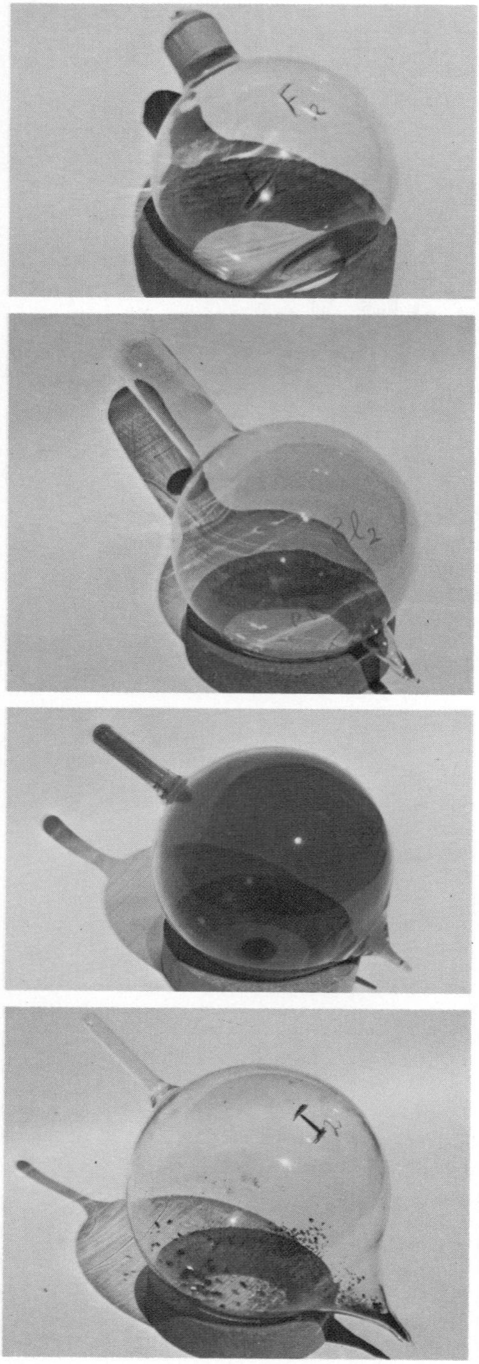

Fig. 29-1. The halogens are colorful elements. Fluorine is a pale-yellow gas; chlorine, a greenish-yellow gas; bromine, a reddish-brown liquid; iodine, a grayish-black crystalline solid.

Fluorine

29.2 Preparation of fluorine

Fluorine is prepared by electrolyzing a mixture of potassium fluoride and hydrogen fluoride. A steel and Monel metal electrolytic cell with a carbon anode is used. The fluoride coating that forms on these metals protects them from further reaction.

Fluorine is the most active nonmetallic element. It unites with hydrogen explosively, even in the dark. It forms compounds with all elements except helium, neon, and argon. There are no known positive oxidation states of fluorine. It forms salts known as *fluorides.* Fluorine reacts with gold and platinum slowly. Special carbon steel containers are used to transport fluorine. These containers become coated with iron fluoride, which resists further action.

29.3 Usefulness of fluorine compounds

The mineral fluorspar, CaF_2, is used in preparing most fluorine compounds. Sodium fluoride is used as a poison for destroying roaches, rats, and other pests. A trace of sodium fluoride, or the less expensive sodium silico-fluoride, is added to drinking water in many areas because fluorides help prevent tooth decay. Fluorides have also been added to some tooth pastes for this reason.

One of the Freons, dichlorodifluoromethane, CCl_2F_2, is used as a refrigerant. It is odorless, nonflammable, and nontoxic. In producing aluminum, melted cryolite, $AlF_3 \cdot 3NaF$, is used as a solvent for aluminum oxide. Uranium is changed to uranium hexafluoride gas, UF_6, for separating the uranium isotopes.

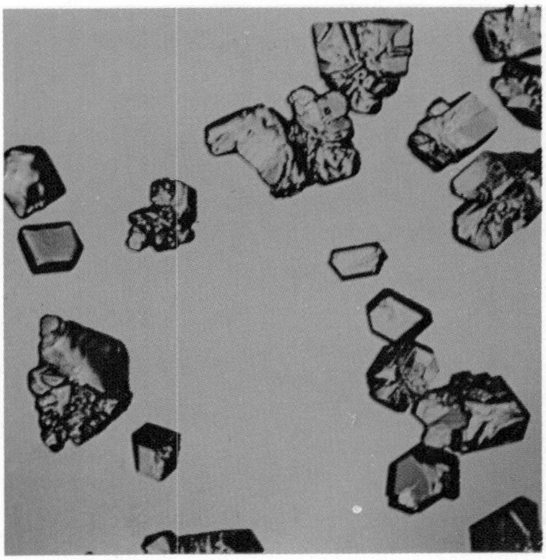

Fig. 29-2. Crystals of xenon tetrafluoride.

Fluorine combines with the noble gases krypton, xenon, and radon. Two fluorides of krypton, KrF_2 and KrF_4, are prepared by passing electricity through krypton-fluorine mixtures. This process is carried out at the temperature of liquid nitrogen. At room temperature the krypton fluorides are not stable and decompose quickly.

Three fluorides of xenon, XeF_2, XeF_4, and XeF_6, have been made. All are white solids at ordinary temperatures; XeF_6 is the most highly reactive. The three compounds each react with hydrogen and produce elemental xenon and hydrogen fluoride. With water, XeF_2 produces xenon, oxygen, and hydrogen fluoride. The other two fluorides react with water and yield xenon trioxide, XeO_3, a colorless, highly explosive solid.

Hydrofluoric acid is used as a catalyst in producing high-octane gasoline. It is also used in making synthetic cryolite for aluminum production. For many years hydrofluoric acid has been used for etching glass. Glassware is given a frosty appearance by exposing it to hydrogen fluoride fumes.

Chlorine

29.4 Wide occurrence of compounds

Chlorine is rarely found uncombined in nature. Elemental chlorine is found in small amounts in some volcanic gases. Chlorides of sodium, potassium, and magnesium are fairly abundant. Common table salt, sodium chloride, is a widely distributed compound. It is found in sea water, in salt brines underground, and in rock salt deposits. Sodium chloride is the commercial source of chlorine.

29.5 Preparation of chlorine

The element chlorine was first isolated in 1774 by Carl Wilhelm Scheele, the codiscoverer of oxygen. The preparation

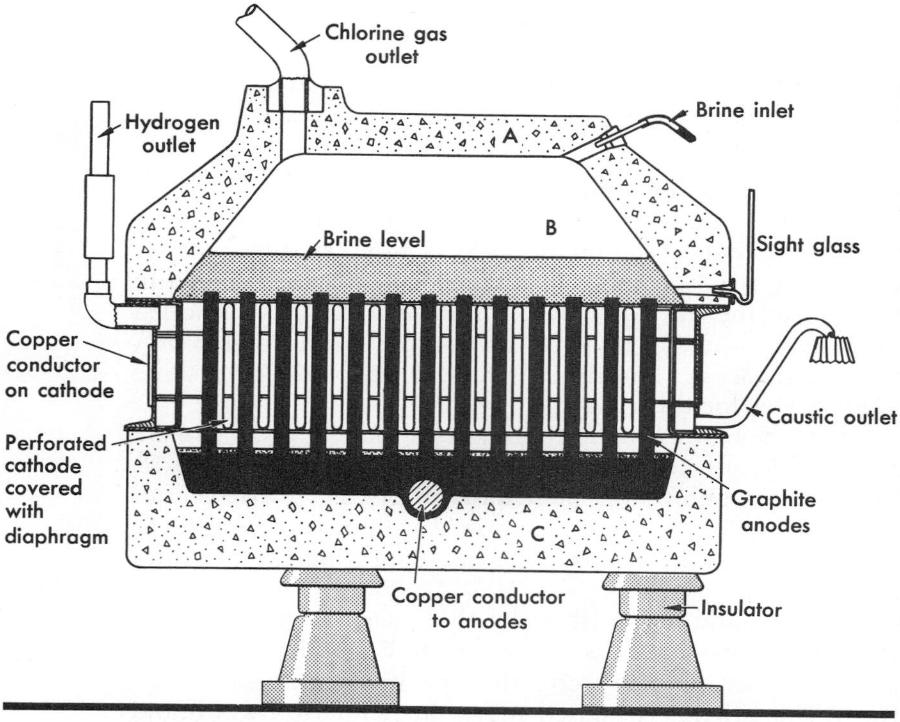

Fig. 29-3. The Hooker cell is used for preparing chlorine by the electrolysis of a solution of sodium chloride.

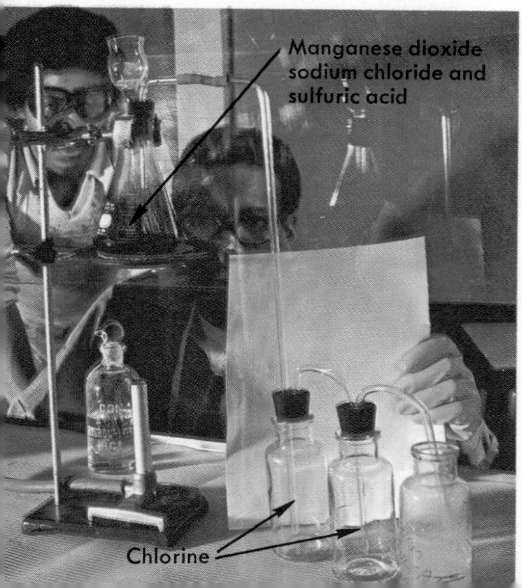

Fig. 29-4. One method of preparing chlorine in the laboratory is by heating a mixture of manganese dioxide and hydrochloric acid. Chlorine is collected by upward displacement of air. The preparation should be performed in a hood.

of elemental chlorine involves the oxidation of chloride ions. Strong oxidizing agents are required.

1. By the electrolysis of sodium chloride. Chlorine is most often prepared by the electrolysis of sodium chloride in water solution. The concentration of the solution is such that hydrogen from the water is released at the cathode, and chlorine is set free at the anode. The hydrogen and chlorine gases are kept separate from each other and from the solution by asbestos partitions. The sodium and hydroxide ions remaining in the solution are recovered as sodium hydroxide.

$$\mathbf{2NaCl(aq) + 2H_2O(l) \xrightarrow{(electricity)} 2NaOH(aq) + H_2(g) + Cl_2(g)}$$

2. By the oxidation of hydrogen chloride. This method involves heating a mixture of manganese dioxide and concentrated hydrochloric acid. The manganese oxidizes half of the chloride ions in the reacting HCl to chlorine atoms. Manganese is reduced during the reaction from the +4 oxidation state to the +2 state.

$$\mathbf{MnO_2(s) + 4HCl(aq) \rightarrow MnCl_2(aq) + 2H_2O(l) + Cl_2(g)}$$

This is the method used by Scheele in first preparing chlorine. It is a useful laboratory preparation.

3. By the action of hydrochloric acid on calcium hypochlorite. Hydrochloric acid is added drop by drop to calcium hypochlorite powder. Chlorine is released and calcium chloride and water are formed.

$$\mathbf{4HCl(aq) + Ca(ClO)_2(s) \rightarrow CaCl_2(aq) + 2Cl_2(g) + 2H_2O(l)}$$

29.6 Physical properties of chlorine

At room temperature, chlorine is a greenish-yellow gas with a disagreeable, suffocating odor. It is about 2.5 times as dense as air and is moderately soluble in water, forming a pale greenish-yellow solution. Chlorine is easily liquefied and is usually marketed in steel cylinders.

When inhaled in small quantities, chlorine affects the mucous membranes of the nose and throat. If inhaled in larger quantities, chlorine is so poisonous that it may cause death.

29.7 Chemical properties of chlorine

The outer shell of a chlorine atom contains seven electrons. There are many reactions by which chlorine atoms may acquire an additional electron and complete the octet.

1. Action with metals. All metals react with chlorine directly. Here are a few specific examples. When powdered antimony is sprinkled into a jar of moist chlorine, the two elements combine spontaneously, emitting a shower of sparks. Antimony trichloride is formed. See Figure 22-1.

$$2Sb(s) + 3Cl_2(g) \rightarrow 2SbCl_3(s)$$

In a similar manner, hot metallic sodium burns in chlorine and forms sodium chloride. See Figure 6-2. Chlorine combines directly with such metals as copper, iron, zinc, and arsenic, if they are heated slightly.

2. Action with hydrogen. If hydrogen and chlorine are mixed in the dark, no reaction occurs. But such a mixture explodes violently if it is heated or exposed to sunlight. The heat or sunlight provides the activation energy. A jet of hydrogen, burning in air, continues to burn if it is inserted into a bottle of chlorine.

$$H_2(g) + Cl_2(g) \rightarrow 2HCl(g)$$

Chlorine does not support the combustion of wood or paper. A paraffin candle, however, continues to burn in chlorine with a smoky flame. In this reaction, the hydrogen of the paraffin combines with the chlorine, forming hydrogen chloride. The carbon is left uncombined.

3. Action with water. A freshly prepared solution of chlorine in water has a greenish-yellow color. If the solution stands in sunlight for a few days, both the color and the strong chlorine odor disappear. The chlorine combines with the water and forms hypochlorous acid and hydrochloric acid. Hypochlorous acid is unstable and decomposes into hydrochloric acid and oxygen.

$$2H_2O(l) + 2Cl_2(g) \rightarrow 2HClO(aq) + 2HCl(aq)$$

$$\searrow 2HCl(aq) + O_2(g)$$

The instability of hypochlorous acid makes chlorine water a good oxidizing agent.

Fig. 29-5. Chlorine has such a great attraction for hydrogen that it can take hydrogen from some of its compounds. A paraffin candle will burn in chlorine. The hydrogen of the paraffin combines with the chlorine and forms hydrogen chloride. The carbon is left uncombined as the smoke.

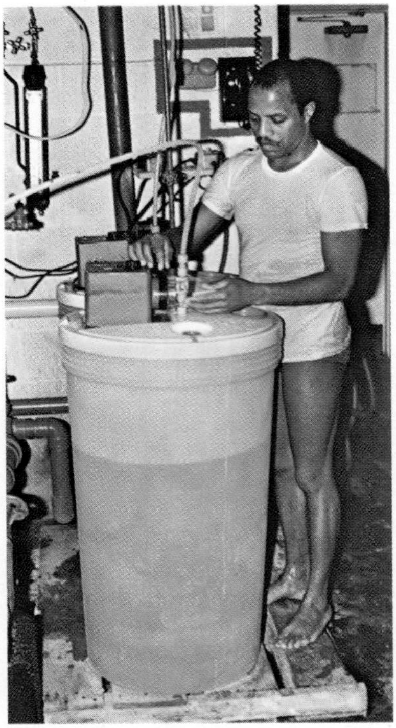

Fig. 29-6. This attendant is regulating the amount of chlorine being added to swimming pool water. Chlorine is used to lower the bacterial content of the water to a safe level.

29.8 Uses of chlorine

1. *For bleaching.* Bleaching solution is usually a solution of sodium hypochlorite. It is made by electrolyzing sodium chloride solution. The released chlorine is allowed to react with the sodium hydroxide being produced at the same time. Sodium hypochlorite is also formed in a reaction between chlorine and sodium carbonate.

CAUTION: Chlorine destroys silk or wool fibers. *Never use commercial bleaches containing hypochlorites on silk or wool.*

2. *As a disinfectant.* Since moist chlorine is a good oxidizing agent, it destroys bacteria. Large quantities of chlorinated lime, Ca(ClO)Cl, are used as a disinfectant.

In city water systems, billions of gallons of water are treated with chlorine to kill disease-producing bacteria. The water in swimming pools is usually treated with chlorine. Chlorine is sometimes used to kill bacteria in sewage as part of the sewage purification process.

3. *For making compounds.* Because chlorine combines directly with many substances, it is used to produce a variety of compounds. Among these are aluminum chloride, Al_2Cl_6, used as a catalyst; carbon tetrachloride, CCl_4, a solvent; 1,1,2-trichloroethene, $CHCl{=}CCl_2$, a cleaning agent; and polyvinyl chloride, the polymer of vinyl chloride, $CH_2{=}CHCl$, a plastic.

29.9 Preparation of hydrogen chloride

In the laboratory, hydrogen chloride can be prepared by treating sodium chloride with concentrated sulfuric acid.

$$\mathbf{NaCl(s) + H_2SO_4(l) \rightarrow NaHSO_4(s) + HCl(g)}$$

This same reaction, carried out at a higher temperature, is used commercially. Under this condition, a second molecule of HCl can be produced per molecule of H_2SO_4 if more NaCl is used.

$$\mathbf{2NaCl(s) + H_2SO_4(l) \rightarrow Na_2SO_4(s) + 2HCl(g)}$$

Another commercial preparation involves the direct union of hydrogen and chlorine. Both are obtained by the electrolysis of concentrated sodium chloride solution. (See Section 29.5.)

A third important commercial source of hydrogen chloride is the chlorination of hydrocarbons. Hydrogen chloride forms as a by-product. (See Sections 18.12 and 18.21.)

Hydrogen chloride dissolved in pure water is sold under the name of hydrochloric acid.

29.10 Physical properties of hydrogen chloride

Hydrogen chloride is a colorless gas with a sharp, penetrating odor. It is denser than air and extremely soluble in water. One volume of water at 0°C dissolves more than 500 volumes of hydrogen chloride at standard pressure. Hydrogen chloride makes a fog with moist air. It is so soluble that it condenses water vapor from the air into tiny drops of hydrochloric acid.

29.11 Chemical properties of hydrogen chloride

Hydrogen chloride is a stable compound that does not burn. Some vigorous oxidizing agents react with it and form water and chlorine. The water solution of hydrogen chloride is a strong acid known as *hydrochloric acid.* Concentrated hydrochloric acid contains about 38% hydrogen chloride by weight and is about 1.2 times as dense as water. Hydrochloric acid reacts with metals above hydrogen in the activity series and with the oxides of metals. It neutralizes hydroxides, forming salts and water.

29.12 Uses of hydrochloric acid

Hydrochloric acid is used in preparing certain chlorides and in cleaning metals. This cleaning involves removing oxides and other forms of tarnish.

Some hydrochloric acid is essential in the process of digestion. The concentration of hydrochloric acid in gastric juice is 0.16 *M*.

Fig. 29-7. A solution used commercially to clean buildings contains hydrofluoric acid.

Bromine

29.13 Bromine from bromides

In the laboratory, bromine can be prepared by using manganese dioxide, sulfuric acid, and sodium bromide.

$$2NaBr(s) + MnO_2(s) + 2H_2SO_4(aq) \rightarrow Na_2SO_4(aq) + MnSO_4(aq) + 2H_2O(l) + Br_2(g)$$

This method is similar to that for preparing chlorine.

The commercial production of bromine from salt-well brines depends on the ability of chlorine to displace bromide ions from solution. Chlorine displaces bromide ions because it is more highly electronegative than bromine.

$$2Br^-(aq) + Cl_2(g) \rightarrow 2Cl^-(aq) + Br_2(l)$$

29.14 Physical properties of bromine

Bromine is a dark-red liquid that is about three times as dense as water. It evaporates readily, forming a vapor which burns the eyes and throat and has a very disagreeable odor. Bromine is moderately soluble in water. The reddish-brown water solution used in the laboratory is known as bromine water.

Fig. 29-8. Bromine can be prepared in the laboratory by heating a mixture of sodium bromide, manganese dioxide, and sulfuric acid in a glass-stoppered retort. This preparation should be performed in a hood.

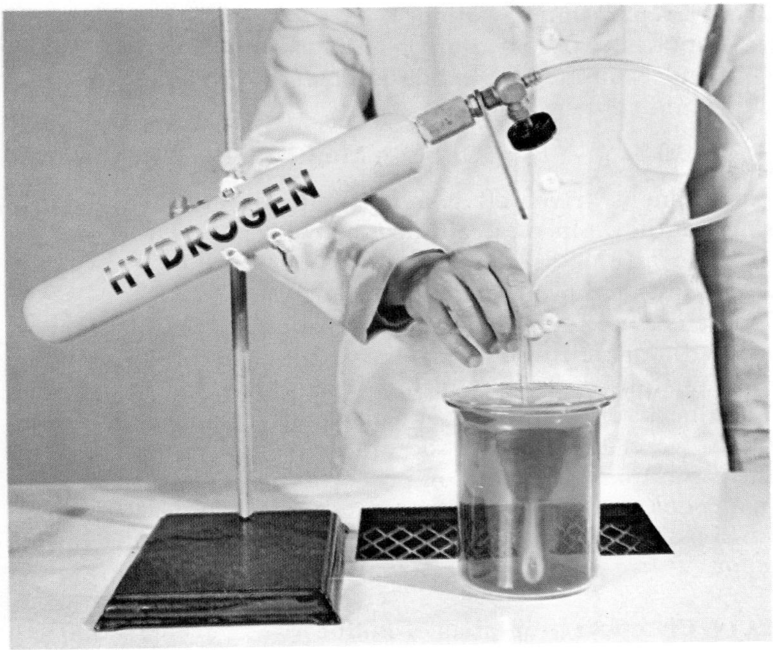

Fig. 29-9. Hydrogen burns in an atmosphere of bromine vapor.

Bromine dissolves readily in carbon tetrachloride, carbon disulfide, and in water solutions of bromides.
CAUTION: *Use great care in handling bromine.* It burns the flesh and forms wounds that heal slowly.

29.15 Chemical properties of bromine

Bromine unites directly with hydrogen and forms hydrogen bromide. It combines with most metals and forms bromides. When it is moist, bromine is a good bleaching agent. Its water solution is a strong oxidizing agent and forms hydrobromic acid and oxygen in sunlight.

29.16 Uses of bromine compounds

Complex bromine-containing organic compounds are added to polyurethane and polystyrene plastics to make them flame retardant. Methyl bromide, CH_3Br, is used by farmers as a soil fumigant. Improved crop yields result from such treatment. Ethylene bromide, $C_2H_4Br_2$, increases the efficiency of lead tetraethyl in antiknock gasoline. Ethylene bromide is also used to control insects in grain and in the soil.

Silver bromide, AgBr, is a yellowish solid. It is highly photosensitive (sensitive to light rays) and is widely used in making photographic film. The bromides of sodium and potassium are used in medicine as sedatives. Such medicines should not be used unless prescribed by a physician. Certain bromine compounds may be used as disinfectants.

Iodine

29.17 Preparation of iodine

The laboratory preparation of iodine is similar to that of chlorine and bromine. An iodide is heated with manganese dioxide and sulfuric acid.

$$2NaI(s) + MnO_2(s) + 2H_2SO_4(aq) \rightarrow Na_2SO_4(aq) + MnSO_4(aq) + 2H_2O(l) + I_2(g)$$

The iodine is driven off as a vapor. It can be condensed as a solid on the walls of a cold dish or beaker.

29.18 Physical properties of iodine

Iodine is a steel-gray solid. When heated, it sublimes (vaporizes without melting) and produces a violet-colored vapor. The odor of this vapor is irritating, resembling that of chlorine.

Iodine is very slightly soluble in water. It is much more soluble in water solutions of sodium or potassium iodide. With these solutions, it forms complex I_3^- ions. It dissolves readily in alcohol, forming a dark-brown solution. It is very soluble in carbon disulfide and carbon tetrachloride, giving a rich purple color.

29.19 Chemical properties of iodine

Iodine is active chemically, though less so than either bromine or chlorine. It combines with metals and forms iodides. It can also form compounds with all nonmetals except sulfur, selenium, and the noble gases. Iodine reacts with organic compounds just as chlorine and bromine do. But since the carbon-iodine bond is not strong, many of the compounds formed decompose readily.

Fig. 29-10. Iodine is prepared in the laboratory by heating sodium iodide and manganese dioxide with sulfuric acid.

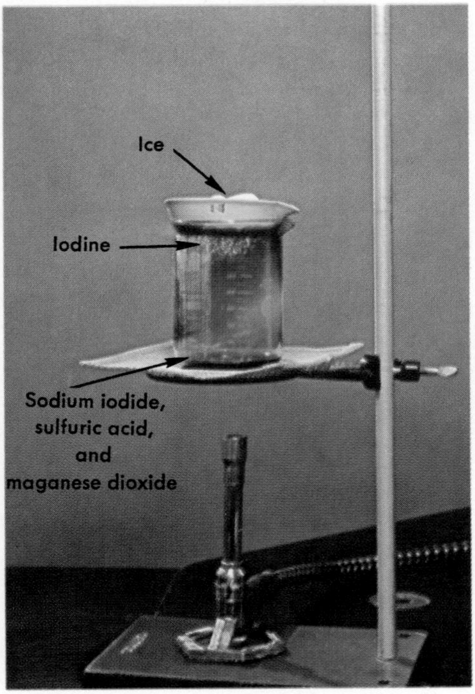

29.20 Uses for iodine

Iodine is most useful as a disinfectant. Iodine complexed (loosely bonded) with certain organic compounds is used as an antiseptic on the skin. Detergents with which iodine is complexed make good combination cleaning and sanitizing agents. Iodine and some iodine compounds are used as catalysts in certain organic reactions.

29.21 Uses of iodides

Silver iodide is a light-sensitive compound used in photographic film. Potassium iodide is added to table salt to provide the iodine necessary for proper nutrition.

SUMMARY

The Halogen Family consists of the highly electronegative elements, fluorine, chlorine, bromine, iodine, and astatine. The atoms of each halogen have seven electrons in the outermost shell. The halogens are very rarely found free in nature. As elements they exist as covalent diatomic molecules.

Fluorine is prepared by the electrolysis of a mixture of potassium fluoride and hydrogen fluoride. The other three common halogens are prepared in the laboratory by oxidizing their binary acids with manganese dioxide. Commercially, chlorine is made by the electrolysis of sodium chloride solution.

Hydrogen chloride is prepared by treating a salt of the acid with sulfuric acid. Each of the hydrogen halides is a colorless gas that is ionized in water solution.

Fluorine compounds are used as (*1*) refrigerants, (*2*) to help prevent tooth decay, (*3*) in aluminum production, (*4*) for separating uranium isotopes, (*5*) in gasoline production, and (*6*) for etching glass. Chlorine is used for bleaching, disinfecting, and for making chlorine-containing compounds. Bromine compounds are used (*1*) to make plastics flame retardant, (*2*) in agriculture, (*3*) in antiknock gasoline, (*4*) as disinfectants, (*5*) in medicine, and (*6*) in photography. Iodine is used as a disinfectant and in synthesizing organic compounds, while iodides are used in photography and as a nutritional supplement.

QUESTIONS

Group A

1. Why are the halogens very rarely found in nature as free elements?
2. List the halogens in order of increasing activity.
3. What does the term *halogen* mean?
4. What kind of container must be used for fluorine?
5. What are the most important uses for hydrofluoric acid?
6. (*a*) What compound is the commercial source of chlorine? (*b*) For what other element is this compound the commercial source?
7. (*a*) Write the equation for the laboratory preparation of chlorine from manganese dioxide and hydrochloric acid. (*b*) Assign oxidation numbers and tell which element is oxidized and which element is reduced.
8. Describe the effects of chlorine on the body.
9. (*a*) List the physical and chemical properties of hydrogen chloride that must be considered in choosing a method of collecting this gas in the laboratory. (*b*) Which method of collection would you choose for a gas with this combination of properties?
10. (*a*) Write the ionic equation for the reaction involved in extracting bromine from salt-well brines. (*b*) What type of reaction is this?
11. List the important physical properties of bromine.
12. Write an equation using electron-dot symbols for the formation of an iodide ion from an iodine atom.
13. Write balanced formula equations for the following:
    (*a*) zinc + chlorine →
    (*b*) calcium + fluorine →
    (*c*) nickel + bromine →
    (*d*) silver + iodine →

Group B

14. If a reaction occurs, complete and balance the following ionic equations.

(*a*) $Br^- + F_2 \rightarrow$
(*b*) $I^- + Br_2 \rightarrow$
(*c*) $F^- + Br_2 \rightarrow$
(*d*) $Cl^- + I_2 \rightarrow$
(*e*) $Cl^- + F_2 \rightarrow$

15. Fluorine does not exhibit any positive oxidation state. Why?
16. Water reacts with xenon difluoride and yields xenon, oxygen, and hydrogen fluoride. (*a*) Write an equation for this reaction. (*b*) Assign oxidation numbers to each element, and balance the equation by a method used to balance oxidation-reduction equations.
17. What properties does dichlorodifluoromethane have that make it useful as a refrigerant?
18. Why must the hydrogen, chlorine, and sodium hydroxide produced in a Hooker cell be kept separated from each other?
19. (*a*) For which does chlorine have greater attraction, carbon or hydrogen? (*b*) What experimental evidence can you give to support your answer?
20. (*a*) Why is freshly prepared chlorine water greenish-yellow in color? (*b*) Why does it become colorless after standing in sunlight?
21. Compare the colors of (*a*) solid iodine; (*b*) iodine in alcohol; (*c*) iodine in carbon tetrachloride; (*d*) iodine vapor.
22. Hydrogen forms binary compounds with each of the four common halogens. (*a*) Write the formulas you would expect for these compounds. (*b*) From electronegativity differences, compare the ionic characters of the bonds in each of these compounds. (*c*) Write equations for the reactions you would expect each to have with water.
23. The chemical reactions between water molecules and molecules of the hydrogen halides are reversible. (*a*) Qualitatively, at equilibrium, what are the relative concentrations of the particles involved? (*b*) What does this indicate about the relative stability of the hydrogen halide molecules compared with the stability of the ions that can be formed from them?
24. Why are sodium chloride and calcium chloride ionic salts, while aluminum chloride is molecular?
25. Which of the halogens is referred to in the caption of the swimming pool scene on page 579, and what is it protecting swimmers against?

PROBLEMS

Group A

1. What mass of sodium hydroxide is formed during the production of $71\bar{0}$ kg of chlorine by the electrolysis of sodium chloride?
2. Bromine (10.0 g) is needed for an experiment. How many grams of sodium bromide are required to produce this bromine?
3. Chlorine reacts with calcium hydroxide and produces bleaching powder, $Ca(ClO)Cl$, and water. (*a*) What mass of calcium hydroxide is required for making $25\bar{0}$ g of bleaching powder? (*b*) What mass of chlorine is also required?
4. How many grams of zinc chloride can be produced from 11.2 liters of chlorine at STP?

Group B

5. What is the percentage of bromine in ethylene bromide, $C_2H_4Br_2$?
6. How many liters of chlorine at STP can be obtained from 468 g of sodium chloride by electrolysis?
7. A laboratory experiment requires five $25\bar{0}$-ml bottles of chlorine, measured at 27°C and $75\bar{0}$ mm pressure. What volume of 38% hydrochloric acid (density 1.20 g/ml) and what mass of manganese dioxide will be required?

chapter 30

RADIO-ACTIVITY

The smaller the particle, the larger the equipment needed to track it down. (See Question 41 on page 611.)

Natural Radioactivity

30.1 Discovery of radioactivity

In 1896, the French scientist Henri Becquerel (bek-*rel*) (1852–1908) was studying the properties of certain minerals. He was particularly interested in their ability to *fluoresce* (give off visible light after being exposed to sunlight). Among these minerals was a sample of uranium ore. By accident, Becquerel found that uranium ore gives off invisible rays. He discovered that these rays penetrate the lightproof covering of a photographic plate and affect the film as if it had been exposed to light rays directly. Substances that give off such invisible rays are *radioactive,* and the property is called *radioactivity.* ***Radioactivity*** *is the spontaneous breakdown of an unstable atomic nucleus with the release of particles and rays.*

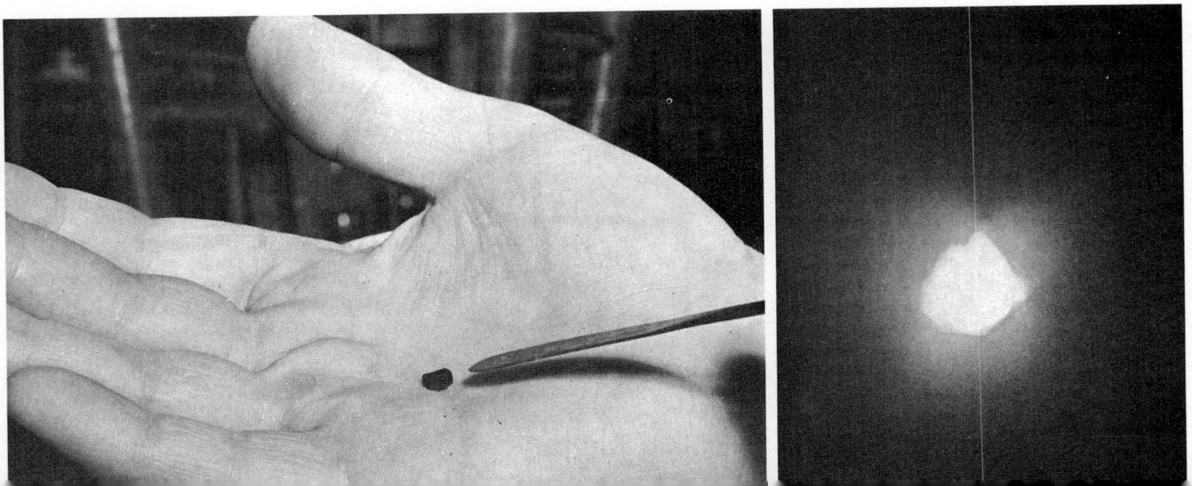

Fig. 30-1. (Left) A fragment of metallic uranium, one of the radioactive elements; (right) a photograph produced when radiation from the same fragment of uranium penetrated the light-tight wrappings of a photographic plate.

Fig. 30-2. The activity of a radioactive material may be measured by the speed with which it discharges a goldleaf electroscope like this one. The material to be tested is placed in the hinged drawer at the bottom.

30.2 Discovery of radium

Becquerel was very interested in the source of radioactivity. At his suggestion, Pierre (1859–1906) and Marie (1867–1934) Curie began to investigate the properties of uranium and its ores. They soon learned that uranium and uranium compounds are mildly radioactive. But they also discovered that one uranium ore (pitchblende) had four times the amount of radioactivity expected on the basis of its uranium content.

In 1898, the Curies discovered two new radioactive metallic elements in pitchblende. These elements, *polonium* and *radium,* accounted for the high radioactivity of pitchblende. Radium is more than 1,000,000 times as radioactive as the same mass of uranium.

Radium is always found in uranium ores. However, it never occurs in such ores in a greater proportion than 1 part of radium to 3×10^6 parts of uranium. The reason for this proportion will be explained in Section 30.7. The production of radium from uranium ore is a long, difficult, and costly procedure. Radium is usually marketed as radium bromide rather than as elemental radium.

30.3 Properties of radium

Radium is the element of highest atomic weight in Group II of the periodic table. Its physical properties were listed in Table 24-1. It is the least electronegative and thus most metallic member of its group. Radium has chemical properties similar to those of barium.

In the expression radium-226, recall that 226 is the mass number of the nuclide. See Section 3.6.

Radium is important not because of its physical or chemical properties but because of its radioactivity. Radium-226 is a naturally occurring radioactive nuclide. Because of its radioactivity, radium-226 and its compounds have several unusual properties. These properties are also observed in other radioactive elements. They include the following:

1. *They affect the light-sensitive emulsion on a photographic film.* Photographic film may be wrapped in heavy black paper and stored in the dark. Even so, radiations from radioactive elements penetrate the wrapping. They affect the film in the same way that light does when the film is exposed to it. When the film is developed, a black spot shows up on the negative where the invisible radiation struck it. The rays from radioactive elements penetrate paper, wood, flesh, and *thin* sheets of metal.

2. *They produce an electric charge in the surrounding air.* The radiation from radioactive elements ionizes the molecules of the gases in the air surrounding it. These ionized molecules conduct electric charges away from the knob of a charged electroscope, thus discharging it. The activity of a radium compound can be measured by the rate at which it discharges an electroscope. Similarly, the radiation given off

by radioactive elements ionizes the low pressure gas in the tube of a Geiger counter. Electricity thus passes through the tube for an instant. The passage of electricity may be registered as a "click" in a set of earphones.

2. They produce fluorescence with certain other compounds. A small quantity of radium bromide added to zinc sulfide causes the zinc sulfide to glow. Since the glow is visible in the dark, the mixture is used in making luminous paint.

4. Their radiations have special physiological effects. The radiation from radium can destroy the germinating power of seed. It can kill bacteria or animals. People who work with radium may be severely burned by the rays that it emits. Such burns heal slowly and can be fatal. However, controlled radiations from radioactive materials are used in the treatment of cancer and certain skin diseases.

5. They undergo radioactive decay. The atoms of all radioactive elements steadily decay into simpler atoms as they release radiation. For example, one half of any number of radium-226 atoms decays into simpler atoms in 1620 years. One half of what remains, or one fourth of the original atoms, decays in the next 1620 years. One half of what is left, or one eighth of the original atoms, decays in the next 1620 years, and so on. This period of 1620 years is called the *half-life of radium-226.* ***Half-life*** *is the length of time during which half of a given number of atoms of a radioactive nuclide decays.* Each radioactive nuclide has its characteristic half-life.

There is some evidence that the half-life of a nuclide can be altered slightly by large changes in its environment. Some of these changes are very low temperature, high pressure, or large variations in a surrounding electric field. Somewhat larger alteration of the half-life of certain nuclides has been found when the decaying nucleus and its valence electrons interact.

30.4 Other natural radioactive elements

The radioactive elements known to Becquerel were uranium and thorium. We have already noted that the Curies discovered two more, polonium and radium. Since that time the natural radioactive nuclides have been identified. See Table 30-1. All nuclides of the elements beyond bismuth in the periodic table are radioactive. However, only polonium, radon, radium, actinium, thorium, protactinium, and uranium have any natural radioactive nuclides. The rest of the elements beyond bismuth have only radioactive nuclides that have been artificially produced.

One important natural radioactive nuclide is the noble gas radon-222. Radon-222 is given off when radium atoms decay. It is collected in tubes and used instead of radium for the treatment of disease.

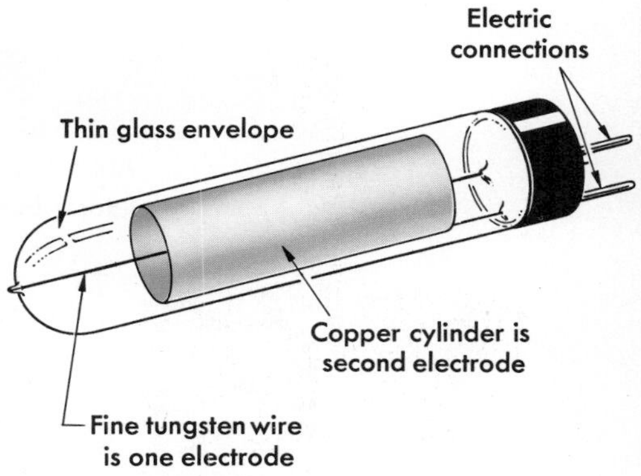

Fig. 30-3. A diagram showing the construction of a Geiger-Müller counter tube. Radiation passing through the tube ionizes the gas it contains and enables current to flow.

Fig. 30-4. A uranium prospector using a Geiger counter in his exploration.

Table 30-1

NATURAL RADIOACTIVE NUCLIDES WITH ATOMIC NUMBERS LESS THAN 83

Nuclide	Abundance in Natural Element (%)	Half-life (years)	Nuclide	Abundance in Natural Element (%)	Half-life (years)
$^{40}_{19}K$	0.0118	1.3×10^{9}	$^{148}_{62}Sm$	11.24	1.2×10^{13}
$^{48}_{20}Ca$	0.18	2×10^{16}	$^{149}_{62}Sm$	13.83	4×10^{14}
$^{50}_{23}V$	0.24	6×10^{14}	$^{152}_{64}Gd$	0.200	1.1×10^{14}
$^{87}_{37}Rb$	27.85	4.7×10^{10}	$^{176}_{71}Lu$	2.59	2.1×10^{10}
$^{115}_{49}In$	95.72	6×10^{14}	$^{174}_{72}Hf$	0.18	4.3×10^{15}
$^{138}_{57}La$	0.089	1.1×10^{11}	$^{187}_{75}Re$	62.93	7×10^{10}
$^{142}_{58}Ce$	11.07	5×10^{15}	$^{190}_{78}Pt$	0.0127	7×10^{11}
$^{144}_{60}Nd$	23.85	5×10^{15}	$^{192}_{78}Pt$	0.78	10^{15}
$^{147}_{62}Sm$	14.97	1.1×10^{11}	$^{204}_{82}Pb$	1.48	1.4×10^{19}

30.5 Nature of the radiation

The radiation given off by such radioactive elements as uranium, thorium, and radium is complex. It consists of three different kinds of particles and rays.

1. The α (alpha) particles are helium nuclei. Their mass is nearly four times that of a protium atom. They have a +2 charge and move at speeds that are near one-tenth the speed of light. They have low penetrating ability mainly because of their relatively low speed. A thin sheet of aluminum foil or a sheet of paper stops them. However, they burn flesh and ionize air easily.

Electrons are described in Section 3.4.

2. The β (beta) particles are electrons. They travel at speeds near the speed of light, with penetrating ability about 100 times greater than that of alpha particles.

Electromagnetic radiation is explained in Section 4.2.

3. The γ (gamma) rays are high-energy electromagnetic waves. They are the same kind of radiation as visible light but of much shorter wavelength and higher frequency. Gamma rays can be produced when nuclear particles undergo transitions in nuclear energy levels. They are the most penetrating of the radiations given off by radioactive elements. Alpha and beta particles are seldom, if ever, given off at the same time from the same nucleus. Gamma rays, however, are often produced along with either alpha or beta particles.

Figure 30-5 shows the effect of a powerful magnetic field

on the complex radiation given off by a small particle of radioactive material. The field is perpendicular to the plane of the paper. The heavy alpha particles are deflected slightly in one direction. The lighter beta particles are deflected more sharply in the opposite direction. The gamma rays, being uncharged, are not affected by the magnet.

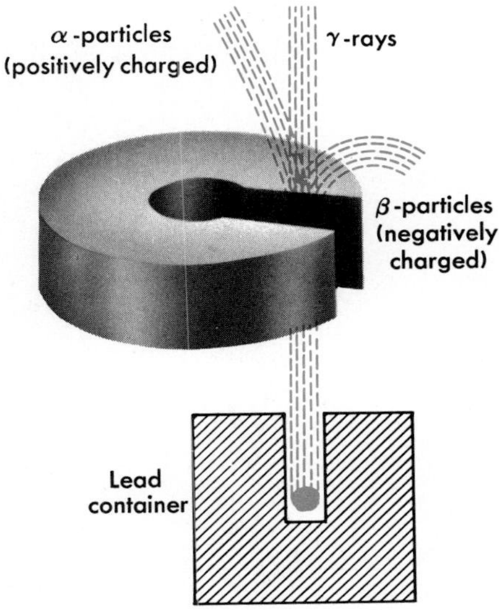

Fig. 30-5. The effect of a magnet on the different types of radiations. The north pole of the magnet is toward the reader and the south pole is away from the reader.

30.6 Decay of atoms of radioactive elements

Radioactive nuclides decay spontaneously, yielding energy. At first it was believed that they did not lose mass and would give off energy forever. However, more careful investigation proved that radioactive materials do lose mass slowly. The presence of electrons and helium nuclei among the radiations is evidence for the loss of mass.

A long series of experiments has shown that this energy results from the decay of nuclei of radium-226 and other radioactive nuclides. Alpha and beta particles are products of such nuclear decay. Certain heavy nuclei break down spontaneously into simpler and lighter nuclei, releasing enormous quantities of energy.

30.7 A series of related radioactive nuclides

All naturally occurring radioactive nuclides with atomic numbers greater than 83 belong to one of three series of related nuclides. The heaviest nuclides of these series are called *parent* nuclides. They are, respectively, uranium-238, uranium-235, and thorium-232. Since radium-226 is in the series

Fig. 30-6. The parent nuclide of the uranium decay series is $^{238}_{92}U$. The final nuclide of the series is $^{206}_{82}Pb$.

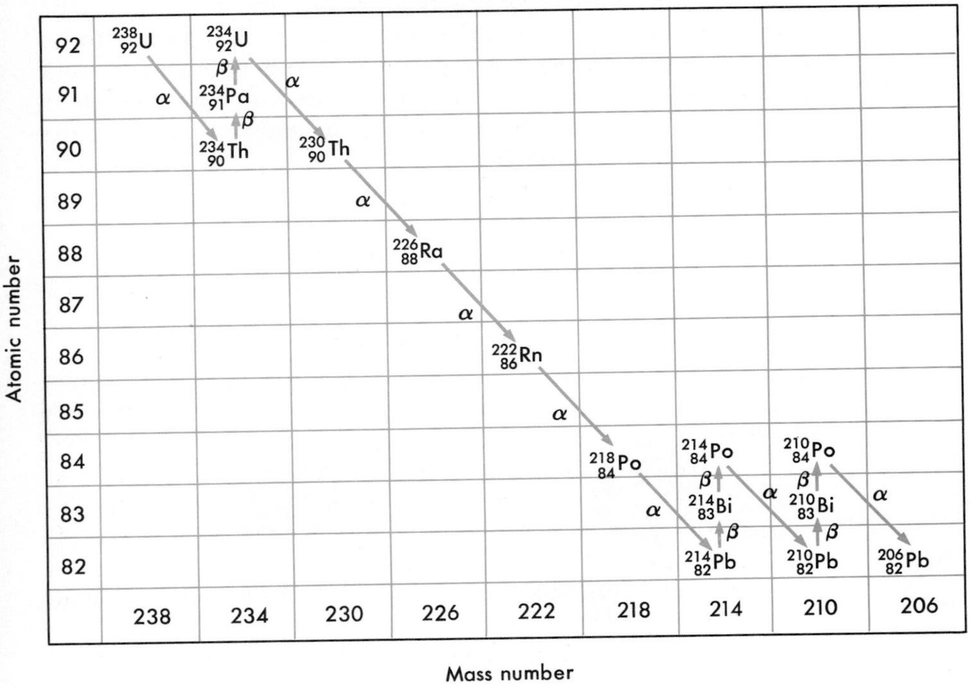

that has uranium-238 as its parent, let us trace this decay series. The various nuclear changes are charted in Figure 30-6.

The nucleus of a uranium-238 atom contains 92 protons (the atomic number of uranium is 92). It has a mass number (number of protons + number of neutrons) of 238. As this nucleus decays, it emits an alpha particle which becomes an atom of helium when its positive charge is neutralized. An alpha particle has a mass number of 4. Since it contains two protons, it has an atomic number of 2. The remainder of the uranium nucleus thus has an atomic number of 90 and a mass number of 234. This nuclide is an isotope of thorium. The *nuclear equation* for this *transmutation reaction* can be written as follows:

$$^{238}_{92}\mathbf{U} \rightarrow {}^{234}_{90}\mathbf{Th} + {}^{4}_{2}\mathbf{He}$$

*A **transmutation** is a change in the identity of a nucleus because of a change in the number of its protons.* Since the above equation is a nuclear equation, only nuclei are represented. The superscript is the mass number. The subscript is the atomic number. Alpha particles are represented as helium nuclei, $^{4}_{2}He$. The total of the mass numbers on the left side of the equation must equal the total of the mass numbers on the right side of the equation. The total of the atomic numbers on the left must equal the total of the atomic numbers on the right.

The half-life of $^{234}_{90}Th$ is about 24 days. It decays by giving off beta particles. The loss of a beta particle from a nucleus increases the number of positive charges in the nucleus (the atomic number) by one. The beta particle is believed to be formed by the change of a neutron into a proton and beta particle (electron). Since the mass of the lost beta particle is so small that it may be neglected, the mass number of the resulting nuclide stays the same.

$$^{234}_{90}\mathbf{Th} \rightarrow {}^{234}_{91}\mathbf{Pa} + {}^{0}_{-1}\mathbf{e}$$

Fig. 30-7. This diagram shows successive alpha and beta particle emissions in the decay of $^{238}_{92}U$.

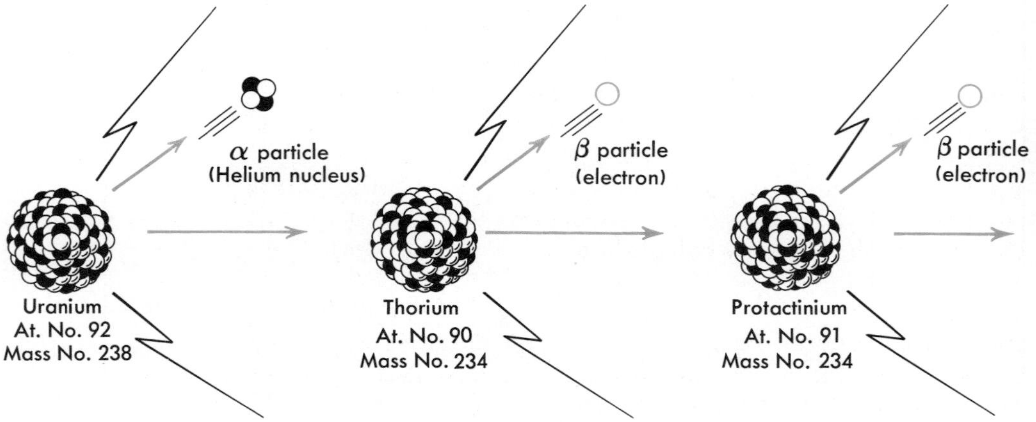

The symbol $_{-1}^{0}e$ represents an electron with an atomic number of -1 and a mass number of 0. $^{234}_{91}Pa$ is an isotope of protactinium. This nuclide decays by releasing beta particles and producing $^{234}_{92}U$.

$$^{234}_{91}\mathbf{Pa} \rightarrow {}^{234}_{92}\mathbf{U} + {}_{-1}^{0}\mathbf{e}$$

The $^{234}_{92}U$ nuclide decays by giving off alpha particles.

$$^{234}_{92}\mathbf{U} \rightarrow {}^{230}_{90}\mathbf{Th} + {}^{4}_{2}\mathbf{He}$$

The isotope of thorium produced also emits alpha particles, forming radium-226.

$$^{230}_{90}\mathbf{Th} \rightarrow {}^{226}_{88}\mathbf{Ra} + {}^{4}_{2}\mathbf{He}$$

Now we can see why ores of uranium contain radium. Radium is one of the products of the decay of uranium atoms. The half-lives of $^{238}_{92}U$ and of $^{226}_{88}Ra$ determine the proportion of uranium atoms to radium atoms in uranium ores.

The decay of $^{226}_{88}Ra$ proceeds according to the chart shown in Figure 30-6. The $^{226}_{88}Ra$ nuclide decays by giving off alpha particles, forming radon-222 as shown by the nuclear equation:

$$^{226}_{88}\mathbf{Ra} \rightarrow {}^{222}_{86}\mathbf{Rn} + {}^{4}_{2}\mathbf{He}$$

The $^{222}_{86}Rn$ nuclei are unstable and have a half-life of about four days. They decay by giving off alpha particles.

$$^{222}_{86}\mathbf{Rn} \rightarrow {}^{218}_{84}\mathbf{Po} + {}^{4}_{2}\mathbf{He}$$

The remaining atomic number and mass number changes shown on the decay chart are also explained in terms of the particles given off. When it loses alpha particles, $^{210}_{84}Po$ forms $^{206}_{82}Pb$. This is a stable, nonradioactive isotope of lead. Thus, a series of spontaneous transmutations begins with $^{238}_{82}U$. It passes through $^{226}_{88}Ra$ and continues on down to $^{206}_{82}Pb$.

30.8 Applications of natural radioactivity

The age of any mineral containing radioactive substances can be estimated with a fair degree of accuracy. Such an estimate is based on the fact that radioactive substances decay at known rates and the assumption that these rates have not changed during the existence of the mineral. The mineral is analyzed to determine the amount of long-lived parent nuclide and the amounts of shorter-lived *daughter* nuclides in the sample. Then, by calculation, scientists can determine how long it must have taken for these amounts of daughter nuclides to be produced. This time is assumed to be the age of the mineral. By this method, the oldest known minerals on earth have been estimated to be about 3.7 billion years old. Dust from sites of moon landings has been found to be about 4.6 billion years old. The ages of moon rocks range from 3.2 to 4.6 billion years.

The age of more recent potassium-containing minerals, 50 thousand to 50 million years old, is determined quite accurately by the proportion of potassium to argon they contain. Some nuclei of $^{40}_{19}K$ decay by capturing an orbital electron and forming $^{40}_{18}Ar$. So, over a period of time, the proportion of argon to potassium in the mineral increases and is used to establish its age.

Some carbon atoms involved in the oxygen-carbon dioxide cycle of living plants and animals are radioactive. Radioactive $^{14}_{6}C$ is continuously being produced from $^{14}_{7}N$ atoms in the atmosphere. This change is brought about by the action of *cosmic rays.* (Cosmic rays are protons and other nuclei of very high energy. These particles come to the earth from outer space.) When living things die, the oxygen-carbon dioxide cycle no longer operates in them. They no longer replace carbon atoms in their cells with other carbon atoms. Thus, the level of radioactivity produced by the radioactive carbon in a given amount of nonliving material slowly diminishes.

Carbon from a wooden beam taken from the tomb of an Egyptian pharaoh yields about half the radiation of carbon in living trees. The half-life of a $^{14}_{6}C$ atom is about 5600 years. Thus, the age of dead wood with half the radioactivity of living wood is about 5600 years. Objects from wood up to about 30,000 years old have been dated by the use of this method. The use of $^{14}_{6}C$ dating has been applied to the study of bone proteins. This technique dates bone material up to about 50,000 years old.

Artificial Radioactivity

30.9 Stability of a nucleus

On the atomic mass scale, the isotope of carbon with six protons and six neutrons in its nucleus is defined as having an *atomic mass* of exactly 12. (See Section 3.12.) On this scale, a $^{4}_{2}He$ nucleus has a mass of 4.0015. The mass of a proton is 1.0073 and the mass of a neutron is 1.0087. A $^{4}_{2}He$ nucleus contains two protons and two neutrons. Thus, we might expect its mass to be the combined mass of these four particles, 4.0320. [$2(1.0073) + 2(1.0087) = 4.0320$.] Note that there is a *difference* of 0.0305 atomic mass unit between the measured mass, 4.0015, and the calculated mass, 4.0320, of a $^{4}_{2}He$ nucleus. *This difference in mass is called the* ***nuclear mass defect.*** *The mass defect, converted into energy units by using Einstein's equation,* $E = mc^2$ (see Section 1.11), *is the energy released when a nucleus is formed from the particles that compose it. This energy is generally referred to as the* ***binding energy.***

Calculations of binding energies of the atoms of the elements show that the lightest and the heaviest elements have the smallest binding energies per nuclear particle. Elements

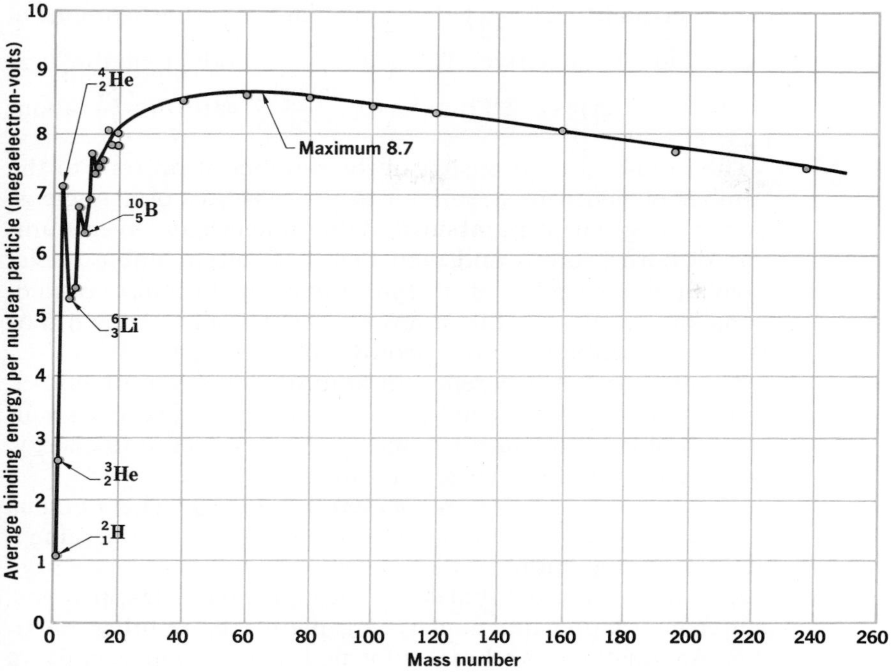

Fig. 30-8. This graph shows the relationship between binding energy per nuclear particle and mass number.

having intermediate atomic weights have the greatest binding energies per nuclear particle. The elements with the greatest binding energies per nuclear particle are the ones with the most stable nuclei. Therefore, the nuclei of the lightest and heaviest atoms are less stable than the nuclei of elements having intermediate atomic weights.

There are factors other than mass that are associated with the stability of atomic nuclei. These are the *ratio of neutrons to protons* and the *even-odd nature* of the number of neutrons and protons.

Many properties of nuclear particles indicate that energy levels exist *within* the atomic nucleus. Among atoms having low atomic numbers, the most stable nuclei are those whose proton-to-neutron ratio is 1 : 1. Nuclei with a greater number of neutrons than protons have lower binding energies and are less stable. In nuclei with an equal number of protons and neutrons, these particles apparently occupy the lowest energy levels in the nucleus. In this way, they give it stability. However, in nuclei that contain an excess of neutrons over protons, some of the neutrons seem to occupy higher energy levels, reducing the binding energy and consequently lowering the stability of the nucleus.

As the atomic number increases, the most stable nuclei have a neutron-to-proton ratio greater than 1 : 1. For example, $^{127}_{53}I$ with a $\frac{\text{neutron}}{\text{proton}}$ ratio of $\frac{74}{53}$ (about 1.40 : 1) is stable. On the other hand, $^{126}_{53}I$ $\left(\frac{73}{53}\right)$, $^{128}_{53}I$ $\left(\frac{75}{53}\right)$, and all other isotopes of iodine, are radioactive. The stable endproduct of the uranium decay series is $^{206}_{82}Pb$. It has a $\frac{\text{neutron}}{\text{proton}}$ ratio of $\frac{124}{82}$ (about 1.51 : 1).

The even-odd relationship of the number of protons to the number of neutrons is related to the stability of a nucleus. By far the greatest number of stable nuclei have even numbers of both protons and neutrons. Less often, stable nuclei have an even number of protons and an odd number of neutrons, or vice versa. Only a few stable nuclei are known that have odd numbers of both protons and neutrons.

Because of the difference in stability of different nuclei, there are four types of nuclear reactions. In each type, a small amount of the mass of the reactants is converted into energy, forming products of greater stability.

1. A nucleus undergoes ***radioactive decay.*** The nucleus releases an alpha or beta particle and gamma rays, forming a slightly lighter, more stable nucleus.

2. A nucleus is bombarded with alpha particles, protons, deuterons (deuterium nuclei, $^{2}_{1}H$), neutrons, or other particles. An unstable nucleus is formed. This nucleus emits a proton or a neutron and becomes more stable. This process is called ***nuclear disintegration.***

3. A very heavy nucleus splits and forms medium-weight nuclei. This process is known as ***fission.***

4. Lightweight nuclei combine and form heavier, more stable nuclei. This process is known as ***fusion.***

30.10 Stable nuclei from radioactive decay

The release of an alpha particle from a radioactive nucleus decreases the mass of the nucleus. The resulting lighter nucleus has higher binding energy per nuclear particle. It is therefore more stable.

The release of an alpha particle decreases the number of protons and neutrons in a nucleus *equally and also by an even number.* Beta particles are released when neutrons change into protons. This change lowers the neutron-to-proton ratio toward the value found for stable nuclei of the same mass number. Both of these changes occur because the product nucleus is more stable than the original nucleus.

30.11 The first artificial nuclear disintegration

After scientists discovered how uranium and radium undergo natural decay and transmutation, they worked to produce artificial transmutations. They had to find a way to add protons to a nucleus of an atom of an element, converting it to the nucleus of an atom of a different element. In 1919, Rutherford produced the first artificial nuclear disintegration. His

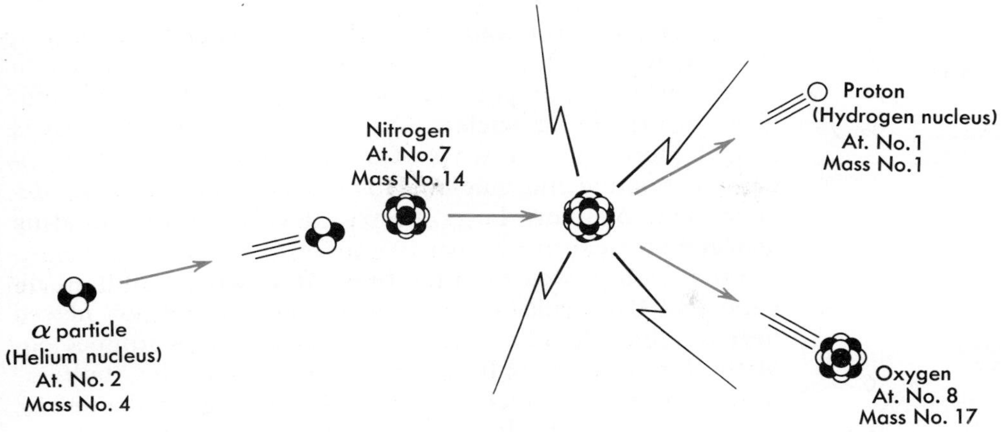

Fig. 30-9. This diagram shows the historic nuclear disintegration performed by Rutherford.

method involved bombarding nitrogen with alpha particles from radium. He obtained protons (hydrogen nuclei) and a stable isotope of oxygen. This nuclear disintegration is represented by the following equation:

$$^{14}_{7}\mathbf{N} + {}^{4}_{2}\mathbf{He} \rightarrow {}^{17}_{8}\mathbf{O} + {}^{1}_{1}\mathbf{H}$$

30.12 Proofs of Einstein's equation

In 1932, two English scientists, J. D. Cockcroft and E. T. S. Walton, experimentally proved Einstein's equation, $E = mc^2$. They bombarded lithium with high-speed protons. Alpha particles and a very large amount of energy were produced.

$$^{7}_{3}\mathbf{Li} + {}^{1}_{1}\mathbf{H} \rightarrow {}^{4}_{2}\mathbf{He} + {}^{4}_{2}\mathbf{He} + \mathbf{energy}$$

There is a loss of matter in this reaction. One lithium nucleus (mass 7.0144) was hit by a proton (mass 1.0073). These formed two alpha particles (helium nuclei) each having a mass of 4.0015. Calculation, (7.0144 + 1.0073) − 2(4.0015), shows that there is a loss of 0.0187 atomic mass unit. Cockcroft and Walton found that the energy released very nearly equaled that predicted by Einstein for such a loss in mass. Later experiments have further supported Einstein's equation.

30.13 Neutron emission in some nuclear disintegrations

We have already stated that neutrons were discovered by Chadwick in 1932. He first detected them in an experiment which involved bombarding beryllium with alpha particles:

Neutrons are described in Section 3.5.

$$^{9}_{4}\mathbf{Be} + {}^{4}_{2}\mathbf{He} \rightarrow {}^{12}_{6}\mathbf{C} + {}^{1}_{0}\mathbf{n}$$

The symbol for a neutron is $^{1}_{0}$n. This symbol indicates a particle with zero atomic number (no protons) and a mass number of 1. The reaction described above proved that neutrons were a second type of particle in the nuclei of atoms.

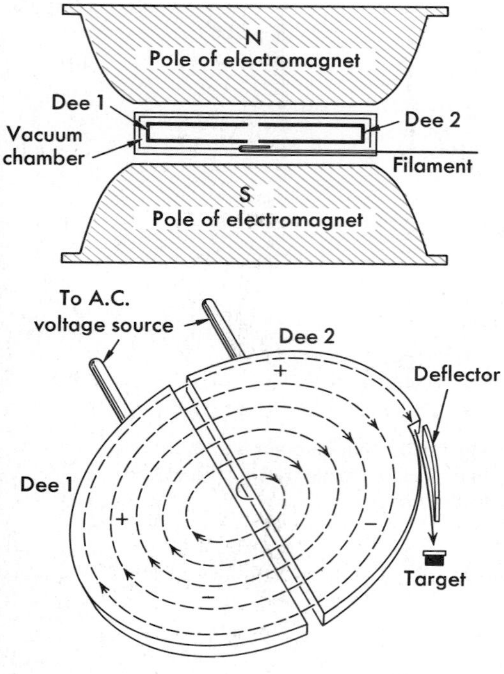

Fig. 30-10. A diagram of the cyclotron used to produce "atomic bullets" of very high energy.

Fig. 30-11. The 60-inch cyclotron of the Brookhaven National Laboratory.

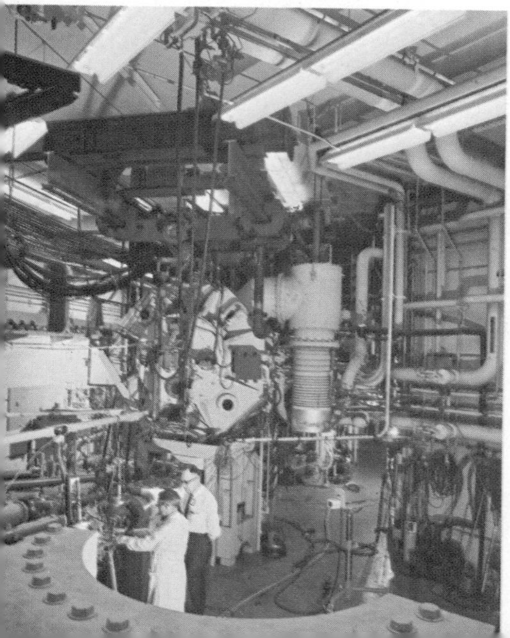

30.14 The cyclotron and other "atom smashers"

Radium was used as a natural source of alpha particles in many early experiments. However, radium is not very efficient in producing nuclear changes. As a result, scientists sought more effective ways of producing high-energy particles for bombarding nuclei. This search resulted in the development of many large electric devices for accelerating charged particles.

The *cyclotron* was invented by E. O. Lawrence of the University of California. It consists of a cylindrical box placed between the poles of a huge electromagnet. Air is pumped out of the box until a high vacuum is produced. The "bullets" used to bombard nuclei are usually protons or deuterons. They enter the cylindrical box through its center.

Inside the box are two hollow, D-shaped electrodes called *dees*. These dees are connected through an oscillator to a source of very high voltage. When the cyclotron is in operation, the oscillator reverses the electric charge on the dees very rapidly. The combined effects of the high-voltage alternating potential and the electromagnetic field cause the protons or deuterons inside to move in a spiral course. They move faster and faster as they near the outside of the box, gaining more and more energy. When they reach the outer rim of the box, they are deflected toward the target. The energy of particles accelerated in a simple cyclotron may reach 15,000,000 electron-volts. This is the energy an electron would have if it were accelerated across a potential difference of 1.5×10^7 volts. By studying the fragments of atoms formed by bombardment, scientists have learned a great deal about atomic structure. They also have discovered much about the products formed when atoms disintegrate. Other machines for bombarding atomic nuclei are the *synchrotron*, the *betatron*, and the *linear accelerator*.

The synchrotron works much like the cyclotron. By varying both the oscillating voltage and the magnetic field, particles are accelerated in a narrow circular path rather than in a spiral. A synchrotron can give an energy of more than 500 billion electron-volts to the protons it accelerates. The betatron accelerates electrons rather than positively charged particles. The accelerated electrons can be used as "bullets" for bombardment or for producing high-energy X rays. Still another type of particle accelerator is the linear accelerator. In this device, the particles travel in a straight line. They are accelerated by passage through many stages of potential difference.

30.15 Neutrons as "bullets"

Before the discovery of neutrons in 1932, alpha particles and protons were used in studying atomic nuclei. But alpha particles and protons are charged particles. It requires great quantities of energy to "fire" these charged "bullets" into a nucleus. Their positive charge causes them to be repelled by the positive nuclear charge. The various kinds of particle accelerators were developed to give charged "bullets" enough energy to overcome this repelling force.

When accelerated positive particles from an atom smasher strike a target material, usually lithium or beryllium, neutrons are produced. Neutrons have no charge. Thus, there is no repelling force, and they can easily penetrate the nucleus of an atom. Some fast neutrons may go through an atom without causing any change in it. Other fast neutrons, however, may cause nuclear disintegration. Slow neutrons, on the other hand, are sometimes trapped by a nucleus. This nucleus is then unstable, and may break apart. Fast neutrons are slowed down by passage through materials composed of elements of low atomic weight. Examples are deuterium oxide or graphite.

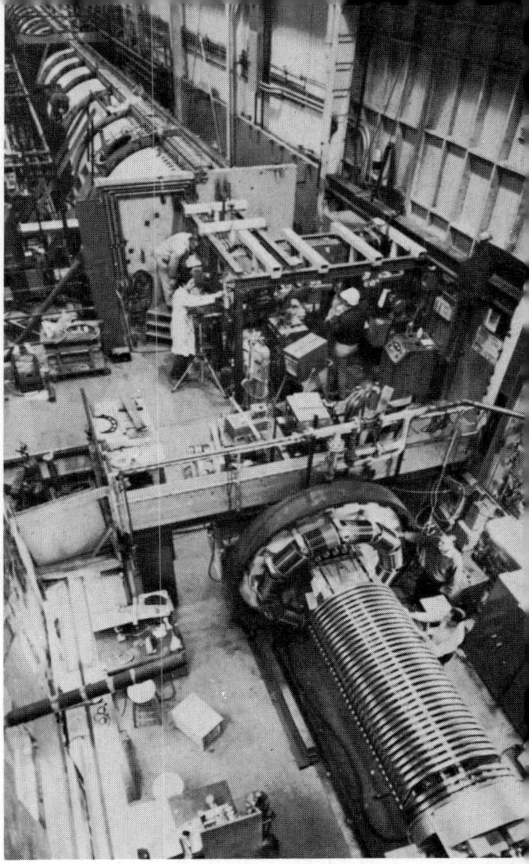

Fig. 30-12. The heavy-ion linear accelerator at the Lawrence Berkeley Laboratory used to synthesize element 106.

30.16 Artificial elements from neutron bombardment

The $^{238}_{92}U$ nuclide is the most plentiful isotope of uranium. When hit by slow neutrons, a $^{238}_{92}U$ nucleus may capture a neutron. This capture produces the nucleus of an atom of an unstable isotope of uranium, $^{239}_{92}U$. This nucleus emits a beta particle. In doing so, it becomes the nucleus of an atom of an artificial radioactive element, neptunium. Neptunium has atomic number 93.

$$^{238}_{92}\mathbf{U} + {}^{1}_{0}\mathbf{n} \rightarrow {}^{239}_{92}\mathbf{U}$$

$$^{239}_{92}\mathbf{U} \rightarrow {}^{239}_{93}\mathbf{Np} + {}^{0}_{-1}\mathbf{e}$$

Neptunium is itself an unstable element. The nucleus of a neptunium atom gives off a beta particle. This change produces the nucleus of an atom of still another artificial element, plutonium, atomic number 94.

$$^{239}_{93}\mathbf{Np} \rightarrow {}^{239}_{94}\mathbf{Pu} + {}^{0}_{-1}\mathbf{e}$$

Neptunium and plutonium were the first artificial *transuranium* elements. ***Transuranium elements*** are those with more than 92 protons in their nuclei. As this is written, 15 artificially prepared transuranium elements have been reported. In addition to neptunium and plutonium, there are americium, curium, berkelium, californium, einsteinium, fermium, mendelevium, nobelium, and lawrencium. Elements 104, 105, 106, and 107 have not yet been officially named. All of these were prepared by bombarding the nuclei of uranium or more complex atoms with neutrons, alpha particles, or other "nuclear bullets." See Table 30-2.

30.17 Artificial radioactive atoms

In 1934, Madame Curie's daughter Irène (1897–1956) and her husband Frédéric Joliot (1900–1958) discovered that stable atoms can be made radioactive by artificial means. This occurs when they are bombarded with deuterons or neutrons. Radioactive isotopes of all the elements have been prepared. For example, radioactive $^{60}_{27}Co$ can be produced from natural nonradioactive $^{59}_{27}Co$ by slow-neutron bombardment. The nuclear equation is

$$^{59}_{27}\mathbf{Co} + {}^{1}_{0}\mathbf{n} \rightarrow {}^{60}_{27}\mathbf{Co}$$

The radiation from $^{60}_{27}Co$ consists of beta particles and gamma rays.

Table 30-2

REACTIONS FOR THE FIRST PREPARATION OF TRANSURANIUM ELEMENTS

Atomic Number	Name	Symbol	Nuclear Reaction
93	neptunium	Np	$^{238}_{92}U + {}^{1}_{0}n \rightarrow {}^{239}_{93}Np + {}^{0}_{-1}e$
94	plutonium	Pu	$^{238}_{92}U + {}^{2}_{1}H \rightarrow {}^{238}_{93}Np + 2{}^{1}_{0}n$
			$^{238}_{93}Np \rightarrow {}^{238}_{94}Pu + {}^{0}_{-1}e$
95	americium	Am	$^{239}_{94}Pu + 2{}^{1}_{0}n \rightarrow {}^{241}_{95}Am + {}^{0}_{-1}e$
96	curium	Cm	$^{239}_{94}Pu + {}^{4}_{2}He \rightarrow {}^{242}_{96}Cm + {}^{1}_{0}n$
97	berkelium	Bk	$^{241}_{95}Am + {}^{4}_{2}He \rightarrow {}^{243}_{97}Bk + 2{}^{1}_{0}n$
98	californium	Cf	$^{242}_{96}Cm + {}^{4}_{2}He \rightarrow {}^{245}_{98}Cf + {}^{1}_{0}n$
99	einsteinium	Es	$^{238}_{92}U + 15{}^{1}_{0}n \rightarrow {}^{253}_{99}Es + 7{}^{0}_{-1}e$
100	fermium	Fm	$^{238}_{92}U + 17{}^{1}_{0}n \rightarrow {}^{255}_{100}Fm + 8{}^{0}_{-1}e$
101	mendelevium	Md	$^{253}_{99}Es + {}^{4}_{2}He \rightarrow {}^{256}_{101}Md + {}^{1}_{0}n$
102	nobelium	No	$^{246}_{96}Cm + {}^{12}_{6}C \rightarrow {}^{254}_{102}No + 4{}^{1}_{0}n$
103	lawrencium	Lr	$^{252}_{98}Cf + {}^{10}_{5}B \rightarrow {}^{258}_{103}Lr + 4{}^{1}_{0}n$
104	kurchatovium	Ku	$^{242}_{94}Pu + {}^{22}_{10}Ne \rightarrow {}^{260}_{104}Ku + 4{}^{1}_{0}n$
104	rutherfordium	Rf	$^{249}_{98}Cf + {}^{12}_{6}C \rightarrow {}^{257}_{104}Rf + 4{}^{1}_{0}n$
105	hahnium	Ha	$^{249}_{98}Cf + {}^{15}_{7}N \rightarrow {}^{260}_{105}Ha + 4{}^{1}_{0}n$
106			$^{249}_{98}Cf + {}^{18}_{8}O \rightarrow {}^{263}_{106}? + 4\,{}^{1}_{0}n$
107			$^{209}_{83}Bi + {}^{54}_{24}Cr \rightarrow {}^{261}_{107}? + 2{}^{1}_{0}n$

Radioactive $^{32}_{15}P$ is prepared by bombardment of $^{32}_{16}S$ with slow neutrons:

$$^{32}_{16}\mathbf{S} + ^{1}_{0}\mathbf{n} \rightarrow ^{32}_{15}\mathbf{P} + ^{1}_{1}\mathbf{H}$$

The radiation from $^{32}_{15}P$ consists only of beta particles.

Radioactive phosphorus, radioactive cobalt, and some other radioactive elements are used to treat certain forms of cancer. Also, many radioactive isotopes are used as *tracers.* Using them, scientists can determine the course of chemical reactions, the cleaning ability of detergents, the wearing ability of various products, the efficiency of fertilizers, the flow of fluids through pipelines, and the movement of sand along sea coasts. Many new radioactive isotopes are made by slow-neutron bombardment in the nuclear reactor at Oak Ridge, Tennessee.

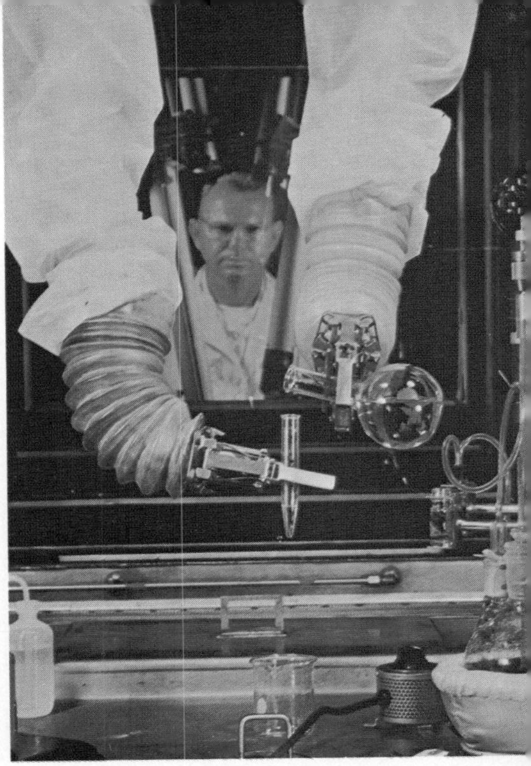

Fig. 30-13. Radioactive materials are handled by remote control in specially designed and shielded "cells."

30.18 Fission of uranium

The element uranium exists as three naturally occurring isotopes, $^{238}_{92}U$, $^{235}_{92}U$, and $^{234}_{92}U$. Most uranium is the nuclide $^{238}_{92}U$. Only 0.7% of natural uranium is $^{235}_{92}U$. The nuclide $^{234}_{92}U$ occurs in only the slightest traces. We have already stated that transuranium elements can be produced when $^{238}_{92}U$ is bombarded with slow neutrons. However, when $^{235}_{92}U$ is bombarded with slow neutrons, each atom may capture one of the neutrons. This extra neutron in the nucleus makes it very unstable. Instead of giving off an alpha or beta particle, as in other radioactive changes, the nucleus splits into medium-weight parts. Neutrons are usually produced during this *fission.* There is a small loss of mass, which appears as a great amount of energy. One equation for the fission of $^{235}_{92}U$ is

The slow-neutron fission of $^{235}_{92}U$ yields products having atomic numbers from 30 to 65 and mass numbers from 72 to 161. See Figure 30-14. Fission into two equal fragments is not the most probable. The highest yield is of particles with mass numbers 95 and 138.

$$^{235}_{92}\mathbf{U} + ^{1}_{0}\mathbf{n} \rightarrow ^{138}_{56}\mathbf{Ba} + ^{95}_{36}\mathbf{Kr} + 3^{1}_{0}\mathbf{n} + \mathbf{energy}$$

The atomic mass of $^{235}_{92}U$ is slightly greater than 235. The atomic masses of the unstable barium and krypton isotopes are slightly less than 138 and 95, respectively. Thus, the masses of the reactants and the masses of the products are not equal. Instead, about 0.2 atomic mass unit of mass is converted to energy for each uranium atom undergoing fission. Plutonium, made from $^{238}_{92}U$, also undergoes fission and produces more neutrons when bombarded with slow neutrons.

Most $^{238}_{92}U$ atoms decay by emitting an alpha particle as described in Section 30.7. But about one out of every 2 million $^{238}_{92}U$ atoms undergoes spontaneous fission.

Uranium atoms exist in very small amounts in many minerals. In the time since their formation, some $^{238}_{92}U$ atoms have undergone spontaneous fission. These fissions have left tracks in certain mineral crystals and in glassy materials. These tracks can be made visible under a microscope by etching. The number of tracks in a given area and the amount of $^{238}_{92}U$ in the specimen are used to indicate the age of the crystal or the time since a glassy material was last heated

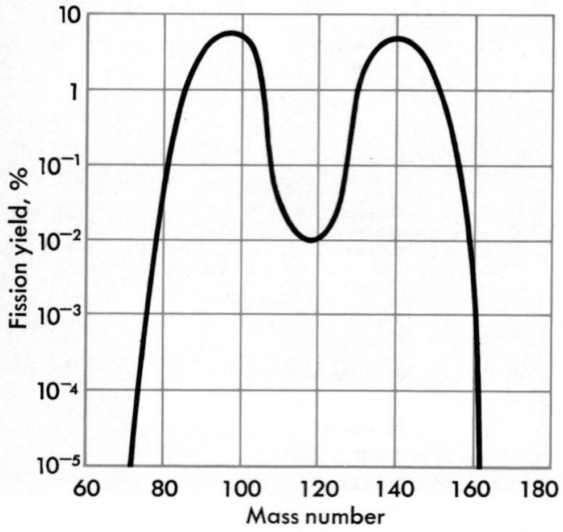

Fig. 30-14. This graph shows the yield of various nuclides that are produced by the slow-neutron fission of uranium-235. The products vary in mass number from 72 to 161. The most probable products have mass numbers of 95 and 138. Observe the low probability of fission products of nearly equal mass numbers.

to a high temperature. This method, called fission-track dating, can establish the age of materials from a few decades old to as old as the solar system.

30.19 Nuclear chain reaction

A ***chain reaction*** *is one in which the material or energy that starts the reaction is also one of the products.* The fissions of $^{235}_{92}U$ and $^{239}_{94}Pu$ can produce chain reactions. One neutron causes the fission of one $^{235}_{92}U$ nucleus. Two or three neutrons are given off when this fission occurs. These neutrons can cause the fission of other $^{235}_{92}U$ nuclei. Again neutrons are emitted. These can cause the fission of still other $^{235}_{92}U$ nuclei. This is a chain reaction. It continues until all the $^{235}_{92}U$ atoms have split or until the neutrons fail to strike $^{235}_{92}U$ nuclei. This is what happens in an uncontrolled chain reaction such as the explosion of a nuclear warhead.

30.20 Action in a nuclear reactor

A ***nuclear reactor*** *is a device in which the controlled fission of radioactive material produces new radioactive substances and energy.* One of the earliest nuclear reactors was built at Oak Ridge, Tennessee, in 1943. This reactor uses natural uranium. It has a lattice-type structure with blocks of graphite forming the framework. Spaced between the blocks of graphite are rods of uranium, encased in aluminum cans for protection. *Control rods* of neutron-absorbing boron steel are inserted into the lattice to limit the number of free neutrons. The reactor is air cooled.

The rods of uranium or uranium oxide are the *nuclear fuel* for the reactor. The energy released in the reactor comes from

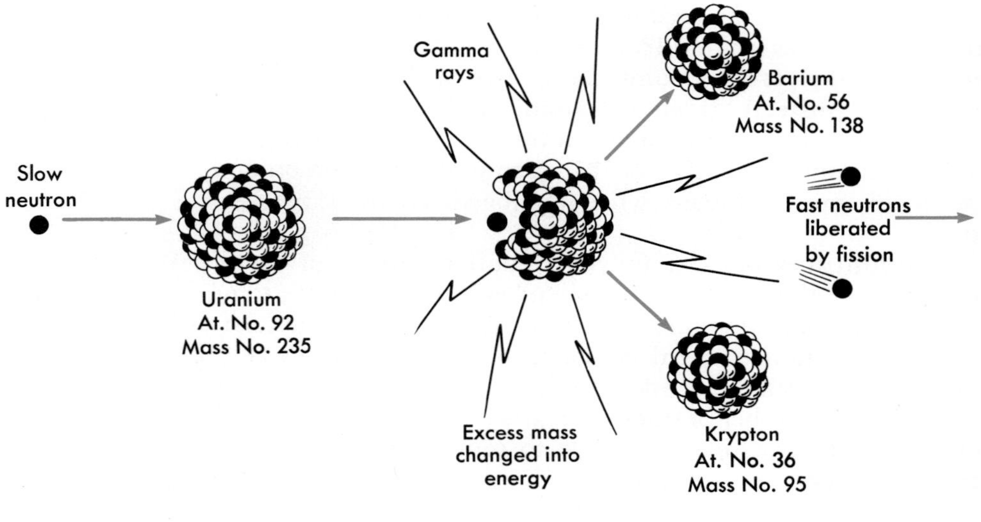

changes in the uranium nuclei. Graphite is said to be the *moderator* because it slows down the fast neutrons produced by fission. By doing so, it makes them more readily captured by a nucleus, and thus more effective for producing additional nuclear changes. The amount of uranium in such a reactor is important. Enough uranium must be present to provide the number of neutrons needed to sustain a chain reaction. This quantity of uranium is called the ***critical size.***

Two types of reactions occur in the fuel in such a reactor. Neutrons cause $^{235}_{92}U$ nuclei to undergo fission. The fast neutrons from this fission are slowed down as they pass through the graphite. Some strike other $^{235}_{92}U$ nuclei and continue the chain reaction. Other neutrons strike $^{238}_{92}U$ nuclei, starting the changes that finally produce plutonium. Great quantities of heat energy are released. For this reason, the reactor has to be cooled continuously by blowing air through tubes in the lattice. The rate of the reaction is controlled by the insertion or removal of the neutron-absorbing control rods. This type of reactor is now used to produce radioactive isotopes.

In nuclear power plants, the reactor is the source of heat energy. The moderator and coolant are pressurized water. The heat from the reactor absorbed by the pressurized water is used to produce steam. This steam turns the turbines, which drive the electric generators. Present problems with nuclear power plant development include questions about location, environmental requirements, and safety of operation. Procurement and enrichment of uranium, as well as methods and policies for storing or reprocessing used nuclear reactor fuel, are also being studied.

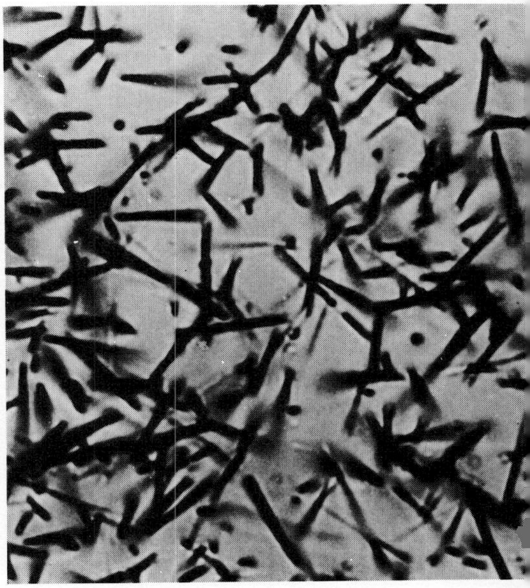

Fig. 30-15. The tracks shown in the photo were caused by the spontaneous fission of uranium-238 atoms. The tracks were enlarged by etching so they would be visible through a light microscope. The tracks are magnified over three thousand times. The crystalline material in which they appear here is zircon.

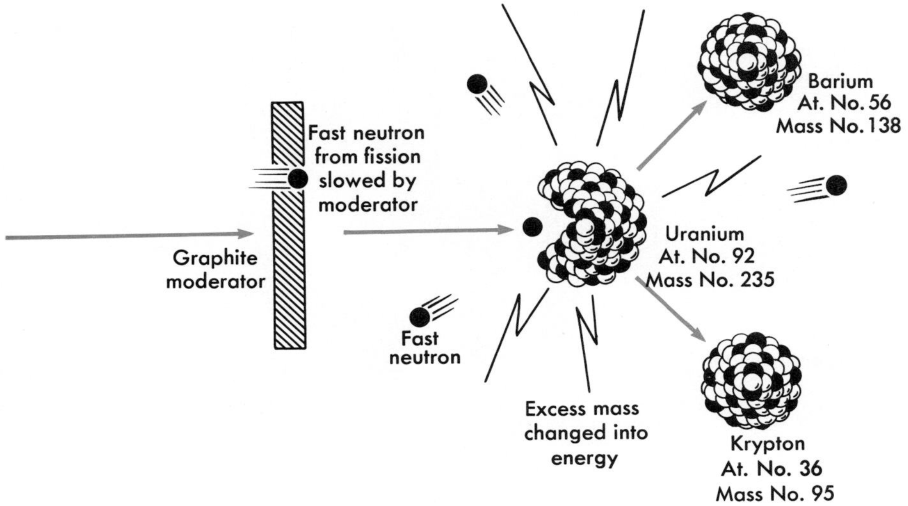

Fig. 30-16. Neutrons from fission of a $^{235}_{92}U$ nucleus, when slowed down by a carbon moderator, can cause fission in a second $^{235}_{92}U$ nucleus. This process makes a chain reaction possible.

30.21 Fusion reactions

We have stated that nuclear stability can be increased by combining lightweight nuclei into heavier nuclei. This process was defined as ***fusion.***

Fusion reactions are the source of the sun's energy. It is believed that there are two series of such reactions going on in the sun. One series occurs at the very hot center of the sun, while the other takes place in the cooler outer portion of the sun. These two reactions proceed by different pathways. However, their net effect is the combination of four hydrogen nuclei into a helium nucleus. A loss of mass occurs and a tremendous amount of energy is released.

The thermonuclear bomb, sometimes called the hydrogen bomb, or H-bomb, produces energy by a fusion reaction. More energy is released per gram of fuel in a fusion reaction than in a fission reaction. For this reason, the H-bomb is much more destructive than the atomic bomb, a fission bomb. Also, the quantities of reacting materials can be made much larger. In theory, there is no limit to the amount of reactants that can be used. Fusion reactions are not chain reactions and thus do not require a critical size of reacting materials.

One possible reaction in a hydrogen bomb involves the formation of alpha particles and tremendous energy from a specific lithium hydride. This special compound may be formed from lithium-6 and deuterium and have the formula

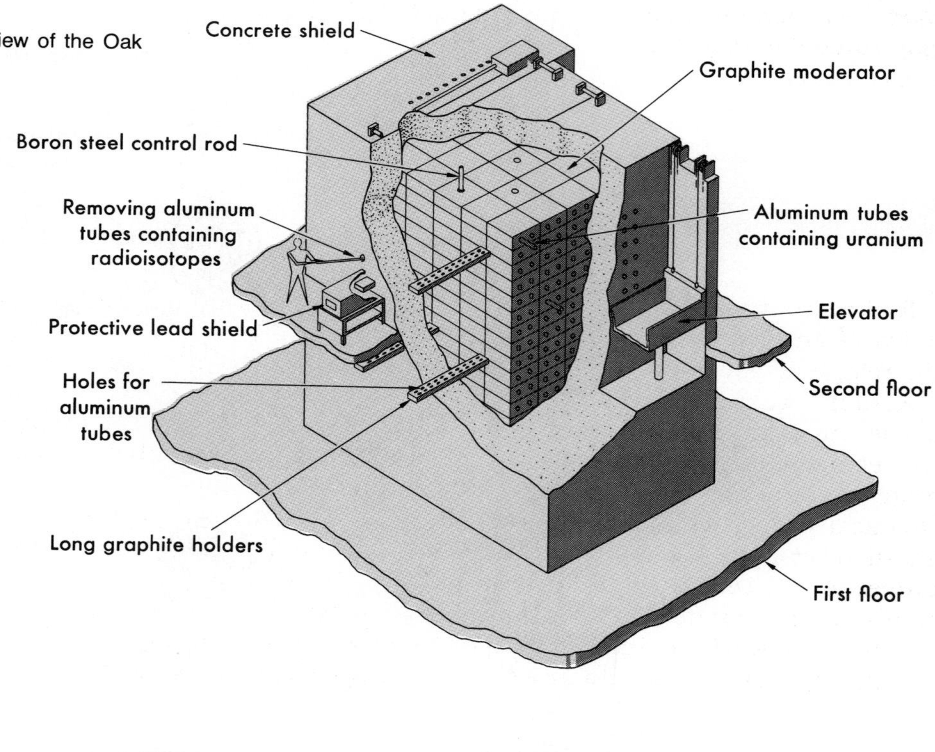

Fig. 30-17. A cutaway view of the Oak Ridge reactor.

Fig. 30-18. This equipment is used in studying laser-induced fusion experiments.

$^{6}_{3}Li^{2}_{1}H$. Such a fusion reaction can be started only by placing $^{6}_{3}Li^{2}_{1}H$ under extremely high temperature and pressure. These conditions are created by using an atomic bomb to set off the hydrogen bomb.

Current research indicates that fusion reactions may be controlled. Scientists are attempting to find ways to confine the nuclear fuel and at the same time make it hot enough and dense enough for fusion to occur. Experiments using high-powered laser light or beams of electrons as ways to start the fusion reaction are being conducted. Such reactions may some day produce useful energy that can be converted to electricity.

SUMMARY

Radioactivity is the spontaneous breakdown of an unstable atomic nucleus with the release of particles and rays.

Radium was discovered by Pierre and Marie Curie in 1898. It is a very radioactive element that is always found in uranium ores. Radium resembles barium in its chemical properties. Radioactive nuclides and their compounds have several unusual properties: (*1*) They affect the light-sensitive emulsion on a photographic film, (*2*) they produce an electric charge in the surrounding air, (*3*) they produce fluorescence with certain other compounds, (*4*) their radiations have special physiological effects, (*5*) they undergo radioactive decay. The half-life of a radioactive nuclide is the length of time that it takes for half of a given number of atoms of the radioactive nuclide to decay.

The radiation given off by radioactive elements consists of three different kinds of particles and rays: (*1*) alpha particles, which are helium nuclei, (*2*) beta particles, which are electrons, and (*3*) gamma rays, which are high-energy X rays. The emission of these particles from the nuclei of radioactive nuclides causes them to decay into simpler nuclides.

All naturally occurring radioactive nuclides with atomic numbers greater than 83 belong to one of three series of related nuclides. Uranium-238 is the parent element of the radioactive series that contains radium. A transmutation is a change in the identity of a nucleus because of a change in the number of its protons.

The age of certain minerals and of carbon-containing materials can be estimated by the amounts of radioactive nuclides they contain.

The difference between the sum of the masses of the separate particles making up a nucleus and the actual mass of a nucleus is the nuclear mass defect. The mass defect, converted into energy units is the energy released when a nucleus is formed from the particles that compose it. This energy is known as the binding energy. The lightest and heaviest elements have the smallest binding energies per nuclear particle and the least stable nuclei. Elements having intermediate atomic weights have the greatest binding energies per nuclear particle and the most stable nuclei. The ratio of neutrons to protons and the even-odd nature of the number of neutrons and protons in a nucleus are also related to its stability.

There are four types of reactions that nuclei undergo and become more stable: (*1*) radioactive decay, (*2*) nuclear disintegration, (*3*) fission, and (*4*) fusion.

The cyclotron is an electromagnetic device for accelerating protons and deuterons in a spiral path. Other particle accelerators are the synchrotron, the betatron, and the linear accelerator.

When bombarded by slow neutrons, a $^{238}_{92}U$ nucleus may capture a neutron and ultimately be transformed into $^{239}_{94}Pu$. Stable atoms may be made artificially radioactive by bombardment with deuterons or neutrons. Artificial radioactive nuclides are used as tracers, in medicine, and in research.

When $^{235}_{92}U$ is bombarded with slow neutrons, it undergoes fission. Fission is the splitting of a very heavy nucleus into medium-weight parts. A chain reaction is one in which the material or energy that starts the reaction is also one of the products.

A nuclear reactor is a device in which the controlled fission of radioactive material produces new radioactive substances and heat energy which may be used to generate electricity.

A fusion reaction is one in which light-weight nuclei are combined into heavier nuclei. Fusion reactions produce the sun's heat and light.

QUESTIONS

Group A

1. (*a*) Who discovered radioactivity? (*b*) How was the discovery made?
2. What evidence led Marie and Pierre Curie to suspect that there were radioactive elements other than uranium in pitchblende?
3. How does the radioactivity of radium compare with that of uranium?
4. What practical use is made of the fluorescence produced in zinc sulfide by a radium compound?
5. What is meant by the *half-life* of a radioactive nuclide?
6. From what part of a radioactive nuclide do the alpha or beta particles come?
7. What change in identity and mass number occurs when a radioactive nuclide gives off an alpha particle?
8. What change in identity and mass number occurs when a radioactive nuclide gives off a beta particle?

9. How is the age of a radioactive mineral estimated?
10. Name the four types of nuclear reactions that produce more stable nuclei.
11. In what ways does natural radioactive decay produce more stable nuclei?
12. How were neutrons first detected as nuclear particles?
13. Why are neutrons more effective particles than protons or alpha particles for bombarding atomic nuclei?
14. What may happen to a neutron that is fired at the nucleus of an atom?
15. For what purposes are radioactive isotopes used?
16. (*a*) What are the naturally occurring isotopes of uranium? (*b*) What is their relative abundance?
17. (*a*) What is fission? (*b*) How is it produced in $^{235}_{92}U$?
18. What is meant by the *critical size* of a reactor?
19. Why must a nuclear reactor be continually cooled?
20. What reaction produces the sun's energy?

Group B

21. Why is radium studied separately rather than with the other elements of Group II?
22. The relative abundance of uranium-238 and radium-226 in uranium ores is proportional to their respective half-lives. The half-life of uranium-238 is 4.51×10^9 years while that of radium-226 is 1.62×10^3 years. What is the proportion of radium atoms to uranium atoms in an uranium ore sample?
23. Why can the radiation from a radioactive material affect photographic film, even though the film is well wrapped in black paper?
24. How does a radioactive material affect the rate of discharge of an electroscope?
25. Where are most of the radioactive nuclides located in the periodic table?
26. Make a chart that compares the following properties of alpha particles and beta particles: identity, mass number, charge, speed, and penetrating ability.
27. What are gamma rays?
28. Write the nuclear equation for the release of an alpha particle by $^{226}_{88}Ra$.
29. Write the nuclear equation for the release of a beta particle by $^{214}_{82}Pb$.
30. Write nuclear equations for successive releases of an alpha particle and a beta particle from $^{214}_{84}Po$.
31. (*a*) Which kinds of elements have the smallest binding energy per nuclear particle? (*b*) Which kind has the greatest binding energy per nuclear particle? (*c*) How does the binding energy per nuclear particle affect the stability of a nucleus?
32. What factors affect the stability of a nucleus?
33. How does each type of nuclear reaction produce more stable nuclei?
34. (*a*) Who produced the first artificial nuclear disintegration? (*b*) Write the equation for this reaction.
35. How was Einstein's equation for the relationship between matter and energy, $E = mc^2$, proved to be correct?
36. (*a*) Describe the path of the accelerated particles in a cyclotron. (*b*) What causes them to take this path?
37. Explain the changes occurring in the nucleus by which $^{239}_{94}Pu$ is produced from $^{238}_{92}U$.
38. (*a*) How are artificially radioactive isotopes prepared? (*b*) Write a nuclear equation to show the preparation of such a nuclide. (*c*) What use is made of the nuclide whose preparation you have shown in this nuclear equation?
39. (*a*) Describe a chain reaction. (*b*) How does the fission of $^{235}_{92}U$ produce a chain reaction?
40. How is a uranium-graphite reactor constructed?
41. The view of the National Accelerator Laboratory shown on page 591 gives some idea of the vast spread of a particle research laboratory. Explain why these facilities must be so spacious.

MATHEMATICS REFRESHER

MR1 Introduction

Chemistry students are frequently required to measure quantities of matter, to record measurement data, and to perform calculations and solve problems which involve measurement values. To perform these tasks competently, some proficiency in the use of significant figures, numbers in exponential form, common logarithms, and mathematical operations with measurement units is essential.

The purpose of this Mathematics Refresher is to provide a review of topics and mathematical operations most commonly used in chemical calculations. It may be helpful to review applicable sections of this refresher before working on chemistry problems or laboratory calculations.

MR2 Significant figures

The measurement of any physical quantity is subject to some uncertainty. The *reliability* of a measurement, or the *measurement detail,* is expressed by recording its magnitude in terms of significant figures.

We use instruments to measure mass, length, time, temperature, etc. A measuring instrument is capable of providing measurement detail within its design limits. A measurement consists of the number detail that can be read from the instrument with certainty, and one final estimated value. All digits in the measurement then have physical significance; they are *significant figures.* Of course, the number expression of the measurement is meaningless unless the measurement unit used is also recorded. ***Significant figures*** *in a measurement expression consist of all digits known with certainty plus the first digit that is uncertain.* The position of the decimal point is irrelevant.

The mean distance to the moon, known to *six significant figures,* is 238,856 miles. This distance is more commonly expressed as 239,000 miles to *three* significant figures, or 240,000 miles to *two* significant figures. The zeros merely serve to locate the (understood) decimal point. Similarly, a measured length of 0.00531 cm is precise to *three* significant figures, the zeros being used to locate the decimal point. However, the measurements 104.06 m and 100.60 m contain *five* significant figures. The question naturally arises: when are zeros significant in a measurement expression?

Rules for determining the number of significant figures are the following:

1. All nonzero digits ***are*** *significant;* 127.34 g contains *five* significant figures.

2. *All zeros between two nonzero digits* ***are*** *significant;* 120.007 m contains *six* significant figures.

3. *Zeros to the right of a nonzero digit, but to the left of an understood decimal point, are not significant unless specifically indicated to be significant.* The rightmost such zero which is significant is indicated by a bar placed above it: 109,000 km contains *three* significant figures; $109{,}0\bar{0}0$ km contains *five* significant figures.

4. *All zeros to the right of a decimal point but to the left of a nonzero digit* ***are not*** *significant:* 0.00476 kg contains *three* significant figures. (The single zero conventionally placed to the left of the decimal point in such an expression is never significant.)

5. *All zeros to the right of a decimal point and to the right of a nonzero digit* ***are*** *significant:* 0.04060 cm and 30.00 mg contain *four* significant figures.

MR3 Operations with significant figures

1. *Addition and subtraction.* Recall that the last significant figure in a measurement is uncertain. The *place* of the last significant figure in a sum or difference is that of the leftmost doubtful figure in any of the measurements involved in the operation.

Addition:

```
27.26  g
         ← leftmost doubtful figure (the 5 in 6.5)
 6.5   g
 4.025 g
--------
37.785 g
   ↑ last significant figure in sum
```

The sum is then rounded to 37.8 g.

Subtraction:

```
20.63 cm
          ← leftmost doubtful figure (the 4 in 11.4)
11.4  cm
--------
 9.23 cm
   ↑ last significant figure in difference
```

The difference is then rounded to 9.2 cm.

2. *Multiplication and division.* The *number* of significant figures in a product or quotient is that of the number of significant figures in the least precise factor. (In the following examples, the number above each term denotes the number of significant figures in the term.)

Multiplication: $\overset{(3)}{\mathbf{9.25\ m}} \times \overset{(2)}{\mathbf{0.52\ m}} = \overset{(2)}{\mathbf{4.8\ m^2}}$

Division: $\overset{(4)}{\mathbf{45.32\ m}} \div \overset{(3)}{\mathbf{3.15\ s}} = \overset{(3)}{\mathbf{14.4\ m/s}}$

MR4 Operations with units

Measurements are always expressed as a significant number of some kind of units: 12.5 g, 6.7 cm, 10.0 s, 42.1° C, 0.09 g/liter, etc. Both the number and the unit are essential parts of the expression since the choice of unit affects the magnitude of the number. A measurement determined to three significant figures to be 1.30 m could be written as $13\bar{0}$ cm.

$$1.30\ \cancel{m} \times \frac{100\ cm}{\cancel{m}} = 13\bar{0}\ cm$$

Observe that the expression 100 cm/m is arrived at by definition, not by measurement. Thus, it is exactly 100 cm per meter and it does not affect the significance of the measurement. A measurement determined to two significant figures to be 1.3 m would be written as 130 cm when converted to the centimeter unit.

$$1.3\ \cancel{m} \times \frac{100\ cm}{\cancel{m}} = 130\ cm$$

Thus, 1.30 m is equivalent to $13\bar{0}$ cm and 1.3 m is equivalent to 130 cm. Similarly, 130.0 cm is equivalent to 1.300 m.

$$130.0\ \cancel{cm} \times \frac{m}{100\ \cancel{cm}} = 1.300\ m$$

Because there are many different units and because the expression of a physical measurement requires *both* a number and a unit, *always* write the unit with the number to which it belongs. Usually the "cancellation" of units in an expression leads directly to the proper unit for the answer. The technique of unit cancellation is referred to as the factor-label method.

SAMPLE PROBLEM

A chemistry student was required to determine the density of an irregularly shaped sample of lead. He first weighed it on a balance sensitive to 0.01 g and found its mass to be 49.33 g. He then immersed the lead in water contained in a cylinder graduated in one-tenth millimeter divisions and observed that it displaced 4.35 ml of water (the 0.05 ml being estimated).

SOLUTION

The student recalled from his study of general science that a body immersed in a liquid displaces its own volume. Since the volume of a solid is normally expressed in cubic measure, he used the equivalency of the milliliter and the cubic centimeter to convert the volume to cubic centimeters.

$$1\ \text{cm}^3 = 1\ \text{ml}$$

$$4.35\ \cancel{\text{ml}} \times \frac{1\ \text{cm}^3}{\cancel{\text{ml}}} = 4.35\ \text{cm}^3$$

By definition:

$$D = \frac{m}{V}$$

$$D = \frac{49.33\ \text{g}}{4.35\ \text{cm}^3} = 11.3\cancel{4}\ \text{g/cm}^3$$

Observe that the indicated division has been carried to the hundredths place. It should next be rounded to the nearest tenth to give the proper number of significant figures in the answer.

A more appropriate way to set up this solution would be as follows:

$$D = \frac{m}{V}$$

$$D = \frac{49.33\ \text{g}}{4.35\ \cancel{\text{ml}} \times 1\ \text{cm}^3/\cancel{\text{ml}}} = 11.3\ \text{g/cm}^3$$

SAMPLE PROBLEM

What is the concentration of sodium chloride (table salt), in grams of salt per gram of solution, if $40\bar{0}$ mg of the salt is dissolved in $10\bar{0}$ ml of water measured at 60° C?

SOLUTION

The problem requires that the concentration be expressed in grams of salt per gram of solution. The mass of solution is the sum of the mass of the water used and the mass of the salt added. As a result, the volume of water must be converted to mass of water. To make this conversion the density of water at 60° C must be known.

Table 10, Appendix B, which gives the density of water over a range of temperatures, shows that water has a density of 0.983 g/ml at 60° C.

By definition: $D = \frac{m}{V}$

Solving for m: $m = DV$

Substituting: $m = 0.983\ \frac{\text{g}}{\cancel{\text{ml}}} \times 10\bar{0}\ \cancel{\text{ml}} = 98.3\ \text{g}$

(Observe that the ml units "cancel," leaving g, which is the proper unit for the result.)

The mass of the salt is given in milligrams and the mass of the water is in grams. Since milligrams and grams cannot be added, the milligrams of salt must be converted to grams.

By definition: $$1\ \mathbf{mg} = 0.001\ \mathbf{g}$$

$$400\bar{0}\ \cancel{\mathbf{mg}} \times \frac{0.001\ \mathbf{g}}{\cancel{\mathbf{mg}}} = 0.400\ \mathbf{g\ of\ salt\ added}$$

(Observe that 0.001 g is derived by definition and is not a measurement precise only to one significant figure.)

$$\mathbf{mass\ of\ solution} = 98.3\ \mathbf{g} + 0.400\ \mathbf{g} = 98.7\ \mathbf{g}$$

(Recall the rule for addition of significant figures to recognize that the sum is 98.7 g and *not* 98.700 g.)

Since 0.400 g of salt is present in 98.7 g of solution, there is

$$\frac{0.400}{98.7}\ \mathbf{g\ of\ salt\ per\ gram\ of\ solution}$$

or

$$0.00405\ \mathbf{g\ salt/g\ solution}$$

MR5 Exponential notation

Scientific work sometimes involves the use of very large or very small numbers. The mass of the earth is about 6,000,000,000,000,000,000,000,000,000 grams. The mass of an electron is 0.000,000,000,000,000,000,000,000,000,910,953,4 gram. Multiplying and dividing with such numbers would be tedious and cumbersome.

It is more convenient to write and use large or small numbers expressed as powers of 10. This *exponential notation* has the form

$$M \times 10^n$$

where M is a number having one digit to the left of the decimal point and n is a positive or negative integer. All digits, zero and nonzero, expressed in M *are significant figures.*

The mass of the earth and the mass of the electron expressed in exponential-notation form become

$$6{,}000{,}000{,}000{,}000{,}000{,}000{,}000{,}000{,}000\ \mathbf{g} = 6 \times 10^{27}\ \mathbf{g}$$

$$0.000{,}000{,}000{,}000{,}000{,}000{,}000{,}000{,}000{,}910{,}953{,}4\ \mathbf{g} = 9.109534 \times 10^{-28}\ \mathbf{g}$$

The distance to the sun is 93,005,000 mi to five significant figures, and is 93,$\bar{0}$00,000 mi to three significant figures. Written in exponential form, these expressions are

$$93{,}005{,}000\ \mathbf{mi} = 9.3005 \times 10^{7}\ \mathbf{mi}$$

$$93{,}\bar{0}00{,}000\ \mathbf{mi} = 9.30 \times 10^{7}\ \mathbf{mi}$$

To change a number into exponential-notation form:

1. Determine M by moving the decimal point to leave only one nonzero digit to the left of it.

2. Determine n by counting the number of places the decimal point has been moved. If moved to the left, n is positive. If moved to the right, n is negative.

$$30{,}000{,}000{,}000 \text{ cm/s} = 3 \times 10^{10} \text{ cm/s}$$

$$30{,}\bar{0}00{,}000{,}000 \text{ cm/s} = 3.00 \times 10^{10} \text{ cm/s}$$

$$0.000059 \text{ g} = 5.9 \times 10^{-5} \text{ g}$$

$$1000 \text{ ml} = 1 \times 10^{3} \text{ ml}$$

$$10\bar{0}0 \text{ ml} = 1.00 \times 10^{3} \text{ ml}$$

$$1005 \text{ ml} = 1.005 \times 10^{3} \text{ ml}$$

MR6 Laws of exponents

Multiplication of exponents is expressed in the general form

$$a^m \times a^n$$

where a is the base and m and n are integers. In multiplication, the exponents are added.

$$a^m \times a^n = a^{m+n}$$

Examples:

$$10^3 \times 10^4 = 10^{3+4} = 10^7$$

$$10^5 \times 10^{-2} = 10^{5+(-2)} = 10^3$$

Division involving exponents is expressed as

$$a^m \div a^n$$

In division, the exponent of the divisor is subtracted from the exponent of the dividend. (Simply change the sign of the exponent of the divisor and add exponents.)

$$a^m \div a^n = a^{m-n}$$

Examples:

$$10^6 \div 10^3 = 10^{6-3} = 10^3$$

$$10^5 \div 10^{-3} = 10^{5-(-3)} = 10^8$$

In multiplication and division computations with numbers expressed in exponential form, the M terms operate according to the multiplication-division rule for significant figures (Section **MR3**). (Reminder: *all* digits are significant.) The laws of exponents govern the multiplication and division of the 10^n terms.

MR7 Equations

1. When an equation is used in solving a problem, sometimes the unknown quantity is not the one isolated. In such a case, the equation should first be solved algebraically to isolate the required unknown quantity.

SAMPLE PROBLEM

Solve the ideal-gas equation $pV = nRT$ for V

SOLUTION

Divide both sides of the equation by p. The result is

$$\boldsymbol{V = \frac{nRT}{p}}$$

SAMPLE PROBLEM

Solve the gas-law equation $V' = V \times \frac{p}{p'} \times \frac{T'}{T}$ for T

SOLUTION

Multiply both sides of the equation by $\frac{T}{V'}$. The result is

$$\boldsymbol{T = \frac{VpT'}{V'p'}}$$

2. Using the equation derived, determine the unit of the answer from the units of the given terms.

SAMPLE PROBLEM

In the equation, $V = \frac{nRT}{p}$, n is given in moles, R in $\frac{\text{liter} \cdot \text{atm}}{\text{mole} \cdot °\text{K}}$, T in °K, and p in atm. Determine the unit for V.

SOLUTION

$$\boldsymbol{V = \frac{\text{moles} \times \frac{\text{liter} \cdot \text{atm}}{\text{mole} \cdot °\text{K}} \times °\text{K}}{\text{atm}} = \text{liter}}$$

3. Substitute the values for the given quantities and estimate the answer.

SAMPLE PROBLEM

Suppose in the equation, $V = \frac{nRT}{p}$, $n = 0.250$ mole, $R = 0.0821 \frac{\text{liter} \cdot \text{atm}}{\text{mole} \cdot {}^\circ\text{K}}$, $T = 273^\circ$ K, and $p = 2.00$ atm. Estimate the value of V.

SOLUTION

$$V = \frac{0.250 \text{ mole} \times 0.0821 \frac{\text{liter} \cdot \text{atm}}{\text{mole} \cdot {}^\circ\text{K}} \times 273^\circ \text{ K}}{2.00 \text{ atm}}$$

$$V_{\text{est}} = \frac{\frac{1}{4} \times 8 \times 10^{-2} \times 3 \times 10^{2}}{2} = 3$$

The form in which the problem is now set up is easily solved on a slide rule. The final slide rule reading is 280. With an estimated answer of 3, the decimal point in the slide rule answer follows the 2. The answer has three significant figures (multiplication-division rule).

$$V = 2.80 \text{ liters}$$

MR8 Calculation of percentage error

The *percentage error* of a measurement experiment can be calculated only if the *observed* value of the quantity being measured can be compared to an *accepted* or known value.

$$\text{percentage error} = \frac{\text{experimental error}}{\text{accepted value}} \times 100\%$$

where the *experimental error* is the difference between the observed value and the accepted value.

MR9 Proportions

1. Direct proportion.

Two variables are said to be directly proportional to one another if their *quotient* has a constant value. Quantities in direct proportion act as follows: if the first quantity is doubled, so is the second; if the first quantity is multiplied by ten, so is the second; if the first quantity is divided by five, so is the second; and so on.

2. Inverse proportion.

Two variables are said to be inversely proportional to one another if their *product* has a constant value. Quantities in inverse proportion act as follows: if the first quantity is doubled, the second is halved; if the first quantity is multiplied by ten, the second is reduced to one-tenth its original value; if the first quantity is divided by five, the second becomes five times its original value; and so on.

MR10 Logarithms

The common logarithm of a number is the exponent or the power to which 10 must be raised in order to obtain the given number. A logarithm is composed of two parts: the *characteristic,* or integral part; and the *mantissa,* or decimal part. The characteristic of the logarithm of any whole or mixed number is one less than the number of digits to the left of its decimal point. The characteristic of the logarithm of a decimal fraction is always negative and is numerically one greater than the number of zeros immediately to the right of the decimal point. Mantissas are read from tables such as Table 17 in Appendix B. Such mantissas are always positive. In determining the mantissa, the decimal point in the original number is ignored since its position is indicated by the characteristic.

Logarithms are exponents and follow the laws of exponents. Specifically, the logarithm of a product equals the sum of the logarithms of the factors.

To find the number whose logarithm is given, determine the digits in the number from the table of mantissas. The characteristic indicates the position of the decimal point. The Sample Problems illustrate the use of logarithms in *Modern Chemistry.*

SAMPLE PROBLEM

Find the logarithm of 10^{-5}.

SOLUTION

Since the logarithm of a number is the power to which 10 must be raised to give the number, the logarithm of 10^{-5} is -5.

SAMPLE PROBLEM

Find the logarithm of 2.5×10^{-3}.

SOLUTION

The characteristic of the logarithm of 2.5 is 0, one less than the number of digits to the left of the decimal point. From Table 17, the mantissa of the logarithm of 2.5 is .40 (to 2 decimal places). So the complete logarithm of 2.5 is 0.40.

The logarithm of 10^{-3} is -3.

The logarithm of a product is the sum of the logarithms of the factors. Therefore,

$$\mathbf{\log 2.5 \times 10^{-3} = \log 2.5 + \log 10^{-3} = 0.40 + (-3) = -2.60}$$

SAMPLE PROBLEM

Express in exponential notation the number whose logarithm is -9.

SOLUTION

The number whose logarithm is -9 is 10^{-9}.

SAMPLE PROBLEM

Express in exponential notation the number whose logarithm is -11.30.

SOLUTION

The number whose logarithm is -11.30 is $10^{-11.30}$. To convert this expression to exponential notation, the exponent must first be changed to the sum of a positive decimal fraction and a negative whole number:

$$\mathbf{10^{-11.30} = 10^{0.70+(-12)}}$$

Since the sum of exponents indicates a product:

$$\mathbf{10^{0.70+(-12)} = 10^{0.70} \times 10^{-12}}$$

From Table 17, 0.70 is the logarithm of 5.0 (to 2 significant figures).

$$\mathbf{10^{0.70} = 5.0}$$

and

$$\mathbf{10^{0.70} \times 10^{-12} = 5.0 \times 10^{-12}}$$

TABLES

Table 1

METRIC-ENGLISH EQUIVALENTS

English to Metric	Metric to English
1 in = 2.54 cm = 2.54×10^{-2} m	1 cm = 0.3937 in = 3.281×10^{-2} ft
1 ft = 30.5 cm = 0.305 m	1 m = 39.37 in = 3.218 ft = 1.094 yd
1 yd = 91.4 cm = 0.914 m	1 cm^3 = 0.0610 in^3 = 3.53×10^{-5} ft^3
1 qt = 946 ml = 0.946 liter	1 liter = 1.06 qt = 3.53×10^{-2} ft^3
1 oz = 2.835×10^4 mg = 28.35 g	1 g = 0.0353 oz = 2.20×10^{-3} lb
1 lb = 453.6 g = 0.4536 kg	1 kg = 2.20 lb = 1.10×10^{-3} tn
1 tn = 907 kg = 0.907 metric tn	1 metric tn (10^3 kg) = $22\bar{0}0$ lb = 1.10 tn

Table 2

ISOTOPES OF SOME ELEMENTS

(Naturally occurring nonradioactive isotopes are given in bold type. Naturally occurring radioactive isotopes are bold-face italics in color. All other radioactive isotopes are in italics. Naturally occurring isotopes are listed in order of their abundance. All other isotopes are listed in order of length of half-life.)

Elements	Mass Numbers of Isotopes
H	**1, 2,** *3*
He	**4, 3,** *6, 7, 5*
Li	**7, 6,** *8, 9, 5*
Be	**9,** *10, 7, 11, 8, 6*
B	**11, 10,** *8, 13, 12, 9*
C	**12, 13,** *14, 11, 10, 15, 16*
N	**14, 15,** *13, 16, 17, 12*
O	**16, 18, 17,** *15, 14, 19, 20*
F	**19,** *18, 17, 20, 21, 16*
Ne	**20, 22, 21,** *24, 23, 19, 18*
Na	**23,** *22, 24, 25, 21, 26, 20*
Mg	**24, 26, 25,** *28, 27, 23*
Al	**27,** *26, 28, 29, 25, 30, 24, 23*
Si	**28, 29, 30,** *32, 31, 27, 26*
P	**31,** *33, 32, 30, 34, 29, 28*
S	**32, 34, 33, 36,** *35, 38, 37, 31, 30*
Cl	**35, 37,** *36, 39, 38, 40, 33, 34, 32*
Ar	**40, 36, 38,** *39, 42, 37, 41, 35*
K	**39, 41,** ***40,*** *43, 42, 44, 45, 38, 37*
Ca	**40, 44, 42,** ***48,*** **43, 46,** *41, 45, 47, 49, 39, 38*
Cr	**52, 53, 50, 54,** *51, 48, 49, 56, 55, 46, 47*
Fe	**56, 54, 57, 58,** *60, 55, 59, 52, 53, 61*
Ni	**58, 60, 62, 61, 64,** *59, 63, 66, 57, 56, 65*
Cu	**63, 65,** *67, 64, 61, 62, 66, 60, 59, 68, 58*
Zn	**64, 66, 68, 67, 70,** *65, 72, 62, 69, 63, 71, 60, 61*
Br	**79, 81,** *77, 82, 83, 76, 75, 74, 84, 80, 78, 85, 88, 87, 89, 90*
Sr	**88, 87, 86, 84,** *90, 85, 89, 82, 83, 91, 92, 80, 81, 93, 94, 95*
Ag	**107, 109,** *105, 111, 113, 112, 104, 103, 106, 115, 102, 116, 108, 117, 110, 114*
Sn	**120, 118, 116, 119, 117, 124, 122, 112, 114, 115,** *126, 113, 125, 121, 110, 127, 123, 111, 109, 108, 129, 128, 130, 132*

Table 2

ISOTOPES OF SOME ELEMENTS (cont'd)

Elements	Mass Numbers of Isotopes
I	**127,** *129, 125, 126, 131, 124, 133, 123, 130, 135, 132, 121, 120, 134, 128, 119, 118, 117, 122, 136, 137, 138, 139*
Ba	**138, 137, 136, 135, 134, 130, 132,** *133, 140, 131, 128, 129, 126, 139, 141, 127, 142, 143*
W	**184, 186, 182, 183, 180,** *181, 185, 188, 178, 187, 177, 176, 179*
Pt	**195, 194, 196, 198,** *192, 190, 193, 188, 191, 197, 200, 189, 184, 186, 187, 199*
Pb	**208, 206, 207,** *204, 205, 202, 210, 203, 200, 212, 201, 209, 198, 199, 196, 211, 214, 195, 194*
Bi	**209,** *208, 207, 205, 206, 210, 203, 204, 202, 201, 212, 213, 200, 199, 214, 215, 196, 211*
Rn	*222, 211, 224, 210, 209, 221, 212, 208, 223, 207, 206, 204, 215, 220, 219, 218, 217, 216*
Ra	*226, 228, 225, 223, 224, 230, 227, 229, 222, 221, 220*
U	*238, 235, 234, 236, 233, 232, 230, 237, 231, 229, 239, 228, 227*
Np	*237, 236, 235, 234, 239, 238, 240, 231, 233, 241, 232*
Pu	*244, 242, 239, 240, 238, 241, 236, 237, 246, 245, 234, 243, 232, 235, 233*
Am	*243, 241, 240, 242, 239, 244, 245, 238, 237, 246, 247*
Cm	*247, 248, 250, 245, 246, 243, 244, 242, 241, 240, 239, 238, 249*
Bk	*247, 248, 249, 245, 246, 243, 244, 250, 251*
Cf	*251, 249, 250, 252, 248, 254, 253, 246, 247, 245, 244, 243, 242*
Es	*254, 252, 255, 253, 251, 250, 249, 256, 248, 246, 247, 245*
Fm	*257, 253, 252, 255, 251, 254, 256, 250, 249, 248, 247, 245, 246, 244*
Md	*258, 257, 256, 255, 252*
No	*255, 253, 254, 257, 256, 252, 251*
Lr	*256, 257, 258, 259*
104	*257, 259, 260*
105	*260*
106	*263*
107	*261*

Table 3

PHYSICAL CONSTANTS

Quantity	Symbol	Value
atomic mass unit	u	$1.6605655 \times 10^{-24}$ g
Avogadro number	N_A	6.022094×10^{23}/mole
electron rest mass	m_e	9.109534×10^{-28} g
gas constant	R	8.20568×10^{-2} liter-atm/mole-°K
ideal gas volume at STP	V_m	22.41383 liters/mole
mechanical equivalent of heat	J	4.1868 joules/cal
neutron rest mass	m_n	$1.6749543 \times 10^{-24}$ g
Planck's constant	h	6.626176×10^{-34} joule-sec
proton rest mass	m_p	$1.6726485 \times 10^{-24}$ g
speed of light in vacuum	c	2.99792458×10^{8} m/sec
temperature of triple point of water		273.16°K = 0.01°C

Table 4

THE ELEMENTS, THEIR SYMBOLS, ATOMIC NUMBERS, AND ATOMIC WEIGHTS

The more common elements are printed in color.

Name of Element	Symbol	Atomic Number	Atomic Weight	Name of Element	Symbol	Atomic Number	Atomic Weight
actinium	Ac	89	[227]	mendelevium	Md	101	[256]
aluminum	Al	13	26.9815	mercury	Hg	80	200.59
americium	Am	95	[243]	molybdenum	Mo	42	95.94
antimony	Sb	51	121.75	neodymium	Nd	60	144.24
argon	Ar	18	39.948	neon	Ne	10	20.179
arsenic	As	33	74.9216	neptunium	Np	93	237.0482
astatine	At	85	[210]	nickel	Ni	28	58.71
barium	Ba	56	137.34	niobium	Nb	41	92.9064
berkelium	Bk	97	[247]	nitrogen	N	7	14.0067
beryllium	Be	4	9.01218	nobelium	No	102	[254]
bismuth	Bi	83	208.9806	osmium	Os	76	190.2
boron	B	5	10.81	oxygen	O	8	15.9994
bromine	Br	35	79.904	palladium	Pd	46	106.4
cadmium	Cd	48	112.40	phosphorus	P	15	30.9738
calcium	Ca	20	40.08	platinum	Pt	78	195.09
californium	Cf	98	[249]	plutonium	Pu	94	[244]
carbon	C	6	12.011	polonium	Po	84	[210]
cerium	Ce	58	140.12	potassium	K	19	39.102
cesium	Cs	55	132.9055	praseodymium	Pr	59	140.9077
chlorine	Cl	17	35.453	promethium	Pm	61	[147]
chromium	Cr	24	51.996	protactinium	Pa	91	231.0359
cobalt	Co	27	58.9332	radium	Ra	88	226.0254
copper	Cu	29	63.546	radon	Rn	86	[222]
curium	Cm	96	[245]	rhenium	Re	75	186.2
dysprosium	Dy	66	162.50	rhodium	Rh	45	102.9055
einsteinium	Es	99	[254]	rubidium	Rb	37	85.4678
erbium	Er	68	167.26	ruthenium	Ru	44	101.07
europium	Eu	63	151.96	rutherfordium	Rf	104	[261]
fermium	Fm	100	[255]	samarium	Sm	62	150.4
fluorine	F	9	18.9984	scandium	Sc	21	44.9559
francium	Fr	87	[223]	selenium	Se	34	78.96
gadolinium	Gd	64	157.25	silicon	Si	14	28.086
gallium	Ga	31	69.72	silver	Ag	47	107.868
germanium	Ge	32	72.59	sodium	Na	11	22.9898
gold	Au	79	196.9665	strontium	Sr	38	87.62
hafnium	Hf	72	178.49	sulfur	S	16	32.06
hahnium	Ha	105	[260]	tantalum	Ta	73	180.9479
helium	He	2	4.00260	technetium	Tc	43	98.9062
holmium	Ho	67	164.9303	tellurium	Te	52	127.60
hydrogen	H	1	1.0080	terbium	Tb	65	158.9254
indium	In	49	114.82	thallium	Tl	81	204.37
iodine	I	53	126.9045	thorium	Th	90	232.0381
iridium	Ir	77	192.22	thulium	Tm	69	168.9342
iron	Fe	26	55.847	tin	Sn	50	118.69
krypton	Kr	36	83.80	titanium	Ti	22	47.90
kurchatovium	Ku	104	[261]	tungsten	W	74	183.85
lanthanum	La	57	138.9055	uranium	U	92	238.029
lawrencium	Lr	103	[257]	vanadium	V	23	50.9414
lead	Pb	82	207.2	xenon	Xe	54	131.30
lithium	Li	3	6.941	ytterbium	Yb	70	173.04
lutetium	Lu	71	174.97	yttrium	Y	39	88.9059
magnesium	Mg	12	24.305	zinc	Zn	30	65.37
manganese	Mn	25	54.9380	zirconium	Zr	40	91.22

A value given in brackets denotes the mass number of the isotope of longest known half-life. The atomic weights of most of these elements are believed to have an error no greater than ±1 in the last digit given.

Table 5

COMMON ELEMENTS

Name	Symbol	Approx. at. wt.	Comm ox. nos.	Name	Symbol	Approx. at. wt.	Common ox. nos.
aluminum	Al	27.0	+3	magnesium	Mg	24.3	+2
antimony	Sb	121.8	+3,+5	manganese	Mn	54.9	+2,+4,+7
arsenic	As	74.9	+3,+5	mercury	Hg	200.6	+1,+2
barium	Ba	137.3	+2	nickel	Ni	58.7	+2
bismuth	Bi	209.0	+3	nitrogen	N	14.0	−3,+3,+5
bromine	Br	79.9	−1,+5	oxygen	O	16.0	−2
calcium	Ca	40.1	+2	phosphorus	P	31.0	+3,+5
carbon	C	12.0	+2,+4	platinum	Pt	195.1	+2,+4
chlorine	Cl	35.5	−1,+5,+7	potassium	K	39.1	+1
chromium	Cr	52.0	+2,+3,+6	silicon	Si	28.1	+4
cobalt	Co	58.9	+2,+3	silver	Ag	107.9	+1
copper	Cu	63.5	+1,+2	sodium	Na	23.0	+1
fluorine	F	19.0	−1	strontium	Sr	87.6	+2
gold	Au	197.0	+1,+3	sulfur	S	32.1	−2,+4,+6
hydrogen	H	1.0	−1,+1	tin	Sn	118.7	+2,+4
iodine	I	126.9	−1,+5	titanium	Ti	47.9	+3,+4
iron	Fe	55.8	+2,+3	tungsten	W	183.8	+6
lead	Pb	207.2	+2,+4	zinc	Zn	65.4	+2

Table 6

COMMON IONS AND THEIR CHARGES

Name	Symbol	Charge	Name	Symbol	Charge
aluminum	Al^{+++}	+3	lead(II)	Pb^{++}	+2
ammonium	NH_4^+	+1	magnesium	Mg^{++}	+2
barium	Ba^{++}	+2	mercury(I)	Hg_2^{++}	+2
calcium	Ca^{++}	+2	mercury(II)	Hg^{++}	+2
chromium(III)	Cr^{+++}	+3	nickel(II)	Ni^{++}	+2
cobalt(II)	Co^{++}	+2	potassium	K^+	+1
copper(I)	Cu^+	+1	silver	Ag^+	+1
copper(II)	Cu^{++}	+2	sodium	Na^+	+1
hydronium	H_3O^+	+1	tin(II)	Sn^{++}	+2
iron(II)	Fe^{++}	+2	tin(IV)	Sn^{++++}	+4
iron(III)	Fe^{+++}	+3	zinc	Zn^{++}	+2
acetate	$C_2H_3O_2^-$	−1	hydrogen sulfate	HSO_4^-	−1
bromide	Br^-	−1	hydroxide	OH^-	−1
carbonate	CO_3^{--}	−2	hypochlorite	ClO^-	−1
chlorate	ClO_3^-	−1	iodide	I^-	−1
chloride	Cl^-	−1	nitrate	NO_3^-	−1
chlorite	ClO_2^-	−1	nitrite	NO_2^-	−1
chromate	CrO_4^{--}	−2	oxide	O^{--}	−2
cyanide	CN^-	−1	perchlorate	ClO_4^-	−1
dichromate	$Cr_2O_7^{--}$	−2	permanganate	MnO_4^-	−1
fluoride	F^-	−1	peroxide	O_2^{--}	−2
hexacyanoferrate(II)	$Fe(CN)_6^{----}$	−4	phosphate	PO_4^{---}	−3
hexacyanoferrate(III)	$Fe(CN)_6^{---}$	−3	sulfate	SO_4^{--}	−2
hydride	H^-	−1	sulfide	S^{--}	−2
hydrogen carbonate	HCO_3^-	−1	sulfite	SO_3^{--}	−2

Table 7

ELECTRON ARRANGEMENT OF THE ELEMENTS

Shells		K	L		M			N				O				P				Q
Sublevels		1*s*	2*s*	2*p*	3*s*	3*p*	3*d*	4*s*	4*p*	4*d*	4*f*	5*s*	5*p*	5*d*	5*f*	6*s*	6*p*	6*d*	6*f*	7*s*
1	hydrogen	1																		
2	helium	2																		
3	lithium	2	1																	
4	beryllium	2	2																	
5	boron	2	2	1																
6	carbon	2	2	2																
7	nitrogen	2	2	3																
8	oxygen	2	2	4																
9	fluorine	2	2	5																
10	neon	2	2	6																
11	sodium	2	2	6	1															
12	magnesium	2	2	6	2															
13	aluminum	2	2	6	2	1														
14	silicon	2	2	6	2	2														
15	phosphorus	2	2	6	2	3														
16	sulfur	2	2	6	2	4														
17	chlorine	2	2	6	2	5														
18	argon	2	2	6	2	6														
19	potassium	2	2	6	2	6		1												
20	calcium	2	2	6	2	6		2												
21	scandium	2	2	6	2	6	1	2												
22	titanium	2	2	6	2	6	2	2												
23	vanadium	2	2	6	2	6	3	2												
24	chromium	2	2	6	2	6	5	1												
25	manganese	2	2	6	2	6	5	2												
26	iron	2	2	6	2	6	6	2												
27	cobalt	2	2	6	2	6	7	2												
28	nickel	2	2	6	2	6	8	2												
29	copper	2	2	6	2	6	10	1												
30	zinc	2	2	6	2	6	10	2												
31	gallium	2	2	6	2	6	10	2	1											
32	germanium	2	2	6	2	6	10	2	2											
33	arsenic	2	2	6	2	6	10	2	3											
34	selenium	2	2	6	2	6	10	2	4											
35	bromine	2	2	6	2	6	10	2	5											
36	krypton	2	2	6	2	6	10	2	6											
37	rubidium	2	2	6	2	6	10	2	6			1								
38	strontium	2	2	6	2	6	10	2	6			2								
39	yttrium	2	2	6	2	6	10	2	6	1		2								
40	zirconium	2	2	6	2	6	10	2	6	2		2								
41	niobium	2	2	6	2	6	10	2	6	4		1								
42	molybdenum	2	2	6	2	6	10	2	6	5		1								
43	technetium	2	2	6	2	6	10	2	6	5		2								
44	ruthenium	2	2	6	2	6	10	2	6	7		1								
45	rhodium	2	2	6	2	6	10	2	6	8		1								
46	palladium	2	2	6	2	6	10	2	6	10										
47	silver	2	2	6	2	6	10	2	6	10		1								
48	cadmium	2	2	6	2	6	10	2	6	10		2								
49	indium	2	2	6	2	6	10	2	6	10		2	1							
50	tin	2	2	6	2	6	10	2	6	10		2	2							
51	antimony	2	2	6	2	6	10	2	6	10		2	3							
52	tellurium	2	2	6	2	6	10	2	6	10		2	4							

Table 7

ELECTRON ARRANGEMENT OF THE ELEMENTS (cont'd)

Shells		K	L		M			N				O				P				Q
Sublevels		1s	2s	2p	3s	3p	3d	4s	4p	4d	4f	5s	5p	5d	5f	6s	6p	6d	6f	7s
53	iodine	2	2	6	2	6	10	2	6	10		2	5							
54	xenon	2	2	6	2	6	10	2	6	10		2	6							
55	cesium	2	2	6	2	6	10	2	6	10		2	6			1				
56	barium	2	2	6	2	6	10	2	6	10		2	6			2				
57	lanthanum	2	2	6	2	6	10	2	6	10		2	6	1		2				
58	cerium	2	2	6	2	6	10	2	6	10	2	2	6			2				
59	praseodymium	2	2	6	2	6	10	2	6	10	3	2	6			2				
60	neodymium	2	2	6	2	6	10	2	6	10	4	2	6			2				
61	promethium	2	2	6	2	6	10	2	6	10	5	2	6			2				
62	samarium	2	2	6	2	6	10	2	6	10	6	2	6			2				
63	europium	2	2	6	2	6	10	2	6	10	7	2	6			2				
64	gadolinium	2	2	6	2	6	10	2	6	10	7	2	6	1		2				
65	terbium	2	2	6	2	6	10	2	6	10	9	2	6			2				
66	dysprosium	2	2	6	2	6	10	2	6	10	10	2	6			2				
67	holmium	2	2	6	2	6	10	2	6	10	11	2	6			2				
68	erbium	2	2	6	2	6	10	2	6	10	12	2	6			2				
69	thulium	2	2	6	2	6	10	2	6	10	13	2	6			2				
70	ytterbium	2	2	6	2	6	10	2	6	10	14	2	6			2				
71	lutetium	2	2	6	2	6	10	2	6	10	14	2	6	1		2				
72	hafnium	2	2	6	2	6	10	2	6	10	14	2	6	2		2				
73	tantalum	2	2	6	2	6	10	2	6	10	14	2	6	3		2				
74	tungsten	2	2	6	2	6	10	2	6	10	14	2	6	4		2				
75	rhenium	2	2	6	2	6	10	2	6	10	14	2	6	5		2				
76	osmium	2	2	6	2	6	10	2	6	10	14	2	6	6		2				
77	iridium	2	2	6	2	6	10	2	6	10	14	2	6	7		2				
78	platinum	2	2	6	2	6	10	2	6	10	14	2	6	9		1				
79	gold	2	2	6	2	6	10	2	6	10	14	2	6	10		1				
80	mercury	2	2	6	2	6	10	2	6	10	14	2	6	10		2				
81	thallium	2	2	6	2	6	10	2	6	10	14	2	6	10		2	1			
82	lead	2	2	6	2	6	10	2	6	10	14	2	6	10		2	2			
83	bismuth	2	2	6	2	6	10	2	6	10	14	2	6	10		2	3			
84	polonium	2	2	6	2	6	10	2	6	10	14	2	6	10		2	4			
85	astatine	2	2	6	2	6	10	2	6	10	14	2	6	10		2	5			
86	radon	2	2	6	2	6	10	2	6	10	14	2	6	10		2	6			
87	francium	2	2	6	2	6	10	2	6	10	14	2	6	10		2	6			1
88	radium	2	2	6	2	6	10	2	6	10	14	2	6	10		2	6			2
89	actinium	2	2	6	2	6	10	2	6	10	14	2	6	10		2	6	1		2
90	thorium	2	2	6	2	6	10	2	6	10	14	2	6	10		2	6	2		2
91	protactinium	2	2	6	2	6	10	2	6	10	14	2	6	10	2	2	6	1		2
92	uranium	2	2	6	2	6	10	2	6	10	14	2	6	10	3	2	6	1		2
93	neptunium	2	2	6	2	6	10	2	6	10	14	2	6	10	4	2	6	1		2
94	plutonium	2	2	6	2	6	10	2	6	10	14	2	6	10	6	2	6			2
95	americium	2	2	6	2	6	10	2	6	10	14	2	6	10	7	2	6			2
96	curium	2	2	6	2	6	10	2	6	10	14	2	6	10	7	2	6	1		2
97	berkelium	2	2	6	2	6	10	2	6	10	14	2	6	10	8	2	6	1		2
98	californium	2	2	6	2	6	10	2	6	10	14	2	6	10	10	2	6			2?
99	einsteinium	2	2	6	2	6	10	2	6	10	14	2	6	10	11	2	6			2?
100	fermium	2	2	6	2	6	10	2	6	10	14	2	6	10	12	2	6			2?
101	mendelevium	2	2	6	2	6	10	2	6	10	14	2	6	10	13	2	6			2?
102	nobelium	2	2	6	2	6	10	2	6	10	14	2	6	10	14	2	6			2?
103	lawrencium	2	2	6	2	6	10	2	6	10	14	2	6	10	14	2	6	1		2?
104		2	2	6	2	6	10	2	6	10	14	2	6	10	14	2	6	2		2?
105		2	2	6	2	6	10	2	6	10	14	2	6	10	14	2	6	3		2?
106		2	2	6	2	6	10	2	6	10	14	2	6	10	14	2	6	4		2?
107		2	2	6	2	6	10	2	6	10	14	2	6	10	14	2	6	5		2?

Table 8

WATER-VAPOR PRESSURE					
Temperature (°C)	Pressure (mm Hg)	Temperature (°C)	Pressure (mm Hg)	Temperature (°C)	Pressure (mm Hg)
0.0	4.6	19.5	17.0	27.0	26.7
5.0	6.5	20.0	17.5	28.0	28.3
10.0	9.2	20.5	18.1	29.0	30.0
12.5	10.9	21.0	18.6	30.0	31.8
15.0	12.8	21.5	19.2	35.0	42.2
15.5	13.2	22.0	19.8	40.0	55.3
16.0	13.6	22.5	20.4	50.0	92.5
16.5	14.1	23.0	21.1	60.0	149.4
17.0	14.5	23.5	21.7	70.0	233.7
17.5	15.0	24.0	22.4	80.0	355.1
18.0	15.5	24.5	23.1	90.0	525.8
18.5	16.0	25.0	23.8	95.0	633.9
19.0	16.5	26.0	25.2	100.0	760.0

Table 9

DENSITY OF GASES AT STP			
Gas	Density (g/liter)	Gas	Density (g/liter)
air, dry	1.2929	hydrogen	0.0899
ammonia	0.771	hydrogen chloride	1.640
carbon dioxide	1.977	hydrogen sulfide	1.539
carbon monoxide	1.250	methane	0.716
chlorine	3.214	nitrogen	1.251
dinitrogen monoxide	1.977	nitrogen monoxide	1.340
ethyne (acetylene)	1.172	oxygen	1.429
helium	0.1785	sulfur dioxide	2.927

Table 10

DENSITY OF WATER			
Temperature (°C)	Density (g/ml)	Temperature (°C)	Density (g/ml)
0	0.99987	15	0.99913
1	0.99993	20	0.99823
2	0.99997	25	0.99707
3	0.99999	30	0.99567
4	1.00000	40	0.99224
5	0.99999	50	0.98807
6	0.99997	60	0.98324
7	0.99993	70	0.97781
8	0.99988	80	0.97183
9	0.99981	90	0.96534
10	0.99973	100	0.95838

Table 11

SOLUBILITY OF GASES IN WATER

Volume of gas (reduced to STP) that can be dissolved in 1 volume of water.

Gas	0°C	10°C	20°C
air	0.0292	0.0228	0.0187
ammonia	1176	902	702
carbon dioxide	1.713	1.194	0.878
chlorine	4.54	3.148	2.299
hydrogen	0.0215	0.0196	0.0182
hydrogen chloride	506.7	473.9	442.0
hydrogen sulfide	4.670	3.399	2.582
nitrogen	0.0235	0.0186	0.0155
oxygen	0.0489	0.0380	0.0310
sulfur dioxide	79.79	56.65	39.37

Table 12

SOLUBILITY CHART

S = soluble in water. A = soluble in acids, insoluble in water. P = partially soluble in water, soluble in dilute acids. I = insoluble in dilute acids and in water. a = slightly soluble in acids, insoluble in water. d = decomposes in water.

	Acetate	Bromide	Carbonate	Chlorate	Chloride	Chromate	Hydroxide	Iodide	Nitrate	Oxide	Phosphate	Silicate	Sulfate	Sulfide
aluminum	S	S	—	S	S	—	A	S	S	a	A	I	S	d
ammonium	S	S	S	S	S	S	—	S	S	—	S	—	S	S
barium	S	S	P	S	S	A	S	S	S	S	A	S	a	d
calcium	S	S	P	S	S	S	S	S	S	P	P	P	P	P
copper(II)	S	S	—	S	S	—	A	—	S	A	A	A	S	A
hydrogen	S	S	—	S	S	—	—	S	S	—	S	I	S	S
iron(II)	S	S	P	S	S	—	A	S	S	A	A	—	S	A
iron(III)	S	S	—	S	S	A	A	S	S	A	P	—	P	d
lead(II)	S	S	A	S	S	A	P	P	S	P	A	A	P	A
magnesium	S	S	P	S	S	S	A	S	S	A	P	A	S	d
manganese(II)	S	S	P	S	S	—	A	S	S	A	P	I	S	A
mercury(I)	P	A	A	S	a	P	—	A	S	A	A	—	P	I
mercury(II)	S	S	—	S	S	P	A	P	S	P	A	—	d	I
potassium	S	S	S	S	S	S	S	S	S	S	S	S	S	S
silver	P	a	A	S	a	P	—	I	S	P	A	—	P	A
sodium	S	S	S	S	S	S	S	S	S	S	S	S	S	S
strontium	S	S	P	S	S	P	S	S	S	S	A	A	P	S
tin(II)	d	S	—	S	S	A	A	S	d	A	A	—	S	A
tin(IV)	S	S	—	—	S	S	P	d	—	A	—	—	S	A
zinc	S	S	P	S	S	P	A	S	S	P	A	A	S	A

Table 13

SOLUBILITY OF COMPOUNDS

Solubilities given in grams of anhydrous compound that can be dissolved in exactly 100 grams of water at the indicated temperatures. Solid phase gives the hydrated form in equilibrium with the saturated solution.

Compound	Formula	Solid Phase	0°C	20°C	60°C	100°
aluminum sulfate	$Al_2(SO_4)_3$	$18H_2O$	31.2	36.4	59.2	89.0
ammonium chloride	NH_4Cl	—	29.4	37.2	55.2	77.3
ammonium nitrate	NH_4NO_3	—	118.3	192.0	421.0	871.0
ammonium sulfate	$(NH_4)_2SO_4$	—	70.6	75.4	88.0	103.3
barium carbonate	$BaCO_3$	—	$0.0016^{8°}$	$0.0022^{18°}$	—	0.0065
barium chloride	$BaCl_2$	$2H_2O$	31.6	35.7	46.4	58.8
barium hydroxide	$Ba(OH)_2$	$8H_2O$	1.67	3.89	20.94	$101.40^{80°}$
barium nitrate	$Ba(NO_3)_2$	—	5.0	9.2	20.3	34.2
barium sulfate	$BaSO_4$	—	1.15×10^{-4}	2.4×10^{-4}	—	4.13×10^{-4}
cadmium sulfate	$CdSO_4$	—	76.48	76.60	83.68	60.77
calcium acetate	$Ca(C_2H_3O_2)_2$	$2H_2O$	37.4	34.7	32.7	—
calcium carbonate	$CaCO_3$	—	—	0.0012	—	0.002
calcium fluoride	CaF_2	—	$0.0016^{18°}$	$0.0017^{25°}$	—	—
calcium hydrogen carbonate	$Ca(HCO_3)_2$	—	16.15	16.60	17.50	18.40
calcium hydroxide	$Ca(OH)_2$	—	0.19	0.17	0.12	0.08
calcium sulfate	$CaSO_4$	$2H_2O$	0.18	0.19	0.20	0.16
cerium sulfate	$Ce_2(SO_4)_3$	$8H_2O$	19.0	9.52	4.04	—
cesium nitrate	$CsNO_3$	—	9.33	23.0	83.8	197.0
copper(II) chloride	$CuCl_2$	$2H_2O$	70.7	77.0	91.2	107.9
copper(II) sulfate	$CuSO_4$	$5H_2O$	14.3	20.7	40.0	75.4
lead(II) chloride	$PbCl_2$	—	0.67	0.99	1.98	3.34
lead(II) nitrate	$Pb(NO_3)_2$	—	38.8	56.5	95	138.8
lithium chloride	$LiCl$	—	67	78.5	103	127.5
lithium sulfate	Li_2SO_4	H_2O	35.3	34.2	31.9	29.9
magnesium hydroxide	$Mg(OH)_2$	—	—	$0.0009^{18°}$	—	—
magnesium sulfate	$MgSO_4$	$6H_2O$	40.8	44.5	53.5	74.0
mercury(I) chloride	Hg_2Cl_2	—	0.00014	0.0002	$0.0007^{40°}$	—
mercury(II) chloride	$HgCl_2$	—	3.6	6.5	16.2	61.3
potassium aluminum sulfate	$KAl(SO_4)_2$	$12H_2O$	3.0	5.9	24.75	$109.0^{90°}$
potassium bromide	KBr	—	53.5	65.2	85.5	104.0
potassium chlorate	$KClO_3$	—	3.3	7.4	24.5	57.0
potassium chloride	KCl	—	27.6	34.0	45.5	56.7
potassium chromate	K_2CrO_4	—	58.2	61.7	68.6	75.6
potassium iodide	KI	—	127.5	144	176	208
potassium nitrate	KNO_3	—	13.3	31.6	110.0	246.0
potassium permanganate	$KMnO_4$	—	2.83	6.4	22.2	—
potassium sulfate	K_2SO_4	—	7.4	11.1	18.2	24.1
silver acetate	$AgC_2H_3O_2$	—	0.72	1.04	1.89	$2.52^{80°}$
silver chloride	$AgCl$	—	8.9×10^{-5} $^{10°}$	1.5×10^{-4}	$0.0005^{50°}$	0.002
silver nitrate	$AgNO_3$	—	122	222	525	952
silver sulfate	Ag_2SO_4	—	0.573	0.796	1.15	1.41
sodium acetate	$NaC_2H_3O_2$	—	119	123.5	139.5	170
sodium chlorate	$NaClO_3$	—	79	101	155	230
sodium chloride	$NaCl$	—	35.7	36.0	37.3	39.8
sodium nitrate	$NaNO_3$	—	73.0	88.0	124.0	180.0
sugar (sucrose)	$C_{12}H_{22}O_{11}$	—	179.2	203.9	287.3	487.2
ytterbium sulfate	$Yb_2(SO_4)_3$	$8H_2O$	44.2	$21.0^{30°}$	10.4	4.67

Table 14

HEAT OF FORMATION

ΔH_f heat of formation of the given substance from its elements. All values of ΔH_f are expressed as kcal/mole at 25° C. Negative values of ΔH_f indicate exothermic reactions. s = solid, l = liquid, g = gas.

Substance	Phase	ΔH_f
aluminum oxide	s	−399.09
ammonia	g	−11.04
ammonium chloride	s	−75.38
ammonium sulfate	s	−281.86
barium chloride	s	−205.56
barium nitrate	s	−237.06
barium sulfate	s	−350.2
benzene	g	+19.82
benzene	l	+11.72
calcium carbonate	s	−288.45
calcium chloride	s	−190.0
calcium hydroxide	s	−235.80
calcium nitrate	s	−224.0
calcium oxide	s	−151.9
calcium sulfate	s	−342.42
carbon (diamond)	s	+0.45
carbon (graphite)	s	0.00
carbon dioxide	g	−94.05
carbon disulfide	g	+27.55
carbon disulfide	l	+21.0
carbon monoxide	g	−26.42
carbon tetrachloride	g	−25.5
carbon tetrachloride	l	−33.3
copper(II) nitrate	s	−73.4
copper(II) oxide	s	−37.1
copper(II) sulfate	s	−184.00
copper(I) sulfide	s	−19.0
copper(II) sulfide	s	−11.6
dinitrogen monoxide	g	+19.49
dinitrogen pentoxide	g	+3.6
dinitrogen pentoxide	l	−10.0
dinitrogen tetroxide	g	+2.31
diphosphorus pentoxide	s	−720.0
ethane	g	−20.24
ethyne (acetylene)	g	+54.19
hydrogen (H_2)	g	0.00
hydrogen bromide	g	−8.66
hydrogen chloride	g	−22.06
hydrogen fluoride	g	−64.2
hydrogen iodide	g	+6.20
hydrogen oxide (water)	g	−57.80
hydrogen oxide (water)	l	−68.32
hydrogen peroxide	g	−31.83
hydrogen peroxide	l	−44.84
hydrogen sulfide	g	−4.82
iodine (I_2)	s	0.00
iodine (I_2)	g	+14.88
iron(III) chloride	s	−96.8
iron(III) oxide	s	−196.5

Substance	Phase	ΔH_f
iron(II,III) oxide	s	−267.0
iron(II) sulfate	s	−220.5
iron(II) sulfide	s	−22.72
lead(II) oxide	s	−52.07
lead(IV) oxide	s	−66.12
lead(II) nitrate	s	−107.35
lead(II) sulfate	s	−219.50
lead(II) sulfide	s	−22.54
lithium chloride	s	−97.70
lithium nitrate	s	−115.28
lithium sulfate	s	−342.83
magnesium chloride	s	−153.40
magnesium oxide	s	−143.84
magnesium sulfate	s	−305.5
manganese(IV) oxide	s	−124.5
mercury(I) chloride	s	−63.32
mercury(II) chloride	s	−55.0
mercury(II) fulminate	s	+64
mercury(II) nitrate	s	−93.0
mercury(II) oxide	s	−21.68
methane	g	−17.89
nitrogen dioxide	g	+8.09
nitrogen monoxide	g	+21.60
oxygen (O_2)	g	0.00
ozone (O_3)	g	+34.00
potassium bromide	s	−93.73
potassium chloride	s	−104.18
potassium hydroxide	s	−101.78
potassium iodide	s	−78.31
potassium nitrate	s	−117.76
potassium sulfate	s	−342.66
silicon dioxide (quartz)	s	−205.4
silver acetate	s	−93.41
silver chloride	s	−30.36
silver nitrate	s	−29.43
silver sulfide	s	−7.69
sodium bromide	s	−86.03
sodium chloride	s	−98.23
sodium hydroxide	s	−101.99
sodium nitrate	s	−101.54
sodium sulfate	s	−330.90
sulfur dioxide	g	−70.96
sulfur trioxide	g	−94.45
tin(IV) chloride	l	−130.3
zinc nitrate	s	−115.12
zinc oxide	s	−83.17
zinc sulfate	s	−233.88
zinc sulfide	s	−48.5
zirconium oxide	s	−258.2

Table 15

HEAT OF COMBUSTION

ΔH_c = heat of combustion of the given substance. All values of ΔH_c are expressed as kcal/mole of substance oxidized to $H_2O(l)$ and/or $CO_2(g)$ at constant pressure and 25°C. s = solid, l = liquid, g = gas.

Substance	Formula	Phase	ΔH_c
hydrogen	H_2	g	−68.32
graphite	C	s	−94.05
carbon monoxide	CO	g	−67.64
methane	CH_4	g	−212.80
ethane	C_2H_6	g	−372.82
propane	C_3H_8	g	−530.60
butane	C_4H_{10}	g	−687.98
pentane	C_5H_{12}	g	−845.16
hexane	C_6H_{14}	l	−995.01
heptane	C_7H_{16}	l	−1151.27
octane	C_8H_{18}	l	−1307.53
ethene (ethylene)	C_2H_4	g	−337.23
propene (propylene)	C_3H_6	g	−491.99
ethyne (acetylene)	C_2H_2	g	−310.62
benzene	C_6H_6	l	−780.98
toluene	C_7H_8	l	−934.50

Table 16

PROPERTIES OF COMMON ELEMENTS

Name	Form/Color at Room Temperature	Density (g/cm^3)	Melting Point (°C)	Boiling Point (°C)	Common Oxidation Numbers
aluminum	silv metal	2.70	660.2	2467	+3
antimony	silv metal	6.69	630.5	1380	+3, +5
argon	colorless gas	1.782*	−189.2	−185.7	0
arsenic	gray metal	5.73	(sublimes)	(sublimes)	+3, +5
barium	silv metal	3.5	725	1140	+2
beryllium	gray metal	1.848	1278	2970	+2
bismuth	silv metal	9.75	271.3	1560	+3
boron	blk solid	2.34	2300	2550 (sublimes)	+3
bromine	red-br liquid	3.12	−7.2	58.8	−1, +5
calcium	silv metal	1.55	842	1487	+2
carbon	diamond	3.51	(sublimes	4827	+2, +4
	graphite	2.26	above 3500° C)	4200	
chlorine	grn-yel gas	3.214*	−101.0	−34.6	−1, +5, +7
chromium	silv metal	7.18	1890	2482	+2, +3, +6
cobalt	silv metal	8.9	1495	2900	+2, +3
copper	red metal	8.96	1083.0	2595	+1, +2
fluorine	yel gas	1.695*	−219.6	−188.1	−1
gold	yel metal	19.32	1063.0	2966	+1, +3
helium	colorless gas	0.1785*	−272.2 (26 atm)	−268.6	0
hydrogen	colorless gas	0.0899*	−259.1	−252.5	−1, +1
iodine	blk solid	4.93	113.5	184.4	−1, +5
iron	silv metal	7.87	1535	3000	+2, +3
lead	silv metal	11.35	327.5	1744	+2, +4
lithium	silv metal	0.534	179	1317	+1
magnesium	silv metal	1.74	651	1107	+2
manganese	silv metal	7.3	1244	2097	+2, +4, +7
mercury	silv liquid	13.55	−38.9	356.6	+1, +2
neon	colorless gas	0.9002*	−248.67	−245.92	0
nickel	silv metal	8.90	1453	2732	+2
nitrogen	colorless gas	1.2506*	−209.9	−195.8	−3, +3, +5
oxygen	colorless gas	1.4290*	−218.4	−183.0	−2
phosphorus	yel solid	1.82	44.1	280	+3, +5
platinum	silv metal	21.45	1769	3800	+2, +4
potassium	silv metal	0.86	63.6	774	+1
radium	silv metal	5(?)	700	<1737	+2
silicon	blk solid	2.33	1410	2355	+4
silver	silv metal	10.50	960.8	2212	+1
sodium	silv metal	0.97	97.8	892	+1
strontium	silv metal	2.54	769	1384	+2
sulfur	yel solid	2.0	114.5	444.6	−2, +4, +6
tin	silv metal	7.31	231.9	2270	+2, +4
titanium	silv metal	4.54	1675	3260	+3, +4
tungsten	gray metal	19.3	3410	5927	+6
uranium	silv metal	19.05	1132.3	3818	+4, +6
zinc	silv metal	7.13	419.4	907	+2

*Densities of gases are given in grams/liter.

Table 17

FOUR-PLACE LOGARITHMS OF NUMBERS

n	0	1	2	3	4	5	6	7	8	9
10	0000	0043	0086	0128	0170	0212	0253	0294	0334	0374
11	0414	0453	0492	0531	0569	0607	0645	0682	0719	0755
12	0792	0828	0864	0899	0934	0969	1004	1038	1072	1106
13	1139	1173	1206	1239	1271	1303	1335	1367	1399	1430
14	1461	1492	1523	1553	1584	1614	1644	1673	1703	1732
15	1761	1790	1818	1847	1875	1903	1931	1959	1987	2014
16	2041	2068	2095	2122	2148	2175	2201	2227	2253	2279
17	2304	2330	2355	2380	2405	2430	2455	2480	2504	2529
18	2553	2577	2601	2625	2648	2672	2695	2718	2742	2765
19	2788	2810	2833	2856	2878	2900	2923	2945	2967	2989
20	3010	3032	3054	3075	3096	3118	3139	3160	3181	3201
21	3222	3243	3263	3284	3304	3324	3345	3365	3385	3404
22	3424	3444	3464	3483	3502	3522	3541	3560	3579	3598
23	3617	3636	3655	3674	3692	3711	3729	3747	3766	3784
24	3802	3820	3838	3856	3874	3892	3909	3927	3945	3962
25	3979	3997	4014	4031	4048	4065	4082	4099	4116	4133
26	4150	4166	4183	4200	4216	4232	4249	4265	4281	4298
27	4314	4330	4346	4362	4378	4393	4409	4425	4440	4456
28	4472	4487	4502	4518	4533	4548	4564	4579	4594	4609
29	4624	4639	4654	4669	4683	4698	4713	4728	4742	4757
30	4771	4786	4800	4814	4829	4843	4857	4871	4886	4900
31	4914	4928	4942	4955	4969	4983	4997	5011	5024	5038
32	5051	5065	5079	5092	5105	5119	5132	5145	5159	5172
33	5185	5198	5211	5224	5237	5250	5263	5276	5289	5302
34	5315	5328	5340	5353	5366	5378	5391	5403	5416	5428
35	5441	5453	5465	5478	5490	5502	5514	5527	5539	5551
36	5563	5575	5587	5599	5611	5623	5635	5647	5658	5670
37	5682	5694	5705	5717	5729	5740	5752	5763	5775	5786
38	5798	5809	5821	5832	5843	5855	5866	5877	5888	5899
39	5911	5922	5933	5944	5955	5966	5977	5988	5999	6010
40	6021	6031	6042	6053	6064	6075	6085	6096	6107	6117
41	6128	6138	6149	6160	6170	6180	6191	6201	6212	6222
42	6232	6243	6253	6263	6274	6284	6294	6304	6314	6325
43	6335	6345	6355	6365	6375	6385	6395	6405	6415	6425
44	6435	6444	6454	6464	6474	6484	6493	6503	6513	6522
45	6532	6542	6551	6561	6571	6580	6590	6599	6609	6618
46	6628	6637	6646	6656	6665	6675	6684	6693	6702	6712
47	6721	6730	6739	6749	6758	6767	6776	6785	6794	6803
48	6812	6821	6830	6839	6848	6857	6866	6875	6884	6893
49	6902	6911	6920	6928	6937	6946	6955	6964	6972	6981
50	6990	6998	7007	7016	7024	7033	7042	7050	7059	7067
51	7076	7084	7093	7101	7110	7118	7126	7135	7143	7152
52	7160	7168	7177	7185	7193	7202	7210	7218	7226	7235
53	7243	7251	7259	7267	7275	7284	7292	7300	7308	7316
54	7324	7332	7340	7348	7356	7364	7372	7380	7388	7396

Table 17

FOUR-PLACE LOGARITHMS OF NUMBERS (cont'd)

n	0	1	2	3	4	5	6	7	8	9
55	7404	7412	7419	7427	7435	7443	7451	7459	7466	7474
56	7482	7490	7497	7505	7513	7520	7528	7536	7543	7551
57	7559	7566	7574	7582	7589	7597	7604	7612	7619	7627
58	7634	7642	7649	7657	7664	7672	7679	7686	7694	7701
59	7709	7716	7723	7731	7738	7745	7752	7760	7767	7774
60	7782	7789	7796	7803	7810	7818	7825	7832	7839	7846
61	7853	7860	7868	7875	7882	7889	7896	7903	7910	7917
62	7924	7931	7938	7945	7952	7959	7966	7973	7980	7987
63	7993	8000	8007	8014	8021	8028	8035	8041	8048	8055
64	8062	8069	8075	8082	8089	8096	8102	8109	8116	8122
65	8129	8136	8142	8149	8156	8162	8169	8176	8182	8189
66	8195	8202	8209	8215	8222	8228	8235	8241	8248	8254
67	8261	8267	8274	8280	8287	8293	8299	8306	8312	8319
68	8325	8331	8338	8344	8351	8357	8363	8370	8376	8382
69	8388	8395	8401	8407	8414	8420	8426	8432	8439	8445
70	8451	8457	8463	8470	8476	8482	8488	8494	8500	8506
71	8513	8519	8525	8531	8537	8543	8549	8555	8561	8567
72	8573	8579	8585	8591	8597	8603	8609	8615	8621	8627
73	8633	8639	8645	8651	8657	8663	8669	8675	8681	8686
74	8692	8698	8704	8710	8716	8722	8727	8733	8739	8745
75	8751	8756	8762	8768	8774	8779	8785	8791	8797	8802
76	8808	8814	8820	8825	8831	8837	8842	8848	8854	8859
77	8865	8871	8876	8882	8887	8893	8899	8904	8910	8915
78	8921	8927	8932	8938	8943	8949	8954	8960	8965	8971
79	8976	8982	8987	8993	8998	9004	9009	9015	9020	9025
80	9031	9036	9042	9047	9053	9058	9063	9069	9074	9079
81	9085	9090	9096	9101	9106	9112	9117	9122	9128	9133
82	9138	9143	9149	9154	9159	9165	9170	9175	9180	9186
83	9191	9196	9201	9206	9212	9217	9222	9227	9232	9238
84	9243	9248	9253	9258	9263	9269	9274	9279	9284	9289
85	9294	9299	9304	9309	9315	9320	9325	9330	9335	9340
86	9345	9350	9355	9360	9365	9370	9375	9380	9385	9390
87	9395	9400	9405	9410	9415	9420	9425	9430	9435	9440
88	9445	9450	9455	9460	9465	9469	9474	9479	9484	9489
89	9494	9499	9504	9509	9513	9518	9523	9528	9533	9538
90	9542	9547	9552	9557	9562	9566	9571	9576	9581	9586
91	9590	9595	9600	9605	9609	9614	9619	9624	9628	9633
92	9638	9643	9647	9652	9657	9661	9666	9671	9675	9680
93	9685	9689	9694	9699	9703	9708	9713	9717	9722	9727
94	9731	9736	9741	9745	9750	9754	9759	9763	9768	9773
95	9777	9782	9786	9791	9795	9800	9805	9809	9814	9818
96	9823	9827	9832	9836	9841	9845	9850	9854	9859	9863
97	9868	9872	9877	9881	9886	9890	9894	9899	9903	9908
98	9912	9917	9921	9926	9930	9934	9939	9943	9948	9952
99	9956	9961	9965	9969	9974	9978	9983	9987	9991	9996

GLOSSARY

absolute zero. The lowest possible temperature, 0°K or −273.15°C.

accuracy. The nearness of a measurement to its accepted value.

acid. (1) A substance that increases the hydronium-ion concentration of its aqueous solution. (2) A proton donor. (3) An electron-pair acceptor.

acid, aqueous. A water solution having acid properties owing to the nature of the solute present.

acid, conjugate. The species formed when a base acquires a proton.

acid anhydride. An oxide that reacts with water and forms an acid, or that is formed by the removal of water from an acid.

actinide series. Rare earth elements of the seventh period following radium, in which the transitional inner building of the *6d* sublevel is interrupted by the inner building of the *5f* sublevel.

activated complex. The transitional structure resulting from an effective collision of reactant particles.

activation energy. See *energy, activation.*

activity series. A table of metals or nonmetals arranged in order of descending activities.

addition. A reaction in which atoms are added to an unsaturated organic molecule.

adsorption. The concentration of a gas, liquid, or solid on the surface of a liquid or solid with which it is in contact.

alcohol. A compound containing a hydrocarbon group and one or more -OH, hydroxyl groups.

aldehyde. A compound that has a hydrocarbon group and one or more 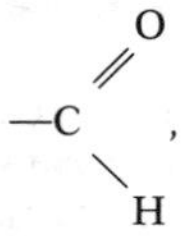, formyl, groups.

alkadiene. A straight- or branched-chain hydrocarbon with two double covalent bonds between carbon atoms in each molecule.

alkali. The hydroxide or carbonate of a Group I metal.

alkali metal. See *metal, alkali.*

alkaline-earth metal. See *metal, alkaline-earth.*

alkane. A straight- or branched-chain hydrocarbon in which the carbon atoms are connected by only single covalent bonds; a member of the paraffin series.

alkene. A straight- or branched-chain hydrocarbon in which two carbon atoms in each molecule are connected by a double covalent bond; a member of the olefin series.

alkyl group. A group derived from an alkane by the loss of a hydrogen atom; frequently symbolized by R-.

alkyl halide. See *halide, alkyl.*

alkylation. The combining of simple hydrocarbons with unsaturated hydrocarbons by heat in the presence of a catalyst.

alkyne. A straight- or branched-chain hydrocarbon in which two carbon atoms in each molecule are connected by a triple covalent bond; a member of the acetylene series.

allotrope. One of the two or more different forms of an element in the same physical phase.

allotropy. The existence of an element in two or more forms in the same physical phase.

alloy. A material composed of two or more metals.

alpha particle. A helium nucleus emitted from the nucleus of a radioactive element.

alum. A double salt of the type $M^{+}M^{+++}(SO_4)_2 \cdot 12H_2O$, $KA1(SO_4)_2 \cdot 12H_2O$ being the most common.

alumina. Anhydrous aluminum oxide, Al_2O_3.

amorphous. Without definite shape.

amphoteric. Capable of acting either as an acid or as a base.

analysis. The separation of a material into its component parts to determine the composition.

angstrom. A unit of linear measure; 1×10^{-8} cm.

anhydrous. Without water of crystallization.

anion. An ion attracted to the anode of an electrolytic cell; a negative ion.

anion hydrolysis. See *hydrolysis, anion.*

anode. A positively charged, or electron-poor electrode.

aqueous acid. See *acid, aqueous.*

aqueous base. See *base, aqueous.*

aromatic hydrocarbon. See *hydrocarbon, aromatic.*

atom. The smallest unit of an element that can exist either alone or in combination with other atoms like it or different from it.

atom, excited. An atom that has absorbed a photon.

atomic mass. See *mass, atomic.*

atomic number. The number of protons in the nucleus of an atom.

atomic theory. See *theory, atomic.*

atomic weight. See *weight, atomic.*

auto-oxidation. Self-oxidizing and reducing. Redox process in which the substance acts both as the oxidizing agent and reducing agent.

Avogadro number. The number of carbon-12 atoms in exactly 12 grams of this nuclide; 6.022094×10^{23}.

baking soda. Sodium hydrogen carbonate, $NaHCO_3$.

barometer. An apparatus for measuring atmospheric pressure.

base. (1) A substance that increases the hydroxide-ion concentration of its aqueous solution. (2) A proton acceptor. (3) An electron-pair donor.

base, aqueous. A water solution having basic properties owing to the nature of the solute present.

base, conjugate. The species that remains after an acid has donated a proton.

basic anhydride. An oxide that reacts with water and forms a solution containing OH^- ions.

beta particle. An electron emitted from the nucleus of a radioactive element.
betatron. A device for accelerating electrons.
binary compound. See *compound, binary.*
binding energy. See *energy, binding.*
blast furnace. A tall cylindrical chamber in which iron oxide is reduced using coke, limestone, and a blast of hot air.
bleaching. The operation by which color is partially or wholly removed from a colored material.
blue vitriol. Hydrated copper(II) sulfate, $CuSO_4$ $5H_2O$.
boiling point. The temperature at which the equilibrium vapor pressure of a liquid is equal to the prevailing atmospheric pressure.
boiling-point constant, molal. The boiling-point elevation of a solvent in a 1-molal solution of a nonvolatile, molecular solute in the solvent.
boiling point, standard. The temperature at which the equilibrium vapor pressure of a liquid is equal to the standard atmospheric pressure, 760 mm of mercury.
bond energy. See *energy, bond.*
borax. Sodium tetraborate, $Na_2B_4O_7 \cdot 10H_2O$.
borax-bead test. An identification test for certain metals whose oxides impart characteristic colors to borax glass beads when fused with them.
borazon. A crystalline form of boron nitride, BN, having about the same hardness as diamond.
bright-line spectrum. See *spectrum, bright-line.*
brine. A concentrated salt-water solution, containing principally sodium chloride.
buffer. A substance that, when added to a solution, causes a resistance to any change in pH.
buffered solution. See *solution, buffered.*

calorie. A unit of heat; the heat required to raise the temperature of 1 gram of water through 1 Celsius degree.
calorimeter. An apparatus for measuring heat of reaction.
carbonyl group. The 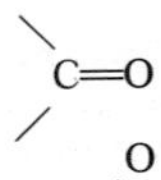 group.
carboxyl group. The 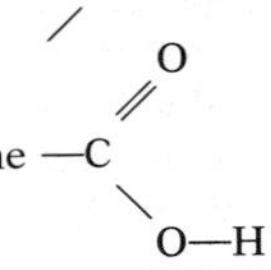 group.
catalyst. A substance or combination of substances that accelerates a chemical reaction without being used up itself.
catalyst, heterogeneous. A catalyst introduced into a reaction system in a different phase from that of the reactants.
catalyst, homogeneous. A catalyst introduced into a reaction system in the same phase as all reactants and products.
catalytic agent. See *catalyst.*
catalytic cracking. See *cracking, catalytic.*
cathode. A negatively charged, or electron-rich, electrode.
cation. An ion attracted to the cathode of an electrolytic cell; a positive ion.
cation hydrolysis. See *hydrolysis, cation.*
caustic. (1) Capable of converting some types of animal and vegetable matter into soluble materials by chemical action. (2) A substance with such properties.
Celsius temperature. See *temperature, Celsius.*
cement. A substance made from limestone and clay which, after mixing with water, sets to a hard mass.
centi-. Metric prefix meaning 0.01.
centigrade scale. The Celsius temperature scale.
chain reaction. A reaction in which the material or energy that starts the reaction is also one of the products.
chemical bond. The linkage between atoms produced by transfer or sharing of electrons.
chemical change. A change in which new substances with new properties are formed.
chemical equilibrium. See *equilibrium, chemical.*
chemical equilibrium law. See *constant, equilibrium.*
chemical equivalent. See *equivalent.*
chemical formula. See *formula, chemical.*
chemical kinetics. The branch of chemistry that deals with reaction rates and reaction mechanisms.
chemical properties. Those properties that pertain to the behavior of a material in changes in which its identity is altered.
chemical symbol. Either a single capital letter, or a capital letter and a small letter used together, as an abbreviation for (1) an element; (2) an atom of an element; (3) a mole of atoms of an element.
chemistry. The science dealing with the structure and composition of substances, the changes in composition, and the mechanisms by which these changes occur.
chemistry, organic. The study of carbon compounds.
colloidal suspension. A two-phase system having dispersed particles suspended in a dispersing medium.
combustion. Any chemical action that occurs so rapidly that both noticeable heat and light are produced.
combustion, heat of. The heat of reaction released by the complete combustion of one mole of a substance.
common-ion effect. The decrease in ionization of a weak electrolyte by the addition of a salt having an ion common to the solution of the electrolyte.
complex ions. See *ions, complex.*
composition reaction. A chemical reaction in which two or more substances combine and form a more complex substance.
compound. A substance that can be decomposed into two or more simpler substances by ordinary chemical means.
compound, binary. A compound consisting of only two elements.
compound, stable. A compound that is not decomposed easily.
compound, unstable. A compound that is decomposed easily.

concentrated. Containing a relatively large amount of solute.

condensation. The process of converting a gas into a liquid or solid.

condensation temperature. See *temperature, condensation.*

conjugate acid. See *acid, conjugate.*

conjugate base. See *base, conjugate.*

constant. A magnitude that does not change in value.

constant, equilibrium. The ratio of the product of the concentrations of the substances produced at equilibrium to the product of the concentrations of reactants, each concentration raised to that power that is the coefficient of the substance in the chemical equation.

constant, gas. The value of the quotient pV/nT; 0.082057 liter·atm/mole·K°.

constant, hydrolysis. The equilibrium constant of a reversible reaction between an ion of a dissolved salt and water.

constant, ionization. The equilibrium constant of a reversible reaction by which ions are produced from molecules.

constant, solubility-product. The product of the molar concentrations of the ions of a sparingly soluble substance in a saturated solution, each concentration raised to the appropriate power.

control rod. A rod of neutron-absorbing material used in regulating the reaction in a nuclear reactor.

coordination number. The number of molecules or ions covalently bonded to (coordinated with) a central ion.

covalence. Covalent bonding.

covalent bonding. Bonding in which atoms share electrons.

covalent molecular crystal. See *crystal, covalent molecular.*

covalent network crystal. See *crystal, covalent network.*

cracking. A process of breaking down complex organic molecules by the action of heat and usually a catalyst.

cracking, catalytic. The breaking up of large molecules into smaller ones by using a catalyst at high temperature.

cracking, thermal. The breaking up of large molecules into smaller ones by the use of high temperature.

critical pressure. See *pressure, critical.*

critical size. The amount of radioactive material required to sustain a chain reaction.

critical temperature. See *temperature, critical.*

critical volume. The volume occupied by one mole of a gas at its critical temperature and critical pressure.

crystal. A homogeneous portion of a substance bounded by plane surfaces making definite angles with each other, giving a regular geometric form.

crystal, covalent molecular. A crystal consisting of molecules arranged in a systematic order.

crystal, covalent network. A crystal consisting of an array of atoms that share electrons with their neighboring atoms and form a giant, compact, interlocking structure.

crystal, ionic. A crystal consisting of ions arranged in a regular pattern.

crystal lattice. The pattern of points that describes the arrangement of particles in a crystal structure.

crystal, metallic. A crystal lattice consisting of positive ions permeated by a cloud of valence electrons.

crystalline. Consisting of or made of crystals.

cyclotron. An electromagnetic device for accelerating protons or deuterons in a spiral path.

decomposition reaction. A chemical reaction in which one substance breaks down and forms two or more simpler substances.

dehydrating agent. A substance that removes water from a material.

dehydration. The removal of oxygen and hydrogen atoms from a substance in the form of water.

deliquescence. The property of certain substances to take up water from the air and form a solution.

density. The mass per unit volume of a material.

destructive distillation. See *distillation, destructive.*

detergent. A substance that removes dirt.

deuterium. The isotope of hydrogen having one proton and one neutron in the nucleus; hydrogen-2.

diatomic. Consisting of two atoms.

diffusion. The process of spreading out spontaneously to fill a space uniformly; the intermingling of the particles of substances.

dilute. Containing a relatively small amount of solute.

dimer. A compound formed by two simpler molecules or radicals.

dimeric. Capable of forming two-fold polymers.

dipole. A polar molecule, one region of which is positive, and another region is negative.

dipole-dipole attraction. A type of van der Waals force which is the attraction between the oppositely charged portions of neighboring polar molecules.

diprotic. Pertaining to an acid capable of donating two protons per molecule.

dispersion interaction. A type of van der Waals force dependent on the number of electrons in the interacting molecules and the tightness with which they are held.

dissociation. The separation of the ions from the crystals of an ionic compound during the solution process.

distillation. The process of evaporation followed by condensation of the vapors in a separate vessel.

distillation, destructive. The process of decomposing materials by heating them in a closed container without access to air or oxygen.

distillation, fractional. The separation of the components of a mixture that have different boiling points by carefully controlled vaporization.

domain. Small magnetized regions formed by groups of properly aligned atoms of ferromagnetic substances.

ductile. Capable of being drawn into a wire.

effervescence. The rapid evolution of a gas from a liquid in which it is dissolved.

efflorescence. The property of hydrated crystals to lose water of crystallization when exposed to the air.
elastic collision. A collision in which there is no net loss of energy.
electrochemical. Pertaining to spontaneous oxidation-reduction reactions used as a source of electric energy.
electrochemical cell. A system of electrodes and electrolyte by which a spontaneous oxidation-reduction reaction can be used as a source of electric current.
electrochemical reaction. A spontaneous oxidation-reduction reaction in which chemical energy can be transformed into electric energy.
electrode. A conductor used to establish electric contact with a nonmetallic part of a circuit.
electrode potential. The potential difference between an electrode and its solution in a half-reaction.
electrolysis. (1) The separation of a compound into simpler substances by an electric current. (2) The process by which an electric current is used to drive an oxidation-reduction reaction.
electrolyte. A substance whose water solution conducts an electric current.
electrolytic. Pertaining to driven oxidation-reduction reactions that utilize electric energy from an external source.
electrolytic cell. A system of electrodes and electrolyte by which an electric current can be used to drive an oxidation-reduction reaction.
electrolytic reaction. A driven oxidation-reduction reaction in which electric energy can be transformed into chemical energy.
electromagnetic radiation. A form of energy, such as light, X rays, or radio waves, which travels through space as waves at the rate of 3.00×10^8 m/sec.
electron. A negatively charged particle found in an atom. It has $\frac{1}{1837}$ of the mass of the simplest type of hydrogen atom.
electron affinity. The energy change that occurs when an electron is acquired by a neutral atom.
electron cloud. The portion of space about a nucleus in which the electrons may most probably be found.
electron pair. Two electrons of opposite spin in the same space orbital.
electron, valence. One of the electrons in an incomplete outer shell of an atom.
electron-volt. The energy required to move an electron across a potential difference of one volt.
electronegativity. The property of an atom of attracting the shared electrons forming a bond between it and another atom.
electroplating. An electrolytic process by which a metal is deposited on a surface.
electroscope. A device for determining the presence of electric charge.
electrovalence. Ionic bonding.
element. A substance that cannot be further decomposed by ordinary chemical means; a substance in which all the atoms have the same number of protons.
element, rare earth. An element that usually differs in electronic configuration from that of next lower or higher atomic number only in the number of *f* electrons in the second-from-outside shell.
element, transition. An element that usually differs in electronic configuration from that of next lower or higher atomic number only in the number of *d* electrons in the next-to-the-outside shell.
element, transuranium. Elements with a higher atomic number than uranium, atomic number 92.
empirical formula. See *formula, empirical.*
endothermic. Pertaining to a process that occurs with the absorption of energy.
energy. The capacity for doing work.
energy, activation. Energy required to transform reactants into an activated complex.
energy, binding. The energy released when a nucleus is formed from its component particles.
energy, bond. The energy required to break chemical bonds.
energy, free. The function of the state of a reaction system that assesses the tendencies toward lowest energy and highest entropy at a given temperature.
energy, heat. The energy transferred between two systems that is associated exclusively with the difference in temperature between the two systems.
energy, ionization. The energy required to remove an electron from an atom.
energy, kinetic. Energy of motion.
energy, potential. Energy of position.
energy level. A region about the nucleus of an atom in which electrons move. A shell.
enthalpy. The heat content of a system at constant pressure.
enthalpy change. A measure of the quantity of heat exchanged by a system and its surroundings (at constant pressure).
entropy. That property that describes the disorder of a system.
enzyme. A catalyst produced by living cells.
equilibrium. A dynamic state in which two opposing processes take place at the same time and at the same rate.
equilibrium, chemical. The state of balance attained in a reversible chemical action in which the rates of the opposing reactions are exactly equal.
equilibrium constant. See *constant, equilibrium.*
equilibrium, ionic. The state of balance attained in a reversible ionization action between un-ionized molecules in solution and their hydrated ions.
equilibrium, physical. A dynamic state in which two opposing physical changes occur at equal rates in the same system.
equilibrium, solution. The physical state attained in which the opposing processes of dissolving and crystallizing of a solute occur at equal rates.
equilibrium, thermal. The condition in which all objects in an isolated system are at the same temperature.
equilibrium vapor pressure. See *pressure, equilibrium vapor.*

equivalence point. That point in acid-base titration in which equivalent quantities of acid and hydroxide are present.

equivalent. (1) The mass in grams of a reactant that contains, replaces, or reacts with (directly or indirectly) the Avogadro number of hydrogen atoms. (2) The mass in grams of a reactant that acquires or supplies the Avogadro number of electrons.

ester. A compound formed by the reaction between an acid and an alcohol.

esterification. The process of producing an ester by reaction of an acid with an alcohol.

ether. An organic oxide.

eudiometer. A gas-measuring tube.

evaporation. The escape of molecules from the surface of liquids and solids.

excited atom. See *atom, excited.*

exothermic. Pertaining to a process that occurs with the liberation of energy.

extensive property. A property of matter that depends on the quantity of matter being considered.

fat. An ester of glycerol and long carbon chain acids.

fermentation. A chemical change produced by the action of an enzyme.

ferromagnetism. The property of certain metals whereby they are strongly attracted by a magnet.

filtration. The process of removing suspended material from a liquid by allowing the liquid to pass through a porous material such as filter paper or a layer of sand.

fission. The breakup of a very heavy nucleus into medium-weight nuclei.

flame test. A test to determine the identity of an element in a compound by the color that the compound imparts to a flame.

flux. A material used to promote the fusion of minerals.

force. The push or pull on a body.

formula. A shorthand method of representing the composition of substances using chemical symbols and numerical subscripts.

formula, chemical. A shorthand method of using chemical symbols and numerical subscripts to represent the composition of a substance.

formula, empirical. A chemical formula that denotes the constituent elements of a substance and the simplest whole-number ratio of atoms of each.

formula, molecular. A chemical formula that denotes the constituent elements of a molecular substance and the number of atoms of each composing one molecule.

formula, simplest. See *formula, empirical.*

formula, structural. A formula that indicates kind, number, arrangement, and valence bonds of the atoms in a molecule.

formula equation. A concise symbolized statement of a chemical change.

formula weight. See *weight, formula.*

formyl group. The 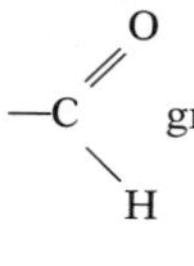 group.

fractional distillation. See *distillation, fractional.*

free energy. See *energy, free.*

free-energy change. The net driving force of a reaction system.

freezing. The process of converting a liquid into a solid.

freezing-point constant, molal. The freezing-point depression of a solvent in a 1-molal solution of a molecular solute in the solvent.

fuel. A material that is burned to provide heat.

fungicide. A chemical material that kills nongreen, microscopic plants known as fungi.

fusion. The combination of light-weight nuclei to form heavier, more stable nuclei.

galvanize. To coat iron or steel with zinc.

gamma ray. A high-energy electromagnetic wave from the nucleus of a radioactive element.

gas. The phase of matter characterized by neither a definite volume nor a definite shape.

gas, ideal. An imaginary gas whose behavior is described by the gas laws.

gas, natural. A mixture of hydrocarbon gases and vapors found in porous formations in the earth's crust.

gas, water. A fuel gas containing mainly CO and H_2 made by blowing a blast of steam through a bed of red-hot coke.

gas constant. See *constant, gas.*

Geiger counter. A device for determining the presence of radiation from radioactive materials.

generator. In chemistry, the vessel in which a reaction occurs to produce a desired gaseous product.

gram. A metric unit of mass equal to one thousandth of the standard kilogram.

gram-atomic weight. See *weight, gram-atomic.*

gram-equivalent weight. See *equivalent.*

gram-formula weight. See *weight, gram-formula.*

gram-molecular weight. See *weight, gram-molecular.*

ground state. The most stable state of an atom.

group. A vertical column of elements in the periodic table.

half-cell. The portion of a voltaic cell consisting of an electrode immersed in a solution of its ions.

half-life. The length of time during which half of a given number of atoms of a radioactive nuclide decays.

half-reaction. The reaction at an electrode in a half-cell of a voltaic cell.

halide. (1) A binary compound of a halogen with a less electronegative element or group of elements. (2) Fluoride, chloride, bromide, iodide, or astatide.

halide, alkyl. An alkane in which a halogen atom is substituted for a hydrogen atom.

halogen. The name given to the family of elements having seven valence electrons.

hard water. Water containing ions such as calcium and magnesium that form precipitates with soap.

heat energy. See *energy, heat.*

heat of combustion. See *combustion, heat of.*

heat of formation. The heat released or absorbed in a composition reaction.

heat of formation, molar. The heat of reaction released or absorbed when one mole of a compound is formed from its elements.

heat of reaction. The quantity of heat evolved or absorbed during a chemical reaction.

heat of solution. See *solution, heat of.*

hematite. A high grade of iron ore consisting principally of Fe_2O_3.

heterogeneous. Having parts with different properties.

heterogeneous catalyst. See *catalyst, heterogeneous.*

heterogeneous reaction. A reaction system in which reactants and products are present in different phases.

hexagonal. A crystalline system in which three equilateral axes intersect at angles of 60° and with a vertical axis of variable length at right angles to the equilateral axes.

homogeneous. Having similar properties throughout.

homogeneous catalyst. See *catalyst, homogeneous.*

homogeneous reaction. A reaction system in which all reactants and products are in the same phase.

homologous series. A series of similar compounds that conform to a general formula.

hybridization. The combining of two or more orbitals of nearly the same energy into new orbitals of equal energy.

hydrate. A crystallized substance that contains water of crystallization.

hydrated ion. See *ion, hydrated.*

hydration. (1) The attachment of water molecules to particles of the solute. (2) The solvation process in which water is the solvent. (3) The addition of hydrogen and oxygen atoms to a substance in the proportion in which they occur in water.

hybride. A compound consisting of hydrogen and one other less electronegative element.

hydrocarbon. A compound containing hydrogen and carbon.

hydrocarbon, aromatic. A hydrocarbon having a resonance structure sometimes represented by alternating single and double bonds in six-membered carbon rings.

hydrogen bond. A weak chemical bond between a hydrogen atom in one polar molecule and a very electronegative atom in a second polar molecule.

hydrogenation. The chemical addition of hydrogen to a material.

hydrolysis. An acid-base reaction between water and ions of a dissolved salt.

hydrolysis, anion. Hydrolysis reaction in which an anion base accepts a proton from a water molecule, increasing the OH^- concentration of the solution.

hydrolysis, cation. Hydrolysis reaction in which a cation acid donates a proton to a water molecule, increasing the H_3O^+ ion concentration of the solution.

hydrolysis constant. See *constant, hydrolysis.*

hydronium ion. See *ion, hydronium.*

hydrous oxide. See *oxide, hydrous.*

hygroscopic. Absorbing and retaining moisture from the atmosphere.

hypothesis. A possible or tentative explanation.

ideal gas. See *gas, ideal.*

immiscible. Not capable of being mixed.

indicator. A substance that changes in color on the passage from acidity to alkalinity, or the reverse.

inertia. Resistance of matter to change in position or motion.

inhibitor. A substance that hinders catalytic action.

inorganic. Pertaining to materials that are not hydrocarbons or their derivatives.

insoluble. (1) Not soluble. (2) So sparingly soluble as to be considered not soluble in the usual sense.

intensive property. A property of matter that is independent of the quantity of matter being considered.

ion. An atom or group of atoms that has a net positive or negative charge resulting from unequal numbers of positively charged protons and negatively charged electrons.

ion, hydrated. An ion of a solute to which molecules of water are attached.

ion, hydronium. A hydrated proton; the H_3O^+ ion.

ion, polyatomic. A charged group of covalently bonded atoms.

ion, spectator. An ion in a reaction system that takes no part in the chemical action.

ion-exchange resin. A resin that can exchange hydronium ions for positive ions; or one that can exchange hydroxide ions for negative ions.

ionic bonding. Bonding in which one or more electrons are transferred from one atom to another.

ionic crystal. See *crystal, ionic.*

ionic equilibrium. See *equilibrium, ionic.*

ionic reaction. A chemical reaction in which ions in solution combine and form a product that leaves the reaction environment.

ionization. The formation of ions from polar solute molecules by the action of the solvent.

ionization constant. See *constant, ionization.*

ionization energy. See *energy, ionization.*

ions, complex. An ionic species composed of a central metal ion combined with a specific number of polar molecules or ions.

isomer. One of two or more compounds having the same molecular formula but different structures.

isometric. A crystalline system in which the three axes are at right angles, as in a cube, and are of equal length.

isotope. One of two or more forms of atoms with the same atomic number but with different atomic masses.

Kelvin temperature. See *temperature, Kelvin.*

kernel. The portion of an atom excluding the valence electrons.

ketone. An organic compound that contains the $>C{=}O$, carbonyl, group.

kiln. A furnace used for producing quicklime, making glass, baking pottery, and so on.
kilo-. Metric prefix meaning 1000.
kilocalorie. The quantity of heat required to raise the temperature of one kilogram of water one Celsius degree.
kinetic energy. See *energy, kinetic.*
kinetic theory. See *theory, kinetic.*
knocking. A pounding sound produced in automobile engines when the mixture of gasoline vapor and air does not burn at a uniform rate.

lanthanide series. Rare earth elements of the sixth period following barium, in which the transitional inner building of the 5*d* sublevel is interrupted by the inner building of the 4*f* sublevel.
law. A generalization that describes behavior in nature.
law, rate. An equation that relates the reaction rate and concentrations of reactants.
leavening agent. A substance that releases carbon dioxide in a dough or batter.
lime. Calcium oxide, CaO; also called quicklime.
lime, slaked. A common name for calcium hydroxide, $Ca(OH)_2$.
limewater. A water solution of calcium hydroxide.
linear accelerator. A particle accelerator in which the particles travel in a straight line through many stages of potential difference.
liquid. The phase of matter characterized by a definite volume but an indefinite shape.
liter. One cubic decimeter.
litmus. A dye extracted from lichens used as an acid-base indicator.
lye. A commercial grade of either sodium hydroxide or potassium hydroxide.

magnetic quantum number. See *quantum number, magnetic.*
malleable. Capable of being shaped by hammering or rolling.
mass. The quantity of matter that a body possesses; a measure of the inertia of a body.
mass, atomic. The mass of an atom expressed relative to the "carbon-12 = exactly 12" scale.
mass action equation. See *constant, equilibrium.*
mass defect. See *nuclear mass defect.*
mass number. (1) The whole number closest to the atomic mass of an atom. (2) The sum of the number of protons and neutrons in the nucleus of an atom.
matter. Anything that occupies space and has mass.
melting. The process of converting a solid into a liquid.
melting point. The temperature at which a solid changes to a liquid.
metal. One of a class of elements that show a luster, are good conductors of heat and electricity, and are electropositive.
metal, alkali. An element of Group I of the periodic table.
metal, alkaline-earth. An element of Group II of the periodic table.
metal, self-protective. A metal that forms a nonporous, nonscaling coat of tarnish.
metallic crystal. See *crystal, metallic.*
metalloid. An element having certain properties characteristic of a metal but which is generally classed as a nonmetal.
metamorphic. Pertains to rocks that have undergone a change in form owing to heat or pressure.
meter. The metric unit of length.
metric system. A decimal system of measurement.
milli-. Metric prefix meaning 0.001.
miscible. Capable of being mixed.
mixture. A material composed of two or more substances each of which retains its own characteristic properties.
moderator. A material that slows down neutrons.
molal boiling-point constant. See *boiling-point constant, molal.*
molal freezing-point constant. See *freezing-point constant, molal.*
molal solution. See *solution, molal.*
molality. The concentration of a solution expressed in moles of solute per 1000 grams of solvent.
molar heat of formation. See *heat of formation, molar.*
molar heat of fusion. The heat energy required to melt one mole of solid at its melting point.
molar heat of vaporization. See *standard molar heat of vaporization.*
molar solution. See *solution, molar.*
molar volume. The volume, in liters, of one mole of a gas at STP; taken as 22.4 liters for ordinary gases, 22.414 liters for the ideal gas.
molarity. The concentration of a solution expressed in moles of solute per liter of solution.
mole. The amount of substance containing the Avogadro number of any kind of chemical unit. In practice, the gram-atomic weight of an element represented as monatomic; the gram-molecular weight of a molecular substance; the gram-formula weight of a nonmolecular substance; and the gram-ionic weight of an ion.
molecular crystal. See *crystal, covalent molecular.*
molecular formula. See *formula, molecular.*
molecular weight. See *weight, molecular.*
molecule. The smallest chemical unit of a substance that is capable of stable independent existence.
molecule, nonpolar. A molecule with all nonpolar bonds or with uniformly spaced polar bonds that are alike and have a uniform exterior electron distribution.
molecule, polar. A molecule containing one or more nonuniformly arranged polar covalent bonds and having a nonuniform exterior electron distribution.
monatomic. Consisting of one atom.
monoclinic. A crystalline system in which there are three unequal axes, with one oblique intersection.
monomer. A simple molecule, or single unit of a polymer.
monoprotic. Pertaining to an acid capable of donating one proton per molecule.
mortar. A mixture of lime, sand, and water that sets to a hard mass.

natural gas. See *gas, natural.*
neutralization. The reaction between hydronium ions and hydroxide ions to form water.
neutron. A neutral particle found in the nucleus of an atom. It has about the same mass as a proton.
nitrogen fixation. The process of converting elemental nitrogen into nitrogen compounds.
nodule. A knob-like swelling on the roots of plants called legumes in which nitrogen-fixing bacteria grow.
nonelectrolyte. A substance whose water solution does not conduct an electric current appreciably.
nonmetal. One of a class of elements that are usually poor conductors of heat and electricity and are electronegative.
nonpolar covalent bond. A covalent bond in which there is an equal attraction for the shared electrons and a resulting balanced distribution of charge.
nonpolar molecule. See *molecule, nonpolar.*
normal solution. See *solution, normal.*
normality. The concentration of a solution expressed in equivalents of solute per liter of solution.
nuclear change. Formation of a new substance through changes in the identity of the atoms involved.
nuclear disintegration. The emission of a proton or neutron from a nucleus as a result of bombarding the nucleus with alpha particles, protons, deuterons, neutrons, and so on.
nuclear equation. An equation representing changes in the nuclei of atoms.
nuclear mass defect. The difference between the mass of a nucleus and the sum of the masses of its constituent particles.
nuclear reactor. A device in which the controlled fission of radioactive material produces new radioactive substances and energy.
nucleus. The positively charged, dense central part of an atom.
nuclide. A variety of atom as determined by the number of protons and number of neutrons in its nucleus.
nuclide, parent. The heaviest, most complex, naturally occurring nuclide in a decay series of radioactive elements.

octane rating. A number indicating how a gasoline behaves with regard to knocking when compared with a test fuel given an arbitrary rating of 100.
octet. An outer shell of an atom having *s* and *p* orbitals filled with eight electrons.
open-hearth. A large reverberatory furnace for making steel.
orbital. See *space orbital.*
orbital quantum number. See *quantum number, orbital.*
ore. A mineral containing an element that can be extracted profitably.
organic. Pertaining to carbon compounds, particularly hydrocarbons and their derivatives.
organic chemistry. See *chemistry, organic.*
orthorhombic. A crystalline system in which there are three unequal axes at right angles.
oxidation. (1) Any chemical reaction that involves the loss of one or more electrons by an atom or an ion. (2) An algebraic increase in the oxidation number of a substance.
oxidation number. A number assigned to each element to indicate the number of electrons assumed to be gained, lost, or shared in compound formation.
oxidation state. See *oxidation number.*
oxidation-reduction reaction. Any chemical process in which there is a transfer of electrons, either partial or complete.
oxide. A compound consisting of oxygen and usually one other element in which oxygen has an oxidation number of -2.
oxide, hydrous. A hydrated metallic oxide.
oxidizing agent. The atom or ion that takes up electrons during an oxidation-reduction reaction.
oxyacid. An acid containing hydrogen, oxygen, and a third element.
oxygen-carbon dioxide cycle. The combination of photosynthesis and the various natural and artificial methods of producing atmospheric carbon dioxide.
ozone. An allotropic form of oxygen containing three atoms per molecule.

paramagnetism. The property of a substance whereby it is weakly attracted into a magnetic field.
parent nuclide. See *nuclide, parent.*
partial pressure. See *pressure, partial.*
period. A horizontal row of elements in the periodic table.
periodic table. A tabular arrangement of the chemical elements based on their atomic structure.
permanent hardness. Hardness in water caused by the sulfates of calcium and magnesium, which can be removed by precipitation or ion-exchange methods.
permutit. A synthetic zeolite, used in softening water.
petroleum. A liquid mixture of hydrocarbons obtained from beneath the surface of the ground.
pH. Hydronium ion index; the common logarithm of the reciprocal of the hydronium-ion concentration.
phlogiston theory. See *theory, phlogiston.*
photon. A quantum (unit) of electromagnetic radiation energy.
photosynthesis. The process by which plants produce carbohydrates and oxygen with the aid of sunlight, using carbon dioxide and water as the raw materials and chlorophyll as the catalyst.
physical change. A change in which the identifying properties of a substance remain unchanged.
physical equilibrium. See *equilibrium, physical.*
physical properties. Those properties that can be determined without causing a change in the identity of a material.
pig iron. Iron recovered from a blast furnace.
plaster of Paris. A form of calcium sulfate, $(CaSO_4)_2 H_2O$, produced by partially dehydrating gypsum.
plastic. A natural or synthetic material that can be

shaped while soft into a required form and then hardened to produce a durable finished article.

polar covalent bond. A covalent bond in which there is an unequal attraction for the shared electrons and a resulting unbalanced distribution of charge.

polar molecule. See *molecule, polar.*

polyatomic ion. See *ion, polyatomic.*

polymer. A compound formed by two or more simpler molecules or radicals with repeating structural units.

polymeric. Capable of forming a polymer.

potential energy. See *energy, potential.*

precipitate. (1) A substance, usually a solid, which separates from a solution as a result of some physical or chemical change. (2) To produce such a substance.

precipitation. The separation of a solid from a solution.

precision. The agreement between the numerical values of two or more measurements made in the same way; the reproducibility of measured data.

pressure. Force per unit area.

pressure, critical. The pressure required to liquefy a gas at its critical temperature.

pressure, equilibrium vapor. The pressure exerted by a vapor in equilibrium with its liquid.

pressure, partial. The pressure each gas of a gaseous mixture would exert if it alone were present.

pressure, standard. The pressure exerted by a column of mercury exactly 760 mm high at 0°C.

pressure, vapor. Pressure owing to the vapor of confined liquids and solids.

principal quantum number. See *quantum number, principal.*

product. An element or compound resulting from chemical action.

product, substitution. A compound in which various atoms or groups have been substituted for one or more atoms.

promoter. A substance that increases the activity of a catalyst when introduced in trace quantities.

protium. The isotope of hydrogen having one proton and no neutrons in the nucleus; hydrogen-1.

protolysis. Proton-transfer reactions.

proton. A positively charged particle found in the nucleus of an atom. It has $\frac{1836}{1837}$ of the mass of the simplest type of hydrogen atom.

proton acceptor. A base according to the Brønsted system.

proton donor. An acid according to the Brønsted system.

pure substance. See *substance.*

quantum number, magnetic. The quantum number that indicates the position about the three axes in space of an orbital.

quantum number, orbital. The quantum number that indicates the shape of an orbital.

quantum number, principal. The quantum number that indicates the most probable distance of an orbital from the nucleus of an atom.

quantum number, spin. The quantum number that indicates the direction of spin of an electron.

quantum numbers. The numbers that describe the distance from the nucleus, the shape, and the position with respect to the three axes in space of an orbital, as well as the direction of spin of the electron(s) in each orbital.

quicklime. A common name for calcium oxide, CaO. Also called lime.

radioactive. Having the property of radioactivity.

radioactive decay. A radioactive change in which a nucleus emits a particle and rays, forming a slightly lighter, more stable nucleus.

radioactive tracer. A radioactive element introduced in small quantities to determine the behavior of chemically similar nonradioactive atoms in various physical or chemical changes.

radioactivity. The spontaneous breakdown of an unstable atomic nucleus with the emission of particles and rays.

rare earth element. See *element, rare earth.*

rate-determining step. The slowest of a sequence of steps along a reaction pathway.

rate law. See *law, rate.*

reactant. An element or compound entering into a chemical reaction.

reaction mechanism. The pathway of a chemical reaction; the sequence of steps by which a reaction occurs.

reaction pathway. See *reaction mechanism.*

reaction rate. A measure of the amount of reactants converted to products per unit of time.

redox. Pertaining to oxidation-reduction reactions.

reducing agent. The atom or ion that supplies electrons during an oxidation-reduction reaction.

reduction. (1) Any chemical reaction that involves the gain of one more more electrons by an atom or an ion. (2) An algebraic decrease in the oxidation number of a substance.

replacement reaction. A chemical reaction in which one substance is displaced from its compound by another substance.

resonance. The bonding situation in substances whose bond properties cannot be satisfactorily represented by any single formula using the electron-dot notation system and keeping the octet rule.

resonance hybrid. A substance whose properties show that its structure is intermediate between several electron-dot structures.

respiration. The process by which a plant or animal absorbs oxygen and gives off products of oxidation in the tissues, especially carbon dioxide.

reversible reaction. A chemical reaction in which the products re-form the original reactants under suitable conditions.

rhombic. See *orthorhombic.*

roasting. Heating in the presence of air.

salt. A compound composed of the positive ions of an aqueous base and the negative ions of an aqueous acid.

saponification. The process of making a soap by hydrolysis of a fat with a strong hydroxide.

saturated. (1) Pertaining to a solution in which the concentration of solute is the maximum possible under existing conditions. (2) Pertaining to an organic compound that has only single covalent bonds between carbon atoms.

saturated solution. See *solution, saturated.*

self-protective metal. See *metal, self-protective.*

semiconductor. A substance with an electric conductivity between that of a metal and an insulator.

shell. A region about the nucleus of an atom in which electrons move. An energy level.

significant figures. The digits in a measurement that represent the number of units counted with reasonable assurance.

simplest formula. See *formula, empirical.*

slag. An easily melted product of the reaction between the flux and the impurities of an ore.

slaked lime. See *lime, slaked.*

slaking. The addition of water to quicklime, CaO, to produce hydrated (slaked) lime, $Ca(OH)_2$.

soft water. (1) Water that lathers readily with soap. (2) Water that is free of hardening agents, or from which these agents have been removed.

solid. The phase of matter characterized by a definite shape.

solubility. The amount of a solute dissolved in a given amount of solvent at equilibrium, under specified conditions.

solubility-product constant. See *constant, solubility product.*

soluble. Capable of being dissolved.

solute. The dissolved substance in a solution.

solution. A homogeneous mixture of two or more substances, the composition of which may be varied within definite limits.

solution, buffered. A solution containing a relatively high concentration of a buffer salt that tends to maintain a constant pH.

solution equilibrium. See *equilibrium, solution.*

solution, heat of. The difference between the heat content of a solution and the heat contents of its components.

solution, molal. A solution containing one mole of solute per 1000 grams of solvent.

solution, molar. A solution containing one mole of solute per liter of solution.

solution, normal. A solution containing one equivalent of solute per liter of solution.

solution, saturated. A solution in which the dissolved and undissolved solutes are in equilibrium.

solution, standard. A solution that contains a definite concentration of solute that is known precisely.

solvation. The clustering of solvent particles about the particles of solute.

solvent. The dissolving medium in a solution.

space orbital. A highly probable location about a nucleus in which an electron may be found.

spectator ion. See *ion, spectator.*

spectroscope. An optical instrument consisting of a collimator tube, a glass prism, and a telescope, used for producing and viewing spectra.

spectrum. The pattern of colors formed by passing light through a prism.

spectrum, bright-line. A spectrum consisting of a series of bright lines having frequencies characteristic of the atoms present.

spin quantum number. See *quantum number, spin.*

stable compound. See *compound, stable.*

standard boiling point. See *boiling point, standard.*

standard molar heat of vaporization. The heat energy required to vaporize one mole of liquid at its standard boiling point.

standard pressure. See *pressure, standard.*

standard solution. See *solution, standard.*

standard temperature. See *temperature, standard.*

stoichiometry. Pertaining to the numerical relationships of elements and compounds and the mathematical proportions of reactants and products in chemical reactions.

STP. The abbreviation for "standard temperature and pressure."

structural formula. See *formula, structural.*

sublimation. The change of phase from a solid to a vapor.

sublime. To pass from the solid to the gaseous phase without liquefying.

subscript. A number written below and to the side of a symbol. If at the left, it represents the atomic number; if at the right, it represents the number of atoms of the element.

substance. A homogeneous material consisting of one particular kind of matter.

substitution. A reaction in which one or more atoms are substituted for hydrogen atoms in a hydrocarbon.

substitution product. See *product, substitution.*

superheated water. Water heated under pressure to a temperature above its normal boiling point.

supersaturated. Pertaining to a solution that contains an amount of solute in excess of that normally possible under existing conditions.

superscript. A number written above and to the side of a symbol. If at the left, it represents the mass number of the atom represented by the symbol.

suspension. See *colloidal suspension.*

symbol. See *chemical symbol.*

synchrotron. A particle accelerator in which particles move in a circular path owing to the varying of the oscillating voltage and the magnetic field.

synthetic. Man-made. Artificial.

taconite. A low grade of iron ore consisting principally of Fe_2O_3 and Fe_3O_4 in a matrix of rock.

temperature. A measure of the ability of a system to transfer heat to, or acquire heat from, other systems.

temperature, Celsius. Temperature on the Celsius scale that has two fixed points, the freezing point and the steam point of water, as 0° and 100°.

temperature, condensation. The lowest temperature at which a substance can exist as a gas at atmospheric pressure.

temperature, critical. The highest temperature at which it is possible to liquefy a gas with any amount of pressure.

temperature, Kelvin. Temperature on the Kelvin scale that is numerically 273° higher than that on the Celsius scale.

temperature, standard. 0° Celsius.

temporary hardness. Hardness in water caused by the presence of hydrogen carbonates of calcium and magnesium, which can be removed by boiling.

tetragonal. A crystalline system in which the three axes are at right angles, but only the two lateral axes are equal.

theory. A plausible explanation of a natural phenomenon in terms of a simple model that has familiar properties.

theory, atomic. A theory that includes information about the structure and properties of atoms, the kinds of compounds they form, and the properties of these compounds. It also includes information about the mass, volume, and energy relationships in reactions between atoms.

theory, kinetic. A theory pertaining to the motion of the ultimate particles of substances, and in particular, of the molecules of gases.

theory, phlogiston. An obsolete theory that explained combustion as being due to the loss of a substance called phlogiston.

thermal cracking. See *cracking, thermal.*

thermal equilibrium. See *equilibrium, thermal.*

thermite reaction. The reaction by which a metal is prepared from its oxide by reduction with aluminum.

titration. The process by which the capacity of a solution of unknown concentration to combine with one of known concentration is measured.

transition. Pertaining to subgroups of elements characterized by the belated filling of the next-to-outermost energy level of the atoms.

transition element. See *element, transition.*

transition interval. The pH range over which the color change of an indicator occurs.

transmutation reaction. A reaction in which the nucleus of an atom undergoes a change in the number of its protons, and consequently in its identity.

transuranium element. See *element, transuranium.*

triclinic. A crystalline system in which there are three unequal axes and oblique intersections.

triple point of water. The single temperature and pressure condition at which water exists in all three phases at the same time.

triprotic. Pertaining to an acid capable of donating three protons per molecule.

tritium. The isotope of hydrogen having one proton and two neutrons in the nucleus; hydrogen-3.

unit cell. The smallest portion of the crystal lattice that exhibits the pattern of the lattice structure.

unsaturated organic compound. An organic compound with one or more double or triple covalent bonds between carbon atoms in each molecule.

unstable compound. See *compound, unstable.*

valence electron. See *electron, valence.*

van der Waals forces. Forces of attraction between molecules.

vapor pressure. See *pressure, vapor.*

vapor pressure, equilibrium. See *pressure, equilibrium vapor.*

vinyl group. The $CH_2{=}CH-$ group.

volatile. Easily vaporized.

voltaic cell. An electrochemical cell arranged to deliver an electric current to an external circuit.

vulcanization. The heating of rubber with other materials to improve its properties.

water gas. See *gas, water.*

water of crystallization. Water that has united with some compounds as they crystallize from solution.

water of hydration. See *water of crystallization.*

water softener. A chemical substance that removes hardness from water.

weight. The measure of the earth's gravitational attraction for a body.

weight, atomic. The average relative mass of the naturally occurring atoms of an element on the "carbon−12 = exactly 12" scale.

weight, formula. The sum of the atomic weights of all the atoms represented in the chemical formula.

weight, gram-atomic. The mass in grams of one mole of naturally occurring atoms of an element.

weight, gram-formula. (1) The mass of a substance in grams equal to its formula weight. (2) The mass of one mole of a substance.

weight, gram-molecular. (1) The mass of a molecular substance in grams equal to its molecular weight. (2) The mass of one mole of molecules of the substance.

weight, molecular. The formula weight of a molecular substance.

word equation. A brief statement that identifies the reactants entering into a chemical reaction and the products formed.

X rays. Electromagnetic radiations of high frequency and short wavelengths.

zeolite. A natural mineral, sodium silico-aluminate, used to soften water.

PICTURE CREDITS

HR&W Photos by Russell Dian appear on pages: **vi-2**, center **3**, bottom left **6**, **10**, bottom **11**, **13**, **15**, figs. 2-9 Photo Essay **21-22**, **35**, top **71**, **93-94**, **98**, **100**, **106**, **133-134**, **146**, **150**, bottom **167**, **173**, **178**, bottom **187**, top **206**, **249**, **251**, **259**, **261**, **264**, **275**, **293**, **299**, **305**, **307**, **309**, **321-322**, **327**, **339**, **355**, **359**, **370** Courtesy Fischer Scientific Company, **403**, **409**, **469**, **474**, right **565**, **582-583**.

HR&W Photos by John King appear on pages: **51**, **74-75**, **129**, **132**, **152-154**, **243**, **255-256**, **285**, **344**, **357**, **430**, **464**, **471**, **473**, top **499**, **503**, **514**, top **557**, **564**, **566**, **573-574**, **588**.

3—top NASA, bottom Simon Trevor-D.B./Bruce Coleman. **4, 5** Photo Essay—1 & 5 Mobil Oil Corp., 2 Texaco, Inc., 3 E. I. DuPont de Nemours & Co., 4 Exxon Research and Engineering Co., 6 FDA, 7 National Bureau of Standards, 8 Dave Woodward/Taurus Photos, 9 Brown Brothers, 10 Courtesy of Dr. Marjorie Horning, Baylor College of Medicine. **6**—top U.S. Steel Corp., 1971 Annual Report, bottom right Courtesy B. F. Goodrich. **7**—Tana Hoban/DPI. **8**—top left Dunn/DPI, top right Courtesy Stanton Magnetics, Inc., bottom T. P. Schmitter. **9**—top left Larry Burrows/Life Magazine © Time, Inc., top center no credit, top right Cenco, bottom NASA. **11**—top Courtesy Goodyear Tire and Rubber Co. **12**—National Bureau of Standards. **14**—Dr. Harold E. Edgerton. **16**—Alex Mulligan. **18**—JOURNAL OF COLLOID AND INTERFACE SCIENCE Vol. 36 No. 4, Aug. 1971—"Anomalous Water-Properties and Factors Affecting Its Yield" by Brummer, Cocks, Entine and Bradspies. **21, 22** Photo Essay—1 ERDA Oakridge, Tenn. **23**—top Culver Pictures, Inc., bottom John Cubitto. **25**—General Electric. **26**—top USAEC Oakridge, Tenn., bottom Lawrence Radiation Laboratory, Univ. of Calif./EBONY-TAN-JET-HUE. **27**—top, bottom Fritz Goro/Life Magazine © Time, Inc., center Alcoa. **29**—Stanford Univ. News and Publications Service. **33**—both Werner Wolff/Black Star. **34**—both From the CHEM Study Film: Molecular Motion. **40** Photo Essay—1 Brown Brothers, 2 Harpers Monthly 1904, 3 & 4 The Granger Collection, 5 Carolyn Polese, 6 National Bureau of Standards. **41**—Professor Erwin W. Mueller, The Penn. State Univ. **42**—top Manfred Kage/Peter Arnold–agent, bottom Dr. A. K. Kleinschmidt. **43**—Professor Erwin W. Mueller, The Penn. State Univ. **57**—NASA. **58**—From the CHEM Study Film: Chemical Bonding. **59**—© 1959 Calif. Institute of Technology and Carnegie Institution of Washington. **60**—Professor Harry Meiners, Rensselaer Polytechnic Institute. **65**—Ferranti, Ltd. **71**—bottom Moscow Technological Institute. **72**—NYPL. **91, 92** Photo Essay—1 & 8 Fred Ward/Black Star, 2 Argonne National Laboratory, 3–6 Eli Lilly & Co., 7 From the CHEM Study Film: Biochemistry and Molecular Structures, 9 Hewlett Packard. **95**—From the CHEM Study Film: Chemical Families. **96**—B. M. Shaub. **110**—L. V. Bergman & Assoc., Inc. **116**—Courtesy Goodyear Tire and Rubber Co. **117**—Courtesy Crazy Glue, Inc. **123**—Darwin Van Campin/DPI. **126**—both John Cubitto. **137**—Courtesy Exxon Research and Engineering Co. **145**—Hans Namuth. **156**—both HR&W Photos by Felix Cooper. **167**—top UPI. **168**—top The Granger Collection, bottom The Bettmann Archive, Inc. **174**—top left Lawrence Fried/The Image Bank, top right American Iron and Steel Institute, bottom Runk–Schoenberger/Grant Heilman. **175**—NASA. **183**—both NASA. **187**—top © David Barnes 1975/Photo Researchers. **188**—From the CHEM Study Film: Molecular Motion.

206—bottom From the CHEM Study Film: Gases and How They Combine. **211**—National Center for Atmospheric Research, Boulder, Col. **225**—Tom Lesley/Black Star. **229**—FOUNDATIONS OF CHEMISTRY, HRW. **232**—Delmar Lipp/DPI. **234**—David Overcash/Bruce Coleman. **235**—Professor Isador Frankuchen, Polytechnic Institute of Brooklyn. **237**—both B. M. Shaub. **339**—JPL/NASA. **241**—The Chemistry Department, Univ. of Iowa. **244**—Calcium Chloride Institute. **250**—Carolyn Polese. **277**—Brown Brothers. **279**—H. Bassow, Germantown Friends School. **289**—Argonne National Laboratory. **301**—Luis Villota/The Image Bank. **338**—From the CHEM Study Film: Acid–Base Indicators. **343**—From the CHEM Study Film: Acid–Base Indicators. **345**—Winterkorn, Hammond & Lillis, Inc./Corning. **349**—Courtesy N. W. Ayer ABH International. **353**—Mel Chior DiGiacomo, Courtesy Union Carbide. **354**—Bethlehem Steel Corporation. **361**—Walter Kidde & Co. **364**—Tana Hoban/DPI. **369**—J. Alex Langley/DPI. **370**—all HR&W Photos by Russell Dian, Courtesy Fischer Scientific Company. **373**—American Gas Assoc. **375**—Courtesy Exxon Research and Engineering Co. **379**—Carolyn Polese. **388**—Mobil Oil Corp. **395**—Courtesy of the New York State Historical Association, Cooperstown. **397**—all E. I. DuPont de Nemours & Co.

401—Carolyn Polese. **405**—W. R. Grace. **406**—Photo Essay—top left, bottom left, bottom left insert E. I. DuPont de Nemours & Co., top right Bruce Roberts 1977/Photo Researchers, bottom right © H. Wendler 1976/The Image Bank, bottom right insert Ivan Massar/Black Star. **439**—Mel Chior DiGiacomo/© The Image Bank. **482**—both From the CHEM Study Film: Electric Interactions. **495**—Calif. Institute of Technology and Carnegie Institution of Washington. **497**—T. P. Schmitter. **499**—bottom B. M. Shaub. **505**—Adapted from the SPECTRUM CHART Sargent Welch Scientific Company. **509**—Stephen Green-Armytage/© The Image Bank. **511**, top **512**—B. M. Shaub. **512**—bottom Courtesy Dow Chemical, U.S.A. **515**—top Lee Boltin, bottom G. R. Roberts. **516**—both The Permutit Co. **523**—Courtesy of the Copper Development Association, Inc. **527**—From the CHEM Study Film: Vanadium, Transition Element. **535**—Inland Steel Company. **536**—U.S. Steel. **537**—Westinghouse. **543**—top Arizona Highways/Color Classics, bottom Courtesy of the Copper Development Association, Inc. **547**—Gazelle Bowl, Courtesy Steuben Glass. **550**—top HR&W Photo by Brian Hammill, bottom David Moore/Black Star. **552**—Anaconda. **553**—Kaiser Aluminum and Chemical Corp. **555**—top Union Carbide, bottom Space Sciences Laboratories, General Electric Co. **556**—top B. M. Shaub, bottom United Aircraft Photo. **557**—All photos (except top one) by James H. Mathews, Univ. of Calif., Riverside. **558**—B. M. Shaub. **561**—© Tony La Tona 1975/Photo Researchers. **563**—U.S. Dept. of Agriculture, Soil Conservation Service. **565**—left Inter Agriculture/Arthur Paulsmeyer. **567**—From the CHEM Study Film: Nitric Acid. **568**—Fritz Henle/Photo Researchers. **571**—Courtesy Freeport Minerals, Inc. **572**—From the CHEM Study Film: Chemical Families. **575**—Carolyn Polese. **579**—Lizabeth Corlett/DPI. **580**—Carolyn Polese. **581**—Argonne National Laboratory. **584**—Sybil Weil. **585**—Courtesy Mike Kupperman, Surface Cleaning Corp. **586**—Carolyn Polese. **587**—From the CHEM Study Film: Bromine–Element from the Sea. **591**—top Fermi National Accelerator Laboratory, bottom left Matt Grimaldi, bottom right Mark Schupack. **592**—Sargent Welch Scientific Company. **593**—EBONY. **602**—ERDA Oakridge, Tenn. **603**—Lawrence Berkeley Laboratory, Univ. of Calif., Berkeley. **605**—ERDA Oakridge, Tenn. **607**—Dr. J. D. Macdougall, Scripps Institution of Oceanography, Univ. of Calif., San Diego. **609**—Lawrence Livermore Laboratory, Univ. of Calif.

Illustrations by Fine Line Studio.

PERIODIC TABLE

METALS

TRANSITION ELEMENTS

Period	I	II								
1	1.0080 H 1 (1)									
2	6.941 Li 3 (2 1)	9.01218 Be 4 (2 2)								
3	22.9898 Na 11 (2 8 1)	24.305 Mg 12 (2 8 2)								
4	39.102 K 19 (2 8 8 1)	40.08 Ca 20 (2 8 8 2)	44.9559 Sc 21 (2 8 9 2)	47.90 Ti 22 (2 8 10 2)	50.9414 V 23 (2 8 11 2)	51.996 Cr 24 (2 8 13 1)	54.9380 Mn 25 (2 8 13 2)	55.847 Fe 26 (2 8 14 2)	58.9332 Co 27 (2 8 15 2)
5	85.4678 Rb 37 (2 8 18 8 1)	87.62 Sr 38 (2 8 18 8 2)	88.9059 Y 39 (2 8 18 9 2)	91.22 Zr 40 (2 8 18 10 2)	92.9064 Nb 41 (2 8 18 12 1)	95.94 Mo 42 (2 8 18 13 1)	98.9062 Tc 43 (2 8 18 13 2)	101.07 Ru 44 (2 8 18 15 1)	102.9055 Rh 45 (2 8 18 16 1)
6	132.9055 Cs 55 (2 8 18 18 8 1)	137.34 Ba 56 (2 8 18 18 8 2)	Lanthanide Series; 174.97 Lu 71 (2 8 18 32 9 2)	178.49 Hf 72 (2 8 18 32 10 2)	180.9479 Ta 73 (2 8 18 32 11 2)	183.85 W 74 (2 8 18 32 12 2)	186.2 Re 75 (2 8 18 32 13 2)	190.2 Os 76 (2 8 18 32 14 2)	192.22 Ir 77 (2 8 18 32 15 2)
7	[223] Fr 87 (2 8 18 32 18 8 1)	226.0254 Ra 88 (2 8 18 32 18 8 2)	Actinide Series; [257] Lr 103 (2 8 18 32 32 9 2)	[261] 104 (2 8 18 32 32 10 2)	[260] 105 (2 8 18 32 32 11 2)	[263] 106 (2 8 18 32 32 12 2)	[261] 107 (2 8 18 32 32 13 2)		

Lanthanide Series						
138.9055 La 57 (2 8 18 18 9 2)	140.12 Ce 58 (2 8 18 20 8 2)	140.9077 Pr 59 (2 8 18 21 8 2)	144.24 Nd 60 (2 8 18 22 8 2)	[147] Pm 61 (2 8 18 23 8 2)	150.4 Sm 62 (2 8 18 24 8 2)	151.96 Eu 63 (2 8 18 25 8 2)

Actinide Series						
[227] Ac 89 (2 8 18 32 18 9 2)	232.0381 Th 90 (2 8 18 32 18 10 2)	231.0359 Pa 91 (2 8 18 32 20 9 2)	238.029 U 92 (2 8 18 32 21 9 2)	237.0482 Np 93 (2 8 18 32 22 9 2)	[244] Pu 94 (2 8 18 32 24 8 2)	[243] Am 95 (2 8 18 32 25 8 2)